with MyEcon|

- **Learning Catalytics**—Generates classroom discussion, guides lectures, and promotes peer-to-peer learning with real-time analytics. Students can use any device to interact in the classroom, engage with content, and even draw and share graphs.

- **Real-Time Data Analysis Exercises**—Using current macro data to help students understand the impact of changes in economic variables, Real-Time Data Analysis Exercises communicate directly with the Federal Reserve Bank of St. Louis's FRED® site and update as new data are available.

- **Current News Exercises**—Every week, current microeconomic and macroeconomic news stories, with accompanying exercises, are posted to MyEconLab. Assignable and auto-graded, these multi-part exercises ask students to recognize and apply economic concepts to real-world events.

- **Experiments**—Flexible, easy-to-assign, auto-graded, and available in Single and Multiplayer versions, Experiments in MyEconLab make learning fun and engaging.

- **Reporting Dashboard**—View, analyze, and report learning outcomes clearly and easily. Available via the Gradebook and fully mobile-ready, the Reporting Dashboard presents student performance data at the class, section, and program levels in an accessible, visual manner.

- **LMS Integration**—Link from any LMS platform to access assignments, rosters, and resources, and synchronize MyLab grades with your LMS gradebook. For students, new direct, single sign-on provides access to all the personalized learning MyLab resources that make studying more efficient and effective.

- **Mobile Ready**—Students and instructors can access multimedia resources and complete assessments right at their fingertips, on any mobile device.

PEARSON

ECONOMICS

TWELFTH EDITION

MICHAEL PARKIN

University of Western Ontario

PEARSON

Boston Columbus Indianapolis New York San Francisco Hoboken
Amsterdam Cape Town Dubai London Madrid Milan Munich Paris Montreal Toronto
Delhi Mexico City Sao Paulo Sydney Hong Kong Seoul Singapore Taipei Tokyo

Vice President, Business Publishing	Donna Battista	**Cover Photos**	FogStock/Alamy, Ingram Publishing/Alamy
Executive Acquisitions Editor	Adrienne D'Ambrosio		
Editorial Assistant	Courtney Turcotte	**Vice President, Director of Digital Strategy and Assessment**	Paul Gentile
Project Manager	Sarah Dumouchelle	**Manager of Learning Applications**	Paul DeLuca
Vice President, Product Marketing	Maggie Moylan	**Digital Editor**	Denise Clinton
Director of Marketing, Digital Services and Products	Jeanette Koskinas	**Director, Digital Studio**	Sacha Laustsen
Senior Product Marketing Manager	Alison Haskins	**Digital Studio Manager**	Diane Lombardo
Executive Field Marketing Manager	Lori DeShazo	**Digital Content Team Lead**	Noel Lotz
Senior Strategic Marketing Manager	Erin Gardner	**Digital Studio Project Manager**	Melissa Honig
Team Lead, Program Management	Ashley Santora	**Text Design, Project Management, and Page Make-up**	Integra Software Services, Inc.
Team Lead, Project Management	Jeff Holcomb	**Copyeditor**	Catherine Baum
Program Manager	Nancy Freihofer	**Technical Illustrator**	Richard Parkin
Supplements Project Manager	Andra Skaalrud	**Printer/Binder**	Courier Kendallville
Operations Specialist	Carol Melville	**Cover Printer**	Courier Kendallville
Cover Designer	Jonathan Boylan	**Text Font**	Adobe Garamond Pro

Library of Congress Cataloging-in-Publication Data

Parkin, Michael
  Economics/Michael Parkin.—Twelfth edition.
    pages cm.
  Includes bibliographical references and index.
  ISBN 978-0-13-387227-9
  1. Economics I. Title.
  HB171.5.P313 2016
  330—dc23

                      2014043488

10 9 8 7 6 5 4 3 2 1

ISBN 10:   0-13-387227-0
ISBN 13: 978-0-13-387227-9

TO ROBIN

Michael Parkin is Professor Emeritus in the Department of Economics at the University of Western Ontario, Canada. Professor Parkin has held faculty appointments at Brown University, the University of Manchester, the University of Essex, and Bond University. He is a past president of the Canadian Economics Association and has served on the editorial boards of the *American Economic Review* and the *Journal of Monetary Economics* and as managing editor of the *Canadian Journal of Economics*. Professor Parkin's research on macroeconomics, monetary economics, and international economics has resulted in over 160 publications in journals and edited volumes, including the *American Economic Review,* the *Journal of Political Economy,* the *Review of Economic Studies,* the *Journal of Monetary Economics,* and the *Journal of Money, Credit and Banking.* He became most visible to the public with his work on inflation that discredited the use of wage and price controls. Michael Parkin also spearheaded the movement toward European monetary union. Professor Parkin is an experienced and dedicated teacher of introductory economics.

BRIEF CONTENTS

PART ONE
INTRODUCTION 1

CHAPTER 1 What Is Economics? 1

CHAPTER 2 The Economic Problem 31

PART TWO
HOW MARKETS WORK 55

CHAPTER 3 Demand and Supply 55

CHAPTER 4 Elasticity 83

CHAPTER 5 Efficiency and Equity 105

CHAPTER 6 Government Actions in Markets 127

CHAPTER 7 Global Markets in Action 151

PART THREE
HOUSEHOLDS' CHOICES 177

CHAPTER 8 Utility and Demand 177

CHAPTER 9 Possibilities, Preferences, and Choices 201

PART FOUR
FIRMS AND MARKETS 223

CHAPTER 10 Organizing Production 223

CHAPTER 11 Output and Costs 247

CHAPTER 12 Perfect Competition 271

CHAPTER 13 Monopoly 297

CHAPTER 14 Monopolistic Competition 323

CHAPTER 15 Oligopoly 341

PART FIVE
MARKET FAILURE AND GOVERNMENT 369

CHAPTER 16 Public Choices, Public Goods, and Healthcare 369

CHAPTER 17 Externalities 391

PART SIX
FACTOR MARKETS, INEQUALITY, AND UNCERTAINTY 419

CHAPTER 18 Markets for Factors of Production 419

CHAPTER 19 Economic Inequality 445

CHAPTER 20 Uncertainty and Information 469

PART SEVEN
MONITORING MACROECONOMIC PERFORMANCE 491

CHAPTER 21 Measuring GDP and Economic Growth 491

CHAPTER 22 Monitoring Jobs and Inflation 515

PART EIGHT
MACROECONOMIC TRENDS 539

CHAPTER 23 Economic Growth 539

CHAPTER 24 Finance, Saving, and Investment 567

CHAPTER 25 Money, the Price Level, and Inflation 589

CHAPTER 26 The Exchange Rate and the Balance of Payments 619

PART NINE
MACROECONOMIC FLUCTUATIONS 649

CHAPTER 27 Aggregate Supply and Aggregate Demand 649

CHAPTER 28 Expenditure Multipliers 673

CHAPTER 29 The Business Cycle, Inflation, and Deflation 703

PART TEN
MACROECONOMIC POLICY 729

CHAPTER 30 Fiscal Policy 729

CHAPTER 31 Monetary Policy 757

Micro Flexibility

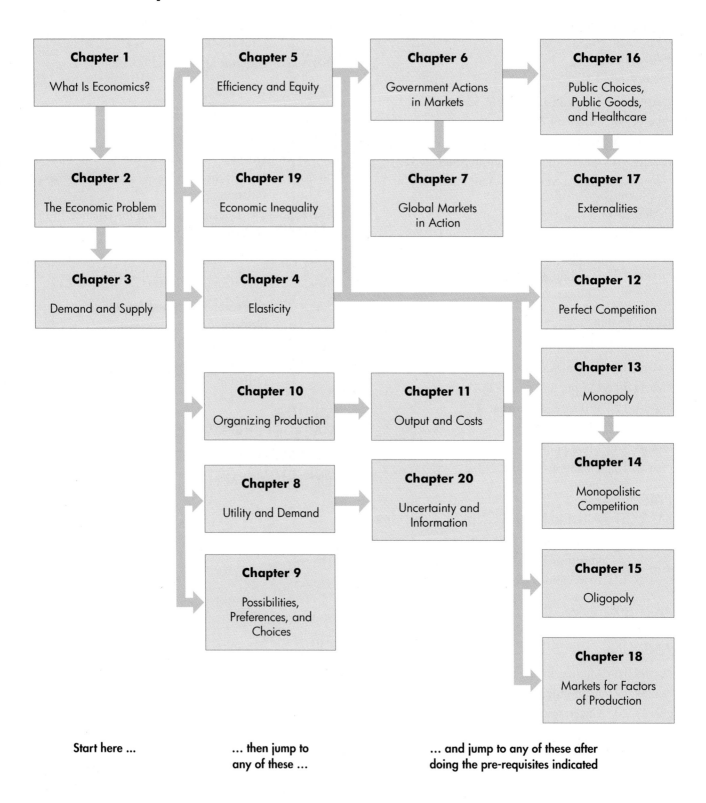

Chapter 1	Chapter 5	Chapter 6	Chapter 16
What Is Economics?	Efficiency and Equity	Government Actions in Markets	Public Choices, Public Goods, and Healthcare

Chapter 2	Chapter 19	Chapter 7	Chapter 17
The Economic Problem	Economic Inequality	Global Markets in Action	Externalities

Chapter 3	Chapter 4	Chapter 12
Demand and Supply	Elasticity	Perfect Competition

Chapter 13 — Monopoly

Chapter 10	Chapter 11
Organizing Production	Output and Costs

Chapter 14 — Monopolistic Competition

Chapter 8	Chapter 20
Utility and Demand	Uncertainty and Information

Chapter 15 — Oligopoly

Chapter 9 — Possibilities, Preferences, and Choices

Chapter 18 — Markets for Factors of Production

Start here ...   ... then jump to any of these ...   ... and jump to any of these after doing the pre-requisites indicated

Macro Flexibility

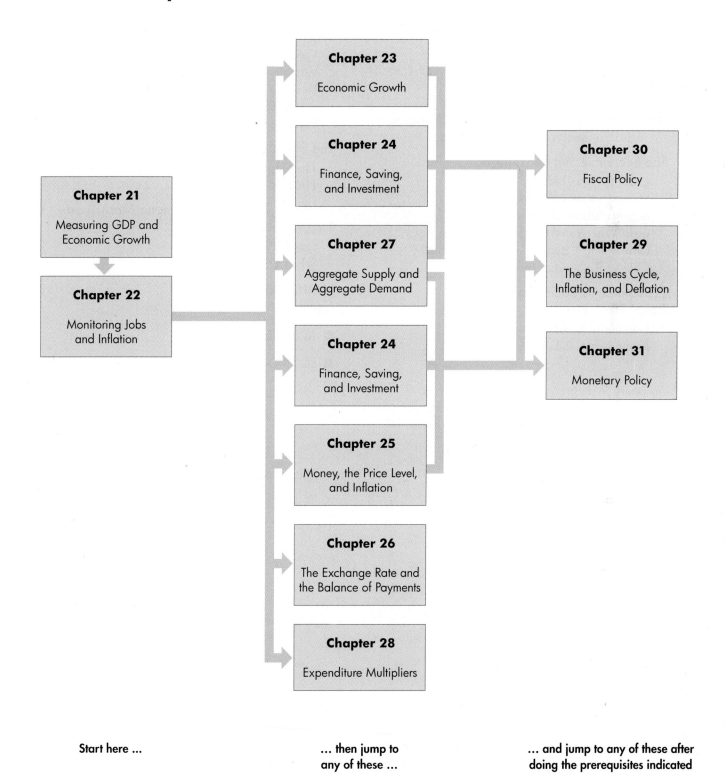

Chapter 23
Economic Growth

Chapter 24
Finance, Saving, and Investment

Chapter 27
Aggregate Supply and Aggregate Demand

Chapter 24
Finance, Saving, and Investment

Chapter 25
Money, the Price Level, and Inflation

Chapter 26
The Exchange Rate and the Balance of Payments

Chapter 28
Expenditure Multipliers

Chapter 21
Measuring GDP and Economic Growth

Chapter 22
Monitoring Jobs and Inflation

Chapter 30
Fiscal Policy

Chapter 29
The Business Cycle, Inflation, and Deflation

Chapter 31
Monetary Policy

Start here ...

... then jump to
any of these ...

... and jump to any of these after
doing the prerequisites indicated

DETAILED CONTENTS

PART ONE
INTRODUCTION 1

CHAPTER **1** ◆ **WHAT IS ECONOMICS?** 1

Definition of Economics 2

Two Big Economic Questions 3
    What, How, and For Whom? 3
    Do Choices Made in the Pursuit of Self-Interest
        also Promote the Social Interest? 5

The Economic Way of Thinking 9
    A Choice Is a Tradeoff 9
    Making a Rational Choice 9
    Benefit: What You Gain 9
    Cost: What You *Must* Give Up 9
    How Much? Choosing at the Margin 10
    Choices Respond to Incentives 10

Economics as Social Science and
Policy Tool 11
    Economist as Social Scientist 11
    Economist as Policy Adviser 11

Summary (Key Points and Key Terms), Worked
Problem, Study Plan Problems and Applications,
and Additional Problems and Applications appear
at the end of each chapter.

APPENDIX Graphs in Economics 15

Graphing Data 15
    Scatter Diagrams 16

Graphs Used in Economic Models 18
    Variables That Move in the Same Direction 18
    Variables That Move in Opposite Directions 19
    Variables That Have a Maximum
        or a Minimum 20
    Variables That Are Unrelated 21

The Slope of a Relationship 22
    The Slope of a Straight Line 22
    The Slope of a Curved Line 23

Graphing Relationships Among More Than
Two Variables 24
    Ceteris Paribus 24
    When Other Things Change 25

MATHEMATICAL NOTE
Equations of Straight Lines 26

■ AT ISSUE, 8

■ ECONOMICS IN THE NEWS, 6, 12

CHAPTER **2** ◆ **THE ECONOMIC PROBLEM** 31

Production Possibilities and Opportunity
Cost 32

Production Possibilities Frontier 32
  Production Efficiency 33
  Tradeoff Along the *PPF* 33
  Opportunity Cost 33

Using Resources Efficiently 35
  The *PPF* and Marginal Cost 35
  Preferences and Marginal Benefit 36
  Allocative Efficiency 37

Economic Growth 38
  The Cost of Economic Growth 38
  A Nation's Economic Growth 39

Gains from Trade 40
  Comparative Advantage and Absolute
    Advantage 40
  Achieving the Gains from Trade 42

Economic Coordination 44
  Firms 44
  Markets 44
  Property Rights 44
  Money 44
  Circular Flows Through Markets 44
  Coordinating Decisions 45

■ ECONOMICS IN ACTION, 39

■ ECONOMICS IN THE NEWS, 34, 46

PART ONE **WRAP-UP** ◆

  Understanding the Scope of Economics
  Your Economic Revolution 53

  Talking with
  Esther Duflo 54

PART TWO
HOW MARKETS WORK 55

CHAPTER **3** ◆ **DEMAND AND SUPPLY** 55

Markets and Prices 56

Demand 57
  The Law of Demand 57
  Demand Curve and Demand Schedule 57
  A Change in Demand 58
  A Change in the Quantity Demanded Versus a
    Change in Demand 60

Supply 62
  The Law of Supply 62
  Supply Curve and Supply Schedule 62
  A Change in Supply 63
  A Change in the Quantity Supplied Versus
    a Change in Supply 64

Market Equilibrium 66
  Price as a Regulator 66
  Price Adjustments 67

Predicting Changes in Price and Quantity 68
  An Increase in Demand 68
  A Decrease in Demand 68
  An Increase in Supply 70
  A Decrease in Supply 70
  Changes in Both Demand and Supply 72

MATHEMATICAL NOTE
Demand, Supply, and Equilibrium 76

■ ECONOMICS IN THE NEWS, 69, 71, 74

CHAPTER 4 ◆ ELASTICITY 83

Price Elasticity of Demand 84
Calculating Price Elasticity of Demand 84
Inelastic and Elastic Demand 85
The Factors that Influence the Elasticity of Demand 86
Elasticity Along a Linear Demand Curve 87
Total Revenue and Elasticity 88
Your Expenditure and Your Elasticity 90

More Elasticities of Demand 91
Income Elasticity of Demand 91
Cross Elasticity of Demand 92

Elasticity of Supply 94
Calculating the Elasticity of Supply 94
The Factors That Influence the Elasticity of Supply 95

■ ECONOMICS IN ACTION, 89, 91, 92

■ ECONOMICS IN THE NEWS, 90, 93, 98

CHAPTER 5 ◆ EFFICIENCY AND EQUITY 105

Resource Allocation Methods 106
Market Price 106
Command 106
Majority Rule 106
Contest 106
First-Come, First-Served 106
Lottery 107
Personal Characteristics 107
Force 107

Benefit, Cost, and Surplus 108
Demand, Willingness to Pay, and Value 108
Individual Demand and Market Demand 108
Consumer Surplus 109
Supply and Marginal Cost 109
Supply, Cost, and Minimum Supply-Price 110
Individual Supply and Market Supply 110
Producer Surplus 111

Is the Competitive Market Efficient? 112
Efficiency of Competitive Equilibrium 112
Market Failure 114
Sources of Market Failure 114
Alternatives to the Market 115

Is the Competitive Market Fair? 116
It's Not Fair if the *Result* Isn't Fair 116
It's Not Fair if the *Rules* Aren't Fair 118
Case Study: A Generator Shortage in a Natural Disaster 118

■ ECONOMICS IN ACTION, 113

■ AT ISSUE, 119

■ ECONOMICS IN THE NEWS, 120

CHAPTER 6 ◆ GOVERNMENT ACTIONS IN MARKETS 127

A Housing Market with a Rent Ceiling 128
A Housing Shortage 128
Increased Search Activity 128
A Black Market 128
Inefficiency of a Rent Ceiling 129
Are Rent Ceilings Fair? 130

A Labor Market with a Minimum Wage 131
Minimum Wage Brings Unemployment 131
Is the Minimum Wage Fair? 131
Inefficiency of a Minimum Wage 132

Taxes 133
Tax Incidence 133
A Tax on Sellers 133
A Tax on Buyers 134
Equivalence of Tax on Buyers and Sellers 134
Tax Incidence and Elasticity of Demand 135
Tax Incidence and Elasticity of Supply 136
Taxes and Efficiency 137
Taxes and Fairness 138

Production Quotas and Subsidies 139
Production Quotas 139
Subsidies 140

Markets for Illegal Goods 142
A Free Market for a Drug 142
A Market for an Illegal Drug 142
Legalizing and Taxing Drugs 143

■ ECONOMICS IN ACTION, 130, 138, 141

■ AT ISSUE, 132

■ ECONOMICS IN THE NEWS, 144

CHAPTER 7 ◆ GLOBAL MARKETS IN ACTION 151

How Global Markets Work 152
International Trade Today 152
What Drives International Trade? 152
Why the United States Imports T-Shirts 153
Why the United States Exports Airplanes 154

Winners, Losers, and the Net Gain from Trade 155
Gains and Losses from Imports 155
Gains and Losses from Exports 156
Gains for All 156

International Trade Restrictions 157
Tariffs 157
Import Quotas 160
Other Import Barriers 163
Export Subsidies 163

The Case Against Protection 164
Helps an Infant Industry Grow 164
Counteracts Dumping 164
Saves Domestic Jobs 164
Allows Us to Compete with Cheap Foreign Labor 164
Penalizes Lax Environmental Standards 165
Prevents Rich Countries from Exploiting Developing Countries 165
Reduces Offshore Outsourcing that Sends Good U.S. Jobs to Other Countries 165
Avoiding Trade Wars 166
Why Is International Trade Restricted? 166
Compensating Losers 167

■ ECONOMICS IN ACTION, 152, 158, 163

■ AT ISSUE, 166

■ ECONOMICS IN THE NEWS, 162, 168

PART TWO WRAP-UP ◆

Understanding How Markets Work
The Amazing Market 175

Talking with
Susan Athey 176

PART THREE
HOUSEHOLDS' CHOICES 177

CHAPTER 8 ◆ UTILITY AND DEMAND   177

Consumption Choices   178
Consumption Possibilities   178
Preferences   179

Utility-Maximizing Choice   181
A Spreadsheet Solution   181
Choosing at the Margin   182
The Power of Marginal Analysis   184
Revealing Preferences   184

Predictions of Marginal Utility Theory   185
A Fall in the Price of a Movie   185
A Rise in the Price of Soda   187
A Rise in Income   188
The Paradox of Value   189
Temperature: An Analogy   190

New Ways of Explaining Consumer Choices   192
Behavioral Economics   192
Neuroeconomics   193
Controversy   193

■ ECONOMICS IN ACTION, 190

■ ECONOMICS IN THE NEWS, 194

CHAPTER 9 ◆ POSSIBILITIES, PREFERENCES, AND CHOICES   201

Consumption Possibilities   202
Budget Line   202
Budget Equation   203

Preferences and Indifference Curves   205
Marginal Rate of Substitution   206
Degree of Substitutability   207

Predicting Consumer Choices   208
Best Affordable Choice   208
A Change in Price   209
A Change in Income   211
Substitution Effect and Income Effect   212

■ ECONOMICS IN ACTION, 210

■ ECONOMICS IN THE NEWS, 214

PART THREE WRAP-UP ◆

Understanding Households' Choices
Making the Most of Life   221

Talking with
Steven D. Levitt   222

PART FOUR
FIRMS AND MARKETS 223

CHAPTER **10** ◆ ORGANIZING PRODUCTION 223

The Firm and Its Economic Problem 224
  The Firm's Goal 224
  Accounting Profit 224
  Economic Accounting 224
  A Firm's Opportunity Cost of Production 224
  Economic Accounting: A Summary 225
  The Firm's Decisions 225
  The Firm's Constraints 226

Technological and Economic Efficiency 227
  Technological Efficiency 227
  Economic Efficiency 227

Information and Organization 229
  Command Systems 229
  Incentive Systems 229
  The Principal–Agent Problem 229
  Coping with the Principal–Agent Problem 229
  Types of Business Organization 230
  Pros and Cons of Different Types of Firms 231

Markets and the Competitive Environment 233
  Measures of Concentration 234
  Limitations of a Concentration Measure 236

Produce or Outsource? Firms and Markets 238
  Firm Coordination 238
  Market Coordination 238
  Why Firms? 238

■ ECONOMICS IN ACTION, 232, 235, 237, 239

■ ECONOMICS IN THE NEWS, 230, 240

CHAPTER **11** ◆ OUTPUT AND COSTS 247

Decision Time Frames 248
  The Short Run 248
  The Long Run 248

Short-Run Technology Constraint 249
  Product Schedules 249
  Product Curves 249
  Total Product Curve 250
  Marginal Product Curve 250
  Average Product Curve 252

Short-Run Cost 253
  Total Cost 253
  Marginal Cost 254
  Average Cost 254
  Marginal Cost and Average Cost 254
  Why the Average Total Cost Curve Is U-Shaped 254
  Cost Curves and Product Curves 256
  Shifts in the Cost Curves 258

Long-Run Cost 260
  The Production Function 260
  Short-Run Cost and Long-Run Cost 260
  The Long-Run Average Cost Curve 262
  Economies and Diseconomies of Scale 262

■ ECONOMICS IN ACTION, 252, 263

■ ECONOMICS IN THE NEWS, 256, 264

CHAPTER **12** ◆ **PERFECT COMPETITION**   271

What Is Perfect Competition?   272
How Perfect Competition Arises   272
Price Takers   272
Economic Profit and Revenue   272
The Firm's Decisions   273

The Firm's Output Decision   274
Marginal Analysis and the Supply Decision   275
Temporary Shutdown Decision   276
The Firm's Supply Curve   277

Output, Price, and Profit in the Short Run   278
Market Supply in the Short Run   278
Short-Run Equilibrium   279
A Change in Demand   279
Profits and Losses in the Short Run   279
Three Possible Short-Run Outcomes   280

Output, Price, and Profit in the Long Run   281
Entry and Exit   281
A Closer Look at Entry   282
A Closer Look at Exit   282
Long-Run Equilibrium   283

Changes in Demand and Supply as Technology Advances   284
An Increase in Demand   284
A Decrease in Demand   285
Technological Advances Change Supply   286

Competition and Efficiency   288
Efficient Use of Resources   288
Choices, Equilibrium, and Efficiency   288

■ ECONOMICS IN ACTION, 281, 283

■ ECONOMICS IN THE NEWS, 285, 287, 290

CHAPTER **13** ◆ **MONOPOLY**   297

Monopoly and How It Arises   298
How Monopoly Arises   298
Monopoly Price-Setting Strategies   299

A Single-Price Monopoly's Output and Price Decision   300
Price and Marginal Revenue   300
Marginal Revenue and Elasticity   301
Price and Output Decision   302

Single-Price Monopoly and Competition Compared   304
Comparing Price and Output   304
Efficiency Comparison   305
Redistribution of Surpluses   306
Rent Seeking   306
Rent-Seeking Equilibrium   306

Price Discrimination   307
Two Ways of Price Discriminating   307
Increasing Profit and Producer Surplus   308
A Price-Discriminating Airline   308
Efficiency and Rent Seeking with Price Discrimination   311

Monopoly Regulation   313
Efficient Regulation of a Natural Monopoly   313
Second-Best Regulation of a Natural Monopoly   314

■ ECONOMICS IN ACTION, 299, 311

■ ECONOMICS IN THE NEWS, 312, 316

CHAPTER **14** ◆ MONOPOLISTIC
               COMPETITION   323

What Is Monopolistic Competition?   324
    Large Number of Firms   324
    Product Differentiation   324
    Competing on Quality, Price, and
        Marketing   324
    Entry and Exit   325
    Examples of Monopolistic Competition   325

Price and Output in Monopolistic
Competition   326
    The Firm's Short-Run Output and Price
        Decision   326
    Profit Maximizing Might Be Loss
        Minimizing   326
    Long Run: Zero Economic Profit   327
    Monopolistic Competition and Perfect
        Competition   328
    Is Monopolistic Competition Efficient?   329

Product Development and Marketing   330
    Product Development   330
    Advertising   330
    Using Advertising to Signal Quality   332
    Brand Names   333
    Efficiency of Advertising and Brand Names   333

■ ECONOMICS IN ACTION, 325, 331

■ ECONOMICS IN THE NEWS, 334

CHAPTER **15** ◆ OLIGOPOLY   341

What Is Oligopoly?   342
    Barriers to Entry   342
    Small Number of Firms   343
    Examples of Oligopoly   343

Oligopoly Games   344
    What Is a Game?   344
    The Prisoners' Dilemma   344
    An Oligopoly Price-Fixing Game   346
    A Game of Chicken   351

Repeated Games and Sequential Games   352
    A Repeated Duopoly Game   352
    A Sequential Entry Game in a Contestable
        Market   354

Antitrust Law   356
    The Antitrust Laws   356
    Price Fixing Always Illegal   357
    Three Antitrust Policy Debates   357
    Mergers and Acquisitions   359

■ ECONOMICS IN ACTION, 343, 350, 358, 359

■ ECONOMICS IN THE NEWS, 353, 360

PART FOUR **WRAP-UP** ◆

Understanding Firms and Markets
Managing Change and Limiting Market
Power   367

Talking with
Thomas Hubbard   368

PART FIVE
MARKET FAILURE AND GOVERNMENT 369

CHAPTER **16** ◆ **PUBLIC CHOICES,
PUBLIC GOODS, AND
HEALTHCARE** 369

Public Choices 370
  Why Governments? 370
  Public Choice and the Political Marketplace 370
  Political Equilibrium 371
  What Is a Public Good? 372
  A Fourfold Classification 372
  The Things Our Governments Buy 372

Providing Public Goods 374
  The Free-Rider Problem 374
  Marginal Social Benefit from a Public Good 374
  Marginal Social Cost of a Public Good 375
  Efficient Quantity of a Public Good 375
  Inefficient Private Provision 375
  Efficient Public Provision 375
  Inefficient Public Overprovision 377

The Economics of Healthcare 378
  Healthcare Market Failure 378
  Alternative Public Choice Solutions 379
  Vouchers a Better Solution? 383

■ ECONOMICS IN ACTION, 370, 373, 376,
   379, 381

■ AT ISSUE, 382

■ ECONOMICS IN THE NEWS, 384

CHAPTER **17** ◆ **EXTERNALITIES** 391

Externalities In Our Lives 392
  Negative Production Externalities 392
  Positive Production Externalities 392
  Negative Consumption Externalities 392
  Positive Consumption Externalities 392

Negative Externality: Pollution 394
  Private, External, and Social Cost 394
  Establish Property Rights 395
  Mandate Clean Technology 396
  Tax or Cap and Price Pollution 397
  Coping with Global Externalities 400

Negative Externality: The Tragedy of the
Commons 401
  Unsustainable Use of a Common Resource 401
  Inefficient Use of a Common Resource 402
  Achieving an Efficient Outcome 404

Positive Externality: Knowledge 406
  Private Benefits and Social Benefits 406
  Government Actions in the Market with External
    Benefits 407
  Illustrating an Efficient Outcome 407
  Bureaucratic Inefficiency and Government
    Failure 408

■ ECONOMICS IN ACTION, 393, 398, 400,
   403, 405, 409

■ AT ISSUE, 399

■ ECONOMICS IN THE NEWS, 410

PART FIVE WRAP-UP ◆

Understanding Market Failure
and Government
We, the People, ... 417

Talking with
Caroline M. Hoxby 418

PART SIX
FACTOR MARKETS, INEQUALITY, AND UNCERTAINTY 419

CHAPTER 18 ◆ MARKETS FOR FACTORS OF PRODUCTION 419

The Anatomy of Factor Markets 420
  Markets for Labor Services 420
  Markets for Capital Services 420
  Markets for Land Services and Natural Resources 420
  Entrepreneurship 420

The Demand for a Factor of Production 421
  Value of Marginal Product 421
  A Firm's Demand for Labor 421
  A Firm's Demand for Labor Curve 422
  Changes in a Firm's Demand for Labor 423

Labor Markets 424
  A Competitive Labor Market 424
  Differences and Trends in Wage Rates 426
  A Labor Market with a Union 428

Capital and Natural Resource Markets 432
  Capital Rental Markets 432
  Land Rental Markets 432
  Nonrenewable Natural Resource Markets 433

MATHEMATICAL NOTE
Present Value and Discounting 438

■ ECONOMICS IN ACTION, 426, 435

■ AT ISSUE, 430

■ ECONOMICS IN THE NEWS, 427, 436

CHAPTER 19 ◆ ECONOMIC INEQUALITY 445

Economic Inequality in the United States 446
  The Distribution of Income 446
  The Income Lorenz Curve 447
  The Distribution of Wealth 448
  Wealth or Income? 448
  Annual or Lifetime Income and Wealth? 449
  Trends in Inequality 449
  Poverty 451

Inequality in the World Economy 453
  Income Distributions in Selected Countries 453
  Global Inequality and Its Trends 454

The Sources of Economic Inequality 455
  Human Capital 455
  Discrimination 456
  Contests Among Superstars 457
  Unequal Wealth 458

Income Redistribution 459
  Income Taxes 459
  Income Maintenance Programs 459
  Subsidized Services 459
  The Big Tradeoff 460

■ ECONOMICS IN ACTION, 450, 452, 460

■ ECONOMICS IN THE NEWS, 462

CHAPTER **20** ◆ UNCERTAINTY AND
                  INFORMATION 469

Decisions in the Face of Uncertainty 470
  Expected Wealth 470
  Risk Aversion 470
  Utility of Wealth 470
  Expected Utility 471
  Making a Choice with Uncertainty 472

Buying and Selling Risk 473
  Insurance Markets 473
  A Graphical Analysis of Insurance 474
  Risk That Can't Be Insured 475

Private Information 476
  Asymmetric Information: Examples and
    Problems 476
  The Market for Used Cars 476
  The Market for Loans 479
  The Market for Insurance 480

Uncertainty, Information, and the Invisible
Hand 481
  Information as a Good 481
  Monopoly in Markets that Cope with
    Uncertainty 481

■ ECONOMICS IN ACTION, 475, 480

■ ECONOMICS IN THE NEWS, 482

PART SIX **WRAP-UP** ◆

  Understanding Factor Markets, Inequality,
  and Uncertainty
  For Whom? 489

  Talking with
  Raj Chetty 490

PART SEVEN
MONITORING MACROECONOMIC
PERFORMANCE 491

CHAPTER **21** ◆ MEASURING GDP AND
                  ECONOMIC GROWTH 491

Gross Domestic Product 492
  GDP Defined 492
  GDP and the Circular Flow of Expenditure
    and Income 492
  Why "Domestic" and Why "Gross"? 494

Measuring U.S. GDP 495
  The Expenditure Approach 495
  The Income Approach 496
  Nominal GDP and Real GDP 497
  Calculating Real GDP 497

The Uses and Limitations of Real GDP 498
  The Standard of Living Over Time 498
  The Standard of Living Across Countries 500
  Limitations of Real GDP 501

APPENDIX Graphs in Macroeconomics 506

The Time-Series Graph 506
  Making a Time-Series Graph 506
  Reading a Time-Series Graph 506
  Ratio Scale Reveals Trend 507
  A Time-Series with a Trend 507
  Using a Ratio Scale 507

MATHEMATICAL NOTE
Chained-Dollar Real GDP 508

■ ECONOMICS IN ACTION, 503

■ AT ISSUE, 502

■ ECONOMICS IN THE NEWS, 504

CHAPTER **22** ◆ MONITORING JOBS
                 AND INFLATION 515

Employment and Unemployment 516
Why Unemployment Is a Problem 516
Current Population Survey 517
Three Labor Market Indicators 517
Other Definitions of Unemployment 519
Most Costly Unemployment 520
Alternative Measures of Unemployment 520

Unemployment and Full Employment 521
Frictional Unemployment 521
Structural Unemployment 521
Cyclical Unemployment 521
"Natural" Unemployment 521
Real GDP and Unemployment Over
  the Cycle 522

The Price Level, Inflation, and Deflation 524
Why Inflation and Deflation are Problems 524
The Consumer Price Index 525
Reading the CPI Numbers 525
Constructing the CPI 525
Measuring the Inflation Rate 526
Distinguishing High Inflation from a High
  Price Level 527
The Biased CPI 527
The Magnitude of the Bias 528
Some Consequences of the Bias 528
Alternative Price Indexes 528
Core Inflation 529
The Real Variables in Macroeconomics 529

■ ECONOMICS IN ACTION, 516, 522

■ ECONOMICS IN THE NEWS, 530

PART SEVEN **WRAP-UP** ◆

Monitoring Macroeconomic Performance
The Big Picture 537

Talking with
Richard Clarida 538

PART EIGHT
MACROECONOMIC TRENDS 539

CHAPTER **23** ◆ ECONOMIC GROWTH 539

The Basics of Economic Growth 540
Calculating Growth Rates 540
Economic Growth Versus Business Cycle
  Expansion 540
The Magic of Sustained Growth 541
Applying the Rule of 70 542

Long-Term Growth Trends 543
Long-Term Growth in the U.S. Economy 543
Real GDP Growth in the World Economy 544

How Potential GDP Grows 546
What Determines Potential GDP? 546
What Makes Potential GDP Grow? 548

Why Labor Productivity Grows 551
Preconditions for Labor Productivity
  Growth 551
Physical Capital Growth 551
Human Capital Growth 552
Technological Advances 552

**Is Economic Growth Sustainable? Theories,
Evidence, and Policies** 555
Classical Growth Theory 555
Neoclassical Growth Theory 555
New Growth Theory 556
New Growth Theory Versus Malthusian
  Theory 558
Sorting Out the Theories 558
The Empirical Evidence on the Causes of
  Economic Growth 558
Policies for Achieving Faster Growth 558

■ ECONOMICS IN ACTION, 545, 552, 553

■ ECONOMICS IN THE NEWS, 554, 560

CHAPTER **24** ◆ FINANCE, SAVING, AND
                  INVESTMENT 567

Financial Institutions and Financial
Markets 568
  Finance and Money 568
  Capital and Financial Capital 568
  Capital and Investment 568
  Wealth and Saving 568
  Financial Capital Markets 569
  Financial Institutions 570
  Insolvency and Illiquidity 572
  Interest Rates and Asset Prices 572

The Loanable Funds Market 573
  Funds that Finance Investment 573
  The Real Interest Rate 574
  The Demand for Loanable Funds 575
  The Supply of Loanable Funds 576
  Equilibrium in the Loanable Funds Market 577
  Changes in Demand and Supply 577

Government in the Loanable Funds
Market 580
  A Government Budget Surplus 580
  A Government Budget Deficit 580

■ ECONOMICS IN ACTION, 570, 574, 575, 578

■ ECONOMICS IN THE NEWS, 582

CHAPTER **25** ◆ MONEY, THE PRICE LEVEL,
                  AND INFLATION 589

What Is Money? 590
  Medium of Exchange 590
  Unit of Account 590
  Store of Value 591
  Money in the United States Today 591

Depository Institutions 593
  Types of Depository Institutions 593
  What Depository Institutions Do 593
  Economic Benefits Provided by Depository
    Institutions 594
  How Depository Institutions Are Regulated 594
  Financial Innovation 596

The Federal Reserve System 597
  The Structure of the Fed 597
  The Fed's Balance Sheet 598
  The Fed's Policy Tools 598

How Banks Create Money 600
  Creating Deposits by Making Loans 600
  The Money Creation Process 601
  The Money Multiplier 602

The Money Market 604
  The Influences on Money Holding 604
  The Demand for Money 605
  Shifts in the Demand for Money Curve 605
  Money Market Equilibrium 606

The Quantity Theory of Money 608

MATHEMATICAL NOTE
The Money Multiplier 612

■ ECONOMICS IN ACTION, 591, 596, 599,
  602, 608

■ AT ISSUE, 595

■ ECONOMICS IN THE NEWS, 603, 610

CHAPTER **26** ◆ **THE EXCHANGE RATE AND THE BALANCE OF PAYMENTS** 619

The Foreign Exchange Market 620
　Trading Currencies 620
　Exchange Rates 620
　Questions About the U.S. Dollar Exchange
　　Rate 620
　An Exchange Rate Is a Price 620
　The Demand for One Money Is the Supply
　　of Another Money 621
　Demand in the Foreign Exchange Market 621
　Demand Curve for U.S. Dollars 622
　Supply in the Foreign Exchange Market 623
　Supply Curve for U.S. Dollars 623
　Market Equilibrium 624
　Changes in the Demand for U.S. Dollars 624
　Changes in the Supply of U.S. Dollars 625
　Changes in the Exchange Rate 626

Arbitrage, Speculation, and Market
Fundamentals 628
　Arbitrage 628
　Speculation 629
　Market Fundamentals 630

Exchange Rate Policy 631
　Flexible Exchange Rate 631
　Fixed Exchange Rate 631
　Crawling Peg 632

Financing International Trade 634
　Balance of Payments Accounts 634
　Borrowers and Lenders 636
　The Global Loanable Funds Market 636
　Debtors and Creditors 637
　Is U.S. Borrowing for Consumption? 637
　Current Account Balance 638
　Net Exports 638
　Where Is the Exchange Rate? 639

■ ECONOMICS IN ACTION, 621, 627, 629,
632, 635, 639

■ ECONOMICS IN THE NEWS, 640

PART EIGHT **WRAP-UP** ◆

Understanding Macroeconomic Trends
Expanding the Frontier 647

Talking with
Xavier Sala-i-Martin 648

PART 9
MACROECONOMIC FLUCTUATIONS 649

CHAPTER **27** ◆ **AGGREGATE SUPPLY AND AGGREGATE DEMAND** 649

Aggregate Supply 650
　Quantity Supplied and Supply 650
　Long-Run Aggregate Supply 650
　Short-Run Aggregate Supply 651
　Changes in Aggregate Supply 652

Aggregate Demand 654
　The Aggregate Demand Curve 654
　Changes in Aggregate Demand 655

Explaining Macroeconomic Trends and
Fluctuations 658
　Short-Run Macroeconomic Equilibrium 658
　Long-Run Macroeconomic Equilibrium 658
　Economic Growth and Inflation in the *AS-AD*
　　Model 659
　The Business Cycle in the *AS-AD* Model 660
　Fluctuations in Aggregate Demand 662
　Fluctuations in Aggregate Supply 663

Macroeconomic Schools of Thought 664
　The Classical View 664
　The Keynesian View 664
　The Monetarist View 665
　The Way Ahead 665

■ ECONOMICS IN ACTION, 656, 659, 660

■ ECONOMICS IN THE NEWS, 666

CHAPTER **28** ◆ **EXPENDITURE MULTIPLIERS** 673

Fixed Prices and Expenditure Plans 674
Expenditure Plans 674
Consumption and Saving Plans 674
Marginal Propensities to Consume and Save 676
Slopes and Marginal Propensities 676
Consumption as a Function of Real GDP 677
Import Function 677

Real GDP with a Fixed Price Level 678
Aggregate Planned Expenditure 678
Actual Expenditure, Planned Expenditure, and Real GDP 679
Equilibrium Expenditure 680
Convergence to Equilibrium 681

The Multiplier 682
The Basic Idea of the Multiplier 682
The Multiplier Effect 682
Why Is the Multiplier Greater Than 1? 683
The Size of the Multiplier 683
The Multiplier and the Slope of the *AE* Curve 684
Imports and Income Taxes 685
The Multiplier Process 685
Business Cycle Turning Points 686

The Multiplier and the Price Level 687
Adjusting Quantities and Prices 687
Aggregate Expenditure and Aggregate Demand 687
Deriving the Aggregate Demand Curve 687
Changes in Aggregate Expenditure and Aggregate Demand 688
Equilibrium Real GDP and the Price Level 689

MATHEMATICAL NOTE
The Algebra of the Keynesian Model 694

■ ECONOMICS IN ACTION, 677, 686

■ ECONOMICS IN THE NEWS, 692

CHAPTER **29** ◆ **THE BUSINESS CYCLE, INFLATION, AND DEFLATION** 703

The Business Cycle 704
Mainstream Business Cycle Theory 704
Real Business Cycle Theory 705

Inflation Cycles 709
Demand-Pull Inflation 709
Cost-Push Inflation 711
Expected Inflation 713
Forecasting Inflation 714
Inflation and the Business Cycle 714

Deflation 715
What Causes Deflation? 715
What are the Consequences of Deflation? 717
How Can Deflation be Ended? 717

The Phillips Curve 718
The Short-Run Phillips Curve 718
The Long-Run Phillips Curve 718

■ ECONOMICS IN ACTION, 706, 716, 719

■ ECONOMICS IN THE NEWS, 720

PART NINE WRAP-UP ◆

Understanding Macroeconomic Fluctuations
Boom and Bust 727

Talking with
Ricardo J. Caballero 728

PART TEN
MACROECONOMIC POLICY 729

CHAPTER 30 ◆ FISCAL POLICY 729

The Federal Budget 730
The Institutions and Laws 730
Highlights of the 2015 Budget 731
The Budget in Historical Perspective 732
Budget Balance and Debt 734
State and Local Budgets 736

Supply-Side Effects of Fiscal Policy 737
Full Employment and Potential GDP 737
The Effects of the Income Tax 737
Taxes on Expenditure and the Tax Wedge 738
Taxes and the Incentive to Save and Invest 739
Tax Revenues and the Laffer Curve 741
The Supply-Side Debate 741

Generational Effects of Fiscal Policy 742
Generational Accounting and Present Value 742
The Social Security Time Bomb 742
Generational Imbalance 743
International Debt 743

Fiscal Stimulus 744
Automatic Fiscal Policy and Cyclical and
    Structural Budget Balances 744
Discretionary Fiscal Stimulus 747

■ ECONOMICS IN ACTION, 736, 738, 746, 748

■ AT ISSUE, 735

■ ECONOMICS IN THE NEWS, 740, 750

CHAPTER 31 ◆ MONETARY POLICY 757

Monetary Policy Objectives and Framework 758
Monetary Policy Objectives 758
Operational "Stable Prices" Goal 759
Operational "Maximum Employment" Goal 759
Responsibility for Monetary Policy 760

The Conduct of Monetary Policy 760
The Monetary Policy Instrument 760
The Fed's Decision-Making Strategy 761

Monetary Policy Transmission 763
Quick Overview 763
Interest Rate Changes 763
Exchange Rate Fluctuations 764
Money and Bank Loans 765
The Long-Term Real Interest Rate 765
Expenditure Plans 765
The Change in Aggregate Demand, Real GDP,
    and the Price Level 766
The Fed Fights Recession 766
The Fed Fights Inflation 768
Loose Links and Long and Variable Lags 769

Extraordinary Monetary Stimulus 772
The Key Elements of the Crisis 772
The Policy Actions 773
Persistently Slow Recovery 773
Policy Strategies and Clarity 775

■ ECONOMICS IN ACTION, 762, 771, 775

■ AT ISSUE, 774

■ ECONOMICS IN THE NEWS, 770, 776

PART TEN WRAP-UP ◆

Understanding Macroeconomic Policy
Tradeoffs and Free Lunches 783

Talking with
Stephanie Schmitt-Grohé 784

Glossary **G-1**
Index **I-1**
Credits **C-1**

The future is always uncertain. But at some times, and now is one such time, the range of possible near-future events is unusually large. Political tensions in the Middle East and Eastern Europe are one source of this uncertainty. But economic policy is another source. There is uncertainty about the way in which international trade policy will evolve as bilateral deals reshape the competitive landscape. There is uncertainty about exchange rate policy as currency fluctuations bring changes in international relative prices. There is extraordinary uncertainty about monetary policy with the Fed having quadrupled the quantity of bank reserves and continuing to delay the return of interest rates to levels considered normal. And there is uncertainty about fiscal policy as an ongoing federal budget deficit interacts with an aging population and rising healthcare costs to create a national debt time bomb.

In the years since the subprime mortgage crisis of August 2007 moved economics from the business report to the front page, a justified fall in confidence has gripped producers, consumers, financial institutions, and governments.

Even the idea that the market is an efficient allocation mechanism has come into question. Many thoughtful people worry about rising income inequality, and some political leaders called for the end of capitalism and the dawn of a new economic order in which tighter regulation reins in unfettered greed.

Rarely do teachers of economics have such a rich feast on which to draw. And rarely are the principles of economics more surely needed to provide the solid foundation on which to think about economic events and navigate the turbulence of economic life.

Although thinking like an economist can bring a clearer perspective to and deeper understanding of today's events, students don't find the economic way of thinking easy or natural. *Economics* seeks to put clarity and understanding in the grasp of the student with a careful and vivid exploration of the tension between self-interest and the social interest, the role and power of incentives—of opportunity cost and marginal benefit—and demonstrating the possibility that markets supplemented by other mechanisms might allocate resources efficiently.

Parkin students begin to think about issues the way real economists do and learn how to explore difficult policy problems and make more informed decisions in their own economic lives.

◆ The Twelfth Edition Revision

Thoroughly updated, intuitive rather than technical, grounded in data and empirical evidence, extensively illustrated with well-chosen examples and photographs, enlivened with applications that focus on issues at play in today's world, focused on learning-by-doing, and seamlessly integrated with MyEconLab: These are the hallmarks of this twelfth edition of *Economics*.

This revision builds on the foundation of the previous edition and retains a thorough and careful presentation of the principles of economics, an emphasis on real-world examples and applications, the development of critical thinking skills, diagrams renowned for pedagogy and clarity, and path-breaking technology.

Highpoints of the Text Revision

This revision has many detailed changes and responses to reviewers, but its highpoints are a new feature and five content changes.

The new feature is a full-page end-of-chapter **worked problem**. As part of the chapter review, the student has an opportunity to work a multi-part problem that covers the core content of the chapter and consists of questions, solutions, and key figures. This new feature increases the incentive for the student to learn-by-doing and actively, rather than passively, review the chapter.

The five main content changes are in the coverage of

- Healthcare
- Externalities
- Financial markets
- The exchange rate
- Cycles, inflation, and deflation

Healthcare A reorganized and renamed Chapter 16, Public Choices, Public Goods, and Healthcare, opens with a new discussion of public choices and the political marketplace and the reasons why healthcare features so prominently in public choices. It presents a revealing pie chart of the allocation of government expenditures, one third of which is on healthcare programs. A new major section on the economics of healthcare describes the healthcare markets, the reasons why they fail, the alternative public choice solutions, the efficiency and equity issues they raise, and the U.S. and international experience. An *At Issue* box looks at Obamacare and one of its critics.

Externalities A reorganized Chapter 17 brings together all the material on externalities (both negative and positive). A major section on negative externalities describes and analyzes the problem of carbon emission and climate change and includes an account of the prisoners' dilemma that arises in coping with global externalities. The chapter includes an *Economics in the News* on the idea of lowering carbon emissions by generating more electricity from gas and less from coal and an *At Issue* on the carbon debate.

Financial Markets Chapter 24, Finance, Saving, and Investment, has an expanded section on the global financial crisis and its aftermath that describes the growth of household debt and house prices. The section on real and nominal interest rates is expanded and illustrated with data. The chapter now contains more on the magnitudes of the sources and uses of loanable funds. The section on loanable funds in the global economy is moved to the chapter on the exchange rate and balance of payments.

The Exchange Rate Chapter 26, The Exchange Rate and the Balance of Payments, contains a heavily revised section entitled Arbitrage, Speculation, and Market Fundamentals that explains the powerful forces that equilibrate the foreign exchange market in the short run and the long run. This section includes a discussion of the Big Mac index. An *Economics in the News* examines the forces at work leading to a strong dollar in the summer of 2014. The section on the global loanable funds market is now integrated into this chapter in the section on the balance of payments.

Cycles, Inflation, and Deflation Chapter 29, The Business Cycle, Inflation, and Deflation, is re-titled, reorganized, and amended. The business cycle material is moved to the beginning of the chapter and a new final section describes and explains the problem of deflation that has gripped Japan for most of the 1990s and the 2000s and is feared in Europe at the present time. Coverage of the Phillips curve is retained but condensed.

Many other chapters have been thoroughly reworked to achieve even greater clarity and to place greater emphasis on applications to current issues. And every chapter now contains a new opening vignette linked directly to an *Economics in the News*, an end-of-chapter problem, and online practice.

All the end-of-chapter *Economics in the News* articles have been updated, and the analysis of the news and the linked problems and applications have been appropriately revised.

Enhanced Pearson eText and New Interactive Features

MyEconLab with Enhanced eText combines digital resources that illuminate content with accessible self-assessment tools to provide students with a comprehensive learning experience—all in one place.

The Enhanced eText's digital resources include animations of figures that bring learning to life, interactive graph drawing exercises, problem solving tools, and news applications.

The results of all the activities in the Enhanced eText feed into the MyEconLab Adaptive Study Plan, which provides an exceptional adaptive learning experience uniquely tailored to the learning challenges of each individual student.

This powerful digital resource enables students to actively use the concepts they're reading about and, through learning-by-doing, achieve deeper understanding of the key economic principles.

 Features to Enhance Teaching and Learning

The changes that I have described are adjustments to an already powerful teaching and learning package. Here, I briefly review the features retained from the previous edition.

Economics in the News

This Parkin hallmark helps students think like economists by connecting chapter tools and concepts to the world around them. In this new edition, *Economics in the News* comes in two formats. One format, as in the previous edition, presents a brief newsclip supplemented by data where needed, and then poses some questions and walks through the answers.

The other format of *Economics in the News* is a rebranding of what I called *Reading Between the Lines* in all the earlier editions. This feature, which appears at the end of every chapter (except the first), shows students how to apply the tools they have learned by analyzing an article from a newspaper or news Web site. The news article connects with the questions first raised in the chapter opener, and the analysis is reinforced with a related end-of-chapter problem.

Diagrams That Show the Action

Through the past eleven editions, this book has set the standard of clarity in its diagrams; the twelfth edition continues to uphold this tradition. My goal is to show "where the economic action is." The diagrams in this book continue to generate an enormously positive response, which confirms my view that graphical analysis is the most powerful tool available for teaching and learning economics at the principles level.

Because many students find graphs hard to work with, I have developed the entire art program with the study and review needs of the student in mind.

The diagrams feature

- Original curves consistently shown in blue
- Shifted curves, equilibrium points, and other important features highlighted in red
- Color-blended arrows to suggest movement
- Graphs paired with data tables
- Diagrams labeled with boxed notes
- Extended captions that make each diagram and its caption a self-contained object for study and review

At Issue

Eleven *At Issue* boxes, three of which are new, engage the student in debate and controversy. An *At Issue* box introduces an issue and then presents two opposing views. It leaves the matter unsettled so that the student and instructor can continue the argument in class and reach their own conclusions.

Economics in Action Boxes

This feature uses boxes within the chapter to provide data and information that links models to real-world economic activity. Some of the issues covered in these boxes include the best affordable choice of recorded music, movies and DVDs; the cost of selling a pair of shoes; how Apple doesn't make the iPhone; opposing trends in air pollution and carbon concentration; structural unemployment in Michigan; how loanable funds fuel a home price bubble; and the size of the fiscal stimulus multipliers.

Chapter Openers

Each chapter opens with a student-friendly vignette that raises questions to motivate the student and focus the chapter. This chapter-opening story is woven into the main body of the chapter and is explored in the *Economics in the News* feature that ends each chapter.

Key Terms

Highlighted terms simplify the student's task of learning the vocabulary of economics. Each highlighted term appears in an end-of-chapter list with its page number, in an end-of-book glossary with its page number, boldfaced in the index, and in MyEconLab in the interactive glossary and the Flash Cards.

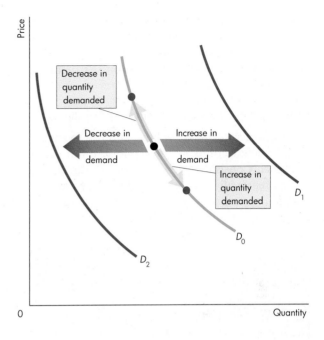

In-Text Review Quizzes

A review quiz at the end of each major section enables students to determine whether a topic needs further study before moving on. This feature includes a reference to the appropriate MyEconLab study plan and a new **Key Terms Quiz** to help students further test their understanding.

End-of-Chapter Study Material

Each chapter closes with a concise summary organized by major topics, a list of key terms with page references, a worked problem, and problems and applications. These learning tools provide students with a summary for review and exam preparation.

Interviews with Economists

Each part closes with an overview of the chapters and a teaser of an interview with a leading economist whose work correlates to what the student is learning. These interviews explore the education and research of these prominent economists and their advice for those who want to continue the study of economics. This edition has new interviews with Esther Duflo (MIT) and Raj Chetty (Harvard). The 65 past and present interviews I have conducted are available in full in MyEconLab.

For the Instructor

This book enables you to focus on the economic way of thinking and choose your own course structure in your principles course.

Focus on the Economic Way of Thinking

As an instructor, you know how hard it is to encourage a student to think like an economist. But that is your goal. Consistent with this goal, the text focuses on and repeatedly uses the central ideas: choice; tradeoff; opportunity cost; the margin; incentives; the gains from voluntary exchange; the forces of demand, supply, and equilibrium; the pursuit of economic rent; the tension between self-interest and the social interest; and the scope and limitations of government actions.

Flexible Structure

You have preferences for how you want to teach your course, and I've organized this book to enable you to choose your teaching path. The charts on pp. vi and vii illustrate the book's flexibility. By following the arrows through the charts you can select the path that best fits your preference for course structure. Whether you want to teach a traditional course that blends theory and policy, or one that takes a fast-track through either theory or policy issues, *Economics* gives you the choice.

Instructor's Supplemental Resources

The supplements for instructors are

- Test Item Files
- PowerPoint Resources
- Instructor's Manuals
- Solutions Manuals

Test Item Files Six separate Test Item Files—three for *Microeconomics* and three for *Macroeconomics*—with nearly 13,000 questions, provide multiple-choice, true/false, numerical, fill-in-the-blank, short-answer, and essay questions. Mark Rush reviewed and edited all the questions to ensure their clarity and consistency.

New questions were written by Svitlana Maksymenko of the University of Pittsburgh, James K. Self of the University of Indiana, Bloomington, Alexandra Nica of the University of Iowa, and Luke Armstrong of Lee College.

Questions follow the style and format of the end-of-chapter text problems. End-of-part tests contain integrative questions that cover all the chapters in the part. News-based application questions are available for each chapter of the text.

Fully networkable and available for Windows® and Macintosh®, TestGen's graphical interface enables instructors to view the Test Item Files; edit and add questions; transfer questions to tests; and print different forms of tests. Tests can be formatted as in any word-processing document with varying fonts, styles, margins, headers, and footers. Search and sort features let the instructor quickly locate questions and arrange them in a preferred order. QuizMaster, working with your school's computer network, automatically grades exams, stores the results, and allows the instructor to view or print a variety of reports.

BlackBoard- and WebCT-ready conversions of the TestGen Test Item Files are available for download from www.pearsonhighered.com/irc.

PowerPoint Resources A set of full-color Microsoft® PowerPoint Presentations, created by Robin Bade, are available. Each chapter contains

- Lecture notes with all the textbook figures animated, tables from the textbook, and speaking notes from the Instructor's Manuals
- Large-scale versions of all the figures and tables in the textbook, animated for instructors to incorporate into their own slide shows
- A student version of the lecture notes with animated textbook figures

The presentations can be used electronically in the classroom or printed to create transparency masters.

Instructor's Manuals Instructor's Manuals, one for *Microeconomics* and one for *Macroeconomics*, integrate the teaching and learning resources and serve as a guide to all the supplements. Written by Laura A. Wolff of Southern Illinois University Edwardsville (microeconomics) and Russ McCullough of Ottawa University (macroeconomics), the Instructor's Manuals are available electronically from MyEconLab or the Instructor's Resource Center.

Each chapter contains an overview, a list of what's new in the twelfth edition, and ready-to-use lecture notes, which enable a new user of Parkin to walk into a classroom and deliver a polished lecture.

Solutions Manuals Comprehensive Solutions Manuals, one for *Microeconomics* and one for *Macroeconomics*, provide instructors with solutions to the Review Quizzes and the end-of-chapter Problems and Applications as well as additional problems and the solutions to these problems. Written by Mark Rush of the University of Florida and reviewed for accuracy by Jeannie Gillmore of the University of Western Ontario, the Solutions Manuals are available electronically from MyEconLab or the Instructor Resource Center.

Getting Your Instructor's Resources

Instructor's Resource Center Instructors can download supplements from a secure, instructor-only source via the Pearson Higher Education Instructor Resource Center Web page, which is found at (www.pearsonhighered.com/irc).

 ## MyEconLab

MyEconLab has been designed and refined with a single purpose in mind: to create those moments of understanding that transform the difficult into the clear and obvious. With comprehensive homework, quiz, test, activity, and tutorial options, instructors can manage all their assessment in one program.

- All of the Review Quiz questions and end-of-chapter Problems and Applications were recreated as assignable auto-graded exercises with targeted feedback and related "Help-me-solve-this" tools by Robin Bade, Jeannie Gillmore of the University of Western Ontario, and Sharmistha Nag of Fairleigh Dickinson University, and were reviewed for accuracy by Trevor Collier of the University of Dayton.
- All of the Review Quiz questions and end-of chapter Problems and Applications are assignable and automatically graded in MyEconLab.
- All of the Review Quiz questions and end-of-chapter Study Plan Problems and Applications are available for students to work in the Adaptive Study Plan.
- All the end-of-chapter Additional Problems and Applications are not available to students in MyEconLab unless assigned by the instructor.
- Many of the problems and applications are algorithmic, draw-graph, and numerical exercises.
- Problems and applications that use real-time data continuously update.
- All *Economics in the News* and Test Item questions are available for instructors to assign as test, quiz, or homework.
- Custom Exercise Builder enables instructors to create their own problems for assignment.
- Gradebook records each student's performance and time spent on the Tests and Study Plan and generates reports by student or by chapter.

Features of the Enhanced eText

The features of the enhanced eText are

- Embedded MyEconLab study plan and assessment
- Figure animations
- Interactive graph-drawing exercises
- More *Economics in the News*
- Worked problems
- Automatic real-time updating
- Key terms quizzes

Embedded MyEconLab Study Plan and Assessment Every Review Quiz question and Study Plan Problem and Application in the enhanced eText can be worked by the student directly from the eText page on which it occurs and receive instant targeted feedback. These exercises are auto-graded and feed into MyEconLab's Adaptive Study Plan, where students receive recommendations based upon their performance. Study Plan links provide opportunities for more practice with exercises similar to those in the eText and give targeted feedback to guide the student in answering the exercises.

Figure Animations Every textbook figure can be worked through using a step-by-step animation, with audio, to help students learn the intuition behind reading and interpreting graphs. These animations may be used for review, or as an instructional aid in the classroom.

Interactive Draw Graph Exercises For each major figure, a graph-drawing exercise accompanies the step-by-step animation. The student builds and interprets the key diagrams and develops understanding by working a multiple-choice question about the figure. Each Draw Graph exercise is auto-graded and feeds into MyEconLab's Adaptive Study Plan.

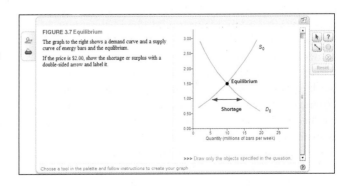

More Economics in the News Each in-text *Economics in the News* is reinforced through an extended application of the same analysis. More *Economics in the News* problems are auto-graded and feed into MyEconLab's Adaptive Study Plan.

Worked Problem Each chapter concludes with a Worked Problem that consists of questions, solutions, and a key figure. These problems can be worked in the enhanced eText directly from the Worked Problem page. As the student works through each problem, feedback and just-in-time learning aids help the student develop proficiency with the concept.

Automatic Real-Time Updating Figures labeled *MyEconLab Real-Time Data* update using the most recent data available from the FRED database maintained by the Federal Reserve Bank of St. Louis.

Key Terms Quiz Key Terms Quiz links provide opportunities for students to check their knowledge of the definitions and uses of the key terms.

Other MyEconLab Features

Adaptive Learning Study Plan Adaptive Learning Study Plan is powered by a sophisticated learning engine that tailors assessment material to the unique needs of each student. The Adaptive Learning Study Plan monitors the student's performance on homework, quizzes, and tests and continuously makes recommendations based on that performance.

If a student is struggling with a concept such as supply and demand, or having trouble calculating a price elasticity of demand, the Adaptive Learning Study Plan provides customized remediation activities—a pathway based on personal proficiencies, the number of attempts, or the difficulty of the questions—to get the student back on track. Students will also receive recommendations for additional practice in the form of rich multimedia learning aids such as videos, an interactive eText, Help Me Solve This tutorials, and graphing tools.

The Adaptive Learning Study Plan can extrapolate a student's future trouble spots and provide learning material and practice to avoid pitfalls. In addition, students who are showing a high degree of success with the assessment material are offered a chance to work on future topics based on the professor's course coverage preferences. This personalized and adaptive feedback and support ensures that your students are optimizing their current and future course work and mastering the concepts, rather than just memorizing and guessing answers.

Dynamic Study Modules The Dynamic Study Modules in MyEconLab engage the student in learning activities, continuously monitor and assess performance in real time, and by analyzing the data, personalize content to reinforce concepts that target each student's strengths and weaknesses. Instructors well-know that not every student learns the same way and at the same rate. And now, thanks to the advances in adaptive learning technology embedded in the Dynamic Study Modules, it is no longer necessary to teach as if they do.

Dynamic Study Modules can be set as homework and the results received right in the gradebook. And, because your students are always on the go, Dynamic Study Modules can be accessed from any computer, tablet, or smartphone.

Real-Time Data Analysis Exercises **FRED** Easy to assign and automatically graded, Real-Time Data Analysis exercises communicate directly with the Federal Reserve Bank of St. Louis's FRED site, so every time FRED posts new data, students can see the most recent data. As a result, Real-Time Data Analysis exercises offer a no-fuss solution for instructors who want to make the most recent data a central part of their macro course.

End-of-chapter exercises accompanied by the Real-Time Data Analysis icon include Real-Time Data versions in MyEconLab. Select in-text figures, labeled Real-time data, update in the eText using FRED data.

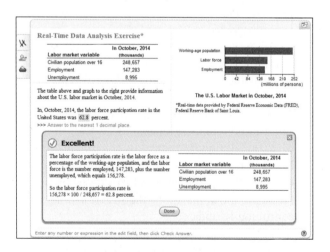

Economics in the News *Economics in the News* is a turn-key solution to bringing daily news into the classroom. Updated daily during the academic year, we upload two relevant articles (one micro, one macro) and provide questions that may be assigned for homework or for classroom discussion.

Current News Each week during the academic year, we upload multi-part microeconomic and macroeconomic exercises, with links to relevant articles, into the MyEconLab assignment manager. These enable instructors to bring current issues and events into the course with easy-to-assign and auto-graded exercises.

Experiments in MyEconLab Experiments are a fun and engaging way to promote active learning and mastery of major economic concepts. Pearson's Experiments program is flexible and easy for instructors to assign and students to use.

- Available experiments cover a competitive market, price floors, price ceilings, taxes, price controls, public goods, and a lemons market.
- Single-player experiments, available to assign, allow your students to play against virtual players from anywhere at any time as long as they have an Internet connection.
- Multi-player experiments allow you to assign and manage a real-time experiment with your class.
- Experiments can be assigned in MyEconLab as homework integrated with pre-questions and post-questions.
- Experiments are auto-graded using algorithms that objectively evaluate a student's economic gain and performance during the experiment.

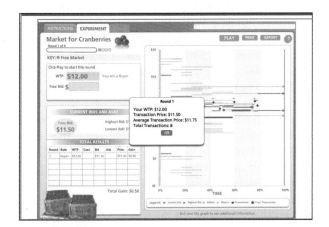

Digital Interactives Digital Interactives immerse the student in an activity that leads to the discovery of a fundamental economic idea or principle. Digital Interactives are designed for use in traditional, online, and hybrid courses, and many incorporate real-time data, as well as data display and analysis tools. A Digital Interactive can be presented in class as a visually stimulating, engaging lecture tool, and can be assigned with assessment questions for grading.

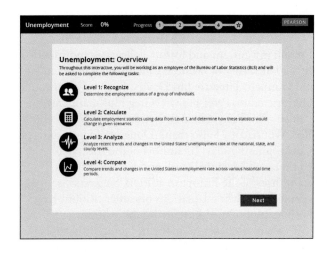

Learning Catalytics MyLab & Mastering with eText now provides Learning Catalytics, a web-based system for managing the interactive classroom that uses students' smartphones, tablets, or laptops to support the peer-instruction teaching method. Instructors can pose a variety of open-ended questions that help students develop critical thinking skills. Real-time monitoring of responses provides data on what students are struggling with and enables instructors to adjust their strategy and try other ways of engaging the students during class. Instructors can also manage student interactions and automatically group students for discussion and teamwork.

AACSB and Learning Outcomes All end-of-chapter and Test Item File questions are tagged in two ways: to AACSB standards and to discipline-specific Learning Outcomes. These two separate tagging systems allow professors to build assessments around desired departmental and course outcomes and track results in MyEconLab's gradebook.

Office Hours Students and instructors can consult the authors using the "Office Hours" links in MyEconLab. The link for students is in Chapter Resources and for Instructors it is in Instructor Resources/Instructor Tools.

Reporting Dashboard View, analyze, and report learning outcomes clearly and easily, and get the information you need to keep your students on track throughout the course, with the new Reporting Dashboard. Available via the Gradebook and fully mobile-ready, the Reporting Dashboard presents student performance data at the class, section, and program levels in an accessible, visual manner.

◆ Acknowledgments

I thank my current and former colleagues and friends at the University of Western Ontario who have taught me so much. They are Jim Davies, Jeremy Greenwood, Ig Horstmann, Peter Howitt, Greg Huffman, David Laidler, Phil Reny, Chris Robinson, John Whalley, and Ron Wonnacott. I also thank Doug McTaggart and Christopher Findlay, co-authors of the Australian edition, and Melanie Powell and Kent Matthews, co-authors of the European edition. Suggestions arising from their adaptations of earlier editions have been helpful to me in preparing this edition.

I thank Rebecca Stein for her thoughtful suggestions and constructive criticism that brought the extensive revision to my treatment of healthcare, public goods, and externalities; Yoram Bauman for careful and helpful reviews of my new coverage of environmental externalities; and Sameh Ajlouni of Yarmouk University for spotting an embarrassing error.

I thank the several thousand students whom I have been privileged to teach. The instant response that comes from the look of puzzlement or enlightenment has taught me how to teach economics.

It is a special joy to thank the many outstanding editors, media specialists, and others at Pearson who contributed to the concerted publishing effort that brought this edition to completion. Denise Clinton, Digital Editor, has played a major role in the evolution of this text since its third edition, and her insights and ideas can still be found in this new edition. Donna Battista, Vice President, Business Publishing, is hugely inspiring and has provided overall direction to the project.

As ever, Adrienne D'Ambrosio, Executive Acquisitions Editor for Economics and my sponsoring editor, played a major role in shaping this revision and the many outstanding supplements that accompany it. Adrienne brings intelligence and insight to her work and is the unchallengeable pre-eminent economics editor. Sarah Dumouchelle, Project Manager, oversaw the production and design process, coordinated the photo research program, and worked with rights and permissions advisors. Andra Skaalrud, Supplements Project Manager, managed our immense supplements program. Nancy Freihofer, Program Manager, provided a steady hand throughout the revision process and helped develop the cover.

Digital Content Team Lead Noel Lotz managed a complex and thorough reviewing process for the content of MyEconLab; and Melissa Honig, Digital Studio Project Manager, ensured that all our media assets were correctly assembled.

Lori DeShazo, Executive Field Marketing Manager, and Alison Haskins, Senior Product Marketing Manager, provided inspired marketing strategy and direction. Jonathan Boylan designed the cover and package and yet again surpassed the challenge of ensuring that we meet the highest design standards.

Catherine Baum provided a careful, consistent, and intelligent copy edit and accuracy check. And Heather Johnson with the other members of an outstanding editorial and production team at Integra-Chicago kept the project on track on an impossibly tight schedule.

I thank all of these wonderful people. It has been inspiring to work with them and to share in creating what I believe is a truly outstanding educational tool.

I thank our talented twelfth edition supplements authors and contributors—Luke Armstrong, Svitlana Maksymenko, Russ McCullough, Alexandra Nica, Jim Self, Laurie Wolff, Jeannie Gillmore, and Sharmistha Nag.

I especially thank Mark Rush, who yet again played a crucial role in creating another edition of this text and package. Mark has been a constant source of good advice and good humor.

I thank the many exceptional reviewers who have shared their insights through the various editions of this book. Their contribution has been invaluable.

I thank the people who work directly with me. Jeannie Gillmore provided outstanding research assistance on many topics, including the *Economics in the News* news articles. Richard Parkin created the electronic art files and offered many ideas that improved the figures in this book. Robin Bade managed an ever-growing and ever more complex MyEconLab database. And Sharmistha Nag has helped me to create *Economics in the News*, Real-Time Data Analysis questions, and Draw Graph exercises.

As with the previous editions, this one owes an enormous debt to Robin Bade. I dedicate this book to her and again thank her for her work. I could not have written this book without the tireless and selfless help she has given me. My thanks to her are unbounded.

Classroom experience will test the value of this book. I would appreciate hearing from instructors and students about how I can continue to improve it in future editions.

Michael Parkin
London, Ontario, Canada
michael.parkin@uwo.ca

◆ Reviewers

Eric Abrams, Hawaii Pacific University
Christopher Adams, Federal Trade Commission
John T. Addison, University of South Carolina
Tajudeen Adenekan, Bronx Community College
Syed Ahmed, Cameron University
Frank Albritton, Seminole Community College
Milton Alderfer, Miami-Dade Community College
William Aldridge, Shelton State Community College
Donald L. Alexander, Western Michigan University
Terence Alexander, Iowa State University
Stuart Allen, University of North Carolina, Greensboro
Sam Allgood, University of Nebraska, Lincoln
Neil Alper, Northeastern University
Alan Anderson, Fordham University
Lisa R. Anderson, College of William and Mary
Jeff Ankrom, Wittenberg University
Fatma Antar, Manchester Community Technical College
Kofi Apraku, University of North Carolina, Asheville
John Atkins, University of West Florida
Moshen Bahmani-Oskooee, University of Wisconsin, Milwaukee
Donald Balch, University of South Carolina
Mehmet Balcilar, Wayne State University
Paul Ballantyne, University of Colorado
Sue Bartlett, University of South Florida
Jose Juan Bautista, Xavier University of Louisiana
Klaus Becker, Texas Tech University
Valerie R. Bencivenga, University of Texas, Austin
Ben Bernanke, Chairman of Federal Reserve
Radha Bhattacharya, California State University, Fullerton
Margot Biery, Tarrant County College, South
John Bittorowitz, Ball State University
David Black, University of Toledo
Kelly Blanchard, Purdue University
S. Brock Blomberg, Claremont McKenna College
William T. Bogart, Case Western Reserve University
Giacomo Bonanno, University of California, Davis
Tan Khay Boon, Nanyard Technological University
Sunne Brandmeyer, University of South Florida
Audie Brewton, Northeastern Illinois University
Baird Brock, Central Missouri State University
Byron Brown, Michigan State University
Imam Bulbul, University of Miami
Jeffrey Buser, Columbus State Community College
Alison Butler, Florida International University
Colleen Callahan, American University
Tania Carbiener, Southern Methodist University
Kevin Carey, American University
Scott Carrell, University of California at Davis

Kathleen A. Carroll, University of Maryland, Baltimore County
Michael Carter, University of Massachusetts, Lowell
Edward Castronova, California State University, Fullerton
Francis Chan, Fullerton College
Ming Chang, Dartmouth College
Subir Chakrabarti, Indiana University-Purdue University
Joni Charles, Texas State University
Adhip Chaudhuri, Georgetown University
Gopal Chengalath, Texas Tech University
Daniel Christiansen, Albion College
Kenneth Christianson, Binghamton University
John J. Clark, Community College of Allegheny County, Allegheny Campus
Cindy Clement, University of Maryland
Meredith Clement, Dartmouth College
Michael B. Cohn, U. S. Merchant Marine Academy
Robert Collinge, University of Texas, San Antonio
Carol Condon, Kean University
Doug Conway, Mesa Community College
Larry Cook, University of Toledo
Bobby Corcoran, retired, Middle Tennessee State University
Kevin Cotter, Wayne State University
James Peery Cover, University of Alabama, Tuscaloosa
Erik Craft, University of Richmond
Eleanor D. Craig, University of Delaware
Jim Craven, Clark College
Jeremy Cripps, American University of Kuwait
Elizabeth Crowell, University of Michigan, Dearborn
Stephen Cullenberg, University of California, Riverside
David Culp, Slippery Rock University
Norman V. Cure, Macomb Community College
Dan Dabney, University of Texas, Austin
Andrew Dane, Angelo State University
James D'Angelo, University of Cincinnati
Joseph Daniels, Marquette University
Gregory DeFreitas, Hofstra University
David Denslow, University of Florida
Shatakshee Dhongde, Rochester Institute of Technology
Mark Dickie, University of Central Florida
James Dietz, California State University, Fullerton
Carol Dole, State University of West Georgia
Ronald Dorf, Inver Hills Community College
John Dorsey, University of Maryland, College Park
Eric Drabkin, Hawaii Pacific University
Amrik Singh Dua, Mt. San Antonio College
Thomas Duchesneau, University of Maine, Orono
Lucia Dunn, Ohio State University
Donald Dutkowsky, Syracuse University
John Edgren, Eastern Michigan University
David J. Eger, Alpena Community College
Harold W. Elder, University of Alabama

Harry Ellis, Jr., University of North Texas
Ibrahim Elsaify, Goldey-Beacom College
Kenneth G. Elzinga, University of Virginia
Patrick Emerson, Oregon State University
Tisha Emerson, Baylor University
Monica Escaleras, Florida Atlantic University
Antonina Espiritu, Hawaii Pacific University
Gwen Eudey, University of Pennsylvania
Barry Falk, Iowa State University
M. Fazeli, Hofstra University
Philip Fincher, Louisiana Tech University
F. Firoozi, University of Texas, San Antonio
Nancy Folbre, University of Massachusetts, Amherst
Kenneth Fong, Temasek Polytechnic (Singapore)
Steven Francis, Holy Cross College
David Franck, University of North Carolina, Charlotte
Mark Frank, Sam Houston State University
Roger Frantz, San Diego State University
Mark Frascatore, Clarkson University
Alwyn Fraser, Atlantic Union College
Connel Fullenkamp, Duke University
Marc Fusaro, East Carolina University
James Gale, Michigan Technological University
Susan Gale, New York University
Roy Gardner, Indiana University
Eugene Gentzel, Pensacola Junior College
Kirk Gifford, Brigham Young University-Idaho
Scott Gilbert, Southern Illinois University, Carbondale
Andrew Gill, California State University, Fullerton
Robert Giller, Virginia Polytechnic Institute and State University
Robert Gillette, University of Kentucky
James N. Giordano, Villanova University
Maria Giuili, Diablo College
Susan Glanz, St. John's University
Robert Gordon, San Diego State University
Richard Gosselin, Houston Community College
John Graham, Rutgers University
John Griffen, Worcester Polytechnic Institute
Wayne Grove, Syracuse University
Robert Guell, Indiana State University
William Gunther, University of Southern Mississippi
Jamie Haag, Pacific University, Oregon
Gail Heyne Hafer, Lindenwood University
Rik W. Hafer, Southern Illinois University, Edwardsville
Daniel Hagen, Western Washington University
David R. Hakes, University of Northern Iowa
Craig Hakkio, Federal Reserve Bank, Kansas City
Bridget Gleeson Hanna, Rochester Institute of Technology
Ann Hansen, Westminster College
Seid Hassan, Murray State University
Jonathan Haughton, Suffolk University
Randall Haydon, Wichita State University

Denise Hazlett, Whitman College
Julia Heath, University of Memphis
Jac Heckelman, Wake Forest University
Jolien A. Helsel, Kent State University
James Henderson, Baylor University
Doug Herman, Georgetown University
Jill Boylston Herndon, University of Florida
Gus Herring, Brookhaven College
John Herrmann, Rutgers University
John M. Hill, Delgado Community College
Jonathan Hill, Florida International University
Lewis Hill, Texas Tech University
Steve Hoagland, University of Akron
Tom Hoerger, Fellow, Research Triangle Institute
Calvin Hoerneman, Delta College
George Hoffer, Virginia Commonwealth University
Dennis L. Hoffman, Arizona State University
Paul Hohenberg, Rensselaer Polytechnic Institute
Jim H. Holcomb, University of Texas, El Paso
Robert Holland, Purdue University
Harry Holzer, Georgetown University
Linda Hooks, Washington and Lee University
Gary Hoover, University of Alabama
Jim Horner, Cameron University
Djehane Hosni, University of Central Florida
Harold Hotelling, Jr., Lawrence Technical University
Calvin Hoy, County College of Morris
Ing-Wei Huang, Assumption University, Thailand
Julie Hunsaker, Wayne State University
Beth Ingram, University of Iowa
Jayvanth Ishwaran, Stephen F. Austin State University
Michael Jacobs, Lehman College
S. Hussain Ali Jafri, Tarleton State University
Dennis Jansen, Texas A&M University
Andrea Jao, University of Pennsylvania
Barbara John, University of Dayton
Barry Jones, Binghamton University
Garrett Jones, Southern Florida University
Frederick Jungman, Northwestern Oklahoma State University
Paul Junk, University of Minnesota, Duluth
Leo Kahane, California State University, Hayward
Veronica Kalich, Baldwin-Wallace College
John Kane, State University of New York, Oswego
Eungmin Kang, St. Cloud State University
Arthur Kartman, San Diego State University
Theresa Kauffman, Chattahoochee Technical College
Gurmit Kaur, Universiti Teknologi (Malaysia)
Louise Keely, University of Wisconsin, Madison
Manfred W. Keil, Claremont McKenna College
Elizabeth Sawyer Kelly, University of Wisconsin, Madison
Rose Kilburn, Modesto Junior College
Amanda King, Georgia Southern University

John King, Georgia Southern University

Robert Kirk, Indiana University-Purdue University, Indianapolis

Norman Kleinberg, City University of New York, Baruch College

Robert Kleinhenz, California State University, Fullerton

John Krantz, University of Utah

Joseph Kreitzer, University of St. Thomas

Patricia Kuzyk, Washington State University

David Lages, Southwest Missouri State University

W. J. Lane, University of New Orleans

Leonard Lardaro, University of Rhode Island

Kathryn Larson, Elon College

Luther D. Lawson, University of North Carolina, Wilmington

Elroy M. Leach, Chicago State University

Jim Lee, Texas A & M, Corpus Christi

Sang Lee, Southeastern Louisiana University

Robert Lemke, Florida International University

Mary Lesser, Iona College

Philip K. Letting, Harrisburg Area Community College

Jay Levin, Wayne State University

Arik Levinson, University of Wisconsin, Madison

Tony Lima, California State University, Hayward

William Lord, University of Maryland, Baltimore County

Nancy Lutz, Virginia Polytechnic Institute and State University

Brian Lynch, Lakeland Community College

Murugappa Madhavan, San Diego State University

K. T. Magnusson, Salt Lake Community College

Mark Maier, Glendale Community College

Svitlana Maksymenko, University of Pittsburgh

Jean Mangan, Staffordshire University Business School

Denton Marks, University of Wisconsin, Whitewater

Michael Marlow, California Polytechnic State University

Akbar Marvasti, University of Houston

Wolfgang Mayer, University of Cincinnati

John McArthur, Wofford College

Katherine McClain, University of Georgia

Amy McCormick, Mary Baldwin College

Russ McCullough, Iowa State University

Catherine McDevitt, Central Michigan University

Gerald McDougall, Wichita State University

Stephen McGary, Brigham Young University-Idaho

Richard D. McGrath, Armstrong Atlantic State University

Richard McIntyre, University of Rhode Island

John McLeod, Georgia Institute of Technology

Mark McLeod, Virginia Polytechnic Institute and State University

B. Starr McMullen, Oregon State University

Sandra McPherson, Millersville University

Mary Ruth McRae, Appalachian State University

Kimberly Merritt, Cameron University

Charles Meyer, Iowa State University

Peter Mieszkowski, Rice University

John Mijares, University of North Carolina, Asheville

Richard A. Miller, Wesleyan University

Judith W. Mills, Southern Connecticut State University

Glen Mitchell, Nassau Community College

Jeannette C. Mitchell, Rochester Institute of Technology

Bagher Modjtahedi, University of California, Davis

Michael A. Mogavero, University of Notre Dame

Khan Mohabbat, Northern Illinois University

Shahruz Mohtadi, Suffolk University

Barbara Moore, University of Central Florida

W. Douglas Morgan, University of California, Santa Barbara

William Morgan, University of Wyoming

James Morley, Washington University in St. Louis

William Mosher, Clark University

Joanne Moss, San Francisco State University

Nivedita Mukherji, Oakland University

Francis Mummery, Fullerton College

Edward Murphy, Southwest Texas State University

Kevin J. Murphy, Oakland University

Kathryn Nantz, Fairfield University

William S. Neilson, Texas A&M University

Paul Nelson, University of Louisiana, Monroe

Bart C. Nemmers, University of Nebraska, Lincoln

Alexandra Nica, University of Iowa

Melinda Nish, Orange Coast College

Anthony O'Brien, Lehigh University

Norman Obst, Michigan State University

Constantin Ogloblin, Georgia Southern University

Neal Olitsky, University of Massachusetts, Dartmouth

Mary Olson, Tulane University

Terry Olson, Truman State University

James B. O'Neill, University of Delaware

Farley Ordovensky, University of the Pacific

Z. Edward O'Relley, North Dakota State University

Donald Oswald, California State University, Bakersfield

Jan Palmer, Ohio University

Michael Palumbo, Chief, Federal Reserve Board

Chris Papageorgiou, Louisiana State University

G. Hossein Parandvash, Western Oregon State College

Randall Parker, East Carolina University

Robert Parks, Washington University

David Pate, St. John Fisher College

James E. Payne, Illinois State University

Donald Pearson, Eastern Michigan University

Steven Peterson, University of Idaho

Mary Anne Pettit, Southern Illinois University, Edwardsville

William A. Phillips, University of Southern Maine

Dennis Placone, Clemson University

Charles Plot, California Institute of Technology, Pasadena

Mannie Poen, Houston Community College

Kathleen Possai, Wayne State University

Ulrika Praski-Stahlgren, University College in Gavle-
Sandviken, Sweden

Edward Price, Oklahoma State University

Rula Qalyoubi, University of Wisconsin, Eau Claire

K. A. Quartey, Talladega College

Herman Quirmbach, Iowa State University

Jeffrey R. Racine, University of South Florida

Ramkishen Rajan, George Mason University

Peter Rangazas, Indiana University-Purdue University,
Indianapolis

Vaman Rao, Western Illinois University

Laura Razzolini, University of Mississippi

Rob Rebelein, University of Cincinnati

J. David Reed, Bowling Green State University

Robert H. Renshaw, Northern Illinois University

Javier Reyes, University of Arkansas

Jeff Reynolds, Northern Illinois University

Rupert Rhodd, Florida Atlantic University

W. Gregory Rhodus, Bentley College

Jennifer Rice, Indiana University, Bloomington

John Robertson, Paducah Community College

Malcolm Robinson, University of North Carolina,
Greensboro

Richard Roehl, University of Michigan, Dearborn

Carol Rogers, Georgetown University

William Rogers, University of Northern Colorado

Thomas Romans, State University of New York, Buffalo

David R. Ross, Bryn Mawr College

Thomas Ross, Baldwin Wallace College

Robert J. Rossana, Wayne State University

Jeffrey Rous, University of North Texas

Rochelle Ruffer, Youngstown State University

John Ruggiero, University of Daytona

Mark Rush, University of Florida

Allen R. Sanderson, University of Chicago

Gary Santoni, Ball State University

Jeffrey Sarbaum, University of North Carolina at Chapel Hill

John Saussy, Harrisburg Area Community College

Don Schlagenhauf, Florida State University

David Schlow, Pennsylvania State University

Paul Schmitt, St. Clair County Community College

Jeremy Schwartz, Hampden-Sydney College

Martin Sefton, University of Nottingham

James K. Self, Indiana University

Esther-Mirjam Sent, University of Notre Dame

Rod Shadbegian, University of Massachusetts, Dartmouth

Neil Sheflin, Rutgers University

Gerald Shilling, Eastfield College

Dorothy R. Siden, Salem State College

Mark Siegler, California State University at Sacramento

Scott Simkins, North Carolina Agricultural and Technical State
University

Jacek Siry, University of Georgia

Chuck Skoro, Boise State University

Phil Smith, DeKalb College

William Doyle Smith, University of Texas, El Paso

Sarah Stafford, College of William and Mary

Rebecca Stein, University of Pennsylvania

Frank Steindl, Oklahoma State University

Jeffrey Stewart, New York University

Rayna Stocheva, University of Miami

Allan Stone, Southwest Missouri State University

Courtenay Stone, Ball State University

Paul Storer, Western Washington University

Richard W. Stratton, University of Akron

Mark Strazicich, Ohio State University, Newark

Michael Stroup, Stephen F. Austin State University

Robert Stuart, Rutgers University

Della Lee Sue, Marist College

Abdulhamid Sukar, Cameron University

Terry Sutton, Southeast Missouri State University

Gilbert Suzawa, University of Rhode Island

David Swaine, Andrews University

Jason Taylor, Central Michigan University

Mark Thoma, University of Oregon

Janet Thomas, Bentley College

Kiril Tochkov, SUNY at Binghamton

Kay Unger, University of Montana

Anthony Uremovic, Joliet Junior College

David Vaughn, City University, Washington

Don Waldman, Colgate University

Francis Wambalaba, Portland State University

Sasiwimon Warunsiri, University of Colorado at Boulder

Rob Wassmer, California State University, Sacramento

Paul A. Weinstein, University of Maryland, College Park

Lee Weissert, St. Vincent College

Robert Whaples, Wake Forest University

David Wharton, Washington College

Mark Wheeler, Western Michigan University

Charles H. Whiteman, University of Iowa

Sandra Williamson, University of Pittsburgh

Brenda Wilson, Brookhaven Community College

Larry Wimmer, Brigham Young University

Mark Witte, Northwestern University

Willard E. Witte, Indiana University

Mark Wohar, University of Nebraska, Omaha

Laura Wolff, Southern Illinois University, Edwardsville

Cheonsik Woo, Vice President, Korea Development Institute

Douglas Wooley, Radford University

Arthur G. Woolf, University of Vermont

John T. Young, Riverside Community College

Michael Youngblood, Rock Valley College

Peter Zaleski, Villanova University

Jason Zimmerman, South Dakota State University

David Zucker, Martha Stewart Living Omnimedia

Supplements Authors

Luke Armstrong, Lee College
Sue Bartlett, University of South Florida
Kelly Blanchard, Purdue University
James Cobbe, Florida State University
Carol Dole, Jacksonville University
Karen Gebhardt, Colorado State University
John Graham, Rutgers University
Jill Herndon, University of Florida
Gary Hoover, University of Alabama
Patricia Kuzyk, Washington State University
Sang Lee, Southeastern Louisiana University
Svitlana Maksymenko, University of Pittsburgh
Robert Martel, University of Connecticut
Katherine McClain, University of Georgia

Russ McCullough, Iowa State University
Barbara Moore, University of Central Florida
James Morley, Washington University in St. Louis
William Mosher, Clark University
Alexandra Nica, University of Iowa
Constantin Ogloblin, Georgia Southern University
Edward Price, Oklahoma State University
Mark Rush, University of Florida
James K. Self, University of Indiana, Bloomington
Rebecca Stein, University of Pennsylvania
Michael Stroup, Stephen F. Austin State University
Della Lee Sue, Marist College
Nora Underwood, University of Central Florida
Laura A. Wolff, Southern Illinois University, Edwardsville

1 WHAT IS ECONOMICS?

After studying this chapter, you will be able to:

- ◆ Define economics and distinguish between microeconomics and macroeconomics
- ◆ Explain the two big questions of economics
- ◆ Explain the key ideas that define the economic way of thinking
- ◆ Explain how economists go about their work as social scientists and policy advisers

Is economics about money: How people make it and spend it? Is it about business, government, and jobs? Is it about why some people and some nations are rich and others poor? Economics is about all these things. But its core is the study of *choices* and their *consequences*.

Your life will be shaped by the choices that you make and the challenges that you face. To face those challenges and seize the opportunities they present, you must understand the powerful forces at play. The economics that you're about to learn will become your most reliable guide. This chapter gets you started by describing the questions that economists try to answer and looking at how economists think as they search for the answers.

◆ Definition of Economics

A fundamental fact dominates our lives: We want more than we can get. Our inability to get everything we want is called **scarcity**. Scarcity is universal. It confronts all living things. Even parrots face scarcity!

Not only do I want a cracker—we all want a cracker!

© The New Yorker Collection 1985
Frank Modell from cartoonbank.com. All Rights Reserved.

Think about the things that *you* want and the scarcity that *you* face. You want to go to a good school, college, or university. You want to live in a well-equipped, spacious, and comfortable home. You want the latest smartphone and the fastest Internet connection for your laptop or iPad. You want some sports and recreational gear—perhaps some new running shoes, or a new bike. You want much more time than is available to go to class, do your homework, play sports and games, read novels, go to the movies, listen to music, travel, and hang out with your friends. And you want to live a long and healthy life.

What you can afford to buy is limited by your income and by the prices you must pay. And your time is limited by the fact that your day has 24 hours.

You want some other things that only governments provide. You want to live in a safe neighborhood in a peaceful and secure world, and enjoy the benefits of clean air, lakes, rivers, and oceans.

What governments can afford is limited by the taxes they collect. Taxes lower people's incomes and compete with the other things they want to buy. What *everyone* can get—what *society* can get—is limited by the productive resources available. These resources are the gifts of nature, human labor and ingenuity, and all the previously produced tools and equipment.

Because we can't get everything we want, we must make *choices*. You can't afford *both* a laptop *and* an iPhone, so you must *choose* which one to buy. You can't spend tonight *both* studying for your next test *and* going to the movies, so again, you must *choose* which one to do. Governments can't spend a tax dollar on *both* national defense *and* environmental protection, so they must *choose* how to spend that dollar.

Your choices must somehow be made consistent with the choices of *others*. If you choose to buy a laptop, someone else must choose to sell it. Incentives reconcile choices. An **incentive** is a reward that encourages an action or a penalty that discourages one. Prices act as incentives. If the price of a laptop is too high, more will be offered for sale than people want to buy. And if the price is too low, fewer will be offered for sale than people want to buy. But there is a price at which choices to buy and sell are consistent.

Economics is the social science that studies the *choices* that individuals, businesses, governments, and entire societies make as they cope with *scarcity* and the *incentives* that influence and reconcile those choices.

The subject has two parts:

- Microeconomics
- Macroeconomics

Microeconomics is the study of the choices that individuals and businesses make, the way these choices interact in markets, and the influence of governments. Some examples of microeconomic questions are: Why are people downloading more movies? How would a tax on e-commerce affect eBay?

Macroeconomics is the study of the performance of the national economy and the global economy. Some examples of macroeconomic questions are: Why does the U.S. unemployment rate fluctuate? Can the Federal Reserve make the unemployment rate fall by keeping interest rates low?

◆ REVIEW QUIZ

1 List some examples of the scarcity that you face.
2 Find examples of scarcity in today's headlines.
3 Find an example of the distinction between microeconomics and macroeconomics in today's headlines.

Work these questions in Study Plan 1.1 and get instant feedback. Do a Key Terms Quiz.   MyEconLab

◆ Two Big Economic Questions

Two big questions summarize the scope of economics:

- How do choices end up determining *what, how*, and *for whom* goods and services are produced?
- Do choices made in the pursuit of *self-interest* also promote the *social interest*?

What, How, and For Whom?

Goods and services are the objects that people value and produce to satisfy wants. *Goods* are physical objects such as cellphones and automobiles. *Services* are tasks performed for people such as cellphone service and auto-repair service.

What? *What* we produce varies across countries and changes over time. In the United States today, agriculture accounts for 1 percent of total production, manufactured goods for 20 percent, and services (retail and wholesale trade, healthcare, and education are the biggest ones) for 79 percent. In contrast, in China today, agriculture accounts for 10 percent of total production, manufactured goods for 45 percent, and services for 45 percent.

Figure 1.1 shows these numbers and also the percentages for Brazil, which fall between those for the United States and China.

What determines these patterns of production? How do choices end up determining the quantities of cellphones, automobiles, cellphone service, auto-repair service, and the millions of other items that are produced in the United States and around the world?

How? *How* we produce is described by the technologies and resources that we use. The resources used to produce goods and services are called **factors of production**, which are grouped into four categories:

- Land
- Labor
- Capital
- Entrepreneurship

Land The "gifts of nature" that we use to produce goods and services are called **land**. In economics, *land* is what in everyday language we call *natural resources*. It includes land in the everyday sense

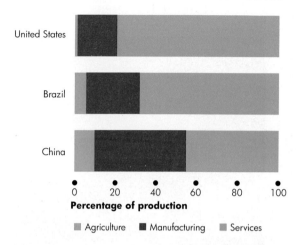

FIGURE 1.1   What Three Countries Produce

Percentage of production

■ Agriculture   ■ Manufacturing   ■ Services

Agriculture and manufacturing are small percentages of production in rich countries such as the United States and large percentages of production in poorer countries such as China. Most of what is produced in the United States is services.

Source of data: CIA Factbook 2014, Central Intelligence Agency.

MyEconLab Animation

together with minerals, oil, gas, coal, water, air, forests, and fish.

Our land surface and water resources are renewable and some of our mineral resources can be recycled. But the resources that we use to create energy are nonrenewable—they can be used only once.

Labor The work time and work effort that people devote to producing goods and services is called **labor**. Labor includes the physical and mental efforts of all the people who work on farms and construction sites and in factories, shops, and offices.

The *quality* of labor depends on **human capital**, which is the knowledge and skill that people obtain from education, on-the-job training, and work experience. You are building your own human capital right now as you work on your economics course, and your human capital will continue to grow as you gain work experience.

Human capital expands over time. Today, 88 percent of the adult population of the United States have completed high school and 32 percent have a college or university degree. Figure 1.2 shows these measures of human capital in the United States and its growth over the past 110 years.

FIGURE 1.2   A Measure of Human Capital

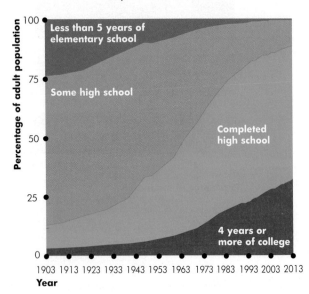

In 2013, 32 percent of the population aged 25 and older had 4 years or more of college, up from 2 percent in 1903. A further 56 percent had completed high school, up from 10 percent in 1903.

Source of data: U.S. Census Bureau, 2014.

MyEconLab Animation

Capital The tools, instruments, machines, buildings, and other constructions that businesses use to produce goods and services are called **capital**.

In everyday language, we talk about money, stocks, and bonds as being "capital." These items are *financial capital*. Financial capital plays an important role in enabling businesses to borrow the funds that they use to buy physical capital. But financial capital is not used to produce goods and services and it is not a factor of production.

Entrepreneurship The human resource that organizes labor, land, and capital is called **entrepreneurship**. Entrepreneurs are the drivers of economic progress. They develop new ideas about what and how to produce, make business decisions, and bear the risks that arise from these decisions.

What determines how the factors of production are used to produce each good and service?

For Whom? *Who* consumes the goods and services that are produced depends on the incomes that people earn. People with large incomes can buy a wide range of goods and services. People with small incomes have fewer options and can afford a smaller range of goods and services.

People earn their incomes by selling the services of the factors of production they own:

- Land earns **rent**.
- Labor earns **wages**.
- Capital earns **interest**.
- Entrepreneurship earns **profit**.

Which factor of production earns the most income? The answer is labor. In 2011, wages were 68 percent of total income and the incomes from land, capital, and entrepreneurship totaled 32 percent. These shares remain remarkably constant over time.

Knowing how income is shared among the factors of production doesn't tell us how it is shared among individuals. And the distribution of income among individuals is extremely unequal. You know of some people who earn very large incomes: Dwayne "The Rock" Johnson (Hercules) earned $46 million in 2013; and Clayton Kershaw has a $215 million 7-year deal with the LA Dodgers.

You know of even more people who earn very small incomes. Servers at McDonald's average around $7.25 an hour; checkout clerks, cleaners, and textile and leather workers all earn less than $10 an hour.

You probably know about other persistent differences in incomes. Men, on average, earn more than women; whites earn more than minorities; college graduates earn more than high-school graduates.

We can get a good sense of who consumes the goods and services produced by looking at the percentages of total income earned by different groups of people. The 20 percent of people with the lowest incomes earn about 5 percent of total income, while the richest 20 percent earn close to 50 percent of total income. So on average, people in the richest 20 percent earn more than 10 times the incomes of those in the poorest 20 percent. There is even huge inequality within the richest 20 percent and the top 1 percent earns almost 15 percent of total income. Why is the distribution of income so unequal?

Economics provides some answers to all these questions about *what, how,* and *for whom* goods and services are produced and much of the rest of this book will help you to understand those answers.

We're now going to look at the second big question of economics: Do choices made in the pursuit of self-interest also promote the social interest?

Do Choices Made in the Pursuit of Self-Interest also Promote the Social Interest?

Every day, you and 320 million other Americans, along with 7.2 billion people in the rest of the world, make economic choices that result in *what, how,* and *for whom* goods and services are produced. These choices are made by people who are pursuing their self-interest.

Self-Interest You make a choice in your self-interest if you think that choice is the best one available for you. All the choices that people make about how to use their time and other resources are made in the pursuit of self-interest. When you allocate your time or your budget, you do what makes the most sense to you. You might think about how your choices affect other people and take into account how you feel about that, but it is how *you* feel that influences your choice. You order a home-delivery pizza because you're hungry, not because the delivery person needs a job. And when the pizza delivery person shows up at your door, he's not doing you a favor. He's pursuing *his* self-interest and hoping for a tip and another call next week.

The big question is: Is it possible that all the choices that each one of us makes in the pursuit of self-interest could end up achieving an outcome that is best for everyone?

Social Interest An outcome is in the social interest if it is best for society as a whole. It is easy to see how you decide what is in *your* self-interest. But how do we decide if something is in the social interest? To help you answer this question, imagine a scene like that in *Economics in the News* on the next page.

Ted, an entrepreneur, creates a new business. He hires a thousand workers and pays them $20 an hour, $1 an hour more than they earned in their old jobs. Ted's business is extremely profitable and his own earnings increase by $1 million per week.

You can see that Ted's decision to create the business is in his self-interest—he gains $1 million a week. You can also see that for Ted's employees, their decisions to work for Ted are in their self-interest— they gain $1 an hour (say $40 a week). And the decisions of Ted's customers must be in their self-interest, otherwise they wouldn't buy from him. But is this outcome in the social interest?

The economist's answer is "Yes." It is in the social interest because it makes everyone better off. There are no losers.

Efficiency and the Social Interest Economists use the everyday word "efficient" to describe a situation that can't be improved upon. Resource use is efficient if it is *not* possible to make someone better off without making someone else worse off. If it *is* possible to make someone better off without making anyone worse off, society can be made better off and the situation is not efficient.

In the Ted story everyone is better off, so it improves efficiency and the outcome is in the social interest. But notice that it would also have been efficient if the workers and customers had gained nothing and Ted had gained even more than $1 million a week. But would that efficient outcome be in the social interest?

Many people have trouble seeing the outcome in which Ted is the only winner as being in the social interest. They say that the social interest requires Ted to share some of his gain either with his workers in higher wages or with his customers in lower prices, or with both groups.

Fair Shares and the Social Interest The idea that the social interest requires "fair shares" is a deeply held one. Think about what you regard as a fair share. To help you, imagine the following game.

I put $100 on the table and tell someone you don't know and who doesn't know you to *propose* a share of the money between the two of you. If you *accept* the proposed share, you each get the agreed upon shares. If you don't accept the proposed share, you both get nothing.

It would be efficient—you would both be better off—if the proposer offered to take $99 and leave you with $1 and you accepted that offer.

But would you accept the $1? If you are like most people, the idea that the other person gets 99 times as much as you is just too much to stomach. "No way," you say and the $100 disappears. That outcome is inefficient. You have both given up something.

When the game I've just described is played in a classroom experiment, about half of the players reject offers of below $30.

So fair shares matter. But what is *fair*? There isn't a crisp definition of fairness to match that of efficiency. Reasonable people have a variety of views about it. Almost everyone agrees that too much inequality is unfair. But how much is too much? And inequality of what: income, wealth, or the *opportunity* to work, earn an income, and accumulate wealth?

You will examine efficiency again in Chapter 2 and efficiency and fairness in Chapter 5.

Questions about the social interest are hard ones to answer and they generate discussion, debate, and disagreement. Four issues in today's world put some flesh on these questions. The issues are:

- Globalization
- Information-age monopolies
- Climate change
- Financial instability

Globalization The term *globalization* means the expansion of international trade, borrowing and lending, and investment.

When Nike produces sports shoes, people in Malaysia get work; and when China Airlines buys new airplanes, Americans who work at Boeing in Seattle build them. While globalization brings expanded production and job opportunities for some workers, it destroys many American jobs. Workers across the manufacturing industries must learn new skills, take service jobs, which are often lower-paid, or retire earlier than previously planned.

Globalization is in the self-interest of those consumers who buy low-cost goods and services produced in other countries; and it is in the self-interest of the multinational firms that produce in low-cost regions and sell in high-price regions. But is globalization in the self-interest of the low-wage worker in Malaysia who sews your new running shoes and the displaced shoemaker in Atlanta? Is it in the social interest?

ECONOMICS IN THE NEWS

The Invisible Hand

From Brewer to Bio-Tech Entrepreneur
Kiran Mazumdar-Shaw trained to become a master brewer and learned about enzymes, the stuff from which bio-pharmaceuticals are made. Discovering it was impossible for a woman in India to become a master brewer, the 25-year-old Kiran decided to create a bio-pharmaceutical business.

Kiran's firm, Biocom, employed uneducated workers who loved their jobs and the living conditions made possible by their high wages. But when a labor union entered the scene and unionized the workers, a furious Kiran fired the workers, automated their jobs, and hired a smaller number of educated workers. Biocom continued to grow and today, Kiran's wealth exceeds $1 billion.

Kiran has become wealthy by developing and producing bio-pharmaceuticals that improve people's lives. But Kiran is sharing her wealth in creative ways. She has opened a cancer treatment center to help thousands of patients who are too poor to pay and created a health insurance scheme.

Source: Ariel Levy, "Drug Test," *The New Yorker*, January 2, 2012

THE QUESTIONS

- Whose decisions in the story were taken in self-interest?
- Whose decisions turned out to be in the social interest?
- Did any of the decisions harm the social interest?

THE ANSWERS

- All the decisions—Kiran's, the workers', the union's, and the firm's customers'—are taken in the pursuit of self-interest.
- Kiran's decisions serve the social interest: She creates jobs that benefit her workers and products that benefit her customers. And her charitable work brings yet further social benefits.
- The labor union's decision might have harmed the social interest because it destroyed the jobs of uneducated workers.

Kiran Mazumdar-Shaw, founder and CEO of Biocom

Information-Age Monopolies The technological change of the past forty years has been called the *Information Revolution*. Bill Gates, a co-founder of Microsoft, held a privileged position in this revolution. For many years, Windows was the only available operating system for the PC. The PC and Mac competed, but the PC had a huge market share.

An absence of competition gave Microsoft the power to sell Windows at prices far above the cost of production. With lower prices, many more people would have been able to afford and buy a computer.

The information revolution has clearly served your self-interest: It has provided your cellphone, laptop, loads of handy applications, and the Internet. It has also served the self-interest of Bill Gates who has seen his wealth soar.

But did the information revolution best serve the social interest? Did Microsoft produce the best possible Windows operating system and sell it at a price that was in the social interest? Or was the quality too low and the price too high?

Climate Change Burning fossil fuels to generate electricity and to power airplanes, automobiles, and trucks pours a staggering 28 billion tons—4 tons per person—of carbon dioxide into the atmosphere each year. These carbon emissions, two thirds of which comes from the United States, China, the European Union, Russia, and India, bring global warming and climate change.

Every day, when you make self-interested choices to use electricity and gasoline, you leave your carbon footprint. You can lessen this footprint by walking, riding a bike, taking a cold shower, or planting a tree.

But can each one of us be relied upon to make decisions that affect the Earth's carbon-dioxide concentration in the social interest? Must governments change the incentives we face so that our self-interested choices are also in the social interest? How can governments change incentives? How can we

encourage the use of wind and solar power to replace the burning of fossil fuels that brings climate change?

Financial Instability In 2008, banks were in trouble. They had made loans that borrowers couldn't repay and they were holding securities the values of which had crashed.

Banks' choices to take deposits and make loans are made in self-interest, but does this lending and borrowing serve the social interest? Do banks lend too much in the pursuit of profit?

When banks got into trouble in 2008, the Federal Reserve (the Fed) bailed them out with big loans backed by taxpayer dollars. Did the Fed's bailout of troubled banks serve the social interest? Or might the Fed's rescue action encourage banks to repeat their dangerous lending in the future?

We've looked at four topics and asked many questions that illustrate the potential conflict between the pursuit of self-interest and the social interest. We've asked questions but not answered them because we've not yet explained the economic principles needed to do so. We will answer these questions in future chapters.

◆ **REVIEW QUIZ**

1 Describe the broad facts about *what, how,* and *for whom* goods and services are produced.
2 Use headlines from the recent news to illustrate the potential for conflict between self-interest and the social interest.

Work these questions in Study Plan 1.2 and get instant feedback. Do a Key Terms Quiz.   MyEconLab

◆ AT **ISSUE**

The Protest Against Market Capitalism

Market capitalism is an economic system in which individuals own land and capital and are free to buy and sell land, capital, and goods and services in markets. Markets for goods and services, along with markets for land and capital, coordinate billions of self-interested choices, which determine what, how, and for whom goods and services are produced. A few people earn enormous incomes, many times the average income. There is no supreme planner guiding the use of scarce resources and the outcome is unintended and unforeseeable.

Centrally planned socialism is an economic system in which the government owns all the land and capital, directs workers to jobs, and decides what, how, and for whom to produce. The Soviet Union, several Eastern European countries, and China have used this system in the past but have now abandoned it. Only Cuba and North Korea use this system today. A few bureaucrats in positions of great power receive huge incomes, many times that of an average person.

Our economy today is a **mixed economy**, which is market capitalism with government regulation.

The **Protest**

The protest against market capitalism takes many forms. Historically, **Karl Marx** and other communist and socialist thinkers wanted to replace it with *socialism* and *central planning*. Today, thousands of people who feel let down by the economic system want less market capitalism and more government regulation. The **Occupy Wall Street** movement, with its focus on the large incomes of the top 1 percent, is a visible example of today's protest. Protesters say:

- Big corporations (especially big banks) have too much power and influence on governments.
- Democratically elected governments can do a better job of allocating resources and distributing income than uncoordinated markets.
- More regulation in the social interest is needed—to serve "human need, not corporate greed."
- In a market, for every winner, there is a loser.
- Big corporations are the winners. Workers and unemployed people are the losers.

The **Economist's Response**

Economists agree that market capitalism isn't perfect. But they argue that it is the best system available and while some government intervention and regulation can help, government attempts to serve the social interest often end up harming it.

Adam Smith (see p. 53), who gave the first systematic account of how market capitalism works, says:

- The self-interest of big corporations is *maximum profit*.
- But an *invisible hand* leads production decisions made in pursuit of self-interest to *unintentionally* promote the social interest.
- Politicians are ill-equipped to regulate corporations or to intervene in markets, and those who think they can improve on the market outcome are most likely wrong.
- In a market, buyers get what they want for less than they would be willing to pay and sellers earn a profit. Both buyers and sellers gain. A market transaction is a "win-win" event.

An Occupy Wall Street protester

"It is not from the benevolence of the butcher, the brewer, or the baker that we expect our dinner, but from their regard to their own interest."
The Wealth of Nations,
1776

Adam Smith

The Economic Way of Thinking

The questions that economics tries to answer tell us about the *scope of economics,* but they don't tell us how economists *think* and go about seeking answers to these questions. You're now going to see how economists go about their work.

We're going to look at six key ideas that define the *economic way of thinking.* These ideas are

- A choice is a *tradeoff.*
- People make *rational choices* by comparing *benefits* and *costs.*
- *Benefit* is what you gain from something.
- *Cost* is what you *must give up* to get something.
- Most choices are "*how-much*" choices made at the *margin.*
- Choices respond to *incentives.*

A Choice Is a Tradeoff

Because we face scarcity, we must make choices. And when we make a choice, we select from the available alternatives. For example, you can spend Saturday night studying for your next economics test or having fun with your friends, but you can't do both of these activities at the same time. You must choose how much time to devote to each. Whatever choice you make, you could have chosen something else.

You can think about your choices as tradeoffs. A tradeoff is an exchange—giving up one thing to get something else. When you choose how to spend your Saturday night, you face a tradeoff between studying and hanging out with your friends.

Making a Rational Choice

Economists view the choices that people make as rational. A rational choice is one that compares costs and benefits and achieves the greatest benefit over cost for the person making the choice.

Only the wants of the person making a choice are relevant to determine its rationality. For example, you might like your coffee black and strong but your friend prefers his milky and sweet. So it is rational for you to choose espresso and for your friend to choose cappuccino.

The idea of rational choice provides an answer to the first question: *What* goods and services will be produced and in what quantities? The answer is those that people rationally choose to buy!

But how do people choose rationally? Why do more people choose an iPad rather than a Microsoft Surface? Why has the U.S. government chosen to build an interstate highway system and not an interstate high-speed railroad system? The answers turn on comparing benefits and costs.

Benefit: What You Gain

The benefit of something is the gain or pleasure that it brings and is determined by preferences—by what a person likes and dislikes and the intensity of those feelings. If you get a huge kick out of "League of Legends," that video game brings you a large benefit. If you have little interest in listening to Yo-Yo Ma playing a Vivaldi cello concerto, that activity brings you a small benefit.

Some benefits are large and easy to identify, such as the benefit that you get from being in school. A big piece of that benefit is the goods and services that you will be able to enjoy with the boost to your earning power when you graduate. Some benefits are small, such as the benefit you get from a slice of pizza.

Economists measure benefit as the most that a person is *willing to give up* to get something. You are willing to give up a lot to be in school. But you would give up only an iTunes download for a slice of pizza.

Cost: What You *Must* Give Up

The opportunity cost of something is the highest-valued alternative that must be given up to get it.

To make the idea of opportunity cost concrete, think about *your* opportunity cost of being in school. It has two components: the things you can't afford to buy and the things you can't do with your time.

Start with the things you can't afford to buy. You've spent all your income on tuition, residence fees, books, and a laptop. If you weren't in school, you would have spent this money on tickets to ball games and movies and all the other things that you enjoy. But that's only the start of your opportunity cost. You've also given up the opportunity to get a job. Suppose that the best job you could get if you weren't in school is working at Citibank as a teller earning $25,000 a year. Another part of your opportunity cost of being in school is all the things that you could buy with the extra $25,000 you would have.

As you well know, being a student eats up many hours in class time, doing homework assignments, preparing for tests, and so on. To do all these school activities, you must give up many hours of what would otherwise be leisure time spent with your friends.

So the opportunity cost of being in school is all the good things that you can't afford and don't have the spare time to enjoy. You might want to put a dollar value on that cost or you might just list all the items that make up the opportunity cost.

The examples of opportunity cost that we've just considered are all-or-nothing costs—you're either in school or not in school. Most situations are not like this one. They involve choosing *how much* of an activity to do.

How Much? Choosing at the Margin

You can allocate the next hour between studying and chatting online with your friends, but the choice is not all or nothing. You must decide how many minutes to allocate to each activity. To make this decision, you compare the benefit of a little bit more study time with its cost—you make your choice at the **margin**.

The benefit that arises from an increase in an activity is called **marginal benefit**. For example, your marginal benefit from one more night of study before a test is the boost it gives to your grade. Your marginal benefit doesn't include the grade you're already achieving without that extra night of work.

The *opportunity cost* of an *increase* in an activity is called **marginal cost**. For you, the marginal cost of studying one more night is the cost of not spending that night on your favorite leisure activity.

To make your decisions, you compare marginal benefit and marginal cost. If the marginal benefit from an extra night of study exceeds its marginal cost, you study the extra night. If the marginal cost exceeds the marginal benefit, you don't study the extra night.

Choices Respond to Incentives

Economists take human nature as given and view people as acting in their self-interest. All people—you, other consumers, producers, politicians, and public servants—pursue their self-interest.

Self-interested actions are not necessarily *selfish* actions. You might decide to use your resources in ways that bring pleasure to others as well as to yourself. But a self-interested act gets the most benefit for *you* based on *your* view about benefit.

The central idea of economics is that we can predict the self-interested choices that people make by looking at the *incentives* they face. People undertake those activities for which marginal benefit exceeds marginal cost; and they reject options for which marginal cost exceeds marginal benefit.

For example, your economics instructor gives you a problem set and tells you these problems will be on the next test. Your marginal benefit from working these problems is large, so you diligently work them. In contrast, your math instructor gives you a problem set on a topic that she says will never be on a test. You get little marginal benefit from working these problems, so you decide to skip most of them.

Economists see incentives as the key to reconciling self-interest and social interest. When our choices are *not* in the social interest, it is because of the incentives we face. One of the challenges for economists is to figure out the incentives that result in self-interested choices being in the social interest.

Economists emphasize the crucial role that institutions play in influencing the incentives that people face as they pursue their self-interest. Laws that protect private property and markets that enable voluntary exchange are the fundamental institutions. You will learn as you progress with your study of economics that where these institutions exist, self-interest can indeed promote the social interest.

◆ REVIEW QUIZ

1 Explain the idea of a tradeoff and think of three tradeoffs that you have made today.
2 Explain what economists mean by rational choice and think of three choices that you've made today that are rational.
3 Explain why opportunity cost is the best forgone alternative and provide examples of some opportunity costs that you have faced today.
4 Explain what it means to choose at the margin and illustrate with three choices at the margin that you have made today.
5 Explain why choices respond to incentives and think of three incentives to which you have responded today.

Work these questions in Study Plan 1.3 and get instant feedback. Do a Key Terms Quiz.   MyEconLab

◆ Economics as Social Science and Policy Tool

Economics is both a social science and a toolkit for advising on policy decisions.

Economist as Social Scientist

As social scientists, economists seek to discover how the economic world works. In pursuit of this goal, like all scientists, economists distinguish between positive and normative statements.

Positive Statements A *positive* statement is about what *is*. It says what is currently believed about the way the world operates. A positive statement might be right or wrong, but we can test it by checking it against the facts. "Our planet is warming because of the amount of coal that we're burning" is a positive statement. We can test whether it is right or wrong.

A central task of economists is to test positive statements about how the economic world works and to weed out those that are wrong. Economics first got off the ground in the late 1700s, so it is a young science compared with, for example, physics, and much remains to be discovered.

Normative Statements A *normative* statement is about what *ought to be*. It depends on values and cannot be tested. Policy goals are normative statements. For example, "We ought to cut our use of coal by 50 percent" is a normative policy statement. You may agree or disagree with it, but you can't test it. It doesn't assert a fact that can be checked.

Unscrambling Cause and Effect Economists are particularly interested in positive statements about cause and effect. Are computers getting cheaper because people are buying them in greater quantities? Or are people buying computers in greater quantities because they are getting cheaper? Or is some third factor causing both the price of a computer to fall and the quantity of computers bought to increase?

To answer such questions, economists create and test economic models. An **economic model** is a description of some aspect of the economic world that includes only those features that are needed for the purpose at hand. For example, an economic model of a cellphone network might include features such as the prices of calls, the number of cellphone users, and the volume of calls. But the model would ignore cellphone colors and ringtones.

A model is tested by comparing its predictions with the facts. But testing an economic model is difficult because we observe the outcomes of the simultaneous change of many factors. To cope with this problem, economists look for natural experiments (situations in the ordinary course of economic life in which the one factor of interest is different and other things are equal or similar); conduct statistical investigations to find correlations; and perform economic experiments by putting people in decision-making situations and varying the influence of one factor at a time to discover how they respond.

Economist as Policy Adviser

Economics is useful. It is a toolkit for advising governments and businesses and for making personal decisions. Some of the most famous economists work partly as policy advisers.

Carmen M. Reinhart at the John F. Kennedy School of Government, Harvard University, has written widely on policy issues arising from government debt and international capital markets.

Maurice Obstfeld of the University of California, Berkeley, and Betsey Stevenson of the University of Michigan are on leave from their academic jobs and serving as economic adviser to President Barack Obama and members of the President's Council of Economic Advisers.

All the policy questions on which economists provide advice involve a blend of the positive and the normative. Economics can't help with the normative part—the policy goal. But it can help to clarify the goal. And for a given goal, economics provides the tools for evaluating alternative solutions—comparing marginal benefits and marginal costs and finding the solution that makes the best use of the available resources.

◆ REVIEW QUIZ

1 Distinguish between a positive statement and a normative statement and provide examples.
2 What is a model? Can you think of a model that you might use in your everyday life?
3 How do economists try to disentangle cause and effect?
4 How is economics used as a policy tool?

Work these questions in Study Plan 1.4 and get instant feedback. Do a Key Terms Quiz.   MyEconLab

◆ ECONOMICS IN THE NEWS

The Internet for Everyone

Mark Zuckerberg's Big Idea: The "Next 5 Billion"
Facebook founder Mark Zuckerberg wants to make it so that anyone, anywhere, can get online. To achieve this goal, he has created internet.org, "a global partnership between technology leaders, nonprofits, local communities, and experts who are working together to bring the Internet to the two thirds of the world's population that doesn't have it."

Sources: *CNN Money,* August 21, 2013 and internet.org

THE DATA

- The figure shows that almost 80 percent of Americans and Canadians have Internet access compared to only 16 percent of Africans and 28 percent of Asians.

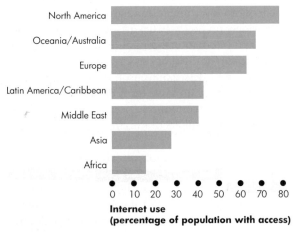

**Internet use
(percentage of population with access)**

Internet Access by Region

- Of the 5 billion people who Mark Zuckerberg wants to have Internet access, 1 billion live in Africa and 2.8 billion live in Asia.
- To figure out what it would take for everyone to have Internet access, we must make an assumption about how many people share resources.
- If four people shared, it would cost about $285 billion for computers and $115 billion a year for Internet access for everyone to get online.
- Satisfying Mark Zuckerberg's want would cost the equivalent of 400 years of Facebook's 2012 profit, or 1,600 Boeing 787 Dreamliners, or 90 aircraft carriers, or 87 billion Big Macs.

THE QUESTIONS

- What is the fundamental economic problem and how does this news clip illustrate it?
- What are some of the things that might be forgone for more people to get online?
- Why don't more people make the tradeoffs needed to get online?
- Why might it be in Mark Zuckerberg's self-interest to get everyone online?
- Why might it not be in the social interest for everyone to get online?

In Africa, 4 in 5 people lack Internet access.

THE ANSWERS

- The fundamental economic problem is scarcity—the fact that wants exceed the resources available to satisfy them. The news clip illustrates scarcity because Mark Zuckerberg's want for everyone to get online *exceeds* the resources available to satisfy it.
- Some of the scarce resources that are used to produce airplanes, war ships, and Big Macs could be reallocated and used to produce more computers and Internet service.
- People don't make the tradeoffs needed to get online because for them, the marginal cost of doing so would exceed the marginal benefit.
- It might be in Mark Zuckerberg's self-interest to get everyone online because that would increase the number of Facebook users and increase the firm's advertising revenues.
- It would not be in the social interest to get everyone online if the marginal cost of an Internet connection exceeded its marginal benefit.

◆ SUMMARY

Key Points

Definition of Economics (p. 2)

- All economic questions arise from scarcity—from the fact that wants exceed the resources available to satisfy them.
- Economics is the social science that studies the choices that people make as they cope with scarcity.
- The subject divides into microeconomics and macroeconomics.

Working Problem 1 will give you a better understanding of the definition of economics.

Two Big Economic Questions (pp. 3–8)

- Two big questions summarize the scope of economics:

  1. How do choices end up determining *what, how*, and *for whom* goods and services are produced?
  2. When do choices made in the pursuit of *self-interest* also promote the *social interest*?

Working Problems 2 and 3 will give you a better understanding of the two big questions of economics.

The Economic Way of Thinking (pp. 9–10)

- Every choice is a tradeoff—exchanging more of something for less of something else.
- People make rational choices by comparing benefit and cost.
- Cost—*opportunity cost*—is what you must give up to get something.
- Most choices are "how much" choices made at the *margin* by comparing marginal benefit and marginal cost.
- Choices respond to incentives.

Working Problems 4 and 5 will give you a better understanding of the economic way of thinking.

Economics as Social Science and Policy Tool (p. 11)

- Economists distinguish between positive statements—what is—and normative statements—what ought to be.
- To explain the economic world, economists create and test economic models.
- Economics is a toolkit used to provide advice on government, business, and personal economic decisions.

Working Problem 6 will give you a better understanding of economics as social science and policy tool.

Key Terms

Benefit, 9	Interest, 4	Profit, 4
Capital, 4	Labor, 3	Rational choice, 9
Economic model, 11	Land, 3	Rent, 4
Economics, 2	Macroeconomics, 2	Scarcity, 2
Efficient, 5	Margin, 10	Self-interest, 5
Entrepreneurship, 4	Marginal benefit, 10	Social interest, 5
Factors of production, 3	Marginal cost, 10	Tradeoff, 9
Goods and services, 3	Microeconomics, 2	Wages, 4
Human capital, 3	Opportunity cost, 9	
Incentive, 2	Preferences, 9	

STUDY PLAN PROBLEMS AND APPLICATIONS

MyEconLab   You can work Problems 1 to 6 in Chapter 1 Study Plan and get instant feedback.

Definition of Economics (Study Plan 1.1)

1. Apple Inc. decides to make iTunes freely available in unlimited quantities.
   a. Does Apple's decision change the incentives that people face?
   b. Is Apple's decision an example of a microeconomic or a macroeconomic issue?

Two Big Economic Questions (Study Plan 1.2)

2. Which of the following pairs does not match?
   a. Labor and wages
   b. Land and rent
   c. Entrepreneurship and profit
   d. Capital and profit

3. Explain how the following news headlines concern self-interest and the social interest.
   a. Starbucks Expands in China
   b. McDonald's Moves into Gourmet Coffee
   c. Food Must Be Labeled with Nutrition Data

The Economic Way of Thinking (Study Plan 1.3)

4. The night before an economics test, you decide to go to the movies instead of staying home and working your MyEconLab Study Plan. You get 50 percent on your test compared with the 70 percent that you normally score.
   a. Did you face a tradeoff?
   b. What was the opportunity cost of your evening at the movies?

5. **Cost of Sochi Winter Olympics**
   The Russian government spent $6.7 billion on Olympic facilities and $16.7 billion upgrading Sochi area infrastructure. Sponsors spent $27.6 billion on hotels and facilities hoping to turn Sochi into a year-round tourist magnet.
   Source: *The Washington Post*, February 11, 2014
   Was the opportunity cost of the Sochi Olympics $6.7, $23.4, or $51 billion? Explain your answer.

Economics as Social Science and Policy Tool

(Study Plan 1.4)

6. Which of the following statements is positive, which is normative, and which can be tested?
   a. The United States should cut its imports.
   b. China is the largest trading partner of the United States.
   c. If the price of antiretroviral drugs increases, HIV/AIDS sufferers will decrease their consumption of the drugs.

 ADDITIONAL PROBLEMS AND APPLICATIONS

MyEconLab   You can work these problems in MyEconLab if assigned by your instructor.

Definition of Economics

7. **Rapper Offers Free Tickets for Concert**
   Eminem will hit the road with Rihanna offering an awesome deal—buy one and get one free!
   Source: *Mstars News*, February 24, 2014
   When Eminem gave away tickets, what was free and what was scarce? Explain your answer.

Two Big Economic Questions

8. How does the creation of a successful movie influence *what*, *how*, and *for whom* goods and services are produced?

9. How does a successful movie illustrate self-interested choices that are also in the social interest?

The Economic Way of Thinking

10. Before starring in *Iron Man*, Robert Downey Jr. had appeared in 45 movies that grossed an average of $5 million on the opening weekend. In contrast, *Iron Man* grossed $102 million.
    a. How will the success of *Iron Man* influence the opportunity cost of hiring Robert Downey Jr.?
    b. How have the incentives for a movie producer to hire Robert Downey Jr. changed?

11. What might be an incentive for you to take a class in summer school? List some of the benefits and costs involved in your decision. Would your choice be rational?

Economics as Social Science and Policy Tool

12. Look at today's *Wall Street Journal*. What is the leading economic news story? With which of the big economic questions does it deal and what tradeoffs does it discuss or imply?

13. Provide two microeconomic statements and two macroeconomic statements. Classify your statements as positive or normative, and explain your classifications.

APPENDIX

Graphs in Economics

After studying this appendix, you will be able to:

◆ Make and interpret a scatter diagram
◆ Identify linear and nonlinear relationships and relationships that have a maximum and a minimum
◆ Define and calculate the slope of a line
◆ Graph relationships among more than two variables

◆ Graphing Data

A graph represents a quantity as a distance on a line. In Fig. A1.1, a distance on the horizontal line represents temperature, measured in degrees Fahrenheit. A movement from left to right shows an increase in temperature. The point 0 represents zero degrees Fahrenheit. To the right of 0, the temperature is positive. To the left of 0, the temperature is negative (as indicated by the minus sign). A distance on the vertical line represents height, measured in thousands of feet. The point 0 represents sea level. Points above 0 represent feet above sea level. Points below 0 represent feet below sea level (indicated by a minus sign).

In Fig. A1.1, the two scale lines are perpendicular to each other and are called *axes*. The vertical line is the *y*-axis, and the horizontal line is the *x*-axis. Each axis has a zero point, which is shared by the two axes and called the *origin*.

To make a two-variable graph, we need two pieces of information: the value of the variable *x* and the value of the variable *y*. For example, off the coast of Alaska, the temperature is 32 degrees—the value of *x*. A fishing boat is located at 0 feet above sea level—the value of *y*. These two bits of information appear as point *A* in Fig. A1.1. A climber at the top of Mount McKinley on a cold day is 20,320 feet above sea level in a zero-degree gale. These two pieces of information appear as point *B*. On a warmer day, a climber might be at the peak of Mt. McKinley when the temperature is 32 degrees, at point *C*.

We can draw two lines, called *coordinates*, from point *C*. One, called the *x*-coordinate, runs from *C* to the vertical axis. This line is called "the *x*-coordinate"

FIGURE A1.1 Making a Graph

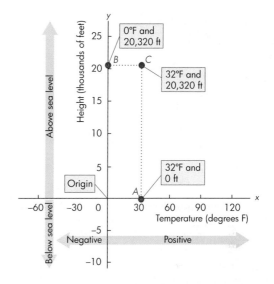

Graphs have axes that measure quantities as distances. Here, the horizontal axis (*x*-axis) measures temperature, and the vertical axis (*y*-axis) measures height. Point *A* represents a fishing boat at sea level (0 on the *y*-axis) on a day when the temperature is 32°F. Point *B* represents a climber at the top of Mt. McKinley, 20,320 feet above sea level at a temperature of 0°F. Point *C* represents a climber at the top of Mt. McKinley, 20,320 feet above sea level at a temperature of 32°F.

MyEconLab Animation

because its length is the same as the value marked off on the *x*-axis. The other, called the *y*-coordinate, runs from *C* to the horizontal axis. This line is called "the *y*-coordinate" because its length is the same as the value marked off on the *y*-axis.

We describe a point on a graph by the values of its *x*-coordinate and its *y*-coordinate. For example, at point *C*, *x* is 32 degrees and *y* is 20,320 feet.

A graph like that in Fig. A1.1 can be made using any quantitative data on two variables. The graph can show just a few points, like Fig. A1.1, or many points. Before we look at graphs with many points, let's reinforce what you've just learned by looking at two graphs made with economic data.

Economists measure variables that describe *what, how,* and *for whom* goods and services are produced. These variables are quantities produced and prices. Figure A1.2 shows two examples of economic graphs.

FIGURE A1.2   Two Graphs of Economic Data

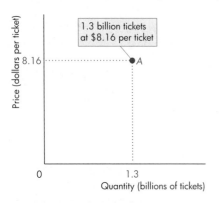

1.3 billion tickets at $8.16 per ticket

(a) Movie tickets: quantity and price

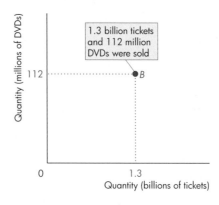

1.3 billion tickets and 112 million DVDs were sold

(b) Movies: tickets and DVDs

The graph in part (a) tells us that in 2013, 1.3 billion movie tickets were sold at an average price of $8.16 per ticket.

The graph in part (b) tells us that in 2013, 1.3 billion movie tickets and 112 million DVDs were sold.

Figure A1.2(a) is a graph about movies in 2013. The *x*-axis measures the quantity of movie tickets sold and the *y*-axis measures the average price of a ticket. Point *A* tells us what the quantity and price were. You can "read" this graph as telling you that in 2013, 1.3 billion movie tickets were sold at an average ticket price of $8.16.

Figure A1.2(b) is a graph about movie-going and DVD buying. The *x*-axis measures the quantity of movie tickets sold in 2013 and the *y*-axis measures the quantity of DVDs sold in the same year. Point *B* tells us what these quantities were. You can "read" this graph as telling you that in 2013, 1.3 billion movie tickets and 112 million DVDs were sold.

The three graphs that you've just seen tell you how to make a graph and how to read a data point on a graph, but they don't improve on the raw data. Graphs become interesting and revealing when they contain a number of data points because then you can visualize the data.

Economists create graphs based on the principles in Figs. A1.1 and A1.2 to reveal, describe, and visualize the relationships among variables. We're now going to look at some examples. These graphs are called scatter diagrams.

Scatter Diagrams

A **scatter diagram** is a graph that plots the value of one variable against the value of another variable for a number of different values of each variable. Such a graph reveals whether a relationship exists between two variables and describes their relationship.

The table in Fig. A1.3 shows some data on two variables: the number of tickets sold at the box office and the number of DVDs sold for nine of the most popular movies in 2013.

What is the relationship between these two variables? Does a big box office success generate a large volume of DVD sales? Or does a box office success mean that fewer DVDs are sold?

We can answer these questions by making a scatter diagram. We do so by graphing the data in the table. In the graph in Fig. A1.3, each point shows the number of box office tickets sold (the *x* variable) and the number of DVDs sold (the *y* variable) of one of the movies. There are nine movies, so there are nine points "scattered" within the graph.

The point labeled *A* tells us that *Monsters University* sold 33 million tickets at the box office and 2.3 million DVDs. The points in the graph don't form a distinct pattern. They suggest that large box office sales do not directly bring large DVD sales. If you want to predict a movie's DVD sales in a given year with any confidence, you need to know more than the number of tickets sold at the box office in that year.

Figure A1.4 shows two scatter diagrams of economic variables. Part (a) shows the relationship between income and expenditure, on average, from 2001 to 2013. Each point represents income and expenditure in a given year. For example, point *A* shows that in 2006, income was $38,000 and expenditure was $31,000. This graph shows that as income increases, so does expenditure, and the relationship is a close one.

FIGURE A1.3   A Scatter Diagram

Movie	Tickets	DVDs
	(millions)	
Iron Man 3	50	1.1
The Hunger Games: Catching Fire	49	1.3
Despicable Me 2	45	1.8
Man of Steel	36	1.2
Frozen	34	0
Monsters University	33	2.3
Gravity	31	0
Fast and Furious 6	29	0
Oz the Great and Powerful	29	1.4

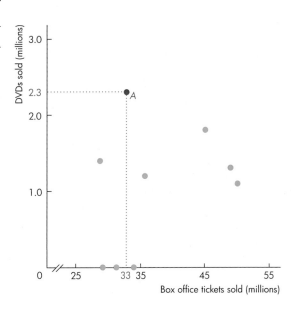

The table lists the number of tickets sold at the box office and the number of DVDs sold for nine popular movies.

The scatter diagram reveals the relationship between these two variables. Each point shows the values of the variables for a specific movie. For example, point A shows the point for *Monsters University*, which sold 33 million tickets and 2.3 million DVDs.

The pattern formed by the points shows no tendency for large box office sales to bring greater DVD sales. You cannot predict how many DVDs of a movie will sell in a given year just by knowing its box office sales in that year.

MyEconLab Animation

Figure A1.4(b) shows a scatter diagram of U.S. inflation and unemployment from 2001 through 2013. Here, the points show no relationship between the two variables. For example, when unemployment was high, the inflation rate was high in 2009 and low in 2010.

You can see that a scatter diagram conveys a wealth of information, and it does so in much less space than we have used to describe only some of its features. But you do have to "read" the graph to obtain all this information.

FIGURE A1.4   Two Economic Scatter Diagrams

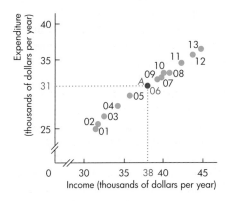

(a) Income and expenditure

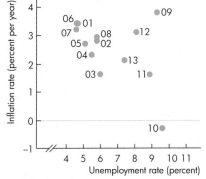

(b) Unemployment and inflation

The scatter diagram in part (a) shows the relationship between income and expenditure from 2001 to 2013. Point A shows that in 2006, income was $38,000 on the x-axis and expenditure was $31,000 on the y-axis. This graph shows that as income rises, so does expenditure and the relationship is a close one.

The scatter diagram in part (b) shows a weak relationship between unemployment and inflation in the United States during most of the years.

MyEconLab Animation

Breaks in the Axes The graph in Fig. A1.4(a) has breaks in its axes, as shown by the small gaps. The breaks indicate that there are jumps from the origin, 0, to the first values recorded.

The breaks are used because the lowest value of income is $30,000 and the lowest value of expenditure exceeds $25,000. If we made this graph with no breaks in its axes, there would be a lot of empty space, the points would be crowded into the top right corner, and it would be difficult to see whether a relationship exists between these two variables. By breaking the axes, we are able to bring the relationship into view.

Putting a break in one or both axes is like using a zoom lens to bring the relationship into the center of the graph and magnify it so that the relationship fills the graph.

Misleading Graphs Breaks can be used to highlight a relationship, but they can also be used to mislead—to make a graph that lies. The most common way of making a graph lie is to put a break in the axis and either to stretch or compress the scale. For example, suppose that in Fig. A1.4(a), we remove the break on the *y*-axis and expenditure ran from zero to $40,000 while the *x*-axis was unchanged. The graph would now create the impression that despite a huge increase in income, expenditure had barely changed.

To avoid being misled, it is a good idea to get into the habit of always looking closely at the values and the labels on the axes of a graph before you start to interpret it.

Correlation and Causation A scatter diagram that shows a clear relationship between two variables, such as Fig. A1.4(a), tells us that the two variables have a high correlation. When a high correlation is present, we can predict the value of one variable from the value of the other variable. But correlation does not imply causation.

Sometimes a high correlation does arise from a causal relationship. It is likely that rising income causes rising expenditure (Fig. A1.4a). But a high correlation can mean that two variables have a common cause. For example, ice cream sales and pool drownings are correlated not because one causes the other, but because both are caused by hot weather.

You've now seen how we can use graphs in economics to show economic data and to reveal relationships. Next, we'll learn how economists use graphs to construct and display economic models.

◆ Graphs Used in Economic Models

The graphs used in economics are not always designed to show real-world data. Often they are used to show general relationships among the variables in an economic model.

An *economic model* is a stripped-down, simplified description of an economy or of a component of an economy such as a business or a household. It consists of statements about economic behavior that can be expressed as equations or as curves in a graph. Economists use models to explore the effects of different policies or other influences on the economy in ways that are similar to the use of model airplanes in wind tunnels and models of the climate.

You will encounter many different kinds of graphs in economic models, but there are some repeating patterns. Once you've learned to recognize these patterns, you will instantly understand the meaning of a graph. Here, we'll look at the different types of curves that are used in economic models, and we'll see some everyday examples of each type of curve. The patterns to look for in graphs are the four cases in which

- Variables move in the same direction.
- Variables move in opposite directions.
- Variables have a maximum or a minimum.
- Variables are unrelated.

Let's look at these four cases.

Variables That Move in the Same Direction

Figure A1.5 shows graphs of the relationships between two variables that move up and down together. A relationship between two variables that move in the same direction is called a **positive relationship** or a **direct relationship**. A line that slopes upward shows such a relationship.

Figure A1.5 shows three types of relationships: one that has a straight line and two that have curved lines. All the lines in these three graphs are called curves. Any line on a graph—no matter whether it is straight or curved—is called a *curve*.

A relationship shown by a straight line is called a **linear relationship**. Figure A1.5(a) shows a linear relationship between the number of miles traveled in

FIGURE A1.5   Positive (Direct) Relationships

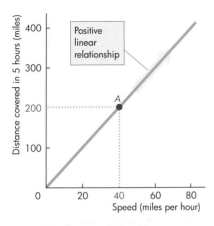

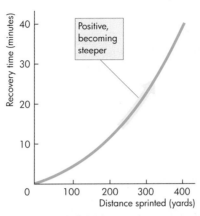

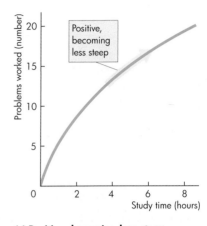

(a) Positive linear relationship   **(b) Positive, becoming steeper**   **(c) Positive, becoming less steep**

Each part shows a positive (direct) relationship between two variables. That is, as the value of the variable measured on the x-axis increases, so does the value of the variable measured on the y-axis. Part (a) shows a linear positive relationship—as the two variables increase together, we move along a straight line.

Part (b) shows a positive relationship such that as the two variables increase together, we move along a curve that becomes steeper.

Part (c) shows a positive relationship such that as the two variables increase together, we move along a curve that becomes flatter.

MyEconLab Animation

5 hours and speed. For example, point *A* shows that you will travel 200 miles in 5 hours if your speed is 40 miles an hour. If you double your speed to 80 miles an hour, you will travel 400 miles in 5 hours.

Figure A1.5(b) shows the relationship between distance sprinted and recovery time (the time it takes the heart rate to return to its normal resting rate). This relationship is an upward-sloping one that starts out quite flat but then becomes steeper as we move along the curve away from the origin. The reason this curve becomes steeper is that the additional recovery time needed from sprinting an additional 100 yards increases. It takes less than 5 minutes to recover from sprinting 100 yards but more than 10 minutes to recover from 200 yards.

Figure A1.5(c) shows the relationship between the number of problems worked by a student and the amount of study time. This relationship is an upward-sloping one that starts out quite steep and becomes flatter as we move along the curve away from the origin. Study time becomes less productive as the student spends more hours studying and becomes more tired.

Variables That Move in Opposite Directions

Figure A1.6 shows relationships between things that move in opposite directions. A relationship between variables that move in opposite directions is called a **negative relationship** or an **inverse relationship**.

Figure A1.6(a) shows the relationship between the hours spent playing squash and the hours spent playing tennis when the total time available is 5 hours. One extra hour spent playing tennis means one hour less spent playing squash and vice versa. This relationship is negative and linear.

Figure A1.6(b) shows the relationship between the cost per mile traveled and the length of a journey. The longer the journey, the lower is the cost per mile. But as the journey length increases, even though the cost per mile decreases, the fall in the cost per mile is smaller the longer the journey. This feature of the relationship is shown by the fact that the curve slopes downward, starting out steep at a short journey length and then becoming flatter as the journey length increases. This relationship arises because some of the costs are fixed, such as auto insurance, and the fixed costs are spread over a longer journey.

FIGURE A1.6   Negative (Inverse) Relationships

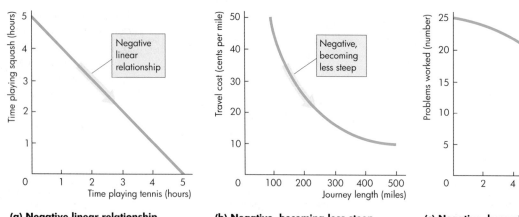

(a) Negative linear relationship   **(b) Negative, becoming less steep**   **(c) Negative, becoming steeper**

Each part shows a negative (inverse) relationship between two variables. Part (a) shows a linear negative relationship. The total time spent playing tennis and squash is 5 hours. As the time spent playing tennis increases, the time spent playing squash decreases, and we move along a straight line.

Part (b) shows a negative relationship such that as the journey length increases, the travel cost decreases as we move along a curve that becomes less steep.

Part (c) shows a negative relationship such that as leisure time increases, the number of problems worked decreases as we move along a curve that becomes steeper.

MyEconLab Animation

Figure A1.6(c) shows the relationship between the amount of leisure time and the number of problems worked by a student. Increasing leisure time produces an increasingly large reduction in the number of problems worked. This relationship is a negative one that starts out with a gentle slope at a small number of leisure hours and becomes steeper as the number of leisure hours increases. This relationship is a different view of the idea shown in Fig. A1.5(c).

Variables That Have a Maximum or a Minimum

Many relationships in economic models have a maximum or a minimum. For example, firms try to make the maximum possible profit and to produce at the lowest possible cost. Figure A1.7 shows relationships that have a maximum or a minimum.

Figure A1.7(a) shows the relationship between rainfall and wheat yield. When there is no rainfall, wheat will not grow, so the yield is zero. As the rainfall increases up to 10 days a month, the wheat yield

increases. With 10 rainy days each month, the wheat yield reaches its maximum at 40 bushels an acre (point *A*). Rain in excess of 10 days a month starts to lower the yield of wheat. If every day is rainy, the wheat suffers from a lack of sunshine and the yield decreases to zero. This relationship is one that starts out sloping upward, reaches a maximum, and then slopes downward.

Figure A1.7(b) shows the reverse case—a relationship that begins sloping downward, falls to a minimum, and then slopes upward. Most economic costs are like this relationship. An example is the relationship between the cost per mile and the speed of the car. At low speeds, the car is creeping in a traffic snarl-up. The number of miles per gallon is low, so the cost per mile is high. At high speeds, the car is traveling faster than its efficient speed, using a large quantity of gasoline, and again the number of miles per gallon is low and the cost per mile is high. At a speed of 55 miles an hour, the cost per mile is at its minimum (point *B*). This relationship is one that starts out sloping downward, reaches a minimum, and then slopes upward.

FIGURE A1.7   Maximum and Minimum Points

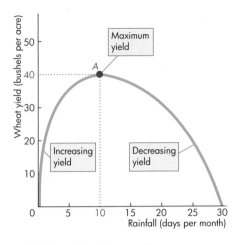

(a) Relationship with a maximum

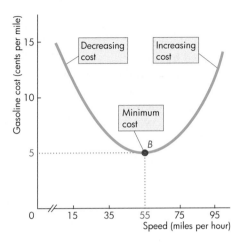

(b) Relationship with a minimum

Part (a) shows a relationship that has a maximum point, *A*. The curve slopes upward as it rises to its maximum point, is flat at its maximum, and then slopes downward.

Part (b) shows a relationship with a minimum point, *B*. The curve slopes downward as it falls to its minimum, is flat at its minimum, and then slopes upward.

MyEconLab Animation

Variables That Are Unrelated

There are many situations in which no matter what happens to the value of one variable, the other variable remains constant. Sometimes we want to show the independence between two variables in a graph, and Fig. A1.8 shows two ways of achieving this.

In describing the graphs in Fig. A1.5 through Fig. A1.7, we have talked about curves that slope upward or slope downward, and curves that become less steep or steeper. Let's spend a little time discussing exactly what we mean by *slope* and how we measure the slope of a curve.

FIGURE A1.8   Variables That Are Unrelated

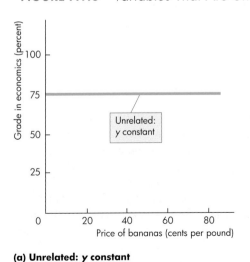

(a) Unrelated: *y* constant

(b) Unrelated: *x* constant

This figure shows how we can graph two variables that are unrelated. In part (a), a student's grade in economics is plotted at 75 percent on the *y*-axis regardless of the price of bananas on the *x*-axis. The curve is horizontal.

In part (b), the output of the vineyards of France on the *x*-axis does not vary with the rainfall in California on the *y*-axis. The curve is vertical.

MyEconLab Animation

◆ The Slope of a Relationship

We can measure the influence of one variable on another by the slope of the relationship. The **slope** of a relationship is the change in the value of the variable measured on the *y*-axis divided by the change in the value of the variable measured on the *x*-axis. We use the Greek letter Δ (*delta*) to represent "change in." Thus Δ*y* means the change in the value of the variable measured on the *y*-axis, and Δ*x* means the change in the value of the variable measured on the *x*-axis. Therefore the slope of the relationship is

$$\text{Slope} = \frac{\Delta y}{\Delta x}.$$

If a large change in the variable measured on the *y*-axis (Δ*y*) is associated with a small change in the variable measured on the *x*-axis (Δ*x*), the slope is large and the curve is steep. If a small change in the variable measured on the *y*-axis (Δ*y*) is associated with a large change in the variable measured on the *x*-axis (Δ*x*), the slope is small and the curve is flat.

We can make the idea of slope clearer by doing some calculations.

The Slope of a Straight Line

The slope of a straight line is the same regardless of where on the line you calculate it. The slope of a straight line is constant. Let's calculate the slope of the positive relationship in Fig. A1.9. In part (a),

---

FIGURE A1.9   The Slope of a Straight Line

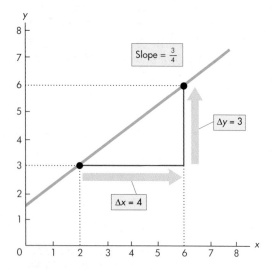

(a) Positive slope

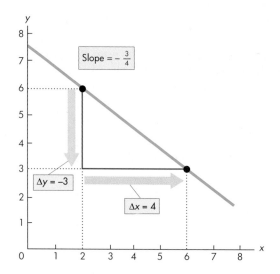

(b) Negative slope

To calculate the slope of a straight line, we divide the change in the value of the variable measured on the *y*-axis (Δ*y*) by the change in the value of the variable measured on the *x*-axis (Δ*x*) as we move along the line.

Part (a) shows the calculation of a positive slope. When *x* increases from 2 to 6, Δ*x* equals 4. That change in *x*

brings about an increase in *y* from 3 to 6, so Δ*y* equals 3. The slope (Δ*y*/Δ*x*) equals 3/4.

Part (b) shows the calculation of a negative slope. When *x* increases from 2 to 6, Δ*x* equals 4. That increase in *x* brings about a decrease in *y* from 6 to 3, so Δ*y* equals −3. The slope (Δ*y*/Δ*x*) equals −3/4.

MyEconLab Animation

FIGURE A1.11   Slope Across an Arc

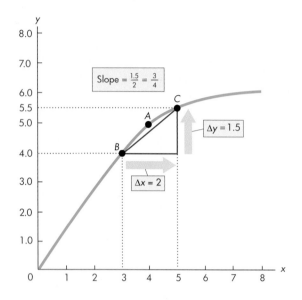

To calculate the average slope of the curve along the arc *BC*, draw a straight line from point *B* to point *C*. The slope of the line *BC* is calculated by dividing the change in *y* by the change in *x*. In moving from *B* to *C*, the increase in *x* is 2 (Δ*x* equals 2) and the change in *y* is 1.5 (Δ*y* equals 1.5). The slope of the line *BC* is 1.5 divided by 2, or 3/4. So the slope of the curve across the arc *BC* is 3/4.

————— MyEconLab *Animation* —————

Therefore the slope is

$$\frac{\Delta y}{\Delta x} = \frac{1.5}{2} = \frac{3}{4}.$$

So the slope of the curve across the arc *BC* is 3/4.

This calculation gives us the slope of the curve between points *B* and *C*. The actual slope calculated is the slope of the straight line from *B* to *C*. This slope approximates the average slope of the curve along the arc *BC*. In this particular example, the slope across the arc *BC* is identical to the slope of the curve at point *A*, but the calculation of the slope of a curve does not always work out so neatly. You might have fun constructing some more examples and a few counterexamples.

You now know how to make and interpret a graph. So far, we've limited our attention to graphs of two variables. We're now going to learn how to graph more than two variables.

◆ Graphing Relationships Among More Than Two Variables

We have seen that we can graph the relationship between two variables as a point formed by the *x*- and *y*-coordinates in a two-dimensional graph. You might be thinking that although a two-dimensional graph is informative, most of the things in which you are likely to be interested involve relationships among many variables, not just two. For example, the amount of ice cream consumed depends on the price of ice cream and the temperature. If ice cream is expensive and the temperature is low, people eat much less ice cream than when ice cream is inexpensive and the temperature is high. For any given price of ice cream, the quantity consumed varies with the temperature; and for any given temperature, the quantity of ice cream consumed varies with its price.

Figure A1.12 shows a relationship among three variables. The table shows the number of gallons of ice cream consumed each day at two different temperatures and at a number of different prices of ice cream. How can we graph these numbers?

To graph a relationship that involves more than two variables, we use the *ceteris paribus* assumption.

Ceteris Paribus

Ceteris paribus (often shortened to *cet par*) means "if all other relevant things remain the same." To isolate the relationship of interest in a laboratory experiment, a scientist holds everything constant except for the variable whose effect is being studied. Economists use the same method to graph a relationship that has more than two variables.

Figure A1.12 shows an example. There, you can see what happens to the quantity of ice cream consumed when the price of ice cream varies but the temperature is held constant.

The curve labeled 70°F shows the relationship between ice cream consumption and the price of ice cream if the temperature remains at 70°F. The numbers used to plot that curve are those in the first two columns of the table. For example, if the temperature is 70°F, 10 gallons are consumed when the price is $2.75 a scoop and 18 gallons are consumed when the price is $2.25 a scoop.

The curve labeled 90°F shows the relationship between ice cream consumption and the price of ice cream if the temperature remains at 90°F. The

FIGURE A1.12 Graphing a Relationship Among Three Variables

Price (dollars per scoop)	Ice cream consumption (gallons per day)	
	70°F	90°F
2.00	25	50
2.25	18	36
2.50	13	26
2.75	**10**	**20**
3.00	7	14
3.25	5	10
3.50	3	6

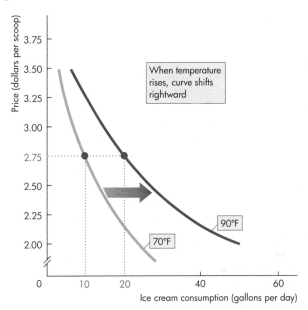

Ice cream consumption depends on its price and the temperature. The table tells us how many gallons of ice cream are consumed each day at different prices and two different temperatures. For example, if the price is $2.75 a scoop and the temperature is 70°F, 10 gallons of ice cream are consumed.

To graph a relationship among three variables, the value of one variable is held constant. The graph shows the relationship between price and consumption when temperature is held constant. One curve holds temperature at 70°F and the other holds it at 90°F.

A change in the price of ice cream brings a movement along one of the curves—along the blue curve at 70°F and along the red curve at 90°F.

When the temperature *rises* from 70°F to 90°F, the curve that shows the relationship between consumption and price *shifts* rightward from the blue curve to the red curve.

MyEconLab Animation

numbers used to plot that curve are those in the first and third columns of the table. For example, if the temperature is 90°F, 20 gallons are consumed when the price is $2.75 a scoop and 36 gallons are consumed when the price is $2.25 a scoop.

When the price of ice cream changes but the temperature is constant, you can think of what happens in the graph as a movement along one of the curves. At 70°F there is a movement along the blue curve and at 90°F there is a movement along the red curve.

When Other Things Change

The temperature is held constant along each of the curves in Fig. A1.12, but in reality the temperature changes. When that event occurs, you can think of what happens in the graph as a shift of the curve. When the temperature rises from 70°F to 90°F, the curve that shows the relationship between ice cream consumption and the price of ice cream shifts rightward from the blue curve to the red curve.

You will encounter these ideas of movements along and shifts of curves at many points in your study of economics. Think carefully about what you've just learned and make up some examples (with assumed numbers) about other relationships.

With what you have learned about graphs, you can move forward with your study of economics. There are no graphs in this book that are more complicated than those that have been explained in this appendix.

MATHEMATICAL NOTE

Equations of Straight Lines

If a straight line in a graph describes the relationship between two variables, we call it a linear relationship. Figure 1 shows the *linear relationship* between a person's expenditure and income. This person spends $100 a week (by borrowing or spending previous savings) when income is zero. Out of each dollar earned, this person spends 50 cents (and saves 50 cents).

All linear relationships are described by the same general equation. We call the quantity that is measured on the horizontal axis (or *x*-axis) *x,* and we call the quantity that is measured on the vertical axis (or *y*-axis) *y.* In the case of Fig. 1, *x* is income and *y* is expenditure.

A Linear Equation

The equation that describes a straight-line relationship between *x* and *y* is

$$y = a + bx.$$

In this equation, *a* and *b* are fixed numbers and they are called *constants*. The values of *x* and *y* vary, so these numbers are called *variables*. Because the equation describes a straight line, the equation is called a *linear equation*.

The equation tells us that when the value of *x* is zero, the value of *y* is *a*. We call the constant *a* the *y*-axis intercept. The reason is that on the graph the straight line hits the *y*-axis at a value equal to *a*. Figure 1 illustrates the *y*-axis intercept.

For positive values of *x*, the value of *y* exceeds *a*. The constant *b* tells us by how much *y* increases above *a* as *x* increases. The constant *b* is the slope of the line.

Slope of Line

As we explain in the chapter, the *slope* of a relationship is the change in the value of *y* divided by the change in the value of *x*. We use the Greek letter Δ (delta) to represent "change in." So Δy means the change in the value of the variable measured on the *y*-axis, and Δx means the change in the value of the variable measured on the *x*-axis. Therefore the slope of the relationship is

$$\text{Slope} = \frac{\Delta y}{\Delta x}.$$

To see why the slope is *b*, suppose that initially the value of *x* is x_1, or $200 in Fig. 2. The corresponding value of *y* is y_1, also $200 in Fig. 2. The equation of the line tells us that

$$y_1 = a + bx_1. \tag{1}$$

Now the value of *x* increases by Δx to $x_1 + \Delta x$ (or $400 in Fig. 2). And the value of *y* increases by Δy to $y_1 + \Delta y$ (or $300 in Fig. 2).

The equation of the line now tells us that

$$y_1 + \Delta y = a + b(x_1 + \Delta x). \tag{2}$$

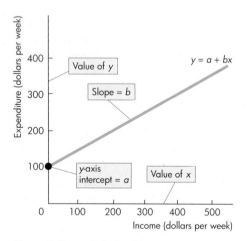

Figure 1 Linear Relationship

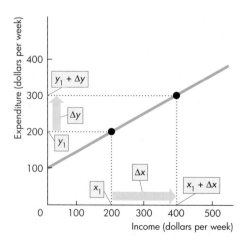

Figure 2 Calculating Slope

To calculate the slope of the line, subtract equation (1) from equation (2) to obtain

$$\Delta y = b\Delta x \qquad (3)$$

and now divide equation (3) by Δx to obtain

$$\Delta y/\Delta x = b.$$

So the slope of the line is b.

Position of Line

The y-axis intercept determines the position of the line on the graph. Figure 3 illustrates the relationship between the y-axis intercept and the position of the line. In this graph, the y-axis measures saving and the x-axis measures income.

When the y-axis intercept, a, is positive, the line hits the y-axis at a positive value of y—as the blue line does. Its y-axis intercept is 100. When the y-axis intercept, a, is zero, the line hits the y-axis at the origin—as the purple line does. Its y-axis intercept is 0. When the y-axis intercept, a, is negative, the line hits the y-axis at a negative value of y—as the red line does. Its y-axis intercept is -100.

As the equations of the three lines show, the value of the y-axis intercept does not influence the slope of the line. All three lines have a slope equal to 0.5.

Positive Relationships

Figure 1 shows a positive relationship—the two variables x and y move in the same direction. All positive

relationships have a slope that is positive. In the equation of the line, the constant b is positive. In this example, the y-axis intercept, a, is 100. The slope b equals $\Delta y/\Delta x$, which in Fig. 2 is 100/200 or 0.5. The equation of the line is

$$y = 100 + 0.5x.$$

Negative Relationships

Figure 4 shows a negative relationship—the two variables x and y move in the opposite direction. All negative relationships have a slope that is negative. In the equation of the line, the constant b is negative. In the example in Fig. 4, the y-axis intercept, a, is 30. The slope, b, equals $\Delta y/\Delta x$, which is $-20/2$ or -10. The equation of the line is

$$y = 30 + (-10)x$$

or

$$y = 30 - 10x.$$

Example

A straight line has a y-axis intercept of 50 and a slope of 2. What is the equation of this line?
The equation of a straight line is

$$y = a + bx$$

where a is the y-axis intercept and b is the slope. So the equation is

$$y = 50 + 2x.$$

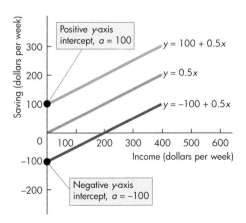

Figure 3 The *y*-Axis Intercept

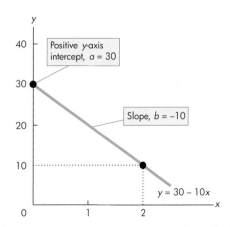

Figure 4 Negative Relationship

REVIEW QUIZ

1 Explain how we "read" the three graphs in Figs. A1.1 and A1.2.
2 Explain what scatter diagrams show and why we use them.
3 Explain how we "read" the three scatter diagrams in Figs. A1.3 and A1.4.
4 Draw a graph to show the relationship between two variables that move in the same direction.
5 Draw a graph to show the relationship between two variables that move in opposite directions.
6 Draw a graph of two variables whose relationship shows (i) a maximum and (ii) a minimum.

7 Which of the relationships in Questions 4 and 5 is a positive relationship and which is a negative relationship?
8 What are the two ways of calculating the slope of a curved line?
9 How do we graph a relationship among more than two variables?
10 Explain what change will bring a *movement along* a curve.
11 Explain what change will bring a *shift* of a curve.

Work these questions in Study Plan 1A and get instant feedback.   MyEconLab

 SUMMARY

Key Points

Graphing Data (pp. 15–18)

- A graph is made by plotting the values of two variables *x* and *y* at a point that corresponds to their values measured along the *x*-axis and the *y*-axis.
- A scatter diagram is a graph that plots the values of two variables for a number of different values of each.
- A scatter diagram shows the relationship between the two variables. It shows whether they are positively related, negatively related, or unrelated.

Graphs Used in Economic Models (pp. 18–21)

- Graphs are used to show relationships among variables in economic models.
- Relationships can be positive (an upward-sloping curve), negative (a downward-sloping curve), positive and then negative (have a maximum point), negative and then positive (have a minimum point), or unrelated (a horizontal or vertical curve).

The Slope of a Relationship (pp. 22–24)

- The slope of a relationship is calculated as the change in the value of the variable measured on the *y*-axis divided by the change in the value of the variable measured on the *x*-axis—that is, $\Delta y/\Delta x$.
- A straight line has a constant slope.
- A curved line has a varying slope. To calculate the slope of a curved line, we calculate the slope at a point or across an arc.

Graphing Relationships Among More Than Two Variables (pp. 24–25)

- To graph a relationship among more than two variables, we hold constant the values of all the variables except two.
- We then plot the value of one of the variables against the value of another.
- A *cet par* change in the value of a variable on an axis of a graph brings a movement along the curve.
- A change in the value of a variable held constant along the curve brings a shift of the curve.

Key Terms

MyEconLab Key Terms Quiz

Ceteris paribus, 24
Direct relationship, 18
Inverse relationship, 19

Linear relationship, 18
Negative relationship, 19
Positive relationship, 18

Scatter diagram, 16
Slope, 22

STUDY PLAN PROBLEMS AND APPLICATIONS

MyEconLab   You can work Problems 1 to 11 in Chapter 1A Study Plan and get instant feedback.

Use the following spreadsheet to work Problems 1 to 3. The spreadsheet provides data on the U.S. economy: Column A is the year, column B is the inflation rate, column C is the interest rate, column D is the growth rate, and column E is the unemployment rate.

	A	B	C	D	E
1	2003	1.6	1.0	2.8	6.0
2	2004	2.3	1.4	3.8	5.5
3	2005	2.7	3.2	3.4	5.1
4	2006	3.4	4.9	2.7	4.6
5	2007	3.2	4.5	1.8	4.6
6	2008	2.9	1.4	−0.3	5.8
7	2009	3.8	0.2	−2.8	9.3
8	2010	−0.3	0.1	2.5	9.6
9	2011	1.6	0.1	1.8	8.9
10	2012	3.1	0.1	2.8	8.1
11	2013	2.1	0.1	1.9	7.4

1. Draw a scatter diagram of the inflation rate and the interest rate. Describe the relationship.
2. Draw a scatter diagram of the growth rate and the unemployment rate. Describe the relationship.
3. Draw a scatter diagram of the interest rate and the unemployment rate. Describe the relationship.

Use the following news clip to work Problems 4 to 6.

LEGO Tops the Box Office

Movie	Theaters (number)	Revenue (dollars per theater)
The LEGO Movie	3,775	$16,551
About Last Night	2,253	$12,356
RoboCop	3,372	$7,432
The Monuments Men	3,083	$5,811

Source: boxofficemojo.com,
Data for weekend of February 14–17, 2014

4. Draw a graph of the relationship between the revenue per theater on the *y*-axis and the number of theaters on the *x*-axis. Describe the relationship.
5. Calculate the slope of the relationship in Problem 4 between 3,775 and 2,253 theaters.
6. Calculate the slope of the relationship in Problem 4 between 2,253 and 3,372 theaters.

7. Calculate the slope of the following relationship.

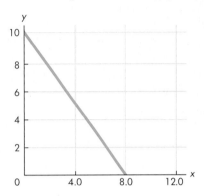

Use the following relationship to work Problems 8 and 9.

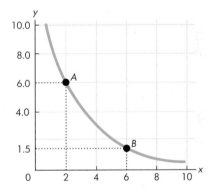

8. Calculate the slope of the relationship at point *A* and at point *B*.
9. Calculate the slope across the arc *AB*.

Use the following table to work Problems 10 and 11. The table gives the price of a balloon ride, the temperature, and the number of rides a day.

Price (dollars per ride)	Balloon rides (number per day)		
	50°F	70°F	90°F
5	32	40	50
10	27	32	40
15	18	27	32

10. Draw a graph to show the relationship between the price and the number of rides when the temperature is 70°F. Describe this relationship.
11. What happens in the graph in Problem 10 if the temperature rises to 90°F?

ADDITIONAL PROBLEMS AND APPLICATIONS

MyEconLab   You can work these problems in MyEconLab if assigned by your instructor.

Use the following spreadsheet to work Problems 12 to 14. The spreadsheet provides data on oil and gasoline: Column A is the year, column B is the price of oil (dollars per barrel), column C is the price of gasoline (cents per gallon), column D is U.S. oil production, and column E is the U.S. quantity of gasoline refined (both in millions of barrels per day).

	A	B	C	D	E
1	2003	31	160	5.7	8.9
2	2004	42	190	5.4	9.1
3	2005	57	231	5.2	9.2
4	2006	66	262	5.1	9.3
5	2007	72	284	5.1	9.3
6	2008	100	330	5.0	9.0
7	2009	62	241	5.4	9.0
8	2010	79	284	5.5	9.0
9	2011	95	354	5.7	9.1
10	2012	94	364	6.5	9.0
11	2013	98	353	7.5	9.1

12. Draw a scatter diagram of the price of oil and the quantity of U.S. oil produced. Describe the relationship.
13. Draw a scatter diagram of the price of gasoline and the quantity of gasoline refined. Describe the relationship.
14. Draw a scatter diagram of the quantity of U.S. oil produced and the quantity of gasoline refined. Describe the relationship.

Use the following data to work Problems 15 to 17. Draw a graph that shows the relationship between the two variables x and y:

x	0	1	2	3	4	5
y	25	24	22	18	12	0

15. a. Is the relationship positive or negative?
    b. Does the slope of the relationship become steeper or flatter as the value of x increases?
    c. Think of some economic relationships that might be similar to this one.
16. Calculate the slope of the relationship between x and y when x equals 3.
17. Calculate the slope of the relationship across the arc as x increases from 4 to 5.
18. Calculate the slope of the curve in the figure in the next column at point A.

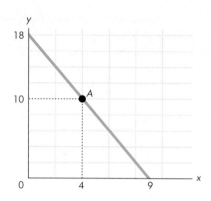

Use the following relationship to work Problems 19 and 20.

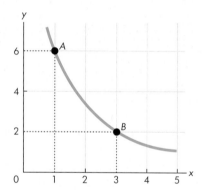

19. Calculate the slope at point A and at point B.
20. Calculate the slope across the arc AB.

Use the following table to work Problems 21 to 23. The table gives information about umbrellas: price, the number purchased, and rainfall in inches.

Price (dollars per umbrella)	Umbrellas (number purchased per day)		
	0 inches	1 inch	2 inches
20	4	7	8
30	2	4	7
40	1	2	4

21. Draw a graph to show the relationship between the price and the number of umbrellas purchased, holding the amount of rainfall constant at 1 inch. Describe this relationship.
22. What happens in the graph in Problem 21 if the price rises and rainfall is constant?
23. What happens in the graph in Problem 21 if the rainfall increases from 1 inch to 2 inches?

2

THE ECONOMIC PROBLEM

After studying this chapter, you will be able to:

◆ Define the production possibilities frontier and use it to calculate opportunity cost

◆ Distinguish between production possibilities and preferences and describe an efficient allocation of resources

◆ Explain how current production choices expand future production possibilities

◆ Explain how specialization and trade expand production possibilities

◆ Describe the economic institutions that coordinate decisions

Hydraulic fracturing, or "fracking," is expanding U.S. oil and gas production and cutting our imports. Should we produce more oil and gas? How do we know when we are using our energy and other resources efficiently?

In this chapter, you study an economic model that answers questions about the efficiency of production and trade.

At the end of the chapter, in *Economics in the News*, we'll apply what you learn to understand how fracking is expanding our production possibilities but why we are still better off importing rather than producing some of our oil and gas.

◆ Production Possibilities and Opportunity Cost

Every working day, in mines, factories, shops, and offices and on farms and construction sites across the United States, 142 million people produce a vast variety of goods and services valued at $60 billion. But the quantities of goods and services that we can produce are limited by our available resources and by technology. And if we want to increase our production of one good, we must decrease our production of something else—we face a tradeoff. You are now going to study the limits to production.

The **production possibilities frontier** (*PPF*) is the boundary between those combinations of goods and services that can be produced and those that cannot. To illustrate the *PPF*, we look at a *model economy* in which the quantities produced of only two goods change, while the quantities produced of all the other goods and services remain the same.

Let's look at the production possibilities frontier for cola and pizza, which represent *any* pair of goods or services.

Production Possibilities Frontier

The *production possibilities frontier* for cola and pizza shows the limits to the production of these two goods, given the total resources and technology available to produce them. Figure 2.1 shows this production possibilities frontier. The table lists combinations of the quantities of pizza and cola that can be produced in a month and the figure graphs these combinations. The *x*-axis shows the quantity of pizzas produced, and the *y*-axis shows the quantity of cola produced.

The *PPF* illustrates *scarcity* because the points outside the frontier are *unattainable*. These points describe wants that can't be satisfied.

We can produce at any point *inside* the *PPF* or *on* the *PPF*. These points are *attainable*. For example, we can produce 4 million pizzas and 5 million cans of cola. Figure 2.1 shows this combination as point *E* on the graph and as possibility *E* in the table.

Moving along the *PPF* from point *E* to point *D* (possibility *D* in the table) we produce more cola and less pizza: 9 million cans of cola and 3 million pizzas. Or moving in the opposite direction from point *E* to point *F* (possibility *F* in the table), we produce more pizza and less cola: 5 million pizzas and no cola.

FIGURE 2.1   Production Possibilities Frontier

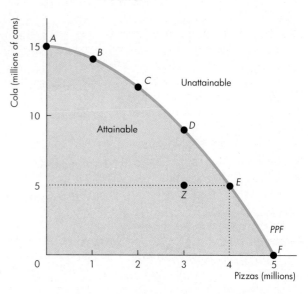

Possibility	Pizzas (millions)		Cola (millions of cans)
A	0	and	15
B	1	and	14
C	2	and	12
D	3	and	9
E	4	and	5
F	5	and	0

The table lists six production possibilities for cola and pizzas. Row *A* tells us that if we produce no pizzas, the maximum quantity of cola we can produce is 15 million cans. Points *A*, *B*, *C*, *D*, *E*, and *F* in the figure represent the rows of the table. The curve passing through these points is the production possibilities frontier (*PPF*).

The *PPF* separates the attainable from the unattainable. Production is possible at any point *inside* the orange area or *on* the frontier. Points outside the frontier are unattainable. Points inside the frontier, such as point *Z*, are inefficient because resources are wasted or misallocated. At such points, it is possible to use the available resources to produce more of either or both goods.

MyEconLab Animation and Draw Graph

Production Efficiency

We achieve **production efficiency** if we produce goods and services at the lowest possible cost. This outcome occurs at all the points *on* the *PPF*. At points *inside* the *PPF*, production is inefficient because we are giving up more than necessary of one good to produce a given quantity of the other good.

For example, at point *Z* in Fig. 2.1, we produce 3 million pizzas and 5 million cans of cola, but we have enough resources to produce 3 million pizzas and 9 million cans of cola. Our pizzas cost more cola than necessary. We can get them for a lower cost. Only when we produce *on* the *PPF* do we incur the lowest possible cost of production.

Production inside the *PPF* is *inefficient* because resources are either *unused* or *misallocated* or both.

Resources are *unused* when they are idle but could be working. For example, we might leave some of the factories idle or some workers unemployed.

Resources are *misallocated* when they are assigned to tasks for which they are not the best match. For example, we might assign skilled pizza chefs to work in a cola factory and skilled cola workers to cook pizza in a pizzeria. We could get more pizzas *and* more cola if we reassigned these workers to the tasks that more closely match their skills.

Tradeoff Along the *PPF*

A choice *along* the *PPF* involves a *tradeoff*. Tradeoffs like that between cola and pizza arise in every imaginable real-world situation in which a choice must be made. At any given time, we have a fixed amount of labor, land, capital, and entrepreneurship and a given state of technology. We can employ these resources and technology to produce goods and services, but we are limited in what we can produce.

When doctors want to spend more on AIDS and cancer research, they face a tradeoff: more medical research for less of some other things. When Congress wants to spend more on education and healthcare, it faces a tradeoff: more education and healthcare for less national defense or homeland security. When an environmental group argues for less logging, it is suggesting a tradeoff: greater conservation of endangered wildlife for less paper. When you want a higher grade on your next test, you face a tradeoff: spend more time studying and less leisure or sleep time.

All the tradeoffs you've just considered involve a cost—an opportunity cost.

Opportunity Cost

The **opportunity cost** of an action is the highest-valued alternative forgone. The *PPF* makes this idea precise and enables us to calculate opportunity cost. Along the *PPF*, there are only two goods, so there is only one alternative forgone: some quantity of the other good. To produce more pizzas we must produce less cola. The opportunity cost of producing an additional pizza is the cola we *must* forgo. Similarly, the opportunity cost of producing an additional can of cola is the quantity of pizza we must forgo.

In Fig. 2.1, if we move from point *C* to point *D*, we produce an additional 1 million pizzas but 3 million fewer cans of cola. The additional 1 million pizzas *cost* 3 million cans of cola. Or 1 pizza costs 3 cans of cola. Similarly, if we move from *D* to *C*, we produce an additional 3 million cans of cola but 1 million fewer pizzas. The additional 3 million cans of cola *cost* 1 million pizzas. Or 1 can of cola costs 1/3 of a pizza.

Opportunity Cost Is a Ratio Opportunity cost is a ratio. It is the decrease in the quantity produced of one good divided by the increase in the quantity produced of another good as we move along the production possibilities frontier.

Because opportunity cost is a ratio, the opportunity cost of producing an additional can of cola is equal to the *inverse* of the opportunity cost of producing an additional pizza. Check this proposition by returning to the calculations we've just done. In the move from *C* to *D*, the opportunity cost of a pizza is 3 cans of cola. And in the move from *D* to *C*, the opportunity cost of a can of cola is 1/3 of a pizza. So the opportunity cost of pizza is the inverse of the opportunity cost of cola.

Increasing Opportunity Cost The opportunity cost of a pizza increases as the quantity of pizzas produced increases. The outward-bowed shape of the *PPF* reflects increasing opportunity cost. When we produce a large quantity of cola and a small quantity of pizza—between points *A* and *B* in Fig. 2.1—the frontier has a gentle slope. An increase in the quantity of pizzas costs a small decrease in the quantity of cola—the opportunity cost of a pizza is a small quantity of cola.

When we produce a large quantity of pizzas and a small quantity of cola—between points *E* and *F* in Fig. 2.1—the frontier is steep. A given increase in the quantity of pizzas *costs* a large decrease in the quantity of cola, so the opportunity cost of a pizza is a large quantity of cola.

◆ ECONOMICS IN THE NEWS

The Opportunity Cost of Cocoa

World's Sweet Tooth Heats Up Cocoa

Chocolate consumption is soaring as people in developing countries are getting wealthier. Cocoa farmers are ramping up production to keep the chocolate flowing, but the price of cocoa keeps rising.

Source: *The Wall Street Journal*, February 13, 2014

THE QUESTIONS

- How does the *PPF* illustrate (1) the limits to cocoa production; (2) the tradeoff we must make to increase cocoa production; and (3) the effect of increased chocolate consumption on the cost of producing cocoa?

THE ANSWERS

- The figure shows the global *PPF* for cocoa and other goods and services. Point *A* on the *PPF* tells us that if 4 million tons of cocoa are produced, a maximum of 96 units of other goods and services can be produced.

- The movement along the *PPF* from *A* to *B* illustrates the tradeoff we must make to increase chocolate and cocoa production.

- The slope of the *PPF* measures the opportunity cost of cocoa. If cocoa production increases from zero to 4 million tons, the production of other goods and services decreases from 100 units to 96 units. The opportunity cost of 1 ton of cocoa is 1 unit of other goods and services.

- But if cocoa production increases from 4 million tons to 8 million tons, the production of other goods and services decreases from 96 units to 80 units. The opportunity cost of 1 ton of cocoa is now 4 units of other goods and services.

- As resources are moved into producing cocoa, labor, land, and capital less suited to the task of cocoa production are used and the cost of the additional cocoa produced increases.

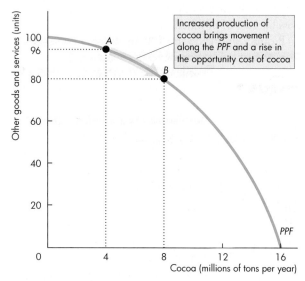

Increased production of cocoa brings movement along the *PPF* and a rise in the opportunity cost of cocoa

PPF for Cocoa and Other Goods and Services

MyEconLab More Economics in the News

The *PPF* is bowed outward because resources are not all equally productive in all activities. People with many years of experience working for PepsiCo are good at producing cola but not very good at making pizzas. So if we move some of these people from PepsiCo to Domino's, we get a small increase in the quantity of pizzas but a large decrease in the quantity of cola.

Similarly, people who have spent years working at Domino's are good at producing pizzas, but they have no idea how to produce cola. So if we move some of these people from Domino's to PepsiCo, we get a small increase in the quantity of cola but a large decrease in the quantity of pizzas. The more of either good we try to produce, the less productive are the additional resources we use to produce that good and the larger is the opportunity cost of a unit of that good.

How do we choose among the points on the *PPF*? How do we know which point is the best?

◆ REVIEW QUIZ

1 How does the production possibilities frontier illustrate scarcity?

2 How does the production possibilities frontier illustrate production efficiency?

3 How does the production possibilities frontier show that every choice involves a tradeoff?

4 How does the production possibilities frontier illustrate opportunity cost?

5 Why is opportunity cost a ratio?

6 Why does the *PPF* bow outward and what does that imply about the relationship between opportunity cost and the quantity produced?

Work these questions in Study Plan 2.1 and get instant feedback. Do a Key Terms Quiz.   MyEconLab

◆ Using Resources Efficiently

We achieve *production efficiency* at every point on the *PPF*, but which of these points is best? The answer is the point on the *PPF* at which goods and services are produced in the quantities that provide the greatest possible benefit. When goods and services are produced at the lowest possible cost and in the quantities that provide the greatest possible benefit, we have achieved **allocative efficiency**.

The questions that we raised when we reviewed the four big issues in Chapter 1 are questions about allocative efficiency. To answer such questions, we must measure and compare costs and benefits.

The *PPF* and Marginal Cost

The **marginal cost** of a good is the opportunity cost of producing one more unit of it. We calculate marginal cost from the slope of the *PPF*. As the quantity of pizzas produced increases, the *PPF* gets steeper and the marginal cost of a pizza increases. Figure 2.2 illustrates the calculation of the marginal cost of a pizza.

Begin by finding the opportunity cost of pizza in blocks of 1 million pizzas. The cost of the first million pizzas is 1 million cans of cola; the cost of the second million pizzas is 2 million cans of cola; the cost of the third million pizzas is 3 million cans of cola, and so on. The bars in part (a) illustrate these calculations.

The bars in part (b) show the cost of an average pizza in each of the 1 million pizza blocks. Focus on the third million pizzas—the move from *C* to *D* in part (a). Over this range, because 1 million pizzas cost 3 million cans of cola, one of these pizzas, on average, costs 3 cans of cola—the height of the bar in part (b).

Next, find the opportunity cost of each additional pizza—the marginal cost of a pizza. The marginal cost of a pizza increases as the quantity of pizzas produced increases. The marginal cost at point *C* is less than it is at point *D*. On average over the range from *C* to *D*, the marginal cost of a pizza is 3 cans of cola. But it exactly equals 3 cans of cola only in the middle of the range between *C* and *D*.

The red dot in part (b) indicates that the marginal cost of a pizza is 3 cans of cola when 2.5 million pizzas are produced. Each black dot in part (b) is interpreted in the same way. The red curve that passes through these dots, labeled *MC*, is the marginal cost curve. It shows the marginal cost of a pizza at each quantity of pizzas as we move along the *PPF*.

FIGURE 2.2 The *PPF* and Marginal Cost

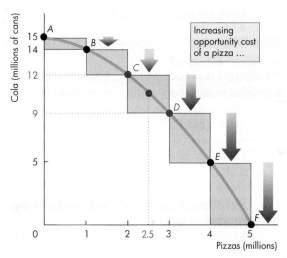

(a) *PPF* **and opportunity cost**

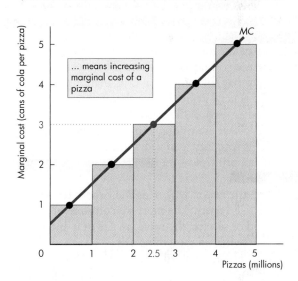

(b) Marginal cost

Marginal cost is calculated from the slope of the *PPF*. As the quantity of pizzas produced increases, the *PPF* gets steeper and the marginal cost of a pizza increases. The bars in part (a) show the opportunity cost of pizza in blocks of 1 million pizzas. The bars in part (b) show the cost of an average pizza in each of these 1 million blocks. The red curve, *MC*, shows the marginal cost of a pizza at each point along the *PPF*. This curve passes through the center of each of the bars in part (b).

MyEconLab Animation

Preferences and Marginal Benefit

The **marginal benefit** from a good or service is the benefit received from consuming one more unit of it. This benefit is subjective. It depends on people's **preferences**—people's likes and dislikes and the intensity of those feelings.

Marginal benefit and *preferences* stand in sharp contrast to *marginal cost* and *production possibilities.* Preferences describe what people like and want and the production possibilities describe the limits or constraints on what is feasible.

We need a concrete way of illustrating preferences that parallels the way we illustrate the limits to production using the *PPF*.

The device that we use to illustrate preferences is the **marginal benefit curve,** which is a curve that shows the relationship between the marginal benefit from a good and the quantity consumed of that good. Note that the *marginal benefit curve* is *unrelated* to the *PPF* and cannot be derived from it.

We measure the marginal benefit from a good or service by the most that people are *willing to pay* for an additional unit of it. The idea is that you are willing to pay less for a good than it is worth to you but you are not willing to pay more: The most you are willing to pay for something is its marginal benefit.

It is a general principle that the more we have of any good or service, the smaller is its marginal benefit and the less we are willing to pay for an additional unit of it. This tendency is so widespread and strong that we call it a principle—the *principle of decreasing marginal benefit.*

The basic reason why marginal benefit decreases is that we like variety. The more we consume of any one good or service, the more we tire of it and would prefer to switch to something else.

Think about your willingness to pay for a pizza. If pizza is hard to come by and you can buy only a few slices a year, you might be willing to pay a high price to get an additional slice. But if pizza is all you've eaten for the past few days, you are willing to pay almost nothing for another slice.

You've learned to think about cost as opportunity cost, not as a dollar cost. You can think about marginal benefit and willingness to pay in the same way. The marginal benefit, measured by what you are willing to pay for something, is the quantity of other goods and services that you are willing to forgo. Let's continue with the example of cola and pizza and illustrate preferences this way.

FIGURE 2.3   Preferences and the Marginal Benefit Curve

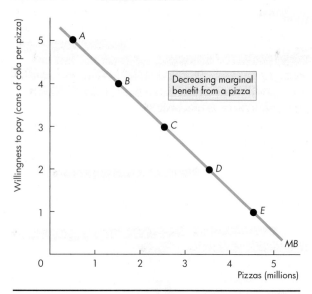

Possibility	Pizzas (millions)	Willingness to pay (cans of cola per pizza)
A	0.5	5
B	1.5	4
C	2.5	3
D	3.5	2
E	4.5	1

The smaller the quantity of pizzas available, the more cola people are willing to give up for an additional pizza. With 0.5 million pizzas available, people are willing to pay 5 cans of cola per pizza. But with 4.5 million pizzas, people are willing to pay only 1 can of cola per pizza. Willingness to pay measures marginal benefit. A universal feature of people's preferences is that marginal benefit decreases.

MyEconLab Animation

Figure 2.3 illustrates preferences as the willingness to pay for pizza in terms of cola. In row *A*, with 0.5 million pizzas available, people are willing to pay 5 cans of cola per pizza. As the quantity of pizzas increases, the amount that people are willing to pay for a pizza falls. With 4.5 million pizzas available, people are willing to pay only 1 can of cola per pizza.

Let's now use the concepts of marginal cost and marginal benefit to describe allocative efficiency.

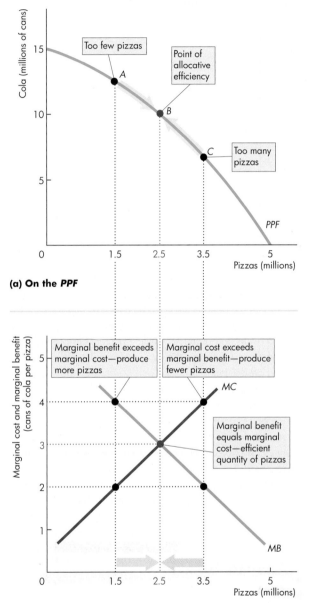

FIGURE 2.4   Efficient Use of Resources

(a) On the PPF

(b) Marginal benefit equals marginal cost

The greater the quantity of pizzas produced, the smaller is the marginal benefit (MB) from pizza—the less cola people are willing to give up to get an additional pizza. But the greater the quantity of pizzas produced, the greater is the marginal cost (MC) of a pizza—the more cola people must give up to get an additional pizza. When marginal benefit equals marginal cost, resources are being used efficiently.

MyEconLab Animation

Allocative Efficiency

At *any* point on the *PPF*, we cannot produce more of one good without giving up some other good. At the *best* point on the *PPF*, we cannot produce more of one good without giving up some other good that provides greater benefit. We are producing at the point of allocative efficiency—the point on the *PPF* that we prefer above all other points.

Suppose in Fig. 2.4, we produce 1.5 million pizzas. In part (b), the marginal cost of a pizza is 2 cans of cola, and the marginal benefit from a pizza is 4 cans of cola. Because someone values an additional pizza more highly than it costs to produce, we can get more value from our resources by moving some of them out of producing cola and into producing pizza.

Now suppose we produce 3.5 million pizzas. The marginal cost of a pizza is now 4 cans of cola, but the marginal benefit from a pizza is only 2 cans of cola. Because the additional pizza costs more to produce than anyone thinks it is worth, we can get more value from our resources by moving some of them away from producing pizza and into producing cola.

Suppose we produce 2.5 million pizzas. Marginal cost and marginal benefit are now equal at 3 cans of cola. This allocation of resources between pizzas and cola is efficient. If more pizzas are produced, the forgone cola is worth more than the additional pizzas. If fewer pizzas are produced, the forgone pizzas are worth more than the additional cola.

◆ REVIEW QUIZ

1 What is marginal cost? How is it measured?
2 What is marginal benefit? How is it measured?
3 How does the marginal benefit from a good change as the quantity produced of that good increases?
4 What is allocative efficiency and how does it relate to the production possibilities frontier?
5 What conditions must be satisfied if resources are used efficiently?

Work these questions in Study Plan 2.2 and get instant feedback. Do a Key Terms Quiz.   MyEconLab

You now understand the limits to production and the conditions under which resources are used efficiently. Your next task is to study the expansion of production possibilities.

Economic Growth

During the past 30 years, production per person in the United States has doubled. The expansion of production possibilities is called **economic growth**. Economic growth increases our *standard of living*, but it doesn't overcome scarcity and avoid opportunity cost. To make our economy grow, we face a tradeoff—the faster we make production grow, the greater is the opportunity cost of economic growth.

The Cost of Economic Growth

Economic growth comes from technological change and capital accumulation. **Technological change** is the development of new goods and of better ways of producing goods and services. **Capital accumulation** is the growth of capital resources, including *human capital*.

Technological change and capital accumulation have vastly expanded our production possibilities. We can produce automobiles that provide us with more transportation than was available when we had only horses and carriages. We can produce satellites that provide global communications on a much larger scale than that available with the earlier cable technology. But if we use our resources to develop new technologies and produce capital, we must decrease our production of consumption goods and services. New technologies and new capital have an opportunity cost. Let's look at this opportunity cost.

Instead of studying the *PPF* of pizzas and cola, we'll hold the quantity of cola produced constant and examine the *PPF* for pizzas and pizza ovens. Figure 2.5 shows this *PPF* as the blue curve PPF_0. If we devote no resources to producing pizza ovens, we produce at point *A*. If we produce 3 million pizzas, we can produce 6 pizza ovens at point *B*. If we produce no pizza, we can produce 10 ovens at point *C*.

The amount by which our production possibilities expand depends on the resources we devote to technological change and capital accumulation. If we devote no resources to this activity (point *A*), our *PPF* remains the blue curve PPF_0 in Fig. 2.5. If we cut the current pizza production and produce 6 ovens (point *B*), then in the future, we'll have more capital and our *PPF* will rotate outward to the position shown by the red curve PPF_1. The fewer resources we use for producing pizza and the more resources we use for producing ovens, the greater is the expansion of our future production possibilities.

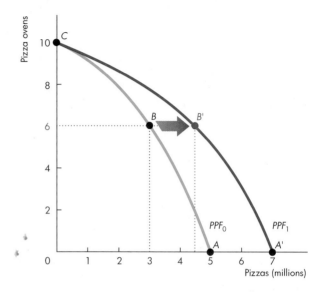

FIGURE 2.5   Economic Growth

PPF_0 shows the limits to the production of pizzas and pizza ovens, with the production of all other goods and services remaining the same. If we devote no resources to producing pizza ovens and produce 5 million pizzas, our production possibilities will remain the same at PPF_0. But if we decrease pizza production to 3 million and produce 6 ovens, at point *B*, our production possibilities expand. After one period, the *PPF* rotates outward to PPF_1 and we can produce at point *B'*, a point outside the original PPF_0. We can rotate the *PPF* outward, but we cannot avoid opportunity cost. The opportunity cost of producing more pizzas in the future is fewer pizzas today.

—— MyEconLab Animation and Draw Graph ——

Economic growth brings enormous benefits in the form of increased consumption in the future, but economic growth is not free and it doesn't abolish scarcity.

In Fig. 2.5, to make economic growth happen we must use some resources to produce new ovens, which leaves fewer resources to produce pizzas. To move to *B'* in the future, we must move from *A* to *B* today. The opportunity cost of more pizzas in the future is fewer pizzas today. Also, on the new *PPF*, we still face a tradeoff and opportunity cost.

The ideas about economic growth that we have explored in the setting of the pizza industry also apply to nations. Hong Kong and the United States provide a striking case study.

ECONOMICS IN ACTION
Hong Kong Catching Up to the United States

In 1963, the production possibilities per person in the United States were more than four times those in Hong Kong (see the figure). The United States devotes one fifth of its resources to accumulating capital, and in 1963, the United States was at point *A* on its *PPF*. Hong Kong devotes one third of its resources to accumulating capital, and in 1963, Hong Kong was at point *A* on its *PPF*.

Since 1963, both economies have experienced economic growth, but because Hong Kong devotes a bigger fraction of its resources to accumulating capital, its production possibilities have expanded more quickly.

By 2013, production possibilities per person in Hong Kong equaled those in the United States. If Hong Kong continues to devote more resources to accumulating capital than the United States does (at point *B* on its 2013 *PPF*), Hong Kong will continue to grow more rapidly. But if Hong Kong decreases its capital accumulation (moving to point *D* on its 2013 *PPF*), then its rate of economic growth will slow.

Hong Kong is typical of the fast-growing Asian economies, which include Taiwan, Thailand, South Korea, China, and India. Production possibilities

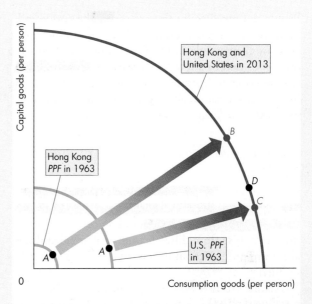

Economic Growth in the United States and Hong Kong

expand in these countries by between 5 percent and almost 10 percent a year.

If such high economic growth rates are maintained, these other Asian countries will continue to close the gap between themselves and the United States, as Hong Kong is doing.

A Nation's Economic Growth

The experiences of the United States and Hong Kong make a striking example of the effects of our choices about consumption and capital accumulation on the rate of economic growth.

If an economy devotes all its factors of production to producing consumption goods and services and none to advancing technology and accumulating capital, its production possibilities in the future will be the same as they are today.

To expand production possibilities in the future, a nation or an economy must devote fewer resources to producing current consumption goods and services and some resources to accumulating capital and developing new technologies. As production possibilities expand, consumption in the future can increase. The decrease in today's consumption is the opportunity cost of tomorrow's increase in consumption.

◆ REVIEW QUIZ

1 What generates economic growth?
2 How does economic growth influence the production possibilities frontier?
3 What is the opportunity cost of economic growth?
4 Explain why Hong Kong has experienced faster economic growth than the United States.
5 Does economic growth overcome scarcity?

Work these questions in Study Plan 2.3 and get instant feedback. Do a Key Terms Quiz.   MyEconLab

Next, we're going to study another way in which we expand our production possibilities—the amazing fact that *both* buyers and sellers gain from specialization and trade.

◆ Gains from Trade

People can produce for themselves all the goods and services that they consume, or they can produce one good or a few goods and trade with others. Producing only one good or a few goods is called *specialization*. We are going to learn how people gain by specializing in the production of the good in which they have a *comparative advantage* and trading with others.

Comparative Advantage and Absolute Advantage

A person has a **comparative advantage** in an activity if that person can perform the activity at a lower opportunity cost than anyone else. Differences in opportunity costs arise from differences in individual abilities and from differences in the characteristics of other resources.

No one excels at everything. One person is an outstanding pitcher but a poor catcher; another person is a brilliant lawyer but a poor teacher. In almost all human endeavors, what one person does easily, someone else finds difficult. The same applies to land and capital. One plot of land is fertile but has no mineral deposits; another plot of land has outstanding views but is infertile. One machine has great precision but is difficult to operate; another is fast but often breaks down.

Although no one excels at everything, some people excel and can outperform others in a large number of activities—perhaps even in all activities. A person who is more productive than others has an **absolute advantage**.

Absolute advantage involves comparing productivities—production per hour—whereas comparative advantage involves comparing opportunity costs.

A person who has an absolute advantage does not have a *comparative* advantage in every activity. John Grisham is a better lawyer and a better author of fast-paced thrillers than most people. He has an absolute advantage in these two activities. But compared to others, he is a better writer than lawyer, so his *comparative* advantage is in writing.

Because ability and resources vary from one person to another, people have different opportunity costs of producing various goods. These differences in opportunity cost are the source of comparative advantage.

Let's explore the idea of comparative advantage by looking at two smoothie bars: one operated by Liz and the other operated by Joe.

Joe's Smoothie Bar   Joe produces smoothies and salads in a small, low-tech bar. He has only one blender, and it's a slow, old machine that keeps stopping. Even if Joe uses all his resources to produce smoothies, he can produce only 6 an hour—see Table 2.1. But Joe is good at making salads, and if he uses all his resources in this activity, he can produce 30 salads an hour.

Joe's ability to make smoothies and salads is the same regardless of how he splits an hour between the two tasks. He can make a salad in 2 minutes or a smoothie in 10 minutes. For each additional smoothie Joe produces, he must decrease his production of salads by 5. And for each additional salad he produces, he must decrease his production of smoothies by 1/5 of a smoothie. So

> Joe's opportunity cost of producing 1 smoothie is 5 salads,

and

> Joe's opportunity cost of producing 1 salad is 1/5 of a smoothie.

Joe's customers buy smoothies and salads in equal quantities. So Joe spends 50 minutes of each hour making smoothies and 10 minutes of each hour making salads. With this division of his time, Joe produces 5 smoothies and 5 salads an hour.

Figure 2.6(a) illustrates the production possibilities at Joe's smoothie bar—Joe's *PPF*.

Joe's *PPF* is linear (not outward bowed) because his ability to produce salads and smoothies is the same no matter how he divides his time between the two activities. Joe's opportunity cost of a smoothie is constant—it is the same at all quantities of smoothies produced.

TABLE 2.1   Joe's Production Possibilities

Item	Minutes to produce 1	Quantity per hour
Smoothies	10	6
Salads	2	30

Liz's Smoothie Bar Liz also produces smoothies and salads but in a high-tech bar that is much more productive than Joe's. Liz can turn out either a smoothie or a salad every 2 minutes—see Table 2.2.

If Liz spends all her time making smoothies, she can produce 30 an hour. And if she spends all her time making salads, she can also produce 30 an hour.

Liz's ability to make smoothies and salads, like Joe's, is the same regardless of how she divides her time between the two tasks. She can make a salad in 2 minutes or a smoothie in 2 minutes. For each additional smoothie Liz produces, she must decrease her production of salads by 1. And for each additional salad she produces, she must decrease her production of smoothies by 1. So

Liz's opportunity cost of producing 1 smoothie is 1 salad,

and

Liz's opportunity cost of producing 1 salad is 1 smoothie.

TABLE 2.2 Liz's Production Possibilities

Item	Minutes to produce 1	Quantity per hour
Smoothies	2	30
Salads	2	30

Liz's customers buy smoothies and salads in equal quantities, so she splits her time equally between the two items and produces 15 smoothies and 15 salads an hour.

Figure 2.6(b) illustrates the production possibilities at Liz's smoothie bar—Liz's *PPF*.

Like Joe's, Liz's *PPF* is linear because her ability to produce salads and smoothies is the same no matter how she divides her time between the two activities. Liz's opportunity cost of a smoothie is 1 salad at all quantities of smoothies produced.

FIGURE 2.6 The Production Possibilities Frontiers

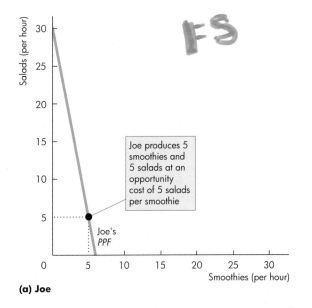

(a) Joe

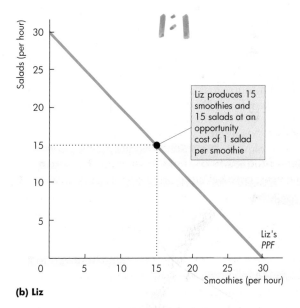

(b) Liz

Joe can produce 30 salads per hour, 1 every two minutes, if he produces no smoothies. Or, he can produce 6 smoothies per hour, 1 every 10 minutes, if he produces no salads. Joe's customers buy equal quantities of salads and smoothies, so Joe produces 5 of each. His opportunity cost of a smoothie is 5 salads.

Liz can produce 30 salads or 30 smoothies per hour, 1 of either item every two minutes. Liz's customers buy equal quantities of salads and smoothies, so she produces 15 of each. Liz's opportunity cost of a smoothie is 1 salad.

MyEconLab Animation

when x increases from 2 to 6, y increases from 3 to 6. The change in x is +4—that is, Δx is 4. The change in y is +3—that is, Δy is 3. The slope of that line is

$$\frac{\Delta y}{\Delta x} = \frac{3}{4}.$$

In part (b), when x increases from 2 to 6, y decreases from 6 to 3. The change in y is *minus* 3—that is, Δy is −3. The change in x is *plus* 4—that is, Δx is 4. The slope of the curve is

$$\frac{\Delta y}{\Delta x} = \frac{-3}{4}.$$

Notice that the two slopes have the same magnitude (3/4), but the slope of the line in part (a) is positive (+3/+4 = 3/4) while that in part (b) is negative (−3/+4 = −3/4). The slope of a positive relationship is positive; the slope of a negative relationship is negative.

The Slope of a Curved Line

The slope of a curved line is trickier. The slope of a curved line is not constant, so the slope depends on where on the curved line we calculate it. There are two ways to calculate the slope of a curved line: You can calculate the slope at a point, or you can calculate the slope across an arc of the curve. Let's look at the two alternatives.

Slope at a Point To calculate the slope at a point on a curve, you need to construct a straight line that has the same slope as the curve at the point in question. Figure A1.10 shows how this is done. Suppose you want to calculate the slope of the curve at point A. Place a ruler on the graph so that the ruler touches point A and no other point on the curve, then draw a straight line along the edge of the ruler. The straight red line is this line, and it is the tangent to the curve at point A. If the ruler touches the curve only at point A, then the slope of the curve at point A must be the same as the slope of the edge of the ruler. If the curve and the ruler do not have the same slope, the line along the edge of the ruler will cut the curve instead of just touching it.

Now that you have found a straight line with the same slope as the curve at point A, you can calculate the slope of the curve at point A by calculating the slope of the straight line. Along the straight line, as x

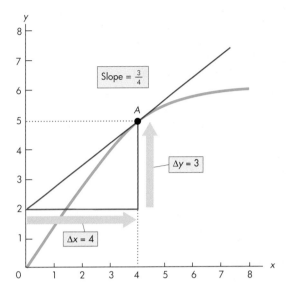

FIGURE A1.10   Slope at a Point

To calculate the slope of the curve at point A, draw the red line that just touches the curve at A—the tangent. The slope of this straight line is calculated by dividing the change in y by the change in x along the red line. When x increases from 0 to 4, Δx equals 4. That change in x is associated with an increase in y from 2 to 5, so Δy equals 3. The slope of the red line is 3/4, so the slope of the curve at point A is 3/4.

—— MyEconLab Animation ——

increases from 0 to 4 (Δx is 4) y increases from 2 to 5 (Δy is 3). Therefore the slope of the straight line is

$$\frac{\Delta y}{\Delta x} = \frac{3}{4}.$$

So the slope of the curve at point A is 3/4.

Slope Across an Arc An arc of a curve is a piece of a curve. Figure A1.11 shows the same curve as in Fig. A1.10, but instead of calculating the slope at point A, we are now going to calculate the slope across the arc from point B to point C. You can see that the slope of the curve at point B is greater than at point C. When we calculate the slope across an arc, we are calculating the average slope between two points. As we move along the arc from B to C, x increases from 3 to 5 and y increases from 4.0 to 5.5. The change in x is 2 (Δx is 2), and the change in y is 1.5 (Δy is 1.5).

Joe's Comparative Advantage In which of the two activities does Joe have a comparative advantage? To answer this question, first recall the definition of comparative advantage. A person has a comparative advantage when that person's opportunity cost of producing a good is lower than another person's opportunity cost of producing that same good.

Joe's opportunity cost of producing a salad is only 1/5 of a smoothie, while Liz's opportunity cost of producing a salad is 1 smoothie. So Joe has a comparative advantage in producing salads.

Liz's Comparative Advantage If Joe has a comparative advantage in producing salads, Liz must have a comparative advantage in producing smoothies. Check the numbers. For Joe, a smoothie costs 5 salads, and for Liz, a smoothie costs only 1 salad. So Liz has a comparative advantage in making smoothies.

Achieving the Gains from Trade

Liz and Joe run into each other one evening in a singles bar. After a few minutes of getting acquainted, Liz tells Joe about her amazing smoothie business. Her only problem, she tells Joe, is that she would like to produce more because potential customers leave when her lines get too long.

Joe doesn't want to risk spoiling a blooming relationship by telling Liz about his own struggling business, but he takes the risk. Joe explains to Liz that he spends 50 minutes of every hour making 5 smoothies and 10 minutes making 5 salads. Liz's eyes pop. "Have I got a deal for you!" she exclaims.

Liz's Proposal Here's the deal that Liz sketches on a paper napkin. Joe stops making smoothies and allocates all his time to producing salads; Liz stops making salads and allocates all her time to producing smoothies. That is, they both specialize in producing the good in which they have a comparative advantage. Together they produce 30 smoothies and 30 salads—see Table 2.3(b).

They then trade. Liz suggests trading at a price of 2 salads per smoothie. For her, that is a good deal because she can produce a smoothie at a cost of 1 salad and sell it to Joe for 2 salads. It is also a good deal for Joe because he can produce a salad at a cost of 1/5 of a smoothie and sell it to Liz for 1/2 a smoothie.

Liz explains that any price above 1 salad per smoothie is good for her and any price below 5 salads per smoothie is good for Joe, so a price of 2 salads per smoothie lets them both gain, as she now describes.

TABLE 2.3   Liz and Joe Gain from Trade

(a) Before trade	Liz	Joe
Smoothies	15	5
Salads	15	5
(b) Specialization	**Liz**	**Joe**
Smoothies	30	0
Salads	0	30
(c) Trade	**Liz**	**Joe**
Smoothies	sell 10	buy 10
Salads	buy 20	sell 20
(d) After trade	**Liz**	**Joe**
Smoothies	20	10
Salads	20	10
(e) Gains from trade	**Liz**	**Joe**
Smoothies	+5	+5
Salads	+5	+5

At the proposed price, Liz offers to sell Joe 10 smoothies in exchange for 20 salads. Equivalently, Joe sells Liz 20 salads in exchange for 10 smoothies.—see Table 2.3(c).

After this trade, Joe has 10 salads—the 30 he produces minus the 20 he sells to Liz. He also has the 10 smoothies that he buys from Liz. So Joe now has increased the quantities of smoothies and salads that he can sell to his customers—see Table 2.3(d).

Liz has 20 smoothies—the 30 she produces minus the 10 she sells to Joe. She also has the 20 salads that she buys from Joe. Liz has increased the quantities of smoothies and salads that she can sell to her customers—see Table 2.3(d). Both Liz and Joe gain 5 smoothies and 5 salads an hour—see Table 2.3(e).

Illustrating Liz's Idea To illustrate her idea, Liz grabs a fresh napkin and draws the graphs in Fig. 2.7. First, she sketches Joe's *PPF* in part (a) and shows the point at which he is producing before they meet.

FIGURE 2.7   The Gains from Trade

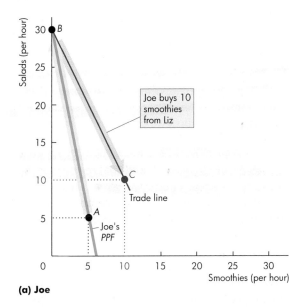

(a) Joe

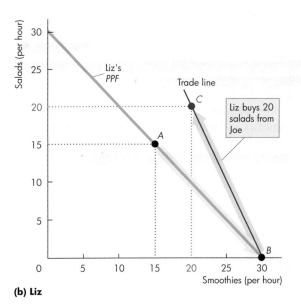

(b) Liz

Initially, Joe produces at point *A* on his *PPF* in part (a), and Liz produces at point *A* on her *PPF* in part (b). Joe's opportunity cost of producing a salad is less than Liz's, so Joe has a comparative advantage in producing salads. Liz's opportunity cost of producing a smoothie is less than Joe's, so Liz has a comparative advantage in producing smoothies.

If Joe specializes in making salads, he produces 30 salads and no smoothies at point *B* on his *PPF*. If Liz specializes in

making smoothies, she produces 30 smoothies and no salads at point *B* on her *PPF*. They exchange salads for smoothies along the red "Trade line." Liz buys salads from Joe for less than her opportunity cost of producing them. Joe buys smoothies from Liz for less than his opportunity cost of producing them. Each goes to point *C*—a point outside his or her *PPF*. With specialization and trade, Joe and Liz gain 5 smoothies and 5 salads each with no extra resources.

MyEconLab Animation and Draw Graph

Recall that he is producing 5 smoothies and 5 salads an hour at point *A*.

She then sketches her own *PPF* in part (b), and marks the point *A* at which she is producing 15 smoothies and 15 salads an hour.

She then shows what happens when they each specialize in producing the good in which they have a comparative advantage. Joe specializes in producing salads and produces 30 salads and no smoothies at point *B* on his *PPF*.

Liz specializes in producing smoothies and produces 30 smoothies and no salads at point *B* on her *PPF*.

They then trade smoothies and salads at a price of 2 salads per smoothie or 1/2 a smoothie per salad. The red "Trade line" that Liz draws on each part of the figure illustrates the tradeoff that each faces at the proposed price.

Liz now shows Joe the amazing outcome of her idea. After specializing and trading, Joe gets 10 smoothies and 10 salads at point *C*—a gain of 5 smoothies and 5 salads. He moves to a point *outside*

his *PPF*. And Liz gets 20 smoothies and 20 salads at point *C*—also a gain of 5 smoothies and 5 salads—and moves to a point *outside* her *PPF*.

Despite Liz being more productive than Joe, both gain from specializing at producing the good in which they have a comparative advantage and trading.

◆ REVIEW QUIZ

1   What gives a person a comparative advantage?
2   Distinguish between comparative advantage and absolute advantage.
3   Why do people specialize and trade?
4   What are the gains from specialization and trade?
5   What is the source of the gains from trade?

Work these questions in Study Plan 2.4 and get instant feedback. Do a Key Terms Quiz.   *MyEconLab*

◆ Economic Coordination

For 7 billion people to specialize and produce millions of different goods and services, individual choices must somehow be coordinated. Two competing coordination systems have been used: central economic planning and markets (see *At Issue*, p. 8).

Central economic planning works badly because economic planners don't know people's production possibilities and preferences, so production ends up *inside* the *PPF* and the wrong things are produced.

Decentralized coordination works best but to do so it needs four complementary social institutions. They are

- Firms
- Markets
- Property rights
- Money

Firms

A **firm** is an economic unit that hires factors of production and organizes them to produce and sell goods and services.

Firms coordinate a huge amount of economic activity. For example, Wal-Mart buys or rents large buildings, equips them with storage shelves and checkout lanes, and hires labor. Wal-Mart directs the labor and decides what goods to buy and sell.

But Sam Walton would not have become one of the wealthiest people in the world if Wal-Mart produced everything that it sells. He became rich by specializing in providing retail services and buying from other firms that specialize in producing goods (just as Liz and Joe did). This trade needs markets.

Markets

In ordinary speech, the word *market* means a place where people buy and sell goods such as fish, meat, fruits, and vegetables.

In economics, a **market** is any arrangement that enables buyers and sellers to get information and to do business with each other. An example is the world oil market, which is not a place but a network of producers, consumers, wholesalers, and brokers who buy and sell oil. In the world oil market, decision makers make deals by using the Internet. Enterprising individuals and firms, each pursuing their own self-interest, have profited by making markets—by standing

ready to buy or sell items in which they specialize. But markets can work only when property rights exist.

Property Rights

The social arrangements that govern the ownership, use, and disposal of anything that people value are called **property rights**. *Real property* includes land and buildings—the things we call property in ordinary speech—and durable goods such as plant and equipment. *Financial property* includes stocks and bonds and money in the bank. *Intellectual property* is the intangible product of creative effort. This type of property includes books, music, computer programs, and inventions of all kinds and is protected by copyrights and patents.

Where property rights are enforced, people have the incentive to specialize and produce the goods and services in which they have a comparative advantage. Where people can steal the production of others, resources are devoted not to production but to protecting possessions.

Money

Money is any commodity or token that is generally acceptable as a means of payment. Liz and Joe don't need money. They can exchange salads and smoothies. In principle, trade in markets can exchange any item for any other item. But you can perhaps imagine how complicated life would be if we exchanged goods for other goods. The "invention" of money makes trading in markets much more efficient.

Circular Flows Through Markets

Trading in markets for goods and services and factors of production creates a circular flow of expenditures and incomes. Figure 2.8 shows the circular flows. Households specialize and choose the quantities of labor, land, capital, and entrepreneurial services to sell or rent to firms. Firms choose the quantities of factors of production to hire. These (red) flows go through the *factor markets*. Households choose the quantities of goods and services to buy, and firms choose the quantities to produce. These (red) flows go through the *goods markets*. Households receive incomes and make expenditures on goods and services (the green flows).

How do markets coordinate all these decisions?

FIGURE 2.8   Circular Flows in the Market Economy

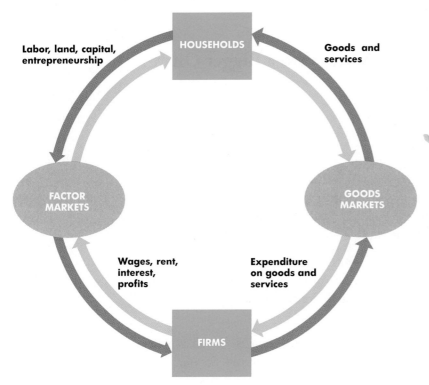

Households and firms make economic choices and markets coordinate these choices.

Households choose the quantities of labor, land, capital, and entrepreneurial services to sell or rent to firms in exchange for wages, rent, interest, and profits. Households also choose how to spend their incomes on the various types of goods and services available.

Firms choose the quantities of factors of production to hire and the quantities of goods and services to produce.

Goods markets and factor markets coordinate these choices of households and firms.

The counterclockwise red flows are real flows—the flow of factors of production from households to firms and the flow of goods and services from firms to households.

The clockwise green flows are the payments for the red flows. They are the flow of incomes from firms to households and the flow of expenditure on goods and services from households to firms.

 MyEconLab Animation

Coordinating Decisions

Markets coordinate decisions through price adjustments. Suppose that some people who want to buy hamburgers are not able to do so. To make buying and selling plans the same, either more hamburgers must be offered for sale or buyers must scale down their appetites (or both). A rise in the price of a hamburger produces this outcome. It encourages producers to offer more hamburgers for sale and encourages some people to change their lunch plans. When the price is right, buying plans and selling plans match.

Alternatively, suppose that more hamburgers are available than people want to buy. In this case, more hamburgers must be bought or fewer hamburgers must be offered for sale (or both). A fall in the price of a hamburger achieves this outcome. It encourages people to buy more hamburgers and it encourages firms to produce a smaller quantity of hamburgers.

◆ REVIEW QUIZ

1 Why are social institutions such as firms, markets, property rights, and money necessary?
2 What are the main functions of markets?
3 What are the flows in the market economy that go from firms to households and the flows from households to firms?

Work these questions in Study Plan 2.5 and get instant feedback. Do a Key Terms Quiz.   MyEconLab

◆ You have now begun to see how economists approach economic questions. You can see all around you the lessons you've learned in this chapter. *Economics in the News* on pp. 46–47 provides an opportunity to apply the *PPF* model to deepen your understanding of why, despite advances in "fracking" technology, we still rely on imports for our energy.

Expanding Production Possibilities

Fracking Is Turning the United States into a Bigger Oil Producer Than Saudi Arabia

The Independent
March 11, 2014

Hector Gallegos sits in the cab of his pick-up enjoying a few hours of calm. A day earlier, workers finished carting off the huge rig that had drilled three new wells beneath this small patch of south Texas farmland and he's now getting ready to prime them for production. He reckons that about three weeks from now each will be producing 1,000 to 2,000 barrels a day. "That's money!" he exclaims with a broad smile.

It's also power, and not in the combustion sense. Thanks to the success of engineers like Mr. Gallegos in pushing the frontiers of hydraulic fracturing, or "fracking," to access reserves of oil trapped in shale formations, notably here in Texas and North Dakota, America is poised to displace Saudi Arabia as the world's top producer. ...

So rapid has been the change in its energy fortunes that even some experts, as well as policy-makers in Washington, are struggling to keep up. Nor are we just talking oil. So much natural gas is being released by the shale also that for now outlandish quantities of it are simply being burned off into the atmosphere.

Even predicting future oil output isn't the precise science you'd expect. "We keep raising our forecasts, and we keep underestimating production," Lejla Alic, an analyst with the International Energy Agency, noted recently. Last year U.S. production reached 7.4 million barrels a day, an increase over 2012 of 15.3 percent. A jump that large hasn't been seen since 1951. This year the United States should produce 8.3 million barrels a day. ...

MyEconLab More Economics in the News

ESSENCE OF THE STORY

- Hydraulic fracturing, or "fracking," is tapping oil and gas reserves trapped in shale formations in Texas, North Dakota, and other areas.

- U.S. oil production in 2013 was 15.3 percent higher than in 2012 at 7.4 million barrels a day.

- U.S. oil production will increase again in 2014 and reach 8.3 million barrels a day.

- Fracking will enable the United States to displace Saudi Arabia as the world's top oil producer.

ECONOMIC ANALYSIS

- The table shows some data on U.S. production and imports in 2000 and 2013.

U.S. production and imports	2000	2013
Oil and gas (million barrels per day)	16	21
Other goods and services (units per day)	34	42
Oil and gas imports (million barrels per day)	13	8

- The news story provides data on oil production and the table adds together the production of oil and natural gas, both of which come from shale formations.

- "Fracking" has increased the production of oil and gas from 16 million barrels per day in 2000 to 21 million barrels per day in 2013, an increase of 31 percent.

- The consumption of oil and gas has remained at 29 million barrels per day, so the increase in production has decreased the imports of oil and gas from 13 million barrels per day in 2000 to 8 million barrels per day in 2013.

- "Fracking" is not the only advance in technology and productivity. Other advances in technology and investment include such items as cellphone networks, Internet services, and industrial robots.

- These advances in technology and investment in capital have increased the production of other goods and services from 34 units in 2000 to 42 units in 2013, an increase of 24 percent. (Think of these "units" as giant shopping carts of goods and services each one of which costs $1 billion in the prices of 2013.)

- We can use the data in the table to make a graph of the U.S. *PPF*, with other goods and services (on the *y*-axis), and oil and gas (on the *x*-axis). Figure 1 shows the *PPF* for 2000 and for 2013 and marks the points on the *PPF*s at which the U.S. economy produced.

- Figure 2 also shows the *PPF* for 2013 and explains why we still import some oil and gas.

- We could easily produce the 29 million barrels per day that we consume. But to increase production from 21 million barrels per day to 29 million barrels, we would incur a higher opportunity cost of energy.

- Recall that the slope of the *PPF* measures opportunity cost. So the slope of the *PPF* at point *A*, the production point in 2013, measures the opportunity cost of producing oil and gas in 2013.

- If our production of oil and gas is efficient, we produce only the quantity at which the opportunity cost equals the cost of buying it from other countries.

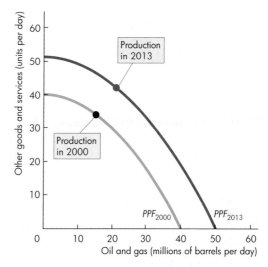

Figure 1 *PPF* **for Oil and Gas and Other Goods and Services: 2000 and 2013**

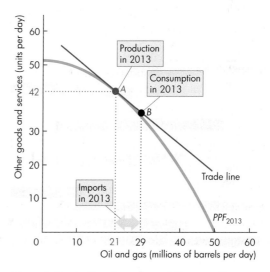

Figure 2 Production, Imports, and Consumption of Oil and Gas in 2013

- The red "Trade line" in Fig. 2 shows our import possibilities. By importing 8 million barrels per day, we can consume 29 million barrels at point *B* outside our *PPF*.

- The opportunity cost of producing more oil and gas in the United States is greater than the opportunity cost of importing it, so it is efficient to limit our production and import some energy.

- With further expansion of "fracking," we might eventually stop importing oil and gas and even start to export it.

SUMMARY

Key Points

Production Possibilities and Opportunity Cost (pp. 32–34)

- The production possibilities frontier is the boundary between production levels that are attainable and those that are not attainable when all the available resources are used to their limits.
- Production efficiency occurs at points on the production possibilities frontier.
- Along the production possibilities frontier, the opportunity cost of producing more of one good is the amount of the other good that must be given up.
- The opportunity cost of all goods increases as the production of the good increases.

Working Problems 1 to 3 will give you a better understanding of production possibilities and opportunity cost.

Using Resources Efficiently (pp. 35–37)

- Allocative efficiency occurs when goods and services are produced at the least possible cost and in the quantities that bring the greatest possible benefit.
- The marginal cost of a good is the opportunity cost of producing one more unit of it.
- The marginal benefit from a good is the benefit received from consuming one more unit of it and is measured by the willingness to pay for it.
- The marginal benefit of a good decreases as the amount of the good available increases.
- Resources are used efficiently when the marginal cost of each good is equal to its marginal benefit.

Working Problems 4 to 6 will give you a better understanding of the efficient use of resources.

Economic Growth (pp. 38–39)

- Economic growth, which is the expansion of production possibilities, results from capital accumulation and technological change.
- The opportunity cost of economic growth is forgone current consumption.
- The benefit of economic growth is increased future consumption.

Working Problem 7 will give you a better understanding of economic growth.

Gains from Trade (pp. 40–43)

- A person has a comparative advantage in producing a good if that person can produce the good at a lower opportunity cost than everyone else.
- People gain by specializing in the activity in which they have a comparative advantage and trading with others.

Working Problems 8 and 9 will give you a better understanding of the gains from trade.

Economic Coordination (pp. 44–45)

- Firms coordinate a large amount of economic activity, but there is a limit to the efficient size of a firm.
- Markets coordinate the economic choices of people and firms.
- Markets can work efficiently only when property rights exist.
- Money makes trading in markets more efficient.

Working Problem 10 will give you a better understanding of economic coordination.

Key Terms

Absolute advantage, 40

Allocative efficiency, 35

Capital accumulation, 38

Comparative advantage, 40

Economic growth, 38

Firm, 44

Marginal benefit, 36

Marginal benefit curve, 36

Marginal cost, 35

Market, 44

Money, 44

Opportunity cost, 33

MyEconLab Key Terms Quiz

Preferences, 36

Production efficiency, 33

Production possibilities frontier, 32

Property rights, 44

Technological change, 38

◆ WORKED PROBLEM

MyEconLab   You can work this problem in Chapter 2 Study Plan.

Leisure Island has 50 hours of labor a day that it can use to produce entertainment and good food. The table shows the maximum quantity of each good that it can produce with different quantities of labor.

Labor (hours)	Entertainment (shows per week)		Good food (meals per week)
0	0	or	0
10	2	or	5
20	4	or	9
30	6	or	12
40	8	or	14
50	10	or	15

Questions

1. Can Leisure Island produce 4 shows and 14 meals a week?
2. If Leisure Island produces 4 shows and 9 meals a week, is production efficient?
3. If Leisure Island produces 8 shows and 5 meals a week, does it face a tradeoff?
4. Suppose that Leisure Island produces 4 shows and 12 meals a week. Calculate the opportunity cost of producing 2 extra shows a week.

Solutions

1. To produce 4 shows it would use 20 hours and to produce 14 meals it would use 40 hours, so to produce 4 shows and 14 meals a week, Leisure Island would use 60 hours of labor. Leisure Island has only 50 hours of labor available, so it cannot produce 4 shows and 14 meals a week.

Key Point: Production is *unattainable* if it uses more resources than are available.

2. When Leisure Island produces 4 shows it uses 20 hours of labor and when it produces 9 meals it uses 20 hours. In total, it uses 40 hours, which is *less than* the 50 hours of labor available. So Leisure Island's production is not efficient.

Key Point: Production is *efficient* only if the economy uses all its resources.

3. When Leisure Island produces 8 shows and 5 meals, it uses 50 hours of labor. Leisure Island is using all its resources, so to produce more of either good, it would face a tradeoff.

Key Point: An economy faces a *tradeoff* only when it uses all the available resources.

4. When Leisure Island produces 4 shows and 12 meals a week, it uses 50 hours of labor. To

produce 2 more shows a week, Leisure Island faces a tradeoff and incurs an opportunity cost.

To produce 2 extra shows a week, Leisure Island moves 10 hours of labor from good food production, which decreases the quantity of meals from 12 to 9 a week—a decrease of 3 meals. That is, to get 2 extra shows a week, Leisure Island *must give up* 3 meals a week. The opportunity cost of the 2 extra shows is 3 meals a week.

Key Point: When an economy is using all its resources and it decides to increase production of one good, it incurs an opportunity cost equal to the quantity of the good that it *must* forgo.

Key Figure

Each row of the following table sets out the combination of shows and meals that Leisure Island can produce in a week when it uses 50 hours of labor.

	Entertainment (shows per week)		Good food (meals per week)
A	0	and	15
B	2	and	14
C	4	and	12
D	6	and	9
E	8	and	5
F	10	and	0

Points A through F plot these combinations in the rows. The blue curve shows Leisure Island's *PPF*. Point X (4 shows and 14 meals in Question 1) is unattainable; Point Y (4 shows and 9 meals in Question 2) is inefficient. Point E (8 shows and 5 meals in Question 3) is on the *PPF*. The arrow illustrates the tradeoff and the calculation of the opportunity cost of 2 extra shows a week.

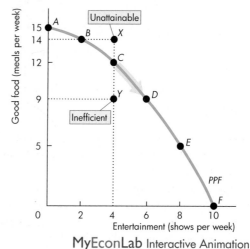

MyEconLab Interactive Animation

STUDY PLAN PROBLEMS AND APPLICATIONS

MyEconLab   You can work Problems 1 to 10 in Chapter 2 Study Plan and get instant feedback.

Production Possibilities and Opportunity Cost

(Study Plan 2.1)

Use the following data to work Problems 1 to 3.

Brazil produces ethanol from sugar, and the land used to grow sugar can be used to grow food crops. The table sets out Brazil's production possibilities for ethanol and food crops:

Ethanol (barrels per day)		Food crops (tons per day)
70	and	0
64	and	1
54	and	2
40	and	3
22	and	4
0	and	5

1. a. Draw a graph of Brazil's *PPF* and explain how your graph illustrates scarcity.
   b. If Brazil produces 40 barrels of ethanol a day, how much food must it produce to achieve production efficiency?
   c. Why does Brazil face a tradeoff on its *PPF*?

2. a. If Brazil increases ethanol production from 40 barrels per day to 54 barrels a day, what is the opportunity cost of the additional ethanol?
   b. If Brazil increases food production from 2 tons per day to 3 tons per day, what is the opportunity cost of the additional food?
   c. What is the relationship between your answers to parts (a) and (b)?

3. Does Brazil face an increasing opportunity cost of ethanol? What feature of Brazil's *PPF* illustrates increasing opportunity cost?

Using Resources Efficiently (Study Plan 2.2)

Use the table above to work Problems 4 and 5.

4. Define marginal cost and calculate Brazil's marginal cost of producing a ton of food when the quantity produced is 2.5 tons per day.

5. Define marginal benefit. Explain how it is measured and why the data in the table does not enable you to calculate Brazil's marginal benefit from food.

6. Distinguish between *production efficiency* and *allocative efficiency*. Explain why many production possibilities achieve production efficiency but only one achieves allocative efficiency.

Economic Growth (Study Plan 2.3)

7. A farm grows wheat and produces pork. The marginal cost of producing each of these products increases as more of it is produced.
   a. Make a graph that illustrates the farm's *PPF*.
   b. The farm adopts a new technology that allows it to use fewer resources to fatten pigs. On your graph sketch the impact of the new technology on the farm's *PPF*.
   c. With the farm using the new technology described in part (b), has the opportunity cost of producing a ton of wheat increased, decreased, or remained the same? Explain and illustrate your answer.
   d. Is the farm more efficient with the new technology than it was with the old one? Why?

Gains from Trade (Study Plan 2.4)

8. In an hour, Sue can produce 40 caps or 4 jackets and Tessa can produce 80 caps or 4 jackets.
   a. Calculate Sue's opportunity cost of producing a cap.
   b. Calculate Tessa's opportunity cost of producing a cap.
   c. Who has a comparative advantage in producing caps?
   d. If Sue and Tessa specialize in producing the good in which they have a comparative advantage, and they trade 1 jacket for 15 caps, who gains from the specialization and trade?

9. Suppose that Tessa buys a new machine that enables her to make 20 jackets an hour. (She can still make only 80 caps per hour.)
   a. Who now has a comparative advantage in producing jackets?
   b. Can Sue and Tessa still gain from trade?
   c. Would Sue and Tessa still be willing to trade 1 jacket for 15 caps? Explain your answer.

Economic Coordination (Study Plan 2.5)

10. For 50 years, Cuba has had a centrally planned economy in which the government makes the big decisions on how resources will be allocated.
    a. Why would you expect Cuba's production possibilities (per person) to be smaller than those of the United States?
    b. What are the social institutions that Cuba might lack that help the United States to achieve allocative efficiency?

ADDITIONAL PROBLEMS AND APPLICATIONS

MyEconLab   You can work these problems in MyEconLab if assigned by your instructor.

Production Possibilities and Opportunity Cost

Use the following table to work Problems 11 and 12. Suppose that Yucatan's production possibilities are

Food (pounds per month)		Sunscreen (gallons per month)
300	and	0
200	and	50
100	and	100
0	and	150

11. a. Draw a graph of Yucatan's *PPF* and explain how your graph illustrates a tradeoff.

   b. If Yucatan produces 150 pounds of food per month, how much sunscreen must it produce if it achieves production efficiency?

   c. What is Yucatan's opportunity cost of producing (i) 1 pound of food and (ii) 1 gallon of sunscreen?

   d. What is the relationship between your answers to part (c)?

12. What feature of a *PPF* illustrates increasing opportunity cost? Explain why Yucatan's opportunity cost does or does not increase.

Using Resources Efficiently

13. In problem 11, what is the marginal cost of 1 pound of food in Yucatan when the quantity produced is 150 pounds per day? What is special about the marginal cost of food in Yucatan?

14. The table describes the preferences in Yucatan.

Sunscreen (gallons per month)	Willingness to pay (pounds of food per gallon)
25	3
75	2
125	1

   a. What is the marginal benefit from sunscreen and how is it measured?

   b. Use the table in Problem 11. What does Yucatan produce to achieve allocative efficiency?

15. **U.K. Music Stores Squeezed off Main Street**
   Music retailing is changing: Sony Music and Amazon are selling online, discount stores are selling at low prices, and Main Street music retailers are all struggling.
   Source: *The Economist*, January 20, 2007

   a. Draw the *PPF* curves for Main Street music retailers and online music retailers before and after the Internet became available.

   b. Draw the marginal cost and marginal benefit curves for Main Street music retailers and online music retailers before and after the Internet became available.

   c. Explain how changes in production possibilities, preferences or both have changed the way in which recorded music is retailed.

Use the following news clip to work Problems 16 and 17.

Malaria Eradication Back on the Table

In response to the Gates Malaria Forum in October 2007, countries are debating the pros and cons of eradication. Dr. Arata Kochi of the World Health Organization believes that with enough money malaria cases could be cut by 90 percent but it would be very expensive to eliminate the remaining 10 percent of cases, so countries should not strive to eradicate malaria.
   Source: *The New York Times*, March 4, 2008

16. Is Dr. Kochi talking about *production efficiency* or *allocative efficiency* or both?

17. Make a graph with the percentage of malaria cases eliminated on the *x*-axis and the marginal cost and marginal benefit of driving down malaria cases on the *y*-axis. On your graph:

   (i) Draw a marginal cost curve and marginal benefit curve that are consistent with Dr. Kochi's opinion.

   (ii) Identify the quantity of malaria eradicated that achieves allocative efficiency.

Economic Growth

18. Capital accumulation and technological change bring economic growth: Production that was unattainable yesterday becomes attainable today; production that is unattainable today will become attainable tomorrow. Why doesn't economic growth bring an end to scarcity one day?

19. **Toyota Plans to Build a Better Company**
   In 2014, Toyota will produce 3 million cars per year and use the balance of its resources to upgrade its workers' skills and create new technology. In three years' time, Toyota plans to produce better cars and be more productive.
   Source: *Financial Post*, April 7, 2014

   a. What is the opportunity cost of upgrading its workers' skills and creating new technology?

b. Sketch Toyota's *PPF* and mark its production point in 2014. Now show on your graph Toyota's *PPF* in 2018.

Gains from Trade

Use the following data to work Problems 20 and 21. Kim can produce 40 pies or 400 cakes an hour. Liam can produce 100 pies or 200 cakes an hour.

20. a. Calculate Kim's opportunity cost of a pie and Liam's opportunity cost of a pie.
    b. If each spends 30 minutes of each hour producing pies and 30 minutes producing cakes, how many pies and cakes does each produce?
    c. Who has a comparative advantage in producing (i) pies and (ii) cakes?

21. a. Draw a graph of Kim's *PPF* and Liam's *PPF* and show the point at which each produces when they spend 30 minutes of each hour producing pies and 30 minutes producing cakes.
    b. On your graph, show what Kim produces and what Liam produces when they specialize.
    c. When they specialize and trade, what are the total gains from trade?
    d. If Kim and Liam share the total gains equally, what trade takes place between them?

22. Tony and Patty produce skis and snowboards. The tables show their production possibilities. Tony produces 5 snowboards and 40 skis a week; Patty produces 10 snowboards and 5 skis a week.

Tony's Production Possibilities

Snowboards (units per week)		Skis (units per week)
25	and	0
20	and	10
15	and	20
10	and	30
5	and	40
0	and	50

Patty's Production Possibilities

Snowboards (units per week)		Skis (units per week)
20	and	0
10	and	5
0	and	10

a. Who has a comparative advantage in producing (i) snowboards and (ii) skis?
b. If Tony and Patty specialize and trade 1 snowboard for 1 ski, what are the gains from trade?

Economic Coordination

23. Indicate on a graph of the circular flows in the market economy, the real and money flows in which the following items belong:
    a. You buy an iPad from the Apple Store.
    b. Apple Inc. pays the designers of the iPad.
    c. Apple Inc. decides to expand and rents an adjacent building.
    d. You buy a new e-book from Amazon.
    e. Apple Inc. hires a student as an intern during the summer.

Economics in the News

24. After you have studied *Economics in the News* on pp. 46–47, answer the following questions.
    a. How has "fracking" changed the U.S. production possibilities?
    b. How have advances in technologies for producing other goods and services changed the U.S. production possibilities?
    c. If "fracking" had been the only technological advance, how would the *PPF* have changed?
    d. If "fracking" had been the only technological advance, how would the opportunity cost of producing oil and gas have changed? Would it have been lower or higher than it actually was?

25. **Lots of Little Screens**

    Inexpensive broadband access has created a generation of television producers for whom the Internet is their native medium. As they redirect the focus from TV to computers, cellphones, and iPods, the video market is developing into an open digital network.

    Source: *The New York Times*, December 2, 2007

    a. How has inexpensive broadband changed the production possibilities of video entertainment and other goods and services?
    b. Sketch a *PPF* for video entertainment and other goods and services before broadband.
    c. Show how the arrival of inexpensive broadband has changed the *PPF*.
    d. Sketch a marginal benefit curve for video entertainment.
    e. Show how the new generation of TV producers for whom the Internet is their native medium might have changed the marginal benefit from video entertainment.
    f. Explain how the efficient quantity of video entertainment has changed.

Your Economic Revolution

Three periods in human history stand out as ones of economic revolution. The first, the *Agricultural Revolution,* occurred 10,000 years ago. In what is today Iraq, people learned to domesticate animals and plant crops. People stopped roaming in search of food and settled in villages, towns, and cities where they specialized in the activities in which they had a comparative advantage and developed markets in which to exchange their products. Wealth increased enormously.

Economics was born during the *Industrial Revolution,* which began in England during the 1760s. For the first time, people began to apply science and create new technologies for the manufacture of textiles and iron, to create steam engines, and to boost the output of farms.

You are studying economics at a time that future historians will call the *Information Revolution.* Over the entire world, people are embracing new information technologies and prospering on an unprecedented scale.

During all three economic revolutions, many have prospered but others have been left behind. It is the range of human progress that poses the greatest question for economics and the one that Adam Smith addressed in the first work of economic science: What causes the differences in wealth among nations?

Many people had written about economics before **Adam Smith***, but he made economics a science. Born in 1723 in Kirkcaldy, a small fishing town near Edinburgh, Scotland, Smith was the only child of the town's customs officer. Lured from his professorship (he was a full professor at 28) by a wealthy Scottish duke who gave him a pension of £300 a year—ten times the average income at that time—Smith devoted ten years to writing his masterpiece:* An Inquiry into the Nature and Causes of the **Wealth of Nations***, published in 1776.*

Why, Adam Smith asked, are some nations wealthy while others are poor? He was pondering these questions at the height of the Industrial Revolution, and he answered by emphasizing the power of the division of labor and free markets in raising labor productivity.

To illustrate his argument, Adam Smith described two pin factories. In the first, one person, using the hand tools available in the 1770s, could make 20 pins a day. In the other, by using those same hand tools but breaking the process into a number of individually small operations in which people specialize—by the division of labor—ten people could make a staggering 48,000 pins a day. One draws

Every individual who intends only his own gain is led by an invisible hand to promote an end (the public good) which was no part of his intention.

ADAM SMITH
The Wealth of Nations

out the wire, another straightens it, a third cuts it, a fourth points it, a fifth grinds it. Three specialists make the head, and a fourth attaches it. Finally, the pin is polished and packaged.

But a large market is needed to support the division of labor: One factory employing ten workers would need to sell more than 15 million pins a year to stay in business!

ESTHER DUFLO is the Abdul Latif Jameel Professor of Poverty Alleviation and Development Economics at the Massachusetts Institute of Technology. Among her many honors are the 2010 John Bates Clark Medal for the best economist under 40 and the Financial Times and Goldman Sachs Business Book of the Year Award in 2011 for her book (with Abhijit Banerjee) *Poor Economics: A Radical Rethinking of the Way to Fight Global Poverty.* Professor Duflo's research seeks to advance our understanding of the economic choices of the extremely poor by conducting massive real-world experiments.

Professor Duflo was an undergraduate student of history and economics at École Normale Supérieure and completed a master's degree at DELTA in Paris before moving to the United States. She earned her PhD in Economics at MIT in 1999.

Michael Parkin talked with her about her work, which advances our understanding of the economic choices and condition of the very poor.

Professor Duflo, what's the story about how you became an economist and in particular the architect of experiments designed to understand the economic choices of the very poor?

When I was a kid, I was exposed to many stories and images of poor children: through my mother's engagement as a doctor in a small NGO dealing with child victims of war and through books and stories about children living all around the world. I remember asking myself how I could justify my luck of being born where I was. I had a very exaggerated idea of what it was to be poor, but this idea caused sufficient discomfort that I knew I had to do something about it, if I could. Quite by accident, I discovered that economics was the way in which I could actually be useful: While spending a year in Russia teaching French and studying History, I realized that academic economists have the ability to intervene in the world while keeping enough sanity to analyze it. I thought this would be ideal for me and I have never regreted it. I have the best job in the world.

> ... imagine living on under a dollar a day after your rent is paid in Seattle or Denver. Not easy!

The very poor who you study are people who live on $1 a day or $2 a day. ... Is $1 a day a true measure that includes everything these poor people consume?

For defining the poverty line, we don't include the cost of housing. The poor also get free goods, sometimes of bad quality (education, healthcare) and the value of those is also not included. Other than that, yes, it is everything.

Moreover, you have to realize this is everything, taking into account the fact that life is much cheaper in many poor countries because salaries are lower, so anything that is made and consumed locally (e.g. a haircut) is cheaper.

For example, in India, the purchasing power of a dollar (in terms of the real goods you can buy) is about 3 times what it is in the United States. So the poverty line we use for India is 33 cents per day, not a dollar.

All told, you really have to imagine living on under a dollar a day after your rent is paid in Seattle or Denver. Not easy!

*Read the full interview with Esther Duflo in MyEconLab.

54

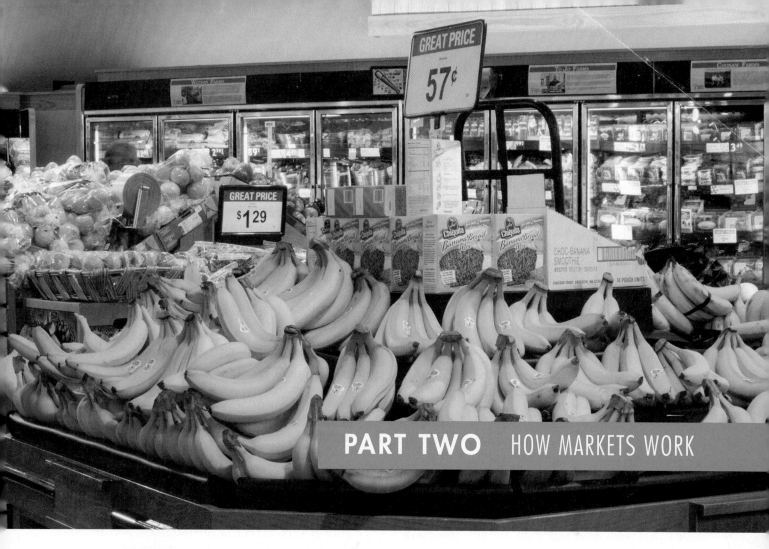

GREAT PRICE
57¢

GREAT PRICE
$1.29

PART TWO HOW MARKETS WORK

3 DEMAND AND SUPPLY

After studying this chapter, you will be able to:

◆ Describe a competitive market and think about a price as an opportunity cost

◆ Explain the influences on demand

◆ Explain the influences on supply

◆ Explain how demand and supply determine prices and quantities bought and sold

◆ Use the demand and supply model to make predictions about changes in prices and quantities

A disease that kills banana trees is jumping continents and left unchecked will bring a big drop in banana production. What will happen to the price of bananas if the disease isn't contained? The demand and supply model answers this question.

This model that you're about to study is the main tool of economics. It explains how prices are determined and how they guide the use of resources to influence *What*, *How*, and *For Whom* goods and services are produced.

Economics in the News at the end of the chapter answers the question about the price of bananas.

◆ Markets and Prices

When you need a new pair of running shoes, want a bagel and a latte, plan to upgrade your cellphone, or need to fly home for Thanksgiving, you must find a place where people sell those items or offer those services. The place in which you find them is a *market*. You learned in Chapter 2 (p. 44) that a market is any arrangement that enables buyers and sellers to get information and to do business with each other.

A market has two sides: buyers and sellers. There are markets for *goods* such as apples and hiking boots, for *services* such as haircuts and tennis lessons, for *factors of production* such as computer programmers and earthmovers, and for other manufactured *inputs* such as memory chips and auto parts. There are also markets for money such as Japanese yen and for financial securities such as Yahoo! stock. Only our imagination limits what can be traded in markets.

Some markets are physical places where buyers and sellers meet and where an auctioneer or a broker helps to determine the prices. Examples of this type of market are the New York Stock Exchange and the wholesale fish, meat, and produce markets.

Some markets are groups of people spread around the world who never meet and know little about each other but are connected through the Internet or by telephone and fax. Examples are the e-commerce markets and the currency markets.

But most markets are unorganized collections of buyers and sellers. You do most of your trading in this type of market. An example is the market for basketball shoes. The buyers in this $3-billion-a-year market are the 45 million Americans who play basketball (or who want to make a fashion statement). The sellers are the tens of thousands of retail sports equipment and footwear stores. Each buyer can visit several different stores, and each seller knows that the buyer has a choice of stores.

Markets vary in the intensity of competition that buyers and sellers face. In this chapter, we're going to study a **competitive market**—a market that has many buyers and many sellers, so no single buyer or seller can influence the price.

Producers offer items for sale only if the price is high enough to cover their opportunity cost. And consumers respond to changing opportunity cost by seeking cheaper alternatives to expensive items.

We are going to study how people respond to *prices* and the forces that determine prices. But to pursue these tasks, we need to understand the relationship between a price and an opportunity cost.

In everyday life, the *price* of an object is the number of dollars that must be given up in exchange for it. Economists refer to this price as the **money price**.

The *opportunity cost* of an action is the highest-valued alternative forgone. If, when you buy a cup of coffee, the highest-valued thing you forgo is some gum, then the opportunity cost of the coffee is the *quantity* of gum forgone. We can calculate the quantity of gum forgone from the money prices of the coffee and the gum.

If the money price of coffee is $1 a cup and the money price of gum is 50¢ a pack, then the opportunity cost of one cup of coffee is two packs of gum. To calculate this opportunity cost, we divide the price of a cup of coffee by the price of a pack of gum and find the *ratio* of one price to the other. The ratio of one price to another is called a **relative price**, and a *relative price is an opportunity cost.*

We can express the relative price of coffee in terms of gum or any other good. The normal way of expressing a relative price is in terms of a "basket" of all goods and services. To calculate this relative price, we divide the money price of a good by the money price of a "basket" of all goods (called a *price index*). The resulting relative price tells us the opportunity cost of the good in terms of how much of the "basket" we must give up to buy it.

The demand and supply model that we are about to study determines *relative prices,* and the word "price" means *relative* price. When we predict that a price will fall, we do not mean that its *money* price will fall—although it might. We mean that its *relative* price will fall. That is, its price will fall *relative* to the average price of other goods and services.

◆ REVIEW QUIZ

1 What is the distinction between a money price and a relative price?
2 Explain why a relative price is an opportunity cost.
3 Think of examples of goods whose relative price has risen or fallen by a large amount.

Work these questions in Study Plan 3.1 and get instant feedback. Do a Key Terms Quiz.   MyEconLab

Let's begin our study of demand and supply, starting with demand.

◆ Demand

If you demand something, then you

1. Want it.
2. Can afford it.
3. Plan to buy it.

Wants are the unlimited desires or wishes that people have for goods and services. How many times have you thought that you would like something "if only you could afford it" or "if it weren't so expensive"? Scarcity guarantees that many—perhaps most—of our wants will never be satisfied. Demand reflects a decision about which wants to satisfy.

The **quantity demanded** of a good or service is the amount that consumers plan to buy during a given time period at a particular price. The quantity demanded is not necessarily the same as the quantity actually bought. Sometimes the quantity demanded exceeds the amount of goods available, so the quantity bought is less than the quantity demanded.

The quantity demanded is measured as an amount per unit of time. For example, suppose that you buy one cup of coffee a day. The quantity of coffee that you demand can be expressed as 1 cup per day, 7 cups per week, or 365 cups per year.

Many factors influence buying plans, and one of them is the price. We look first at the relationship between the quantity demanded of a good and its price. To study this relationship, we keep all other influences on buying plans the same and we ask: How, other things remaining the same, does the quantity demanded of a good change as its price changes?

The law of demand provides the answer.

The Law of Demand

The **law of demand** states:

Other things remaining the same, the higher the price of a good, the smaller is the quantity demanded; and the lower the price of a good, the greater is the quantity demanded.

Why does a higher price reduce the quantity demanded? For two reasons:

- Substitution effect
- Income effect

Substitution Effect When the price of a good rises, other things remaining the same, its *relative* price—its opportunity cost—rises. Although each good is unique, it has *substitutes*—other goods that can be used in its place. As the opportunity cost of a good rises, the incentive to economize on its use and switch to a substitute becomes stronger.

Income Effect When a price rises, other things remaining the same, the price rises *relative* to income. Faced with a higher price and an unchanged income, people cannot afford to buy all the things they previously bought. They must decrease the quantities demanded of at least some goods and services. Normally, the good whose price has increased will be one of the goods that people buy less of.

To see the substitution effect and the income effect at work, think about the effects of a change in the price of an energy bar. Several different goods are substitutes for an energy bar. For example, an energy drink could be consumed instead of an energy bar.

Suppose that an energy bar initially sells for $3 and then its price falls to $1.50. People now substitute energy bars for energy drinks—the substitution effect. And with a budget that now has some slack from the lower price of an energy bar, people buy even more energy bars—the income effect. The quantity of energy bars demanded increases for these two reasons.

Now suppose that an energy bar initially sells for $3 and then the price doubles to $6. People now buy fewer energy bars and more energy drinks—the substitution effect. And faced with a tighter budget, people buy even fewer energy bars—the income effect. The quantity of energy bars demanded decreases for these two reasons.

Demand Curve and Demand Schedule

You are now about to study one of the two most used curves in economics: the demand curve. You are also going to encounter one of the most critical distinctions: the distinction between *demand* and *quantity demanded*.

The term **demand** refers to the entire relationship between the price of a good and the quantity demanded of that good. Demand is illustrated by the demand curve and the demand schedule. The term *quantity demanded* refers to a point on a demand curve—the quantity demanded at a particular price.

Figure 3.1 shows the demand curve for energy bars. A **demand curve** shows the relationship between the quantity demanded of a good and its price when all other influences on consumers' planned purchases remain the same.

The table in Fig. 3.1 is the demand schedule for energy bars. A *demand schedule* lists the quantities demanded at each price when all the other influences on consumers' planned purchases remain the same. For example, if the price of a bar is 50¢, the quantity demanded is 22 million a week. If the price is $2.50, the quantity demanded is 5 million a week. The other rows of the table show the quantities demanded at prices of $1.00, $1.50, and $2.00.

We graph the demand schedule as a demand curve with the quantity demanded on the *x*-axis and the price on the *y*-axis. The points on the demand curve labeled *A* through *E* correspond to the rows of the demand schedule. For example, point *A* on the graph shows a quantity demanded of 22 million energy bars a week at a price of 50¢ a bar.

Willingness and Ability to Pay Another way of looking at the demand curve is as a willingness-and-ability-to-pay curve. The willingness and ability to pay is a measure of *marginal benefit.*

If a small quantity is available, the highest price that someone is willing and able to pay for one more unit is high. But as the quantity available increases, the marginal benefit of each additional unit falls and the highest price that someone is willing and able to pay also falls along the demand curve.

In Fig. 3.1, if only 5 million energy bars are available each week, the highest price that someone is willing to pay for the 5 millionth bar is $2.50. But if 22 million energy bars are available each week, someone is willing to pay 50¢ for the last bar bought.

A Change in Demand

When any factor that influences buying plans changes, other than the price of the good, there is a **change in demand.** Figure 3.2 illustrates an increase in demand. When demand increases, the demand curve shifts rightward and the quantity demanded at each price is greater. For example, at $2.50 a bar, the quantity demanded on the original (blue) demand curve is 5 million energy bars a week. On the new (red) demand curve, at $2.50 a bar, the quantity demanded is 15 million bars a week. Look closely at the numbers in the table and check that the quantity demanded at each price is greater.

FIGURE 3.1 The Demand Curve

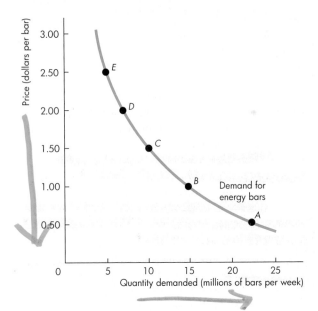

	Price (dollars per bar)	Quantity demanded (millions of bars per week)
A	0.50	22
B	1.00	15
C	1.50	10
D	2.00	7
E	2.50	5

The table shows a demand schedule for energy bars. At a price of 50¢ a bar, 22 million bars a week are demanded; at a price of $1.50 a bar, 10 million bars a week are demanded. The demand curve shows the relationship between quantity demanded and price, other things remaining the same. The demand curve slopes downward: As the price falls, the quantity demanded increases.

The demand curve can be read in two ways. For a given price, the demand curve tells us the quantity that people plan to buy. For example, at a price of $1.50 a bar, people plan to buy 10 million bars a week. For a given quantity, the demand curve tells us the maximum price that consumers are willing and able to pay for the last bar available. For example, the maximum price that consumers will pay for the 15 millionth bar is $1.00.

MyEconLab Animation

FIGURE 3.2   An Increase in Demand

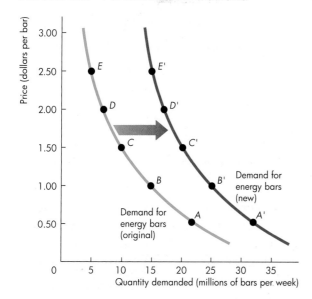

Original demand schedule Original income			New demand schedule New higher income		
	Price (dollars per bar)	Quantity demanded (millions of bars per week)		Price (dollars per bar)	Quantity demanded (millions of bars per week)
A	0.50	22	A'	0.50	32
B	1.00	15	B'	1.00	25
C	1.50	10	C'	1.50	20
D	2.00	7	D'	2.00	17
E	2.50	5	E'	2.50	15

A change in any influence on buying plans other than the price of the good itself results in a new demand schedule and a shift of the demand curve. A change in income changes the demand for energy bars. At a price of $1.50 a bar, 10 million bars a week are demanded at the original income (row C of the table) and 20 million bars a week are demanded at the new higher income (row C'). A rise in income increases the demand for energy bars. The demand curve shifts *rightward*, as shown by the shift arrow and the resulting red curve.

—— **MyEconLab** Animation ——

Six main factors bring changes in demand. They are changes in

- The prices of related goods
- Expected future prices
- Income
- Expected future income and credit
- Population
- Preferences

Prices of Related Goods The quantity of energy bars that consumers plan to buy depends in part on the prices of substitutes for energy bars. A substitute is a good that can be used in place of another good. For example, a bus ride is a substitute for a train ride; a hamburger is a substitute for a hot dog; and an energy drink is a substitute for an energy bar. If the price of a substitute for an energy bar rises, people buy less of the substitute and more energy bars. For example, if the price of an energy drink rises, people buy fewer energy drinks and more energy bars. The demand for energy bars increases.

The quantity of energy bars that people plan to buy also depends on the prices of complements with energy bars. A complement is a good that is used in conjunction with another good. Hamburgers and fries are complements, and so are energy bars and exercise. If the price of an hour at the gym falls, people buy more gym time *and more* energy bars.

Expected Future Prices If the expected future price of a good rises and if the good can be stored, the opportunity cost of obtaining the good for future use is lower today than it will be in the future when people expect the price to be higher. So people retime their purchases—they substitute over time. They buy more of the good now before its price is expected to rise (and less afterward), so the demand for the good today increases.

For example, suppose that a Florida frost damages the season's orange crop. You expect the price of orange juice to rise, so you fill your freezer with enough frozen juice to get you through the next six months. Your current demand for frozen orange juice has increased, and your future demand has decreased.

Similarly, if the expected future price of a good falls, the opportunity cost of buying the good today is high relative to what it is expected to be in the future. So again, people retime their purchases. They buy less of the good now before its price is expected to fall, so the demand for the good decreases today and increases in the future.

Computer prices are constantly falling, and this fact poses a dilemma. Will you buy a new computer now, in time for the start of the school year, or will you wait until the price has fallen some more? Because people expect computer prices to keep falling, the current demand for computers is less (and the future demand is greater) than it otherwise would be.

Income Consumers' income influences demand. When income increases, consumers buy more of most goods; and when income decreases, consumers buy less of most goods. Although an increase in income leads to an increase in the demand for *most* goods, it does not lead to an increase in the demand for *all* goods. A **normal good** is one for which demand increases as income increases. An **inferior good** is one for which demand decreases as income increases. As incomes increase, the demand for air travel (a normal good) increases and the demand for long-distance bus trips (an inferior good) decreases.

Expected Future Income and Credit When expected future income increases or credit becomes easier to get, demand for a good might increase now. For example, a salesperson gets the news that she will receive a big bonus at the end of the year, so she goes into debt and buys a new car right now, rather than waiting until she receives the bonus.

Population Demand also depends on the size and the age structure of the population. The larger the population, the greater is the demand for all goods and services; the smaller the population, the smaller is the demand for all goods and services.

For example, the demand for parking spaces, running shoes, movies, or just about anything that you can imagine is much greater in New York City (population 8.3 million) than it is in Boise, Idaho (population 212,000).

Also, the larger the proportion of the population in a given age group, the greater is the demand for the goods and services used by that age group.

For example, during the 1990s, a decrease in the college-age population decreased the demand for college places. During those same years, the number of Americans aged 85 years and over increased by more than 1 million. As a result, the demand for nursing home services increased.

TABLE 3.1 The Demand for Energy Bars

The Law of Demand

The quantity of energy bars demanded

Decreases if:	Increases if:
■ The price of an energy bar rises	■ The price of an energy bar falls

Changes in Demand

The demand for energy bars

Decreases if:	Increases if:
■ The price of a substitute falls	■ The price of a substitute rises
■ The price of a complement rises	■ The price of a complement falls
■ The expected future price of an energy bar falls	■ The expected future price of an energy bar rises
■ Income falls*	■ Income rises*
■ Expected future income falls or credit becomes harder to get*	■ Expected future income rises or credit becomes easier to get*
■ The population decreases	■ The population increases

*An energy bar is a normal good.

Preferences Demand depends on preferences. *Preferences* determine the value that people place on each good and service. Preferences depend on such things as the weather, information, and fashion. For example, greater health and fitness awareness has shifted preferences in favor of energy bars, so the demand for energy bars has increased.

Table 3.1 summarizes the influences on demand and the direction of those influences.

A Change in the Quantity Demanded Versus a Change in Demand

Changes in the influences on buying plans bring either a change in the quantity demanded or a change in demand. Equivalently, they bring either a movement along the demand curve or a shift of the demand curve. The distinction between a change in the quantity demanded and a change in demand is the same as that between a movement along the demand curve and a shift of the demand curve.

A point on the demand curve shows the quantity demanded at a given price, so a movement along the demand curve shows a **change in the quantity demanded**. The entire demand curve shows demand, so a shift of the demand curve shows a *change in demand.* Figure 3.3 illustrates these distinctions.

Movement Along the Demand Curve If the price of the good changes but no other influence on buying plans changes, we illustrate the effect as a movement along the demand curve.

A fall in the price of a good increases the quantity demanded of it. In Fig. 3.3, we illustrate the effect of a fall in price as a movement down along the demand curve D_0.

A rise in the price of a good decreases the quantity demanded of it. In Fig. 3.3, we illustrate the effect of a rise in price as a movement up along the demand curve D_0.

A Shift of the Demand Curve If the price of a good remains constant but some other influence on buying plans changes, there is a change in demand for that good. We illustrate a change in demand as a shift of the demand curve. For example, if more people work out at the gym, consumers buy more energy bars regardless of the price of a bar. That is what a rightward shift of the demand curve shows—more energy bars are demanded at each price.

In Fig. 3.3, there is a *change in demand,* and the demand curve shifts when any influence on buying plans changes, other than the price of the good. Demand *increases* and the demand curve *shifts rightward* (to the red demand curve D_1) if the price of a substitute rises, the price of a complement falls, the expected future price of the good rises, income increases (for a normal good), expected future income or credit increases, or the population increases. Demand *decreases* and the demand curve *shifts leftward* (to the red demand curve D_2) if the price of a substitute falls, the price of a complement rises, the expected future price of the good falls, income decreases (for a normal good), expected future income or credit decreases, or the population decreases. (For an inferior good, the effects of changes in income are in the opposite direction to those described above.)

FIGURE 3.3   A Change in the Quantity Demanded Versus a Change in Demand

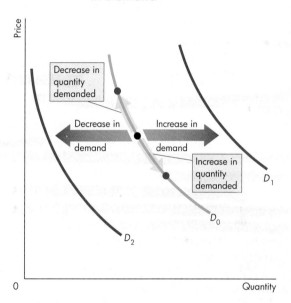

When the price of the good changes, there is a movement along the demand curve and a *change in the quantity demanded,* shown by the blue arrows on demand curve D_0. When any other influence on buying plans changes, there is a shift of the demand curve and a *change in demand.* An increase in demand shifts the demand curve rightward (from D_0 to D_1). A decrease in demand shifts the demand curve leftward (from D_0 to D_2).

MyEconLab Animation and Draw Graph

◆ **REVIEW QUIZ**

1 Define the quantity demanded of a good or service.
2 What is the law of demand and how do we illustrate it?
3 What does the demand curve tell us about the price that consumers are willing to pay?
4 List all the influences on buying plans that change demand, and for each influence, say whether it increases or decreases demand.
5 Why does demand not change when the price of a good changes with no change in the other influences on buying plans?

Work these questions in Study Plan 3.2 and get instant feedback. Do a Key Terms Quiz.   MyEconLab

◆ Supply

If a firm supplies a good or service, the firm

1. Has the resources and technology to produce it.
2. Can profit from producing it.
3. Plans to produce it and sell it.

A supply is more than just having the *resources* and the *technology* to produce something. *Resources and technology* are the constraints that limit what is possible.

Many useful things can be produced, but they are not produced unless it is profitable to do so. Supply reflects a decision about which technologically feasible items to produce.

The **quantity supplied** of a good or service is the amount that producers plan to sell during a given time period at a particular price. The quantity supplied is not necessarily the same amount as the quantity actually sold. Sometimes the quantity supplied is greater than the quantity demanded, so the quantity sold is less than the quantity supplied.

Like the quantity demanded, the quantity supplied is measured as an amount per unit of time. For example, suppose that GM produces 1,000 cars a day. The quantity of cars supplied by GM can be expressed as 1,000 a day, 7,000 a week, or 365,000 a year. Without the time dimension, we cannot tell whether a particular quantity is large or small.

Many factors influence selling plans, and again one of them is the price of the good. We look first at the relationship between the quantity supplied of a good and its price. Just as we did when we studied demand, to isolate the relationship between the quantity supplied of a good and its price, we keep all other influences on selling plans the same and ask: How does the quantity supplied of a good change as its price changes when other things remain the same?

The law of supply provides the answer.

The Law of Supply

The **law of supply** states:

> Other things remaining the same, the higher the price of a good, the greater is the quantity supplied; and the lower the price of a good, the smaller is the quantity supplied.

Why does a higher price increase the quantity supplied? It is because *marginal cost increases*. As the quantity produced of any good increases, the marginal cost of producing the good increases. (See Chapter 2, p. 35 to review marginal cost.)

It is never worth producing a good if the price received for the good does not at least cover the marginal cost of producing it. When the price of a good rises, other things remaining the same, producers are willing to incur a higher marginal cost, so they increase production. The higher price brings forth an increase in the quantity supplied.

Let's now illustrate the law of supply with a supply curve and a supply schedule.

Supply Curve and Supply Schedule

You are now going to study the second of the two most used curves in economics: the supply curve. You're also going to learn about the critical distinction between *supply* and *quantity supplied*.

The term **supply** refers to the entire relationship between the price of a good and the quantity supplied of it. Supply is illustrated by the supply curve and the supply schedule. The term *quantity supplied* refers to a point on a supply curve—the quantity supplied at a particular price.

Figure 3.4 shows the supply curve of energy bars. A **supply curve** shows the relationship between the quantity supplied of a good and its price when all other influences on producers' planned sales remain the same. The supply curve is a graph of a supply schedule.

The table in Fig. 3.4 sets out the supply schedule for energy bars. A *supply schedule* lists the quantities supplied at each price when all the other influences on producers' planned sales remain the same. For example, if the price of an energy bar is 50¢, the quantity supplied is zero—in row *A* of the table. If the price of an energy bar is $1.00, the quantity supplied is 6 million energy bars a week—in row *B*. The other rows of the table show the quantities supplied at prices of $1.50, $2.00, and $2.50.

To make a supply curve, we graph the quantity supplied on the *x*-axis and the price on the *y*-axis. The points on the supply curve labeled *A* through *E* correspond to the rows of the supply schedule. For example, point *A* on the graph shows a quantity supplied of zero at a price of 50¢ an energy bar. Point *E* shows a quantity supplied of 15 million bars at $2.50 an energy bar.

FIGURE 3.4   The Supply Curve

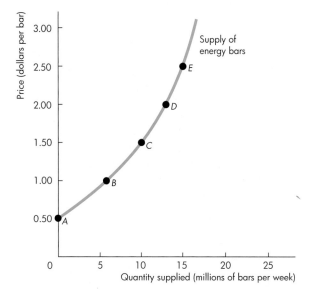

	Price (dollars per bar)	Quantity supplied (millions of bars per week)
A	0.50	0
B	1.00	6
C	1.50	10
D	2.00	13
E	2.50	15

The table shows the supply schedule of energy bars. For example, at a price of $1.00, 6 million bars a week are supplied; at a price of $2.50, 15 million bars a week are supplied. The supply curve shows the relationship between the quantity supplied and the price, other things remaining the same. The supply curve slopes upward: As the price of a good increases, the quantity supplied increases.

A supply curve can be read in two ways. For a given price, the supply curve tells us the quantity that producers plan to sell at that price. For example, at a price of $1.50 a bar, producers are planning to sell 10 million bars a week. For a given quantity, the supply curve tells us the minimum price at which producers are willing to sell one more bar. For example, if 15 million bars are produced each week, the lowest price at which a producer is willing to sell the 15 millionth bar is $2.50.

MyEconLab Animation

Minimum Supply Price The supply curve can be interpreted as a minimum-supply-price curve—a curve that shows the lowest price at which someone is willing to sell. This lowest price is the *marginal cost*.

If a small quantity is produced, the lowest price at which someone is willing to sell one more unit is low. But as the quantity produced increases, the marginal cost of each additional unit rises, so the lowest price at which someone is willing to sell an additional unit rises along the supply curve.

In Fig. 3.4, if 15 million bars are produced each week, the lowest price at which someone is willing to sell the 15 millionth bar is $2.50. But if 10 million bars are produced each week, someone is willing to accept $1.50 for the last bar produced.

A Change in Supply

When any factor that influences selling plans other than the price of the good changes, there is a **change in supply**. Six main factors bring changes in supply. They are changes in

- The prices of factors of production
- The prices of related goods produced
- Expected future prices
- The number of suppliers
- Technology
- The state of nature

Prices of Factors of Production The prices of the factors of production used to produce a good influence its supply. To see this influence, think about the supply curve as a minimum-supply-price curve. If the price of a factor of production rises, the lowest price that a producer is willing to accept for that good rises, so supply decreases. For example, during 2008, as the price of jet fuel increased, the supply of air travel decreased. Similarly, a rise in the minimum wage decreases the supply of hamburgers.

Prices of Related Goods Produced The prices of related goods that firms produce influence supply. For example, if the price of an energy drink rises, firms switch production from bars to drinks. The supply of energy bars decreases. Energy bars and energy drinks are *substitutes in production*—goods that can be produced by using the same resources. If the price of beef rises, the supply of cowhide increases. Beef and cowhide are *complements in production*—goods that must be produced together.

Expected Future Prices If the expected future price of a good rises, the return from selling the good in the future increases and is higher than it is today. So supply decreases today and increases in the future.

The Number of Suppliers The larger the number of firms that produce a good, the greater is the supply of the good. As new firms enter an industry, the supply in that industry increases. As firms leave an industry, the supply in that industry decreases.

Technology The term "technology" is used broadly to mean the way that factors of production are used to produce a good. A technology change occurs when a new method is discovered that lowers the cost of producing a good. For example, new methods used in the factories that produce computer chips have lowered the cost and increased the supply of chips.

The State of Nature The state of nature includes all the natural forces that influence production. It includes the state of the weather and, more broadly, the natural environment. Good weather can increase the supply of many agricultural products and bad weather can decrease their supply. Extreme natural events such as earthquakes, tornadoes, and hurricanes can also influence supply.

Figure 3.5 illustrates an increase in supply. When supply increases, the supply curve shifts rightward and the quantity supplied at each price is larger. For example, at $1.00 per bar, on the original (blue) supply curve, the quantity supplied is 6 million bars a week. On the new (red) supply curve, the quantity supplied is 15 million bars a week. Look closely at the numbers in the table in Fig. 3.5 and check that the quantity supplied is larger at each price.

Table 3.2 summarizes the influences on supply and the directions of those influences.

A Change in the Quantity Supplied Versus a Change in Supply

Changes in the influences on selling plans bring either a change in the quantity supplied or a change in supply. Equivalently, they bring either a movement along the supply curve or a shift of the supply curve.

A point on the supply curve shows the quantity supplied at a given price. A movement along the supply curve shows a **change in the quantity supplied.** The entire supply curve shows supply. A shift of the supply curve shows a *change in supply*.

FIGURE 3.5   An Increase in Supply

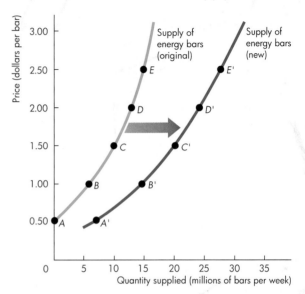

Original supply schedule Old technology			New supply schedule New technology		
	Price (dollars per bar)	Quantity supplied (millions of bars per week)		Price (dollars per bar)	Quantity supplied (millions of bars per week)
A	0.50	0	A'	0.50	7
B	1.00	6	B'	1.00	15
C	1.50	10	C'	1.50	20
D	2.00	13	D'	2.00	25
E	2.50	15	E'	2.50	27

A change in any influence on selling plans other than the price of the good itself results in a new supply schedule and a shift of the supply curve. For example, a new, cost-saving technology for producing energy bars changes the supply of energy bars. At a price of $1.50 a bar, 10 million bars a week are supplied when producers use the old technology (row C of the table) and 20 million energy bars a week are supplied when producers use the new technology (row C'). An advance in technology *increases* the supply of energy bars. The supply curve shifts *rightward*, as shown by the shift arrow and the resulting red curve.

MyEconLab Animation

Figure 3.6 illustrates and summarizes these distinctions. If the price of the good changes and other things remain the same, there is a *change in the quantity supplied* of that good. If the price of the good falls, the quantity supplied decreases and there is a movement down along the supply curve S_0. If the price of the good rises, the quantity supplied increases and there is a movement up along the supply curve S_0. When any other influence on selling plans changes, the supply curve shifts and there is a *change in supply*. If supply increases, the supply curve shifts rightward to S_1. If supply decreases, the supply curve shifts leftward to S_2.

TABLE 3.2   The Supply of Energy Bars

The Law of Supply

The quantity of energy bars supplied

Decreases if:	Increases if:
■ The price of an energy bar falls	■ The price of an energy bar rises

Changes in Supply

The supply of energy bars

Decreases if:	Increases if:
■ The price of a factor of production used to produce energy bars rises	■ The price of a factor of production used to produce energy bars falls
■ The price of a substitute in production rises	■ The price of a substitute in production falls
■ The price of a complement in production falls	■ The price of a complement in production rises
■ The expected future price of an energy bar rises	■ The expected future price of an energy bar falls
■ The number of suppliers of bars decreases	■ The number of suppliers of bars increases
■ A technology change decreases energy bar production	■ A technology change increases energy bar production
■ A natural event decreases energy bar production	■ A natural event increases energy bar production

FIGURE 3.6   A Change in the Quantity Supplied Versus a Change in Supply

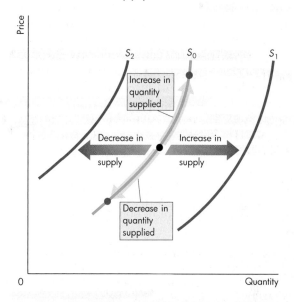

When the price of the good changes, there is a movement along the supply curve and a *change in the quantity supplied*, shown by the blue arrows on supply curve S_0. When any other influence on selling plans changes, there is a shift of the supply curve and a *change in supply*. An increase in supply shifts the supply curve rightward (from S_0 to S_1), and a decrease in supply shifts the supply curve leftward (from S_0 to S_2).

—— MyEconLab Animation and Draw Graph ——

◆ REVIEW QUIZ

1 Define the quantity supplied of a good or service.
2 What is the law of supply and how do we illustrate it?
3 What does the supply curve tell us about the producer's minimum supply price?
4 List all the influences on selling plans, and for each influence, say whether it changes supply.
5 What happens to the quantity of cellphones supplied and the supply of cellphones if the price of a cellphone falls?

Work these questions in Study Plan 3.3 and get instant feedback. Do a Key Terms Quiz.   MyEconLab

Now we're going to combine demand and supply and see how prices and quantities are determined.

◆ Market Equilibrium

We have seen that when the price of a good rises, the quantity demanded *decreases* and the quantity supplied *increases*. We are now going to see how the price adjusts to coordinate buying plans and selling plans and achieve an equilibrium in the market.

An *equilibrium* is a situation in which opposing forces balance each other. Equilibrium in a market occurs when the price balances buying plans and selling plans. The **equilibrium price** is the price at which the quantity demanded equals the quantity supplied. The **equilibrium quantity** is the quantity bought and sold at the equilibrium price. A market moves toward its equilibrium because

- Price regulates buying and selling plans.
- Price adjusts when plans don't match.

Price as a Regulator

The price of a good regulates the quantities demanded and supplied. If the price is too high, the quantity supplied exceeds the quantity demanded. If the price is too low, the quantity demanded exceeds the quantity supplied. There is one price at which the quantity demanded equals the quantity supplied. Let's work out what that price is.

Figure 3.7 shows the market for energy bars. The table shows the demand schedule (from Fig. 3.1) and the supply schedule (from Fig. 3.4). If the price is 50¢ a bar, the quantity demanded is 22 million bars a week but no bars are supplied. There is a shortage of 22 million bars a week. The final column of the table shows this shortage. At a price of $1.00 a bar, there is still a shortage but only of 9 million bars a week.

If the price is $2.50 a bar, the quantity supplied is 15 million bars a week but the quantity demanded is only 5 million. There is a surplus of 10 million bars a week.

The one price at which there is neither a shortage nor a surplus is $1.50 a bar. At that price, the quantity demanded equals the quantity supplied: 10 million bars a week. The equilibrium price is $1.50 a bar, and the equilibrium quantity is 10 million bars a week.

Figure 3.7 shows that the demand curve and the supply curve intersect at the equilibrium price of $1.50 a bar. At each price *above* $1.50 a bar, there is a surplus of bars. For example, at $2.00 a bar, the surplus is 6

FIGURE 3.7   Equilibrium

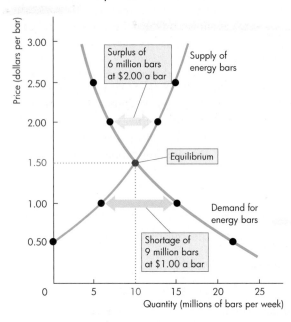

Price (dollars per bar)	Quantity demanded	Quantity supplied	Shortage (−) or surplus (+)
	(millions of bars per week)		
0.50	22	0	−22
1.00	15	6	−9
1.50	**10**	**10**	**0**
2.00	7	13	+6
2.50	5	15	+10

The table lists the quantity demanded and the quantity supplied as well as the shortage or surplus of bars at each price. If the price is $1.00 a bar, 15 million bars a week are demanded and 6 million bars are supplied. There is a shortage of 9 million bars a week, and the price rises.

If the price is $2.00 a bar, 7 million bars a week are demanded and 13 million bars are supplied. There is a surplus of 6 million bars a week, and the price falls.

If the price is $1.50 a bar, 10 million bars a week are demanded and 10 million bars are supplied. There is neither a shortage nor a surplus, and the price does not change. The price at which the quantity demanded equals the quantity supplied is the equilibrium price, and 10 million bars a week is the equilibrium quantity.

MyEconLab Animation and Draw Graph

million bars a week, as shown by the blue arrow. At each price *below* $1.50 a bar, there is a shortage of bars. For example, at $1.00 a bar, the shortage is 9 million bars a week, as shown by the red arrow.

Price Adjustments

You've seen that if the price is below equilibrium, there is a shortage; and if the price is above equilibrium, there is a surplus. But can we count on the price to change and eliminate a shortage or a surplus? We can, because such price changes are beneficial to both buyers and sellers. Let's see why the price changes when there is a shortage or a surplus.

A Shortage Forces the Price Up Suppose the price of an energy bar is $1. Consumers plan to buy 15 million bars a week, and producers plan to sell 6 million bars a week. Consumers can't force producers to sell more than they plan, so the quantity that is actually offered for sale is 6 million bars a week. In this situation, powerful forces operate to increase the price and move it toward the equilibrium price. Some producers, noticing lines of unsatisfied consumers, raise the price. Some producers increase their output. As producers push the price up, the price rises toward its equilibrium. The rising price reduces the shortage because it decreases the quantity demanded and increases the quantity supplied. When the price has increased to the point at which there is no longer a shortage, the forces moving the price stop operating and the price comes to rest at its equilibrium.

A Surplus Forces the Price Down Suppose the price of a bar is $2. Producers plan to sell 13 million bars a week, and consumers plan to buy 7 million bars a week. Producers cannot force consumers to buy more than they plan, so the quantity that is actually bought is 7 million bars a week. In this situation, powerful forces operate to lower the price and move it toward the equilibrium price. Some producers, unable to sell the quantities of energy bars they planned to sell, cut their prices. In addition, some producers scale back production. As producers cut the price, the price falls toward its equilibrium. The falling price decreases the surplus because it increases the quantity demanded and decreases the quantity supplied. When the price has fallen to the point at which there is no longer a surplus, the forces moving the price stop operating and the price comes to rest at its equilibrium.

The Best Deal Available for Buyers and Sellers

When the price is below equilibrium, it is forced upward. Why don't buyers resist the increase and refuse to buy at the higher price? The answer is because they value the good more highly than its current price and they can't satisfy their demand at the current price. In some markets—for example, the markets that operate on eBay—the buyers might even be the ones who force the price up by offering to pay a higher price.

When the price is above equilibrium, it is bid downward. Why don't sellers resist this decrease and refuse to sell at the lower price? The answer is because their minimum supply price is below the current price and they cannot sell all they would like to at the current price. Sellers willingly lower the price to gain market share.

At the price at which the quantity demanded and the quantity supplied are equal, neither buyers nor sellers can do business at a better price. Buyers pay the highest price they are willing to pay for the last unit bought, and sellers receive the lowest price at which they are willing to supply the last unit sold.

When people freely make offers to buy and sell and when demanders try to buy at the lowest possible price and suppliers try to sell at the highest possible price, the price at which trade takes place is the equilibrium price—the price at which the quantity demanded equals the quantity supplied. The price coordinates the plans of buyers and sellers, and no one has an incentive to change it.

◆ REVIEW QUIZ

1 What is the equilibrium price of a good or service?
2 Over what range of prices does a shortage arise? What happens to the price when there is a shortage?
3 Over what range of prices does a surplus arise? What happens to the price when there is a surplus?
4 Why is the price at which the quantity demanded equals the quantity supplied the equilibrium price?
5 Why is the equilibrium price the best deal available for both buyers and sellers?

Work these questions in Study Plan 3.4 and get instant feedback. Do a Key Terms Quiz.   MyEconLab

◆ Predicting Changes in Price and Quantity

The demand and supply model that we have just studied provides us with a powerful way of analyzing influences on prices and the quantities bought and sold. According to the model, a change in price stems from a change in demand, a change in supply, or a change in both demand and supply. Let's look first at the effects of a change in demand.

An Increase in Demand

If more people join health clubs, the demand for energy bars increases. The table in Fig. 3.8 shows the original and new demand schedules for energy bars as well as the supply schedule of energy bars.

The increase in demand creates a shortage at the original price, and to eliminate the shortage the price must rise.

Figure 3.8 shows what happens. The figure shows the original demand for and supply of energy bars. The original equilibrium price is $1.50 an energy bar, and the equilibrium quantity is 10 million energy bars a week. When demand increases, the demand curve shifts rightward. The equilibrium price rises to $2.50 an energy bar, and the quantity supplied increases to 15 million energy bars a week, as highlighted in the figure. There is an *increase in the quantity supplied* but *no change in supply*—a movement along, but no shift of, the supply curve.

A Decrease in Demand

We can reverse this change in demand. Start at a price of $2.50 a bar with 15 million energy bars a week being bought and sold, and then work out what happens if demand decreases to its original level. Such a decrease in demand might arise if people switch to energy drinks (a substitute for energy bars). The decrease in demand shifts the demand curve leftward. The equilibrium price falls to $1.50 a bar, the quantity supplied decreases, and the equilibrium quantity decreases to 10 million bars a week.

We can now make our first two predictions:

1. When demand increases, the price rises and the quantity increases.
2. When demand decreases, the price falls and the quantity decreases.

FIGURE 3.8   The Effects of a Change in Demand

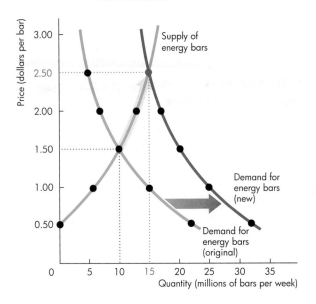

Price (dollars per bar)	Quantity demanded (millions of bars per week)		Quantity supplied (millions of bars per week)
	Original	New	
0.50	22	32	0
1.00	15	25	6
1.50	**10**	20	**10**
2.00	7	17	13
2.50	5	**15**	**15**

Initially, the demand for energy bars is the blue demand curve. The equilibrium price is $1.50 a bar, and the equilibrium quantity is 10 million bars a week. When more health-conscious people do more exercise, the demand for energy bars increases and the demand curve shifts rightward to become the red curve.

At $1.50 a bar, there is now a shortage of 10 million bars a week. The price of a bar rises to a new equilibrium of $2.50. As the price rises to $2.50, the quantity supplied increases—shown by the blue arrow on the supply curve—to the new equilibrium quantity of 15 million bars a week. Following an increase in demand, the quantity supplied increases but supply does not change—the supply curve does not shift.

MyEconLab Animation and Draw Graph

◆ ECONOMICS IN THE NEWS

The Market for College Education

Obama Decries Rising Cost of College Education

President Obama told colleges, "You can't assume that you'll just jack up tuition every single year. ... In the coming decade, 60 percent of new jobs will require more than a high school diploma ... Higher education is not a luxury. It's an economic imperative that every family in America should be able to afford."

Source: *The Associated Press*, January 27, 2012

THE DATA

The scatter diagram provides data on college enrollments and tuition from 1994 through 2013.

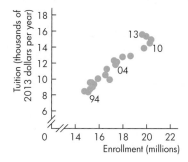

THE QUESTIONS

- What does the scatter diagram tell us?
- Why has college tuition increased? Is it because demand increased or supply increased?

THE ANSWERS

- The scatter diagram tells us that in most years through 2010, both tuition and enrollments increased. Since 2010, tuition has increased and enrollments have decreased.
- An increase in demand brings a rise in the price (tuition) and an increase in the quantity (enrollments).
- Because both the price and quantity increased through 2010, the demand for college education increased during those years.
- A decrease in supply brings a rise in price and a decrease in the quantity.
- Because the price increased and the quantity decreased after 2010, the supply of college education decreased during those recent years.
- The figure shows the market for college education.

- The supply curve of college education, *S*, slopes upward because the principle of increasing opportunity cost applies to college education just as it does to other goods and services.
- In 1994, the demand for college education was D_{1994}. The equilibrium tuition was $8,000 and 15 million students were enrolled in college.
- Between 1994 and 2010:
  1) Income per person increased
  2) Population increased, and
  3) More new jobs required higher education.
- These (and possibly other) factors increased the demand for a college education. The demand curve shifted rightward to D_{2010}. Equilibrium tuition increased to $15,000 and the quantity supplied increased to 20 million students.

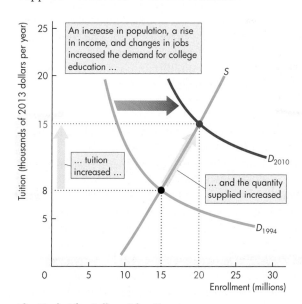

The Market for College Education

An Increase in Supply

When Nestlé (the producer of PowerBar) and other energy bar producers switch to a new cost-saving technology, the supply of energy bars increases. Figure 3.9 shows the new supply schedule (the same one that was shown in Fig. 3.5). What are the new equilibrium price and quantity? The price falls to $1.00 a bar, and the quantity increases to 15 million bars a week. You can see why by looking at the quantities demanded and supplied at the old price of $1.50 a bar. The new quantity supplied at that price is 20 million bars a week, and there is a surplus. The price falls. Only when the price is $1.00 a bar does the quantity supplied equal the quantity demanded.

Figure 3.9 illustrates the effect of an increase in supply. It shows the demand curve for energy bars and the original and new supply curves. The initial equilibrium price is $1.50 a bar, and the equilibrium quantity is 10 million bars a week. When supply increases, the supply curve shifts rightward. The equilibrium price falls to $1.00 a bar, and the quantity demanded increases to 15 million bars a week, highlighted in the figure. There is an *increase in the quantity demanded* but *no change in demand*—a movement along, but no shift of, the demand curve.

A Decrease in Supply

Start out at a price of $1.00 a bar with 15 million bars a week being bought and sold. Then suppose that the cost of labor or raw materials rises and the supply of energy bars decreases. The decrease in supply shifts the supply curve leftward. The equilibrium price rises to $1.50 a bar, the quantity demanded decreases, and the equilibrium quantity decreases to 10 million bars a week.

We can now make two more predictions:

1. When supply increases, the price falls and the quantity increases.
2. When supply decreases, the price rises and the quantity decreases.

You've now seen what happens to the price and the quantity when either demand or supply changes while the other one remains unchanged. In real markets, both demand and supply can change together. When this happens, to predict the changes in price and quantity, we must combine the effects that you've just seen. That is your final task in this chapter.

FIGURE 3.9   The Effects of a Change in Supply

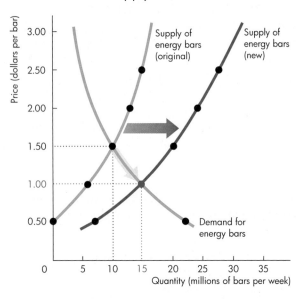

Price (dollars per bar)	Quantity demanded (millions of bars per week)	Quantity supplied (millions of bars per week)	
		Original	New
0.50	22	0	7
1.00	15	6	15
1.50	10	10	20
2.00	7	13	25
2.50	5	15	27

Initially, the supply of energy bars is shown by the blue supply curve. The equilibrium price is $1.50 a bar, and the equilibrium quantity is 10 million bars a week. When the new cost-saving technology is adopted, the supply of energy bars increases and the supply curve shifts rightward to become the red curve.

At $1.50 a bar, there is now a surplus of 10 million bars a week. The price of an energy bar falls to a new equilibrium of $1.00 a bar. As the price falls to $1.00, the quantity demanded increases—shown by the blue arrow on the demand curve—to the new equilibrium quantity of 15 million bars a week. Following an increase in supply, the quantity demanded increases but demand does not change—the demand curve does not shift.

MyEconLab Animation and Draw Graph

ECONOMICS IN THE NEWS

The Market for Coffee

Coffee Price Slides

With plentiful crops in Brazil and a recovery in Colombian production, the price of arabica beans has fallen.

Source: *The Financial Times*, October 24, 2013

THE DATA

	Quantity (millions of tons per year)	Price (dollars per pound)
2013	134	6.00
2014	145	5.00

THE QUESTIONS

- What does the data table tell us?
- Why did the price of coffee decrease? Is it because demand changed or because supply changed, and in which direction?

THE ANSWERS

- The data table tells us that during 2014, the quantity of coffee produced increased and the price of coffee fell.
- An increase in demand brings an increase in the quantity and a rise in the price.
- An increase in supply brings an increase in the quantity and a fall in the price.
- Because the quantity of coffee increased and the average price fell, there must have been an increase in the supply of coffee.
- The supply of coffee increases if the crop yields increase or if producers increase their plantings.
- The news clip says the Brazilian crop was plentiful and that the Colombian production recovered. These increases in production brought an increase in the supply of coffee.
- The figure illustrates the market for coffee in 2013 and 2014. The demand curve *D* shows the demand for coffee.
- In 2013, the supply curve was S_{13}, the average price was $6.00 per pound and the quantity of coffee traded was 134 million tons.
- In 2014, the increased coffee production in Brazil and Colombia increased the supply of coffee to S_{14}.

- The price fell to $5.00 per pound and the quantity traded increased to 145 million tons.
- The lower price brought an increase in the quantity of coffee demanded, which is shown by the movement along the demand curve.

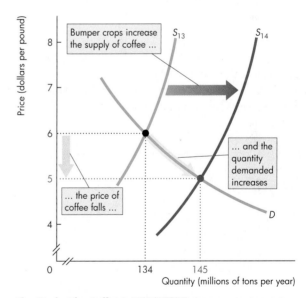

The Market for Coffee in 2013–2014

MyEconLab More Economics in the News

Changes in Both Demand and Supply

You now know how a change in demand or a change in supply changes the equilibrium price and quantity. But sometimes, events occur that change both demand and supply. When both demand and supply change, we find the resulting change in the equilibrium price and equilibrium quantity by combining the separate cases you've just studied.

Four cases need to be considered. Both demand and supply might increase or decrease, and demand or supply might increase and the other decrease.

Both Demand and Supply Change in the Same Direction

When demand and supply change in the same direction, the equilibrium quantity changes in that same direction, but to predict whether the price rises or falls, we need to know the magnitudes of the changes in demand and supply.

If demand increases by more than supply increases, the price rises. But if supply increases by more than demand increases, the price falls.

Figure 3.10(a) shows the case when both demand and supply increase and by the same amount. The equilibrium quantity increases. But because the increase in demand equals the increase in supply, neither a shortage nor a surplus arises so the price doesn't change. A bigger increase in demand would have created a shortage and a rise in the price; a bigger increase in supply would have created a surplus and a fall in the price.

Figure 3.10(b) shows the case when both demand and supply decrease by the same amount. Here the equilibrium quantity decreases and again the price might either rise or fall.

Both Demand and Supply Change in Opposite Directions

When demand and supply change in opposite directions, we can predict how the price changes, but we need to know the magnitudes of the changes in demand and supply to say whether the equilibrium quantity increases or decreases.

If demand changes by more than supply, the equilibrium quantity changes in the same direction as the change in demand. But if supply changes by more than demand, the equilibrium quantity changes in the same direction as the change in supply.

FIGURE 3.10   The Effects of Changes in Both Demand and Supply in the Same Direction

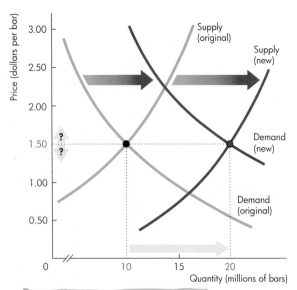

(a) Increase in both demand and supply

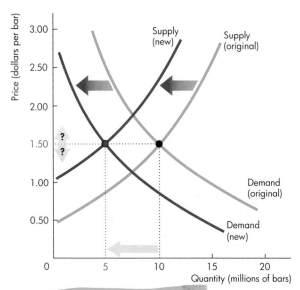

(b) Decrease in both demand and supply

An increase in demand shifts the demand curve rightward to become the red new demand curve and an increase in supply shifts the supply curve rightward to become the red new supply curve. The price might rise or fall, but the quantity increases.

A decrease in demand shifts the demand curve leftward to become the red new demand curve and a decrease in supply shifts the supply curve leftward to become the red new supply curve. The price might rise or fall, but the quantity decreases.

FIGURE 3.11   The Effects of Changes in Both Demand and Supply in Opposite Directions

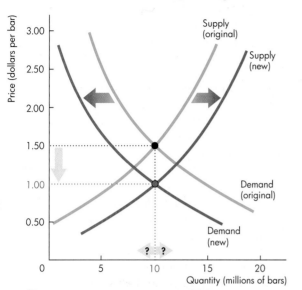

(a) Decrease in demand; increase in supply

A decrease in demand shifts the demand curve leftward to become the red new demand curve and an increase in supply shifts the supply curve rightward to become the red new supply curve. The price falls, but the quantity might increase or decrease.

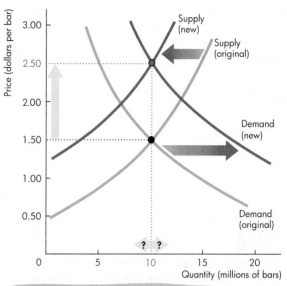

(b) Increase in demand; decrease in supply

An increase in demand shifts the demand curve rightward to become the red new demand curve and a decrease in supply shifts the supply curve leftward to become the red new supply curve. The price rises, but the quantity might increase or decrease.

——— MyEconLab Animation ———

Figure 3.11(a) illustrates what happens when demand decreases and supply increases by the same amount. At the initial price, there is a surplus, so the price falls. A decrease in demand decreases the quantity and an increase in supply increases the quantity, so when these changes occur together, we can't say what happens to the quantity unless we know the magnitudes of the changes.

Figure 3.11(b) illustrates what happens when demand increases and supply decreases by the same amount. In this case, at the initial price, there is a shortage, so the price rises. An increase in demand increases the quantity and a decrease in supply decreases the quantity, so again, when these changes occur together, we can't say what happens to the quantity unless we know the magnitudes of the changes in demand and supply.

For all the cases in Fig. 3.10 and Fig. 3.11 where you "can't say" what happens to the price or the quantity, draw some examples that go in each direction.

◆ **REVIEW QUIZ**

What is the effect on the price and quantity of MP3 players (such as the iPod) if

1   The price of a PC falls or the price of an MP3 download rises? (Draw the diagrams!)
2   More firms produce MP3 players or electronics workers' wages rise? (Draw the diagrams!)
3   Any two of the events in questions 1 and 2 occur together? (Draw the diagrams!)

Work these questions in Study Plan 3.5 and get instant feedback.   MyEconLab

◆   To complete your study of demand and supply, take a look at *Economics in the News* on pp. 74–75, which explains what would happen to the price of bananas if a disease that kill plants were to jump continents to Central America. Try to get into the habit of using the demand and supply model to understand the changes in prices in your everyday life.

Demand and Supply: The Market for Bananas

Banana Supply Seen at Risk as Disease Spreads

Bloomberg News
April 9, 2014

A disease damaging banana crops in Southeast Asia has spread to the Middle East and Africa, posing risks to world supply and trade totaling $8.9 billion, according to the United Nations' Food and Agriculture Organization.

The TR4 strain of Panama disease, a soil-born fungus that attacks plant roots, is deadly for the Cavendish banana that makes up about 95 percent of supplies to importers, including North America and Europe, Fazil Dusunceli, an agriculture officer at the FAO, said. …

While the disease hasn't reached top Latin America exporters such as Ecuador, Costa Rica, or Colombia, TR4 was discovered in Jordan and Mozambique, indicating it moved beyond Asia, he said.

"The export market is dominated by the Cavendish, and it is unfortunately susceptible to this particular race of the disease," Dusunceli said. "This is serious for the medium term, but at the same time we should avoid panicking too."

Global exports reached a record value in 2011 and totaled 18.7 million metric tons, making bananas the world's most widely-traded fruit, according to the most recent FAO data. The United States is the top importer, followed by Belgium, the data show. Belgium's Port of Antwerp is the world's largest banana port, it says.

U.S. consumer prices for bananas were 59.9 cents a pound in February, 2.2 percent higher than an almost three-year low reached in October at 58.6 cents a pound, according to data from the Bureau of Labor Statistics. The export price of bananas from Ecuador, the world's biggest shipper, and Central America for U.S. destinations was $966.85 a ton in March, the highest in 18 months, according to the International Monetary Fund. …

Whitney McFerron, "Banana Supply Seen by UN's FAO at Risk as Disease Spreads," Bloomberg News, April 4, 2014. Copyright © by Jessica Stremmel. Used by permission of Jessica Stremmel.

ESSENCE OF THE STORY

- The U.S. consumer price of bananas was 59.9 cents a pound in February 2014.

- About 95 percent of bananas traded are a variety called Cavendish.

- Cavendish banana plants can be destroyed by the TR4 strain of Panama disease.

- TR4 hasn't reached Latin America but it has jumped from Asia to the Middle East and Africa.

- Fazil Dusunceli of the United Nations' Food and Agriculture Organization says "This is serious for the medium term, but at the same time we should avoid panicking too."

MyEconLab More Economics in the News

ECONOMIC ANALYSIS

- In the market for bananas, a decrease in world production would decrease supply.

- A decrease in the supply of bananas would raise their price, decrease the equilibrium quantity, and decrease the quantity of bananas demanded.

- We can see the likely price increase by looking at previous events in the banana market.

- Figure 1 shows the price of bananas since 2004. You can see that there was a big temporary jump in the price in 2008.

- That jump in price was *not* caused by a decrease in banana production because as Fig. 2 shows, banana production has increased every year since 2004 except for 2012.

- What happened in 2008? The answer is a spike in the price of oil.

- Transporting bananas from plantations in Central and South America to your neighborhood grocery store uses a lot of fuel. So when the cost of fuel increased in 2008, the cost of delivering bananas increased, and the U.S. consumer price of bananas increased.

- A decrease in supply caused by the TR4 disease would have a similar effect on the banana market to what happened in 2008.

- Figure 3 illustrates this effect. The supply of bananas decreases from S_N (normal) to S_D (disease), the price rises, the equilibrium quantity decreases, and the quantity of bananas demanded decreases.

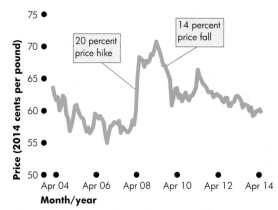

Figure 1 The Price of Bananas: 2004–2014

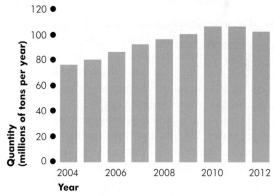

Figure 2 Banana Production: 2004–2012

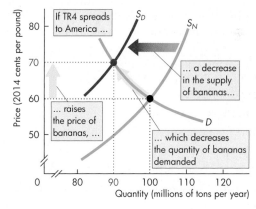

Figure 3 The Market for Bananas

75

MATHEMATICAL NOTE

Demand, Supply, and Equilibrium

Demand Curve

The law of demand says that as the price of a good or service falls, the quantity demanded of that good or service increases. We can illustrate the law of demand by drawing a graph of the demand curve or writing down an equation. When the demand curve is a straight line, the following equation describes it:

$$P = a - bQ_D,$$

where P is the price and Q_D is the quantity demanded. The a and b are positive constants.

The demand equation tells us three things:

1. The price at which no one is willing to buy the good (Q_D is zero). That is, if the price is a, then the quantity demanded is zero. You can see the price a in Fig. 1. It is the price at which the demand curve hits the y-axis—what we call the demand curve's "y-intercept."
2. As the price falls, the quantity demanded increases. If Q_D is a positive number, then the price P must be less than a. As Q_D gets larger, the price P becomes smaller. That is, as the quantity increases, the maximum price that buyers are willing to pay for the last unit of the good falls.
3. The constant b tells us how fast the maximum price that someone is willing to pay for the good falls as the quantity increases. That is, the constant b tells us about the steepness of the demand curve. The equation tells us that the slope of the demand curve is $-b$.

Supply Curve

The law of supply says that as the price of a good or service rises, the quantity supplied of that good or service increases. We can illustrate the law of supply by drawing a graph of the supply curve or writing down an equation. When the supply curve is a straight line, the following equation describes it:

$$P = c + dQ_S,$$

where P is the price and Q_S is the quantity supplied. The c and d are positive constants.

The supply equation tells us three things:

1. The price at which sellers are not willing to supply the good (Q_S is zero). That is, if the price is c, then no one is willing to sell the good. You can see the price c in Fig. 2. It is the price at which the supply curve hits the y-axis—what we call the supply curve's "y-intercept."
2. As the price rises, the quantity supplied increases. If Q_S is a positive number, then the price P must be greater than c. As Q_S increases, the price P becomes larger. That is, as the quantity increases, the minimum price that sellers are willing to accept for the last unit rises.
3. The constant d tells us how fast the minimum price at which someone is willing to sell the good rises as the quantity increases. That is, the constant d tells us about the steepness of the supply curve. The equation tells us that the slope of the supply curve is d.

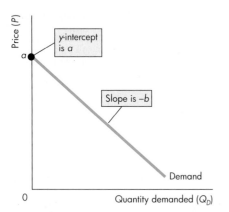

Figure 1 Demand Curve

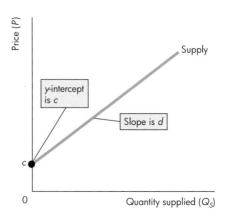

Figure 2 Supply Curve

Market Equilibrium

Demand and supply determine market equilibrium. Figure 3 shows the equilibrium price (P^*) and equilibrium quantity (Q^*) at the intersection of the demand curve and the supply curve.

We can use the equations to find the equilibrium price and equilibrium quantity. The price of a good adjusts until the quantity demanded Q_D equals the quantity supplied Q_S. So at the equilibrium price (P^*) and equilibrium quantity (Q^*),

$$Q_D = Q_S = Q^*.$$

To find the equilibrium price and equilibrium quantity, substitute Q^* for Q_D in the demand equation and Q^* for Q_S in the supply equation. Then the price is the equilibrium price (P^*), which gives

$$P^* = a - bQ^*$$
$$P^* = c + dQ^*.$$

Notice that

$$a - bQ^* = c + dQ^*.$$

Now solve for Q^*:

$$a - c = bQ^* + dQ^*$$
$$a - c = (b + d)Q^*$$
$$Q^* = \frac{a - c}{b + d}.$$

To find the equilibrium price P^*, substitute for Q^* in either the demand equation or the supply equation.

Using the demand equation, we have

$$P^* = a - b\left(\frac{a - c}{b + d}\right)$$
$$P^* = \frac{a(b + d) - b(a - c)}{b + d}$$
$$P^* = \frac{ad + bc}{b + d}.$$

Alternatively, using the supply equation, we have

$$P^* = c + d\left(\frac{a - c}{b + d}\right)$$
$$P^* = \frac{c(b + d) + d(a - c)}{b + d}$$
$$P^* = \frac{ad + bc}{b + d}.$$

An Example

The demand for ice-cream cones is

$$P = 800 - 2Q_D.$$

The supply of ice-cream cones is

$$P = 200 + 1Q_S.$$

The price of a cone is expressed in cents, and the quantities are expressed in cones per day.

To find the equilibrium price (P^*) and equilibrium quantity (Q^*), substitute Q^* for Q_D and Q_S and P^* for P. That is,

$$P^* = 800 - 2Q^*$$
$$P^* = 200 + 1Q^*$$

Now solve for Q^*:

$$800 - 2Q^* = 200 + 1Q^*$$
$$600 = 3Q^*$$
$$Q^* = 200.$$

And

$$P^* = 800 - 2(200)$$
$$= 400.$$

The equilibrium price is $4 a cone, and the equilibrium quantity is 200 cones per day.

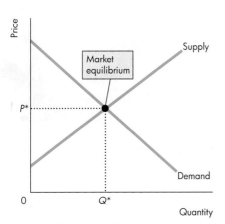

Figure 3 Market Equilibrium

SUMMARY

Key Points

Markets and Prices (p. 56)

- A competitive market is one that has so many buyers and sellers that no single buyer or seller can influence the price.
- Opportunity cost is a relative price.
- Demand and supply determine relative prices.

Working Problem 1 will give you a better understanding of markets and prices.

Demand (pp. 57–61)

- Demand is the relationship between the quantity demanded of a good and its price when all other influences on buying plans remain the same.
- The higher the price of a good, other things remaining the same, the smaller is the quantity demanded—the law of demand.
- Demand depends on the prices of related goods (substitutes and complements), expected future prices, income, expected future income and credit, the population, and preferences.

Working Problems 2 to 4 will give you a better understanding of demand.

Supply (pp. 62–65)

- Supply is the relationship between the quantity supplied of a good and its price when all other influences on selling plans remain the same.
- The higher the price of a good, other things remaining the same, the greater is the quantity supplied—the law of supply.

- Supply depends on the prices of factors of production used to produce a good, the prices of related goods produced, expected future prices, the number of suppliers, technology, and the state of nature.

Working Problems 5 and 6 will give you a better understanding of supply.

Market Equilibrium (pp. 66–67)

- At the equilibrium price, the quantity demanded equals the quantity supplied.
- At any price above the equilibrium price, there is a surplus and the price falls.
- At any price below the equilibrium price, there is a shortage and the price rises.

Working Problem 7 will give you a better understanding of market equilibrium.

Predicting Changes in Price and Quantity (pp. 68–73)

- An increase in demand brings a rise in the price and an increase in the quantity supplied. A decrease in demand brings a fall in the price and a decrease in the quantity supplied.
- An increase in supply brings a fall in the price and an increase in the quantity demanded. A decrease in supply brings a rise in the price and a decrease in the quantity demanded.
- An increase in demand and an increase in supply bring an increased quantity but an uncertain price change. An increase in demand and a decrease in supply bring a higher price but an uncertain change in quantity.

Working Problems 8 to 10 will give you a better understanding of predicting changes in price and quantity.

Key Terms

Change in demand, 58

Change in supply, 63

Change in the quantity demanded, 61

Change in the quantity supplied, 64

Competitive market, 56

Complement, 59

Demand, 57

Demand curve, 58

Equilibrium price, 66

Equilibrium quantity, 66

Inferior good, 60

Law of demand, 57

Law of supply, 62

Money price, 56

Normal good, 60

MyEconLab Key Terms Quiz

Quantity demanded, 57

Quantity supplied, 62

Relative price, 56

Substitute, 59

Supply, 62

Supply curve, 62

WORKED PROBLEM

MyEconLab   You can work this problem in Chapter 3 Study Plan.

The table sets out the demand and supply schedules for roses on a normal weekend.

Price (dollars per rose)	Quantity demanded	Quantity supplied
	(roses per week)	
6.00	150	60
7.00	100	100
8.00	70	130
9.00	50	150

Questions

1. If the price of a rose is $6, describe the situation in the rose market. Explain how the price adjusts.

2. If the price of a rose is $9, describe the situation in the rose market. Explain how the price adjusts.

3. What is the market equilibrium?

4. Rose sellers know that Mother's Day is next weekend and they expect the price to be higher, so they withhold 60 roses from the market this weekend. What is the price this weekend?

5. On Mother's Day, demand increases by 160 roses. What is the price of a rose on Mother's Day?

Solutions

1. At $6 a rose, the quantity demanded is 150 and the quantity supplied is 60. The quantity demanded exceeds the quantity supplied and there is a *shortage* of 90 roses. With people lining up and a shortage, the price rises above $6 a rose.

Key Point: When a shortage exists, the price rises.

2. At $9 a rose, the quantity demanded is 50 and the quantity supplied is 150. The quantity supplied exceeds the quantity demanded and there is a *surplus* of 100 roses. With slow sales of roses and a surplus, the price falls to below $9 a rose.

Key Point: When a surplus exists, the price falls.

3. Market equilibrium occurs at the price at which the quantity demanded *equals* the quantity supplied. That price is $7 a rose. The market equilibrium is a price is $7 a rose and 100 roses a week. Point *A* on the figure.

Key Point: At market equilibrium, there is no shortage or surplus.

4. Sellers expect a higher price next weekend, so they decrease the quantity supplied this weekend by 60 roses at each price. Create the new table:

Price (dollars per rose)	Quantity demanded	Quantity supplied
	(roses per week)	
6.00	150	0
7.00	**100**	**40**
8.00	70	70
9.00	50	90

At $7 a rose, there is a shortage of 60 roses, so the price rises to $8 a rose, where the quantity demanded equals the quantity supplied. (Point *B*)

Key Point: When supply decreases, the price rises.

5. Demand increases by 160 roses. Sellers plan to increase the normal supply by the 60 roses withheld last weekend. Create the new table:

Price (dollars per rose)	Quantity demanded	Quantity supplied
	(roses per week)	
6.00	310	120
7.00	**260**	**160**
8.00	230	190
9.00	**210**	**210**

At $7 a rose, there is a shortage of 100 roses, so the price rises until, at $9 a rose, the quantity demanded equals the quantity supplied. The price on Mother's Day is $9 a rose. (Point *C*)

Key Point: When demand increases by more than supply, the price rises.

Key Figure

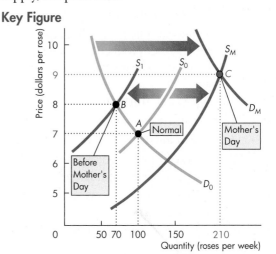

STUDY PLAN PROBLEMS AND APPLICATIONS

MyEconLab   You can work Problems 1 to 10 in Chapter 3 Study Plan and get instant feedback.

Markets and Prices (Study Plan 3.1)

1. In April 2014, the money price of a carton of milk was $2.01 and the money price of a gallon of gasoline was $3.63. Calculate the relative price of a gallon of gasoline in terms of milk.

Demand (Study Plan 3.2)

2. The price of food increased during the past year.
   a. Explain why the law of demand applies to food just as it does to other goods and services.
   b. Explain how the substitution effect influences food purchases when the price of food rises and other things remain the same.
   c. Explain how the income effect influences food purchases and provide some examples of the income effect.

3. Which of the following goods are likely substitutes and which are likely complements? (You may use an item more than once):

   coal, oil, natural gas, wheat, corn, pasta, pizza, sausage, skateboard, roller blades, video game, laptop, iPad, cellphone, text message, email

4. As the average income in China continues to increase, explain how the following will change:
   a. The demand for beef
   b. The demand for rice

Supply (Study Plan 3.3)

5. In 2013, the price of corn fell and some corn farmers will switch from growing corn in 2014 to growing soybeans.
   a. Does this fact illustrate the law of demand or the law of supply? Explain your answer.
   b. Why would a corn farmer grow soybeans?

6. Dairies make low-fat milk from full-cream milk, and in the process they produce cream, which is made into ice cream. The following events occur one at a time:
   (i) The wage rate of dairy workers rises.
   (ii) The price of cream rises.
   (iii) The price of low-fat milk rises.
   (iv) With a drought forecasted, dairies raise their expected price of low-fat milk next year.
   (v) New technology lowers the cost of producing ice cream.
   Explain the effect of each event on the supply of low-fat milk.

Market Equilibrium (Study Plan 3.4)

7. The demand and supply schedules for gum are

Price (cents per pack)	Quantity demanded	Quantity supplied
	(millions of packs a week)	
20	180	60
40	140	100
60	100	140
80	60	180

   a. Suppose that the price of gum is 70¢ a pack. Describe the situation in the gum market and explain how the price adjusts.
   b. Suppose that the price of gum is 30¢ a pack. Describe the situation in the gum market and explain how the price adjusts.

Predicting Changes in Price and Quantity (Study Plan 3.5)

8. The following events occur one at a time:
   (i) The price of crude oil rises.
   (ii) The price of a car rises.
   (iii) All speed limits on highways are abolished.
   (iv) Robots cut car production costs.
   Explain the effect of each of these events on the market for gasoline.

9. In Problem 7, a fire destroys some factories that produce gum and the quantity of gum supplied decreases by 40 million packs a week at each price.
   a. Explain what happens in the market for gum and draw a graph to illustrate the changes.
   b. At the same time as the fire, the teenage population increases and the quantity of gum demanded increases by 40 million packs a week at each price. What is the new market equilibrium? Show the changes on your graph.

10. **Frigid Florida Winter is Bad News for Tomato Lovers**
    An unusually cold January in Florida destroyed entire fields of tomatoes. Florida's growers are shipping only a quarter of their usual 5 million pounds a week. The price has risen from $6.50 for a 25-pound box a year ago to $30 now.
    Source: *USA Today*, March 3, 2010
    a. Make a graph to illustrate the market for tomatoes before the unusually cold January and show how the events in the news clip influence the market for tomatoes.
    b. Why is the news "bad for tomato lovers"?

ADDITIONAL PROBLEMS AND APPLICATIONS

MyEconLab   You can work these problems in MyEconLab if assigned by your instructor.

Markets and Prices

11. What features of the world market for crude oil make it a competitive market?

12. The money price of a textbook is $90 and the money price of the Wii game *Super Mario Galaxy* is $45.
    a. What is the opportunity cost of a textbook in terms of the Wii game?
    b. What is the relative price of the Wii game in terms of textbooks?

Demand

13. The price of gasoline has increased during the past year.
    a. Explain why the law of demand applies to gasoline just as it does to all other goods and services.
    b. Explain how the substitution effect influences gasoline purchases and provide some examples of substitutions that people might make when the price of gasoline rises and other things remain the same.
    c. Explain how the income effect influences gasoline purchases and provide some examples of the income effects that might occur when the price of gasoline rises and other things remain the same.

14. Think about the demand for the three game consoles: Xbox One, PlayStation 4, and Wii U. Explain the effect of each of the following events on the demand for Xbox One games and the quantity of Xbox One games demanded, other things remaining the same. The events are
    a. The price of an Xbox One falls.
    b. The prices of a PlayStation 4 and a Wii U fall.
    c. The number of people writing and producing Xbox One games increases.
    d. Consumers' incomes increase.
    e. Programmers who write code for Xbox One games become more costly to hire.
    f. The expected future price of an Xbox One game falls.
    g. A new game console that is a close substitute for Xbox One comes onto the market.

Supply

15. Classify the following pairs of goods and services as substitutes in production, complements in production, or neither.
    a. Bottled water and health club memberships
    b. French fries and baked potatoes
    c. Leather boots and leather shoes
    d. Hybrids and SUVs
    e. Diet coke and regular coke

16. When a timber mill makes logs from trees it also produces sawdust, which is used to make plywood.
    a. Explain how a rise in the price of sawdust influences the supply of logs.
    b. Explain how a rise in the price of sawdust influences the supply of plywood.

17. **New Maple Syrup Sap Method**
    With the new way to tap maple trees, farmers could produce 10 times as much maple syrup per acre.
    Source: cbc.ca, February 5, 2014
    Will the new method change the supply of maple syrup or the quantity supplied of maple syrup, other things remaining the same? Explain.

Market Equilibrium

Use the following figure to work Problems 18 and 19.

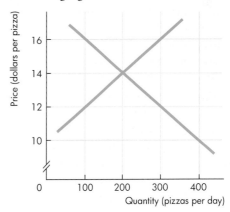

18. a. Label the curves. Which curve shows the willingness to pay for a pizza?
    b. If the price of a pizza is $16, is there a shortage or a surplus and does the price rise or fall?

c. Sellers want to receive the highest possible price, so why would they be willing to accept less than $16 a pizza?

19. a. If the price of a pizza is $12, is there a shortage or a surplus and does the price rise or fall?

   b. Buyers want to pay the lowest possible price, so why would they be willing to pay more than $12 for a pizza?

20. The demand and supply schedules for potato chips are

Price (cents per bag)	Quantity demanded	Quantity supplied
	(millions of bags per week)	
50	160	130
60	150	140
70	140	150
80	130	160
90	120	170
100	110	180

a. Draw a graph of the potato chip market and mark in the equilibrium price and quantity.

b. If the price is 60¢ a bag, is there a shortage or a surplus, and how does the price adjust?

Predicting Changes in Price and Quantity

21. In Problem 20, a new dip increases the quantity of potato chips that people want to buy by 30 million bags per week at each price.
   a. Does the demand for chips change? Does the supply of chips change? Describe the change.
   b. How do the equilibrium price and equilibrium quantity of chips change?

22. In Problem 20, if a virus destroys potato crops and the quantity of potato chips produced decreases by 40 million bags a week at each price, how does the supply of chips change?

23. If the virus in Problem 22 hits just as the new dip in Problem 28 comes onto the market, how do the equilibrium price and equilibrium quantity of chips change?

24. **Strawberry Prices Drop as Late Harvest Hits Market**

   Shoppers bought strawberries in March for $1.25 a pound rather than the $3.49 a pound they paid last year. With the price so low, some growers plowed over their strawberry plants to make way for spring melons; others froze their harvests and sold them to juice and jam makers.

   Source: *USA Today*, April 5, 2010

   a. Explain how the market for strawberries would have changed if growers had not plowed in their plants but offered locals "you pick for free."

   b. Describe the changes in demand and supply in the market for strawberry jam.

25. **"Popcorn Movie" Experience Gets Pricier**

   Cinemas are raising the price of popcorn. Demand for field corn, which is used for animal feed, corn syrup, and ethanol, has increased and its price has exploded. That's caused some farmers to shift from growing popcorn to easier-to-grow field corn.

   Source: *USA Today*, May 24, 2008

   Explain and illustrate graphically the events described in the news clip in the market for
   a. Popcorn
   b. Movie tickets

26. **Watch Out for Rising Dry-Cleaning Bills**

   In the past year, the price of dry-cleaning solvent doubled. More than 4,000 dry cleaners across the United States disappeared as budget-conscious consumers cut back. This year the price of hangers used by dry cleaners is expected to double.

   Source: CNN Money, June 4, 2012

   a. Explain the effect of rising solvent prices on the market for dry cleaning.

   b. Explain the effect of consumers becoming more budget conscious along with the rising price of solvent on the price of dry cleaning.

   c. If the price of hangers does rise this year, do you expect additional dry cleaners to disappear? Explain why or why not.

Economics in the News

27. After you have studied *Economics in the News* on pp. 74–75, answer the following questions.

   a. What would happen to the price of bananas if TR4 spread to Central America?

   b. What are some of the substitutes for bananas and what would happen to demand, supply, price, and quantity in the markets for these items if TR4 were to come to America?

   c. What are some of the complements of bananas and what would happen to demand, supply, price, and quantity in the markets for these items if TR4 were to come to America?

   d. When the price of bananas increased in 2008, did it rise by as much as the rise in the price of oil? Why or why not?

   e. Why would the expectation of the future arrival of TR4 in the Americas have little or no effect on today's price of bananas?

4 ELASTICITY

After studying this chapter, you will be able to:

◆ Define, calculate, and explain the factors that influence the price elasticity of demand

◆ Define, calculate, and explain the factors that influence the income elasticity of demand and the cross elasticity of demand

◆ Define, calculate, and explain the factors that influence the elasticity of supply

In 2013, coffee production soared and the price tumbled. Despite the increased production, coffee producers saw their revenue fall. How does the quantity of coffee produced influence the price of coffee and the revenue of coffee producers?

To answer this and similar questions, we use the neat tool that you study in this chapter: elasticity.

At the end of the chapter, in *Economics in the News*, we use the concept of elasticity to answer the question about the market for coffee. But we begin by explaining elasticity in another familiar setting: the market for pizza.

◆ Price Elasticity of Demand

You know that when supply decreases, the equilibrium price rises and the equilibrium quantity decreases. But does the price rise by a large amount and the quantity decrease by a little? Or does the price barely rise and the quantity decrease by a large amount?

The answer depends on the responsiveness of the quantity demanded of a good to a change in its price. If the quantity demanded is not very responsive to a change in the price, the price rises a lot and the equilibrium quantity doesn't change much. If the quantity demanded *is* very responsive to a change in the price, the price barely rises and the equilibrium quantity changes a lot.

You might think about the responsiveness of the quantity demanded of a good to a change in its price in terms of the slope of the demand curve. If the demand curve is steep, the quantity demanded of the good isn't very responsive to a change in the price. If the demand curve is almost flat, the quantity demanded *is* very responsive to a change in the price.

But the slope of a demand curve depends on the units in which we measure the price and the quantity—we can make the curve steep or almost flat just by changing the units in which we measure the price and the quantity. Also we often want to compare the demand for different goods and services and quantities of these goods are measured in unrelated units. For example, a pizza producer might want to compare the demand for pizza with the demand for soft drinks. Which quantity demanded is more responsive to a price change? This question can't be answered by comparing the slopes of two demand curves. The units of measurement of pizza and soft drinks are unrelated. But the question *can* be answered with a measure of responsiveness that is *independent* of units of measurement. Elasticity is such a measure.

The **price elasticity of demand** is a units-free measure of the responsiveness of the quantity demanded of a good to a change in its price when all other influences on buying plans remain the same.

Calculating Price Elasticity of Demand

We calculate the *price elasticity of demand* by using the formula:

$$\text{Price elasticity of demand} = \frac{\text{Percentage change in quantity damanded}}{\text{Percentage change in price}}.$$

To calculate the price elasticity of demand for pizza, we need to know the quantity demanded of pizza at two different prices, when all other influences on buying plans remain the same.

Figure 4.1 zooms in on a section of the demand curve for pizza and shows how the quantity demanded responds to a small change in price. Initially, the price is $20.50 a pizza and 9 pizzas an hour are demanded—the original point. The price then falls to $19.50 a pizza, and the quantity demanded increases to 11 pizzas an hour—the new point. When the price falls by $1 a pizza, the quantity demanded increases by 2 pizzas an hour.

To calculate the price elasticity of demand, we express the change in price as a percentage of the *average price* and the change in the quantity demanded as a percentage of the *average quantity*. By using the average price and average quantity, we calculate the elasticity at a point on the demand curve midway between the original point and the new point.

The original price is $20.50 and the new price is $19.50, so the price change is $1 and the average price is $20 a pizza. Call the percentage change in the price $\%\Delta P$, then

$$\%\Delta P = \Delta P / P_{ave} \times 100 = (\$1/\$20) \times 100 = 5\%.$$

The original quantity demanded is 9 pizzas and the new quantity demanded is 11 pizzas, so the quantity change is 2 pizzas and the average quantity demanded is 10 pizzas. Call the percentage change in the quantity demanded $\%\Delta Q$, then

$$\%\Delta Q = \Delta Q / Q_{ave} \times 100 = (2/10) \times 100 = 20\%.$$

The price elasticity of demand equals the percentage change in the quantity demanded (20 percent) divided by the percentage change in price (5 percent) and is 4. That is,

$$\text{Price elasticity of demand} = \frac{\%\Delta Q}{\%\Delta P}$$

$$= \frac{20\%}{5\%} = 4.$$

Average Price and Quantity Notice that we use the *average* price and *average* quantity. We do this because it gives the most precise measurement of elasticity—at the *midpoint* between the original price and the new price. If the price falls from $20.50 to $19.50, the $1 price change is 4.9 percent of $20.50. The change in quantity of 2 pizzas is 22.2 percent of 9 pizzas, the original quantity. So if we use these

FIGURE 4.1 Calculating the Elasticity of Demand

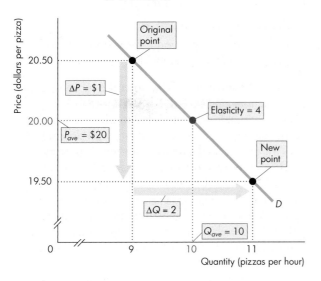

The elasticity of demand is calculated by using the formula:*

$$\text{Price elasticity of demand} = \frac{\text{Percentage change in quantity demanded}}{\text{Percentage change in price}}$$

$$= \frac{\%\Delta Q}{\%\Delta P}$$

$$= \frac{\Delta Q/Q_{ave}}{\Delta P/P_{ave}}$$

$$= \frac{2/10}{1/20} = 4.$$

This calculation measures the elasticity at an average price of $20 a pizza and an average quantity of 10 pizzas an hour.

* In the formula, the Greek letter delta (Δ) stands for "change in" and %Δ stands for "percentage change in."

MyEconLab Animation and Draw Graph

numbers, the price elasticity of demand is 22.2 divided by 4.9, which equals 4.5. But if the price rises from $19.50 to $20.50, the $1 price change is 5.1 percent of $19.50. The change in quantity of 2 pizzas is 18.2 percent of 11 pizzas, the original quantity. So if we use these numbers, the price elasticity of demand is 18.2 divided by 5.1, which equals 3.6.

By using percentages of the *average* price and *average* quantity, we get the *same value* for the elasticity regardless of whether the price falls from $20.50 to $19.50 or rises from $19.50 to $20.50.

Percentages and Proportions Elasticity is the ratio of two percentage changes, so when we divide one percentage change by another, the 100s cancel. A percentage change is a *proportionate* change multiplied by 100. The proportionate change in price is $\Delta P/P_{ave}$, and the proportionate change in quantity demanded is $\Delta Q/Q_{ave}$. So if we divide $\Delta Q/Q_{ave}$ by $\Delta P/P_{ave}$ we get the same answer as we get by using percentage changes.

A Units-Free Measure Now that you've calculated a price elasticity of demand, you can see why it is a *units-free measure*. Elasticity is a units-free measure because the percentage change in each variable is independent of the units in which the variable is measured. The ratio of the two percentages is a number without units.

Minus Sign and Elasticity When the price of a good *rises*, the quantity demanded *decreases*. Because a *positive* change in price brings a *negative* change in the quantity demanded, the price elasticity of demand is a negative number. But it is the magnitude, or *absolute value*, of the price elasticity of demand that tells us how responsive the quantity demanded is. So to compare price elasticities of demand, we use the *magnitude* of the elasticity and ignore the minus sign.

Inelastic and Elastic Demand

If the quantity demanded remains constant when the price changes, then the price elasticity of demand is zero and the good is said to have a **perfectly inelastic demand**. One good that has a very low price elasticity of demand (perhaps zero over some price range) is insulin. Insulin is of such importance to some diabetics that if the price rises or falls, they do not change the quantity they buy.

If the percentage change in the quantity demanded equals the percentage change in the price, then the price elasticity equals 1 and the good is said to have a **unit elastic demand**.

Between perfectly inelastic demand and unit elastic demand is a general case in which *the percentage change in the quantity demanded is less than the percentage change in the price*. In this case, the price elasticity of demand is between zero and 1 and the good is said to have an **inelastic demand**. Food and shelter are examples of goods with inelastic demand.

If the quantity demanded changes by an infinitely large percentage in response to a tiny price change, then the price elasticity of demand is infinity and the good is said to have a **perfectly elastic demand**. An example of a good that has a very high elasticity of demand (almost infinite) is a soft drink from two campus machines located side by side. If the two machines offer the same soft drinks for the same price, some people buy from one machine and some from the other. But if one machine's price is higher than the other's, by even a small amount, no one buys from the machine with the higher price. Drinks from the two machines are perfect substitutes. The demand for a good that has a perfect substitute is perfectly elastic.

Between unit elastic demand and perfectly elastic demand is another general case in which *the percentage change in the quantity demanded exceeds the percentage change in price*. In this case, the price elasticity of demand is greater than 1 and the good is said to have an **elastic demand**. Automobiles and furniture are examples of goods that have elastic demand.

Figure 4.2 shows three demand curves that cover the entire range of possible elasticities of demand that you've just reviewed. In Fig. 4.2(a), the quantity demanded is constant regardless of the price, so this demand is perfectly inelastic. In Fig. 4.2(b), the percentage change in the quantity demanded equals the percentage change in price, so this demand is unit elastic. In Fig. 4.2(c), the price is constant regardless of the quantity demanded, so this figure illustrates a perfectly elastic demand.

You now know the distinction between elastic and inelastic demand. But what determines whether the demand for a good is elastic or inelastic?

The Factors that Influence the Elasticity of Demand

The elasticity of demand for a good depends on

- The closeness of substitutes
- The proportion of income spent on the good
- The time elapsed since the price change

Closeness of Substitutes The closer the substitutes for a good, the more elastic is the demand for it. Oil as fuel or raw material for chemicals has no close substitutes so the demand for oil is inelastic. Plastics are close substitutes for metals, so the demand for metals is elastic.

The degree of substitutability depends on how narrowly (or broadly) we define a good. For example, a smartphone has no close substitutes, but an Apple iPhone is a close substitute for a Samsung Galaxy. So the elasticity of demand for smartphones is lower than the elasticity of demand for an iPhone or a Galaxy.

In everyday language we call goods such as food and shelter *necessities* and goods such as exotic vacations *luxuries*. A necessity has poor substitutes, so it generally has an inelastic demand. A luxury usually has many substitutes, one of which is not buying it. So a luxury generally has an elastic demand.

Proportion of Income Spent on the Good Other things remaining the same, the greater the proportion of income spent on a good, the more elastic (or less inelastic) is the demand for it.

FIGURE 4.2   Inelastic and Elastic Demand

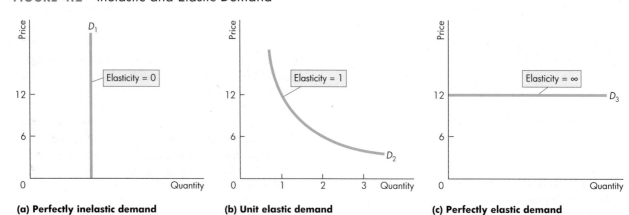

(a) Perfectly inelastic demand   **(b) Unit elastic demand**   **(c) Perfectly elastic demand**

Each demand illustrated here has a constant elasticity. The demand curve in part (a) illustrates the demand for a good that has a zero elasticity of demand. The demand curve in part (b) illustrates the demand for a good with a unit elasticity of demand. And the demand curve in part (c) illustrates the demand for a good with an infinite elasticity of demand.

MyEconLab Animation

Think about your own elasticity of demand for chewing gum and housing. If the price of gum rises, you consume almost as much as before. Your demand for gum is inelastic. If apartment rents rise, you look for someone to share with. Your demand for housing is not as inelastic as your demand for gum. Why the difference? Housing takes a big chunk of your budget, and gum takes little. You barely notice the higher price of gum, while the higher rent puts your budget under severe strain.

Time Elapsed Since Price Change The longer the time that has elapsed since a price change, the more elastic is demand. When the price of oil increased by 400 percent during the 1970s, people barely changed the quantity of oil and gasoline they bought. But gradually, as more efficient auto and airplane engines were developed, the quantity bought decreased. The demand for oil became more elastic as more time elapsed following the huge price hike.

Elasticity Along a Linear Demand Curve

Elasticity of demand is not the same as slope. And a good way to see this fact is by studying a demand curve that has a constant slope but a varying elasticity.

The demand curve in Fig. 4.3 is linear, which means that it has a constant slope. Along this demand curve, a $5 rise in the price brings a decrease of 10 pizzas an hour.

But the price elasticity of demand is not constant along this demand curve. To see why, let's calculate some elasticities.

At the midpoint of the demand curve, the price is $12.50 and the quantity is 25 pizzas per hour. If the price rises from $10 to $15 a pizza, the quantity demanded decreases from 30 to 20 pizzas an hour and the average price and average quantity are at the midpoint of the demand curve. So

$$\text{Price elasticity of demand} = \frac{10/25}{5/12.50}$$
$$= 1.$$

That is, at the midpoint of a linear demand curve, the price elasticity of demand is 1.

At prices *above* the midpoint, the price elasticity of demand is greater than 1: Demand is elastic. To see that demand is elastic, let's calculate the elasticity when the price rises from $15 to $25 a pizza. You can see that quantity demanded decreases from 20 to zero pizzas an hour. The average price is $20 a pizza, and

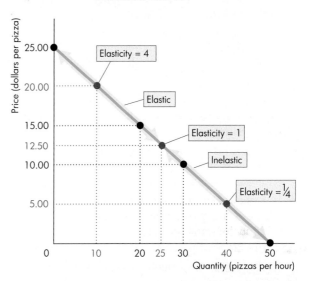

FIGURE 4.3   Elasticity Along a Linear Demand Curve

On a linear demand curve, demand is unit elastic at the midpoint (elasticity is 1), elastic above the midpoint, and inelastic below the midpoint.

————— MyEconLab Animation and Draw Graph —————

the average quantity is 10 pizzas. Putting these numbers into the elasticity formula:

$$\text{Price elasticity of demand} = \frac{\Delta Q/Q_{ave}}{\Delta P/P_{ave}}$$
$$= \frac{20/10}{10/20}$$
$$= 4.$$

That is, the price elasticity of demand at an average price of $20 a pizza is 4.

At prices *below* the midpoint, the price elasticity of demand is less than 1: Demand is inelastic. For example, if the price rises from zero to $10 a pizza, the quantity demanded decreases from 50 to 30 pizzas an hour. The average price is now $5 and the average quantity is 40 pizzas an hour. So

$$\text{Price elasticity of demand} = \frac{20/40}{10/5}$$
$$= 1/4.$$

That is, the price elasticity of demand at an average price of $5 a pizza is 1/4.

Total Revenue and Elasticity

The **total revenue** from the sale of a good equals the price of the good multiplied by the quantity sold. When a price changes, total revenue also changes. But a cut in the price does not always decrease total revenue. The change in total revenue depends on the elasticity of demand in the following way:

- If demand is elastic, a 1 percent price cut increases the quantity sold by more than 1 percent and total revenue increase s.
- If demand is inelastic, a 1 percent price cut increases the quantity sold by less than 1 percent and total revenue decreases.
- If demand is unit elastic, a 1 percent price cut increases the quantity sold by 1 percent and total revenue does not change.

In Fig. 4.4(a), over the price range $25 to $12.50 a pizza, demand is elastic. At a price of $12.50 a pizza, demand is unit elastic. Over the price range from $12.50 a pizza to zero, demand is inelastic.

Figure 4.4(b) shows total revenue. At a price of $25, the quantity sold is zero, so total revenue is zero. At a price of zero, the quantity demanded is 50 pizzas an hour and total revenue is again zero. A price cut in the elastic range brings an increase in total revenue—the percentage increase in the quantity demanded is greater than the percentage decrease in price. A price cut in the inelastic range brings a decrease in total revenue—the percentage increase in the quantity demanded is less than the percentage decrease in price. At unit elasticity, total revenue is at a maximum.

Figure 4.4 shows how we can use this relationship between elasticity and total revenue to estimate elasticity using the total revenue test. The **total revenue test** is a method of estimating the price elasticity of demand by observing the change in total revenue that results from a change in the price, when all other influences on the quantity sold remain the same.

- If a price cut increases total revenue, demand is elastic.
- If a price cut decreases total revenue, demand is inelastic.
- If a price cut leaves total revenue unchanged, demand is unit elastic.

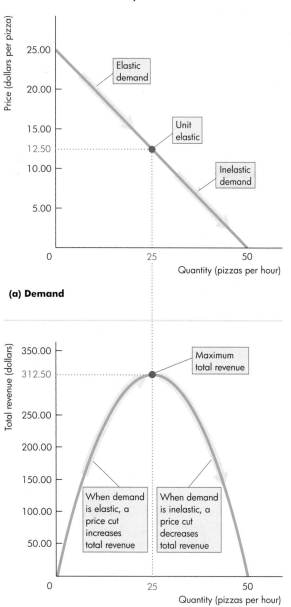

FIGURE 4.4 Elasticity and Total Revenue

(a) Demand

(b) Total revenue

When demand is elastic, in the price range from $25 to $12.50, a decrease in price (part a) brings an increase in total revenue (part b). When demand is inelastic, in the price range from $12.50 to zero, a decrease in price (part a) brings a decrease in total revenue (part b). When demand is unit elastic, at a price of $12.50 (part a), total revenue is at a maximum (part b).

MyEconLab Animation

ECONOMICS IN ACTION
Elastic and Inelastic Demand

The real-world price elasticities of demand in the table range from 1.52 for metals, the item with the most elastic demand in the table, to 0.05 for oil, the item with the most inelastic demand in the table. The demand for food is also inelastic.

Oil and food, which have poor substitutes and inelastic demand, might be classified as necessities. Furniture and motor vehicles, which have good substitutes and elastic demand, might be classified as luxuries.

Price Elasticities of Demand

Good or Service	Elasticity
Elastic Demand	
Metals	1.52
Electrical engineering products	1.39
Mechanical engineering products	1.30
Furniture	1.26
Motor vehicles	1.14
Instrument engineering products	1.10
Transportation services	1.03
Inelastic Demand	
Gas, electricity, and water	0.92
Chemicals	0.89
Clothing	0.64
Banking and insurance services	0.56
Housing services	0.55
Agricultural and fish products	0.42
Books, magazines, and newspapers	0.34
Food	0.12
Cigarettes	0.11
Soft drinks	0.05
Oil	0.05

Sources of data: Ahsan Mansur and John Whalley, "Numerical Specification of Applied General Equilibrium Models: Estimation, Calibration, and Data," in *Applied General Equilibrium Analysis*, eds. Herbert E. Scarf and John B. Shoven (New York: Cambridge University Press, 1984), 109, Henri Theil, Ching-Fan Chung, and James L. Seale, Jr., *Advances in Econometrics, Supplement I, 1989, International Evidence on Consumption Patterns* (Greenwich, Conn.: JAI Press Inc., 1989), and Emilio Pagoulatos and Robert Sorensen, "What Determines the Elasticity of Industry Demand," *International Journal of Industrial Organization*, 1986, and Geoffrey Heal, Columbia University, Web site.

Price Elasticities of Demand for Food

The price elasticity of demand for food in the United States is estimated to be 0.12. This elasticity is an average over all types of food. The demand for most food items is inelastic, but there is a wide range of elasticities as the figure below shows for a range of fruits, vegetables, and meats.

The demand for grapes and the demand for beef are elastic. The demand for oranges is unit elastic. These food items, especially grapes and beef, have many good substitutes. Florida winter tomatoes have closer substitutes than tomatoes in general, so the demand for the Florida winter variety is more elastic (less inelastic) than the demand for tomatoes.

Carrots and cabbage, on which we spend a very small proportion of income, have an almost zero elastic demand.

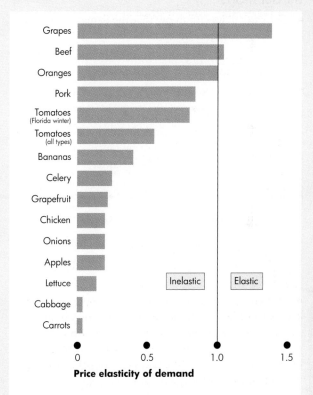

Price Elasticities of Demand for Food

Sources of data: Kuo S. Huang, *U.S. demand for food: A complete system of price and income effects* U.S. Dept. of Agriculture, Economic Research Service, Washington, DC, 1985; J. Scott Shonkwiler and Robert D. Emerson, "Imports and the Supply of Winter Tomatoes: An Application of Rational Expectations," *American Journal of Agricultural Economics*, Vol. 64, No. 4 (Nov., 1982), pp. 634–641; and Kuo S. Huang, "A Further Look at Flexibilities and Elasticities," *American Journal of Agricultural Economics*, Vol. 76, No. 2 (May, 1994), pp. 313–317.

ECONOMICS IN THE NEWS

The Elasticity of Demand for Peanut Butter

Peanut Butter Prices to Rise 30 to 40 Percent
Scott Karns, president and CEO of Karns Foods, said "People are still going to need it for their family. It's still an extremely economical item." Patty Nolan, who is on a fixed income, said "I love peanut butter so I'm using a little less so I don't go through it."

Source: *The Patriot-News*, November 2, 2011

THE DATA

	Quantity (millions of tons per year)	Price (dollars per pound)
2011	350	2.00
2012	300	2.80

THE QUESTIONS

- Does the news clip imply that the demand for peanut butter is elastic or inelastic?
- If the data are two points on the demand curve for peanut butter, what is the price elasticity of demand?

THE ANSWERS

- The two remarks in the news clip suggest that the quantity of peanut butter demanded will decrease when the price rises, but not by much. The demand for peanut butter is inelastic.

- The data table says the price of peanut butter increased by $0.80 with an average price of $2.40, so the price increased by 33.3 percent. The quantity demanded decreased by 50 million tons with an average quantity of 325 million tons, so the quantity demanded decreased by 15.4 percent. The price elasticity of demand equals 15.4 percent divided by 33.3 percent, which is 0.46.

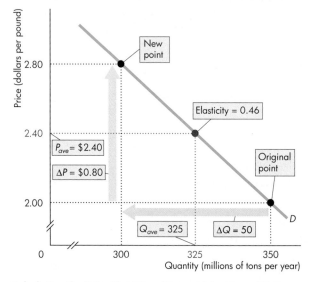

Calculating the Price Elasticity of Demand for Peanut Butter

MyEconLab More Economics in the News

Your Expenditure and Your Elasticity

When the price of a good changes, the change in your expenditure on the good depends on *your* elasticity of demand.

- If your demand for the good is elastic, a 1 percent price cut increases the quantity you buy by more than 1 percent and your expenditure on the item increases.
- If your demand for the good is inelastic, a 1 percent price cut increases the quantity you buy by less than 1 percent and your expenditure on the item decreases.
- If your demand for the good is unit elastic, a 1 percent price cut increases the quantity you buy by 1 percent and your expenditure on the item does not change.

So if you spend more on an item when its price falls, your demand for that item is elastic; if you spend the same amount, your demand is unit elastic; and if you spend less, your demand is inelastic.

You've now completed your study of the *price* elasticity of demand. Two other elasticity concepts tell us about the effects of other influences on demand. Let's look at these other elasticities of demand.

◆ More Elasticities of Demand

Suppose the economy is expanding and people are enjoying rising incomes. You know that a change in income changes demand. So this increased prosperity brings an increase in the demand for most types of goods and services. By how much will a rise in income increase the demand for pizza? This question is answered by the income elasticity of demand.

Income Elasticity of Demand

The **income elasticity of demand** is a measure of the responsiveness of the demand for a good or service to a change in income, other things remaining the same. It tells us by how much a demand curve shifts at a given price.

The income elasticity of demand is calculated by using the formula:

$$\text{Income elasticity of demand} = \frac{\text{Percentage change in quantity demanded}}{\text{Percentage change in income}}.$$

Income elasticities of demand can be positive or negative and they fall into three interesting ranges:

- Positive and greater than 1 (*normal* good, income elastic)
- Positive and less than 1 (*normal* good, income inelastic)
- Negative (*inferior* good)

Income Elastic Demand Suppose that the price of pizza is constant and 9 pizzas an hour are bought. Then incomes rise from $975 to $1,025 a week. No other influence on buying plans changes and the quantity of pizzas sold increases to 11 an hour.

The change in the quantity demanded is +2 pizzas. The average quantity is 10 pizzas, so the quantity demanded increases by 20 percent. The change in income is +$50 and the average income is $1,000, so incomes increase by 5 percent. The income elasticity of demand for pizza is

$$\frac{20\%}{5\%} = 4.$$

The demand for pizza is income elastic. The percentage increase in the quantity of pizza demanded exceeds the percentage increase in income.

ECONOMICS IN ACTION
Necessities and Luxuries

The demand for a necessity such as food or clothing is income inelastic, while the demand for a luxury such as airline and foreign travel is income elastic. But what is a necessity and what is a luxury depends on the level of income. For people with a low income, food and clothing can be luxuries. So the level of income has a big effect on income elasticities of demand.

The figure shows this effect on the income elasticity of demand for food in 10 countries. In countries with low incomes, such as Tanzania and India, the income elasticity of demand for food is high. In countries with high incomes, such as Canada, the income elasticity of demand for food is low. That is, as income increases, the income elasticity of demand for food decreases. Low-income consumers spend a larger percentage of any increase in income on food than do high-income consumers.

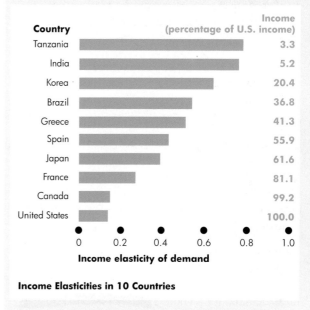

Country	Income (percentage of U.S. income)
Tanzania	3.3
India	5.2
Korea	20.4
Brazil	36.8
Greece	41.3
Spain	55.9
Japan	61.6
France	81.1
Canada	99.2
United States	100.0

Income elasticity of demand

Income Elasticities in 10 Countries

Income Inelastic Demand If the income elasticity of demand is positive but less than 1, demand is income inelastic. The percentage increase in the quantity demanded is positive but less than the percentage increase in income.

Whether demand is income elastic or income inelastic has an important implication for the percentage of income spent on a good. If the demand for a good is *income elastic,* the percentage of income spent on that good *increases* as income increases. And

ECONOMICS IN ACTION

Income Elastic and Inelastic Demand

The table shows some real-world income elasticites of demand and confirms that a necessity such as food or clothing is income inelastic, while the demand for a luxury such as airline travel is income elastic.

Some Real-World Income Elasticities of Demand

Income Elastic Demand

Airline travel	5.82
Movies	3.41
Foreign travel	3.08
Electricity	1.94
Restaurant meals	1.61
Local buses and trains	1.38
Haircuts	1.36
Automobiles	1.07

Income Inelastic Demand

Tobacco	0.86
Alcoholic drinks	0.62
Furniture	0.53
Clothing	0.51
Newspapers and magazines	0.38
Telephone	0.32
Food	0.14

Sources of data: H.S. Houthakker and Lester D. Taylor, *Consumer Demand in the United States* (Cambridge, Mass.: Harvard University Press, 1970), and Henri Theil, Ching-Fan Chung, and James L. Seale, Jr., *Advances in Econometrics, Supplement 1, 1989, International Evidence on Consumption Patterns* (Greenwich, Conn.: JAI Press, Inc., 1989).

if the demand for a good is *income inelastic*, the percentage of income spent on that good *decreases* as income increases.

Inferior Goods If the income elasticity of demand is negative, the good is an *inferior* good. The quantity demanded of an inferior good and the amount spent on it *decrease* when income increases. Goods in this category include small motorcycles, potatoes, and rice. Low-income consumers buy these goods and spend a large percentage of their incomes on them.

Cross Elasticity of Demand

The burger shop next to your pizzeria has just raised its price of a burger. You know that pizzas and burgers are substitutes. You also know that when the price of a substitute for pizza *rises*, the demand for pizza *increases*. But how big is the influence of the price of a burger on the demand for pizza?

You know, too, that pizza and soft drinks are complements. And you know that if the price of a complement of pizza *rises*, the demand for pizza *decreases*. So you wonder, by how much will a rise in the price of a soft drink decrease the demand for your pizza?

To answer this question, you need to know about the cross elasticity of demand for pizza. Let's examine this elasticity measure.

We measure the influence of a change in the price of a substitute or complement by using the concept of the cross elasticity of demand. The **cross elasticity of demand** is a measure of the responsiveness of the demand for a good to a change in the price of a substitute or complement, other things remaining the same.

We calculate the *cross elasticity of demand* by using the formula:

$$\text{Cross elasticity of demand} = \frac{\text{Percentage change in quantity demanded}}{\text{Percentage change in price of a substitute or complement}}.$$

The cross elasticity of demand can be positive or negative. If the cross elasticity of demand is *positive*, demand and the price of the other good change in the *same* direction, so the two goods are *substitutes*. If the cross elasticity of demand is *negative*, demand and the price of the other good change in *opposite* directions, so the two goods are *complements*.

Substitutes Suppose that the price of pizza is constant and people buy 9 pizzas an hour. Then the price of a burger rises from $1.50 to $2.50. No other influence on buying plans changes and the quantity of pizzas bought increases to 11 an hour.

The change in the quantity demanded at the current price is +2 pizzas—the new quantity, 11 pizzas, minus the original quantity, 9 pizzas. The average quantity is 10 pizzas. So the quantity of pizzas demanded increases by 20 percent. That is,

$$\Delta Q/Q_{ave} \times 100 = (+2/10) \times 100 = +20\%.$$

The change in the price of a burger, a substitute for pizza, is +$1—the new price, $2.50, minus the original price, $1.50. The average price is $2 a burger. So the price of a burger rises by 50 percent. That is,

$$\Delta P/P_{ave} \times 100 = (+\$1/\$2) \times 100 = +50\%.$$

So the cross elasticity of demand for pizza with respect to the price of a burger is

$$\frac{+20\%}{+50\%} = 0.4.$$

Figure 4.5 illustrates the cross elasticity of demand. Because pizza and burgers are substitutes, when the price of a burger rises, the demand for pizza increases. The demand curve for pizza shifts rightward from D_0 to D_1. Because a *rise* in the price of a burger brings an *increase* in the demand for pizza, the cross elasticity of demand for pizza with respect to the price of a burger is *positive*. Both the price and the quantity change in the same direction.

Complements Now suppose that the price of pizza is constant and 11 pizzas an hour are bought. Then the price of a soft drink rises from $1.50 to $2.50. No other influence on buying plans changes and the quantity of pizzas bought falls to 9 an hour.

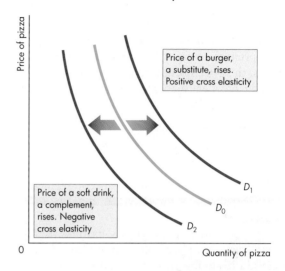

FIGURE 4.5 Cross Elasticity of Demand

A burger is a *substitute* for pizza. When the price of a burger rises, the demand for pizza increases and the demand curve for pizza shifts rightward from D_0 to D_1. The cross elasticity of demand is *positive*.

A soft drink is a *complement* of pizza. When the price of a soft drink rises, the demand for pizza decreases and the demand curve for pizza shifts leftward from D_0 to D_2. The cross elasticity of demand is *negative*.

MyEconLab Animation and Draw Graph

ECONOMICS IN THE NEWS

More Peanut Butter Demand Elasticities

Peanut Butter Related Markets
Professor Timothy Mathews teaches economics at Kennesaw State University, Georgia, the nation's number one peanut-producing state. The data table below shows his guesses about some demand elasticities for peanut butter.

Source: Timothy Mathews

THE DATA

Income elasticity	−0.31
Cross elasticity peanut butter and grape jelly	−0.27
Cross elasticity peanut butter and American cheese	+0.18

THE QUESTIONS
- What do the data provided tell us about the demand for peanut butter? Is it a normal good?
- Is grape jelly a substitute for or a complement of peanut butter? Is American cheese a substitute for or a complement of peanut butter?

THE ANSWERS
- The income elasticity of demand for peanut butter is *negative*, which means that peanut butter is an *inferior good*. People buy less peanut butter as income rises.
- The cross elasticity of demand of peanut butter with respect to the price of grape jelly is *negative*, which means that peanut butter and grape jelly are *complements*.
- The cross elasticity of demand of peanut butter with respect to the price of American cheese is *positive*, which means that peanut butter and American cheese are *substitutes*.

MyEconLab More Economics in the News

The change in the quantity demanded is the opposite of what we've just calculated: The quantity of pizzas demanded decreases by 20 percent (−20%).

The change in the price of a soft drink, a rise of $1 from $1.50 to $2.50, is the same as the change in the price of a burger that we've just calculated. That is, the price rises by 50 percent (+50%).

So the cross elasticity of demand for pizza with respect to the price of a soft drink is

$$\frac{-20\%}{+50\%} = -0.4.$$

Because pizza and soft drinks are complements, when the price of a soft drink rises, the demand for pizza decreases.

In Fig. 4.5, when the price of soft drinks rises the demand curve for pizza shifts leftward from D_0 to D_2. Because a *rise* in the price of a soft drink brings a *decrease* in the demand for pizza, the cross elasticity of demand for pizza with respect to the price of a soft drink is *negative*. The price and quantity change in *opposite* directions.

The magnitude of the cross elasticity of demand determines how far the demand curve shifts. The larger the cross elasticity (absolute value), the greater is the change in demand and the larger is the shift in the demand curve.

If two items are close substitutes, such as two brands of spring water, the cross elasticity is large. If two items are close complements, such as movies and popcorn, the cross elasticity is large.

If two items are somewhat unrelated to each other, such as newspapers and orange juice, the cross elasticity is small—perhaps even zero.

◆ REVIEW QUIZ

1 What does the income elasticity of demand measure?
2 What does the sign (positive/negative) of the income elasticity tell us about a good?
3 What does the cross elasticity of demand measure?
4 What does the sign (positive/negative) of the cross elasticity of demand tell us about the relationship between two goods?

Work these questions in Study Plan 4.2 and get instant feedback. Do a Key Terms Quiz.   MyEconLab

◆ Elasticity of Supply

You know that when demand increases, the equilibrium price rises and the equilibrium quantity increases. But does the price rise by a large amount and the quantity increase by a little? Or does the price barely rise and the quantity increase by a large amount?

The answer depends on the responsiveness of the quantity supplied to a change in the price. If the quantity supplied is not very responsive to price, then an increase in demand brings a large rise in the price and a small increase in the equilibrium quantity. If the quantity supplied is highly responsive to price, then an increase in demand brings a small rise in the price and a large increase in the equilibrium quantity.

The problems that arise from using the slope of the supply curve to indicate responsiveness are the same as those we considered when discussing the responsiveness of the quantity demanded, so we use a units-free measure—the elasticity of supply.

Calculating the Elasticity of Supply

The **elasticity of supply** measures the responsiveness of the quantity supplied to a change in the price of a good when all other influences on selling plans remain the same. It is calculated by using the formula:

$$\text{Elasticity of supply} = \frac{\text{Percentage change in quantity supplied}}{\text{Percentage change in price}}.$$

We use the same method that you learned when you studied the elasticity of demand. (Refer back to p. 84 to check this method.)

Elastic and Inelastic Supply If the elasticity of supply is greater than 1, we say that supply is elastic; and if the elasticity of supply is less than 1, we say that supply is inelastic.

Suppose that when the price rises from $20 to $21, the quantity supplied increases from 10 to 20 pizzas per hour. The price rise is $1 and the average price is $20.50, so the price rises by 4.9 percent of the average price. The quantity increases from 10 to 20 pizzas an hour, so the increase is 10 pizzas, the average quantity is 15 pizzas, and the quantity increases by 67 percent. The elasticity of supply is equal to 67 percent divided by 4.9 percent, which equals 13.67. Because the elasticity of supply exceeds 1 (in this case by a lot), supply is elastic.

In contrast, suppose that when the price rises from $20 to $30, the quantity of pizza supplied increases from 10 to 13 per hour. The price rise is $10 and the average price is $25, so the price rises by 40 percent of the average price. The quantity increases from 10 to 13 pizzas an hour, so the increase is 3 pizzas, the average quantity is 11.5 pizzas an hour, and the quantity increases by 26 percent. The elasticity of supply is equal to 26 percent divided by 40 percent, which equals 0.65. Now, because the elasticity of supply is less than 1, supply is inelastic.

Figure 4.6 shows the range of elasticities of supply. If the quantity supplied is fixed regardless of the price, the supply curve is vertical and the elasticity of supply is zero. Supply is perfectly inelastic. This case is shown in Fig. 4.6(a). A special intermediate case occurs when the percentage change in price equals the percentage change in quantity. Supply is then unit elastic. This case is shown in Fig. 4.6(b). No matter how steep the supply curve is, if it is linear and passes through the origin, supply is unit elastic. If there is a price at which sellers are willing to offer any quantity for sale, the supply curve is horizontal and the elasticity of supply is infinite. Supply is perfectly elastic. This case is shown in Fig. 4.6(c).

The Factors That Influence the Elasticity of Supply

The elasticity of supply of a good depends on

- Resource substitution possibilities
- Time frame for the supply decision

Resource Substitution Possibilities Some goods and services can be produced only by using unique or rare productive resources. These items have a low, perhaps even a zero, elasticity of supply. Other goods and services can be produced by using commonly available resources that could be allocated to a wide variety of alternative tasks. Such items have a high elasticity of supply.

A van Gogh painting is an example of a good with a vertical supply curve and a zero elasticity of supply. At the other extreme, wheat can be grown on land that is almost equally good for growing corn, so it is just as easy to grow wheat as corn. The opportunity cost of wheat in terms of forgone corn is almost constant. As a result, the supply curve of wheat is almost horizontal and its elasticity of supply is very large. Similarly, when a good is produced in many different countries (for example, sugar and beef), the supply of the good is highly elastic.

The supply of most goods and services lies between these two extremes. The quantity produced

---

FIGURE 4.6   Inelastic and Elastic Supply

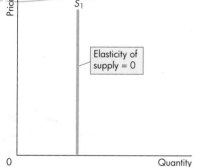

(a) Perfectly inelastic supply

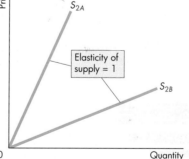

(b) Unit elastic supply

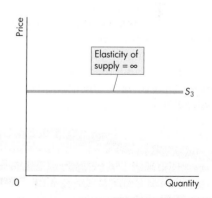

(c) Perfectly elastic supply

Each supply illustrated here has a constant elasticity. The supply curve in part (a) illustrates the supply of a good that has a zero elasticity of supply. Each supply curve in part (b) illustrates the supply of a good with a unit elasticity of supply. All linear supply curves that pass through the origin illustrate supplies that are unit elastic. The supply curve in part (c) illustrates the supply of a good with an infinite elasticity of supply.

can be increased but only by incurring a higher cost. If a higher price is offered, the quantity supplied increases. Such goods and services have an elasticity of supply between zero and infinity.

Time Frame for the Supply Decision To study the influence of the amount of time elapsed since a price change, we distinguish three time frames of supply:

- Momentary supply
- Short-run supply
- Long-run supply

Momentary Supply When the price of a good changes, the immediate response of the quantity supplied is determined by the *momentary supply* of that good.

Some goods, such as fruits and vegetables, have a perfectly inelastic momentary supply—a vertical supply curve. The quantities supplied depend on crop-planting decisions made earlier. In the case of oranges, for example, planting decisions have to be made many years in advance of the crop being available. Momentary supply is perfectly inelastic because, on a given day, no matter what the price of oranges, producers cannot change their output. They have picked, packed, and shipped their crop to market, and the quantity available for that day is fixed.

In contrast, some goods have a perfectly elastic momentary supply. Long-distance phone calls are an example. When many people simultaneously make a call, there is a big surge in the demand for telephone cables, computer switching, and satellite time. The quantity supplied increases, but the price remains constant. Long-distance carriers monitor fluctuations in demand and reroute calls to ensure that the quantity supplied equals the quantity demanded without changing the price.

Short-Run Supply The response of the quantity supplied to a price change when only *some* of the possible adjustments to production can be made is determined by *short-run supply*. Most goods have an inelastic short-run supply. To increase output in the short run, firms must work their labor force overtime and perhaps hire additional workers. To decrease their output in the short run, firms either lay off workers or reduce their hours of work. With the passage of time, firms can make more adjustments, perhaps training additional workers or buying additional tools and other equipment.

For the orange grower, if the price of oranges falls, some pickers can be laid off and oranges left on the trees to rot. Or if the price of oranges rises, the grower can use more fertilizer and improved irrigation to increase the yield of the existing trees.

But an orange grower can't change the number of trees producing oranges in the short run.

Long-Run Supply The response of the quantity supplied to a price change after *all* the technologically possible ways of adjusting supply have been exploited is determined by *long-run supply.* For most goods and services, long-run supply is elastic and perhaps perfectly elastic.

For the orange grower, the long run is the time it takes new tree plantings to grow to full maturity—about 15 years. In some cases, the long-run adjustment occurs only after a completely new production plant has been built and workers have been trained to operate it—typically a process that might take several years.

REVIEW QUIZ

1 Why do we need a units-free measure of the responsiveness of the quantity supplied of a good or service to a change in its price?
2 Define the elasticity of supply and show how it is calculated.
3 What are the main influences on the elasticity of supply that make the supply of some goods elastic and the supply of other goods inelastic?
4 Provide examples of goods or services whose elasticities of supply are (a) zero, (b) greater than zero but less than infinity, and (c) infinity.
5 How does the time frame over which a supply decision is made influence the elasticity of supply? Explain your answer.

Work these questions in Study Plan 4.3 and get instant feedback. Do a Key Terms Quiz.   MyEconLab

◆ You have now learned about the elasticities of demand and supply. Table 4.1 summarizes all the elasticities that you've met in this chapter. In the next chapter, we study the efficiency of competitive markets. But first study *Economics in the News* on pp. 98–99, which puts the elasticity of demand to work and looks at the market for coffee.

TABLE 4.1   A Compact Glossary of Elasticities

Price Elasticities of Demand

A relationship is described as	When its magnitude is	Which means that
Perfectly elastic	Infinity	The smallest possible increase in price causes an infinitely large decrease in the quantity demanded*
Elastic	Less than infinity but greater than 1	The percentage decrease in the quantity demanded exceeds the percentage increase in price
Unit elastic	1	The percentage decrease in the quantity demanded equals the percentage increase in price
Inelastic	Less than 1 but greater than zero	The percentage decrease in the quantity demanded is less than the percentage increase in price
Perfectly inelastic	Zero	The quantity demanded is the same at all prices

Cross Elasticities of Demand

A relationship is described as	When its value is	Which means that
Close substitutes	Large	The smallest possible increase in the price of one good causes an infinitely large increase in the quantity demanded* of the other good
Substitutes	Positive	If the price of one good increases, the quantity demanded of the other good also increases
Unrelated goods	Zero	If the price of one good increases, the quantity demanded of the other good remains the same
Complements	Negative	If the price of one good increases, the quantity demanded of the other good decreases

Income Elasticities of Demand

A relationship is described as	When its value is	Which means that
Income elastic (normal good)	Greater than 1	The percentage increase in the quantity demanded is greater than the percentage increase in income*
Income inelastic (normal good)	Less than 1 but greater than zero	The percentage increase in the quantity demanded is greater than zero but less than the percentage increase in income
Negative (inferior good)	Less than zero	When income increases, quantity demanded decreases

Elasticities of Supply

A relationship is described as	When its magnitude is	Which means that
Perfectly elastic	Infinity	The smallest possible increase in price causes an infinitely large increase in the quantity supplied*
Elastic	Less than infinity but greater than 1	The percentage increase in the quantity supplied exceeds the percentage increase in the price
Unit elastic	1	The percentage increase in the quantity supplied equals the percentage increase in the price
Inelastic	Greater than zero but less than 1	The percentage increase in the quantity supplied is less than the percentage increase in the price
Perfectly inelastic	Zero	The quantity supplied is the same at all prices

*In each description, the directions of change may be reversed. For example, in the case of a perfectly elastic demand, the smallest possible *decrease* in price causes an infinitely large *increase* in the quantity demanded.

The Elasticity of Demand for Coffee

Drop in Global Coffee Prices Shrinks Farmers' Revenue

Daily Monitor
November 6, 2013

Global coffee prices have continued on a downward trend, casting a gloomy picture on … farmers' income.

Latest records from the International Coffee Organization (ICO) show the drop has continued even as the new coffee calendar begins.

By close of October, ICO [average price] dropped to 100.38 cents, down from the 111.82 cents per pound in September. …

In an interview with the *Daily Monitor*, Mr. David Barry, the managing director of Kyagalanyi Coffee Ltd., Uganda's leading coffee exporting company, said: "We may not know what's ahead of us but trends show a further fall in prices and everyone has to brave this."

The drop in price has been attributed to increased production, with the biggest producers being Brazil and Vietnam. … [Their] combined production reached 90 million bags, with the latter posting 60 million bags and the former 30 million.

Crop year 2012/13 has now closed in all exporting countries and according to available information, total production is estimated at 145.2 million bags. This is 12.8 million bags more than 2011/12, representing a 9.6 percent increase. …

MyEconLab More Economics in the News

ESSENCE OF THE STORY

- Global coffee prices fell from 111.82 cents per pound in September 2013 to 100.38 cents per pound in November 2013.

- The fall in price was the result of increased production.

- Output in Brazil, the world's largest producer, was 60 million bags, and in Vietnam, the second-largest producer, it was 30 million bags.

- For the crop year 2012/13, total production was estimated at 145.2 million bags.

- Production in 2012/13 was 12.8 million bags more than 2011/12, a 9.6 percent increase.

ECONOMIC ANALYSIS

- The table below summarizes data provided by the International Coffee Organization, which supplements and updates some of the information in this news article.

Summary of Coffee Data

Year	Quantity produced (millions of bags)	Price (U.S. cents per pound)
2012	134	135
2013	145	100

- Figure 1 provides yet more data and shows that after falling through 2013, the price of coffee climbed steeply in 2014.

- The price of coffee fluctuates because the supply of coffee fluctuates. And the price fluctuates by much more than the quantity of coffee produced because the demand for coffee is inelastic.

- The news headline provides the first clue that demand is inelastic: When the price falls, revenue shrinks. This information enables us to use the *total revenue test*, "If a price cut decreases total revenue, then demand is inelastic."

- We can estimate the price elasticity of demand for coffee, assuming that demand didn't change, by using the events in the market in 2012 and 2013.

- Figure 2 illustrates the global market for coffee in these two years. The demand curve for coffee is *D* and in 2012, the supply curve of coffee was S_{12}. The equilibrium price was 135 cents per pound, and the equilibrium quantity was 134 million bags.

- In 2013, supply increased to S_{13}, the price fell to 100 cents per pound, and the quantity increased to 145 million bags.

- Figure 3 focuses on the demand curve and summarizes the elasticity calculation. The price fell by 35 cents, which is 30 percent of the average price of 117 cents. The quantity demanded increased by 11 million bags, which is 7.9 percent of the average quantity.

- The price elasticity of demand is 7.9 percent/30 percent, which equals 0.26. A 1 percent fall in price brings a 0.26 percent increase in the quantity demanded. And a 1 percent increase in the quantity brings a fall in price equal to 1/0.26, or almost 4 percent.

- When demand is inelastic, a small percentage change in the supply brings a large percentage change in the price.

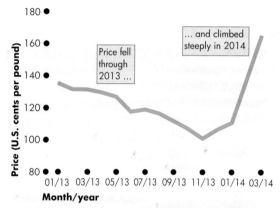

Figure 1 The Coffee-Price Roller Coaster

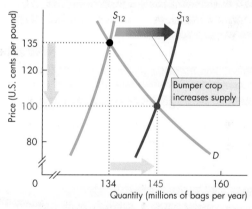

Figure 2 The Market for Coffee: 2012 and 2013

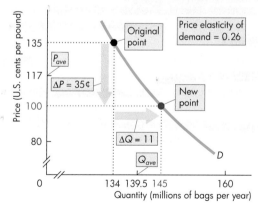

Figure 3 The Price Elasticity of Demand for Coffee

99

SUMMARY

Key Points

Price Elasticity of Demand (pp. 84–90)

- Elasticity is a measure of the responsiveness of the quantity demanded of a good to a change in its price, other things remaining the same.
- Price elasticity of demand equals the percentage change in the quantity demanded divided by the percentage change in the price.
- The larger the magnitude of the price elasticity of demand, the greater is the responsiveness of the quantity demanded to a given price change.
- If demand is elastic, a cut in price leads to an increase in total revenue. If demand is unit elastic, a cut in price leaves total revenue unchanged. And if demand is inelastic, a cut in price leads to a decrease in total revenue.
- Price elasticity of demand depends on how easily one good serves as a substitute for another, the proportion of income spent on the good, and the length of time elapsed since the price change.

Working Problems 1 to 5 will give you a better understanding of the price elasticity of demand.

More Elasticities of Demand (pp. 91–94)

- Income elasticity of demand measures the responsiveness of demand to a change in income, other things remaining the same. For a normal good, the income elasticity of demand is positive. For an inferior good, the income elasticity of demand is negative.
- When the income elasticity of demand is greater than 1 (income elastic), the percentage of income spent on the good increases as income increases.
- When the income elasticity of demand is less than 1 (income inelastic or inferior), the percentage of income spent on the good decreases as income increases.
- Cross elasticity of demand measures the responsiveness of the demand for one good to a change in the price of a substitute or a complement, other things remaining the same.
- The cross elasticity of demand with respect to the price of a substitute is positive. The cross elasticity of demand with respect to the price of a complement is negative.

Working Problems 6 to 8 will give you a better understanding of cross and income elasticities of demand.

Elasticity of Supply (pp. 94–96)

- Elasticity of supply measures the responsiveness of the quantity supplied of a good to a change in its price, other things remaining the same.
- The elasticity of supply is usually positive and ranges between zero (vertical supply curve) and infinity (horizontal supply curve).
- Supply decisions have three time frames: momentary, short run, and long run.
- Momentary supply refers to the response of the quantity supplied to a price change at the instant that the price changes.
- Short-run supply refers to the response of the quantity supplied to a price change after some of the technologically feasible adjustments in production have been made.
- Long-run supply refers to the response of the quantity supplied to a price change when all the technologically feasible adjustments in production have been made.

Working Problem 9 will give you a better understanding of the elasticity of supply.

Key Terms

MyEconLab Key Terms Quiz

Cross elasticity of demand, 92
Elastic demand, 86
Elasticity of supply, 94
Income elasticity of demand, 91

Inelastic demand, 85
Perfectly elastic demand, 85
Perfectly inelastic demand, 85
Price elasticity of demand, 84

Total revenue, 88
Total revenue test, 88
Unit elastic demand, 85

WORKED PROBLEM

MyEconLab   You can work this problem in Chapter 4 Study Plan.

A rise in the price of a smoothie from $2 to $3 results in a fall in the quantity of smoothies demanded from 220 million to 180 million a day and at today's price of a muffin, $1.50, the quantity of muffins demanded increases from 80 million to 100 million a day.

Questions

1. Calculate the percentage change in the price of a smoothie and the percentage change in the quantity demanded of smoothies.
2. Calculate the price elasticity of demand for smoothies.
3. Is the demand for smoothies elastic or inelastic?
4. Calculate the cross elasticity of demand for muffins with respect to the price of a smoothie.

Solutions

1. The price of a smoothie rises by $1 and the quantity demanded falls by 40 million a day.

   To calculate the percentage changes in the price and quantity demanded, use the average price and average quantity. The figure illustrates the calculations.

   The average price of a smoothie is $2.50, so the percentage change in the price was ($1/$2.50) × 100, or 40 percent.

   The average quantity of smoothies is 200 million, so the percentage change in the quantity demanded was (40 million/200 million) × 100, or 20 percent.

Key Point: When working with elasticity, the percentage change in the price and quantity is the percentage of the average price and average quantity.

2. The price elasticity of demand is the ratio of the percentage change in the quantity to the percentage change in price.

   To calculate the price elasticity of demand for smoothies, divide the percentage change in quantity by the percentage change in the price. The ratio of two percentage changes has no units.

Key Point: The price elasticity calculated is the price elasticity of demand at the price midway between the original and the new prices. That is, it calculates the elasticity at the average price.

3. The price elasticity of demand for smoothies is *less than* 1, so the demand is inelastic.

Key Point: When the percentage change in the quantity demanded is *less than* the percentage change in the price, demand is inelastic and the price elasticity of demand is less than 1.

4. To calculate the cross elasticity of demand for muffins with respect to the price of a smoothie, divide the percentage change in quantity of muffins demanded by the percentage change in the price of a smoothie.

   When the price of a smoothie rises by 40 percent, the quantity of muffins demanded increases from 80 million to 100 million, a change of 20 million.

   The average quantity of muffins is 90 million, so the percentage change in the quantity of muffins is (20 million/90 million) × 100, which equals 22.2 percent.

   The cross elasticity of the demand for muffins with respect to the price of a smoothie equals 22.2 percent/40 percent, which equals 0.55.

   The cross elasticity of demand for muffins with respect to the price of a smoothie is *positive*, which means that muffins and smoothies are substitutes—just as you thought!

Key Point: The cross elasticity of demand is positive for substitutes and negative for complements.

Key Figure

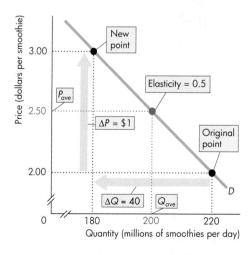

MyEconLab Interactive Animation

◆ STUDY PLAN PROBLEMS AND APPLICATIONS

MyEconLab   You can work Problems 1 to 9 in Chapter 4 Study Plan and get instant feedback.

Price Elasticity of Demand (Study Plan 4.1)

1. Rain spoils the strawberry crop, the price rises from $4 to $6 a box, and the quantity demanded decreases from 1,000 to 600 boxes a week.
    a. Calculate the price elasticity of demand over this price range.
    b. Describe the demand for strawberries.

2. If the quantity of dental services demanded increases by 10 percent when the price of dental services falls by 10 percent, is the demand for dental services inelastic, elastic, or unit elastic?

3. The demand schedule for hotel rooms is

Price (dollars per room per night)	Quantity demanded (millions of rooms per night)
200	100
250	80
400	50
500	40
800	25

    a. What happens to total revenue when the price falls from $400 to $250 a room per night and from $250 to $200 a room per night?
    b. Is the demand for hotel rooms elastic, inelastic, or unit elastic?

4. The figure shows the demand for pens.

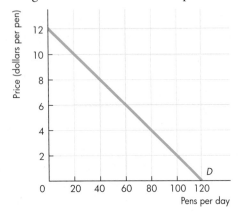

    Calculate the elasticity of demand when the price rises from $4 to $6 a pen. Over what price range is the demand for pens elastic?

5. In 2003, when music downloading first took off, Universal Music slashed the average price of a CD from $21 to $15. The company expected the price cut to boost the quantity of CDs sold by 30 percent, other things remaining the same.
    a. What was Universal Music's estimate of the price elasticity of demand for CDs?
    b. If you were making the pricing decision at Universal Music, what would be your pricing decision? Explain your decision.

More Elasticities of Demand (Study Plan 4.2)

6. When Judy's income increased from $130 to $170 a week, she increased her demand for concert tickets by 15 percent and decreased her demand for bus rides by 10 percent. Calculate Judy's income elasticity of demand for (a) concert tickets and (b) bus rides.

7. If a 12 percent rise in the price of orange juice decreases the quantity of orange juice demanded by 22 percent and increases the quantity of apple juice demanded by 14 percent, calculate the
    a. Price elasticity of demand for orange juice.
    b. Cross elasticity of demand for apple juice with respect to the price of orange juice.

8. If a rise in the price of sushi from 98¢ to $1.02 a piece decreases the quantity of soy sauce demanded from 101 units to 99 units an hour and decreases the quantity of sushi demanded by 1 percent an hour, calculate the:
    a. Price elasticity of demand for sushi.
    b. Cross elasticity of demand for soy sauce with respect to the price of sushi.

Elasticity of Supply (Study Plan 4.3)

9. The table sets out the supply schedule of jeans.

Price (dollars per pair)	Quantity supplied (millions of pairs per year)
120	24
125	28
130	32
135	36

    a. Calculate the elasticity of supply when the price rises from $125 to $135 a pair.
    b. Calculate the elasticity of supply when the average price is $125 a pair.
    c. Is the supply of jeans elastic, inelastic, or unit elastic?

◆ ADDITIONAL PROBLEMS AND APPLICATIONS

MyEconLab   You can work these problems in MyEconLab if assigned by your instructor.

Price Elasticity of Demand

10. With higher fuel costs, airlines raised their average fare from 75¢ to $1.25 per passenger mile and the number of passenger miles decreased from 2.5 million a day to 1.5 million a day.
    a. What is the price elasticity of demand for air travel over this price range?
    b. Describe the demand for air travel.

11. The figure shows the demand for DVD rentals.

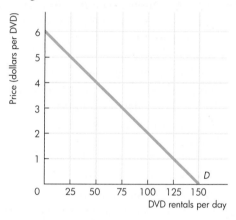

    a. Calculate the elasticity of demand when the price of a DVD rental rises from $3 to $5.
    b. At what price is the elasticity of demand for DVD rentals equal to 1?

Use the following table to work Problems 12 to 14.
The demand schedule for computer chips is

Price (dollars per chip)	Quantity demanded (millions of chips per year)
200	50
250	45
300	40
350	35
400	30

12. a. What happens to total revenue if the price falls from $400 to $350 a chip and from $350 to $300 a chip?
    b. At what price is total revenue at a maximum?

13. At an average price of $350, is the demand for chips elastic, inelastic, or unit elastic? Use the total revenue test to answer this question.

14. At $250 a chip, is the demand for chips elastic or inelastic? Use the total revenue test to answer this question.

15. Your price elasticity of demand for bananas is 4. If the price of bananas rises by 5 percent, what is
    a. The percentage change in the quantity of bananas you buy?
    b. The change in your expenditure on bananas?

16. **As Gasoline Prices Soar, Americans Slowly Adapt**
    As gas prices rose in March 2008, Americans drove 11 billion fewer miles than in March 2007. Realizing that prices were not going down, Americans adapted to higher energy costs. Americans spent 3.7 percent of their disposable income on transportation fuels. How much we spend on gasoline depends on the choices we make: what car we drive, where we live, how much time we spend driving, and where we choose to go. For many people, higher energy costs mean fewer restaurant meals, deferred weekend outings with the kids, less air travel, and more time closer to home.
    Source: *International Herald Tribune*, May 23, 2008
    a. List and explain the elasticities of demand that are implicitly referred to in the news clip.
    b. Why, according to the news clip, is the demand for gasoline inelastic?

More Elasticities of Demand

Use this information to work Problems 17 and 18.
Economy Forces Many to Shorten Holiday Plans
This year Americans are taking fewer exotic holidays by air and instead are visiting local scenic places by car. The global financial crisis has encouraged many Americans to cut their holiday budgets.
Source: *USA Today*, May 22, 2009

17. Given the prices of the two holidays, is the income elasticity of demand for exotic holidays positive or negative? Are exotic holidays a normal good or an inferior good? Are local holidays a normal good or an inferior good?

18. Are exotic holidays and local holidays substitutes? Explain your answer.

19. When Alex's income was $3,000, he bought 4 bagels and 12 donuts a month. Now his income is $5,000 and he buys 8 bagels and 6 donuts a month. Calculate Alex's income elasticity of demand for (a) bagels and (b) donuts.

20. **Walmart's Recession-Time Pet Project**

    During the recession, Walmart moved its pet food and supplies to the front with its other fast-growing business, baby products. Retail experts point out that kids and pets tend to be fairly recession-resistant businesses—even in a recession, dogs will be fed and kids will get their toys.

    Source: *CNN*, May 13, 2008

    a. What does this news clip imply about the income elasticity of demand for pet food and baby products?

    b. Would the income elasticity of demand be greater or less than 1? Explain.

21. If a 5 percent fall in the price of chocolate sauce increases the quantity demanded of chocolate sauce by 10 percent and increases the quantity of ice cream demanded by 15 percent, calculate the

    a. Price elasticity of demand for chocolate sauce.

    b. Cross elasticity of demand for ice cream with respect to the price of chocolate sauce.

22. **To Love, Honor, and Save Money**

    In a survey of caterers and event planners, nearly half of them said that they were seeing declines in wedding spending in response to the economic slowdown; 12% even reported wedding cancellations because of financial concerns.

    Source: *Time*, June 2, 2008

    a. Based upon this news clip, are wedding events a normal good or an inferior good? Explain.

    b. Are wedding events more a necessity or a luxury? Would the income elasticity of demand be greater than 1, less than 1, or equal to 1? Explain.

Elasticity of Supply

23. The table sets out the supply schedule of long-distance phone calls.

Price (cents per minute)	Quantity supplied (millions of minutes per day)
10	200
20	400
30	600
40	800

Calculate the elasticity of supply when

a. The price falls from 40¢ to 30¢ a minute.

b. The average price is 20¢ a minute.

24. **Weak Coal Prices Hit China's Third-Largest Coal Miner**

    The chairman of Yanzhou Coal Mining reported that the recession had decreased the demand for coal, with its sales falling by 11.9 percent to 7.92 million tons from 8.99 million tons a year earlier, despite a 10.6 percent cut in the price.

    Source: *Dow Jones*, April 27, 2009

    Calculate the price elasticity of supply of coal. Is the supply of coal elastic or inelastic?

Economics in the News

25. After you have studied *Economics in the News* on pp. 98–99, answer the following questions.

    a. Looking at Fig. 1 on p. 99, explain what must have happened in 2014 to the supply of coffee.

    b. Given the information in Fig. 1 and the estimated elasticity of demand for coffee, by what percentage did the quantity of coffee change in 2014 and in which direction?

    c. The news article says that farmers' revenue shrank as the price of coffee fell. Explain why this fact tells us that the demand for coffee is inelastic.

    d. How does the total revenue test work for a rise in the price? What do you predict happened to total revenue in 2014? Why?

    e. Coffee isn't just coffee. It comes in different varieties, the main two being Arabica and Robusta. Would you expect the elasticity of demand for Arabica to be the same as the elasticity of demand for coffee? Explain why or why not.

26. **Comcast Deal Won't Lead to Netflix Price Hike**

    Under the deal, Netflix will buy Internet service from Comcast, rather than connect directly for free with some smaller ISPs like Cablevision as it does now.

    Source: *CNN*, April 24, 2014

    a. How will Netflix's decision to buy more expensive Internet service influence Netflix's supply of online movie viewing?

    b. Given your answer to part (a), explain why Netflix says it will not hike its price.

    c. What can you say about the price elasticity of demand for Netflix online movie viewing?

5

EFFICIENCY AND EQUITY

After studying this chapter, you will be able to:

- Describe the alternative methods of allocating scarce resources

- Explain the connection between demand and marginal benefit and define consumer surplus; and explain the connection between supply and marginal cost and define producer surplus

- Explain the conditions under which markets are efficient and inefficient

- Explain the main ideas about fairness and evaluate claims that markets result in unfair outcomes

Every day, millions of people make self-interested choices to drive to work rather than take the bus or train. The outcome of these choices is gridlock and a lot of lost time. Are we using our highways and our time efficiently?

One way of eliminating traffic jams is to make people pay for road use—to make all the highways toll-roads. Rich people can easily pay a toll, but poor people can't afford to pay. Would tolls be fair?

We'll answer these questions about highway use in *Economics in the News* at the end of the chapter. But first, we examine the efficiency and fairness of alternative ways of allocating scarce resources.

◆ Resource Allocation Methods

If resources were abundant, and not scarce, we would not need to allocate them among alternative uses. But resources *are* scarce: They must be allocated somehow. Our goal is to discover how resources might be allocated efficiently and fairly. So what are the alternative methods of allocating scarce resources?

Eight alternative methods that might be used are

- Market price
- Command
- Majority rule
- Contest
- First-come, first-served
- Lottery
- Personal characteristics
- Force

Let's briefly examine each method.

Market Price

When a market price allocates a scarce resource, the people who are willing and able to pay that price get the resource. Two kinds of people decide not to pay the market price: those who can afford to pay but choose not to buy and those who are too poor and simply can't afford to buy.

For many goods and services, distinguishing between those who choose not to buy and those who can't afford to buy doesn't matter. But for a few items, it does matter. For example, poor people can't afford to pay school fees and doctors' fees. Because poor people can't afford items that most people consider to be essential, these items are usually allocated by one of the other methods.

Command

A **command system** allocates resources by the order (command) of someone in authority. In the U.S. economy, the command system is used extensively inside firms and government departments. For example, if you have a job, most likely someone tells you what to do. Your labor is allocated to specific tasks by a command.

A command system works well in organizations in which the lines of authority and responsibility are clear and it is easy to monitor the activities being per-

formed. But a command system works badly when the range of activities to be monitored is large and when it is easy for people to fool those in authority. North Korea uses a command system and it works so badly that it even fails to deliver an adequate supply of food.

Majority Rule

Majority rule allocates resources in the way that a majority of voters choose. Societies use majority rule to elect representative governments that make some of the biggest decisions. For example, majority rule decides the tax rates that end up allocating scarce resources between private use and public use. And majority rule decides how tax dollars are allocated among competing uses such as education and healthcare.

Majority rule works well when the decisions being made affect large numbers of people and self-interest must be suppressed to use resources most effectively.

Contest

A contest allocates resources to a winner (or a group of winners). Sporting events use this method. Serena Williams competes with other tennis professionals, and the winner gets the biggest payoff. But contests are more general than those in a sports arena, though we don't normally call them contests. For example, Bill Gates won a contest to provide the world's personal computer operating system.

Contests do a good job when the efforts of the "players" are hard to monitor and reward directly. When a manager offers everyone in the company the opportunity to win a big prize, people are motivated to work hard and try to become the winner. Only a few people end up with a big prize, but many people work harder in the process of trying to win. The total output produced by the workers is much greater than it would be without the contest.

First-Come, First-Served

A first-come, first-served method allocates resources to those who are first in line. Many casual restaurants won't accept reservations. They use first-come, first-served to allocate their scarce tables. Highway space is allocated in this way too: The first to arrive at the on-ramp gets the road space. If too many vehicles enter the highway, the speed slows and people wait in line for some space to become available.

First-come, first-served works best when, as in the above examples, a scarce resource can serve just one user at a time in a sequence. By serving the user who arrives first, this method minimizes the time spent waiting for the resource to become free.

Lottery

Lotteries allocate resources to those who pick the winning number, draw the lucky cards, or come up lucky on some other gaming system. State lotteries and casinos reallocate millions of dollars' worth of goods and services every year.

But lotteries are more widespread than jackpots and roulette wheels in casinos. They are used to allocate landing slots to airlines at some airports and places in the New York and Boston marathons, and have been used to allocate fishing rights and the electromagnetic spectrum used by cellphones.

Lotteries work best when there is no effective way to distinguish among potential users of a scarce resource.

Personal Characteristics

When resources are allocated on the basis of personal characteristics, people with the "right" characteristics get the resources. Some of the resources that matter most to you are allocated in this way. For example, you will choose a marriage partner on the basis of personal characteristics. But this method can also be used in unacceptable ways. Allocating the best jobs to white, Anglo-Saxon males and discriminating against visible minorities and women is an example.

Force

Force plays a crucial role, for both good and ill, in allocating scarce resources. Let's start with the ill.

War, the use of military force by one nation against another, has played an enormous role historically in allocating resources. The economic supremacy of European settlers in the Americas and Australia owes much to the use of this method.

Theft, the taking of the property of others without their consent, also plays a large role. Both large-scale organized crime and small-scale petty crime collectively allocate billions of dollars worth of resources annually.

But force plays a crucial positive role in allocating resources. It provides the state with an effective method of transferring wealth from the rich to the poor, and it provides the legal framework in which voluntary exchange in markets takes place.

A legal system is the foundation on which our market economy functions. Without courts to enforce contracts, it would not be possible to do business. But the courts could not enforce contracts without the ability to apply force if necessary. The state provides the ultimate force that enables the courts to do their work.

More broadly, the force of the state is essential to uphold the principle of the rule of law. This principle is the bedrock of civilized economic (and social and political) life. With the rule of law upheld, people can go about their daily economic lives with the assurance that their property will be protected—that they can sue for violations against their property (and be sued if they violate the property of others).

Free from the burden of protecting their property and confident in the knowledge that those with whom they trade will honor their agreements, people can get on with focusing on the activity in which they have a comparative advantage and trading for mutual gain.

REVIEW QUIZ

1 Why do we need methods of allocating scarce resources?
2 Describe the alternative methods of allocating scarce resources.
3 Provide an example of each allocation method that illustrates when it works well.
4 Provide an example of each allocation method that illustrates when it works badly.

Work these questions in Study Plan 5.1 and get instant feedback. Do a Key Terms Quiz.   MyEconLab

In the next sections, we're going to see how a market can achieve an efficient use of resources, examine the obstacles to efficiency, and see how sometimes an alternative method might improve on the market. After looking at efficiency, we'll turn our attention to the more difficult issue of fairness.

◆ Benefit, Cost, and Surplus

Resources are allocated efficiently and in the *social interest* when they are used in the ways that people value most highly. You saw in Chapter 2 that this outcome occurs when the quantities produced are at the point on the *PPF* at which marginal benefit equals marginal cost (see pp. 35–37). We're now going to see whether competitive markets produce the efficient quantities.

We begin on the demand side of a market.

Demand, Willingness to Pay, and Value

In everyday life, we talk about "getting value for money." When we use this expression, we are distinguishing between *value* and *price*. Value is what we get, and price is what we pay.

The value of one more unit of a good or service is its marginal benefit. We measure marginal benefit by the maximum price that is willingly paid for another unit of the good or service. But willingness to pay determines demand. *A demand curve is a marginal benefit curve.*

In Fig. 5.1(a), Lisa is willing to pay $1 for the 30th slice of pizza and $1 is her marginal benefit from that slice. In Fig. 5.1(b), Nick is willing to pay $1 for the 10th slice of pizza and $1 is his marginal benefit from that slice. But at what quantity is the market willing to pay $1 for the marginal slice? The answer is provided by the *market demand curve*.

Individual Demand and Market Demand

The relationship between the price of a good and the quantity demanded by one person is called *individual demand*. And the relationship between the price of a good and the quantity demanded by all buyers is called *market demand*.

> The market demand curve is the horizontal sum of the individual demand curves and is formed by adding the quantities demanded by all the individuals at each price.

Figure 5.1(c) illustrates the market demand for pizza if Lisa and Nick are the only people in the market. Lisa's demand curve in part (a) and Nick's demand curve in part (b) sum horizontally to the market demand curve in part (c).

FIGURE 5.1   Individual Demand, Market Demand, and Marginal Social Benefit

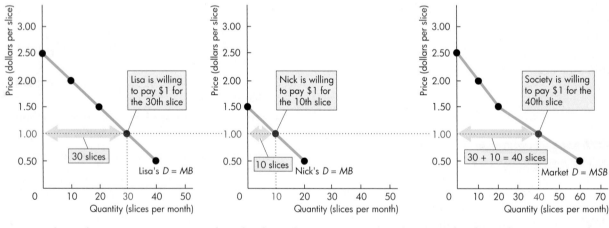

(a) Lisa's demand   **(b) Nick's demand**   **(c) Market demand**

At a price of $1 a slice, the quantity demanded by Lisa is 30 slices and the quantity demanded by Nick is 10 slices, so the quantity demanded by the market is 40 slices. Lisa's demand curve in part (a) and Nick's demand curve in part (b) sum horizontally to the market demand curve in part (c). The market demand curve is the marginal social benefit (*MSB*) curve.

MyEconLab Animation

At a price of $1 a slice, Lisa demands 30 slices and Nick demands 10 slices, so the market quantity demanded at $1 a slice is 40 slices.

For Lisa and Nick, their demand curves are their marginal benefit curves. For society, the market demand curve is the marginal benefit curve. We call the marginal benefit to the entire society *marginal social benefit*. So the market demand curve is also the *marginal social benefit (MSB) curve*.

Consumer Surplus

We don't always have to pay as much as we are willing to pay. We get a bargain. When people buy something for less than it is worth to them, they receive a consumer surplus. **Consumer surplus** is the excess of the benefit received from a good over the amount paid for it. We can calculate consumer surplus as the marginal benefit (or value) of a good minus its price, summed over the quantity bought.

Figure 5.2(a) shows Lisa's consumer surplus from pizza when the price is $1 a slice. At this price, she buys 30 slices a month because the 30th slice is worth exactly $1 to her. But Lisa is willing to pay $2 for the 10th slice, so her marginal benefit from this slice is

$1 more than she pays for it—she receives a surplus of $1 on the 10th slice.

Lisa's consumer surplus is the sum of the surpluses on *all of the slices she buys*. This sum is the area of the green triangle—the area below the demand curve and above the market price line. The area of this triangle is equal to its base (30 slices) multiplied by its height ($1.50) divided by 2, which is $22.50. The area of the blue rectangle in Fig. 5.2(a) shows what Lisa pays for 30 slices of pizza.

Figure 5.2(b) shows Nick's consumer surplus, and part (c) shows the consumer surplus for the market. The consumer surplus for the market is the sum of the consumer surpluses of Lisa and Nick.

All goods and services have decreasing marginal benefit, so people receive more benefit from their consumption than the amount they pay.

Supply and Marginal Cost

Your next task is to see how market supply reflects marginal cost. The connection between supply and cost closely parallels the related ideas about demand and benefit that you've just studied. Firms are in business to make a profit. To do so, they must sell

FIGURE 5.2 Demand and Consumer Surplus

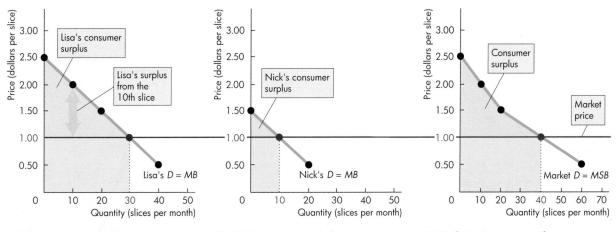

(a) Lisa's consumer surplus   **(b) Nick's consumer surplus**   **(c) Market consumer surplus**

Lisa is willing to pay $2 for her 10th slice of pizza in part (a). At a market price of $1 a slice, Lisa receives a surplus of $1 on the 10th slice. The green triangle shows her consumer surplus on the 30 slices she buys at $1 a slice. The

green triangle in part (b) shows Nick's consumer surplus on the 10 slices that he buys at $1 a slice. The green area in part (c) shows the consumer surplus for the market. The blue rectangles show the amounts spent on pizza.

MyEconLab Animation and Draw Graph

their output for a price that exceeds the cost of production. Let's investigate the relationship between cost and price.

Supply, Cost, and Minimum Supply-Price

Firms make a profit when they receive more from the sale of a good or service than the cost of producing it. Just as consumers distinguish between value and price, so producers distinguish between *cost* and *price*. Cost is what a firm gives up when it produces a good or service and price is what a firm receives when it sells the good or service.

The cost of producing one more unit of a good or service is its marginal cost. Marginal cost is the minimum price that producers must receive to induce them to offer one more unit of a good or service for sale. But the minimum supply-price determines supply. *A supply curve is a marginal cost curve.*

In Fig. 5.3(a), Maria is willing to produce the 100th pizza for $15, her marginal cost of that pizza. In Fig. 5.3(b), Max is willing to produce the 50th pizza for $15, his marginal cost.

What quantity is this market willing to produce for $15 a pizza? The answer is provided by the *market supply curve*.

Individual Supply and Market Supply

The relationship between the price of a good and the quantity supplied by one producer is called *individual supply*. And the relationship between the price of a good and the quantity supplied by all producers is called *market supply*.

The market supply curve is the horizontal sum of the individual supply curves and is formed by adding the quantities supplied by all the producers at each price.

Figure 5.3(c) illustrates the market supply of pizzas if Maria and Max are the only producers. Maria's supply curve in part (a) and Max's supply curve in part (b) sum horizontally to the market supply curve in part (c).

At a price of $15 a pizza, Maria supplies 100 pizzas and Max supplies 50 pizzas, so the quantity supplied by the market at $15 a pizza is 150 pizzas.

For Maria and Max, their supply curves are their marginal cost curves. For society, the market supply curve is its marginal cost curve. We call the society's marginal cost *marginal social cost*. So the market supply curve is also the *marginal social cost (MSC) curve*.

FIGURE 5.3 Individual Supply, Market Supply, and Marginal Social Cost

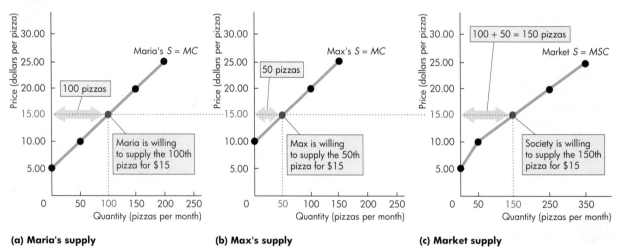

(a) Maria's supply   **(b) Max's supply**   **(c) Market supply**

At a price of $15 a pizza, the quantity supplied by Maria is 100 pizzas and the quantity supplied by Max is 50 pizzas, so the quantity supplied by the market is 150 pizzas. Maria's supply curve in part (a) and Max's supply curve in part (b) sum horizontally to the market supply curve in part (c). The market supply curve is the marginal social cost (MSC) curve.

MyEconLab Animation

Producer Surplus

When price exceeds marginal cost, the firm receives a producer surplus. **Producer surplus** is the excess of the amount received from the sale of a good or service over the cost of producing it. We calculate producer surplus as the price received minus the marginal cost (or minimum supply-price), summed over the quantity sold.

Figure 5.4(a) shows Maria's producer surplus from pizza when the price is $15 a pizza. At this price, she sells 100 pizzas a month because the 100th pizza costs her $15 to produce. But Maria is willing to produce the 50th pizza for her marginal cost, which is $10, so she receives a surplus of $5 on this pizza.

Maria's producer surplus is the sum of the surpluses on the pizzas she sells. This sum is the area of the blue triangle—the area below the market price and above the supply curve. The area of this triangle is equal to its base (100) multiplied by its height ($10) divided by 2, which is $500.

The red area below the supply curve in Fig. 5.4(a) shows what it costs Maria to produce 100 pizzas.

The area of the blue triangle in Fig. 5.4(b) shows Max's producer surplus and the blue area in Fig. 5.4(c) shows the producer surplus for the market.

The producer surplus for the market is the sum of the producer surpluses of Maria and Max.

◆ **REVIEW QUIZ**

1 What is the relationship between the marginal benefit, value, and demand?
2 What is the relationship between individual demand and market demand?
3 What is consumer surplus? How is it measured?
4 What is the relationship between the marginal cost, minimum supply-price, and supply?
5 What is the relationship between individual supply and market supply?
6 What is producer surplus? How is it measured?

Work these questions in Study Plan 5.2 and get instant feedback. Do a Key Terms Quiz.   MyEconLab

Consumer surplus and producer surplus can be used to measure the efficiency of a market. Let's see how we can use these concepts to study the efficiency of a competitive market.

FIGURE 5.4 Supply and Producer Surplus

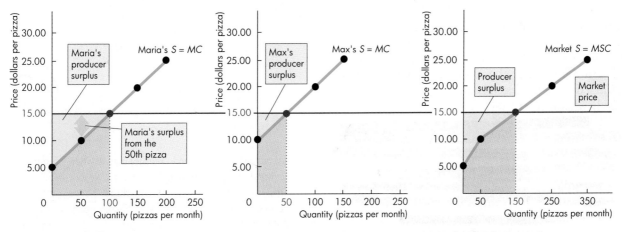

(a) Maria's producer surplus

(b) Max's producer surplus

(c) Market producer surplus

Maria is willing to produce the 50th pizza for $10 in part (a). At a market price of $15 a pizza, Maria gets a surplus of $5 on the 50th pizza. The blue triangle shows her producer surplus on the 100 pizzas she sells at $15 each.

The blue triangle in part (b) shows Max's producer surplus on the 50 pizzas that he sells at $15 each. The blue area in part (c) shows producer surplus for the market. The red areas show the cost of producing the pizzas sold.

MyEconLab Animation and Draw Graph

◆ Is the Competitive Market Efficient?

Figure 5.5(a) shows the market for pizza. The market forces that you studied in Chapter 3 (pp. 66–67) pull the pizza market to its equilibrium price of $15 a pizza and equilibrium quantity of 10,000 pizzas a day. Buyers enjoy a consumer surplus (green area) and sellers enjoy a producer surplus (blue area), but is this competitive equilibrium efficient?

Efficiency of Competitive Equilibrium

You've seen that the market demand curve for a good or service tells us the marginal social benefit from it. You've also seen that the market supply curve of a good or service tells us the marginal social cost of producing it.

Equilibrium in a competitive market occurs when the quantity demanded equals the quantity supplied at the intersection of the demand curve and the supply curve. At this intersection point, marginal social benefit on the demand curve equals marginal social cost on the supply curve. This equality is the condition for allocative efficiency. So in equilibrium, a competitive market achieves allocative efficiency.

Figure 5.5 illustrates the efficiency of competitive equilibrium. The demand curve and the supply curve intersect in part (a) and marginal social benefit equals marginal social cost in part (b).

If production is less than 10,000 pizzas a day, the marginal pizza is valued more highly than it costs to produce. If production exceeds 10,000 pizzas a day, the marginal pizza costs more to produce than the value that consumers place on it. Only when 10,000 pizzas a day are produced is the marginal pizza worth exactly what it costs.

The competitive market pushes the quantity of pizzas produced to its efficient level of 10,000 a day. If production is less than 10,000 pizzas a day, a shortage raises the price, which increases production. If production exceeds 10,000 pizzas a day, a surplus of pizzas lowers the price, which decreases production. So a competitive pizza market is efficient.

Figure 5.5(a) also shows the consumer surplus and producer surplus. The sum of consumer surplus and producer surplus is called **total surplus**. When the efficient quantity is produced, total surplus is maximized. Buyers and sellers acting in their self-interest end up promoting the social interest.

FIGURE 5.5   An Efficient Market for Pizza

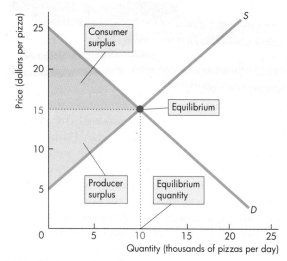

(a) Equilibrium and surpluses

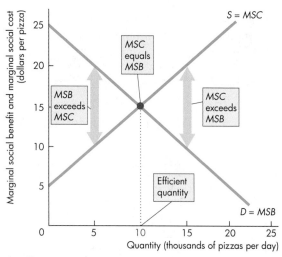

(b) Efficiency

Competitive equilibrium in part (a) occurs when the quantity demanded equals the quantity supplied. Resources are used efficiently in part (b) when marginal social benefit, *MSB*, equals marginal social cost, *MSC*. Total surplus, which is the sum of consumer surplus (the green triangle) and producer surplus (the blue triangle) is maximized.

The efficient quantity in part (b) is the same as the equilibrium quantity in part (a). The competitive pizza market produces the efficient quantity of pizzas.

_____ MyEconLab Animation and Draw Graph _____

ECONOMICS IN ACTION

Seeing the Invisible Hand

Adam Smith said that a seller in a competitive market is "led by *an invisible hand* to promote an end which was no part of his intention" (see p. 8). Smith believed that the invisible hand sends resources to the uses in which they have the highest value.

You can't *see* the invisible hand, but you can imagine it, and you can see its consequences in the cartoon and in today's world.

Umbrella for Sale The cold drinks vendor has cold drinks and shade and he has a marginal cost and a minimum supply-price of each. The reader on the park bench has a marginal benefit and willingness to pay for each. The reader's marginal benefit from shade exceeds the vendor's marginal cost; but the vendor's marginal cost of a cold drink exceeds the reader's marginal benefit. They trade the umbrella. The vendor gets a producer surplus from selling the shade for more than its marginal cost, and the reader gets a consumer surplus from buying the shade for less than its marginal benefit. Both are better off and the umbrella has moved to a higher-valued use.

The Invisible Hand at Work Today Many of the markets in which you trade work like that in the cartoon to achieve an efficient allocation of resources.

When you order a pizza for home delivery, you make a choice about how scarce resources will be used. You make your choice in your self-interest. The pizza cook and the person who delivers your pizza also make their choices in their self-interest.

The pizza market coordinates these choices. You buy the quantity of pizza that makes the price you pay equal to your marginal benefit. And the pizza producer sells the quantity at which the price equals his marginal cost. Total surplus is maximized in an efficient pizza market.

© The New Yorker Collection 1985 Mike Twohy from cartoonbank.com. All Rights Reserved.

Market Failure

Markets are not always efficient, and when a market is inefficient, we call the outcome **market failure**. In a market failure, either too little (underproduction) or too much (overproduction) of an item is produced.

Underproduction In Fig. 5.6(a), the quantity of pizzas produced is 5,000 a day. At this quantity, consumers are willing to pay $20 for a pizza that costs only $10 to produce. The quantity produced is inefficient—there is underproduction—and total surplus is smaller than its maximum possible level.

We measure the scale of inefficiency by **deadweight loss**, which is the decrease in total surplus that results from an inefficient level of production. The gray triangle in Fig. 5.6(a) shows the deadweight loss.

Overproduction In Fig. 5.6(b), the quantity of pizzas produced is 15,000 a day. At this quantity, consumers are willing to pay only $10 for a pizza that costs $20 to produce. By producing the 15,000th pizza, $10 of resources are wasted. Again, the gray triangle shows the deadweight loss, which reduces the total surplus to less than its maximum.

Inefficient production creates a deadweight loss that is borne by the entire society: It is a social loss.

Sources of Market Failure

Obstacles to efficiency that bring market failure are

- Price and quantity regulations
- Taxes and subsidies
- Externalities
- Public goods and common resources
- Monopoly
- High transactions costs

Price and Quantity Regulations A *price regulation*, either a price cap or a price floor, blocks the price adjustments that balance the quantity demanded and the quantity supplied and lead to underproduction. A *quantity regulation* that limits the amount that a farm is permitted to produce also leads to underproduction.

Taxes and Subsidies *Taxes* increase the prices paid by buyers, lower the prices received by sellers, and lead to underproduction. *Subsidies*, which are payments by the government to producers, decrease the prices paid by buyers, increase the prices received by sellers, and lead to overproduction.

FIGURE 5.6 Underproduction and Overproduction

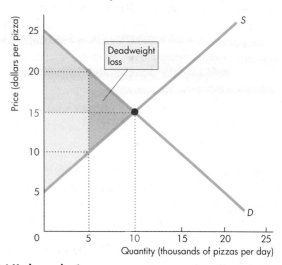

(a) Underproduction

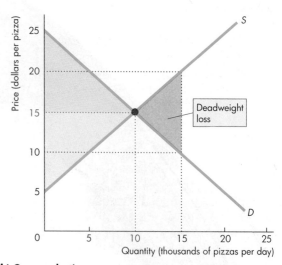

(b) Overproduction

If 5,000 pizzas a day are produced, in part (a), total surplus (the sum of the green and blue areas) is smaller than its maximum by the amount of the deadweight loss (the gray triangle). At all quantities below 10,000 pizzas a day, the benefit from one more pizza exceeds its cost.

If 15,000 pizzas a day are produced, in part (b), total surplus is also smaller than its maximum by the amount of the deadweight loss. At all quantities in excess of 10,000 pizzas a day, the cost of one more pizza exceeds its benefit.

MyEconLab Animation and Draw Graph

Externalities An *externality* is a cost or a benefit that affects someone other than the seller or the buyer. An *external cost* arises when an electric utility burns coal and emits carbon dioxide. The utility doesn't consider the cost of climate change when it decides how much power to produce. The result is overproduction. An *external benefit* arises when an apartment owner installs a smoke detector and decreases her neighbor's fire risk. She doesn't consider the benefit to her neighbor when she decides how many detectors to install. The result is underproduction.

Public Goods and Common Resources A *public good* is a good or service from which everyone benefits and no one can be excluded. National defense is an example. A competitive market would underproduce national defense because everyone would try to free ride on everyone else.

A *common resource* is owned by no one but is available to be used by everyone. Atlantic salmon is an example. It is in everyone's self-interest to ignore the costs they impose on others when they decide how much of a common resource to use: It is overused.

Monopoly A *monopoly* is a firm that is the sole provider of a good or service. Local water supply and cable television are supplied by firms that are monopolies. The monopoly's self-interest is to maximize its profit, and because it has no competitors, it produces too little and charges too high a price: It underproduces.

High Transactions Costs When you buy your first house, you will also buy the services of an agent and a lawyer to do the transaction. Economists call the costs of the services that enable a market to bring buyers and sellers together **transactions costs**. It is costly to operate *any* market, but some markets are so costly to operate that they simply don't. For example, there's no market in time slots on a local tennis court. Instead, the court uses first-come, first-served: You hang around until the court becomes vacant and "pay" with your waiting time. When transactions costs are high, the market might underproduce.

You now know the conditions under which resource allocation is efficient. You've seen how a competitive market can be efficient, and you've seen some obstacles to efficiency. Can alternative allocation methods improve on the market?

Alternatives to the Market

When a market is inefficient, can one of the alternative nonmarket methods that we described at the beginning of this chapter do a better job? Sometimes it can.

Often, majority rule might be used in an attempt to improve the allocation of resources. But majority rule has its own shortcomings. A group that pursues the self-interest of its members can become the majority. For example, a price or quantity regulation that creates inefficiency is almost always the result of a self-interested group becoming the majority and imposing costs on the minority. Also, with majority rule, votes must be translated into actions by bureaucrats who have their own agendas based on their self-interest.

Managers in firms issue commands and avoid the transactions costs that they would incur if they went to a market every time they needed a job done.

First-come, first-served works best in some situations. Think about the scene at a busy ATM. Instead of waiting in line people might trade places at a "market" price. But someone would need to ensure that trades were honored. At a busy ATM, first-come, first-served is the most efficient arrangement.

There is no one efficient mechanism that allocates all resources efficiently. But markets, when supplemented by other mechanisms such as majority rule, command systems, and first-come, first-served, do an amazingly good job.

◆ REVIEW QUIZ

1 Do competitive markets use resources efficiently? Explain why or why not.
2 What is deadweight loss and under what conditions does it occur?
3 What are the obstacles to achieving an efficient allocation of resources in the market economy?

Work these questions in Study Plan 5.3 and get instant feedback. Do a Key Terms Quiz.   MyEconLab

Is an efficient allocation of resources also a fair allocation? Does the competitive market provide people with fair incomes for their work? Do people always pay a fair price for the things they buy? Don't we need the government to step into some competitive markets to prevent the price from rising too high or falling too low? Let's now study these questions.

◆ Is the Competitive Market Fair?

When a natural disaster strikes, such as a severe winter storm or a hurricane, the prices of many essential items jump. The reason prices jump is that the demand and willingness to pay for these items has increased, but the supply has not changed. So the higher prices achieve an efficient allocation of scarce resources. News reports of these price hikes almost never talk about efficiency. Instead, they talk about equity or fairness. The claim that is often made is that it is unfair for profit-seeking dealers to cheat the victims of natural disaster.

Similarly, when low-skilled people work for a wage that is below what most would regard as a "living wage," the media and politicians talk of employers taking unfair advantage of their workers.

How do we decide whether something is fair or unfair? You know when you *think* something is unfair, but how do you *know*? What are the *principles* of fairness?

Philosophers have tried for centuries to answer this question. Economists have offered their answers too. But before we look at the proposed answers, you should know that there is no universally agreed upon answer.

Economists agree about efficiency. That is, they agree that it makes sense to make the economic pie as large as possible and to produce it at the lowest possible cost. But they do not agree about equity. That is, they do not agree about what are fair shares of the economic pie for all the people who make it. The reason is that ideas about fairness are not exclusively economic ideas. They touch on politics, ethics, and religion. Nevertheless, economists have thought about these issues and have a contribution to make. Let's examine the views of economists on this topic.

To think about fairness, think of economic life as a game—a serious game. All ideas about fairness can be divided into two broad groups. They are

- It's not fair if the *result* isn't fair.
- It's not fair if the *rules* aren't fair.

It's Not Fair if the *Result* Isn't Fair

The earliest efforts to establish a principle of fairness were based on the view that the result is what matters. The general idea was that it is unfair if people's incomes are too unequal. For example, it is unfair

that a bank president earns millions of dollars a year while a bank teller earns only thousands of dollars. It is unfair that a store owner makes a larger profit and her customers pay higher prices in the aftermath of a winter storm.

During the nineteenth century, economists thought they had made an incredible discovery: Efficiency requires equality of incomes. To make the economic pie as large as possible, it must be cut into equal pieces, one for each person. This idea turns out to be wrong. But there is a lesson in the reason that it is wrong, so this idea is worth a closer look.

Utilitarianism The nineteenth-century idea that only equality brings efficiency is called *utilitarianism*. **Utilitarianism** is a principle that states that we should strive to achieve "the greatest happiness for the greatest number." The people who developed this idea were known as utilitarians. They included the most eminent thinkers, such as Jeremy Bentham and John Stuart Mill.

Utilitarians argued that to achieve "the greatest happiness for the greatest number," income must be transferred from the rich to the poor up to the point of complete equality—to the point at which there are no rich and no poor.

They reasoned in the following way: First, everyone has the same basic wants and a similar capacity to enjoy life. Second, the greater a person's income, the smaller is the marginal benefit of a dollar. The millionth dollar spent by a rich person brings a smaller marginal benefit to that person than the marginal benefit that the thousandth dollar spent brings to a poorer person. So by transferring a dollar from the millionaire to the poorer person, more is gained than is lost. The two people added together are better off.

Figure 5.7 illustrates this utilitarian idea. Tom and Jerry have the same marginal benefit curve, *MB*. (Marginal benefit is measured on the same scale of 1 to 3 for both Tom and Jerry.) Tom is at point *A*. He earns $5,000 a year, and his marginal benefit from a dollar is 3 units. Jerry is at point *B*. He earns $45,000 a year, and his marginal benefit from a dollar is 1 unit. If a dollar is transferred from Jerry to Tom, Jerry loses 1 unit of marginal benefit and Tom gains 3 units. So together, Tom and Jerry are better off—they are sharing the economic pie more efficiently. If a second dollar is transferred, the same thing happens: Tom gains more than Jerry loses. And the same is true for every dollar transferred until they both reach point *C*. At point *C*, Tom and Jerry have $25,000

FIGURE 5.7   Utilitarian Fairness

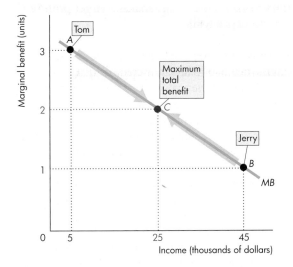

Tom earns $5,000 and has 3 units of marginal benefit at point A. Jerry earns $45,000 and has 1 unit of marginal benefit at point B. If income is transferred from Jerry to Tom, Jerry's loss is less than Tom's gain. Only when each of them has $25,000 and 2 units of marginal benefit (at point C) can the sum of their total benefit increase no further.

MyEconLab Animation

each and a marginal benefit of 2 units. Now they are sharing the economic pie in the most efficient way. It brings the greatest happiness to Tom and Jerry.

The Big Tradeoff One big problem with the utilitarian ideal of complete equality is that it ignores the costs of making income transfers. Recognizing the costs of making income transfers leads to what is called the **big tradeoff**, which is a tradeoff between efficiency and fairness.

The big tradeoff is based on the following facts. Income can be transferred from people with high incomes to people with low incomes only by taxing the high incomes. Taxing people's income from employment makes them work less. It results in the quantity of labor being less than the efficient quantity. Taxing people's income from capital makes them save less. It results in the quantity of capital being less than the efficient quantity. With smaller quantities of both labor and capital, the quantity of goods and services produced is less than the efficient quantity. The economic pie shrinks.

The tradeoff is between the size of the economic pie and the degree of equality with which it is shared. The greater the amount of income redistribution through income taxes, the greater is the inefficiency—the smaller is the economic pie.

There is a second source of inefficiency. A dollar taken from a rich person does not end up as a dollar in the hands of a poorer person. Some of the dollar is spent on administration of the tax and transfer system. The cost of tax-collecting agencies, such as the Internal Revenue Service (IRS), and welfare-administering agencies, such as the Centers for Medicare & Medicaid Services (CMS), must be paid with some of the taxes collected. Also, taxpayers hire accountants, auditors, and lawyers to help them ensure that they pay the correct amount of taxes. These activities use skilled labor and capital resources that could otherwise be used to produce goods and services that people value.

When all these costs are taken into account, taking a dollar from a rich person does not give a dollar to a poor person. It is possible that with high taxes, people with low incomes might end up being worse off. Suppose, for example, that highly taxed entrepreneurs decide to work less hard and shut down some of their businesses. Low-income workers get fired and must seek other, perhaps even lower-paid, work.

Today, because of the big tradeoff, no one says that fairness requires complete equality of incomes.

Make the Poorest as Well Off as Possible A new solution to the big-tradeoff problem was proposed by philosopher John Rawls in a classic book entitled *A Theory of Justice*, published in 1971. Rawls says that, taking all the costs of income transfers into account, the fair distribution of the economic pie is the one that makes the poorest person as well off as possible. The incomes of rich people should be taxed, and after paying the costs of administering the tax and transfer system, what is left should be transferred to the poor. But the taxes must not be so high that they make the economic pie shrink to the point at which the poorest person ends up with a smaller piece. A bigger share of a smaller pie can be less than a smaller share of a bigger pie. The goal is to make the piece enjoyed by the poorest person as big as possible. Most likely, this piece will not be an equal share.

The "fair results" idea requires a change in the results after the game is over. Some economists say that these changes are themselves unfair and propose a different way of thinking about fairness.

It's Not Fair if the *Rules* Aren't Fair

The idea that it's not fair if the rules aren't fair is based on a fundamental principle that seems to be hardwired into the human brain: the symmetry principle. The **symmetry principle** is the requirement that people in similar situations be treated similarly. It is the moral principle that lies at the center of all the big religions and that says, in some form or other, "Behave toward other people in the way you expect them to behave toward you."

In economic life, this principle translates into *equality of opportunity*. But equality of opportunity to do what? This question is answered by the philosopher Robert Nozick in a book entitled *Anarchy, State, and Utopia*, published in 1974.

Nozick argues that the idea of fairness as an outcome or result cannot work and that fairness must be based on the fairness of the rules. He suggests that fairness obeys two rules:

1. The state must enforce laws that establish and protect private property.
2. Private property may be transferred from one person to another only by voluntary exchange.

The first rule says that everything that is valuable must be owned by individuals and that the state must ensure that theft is prevented. The second rule says that the only legitimate way a person can acquire property is to buy it in exchange for something else that the person owns. If these rules, which are the only fair rules, are followed, then the result is fair. It doesn't matter how unequally the economic pie is shared, provided that the pie is made by people, each one of whom voluntarily provides services in exchange for the share of the pie offered in compensation.

These rules satisfy the symmetry principle. If these rules are not followed, the symmetry principle is broken. You can see these facts by imagining a world in which the laws are not followed.

First, suppose that some resources or goods are not owned. They are common property. Then everyone is free to participate in a grab to use them. The strongest will prevail. But when the strongest prevails, the strongest effectively *owns* the resources or goods in question and prevents others from enjoying them.

Second, suppose that we do not insist on voluntary exchange for transferring ownership of resources from one person to another. The alternative is *involuntary* transfer. In simple language, the alternative is theft.

Both of these situations violate the symmetry principle. Only the strong acquire what they want. The weak end up with only the resources and goods that the strong don't want.

In a majority-rule political system, the strong are those in the majority or those with enough resources to influence opinion and achieve a majority.

In contrast, if the two rules of fairness are followed, everyone, strong and weak, is treated in a similar way. All individuals are free to use their resources and human skills to create things that are valued by themselves and others and to exchange the fruits of their efforts with all others. This set of arrangements is the only one that obeys the symmetry principle.

Fair Rules and Efficiency If private property rights are enforced and if voluntary exchange takes place in a competitive market with none of the obstacles described above (p. 114), resources will be allocated efficiently.

According to the Nozick fair-rules view, no matter how unequal is the resulting distribution of income and wealth, it will be fair.

It would be better if everyone were as well off as those with the highest incomes, but scarcity prevents that outcome and the best attainable outcome is the efficient one.

Case Study: A Generator Shortage in a Natural Disaster

Hurricane Katrina shut down electricity supplies over a wide area and increased the demand for portable generators. What is the fair way to allocate the available generators?

If the market price is used, the outcome is efficient. Sellers *and buyers* are better off and no one is worse off. But people who own generators make a larger profit and the generators go to those who want them most and can afford them. Is that fair?

On the Nozick rules view, the outcome is fair. On the fair outcome view, the outcome might be considered unfair. But what are the alternatives? They are command; majority rule; contest; first-come, first-served; lottery; personal characteristics; and force. Except by chance, none of these methods delivers an allocation of generators that is either fair or efficient. It is unfair in the rules view because the distribution involves involuntary transfers of resources among citizens. It is unfair in the results view because the poorest don't end up being made as well off as possible.

◆ AT **ISSUE**

Price Gouging

Price gouging is the practice of offering an essential item for sale following a natural disaster at a price much higher than its normal price.

In the aftermath of Hurricane Katrina, John Shepperson bought 19 generators and rented a U-Haul truck to transport them from his Kentucky home to a town in Mississippi that had lost its electricity supply. He offered the generators to eager buyers at twice the price he had paid for them. But before Mr. Shepperson had made a sale, the Mississippi police confiscated the generators and put him in jail for four days for price gouging.

In **Favor of a Law Against Price Gouging**

Supporters of laws against price gouging say

- It unfairly exploits vulnerable needy buyers.
- It unfairly rewards unscrupulous sellers.
- In situations of extraordinary shortage, prices should be regulated to prevent these abuses and scarce resources should be allocated by one of the non-market mechanisms such as majority vote or equal shares for all.

Should the price that this seller of generators may charge be regulated?

The **Economist's Response**

Economists say that preventing a voluntary market transaction leads to inefficiency—it makes some people worse off without making anyone better off.

- In the figure below, when the demand for generators increases from D_0 to D_1, the equilibrium price rises from \$200 to \$600.
- Calling the price rise "gouging" and blocking it with a law prevents additional units from being made available and creates a deadweight loss.

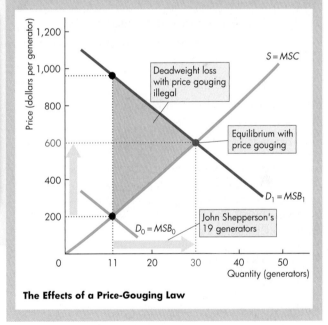

The Effects of a Price-Gouging Law

◆ REVIEW QUIZ

1. What are the two big approaches to thinking about fairness?
2. What is the utilitarian idea of fairness and what is wrong with it?
3. Explain the big tradeoff. What idea of fairness has been developed to deal with it?
4. What is the idea of fairness based on fair rules?

Work these questions in Study Plan 5.4 and get instant feedback. Do a Key TermsQuiz.   MyEconLab

◆ You've now studied efficiency and equity (fairness), the two biggest issues that run through the whole of economics. *Economics in the News* on pp. 120–121 looks at an example of an *inefficiency* in our economy today. At many points throughout this book—and in your life—you will return to and use the ideas you've learned in this chapter. We start to apply these ideas in the next chapter where we study some sources of *in*efficiency and *un*fairness.

Making Traffic Flow Efficiently

A Fundamental Law of Road Congestion

American Economic Review
October, 2011

It is not an everyday occurrence for economic research to make the news. But an article in the *American Economic Review* by Gilles Duranton and Matthew A. Turner of the University of Toronto entitled "The Fundamental Law of Road Congestion: Evidence from U.S. Cities," caught the attention of several newspapers and magazines for its eyepopping findings and implicit recommendation.

Noting that an average American household spends almost 3 hours a day in a passenger vehicle achieving an average speed of less than 30 miles per hour, Professors Duranton and Turner wanted to find out how it might be possible to end the rush-hour crawl, ease traffic congestion, and make the nation's highways more productive.

To get the answers, they studied traffic flows and highways in all the major U.S. cities in 1983, 1993, and 2003 to determine the effect of adding highway capacity on traffic volumes and flows.

Their startling discovery is that on interstate highways, increasing highway capacity increases vehicle miles traveled by the same percentage. Residents and businesses drive more, and better highways attract inward migration.

Durant and Turner also found that increasing the capacity of one type of road diverts little traffic from other types of roads.

And they found that increasing the provision of public transportation does not lower congestion.

They concluded that the only candidate for improving traffic flow is to use a congestion pricing system.

Source of information: "The Fundamental Law of Road Congestion: Evidence from US Cities", *American Economic Review*, 101(6): 2616-52, (October, 2011).

MyEconLab More Economics in the News

ESSENCE OF THE STORY

- Economists Gilles Duranton and Matthew Turner discovered that adding a lane to a highway does not ease congestion.

- Highway use increases in proportion to the available roadways.

- Increasing the capacity of one road does not reduce congestion on others.

- Duranton and Turner say that congestion pricing is the only available solution to overcrowded highways.

ECONOMIC ANALYSIS

- The discovery that adding a highway does not ease congestion points to congestion pricing as a solution. Let's see how a congestion price works.

- A highway has the marginal social cost curve *MSC* in the figures. The highway can carry only 10,000 vehicles per hour with no congestion.

- At off-peak times, the demand curve and marginal benefit curve is $D_o = MSB_o$; and the peak time demand curve and marginal benefit curve is $D_p = MSB_p$.

- Figure 1 illustrates inefficient road use. At off-peak, the outcome is efficient but at the peak demand time, at a zero price, 40,000 vehicles per hour enter the road. The marginal social cost is $6 per vehicle-hour and there is a deadweight loss (of time and gasoline) shown by the gray triangle.

- Figure 2 illustrates efficient road use at the peak period. Imposing a congestion charge of $3 per vehicle-hour brings an equilibrium at 25,000 vehicles per hour, which is the efficient quantity. Total surplus, the sum of consumer surplus (green) *plus* producer surplus (blue), is maximized.

- Congestion charges would be paid by all road users, regardless of whether they are rich or poor, but they don't have to leave the poor worse off.

- Revenue raised from congestion charges can be redistributed to low-income households if there is a fairness problem.

- So long as road users pay the marginal social cost of their decision, road use is efficient.

- London has a simple system of congestion pricing that imposes a charge when a vehicle enters a central congestion zone.

- Singapore has the world's most sophisticated congestion pricing with the price displayed on gantries (see photo), and the price rises as congestion increases and falls as congestion eases.

- Advances in technology make congestion pricing an attractive alternative to congestion.

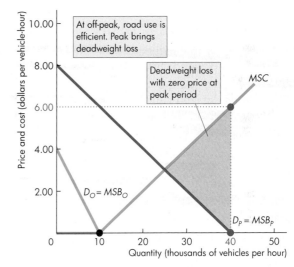

Figure 1 Inefficient Rush-Hour Road Use

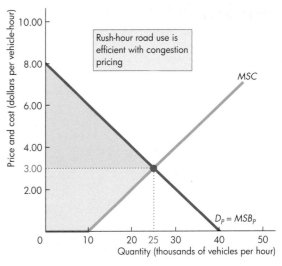

While traffic grinds to a halt on U.S. freeways, Electronic Road Pricing (ERP) keeps vehicles moving in Singapore.

Figure 2 Efficient Rush-Hour Road Use

SUMMARY

Key Points

Resource Allocation Methods (pp. 106–107)

■ Because resources are scarce, some mechanism must allocate them.

■ The alternative allocation methods are market price; command; majority rule; contest; first-come, first-served; lottery; personal characteristics; and force.

Working Study Plan Problem 1 will give you a better understanding of resource allocation methods.

Benefit, Cost, and Surplus (pp. 108–111)

■ The maximum price willingly paid is marginal benefit, so a demand curve is also a marginal benefit curve.

■ The market demand curve is the horizontal sum of the individual demand curves and is the marginal social benefit curve.

■ Value is what people are *willing to* pay; price is what people *must* pay.

■ Consumer surplus is the excess of the benefit received from a good or service over the amount paid for it.

■ The minimum supply-price is marginal cost, so a supply curve is also a marginal cost curve.

■ The market supply curve is the horizontal sum of the individual supply curves and is the marginal social cost curve.

■ Cost is what producers pay; price is what producers receive.

■ Producer surplus is the excess of the amount received from the sale of a good or service over the cost of producing it.

Working Study Plan Problems 2 to 7 will give you a better understanding of benefit, cost, and surplus.

Is the Competitive Market Efficient? (pp. 112–115)

■ In a competitive equilibrium, marginal social benefit equals marginal social cost and resource allocation is efficient.

■ Buyers and sellers acting in their self-interest end up promoting the social interest.

■ Total surplus, consumer surplus plus producer surplus, is maximized.

■ Producing less than or more than the efficient quantity creates deadweight loss.

■ Price and quantity regulations; taxes and subsidies; externalities; public goods and common resources; monopoly; and high transactions costs can lead to market failure.

Working Study Plan Problem 8 will give you a better understanding of the efficiency of competitive markets.

Is the Competitive Market Fair? (pp. 116–119)

■ Ideas about fairness can be divided into two groups: fair *results* and fair *rules*.

■ Fair-results ideas require income transfers from the rich to the poor.

■ Fair-rules ideas require property rights and voluntary exchange.

Working Study Plan Problems 9 and 10 will give you a better understanding of the fairness of competitive markets.

Key Terms

Big tradeoff, 117
Command system, 106
Consumer surplus, 109
Deadweight loss, 114

Market failure, 114
Producer surplus, 111
Symmetry principle, 118 ✓
Total surplus, 112

Transactions costs, 115
Utilitarianism, 116

MyEconLab Key Terms Quiz

WORKED PROBLEM

MyEconLab   You can work this problem in Chapter 5 Study Plan.

The figure illustrates the market for sunscreen.

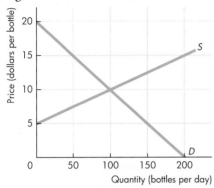

Questions

1. At the market equilibrium, calculate
   (a) consumer surplus and (b) producer surplus.
2. Is the market for sunscreen efficient? Why?
3. What is deadweight loss? Calculate it if factories produce only 50 bottles of sunscreen.

Solutions

1. (a) Consumer surplus is the excess of the benefit received over the amount buyers paid for it. The demand curve tells us the benefit, so consumer surplus equals the area under the demand curve above the market price, summed over the quantity bought. The price paid is $10 a bottle, the quantity bought is 100 bottles, so consumer surplus equals the area of the green triangle in the figure below.

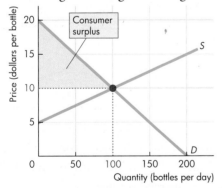

Area of the triangle = (Base × Height) ÷ 2. The base is the quantity bought (100 bottles) and the height the maximum price ($20 a bottle) *minus* the market price ($10 a bottle). Consumer surplus equals 100 × ($20 − $10) ÷ 2, which is $500.

Key Point: Consumer surplus equals the area under the demand curve above the market price.

1. (b) Producer surplus is the excess of the amount received by sellers over the cost of production.

The supply curve tells us the cost of producing the good, so producer surplus is equal to the area under the market price above the supply curve, summed over the quantity sold.
Producer surplus is equal to the area of the blue triangle in the following figure.

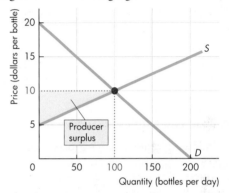

In this triangle, the base is the quantity sold (100 bottles), the height is the market price ($10 a bottle) *minus* the minimum cost ($5 a bottle), so producer surplus is 100 × ($10 − $5) ÷ 2, or $250.

Key Point: Producer surplus equals the area under the market price above the supply curve.

2. Total surplus (consumer surplus plus producer surplus) is a maximum, so the market is efficient.

Key Point: A competitive market is always efficient.

3. When factories produce *less* than the efficient quantity (100 bottles), some total surplus is lost. This loss is called the deadweight loss and it is equal to the area of the gray triangle in the following figure.

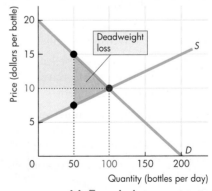

MyEconLab Interactive Animation

The base is the benefit of the 50th bottle *minus* the cost of producing it ($7.50), the height is quantity not produced (50 bottles), so deadweight loss equals ($15 − $7.50) × 50 ÷ 2, which is $187.50.

Key Point: Underproduction creates a deadweight loss.

STUDY PLAN PROBLEMS AND APPLICATIONS

MyEconLab   You can work Problems 1 to 10 in Chapter 5 Study Plan and get instant feedback.

Resource Allocation Methods (Study Plan 5.1)

1. At Chez Panisse, a restaurant in Berkeley, reservations are essential. At Mandarin Dynasty, a restaurant near the University of California San Diego, reservations are recommended. At Eli Cannon's, a restaurant in Middletown, Connecticut, reservations are not accepted.

   Describe the method of allocating scarce table resources at these three restaurants. Why do you think restaurants don't use the market price to allocate their tables?

Benefit, Cost, and Surplus (Study Plan 5.2)

Use the following table to work Problems 2 to 4.
The table gives the demand schedules for train travel for the only buyers in the market, Ann, Beth, and Cy.

Price (dollars per mile)	Quantity demanded (miles)		
	Ann	Beth	Cy
3	30	25	20
4	25	20	15
5	20	15	10
6	15	10	5
7	10	5	0
8	5	0	0
9	0	0	0

2. a. Construct the market demand schedule.
   b. What is the maximum price that each traveler is willing to pay to travel 20 miles? Why?

3. a. What is the marginal social benefit when the total distance traveled is 60 miles?
   b. When the total distance traveled is 60 miles, how many miles does each travel and what is their marginal private benefit?

4. What is each traveler's consumer surplus when the price is $4 a mile? What is the market consumer surplus when the price is $4 a mile?

Use the table in the next column to work Problems 5 to 7.

The table gives the supply schedules of the only sellers of hot air balloon rides: Xavier, Yasmin, and Zack.

5. a. Construct the market supply schedule.
   b. What are the minimum prices that Xavier, Yasmin, and Zack are willing to accept to supply 20 rides? Why?

Price (dollars per ride)	Quantity supplied (rides per week)		
	Xavier	Yasmin	Zack
100	30	25	20
90	25	20	15
80	20	15	10
70	15	10	5
60	10	5	0
50	5	0	0
40	0	0	0

6. a. What is the marginal social cost when the total number of rides is 30?
   b. What is the marginal cost for each supplier when the total number of rides is 30 and how many rides does each of the sellers supply?

7. When the price is $70 a ride, what is each seller's producer surplus? What is the market producer surplus?

Is the Competitive Market Efficient? (Study Plan 5.3)

8. The figure shows the competitive market for cellphones.

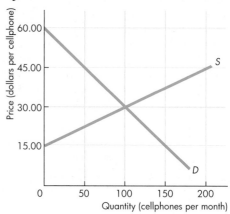

   a. What is the market equilibrium?
   b. Shade in the consumer surplus and label it.
   c. Shade in the producer surplus and label it.
   d. Calculate total surplus.
   e. Is the market for cellphones efficient?

Is the Competitive Market Fair? (Study Plan 5.4)

9. Explain why the allocation method used by each restaurant in Problem 1 is fair or not fair.

10. In the Worked Problem (p. 123), how can the 50 bottles available be allocated to beach-goers? Would the possible methods be fair or unfair?

ADDITIONAL PROBLEMS AND APPLICATIONS

MyEconLab   You can work these problems in MyEconLab if assigned by your instructor.

Resource Allocation Methods

11. At McDonald's, no reservations are accepted; at Panorama at St. Louis Art Museum, reservations are accepted; at the Bissell Mansion restaurant, reservations are essential. Describe the method of allocating tables in these three restaurants. Why do restaurants have different reservations policies?

Benefit, Cost, and Surplus

Use the following table to work Problems 12 to 15. The table gives the supply schedules for jet-ski rides by the only suppliers: Rick, Sam, and Tom.

Price (dollars per ride)	Quantity supplied (rides per day)		
	Rick	Sam	Tom
10.00	0	0	0
12.50	5	0	0
15.00	10	5	0
17.50	15	10	5
20.00	20	15	10

12. What is each owner's minimum supply-price of 10 rides a day?

13. Which owner has the largest producer surplus when the price of a ride is $17.50? Explain.

14. What is the marginal social cost of 45 rides a day?

15. Construct the market supply schedule of jet-ski rides.

16. The table gives the demand and supply schedules for sandwiches.

Price (dollars per sandwich)	Quantity demanded	Quantity supplied
	(sandwiches per hour)	
0	300	0
1	250	50
2	200	100
3	150	150
4	100	200
5	50	250
6	0	300

a. What is the maximum price that consumers are willing to pay for the 200th sandwich?

b. What is the minimum price that producers are willing to accept for the 200th sandwich?

c. If 200 sandwiches a day are available, what is the total surplus?

17. **Home Heating Bills Surge Amid Record Cold**
    If there's one thing that can set home heating costs soaring, it's a long, frigid blast from one of the coldest winters in 20 years and people are going to use 10 to 12 percent more natural gas this year than they have normally.
    Source: CBC News, March 3, 2014

    a. How is the price of natural gas determined?

    b. When demand increases, explain the process by which the market adjusts.

    c. On a graph, show the effect of the increase in demand on consumer surplus and producer surplus.

Is the Competitive Market Efficient?

18. Use the data in the table in Problem 16.
    a. If the sandwich market is efficient, what is the consumer surplus, what is the producer surplus, and what is the total surplus?

    b. If the demand for sandwiches increases and sandwich makers produce the efficient quantity, what happens to producer surplus and deadweight loss?

Use the following news clip to work Problems 19 to 21.

The Right Price for Digital Music
Apple's $1.29-for-the-latest-songs model isn't perfect and isn't it too much to pay for music that appeals to just a few people? We need a system that will be profitable but fair to music lovers. The solution: Price song downloads according to demand. The more people who download a particular song, the higher will be the price of that song; the fewer people who buy a particular song, the lower will be the price of that song. That is a free-market solution—the market would determine the price.
Source: *Slate*, December 5, 2005

Assume that the marginal social cost of downloading a song from the iTunes Store is zero. (This assumption means that the cost of operating the iTunes Store doesn't change if people download more songs.)

19. a. Draw a graph of the market for downloadable music with a price of $1.29 for all the latest songs. On your graph, show consumer surplus and producer surplus.

b. With a price of $1.29 for all the latest songs, is the market efficient or inefficient? If it is inefficient, show the deadweight loss on your graph.

20. If the pricing scheme described in the news clip were adopted, how would consumer surplus, producer surplus, and the deadweight loss change?

21. a. If the pricing scheme described in the news clip were adopted, would the market be efficient or inefficient? Explain.

b. Is the pricing scheme described in the news clip a "free-market solution"? Explain.

22. Only 1 percent of the world supply of water is fit for human consumption. Some places have more water than they can use; some could use much more than they have. The 1 percent available would be sufficient if only it were in the right place.

a. What is the major problem in achieving an efficient use of the world's water?

b. If there were a global market in water, like there is in oil, how do you think the market would be organized?

c. Would a free world market in water achieve an efficient use of the world's water resources? Explain why or why not.

Is the Competitive Market Fair?

23. Use the information in Problem 22. Would a free world market in water achieve a fair use of the world's water resources? Explain why or why not and be clear about the concept of fairness that you are using.

24. The winner of the men's and women's tennis singles at the U.S. Open is paid twice as much as the runner-up, but it takes two players to have a singles final. Is the compensation arrangement fair?

25. **The Scandal of Phone Call Price Gouging by Prisons**

In most U.S. states, the phone company guarantees the prison a commission of a percentage on every call. The average commission is 42% of the cost of the call, but in some states it is 60%. So 60% of what families pay to receive a collect call from their imprisoned relative has nothing to do with the cost of the phone service. Also, the phone company that offers the highest commission is often the company to get the prison contract.

Source: *The Guardian*, May 23, 2012

a. Who is practicing price gouging: the prison, the phone company, or both? Explain.

b. Evaluate the "fairness" of the prison's commission.

Economics in the News

26. After you have studied *Economics in the News* on pp. 120–121, answer the following questions.

a. What is the method used to allocate highway space in the United States and what is the method used in Singapore?

b. Who benefits from the U.S. method of highway resource allocation? Explain your answer using the ideas of marginal social benefit, marginal social cost, consumer surplus, and producer surplus.

c. Who benefits from the Singaporean method of highway resource allocation? Explain your answer using the ideas of marginal social benefit, marginal social cost, consumer surplus, and producer surplus.

d. If road use were rationed by limiting drivers with even-date birthdays to drive only on even days (and odd-date birthdays to drive only on odd days), would highway use be more efficient? Explain your answer.

27. **Fight over Water Rates; Escondido Farmers Say Increase Would Put Them Out of Business**

Agricultural users of water pay less than residential and business users. Since 1993, water rates have increased by more than 90 percent for residential customers and by only 50 percent for agricultural users.

Source: *The San Diego Union-Tribune*, June 14, 2006

a. Do you think that the allocation of water between agricultural and residential users is likely to be efficient? Explain your answer.

b. If agricultural users paid a higher price, would the allocation of resources be more efficient?

c. If agricultural users paid a higher price, what would happen to consumer surplus and producer surplus from water?

d. Is the difference in price paid by agricultural and residential users fair?

6 GOVERNMENT ACTIONS IN MARKETS

After studying this chapter, you will be able to:

◆ Explain how a rent ceiling creates a housing shortage

◆ Explain how a minimum wage law creates unemployment

◆ Explain the effects of a tax

◆ Explain the effects of production quotas and subsidies

◆ Explain how markets for illegal goods work

In New York City, where food servers and grocery clerks earn the minimum wage of $7.25 an hour, a budget one-bedroom apartment rents for $1,000 a month. For the lowest paid, that leaves $160 a month for food, clothing, and other necessities. What can governments do to help these people?

This chapter explains the effects of minimim wage laws and rent ceilings, and *Economics in the News* at the end of the chapter looks at some recent changes in state minimum wages. The chapter also explains the effects of taxes, production quotas and subsidies, and laws that make trading in some things illegal.

◆ A Housing Market with a Rent Ceiling

We spend more of our income on housing than on any other good or service, so it isn't surprising that rents can be a political issue. When rents are high, or when they jump by a large amount, renters might lobby the government for limits on rents.

A government regulation that makes it illegal to charge a price higher than a specified level is called a **price ceiling** or **price cap.**

The effects of a price ceiling on a market depend crucially on whether the ceiling is imposed at a level that is above or below the equilibrium price.

A price ceiling set *above the equilibrium price* has no effect. The reason is that the price ceiling does not constrain the market forces. The force of the law and the market forces are not in conflict. But a price ceiling *below the equilibrium price* has powerful effects on a market. The reason is that the price ceiling attempts to prevent the price from regulating the quantities demanded and supplied. The force of the law and the market forces are in conflict.

When a price ceiling is applied to a housing market, it is called a **rent ceiling**. A rent ceiling set below the equilibrium rent creates

- A housing shortage
- Increased search activity
- A black market

A Housing Shortage

At the equilibrium price, the quantity demanded equals the quantity supplied. In a housing market, when the rent is at the equilibrium level, the quantity of housing supplied equals the quantity of housing demanded and there is neither a shortage nor a surplus of housing.

But at a rent set below the equilibrium rent, the quantity of housing demanded exceeds the quantity of housing supplied—there is a shortage. So if a rent ceiling is set below the equilibrium rent, there will be a shortage of housing.

When there is a shortage, the quantity available is the quantity supplied, and somehow this quantity must be allocated among the frustrated demanders. One way in which this allocation occurs is through increased search activity.

Increased Search Activity

The time spent looking for someone with whom to do business is called **search activity**. We spend some time in search activity almost every time we make a purchase. When you're shopping for the latest hot new cellphone, and you know four stores that stock it, how do you find which store has the best deal? You spend a few minutes on the Internet, checking out the various prices. In some markets, such as the housing market, people spend a lot of time checking the alternatives available before making a choice.

When a price is regulated and there is a shortage, search activity increases. In the case of a rent-controlled housing market, frustrated would-be renters scan the newspapers, not only for housing ads but also for death notices! Any information about newly available housing is useful, and apartment seekers race to be first on the scene when news of a possible supplier breaks.

The *opportunity cost* of a good is equal not only to its price but also to the value of the search time spent finding the good. So the opportunity cost of housing is equal to the rent (a regulated price) plus the time and other resources spent searching for the restricted quantity available. Search activity is costly. It uses time and other resources, such as phone calls, automobiles, and gasoline that could have been used in other productive ways.

A rent ceiling controls only the rent portion of the cost of housing. The cost of increased search activity might end up making the full cost of housing *higher* than it would be without a rent ceiling.

A Black Market

A rent ceiling also encourages illegal trading in a **black market**, an illegal market in which the equilibrium price exceeds the price ceiling. Black markets occur in rent-controlled housing and many other markets. For example, scalpers run black markets in tickets for big sporting events and rock concerts.

When a rent ceiling is in force, frustrated renters and landlords constantly seek ways of increasing rents. One common way is for a new tenant to pay a high price for worthless fittings, such as charging $2,000 for threadbare drapes. Another is for the tenant to pay an exorbitant price for new locks and keys—called "key money."

The level of a black market rent depends on how tightly the rent ceiling is enforced. With loose enforcement, the black market rent is close to the unregulated rent. But with strict enforcement, the black market rent is equal to the maximum price that a renter is willing to pay.

Figure 6.1 illustrates the effects of a rent ceiling. The demand curve for housing is *D* and the supply curve is *S*. A rent ceiling is imposed at $800 a month. Rents that exceed $800 a month are in the gray-shaded illegal region in the figure. You can see that the equilibrium rent, where the demand and supply curves intersect, is in the illegal region.

At a rent of $800 a month, the quantity of housing supplied is 60,000 units and the quantity demanded is 100,000 units. So with a rent of $800 a month, there is a shortage of 40,000 units of housing.

To rent the 60,000th unit, someone is willing to pay $1,200 a month. They might pay this amount by incurring search costs that bring the total cost of housing to $1,200 a month, or they might pay a black market price of $1,200 a month. Either way, they end up incurring a cost that exceeds what the equilibrium rent would be in an unregulated market.

Inefficiency of a Rent Ceiling

A rent ceiling set below the equilibrium rent results in an inefficient underproduction of housing services. The *marginal social benefit* of housing exceeds its *marginal social cost* and a deadweight loss shrinks the producer surplus and consumer surplus (Chapter 5, pp. 112–114).

Figure 6.2 shows this inefficiency. The rent ceiling ($800 per month) is below the equilibrium rent ($1,000 per month) and the quantity of housing supplied (60,000 units) is less than the efficient quantity (80,000 units).

Because the quantity of housing supplied (the quantity available) is less than the efficient quantity, there is a deadweight loss, shown by the gray triangle. Producer surplus shrinks to the blue triangle and consumer surplus shrinks to the green triangle. The red rectangle represents the potential loss from increased search activity. This loss is borne by consumers and the full loss from the rent ceiling is the sum of the deadweight loss and the increased cost of search.

FIGURE 6.1   A Rent Ceiling

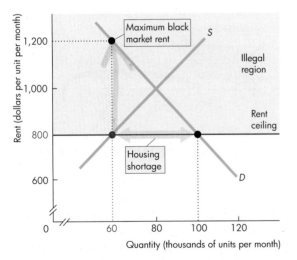

A rent above the rent ceiling of $800 a month is illegal (in the gray-shaded illegal region). At a rent of $800 a month, the quantity of housing supplied is 60,000 units. Frustrated renters spend time searching for housing and they make deals with landlords in a black market. Someone is willing to pay $1,200 a month for the 60,000th unit.

MyEconLab Animation and Draw Graph

FIGURE 6.2   The Inefficiency of a Rent Ceiling

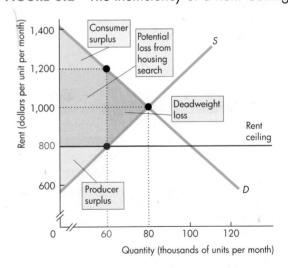

Without a rent ceiling, the market produces an efficient 80,000 units of housing at a rent of $1,000 a month. A rent ceiling of $800 a month decreases the quantity of housing supplied to 60,000 units. Producer surplus and consumer surplus shrink and a deadweight loss arises. The red rectangle represents the cost of resources used in increased search activity. The full loss from the rent ceiling equals the sum of the red rectangle and gray triangle.

MyEconLab Animation and Draw Graph

Are Rent Ceilings Fair?

Rent ceilings might be inefficient, but don't they achieve a fairer allocation of scarce housing? Let's explore this question.

Chapter 5 (pp. 116–118) reviews two key ideas about fairness. According to the *fair-rules* view, anything that blocks voluntary exchange is unfair, so rent ceilings are unfair. But according to the *fair-result* view, a fair outcome is one that benefits the less well off. So according to this view, the fairest outcome is the one that allocates scarce housing to the poorest. To see whether rent ceilings help to achieve a fairer outcome in this sense, we need to consider how the market allocates scarce housing resources in the face of a rent ceiling.

Blocking rent adjustments doesn't eliminate scarcity. Rather, because it decreases the quantity of housing available, it creates an even bigger challenge for the housing market. Somehow, the market must ration a smaller quantity of housing and allocate that housing among the people who demand it.

When the rent is not permitted to allocate scarce housing, what other mechanisms are available, and are *they* fair? Some possible mechanisms are:

- A lottery
- First-come, first-served
- Discrimination

A lottery allocates housing to those who are lucky, not to those who are poor. First-come, first-served (a method used to allocate housing in England after World War II) allocates housing to those who have the greatest foresight and who get their names on a list first, not to the poorest. Discrimination allocates scarce housing based on the views and self-interest of the owner of the housing. In the case of public housing, what counts is the self-interest of the bureaucracy that administers the allocation.

In principle, self-interested owners and bureaucrats could allocate housing to satisfy some criterion of fairness, but they are not likely to do so. Discrimination based on friendship, family ties, and criteria such as race, ethnicity, or sex is more likely to enter the equation. We might make such discrimination illegal, but we cannot prevent it from occurring.

It is hard, then, to make a case for rent ceilings on the basis of fairness. When rent adjustments are blocked, other methods of allocating scarce housing resources operate that do not produce a fair outcome.

ECONOMICS IN ACTION

Rent Control Winners: The Rich and Famous

New York, San Francisco, London, and Paris, four of the world's great cities, have rent ceilings in some part of their housing markets. Boston had rent ceilings for many years but abolished them in 1997. Many other U.S. cities do not have, and have never had, rent ceilings. Among them are Atlanta, Baltimore, Chicago, Dallas, Philadelphia, Phoenix, and Seattle.

To see the effects of rent ceilings in practice we can compare the housing markets in cities with ceilings with those without ceilings. We learn two main lessons from such a comparison.

First, rent ceilings definitely create a housing shortage. Second, they do lower the rents for some but raise them for others.

A survey* conducted in 1997 showed that the rents of housing units *actually available for rent* were 2.5 times the average of all rents in New York but equal to the average rent in Philadelphia. The winners from rent ceilings are the families that have lived in a city for a long time. In New York, these families include some rich and famous ones. The voting power of the winners keeps the rent ceilings in place. Mobile newcomers are the losers in a city with rent ceilings.

The bottom line is that, in principle and in practice, rent ceilings are inefficient and unfair.

---

* William Tucker, "How Rent Control Drives Out Affordable Housing," Cato Policy Analysis No. 274, May 21, 1997, Cato Institute.

◆ REVIEW QUIZ

1 What is a rent ceiling and what are its effects if it is set above the equilibrium rent?
2 What are the effects of a rent ceiling that is set below the equilibrium rent?
3 How are scarce housing resources allocated when a rent ceiling is in place?
4 Why does a rent ceiling create an inefficient and unfair outcome in the housing market?

Work these questions in Study Plan 6.1 and get instant feedback. Do a Key Terms Quiz.   MyEconLab

You now know how a price ceiling (rent ceiling) works. Next, we'll learn about the effects of a price floor by studying a minimum wage in a labor market.

A Labor Market with a Minimum Wage

For each one of us, the labor market is the market that influences the jobs we get and the wages we earn. Firms decide how much labor to demand, and the lower the wage rate, the greater is the quantity of labor demanded. Households decide how much labor to supply, and the higher the wage rate, the greater is the quantity of labor supplied. The wage rate adjusts to make the quantity of labor demanded equal to the quantity supplied.

When wage rates are low, or when they fail to keep up with rising prices, labor unions might turn to governments and lobby for a higher wage rate.

A government regulation that makes it illegal to charge a price lower than a specified level is called a **price floor**.

The effects of a price floor on a market depend crucially on whether the floor is imposed at a level that is above or below the equilibrium price.

A price floor set *below the equilibrium price* has no effect. The reason is that the price floor does not constrain the market forces. The force of the law and the market forces are not in conflict. But a price floor set *above the equilibrium price* has powerful effects on a market. The reason is that the price floor attempts to prevent the price from regulating the quantities demanded and supplied. The force of the law and the market forces are in conflict.

When a price floor is applied to a labor market, it is called a **minimum wage**. A minimum wage imposed at a level that is above the equilibrium wage creates unemployment. Let's look at the effects of a minimum wage.

Minimum Wage Brings Unemployment

At the equilibrium price, the quantity demanded equals the quantity supplied. In a labor market, when the wage rate is at the equilibrium level, the quantity of labor supplied equals the quantity of labor demanded: There is neither a shortage of labor nor a surplus of labor.

But at a wage rate above the equilibrium wage, the quantity of labor supplied exceeds the quantity of labor demanded—there is a surplus of labor. So when a minimum wage is set above the equilibrium wage, there is a surplus of labor. The demand for labor determines the level of employment, and the surplus of labor is unemployed.

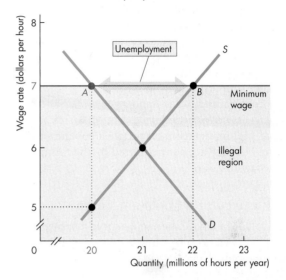

FIGURE 6.3   Minimum Wage and Unemployment

The minimum wage rate is set at $7 an hour. Any wage rate below $7 an hour is illegal (in the gray-shaded illegal region). At the minimum wage of $7 an hour, 20 million hours are hired but 22 million hours are available. Unemployment—AB—of 2 million hours a year is created. With only 20 million hours demanded, someone is willing to supply the 20 millionth hour for $5.

MyEconLab Animation and Draw Graph

Figure 6.3 illustrates the effect of the minimum wage on unemployment. The demand for labor curve is D and the supply of labor curve is S. The horizontal red line shows the minimum wage set at $7 an hour. A wage rate below this level is illegal, in the gray-shaded illegal region of the figure. At the minimum wage rate, 20 million hours of labor are demanded (point A) and 22 million hours of labor are supplied (point B), so 2 million hours of available labor are unemployed.

With only 20 million hours demanded, someone is willing to supply that 20 millionth hour for $5. Frustrated unemployed workers spend time and other resources searching for hard-to-find jobs.

Is the Minimum Wage Fair?

The minimum wage is unfair on both views of fairness: It delivers an unfair *result* and imposes an unfair *rule*.

The *result* is unfair because only those people who have jobs and keep them benefit from the minimum wage. The unemployed end up worse off than they would be with no minimum wage. Some of those who search for jobs and find them end up worse off because of the increased cost of job search they incur. Also those who search and find jobs aren't always the least well off. When the wage rate doesn't allocate labor, other mechanisms determine who finds a job. One such mechanism is discrimination, which is yet another source of unfairness.

The minimum wage imposes an unfair *rule* because it blocks voluntary exchange. Firms are willing to hire more labor and people are willing to work more, but they are not permitted by the minimum wage law to do so.

Inefficiency of a Minimum Wage

In the labor market, the supply curve measures the marginal social cost of labor to workers. This cost is leisure forgone. The demand curve measures the marginal social benefit from labor. This benefit is the value of the goods and services produced. An

unregulated labor market allocates the economy's scarce labor resources to the jobs in which they are valued most highly. The market is efficient.

The minimum wage frustrates the market mechanism and results in unemployment and increased job search. At the quantity of labor employed, the marginal social benefit of labor exceeds its marginal social cost and a deadweight loss shrinks the firms' surplus and the workers' surplus.

Figure 6.4 shows this inefficiency. The minimum wage ($7 an hour) is above the equilibrium wage ($6 an hour) and the quantity of labor demanded and employed (20 million hours) is less than the efficient quantity (21 million hours).

Because the quantity of labor employed is less than the efficient quantity, there is a deadweight loss, shown by the gray triangle. The firms' surplus shrinks to the blue triangle and the workers' surplus shrinks to the green triangle. The red rectangle shows the potential loss from increased job search, which is borne by workers. The full loss from the minimum wage is the sum of the deadweight loss and the increased cost of job search.

◆ AT **ISSUE**

Does the Minimum Wage Cause Unemployment?

In the United States, the federal government's Fair Labor Standards Act sets the minimum wage, which has fluctuated between 35 percent and 50 percent of the average wage, and in 2014 it was $7.25 an hour, a level set in 2009. Most states have minimum wages that exceed the federal minimum.

Does the minimum wage result in unemployment, and if so, how much unemployment does it create?

No, It Doesn't

David Card of the University of California at Berkeley and Alan Krueger of Princeton University say:

- An increase in the minimum wage *increases teenage employment* and *decreases unemployment*.
- Their study of minimum wages in California, New Jersey, and Texas found that the employment rate of low-income workers increased following an increase in the minimum wage.
- A higher wage *increases* employment by making workers more conscientious and productive as well as less likely to quit, which lowers unproductive labor turnover.
- A higher wage rate also encourages managers to seek ways to increase labor productivity.

Yes, It Does

Most economists are skeptical about Card and Krueger's conclusion.

- The consensus view is that a 10 percent rise in the minimum wage *decreases teenage employment* by between 1 and 3 percent.
- Firms freely pay wage rates above the equilibrium wage to encourage more productive work habits.
- Daniel Hamermesh of the University of Texas at Austin says that firms anticipate the rise and cut employment *before* the minimum wage goes up.
- Finis Welch of Texas A&M University and Kevin Murphy of the University of Chicago say the employment effects that Card and Krueger found are caused by regional differences in economic growth and not by a rise in the minimum wage.

FIGURE 6.4   The Inefficiency of a Minimum Wage

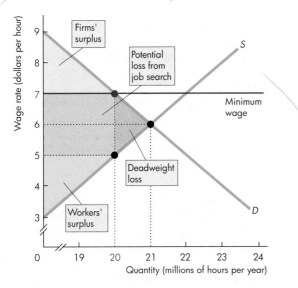

A minimum wage decreases employment. Firms' surplus (blue area) and workers' surplus (green area) shrink and a deadweight loss (gray area) arises. Job search increases and the red area shows the loss from this activity.

MyEconLab Animation

REVIEW QUIZ

1 What is a minimum wage and what are its effects if it is set above the equilibrium wage?
2 What are the effects of a minimum wage set below the equilibrium wage?
3 Explain how scarce jobs are allocated when a minimum wage is in place.
4 Explain why a minimum wage creates an inefficient allocation of labor resources.
5 Explain why a minimum wage is unfair.

Work these questions in Study Plan 6.2 and get instant feedback. Do a Key Terms Quiz.   MyEconLab

Next we're going to study a more widespread government action in markets: taxes. We'll see how taxes change prices and quantities. You will discover the surprising fact that while the government can impose a tax, it can't decide who will pay the tax! You will also see that a tax creates a deadweight loss.

◆ Taxes

Everything you earn and almost everything you buy is taxed. Income taxes and Social Security taxes are deducted from your earnings and sales taxes are added to the bill when you buy something. Employers also pay a Social Security tax for their workers, and producers of tobacco products, alcoholic drinks, and gasoline pay a tax every time they sell something.

Who *really* pays these taxes? Because the income tax and Social Security tax are deducted from your pay, and the sales tax is added to the prices that you pay, isn't it obvious that *you* pay these taxes? And isn't it equally obvious that your employer pays the employer's contribution to the Social Security tax and that tobacco producers pay the tax on cigarettes?

You're going to discover that it isn't obvious who *really* pays a tax and that lawmakers don't make that decision. We begin with a definition of tax incidence.

Tax Incidence

Tax incidence is the division of the burden of a tax between buyers and sellers. When the government imposes a tax on the sale of a good,* the price paid by buyers might rise by the full amount of the tax, by a lesser amount, or not at all. If the price paid by buyers rises by the full amount of the tax, then the burden of the tax falls entirely on buyers—the buyers pay the tax. If the price paid by buyers rises by a lesser amount than the tax, then the burden of the tax falls partly on buyers and partly on sellers. And if the price paid by buyers doesn't change at all, then the burden of the tax falls entirely on sellers.

Tax incidence does not depend on the tax law. The law might impose a tax on sellers or on buyers, but the outcome is the same in either case. To see why, let's look at the tax on cigarettes in New York City.

A Tax on Sellers

On July 1, 2002, Mayor Bloomberg put a tax of $1.50 a pack on cigarettes sold in New York City. To work out the effects of this tax on the sellers of cigarettes, we begin by examining the effects on demand and supply in the market for cigarettes.

---

*These outcomes also apply to services and factors of production (land, labor, and capital).

In Fig. 6.5, the demand curve is D, and the supply curve is S. With no tax, the equilibrium price is $3 per pack and 350 million packs a year are bought and sold.

A tax on sellers is like an increase in cost, so it decreases supply. To determine the position of the new supply curve, we add the tax to the minimum price that sellers are willing to accept for each quantity sold. You can see that without the tax, sellers are willing to offer 350 million packs a year for $3 a pack. So with a $1.50 tax, they will offer 350 million packs a year only if the price is $4.50 a pack. The supply curve shifts to the red curve labeled $S + tax on sellers$.

Equilibrium occurs where the new supply curve intersects the demand curve at 325 million packs a year. The price paid by buyers rises by $1 to $4 a pack. And the price received by sellers falls by 50¢ to $2.50 a pack. So buyers pay $1 of the tax and sellers pay the other 50¢.

A Tax on Buyers

Suppose that instead of taxing sellers, New York City taxes cigarette buyers $1.50 a pack.

A tax on buyers lowers the amount they are willing to pay sellers, so it decreases demand and shifts the demand curve leftward. To determine the position of this new demand curve, we subtract the tax from the maximum price that buyers are willing to pay for each quantity bought. You can see, in Fig. 6.6, that without the tax, buyers are willing to buy 350 million packs a year for $3 a pack. So with a $1.50 tax, they are willing to buy 350 million packs a year only if the price including the tax is $3 a pack, which means that they're willing to pay sellers only $1.50 a pack. The demand curve shifts to become the red curve labeled $D - tax on buyers$.

Equilibrium occurs where the new demand curve intersects the supply curve at a quantity of 325 million packs a year. The price received by sellers is $2.50 a pack, and the price paid by buyers is $4.

Equivalence of Tax on Buyers and Sellers

You can see that the tax on buyers in Fig. 6.6 has the same effects as the tax on sellers in Fig. 6.5. In both cases, the equilibrium quantity decreases to 325 million packs a year, the price paid by buyers rises to $4 a pack, and the price received by sellers falls to $2.50 a pack. Buyers pay $1 of the $1.50 tax, and sellers pay the other 50¢ of the tax.

FIGURE 6.5   A Tax on Sellers

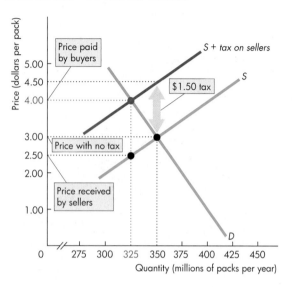

With no tax, 350 million packs a year are bought and sold at $3 a pack. A tax on sellers of $1.50 a pack shifts the supply curve from S to $S + tax on sellers$. The equilibrium quantity decreases to 325 million packs a year, the price paid by buyers rises to $4 a pack, and the price received by sellers falls to $2.50 a pack. The tax raises the price paid by buyers by less than the tax and lowers the price received by sellers, so buyers and sellers share the burden of the tax.

―――― MyEconLab Animation and Draw Graph ――――

Can We Share the Burden Equally? Suppose that Mayor Bloomberg wants the burden of the cigarette tax to fall equally on buyers and sellers and declares that a 75¢ tax be imposed on each. Is the burden of the tax then shared equally?

You can see that it is not. The tax is still $1.50 a pack. You've seen that the tax has the same effect regardless of whether it is imposed on sellers or buyers. So imposing half the tax on sellers and half on buyers is like an average of the two cases you've just examined. (Draw the demand-supply graph and work out what happens in this case. The demand curve shifts downward by 75¢ and the supply curve shifts upward by 75¢. The new equilibrium quantity is still 325 million packs a year. Buyers pay $4 a pack, of which 75¢ is tax. Sellers receive $3.25 from buyers, but pay a 75¢ tax, so sellers net $2.50 a pack.)

When a transaction is taxed, there are two prices: the price paid by buyers, which includes the tax; and the price received by sellers, which excludes the tax.

FIGURE 6.6   A Tax on Buyers

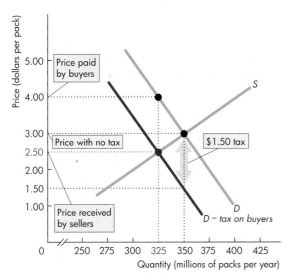

With no tax, 350 million packs a year are bought and sold at $3 a pack. A tax on buyers of $1.50 a pack shifts the demand curve from *D* to *D – tax on buyers*. The equilibrium quantity decreases to 325 million packs a year, the price paid by buyers rises to $4 a pack, and the price received by sellers falls to $2.50 a pack. The tax raises the price paid by buyers by less than the tax and lowers the price received by sellers, so buyers and sellers share the burden of the tax.

MyEconLab Animation

Buyers respond to the price that *includes* the tax and sellers respond to the price that *excludes* the tax.

A tax is like a wedge between the price buyers pay and the price sellers receive. The size of the wedge determines the effects of the tax, not the side of the market on which the government imposes the tax.

The Social Security Tax The Social Security tax is an example of a tax that Congress imposes equally on both buyers and sellers. But the principles you've just learned apply to this tax too. The market for labor, not Congress, decides how the burden of the Social Security tax is divided between firms and workers.

In the New York City cigarette tax example, buyers bear twice the burden of the tax borne by sellers. In special cases, either buyers or sellers bear the entire burden. The division of the burden of a tax between buyers and sellers depends on the elasticities of demand and supply, as you will now see.

Tax Incidence and Elasticity of Demand

The division of the tax between buyers and sellers depends in part on the elasticity of demand. There are two extreme cases:

- Perfectly inelastic demand—buyers pay.
- Perfectly elastic demand—sellers pay.

Perfectly Inelastic Demand Figure 6.7 shows the market for insulin, a vital daily medication for those with diabetes. Demand is perfectly inelastic at 100,000 doses a day, regardless of the price, as shown by the vertical demand curve *D*. That is, a diabetic would sacrifice all other goods and services rather than not consume the insulin dose that provides good health. The supply curve of insulin is *S*. With no tax, the price is $2 a dose and the quantity is 100,000 doses a day.

If insulin is taxed at 20¢ a dose, we must add the tax to the minimum price at which drug companies are willing to sell insulin. The result is the new supply curve *S + tax*. The price rises to $2.20 a dose, but the quantity does not change. Buyers pay the entire tax of 20¢ a dose.

FIGURE 6.7   Tax with Perfectly Inelastic Demand

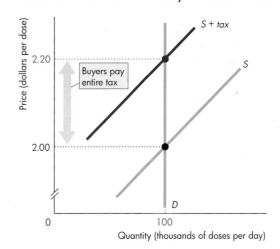

In this market for insulin, demand is perfectly inelastic. With no tax, the price is $2 a dose and the quantity is 100,000 doses a day. A tax of 20¢ a dose shifts the supply curve to *S + tax*. The price rises to $2.20 a dose, but the quantity bought does not change. Buyers pay the entire tax.

MyEconLab Animation

Perfectly Elastic Demand Figure 6.8 shows the market for pink marker pens. Demand is perfectly elastic at $1 a pen, as shown by the horizontal demand curve *D*. If pink pens are less expensive than the other colors, everyone uses pink. If pink pens are more expensive than other colors, no one uses pink. The supply curve is *S*. With no tax, the price of a pink pen is $1 and the quantity is 4,000 pens a week.

Suppose that the government imposes a tax of 10¢ a pen on pink marker pens but not on other colors. The new supply curve is *S + tax*. The price remains at $1 a pen, and the quantity decreases to 1,000 pink pens a week. The 10¢ tax leaves the price paid by buyers unchanged but lowers the amount received by sellers by the full amount of the tax. Sellers pay the entire tax of 10¢ a pink pen.

We've seen that when demand is perfectly inelastic, buyers pay the entire tax and when demand is perfectly elastic, sellers pay the entire tax. In the usual case, demand is neither perfectly inelastic nor perfectly elastic and the tax is split between buyers and sellers. But the division depends on the elasticity of demand: The more inelastic the demand, the larger is the amount of the tax paid by buyers.

FIGURE 6.8   Tax with Perfectly Elastic Demand

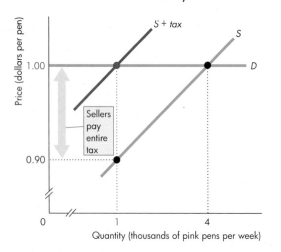

In this market for pink pens, demand is perfectly elastic. With no tax, the price of a pen is $1 and the quantity is 4,000 pens a week. A tax of 10¢ a pink pen shifts the supply curve to *S + tax*. The price remains at $1 a pen, and the quantity of pink pens sold decreases to 1,000 a week. Sellers pay the entire tax.

—————— MyEconLab Animation ——————

Tax Incidence and Elasticity of Supply

The division of the tax between buyers and sellers also depends, in part, on the elasticity of supply. Again, there are two extreme cases:

- Perfectly inelastic supply—sellers pay.
- Perfectly elastic supply—buyers pay.

Perfectly Inelastic Supply Figure 6.9(a) shows the market for water from a mineral spring that flows at a constant rate that can't be controlled. Supply is perfectly inelastic at 100,000 bottles a week, as shown by the supply curve *S*. The demand curve for the water from this spring is *D*. With no tax, the price is 50¢ a bottle and the quantity is 100,000 bottles.

Suppose this spring water is taxed at 5¢ a bottle. The supply curve does not change because the spring owners still produce 100,000 bottles a week, even though the price they receive falls. But buyers are willing to buy the 100,000 bottles only if the price is 50¢ a bottle, so the price remains at 50¢ a bottle. The tax reduces the price received by sellers to 45¢ a bottle, and sellers pay the entire tax.

Perfectly Elastic Supply Figure 6.9(b) shows the market for sand from which computer-chip makers extract silicon. Supply of this sand is perfectly elastic at a price of 10¢ a pound, as shown by the supply curve *S*. The demand curve for sand is *D*. With no tax, the price is 10¢ a pound and 5,000 pounds a week are bought.

If this sand is taxed at 1¢ a pound, we must add the tax to the minimum supply-price. Sellers are now willing to offer any quantity at 11¢ a pound along the curve *S + tax*. A new equilibrium is determined where the new supply curve intersects the demand curve: at a price of 11¢ a pound and a quantity of 3,000 pounds a week. The tax has increased the price buyers pay by the full amount of the tax—1¢ a pound—and has decreased the quantity sold. Buyers pay the entire tax.

We've seen that when supply is perfectly inelastic, sellers pay the entire tax, and when supply is perfectly elastic, buyers pay the entire tax. In the usual case, supply is neither perfectly inelastic nor perfectly elastic and the tax is split between buyers and sellers. But how the tax is split depends on the elasticity of supply: The more elastic the supply, the larger is the amount of the tax paid by buyers.

FIGURE 6.9   Tax and the Elasticity of Supply

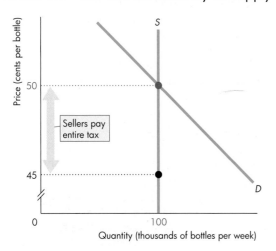

(a) Perfectly inelastic supply

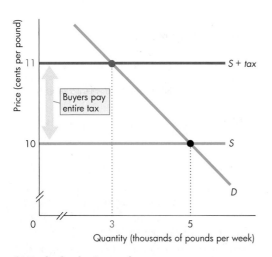

(b) Perfectly elastic supply

Part (a) shows the market for water from a mineral spring. Supply is perfectly inelastic. With no tax, the price is 50¢ a bottle. With a tax of 5¢ a bottle, the price remains at 50¢ a bottle. The number of bottles bought remains the same, but the price received by sellers decreases to 45¢ a bottle. Sellers pay the entire tax.

Part (b) shows the market for sand. Supply is perfectly elastic. With no tax, the price is 10¢ a pound. A tax of 1¢ a pound increases the minimum supply-price to 11¢ a pound. The supply curve shifts to *S + tax*. The price increases to 11¢ a pound. Buyers pay the entire tax.

MyEconLab Animation

Taxes and Efficiency

A tax drives a wedge between the buying price and the selling price and results in inefficient underproduction. The price buyers pay is also the buyers' willingness to pay, which measures *marginal social benefit*. The price sellers receive is also the sellers' minimum supply-price, which equals *marginal social cost*.

A tax makes marginal social benefit exceed marginal social cost, shrinks the producer surplus and consumer surplus, and creates a deadweight loss.

Figure 6.10 shows the inefficiency of a tax on MP3 players. The demand curve, *D*, shows marginal social benefit, and the supply curve, *S*, shows marginal social cost. Without a tax, the market produces the efficient quantity (5,000 players a week).

With a tax, the sellers' minimum supply-price rises by the amount of the tax and the supply curve shifts to *S + tax*. This supply curve does *not* show marginal social cost. The tax component isn't a *social* cost of

FIGURE 6.10   Taxes and Efficiency

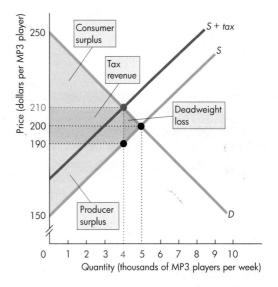

With no tax, 5,000 players a week are produced. With a $20 tax, the buyers' price rises to $210, the sellers' price falls to $190, and the quantity decreases to 4,000 players a week. Consumer surplus shrinks to the green area, and the producer surplus shrinks to the blue area. Part of the loss of consumer surplus and producer surplus goes to the government as tax revenue (the purple area) and part becomes a deadweight loss (the gray area).

MyEconLab Animation

production. It is a transfer of resources to the government. At the new equilibrium quantity (4,000 players a week), both consumer surplus and producer surplus shrink. Part of each surplus goes to the government in tax revenue—the purple area; part becomes a deadweight loss—the gray area.

Only in the extreme cases of perfectly inelastic demand and perfectly inelastic supply does a tax not change the quantity bought and sold so that no deadweight loss arises.

Taxes and Fairness

We've examined the incidence and the efficiency of taxes. But when political leaders debate tax issues, it is fairness, not incidence and efficiency, that gets the most attention. Democrats complain that Republican tax cuts are unfair because they give the benefits of lower taxes to the rich. Republicans counter that it is fair that the rich get most of the tax cuts because they pay most of the taxes. No easy answers are available to the questions about the fairness of taxes.

Economists have proposed two conflicting principles of fairness to apply to a tax system:

- The benefits principle
- The ability-to-pay principle

The Benefits Principle The *benefits principle* is the proposition that people should pay taxes equal to the benefits they receive from the services provided by government. This arrangement is fair because it means that those who benefit most pay the most taxes. It makes tax payments and the consumption of government-provided services similar to private consumption expenditures.

The benefits principle can justify high fuel taxes to pay for freeways, high taxes on alcoholic beverages and tobacco products to pay for public healthcare services, and high rates of income tax on high incomes to pay for the benefits from law and order and from living in a secure environment, from which the rich might benefit more than the poor.

The Ability-to-Pay Principle The *ability-to-pay principle* is the proposition that people should pay taxes according to how easily they can bear the burden of the tax. A rich person can more easily bear the burden than a poor person can, so the ability-to-pay principle can reinforce the benefits principle to justify high rates of income tax on high incomes.

ECONOMICS IN ACTION

Workers and Consumers Pay the Most Tax

Because the elasticity of the supply of labor is low and the elasticity of demand for labor is high, workers pay most of the personal income taxes and most of the Social Security taxes. Because the elasticities of demand for alcohol, tobacco, and gasoline are low and the elasticities of supply are high, the burden of these taxes (excise taxes) falls more heavily on buyers than on sellers.

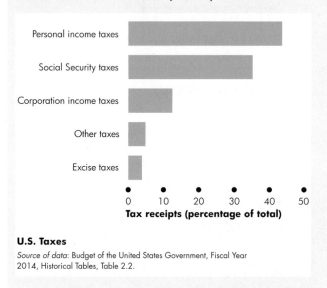

U.S. Taxes

Source of data: Budget of the United States Government, Fiscal Year 2014, Historical Tables, Table 2.2.

◆ REVIEW QUIZ

1 How does the elasticity of demand influence the incidence of a tax, the tax revenue, and the deadweight loss?
2 How does the elasticity of supply influence the incidence of a tax, the quantity bought, the tax revenue, and the deadweight loss?
3 Why is a tax inefficient?
4 When would a tax be efficient?
5 What are the two principles of fairness that are applied to tax systems?

Work these questions in Study Plan 6.3 and get instant feedback. Do a Key Terms Quiz.   MyEconLab

Your next task is to study production quotas and subsidies, tools that are used to influence the markets for farm products.

◆ Production Quotas and Subsidies

An early or late frost, a hot dry summer, and a wet spring present just a few of the challenges that fill the lives of farmers with uncertainty and sometimes with economic hardship. Fluctuations in the weather bring fluctuations in farm output and prices and sometimes leave farmers with low incomes. To help farmers avoid low prices and low incomes, governments intervene in the markets for farm products.

Price floors that work a bit like the minimum wage that you've already studied might be used. But as you've seen, this type of government action creates a surplus and is inefficient. These same conclusions apply to the effects of a price floor for farm products.

Governments often use two other methods of intervention in the markets for farm products:

- Production quotas
- Subsidies

Production Quotas

In the markets for sugarbeets, tobacco leaf, and cotton (among others), governments have, from time to time, imposed production quotas. A **production quota** is an upper limit to the quantity of a good that may be produced in a specified period. To discover the effects of a production quota, let's look at what a quota does to the market for sugarbeets.

Suppose that the growers of sugarbeets want to limit total production to get a higher price. They persuade the government to introduce a production quota on sugarbeets.

The effect of the production quota depends on whether it is set below or above the equilibrium quantity. If the government introduced a production quota above the equilibrium quantity, nothing would change because sugarbeet growers would already be producing less than the quota. But a production quota set *below the equilibrium quantity* has big effects, which are

- A decrease in supply
- A rise in price
- A decrease in marginal cost
- Inefficient underproduction
- An incentive to cheat and overproduce

Figure 6.11 illustrates these effects.

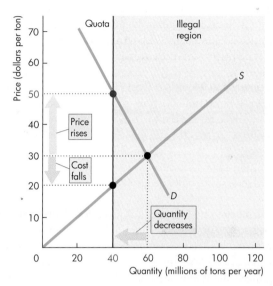

FIGURE 6.11 The Effects of a Production Quota

With no quota, growers produce 60 million tons a year and the price is $30 a ton. A production quota of 40 million tons a year restricts total production to that amount. The quantity produced decreases to 40 million tons a year, the price rises to $50 a ton, and the farmers' marginal cost falls to $20 a ton. Because marginal social cost (on the supply curve) is less than marginal social benefit (on the demand curve), a deadweight loss arises from the underproduction.

MyEconLab Animation

A Decrease in Supply A production quota on sugarbeets decreases the supply of sugarbeets. Each grower is assigned a production limit that is less than the amount that would be produced—and supplied—without the quota. The total of the growers' limits equals the quota, and any production in excess of the quota is illegal.

The quantity supplied becomes the amount permitted by the production quota, and this quantity is fixed. The supply of sugarbeets becomes perfectly inelastic at the quantity permitted under the quota.

In Fig. 6.11, with no quota, growers would produce 60 million tons of sugarbeets a year—the market equilibrium quantity. With a production quota set at 40 million tons a year, the gray-shaded area shows the illegal region. As in the case of price ceilings and price floors, market forces and political forces are in conflict in this illegal region.

The vertical red line labeled "Quota" becomes the supply curve of sugarbeets at prices above $20 a ton.

A Rise in Price The production quota raises the price of sugarbeets. When the government sets a production quota, it leaves market forces free to determine the price. Because the quota decreases the supply of sugarbeets, it raises the price. In Fig. 6.11, with no quota, the price is $30 a ton. With a quota of 40 million tons, the price rises to $50 a ton.

A Decrease in Marginal Cost The production quota lowers the marginal cost of growing sugarbeets. Marginal cost decreases because growers produce less and stop using the resources with the highest marginal cost. Sugarbeet growers slide down their supply (and marginal cost) curves. In Fig. 6.11, marginal cost decreases to $20 a ton.

Inefficiency The production quota results in inefficient underproduction. Marginal social benefit at the quantity produced is equal to the market price, which has increased. Marginal social cost at the quantity produced has decreased and is less than the market price. So marginal social benefit exceeds marginal social cost and a deadweight loss arises.

An Incentive to Cheat and Overproduce The production quota creates an incentive for growers to cheat and produce more than their individual production limit. With the quota, the price exceeds marginal cost, so the grower can get a larger profit by producing one more unit. Of course, if all growers produce more than their assigned limit, the production quota becomes ineffective, and the price falls to the equilibrium (no quota) price.

To make the production quota effective, growers must set up a monitoring system to ensure that no one cheats and overproduces. But it is costly to set up and operate a monitoring system and it is difficult to detect and punish producers who violate their quotas.

Because of the difficulty of operating a quota, producers often lobby governments to establish a quota and provide the monitoring and punishment systems that make it work.

Subsidies

In the United States, the producers of peanuts, sugarbeets, milk, wheat, and many other farm products receive subsidies. A **subsidy** is a payment made by the government to a producer. A large and controversial Farm Bill passed by Congress in 2008 renewed and extended a wide range of subsidies.

The effects of a subsidy are similar to the effects of a tax but they go in the opposite directions. These effects are

- An increase in supply
- A fall in price and increase in quantity produced
- An increase in marginal cost
- Payments by government to farmers
- Inefficient overproduction

Figure 6.12 illustrates the effects of a subsidy to peanut farmers.

An Increase in Supply In Fig. 6.12, with no subsidy, the demand curve D and the supply curve S determine the price of peanuts at $40 a ton and the quantity of peanuts at 40 million tons a year.

Suppose that the government introduces a subsidy of $20 a ton to peanut farmers. A subsidy is like a negative tax. A tax is equivalent to an increase in cost, so a subsidy is equivalent to a decrease in cost. The subsidy brings an increase in supply.

To determine the position of the new supply curve, we subtract the subsidy from the farmers' minimum supply-price. In Fig. 6.12, with no subsidy, farmers are willing to offer 40 million tons a year at a price of $40 a ton. With a subsidy of $20 a ton, they will offer 40 million tons a year if the price is as low as $20 a ton. The supply curve shifts to the red curve labeled $S - subsidy$.

A Fall in Price and Increase in Quantity Produced The subsidy lowers the price of peanuts and increases the quantity produced. In Fig. 6.12, equilibrium occurs where the new supply curve intersects the demand curve at a price of $30 a ton and a quantity of 60 million tons a year.

An Increase in Marginal Cost The subsidy lowers the price paid by consumers but increases the marginal cost of producing peanuts. Marginal cost increases because farmers grow more peanuts, which means that they must begin to use some resources that are less ideal for growing peanuts. Peanut farmers slide up their supply (and marginal cost) curves. In Fig. 6.12, marginal cost increases to $50 a ton.

Payments by Government to Farmers The government pays a subsidy to peanut farmers on each ton of peanuts produced. In this example, farmers increase production to 60 million tons a year and receive a

FIGURE 6.12 The Effects of a Subsidy

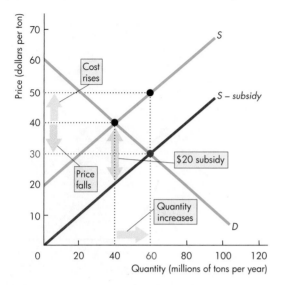

With no subsidy, farmers produce 40 million tons a year at $40 a ton. A subsidy of $20 a ton shifts the supply curve rightward to *S – subsidy*. The equilibrium quantity increases to 60 million tons a year, the price falls to $30 a ton, and the price plus the subsidy received by farmers rises to $50 a ton. In the new equilibrium, marginal social cost (on the supply curve) exceeds marginal social benefit (on the demand curve) and the subsidy results in inefficient overproduction.

MyEconLab Animation

subsidy of $20 a ton. So peanut farmers receive payments from the government that total $1,200 million a year.

Inefficient Overproduction The subsidy results in inefficient overproduction. At the quantity produced with the subsidy, marginal social benefit is equal to the market price, which has fallen. Marginal social cost has increased and it exceeds the market price. Because marginal social cost exceeds marginal social benefit, the increased production brings inefficiency.

Subsidies spill over to the rest of the world. Because a subsidy lowers the domestic market price, subsidized farmers will offer some of their output for sale on the world market. The increase in supply on the world market lowers the price in the rest of the world. Faced with lower prices, farmers in other countries decrease production and receive smaller revenues.

ECONOMICS IN ACTION
Rich High-Cost Farmers the Winners

Farm subsidies are a major obstacle to achieving an efficient use of resources in the global markets for farm products and are a source of tension between the United States, Europe, and developing nations.

The United States and the European Union are the world's two largest and richest economies. They also pay their farmers the biggest subsidies, which create inefficient overproduction of food in these rich economies.

At the same time, U.S. and European subsidies make it more difficult for farmers in the developing nations of Africa, Asia, and Central and South America to compete in global food markets. Farmers in these countries can often produce at a lower opportunity cost than the U.S. and European farmers.

Two rich countries, Australia and New Zealand, have stopped subsidizing farmers. The result has been an improvement in the efficiency of farming in these countries. New Zealand is so efficient at producing lamb and dairy products that it has been called the Saudi Arabia of milk (an analogy with Saudi Arabia's huge oil reserve and production.)

International opposition to U.S. and European farm subsidies is strong. Opposition to farm subsidies inside the United States and Europe is growing, but it isn't as strong as the pro-farm lobby, so don't expect an early end to these subsidies.

◆ REVIEW QUIZ

1 Summarize the effects of a production quota on the market price and the quantity produced.
2 Explain why a production quota is inefficient.
3 Explain why a voluntary production quota is difficult to operate.
4 Summarize the effects of a subsidy on the market price and the quantity produced.
5 Explain why a subsidy is inefficient.

Work these questions in Study Plan 6.4 and get instant feedback. Do a Key Terms Quiz.   MyEconLab

Governments intervene in some markets by making it illegal to trade in a good. Let's now see how these markets work.

◆ Markets for Illegal Goods

The markets for many goods and services are regulated, and buying and selling some goods is illegal. The best-known examples of such goods are drugs such as marijuana, cocaine, ecstasy, and heroin.

Despite the fact that these drugs are illegal, trade in them is a multibillion-dollar business. This trade can be understood by using the same economic model and principles that explain trade in legal goods. To study the market for illegal goods, we're first going to examine the prices and quantities that would prevail if these goods were not illegal. Next, we'll see how prohibition works. Then we'll see how a tax might be used to limit the consumption of these goods.

A Free Market for a Drug

Figure 6.13 shows the market for a drug. The demand curve, D, shows that, other things remaining the same, the lower the price of the drug, the larger is the quantity of the drug demanded. The supply curve, S, shows that, other things remaining the same, the lower the price of the drug, the smaller is the quantity supplied. If the drug were not illegal, the quantity bought and sold would be Q_C and the price would be P_C.

A Market for an Illegal Drug

When a good is illegal, the cost of trading in the good increases. By how much the cost increases and who bears the cost depend on the penalties for violating the law and the degree to which the law is enforced. The larger the penalties and the better the policing, the higher are the costs. Penalties might be imposed on sellers, buyers, or both.

Penalties on Sellers   Drug dealers in the United States face large penalties if their activities are detected. Penalties for convicted dealers range from jail terms of 10 years to life and fines that might be as large as $2 million.

These penalties are part of the cost of supplying illegal drugs, and they bring a decrease in supply—a leftward shift in the supply curve. To determine the new supply curve, we add the cost of breaking the law to the minimum price that drug dealers are willing to accept.

In Fig. 6.13, the cost of breaking the law by selling drugs (*CBL*) is added to the minimum price

FIGURE 6.13   A Market for an Illegal Good

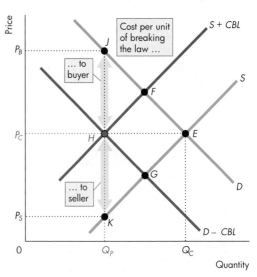

The demand curve for drugs is D, and the supply curve is S. If drugs are not illegal, the quantity bought and sold is Q_C at a price of P_C—point E. If selling drugs is illegal, the cost of breaking the law by selling drugs (*CBL*) is added to the minimum supply-price and supply decreases to $S + CBL$. The market moves to point F. If buying drugs is illegal, the cost of breaking the law is subtracted from the maximum price that buyers are willing to pay, and demand decreases to $D - CBL$. The market moves to point G. With both buying and selling illegal, the supply curve and the demand curve shift and the market moves to point H. The market price remains at P_C, but the market price plus the penalty for buying rises—point J—and the market price minus the penalty for selling falls—point K.

—— **MyEconLab** Animation——

that dealers will accept and the supply curve shifts leftward to $S + CBL$. If penalties were imposed only on sellers, the market equilibrium would move from point E to point F.

Penalties on Buyers   In the United States, it is illegal to *possess* drugs such as marijuana, cocaine, ecstasy, and heroin. Possession of marijuana can bring a prison term of 1 year, and possession of heroin can bring a prison term of 2 years. Penalties fall on buyers, and the cost of breaking the law must be subtracted from the value of the good to determine the maximum price buyers are willing to pay for the drugs. Demand decreases, and the demand curve shifts leftward. In Fig. 6.13, the demand curve shifts to $D - CBL$. If penalties were imposed only on buyers, the market equilibrium would move from point E to point G.

Penalties on Both Sellers and Buyers If penalties are imposed on both sellers *and* buyers, both supply and demand decrease and both the supply curve and the demand curve shift. In Fig. 6.13, the costs of breaking the law are the same for both buyers and sellers, so both curves shift leftward by the same amount. The market equilibrium moves to point H. The market price remains at the competitive market price P_C, but the quantity bought decreases to Q_P. Buyers pay P_C plus the cost of breaking the law, which equals P_B. Sellers receive P_C minus the cost of breaking the law, which equals P_S.

The larger the penalties and the greater the degree of law enforcement, the larger is the decrease in demand and/or supply. If the penalties are heavier on sellers, the supply curve shifts farther than the demand curve and the market price rises above P_C. If the penalties are heavier on buyers, the demand curve shifts farther than the supply curve and the market price falls below P_C. In the United States, the penalties on sellers are larger than those on buyers, so the quantity of drugs traded decreases and the market price increases compared with a free market.

With high enough penalties and effective law enforcement, it is possible to decrease demand and/or supply to the point at which the quantity bought is zero. But in reality, such an outcome is unusual. It does not happen in the United States in the case of illegal drugs. The key reason is the high cost of law enforcement and insufficient resources for the police to achieve effective enforcement. Because of this situation, some people suggest that drugs (and other illegal goods) should be legalized and sold openly but also taxed at a high rate in the same way that legal drugs such as alcohol are taxed. How would such an arrangement work?

Legalizing and Taxing Drugs

From your study of the effects of taxes, it is easy to see that the quantity bought of a drug could be decreased if the drug were legalized and taxed. Imposing a sufficiently high tax could decrease the supply, raise the price, and achieve the same decrease in the quantity bought as does a prohibition on drugs. The government would collect a large tax revenue.

Illegal Trading to Evade the Tax It is likely that an extremely high tax rate would be needed to cut the quantity of drugs bought to the level prevailing with a prohibition. It is also likely that many drug dealers and consumers would try to cover up their activities to evade the tax. If they did act in this way, they would face the cost of breaking the law—the tax law. If the penalty for tax law violation is as severe and as effectively policed as drug-dealing laws, the analysis we've already conducted applies also to this case. The quantity of drugs bought would depend on the penalties for law breaking and on the way in which the penalties are assigned to buyers and sellers.

Taxes Versus Prohibition: Some Pros and Cons Which is more effective: prohibition or taxes? In favor of taxes and against prohibition is the fact that the tax revenue can be used to make law enforcement more effective. It can also be used to run a more effective education campaign against illegal drug use. In favor of prohibition and against taxes is the fact that prohibition sends a signal that might influence preferences, decreasing the demand for illegal drugs. Also, some people intensely dislike the idea of the government profiting from trade in harmful substances.

◆ REVIEW QUIZ

1 How does the imposition of a penalty for selling an illegal drug influence demand, supply, price, and the quantity of the drug consumed?
2 How does the imposition of a penalty for possessing an illegal drug influence demand, supply, price, and the quantity of the drug consumed?
3 How does the imposition of a penalty for selling *or* possessing an illegal drug influence demand, supply, price, and the quantity of the drug consumed?
4 Is there any case for legalizing drugs?

Work these questions in Study Plan 6.5 and get instant feedback.   MyEconLab

---

◆ You now know how to use the demand and supply model to predict prices, to study government actions in markets, and to study the sources and costs of inefficiency. In *Economics in the News* on pp. 144–145, you will see how to apply what you've learned by looking at the effects of the minimum wage rate in the market for low-skilled labor.

Push to Raise the Minimum Wage

Most State Minimum Wages Rising to Exceed the Federal Minimum

Bureau of Labor Statistics and National Conference of State Legislatures

The recovery from the 2008–2009 recession has not seen much growth in wage rates, and the spread between the top and bottom earnings has widened. Budget-strained low-paid workers and their political supporters think the minimum wage should rise.

The Bureau of Labor Statistics (BLS) reports that in 2013, 1.5 million earned the federal minimum wage of $7.25 an hour and about 1.8 million had wages below the federal minimum. These 3.3 million workers represented 4.3 percent of hourly paid workers, which compares to 4.7 percent in 2012 and 13.4 percent in 1979.

Federal law-makers are not moving, but most state legislatures agree that the minimum wage should rise. According to the National Conference of State Legislatures, 38 states introduced minimum wage bills during the 2014 session and 34 states considered increases to the state minimum wage rate. Ten states (Connecticut, Delaware, Hawaii, Maryland, Massachusetts, Michigan, Minnesota, Rhode Island, Vermont, and West Virginia) and D.C. have increased their minimum wage rate during the 2014 session.

As of August 1, 2014, 23 states and D.C. have minimum wage rates above the federal minimum wage and 18 states have minimum wage rates the same as the federal minimum wage of $7.25 an hour. A few states have minimum wage rates below the federal minimum wage, so the federal minimum thus applies in these cases.

Most economists think that a higher minimum wage will lower employment.

BLS Reports March 2014 Report 1048 *Characteristics of Minimum Wage Workers, 2013*, http://www.bls.gov/cps/minwage2013.pdf, and National Conference of State Legislatures, http://www.ncsl.org/research/labor-and-employment/state-minimum-wage-chart.aspx#1

MyEconLab More Economics in the News

ESSENCE OF THE STORY

- In 2014, 34 states considered raising the state minimum wage rate.

- In 2014, state minimum wage rates were higher than the federal rate of $7.25 an hour in 23 states and DC.

- Another 18 states have a minimum wage rate equal to the federal minimum.

- The Bureau of Labor Statistics reports that 3.3 million or 4.3 percent of hourly- paid workers were paid at or below the federal minimum in 2013.

- Supporters of minimum-wage hikes say that low-paid workers have fallen further behind.

- Economists say a higher minimum wage will cost jobs.

ECONOMIC ANALYSIS

- The state minimum wage rate exceeds the federal minimum wage rate in 23 states.

- The state average minimum wage in 2014 was $8.25 an hour, $1 more than the federal minimum of $7.25 an hour, set in 2009.

- Other wage rates have risen and the cost of living has increased, and there was a widely held view that the minimum wage rate needed to rise.

- With disagreement leading to inaction in Washington, an increasing number of state governments began to raise their state minimum wage rates to levels that exceeded the federal minimum wage.

- Supporters of the increases believed that employment would not be adversely affected, while opponents argued that the higher minimum wage would bring job losses.

- The figures illustrate these two opinions about the effect of a higher minimum wage rate.

- Figure 1 illustrates a market for low-skilled labor in which the equilibrium wage rate exceeds the minimum wage.

- The demand for labor is D_0 and the supply of labor is S_0, so the equilibrium wage rate is $8.75 an hour.

- The minimum wage rate is $8.25 an hour, so no one earns the minimum wage.

- Because the equilibrium wage rate exceeds the minimum wage rate, the quantity of labor demanded equals the quantity of labor supplied and the minimum wage rate has no effect on the market outcome.

- Figure 2 illustrates a market for low-skilled labor in which the equilibrium wage rate is lower than the minimum wage rate.

- The demand for labor is D_1 and the supply of labor is S_1, so the equilibrium wage rate is $7.75 an hour.

- The minimum wage rate is $8.25 an hour, and the quantity of labor employed equals the quantity demanded at the minimum wage rate.

- The quantity of labor demanded and employed is 3.6 million—the quantity estimated by the Bureau of Labor Statistics.

- At the equilibrium wage rate, the quantity of labor supplied is 3.7 million (an assumed quantity) and 0.1 million workers are unemployed.

- With the equilibrium wage rate less than the minimum wage rate, the quantity of labor demanded is less than the quantity of labor supplied and the minimum wage rate brings an increase in unemployment.

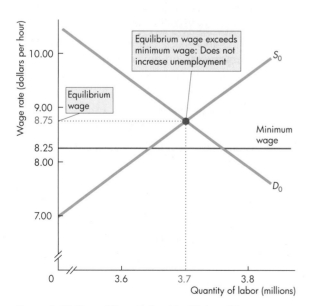

Figure 1 Minimum Wage Below Equilibrium Wage

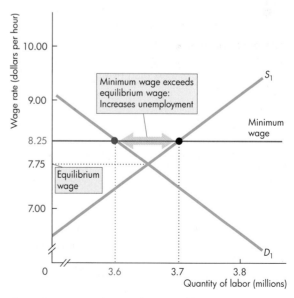

Figure 2 Minimum Wage Above Equilibrium Wage

ᴹMARY

Key Points

A Housing Market with a Rent Ceiling (pp. 128–130)

- A rent ceiling that is set above the equilibrium rent has no effect.
- A rent ceiling that is set below the equilibrium rent creates a housing shortage, increased search activity, and a black market.
- A rent ceiling that is set below the equilibrium rent is inefficient and unfair.

Working Problems 1 and 2 will give you a better understanding of a housing market with a rent ceiling.

A Labor Market with a Minimum Wage (pp. 131–133)

- A minimum wage set below the equilibrium wage rate has no effect.
- A minimum wage set above the equilibrium wage rate creates unemployment and increases the amount of time people spend searching for a job.
- A minimum wage set above the equilibrium wage rate is inefficient, unfair, and hits low-skilled young people hardest.

Working Problems 3 and 4 will give you a better understanding of a labor market with a minimum wage.

Taxes (pp. 133–138)

- A tax raises the price paid by buyers, but usually by less than the tax.
- The elasticity of demand and the elasticity of supply determine the share of a tax paid by buyers and sellers.

- The less elastic the demand or the more elastic the supply, the larger is the share of the tax paid by buyers.
- If demand is perfectly elastic or supply is perfectly inelastic, sellers pay the entire tax. And if demand is perfectly inelastic or supply is perfectly elastic, buyers pay the entire tax.

Working Problem 5 will give you a better understanding of taxes.

Production Quotas and Subsidies (pp. 139–141)

- A production quota leads to inefficient underproduction, which raises the price.
- A subsidy is like a negative tax. It lowers the price, increases the cost of production, and leads to inefficient overproduction.

Working Problems 6 and 7 will give you a better understanding of production quotas and subsidies.

Markets for Illegal Goods (pp. 142–143)

- Penalties on sellers increase the cost of selling the good and decrease the supply of the good.
- Penalties on buyers decrease their willingness to pay and decrease the demand for the good.
- Penalties on buyers and sellers decrease the quantity of the good, raise the price buyers pay, and lower the price sellers receive.
- Legalizing and taxing can achieve the same outcome as penalties on buyers and sellers.

Working Problem 8 will give you a better understanding of markets for illegal goods.

Key Terms

MyEconLab Key Terms Quiz

Black market, 128
Minimum wage, 131
Price cap, 128
Price ceiling, 128

Price floor, 131
Production quota, 139
Rent ceiling, 128
Search activity, 128

Subsidy, 140
Tax incidence, 133

◆ WORKED PROBLEM

MyEconLab   You can work this problem in Chapter 6 Study Plan.

The table shows the demand and supply schedules for tickets to a concert in the park.

Price (dollars per ticket)	Quantity demanded	Quantity supplied
	(tickets per concert)	
5	600	200
6	500	300
7	400	400
8	300	500
9	200	600
10	100	700

Questions

1. If there is no tax on concert tickets, what is the price of a ticket and how many tickets are bought?

If a sales tax of $2 a ticket is imposed on sellers of concert tickets

2. What is the price a concert-goer pays for a ticket and how many tickets are bought?
3. Who pays the tax and what is the government's tax revenue?
4. Is the market for concert tickets efficient? Explain.

Solutions

1. With no sales tax on concert tickets, the price of a ticket is the market equilibrium price, which is $7 a ticket. At $7 a ticket, the quantity of tickets bought is 400 per concert.
2. With a sales tax of $2 a ticket imposed on sellers, the supply of tickets decrease. The reason it that at any ticket price paid by buyers, concert organizers will receive $2 less per ticket.

   For example, concert organizers are willing to supply 700 tickets per concert if they receive $10 a ticket. But with a tax of $2 a ticket, concert organizers will receive only $8 a ticket after paying the government the $2 tax per ticket. So concert organizers will not be willing to supply 700 tickets at the after-tax price of $8 a ticket. The table above tells us that concert organizers are willing to supply only 500 tickets per concert when they receive $8 a ticket.

   We need to create the new supply schedule. We have already found one point on the new supply schedule: At a market price of $10 a ticket, concert organizers are willing to supply 500 tickets.

   The table in the next column shows the new supply schedule.

Price (dollars per ticket)	Quantity demanded	New quantity supplied
	(tickets per concert)	
6	500	
7	400	200
8	300	300
9	200	400
10	100	500

Check that you can explain why, at a market price of $7 a ticket, concert organizers are willing to supply 400 tickets when tickets are not taxed but only 200 tickets when tickets are taxed $2 per ticket.

With the $2 tax, concert-goers pay $8 a ticket and buy 300 tickets.

Key Point: A sales tax raises the market price and the quantity bought decreases.

3. If a sales tax of $2 a ticket is imposed on concert tickets, the price concert-goers pay rises from $7 a ticket to $8 a ticket. So concert-goers pay $1 of the $2 tax. Concert organizers pay the other $1 of tax. The government's tax revenue is $2 × 300, or $600.

Key Point: Some of the tax is paid by buyers and some by sellers.

4. With no tax, 400 tickets per concert is efficient. With the tax, the ticket price rises and the quantity bought decreases to 300 per concert. The outcome is inefficient and a deadweight loss arises.

Key Point: A sales tax that decreases the quantity sold is inefficient and creates a deadweight loss.

Key Figure

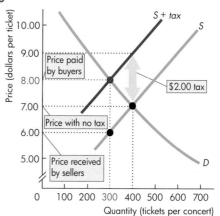

MyEconLab Interactive Animation

STUDY PLAN PROBLEMS AND APPLICATIONS

MyEconLab   You can work Problems 1 to 8 in Chapter 6 Study Plan and get instant feedback.

A Housing Market with a Rent Ceiling (Study Plan 6.1)

Use the following graph of the market for rental housing in Townsville to work Problems 1 and 2.

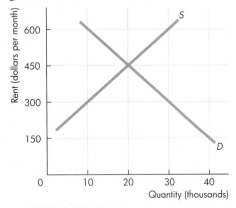

1. a. What are the equilibrium rent and the quantity of housing rented?

   b. If a rent ceiling is set at $600 a month, what is the rent paid? What is the shortage of housing?

2. If the rent ceiling is $300 a month, what is the quantity rented, the shortage of housing, and the maximum price that someone is willing to pay for the last unit of housing available?

A Labor Market with a Minimum Wage (Study Plan 6.2)

Use the following data on the demand and supply schedules of teenage labor to work Problems 3 and 4.

Wage rate (dollars per hour)	Quantity demanded	Quantity supplied
	(hours per month)	
5	2,500	1,500
6	2,000	2,000
7	1,500	2,500
8	1,000	3,000

3. Calculate the equilibrium wage rate, the hours worked, and the quantity of unemployment.

4. The minimum wage for teenagers is $7 an hour.

   a. How many hours are unemployed?

   b. If the demand for teenage labor increases by 500 hours a month, what is the wage rate and how many hours are unemployed?

Taxes (Study Plan 6.3)

5. The table in the next column sets out the demand and supply schedules for chocolate brownies.

Price (cents per brownie)	Quantity demanded	Quantity supplied
	(millions per day)	
50	5	3
60	4	4
70	3	5
80	2	6

   a. If sellers are taxed 20¢ a brownie, what is the price and who pays the tax?

   b. If buyers are taxed 20¢ a brownie, what is the price and who pays the tax?

Production Quotas and Subsidies (Study Plan 6.4)

Use the following data to work Problems 6 and 7. The demand and supply schedules for rice are

Price (dollars per box)	Quantity demanded	Quantity supplied
	(boxes per week)	
1.20	3,000	1,500
1.30	2,750	2,000
1.40	2,500	2,500
1.50	2,250	3,000
1.60	2,000	3,500

Calculate the price, the marginal cost of rice, and the quantity produced if the government

6. Sets a production quota of 2,000 boxes a week.

7. Introduces a subsidy of $0.30 a box.

Markets for Illegal Goods (Study Plan 6.5)

8. The figure shows the market for an illegal good.

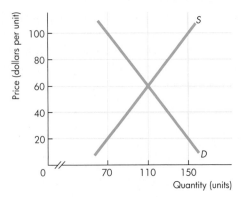

Calculate the market price and the quantity bought if a penalty of $20 a unit is imposed on

a. Sellers only or buyers only.

b. Both sellers and buyers.

ADDITIONAL PROBLEMS AND APPLICATIONS

MyEconLab   You can work these problems in MyEconLab if assigned by your instructor.

A Housing Market with a Rent Ceiling

Use the following table to work Problems 9 and 10. The table sets out the demand and supply schedules for college meals:

Price (dollars per meal)	Quantity demanded	Quantity supplied
	(meals per week)	
4	3,000	1,500
5	2,750	2,000
6	2,500	2,500
7	2,250	3,000
8	2,000	3,500

9. a. What are the equilibrium meal price and equilibrium quantity of meals?

   b. If the college put a price ceiling on meals at $7 a meal, what is the price students pay for a meal? How many meals do they buy?

10. If the college put a price ceiling on meals at $4 a meal, what is the quantity bought, the shortage of meals, and the maximum price that someone is willing to pay for the last meal available?

A Labor Market with a Minimum Wage

Use the following news clip to work Problems 11 and 12.

Malaysia Passes Its First Minimum Wage Law

About 3.2 million low-income workers across Malaysia are expected to benefit from the country's first minimum wage, which the government says will transform Malaysia into a high-income nation. Employer groups argue that paying the minimum wage, which is not based on productivity or performance, would raise their costs and reduce business profits.

Source: *The New York Times*, May 1, 2012

11. On a graph of the market for low-skilled labor, show the effect of the minimum wage on the quantity of labor employed.

12. Explain the effects of the minimum wage on the workers' surplus, the firms' surplus, and the efficiency of the market for low-skilled workers.

Taxes

13. Use the news clip in Problem 11.
    a. If the Malaysian government cut the tax on business profits, would it offset the effect of the minimum wage on employment? Explain.

    b. Would a cut in the Social Security tax that small businesses pay offset the effect of the higher minimum wage on employment? Explain.

14. The demand and supply schedules for tulips are

Price (dollars per bunch)	Quantity demanded	Quantity supplied
	(bunches per week)	
10	100	40
12	90	60
14	80	80
16	70	100
18	60	120

   a. If tulips are not taxed, what is the price and how many bunches are bought?

   b. If tulips are taxed $6 a bunch, what are the price and quantity bought? Who pays the tax?

15. **Cigarette Taxes, Black Markets, and Crime: Lessons from New York's 50-Year Losing Battle**

New York City has the highest cigarette taxes in the country. During the four months following the recent tax hike, sales of taxed cigarettes in the city fell by more than 50 percent as consumers turned to the city's bustling black market. The thriving illegal market for cigarettes has diverted billions of dollars from legitimate businesses and governments to criminals.

Source: Cato Institute, February 6, 2003

   a. How has the market for cigarettes in New York City responded to the high cigarette taxes?

   b. How does the emergence of a black market impact the elasticity of demand in a legal market?

   c. Why might an increase in the tax rate actually cause a decrease in the tax revenue?

Production Quotas and Subsidies

Use the following news clip to work Problems 16 to 18.

Crop Prices Erode Farm Subsidy Program

High corn and soybean prices mean farmers are making the most money in their lives. The reason: Grain prices are far too high to trigger payouts under the U.S. primary farm-subsidy program's "price support" formula. The market has done what Congress couldn't do and that is "slash farm subsidies."

Source: *The Wall Street Journal*, July 25, 2011

16. a. Why are U.S. soybean farmers subsidized?

b. Explain how a subsidy paid to soybean farmers affects the price of soybean and the marginal cost of producing it.

17. Show in a graph how a subsidy paid to soybean farmers affects the consumer surplus and the producer surplus from soybean. Does the subsidy make the soybean market more efficient or less efficient? Explain.

18. In the market for corn with a price support, explain why the corn price has risen and ended up being too high to "trigger payouts."

Use the following figure, which shows the market for tomatoes, to work Problems 19 and 20.

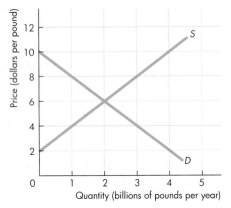

19. If the government subsidizes growers at $4 a pound, what is the quantity produced, the quantity demanded, and the subsidy paid to growers?

20. If the government subsidizes growers at $4 a pound, who gains and who loses from the subsidy? What is the deadweight loss? Could the subsidy be regarded as being fair?

Markets for Illegal Goods

21. The table gives the demand and supply schedules for an illegal drug.

Price (dollars per unit)	Quantity demanded	Quantity supplied
	(units per day)	
50	500	300
60	400	400
70	300	500
80	200	600
90	100	700

a. What is the price and how many units are bought if there is no penalty on drugs?

b. If the penalty on sellers is $20 a unit, what are the price and quantity consumed?

c. If the penalty on buyers is $20 a unit, what are the price and quantity consumed?

Economics in the News

22. After you have studied *Economics in the News* on pp. 144–145, answer the following questions.

a. When a state raises its minimum wage above the federal minimum, what would you expect to happen to unemployment in that state? Illustrate your answer with a graph.

b. The news article reports that the percentage of hourly paid workers paid the minimum wage or less decreased from 13.4 percent in 1979 to 4.3 percent in 2013. Would you expect the rise in the minimum wage to have a smaller effect on unemployment today than in 1979?

c. The news article reports that during the recovery from the 2008–2009 recession, wage rates grew slowly and the bottom wage rates grew slower than top wage rates, straining the budgets of low-paid workers. How would you expect this fact to have influenced the effect of the minimum wage on unemployment?

23. **Hollywood: Organized Crime Hits the Movies**

The Mexican army seized 1,180 disc burners and 3.14 million copies of movies and TV shows from 23 warehouses in a move to fight piracy that costs Hollywood about $590 million a year.

Source: Bloomberg *Businessweek,* April 7, 2011

Assume that the marginal cost of producing a DVD (legal or illegal) is a constant $3 and that legal DVDs bear an additional marginal cost of $5 each in royalty payments to film studios.

a. Draw a graph of the market for counterfeit DVDs, assuming that there are no effective penalties on either buyers or sellers for breaking the law.

b. How do the events reported in the news clip change the market outcome? Show the effects in your graph.

c. With no penalty on buyers, if a penalty for breaking the law is imposed on sellers at more than $5 a disc, how does the market work and what is the equilibrium price?

d. With no penalty on sellers, if a penalty for breaking the law is imposed on buyers at more than $5 a disc, how does the market work and what is the equilibrium price?

e. What is the marginal benefit of an illegal DVD in the situations described in parts (c) and (d)?

f. In light of your answer to part (e), why does law enforcement usually focus on sellers rather than buyers?

7
GLOBAL MARKETS IN ACTION

After studying this chapter, you will be able to:

◆ Explain how markets work with international trade

◆ Identify the gains from international trade and its winners and losers

◆ Explain the effects of international trade barriers

◆ Explain and evaluate arguments used to justify restricting international trade

iPhones, Wii games, and Nike shoes are just three of the items that you might buy that are not produced in the United States. Why don't we produce phones, games, and shoes in America? Isn't the globalization of production killing good American jobs?

You will find the answers in this chapter. And you will see why global trade is a win-win deal for buyers and sellers. You will also see why governments restrict trade, and in *Economics in the News* at the end of the chapter, why it is difficult for the United States to make a free-trade deal with Japan.

But first, we study the gains from international trade.

◆ How Global Markets Work

Because we trade with people in other countries, the goods and services that we can buy and consume are not limited by what we can produce. The goods and services that we buy from other countries are our **imports**; and the goods and services that we sell to people in other countries are our **exports**.

International Trade Today

Global trade today is enormous. In 2013, global exports and imports were $23 trillion, which is one third of the value of global production. The United States is the world's largest international trader and accounts for 10 percent of world exports and 12 percent of world imports. Germany and China, which rank 2 and 3 behind the United States, lag by a large margin.

In 2013, total U.S. exports were $2.3 trillion, which is about 14 percent of the value of U.S. production. Total U.S. imports were $2.7 trillion, which is about 17 percent of total expenditure in the United States.

We trade both goods and services. In 2013, exports of services were about one third of total exports and imports of services were about one fifth of total imports.

What Drives International Trade?

Comparative advantage is the fundamental force that drives international trade. Comparative advantage (see Chapter 2, p. 40) is a situation in which a person can perform an activity or produce a good or service at a lower opportunity cost than anyone else. This same idea applies to nations. We can define *national comparative advantage* as a situation in which a nation can perform an activity or produce a good or service at a lower opportunity cost than any other nation.

The opportunity cost of producing a T-shirt is lower in China than in the United States, so China has a comparative advantage in producing T-shirts. The opportunity cost of producing an airplane is lower in the United States than in China, so the United States has a comparative advantage in producing airplanes.

You saw in Chapter 2 how Liz and Joe reap gains from trade by specializing in the production of the good at which they have a comparative advantage and then trading with each other. Both are better off.

ECONOMICS IN ACTION

We Trade Services for Oil

We import huge amounts of oil—about $300 billion in 2012. How do we pay for all this oil? The answer is by exporting business, professional, and technical services, airplanes, food and drinks, and chemicals. We also trade a large quantity of automobiles, but we both export and import them (mainly in trade with Canada).

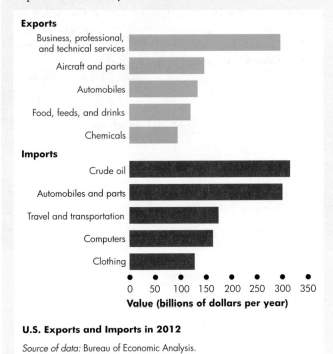

U.S. Exports and Imports in 2012

Source of data: Bureau of Economic Analysis.

This same principle applies to trade among nations. Because China has a comparative advantage at producing T-shirts and the United States has a comparative advantage at producing airplanes, the people of both countries can gain from specialization and trade. China can buy airplanes from the United States at a lower opportunity cost than that at which Chinese firms can produce them. And Americans can buy T-shirts from China for a lower opportunity cost than that at which U.S. firms can produce them. Also, through international trade, Chinese producers can get higher prices for their T-shirts and Boeing can sell airplanes for a higher price. Both countries gain from international trade.

Let's now illustrate the gains from trade that we've just described by studying demand and supply in the global markets for T-shirts and airplanes.

Why the United States Imports T-Shirts

The United States imports T-shirts because the rest of the world has a comparative advantage in producing T-shirts. Figure 7.1 illustrates how this comparative advantage generates international trade and how trade affects the price of a T-shirt and the quantities produced and bought.

The demand curve D_{US} and the supply curve S_{US} show the demand and supply in the U.S. domestic market only. The demand curve tells us the quantity of T-shirts that Americans are willing to buy at various prices. The supply curve tells us the quantity of T-shirts that U.S. garment makers are willing to sell at various prices—that is, the quantity supplied at each price when all T-shirts sold in the United States are produced in the United States.

Figure 7.1(a) shows what the U.S. T-shirt market would be like with no international trade. The price of a shirt would be $8 and 40 million shirts a year would be produced by U.S. garment makers and bought by U.S. consumers.

Figure 7.1(b) shows the market for T-shirts with international trade. Now the price of a T-shirt is determined in the world market, not the U.S. domestic market. The world price of a T-shirt is less than $8, which means that the rest of the world has a comparative advantage in producing T-shirts. The world price line shows the world price at $5 a shirt.

The U.S. demand curve, D_{US}, tells us that at $5 a shirt, Americans buy 60 million shirts a year. The U.S. supply curve, S_{US}, tells us that at $5 a shirt, U.S. garment makers produce 20 million T-shirts a year. To buy 60 million T-shirts when only 20 million are produced in the United States, we must import T-shirts from the rest of the world. The quantity of T-shirts imported is 40 million a year.

FIGURE 7.1   A Market with Imports

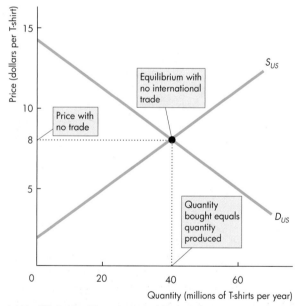

(a) Equilibrium with no international trade

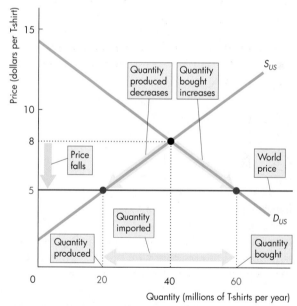

(b) Equilibrium in a market with imports

Part (a) shows the U.S. market for T-shirts with no international trade. The U.S. domestic demand curve D_{US} and U.S. domestic supply curve S_{US} determine the price of a T-shirt at $8 and the quantity of T- shirts produced and bought in the United States at 40 million a year.

Part (b) shows the U.S. market for T-shirts with

international trade. World demand for and world supply of T-shirts determine the world price of a T-shirt, which is $5. The price in the U.S. market falls to $5 a shirt. U.S. purchases of T-shirts increase to 60 million a year, and U.S. production of T-shirts decreases to 20 million a year. The United States imports 40 million T-shirts a year.

Why the United States Exports Airplanes

Figure 7.2 illustrates international trade in airplanes. The demand curve D_{US} and the supply curve S_{US} show the demand and supply in the U.S. domestic market only. The demand curve tells us the quantity of airplanes that U.S. airlines are willing to buy at various prices. The supply curve tells us the quantity of airplanes that U.S. aircraft makers are willing to sell at various prices.

Figure 7.2(a) shows what the U.S. airplane market would be like with no international trade. The price of an airplane would be $100 million and 400 airplanes a year would be produced by U.S. aircraft makers and bought by U.S. airlines.

Figure 7.2(b) shows the U.S. airplane market with international trade. Now the price of an airplane is determined in the world market and the world price of an airplane is higher than $100 million, which means that the United States has a comparative advantage in producing airplanes. The world price line shows the world price at $150 million.

The U.S. demand curve, D_{US}, tells us that at $150 million an airplane, U.S. airlines buy 200 airplanes a year. The U.S. supply curve, S_{US}, tells us that at $150 million an airplane, U.S. aircraft makers produce 700 airplanes a year. The quantity produced in the United States (700 a year) minus the quantity purchased by U.S. airlines (200 a year) is the quantity of airplanes exported, which is 500 airplanes a year.

◆ REVIEW QUIZ

1 Describe the situation in the market for a good or service that the United States imports.
2 Describe the situation in the market for a good or service that the United States exports.

You can work these questions in Study Plan 7.1 and get instant feedback. Do a Key Terms Quiz.   MyEconLab

---

FIGURE 7.2   A Market with Exports

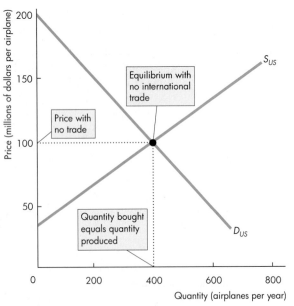

(a) Equilibrium without international trade

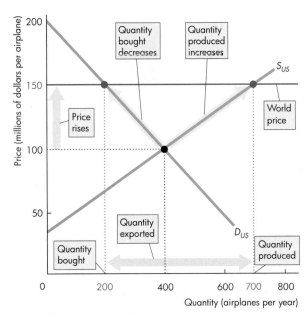

(b) Equilibrium in a market with exports

In part (a), the U.S. market with no international trade, the U.S. domestic demand curve D_{US} and the U.S. domestic supply curve S_{US} determine the price of an airplane at $100 million and 400 airplanes are produced and bought each year.

In part (b), the U.S. market with international trade, world demand and world supply determine the world price, which is $150 million per airplane. The price in the U.S. market rises. U.S. airplane production increases to 700 a year, and U.S. purchases of airplanes decrease to 200 a year. The United States exports 500 airplanes a year.

MyEconLab Animation

Winners, Losers, and the Net Gain from Trade

In Chapter 1 (see p. 6), we asked whether globalization is in the self-interest of the low-wage worker in Malaysia who sews your new running shoes and the displaced shoemaker in Atlanta? Is it in the social interest? We're now going to answer these questions. You will learn why producers complain about cheap foreign imports, but consumers of imports never complain.

Gains and Losses from Imports

We measure the gains and losses from imports by examining their effect on consumer surplus, producer surplus, and total surplus. In the importing country the winners are those whose surplus increases and the losers are those whose surplus decreases.

Figure 7.3(a) shows what consumer surplus and producer surplus would be with no international trade in T-shirts. U.S. domestic demand, D_{US}, and U.S. domestic supply, S_{US}, determine the price and quantity. The green area shows consumer surplus and the blue area shows producer surplus. Total surplus is the sum of consumer surplus and producer surplus.

Figure 7.3(b) shows how these surpluses change when the U.S. market opens to imports. The U.S. price falls to the world price. The quantity bought increases to the quantity demanded at the world price and consumer surplus expands from A to the larger green area $A + B + D$. The quantity produced in the United States decreases to the quantity supplied at the world price and producer surplus shrinks to the smaller blue area C.

Part of the gain in consumer surplus, the area B, is a loss of producer surplus—a redistribution of total surplus. But the other part of the increase in consumer surplus, the area D, is a net gain. This increase in total surplus results from the lower price and increased purchases and is the gain from imports.

FIGURE 7.3   Gains and Losses in a Market with Imports

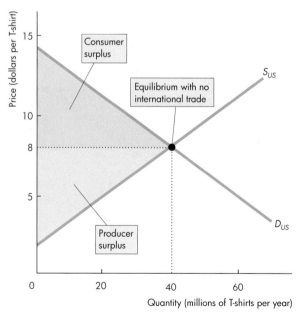

(a) Consumer surplus and producer surplus with no international trade

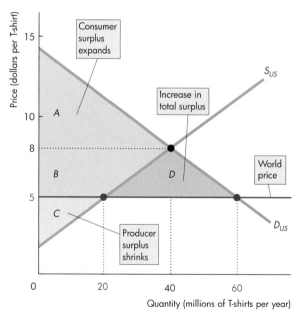

(b) Gains and losses from imports

In part (a), with no international trade, the green area shows the consumer surplus and the blue area shows the producer surplus.

In part (b), with international trade, the price falls to the world price of $5 a shirt. Consumer surplus expands from area A to the area $A + B + D$. Producer surplus shrinks to area C. Area B is a transfer of surplus from producers to consumers. Area D is an increase in total surplus—the gain from imports.

MyEconLab Animation and Draw Graph

Gains and Losses from Exports

We measure the gains and losses from exports just like we measured those from imports, by their effect on consumer surplus, producer surplus, and total surplus.

Figure 7.4(a) shows the situation with no international trade. Domestic demand, D_{US}, and domestic supply, S_{US}, determine the price and quantity, the consumer surplus, and the producer surplus.

Figure 7.4(b) shows how the consumer surplus and producer surplus change when the good is exported. The price rises to the world price. The quantity bought decreases to the quantity demanded at the world price and the consumer surplus shrinks to the green area A. The quantity produced increases to the quantity supplied at the world price and the producer surplus expands to the blue area $B + C + D$.

Part of the gain in producer surplus, the area B, is a loss in consumer surplus—a redistribution of the total surplus. But the other part of the increase in producer surplus, the area D, is a net gain. This increase in total

surplus results from the higher price and increased production and is the gain from exports.

Gains for All

You've seen that both imports and exports bring gains. Because one country's exports are other countries' imports, international trade brings gain for all countries. International trade is a win-win game.

◆ REVIEW QUIZ

1 How is the gain from imports distributed between consumers and domestic producers?
2 How is the gain from exports distributed between consumers and domestic producers?
3 Why is the net gain from international trade positive?

Work these questions in Study Plan 7.2 and get instant feedback.   MyEconLab

---

FIGURE 7.4   Gains and Losses in a Market with Exports

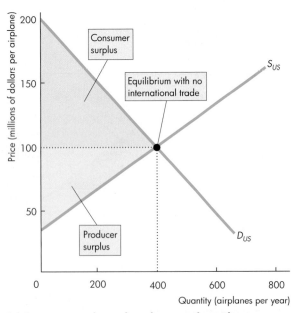

(a) Consumer surplus and producer surplus with no international trade

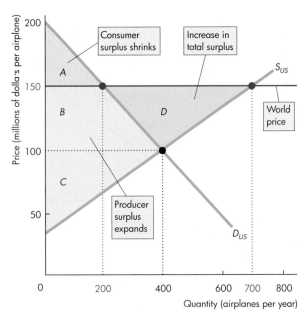

(b) Gains and losses from exports

In part (a), the U.S. market with no international trade, the green area shows the consumer surplus and the blue area shows the producer surplus. In part (b), the U.S. market with international trade, the price rises to the world price.

Consumer surplus shrinks to area A. Producer surplus expands from area C to the area $B + C + D$. Area B is a transfer of surplus from consumers to producers. Area D is an increase in total surplus—the gain from exports.

MyEconLab Animation and Draw Graph

◆ International Trade Restrictions

Governments use four sets of tools to influence international trade and protect domestic industries from foreign competition. They are

- Tariffs
- Import quotas
- Other import barriers
- Export subsidies

Tariffs

A **tariff** is a tax on a good that is imposed by the importing country when an imported good crosses its international boundary. For example, the government of India imposes a 100 percent tariff on wine imported from California. So when an Indian imports a $10 bottle of Californian wine, he pays the Indian government a $10 import duty.

Tariffs raise revenue for governments and serve the self-interest of people who earn their incomes in import-competing industries. But as you will see, restrictions on free international trade decrease the gains from trade and are not in the social interest.

The Effects of a Tariff To see the effects of a tariff, let's return to the example in which the United States imports T-shirts. With free trade, the T-shirts are imported and sold at the world price. Then, under pressure from U.S. garment makers, the U.S. government imposes a tariff on imported T-shirts. Buyers of T-shirts must now pay the world price plus the tariff. Several consequences follow and Fig. 7.5 illustrates them.

Figure 7.5(a) shows the situation with free international trade. The United States produces 20 million T-shirts a year and imports 40 million a year at the world price of $5 a shirt. Figure 7.5(b) shows what happens with a tariff set at $2 per T-shirt.

FIGURE 7.5   The Effects of a Tariff

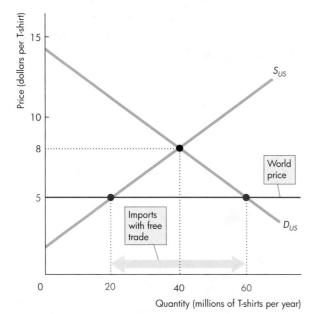

(a) Free trade

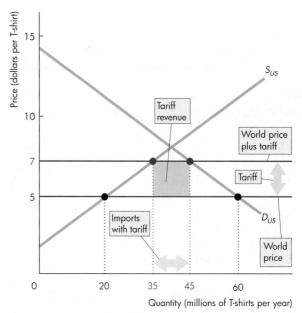

(b) Market with tariff

The world price of a T-shirt is $5. With free trade in part (a), Americans buy 60 million T-shirts a year. U.S. garment makers produce 20 million T-shirts a year and the United States imports 40 million a year.

With a tariff of $2 per T-shirt in part (b), the price in

the U.S. market rises to $7 a T-shirt. U.S. production increases, U.S. purchases decrease, and the quantity imported decreases. The U.S. government collects a tariff revenue of $2 on each T-shirt imported, which is shown by the purple rectangle.

The following changes occur in the market for T-shirts:

- The price of a T-shirt in the United States rises by $2.
- The quantity of T-shirts bought in the United States decreases.
- The quantity of T-shirts produced in the United States increases.
- The quantity of T-shirts imported into the United States decreases.
- The U.S. government collects a tariff revenue.

Rise in Price of a T-Shirt To buy a T-shirt, Americans must pay the world price plus the tariff, so the price of a T-shirt rises by the $2 tariff to $7. Figure 7.5(b) shows the new domestic price line, which lies $2 above the world price line. The price rises by the full amount of the tariff. The buyer pays the entire tariff because supply from the rest of the world is perfectly elastic (see Chapter 6, pp. 136–137).

Decrease in Purchases The higher price of a T-shirt brings a decrease in the quantity demanded along the demand curve. Figure 7.5(b) shows the decrease from 60 million T-shirts a year at $5 a shirt to 45 million a year at $7 a shirt.

Increase in Domestic Production The higher price of a T-shirt stimulates domestic production, and U.S. garment makers increase the quantity supplied along the supply curve. Figure 7.5(b) shows the increase from 20 million T-shirts at $5 a shirt to 35 million a year at $7 a shirt.

Decrease in Imports T-shirt imports decrease by 30 million, from 40 million to 10 million a year. Both the decrease in purchases and the increase in domestic production contribute to this decrease in imports.

Tariff Revenue The government's tariff revenue is $20 million—$2 per shirt on 10 million imported shirts—shown by the purple rectangle.

Winners, Losers, and the Social Loss from a Tariff A tariff on an imported good creates winners and losers and a social loss. When the U.S. government imposes a tariff on an imported good,

- U.S. consumers of the good lose.
- U.S. producers of the good gain.
- U.S. consumers lose more than U.S. producers gain.
- Society loses: a deadweight loss arises.

U.S. Consumers of the Good Lose Because the price of a T-shirt in the United States rises, the quantity of T-shirts demanded decreases. The combination of a higher price and smaller quantity bought decreases consumer surplus—the loss to U.S. consumers that arises from a tariff.

ECONOMICS IN ACTION

U.S. Tariffs Almost Gone

The Smoot-Hawley Act, which was passed in 1930, took U.S. tariffs to a peak average rate of 20 percent in 1933. (One third of imports was subject to a 60 percent tariff.) The **General Agreement on Tariffs and Trade (GATT)** was established in 1947. Since then tariffs have fallen in a series of negotiating rounds, the most significant of which are identified in the figure. Tariffs are now as low as they have ever been but import quotas and other trade barriers persist.

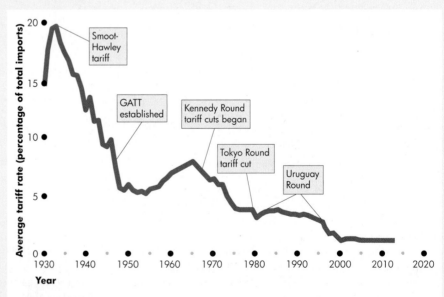

Tariffs: 1930–2013

Sources of data: U.S. Bureau of the Census, *Historical Statistics of the United States, Colonial Times to 1970,* Bicentennial Edition, Part 1 (Washington, D.C., 1975); Series U-212: updated from *Statistical Abstract of the United States:* various editions.

U.S. Producers of the Good Gain Because the price of an imported T-shirt rises by the amount of the tariff, U.S. T-shirt producers are now able to sell their T-shirts for the world price plus the tariff. At the higher price, the quantity of T-shirts supplied by U.S. producers increases. The combination of a higher price and larger quantity produced increases producer surplus—the gain to U.S. producers from the tariff.

U.S. Consumers Lose More Than U.S. Producers Gain Consumer surplus decreases for four reasons: Some becomes producer surplus, some is lost in a higher cost of production (domestic producers have higher costs than foreign producers), some is lost because imports decrease, and some goes to the government as tariff revenue. Figure 7.6 shows these sources of lost consumer surplus.

Figure 7.6(a) shows the consumer surplus and producer surplus with free international trade in T-shirts. Figure 7.6(b) shows the consumer surplus and producer surplus with a $2 tariff on imported T-shirts. By comparing Fig. 7.6(b) with Fig. 7.6(a), you can see how a tariff changes these surpluses.

Consumer surplus—the green area—shrinks for four reasons. First, the higher price transfers surplus from consumers to producers. The blue area B represents this loss (and gain of producer surplus). Second, domestic production costs more than imports. The supply curve S_{US} shows the higher cost of production and the gray area C shows this loss of consumer surplus. Third, some of the consumer surplus is transferred to the government. The purple area D shows this loss (and gain of government revenue). Fourth, some of the consumer surplus is lost because imports decrease. The gray area E shows this loss.

Society Loses: A Deadweight Loss Arises Some of the loss of consumer surplus is transferred to producers and some is transferred to the government and spent on government programs that people value. But the increase in production cost and the loss from decreased imports is transferred to no one: It is a social loss—a deadweight loss. The gray areas labeled C and E represent this deadweight loss. Total surplus decreases by the area $C + E$.

FIGURE 7.6 The Winners and Losers from a Tariff

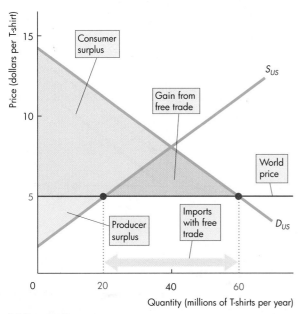

(a) Free trade

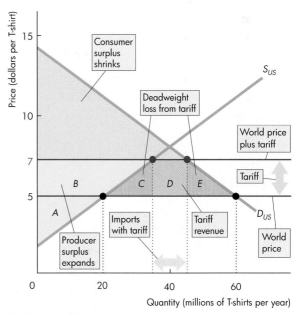

(b) Market with tariff

The world price of a T-shirt is $5. In part (a), with free trade, the United States imports 40 million T-shirts. Consumer surplus, producer surplus, and the gains from free trade are as large as possible.

In part (b), a tariff of $2 per T-shirt raises the U.S. price

of a T-shirt to $7. The quantity imported decreases. Consumer surplus shrinks by the areas B, C, D, and E. Producer surplus expands by area B. The government's tariff revenue is area D, and the tariff creates a deadweight loss equal to the area $C + E$.

Import Quotas

We now look at the second tool for restricting trade: import quotas. An **import quota** is a restriction that limits the quantity of a good that may be imported in a given period.

Most countries impose import quotas on a wide range of items. The United States imposes them on food products such as sugar and bananas and manufactured goods such as textiles and paper.

Import quotas enable the government to satisfy the self-interest of the people who earn their incomes in the import-competing industries. But you will discover that, like a tariff, an import quota decreases the gains from trade and is not in the social interest.

The Effects of an Import Quota The effects of an import quota are similar to those of a tariff. The price rises, the quantity bought decreases, and the quantity produced in the United States increases. Figure 7.7 illustrates the effects.

Figure 7.7(a) shows the situation with free international trade. Figure 7.7(b) shows what happens with an import quota of 10 million T-shirts a year. The U.S. supply curve of T-shirts becomes the domestic supply curve, S_{US}, plus the quantity that the import quota permits. So the supply curve becomes $S_{US} + quota$. The price of a T-shirt rises to $7, the quantity of T-shirts bought in the United States decreases to 45 million a year, the quantity of T-shirts produced in the United States increases to 35 million a year, and the quantity of T-shirts imported into the United States decreases to the quota quantity of 10 million a year. All the effects of this quota are identical to the effects of a $2 per shirt tariff, as you can check in Fig. 7.5(b).

Winners, Losers, and the Social Loss from an Import Quota An import quota creates winners and losers that are similar to those of a tariff but with an interesting difference.

FIGURE 7.7   The Effects of an Import Quota

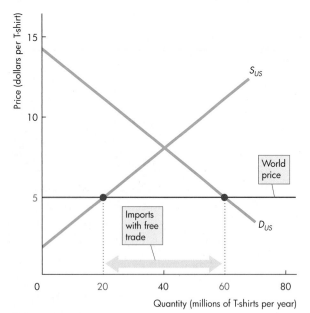

(a) Free trade

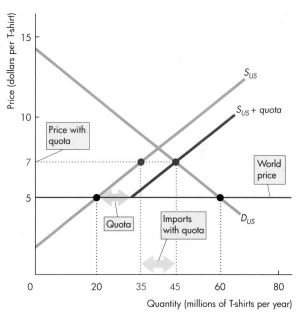

(b) Market with import quota

With free international trade, in part (a), Americans buy 60 million T-shirts at the world price. The United States produces 20 million T-shirts and imports 40 million a year. With an import quota of 10 million T-shirts a year, in part (b),

the supply of T-shirts in the United States is shown by the curve $S_{US} + quota$. The price in the United States rises to $7 a T-shirt. U.S. production increases, U.S. purchases decrease, and the quantity of T-shirts imported decreases.

When the government imposes an import quota,

- U.S. consumers of the good lose.
- U.S. producers of the good gain.
- Importers of the good gain.
- Society loses: a deadweight loss arises.

Figure 7.8 shows these gains and losses from a quota. By comparing Fig. 7.8(b) with a quota and Fig. 7.8(a) with free trade, you can see how an import quota of 10 million T-shirts a year changes the consumer and producer surpluses.

Consumer surplus—the green area—shrinks. This decrease is the loss to consumers from the import quota. The decrease in consumer surplus is made up of four parts. First, some of the consumer surplus is transferred to producers. The blue area B represents this loss of consumer surplus (and gain of producer surplus). Second, part of the consumer surplus is lost because the domestic cost of production is higher than the world price. The gray area C represents this loss. Third, part of the consumer surplus is transferred to importers who buy T-shirts for $5 (the world price) and sell them for $7 (the U.S. domestic price). The two blue areas D represent this loss of consumer surplus and profit for importers. Fourth, part of the consumer surplus is lost because imports decrease. The gray area E represents this loss.

The loss of consumer surplus from the higher cost of production and the decrease in imports is a social loss—a deadweight loss. The gray areas labeled C and E represent this deadweight loss. Total surplus decreases by the area $C + E$.

You can now see the one difference between a quota and a tariff. A tariff brings in revenue for the government while a quota brings a profit for the importers. All the other effects are the same, provided the quota is set at the same quantity of imports that results from the tariff.

FIGURE 7.8   The Winners and Losers from an Import Quota

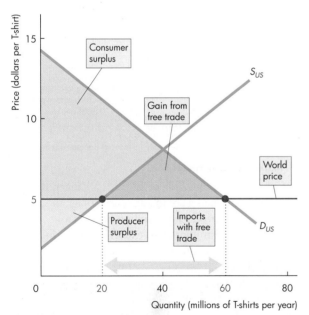

(a) Free trade

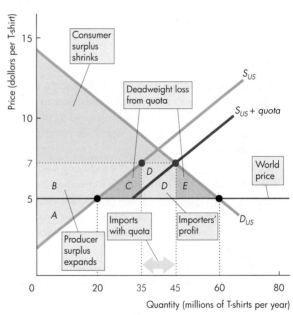

(b) Market with import quota

The world price of a T-shirt is $5. In part (a), with free trade, the United States produces 20 million T-shirts a year and imports 40 million T-shirts. Consumer surplus, producer surplus, and the gain from free international trade (darker green area) are as large as possible.

In part (b), the import quota raises the price of a T-shirt to $7. The quantity imported decreases. Consumer surplus shrinks by the areas B, C, D, and E. Producer surplus expands by area B. Importers' profit is the two areas D, and the quota creates a deadweight loss equal to $C + E$.

MyEconLab Animation and Draw Graph

ECONOMICS IN THE NEWS

The Changing Market for Coat Hangers

Your Dry Cleaning Bill Is About to Get Worse
The price of wire hangers is a big deal for a dry cleaner, and that price will rise when the Commerce Department puts a 21 percent tariff on hangers made in Vietnam. The tariff is in response to a wire-hanger export subsidy paid to producers in Vietnam.

Source: CNN Money, June 4, 2012

SOME FACTS

Albert J. Parkhouse invented the wire hanger in Jackson, Michigan, in 1903 and for almost 100 years, the United States produced and exported wire hangers. During the past 20 years, China and Vietnam have become the major lowest-cost producers.

THE PROBLEM

Explain why the United States has switched from exporting to importing wire hangers. Also explain the effects of the 21 percent tariff. Does Vietnam's export subsidy make the tariff efficient? Illustrate your explanations with a graph.

THE SOLUTION

■ Initially, the opportunity cost of producing a wire hanger was lower in the United States than in the rest of the world. The United States had a comparative advantage in producing wire hangers and exported them.

■ Today, the opportunity cost of producing a wire hanger is lower in China and Vietnam than in the United States (and other countries). China and Vietnam have a comparative advantage in producing wire hangers, so the United States imports them.

■ By imposing a 21 percent tariff on wire hangers, the price in the United States rises above the world price by this percentage.

■ The higher price decreases the quantity of wire hangers demanded in the United States, increases the quantity that U.S. producers supply, and decreases U.S. imports of wire hangers.

■ The figure illustrates the U.S. market for wire hangers. The demand curve D_{US} and the supply curve S_{US} are assumed not to change. The U.S. price with no international trade is 10 cents per hanger.

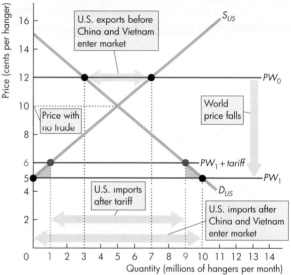

U.S. Market for Wire Hangers

■ With a world price PW_0 of 12 cents a hanger, the United States had a comparative advantage in hangers, so it produced 7 million hangers a month, used 3 million, and exported 4 million. The figure shows the quantity of U.S. exports.

■ When the world price falls to PW_1 at 5 cents a hanger, the United States stops producing hangers and imports 10 million a month.

■ With a 21 percent tariff, the price in the United States rises to $PW_1 + tariff$. U.S. hanger production now becomes 1 million a month, the quantity used decreases to 9 million, and imports decrease to 8 million.

■ The fact that the tariff is a response to Vietnam's export subsidy does not make the tariff efficient. It creates a deadweight loss shown by the two gray triangles.

MyEconLab More Economics in the News

Other Import Barriers

Two sets of policies that influence imports are

- Health, safety, and regulation barriers
- Voluntary export restraints

Health, Safety, and Regulation Barriers Thousands of detailed health, safety, and other regulations restrict international trade. For example, U.S. food imports are examined by the Food and Drug Administration to determine whether the food is "pure, wholesome, safe to eat, and produced under sanitary conditions." The discovery of BSE (mad cow disease) in just one U.S. cow in 2003 was enough to close down international trade in U.S. beef. The European Union bans imports of most genetically modified foods, such as U.S.-produced soybeans. Although regulations of the type we've just described are not designed to limit international trade, they have that effect.

Voluntary Export Restraints A *voluntary export restraint* is like a quota allocated to a foreign exporter of a good. This type of trade barrier isn't common. It was initially used during the 1980s when Japan voluntarily limited its exports of car parts to the United States.

Export Subsidies

A *subsidy* is a payment by the government to a producer. You studied the effects of a subsidy on the quantity produced and the price of a subsidized farm product in Chapter 6, pp. 140–141.

An *export subsidy* is a payment by the government to the producer of an exported good. Export subsidies are illegal under a number of international agreements, including the North American Free Trade Agreement (NAFTA), and the rules of the World Trade Organization (WTO).

Although export subsidies are illegal, the subsidies that the U.S. and European Union governments pay to farmers end up increasing domestic production, some of which gets exported. These exports of subsidized farm products make it harder for producers in other countries, notably in Africa and Central and South America, to compete in global markets. Export subsidies bring gains to domestic producers, but they result in inefficient underproduction in the rest of the world and create a deadweight loss.

ECONOMICS IN ACTION

Self-Interest Beats the Social Interest

The **World Trade Organization** (**WTO**) is an international body established by the world's major trading nations for the purpose of supervising international trade and lowering the barriers to trade.

In 2001, at a meeting of trade ministers from all the WTO member-countries held in Doha, Qatar, an agreement was made to begin negotiations to lower tariff barriers and quotas that restrict international trade in farm products and services. These negotiations are called the **Doha Development Agenda** or the **Doha Round**.

In the period since 2001, thousands of hours of conferences in Cancún in 2003, Geneva in 2004, and Hong Kong in 2005, and ongoing meetings at WTO headquarters in Geneva, costing millions of taxpayers' dollars, have made disappointing progress.

Rich nations, led by the United States, the European Union, and Japan, want greater access to the markets of developing nations in exchange for allowing those nations greater access to the markets of the rich world, especially those for farm products.

Developing nations, led by Brazil, China, India, and South Africa, want access to the markets of farm products of the rich world, but they also want to protect their infant industries.

With two incompatible positions, these negotiations are stalled and show no signs of a breakthrough. The self-interests of rich nations and developing nations are preventing the achievement of the social interest.

◆ REVIEW QUIZ

1 What are the tools that a country can use to restrict international trade?
2 Explain the effects of a tariff on domestic production, the quantity bought, and the price.
3 Explain who gains and who loses from a tariff and why the losses exceed the gains.
4 Explain the effects of an import quota on domestic production, consumption, and price.
5 Explain who gains and who loses from an import quota and why the losses exceed the gains.

Work these questions in Study Plan 7.3 and get instant feedback. Do a Key Terms Quiz.   MyEconLab

◆ The Case Against Protection

You've just seen that free trade promotes prosperity and protection is inefficient. Yet trade is restricted with tariffs, quotas, and other barriers. Why? Seven arguments for trade restrictions are that protecting domestic industries from foreign competition

- Helps an infant industry grow.
- Counteracts dumping.
- Saves domestic jobs.
- Allows us to compete with cheap foreign labor.
- Penalizes lax environmental standards.
- Prevents rich countries from exploiting developing countries.
- Reduces offshore outsourcing that sends good U.S. jobs to other countries.

Helps an Infant Industry Grow

Comparative advantages change with on-the-job experience—*learning-by-doing*. When a new industry or a new product is born—an *infant industry*—it is not as productive as it will become with experience. It is argued that such an industry should be protected from international competition until it can stand alone and compete.

It is true that learning-by-doing can change comparative advantage, but this fact doesn't justify protecting an infant industry. Firms anticipate and benefit from learning-by-doing without protection from foreign competition.

When Boeing started to build airplanes, productivity was at first low. But after a period of learning-by-doing, huge productivity gains followed. Boeing didn't need a tariff to achieve these productivity gains.

Counteracts Dumping

Dumping occurs when a foreign firm sells its exports at a lower price than its cost of production. Dumping might be used by a firm that wants to gain a global monopoly. In this case, the foreign firm sells its output at a price below its cost to drive domestic firms out of business. When the domestic firms have gone, the foreign firm takes advantage of its monopoly position and charges a higher price for its product. Dumping is illegal under the rules of the World Trade Organization and is usually regarded as a justification for temporary tariffs, which are called *countervailing duties*.

But it is virtually impossible to detect dumping because it is hard to determine a firm's costs. As a result, the test for dumping is whether a firm's export price is below its domestic price. But this test is weak because it is rational for a firm to charge a low price in a market in which the quantity demanded is highly sensitive to price and a higher price in a market in which demand is less price-sensitive.

Saves Domestic Jobs

First, free trade does destroy some jobs, but it also creates other jobs. It brings about a global rationalization of labor and allocates labor resources to their highest-valued activities. International trade in textiles has cost tens of thousands of U.S. jobs as U.S. textile mills and other factories closed. But tens of thousands of jobs have been created in other countries as textile mills opened. And tens of thousands of U.S. workers have better-paying jobs than as textile workers because U.S. export industries have expanded and created new jobs. More jobs have been created than destroyed.

Although protection can save particular jobs, it does so at a high cost. For example, until 2005, U.S. textile jobs were protected by an international agreement called the Multifiber Arrangement. The U.S. International Trade Commission (ITC) has estimated that because of import quotas, 72,000 jobs existed in the textile industry that would otherwise have disappeared and that the annual clothing expenditure in the United States was $15.9 billion ($160 per family) higher than it would have been with free trade. Equivalently, the ITC estimated that each textile job saved cost $221,000 a year.

Imports don't only destroy jobs. They create jobs for retailers that sell imported goods and for firms that service those goods. Imports also create jobs by creating income in the rest of the world, some of which is spent on U.S.-made goods and services.

Allows Us to Compete with Cheap Foreign Labor

With the removal of tariffs on trade between the United States and Mexico, people said we would hear a "giant sucking sound" as jobs rushed to Mexico. That didn't happen. Why?

It didn't happen because low-wage labor is low-productivity labor. If a U.S. autoworker earns $30 an hour and produces 15 units of output an hour, the average labor cost of a unit of output is $2. If a Mexican auto-worker earns $3 an hour and produces 1 unit of output an hour, the average labor cost of a unit of output is $3. Other things remaining the same, the higher a worker's productivity, the higher is the worker's wage rate. High-wage workers have high productivity; low-wage workers have low productivity.

It is *comparative advantage*, not wage differences, that drive international trade and that enable us to compete with Mexico and Mexico to compete with us.

Penalizes Lax Environmental Standards

Another argument for protection is that it provides an incentive to poor countries to raise their environmental standards—free trade with the richer and "greener" countries is a reward for improved environmental standards.

This argument for protection is weak. First, a poor country cannot afford to be as concerned about its environmental standard as a rich country can. Today, some of the worst pollution of air and water is found in China, Mexico, and the former communist countries of Eastern Europe. But only a few decades ago, London and Los Angeles topped the pollution league chart. The best hope for cleaner air in Beijing and Mexico City is rapid income growth, which free trade promotes. As incomes in developing countries grow, they have the *means* to match their desires to improve their environment. Second, a poor country may have a comparative advantage at doing "dirty" work, which helps it to raise its income and at the same time enables the global economy to achieve higher environmental standards than would otherwise be possible.

Prevents Rich Countries from Exploiting Developing Countries

Another argument for protection is that international trade must be restricted to prevent the people of the rich industrial world from exploiting the poorer people of the developing countries and forcing them to work for slave wages.

Child labor and near-slave labor are serious problems. But by trading with poor countries, we increase the demand for the goods that these countries produce and increase the demand for their labor. When the demand for labor in developing countries increases, the wage rate rises. So, rather than exploiting people in developing countries, trade can improve their opportunities and increase their incomes.

Reduces Offshore Outsourcing that Sends Good U.S. Jobs to Other Countries

Offshore outsourcing—buying goods, components, or services from firms in other countries—brings gains from trade identical to those of any other type of trade. We could easily change the names of the items traded from T-shirts and airplanes (the examples in the previous sections of this chapter) to banking services and call-center services (or any other pair of services). A U.S. bank might export banking services to Indian firms, and Indians might provide call-center services to U.S. firms. This type of trade would benefit both Americans and Indians, provided the United States has a comparative advantage in banking services and India has a comparative advantage in call-center services.

Despite the gain from specialization and trade that offshore outsourcing brings, many people believe that it also brings costs that eat up the gains. Why?

A major reason is that it seems to send good U.S. jobs to other countries. It is true that some manufacturing and service jobs are going overseas. But others are expanding at home. The United States imports call-center services, but it exports education, healthcare, legal, financial, and a host of other types of services. The number of jobs in these sectors is expanding and will continue to expand.

The exact number of jobs that have moved to lower-cost offshore locations is not known, and estimates vary. But even the highest estimate is small compared to the normal rate of job creation and labor turnover.

Gains from trade do not bring gains for every single person. Americans, on average, gain from offshore outsourcing, but some people lose. The losers are those who have invested in the human capital to do a specific job that has now gone offshore.

Unemployment benefits provide short-term temporary relief for these displaced workers. But the long-term solution requires retraining and the acquisition of new skills.

Beyond bringing short-term relief through unemployment benefits, government has a larger role to play. By providing education and training, it can enable the labor force of the twenty-first century to engage in the ongoing learning and sometimes rapid retooling that jobs we can't foresee today will demand.

Schools, colleges, and universities will expand and become better at doing their job of producing a more highly educated and flexible labor force.

◆ AT **ISSUE**

Is Offshore Outsourcing Bad or Good for America?

Citibank, Bank of America, Apple, Nike, and Wal-Mart engage in offshore outsourcing when they buy finished goods, components, or services from firms in other countries. Buying goods and components has been going on for centuries, but buying *services* such as customer support call-center services, is new and is made possible by the development of low-cost telephone and Internet service.

Should this type of offshore outsourcing be discouraged and penalized with taxes and regulations?

Bad	Good
■ In his 2012 *State of the Union Address*, President Obama said, "A business that wants to outsource jobs shouldn't get a tax deduction for doing it. … It is time to stop rewarding businesses that ship jobs overseas, and start rewarding companies that create jobs right here in America."	■ Economist N. Gregory Mankiw, when Chair of President George W. Bush's Council of Economic Advisers, said, "I think outsourcing … is probably a plus for the economy in the long run."
■ A survey conducted in 2004 found that 69 percent of Americans think outsourcing hurts the U.S. economy and only 17 percent think it helps.	■ Mankiw went on to say that it doesn't matter whether "items produced abroad come on planes, ships, or over fiber-optic cables … the economics is basically the same."
	■ What Greg Mankiw is saying is that the economic analysis of the gains from international trade—exactly the same as what you have studied on pp. 153–156—applies to all types of international trade.
	■ Offshore outsourcing, like all other forms of international trade, is a source of gains for all.

Have these Indian call-center workers destroyed American jobs? Or does their work benefit American workers?

Avoiding Trade Wars

We have reviewed the arguments commonly heard in favor of protection and the counterarguments against it. But one counterargument to protection that is general and quite overwhelming is that protection invites retaliation and can trigger a trade war.

A trade war is a contest in which when one country raises its import tariffs, other countries retaliate with increases of their own, which trigger yet further increases from the first country.

A trade war occurred during the Great Depression of the 1930s when the United States introduced the Smoot-Hawley tariff. Country after country retaliated with its own tariff, and in a short period, world trade had almost disappeared. The costs to all countries were large and led to a renewed international resolve to avoid such self-defeating moves in the future. The costs also led to attempts to liberalize trade following World War II.

Why Is International Trade Restricted?

Why, despite all the arguments against protection, is trade restricted? There are two key reasons:

■ Tariff revenue
■ Rent seeking

Tariff Revenue Government revenue is costly to collect. In developed countries such as the United States, a well-organized tax collection system is in place that can generate billions of dollars of income tax and sales tax revenues.

But governments in developing countries have a difficult time collecting taxes from their citizens. Much economic activity takes place in an informal economy with few financial records. The one area in which economic transactions are well recorded is international trade. So tariffs on international trade are a convenient source of revenue in these countries.

Rent Seeking Rent seeking is the major reason why international trade is restricted. **Rent seeking** is lobbying for special treatment by the government to create economic profit or to divert consumer surplus or producer surplus away from others. Free trade increases consumption possibilities *on average*, but not everyone shares in the gain and some people even lose. Free trade brings benefits to some and imposes costs on others, with total benefits exceeding total costs. The uneven distribution of costs and benefits is the principal obstacle to achieving more liberal international trade.

Returning to the example of trade in T-shirts and airplanes, the benefits from free trade accrue to all the producers of airplanes and to those producers of T-shirts that do not bear the costs of adjusting to a smaller garment industry. These costs are transition costs, not permanent costs. The costs of moving to free trade are borne by the garment producers and their employees who must become producers of other goods and services in which the United States has a comparative advantage.

The number of winners from free trade is large, but because the gains are spread thinly over a large number of people, the gain per person is small. The winners could organize and become a political force lobbying for free trade. But political activity is costly. It uses time and other scarce resources and the gains per person are too small to make the cost of political activity worth bearing.

In contrast, the number of losers from free trade is small, but the loss per person is large. Because the loss per person is large, the people who lose *are* willing to incur considerable expense to lobby against free trade.

Both the winners and losers weigh benefits and costs. Those who gain from free trade weigh the benefits it brings against the cost of achieving it. Those who lose from free trade and gain from protection weigh the benefit of protection against the cost of maintaining it. The protectionists undertake a larger quantity of political lobbying than the free traders.

Compensating Losers

If, in total, the gains from free international trade exceed the losses, why don't those who gain compensate those who lose so that everyone is in favor of free trade?

Some compensation does take place. When Congress approved the North American Free Trade

Agreement (NAFTA) with Canada and Mexico, it set up a $56 million fund to support and retrain workers who lost their jobs as a result of the new trade agreement. During NAFTA's first six months, only 5,000 workers applied for benefits under this scheme. The losers from international trade are also compensated indirectly through the normal unemployment compensation arrangements. But only limited attempts are made to compensate those who lose.

The main reason full compensation is not attempted is that the costs of identifying all the losers and estimating the value of their losses would be enormous. Also, it would never be clear whether a person who has fallen on hard times is suffering because of free trade or for other reasons that might be largely under her or his control. Furthermore, some people who look like losers at one point in time might, in fact, end up gaining. The young autoworker who loses his job in Michigan and becomes a computer assembly worker in Minneapolis might resent the loss of work and the need to move. But a year later, looking back on events, he counts himself fortunate.

Because we do not, in general, compensate the losers from free international trade, protectionism is a popular and permanent feature of our national economic and political life.

◆ REVIEW QUIZ

1 What are the infant industry and dumping arguments for protection? Are they correct?
2 Can protection save jobs and the environment and prevent workers in developing countries from being exploited?
3 What is offshore outsourcing? Who benefits from it and who loses?
4 What are the main reasons for imposing a tariff?
5 Why don't the winners from free trade win the political argument?

Work these questions in Study Plan 7.4 and get instant feedback. Do a Key Terms Quiz.   MyEconLab

◆ We end this chapter on global markets in action with *Economics in the News* on pp. 168–169, where we apply what you've learned by looking at the benefits of and obstacles to a U.S. free-trade deal with Japan.

Obstacles to Free Trade

Obama and Abe Fail to Reach Trade Deal

Thw Financial Times
April 25, 2014

… Despite encouraging statements from Mr. Obama and Japanese prime minister Shinzo Abe, negotiators failed to overcome differences on Japanese agricultural tariffs and the automobile trade. …

In their joint statement, Mr. Obama and Mr. Abe said the progress made marked a "key milestone in the Trans Pacific Partnership (TPP) negotiations and will inject fresh momentum into the broader talks." But neither side provided any details about what was achieved. …

"All of us have to move out of our comfort zones and not just expect that we are going to get access to somebody else's market without providing access to our own," Mr. Obama said on Thursday.

The talks between the United States and Japan have been focused on agriculture and cars. The United States has been seeking greater access to Japan's automotive and agricultural markets although Japan has vowed to do what it can to protect politically sensitive products such as beef, pork, and rice. In exchange, Japan wants the United States to remove its existing tariffs on imported cars and light trucks.

The significance of a breakthrough, however, would be much broader, said Jeffrey Schott, a close watcher of the TPP and U.S. trade policy at the Washington-based Peterson Institute for International Economics.

Chief negotiators from all 12 TPP countries are due to gather in Vietnam in May and their trade ministers are expected to meet shortly afterwards in China. Both encounters are seen as important for efforts to wrap up the TPP. Not having a U.S.-Japan deal before then would be a setback.

Any deal with Japan would also help the Obama administration in its efforts to secure so-called "fast track" negotiating authority from Congress. Senior Democrats have been reluctant to back the U.S. president's plan.

Jonathan Soble and Shawn Donnan, "Obama and Abe Fail to Reach Trade Deal," *The Financial Times*, April 25, 2014.

MyEconLab More Economics in the News

ESSENCE OF THE STORY

- The United States and Japan are attempting to make a trade agreement as a component of the broad TPP.

- Negotiations have focused on agriculture and cars.

- The United States wants greater access to Japan's auto and agricultural markets.

- Japan wants to protect beef, pork, and rice.

- Japan wants the United States to remove tariffs on imported cars and light trucks.

- Not having a U.S.-Japan deal before broader negotiations among the 12 TPP nations would be a setback.

ECONOMIC ANALYSIS

- Twelve Pacific-rim nations are attempting to reach a trade deal that lowers barriers to trade.

- The United States and Japan, the two largest of the economies, are seeking agreement ahead of the broader negotiations, but obstacles stand in the way of a deal.

- The core of the problem is Japan's wish to protect its farmers, and especially its rice farmers.

- Figure 1 shows how Japan is protecting its rice farmers but damaging its consumers' interest.

- The demand curve is D_J and the supply curve is S_J. With a total ban on rice imports (an import quota of zero), the price of rice is $4,000 per ton and 10 million tons are produced and consumed per year.

- If Japan opened up its rice market to free international trade, the price of rice would fall. In Fig. 1, the price falls to the world price (assumed) of $2,800 per ton, shown by the line PW.

- With free trade, Japan can buy rice for $2,800 per ton and the price in Japan falls to that level. The quantity of rice demanded increases to 16 million tons, the quantity supplied decreases to 6 million tons, and 10 million tons are imported. (Assumed quantities.)

- The Japanese rice producers' surplus shrinks and the Japanese consumer surplus expands by the amount of the light green area. Consumer surplus also increases and total surplus increases by the darker green area.

- The farm lobby in Japan is strong and the government is unwilling to risk losing votes by permitting free trade in rice. But it has moved in that direction in its deal with Australia, and it is expected to move further in a deal with the United States.

- Figure 2 shows why the United States is interested in this deal. The demand curve for rice is D_{US} and the supply curve is S_{US}. If there were no international trade in rice, the price in the United States would be $1,600 per ton and 4 million tons would be produced and consumed each year.

- With free trade, the United States can sell rice at the world price of $2,800 per ton and the price in the United States rises to that level. The quantity of rice demanded decreases to 2 million tons, the quantity supplied increases to 8 million tons, and 6 million tons are exported. (Assumed quantities.)

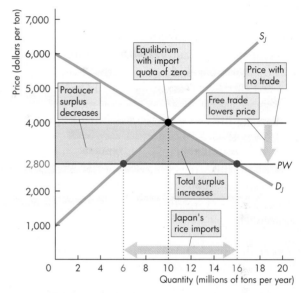

Figure 1 The Market for Rice in Japan

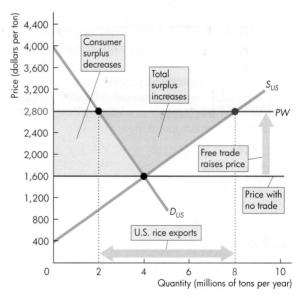

Figure 2 The Market for Rice in the United States

- The U.S. consumer surplus shrinks and the U.S. rice producers' surplus expands by the amount of the light blue area. Producer surplus also increases and total surplus increases by the darker blue area.

169

SUMMARY

Key Points

How Global Markets Work (pp. 152–154)

- Comparative advantage drives international trade.
- If the world price of a good is lower than the domestic price, the rest of the world has a comparative advantage in producing that good and the domestic country gains by producing less, consuming more, and importing the good.
- If the world price of a good is higher than the domestic price, the domestic country has a comparative advantage in producing that good and gains by producing more, consuming less, and exporting the good.

Working Problems 1 to 3 will give you a better understanding of how global markets work.

Winners, Losers, and the Net Gain from Trade (pp. 155–156)

- Compared to a no-trade situation, in a market with imports, consumer surplus is larger, producer surplus is smaller, and total surplus is larger with free international trade.
- Compared to a no-trade situation, in a market with exports, consumer surplus is smaller, producer surplus is larger, and total surplus is larger with free international trade.

Working Problem 4 will give you a better understanding of winners, losers, and the net gains from trade.

International Trade Restrictions (pp. 157–163)

- Countries restrict international trade by imposing tariffs, import quotas, and other import barriers.
- Trade restrictions raise the domestic price of imported goods, lower the quantity imported, decrease consumer surplus, increase producer surplus, and create a deadweight loss.

Working Problems 5 to 11 will give you a better understanding of international trade restrictions.

The Case Against Protection (pp. 164–167)

- Arguments that protection helps an infant industry to grow and counteracts dumping are weak.
- Arguments that protection saves jobs, allows us to compete with cheap foreign labor, is needed to penalize lax environmental standards, and prevents exploitation of developing countries are flawed.
- Offshore outsourcing is just a new way of reaping gains from trade and does not justify protection.
- Trade restrictions are popular because protection brings a small loss per person to a large number of people and a large gain per person to a small number of people. Those who gain have a stronger political voice than those who lose and it is too costly to identify and compensate losers.

Working Problem 12 will give you a better understanding of the case against protection.

Key Terms

MyEconLab Key Terms Quiz

Dumping, 164

Exports, 152

Import quota, 160

Imports, 152

Offshore outsourcing, 165

Rent seeking, 167

Tariff, 157

WORKED PROBLEM

MyEconLab   You can work this problem in Chapter 7 Study Plan.

The table shows the U.S. demand schedule for honey and the supply schedule of honey by U.S. producers. The world price of honey is $8 a jar.

Price (dollars per jar)	Quantity demanded	Quantity supplied
	(millions of jars per year)	
5	10	0
6	8	3
7	6	6
8	4	9
9	2	12
10	0	15

Questions

1. With no international trade, what is the price of honey and the quantity bought and sold in the United States? Does the United States have a comparative advantage in producing honey and with free international trade, does the United States export or import honey?

2. With free international trade, what is the U.S. price of honey, the quantity bought by Americans, the quantity produced in the United States, and the quantity of honey exported or imported?

3. Do Americans gain from international trade in honey? Do all Americans gain? If not, who loses and do the gains exceed the losses?

Solutions

1. With no international trade, the price of honey is that at which the U.S. quantity demanded equals the U.S quantity supplied. The table shows that this price is $7 a jar at which the equilibrium quantity is 6 million jars a year.

   The price of honey in the United States is less than the world price, which means that the opportunity cost of producing a jar of honey in the United States is *less* than the opportunity cost of producing it in the rest of the world. So U.S. producers have a comparative advantage in producing honey and with free international trade, the United States exports honey.

Key Point: Comparative advantage is determined by comparing the opportunity cost of producing the good in the United States to the world price.

2. With free international trade, the price of honey in the United States rises to the world price of $8 a jar. Americans cut their consumption of honey

to 4 million jars a year while U.S. honey producers expand production to 9 million jars a year. The United States exports 5 million jars a year.

The figure shows the quantities bought and produced in the United States and the quantity exported.

Key Point: As the domestic price rises to the world price, the quantity demanded decreases and the quantity supplied increases, and the difference is exported.

3. With free international trade, the United States gains from exporting honey because the higher price and the larger quantity of honey produced increase U.S. total surplus from honey.

   Consumers lose because the price of honey rises and they buy less honey. Consumer surplus from honey decreases. But the higher price and the larger quantity produced increase producer surplus from honey. The United States gains because the increase in producer surplus is greater than the loss in consumer surplus.

   The figure shows that with no trade, consumer surplus equals area $A + B$ and producer surplus equals area C. With free trade, consumer surplus shrinks to area A, producer surplus expands to area $B + C + D$, and total surplus (the gains from trade in honey) increases by area D.

Key Point: Free trade increases the total surplus, but for an exporting country some consumer surplus is transferred to producers of the exported good.

Key Figure

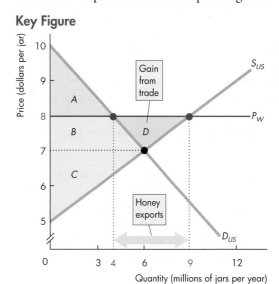

MyEconLab Interactive Graph

STUDY PLAN PROBLEMS AND APPLICATIONS

MyEconLab   You can work Problems 1 to 11 in Chapter 7 Study Plan and get instant feedback.

How Global Markets Work (Study Plan 7.1)

Use the following data to work Problems 1 to 3. Wholesalers buy and sell roses in containers that hold 120 stems. The table provides information about the wholesale market for roses in the United States. The demand schedule is the wholesalers' demand and the supply schedule is the U.S. rose growers' supply.

Price (dollars per container)	Quantity demanded	Quantity supplied
	(millions of containers per year)	
100	15	0
125	12	2
150	9	4
175	6	6
200	3	8
225	0	10

Wholesalers can buy roses at auction in Aalsmeer, Holland, for $125 per container.

1. a. Without international trade, what would be the price of a container of roses and how many containers of roses a year would be bought and sold in the United States?

    b. At the price in your answer to part (a), does the United States or the rest of the world have a comparative advantage in producing roses?

2. If U.S. wholesalers buy roses at the lowest possible price, how many do they buy from U.S. growers and how many do they import?

3. Draw a graph to illustrate the U.S. wholesale market for roses. Show the equilibrium in that market with no international trade and the equilibrium with free trade. Mark the quantity of roses produced in the United States, the quantity imported, and the total quantity bought.

Winners, Losers, and the Net Gain from Trade
(Study Plan 7.2)

4. Use the information on the U.S. wholesale market for roses in Problem 1 to

    a. Explain who gains and who loses from free international trade in roses compared to a situation in which Americans buy only roses grown in the United States.

    b. Draw a graph to illustrate the gains and losses from free trade.

    c. Calculate the gain from international trade.

International Trade Restrictions (Study Plan 7.3)

Use the information on the U.S. wholesale market for roses in Problem 1 to work Problems 5 to 10.

5. If the United States puts a tariff of $25 per container on imports of roses, explain how the U.S. price of roses, the quantity of roses bought, the quantity produced in the United States, and the quantity imported change.

6. Who gains and who loses from this tariff?

7. Draw a graph of the U.S. market for roses to illustrate the gains and losses from the tariff and on the graph identify the gains and losses, the tariff revenue, and the deadweight loss created.

8. If the United States puts an import quota on roses of 5 million containers, what happens to the U.S. price of roses, the quantity of roses bought, the quantity produced in the United States, and the quantity imported?

9. Who gains and who loses from this quota?

10. Draw a graph to illustrate the gains and losses from the import quota and on the graph identify the gains and losses, the importers' profit, and the deadweight loss.

The Case Against Protection (Study Plan 7.4)

11. **Chinese Tire Maker Rejects Charge of Defects**
    U.S. regulators ordered the recall of more than 450,000 faulty tires. The Chinese producer of the tires disputed the allegations and hinted that the recall might be an effort to hamper Chinese exports to the United States.

    Source: *International Herald Tribune,*
    June 26, 2007

    a. What does the news clip imply about the comparative advantage of producing tires in the United States and China?

    b. Could product quality be a valid argument against free trade? If it could, explain how.

ADDITIONAL PROBLEMS AND APPLICATIONS

MyEconLab   You can work these problems in MyEconLab if assigned by your instructor.

How Global Markets Work

12. Suppose that the world price of sugar is 10 cents a pound, the United States does not trade internationally, and the equilibrium price of sugar in the United States is 20 cents a pound. The United States then begins to trade internationally.
    a. How does the price of sugar in the United States change?
    b. Do U.S. consumers buy more or less sugar?
    c. Do U.S. sugar growers produce more or less sugar?
    d. Does the United States export or import sugar and why?

13. Suppose that the world price of steel is $100 a ton, India does not trade internationally, and the equilibrium price of steel in India is $60 a ton. India then begins to trade internationally.
    a. How does the price of steel in India change?
    b. How does the quantity of steel produced in India change?
    c. How does the quantity of steel bought by India change?
    d. Does India export or import steel and why?

14. A semiconductor is a key component in your laptop, cellphone, and iPod. The table provides information about the market for semiconductors in the United States.

Price (dollars per unit)	Quantity demanded	Quantity supplied
	(billions of units per year)	
10	25	0
12	20	20
14	15	40
16	10	60
18	5	80
20	0	100

Producers of semiconductors can get $18 a unit on the world market.
    a. With no international trade, what would be the price of a semiconductor and how many semiconductors a year would be bought and sold in the United States?
    b. Does the United States have a comparative advantage in producing semiconductors?

15. **Act Now, Eat Later**
    The hunger crisis in poor countries has its roots in U.S. and European policies of subsidizing the diversion of food crops to produce biofuels like corn-based ethanol. That is, doling out subsidies to put the world's dinner into the gas tank.

    Source: *Time*, May 5, 2008

    a. What is the effect on the world price of corn of the increased use of corn to produce ethanol in the United States and Europe?
    b. How does the change in the world price of corn affect the quantity of corn produced in a poor developing country with a comparative advantage in producing corn, the quantity it consumes, and the quantity that it either exports or imports?

Winners, Losers, and the Net Gain from Trade

16. Draw a graph of the market for corn in the poor developing country in Problem 15(b) to show the changes in consumer surplus, producer surplus, and deadweight loss.

Use the following news clip to work Problems 17 and 18.

South Korea to Resume U.S. Beef Imports
South Korea will reopen its market to most U.S. beef. South Korea banned imports of U.S. beef in 2003 amid concerns over a case of mad cow disease in the United States. The ban closed what was then the third-largest market for U.S. beef exporters.

Source: CNN, May 29, 2008

17. a. Explain how South Korea's import ban on U.S. beef affected beef producers and consumers in South Korea.
    b. Draw a graph of the market for beef in South Korea to illustrate your answer to part (a). Identify the changes in consumer surplus, producer surplus, and deadweight loss.

18. a. Assuming that South Korea is the only importer of U.S. beef, explain how South Korea's import ban on U.S. beef affected beef producers and consumers in the United States.
    b. Draw a graph of the market for beef in the United States to illustrate your answer to part (a). Identify the changes in consumer surplus, producer surplus, and deadweight loss.

International Trade Restrictions

Use the following information to work Problems 19 to 21.

Before 1995, trade between the United States and Mexico was subject to tariffs. In 1995, Mexico joined NAFTA and all U.S. and Mexican tariffs have gradually been removed.

19. Explain how the price that U.S. consumers pay for goods from Mexico and the quantity of U.S. imports from Mexico have changed. Who are the winners and who are the losers from this free trade?

20. Explain how the quantity of U.S. exports to Mexico and the U.S. government's tariff revenue from trade with Mexico have changed.

21. Suppose that this year tomato growers in Florida lobby the U.S. government to impose an import quota on Mexican tomatoes. Explain who in the United States would gain and who would lose from such a quota.

Use the following information to work Problems 22 and 23.

Suppose that in response to huge job losses in the U.S. textile industry, Congress imposes a 100 percent tariff on imports of textiles from China.

22. Explain how the tariff on textiles will change the price that U.S. buyers pay for textiles, the quantity of textiles imported, and the quantity of textiles produced in the United States.

23. Explain how the U.S. and Chinese gains from trade will change. Who in the United States will lose and who will gain?

Use the following information to work Problems 24 and 25.

With free trade between Australia and the United States, Australia would export beef to the United States. But the United States imposes an import quota on Australian beef.

24. Explain how this quota influences the price that U.S. consumers pay for beef, the quantity of beef produced in the United States, and the U.S. and the Australian gains from trade.

25. Explain who in the United States gains from the quota on beef imports and who loses.

The Case Against Protection

26. **Trading Up**

The cost of protecting jobs in uncompetitive sectors through tariffs is high: Saving a job in the sugar industry costs American consumers $826,000 in higher prices a year; saving a dairy industry job costs $685,000 per year; and saving a job in the manufacturing of women's handbags costs $263,000.

Source: *The New York Times*, June 26, 2006

a. What are the arguments for saving the jobs mentioned in this news clip? Explain why these arguments are faulty.

b. Is there any merit to saving these jobs?

Economics in the News

27. After you have studied *Economics in the News* on pp. 168–169, answer the following questions.

a. What is the TPP?

b. Who in the United States would benefit and who would lose from a successful TPP?

c. Illustrate your answer to part (b) with an appropriate graphical analysis assuming that tariffs are not completely eliminated.

d. Who in Japan and other TPP nations would benefit and who would lose from a successful TPP?

e. Illustrate with an appropriate graphical analysis who in Japan would benefit and who would lose from a successful TPP, assuming that all Japan's import quotas and tariffs are completely eliminated.

28. E.U. Agrees to Trade Deal with South Korea

Italy has dropped its resistance to a E.U. trade agreement with South Korea, which will wipe out $2 billion in annual duties on E.U. exports. Italians argued that the agreement, which eliminates E.U. duties on South Korean cars, would put undue pressure on its own automakers.

Source: *The Financial Times*, September 16, 2010

a. What is a free trade agreement? What is its aim?

b. Explain how a tariff on E.U. car imports changes E.U. production of cars, purchases of cars, and imports of cars. Illustrate your answer with an appropriate graphical analysis.

c. Show on your graph the changes in consumer surplus and producer surplus that result from free trade in cars.

d. Explain why Italian automakers opposed cuts in car import tariffs.

The Amazing Market

PART TWO

The five chapters that you've just studied explain how markets work. The market is an amazing instrument. It enables people who have never met and who know nothing about each other to interact and do business. It also enables us to allocate our scarce resources to the uses that we value most highly. Markets can be very simple or highly organized. Markets are ancient and they are modern.

A simple and ancient market is one that the American historian Daniel J. Boorstin describes in *The Discoverers* (p. 161). In the late fourteenth century,

> *The Muslim caravans that went southward from Morocco across the Atlas Mountains arrived after twenty days at the shores of the Senegal River. There the Moroccan traders laid out separate piles of salt, of beads from Ceutan coral, and cheap manufactured goods. Then they retreated out of sight. The local tribesmen, who lived in the strip mines where they dug their gold, came to the shore and put a heap of gold beside each pile of Moroccan goods. Then they, in turn, went out of view, leaving the Moroccan traders either to take the gold offered for a particular pile or to reduce the pile of their merchandise to suit the offered price in gold. Once again the Moroccan traders withdrew, and the process went on. By this system of commercial etiquette, the Moroccans collected their gold.*

Auctions on eBay and U.S. government auctions of the airwaves that cellphone companies use are examples of organized and modern markets. Susan Athey, whom you will meet on the following page, is a world-renowned expert on the design of auctions.

Everything and anything that can be exchanged is traded in markets to the benefit of both buyers and sellers.

Alfred Marshall *(1842–1924) grew up in an England that was being transformed by the railroad and by the expansion of manufacturing. Mary Paley was one of Marshall's students at Cambridge, and when Alfred and Mary married, in 1877, celibacy rules barred Alfred from continuing to teach at Cambridge. By 1884, with more liberal rules, the Marshalls returned to Cambridge, where Alfred became Professor of Political Economy.*

Many economists had a hand in refining the demand and supply model, but the first thorough and complete statement of the model as we know it today was set out by Alfred Marshall, with the help of Mary Paley Marshall. Published in 1890, this monumental treatise, The Principles of Economics, *became the textbook on economics on both sides of the Atlantic for almost half a century.*

"The forces to be dealt with are ... so numerous, that it is best to take a few at a time. ... Thus we begin by isolating the primary relations of supply, demand, and price."

ALFRED MARSHALL
The Principles of Economics

SUSAN ATHEY is Professor of Economics at Harvard University. Born in 1970, she completed high school in three years, wrapped up three majors—in economics, mathematics, and computer science—at Duke University at 20, completed her Ph.D. at Stanford University at 24, and was voted tenure at MIT and Stanford at 29. After teaching at MIT for six years and Stanford for five years, she moved to Harvard in 2006. Among her many honors and awards, the most prestigious is the John Bates Clark Medal given to the best economist under 40. She is the first woman to receive this award.

Professor Athey's research is broad both in scope and style. A government that wants to auction natural resources will turn to her fundamental discoveries (and possibly consult with her) before deciding how to organize the auction. An economist who wants to test a theory using a large data set will use her work on statistics and econometrics.

Michael Parkin talked with Susan Athey about her research, what economists have learned about designing markets, and her advice to students.

Professor Athey, what sparked your interest in economics?

I was studying mathematics and computer science, but I felt that the subjects were not as relevant as I would like. I discovered economics through a research project with a professor who was working on auctions. I had a summer job working for a firm that sold computers to the government through auctions. Eventually my professor, Bob Marshall, wrote two articles on the topic and testified before Congress to help reform the system for government procurement of computers. That really inspired me and showed me the power of economic ideas to change the world and to make things work more efficiently.

What is the connection between an auction and the supply and demand model?

The basic laws of supply and demand can be seen in evidence in an auction market like eBay. The more sellers that are selling similar products, the lower the prices they can expect to achieve. Similarly, the more buyers there are demanding those objects, the higher the prices the sellers can achieve.

*Read the full interview with Susan Athey in MyEconLab.

An important thing for an auction marketplace is to attract a good balance of buyers and sellers so that both the buyers and the sellers find it more profitable to transact in that marketplace rather than using some other mechanism. From a seller's perspective, the more bidders there are on the platform, the greater the demand and the higher the prices. And from the buyer's perspective, the more sellers there are on the platform, the greater the supply and the lower the prices.

> The basic laws of supply and demand can be seen in evidence in an auction market like eBay.

Can we think of an auction as a mechanism for finding the equilibrium price and quantity?

Exactly. We can think of the whole collection of auctions on eBay as being a mechanism to discover a market clearing price, and individual items might sell a little higher or a little lower but over all we believe that the prices on eBay auctions will represent equilibrium prices.

8

UTILITY AND DEMAND

After studying this chapter, you will be able to:

◆ Explain the limits to consumption and describe preferences using the concept of utility

◆ Explain the marginal utility theory of consumer choice

◆ Use marginal utility theory to predict the effects of changes in prices and incomes and to explain the paradox of value

◆ Describe some new ways of explaining consumer choices

You enjoy sugary drinks and sometimes, perhaps, drink more than is good for your health. What determines our choices about the quantity of sugary drinks we consume?

You know that diamonds are expensive and water is cheap. Doesn't that seem odd? Why do we place a higher value on useless diamonds than on essential-to-life water?

The theory of consumer choice that you're going to study in this chapter answers questions like the ones we've just posed. *Economics in the News* at the end of the chapter applies what you learn to a debate about whether sugary drinks should be banned or taxed to discourge their consumption.

◆ Consumption Choices

The choices that you make as a buyer of goods and services—your consumption choices—are influenced by many factors. We can summarize them under two broad headings:

- Consumption possibilities
- Preferences

Consumption Possibilities

Your consumption possibilities are all the things that you can afford to buy. You can afford many different combinations of goods and services, but they are all limited by your income and by the prices that you must pay. For example, you might decide to spend a big part of your income on a gym membership and personal trainer and little on movies and music, or you might spend lots on movies and music and use the free gym at school.

The easiest way to describe consumption possibilities is to consider a model consumer who buys only two items. That's what we'll now do. We'll study the consumption possibilities of Lisa, who buys only movies and soda.

A Consumer's Budget Line Consumption possibilities are limited by income and by the prices of movies and soda. When Lisa spends all her income, she reaches the limits to her consumption possibilities. We describe this limit with a **budget line,** which marks the boundary between those combinations of goods and services that a household can afford to buy and those that it cannot afford.

Figure 8.1 illustrates Lisa's consumption possibilities of movies and soda and her budget line. Lisa has an income of $40 a month, the price of a movie is $8, and the price of soda is $4 a case. Rows A through F in the table show six possible ways of allocating $40 to these two goods. For example, in row A Lisa buys 10 cases of soda and sees no movies; in row F she sees 5 movies and buys no soda; and in row C she sees 2 movies and buys 6 cases of soda.

Points A through F in the graph illustrate the possibilities presented in the table, and the line passing through these points is Lisa's budget line.

The budget line constrains choices: It marks the boundary between what is affordable and unaffordable. Lisa can afford all the points on the budget line and inside it. Points outside the line are unaffordable.

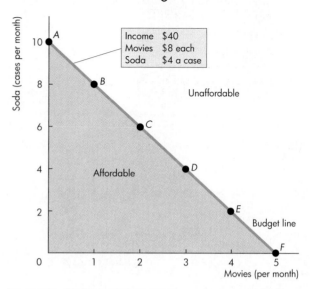

FIGURE 8.1   Lisa's Budget Line

Income	$40
Movies	$8 each
Soda	$4 a case

	Movies		Soda	
Possibility	Quantity	Expenditure (dollars)	Cases	Expenditure (dollars)
A	0	0	10	40
B	1	8	8	32
C	**2**	**16**	**6**	**24**
D	3	24	4	16
E	4	32	2	8
F	5	40	0	0

The graph and the table show six possible ways in which Lisa can allocate $40 to movies and soda. In row C and at point C, she sees 2 movies and buys 6 cases of soda. The line AF is Lisa's budget line and is a boundary between what she can afford and what she cannot afford. Her choices must lie along the line AF or inside the orange area.

MyEconLab Animation and Draw Graph

Changes in Consumption Possibilities Consumption possibilities change when income or prices change. A rise in income shifts the budget line outward but leaves its slope unchanged. A change in a price changes the slope[1] of the line. Our goal is to predict the effects of such changes on consumption choices. To do so, we must determine the choice a consumer makes. The budget line shows what is possible; preferences determine which possibility is chosen. We'll now describe a consumer's preferences.

_____
[1] Chapter 9 explains an alternative model of consumer choice and pp. 203–204 provides some detail on how changes in income and prices change the budget line.

Preferences

Lisa's income and the prices that she faces limit her consumption choices, but she still has lots of choice. The choice that she makes depends on her **preferences**—a description of her likes and dislikes.

You saw one way that economists use to describe preferences in Chapter 2 (p. 36), the concept of *marginal benefit* and the *marginal benefit curve*. But you also saw in Chapter 5 (p. 108) that a marginal benefit curve is also a demand curve. The goal of a theory of consumer choice is to derive the demand curve from a deeper account of how consumers make their buying plans. That is, we want to *explain what determines demand and marginal benefit.*

To achieve this goal, we need a deeper way of describing preferences. One approach to this problem uses the idea of utility, and defines **utility** as the benefit or satisfaction that a person gets from the consumption of goods and services. We distinguish two utility concepts:

- Total utility
- Marginal utility

Total Utility The total benefit that a person gets from the consumption of all the different goods and services is called **total utility.** Total utility depends on the level of consumption—more consumption generally gives more total utility.

To illustrate the concept of total utility, think about Lisa's choices. We tell Lisa that we want to measure her utility from movies and soda. We can use any scale that we wish to measure her total utility and we give her two starting points: (1) We will call the total utility from no movies and no soda zero utility; and (2) we will call the total utility she gets from seeing 1 movie a month 50 units.

We then ask Lisa to tell us, using the same scale, how much she would like 2 movies, and more, up to 10 movies a month. We also ask her to tell us, on the same scale, how much she would like 1 case of soda a month, 2 cases, and more, up to 10 cases a month.

In Table 8.1, the columns headed "Total utility" show Lisa's answers. Looking at those numbers, you can say a lot about how much Lisa likes soda and movies. She says that 1 case of soda gives her 75 units of utility—50 percent more than the utility that she gets from seeing 1 movie. You can also see that her total utility from soda climbs more slowly than her total utility from movies. This difference turns on the second utility concept: *marginal utility.*

TABLE 8.1   Lisa's Utility from Movies and Soda

Movies			Soda		
Quantity (per month)	Total utility	Marginal utility	Cases (per month)	Total utility	Marginal utility
0	0		0	0	
		 50			 75
1	50		1	75	
		 40			 48
2	90		2	123	
		 32			 36
3	122		3	159	
		 28			 24
4	150		4	183	
		 26			 22
5	176		5	205	
		 24			 20
6	200		6	225	
		 22			 13
7	222		7	238	
		 20			 10
8	242		8	248	
		 17			 7
9	259		9	255	
		 16			 5
10	275		10	260	

Marginal Utility We define **marginal utility** as the *change* in total utility that results from a one-unit increase in the quantity of a good consumed.

In Table 8.1, the columns headed "Marginal utility" show Lisa's marginal utility from movies and soda. You can see that if Lisa increases the soda she buys from 1 to 2 cases a month, her total utility from soda increases from 75 units to 123 units. For Lisa, the marginal utility from the second case each month is 48 units (123 – 75).

The marginal utility numbers appear midway between the quantities of soda because it is the *change* in the quantity she buys from 1 to 2 cases that produces the marginal utility of 48 units.

Marginal utility is *positive,* but it *diminishes* as the quantity of a good consumed increases.

Positive Marginal Utility All the things that people enjoy and want more of have a positive marginal utility. Some objects and activities can generate negative marginal utility—and lower total utility. Two examples are hard labor and polluted air. But all the goods and services that people value and that we are thinking about here have positive marginal utility: Total utility increases as the quantity consumed increases.

Diminishing Marginal Utility As Lisa sees more movies, her total utility from movies increases but her marginal utility from movies decreases. Similarly, as she

FIGURE 8.2 Total Utility and Marginal Utility

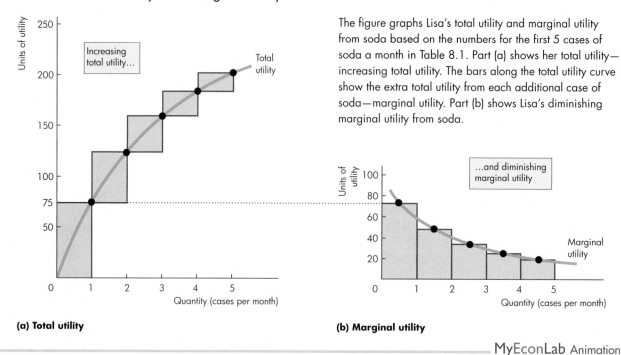

(a) Total utility

(b) Marginal utility

The figure graphs Lisa's total utility and marginal utility from soda based on the numbers for the first 5 cases of soda a month in Table 8.1. Part (a) shows her total utility—increasing total utility. The bars along the total utility curve show the extra total utility from each additional case of soda—marginal utility. Part (b) shows Lisa's diminishing marginal utility from soda.

consumes more soda, her total utility from soda increases but her marginal utility from soda decreases.

The tendency for marginal utility to decrease as the consumption of a good increases is so general and universal that we give it the status of a *principle*—the principle of **diminishing marginal utility.**

You can see Lisa's diminishing marginal utility by calculating a few numbers. Her marginal utility from soda decreases from 75 units from the first case to 48 units from the second case and to 36 units from the third. Her marginal utility from movies decreases from 50 units for the first movie to 40 units for the second and 32 units for the third. Lisa's marginal utility diminishes as she buys more of each good.

Your Diminishing Marginal Utility You've been studying all day and into the evening, and you've been too busy finishing an assignment to shop for soda. A friend drops by with a can of soda. The utility you get from that soda is the marginal utility from your first soda of the day—from *one* can. On another day you've been on a soda binge. You've been working on an assignment, but you've guzzled 10 cans of soda while doing so, and are now totally wired. You are happy enough to have one more can, but the thrill that you get from it is not very large. It is the marginal utility from the *eleventh* can in a day.

Graphing Lisa's Utility Schedules Figure 8.2(a) illustrates Lisa's total utility from soda. The more soda Lisa consumes in a month, the more total utility she gets. Her total utility curve slopes upward.

Figure 8.2(b) illustrates Lisa's marginal utility from soda. It is a graph of the marginal utility numbers in Table 8.1. This graph shows Lisa's diminishing marginal utility from soda. Her marginal utility curve slopes downward as she consumes more soda.

We've described Lisa's consumption possibilities and preferences. Your next task is to see how Lisa chooses what to consume.

◆ REVIEW QUIZ

1 Explain how a consumer's income and the prices of goods limit consumption possibilities.
2 What is utility and how do we use the concept of utility to describe a consumer's preferences?
3 What is the distinction between total utility and marginal utility?
4 What is the key assumption about marginal utility?

Work these questions in Study Plan 8.1 and get instant feedback. Do a Key Terms Quiz.   MyEconLab

◆ Utility-Maximizing Choice

Consumers want to get the most utility possible from their limited resources. They make the choice that maximizes utility. To discover this choice, we combine the constraint imposed by the budget and the consumer's preferences and find the point on the budget line that gives the consumer the maximum attainable utility. Let's find Lisa's utility-maximizing choice.

A Spreadsheet Solution

Lisa's most direct way of finding the quantities of movies and soda that maximize her utility is to make a table in a spreadsheet with the information and calculations shown in Table 8.2. Let's see what that table tells us.

Find the Just-Affordable Combinations Table 8.2 shows the combinations of movies and soda that Lisa can afford and that exhaust her $40 income. For example, in row A, Lisa buys only soda and at $4 a case she can buy 10 cases. In row B, Lisa sees 1 movie and buys 8 cases of soda. She spends $8 on the movie. At $4 a case, she spends $32 on soda and can buy 8 cases. The combination in row B just exhausts her $40. The combinations shown in the table are the same as those plotted on her budget line in Fig. 8.1.

We noted that the budget line shows that Lisa can also afford any combination *inside* the budget line. The quantities in those combinations would be smaller than the ones shown in Table 8.2 and they do not exhaust her $40. But smaller quantities don't maximize her utility. Why? The marginal utilities of movies and soda are positive, so the more of each that Lisa buys, the more total utility she gets.

Find the Total Utility for Each Just-Affordable Combination Table 8.2 shows the total utility that Lisa gets from the just-affordable quantities of movies and soda. The second and third columns show the numbers for movies and the fourth and fifth columns show those for soda. The center column adds the total utility from movies to the total utility from soda. This number, the total utility from movies *and* soda, is what Lisa wants to maximize.

In row A of the table, Lisa sees no movies and buys 10 cases of soda. She gets no utility from movies and 260 units of utility from soda. Her total utility from movies and soda (the center column) is 260 units.

TABLE 8.2 Lisa's Utility-Maximizing Choice

	Movies $8		Total utility from movies and soda	Soda $4	
	Quantity (per month)	Total utility		Total utility	Cases (per month)
A	0	0	260	260	10
B	1	50	298	248	8
C	2	90	315	225	6
D	3	122	305	183	4
E	4	150	273	123	2
F	5	176	176	0	0

In row C of the table, Lisa sees 2 movies and buys 6 cases of soda. She gets 90 units of utility from movies and 225 units of utility from soda. Her total utility from movies and soda is 315 units. This combination of movies and soda maximizes Lisa's total utility. That is, given the prices of movies and soda, Lisa's best choice when she has $40 to spend is to see 2 movies and buy 6 cases of soda.

If Lisa sees 1 movie, she can buy 8 cases of soda, but she gets only 298 units of total utility—17 units less than the maximum attainable. If Lisa sees 3 movies, she can buy only 4 cases of soda. She gets 305 units of total utility—10 units less than the maximum attainable.

Consumer Equilibrium We've just described Lisa's consumer equilibrium. A **consumer equilibrium** is a situation in which a consumer has allocated all of his or her available income in the way that maximizes his or her total utility, given the prices of goods and services. Lisa's consumer equilibrium is 2 movies and 6 cases of soda.

To find Lisa's consumer equilibrium, we did something that an economist might do but that a consumer is not likely to do: We measured her total utility from all the affordable combinations of movies and soda and then, by inspection of the numbers, selected the combination that gives the highest total utility. There is a more natural way of finding a consumer's equilibrium—a way that uses the idea that choices are made at the margin, as you first met in Chapter 1. Let's look at this approach.

Choosing at the Margin

When you go shopping you don't do utility calculations. But you do decide how to allocate your budget, and you do so in a way that you think is best for you. If you could make yourself better off by spending a few more dollars on an extra unit of one item and the same number of dollars less on something else, you would make that change. So, when you've allocated your budget in the best possible way, you can't make yourself better off by spending more on one item and less on others.

Marginal Utility per Dollar Economists interpret your best possible choice by using the idea of marginal utility per dollar. *Marginal utility* is the increase in total utility that results from consuming *one more unit* of a good. **Marginal utility per dollar** is the *marginal utility* from a good that results from spending *one more dollar* on it.

The distinction between these two marginal concepts is clearest for a good that is infinitely divisible, such as gasoline. You can buy gasoline by the smallest fraction of a gallon and literally choose to spend one more or one less dollar at the pump. The increase in total utility that results from spending one more dollar at the pump is the marginal utility per dollar from gasoline. When you buy a movie ticket or a case of soda, you must spend your dollars in bigger lumps. To buy our marginal movie ticket or case of soda, you must spend the price of one unit and your total utility increases by the marginal utility from that item. So to calculate the marginal utility per dollar for movies (or soda), we must divide marginal utility from the good by its price.

Call the marginal utility from movies MU_M and the price of a movie P_M. Then the *marginal utility per dollar from movies* is

$$MU_M/P_M.$$

Call the marginal utility from soda MU_S and the price of a case of soda P_S. Then the *marginal utility per dollar from soda* is

$$MU_S/P_S.$$

By comparing the marginal utility per dollar from all the goods that a person buys, we can determine whether the budget has been allocated in the way that maximizes total utility.

Let's see how we use the marginal utility per dollar to define a utility-maximizing rule.

Utility-Maximizing Rule A consumer's total utility is maximized by following the rule:

- Spend all the available income.
- Equalize the marginal utility per dollar for all goods.

Spend All the Available Income Because more consumption brings more utility, only those choices that exhaust income can maximize utility. For Lisa, combinations of movies and soda that leave her with money to spend don't give her as much total utility as those that exhaust her $40 per month income.

Equalize the Marginal Utility per Dollar The basic idea behind this rule is to move dollars from good B to good A if doing so increases the utility from good A by more than it decreases the utility from good B. Such a utility-increasing move is possible if the marginal utility per dollar from good A *exceeds* that from good B.

But buying more of good A decreases its marginal utility. And buying less of good B increases its marginal utility. So by moving dollars from good B to good A, total utility rises, and the gap between the marginal utilities per dollar gets smaller.

As long as the gap exists—as long as the marginal utility per dollar from good A exceeds that from good B—total utility can be increased by spending more on A and less on B. But when enough dollars have been moved from B to A to make the two marginal utilities per dollar equal, total utility cannot be increased further. Total utility is maximized.

Lisa's Marginal Calculation Let's apply the basic idea to Lisa. To calculate Lisa's marginal utility per dollar, we divide her marginal utility numbers for each quantity of each good by the price of the good. The table in Fig. 8.3 shows these calculations for Lisa, and the graph illustrates the situation on Lisa's budget line. The rows of the table are three of her affordable combinations of movies and soda.

Too Much Soda and Too Few Movies In row B, Lisa sees 1 movie a month and consumes 8 cases of soda a month. Her marginal utility from seeing 1 movie a month is 50 units. Because the price of a movie is $8, Lisa's marginal utility per dollar from movies is 50 units divided by $8, or 6.25 units of utility per dollar.

Lisa's marginal utility from soda when she consumes 8 cases of soda a month is 10 units. Because the price of soda is $4 a case, Lisa's marginal utility per dollar from soda is 10 units divided by $4, or 2.50 units of utility per dollar.

When Lisa sees 1 movie and consumes 8 cases of soda a month, her marginal utility per dollar from soda is *less than* her marginal utility per dollar from movies. That is,

$$MU_S/P_S < MU_M/P_M.$$

If Lisa spent an extra dollar on movies and a dollar less on soda, her total utility would increase. She would get 6.25 units from the extra dollar spent on movies and lose 2.50 units from the dollar less spent on soda. Her total utility would increase by 3.75 units (6.25 − 2.50).

Too Little Soda and Too Many Movies In row *D*, Lisa sees 3 movies a month and consumes 4 cases of soda. Her marginal utility from seeing the third movie a month is 32 units. At a price of $8 a movie, Lisa's marginal utility per dollar from movies is 32 units divided by $8, or 4 units of utility per dollar.

Lisa's marginal utility from soda when she buys 4 cases a month is 24 units. At a price of $4 a case, Lisa's marginal utility per dollar from soda is 24 units divided by $4, or 6 units of utility per dollar.

When Lisa sees 3 movies and consumes 4 cases of soda a month, her marginal utility per dollar from soda *exceeds* her marginal utility per dollar from movies. That is,

$$MU_S/P_S > MU_M/P_M.$$

If Lisa spent an extra dollar on soda and a dollar less on movies, her total utility would increase. She would get 6 units from the extra dollar spent on soda and she would lose 4 units from the dollar less spent on movies. Her total utility would increase by 2 units (6 − 4).

Utility-Maximizing Movies and Soda In Fig. 8.3, if Lisa moves from row *B* to row *C*, she increases the movies she sees from 1 to 2 a month and decreases the soda she consumes from 8 to 6 cases a month. Her marginal utility per dollar from movies falls to 5 and her marginal utility per dollar from soda rises to 5.

Similarly, if Lisa moves from row *D* to row *C*, she decreases the movies she sees from 3 to 2 a month and increases the soda she consumes from 4 to 6 cases a month. Her marginal utility per dollar from movies rises to 5 and her marginal utility per dollar from soda falls to 5.

When Lisa sees 2 movies and consumes 6 cases of soda a month, her marginal utility per dollar from soda *equals* her marginal utility per dollar from

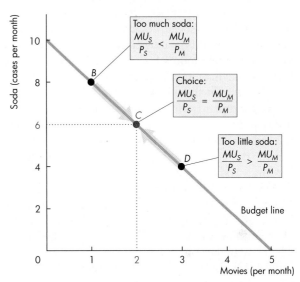

FIGURE 8.3   Equalizing Marginal Utilities per Dollar

	Movies ($8 each)			Soda ($4 per case)		
	Quantity	Marginal utility	Marginal utility per dollar	Cases	Marginal utility	Marginal utility per dollar
B	1	50	6.25	8	10	2.50
C	2	40	**5.00**	6	20	**5.00**
D	3	32	4.00	4	24	6.00

The graph shows Lisa's budget line and identifies three points on it. The rows of the table describe these points.

At point *B* (row *B*), with 1 movie and 8 cases of soda, Lisa's marginal utility per dollar from soda is less than that from movies: Buy less soda and see more movies.

At point *D* (row *D*), with 3 movies and 4 cases of soda, Lisa's marginal utility per dollar from soda is greater than that from movies: Buy more soda and see fewer movies.

At point *C* (row *C*), with 2 movies and 6 cases of soda, Lisa's marginal utility per dollar from soda is equal to that from movies: Lisa's utility is maximized.

—— **MyEconLab** Animation and Draw Graph ——

movies. That is,

$$MU_S/P_S = MU_M/P_M.$$

Lisa can't move from this allocation of her budget without making herself worse off.

The Power of Marginal Analysis

The method we've just used to find Lisa's utility-maximizing choice of movies and soda is an example of the power of marginal analysis. Lisa doesn't need a computer and a spreadsheet program to maximize utility. She can achieve this goal by comparing the marginal gain from having more of one good with the marginal loss from having less of another good.

The rule that she follows is simple: If the marginal utility per dollar from movies exceeds the marginal utility per dollar from soda, see more movies and buy less soda; if the marginal utility per dollar from soda exceeds the marginal utility per dollar from movies, buy more soda and see fewer movies.

More generally, if the marginal gain from an action exceeds the marginal loss, take the action. You will meet this principle time and again in your study of economics, and you will find yourself using it when you make your own economic choices, especially when you must make big decisions.

Revealing Preferences

When we introduced the idea of utility, we arbitrarily chose 50 units as Lisa's total utility from 1 movie, and we pretended that we asked Lisa to tell us how many units of utility she got from different quantities of soda and movies.

You're now about to discover that we don't need to ask Lisa to tell us her preferences. We can figure them out for ourselves by observing what she buys at various prices.

Also, the units in which we measure Lisa's preferences don't matter. Any arbitrary units will work. In this respect, utility is like temperature. Predictions about the freezing point of water don't depend on the temperature scale; and predictions about a household's consumption choice don't depend on the units of utility.

Lisa's Preferences In maximizing total utility by making the marginal utility per dollar equal for all goods, the units in which utility is measured do not matter.

You've seen that when Lisa maximizes her total utility, her marginal utility per dollar from soda, MU_S/P_S, equals her marginal utility per dollar from movies, MU_M/P_M. That is,

$$MU_S/P_S = MU_M/P_M.$$

Multiply both sides of this equation by the price of soda, P_S, to obtain

$$MU_S = MU_M \times (P_S/P_M).$$

This equation says that the marginal utility from soda, MU_S, is equal to the marginal utility from movies, MU_M, multiplied by the ratio of the price of soda, P_S, to the price of a movie, P_M.

The ratio P_S/P_M is the relative price of soda in terms of movies: It is the number of movies that must be forgone to get 1 case of soda. It is also the opportunity cost of soda. (See Chapter 2, p. 33 and Chapter 3, p. 56.)

For Lisa, when $P_M = \$8$ and $P_S = \$4$ we observe that in a month she goes to the movies twice and buys 6 cases of soda. So we know that her MU_S from 6 cases of soda equals her MU_M from 2 movies multiplied by $\$4/\$8$ or 0.5. That is, for Lisa, the marginal utility from 6 cases of soda equals one-half of the marginal utility from 2 movies.

If we observe the choices that Lisa makes at more prices, we can find more rows in her utility schedule. By her choices, Lisa reveals her preferences.

Units of Utility Don't Matter Lisa's marginal utility from 6 cases of soda is one-half of her marginal utility from 2 movies. So if the marginal utility from the second movie is 40 units, then the marginal utility from the sixth case of soda is 20 units. But if we call the marginal utility from the second movie 50 units, then the marginal utility from the sixth case of soda is 25 units. The units of utility are arbitrary.

◆ REVIEW QUIZ

1 Why does a consumer spend the entire budget?
2 What is the marginal utility per dollar and how is it calculated?
3 What two conditions are met when a consumer is maximizing utility?
4 Explain why equalizing the marginal utility per dollar for all goods maximizes utility.

Work these questions in Study Plan 8.2 and get instant feedback. Do a Key Terms Quiz.   MyEconLab

You now understand the marginal utility theory of consumer choices. Your next task is to see what the theory predicts.

Predictions of Marginal Utility Theory

We're now going to use marginal utility theory to make some predictions. You will see that marginal utility theory predicts the law of demand. The theory also predicts that a fall in the price of a substitute of a good decreases the demand for the good and that for a normal good, a rise in income increases demand. All these effects, which in Chapter 3 we simply assumed, are predictions of marginal utility theory.

To derive these predictions, we will study the effects of three events:

- A fall in the price of a movie
- A rise in the price of soda
- A rise in income

A Fall in the Price of a Movie

With the price of a movie at $8 and the price of soda at $4, Lisa is maximizing utility by seeing 2 movies and buying 6 cases of soda each month. Then, with no change in her $40 income and no change in the price of soda, the price of a movie falls from $8 to $4. How does Lisa change her buying plans?

Finding the New Quantities of Movies and Soda

You can find the effect of a fall in the price of a movie on the quantities of movies and soda that Lisa buys in a three-step calculation.

1. Determine the just-affordable combinations of movies and soda at the new prices.
2. Calculate the new marginal utilities per dollar from the good whose price has changed.
3. Determine the quantities of movies and soda that make their marginal utilities per dollar equal.

Affordable Combinations The lower price of a movie means that Lisa can afford more movies or more soda. Table 8.3 shows her new affordable combinations. In row *A*, if she continues to see 2 movies a month, she can now afford 8 cases of soda and in row *B*, if she continues to buy 6 cases of soda, she can now afford 4 movies. Lisa can afford any of the combinations shown in the rows of Table 8.3.

The next step is to find her new marginal utilities per dollar from movies.

New Marginal Utilities per Dollar from Movies A person's preferences don't change just because a price has changed. With no change in her preferences, Lisa's marginal utilities in Table 8.3 are the same as those in Table 8.1. But because the price of a movie has changed, the marginal utility *per dollar* from movies changes. In fact, with a halving of the price of a movie from $8 to $4, the marginal utility per dollar from movies has doubled.

The numbers in Table 8.3 show Lisa's new marginal utility per dollar from movies for each quantity of movies. The table also shows Lisa's marginal utility per dollar from soda for each quantity.

Equalizing the Marginal Utilities per Dollar You can see that if Lisa continues to see 2 movies a month and buy 6 cases of soda, her marginal utility per dollar from movies (row *A*) is 10 units and her marginal utility per dollar from soda (row *B*) is 5 units. Lisa is buying too much soda and too few movies. If she spends a dollar more on movies and a dollar less on soda, her total utility increases by 5 units (10 − 5).

If Lisa continues to buy 6 cases of soda and increases the number of movies to 4 (row *B*), her

---

TABLE 8.3 How a Change in the Price of Movies Affects Lisa's Choices

	Movies ($4 each)			Soda ($4 per case)		
	Quantity	Marginal utility	Marginal utility per dollar	Cases	Marginal utility	Marginal utility per dollar
	0	0		10	5	1.25
	1	50	12.50	9	7	1.75
A	2	40	**10.00**	8	10	2.50
	3	32	8.00	7	13	3.25
B	4	28	7.00	**6**	20	**5.00**
	5	26	6.50	5	22	5.50
C	6	24	**6.00**	4	24	**6.00**
	7	22	5.50	3	36	9.00
	8	20	5.00	2	48	12.00
	9	17	4.25	1	75	18.75
	10	16	4.00	0	0	

marginal utility per dollar from movies falls to 7 units, but her marginal utility per dollar from soda is 5 units. Lisa is still buying too much soda and seeing too few movies. If she spends a dollar more on movies and a dollar less on soda, her total utility increases by 2 units (7 − 5).

But if Lisa sees 6 movies and buys 4 cases of soda a month (row C), her marginal utility per dollar from movies (6 units) equals her marginal utility per dollar from soda and she is maximizing utility. If Lisa moves from this allocation of her budget in either direction, her total utility decreases.

Lisa's increased purchases of movies results from a substitution effect—she substitutes the now lower-priced movies for soda—and an income effect—she can afford more movies.

A Change in the Quantity Demanded Lisa's increase in the quantity of movies that she sees is a change in the quantity demanded. It is the change in the quantity of movies that she plans to see each month when the price of a movie changes and all other influences on buying plans remain the same. We illustrate a change in the quantity demanded by a movement along a demand curve.

Figure 8.4(a) shows Lisa's demand curve for movies. When the price of a movie is $8, Lisa sees 2 movies a month. When the price of a movie falls to $4, she sees 6 movies a month. Lisa moves downward along her demand curve for movies.

The demand curve traces the quantities that maximize utility at each price, with all other influences remaining the same. You can also see that utility-maximizing choices generate a downward-sloping demand curve. Utility maximization with diminishing marginal utility implies the law of demand.

A Change in Demand The decrease in the quantity of soda that Lisa buys is the change in the quantity of soda that she plans to buy at a given price of soda when the price of a movie changes. It is a change in her demand for soda. We illustrate a change in demand by a shift of a demand curve.

Figure 8.4(b) shows Lisa's demand curve for soda. The price of soda is fixed at $4 a case. When the price of a movie is $8, Lisa buys 6 cases of soda on demand curve D_0. When the price of a movie falls to $4, Lisa buys 4 cases of soda on demand curve D_1. The fall in the price of a movie decreases Lisa's demand for soda. Her demand curve for soda shifts leftward. For Lisa, soda and movies are substitutes.

FIGURE 8.4   A Fall in the Price of a Movie

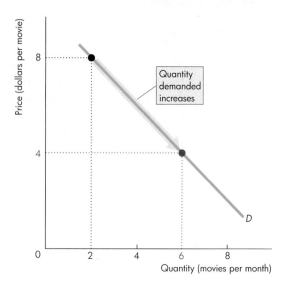

(a) Demand for movies

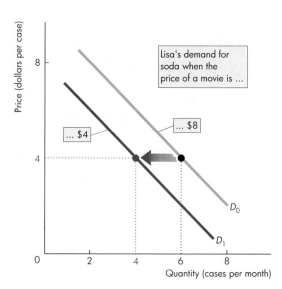

(b) Demand for soda

When the price of a movie falls and the price of soda remains the same, the quantity of movies demanded by Lisa increases, and in part (a), Lisa moves along her demand curve for movies. Also, when the price of a movie falls, Lisa's demand for soda decreases, and in part (b), her demand curve for soda shifts leftward. For Lisa, soda and movies are substitutes.

MyEconLab Animation

A Rise in the Price of Soda

Now suppose that with the price of a movie at $4, the price of soda rises from $4 to $8 a case. How does this price change influence Lisa's buying plans? We find the answer by repeating the three-step calculation with the new price of soda.

Table 8.4 shows Lisa's new affordable combinations. In row *A*, if she continues to buy 4 cases of soda a month she can afford to see only 2 movies; and in row *B*, if she continues to see 6 movies a month, she can afford only 2 cases of soda.

Table 8.4 show Lisa's marginal utility per dollar from soda for each quantity of soda when the price is $8 a case. The table also shows Lisa's marginal utility per dollar from movies for each quantity.

If Lisa continues to buy 4 cases of soda (row *A*), her marginal utility per dollar from soda is 3. But she must cut the movies she sees to 2, which increases her marginal utility per dollar from movies to 10. Lisa is buying too much soda and too few movies. If she spends a dollar less on soda and a dollar more on movies, her utility increases by 7 units (10 − 3).

But if Lisa sees 6 movies a month and cuts her soda to 2 cases (row *B*), her marginal utility per dollar from movies (6 units) equals her marginal utility per dollar from soda. She is maximizing utility.

Lisa's decreased purchases of soda results from an income effect—she can afford fewer cases and she buys fewer cases. But she continues to buy the same quantity of movies.

Lisa's Demand for Soda Now that we've calculated the effect of a change in the price of soda on Lisa's buying plans when income and the price of movies remain the same, we have found two points on her demand curve for soda: When the price of soda is $4 a case, Lisa buys 4 cases a month; and when the price of soda is $8 a case, she buys 2 cases a month.

Figure 8.5 shows these points on Lisa's demand curve for soda. It also shows the change in the quantity of soda demanded when the price of soda rises and all other influences on Lisa's buying plans remain the same.

In this example, Lisa continues to buy the same quantity of movies, but this outcome does not always occur. It is a consequence of Lisa's preferences. With different marginal utilities, she might have decreased or increased the quantity of movies that she sees when the price of soda changes.

You've seen that marginal utility theory predicts the law of demand—the way in which the quantity demanded of a good changes when its price changes. Next, we'll see how marginal utility theory predicts the effect of a change in income on demand.

TABLE 8.4 How a Change in the Price of Soda Affects Lisa's Choices

	Movies ($4 each)			Soda ($8 per case)		
	Quantity	Marginal utility	Marginal utility per dollar	Cases	Marginal utility	Marginal utility per dollar
	0	0		5	22	2.75
A	2	40	10.00	**4**	24	**3.00**
	4	28	7.00	3	36	4.50
B	6	24	**6.00**	**2**	48	**6.00**
	8	20	5.00	1	75	9.38
	10	16	4.00	0	0	

FIGURE 8.5 A Rise in the Price of Soda

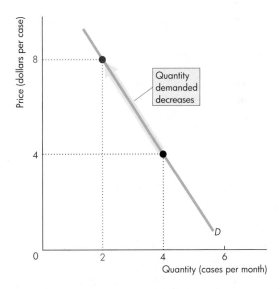

When the price of soda rises and the price of a movie and Lisa's income remain the same, the quantity of soda demanded by Lisa decreases. Lisa moves along her demand curve for soda.

MyEconLab Animation

A Rise in Income

Suppose that Lisa's income increases from $40 to $56 a month and that the price of a movie is $4 and the price of soda is $4 a case. With these prices and with an income of $40 a month, Lisa sees 6 movies and buys 4 cases of soda a month (Table 8.3). How does the increase in Lisa's income from $40 to $56 change her buying plans?

Table 8.5 shows the calculations needed to answer this question. If Lisa continues to see 6 movies a month, she can now afford to buy 8 cases of soda (row A); if she continues to buy 4 cases of soda, she can now afford to see 10 movies (row C).

In row A, Lisa's marginal utility per dollar from movies is greater than her marginal utility per dollar from soda. She is buying too much soda and too few movies. In row C, Lisa's marginal utility per dollar from movies is less than her marginal utility per dollar from soda. She is buying too little soda and too many movies. But in row B, when Lisa sees 8 movies a month and buys 6 cases of soda, her marginal utility per dollar from movies equals that from soda. She is maximizing utility.

Figure 8.6 shows the effects of the rise in Lisa's income on her demand curves for movies and soda. The price of each good is $4. When Lisa's income

TABLE 8.5   Lisa's Choices with an Income of $56 a Month

Movies ($4 each)			Soda ($4 per case)		
Quantity	Marginal utility	Marginal utility per dollar	Cases	Marginal utility	Marginal utility per dollar
4	28	7.00	10	5	1.25
5	26	6.50	9	7	1.75
A 6	24	**6.00**	8	10	2.50
7	22	5.50	7	13	3.25
B 8	20	**5.00**	6	20	**5.00**
9	17	4.25	5	22	5.50
C 10	16	4.00	**4**	24	**6.00**

rises to $56 a month, she sees 2 more movies and buys 2 more cases of soda. Her demand curves for both movies and soda shift rightward—her demand for both movies and soda increases. With a larger income, the consumer always buys more of a *normal* good. For Lisa, movies and soda are normal goods.

FIGURE 8.6   The Effects of a Rise in Income

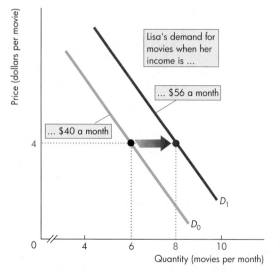

(a) Demand for movies

When Lisa's income increases, her demand for movies and her demand for soda increase. Lisa's demand curves

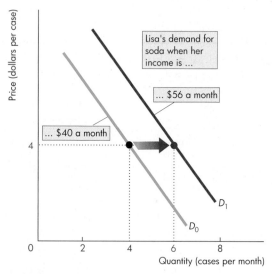

(b) Demand for soda

for movies, in part (a), and for soda, in part (b), shift rightward. For Lisa, movies and soda are normal goods.

MyEconLab Animation

The Paradox of Value

The price of water is low and the price of a diamond is high, but water is essential to life while diamonds are used mostly for decoration. How can valuable water be so cheap while a relatively useless diamond is so expensive? This so-called *paradox of value* has puzzled philosophers for centuries. Not until the theory of marginal utility had been developed could anyone give a satisfactory answer.

The Paradox Resolved The paradox is resolved by distinguishing between *total* utility and *marginal* utility. The total utility that we get from water is enormous. But remember, the more we consume of something, the smaller is its marginal utility.

We use so much water that its marginal utility—the benefit we get from one more glass of water or another 30 seconds in the shower—diminishes to a small value.

Diamonds, on the other hand, have a small total utility relative to water, but because we buy few diamonds, they have a high marginal utility.

When a household has maximized its total utility, it has allocated its income in the way that makes the marginal utility per dollar equal for all goods. That is, the marginal utility from a good divided by the price of the good is equal for all goods.

This equality of marginal utilities per dollar holds true for diamonds and water: Diamonds have a high price and a high marginal utility. Water has a low price and a low marginal utility. When the high marginal utility from diamonds is divided by the high price of a diamond, the result is a number that equals the low marginal utility from water divided by the low price of water. The marginal utility per dollar is the same for diamonds and water.

Value and Consumer Surplus Another way to think about the paradox of value and illustrate how it is resolved uses *consumer surplus*. Figure 8.7 explains the paradox of value by using this idea. The supply of water in part (a) is perfectly elastic at price P_W, so the quantity of water consumed is Q_W and the large green area shows the consumer surplus from water. The supply of diamonds in part (b) is perfectly inelastic at the quantity Q_D, so the price of a diamond is P_D and the small green area shows the consumer surplus from diamonds. Water is cheap, but brings a large consumer surplus; diamonds are expensive, but bring a small consumer surplus.

FIGURE 8.7 The Paradox of Value

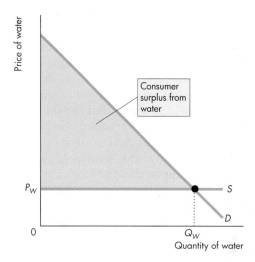

(a) Water

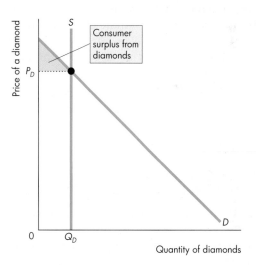

(b) Diamonds

Part (a) shows the demand for and supply of water. Supply is perfectly elastic at the price P_W. At this price, the quantity of water consumed is Q_W and the large green triangle shows consumer surplus. Part (b) shows the demand for and supply of diamonds. Supply is perfectly inelastic at the quantity Q_D. At this quantity, the price of a diamond is P_D and the small green triangle shows consumer surplus. Water is valuable—has a large consumer surplus—but cheap. Diamonds are less valuable than water—have a smaller consumer surplus—but are expensive.

MyEconLab Animation and Draw Graph

Temperature: An Analogy

Utility is similar to temperature—both are abstract concepts. You can't *observe* temperature. You can observe water turning to steam if it is hot enough or turning to ice if it is cold enough. You can also construct an instrument—a thermometer—that can help you to predict when such changes will occur. We call the scale on the thermometer *temperature* and we call the units of temperature *degrees*. But like the units of utility, these degree units are arbitrary. We can use Celsius units or Fahrenheit units or some other units.

The concept of utility helps us to make predictions about consumption choices in much the same way that the concept of temperature helps us to make predictions about physical phenomena.

Admittedly, marginal utility theory does not enable us to predict how buying plans change with the same precision that a thermometer enables us to predict when water will turn to ice or steam. But the theory provides important insights into buying plans and has some powerful implications. It helps us to understand why people buy more of a good or service when its price falls and why people buy more of most goods when their incomes increase. It also resolves the paradox of value.

We're going to end this chapter by looking at some new ways of studying individual economic choices and consumer behavior.

◆ REVIEW QUIZ

1 When the price of a good falls and the prices of other goods and a consumer's income remain the same, explain what happens to the consumption of the good whose price has fallen and to the consumption of other goods.

2 Elaborate on your answer to the previous question by using demand curves. For which good does demand change and for which good does the quantity demanded change?

3 If a consumer's income increases and if all goods are normal goods, explain how the quantity bought of each good changes.

4 What is the paradox of value and how is the paradox resolved?

5 What are the similarities between utility and temperature?

Work these questions in Study Plan 8.3 and get instant feedback.   MyEconLab

ECONOMICS IN ACTION

Maximizing Utility from Recorded Music

In 2012, Americans spent $7 billion on recorded music, down from more than $14 billion in 2000. But the combined quantity of discs and downloads bought increased from 1 billion in 2000 to 1.6 billion in 2012 and the average price of a unit of recorded music fell from $14.00 to $3.90.

The average price fell because the mix of formats bought changed dramatically. In 2001, we bought 900 million CDs; in 2012, we bought only 211 million CDs and downloaded 1.4 billion music files. Figure 1 shows the longer history of the changing formats of recorded music.

The music that we buy isn't just one good—it is several goods. Singles and albums are different goods; downloads and discs are different goods; and downloads to a computer and downloads to a cellphone are different goods. There are five major categories and the table shows the quantities of each that we bought in 2012 (excluding DVDs and cassettes).

Format	Singles	Albums
	(millions in 2012)	
Disc	211	241
Download	1,400	105
Mobile	116	–

Source of data: Recording Industry Association of America.

Most people buy all their music in digital form, but many still buy physical CDs and some people buy both downloads and CDs.

We get utility from the singles and albums that we buy, and the more songs and albums we have, the more utility we get. But our marginal utility from songs and albums decreases as the quantity that we own increases.

We also get utility from convenience. A song that we can buy with a mouse click and play with the spin of a wheel is more convenient both to buy and to use than a song on a CD. The convenience of songs downloaded over the Internet means that, song for song, we get more utility from a song downloaded than we get from a song on a physical CD.

But most albums are still played at home on a CD player. So for most people, a physical CD is a more convenient medium for delivering an album. Album for album, people on average get more utility from a CD than from a download.

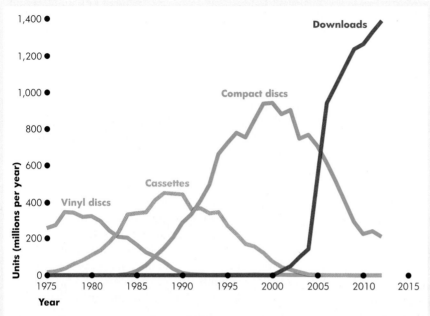

In the 1970s, recorded music came on vinyl discs. Cassettes gradually replaced vinyl, then compact discs (CDs) gradually replaced cassettes, and today, digital files downloaded to computers and mobile devices are replacing physical CDs.

Figure 1 Changing Formats of Recorded Music

Sources of data: U.S. Census Bureau, *The 2012 Statistical Abstract*, Table 1140; and the Recording Industry Association of America.

When we decide how many singles and albums to download and how many to buy on CD, we compare the marginal utility per dollar from each type of music in each format. We make the marginal utility per dollar from each type of music in each format equal, as the equations below show.

The market for single downloads has created an enormous consumer surplus. Figure 2 shows the demand curve for singles. One point on the demand curve is the 2001 price and quantity—100 million singles were bought at an average price of $5.00. Another point on the demand curve is that for 2012—1,400 million singles downloaded at $1.20 each.

If the demand curve has not shifted and is linear (assumed here), we can calculate the increase in consumer surplus generated by the fall in the price and the increase in the quantity demanded. The green area of the figure shows this increase in consumer surplus.

Consumer surplus increases by ($5.00 − $1.20) = $3.80 on the first 100 million and by $3.80 × 1,300/2 on the additional 1,300 singles. So the increase in consumer surplus is $2.85 billion.

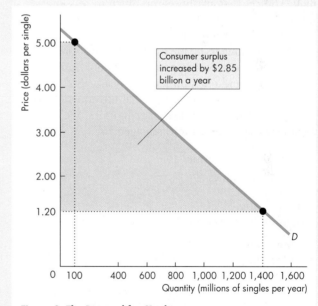

Figure 2 The Demand for Singles

$$\frac{MU_{single\ downloads}}{P_{single\ downloads}} = \frac{MU_{album\ downloads}}{P_{album\ downloads}} = \frac{MU_{physical\ singles}}{P_{physical\ singles}} = \frac{MU_{physical\ albums}}{P_{physical\ albums}} = \frac{MU_{mobile}}{P_{mobile}}$$

$$\frac{MU_{single\ downloads}}{\$1.20} = \frac{MU_{album\ downloads}}{\$10.99} = \frac{MU_{physical\ singles}}{\$4.76} = \frac{MU_{physical\ albums}}{\$9.99} = \frac{MU_{mobile}}{\$2.39}$$

◆ New Ways of Explaining Consumer Choices

When William Stanley Jevons developed marginal utility theory in the 1860s, he would have loved to look inside people's brains and "see" their utility. But he believed that the human brain was the ultimate black box that could never be observed directly. For Jevons, and for most economists today, the purpose of marginal utility theory is to explain our *actions*, not what goes on inside our brains.

Economics has developed over the past 150 years with little help from and paying little attention to advances being made in psychology. Both economics and psychology seek to explain human behavior, but they have developed different ways of attacking the challenge.

A few researchers *have* paid attention to the potential payoff from exploring economic problems by using the tools of psychology. These researchers, some economists and some psychologists, think that marginal utility theory is based on a view of how people make choices that attributes too much to reason and rationality. They propose an alternative approach based on the methods of psychology.

Other researchers, some economists and some neuroscientists, are using new tools to look inside the human brain and open up Jevons' "black box."

This section provides a very brief introduction to these new and exciting areas of economics. We'll explore the two related research agendas:

- Behavioral economics
- Neuroeconomics

Behavioral Economics

Behavioral economics studies the ways in which limits on the human brain's ability to compute and implement rational decisions influences economic behavior—both the decisions that people make and the consequences of those decisions for the way markets work.

Behavioral economics starts with observed behavior. It looks for anomalies—choices that do not seem to be rational. It then tries to account for the anomalies by using ideas developed by psychologists that emphasize features of the human brain that limit rational choice.

In behavioral economics, instead of being rational utility maximizers, people are assumed to have three impediments that prevent rational choice: bounded rationality, bounded willpower, and bounded self-interest.

Bounded Rationality Bounded rationality is rationality that is limited by the computing power of the human brain. We can't always work out the rational choice.

For Lisa, choosing between movies and soda, it seems unlikely that she would have much trouble figuring out what to buy. But toss Lisa some uncertainty and the task becomes harder. She's read the reviews of *Ironman 2* on Fandango, but does she really want to see that movie? How much marginal utility will it give her? Faced with uncertainty, people might use rules of thumb, listen to the views of others, and make decisions based on gut instinct rather than on rational calculation.

Bounded Willpower Bounded willpower is the less-than-perfect willpower that prevents us from making a decision that we know, at the time of implementing the decision, we will later regret.

Lisa might be feeling particularly thirsty when she passes a soda vending machine. Under Lisa's rational utility-maximizing plan, she buys her soda at the discount store, where she gets it for the lowest possible price. Lisa has already bought her soda for this month, but it is at home. Spending $1 on a can now means giving up a movie later this month.

Lisa's rational choice is to ignore the temporary thirst and stick to her plan. But she might not possess the willpower to do so—sometimes she will and sometimes she won't.

Bounded Self-Interest Bounded self-interest is the limited self-interest that results in sometimes suppressing our own interests to help others.

A hurricane hits the Florida coast and Lisa, feeling sorry for the victims, donates $10 to a fund-raiser. She now has only $30 to spend on movies and soda this month. The quantities that she buys are not, according to her utility schedule, the ones that maximize her utility.

The main applications of behavioral economics are in two areas: finance, where uncertainty is a key factor in decision making, and savings, where the future is a key factor. But one behavior observed by behavioral economists is more general and might affect your choices. It is called the endowment effect.

The Endowment Effect The endowment effect is the tendency for people to value something more highly simply because they own it. If you have allocated your income to maximize utility, then the price you would be willing to accept to give up something that you own (for example, your coffee mug) should be the same as the price you are willing to pay for an identical one.

In experiments, students seem to display the endowment effect: The price they are willing to pay for a coffee mug that is identical to the one they own is less than the price they would be willing to accept to give up the coffee mug that they own. Behavioral economists say that this behavior contradicts marginal utility theory.

Neuroeconomics

Neuroeconomics is the study of the activity of the human brain when a person makes an economic decision. The discipline uses the observational tools and ideas of neuroscience to obtain a better understanding of economic decisions.

Neuroeconomics is an experimental discipline. In an experiment, a person makes an economic decision and the electrical or chemical activity of the person's brain is observed and recorded using the same type of equipment that neurosurgeons use to diagnose brain disorders.

The observations provide information about which regions of the brain are active at different points in the process of making an economic decision.

Observations show that some economic decisions generate activity in the area of the brain (called the prefrontal cortex) where we store memories, analyze data, and anticipate the consequences of our actions. If people make rational utility-maximizing decisions, it is in this region of the brain that the decision occurs.

But observations also show that some economic decisions generate activity in the region of the brain (called the hippocampus) where we store memories of anxiety and fear. Decisions that are influenced by activity in this part of the brain might not be rational but instead be driven by fear or panic.

Neuroeconomists are also able to observe the amount of a brain hormone (called dopamine), the quantity of which increases in response to pleasurable events and decreases in response to disappointing events. These observations might one day enable neuroeconomists to actually measure utility and shine a bright light inside what was once believed to be the ultimate black box.

Controversy

The new ways of studying consumer choice that we've briefly described here are being used more widely to study business decisions and decisions in financial markets, and this type of research is surely going to become more popular.

But behavioral economics and neuroeconomics generate controversy. Most economists hold the view of Jevons that the goal of economics is to explain the decisions that we observe people making and not to explain what goes on inside people's heads.

Most economists would prefer to probe apparent anomalies more deeply and figure out why they are not anomalies after all.

Economists also point to the power of marginal utility theory and its ability to explain consumer choice and demand as well as resolve the paradox of value.

◆ REVIEW QUIZ

1 Define behavioral economics.
2 What are the three limitations on human rationality that behavioral economics emphasizes?
3 Define neuroeconomics.
4 What do behavioral economics and neuroeconomics seek to achieve?

Work these questions in Study Plan 8.4 and get instant feedback. Do a Key Terms Quiz.   MyEconLab

---

◆   You have now completed your study of marginal utility theory and some new ideas about how people make economic choices. You can see marginal utility theory in action once again in *Economics in the News* on pp. 194–195, where it is used to compare the effects of a tax on big cups of sugary soft drinks versus an outright ban.

Influencing Consumer Choice for Sugary Drinks

Drinks Groups Sue Over NY "Supersize" Ban

The Financial Times
October 13, 2012

The U.S. beverage industry is taking the administration of Michael Bloomberg, New York mayor, to court over its decision to ban sales of "supersized" sugary drinks.

Trade groups led by the American Beverage Association filed a lawsuit late on Friday in New York state court attempting to block the rule, which is set to be imposed next spring.

Last month, New York's board of health voted to approve a proposal made by Mr. Bloomberg in May that would prohibit restaurants, theaters, and stadiums from selling sugary drinks in portions bigger than 16 fl oz. ...

The lawsuit comes as the soda industry is locked in an increasingly contentious battle with regulators over labeling and taxation of their products. Industry groups are currently fighting soda tax proposals in two California cities and have successfully pushed back several other similar efforts. ...

Marc La Vorgna, a spokesman for Mr. Bloomberg, called the lawsuit baseless and suggested that the drinks industry would fail to stop the ban.

"For 100 years, major public health decisions—the posting of calorie counts, the ban of transfats, the sanitation of the sewage system, the fluoridation of the water system, and much more—have been left to a board of health professionals and it has benefited the health of New Yorkers," he said. "The mayor's plan to limit the size of sugary beverages—the leading contributor to the obesity epidemic—has spurred a long overdue national dialogue on obesity."

Alan Rappeport, "Drinks Groups Sue Over NY 'Supersize' Ban," *The Financial Times*, October 13, 2012.

ESSENCE OF THE STORY

- New York City mayor Michael Bloomberg has banned the sale of sweetened drinks larger than 16 ounces at many venues.

- Two cities in California are considering placing a tax on sugar-sweetened beverages.

- Trade groups that sell these drinks are seeking court orders to block the ban and taxes.

- A spokesman for mayor Bloomberg says sugary drinks are the leading contributor to obesity and the ban is a public health measure like the sanitation system.

MyEconLab More Economics in the News

ECONOMIC ANALYSIS

- Concerned that people are choosing to consume more sugary soda than is healthy, New York mayor Michael Bloomberg wants to ban large servings and the city of Richmond, CA, is considering a 1-penny-per-ounce tax.

- Consumers choose to buy the quantity of sugary drinks that maximizes utility.

- To do so, they make the marginal utility per dollar for all other goods and services equal to the marginal utility per dollar for sugary drinks. That is:

$$\frac{MU_O}{P_O} = \frac{MU_S}{P_S}.$$

- Because of the way in which drinks are sold, there isn't a single price. The table shows some prices in St. Louis in June 2012.

Prices of Sugary Drinks

Size (ounces)	At the movies	At a 7-Eleven
20	4.00	1.09
32	4.50	1.29
44	5.00	1.49
52	5.50	1.69
104	[free refill]	

- These prices tell us that people who buy their drinks in big cups pay a lower price per ounce.

- Because a person who buys a 52-ounce cup gets a free refill, the price of the marginal ounce for that person is zero. With a price of zero, the buyer drinks the quantity at which marginal utility is also zero.

- The suggestions for decreasing the consumption of sugary drinks are ways of raising the price.

- A tax raises the price because the tax is added to the price received by the seller. A ban on large cups raises the price because the price per ounce is higher for small cups than for large cups. Both have a similar outcome.

- Faced with a higher price of sugary drinks, a consumer maximizes utility by consuming a smaller quantity of sugary drinks.

- The reason is that consumer equilibrium becomes

$$\frac{MU_O}{P_O} = \frac{MU_S}{(P_S + tax)}.$$

- When a tax is imposed, the price doesn't rise by the entire amount of the tax, but generally $P_S + tax$ is greater than the price before that tax was imposed.

- Because $P_S + tax$ is greater than P_S, MU_S must rise to restore the equality of the marginal utilities per dollar. But to increase MU_S, the quantity of sugary drinks consumed must decrease.

- Figure 1 illustrates and makes clear why consumption of sugary drinks decreases.

- Suppose that with no tax, the budget line is BL_0 and to make the marginal utilities per dollar equal, the consumer buys 60 ounces of drinks and 100 units of other goods and services per day.

- A tax raises the price to $P_S + tax$ and the budget line becomes steeper as BL_1.

- If the consumer continues to drink 60 ounces per day, the quantity of other items bought must fall to 50 units a day. MU_O rises and

$$\frac{MU_O}{P_O} > \frac{MU_S}{(P_S + tax)}.$$

- To restore maximum utility, the consumer buys a smaller quantity of sugary drinks, which increases MU_S, and a greater quantity of other goods, which decreases MU_O. A movement up along the budget line BL_1 shows these changes in quantities consumed.

- The consumer substitutes other goods and services for sugary drinks until

$$\frac{MU_O}{P_O} = \frac{MU_S}{(P_S + tax)}.$$

- At this point, the consumer is again maximizing utility.

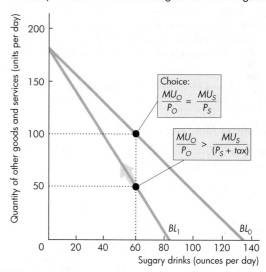

Figure 1 The Effect of a Tax

SUMMARY

Key Points

Consumption Choices (pp. 178–180)

- A household's consumption choices are determined by its consumption possibilities and preferences.
- A budget line defines a household's consumption possibilities.
- A household's preferences can be described by a utility schedule that lists the total utility and marginal utility derived from various quantities of goods and services consumed.
- The principle of diminishing marginal utility is that the marginal utility from a good or service decreases as consumption of the good or service increases.

Working Problems 1 to 5 will give you a better understanding of consumption choices.

Utility-Maximizing Choice (pp. 181–184)

- A consumer's objective is to maximize total utility.
- Total utility is maximized when all the available income is spent and when the marginal utility per dollar from all goods is equal.
- If the marginal utility per dollar for good A exceeds that for good B, total utility increases if the quantity purchased of good A increases and the quantity purchased of good B decreases.

Working Problems 6 to 8 will give you a better understanding of a consumer's utility-maximizing choice.

Predictions of Marginal Utility Theory (pp. 185–191)

- Marginal utility theory predicts the law of demand. That is, other things remaining the same, the

higher the price of a good, the smaller is the quantity demanded of that good.
- Marginal utility theory also predicts that, other things remaining the same, an increase in the consumer's income increases the demand for a normal good.
- Marginal utility theory resolves the paradox of value.
- Total value is *total* utility or consumer surplus. But price is related to *marginal* utility.
- Water, which we consume in large amounts, has a high total utility and a large consumer surplus, but the price of water is low and the marginal utility from water is low.
- Diamonds, which we buy in small quantities, have a low total utility and a small consumer surplus, but the price of a diamond is high and the marginal utility from diamonds is high.

Working Problems 9 to 13 will give you a better understanding of the predictions of marginal utility theory.

New Ways of Explaining Consumer Choices

(pp. 192–193)

- Behavioral economics studies limits on the ability of the human brain to compute and implement rational decisions.
- Bounded rationality, bounded willpower, and bounded self-interest are believed to explain some choices.
- Neuroeconomics uses the ideas and tools of neuroscience to study the effects of economic events and choices inside the human brain.

Working Problems 14 and 15 will give you a better understanding of the new ways of explaining consumer choices.

Key Terms

MyEconLab Key Terms Quiz

Behavioral economics, 192
Budget line, 178
Consumer equilibrium, 181
Diminishing marginal utility, 180

Marginal utility, 179
Marginal utility per dollar, 182
Neuroeconomics, 193
Preferences, 179

Total utility, 179
Utility, 179

WORKED PROBLEM

MyEconLab   You can work this problem in Chapter 8 Study Plan.

Jake has a budget of $10 per week to spend on song downloads and cookies. The table shows his marginal utility from each good.

Quantity per week	Marginal utility from a song	Marginal utility from a cookie
1	14	20
2	12	16
3	11	12
4	10	8
5	9	4
6	8	3
7	7	2
8	6	1

Questions

1. If the price of a song is $1 and the price of a cookie is $2, what are the quantities of songs and cookies that exhaust Jake's budget?

2. How does Jake allocate his $10 between songs and cookies?

3. If the price of a song rises to $2 and the price of a cookie remains at $2, does Jake buy fewer songs and cookies, or only fewer songs?

Solutions

1. The price of a cookie is twice that of a song, so each additional cookie Jake buys costs him 2 fewer songs—the opportunity cost of a cookie is 2 songs. So Jake can buy either 8 songs and 1 cookie, or 6 songs and 2 cookies, or 4 songs and 3 cookies, or 2 songs and 4 cookies, or 0 songs and 5 cookies.

Key Point: To exhaust the budget, all income is spent.

2. Jake buys the quantities of songs and cookies that maximize his total utility. He buys the quantities that make the marginal utility per dollar the same for the two goods.

   To calculate the marginal utility per dollar, make a table in which each row is an affordable combination of songs and cookies. Show the marginal utility for each good and then calculate the marginal utility per dollar for each row.

   The table in the next column shows the calculations. Check the calculation on row *B*, with 4 songs and 3 cookies. The marginal utility of a song is 10 units and because the price of a song is $1, the marginal utility per dollar is also 10 units.

	Songs ($1 each)			Cookies ($2 each)		
	Quantity	Marginal utility	Marginal utility per dollar	Quantity	Marginal utility	Marginal utility per dollar
A	2	12	12	4	8	4
B	4	10	10	3	12	6
C	6	8	8	2	16	8
D	8	6	6	1	20	10

The marginal utility of a cookie is 12 units and because the price of a cookie is $2, the marginal utility per dollar is 6 units.

Because the marginal utility per dollar from 4 songs *exceeds* that from 3 cookies, Jake can increase his total utility by buying more songs and fewer cookies.

In the highlighted row *C*, the marginal utilities per dollar are equal and total utility is maximized. So Jake buys 6 songs and 2 cookies to maximize utility.

Key Point: Total utility is maximized when the marginal utility per dollar is the same for all goods.

3. If the price of a song rises to $2, the affordable combinations shrink. Jake can now afford combinations of quantities that total 5. The table below shows the new combinations that exhaust Jake's budget and the marginal utility per dollar for each possibility.

	Songs ($2 each)			Cookies ($2 each)		
	Quantity	Marginal utility	Marginal utility per dollar	Quantity	Marginal utility	Marginal utility per dollar
A	1	14	7	4	8	4
B	2	12	6	3	12	6
C	3	11	5.5	2	16	8
D	4	10	5	1	20	10

To maximize his utility, Jake now buys only 2 songs and increases his consumption of cookies to 3 per week in row *B*.

Key Point: When the price of a good rises, the utility-maximizing quantity of that good decreases, but the quantity of other goods bought might increase or decrease.

STUDY PLAN PROBLEMS AND APPLICATIONS

MyEconLab   You can work Problems 1 to 15 in Chapter 8 Study Plan and get instant feedback.

Consumption Choices (Study Plan 8.1)

Jerry has $12 a week to spend on yogurt and berries. The price of yogurt is $2, and berries are $4 a box.

1. List the combinations of yogurt and berries that Jerry can afford. Draw a graph of his budget line with the quantity of berries plotted on the *x*-axis.

2. How do Jerry's consumption possibilities change if, other things remaining the same, (i) the price of berries falls and (ii) Jerry's income increases?

Use the following data to work Problems 3 to 5.

Max has $35 a day to spend on windsurfing and snorkeling and he can spend as much time as he likes doing them. The price of renting equipment for windsurfing is $10 an hour and for snorkeling is $5 an hour. The table shows the total utility Max gets from each activity.

Hours per day	Total utility from windsurfing	Total utility from snorkeling
1	120	40
2	220	76
3	300	106
4	360	128
5	396	140
6	412	150
7	422	158

3. Calculate Max's marginal utility from windsurfing at each number of hours per day. Does Max's marginal utility from windsurfing obey the principle of diminishing marginal utility?

4. Calculate Max's marginal utility from snorkeling at each number of hours per day. Does Max's marginal utility from snorkeling obey the principle of diminishing marginal utility?

5. Which does Max enjoy more: his 6th hour of windsurfing or his 6th hour of snorkeling?

Utility-Maximizing Choice (Study Plan 8.2)

Use the data in Problem 3 to work Problems 6 to 8.

6. Make a table of the combinations of hours spent windsurfing and snorkeling that Max can afford.

7. Add two columns to your table in Problem 6 and list Max's marginal utility per dollar from windsurfing and from snorkeling.

8. a. To maximize his utility, how many hours a day does Max spend on each activity?

   b. If Max spent a dollar more on windsurfing

and a dollar less on snorkeling than in part (a), how would his total utility change?

   c. If Max spent a dollar less on windsurfing and a dollar more on snorkeling than in part (a), how would his total utility change?

Predictions of Marginal Utility Theory (Study Plan 8.3)

Use the data in Problem 3 to work Problems 9 to 13.

9. If the price of renting windsurfing equipment is cut to $5 an hour, how many hours a day does Max spend on each activity?

10. Draw Max's demand curve for rented windsurfing equipment. Over the price range $5 to $10 an hour, is Max's demand elastic or inelastic?

11. How does Max's demand for snorkeling equipment change when the price of windsurfing equipment falls? What is Max's cross elasticity of demand for snorkeling with respect to the price of windsurfing? Are windsurfing and snorkeling substitutes or complements for Max?

12. If Max's income increases from $35 to $55 a day, how does his demand for windsurfing equipment change? Is windsurfing a normal good? Explain.

13. If Max's income increases from $35 to $55 a day, how does his demand for snorkeling equipment change? Is snorkeling a normal good? Explain.

New Ways of Explaining Consumer Choices
(Study Plan 8.4)

Use the following news clip to work Problems 14 and 15.

Eating Away the Innings in Baseball's Cheap Seats

Baseball and gluttony, two of America's favorite pastimes, are merging, with Major League Baseball stadiums offering all-you-can-eat seats. Some fans try to "set personal records" during their first game, but by the third time in such seats they eat normally.

Source: *USA Today*, March 6, 2008

14. What conflict might exist between utility-maximization and setting "personal records" for eating? What does the fact that fans eat less at subsequent games indicate about their marginal utility from ballpark food as they consume more?

15. How can setting personal records for eating be reconciled with marginal utility theory? Which ideas of behavioral economics are consistent with the information in the news clip?

◆ ADDITIONAL PROBLEMS AND APPLICATIONS

MyEconLab   You can work these problems in MyEconLab if assigned by your instructor.

Consumption Choices

16. Tim buys 2 pizzas and sees 1 movie a week when he has $16 to spend, a movie ticket is $8, and a pizza is $4. Draw Tim's budget line. If the price of a movie ticket falls to $4, describe how Tim's consumption possibilities change.

17. Cindy has $70 a month to spend, and she can spend as much time as she likes playing golf and tennis. The price of an hour of golf is $10, and the price of an hour of tennis is $5. The table shows Cindy's marginal utility from each sport.

Hours per month	Marginal utility from golf	Marginal utility from tennis
1	80	40
2	60	36
3	40	30
4	30	10
5	20	5
6	10	2
7	6	1

Make a table that shows Cindy's affordable combinations of hours playing golf and tennis. If Cindy increases her expenditure to $100, describe how her consumption possibilities change.

Utility-Maximizing Choice

Use the information in Problem 17 to work Problems 18 to 24.

18. a. How many hours of golf and how many hours of tennis does Cindy play to maximize her utility?

   b. Compared to part (a), if Cindy spent a dollar more on golf and a dollar less on tennis, by how much would her total utility change?

   c. Compared to part (a), if Cindy spent a dollar less on golf and a dollar more on tennis, by how much would her total utility change?

19. Explain why, if Cindy equalized the marginal utility per hour of golf and tennis, she would *not* maximize her utility.

Predictions of Marginal Utility Theory

Cindy's tennis club raises its price of an hour of tennis from $5 to $10, other things remaining the same.

20. a. List the combinations of hours spent playing golf and tennis that Cindy can now afford and her marginal utility per dollar from golf and from tennis.

   b. How many hours does Cindy now spend playing golf and how many hours does she spend playing tennis?

21. Use the information in Problem 20 to draw Cindy's demand curve for tennis. Over the price range of $5 to $10 an hour of tennis, is Cindy's demand for tennis elastic or inelastic?

22. Explain how Cindy's demand for golf changed when the price of an hour of tennis increased from $5 to $10 in Problem 20. What is Cindy's cross elasticity of demand for golf with respect to the price of tennis? Are tennis and golf substitutes or complements for Cindy?

23. Cindy loses her math tutoring job and the amount she has to spend on golf and tennis falls from $70 to $35 a month. With the price of an hour of golf at $10 and of tennis at $5, calculate the change in the hours she spends playing golf. For Cindy, is golf a normal good or an inferior good? Is tennis a normal good or an inferior good?

24. Cindy takes a Club Med vacation, the cost of which includes unlimited sports activities. With no extra charge for golf and tennis, Cindy allocates a total of 4 hours a day to these activities.

   a. How many hours does Cindy play golf and how many hours does she play tennis?

   b. What is Cindy's marginal utility from golf and from tennis?

   c. Why does Cindy equalize the marginal utilities rather than the marginal utility per dollar from golf and from tennis?

25. Jim has made his best affordable choice of muffins and coffee. He spends all of his income on 10 muffins at $1 each and 20 cups of coffee at $2 each. Now the price of a muffin rises to $1.50 and the price of coffee falls to $1.75 a cup.

   a. Will Jim now be able to buy 10 muffins and 20 coffees?

b. If Jim changes the quantities he buys, will he buy more or fewer muffins and more or less coffee? Expain your answer.

26. Ben spends $50 a year on 2 bunches of flowers and $50 a year on 10,000 gallons of tap water. Ben is maximizing utility and his marginal utility from water is 0.5 unit per gallon.

    a. Are flowers or water more valuable to Ben?

    b. Explain how Ben's expenditure on flowers and water illustrates the paradox of value.

New Ways of Explaining Consumer Choices

Use the following news clip to work Problems 27 to 29.

Putting a Price on Human Life

Researchers at Stanford and the University of Pennsylvania estimated that a healthy human life is worth about $129,000. Using Medicare records on treatment costs for kidney dialysis as a benchmark, the authors tried to pinpoint the threshold beyond which ensuring another "quality" year of life was no longer financially worthwhile. The study comes amid debate over whether Medicare should start rationing healthcare on the basis of cost effectiveness.

Source: *Time*, June 9, 2008

27. Why might Medicare ration healthcare according to treatment that is "financially worthwhile" as opposed to providing as much treatment as is needed by a patient, regardless of costs?

28. What conflict might exist between a person's valuation of his or her own life and the rest of society's valuation of that person's life?

29. How does the potential conflict between self-interest and the social interest complicate setting a financial threshold for Medicare treatments?

Economics in the News

30. After you have studied *Economics in the News* (pp. 194–195), answer the following questions.

    a. If big cups of sugary drinks are banned at restaurants, theaters, and stadiums,

        (i) How will the price of an ounce of sugary drink change?

        (ii) How will consumers respond to the change in price?

    b. If a tax is imposed on sugary drinks, how does

        (i) The marginal utility of a sugary drink change?

        (ii) The consumer surplus in the market for sugary drinks change?

31. **Five Signs You Have Too Much Money**
    When a bottle of water costs $38, it's hard not to agree that bottled water is a fool's drink. The drink of choice among image-conscious status seekers and high-end tee-totalers in L.A. is Bling H_2O. It's not the water that accounts for the cost of the $38, but the "limited edition" bottle decked out in Swarovski crystals.

    Source: CNN, January 17, 2006

    a. Assuming that the price of a bottle of Bling H_2O is $38 in all the major U.S. cities, what might its popularity in Los Angeles reveal about consumers' incomes or preferences in Los Angeles relative to other major U.S. cities?

    b. Why might the marginal utility from a bottle of Bling H_2O decrease more rapidly than the marginal utility from ordinary bottled water?

32. **How to Buy Happiness. Cheap**
    On any day, the rich tend to be a bit happier than the poor, but increases in average living standards don't seem to make people happier. The average American's income is up 80% since 1972, but the percentage describing themselves as "very happy" (roughly a third) hasn't changed. As living standards increase, most of us respond by raising our own standards: Things that once seemed luxuries now are necessities and we work harder to buy stuff that satisfies us less and less.

    Source: CNN, October 1, 2004

    According to the news clip,

    a. How do widespread increases in living standards influence total utility?

    b. How do total utility and marginal utility from consumption change over time?

9 POSSIBILITIES, PREFERENCES, AND CHOICES

After studying this chapter, you will be able to:

◆ Describe a household's budget line and show how it changes when prices or income change

◆ Use indifference curves to map preferences and explain the principle of diminishing marginal rate of substitution

◆ Predict the effects of changes in prices and income on consumption choices

The iPad has revolutionized the way we read magazines and books and check our grades. Yet the magazine racks and bookstore shelves are still stuffed with traditional printed paper. Similarly, low-priced on-demand movies and DVD rentals have made it easier to watch a movie at home. Yet we're also going to movie theaters in ever-greater numbers.

In this chapter, we're going to study a model that explains the choices we make and applies it to choices about using new and old technologies. At the end of the chapter in *Economics in the News*, we use the model to explain why e-books are taking off and replacing printed books.

◆ Consumption Possibilities

Consumption choices are limited by income and by prices. A household has a given amount of income to spend and cannot influence the prices of the goods and services it buys. A household's **budget line** describes the limits to its consumption choices. Let's look at Lisa's budget line.*

Budget Line

Lisa has an income of $40 a month to spend. She buys two goods: movies and soda. The price of a movie is $8, and the price of soda is $4 a case.

Figure 9.1 shows alternative combinations of movies and soda that Lisa can afford. In row *A*, she sees no movies and buys 10 cases of soda. In row *F*, she sees 5 movies and buys no soda. Both of these combinations of movies and soda exhaust the $40 available. Check that the combination of movies and soda in each of the other rows also exhausts Lisa's $40 of income. The numbers in the table and the points *A* through *F* in the graph describe Lisa's consumption possibilities.

Divisible and Indivisible Goods Some goods—called divisible goods—can be bought in any quantity desired. Examples are gasoline and electricity. We can best understand household choice if we suppose that all goods and services are divisible. For example, Lisa can see half a movie a month on average by seeing one movie every two months. When we think of goods as being divisible, the consumption possibilities are not only the points *A* through *F* shown in Fig. 9.1, but also all the intermediate points that form the line running from *A* to *F*. This line is Lisa's budget line.

Affordable and Unaffordable Quantities Lisa's budget line is a constraint on her choices. It marks the boundary between what is affordable and what is unaffordable. She can afford any point on the line and inside it. She cannot afford any point outside the line. The constraint on her consumption depends on the prices and her income, and the constraint changes when the price of a good or her income changes. To see how, we use a budget equation.

---

*If you have studied Chapter 8 on marginal utility theory, you have already met Lisa. This tale of her thirst for soda and zeal for movies will sound familiar to you—up to a point. In this chapter, we're going to explore her budget line in more detail and use a different method for representing preferences—one that does not require the idea of utility.

FIGURE 9.1   The Budget Line

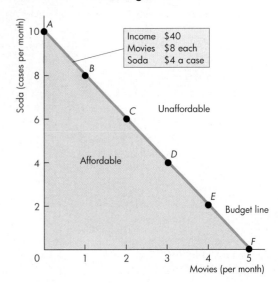

Consumption possibility	Movies (per month)	Soda (cases per month)
A	0	10
B	1	8
C	2	6
D	3	4
E	4	2
F	5	0

Lisa's budget line shows the boundary between what she can and cannot afford. The rows of the table list Lisa's affordable combinations of movies and soda when her income is $40, the price of soda is $4 a case, and the price of a movie is $8. For example, row *A* tells us that Lisa spends all of her $40 income when she buys 10 cases of soda and sees no movies. The figure graphs Lisa's budget line. Points *A* through *F* in the graph represent the rows of the table. For divisible goods, the budget line is the continuous line *AF*. To calculate the equation for Lisa's budget line, start with expenditure equal to income:

$$\$4Q_S + \$8Q_M = \$40.$$

Divide by $4 to obtain

$$Q_S + 2Q_M = 10.$$

Subtract $2Q_M$ from both sides to obtain

$$Q_S = 10 - 2Q_M.$$

MyEconLab Animation

Budget Equation

We can describe the budget line by using a *budget equation*. The budget equation starts with the fact that

$$\text{Expenditure} = \text{Income}.$$

Expenditure is equal to the sum of the price of each good multiplied by the quantity bought. For Lisa,

$$\text{Expenditure} = (\text{Price of soda} \times \text{Quantity of soda})$$
$$+ (\text{Price of a movie} \times \text{Quantity of movies}).$$

Call the price of soda P_S, the quantity of soda Q_S, the price of a movie P_M, the quantity of movies Q_M, and income Y. We can now write Lisa's budget equation as

$$P_S Q_S + P_M Q_M = Y.$$

Or, using the prices Lisa faces, $4 a case of soda and $8 a movie, and Lisa's income, $40, we get

$$\$4 Q_S + \$8 Q_M = \$40.$$

Lisa can choose any quantities of soda (Q_S) and movies (Q_M) that satisfy this equation. To find the relationship between these quantities, divide both sides of the equation by the price of soda (P_S) to get

$$Q_S + \frac{P_M}{P_S} \times Q_M = \frac{Y}{P_S}.$$

Now subtract the term $(P_M/P_S) \times Q_M$ from both sides of this equation to get

$$Q_S = \frac{Y}{P_S} - \frac{P_M}{P_S} \times Q_M.$$

For Lisa, income (Y) is $40, the price of a movie (P_M) is $8, and the price of soda (P_S) is $4 a case. So Lisa must choose the quantities of movies and soda to satisfy the equation

$$Q_S = \frac{\$40}{\$4} - \frac{\$8}{\$4} \times Q_M,$$

or

$$Q_S = 10 - 2 Q_M.$$

To interpret the equation, look at the budget line in Fig. 9.1 and check that the equation delivers that budget line. First, set Q_M equal to zero. The budget equation tells us that Q_S, the quantity of soda, is Y/P_S, which is 10 cases. This combination of Q_M and Q_S is the one shown in row A of the table in Fig. 9.1. Next set Q_M equal to 5. Q_S now equals zero (row F of the table). Check that you can derive the other rows.

The budget equation contains two variables chosen by the household (Q_M and Q_S) and two variables that the household takes as given (Y/P_S and P_M/P_S). Let's look more closely at these variables.

Real Income A household's **real income** is its income expressed as a quantity of goods that the household can afford to buy. Expressed in terms of soda, Lisa's real income is Y/P_S. This quantity is the maximum quantity of soda that she can buy. It is equal to her money income divided by the price of soda. Lisa's money income is $40 and the price of soda is $4 a case, so her real income in terms of soda is 10 cases, which is shown in Fig. 9.1 as the point at which the budget line intersects the y-axis.

Relative Price A **relative price** is the price of one good divided by the price of another good. In Lisa's budget equation, the variable P_M/P_S is the relative price of a movie in terms of soda. For Lisa, P_M is $8 a movie and P_S is $4 a case, so P_M/P_S is equal to 2 cases of soda per movie. That is, to see 1 movie, Lisa must give up 2 cases of soda.

You've just calculated Lisa's opportunity cost of seeing a movie. Recall that the opportunity cost of an action is the best alternative forgone. For Lisa to see 1 more movie a month, she must forgo 2 cases of soda. You've also calculated Lisa's opportunity cost of soda. For Lisa to buy 2 more cases of soda a month, she must forgo seeing 1 movie. So her opportunity cost of 2 cases of soda is 1 movie.

The relative price of a movie in terms of soda is the magnitude of the slope of Lisa's budget line. To calculate the slope of the budget line, recall the formula for slope (see the Chapter 1 Appendix): Slope equals the change in the variable measured on the y-axis divided by the change in the variable measured on the x-axis as we move along the line. In Lisa's case (Fig. 9.1), the variable measured on the y-axis is the quantity of soda and the variable measured on the x-axis is the quantity of movies. Along Lisa's budget line, as soda decreases from 10 to 0 cases, movies increase from 0 to 5. So the magnitude of the slope of the budget line is 10 cases divided by 5 movies, or 2 cases of soda per movie. The magnitude of this slope is exactly the same as the relative price we've just calculated. It is also the opportunity cost of a movie.

A Change in Prices When prices change, so does the budget line. The lower the price of the good measured on the x-axis, other things remaining the same, the flatter is the budget line. For example, if the price of a movie falls from $8 to $4, real income

FIGURE 9.2   Changes in Prices and Income

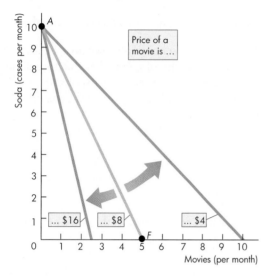

(a) A change in price

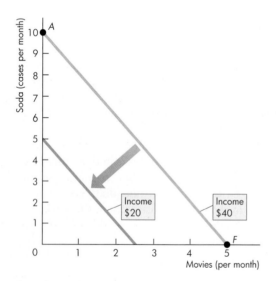

(b) A change in income

In part (a), the price of a movie changes. A fall in the price from $8 to $4 rotates the budget line outward and makes it flatter. A rise in the price from $8 to $16 rotates the budget line inward and makes it steeper.

In part (b), income falls from $40 to $20 while the prices of movies and soda remain the same. The budget line shifts leftward, but its slope does not change.

MyEconLab Animation and Draw Graph

in terms of soda does not change but the relative price of a movie falls. The budget line rotates outward and becomes flatter, as Fig. 9.2(a) illustrates. The higher the price of the good measured on the *x*-axis, other things remaining the same, the steeper is the budget line. For example, if the price of a movie rises from $8 to $16, the relative price of a movie increases. The budget line rotates inward and becomes steeper, as Fig. 9.2(a) illustrates.

A Change in Income A change in money income changes real income but does not change the relative price. The budget line shifts, but its slope does not change. An increase in money income increases real income and shifts the budget line rightward. A decrease in money income decreases real income and shifts the budget line leftward.

Figure 9.2(b) shows the effect of a change in money income on Lisa's budget line. The initial budget line when Lisa's income is $40 is the same as in Fig. 9.1. The new budget line shows how much Lisa can buy if her income falls to $20 a month. The two budget lines have the same slope because the relative price is the same. The new budget line is closer to the origin because Lisa's real income has decreased.

◆ REVIEW QUIZ

1 What does a household's budget line show?
2 How does the relative price and a household's real income influence its budget line?
3 If a household has an income of $40 and buys only bus rides at $2 each and magazines at $4 each, what is the equation of the household's budget line?
4 If the price of one good changes, what happens to the relative price and the slope of the household's budget line?
5 If a household's money income changes and prices do not change, what happens to the household's real income and budget line?

Work these questions in Study Plan 9.1 and get instant feedback. Do a Key Terms Quiz.   *MyEconLab*

We've studied the limits to what a household can consume. Let's now learn how we can describe preferences and make a map that contains a lot of information about a household's preferences.

◆ Preferences and Indifference Curves

You are going to discover a very cool idea: that of drawing a map of a person's preferences. A preference map is based on the intuitively appealing idea that people can sort all the possible combinations of goods into three groups: preferred, not preferred, and indifferent. To make this idea more concrete, let's ask Lisa to tell us how she ranks various combinations of movies and soda.

Figure 9.3 shows part of Lisa's answer. She tells us that she currently sees 2 movies and buys 6 cases of soda a month at point C. She then lists all the combinations of movies and soda that she says are just as acceptable to her as her current situation. When we plot these combinations of movies and soda, we get the green curve in Fig. 9.3(a). This curve is the key element in a preference map and is called an indifference curve.

An **indifference curve** is a line that shows combinations of goods among which a consumer is *indifferent*. The indifference curve in Fig. 9.3(a) tells us that Lisa is just as happy to see 2 movies and buy 6 cases of soda a month at point C as she is to have the combination of movies and soda at point G or at any other point along the curve.

Lisa also says that she prefers all the combinations of movies and soda above the indifference curve in Fig. 9.3(a)—the yellow area—to those on the indifference curve. And she prefers any combination on the indifference curve to any combination in the gray area below the indifference curve.

The indifference curve in Fig. 9.3(a) is just one of a whole family of such curves. This indifference curve appears again in Fig. 9.3(b), labeled I_1. The curves labeled I_0 and I_2 are two other indifference curves. Lisa prefers any point on indifference curve I_2 to any point on indifference curve I_1, and she prefers any point on I_1 to any point on I_0. We refer to I_2 as being a higher indifference curve than I_1 and I_1 as being higher than I_0.

A preference map is a series of indifference curves that resemble the contour lines on a map. By looking at the shape of the contour lines on a map, we can draw conclusions about the terrain. Similarly, by looking at the shape of the indifference curves, we can draw conclusions about a person's preferences.

Let's learn how to "read" a preference map.

FIGURE 9.3   A Preference Map

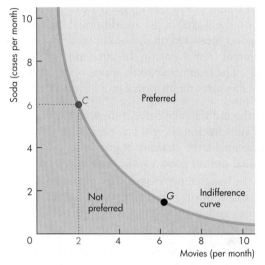

(a) An indifference curve

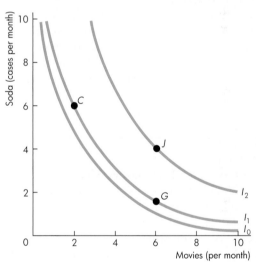

(b) Lisa's preference map

Part (a) shows one of Lisa's indifference curves. She is indifferent between point C (with 2 movies and 6 cases of soda) and all other points on the green indifference curve, such as G. She prefers points above the indifference curve (in the yellow area) to points on it, and she prefers points on the indifference curve to points below it (in the gray area).
Part (b) shows three of the indifference curves—I_0, I_1, and I_2—in Lisa's preference map. She prefers point J to point C or G, and she prefers all the points on I_2 to those on I_1.

───── MyEconLab Animation ─────

Marginal Rate of Substitution

The **marginal rate of substitution** (*MRS*) is the rate at which a person will give up good *y* (the good measured on the *y*-axis) to get an additional unit of good *x* (the good measured on the *x*-axis) while remaining indifferent (remaining on the same indifference curve). The magnitude of the slope of an indifference curve measures the marginal rate of substitution.

■ If the indifference curve is *steep*, the marginal rate of substitution is *high*. The person is willing to give up a large quantity of good *y* to get an additional unit of good *x* while remaining indifferent.

■ If the indifference curve is *flat*, the marginal rate of substitution is *low*. The person is willing to give up a small amount of good *y* to get an additional unit of good *x* while remaining indifferent.

Figure 9.4 shows you how to calculate the marginal rate of substitution.

At point *C* on indifference curve I_1, Lisa buys 6 cases of soda and sees 2 movies. Her marginal rate of substitution is the magnitude of the slope of the indifference curve at point *C*. To measure this magnitude, place a straight line against, or tangent to, the indifference curve at point *C*. Along that line, as the quantity of soda decreases by 10 cases, the number of movies increases by 5—or 2 cases per movie. At point *C*, Lisa is willing to give up soda for movies at the rate of 2 cases per movie—a marginal rate of substitution of 2.

At point *G* on indifference curve I_1, Lisa buys 1.5 cases of soda and sees 6 movies. Her marginal rate of substitution is measured by the slope of the indifference curve at point *G*. That slope is the same as the slope of the tangent to the indifference curve at point *G*. Now, as the quantity of soda decreases by 4.5 cases, the number of movies increases by 9—or 1/2 case per movie. At point *G*, Lisa is willing to give up soda for movies at the rate of 1/2 case per movie—a marginal rate of substitution of 1/2.

As Lisa sees more movies and buys less soda, her marginal rate of substitution diminishes. Diminishing marginal rate of substitution is the key assumption about preferences. A **diminishing marginal rate of substitution** is a general tendency for a person to be willing to give up less of good *y* to get one more unit of good *x*, while at the same time remaining indifferent as the quantity of *x* increases. In Lisa's case, she is less willing to give up soda to see one more movie as the number of movies she sees increases.

FIGURE 9.4   The Marginal Rate of Substitution

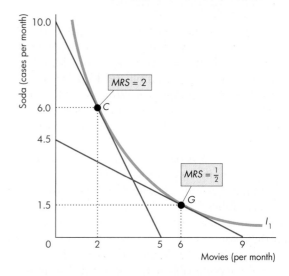

The magnitude of the slope of an indifference curve is called the marginal rate of substitution (*MRS*). The red line at point *C* tells us that Lisa is willing to give up 10 cases of soda to see 5 movies. Her marginal rate of substitution at point *C* is 10 divided by 5, which equals 2. The red line at point *G* tells us that Lisa is willing to give up 4.5 cases of soda to see 9 movies. Her marginal rate of substitution at point *G* is 4.5 divided by 9, which equals 1/2.

MyEconLab Animation and Draw Graph

Your Diminishing Marginal Rate of Substitution

Think about your own diminishing marginal rate of substitution. Imagine that in a week, you drink 10 cases of soda and see no movies. Most likely, you are willing to give up a lot of soda so that you can see just 1 movie. But now imagine that in a week, you buy 1 case of soda and see 6 movies. Most likely, you will now not be willing to give up much soda to see a seventh movie. As a general rule, the greater the number of movies you see, the smaller is the quantity of soda you are willing to give up to see one additional movie.

The shape of a person's indifference curves incorporates the principle of the diminishing marginal rate of substitution because the curves are bowed toward the origin. The tightness of the bend of an indifference curve tells us how willing a person is to substitute one good for another while remaining indifferent. Let's look at some examples that make this point clear.

Degree of Substitutability

Most of us would not regard movies and soda as being *close* substitutes, but they are substitutes. No matter how much you love soda, some increase in the number of movies you see will compensate you for being deprived of a can of soda. Similarly, no matter how much you love going to the movies, some number of cans of soda will compensate you for being deprived of seeing one movie. A person's indifference curves for movies and soda might look something like those for most ordinary goods and services shown in Fig. 9.5(a).

Close Substitutes Some goods substitute so easily for each other that most of us do not even notice which we are consuming. The different brands of marker pens and pencils are examples. Most people don't care which brand of these items they use or where they buy them. A marker pen from the campus bookstore is just as good as one from the local grocery store. You would be willing to forgo a pen from the campus store if you could get one more pen from the local grocery store. When two goods are perfect substitutes, their indifference curves are straight lines that slope downward, as Fig. 9.5(b) illustrates. The marginal rate of substitution is constant.

Complements Some goods do not substitute for each other at all. Instead, they are complements. The complements in Fig. 9.5(c) are left and right running shoes. Indifference curves of perfect complements are L-shaped. One left running shoe and one right running shoe are as good as one left shoe and two right shoes. Having two of each is preferred to having one of each, but having two of one and one of the other is no better than having one of each.

The extreme cases of perfect substitutes and perfect complements shown here don't often happen in reality, but they do illustrate that the shape of the indifference curve shows the degree of substitutability between two goods. The closer the two goods are to perfect substitutes, the closer the marginal rate of substitution is to being constant (a straight line), rather than diminishing (a curved line). Indifference

---

FIGURE 9.5 The Degree of Substitutability

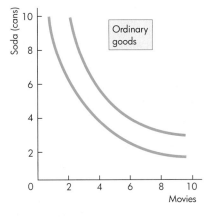

(a) Ordinary goods

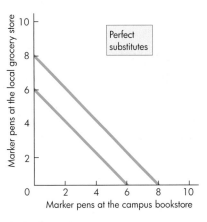

(b) Perfect substitutes

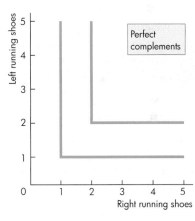

(c) Perfect complements

The shape of the indifference curves reveals the degree of substitutability between two goods. Part (a) shows the indifference curves for two ordinary goods: movies and soda. To drink less soda and remain indifferent, one must see more movies. The number of movies that compensates for a reduction in soda increases as less soda is consumed. Part (b) shows the indifference curves for two perfect substitutes. For the consumer to remain indifferent, one fewer marker pen from the local grocery store must be replaced by one extra marker pen from the campus bookstore. Part (c) shows two perfect complements—goods that cannot be substituted for each other at all. Having two left running shoes with one right running shoe is no better than having one of each. But having two of each is preferred to having one of each.

MyEconLab Animation

"With the pork I'd recommend an Alsatian white or a Coke."

© The New Yorker Collection 1988
Robert Weber from cartoonbank.com. All Rights Reserved.

curves for poor substitutes are tightly curved and lie between the shapes of those shown in Figs. 9.5(a) and 9.5(c).

As you can see in the cartoon, according to the waiter's preferences, Coke and Alsatian white wine are perfect substitutes and each is a complement of pork. We hope the customers agree with him.

◆ REVIEW QUIZ

1 What is an indifference curve and how does a preference map show preferences?
2 Why does an indifference curve slope downward and why is it bowed toward the origin?
3 What do we call the magnitude of the slope of an indifference curve?
4 What is the key assumption about a consumer's marginal rate of substitution?

Work these questions in Study Plan 9.2 and get instant feedback. Do a Key Terms Quiz.   MyEconLab

The two components of the model of household choice are now in place: the budget line and the preference map. We will now use these components to work out a household's choice and to predict how choices change when prices and income change.

◆ Predicting Consumer Choices

We are now going to predict the quantities of movies and soda that Lisa chooses to buy. We're also going to see how these quantities change when a price changes or when Lisa's income changes. Finally, we're going to see how the *substitution effect* and the *income effect*, two ideas that you met in Chapter 3 (see p. 57), guarantee that for a normal good, the demand curve slopes downward.

Best Affordable Choice

When Lisa makes her best affordable choice of movies and soda, she spends all her income and is on her highest attainable indifference curve. Figure 9.6 illustrates this choice: The budget line is from Fig. 9.1 and the indifference curves are from Fig. 9.3(b). Lisa's best affordable choice is 2 movies and 6 cases of soda at point *C*—the *best affordable point.*

FIGURE 9.6   The Best Affordable Choice

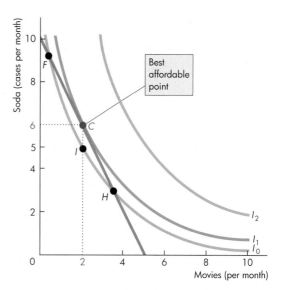

Lisa's best affordable choice is at point *C*, the point on her budget line and on her highest attainable indifference curve. At point *C*, Lisa's marginal rate of substitution between movies and soda (the magnitude of the slope of the indifference curve I_1) equals the relative price of movies and soda (the slope of the budget line).

MyEconLab Animation and Draw Graph

On the Budget Line The best affordable point is on the budget line. For every point inside the budget line, such as point *I*, there are points on the budget line that Lisa prefers. For example, she prefers all the points on the budget line between *F* and *H* to point *I*, so she chooses a point on the budget line.

On the Highest Attainable Indifference Curve Every point on the budget line lies on an indifference curve. For example, points *F* and *H* lie on the indifference curve I_0. By moving along her budget line from either *F* or *H* toward *C*, Lisa reaches points on ever-higher indifference curves that she prefers to points *F* or *H*. When Lisa gets to point *C*, she is on the highest attainable indifference curve.

Marginal Rate of Substitution Equals Relative Price At point *C*, Lisa's marginal rate of substitution between movies and soda (the magnitude of the slope of the indifference curve) is equal to the relative price of movies and soda (the magnitude of the slope of the budget line). Lisa's willingness to pay for a movie equals her opportunity cost of a movie.

Let's now see how Lisa's choices change when a price changes.

A Change in Price

The effect of a change in the price of a good on the quantity of the good consumed is called the **price effect**. We will use Fig. 9.7(a) to work out the price effect of a fall in the price of a movie. We start with the price of a movie at $8, the price of soda at $4 a case, and Lisa's income at $40 a month. In this situation, she buys 6 cases of soda and sees 2 movies a month at point *C*.

Now suppose that the price of a movie falls to $4. With a lower price of a movie, the budget line rotates outward and becomes flatter. The new budget line is the darker orange one in Fig. 9.7(a). For a refresher on how a price change affects the budget line, check back to Fig. 9.2(a).

Lisa's best affordable point is now point *J*, where she sees 6 movies and drinks 4 cases of soda. Lisa drinks less soda and watches more movies now that movies are cheaper. She cuts her soda purchases from 6 to 4 cases and increases the number of movies she sees from 2 to 6 a month. When the price of a movie falls and the price of soda and her income remain constant, Lisa substitutes movies for soda.

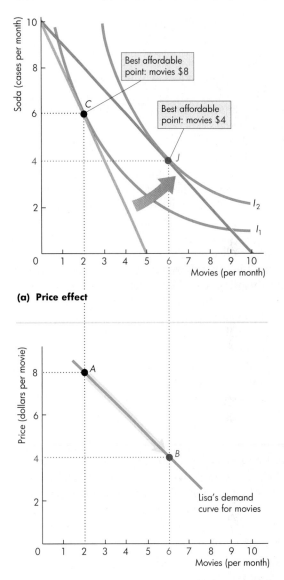

FIGURE 9.7 Price Effect and Demand Curve

(a) Price effect

(b) Demand curve

Initially, Lisa's best affordable point is *C* in part (a). If the price of a movie falls from $8 to $4, Lisa's best affordable point is *J*. The move from *C* to *J* is the price effect.

At a price of $8 a movie, Lisa sees 2 movies a month, at point *A* in part (b). At a price of $4 a movie, she sees 6 movies a month, at point *B*. Lisa's demand curve for movies traces out her best affordable quantity of movies as the price of a movie varies.

MyEconLab Animation

ECONOMICS IN ACTION

Best Affordable Choice of Movies and DVDs

Between 2005 and 2014, box-office receipts rose by more than ticket prices, which means that moviegoing has increased.

Why has moviegoing increased? One answer is that the consumer's experience has improved. Movies in 3-D such as *Godzilla* play better on the big screen than at home. Also, movie theaters are able to charge a higher price for 3-D films and other big hits, which further boosts receipts. But there is another answer, and at first thought an unlikely one: Events in the market for DVD rentals have impacted going to the movies. To see why, let's look at the recent history of the DVD rentals market.

Back in 2005, Blockbuster was the main player and the price of a DVD rental was around $4 a night. Redbox was a fledgling. It had started a year earlier with just 140 kiosks in selected McDonald's restaurants. But Redbox expanded rapidly and in 2014 had outlets across the nation renting DVDs at a price of $1.20 a night. Blockbuster was history.

The easy access to DVDs at $1.20 a night transformed the markets for movie watching and the figure shows why.

A student has a budget of $50 a month to allocate to movies. To keep the story clear, we'll suppose that it cost $10 to go to a movie in both 2005 and 2014. The price of a DVD rental in 2005 was $4, so the student's budget line is the one that runs from 5 movies on the *y*-axis to 12.5 DVD rentals on the *x*-axis. The student's best affordable point is 7 rentals and 2 movies a month.

In 2014, the price of a rental falls to $1.20 a night but the price of a movie ticket remains at $10. So the budget line rotates outward. The student's best affordable point is now at 17 rentals and 3 movies a month. (This student loves movies!)

Many other things changed between 2005 and 2014 that influenced the markets for movies and DVD rentals, but the fall in the price of a DVD rental was the biggest influence.

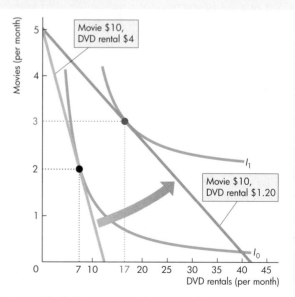

Best Affordable Movies and DVD Rentals

The Demand Curve In Chapter 3, we asserted that the demand curve slopes downward. We can now derive a demand curve from a consumer's budget line and indifference curves. By doing so, we can see that the law of demand and the downward-sloping demand curve are consequences of a consumer's choosing her or his best affordable combination of goods.

To derive Lisa's demand curve for movies, lower the price of a movie and find her best affordable point at different prices. We've just done this for two movie prices in Fig. 9.7(a). Figure 9.7(b) highlights these two prices and two points that lie on Lisa's demand curve for movies. When the price of a movie is $8, Lisa sees 2 movies a month at point A. When the price falls to $4, she increases the number of movies she sees to 6 a month at point B. The demand curve is made up of these two points plus all the other points that tell us Lisa's best affordable quantity of movies at each movie price, with the price of soda and Lisa's income remaining the same. As you can see, Lisa's demand curve for movies slopes downward—the lower the price of a movie, the more movies she sees. This is the law of demand.

Next, let's see how Lisa changes her purchases of movies and soda when her income changes.

A Change in Income

The effect of a change in income on buying plans is called the **income effect**. Let's work out the income effect by examining how buying plans change when income changes and prices remain constant. Figure 9.8 shows the income effect when Lisa's income falls. With an income of $40, the price of a movie at $4, and the price of soda at $4 a case, Lisa's best affordable point is J—she buys 6 movies and 4 cases of soda. If her income falls to $28, her best affordable point is K—she sees 4 movies and buys 3 cases of soda. When Lisa's income falls, she buys less of both goods. Movies and soda are normal goods.

The Demand Curve and the Income Effect A change in income leads to a shift in the demand curve, as shown in Fig. 9.8(b). With an income of $40, Lisa's demand curve for movies is D_0, the same as in Fig. 9.7(b). But when her income falls to $28, she plans to see fewer movies at each price, so her demand curve shifts leftward to D_1.

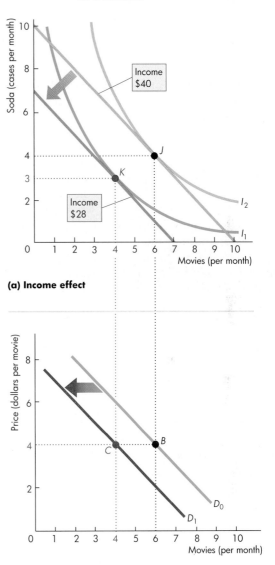

FIGURE 9.8   Income Effect and Change in Demand

(a) Income effect

(b) Demand curve for movies

A change in income shifts the budget line, changes the best affordable point, and changes demand.

In part (a), when Lisa's income decreases from $40 to $28, she sees fewer movies and buys less soda.

In part (b), when Lisa's income is $40, her demand curve for movies is D_0. When Lisa's income falls to $28, her demand curve for movies shifts leftward to D_1. For Lisa, going to the movies is a normal good. Her demand for movies decreases because she now sees fewer movies at each price.

MyEconLab Animation

Substitution Effect and Income Effect

For a normal good, a fall in its price *always* increases the quantity bought. We can prove this assertion by dividing the price effect into two parts:

- Substitution effect
- Income effect

Figure 9.9(a) shows the price effect and Figs. 9.9(b) and 9.9(c) show the two parts into which we separate the price effect.

Substitution Effect The **substitution effect** is the effect of a change in price on the quantity bought when the consumer (hypothetically) remains indifferent between the original situation and the new one. To work out Lisa's substitution effect when the price of a movie falls, we must lower her income by enough to keep her on the same indifference curve as before.

Figure 9.9(a) shows the price effect of a fall in the price of a movie from $8 to $4. The number of movies increases from 2 to 6 a month. When the price falls, suppose (hypothetically) that we cut Lisa's income to $28. What's special about $28? It is the

income that is just enough, at the new price of a movie, to keep Lisa's best affordable point on the same indifference curve (I_1) as her original point C. Lisa's budget line is now the medium orange line in Fig. 9.9(b). With the lower price of a movie and a smaller income, Lisa's best affordable point is K. The move from C to K along indifference curve I_1 is the substitution effect of the price change. The substitution effect of the fall in the price of a movie is an increase in the quantity of movies from 2 to 4. The direction of the substitution effect never varies: When the relative price of a good falls, the consumer substitutes more of that good for the other good.

Income Effect To calculate the substitution effect, we gave Lisa a $12 pay cut. To calculate the income effect, we give Lisa back her $12. The $12 increase in income shifts Lisa's budget line outward, as shown in Fig. 9.9(c). The slope of the budget line does not change because both prices remain the same. This change in Lisa's budget line is similar to the one illustrated in Fig. 9.8. As Lisa's budget line shifts outward, her consumption possibilities expand and her best afford-

FIGURE 9.9   Substitution Effect and Income Effect

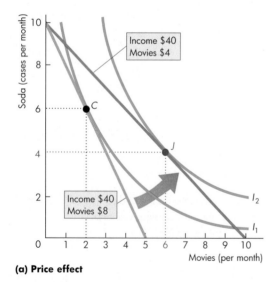

(a) Price effect

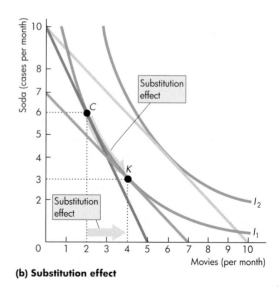

(b) Substitution effect

When the price of a movie falls from $8 to $4, Lisa moves from point C to point J in part (a). The price effect is an increase in the number of movies from 2 to 6 a month. This price effect is separated into a substitution effect in part (b) and an income effect in part (c).

To isolate the substitution effect, we confront Lisa with the new price but keep her on her original indifference curve, I_1. The substitution effect is the move from C to K along indifference curve I_1—an increase from 2 to 4 movies a month.

able point becomes *J* on indifference curve I_2. The move from *K* to *J* is the income effect of the price change.

As Lisa's income increases, she sees more movies. For Lisa, a movie is a normal good. For a normal good, the income effect *reinforces* the substitution effect. Because the two effects work in the same direction, we can be sure that the demand curve slopes downward. But some goods are inferior goods. What can we say about the demand for an inferior good?

Inferior Goods Recall that an *inferior good* is a good for which *demand decreases* when *income increases*. For an inferior good, the income effect is negative, which means that a lower price does not inevitably lead to an increase in the quantity demanded. The substitution effect of a fall in the price increases the quantity demanded, but the negative income effect works in the opposite direction and offsets the substitution effect to some degree. The key question is to what degree.

If the negative income effect *equals* the positive substitution effect, a fall in price leaves the quantity bought the same. When a fall in price leaves the quantity demanded unchanged, the demand curve is vertical and demand is perfectly inelastic.

If the negative income effect *is smaller than* the positive substitution effect, a fall in price increases the quantity bought and the demand curve still slopes downward like that for a normal good. But the demand for an inferior good might be less elastic than that for a normal good.

If the negative income effect *exceeds* the positive substitution effect, a fall in the price *decreases* the quantity bought and the demand curve *slopes upward*. This case does not appear to occur in the real world.

You can apply the indifference curve model that you've studied in this chapter to explain the changes in the way we buy recorded music, see movies, and make all our other consumption choices. We allocate our budgets to make our best affordable choices. Changes in prices and incomes change our best affordable choices and change consumption patterns.

◆ REVIEW QUIZ

1 When a consumer chooses the combination of goods and services to buy, what is she or he trying to achieve?
2 Explain the conditions that are met when a consumer has found the best affordable combination of goods to buy. (Use the terms *budget line*, *marginal rate of substitution*, and *relative price* in your explanation.)
3 If the price of a normal good falls, what happens to the quantity demanded of that good?
4 Into what two effects can we divide the effect of a price change?
5 For a normal good, does the income effect reinforce the substitution effect or does it partly offset the substitution effect?

Work these questions in Study Plan 9.3 and get instant feedback. Do a Key Terms Quiz.   MyEconLab

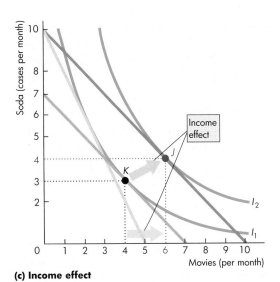

(c) Income effect

To isolate the income effect, we confront Lisa with the new price of movies but increase her income so that she can move from the original indifference curve, I_1, to the new one, I_2. The income effect is the move from *K* to *J*—an increase from 4 to 6 movies a month.

MyEconLab Animation and Draw Graph

◆ *Economics in the News* on pp. 214–215 applies the theory of household choice to explain how people chose whether to buy their books in electronic or paper format and why e-books boomed in 2011.

In the chapters that follow, we study the choices that firms make in their pursuit of profit and how those choices determine the supply of goods and services and the demand for productive resources.

Paper Books Versus e-Books

It's the End of Books As You Knew Them: e-Books Out-Sell Hardbound

ZDNet
June 18, 2012

If you follow the book trade, you knew this was coming. e-books, no matter whether you read them on an Amazon Kindle, a Barnes & Noble Nook, or your iPad are selling like crazy. We may complain about their high prices and even take e-book publishers to court for their prices and hardware lock-in, but we love our e-books. In fact, we love them so much that for the first time adult e-book sales were higher than adult hardcover sales.

It wasn't even close. The Association of American Publishers reported that in the first quarter of 2012, adult e-book sales were up to $282.3 million while adult hardcover sales came to only $229.6 million. In last year's first quarter, hardcover sales accounted for $223 million in sales while e-books logged $220.4 million.

So where are the e-book buyers coming from? The answer is trade and mass-market paperbacks. Trade paperback sales fell from $335-million to $299.8-million. That's a drop of 10.5%. Mass market paperbacks sales had it even worse. They plummeted $124.8-million to $98.9-million in the same quarter last year. That's a fall of 20.8%.

The conventional wisdom had been that e-books would eat up hardbound book sales. That's not happening. Instead, while e-books will certainly by year's end be the most popular book format, it's paperback books that are really taking a hit. Perhaps that's because when you're buying a hardcover, you're buying not just a story, but an artifact, an object with more value than just as a way to get to the story. ...

© 2012 ZDNet.

ESSENCE OF THE STORY

- In the first quarter of 2012, adult e-books out-sold adult hardcover books for the first time.

- The Association of American Publishers reported first quarter 2012, adult e-book sales at $282.3 million and adult hardcover sales at $229.6 million.

- First quarter 2011 numbers were e-books $220.4 million and hardcovers $223 million.

- Trade paperback sales fell from $335 million to $299.8 million—a 10.5 percent fall.

- Mass market paperback sales fell from $124.8 million to $98.9 million—a 20.8 percent fall.

MyEconLab More Economics in the News

ECONOMIC ANALYSIS

- Sales of e-books are growing rapidly because of the choices that millions of consumers are making. One of these consumers is Andy.

- Andy loves reading, but he also enjoys music. His budget for books and music is limited. So he must choose among the many alternative combinations of books and albums that he can afford.

- Figure 1 shows Andy's indifference curves for books (of all types) and albums.

- Andy's annual budget for albums and books is $600. The price of an album is $10, the price of a print book is $20, and the price of an e-book is $10.

- Figure 1 shows two budget lines: one if Andy buys print books and albums and another if he buys e-books and albums.

- In Fig. 1, the price of an e-book reader is $200. Andy must spend this amount on a reader if he is to buy e-books, which leaves him with $400 for albums and e-books. If he buys 15 e-books, he can afford 25 albums [(15 × $10) + (25 × $10) = $400].

- If Andy buys print books and albums, he can afford 15 print books and 30 albums [(15 × $20) + (30 × $10) = $600].

- This combination is Andy's best affordable choice—15 print books and 30 albums shown at point A. Andy doesn't buy e-books.

- Now the price of an e-book reader falls, and today Andy can buy a reader that previously cost $200 for $100.

- Figure 2 shows what happens to Andy's budget line and his choices.

- If Andy buys print books and albums, nothing changes. He can still afford 15 print books and 30 albums [(15 × $20) + (30 × $10) = $600].

- But if he buys e-books, his situation has changed. After spending $100 on an e-book reader, Andy is left with $500 for albums and e-books. If he buys 15 e-books he can now afford 35 albums [(15 × $10) + (35 × $10) = $500].

- Andy can now afford more albums if he buys the same number of books that he bought when the reader cost $200. But that's not Andy's best affordable combination of albums and books.

- The price of an e-book is lower than the price of a print book, so for Andy the relative price of a book has fallen and he can benefit by substituting books for albums.

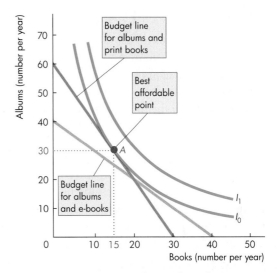

Figure 1 When the Price of a Reader Is $200

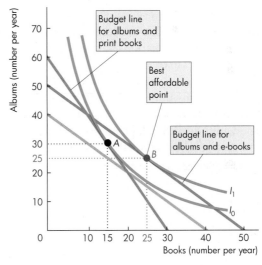

Figure 2 When the Price of a Reader Is $100

- Andy moves along his budget line to the point at which his marginal rate of substitution of books for albums equals the relative price.

- This point occurs at B where Andy buys 25 e-books and 25 albums [(25 × $10) + (25 × $10) = $500].

- The surge in e-book sales is the consequence of Andy and other rational consumers responding to the incentive of a change in relative prices and, in particular, a fall in the price of an e-book reader.

215

SUMMARY

Key Points

Consumption Possibilities (pp. 202–204)

- The budget line is the boundary between what a household can and cannot afford, given its income and the prices of goods.
- The point at which the budget line intersects the *y*-axis is the household's real income in terms of the good measured on that axis.
- The magnitude of the slope of the budget line is the relative price of the good measured on the *x*-axis in terms of the good measured on the *y*-axis.
- A change in the price of one good changes the slope of the budget line. A change in income shifts the budget line but does not change its slope.

Working Problems 1 to 5 will give you a better understanding of consumption possibilities.

Preferences and Indifference Curves (pp. 205–208)

- A consumer's preferences can be represented by indifference curves. The consumer is indifferent among all the combinations of goods that lie on an indifference curve.
- A consumer prefers any point above an indifference curve to any point on it and prefers any point on an indifference curve to any point below it.
- The magnitude of the slope of an indifference curve is called the marginal rate of substitution.
- The marginal rate of substitution diminishes as consumption of the good measured on the *y*-axis

decreases and consumption of the good measured on the *x*-axis increases.

Working Problems 6 and 7 will give you a better understanding of preferences and indifference curves.

Predicting Consumer Choices (pp. 208–213)

- A household consumes at its best affordable point. This point is on the budget line and on the highest attainable indifference curve and has a marginal rate of substitution equal to relative price.
- The effect of a price change (the price effect) can be divided into a substitution effect and an income effect.
- The substitution effect is the effect of a change in price on the quantity bought when the consumer (hypothetically) remains indifferent between the original choice and the new choice.
- The substitution effect always results in an increase in consumption of the good whose relative price has fallen.
- The income effect is the effect of a change in income on consumption.
- For a normal good, the income effect reinforces the substitution effect. For an inferior good, the income effect works in the opposite direction to the substitution effect.

Working Problems 8 to 11 will give you a better understanding of predicting consumer choices.

Key Terms

MyEconLab Key Terms Quiz

Budget line, 202
Diminishing marginal rate of
    substitution, 206
Income effect, 211

Indifference curve, 205
Marginal rate of substitution, 206
Price effect, 209
Real income, 203

Relative price, 203
Substitution effect, 212

WORKED PROBLEM

MyEconLab   You can work this problem in Chapter 9 Study Plan.

Wendy drinks 10 sugary drinks and 4 smoothies a week. Smoothies are $5 each and sugary drinks were $2 each. This week, things are different: The government has slapped a tax on sugary drinks and their price has doubled to $4. But it's not all bad news for Wendy. The government has also revised the income tax, so Wendy's drinks budget has increased. She can now just afford to buy her usual 10 sugary drinks and 4 smoothies a week.

Questions

1. What was Wendy's drinks budget last week and what is it this week?
2. What was Wendy's opportunity cost of a sugary drink last week and what is it this week?
3. Does Wendy buy 10 sugary drinks and 4 smoothies this week? Explain.
4. Is Wendy better off this week than last week? Explain.

Solutions

1. To find Wendy's drinks budget, use the fact that Income (available for drinks) = Expenditure.

   Expenditure = (Price of a sugary drink × Quantity of sugary drinks) + (Price of a smoothie × Quantity of smoothies).

   Last week, her income was ($2 × 10) + ($5 × 4) = $40.

   This week, her income is ($4 × 10) + ($5 × 4) = $60.

Key Point: Income limits expenditure and expenditure equals price multiplied by quantity, summed over the goods consumed.

2. Wendy's opportunity cost of a sugary drink is the number of smoothies she must forgo to get 1 sugary drink. Wendy's opportunity cost equals the relative price of a sugary drink, which is the price of a sugary drink divided by the price of a smoothie.

   Last week, Wendy's opportunity cost of a sugary drink was $2 ÷ $5 = 2/5 or 0.4 smoothies.

   This week, it is $4 ÷ $5 = 4/5 or 0.8 smoothies.

Key Point: A relative price is an opportunity cost.

3. Wendy does not buy 10 sugary drinks and 4 smoothies this week because it is not her best affordable choice.

At her best affordable choice, Wendy's marginal rate of substitution (*MRS*) between sugary drinks and smoothies is equal to the relative price of sugary drinks and smoothies.

Last week, when she chose 10 sugary drinks and 4 smoothies, her *MRS* was 0.4, equal to last week's relative price of 0.4 smoothies per sugary drink. This week, the relative price is 0.8 smoothies per sugary drink, so Wendy changes her choice to make her *MRS* equal 0.8.

To increase her *MRS* from 0.4 to 0.8, Wendy buys fewer sugary drinks and more smoothies. We know how she changes her choice but not the new quantities she buys. To get the quantities, we would need to know Wendy's preferences as described by her indifference curves.

Key Point: When the relative price of a good rises, the consumer buys less of that good to make the *MRS* increase to equal the higher relative price.

4. Wendy is better off! She can still buy her last week's choice but, at that choice, she is not at her best affordable point. So by buying more smoothies, she moves along her budget line to a higher indifference curve at which *MRS* equals 0.8.

Key Point: When both income and the relative price of a good change so that the old choice is still available, the consumer's best affordable choice changes.

Key Figure

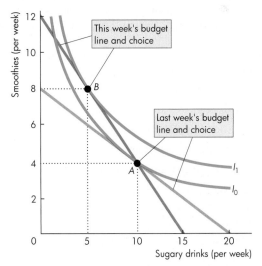

MyEconLab Interactive Animation

STUDY PLAN PROBLEMS AND APPLICATIONS

MyEconLab   You can work Problems 1 to 11 in Chapter 9 Study Plan and get instant feedback.

Consumption Possibilities (Study Plan 9.1)

Use the following data to work Problems 1 and 2.
Sara's income is $12 a week. The price of popcorn is $3 a bag, and the price of a smoothie is $3.

1. Calculate Sara's real income in terms of smoothies. Calculate her real income in terms of popcorn. What is the relative price of smoothies in terms of popcorn? What is the opportunity cost of a smoothie?

2. Calculate the equation for Sara's budget line (with bags of popcorn on the left side). Draw a graph of Sara's budget line with the quantity of smoothies on the *x*-axis. What is the slope of Sara's budget line? What determines its value?

Use the following data to work Problems 3 and 4.
Sara's income falls from $12 to $9 a week, while the price of popcorn is unchanged at $3 a bag and the price of a smoothie is unchanged at $3.

3. What is the effect of the fall in Sara's income on her real income in terms of (a) smoothies and (b) popcorn?

4. What is the effect of the fall in Sara's income on the relative price of a smoothie in terms of popcorn? What is the slope of Sara's new budget line if it is drawn with smoothies on the *x*-axis?

5. Sara's income is $12 a week. The price of popcorn rises from $3 to $6 a bag, and the price of a smoothie is unchanged at $3. Explain how Sara's budget line changes with smoothies on the *x*-axis.

Preferences and Indifference Curves (Study Plan 9.2)

6. Draw figures that show your indifference curves for the following pairs of goods:
   - Right gloves and left gloves
   - Coca-Cola and Pepsi
   - Desktop computers and laptop computers
   - Strawberries and ice cream

For each pair, are the goods perfect substitutes, perfect complements, substitutes, complements, or unrelated?

7. Discuss the shape of the indifference curve for each of the following pairs of goods:
   - Orange juice and smoothies
   - Baseballs and baseball bats

   - Left running shoe and right running shoe
   - Eyeglasses and contact lenses

   Explain the relationship between the shape of the indifference curve and the marginal rate of substitution as the quantities of the two goods change.

Predicting Consumer Choices (Study Plan 9.3)

Use the following data to work Problems 8 and 9.
Pam has made her best affordable choice of cookies and granola bars. She spends all of her weekly income on 30 cookies at $1 each and 5 granola bars at $2 each. Next week, she expects the price of a cookie to fall to 50¢ and the price of a granola bar to rise to $5.

8. a. Will Pam be able to buy and want to buy 30 cookies and 5 granola bars next week?

   b. Which situation does Pam prefer: cookies at $1 and granola bars at $2 or cookies at 50¢ and granola bars at $5?

9. a. If Pam changes how she spends her weekly income, will she buy more or fewer cookies and more or fewer granola bars?

   b. When the prices change next week, will there be an income effect, a substitution effect, or both at work?

Use the following news clip to work Problems 10 and 11.

Boom Time for "Gently Used" Clothes

Most retailers are blaming the economy for their poor sales, but one store chain that sells used name-brand children's clothes, toys, and furniture is boldly declaring that an economic downturn can actually be a boon for its business. Last year, the company took in $20 million in sales, up 5% from the previous year.

Source: CNN, April 17, 2008

10. a. According to the news clip, is used clothing a normal good or an inferior good? If the price of used clothing falls and income remains the same, explain how the quantity of used clothing bought changes.

   b. Describe the substitution effect and the income effect that occur.

11. Use a graph of a family's indifference curves for used clothing and other goods. Then draw two budget lines to show the effect of a fall in income on the quantity of used clothing purchased.

ADDITIONAL PROBLEMS AND APPLICATIONS

MyEconLab   You can work these problems in MyEconLab if assigned by your instructor.

Consumption Possibilities

Use the following data to work Problems 12 to 15.

Marc has a budget of $20 a month to spend on root beer and DVDs. The price of root beer is $5 a bottle, and the price of a DVD is $10.

12. What is the relative price of root beer in terms of DVDs and what is the opportunity cost of a bottle of root beer?

13. Calculate Marc's real income in terms of root beer. Calculate his real income in terms of DVDs.

14. Calculate the equation for Marc's budget line (with the quantity of root beer on the left side).

15. Draw a graph of Marc's budget line with the quantity of DVDs on the *x*-axis. What is the slope of Marc's budget line? What determines its value?

Use the following data to work Problems 16 to 19.

Amy has $20 a week to spend on coffee and cake. The price of coffee is $4 a cup, and the price of cake is $2 a slice.

16. Calculate Amy's real income in terms of cake. Calculate the relative price of cake in terms of coffee.

17. Calculate the equation for Amy's budget line (with cups of coffee on the left side).

18. If Amy's income increases to $24 a week and the prices of coffee and cake remain unchanged, describe the change in her budget line.

19. If the price of cake doubles while the price of coffee remains at $4 a cup and Amy's income remains at $20, describe the change in her budget line.

Use the following news clip to work Problems 20 and 21.

Gas Prices Straining Budgets

With gas prices rising, many people say they are staying in and scaling back spending to try to keep within their budget. They are driving as little as possible, cutting back on shopping and eating out, and reducing other discretionary spending.

         Source: CNN, February 29, 2008

20. a. Sketch a budget line for a household that spends its income on only two goods: gasoline and restaurant meals. Identify the combinations of gasoline and restaurant meals that are affordable and those that are unaffordable.

    b. Sketch a second budget line to show how a rise in the price of gasoline changes the affordable and unaffordable combinations of gasoline and restaurant meals. Describe how the household's consumption possibilities change.

21. How does a rise in the price of gasoline change the relative price of a restaurant meal? How does a rise in the price of gasoline change real income in terms of restaurant meals?

Preferences and Indifference Curves

Use the following information to work Problems 22 and 23.

Rashid buys only books and CDs and the figure shows his preference map.

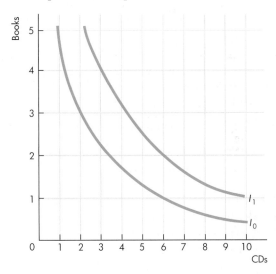

22. a. If Rashid chooses 3 books and 2 CDs, what is his marginal rate of substitution?

    b. If Rashid chooses 2 books and 6 CDs, what is his marginal rate of substitution?

23. Do Rashid's indifference curves display diminishing marginal rate of substitution? Explain why or why not.

24. **You May Be Paid More (or Less) Than You Think**

It's so hard to put a price on happiness, isn't it? But if you've ever had to choose between a job you like and a better-paying one that you like less, you probably wished some economist would tell you how much job satisfaction is worth. Trust in management is by far the biggest component to consider. Say you get a new boss and your trust in management goes up a bit (say, up 1 point on a 10-point scale). That's like getting a 36-percent pay raise. In other words, that increased level of trust will boost your level of overall satisfaction in life by about the same amount as a 36-percent raise would.

Source: CNN, March 29, 2006

a. Measure trust in management on a 10-point scale, measure pay on the same 10-point scale, and think of them as two goods. Sketch an indifference curve (with trust on the *x*-axis) that is consistent with the news clip.

b. What is the marginal rate of substitution between trust in management and pay according to this news clip?

c. What does the news clip imply about the principle of diminishing marginal rate of substitution? Is that implication likely to be correct?

Predicting Consumer Choices

Use the following data to work Problems 25 and 26.
Jim has made his best affordable choice of muffins and coffee. He spends all of his income on 10 muffins at $1 each and 20 cups of coffee at $2 each. Now the price of a muffin rises to $1.50 and the price of coffee falls to $1.75 a cup.

25. a. Will Jim now be able and want to buy 10 muffins and 20 coffees?

b. Which situation does Jim prefer: muffins at $1 and coffee at $2 a cup or muffins at $1.50 and coffee at $1.75 a cup?

26. a. If Jim changes the quantities that he buys, will he buy more or fewer muffins and more or less coffee? Explain your answer.

b. When the prices change, will there be an income effect, a substitution effect, or both at work? Explain your answer.

Use the following data and figure to work Problems 27 to 29.
Sara's income is $12 a week. The price of popcorn is $3 a bag, and the price of cola is $1.50 a can. The figure shows Sara's preference map for popcorn and cola.

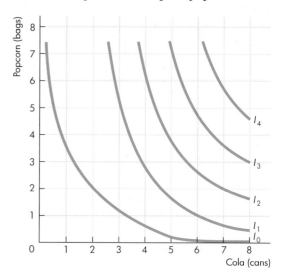

27. What quantities of popcorn and cola does Sara buy? What is Sara's marginal rate of substitution at the point at which she consumes?

28. Suppose that the price of cola rises from $1.50 to $3.00 a can while the price of popcorn and Sara's income remain the same. What quantities of cola and popcorn does Sara now buy? What are two points on Sara's demand curve for cola? Draw Sara's demand curve.

29. Suppose that the price of cola rises to $3.00 a can and the price of popcorn and Sara's income remain the same.

a. What is the substitution effect of this price change and what is the income effect of the price change?

b. Is cola a normal good or an inferior good? Explain.

Economics in the News

30. After you have studied *Economics in the News* on pp. 214–215, answer the following questions.

a. How do you buy books?

b. Sketch your budget line for books and other goods.

c. Sketch your indifference curves for books and other goods.

d. Identify your best affordable point.

Making the Most of Life

The powerful forces of demand and supply shape the fortunes of families, businesses, nations, and empires in the same unrelenting way that the tides and winds shape rocks and coastlines. You saw in Chapters 3 through 7 how these forces raise and lower prices, increase and decrease quantities bought and sold, cause revenues to fluctuate, and send resources to their most valuable uses.

These powerful forces begin quietly and privately with the choices that each one of us makes. Chapters 8 and 9 probe these individual choices, offering two alternative approaches to explaining both consumption plans and the allocation of time. These explanations of consumption plans can also explain "non-economic" choices, such as whether to marry and how many children to have. In a sense, there are no non-economic choices. If there is scarcity, there must be choice, and economics studies all choices.

The earliest economists (Adam Smith and his contemporaries) did not have a very deep understanding of households' choices. It was not until the nineteenth century that progress was made in this area when Jeremy Bentham (below) introduced the concept of utility and applied it to the study of human choices. Today, Steven Levitt, whom you will meet on the following page, is one of the most influential students of human behavior.

Jeremy Bentham *(1748–1832), who lived in London, was the son and grandson of lawyers and was himself trained as a barrister. But Bentham rejected the opportunity to maintain the family tradition and, instead, spent his life as a writer, activist, and Member of Parliament in the pursuit of rational laws that would bring the greatest happiness to the greatest number of people.*

Bentham, whose embalmed body is preserved to this day in a glass cabinet in the University of London, was the first person to use the concept of utility to explain human choices. But in Bentham's day, the distinction between explaining and prescribing was not a sharp one, and Bentham was ready to use his ideas to tell people how they ought to behave. He was one of the first to propose pensions for the retired, guaranteed employment, minimum wages, and social benefits such as free education and free medical care.

"... It is the greatest happiness of the greatest number that is the measure of right and wrong."

JEREMY BENTHAM
Fragment on Government

I think of economics as being primarily about a way of looking at the world and a set of tools for thinking clearly.

STEVEN D. LEVITT is William B. Ogden Distinguished Service Professor of Economics at the University of Chicago. Born in Minneapolis, he was an undergraduate at Harvard and a graduate student at MIT. Among his many honors, he was recently awarded the John Bates Clark Medal, given to the best economist under 40.

Professor Levitt has studied an astonishingly wide range of human choices and their outcomes. He has examined the effects of policing on crime, shown that real estate agents get a higher price when they sell their own homes than when they sell other people's, devised a test to detect cheating teachers, and studied the choices of drug dealers and gang members. Much of this research has been popularized in *Freakonomics* (Steven D. Levitt and Stephen J. Dubner, HarperCollins, 2005). What unifies this apparently diverse body of research is the use of natural experiments. Professor Levitt has an incredible ability to find just the right set of events and the data the events have generated to enable him to isolate the effect he's looking for.

Michael Parkin talked with Steven Levitt about his work and what economists have discovered about how people respond to incentives.

Why did you become an economist?

As a freshman in college, I took introductory economics. All the ideas made perfect sense to me—it was the way I naturally thought. My friends were befuddled. I thought, "This is the field for me!"

The idea of rational choice made at the margin lies at the heart of economics. Would you say that your work generally supports that idea or challenges it? Can you provide some examples?

I don't like the word "rational" in this context. I think economists model agents as being rational just for convenience. What really matters is whether people respond to incentives. My work very much supports the idea that humans in all types of circumstances respond strongly to incentives. I've seen it with drug dealers, auto thieves, sumo wrestlers, real estate agents, and elementary school teachers, just to name a few examples.

*Read the full interview with Steven Levitt in MyEconLab.

Drug dealers, for instance, want to make money, but they also want to avoid being arrested or even killed. In the data we have on drug sellers, we see that when the drug trade is more lucrative, dealers are willing to take greater risks of arrest to carve out a share of the market…. Sumo wrestlers, on the other hand, care mostly about their official ranking. Sometimes matches occur where one wrestler has more to lose or gain than the other wrestler. We find that sumo wrestlers make corrupt deals to make sure the wrestler who wins is the one who needs to win.

Why is an economist interested in crime and cheating?

I think of economics as being primarily about a way of looking at the world and a set of tools for thinking clearly. The topics you apply these tools to are unlimited. That is why I think economics has been so powerful. If you understand economics and use the tools wisely, you will be a better business person, doctor, public servant, parent.

10 ORGANIZING PRODUCTION

After studying this chapter, you will be able to:

◆ Explain the economic problem that all firms face

◆ Distinguish between technological efficiency and economic efficiency

◆ Define and explain the principal–agent problem

◆ Distinguish among different types of markets

◆ Explain why markets coordinate some economic activities and why firms coordinate others

In 1990, a British scientist named Tim Berners-Lee invented the World Wide Web, a remarkable idea that paved the way for the creation of thousands of profitable firms among which are Facebook, Twitter, Google, Amazon, and eBay.

What are the decisions that firms must make? That's the question you study in this chapter. In *Economics in the News* at the end of the chapter, we'll look at some decisions made by Facebook and Google in the Internet advertising market.

◆ The Firm and Its Economic Problem

The 20 million firms in the United States differ in size and in the scope of what they do, but they all perform the same basic economic functions. Each **firm** is an institution that hires factors of production and organizes those factors to produce and sell goods and services. Our goal is to predict firms' behavior. To do so, we need to know a firm's goal and the constraints it faces. We start with the goal.

The Firm's Goal

When economists ask entrepreneurs what they are trying to achieve, they get many different answers. Some talk about making a high-quality product, others about business growth, others about market share, others about the job satisfaction of their workforce, and an increasing number today talk about social and environmental responsibility. All of these goals are pursued by firms, but they are not the fundamental goal: They are the means to that goal.

A firm's goal is to maximize profit. A firm that does not seek to maximize profit is either eliminated or taken over by a firm that does seek that goal.

What is the profit that a firm seeks to maximize? To answer this question, we'll look at Campus Sweaters, Inc., a small producer of knitted sweaters owned and operated by Cindy.

Accounting Profit

In 2012, Campus Sweaters received $400,000 for the sweaters it sold and paid out $80,000 for wool, $20,000 for utilities, $120,000 for wages, $5,000 for the lease of a computer, and $5,000 in interest on a bank loan. These expenses total $230,000, so the firm had a cash surplus of $170,000.

To measure the profit of Campus Sweaters, Cindy's accountant subtracted $20,000 for the depreciation of buildings and knitting machines from the $170,000 cash surplus. *Depreciation* is the fall in the value of a firm's capital. To calculate depreciation, accountants use Internal Revenue Service rules based on standards established by the Financial Accounting Standards Board. Using these rules, Cindy's accountant calculated that Campus Sweaters made a profit of $150,000 in 2012.

Economic Accounting

Accountants measure a firm's profit to ensure that the firm pays the correct amount of income tax and to show its investors how their funds are being used.

Economists measure a firm's profit to enable them to predict the firm's decisions, and the goal of these decisions is to maximize *economic profit*. **Economic profit** is equal to total revenue minus total cost, with total cost measured as the *opportunity cost of production*.

A Firm's Opportunity Cost of Production

The *opportunity cost* of any action is the highest-valued alternative forgone. The *opportunity cost of production* is the value of the best alternative use of the resources that a firm uses in production.

A firm's opportunity cost of production is the value of real alternatives forgone. We express opportunity cost in money units so that we can compare and add up the value of the alternatives forgone.

A firm's opportunity cost of production is the sum of the cost of using resources

- Bought in the market
- Owned by the firm
- Supplied by the firm's owner

Resources Bought in the Market A firm incurs an opportunity cost when it buys resources in the market. The amount spent on these resources is an opportunity cost of production because the firm could have bought different resources to produce some other good or service. For Campus Sweaters, the resources bought in the market are wool, utilities, labor, a leased computer, and a bank loan. The $230,000 spent on these items in 2012 could have been spent on something else, so it is an opportunity cost of producing sweaters.

Resources Owned by the Firm A firm incurs an opportunity cost when it uses its own capital. The cost of using capital owned by the firm is an opportunity cost of production because the firm could sell the capital that it owns and rent capital from another firm. When a firm uses its own capital, it implicitly rents it from itself. In this case, the firm's opportunity cost of using the capital it owns is called the **implicit rental rate** of capital. The implicit rental rate of capital has two components: economic depreciation and forgone interest.

Economic Depreciation Accountants measure *depreciation*, the fall in the value of a firm's capital, using formulas that are unrelated to the change in the market value of capital. **Economic depreciation** is the fall in the *market value* of a firm's capital over a given period. It equals the market price of the capital at the beginning of the period minus the market price of the capital at the end of the period.

Suppose that Campus Sweaters could have sold its buildings and knitting machines on January 1, 2012, for $400,000 and that it can sell the same capital on December 31, 2012, for $375,000. The firm's economic depreciation during 2012 is $25,000 ($400,000 – $375,000). This forgone $25,000 is an opportunity cost of production.

Forgone Interest The funds used to buy capital could have been used for some other purpose, and in their next best use, they would have earned interest. This forgone interest is an opportunity cost of production.

Suppose that Campus Sweaters used $300,000 of its own funds to buy capital. If the firm invested its $300,000 in bonds instead of a knitting factory (and rented the capital it needs to produce sweaters), it would have earned $15,000 a year in interest. This forgone interest is an opportunity cost of production.

Resources Supplied by the Firm's Owner A firm's owner might supply *both* entrepreneurship and labor.

Entrepreneurship The factor of production that organizes a firm and makes its decisions might be supplied by the firm's owner or by a hired entrepreneur. The return to entrepreneurship is profit, and the profit that an entrepreneur earns *on average* is called **normal profit**. Normal profit is the cost of entrepreneurship and is an opportunity cost of production.

If Cindy supplies entrepreneurial services herself, and if the normal profit she can earn on these services is $45,000 a year, this amount is an opportunity cost of production at Campus Sweaters.

Owner's Labor Services *In addition* to supplying entrepreneurship, the owner of a firm might supply labor but not take a wage. The opportunity cost of the owner's labor is the wage income forgone by not taking the best alternative job.

If Cindy supplies labor to Campus Sweaters, and if the wage she can earn on this labor at another firm is $55,000 a year, this amount of wages forgone is an opportunity cost of production at Campus Sweaters.

Economic Accounting: A Summary

Table 10.1 summarizes the economic accounting. Campus Sweaters' total revenue is $400,000; its opportunity cost of production is $370,000; and its economic profit is $30,000.

Cindy's personal income is the $30,000 of economic profit plus the $100,000 that she earns by supplying resources to Campus Sweaters.

The Firm's Decisions

To achieve the objective of maximum economic profit, a firm must make five decisions:

1. What to produce and in what quantities
2. How to produce
3. How to organize and compensate its managers and workers
4. How to market and price its products
5. What to produce itself and buy from others

In all these decisions, a firm's actions are limited by the constraints that it faces. Your next task is to learn about these constraints.

TABLE 10.1   Economic Accounting

Item		Amount
Total Revenue		**$400,000**
Cost of Resources Bought in Market		
Wool	$80,000	
Utilities	20,000	
Wages	120,000	
Computer lease	5,000	
Bank interest	5,000	$230,000
Cost of Resources Owned by Firm		
Economic depreciation	$25,000	
Forgone interest	15,000	$40,000
Cost of Resources Supplied by Owner		
Cindy's normal profit	$45,000	
Cindy's forgone wages	55,000	$100,000
Opportunity Cost of Production		**$370,000**
Economic Profit		**$30,000**

The Firm's Constraints

Three features of a firm's environment limit the maximum economic profit it can make. They are

- Technology constraints
- Information constraints
- Market constraints

Technology Constraints Economists define technology broadly. A **technology** is any method of producing a good or service. Technology includes the detailed designs of machines and the layout of the workplace. It includes the organization of the firm. For example, the shopping mall is one technology for producing retail services. It is a different technology from the catalog store, which in turn is different from the downtown store.

It might seem surprising that a firm's profit is limited by technology because it seems that technological advances are constantly increasing profit opportunities. Almost every day, we learn about some new technological advance that amazes us. With computers that speak and recognize our own speech and cars that can find the address we need in a city we've never visited, we can accomplish more than ever.

Technology advances over time. But at each point in time, to produce more output and gain more revenue, a firm must hire more resources and incur greater costs. The increase in profit that a firm can achieve is limited by the technology available. For example, by using its current plant and workforce, Ford can produce some maximum number of cars per day. To produce more cars per day, Ford must hire more resources, which increases its costs and limits the increase in profit that it can make by selling the additional cars.

Information Constraints We never possess all the information we would like to have to make decisions. We lack information about both the future and the present. For example, suppose you plan to buy a new computer. When should you buy it? The answer depends on how the price is going to change in the future. Where should you buy it? The answer depends on the prices at hundreds of different computer stores. To get the best deal, you must compare the quality and prices in every store. But the opportunity cost of this comparison exceeds the cost of the computer!

A firm is constrained by limited information about the quality and efforts of its workforce, the current and future buying plans of its customers, and the plans of its competitors. Workers might make too little effort, customers might switch to competing suppliers, and a competitor might enter the market and take some of the firm's business.

To address these problems, firms create incentives to boost workers' efforts even when no one is monitoring them; conduct market research to lower uncertainty about customers' buying plans; and "spy" on each other to anticipate competitive challenges. But these efforts don't eliminate incomplete information and uncertainty, which limit the economic profit that a firm can make.

Market Constraints The quantity each firm can sell and the price it can obtain are constrained by its customers' willingness to pay and by the prices and marketing efforts of other firms. Similarly, the resources that a firm can buy and the prices it must pay for them are limited by the willingness of people to work for and invest in the firm. Firms spend billions of dollars a year marketing and selling their products. Some of the most creative minds strive to find the right message that will produce a knockout television advertisement. Market constraints and the expenditures firms make to overcome them limit the profit a firm can make.

◆ REVIEW QUIZ

1 What is a firm's fundamental goal and what happens if the firm doesn't pursue this goal?
2 Why do accountants and economists calculate a firm's costs and profit in different ways?
3 What are the items that make opportunity cost differ from the accountant's measure of cost?
4 Why is normal profit an opportunity cost?
5 What are the constraints that a firm faces? How does each constraint limit the firm's profit?

Work these questions in Study Plan 10.1 and get instant feedback. Do a Key Terms Quiz.   MyEconLab

---

In the rest of this chapter and in Chapters 11 through 14, we study the choices that firms make. You're going to learn how we can predict a firm's decisions as those that maximize profit given the constraints the firm faces. We begin by taking a closer look at a firm's technology constraints.

Technological and Economic Efficiency

Microsoft employs a large workforce, and most Microsoft workers possess a large amount of human capital. But the firm uses a small amount of physical capital. In contrast, a coal-mining company employs a huge amount of mining equipment (physical capital) and almost no labor. Why? The answer lies in the concept of efficiency. There are two concepts of production efficiency: technological efficiency and economic efficiency. **Technological efficiency** occurs when the firm produces a given output by using the least amount of inputs. **Economic efficiency** occurs when the firm produces a given output at the least cost. Let's explore the two concepts of efficiency by studying an example.

Suppose that there are four alternative techniques for making TVs:

A. *Robot production.* One person monitors the entire computer-driven process.

B. *Production line.* Workers specialize in a small part of the job as the emerging TV passes them on a production line.

C. *Hand-tool production.* A single worker uses a few hand tools to make a TV.

D. *Bench production.* Workers specialize in a small part of the job but walk from bench to bench to perform their tasks.

Table 10.2 sets out the amounts of labor and capital required by each of these four methods to make 10 TVs a day.

Which of these alternative methods are technologically efficient?

Technological Efficiency

Recall that *technological efficiency* occurs when the firm produces a given output by using the least amount of inputs. Look at the numbers in the table and notice that method *A* uses the most capital and the least labor. Method *C* uses the most labor and the least capital. Method *B* and method *D* lie between the two extremes. They use less capital and more labor than method *A* and less labor but more capital than method *C*.

Compare methods *B* and *D*. Method *D* requires 100 workers and 10 units of capital to produce 10

TABLE 10.2 Four Ways of Making 10 TVs a Day

| | | Quantities of inputs | |
	Method	Labor	Capital
A	Robot production	1	1,000
B	Production line	10	10
C	Hand-tool production	1,000	1
D	Bench production	100	10

TVs. Method *B* can produce those same 10 TVs by using 10 workers and the same 10 units of capital. Because method *D* uses the same amount of capital and more labor than method *B*, method *D* is not technologically efficient.

Are any of the other methods not technologically efficient? The answer is no. Each of the other methods is technologically efficient. Method *A* uses more capital but less labor than method *B*, and method *C* uses more labor but less capital than method *B*.

Which of the methods are economically efficient?

Economic Efficiency

Recall that *economic efficiency* occurs when the firm produces a given output at the least cost.

Method *D*, which is technologically inefficient, is also economically inefficient. It uses the same amount of capital as method *B* but 10 times as much labor, so it costs more. A technologically inefficient method is never economically efficient.

One of the three technologically efficient methods is economically efficient. The other two are economically inefficient. But which method is economically efficient depends on factor prices.

In Table 10.3(a), the wage rate is $75 per day and the rental rate of capital is $250 per day. By studying Table 10.3(a), you can see that method *B* has the lowest cost and is the economically efficient method.

In Table 10.3(b), the wage rate is $150 a day and the rental rate of capital is $1 a day. Looking at Table 10.3(b), you can see that method *A* has the lowest cost and is the economically efficient method. In this case, capital is so cheap relative to labor that the

TABLE 10.3   The Costs of Different Ways of Making 10 TVs a Day

(a) Wage rate $75 per day; Capital rental rate $250 per day

Method	Inputs Labor	Capital	Labor cost ($75 per day)		Capital cost ($250 per day)		Total cost
A	1	1,000	$75	+	$250,000	=	$250,075
B	10	10	750	+	2,500	=	3,250
C	1,000	1	75,000	+	250	=	75,250

(b) Wage rate $150 per day; Capital rental rate $1 per day

Method	Inputs Labor	Capital	Labor cost ($150 per day)		Capital cost ($1 per day)		Total cost
A	1	1,000	$150	+	$1,000	=	$1,150
B	10	10	1,500	+	10	=	1,510
C	1,000	1	150,000	+	1	=	150,001

(c) Wage rate $1 per day; Capital rental rate $1,000 per day

Method	Inputs Labor	Capital	Labor cost ($1 per day)		Capital cost ($1,000 per day)		Total cost
A	1	1,000	$1	+	$1,000,000	=	$1,000,001
B	10	10	10	+	10,000	=	10,010
C	1,000	1	1,000	+	1,000	=	2,000

method that uses the most capital is the economically efficient method.

In Table 10.3(c), the wage rate is $1 a day and the rental rate of capital is $1,000 a day. You can see that method C has the lowest cost and is the economically efficient method. In this case, labor is so cheap relative to capital that the method that uses the most labor is the economically efficient method.

Economic efficiency depends on the relative costs of resources. The economically efficient method is the one that uses a smaller amount of the more expensive resource and a larger amount of the less expensive resource.

A firm that is not economically efficient does not maximize profit. Natural selection favors efficient firms and inefficient firms disappear. Inefficient firms go out of business or are taken over by firms that produce at lower costs.

◆ REVIEW QUIZ

1 Is a firm technologically efficient if it uses the latest technology? Why or why not?
2 Is a firm economically inefficient if it can cut its costs by producing less? Why or why not?
3 Explain the key distinction between technological efficiency and economic efficiency.
4 Why do some firms use large amounts of capital and small amounts of labor while others use small amounts of capital and large amounts of labor?

Work these questions in Study Plan 10.2 and get instant feedback. Do a Key Terms Quiz.   MyEconLab

Next we study the information constraints that firms face and the wide array of organization structures these constraints generate.

◆ Information and Organization

Each firm organizes the production of goods and services using a combination of two systems:

- Command systems
- Incentive systems

Command Systems

A **command system** is a method of organizing production that uses a managerial hierarchy. Commands pass downward through the hierarchy, and information passes upward.

The military uses the purest form of command system. A commander-in-chief makes the big decisions about strategic goals. Beneath this highest level, generals organize their military resources. Beneath the generals, successively lower ranks organize smaller and smaller units but pay attention to ever-increasing degrees of detail. At the bottom of the hierarchy are the people who operate weapons systems.

Command systems in firms are not as rigid as those in the military, but they share some similar features. A chief executive officer (CEO) sits at the top of a firm's command system. Senior executives specialize in managing production, marketing, finance, and personnel. Beneath these senior managers are the people who supervise the day-to-day operations of the business and beneath them, the people who operate the firm's machines and who make and sell the firm's products.

Managers try to be well informed, but they almost always have incomplete information about what is happening in the divisions for which they are responsible. For this reason, firms also use incentive systems.

Incentive Systems

An **incentive system** is a method of organizing production that uses a market-like mechanism inside the firm. Instead of issuing commands, senior managers create compensation schemes to induce workers to perform in ways that maximize the firm's profit.

Incentive systems operate at all levels in a firm. The compensation plan of a CEO might include a share in the firm's profit, factory floor workers sometimes receive compensation based on the quantity they produce, and salespeople, who spend most of their working time alone, are induced to work hard by being paid a small salary and a large performance-related bonus.

The Principal–Agent Problem

The **principal–agent problem** is the problem of devising compensation rules that induce an *agent* to act in the best interest of a *principal*. For example, the stockholders of Texaco are *principals,* and the firm's managers are *agents*. The stockholders (the principals) must induce the managers (agents) to act in the stockholders' best interest. Similarly, Mark Zuckerberg (a principal) must induce the designers who are working on the next generation Facebook (agents) to work efficiently.

Agents, whether they are managers or workers, pursue their own goals and often impose costs on a principal. For example, the goal of stockholders of Citicorp (principals) is to maximize the firm's profit—its true profit, not some fictitious paper profit. But the firm's profit depends on the actions of its managers (agents), and they have their own goals. Perhaps a bank manager takes a customer to a ball game on the pretense that she is building customer loyalty, when in fact she is simply enjoying on-the-job leisure. This same manager is also a principal, and her tellers are agents. The manager wants the tellers to work hard and attract new customers so that she can meet her operating targets. But the workers slack off and take on-the-job leisure.

Coping with the Principal–Agent Problem

A principal must create incentives that induce each agent to work in the interests of the principal. Three ways of coping with the principal–agent problem are

- Ownership
- Incentive pay
- Long-term contracts

Ownership By assigning ownership (or part-ownership) of a business to managers or workers, it is sometimes possible to induce a job performance that increases a firm's profits. Part-ownership is quite common for senior managers but less common for workers. When United Airlines was running into problems a few years ago, it made most of its employees owners of the company.

Incentive Pay Incentive pay—pay related to performance—is very common. Incentives are based on a variety of performance criteria such as profits, production, or sales targets. Promoting an employee for good performance is another example of the use of incentive pay.

Long-Term Contracts Long-term contracts tie the long-term fortunes of managers and workers (agents) to the success of the principal(s)—the owner(s) of the firm. For example, a multiyear employment contract for a CEO encourages that person to take a long-term view and devise strategies that achieve maximum profit over a sustained period.

These three ways of coping with the principal–agent problem give rise to different types of business organization.

Types of Business Organization

The three main types of business organization are

- Proprietorship
- Partnership
- Corporation

Proprietorship A *proprietorship* is a firm with a single owner—a proprietor—who has unlimited liability. *Unlimited liability* is the legal responsibility for all the

---

◆ ECONOMICS IN THE NEWS

Principals and Agents Get It Wrong

JPMorgan Pay May Be Clawed Back
In May 2012, JPMorgan Chase announced that traders in London had incurred losses of $2 billion. CEO Jamie Dimon said the losses arose from a "flawed, complex, poorly reviewed, poorly executed, and poorly monitored" trading strategy.
JPMorgan Chase's stock price fell on the news. One top executive took early retirement. JPMorgan executives and traders are compensated by results with bonus payments in cash and stock options. Dimon said "It's likely that there will be clawbacks" of compensation.

Sources: *AP, Bloomberg,* and *Reuters,* May/June, 2012

THE QUESTIONS

- Who are the principals and who are the agents?
- How did JPMorgan try to cope with its principal–agent problem?
- On the occasion reported here, how did JPMorgan get it wrong?
- What role did JPMorgan's share price play?

THE ANSWERS

- The JPMorgan stockholders are principals and Jamie Dimon is their agent.
- Jamie Dimon, as CEO, is a principal and the top executives are agents.
- JPMorgan top executives are principals, and the traders who incurred the losses are agents.
- JPMorgan tried to cope with the principal–agent problem by compensating agents with performance bonuses, profit shares through stock options, and with the possibility of clawbacks for poor performance.
- We don't know the details but, based on what

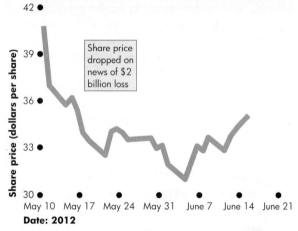

Figure 1 JPMorgan Share Price

Jamie Dimon said, it seems that the specific trading activities that incurred a $2 billion loss were complex and not properly understood either by the traders (the agents at the end of the line) or the managers who designed the trading activities.

- The fall in JPMorgan's stock price not only lowered the wealth of stockholders but also lowered the compensation of Jamie Dimon and the other executives compensated with stock options.

MyEconLab More Economics in the News

debts of a firm up to an amount equal to the entire personal wealth of the owner. Farmers, computer programmers, and artists are often proprietorships.

The proprietor makes management decisions, receives the firm's profits, and is responsible for its losses. Profits from a proprietorship are taxed at the same rate as other sources of the proprietor's personal income.

Partnership A *partnership* is a firm with two or more owners who have unlimited liability. Partners must agree on an appropriate management structure and on how to divide the firm's profits among themselves. The profits of a partnership are taxed as the personal income of the owners, but each partner is legally liable for all the debts of the partnership (limited only by the wealth of that individual partner). Liability for the full debts of the partnership is called *joint unlimited liability*. Most law firms are partnerships.

Corporation A *corporation* is a firm owned by one or more limited liability stockholders. *Limited liability* means that the owners have legal liability only for the value of their initial investment. This

limitation of liability means that if the corporation becomes bankrupt, its owners do not use their personal wealth to pay the corporation's debts.

Corporations' profits are taxed independently of stockholders' incomes. Stockholders pay a capital gains tax on the profit they earn when they sell a stock for a higher price than they paid for it. Corporate stocks generate capital gains when a corporation retains some of its profit and reinvests it in profitable activities. So retained earnings are taxed twice because the capital gains they generate are taxed. Dividend payments are also taxed but at a lower rate than other sources of income.

Pros and Cons of Different Types of Firms

The different types of business organization arise from firms trying to cope with the principal–agent problem. Each type has advantages in particular situations and because of its special advantages, each type continues to exist. Each type of business organization also has disadvantages.

Table 10.4 summarizes these and other pros and cons of the different types of firms.

TABLE 10.4 The Pros and Cons of Different Types of Firms

Type of Firm	Pros	Cons
Proprietorship	■ Easy to set up ■ Simple decision making ■ Profits taxed only once as owner's income	■ Bad decisions not checked; no need for consensus ■ Owner's entire wealth at risk ■ Firm dies with owner ■ Cost of capital and labor is high relative to that of a corporation
Partnership	■ Easy to set up ■ Diversified decision making ■ Can survive withdrawal of partner ■ Profits taxed only once as owners' incomes	■ Achieving consensus may be slow and expensive ■ Owners' entire wealth at risk ■ Withdrawal of partner may create capital shortage ■ Cost of capital and labor is high relative to that of a corporation
Corporation	■ Owners have limited liability ■ Large-scale, low-cost capital available ■ Professional management not restricted by ability of owners ■ Perpetual life ■ Long-term labor contracts cut labor costs	■ Complex management structure can make decisions slow and expensive ■ Retained profits taxed twice: as company profit and as stockholders' capital gains

ECONOMICS IN ACTION

Types of Firms in the Economy

Three types of firms operate in the United States: proprietorships, partnerships, and corporations.

Which type of firm dominates? Which produces most of the output of the U.S. economy?

Proprietorships Most Common Three quarters of the firms in the United States are proprietorships and they are mainly small businesses. Almost one fifth of the firms are corporations, and only a twentieth are partnerships (see Fig.1).

Corporations Produce Most Corporations generate almost 90 percent of business revenue. Revenue is a measure of the value of production, so corporations produce most of the output in the U.S. economy.

Variety Across Industries In agriculture, forestry, and fishing, proprietorships generate about 40 percent of the total revenue. Proprietorships also generate a significant percentage of the revenue in services, construction, and retail trade. Partnerships account for a small percentage of revenue in all sectors and feature most in agriculture, forestry, and fishing; services; and mining. Corporations dominate all sectors and have the manufacturing industries almost to themselves.

Why do corporations dominate the business scene? Why do the other types of businesses survive? And why are proprietorships and partnerships more prominent in some sectors? The answers lie in the pros and cons of the different types of business organization. Corporations dominate where a large amount of capital is used; proprietorships dominate where flexibility in decision making is critical.

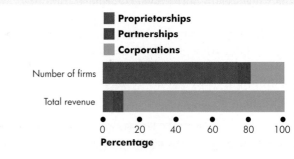

Figure 1 Number of Firms and Total Revenue

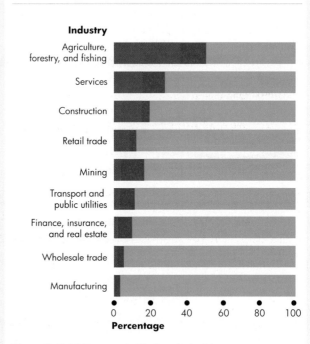

Figure 2 Total Revenue in Various Industries
Source of data: U.S. Bureau of the Census, *Statistical Abstract of the United States,* 2001.

◆ REVIEW QUIZ

1 Explain the distinction between a command system and an incentive system.
2 What is the principal–agent problem? What are three ways in which firms try to cope with it?
3 What are the three types of firms? Explain the major advantages and disadvantages of each.

Work these questions in Study Plan 10.3 and get instant feedback. Do a Key Terms Quiz.   MyEconLab

You've now seen how technology constraints and information constraints influence the way firms operate. You've seen why some firms operate with a large amount of labor and human capital and a small amount of physical capital. You've also seen how firms use a mixture of command and incentive systems and employ different types of business organization to cope with the principal–agent problem.

Your next task is to look at the variety of market situations in which firms operate and classify the different market environments in which firms do business.

Markets and the Competitive Environment

The markets in which firms operate vary a great deal. Some are highly competitive, and profits in these markets are hard to come by. Some appear to be almost free from competition, and firms in these markets earn large profits. Some markets are dominated by fierce advertising campaigns in which each firm seeks to persuade buyers that it has the best products. And some markets display the character of a strategic game.

Economists identify four market types:

1. Perfect competition
2. Monopolistic competition
3. Oligopoly
4. Monopoly

Perfect competition arises when there are many firms, each selling an identical product, many buyers, and no restrictions on the entry of new firms into the industry. The many firms and buyers are all well informed about the prices of the products of each firm in the industry. The worldwide markets for wheat, corn, rice, and other grain crops are examples of perfect competition.

Monopolistic competition is a market structure in which a large number of firms compete by making similar but slightly different products. Making a product slightly different from the product of a competing firm is called **product differentiation**. Product differentiation gives a firm in monopolistic competition an element of market power. The firm is the sole producer of the particular version of the good in question. For example, in the market for pizzas, hundreds of firms make their own version of the perfect pizza. Each of these firms is the sole producer of a particular brand. Differentiated products are not necessarily different products. What matters is that consumers perceive them to be different. For example, different brands of potato chips and ketchup might be almost identical but be perceived by consumers to be different.

Oligopoly is a market structure in which a small number of firms compete. Computer software, airplane manufacture, and international air transportation are examples of oligopolistic industries. Oligopolies might produce almost identical products, such as the colas produced by Coke and Pepsi. Or they might produce differentiated products such as Boeing and Airbus aircraft.

Monopoly arises when there is one firm, which produces a good or service that has no close substitutes and in which the firm is protected by a barrier preventing the entry of new firms. In some places, the phone, gas, electricity, cable television, and water suppliers are local monopolies—monopolies restricted to a given location. Microsoft Corporation, the software developer that created Windows, the operating system for the personal computer, is an example of a global monopoly.

Perfect competition is the most extreme form of competition. Monopoly is the most extreme absence of competition. The other two market types fall between these extremes.

Many factors must be taken into account to determine which market structure describes a particular real-world market. One of these factors is the extent to which a small number of firms dominates the market. To measure this feature of markets, economists use indexes called measures of concentration. Let's look at these measures.

Measures of Concentration

Economists use two measures of concentration:

- The four-firm concentration ratio
- The Herfindahl-Hirschman Index

The Four-Firm Concentration Ratio The **four-firm concentration ratio** is the percentage of the value of sales accounted for by the four largest firms in an industry. The range of the concentration ratio is from almost zero for perfect competition to 100 percent for monopoly. This ratio is the main measure used to assess market structure.

Table 10.5 shows two calculations of the four-firm concentration ratio: one for tire makers and one for printers. In this example, 14 firms produce tires. The largest four have 80 percent of the sales, so the four-firm concentration ratio is 80 percent. In the printing industry, with 1,004 firms, the largest four firms have only 0.5 percent of the sales, so the four-firm concentration ratio is 0.5 percent.

A low concentration ratio indicates a high degree of competition, and a high concentration ratio indicates an absence of competition. A monopoly has a concentration ratio of 100 percent—the largest (and only) firm has 100 percent of the sales. A four-firm concentration ratio that exceeds 60 percent is regarded as an indication of a market that is highly concentrated and dominated by a few firms in an oligopoly. A ratio of less than 60 percent is regarded as an indication of a competitive market.

The Herfindahl-Hirschman Index The **Herfindahl-Hirschman Index**—also called the HHI—is the square of the percentage market share of each firm summed over the largest 50 firms (or summed over all the firms if there are fewer than 50) in a market. For example, if there are four firms in a market and the market shares of the firms are 50 percent, 25 percent, 15 percent, and 10 percent, the Herfindahl-Hirschman Index is:

$$\text{HHI} = 50^2 + 25^2 + 15^2 + 10^2 = 3,450.$$

TABLE 10.5   Calculating the Four-Firm Concentration Ratio

Tire makers		Printers	
Firm	**Sales** (millions of dollars)	**Firm**	**Sales** (millions of dollars)
Top, Inc.	200	Fran's	2.5
ABC, Inc.	250	Ned's	2.0
Big, Inc.	150	Tom's	1.8
XYZ, Inc.	100	Jill's	1.7
Largest 4 firms	700	Largest 4 firms	8.0
Other 10 firms	175	Other 1,000 firms	1,592.0
Industry	875	Industry	1,600.0

Four-firm concentration ratios:

Tire makers: $\dfrac{700}{875} \times 100 = 80$ percent   Printers: $\dfrac{8}{1,600} \times 100 = 0.5$ percent

ECONOMICS IN ACTION

Concentration in the U.S. Economy

The U.S. Department of Commerce calculates and publishes data showing concentration ratios and the HHI for each industry in the United States. The bars in the figure show the four-firm concentration ratio and the number at the end of each bar is the HHI.

Cigarette and battery manufacturing are two of the most concentrated industries. A very small number of firms dominate the markets for these products and their competitors are small firms that have small market shares.

Glass containers, trucks, breakfast cereals, and major appliances are highly concentrated industries. They are oligopolies.

Cookies and crackers, motor vehicles, and soft drinks are moderately concentrated industries. They are examples of monopolistic competition.

Snack food, ice cream, milk, cheese, commercial printing, canvas bags manufacturing, quick printers, and bakers have low concentration measures and are highly competitive industries.

Concentration measures are useful indicators of the degree of competition in a market, but they must be supplemented by other information to determine the structure of the market.

Newspapers and automobiles are examples of how the concentration measures give a misleading reading of the degree of competition. Most newspapers are local. They serve a single city or even a smaller area. So despite the low concentration measure, newspapers are concentrated in their own local areas. Automobiles are traded internationally and foreign cars are freely imported into the United States. Despite the moderately high U.S. concentration measure, the automobile industry is competitive.

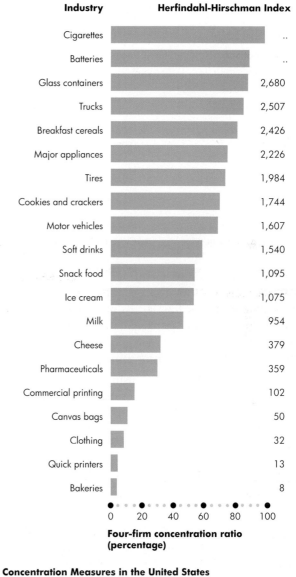

Concentration Measures in the United States

Source of data: Concentration Ratios in Manufacturing (Washington, D.C.: U.S. Department of Commerce, 2007).

In perfect competition, the HHI is small. For example, if each of the largest 50 firms in an industry has a market share of 0.1 percent, then the HHI is $0.1^2 \times 50 = 0.5$. In a monopoly, the HHI is 10,000. The firm has 100 percent of the market: $100^2 = 10,000$.

The HHI became a popular measure of the degree of competition during the 1980s, when the Justice Department used it to classify markets. A market in

which the HHI is less than 1,500 is regarded as being competitive. A market in which the HHI lies between 1,500 and 2,500 is regarded as being moderately competitive. But a market in which the HHI exceeds 2,500 is regarded as being uncompetitive.

Table 10.6 summarizes the characteristics of the types of market structure, along with the measures of concentration and some examples of each type.

TABLE 10.6 Market Structure

Characteristics	Perfect competition	Monopolistic competition	Oligopoly	Monopoly
Number of firms in industry	Many	Many	Few	One
Product	Identical	Differentiated	Either identical or differentiated	No close substitutes
Barriers to entry	None	None	Moderate	High
Firm's control over price	None	Some	Considerable	Considerable or regulated
Concentration ratio	0	Low	High	100
HHI (approx. ranges)	Close to 0	Less than 2,500	More than 2,500	10,000
Examples	Wheat, corn	Food, clothing	Computer chips	Local water supply

Limitations of a Concentration Measure

The three main limitations of using only concentration measures as determinants of market structure are their failure to take proper account of

- The geographical scope of the market
- Barriers to entry and firm turnover
- The correspondence between a market and an industry

Geographical Scope of the Market Concentration measures take a national view of the market. Many goods are sold in a *national* market, but some are sold in a *regional* market and some in a *global* one. The concentration measures for newspapers are low, indicating competition, but in most cities the newspaper industry is highly concentrated. The concentration measures for automobiles are high, indicating little competition, but the three biggest U.S. car makers compete with foreign car makers in a highly competitive global market.

Barriers to Entry and Firm Turnover Some markets are highly concentrated but entry is easy and the turnover of firms is large. For example, small towns have few restaurants, but no restrictions hinder a new restaurant from opening and many attempt to do so.

Also, a market with only a few firms might be competitive because of *potential entry*. The few firms in a market face competition from the many potential firms that will enter the market if economic profit opportunities arise.

Market and Industry Correspondence To calculate concentration ratios, the Department of Commerce classifies each firm as being in a particular industry. But markets do not always correspond closely to industries for three reasons.

First, markets are often narrower than industries. For example, the pharmaceutical industry, which has a low concentration ratio, operates in many separate markets for individual products—for example, measles vaccine and AIDS-fighting drugs. These drugs do not compete with each other, so this industry, which looks competitive, includes firms that are monopolies (or near monopolies) in markets for individual drugs.

Second, most firms make several products. For example, Westinghouse makes electrical equipment and, among other things, gas-fired incinerators and plywood. So this one firm operates in at least three separate markets, but the Department of Commerce classifies Westinghouse as being in the electrical goods and equipment industry. The fact that Westinghouse competes with other producers of plywood does not

ECONOMICS IN ACTION
A Competitive Environment

How competitive are markets in the United States? Do most U.S. firms operate in competitive markets, in monopolistic competition, in oligopoly, or in monopoly markets?

The data needed to answer these questions are hard to get. The last attempt to answer the questions, in a study by William G. Shepherd, an economics professor at the University of Massachusetts at Amherst, covered the years from 1939 to 1980. The figure shows what he discovered.

In 1980, three quarters of the value of goods and services bought and sold in the United States was traded in markets that are essentially competitive—markets that have almost perfect competition or monopolistic competition. Monopoly and the dominance of a single firm accounted for about 5 percent of sales. Oligopoly, which is found mainly in manufacturing, accounted for about 18 percent of sales.

Over the period studied, the U.S. economy became increasingly competitive. The percentage of output sold by firms operating in competitive markets (blue bars) has expanded most, and has shrunk most in oligopoly markets (red bars).

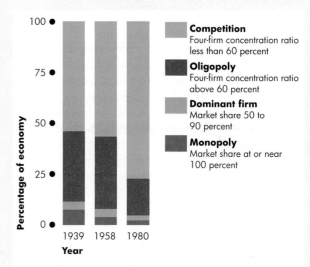

The Market Structure of the U.S. Economy

Source of data: William G. Shepherd, "Causes of Increased Competition in the U.S. Economy, 1939–1980," *Review of Economics and Statistics,* Vol 64, No 4 (November, 1982), pp. 613–626. © 1982 by the President and Fellows of Harvard College. Reprinted with permission.

But also during the past decades, the U.S. economy has become much more exposed to competition from the rest of the world. The data used by William G. Shepherd don't capture this international competition, so the data probably understate the degree of true competition in the U.S. economy.

show up in the concentration numbers for the plywood market.

Third, firms switch from one market to another depending on profit opportunities. For example, Motorola, which today produces cellular telephones and other communications products, has diversified from being a TV and computer chip maker. Motorola no longer produces TVs. Publishers of newspapers, magazines, and textbooks are today rapidly diversifying into Internet and multimedia products. These switches among markets show that there is much scope for entering and exiting a market, and so measures of concentration have limited usefulness.

Despite their limitations, concentration measures do provide a basis for determining the degree of competition in a market when they are combined with information about the geographical scope of the market, barriers to entry, and the extent to which large, multiproduct firms straddle a variety of markets.

◆ REVIEW QUIZ

1 What are the four market types? Explain the distinguishing characteristics of each.
2 What are the two measures of concentration? Explain how each measure is calculated.
3 Under what conditions do the measures of concentration give a good indication of the degree of competition in a market?
4 Is the U.S. economy competitive? Is it becoming more competitive or less competitive?

Work these questions in Study Plan 10.4 and get instant feedback. Do a Key Terms Quiz.   MyEconLab

You now know the variety of market types and how we identify them. Our final question in this chapter is: What determines the things that firms decide to buy from other firms rather than produce for themselves?

◆ Produce or Outsource? Firms and Markets

To produce a good or service, even a simple one such as a shirt, factors of production must be hired and their activities coordinated. To produce a good as complicated as an iPhone, an enormous range of specialist factors of production must be coordinated.

Factors of production can be coordinated either by firms or markets. We'll describe these two ways of organizing production and then see why firms play a crucial role in achieving an efficient use of resources.

Firm Coordination

Firms hire labor, capital, and land, and by using a mixture of command systems and incentive systems (see p. 229) organize and coordinate their activities to produce goods and services.

Firm coordination occurs when you take your car to the garage for service such as an oil change and brake check. The garage owner hires a mechanic and tools and coordinates all the activities that get your car serviced. Firms also coordinate the production of cornflakes, golf clubs, and a host of other items.

Market Coordination

Markets coordinate production by adjusting prices and making the decisions of buyers and sellers of factors of production and components consistent.

Market coordination occurs to produce a rock concert. A promoter books a stadium, rents some stage equipment, hires some audio and video recording engineers and technicians, and engages some rock groups, a superstar, a publicity agent, and a ticket agent. The promoter sells tickets to thousands of rock fans, audio rights to a recording company, and video and broadcasting rights to a television network. All these transactions take place in markets that coordinate the buying and selling of this huge variety of factors of production.

Outsourcing, buying parts or products from other firms, is another example of market coordination. Dell outsources the production of all the components of its computers. Automakers outsource the production of windshields, windows, transmission systems, engines, tires, and many other auto parts. Apple outsources the entire production of iPods, iPads, and iPhones.

Why Firms?

What determines whether a firm or a market coordinates a particular set of activities? How does a firm decide whether to buy an item from another firm or manufacture it itself? The answer is cost. Taking account of the opportunity cost of time as well as the costs of the other inputs, a firm uses the method that costs least. In other words, it uses the economically efficient method.

If a task can be performed at a lower cost by markets than by a firm, markets will do the job, and any attempt to set up a firm to replace such market activity will be doomed to failure.

Firms coordinate economic activity when a task can be performed more efficiently by a firm than by markets. In such a situation, it is profitable to set up a firm. Firms are often more efficient than markets as coordinators of economic activity because they can achieve

- Lower transactions costs
- Economies of scale
- Economies of scope
- Economies of team production

Lower Transactions Costs Firms eliminate transactions costs. **Transactions costs** are the costs that arise from finding someone with whom to do business, of reaching an agreement about the price and other aspects of the exchange, and of ensuring that the terms of the agreement are fulfilled. Market transactions require buyers and sellers to get together and to negotiate the terms and conditions of their trading. Sometimes, lawyers have to be hired to draw up contracts. A broken contract leads to still more expense. A firm can lower such transactions costs by reducing the number of individual transactions undertaken.

Imagine getting your car fixed using market coordination. You hire a mechanic to diagnose the problems and make a list of the parts and tools needed to fix them. You buy the parts from several dealers, rent the tools from ABC Rentals, hire an auto mechanic, return the tools, and pay your bills. You can avoid all these transactions and the time they cost you by letting your local garage fix the car.

Economies of Scale When the cost of producing a unit of a good falls as its output rate increases, **economies of scale** exist. An automaker experiences economies of scale because as the scale of production increases, the firm can use cost-saving equipment and

ECONOMICS IN ACTION

Apple Doesn't Make the iPhone!

Apple designed the iPhone and markets it, but Apple doesn't manufacture it. Why? Apple wants to produce the iPhone at the lowest possible cost. Apple achieves its goal by assigning the production task to more than 30 firms, some of which are listed in the table opposite. These 30 firms produce the components in Asia, Europe, and North America and then the components are assembled in its sleek, iconic case by Foxconn and Quanta in Taiwan.

Most electronic products—TVs, DVD players, iPods and iPads, and personal computers—are produced in a similar way to the iPhone with a combination of firm and market coordination. Hundreds of little-known firms compete fiercely to get their components into well-known consumer products.

Altus Technology	Taiwan
Balda	Germany
Broadcom	United States
Cambridge Silicon Radio	UK
Catcher	Taiwan
Cyntec	Taiwan
Delta Electronics	Taiwan
Epson	Japan
Foxconn	Taiwan
Infineon Technologies	Germany
Intel	United States
Largan Precision	Taiwan
Lite-On	Taiwan
Marvell	United States
Micron	United States
National Semiconductor	United States
Novatek	Taiwan
Primax	Taiwan
Quanta	Taiwan
Samsung	Korea
Sanyo	Japan
Sharp	Japan
Taiwan Semiconductor	Taiwan
TMD	Japan

highly specialized labor. An automaker that produces only a few cars a year must use hand-tool methods that are costly. Economies of scale arise from specialization and the division of labor that can be reaped more effectively by firm coordination rather than market coordination.

Economies of Scope A firm experiences **economies of scope** when it uses specialized (and often expensive) resources to produce a *range of goods and services*. For example, Toshiba uses its designers and specialized equipment to make the hard drive for the iPod. But it makes many different types of hard drives and other related products. As a result, Toshiba produces the iPod hard drive at a lower cost than a firm making only the iPod hard drive could achieve.

Economies of Team Production A production process in which the individuals in a group specialize in mutually supportive tasks is *team production*. Sports provide the best examples of team activity. In baseball, some team members specialize in pitching and others in fielding. In basketball, some team members specialize in defense and some in offense. The production of goods and services offers many examples of team activity. For example, production lines in a TV manufacturing plant work most efficiently when individual activity is organized in teams, each worker specializing in a few tasks. You can also think of an entire firm as being a team. The team has buyers of raw materials and other inputs, production workers, and salespeople. Each individual member of the team

specializes, but the value of the output of the team and the profit that it earns depend on the coordinated activities of all the team's members.

Because firms can economize on transactions costs, reap economies of scale and economies of scope, and organize efficient team production, it is firms rather than markets that coordinate most of our economic activity.

◆ REVIEW QUIZ

1 What are the two ways in which economic activity can be coordinated?

2 What determines whether a firm or markets coordinate production?

3 What are the main reasons why firms can often coordinate production at a lower cost than markets can?

Work these questions in Study Plan 10.5 and get instant feedback. Do a Key Terms Quiz.   MyEconLab

Economics in the News on pp. 240–241 explores the market for Internet advertising. In the next four chapters, we continue to study firms and the decisions they make. In Chapter 11, we learn about the relationships between cost and output at different output levels. These relationships are common to all types of firms in all types of markets. We then turn to problems that are specific to firms in different types of markets.

Battling for Markets in Internet Advertising

Facebook Rolls Out Real-Time Ad Platform

The Financial Times
September 13, 2012

Some of the world's largest advertising companies have signed up to Facebook's new real-time advertising platform, in a move that the social network hopes will bolster its revenue streams.

On Thursday, Facebook officially launched the platform, called Facebook Ad Exchange, or FBX, following months of testing. The system allows marketers to bid in real-time to buy ad impressions on the social networking site, and deliver their ads to users based on their immediate web-browsing habits, or linked to current events, such as sports results.

"Real-time marketing is getting to be a really important component of digital advertising," said Rebecca Lieb, an analyst with the Altimeter Group. "We'll see a lot of event-triggered marketing in the upcoming election cycle."

The ads use information gathered from computer browsing histories to target individual Facebook users, and the ad prices fluctuate as in an auction-style bidding system. So a user who looks at shoes on a retail site could then see an ad for the same brand when clicking back to Facebook.

The capacity will help Facebook compete more directly with advertising rivals Google and Yahoo, which have long provided real-time bidding to advertisers....

Within one tenth of a second, the system notifies when an ad space is available, evaluates 2,000 data points to determine the most relevant ad, calculates a price and prompts the ad to appear.

The global real-time bidding sector is estimated to be worth some $3bn–$4bn, but industry observers expect this to reach as much as $20bn by 2015....

Mark Wembridge and April Dembosky, "Facebook Rolls Out Real-Time Ad Platform," *The Financial Times*, September 13, 2012.

MyEconLab More Economics in the News

ESSENCE OF THE STORY

- Facebook is under pressure to generate advertising revenue.
- Real-time bidding is widely used for Internet advertising and its market share is growing rapidly.
- Facebook and Google are getting better at capturing user activity.
- A new Facebook system will target ads at the user's current interests.
- Advertisers will bid to get their ads in front of the right users.

ECONOMIC ANALYSIS

- Like all firms, Facebook and Google aim to maximize profit.

- Facebook provides social networking services and Google provides search services, a variety of other services, and with Google+ is offering a social networking service.

- Facebook and Google face constraints imposed by the market and technology.

- People who use social networks demand their services, and at the latest count Facebook and another 200-odd firms supply social networking services.

- People looking for information demand Internet search services, and Google and more than 100 other firms supply Internet search services.

- The equilibrium price of social networking services and of Internet search services is zero, and the equilibrium quantity of each is the quantity demanded at a zero price.

- Social network and Internet search providers enjoy economies of scope: They produce advertising services as well as their other service.

- Unlike social networking and search, Internet advertising is a big revenue and profit generator.

- Because the providers of social networking and search know a lot about their users, they can offer advertisers access to potential customers and charge a high price for this precision.

- Google has been enormously successful at delivering advertising based on a user's search activity, and its revenue has grown from $1 billion in 2003 to $56 billion in 2013 (see Fig.1). Google's profit in 2013 was $13 billion (see Fig. 2).

- Facebook is still learning how to tap its advertising potential and the news article describes its innovation in 2012: real-time bidding for advertising based on a user's browsing.

- Facebook's revenue is beginning to grow, but by 2013 it had reached only $8 billion (see Fig. 1).

- Providing a social networking service or search service doesn't guarantee success in generating advertising revenue and profit.

- Yahoo is an example of a firm that hasn't performed as well as its owners would wish.

- As Google and Facebook have seen explosive growth in users and revenues, Yahoo has struggled.

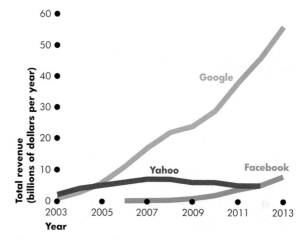

Figure 1 Total Revenue Comparison

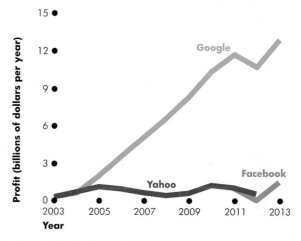

Figure 2 Profit Comparison

- Figure 1 shows that Yahoo's revenue peaked in 2008 and has been falling while Google's has soared and Facebook's has grown to overtake that of Yahoo.

- Figure 2 shows that Yahoo's profit has been flat while Google's has soared. Facebook's profit remains modest.

- The data shown in Figs.1 and 2 suggest that so far, Internet search is a more effective tool for generating revenue and profit than social networking. Perhaps Facebook's new revenue model will change that.

- The data also suggest that Facebook's and Google's expansion is tightening the market constraint that Yahoo faces.

241

SUMMARY

Key Points

The Firm and Its Economic Problem (pp. 224–226)

- Firms hire and organize factors of production to produce and sell goods and services.
- A firm's goal is to maximize economic profit, which is total revenue minus total cost measured as the opportunity cost of production.
- A firm's opportunity cost of production is the sum of the cost of resources bought in the market, using the firm's own resources, and resources supplied by the firm's owner.
- Normal profit is the opportunity cost of entrepreneurship and is part of the firm's opportunity cost.
- Technology, information, and markets limit the economic profit that a firm can make.

Working Problems 1 and 2 will give you a better understanding of the firm and its economic problem.

Technological and Economic Efficiency (pp. 227–228)

- A method of production is technologically efficient when a firm uses the least amount of inputs to produce a given output.
- A method of production is economically efficient when the cost of producing a given output is as low as possible.

Working Problem 3 will give you a better understanding of technological and economic efficiency.

Information and Organization (pp. 229–232)

- Firms use a combination of command systems and incentive systems to organize production.
- Faced with incomplete information and uncertainty, firms induce managers and workers to perform in ways that are consistent with the firms' goals.
- Proprietorships, partnerships, and corporations use ownership, incentive pay, and long-term contracts to cope with the principal–agent problem.

Working Problem 4 will give you a better understanding of information and organization.

Markets and the Competitive Environment (pp. 233–237)

- In perfect competition, many sellers offer an identical product to many buyers and entry is free.
- In monopolistic competition, many sellers offer slightly different products to many buyers and entry is free.
- In oligopoly, a small number of sellers compete and barriers to entry limit the number of firms.
- In monopoly, one firm produces an item that has no close substitutes and the firm is protected by a barrier to entry that prevents the entry of competitors.

Working Problems 5 and 6 will give you a better understanding of markets and the competitive environment.

Produce or Outsource? Firms and Markets (pp. 238–239)

- Firms coordinate economic activities when they can perform a task more efficiently—at lower cost—than markets can.
- Firms economize on transactions costs and achieve the benefits of economies of scale, economies of scope, and economies of team production.

Working Problem 7 will give you a better understanding of firms and markets.

Key Terms   MyEconLab Key Terms Quiz

Command system, 229	Four-firm concentration ratio, 234	Oligopoly, 233
Economic depreciation, 225	Herfindahl-Hirschman Index, 234	Perfect competition, 233
Economic efficiency, 227	Implicit rental rate, 224	Principal–agent problem, 229
Economic profit, 224	Incentive system, 229	Product differentiation, 233
Economies of scale, 238	Monopolistic competition, 233	Technological efficiency, 227
Economies of scope, 239	Monopoly, 233	Technology, 226
Firm, 224	Normal profit, 225	Transactions costs, 238

WORKED PROBLEM

MyEconLab   You can work this problem in Chapter 10 Study Plan.

Mike operates a bike retail store and repair shop, Mike's Bikes.

Some data about the firm and industry:

- Last year, the market value of the firm's showroom and workshop increased from $600,000 to $675,000; the market value of the inventory of unsold bikes decreased from $400,000 to $320,000; and the market value of the firm's tools remained constant at $5,000.
- The firm paid manufacturers $770,000 for bikes.
- The cost of electricity and IT services was $25,000.
- The wages paid to shop assistants were $50,000.
- Mike is the firm's entrepreneur. He also works part-time at a bike manufacturer that pays $40 per hour. The manufacturer wants Mike to work full time, but instead he does repairs at Mike's Bikes for 10 hours a week.
- Normal profit in bike retailing is $40,000 per year.
- The interest rate is 5 percent per year.

Questions

1. What was the cost of the resources Mike's Bikes bought in the marketplace last year?
2. What was Mike's Bikes' opportunity cost of using resources owned by the firm last year?
3. What was Mike's Bikes' opprtunity cost of using resources supplied by Mike last year?
4. What was Mike's Bikes' opportunity cost of production last year?

Solutions

1. The firm bought bikes for $770,000; electricity and IT services for $25,000; and paid wages to shop assistants of $50,000. The total cost of these resources bought in the marketplace was $845,000.

Key Point: The cost of resources bought in the market is the total amount paid for them.

2. The resources owned by Mike's Bikes are the tools, the inventory of bikes, and the showroom and workshop.

The opportunity cost of using these resources is economic depreciation and forgone interest.

Economic depreciation is the change in the market value of the firm's resources. The market value of the inventory of bikes fell by $80,000 but the market value of the showroom and workshop increased by

$75,000, so the total economic depreciation was $80,000 − $75,000, or $5,000.

Forgone interest is the interest that could be earned on the market value of the firm's resources. That value is $675,000 (showroom and workshop), $320,000 (bikes), and $5,000 (tools), which total $1,000,000. The interest forgone is 5 percent of the $1,000,000, which equals $50,000.

So the opportunity cost of using resources owned by the firm was $5,000 + $50,000, or $55,000.

Key Point: The cost of using resources owned by the firm is part of the firm's opportunity costs.

3. The resources supplied by Mike are his entrepreneurial services and his labor. The opportunity cost of his entrepreneurial services is normal profit of $40,000 and of his labor is $20,000 (10 hours a week at his opportunity cost of $40 per hour, for 50 weeks). These two items total $60,000.

Key Point: The cost of using resources supplied by the owner is part of the firm's opportunity costs.

4. The opportunity cost of production is the sum of three components of the opportunity cost of the resources used, $845,000 + $55,000 + $60,000, which was $960,000.

Key Point: The firm's opportunity cost of production is the sum of the cost of all the resources used.

Key Table

Item		Amount
Cost of Resources Bought in Market		
Bikes	$770,000	
Electricity and IT services	25,000	
Wages	50,000	845,000
Cost of Resources Owned by Firm		
Economic depreciation	$5,000	
Forgone interest	50,000	$55,000
Cost of Resources Supplied by Owner		
Mike's normal profit	$40,000	
Mike's forgone wages	20,000	$60,000
Opportunity Cost of Production		**$960,000**

MyEconLab Interactive Animation

STUDY PLAN PROBLEMS AND APPLICATIONS

MyEconLab   You can work Problems 1 to 7 in Chapter 10 Study Plan and get instant feedback.

The Firm and Its Economic Problem (Study Plan 10.1)

1. One year ago, Jack and Jill set up a vinegar-bottling firm (called JJVB). Use the following data to calculate JJVB's opportunity cost of production during its first year of operation:
   - Jack and Jill put $50,000 of their own money into the firm and bought equipment for $30,000.
   - They hired one worker at $20,000 a year.
   - Jack quit his old job, which paid $30,000 a year, and worked full-time for JJVB.
   - Jill kept her old job, which paid $30 an hour, but gave up 500 hours of leisure a year to work for JJVB.
   - JJVB bought $10,000 of goods and services.
   - The market value of the equipment at the end of the year was $28,000.
   - Jack and Jill have a $100,000 home loan on which they pay interest of 6 percent a year.

2. Joe, who has no skills, no job experience, and no alternative employment, runs a shoeshine stand. Other operators of shoeshine stands earn $10,000 a year. Joe pays rent of $2,000 a year, and his total revenue is $15,000 a year. Joe spent $1,000 on equipment, which he used his credit card to buy. The interest on a credit card balance is 20 percent a year. At the end of the year, Joe was offered $500 for his business and all its equipment. Calculate Joe's opportunity cost of production and his economic profit.

Technological and Economic Efficiency (Study Plan 10.2)

3. Four ways of laundering 100 shirts are:

Method	Labor (hours)	Capital (machines)
A	1	10
B	5	8
C	20	4
D	50	1

   a. Which methods are technologically efficient?
   b. Which method is economically efficient if the hourly wage rate and the implicit rental rate of capital are (i) wage rate $1, rental rate $100; (ii) wage rate $5, rental rate $50; and (iii) wage rate $50, rental rate $5?

Information and Organization (Study Plan 10.3)

4. **Executive Pay**

   Executive compensation, based on performance, can theoretically constrain pay, but companies are paying their top executives more and more. The median compensation of a CEO in 2013 was $13.9 million, up 9 percent from 2012.

   Source: CNBC, April 28, 2014

   What is the economic problem that CEO compensation schemes are designed to solve? Would paying executives with stock align their interests with shareholders'?

Markets and the Competitive Environment

(Study Plan 10.4)

5. Sales of the firms in the tattoo industry are:

Firm	Sales (dollars per year)
Bright Spots	450
Freckles	325
Love Galore	250
Native Birds	200
Other 15 firms	800

   Calculate the four-firm concentration ratio. What is the structure of the tattoo industry?

6. **GameStop Racks Up the Points**

   No retailer has more cachet among gamers than GameStop. For now, only Wal-Mart has a larger share—21.3% last year. GameStop's share was 21.1% last year, and may well overtake Wal-Mart this year. But if new women gamers prefer shopping at Target to GameStop, Wal-Mart and Target might erode GameStop's market share.

   Source: *Fortune*, June 9, 2008

   Estimate a range for the four-firm concentration ratio and the HHI for the U.S. game market based on the data provided in this news clip.

Produce or Outsource? Firms and Markets

(Study Plan 10.5)

7. FedEx contracts independent truck operators to pick up and deliver its packages and pays them on the volume of packages carried. Why doesn't FedEx buy more trucks and hire more drivers? What incentive problems might arise from this arrangement?

ADDITIONAL PROBLEMS AND APPLICATIONS

MyEconLab You can work these problems in MyEconLab if assigned by your instructor.

The Firm and Its Economic Problem

Use the following data to work Problems 8 and 9.
Lee is a computer programmer who earned $35,000 in 2011. But on January 1, 2012, Lee opened a body board manufacturing business. At the end of the first year of operation, he submitted the following information to his accountant:

- He stopped renting out his cottage for $3,500 a year and used it as his factory. The market value of the cottage increased from $70,000 to $71,000.

- He spent $50,000 on materials, phone, etc.

- He leased machines for $10,000 a year.

- He paid $15,000 in wages.

- He used $10,000 from his savings account, which earns 5 percent a year interest.

- He borrowed $40,000 at 10 percent a year.

- He sold $160,000 worth of body boards.

- Normal profit is $25,000 a year.

8. Calculate Lee's opportunity cost of production and his economic profit.

9. Lee's accountant recorded the depreciation on his cottage during 2012 as $7,000. According to the accountant, what profit did Lee make?

10. In 2011, Toni taught music and earned $20,000. She also earned $4,000 by renting out her basement. On January 1, 2012, she quit teaching, stopped renting out her basement, and began to use it as the office for her new Web site design business. She took $2,000 from her savings account to buy a computer. During 2012, she paid $1,500 for the lease of a Web server and $1,750 for high-speed Internet service. She received a total revenue from Web site designing of $45,000 and earned interest at 5 percent a year on her savings account balance. Normal profit is $55,000 a year. At the end of 2012, Toni could have sold her computer for $500. Calculate Toni's opportunity cost of production and her economic profit in 2012.

11. **The Colvin Interview: Chrysler**
    The key driver of profitability will be that the focus of the company isn't on profitability. Our focus is on the customer. If we can find a way to give customers what they want better than anybody else, then what can stop us?
    Source: *Fortune*, April 14, 2008

a. In spite of what Chrysler's vice chairman and co-president claims, why is Chrysler's focus actually on profitability?

b. What would happen to Chrysler if it didn't focus on maximizing profit, but instead focused its production and pricing decisions to "give customers what they want"?

12. **Must Watches**
    Stocks too volatile? Bonds too boring? Then try an alternative investment—one you can wear on your wrist. ... [The] typical return on a watch over five to ten years is roughly 10%. [One could] do better in an index fund, but ... what other investment is so wearable?
    Source: *Fortune*, April 14, 2008

a. What is the cost of buying a watch?

b. What is the opportunity cost of owning a watch?

c. Does owning a watch create an economic profit opportunity?

Technological and Economic Efficiency

Use the following data to work Problems 13 and 14.
Four methods of completing a tax return and the time taken by each method are with a PC, 1 hour; with a pocket calculator, 12 hours; with a pocket calculator and paper and pencil, 12 hours; and with a pencil and paper, 16 hours. The PC and its software cost $1,000, the pocket calculator costs $10, and the pencil and paper cost $1.

13. Which, if any, of the methods is technologically efficient?

14. Which method is economically efficient if the wage rate is (i) $5 an hour, (ii) $50 an hour, and (iii) $500 an hour?

15. **A Medical Sensation**
    Hospitals are buying da Vinci surgical robots. Surgeons, sitting comfortably at a da Vinci console, can use various robotic attachments to perform even the most complex procedures.
    Source: *Fortune*, April 28, 2008

a. Assume that performing a surgery with a surgical robot requires fewer surgeons and nurses. Is using the surgical robot technologically efficient?

b. What additional information would you need to be able to say that switching to surgical robots is economically efficient for a hospital?

Information and Organization

16. Wal-Mart has more than 3,700 stores, more than one million employees, and total revenues of close to a quarter of a trillion dollars in the United States alone. Sarah Frey-Talley runs the family-owned Frey Farms in Illinois and supplies Wal-Mart with pumpkins and other fresh produce.

   a. How does Wal-Mart coordinate its activities? Is it likely to use mainly a command system or also to use incentive systems? Explain.

   b. How do you think Sarah Frey-Talley coordinates the activities of Frey Farms? Is she likely to use mainly a command system or also to use incentive systems? Explain.

   c. Describe, compare, and contrast the principal–agent problems faced by Wal-Mart and Frey Farms. How might these firms cope with their principal–agent problems?

17. **Where Does Google Go Next?**

   Google gives its engineers one day a week to work on whatever project they want. A couple of colleagues did what many of the young geniuses do at Google: They came up with a cool idea. At Google, you often end up with a laissez-faire mess instead of resource allocation.

   Source: *Fortune*, May 26, 2008

   a. Describe Google's method of organizing production with their software engineers.

   b. What are the potential gains and opportunity costs associated with this method?

Markets and the Competitive Environment

18. Market shares of chocolate makers are:

Firm	Market share (percent)
Truffles, Inc.	25
Magic, Inc.	20
Mayfair, Inc.	15
All Natural, Inc.	15
Gold, Inc.	15
Bond, Inc.	10

Calculate the Herfindahl-Hirschman Index. What is the structure of the chocolate industry?

Produce or Outsource? Firms and Markets

Use the following information to work Problems 19 to 21.

Two leading design firms, Astro Studios of San Francisco and Hers Experimental Design Laboratory, Inc. of Osaka, Japan, worked with Microsoft to design the Xbox 360 video game console. IBM, ATI, and SiS designed the Xbox 360's hardware. Three firms—Flextronics, Wistron, and Celestica—manufactured the Xbox 360 at their plants in China and Taiwan.

19. Describe the roles of market coordination and coordination by firms in the design, manufacture, and marketing of the Xbox 360.

20. a. Why do you think Microsoft works with a large number of other firms, rather than performing all the required tasks itself?

   b. What are the roles of transactions costs, economies of scale, economies of scope, and economies of team production in the design, manufacture, and marketing of the Xbox?

21. Why do you think the Xbox is designed in the United States and Japan but built in China?

Economics in the News

22. After you have studied *Economics in the News* on pp. 240–241, answer the following questions.

   a. What products do Facebook and Google sell?

   b. In what types of markets do Facebook and Google compete?

   c. How do social networks and Internet search providers generate revenue?

   d. What is special about social networking sites that make them attractive to advertisers?

   e. What is special about Internet search providers that make them attractive to advertisers?

   f. What technological changes might increase the profitability of social networks compared to Internet search providers?

23. **Long Reviled, Merit Pay Gains Among Teachers**

   School districts in many states experiment with plans that compensate teachers partly based on classroom performance, rather than their years on the job and coursework completed. Working with mentors to improve their instruction and getting bonuses for raising student achievement encourages efforts to raise teaching quality.

   Source: *The New York Times*, June 18, 2007

   How does "merit pay" attempt to cope with the principal–agent problem in public education?

11 OUTPUT AND COSTS

After studying this chapter, you will be able to:

◆ Distinguish between the short run and the long run

◆ Explain and illustrate a firm's short-run product curves

◆ Explain and derive a firm's short-run cost curves

◆ Explain and derive a firm's long-run average cost curve

Behind the scenes of your favorite Starbucks coffee shop, many economic decisions have been made that affect the firm's cost of production. Starbucks has decided how much to produce, how many people to employ, and how much and what type of equipment to use. How does a firm make these decisions?

We are going to answer this question in this chapter. And in *Economics in the News* at the end of the chapter, we'll look at how recent expansion decisions by Starbucks affect the firm's production costs. But first, we'll study the costs of a simpler, smaller firm, Campus Sweaters, a (fictional) producer of knitwear.

◆ Decision Time Frames

People who operate firms make many decisions, and all of their decisions are aimed at achieving one over-riding goal: maximum attainable profit. But not all decisions are equally critical. Some decisions are big ones. Once made, they are costly (or impossible) to reverse. If such a decision turns out to be incorrect, it might lead to the failure of the firm. Other decisions are small. They are easily changed. If one of these decisions turns out to be incorrect, the firm can change its actions and survive.

The biggest decision that an entrepreneur makes is in what industry to establish a firm. For most entre-preneurs, their background knowledge and interests drive this decision. But the decision also depends on profit prospects—on the expectation that total rev-enue will exceed total cost.

Cindy has decided to set up Campus Sweaters. She has also decided the most effective method of organiz-ing the firm. But she has not decided the quantity to produce, the factors of production to hire, or the price to charge for sweaters.

Decisions about the quantity to produce and the price to charge depend on the type of market in which the firm operates. Perfect competition, monopolistic competition, oligopoly, and monopoly all confront the firm with *different* problems. Decisions about *how* to produce a given output do not depend on the type of market in which the firm operates. *All* types of firms in *all* types of markets make similar decisions about how to produce.

The actions that a firm can take to influence the relationship between output and cost depend on how soon the firm wants to act. A firm that plans to change its output rate tomorrow has fewer options than one that plans to change its output rate six months or six years in the future.

To study the relationship between a firm's output decision and its costs, we distinguish between two decision time frames:

- The short run
- The long run

The Short Run

The **short run** is a time frame in which the quantity of at least one factor of production is fixed. For most firms, capital, land, and entrepreneurship are fixed fac-tors of production and labor is the variable factor of

production. We call the fixed factors of production the firm's *plant*: In the short run, a firm's plant is fixed.

For Campus Sweaters, the fixed plant is its factory building and its knitting machines. For an electric power utility, the fixed plant is its buildings, genera-tors, computers, and control systems.

To increase output in the short run, a firm must increase the quantity of a variable factor of production, which is usually labor. So to produce more output, Campus Sweaters must hire more labor and operate its knitting machines for more hours a day. Similarly, an electric power utility must hire more labor and operate its generators for more hours a day.

Short-run decisions are easily reversed. The firm can increase or decrease its output in the short run by increasing or decreasing the amount of labor it hires.

The Long Run

The **long run** is a time frame in which the quantities of *all* factors of production can be varied. That is, the long run is a period in which the firm can change its *plant*.

To increase output in the long run, a firm can change its plant as well as the quantity of labor it hires. Campus Sweaters can decide whether to install more knitting machines, use a new type of machine, reorgan-ize its management, or hire more labor. Long-run deci-sions are *not* easily reversed. Once a plant decision is made, the firm usually must live with it for some time. To emphasize this fact, we call the past expendi-ture on a plant that has no resale value a **sunk cost**. A sunk cost is irrelevant to the firm's current decisions. The only costs that influence its current decisions are the short-run cost of changing its labor inputs and the long-run cost of changing its plant.

◆ REVIEW QUIZ

1 Distinguish between the short run and the long run.
2 Why is a sunk cost irrelevant to a firm's current decisions?

Work these questions in Study Plan 11.1 and get instant feedback. Do a Key Terms Quiz. MyEconLab

We're going to study costs in the short run and the long run. We begin with the short run and describe a firm's technology constraint.

Short-Run Technology Constraint

To increase output in the short run, a firm must increase the quantity of labor employed. We describe the relationship between output and the quantity of labor employed by using three related concepts:

1. Total product
2. Marginal product
3. Average product

These product concepts can be illustrated either by product schedules or by product curves. Let's look first at the product schedules.

Product Schedules

Table 11.1 shows some data that describe Campus Sweaters' total product, marginal product, and average product. The numbers tell us how the quantity of sweaters produced increases as Campus Sweaters employs more workers. The numbers also tell us about the productivity of the labor that Campus Sweaters employs.

Focus first on the columns headed "Labor" and "Total product." **Total product** is the maximum output that a given quantity of labor can produce. You can see from the numbers in these columns that as Campus Sweaters employs more labor, total product increases. For example, when 1 worker is employed, total product is 4 sweaters a day, and when 2 workers are employed, total product is 10 sweaters a day. Each increase in employment increases total product.

The **marginal product** of labor is the increase in total product that results from a one-unit increase in the quantity of labor employed, with all other inputs remaining the same. For example, in Table 11.1, when Campus Sweaters increases employment from 2 to 3 workers and does not change its capital, the marginal product of the third worker is 3 sweaters—total product increases from 10 to 13 sweaters.

Average product tells how productive workers are on average. The **average product** of labor is equal to total product divided by the quantity of labor employed. For example, in Table 11.1, the average product of 3 workers is 4.33 sweaters per worker—13 sweaters a day divided by 3 workers.

If you look closely at the numbers in Table 11.1, you can see some patterns. As Campus Sweaters hires more labor, marginal product increases initially, and

TABLE 11.1 Total Product, Marginal Product, and Average Product

	Labor (workers per day)	Total product (sweaters per day)	Marginal product (sweaters per additional worker)	Average product (sweaters per worker)
A	0	0		
			 4	
B	1	4		4.00
			 6	
C	2	10		5.00
			 3	
D	3	13		4.33
			 2	
E	4	15		3.75
			 1	
F	5	16		3.20

Total product is the total amount produced. Marginal product is the change in total product that results from a one-unit increase in labor. For example, when labor increases from 2 to 3 workers a day (row C to row D), total product increases from 10 to 13 sweaters a day. The marginal product of going from 2 to 3 workers is 3 sweaters. Average product is total product divided by the quantity of labor employed. For example, the average product of 3 workers is 4.33 sweaters per worker (13 sweaters a day divided by 3 workers).

then begins to decrease. For example, marginal product increases from 4 sweaters a day for the first worker to 6 sweaters a day for the second worker and then decreases to 3 sweaters a day for the third worker. Average product also increases at first and then decreases. You can see the relationships between the quantity of labor hired and the three product concepts more clearly by looking at the product curves.

Product Curves

The product curves are graphs of the relationships between employment and the three product concepts you've just studied. They show how total product, marginal product, and average product change as employment changes. They also show the relationships among the three concepts. Let's look at the product curves.

Total Product Curve

Figure 11.1 shows Campus Sweaters' total product curve, *TP*, which is a graph of the total product schedule. Points *A* through *F* correspond to rows *A* through *F* in Table 11.1. To graph the entire total product curve, we vary labor by hours rather than whole days.

Notice the shape of the total product curve. As employment increases from zero to 1 worker a day, the curve becomes steeper. Then, as employment increases to 3, 4, and 5 workers a day, the curve becomes less steep.

The total product curve is similar to the *production possibilities frontier* (explained in Chapter 2). It separates the attainable output levels from those that are unattainable. All the points that lie above the curve are unattainable. Points that lie below the curve, in the orange area, are attainable, but they are inefficient—they use more labor than is necessary to produce a given output. Only the points *on* the total product curve are technologically efficient.

FIGURE 11.1 Total Product Curve

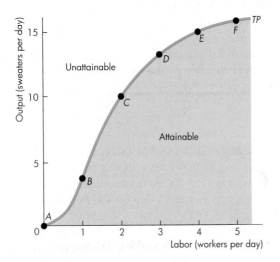

The total product curve, *TP*, is based on the data in Table 11.1. The total product curve shows how the quantity of sweaters produced changes as the quantity of labor employed changes. For example, 2 workers can produce 10 sweaters a day (point *C*). Points *A* through *F* on the curve correspond to the rows of Table 11.1. The total product curve separates attainable outputs from unattainable outputs. Points below the *TP* curve are inefficient.

MyEconLab Animation

Marginal Product Curve

Figure 11.2 shows Campus Sweaters' marginal product of labor. Part (a) reproduces the total product curve from Fig. 11.1 and part (b) shows the marginal product curve, *MP*.

In part (a), the orange bars illustrate the marginal product of labor. The height of a bar measures marginal product. Marginal product is also measured by the slope of the total product curve. Recall that the slope of a curve is the change in the value of the variable measured on the *y*-axis—output—divided by the change in the variable measured on the *x*-axis—labor—as we move along the curve. A one-unit increase in labor, from 2 to 3 workers, increases output from 10 to 13 sweaters, so the slope from point *C* to point *D* is 3 sweaters per additional worker, the same as the marginal product we've just calculated.

Again varying the amount of labor in the smallest units possible, we can draw the marginal product curve shown in Fig. 11.2(b). The *height* of this curve measures the *slope* of the total product curve at a point. Part (a) shows that an increase in employment from 2 to 3 workers increases output from 10 to 13 sweaters (an increase of 3). The increase in output of 3 sweaters appears on the *y*-axis of part (b) as the marginal product of going from 2 to 3 workers. We plot that marginal product at the midpoint between 2 and 3 workers. Notice that the marginal product shown in Fig. 11.2(b) reaches a peak at 1.5 workers, and at that point, marginal product is 6 sweaters per additional worker. The peak occurs at 1.5 workers because the total product curve is steepest when employment increases from 1 worker to 2 workers.

The total product and marginal product curves differ across firms and types of goods. GM's product curves are different from those of PennPower, whose curves in turn are different from those of Campus Sweaters. But the shapes of the product curves are similar because almost every production process has two features:

- Increasing marginal returns initially
- Diminishing marginal returns eventually

Increasing Marginal Returns Increasing marginal returns occur when the marginal product of an additional worker exceeds the marginal product of the previous worker. Increasing marginal returns arise from increased specialization and division of labor in the production process.

FIGURE 11.2   Total Product and Marginal Product

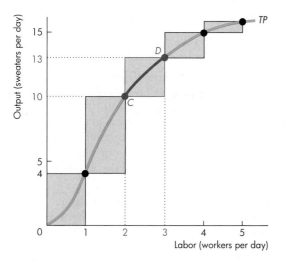

(a) Total product

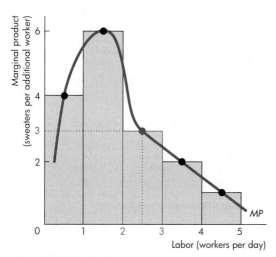

(b) Marginal product

Marginal product is illustrated by the orange bars. For example, when labor increases from 2 to 3 workers a day, marginal product is the orange bar whose height is 3 sweaters. (Marginal product is shown midway between the quantities of labor to emphasize that marginal product results from *changing* the quantity of labor.) The steeper the slope of the total product curve (*TP*) in part (a), the larger is marginal product (*MP*) in part (b). Marginal product increases to a maximum (in this example when 1.5 workers a day are employed) and then declines—diminishing marginal product.

MyEconLab Animation

For example, if Campus Sweaters employs one worker, that person must learn all the aspects of sweater production: running the knitting machines, fixing breakdowns, packaging and mailing sweaters, buying and checking the type and color of the wool. All these tasks must be performed by that one person.

If Campus Sweaters hires a second person, the two workers can specialize in different parts of the production process and can produce more than twice as much as one worker. The marginal product of the second worker is greater than the marginal product of the first worker. Marginal returns are increasing.

Diminishing Marginal Returns Most production processes experience increasing marginal returns initially, but all production processes eventually reach a point of *diminishing* marginal returns. **Diminishing marginal returns** occur when the marginal product of an additional worker is less than the marginal product of the previous worker.

Diminishing marginal returns arise from the fact that more and more workers are using the same capital and working in the same space. As more workers are added, there is less and less for the additional workers to do that is productive. For example, if Campus Sweaters hires a third worker, output increases but not by as much as it did when it hired the second worker. In this case, after two workers are hired, all the gains from specialization and the division of labor have been exhausted. By hiring a third worker, the factory produces more sweaters, but the equipment is being operated closer to its limits. There are even times when the third worker has nothing to do because the machines are running without the need for further attention. Hiring more and more workers continues to increase output but by successively smaller amounts. Marginal returns are diminishing. This phenomenon is such a pervasive one that it is called a "law"—the law of diminishing returns. The **law of diminishing returns** states that

> As a firm uses more of a variable factor of production with a given quantity of the fixed factor of production, the marginal product of the variable factor eventually diminishes.

You are going to return to the law of diminishing returns when we study a firm's costs, but before we do that, let's look at the average product of labor and the average product curve.

Average Product Curve

Figure 11.3 illustrates Campus Sweaters' average product of labor and shows the relationship between average product and marginal product. Points *B* through *F* on the average product curve *AP* correspond to those same rows in Table 11.1. Average product increases from 1 to 2 workers (its maximum value at point *C*) but then decreases as yet more workers are employed. Notice also that average product is largest when average product and marginal product are equal. That is, the marginal product curve cuts the average product curve at the point of maximum average product. For the number of workers at which marginal product exceeds average product, average product is *increasing*. For the number of workers at which marginal product is less than average product, average product is *decreasing*.

The relationship between the average product and marginal product is a general feature of the relationship between the average and marginal values of any variable—even your grades.

How to Pull Up Your Average

Do you want to pull up your average grade? Then make sure that your grade this semester is better than your current average! This semester is your marginal semester. If your marginal grade exceeds your average grade (like the second semester in the figure), your average will rise. If your marginal grade equals your average grade (like the third semester in the figure), your average won't change. If your marginal grade is below your average grade (like the fourth semester in the figure), your average will fall.

The relationship between your marginal and average grades is exactly the same as that between marginal product and average product.

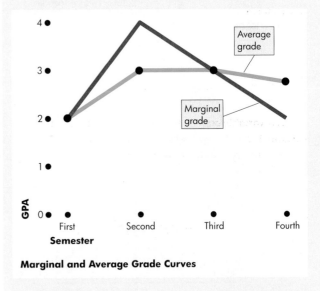

Marginal and Average Grade Curves

FIGURE 11.3   Average Product

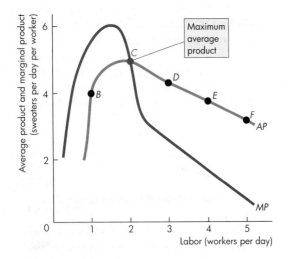

The figure shows the average product of labor and the connection between average product and marginal product. With 1 worker, marginal product exceeds average product, so average product is increasing. With 2 workers, marginal product equals average product, so average product is at its maximum. With more than 2 workers, marginal product is less than average product, so average product is decreasing.

MyEconLab Animation

◆ REVIEW QUIZ

1 Explain how the marginal product and average product of labor change as the labor employed increases (a) initially and (b) eventually.
2 What is the law of diminishing returns? Why does marginal product eventually diminish?
3 Explain the relationship between marginal product and average product.

Work these questions in Study Plan 11.2 and get instant feedback. Do a Key Terms Quiz.   *MyEconLab*

Campus Sweaters' product curves influence its costs, as you are now going to see.

◆ Short-Run Cost

To produce more output in the short run, a firm must employ more labor, which means that it must increase its costs. We describe the relationship between output and cost by using three cost concepts:

- Total cost
- Marginal cost
- Average cost

Total Cost

A firm's **total cost** (*TC*) is the cost of *all* the factors of production it uses. We separate total cost into total *fixed* cost and total *variable* cost.

Total fixed cost (*TFC*) is the cost of the firm's fixed factors. For Campus Sweaters, total fixed cost includes the cost of renting knitting machines and *normal profit*, which is the opportunity cost of Cindy's entrepreneurship (see Chapter 10, p. 225). The quantities of fixed factors don't change as output changes, so total fixed cost is the same at all outputs.

Total variable cost (*TVC*) is the cost of the firm's variable factors. For Campus Sweaters, labor is the variable factor, so this component of cost is its wage bill. Total variable cost changes as output changes.

Total cost is the sum of total fixed cost and total variable cost. That is,

$$TC = TFC + TVC.$$

The table in Fig. 11.4 shows total costs. Campus Sweaters rents one knitting machine for $25 a day, so its *TFC* is $25. To produce sweaters, the firm hires labor, which costs $25 a day. *TVC* is the number of workers multiplied by $25. For example, to produce 13 sweaters a day, in row *D*, the firm hires 3 workers and *TVC* is $75. *TC* is the sum of *TFC* and *TVC*, so to produce 13 sweaters a day, *TC* is $100. Check the calculations in the other rows of the table.

Figure 11.4 shows Campus Sweaters' total cost curves, which graph total cost against output. The green *TFC* curve is horizontal because total fixed cost ($25 a day) does not change when output changes. The purple *TVC* curve and the blue *TC* curve both slope upward because to increase output, more labor must be employed, which increases total variable cost. Total fixed cost equals the vertical distance between the *TVC* and *TC* curves.

Let's now look at a firm's marginal cost.

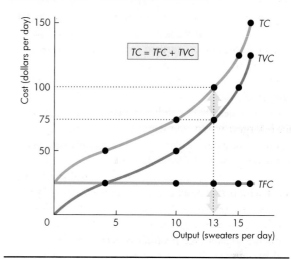

FIGURE 11.4   Total Cost Curves

$$TC = TFC + TVC$$

Labor (workers per day)	Output (sweaters per day)	Total fixed cost (*TFC*)	Total variable cost (*TVC*)	Total cost (*TC*)
		(dollars per day)		
A 0	0	25	0	25
B 1	4	25	25	50
C 2	10	25	50	75
D 3	**13**	**25**	**75**	**100**
E 4	15	25	100	125
F 5	16	25	125	150

Campus Sweaters rents a knitting machine for $25 a day, so this cost is the firm's total fixed cost. The firm hires workers at a wage rate of $25 a day, and this cost is its total variable cost. For example, in row *D*, Campus Sweaters employs 3 workers and its total variable cost is 3 × $25, which equals $75. Total cost is the sum of total fixed cost and total variable cost. For example, when Campus Sweaters employs 3 workers, total cost is $100—total fixed cost of $25 plus total variable cost of $75.

The graph shows Campus Sweaters' total cost curves. Total fixed cost is constant—the *TFC* curve is a horizontal line. Total variable cost increases as output increases, so the *TVC* curve and the *TC* curve increase as output increases. The vertical distance between the *TC* curve and the *TVC* curve equals total fixed cost, as illustrated by the two arrows.

MyEconLab Animation

Marginal Cost

Figure 11.4 shows that total variable cost and total cost increase at a decreasing rate at small outputs, but eventually, as output increases, total variable cost and total cost increase at an increasing rate. To understand this pattern in the change in total cost as output increases, we need to use the concept of *marginal cost.*

A firm's **marginal cost** is the increase in total cost that results from a one-unit increase in output. We calculate marginal cost as the increase in total cost divided by the increase in output. The table in Fig. 11.5 shows this calculation. When, for example, output increases from 10 sweaters to 13 sweaters, total cost increases from $75 to $100. The change in output is 3 sweaters, and the change in total cost is $25. The marginal cost of one of those 3 sweaters is ($25 ÷ 3), which equals $8.33.

Figure 11.5 graphs the marginal cost data in the table as the red marginal cost curve, *MC*. This curve is U-shaped because when Campus Sweaters hires a second worker, marginal cost decreases, but when it hires a third, a fourth, and a fifth worker, marginal cost successively increases.

At small outputs, marginal cost decreases as output increases because of greater specialization and the division of labor. But as output increases further, marginal cost eventually increases because of the *law of diminishing returns.* The law of diminishing returns means that the output produced by each additional worker is successively smaller. To produce an additional unit of output, ever more workers are required, and the cost of producing the additional unit of output—marginal cost—must eventually increase.

Marginal cost tells us how total cost changes as output increases. The final cost concept tells us what it costs, on average, to produce a unit of output. Let's now look at Campus Sweaters' average costs.

Average Cost

Ther are three average costs of production:

1. Average fixed cost
2. Average variable cost
3. Average total cost

Average fixed cost (*AFC*) is total fixed cost per unit of output. **Average variable cost** (*AVC*) is total variable cost per unit of output. **Average total cost** (*ATC*) is total cost per unit of output. The average cost concepts are calculated from the total cost concepts as follows:

$$TC = TFC + TVC.$$

Divide each total cost term by the quantity produced, *Q*, to get

$$\frac{TC}{Q} = \frac{TFC}{Q} + \frac{TVC}{Q},$$

or

$$ATC = AFC + AVC.$$

The table in Fig. 11.5 shows the calculation of average total cost. For example, in row *C*, output is 10 sweaters. Average fixed cost is ($25 ÷ 10), which equals $2.50, average variable cost is ($50 ÷ 10), which equals $5.00, and average total cost is ($75 ÷ 10), which equals $7.50. Note that average total cost is equal to average fixed cost ($2.50) plus average variable cost ($5.00).

Figure 11.5 shows the average cost curves. The green average fixed cost curve (*AFC*) slopes downward. As output increases, the same constant total fixed cost is spread over a larger output. The blue average total cost curve (*ATC*) and the purple average variable cost curve (*AVC*) are U-shaped. The vertical distance between the average total cost and average variable cost curves is equal to average fixed cost—as indicated by the two arrows. That distance shrinks as output increases because average fixed cost declines with increasing output.

Marginal Cost and Average Cost

The marginal cost curve (*MC*) intersects the average variable cost curve and the average total cost curve *at their minimum points.* When marginal cost is less than average cost, average cost is decreasing, and when marginal cost exceeds average cost, average cost is increasing. This relationship holds for both the *ATC* curve and the *AVC* curve. It is another example of the relationship you saw in Fig. 11.3 for average product and marginal product and in your average and marginal grades.

Why the Average Total Cost Curve Is U-Shaped

Average total cost is the sum of average fixed cost and average variable cost, so the shape of the *ATC* curve

FIGURE 11.5   Marginal Cost and Average Costs

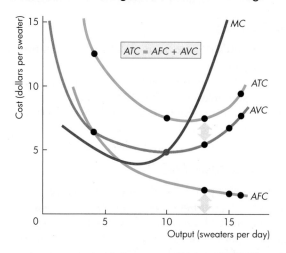

ATC = AFC + AVC

Marginal cost is calculated as the change in total cost divided by the change in output. When output increases from 4 to 10 sweaters, an increase of 6 sweaters, total cost increases by $25. Marginal cost is $25 ÷ 6, which is $4.17.

Each average cost concept is calculated by dividing the related total cost by output. When 10 sweaters are produced, AFC is $2.50 ($25 ÷ 10), AVC is $5 ($50 ÷ 10), and ATC is $7.50 ($75 ÷ 10).

The graph shows that the MC curve is U-shaped and intersects the AVC curve and the ATC curve at their minimum points. The average fixed cost curve (AFC) is downward sloping. The ATC curve and AVC curve are U-shaped. The vertical distance between the ATC curve and the AVC curve is equal to average fixed cost, as illustrated by the two arrows.

	Labor (workers per day)	Output (sweaters per day)	Total fixed cost (TFC)	Total variable cost (TVC)	Total cost (TC)	Marginal cost (MC) (dollars per additional sweater)	Average fixed cost (AFC)	Average variable cost (AVC)	Average total cost (ATC)
				(dollars per day)				(dollars per sweater)	
A	0	0	25	0	25		—	—	—
						.... 6.25			
B	1	4	25	25	50		6.25	6.25	12.50
						.... 4.17			
C	2	10	25	50	75		2.50	5.00	7.50
						.... 8.33			
D	3	13	25	75	100		1.92	5.77	7.69
						.......12.50			
E	4	15	25	100	125		1.67	6.67	8.33
						.......25.00			
F	5	16	25	125	150		1.56	7.81	9.38

MyEconLab Animation and Draw Graph

combines the shapes of the *AFC* and *AVC* curves. The U shape of the *ATC* curve arises from the influence of two opposing forces:

1. Spreading total fixed cost over a larger output
2. Eventually diminishing returns

When output increases, the firm spreads its total fixed cost over a larger output and so its average fixed cost decreases—its *AFC* curve slopes downward.

Diminishing returns means that as output increases, ever-larger amounts of labor are needed to produce an additional unit of output. So as output increases, average variable cost decreases initially but

eventually increases, and the *AVC* curve slopes upward. The *AVC* curve is U-shaped.

The shape of the *ATC* curve combines these two effects. Initially, as output increases, both average fixed cost and average variable cost decrease, so average total cost decreases. The *ATC* curve slopes downward.

But as output increases further and diminishing returns set in, average variable cost starts to increase. With average fixed cost decreasing more quickly than average variable cost is increasing, the *ATC* curve continues to slope downward. Eventually, average variable cost starts to increase more quickly than average fixed cost decreases, so average total cost starts to increase. The *ATC* curve slopes upward.

Cost Curves and Product Curves

The technology that a firm uses determines its costs. A firm's cost curves come directly from its product curves. You've used this link in the tables in which we have calculated total cost from the total product schedule and information about the prices of the factors of production. We're now going to get a clearer view of the link between the product curves and the cost curves. We'll look first at the link between total cost and total product and then at the links between the average and marginal product and cost curves.

Total Product and Total Variable Cost Figure 11.6 shows the links between the firm's total product curve, *TP*, and its total *variable* cost curve, *TVC*. The graph is a bit unusual in two ways. First, it measures two variables on the *x*-axis—labor and variable cost. Second, it graphs the *TVC* curve but with variable cost on the *x*-axis and output on the *y*-axis. The graph can show labor and cost on the *x*-axis because variable cost is proportional to labor. One worker costs $25 a day. Graphing output against labor gives the *TP* curve and graphing variable cost against output gives the *TVC* curve.

FIGURE 11.6   Total Product and Total Variable Cost

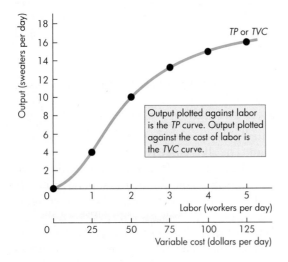

The figure shows the total product curve, *TP*, as a graph of output (sweaters per day) plotted against labor (workers per day). It also shows the total variable cost curve, *TVC*, as a graph of total variable cost (dollars per day) against output. The only difference between the *TVC* curve here and that in Fig. 11.4 is that we've switched the *x*-axis and *y*-axis.

MyEconLab Animation

ECONOMICS IN THE NEWS

Checkout Cost Curves

Walmart Adds iPhone Scan-and-Checkout Feature to 12 More Markets

Walmart is tripling the number of stores that lets shoppers scan items with their iPhones and pay at self-checkout counters. Walmart's "Scan & Go" program will soon be in more than 200 stores.

Source: Reuters, March 20, 2013

DATA AND ASSUMPTIONS

A grocery store paid $20,000 to install 5 worker-operated checkout lines. With a life of 9 years and operating for 10 hours a day, these machines have an *implicit rental rate* of $1.00 an hour. Checkout clerks can be hired for $10 an hour. The total product schedule (checkouts per hour) for this store is

Checkout clerks	1	2	3	4	5
Checkouts per hour	12	22	30	36	40

Another grocery store has converted to all self-checkout. It paid $100,000 to install a 5-line self-operated system. With a 5-year life and operating for 10 hours a day, the system has an *implicit rental rate* of $7.00 an hour. It hires checkout assistants to help customers at $10 an hour—the same wage as paid to checkout clerks. The total product schedule for this store is

Checkout assistants	1	1	1	2
Checkouts per hour	12	22	30	36

That is, one checkout assistant can help shoppers check out up to a rate of 30 an hour and a second assistant can boost output to 36 an hour. (Shoppers using self-checkout aren't as quick as clerks, so the fastest rate at which this store can check out customers is 36 an hour.)

THE PROBLEM

- Which checkout system has the lower average total cost (*ATC*)? Which system has the lower marginal cost (*MC*)? Sketch the *ATC* and *MC* curves for the two systems.

THE SOLUTION

- Start with the worker-operated checkout system. Fixed cost is $1.00 per hour and variable cost is $10.00 per clerk. So the total cost schedule is

Checkout clerks	1	2	3	4	5
Checkouts per hour	12	22	30	36	40
Total cost (*TC*) per hour	11	21	31	41	51

- Calculate *MC* as the change in *TC* divided by the change in output (change in number of checkouts) and calculate *ATC* as *TC* divided by output to get

Checkouts per hour	12	22	30	36	40
Marginal cost (MC)	0.83	1.00	1.25	1.67	2.50
Average total cost (ATC)	0.92	0.95	1.03	1.14	1.28

- Figure 1 graphs the *MC* and *ATC* values at each output rate.

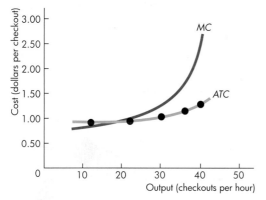

Figure 1 Operator Checkout

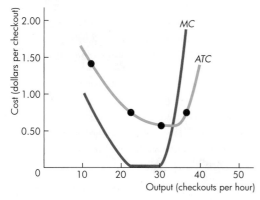

Figure 2 Self-Checkout

- Now do similar calculations for the self-checkout system. Fixed cost is $7.00 per hour and variable cost is $10.00 per clerk hour. So the total cost schedule is

Checkout assistants	1	1	1	2
Checkouts per hour	12	22	30	36
Total cost (TC) per hour	17	17	17	27

- Calculate *MC* and *ATC* in the same way as before to get

Checkouts per hour	12	22	30	36
Marginal cost (MC)	0.83	0	0	1.67
Average total cost (ATC)	1.42	0.77	0.57	0.75

- Figure 2 graphs the *MC* and *ATC* values at each output rate.

- Figure 3 compares the *ATC* of the two systems. You can see that the self-checkout system has higher *ATC* at low output rates and lower *ATC* at higher output rates. The reason is that self-checkout has a higher fixed cost and lower variable cost than the worker-operated system.

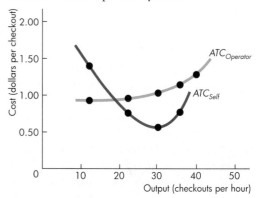

Figure 3 *ATC* Compared

MyEconLab More Economics in the News

Average and Marginal Product and Cost Figure 11.7 shows the links between the firm's average and marginal product curves and its average and marginal cost curves. The upper graph shows the average product curve, *AP*, and the marginal product curve, *MP*—like those in Fig. 11.3. The lower graph shows the average variable cost curve, *AVC*, and the marginal cost curve, *MC*—like those in Fig. 11.5.

As labor increases up to 1.5 workers a day (upper graph), output increases to 6.5 sweaters a day (lower graph). Marginal product and average product rise and marginal cost and average variable cost fall. At the point of maximum marginal product, marginal cost is at a minimum.

As labor increases from 1.5 workers to 2 workers a day (upper graph), output increases from 6.5 sweaters to 10 sweaters a day (lower graph). Marginal product falls and marginal cost rises, but average product continues to rise and average variable cost continues to fall. At the point of maximum average product, average variable cost is at a minimum. As labor increases further, output increases. Average product diminishes and average variable cost increases.

Shifts in the Cost Curves

The position of a firm's short-run cost curves depends on two factors:

- Technology
- Prices of factors of production

Technology A technological change that increases productivity increases the marginal product and average product of labor. With a better technology, the same factors of production can produce more output, so the technological advance lowers the costs of production and shifts the cost curves downward.

For example, advances in robot production techniques have increased productivity in the automobile industry. As a result, the product curves of Chrysler, Ford, and GM have shifted upward and their cost curves have shifted downward. But the relationships between their product curves and cost curves have not changed. The curves are still linked in the way shown in Figs. 11.6 and 11.7.

Often, as in the case of robots producing cars, a technological advance results in a firm using more capital, a fixed factor, and less labor, a variable factor.

FIGURE 11.7   Average and Marginal Product Curves and Cost Curves

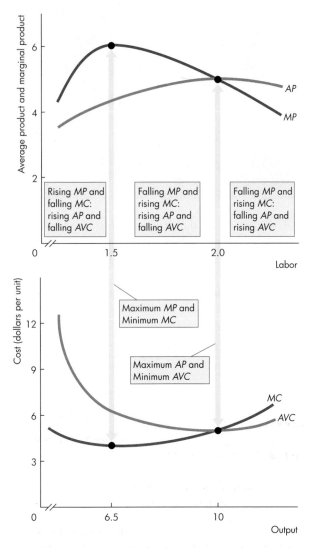

A firm's *MP* curve is linked to its *MC* curve. If, as the firm increases its labor from 0 to 1.5 workers a day, the firm's marginal product rises, its marginal cost falls. If marginal product is at a maximum, marginal cost is at a minimum. If, as the firm hires more labor, its marginal product diminishes, its marginal cost rises.

A firm's *AP* curve is linked to its *AVC* curve. If, as the firm increases its labor to 2 workers a day, its average product rises, its average variable cost falls. If average product is at a maximum, average variable cost is at a minimum. If, as the firm hires more labor, its average product diminishes, its average variable cost rises.

MyEconLab Animation

TABLE 11.2   A Compact Glossary of Costs

Term	Symbol	Definition	Equation
Fixed cost		Cost that is independent of the output level; cost of a fixed factor of production	
Variable cost		Cost that varies with the output level; cost of a variable factor of production	
Total fixed cost	TFC	Cost of the fixed factors of production	
Total variable cost	TVC	Cost of the variable factors of production	
Total cost	TC	Cost of all factors of production	$TC = TFC + TVC$
Output (total product)	TP	Total quantity produced (output Q)	
Marginal cost	MC	Change in total cost resulting from a one-unit increase in total product	$MC = \Delta TC \div \Delta Q$
Average fixed cost	AFC	Total fixed cost per unit of output	$AFC = TFC \div Q$
Average variable cost	AVC	Total variable cost per unit of output	$AVC = TVC \div Q$
Average total cost	ATC	Total cost per unit of output	$ATC = AFC + AVC$

Another example is the use of ATMs by banks to dispense cash. ATMs, which are fixed capital, have replaced tellers, which are variable labor. Such a technological change decreases total cost but increases fixed costs and decreases variable cost. This change in the mix of fixed cost and variable cost means that at small outputs, average total cost might increase, while at large outputs, average total cost decreases.

Prices of Factors of Production An increase in the price of a factor of production increases the firm's costs and shifts its cost curves. How the curves shift depends on which factor price changes.

An increase in rent or some other component of *fixed* cost shifts the TFC and AFC curves upward and shifts the TC curve upward but leaves the AVC and TVC curves and the MC curve unchanged. For example, if the interest expense paid by a trucking company increases, the fixed cost of transportation services increases.

An increase in wages, gasoline, or another component of *variable* cost shifts the TVC and AVC curves upward and shifts the MC curve upward but leaves the AFC and TFC curves unchanged. For example, if truck drivers' wages or the price of gasoline increases, the variable cost and marginal cost of transportation services increase.

You've now completed your study of short-run costs. All the concepts that you've met are summarized in a compact glossary in Table 11.2.

REVIEW QUIZ

1 What relationships do a firm's short-run cost curves show?
2 How does marginal cost change as output increases (a) initially and (b) eventually?
3 What does the law of diminishing returns imply for the shape of the marginal cost curve?
4 What is the shape of the AFC curve and why does it have this shape?
5 What are the shapes of the AVC curve and the ATC curve and why do they have these shapes?

Work these questions in Study Plan 11.3 and get instant feedback. Do a Key Terms Quiz.   MyEconLab

Long-Run Cost

We are now going to study the firm's long-run costs. In the long run, a firm can vary both the quantity of labor and the quantity of capital, so in the long run, all the firm's costs are variable.

The behavior of long-run cost depends on the firm's *production function*, which is the relationship between the maximum output attainable and the quantities of both labor and capital.

The Production Function

Table 11.3 shows Campus Sweaters' production function. The table lists total product schedules for four different quantities of capital. The quantity of capital identifies the plant size. The numbers for plant 1 are for a factory with 1 knitting machine—the case we've just studied. The other three plants have 2, 3, and 4 machines. If Campus Sweaters uses plant 2 with 2 knitting machines, the various amounts of labor can produce the outputs shown in the second column of the table. The other two columns show the outputs of yet larger quantities of capital. Each column of the table could be graphed as a total product curve for each plant.

Diminishing Returns Diminishing returns occur with each of the four plant sizes as the quantity of labor increases. You can check that fact by calculating the marginal product of labor in each of the plants with 2, 3, and 4 machines. With each plant size, as the firm increases the quantity of labor employed, the marginal product of labor (eventually) diminishes.

Diminishing Marginal Product of Capital
Diminishing returns also occur with each quantity of labor as the quantity of capital increases. You can check that fact by calculating the marginal product of capital at a given quantity of labor. The *marginal product of capital* is the change in total product divided by the change in capital when the quantity of labor is constant—equivalently, the change in output resulting from a one-unit increase in the quantity of capital. For example, if Campus Sweaters has 3 workers and increases its capital from 1 machine to 2 machines, output increases from 13 to 18 sweaters a day. The marginal product of the second machine is 5 sweaters a day. If Campus Sweaters continues to employ 3 workers

TABLE 11.3 The Production Function

Labor (workers per day)	Output (sweaters per day)			
	Plant 1	Plant 2	Plant 3	Plant 4
1	4	10	13	15
2	10	15	18	20
3	13	18	22	24
4	15	20	24	26
5	16	21	25	27
Knitting machines (number)	1	2	3	4

The table shows the total product data for four quantities of capital (plant sizes). The greater the plant size, the larger is the output produced by any given quantity of labor. For a given plant size, the marginal product of labor diminishes as more labor is employed. For a given quantity of labor, the marginal product of capital diminishes as the quantity of capital used increases.

and increases the number of machines from 2 to 3, output increases from 18 to 22 sweaters a day. The marginal product of the third machine is 4 sweaters a day, down from 5 sweaters a day for the second machine.

Let's now see what the production function implies for long-run costs.

Short-Run Cost and Long-Run Cost

As before, Campus Sweaters can hire workers for $25 a day and rent knitting machines for $25 a day. Using these factor prices and the data in Table 11.3, we can calculate the average total cost and graph the *ATC* curves for factories with 1, 2, 3, and 4 knitting machines. We've already studied the costs of a factory with 1 machine in Figs. 11.4 and 11.5. In Fig. 11.8, the average total cost curve for that case is ATC_1. Figure 11.8 also shows the average total cost curve for a factory with 2 machines, ATC_2, with 3 machines, ATC_3, and with 4 machines, ATC_4.

You can see, in Fig. 11.8, that the plant size has a big effect on the firm's average total cost.

FIGURE 11.8   Short-Run Costs of Four Different Plants

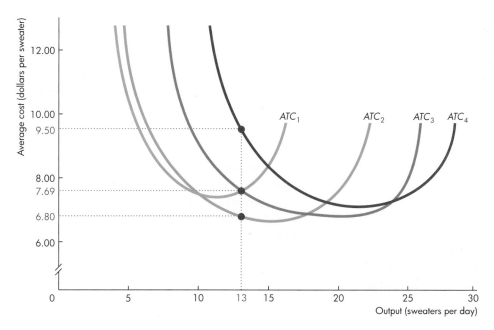

The figure shows short-run average total cost curves for four different quantities of capital at Campus Sweaters. The firm can produce 13 sweaters a day with 1 knitting machine on ATC_1 or with 3 knitting machines on ATC_3 for an average cost of $7.69 a sweater. The firm can produce 13 sweaters a day by using 2 machines on ATC_2 for $6.80 a sweater or by using 4 machines on ATC_4 for $9.50 a sweater.

If the firm produces 13 sweaters a day, the least-cost method of production, *the long-run method*, is with 2 machines on ATC_2.

In Fig. 11.8, two things stand out:

1. Each short-run *ATC* curve is U-shaped.
2. For each short-run *ATC* curve, the larger the plant, the greater is the output at which average total cost is at a minimum.

Each short-run *ATC* curve is U-shaped because, as the quantity of labor increases, its marginal product initially increases and then diminishes. This pattern in the marginal product of labor, which we examined in some detail for the plant with 1 knitting machine on pp. 254–255, occurs at all plant sizes.

The minimum average total cost for a larger plant occurs at a greater output than it does for a smaller plant because the larger plant has a higher total fixed cost and therefore, for any given output, a higher average fixed cost.

Which short-run *ATC* curve a firm operates on depends on the plant it has. In the long run, the firm can choose its plant and the plant it chooses is the one that enables it to produce its planned output at the lowest average total cost.

To see why, suppose that Campus Sweaters plans to produce 13 sweaters a day. In Fig. 11.8, with 1 machine, the average total cost curve is ATC_1 and the average total cost of 13 sweaters a day is $7.69 a sweater. With 2 machines, on ATC_2, average total cost is $6.80 a sweater. With 3 machines, on ATC_3, average total cost is $7.69 a sweater, the same as with 1 machine. Finally, with 4 machines, on ATC_4, average total cost is $9.50 a sweater.

The economically efficient plant for producing a given output is the one that has the lowest average total cost. For Campus Sweaters, the economically efficient plant to use to produce 13 sweaters a day is the one with 2 machines.

In the long run, Cindy chooses the plant that minimizes average total cost. When a firm is producing a given output at the least possible cost, it is operating on its *long-run average cost curve*.

The **long-run average cost curve** is the relationship between the lowest attainable average total cost and output when the firm can change both the plant it uses and the quantity of labor it employs.

The long-run average cost curve is a planning curve. It tells the firm the plant and the quantity of labor to use at each output to minimize average cost. Once the firm chooses a plant, the firm operates on the short-run cost curves that apply to that plant.

The Long-Run Average Cost Curve

Figure 11.9 shows how a long-run average cost curve is derived. The long-run average cost curve *LRAC* consists of pieces of the four short-run *ATC* curves. For outputs up to 10 sweaters a day, average total cost is the lowest on ATC_1. For outputs between 10 and 18 sweaters a day, average total cost is the lowest on ATC_2. For outputs between 18 and 24 sweaters a day, average total cost is the lowest on ATC_3. And for outputs in excess of 24 sweaters a day, average total cost is the lowest on ATC_4. The piece of each *ATC* curve with the lowest average total cost is highlighted in dark blue in Fig. 11.9. This dark blue scallop-shaped curve made up of the pieces of the four *ATC* curves is the *LRAC* curve.

Economies and Diseconomies of Scale

Economies of scale are features of a firm's technology that make average total cost *fall* as output increases. When economies of scale are present, the *LRAC* curve slopes downward. In Fig. 11.9, Campus Sweaters has economies of scale for outputs up to 15 sweaters a day.

Greater specialization of both labor and capital is the main source of economies of scale. For example, if

GM produces 100 cars a week, each worker must perform many different tasks and the capital must be general-purpose machines and tools. But if GM produces 10,000 cars a week, each worker specializes in a small number of tasks, uses task-specific tools, and becomes highly proficient.

Diseconomies of scale are features of a firm's technology that make average total cost *rise* as output increases. When diseconomies of scale are present, the *LRAC* curve slopes upward. In Fig. 11.9, Campus Sweaters experiences diseconomies of scale at outputs greater than 15 sweaters a day.

The challenge of managing a large enterprise is the main source of diseconomies of scale.

Constant returns to scale are features of a firm's technology that keep average total cost constant as output increases. When constant returns to scale are present, the *LRAC* curve is horizontal.

Economies of Scale at Campus Sweaters The economies of scale and diseconomies of scale at Campus Sweaters arise from the firm's production function in Table 11.3. With 1 machine and 1 worker, the firm produces 4 sweaters a day. With 2 machines and 2 workers, total cost doubles but

FIGURE 11.9   Long-Run Average Cost Curve

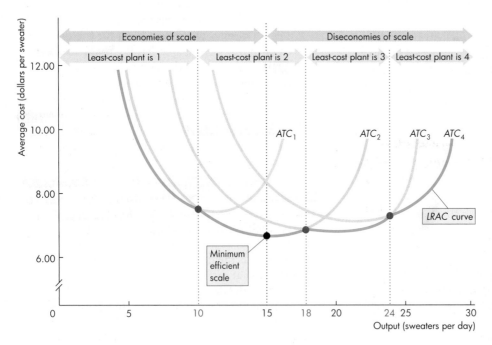

The long-run average cost curve traces the lowest attainable *ATC* when both labor and capital change. The green arrows highlight the output range over which each plant achieves the lowest *ATC*. Within each range, to change the quantity produced, the firm changes the quantity of labor it employs.

Along the *LRAC* curve, economies of scale occur if average cost falls as output increases; diseconomies of scale occur if average cost rises as output increases. Minimum efficient scale is the output at which average cost is lowest, 15 sweaters a day.

ECONOMICS IN ACTION

Produce More to Cut Cost

Why do GM, Ford, and the other automakers have expensive equipment lying around that isn't fully used? You can answer this question with what you've learned in this chapter.

The basic answer is that auto production enjoys economies of scale. A larger output rate brings a lower long-run average cost—the firm's $LRAC$ curve slopes downward.

An auto producer's average total cost curves look like those in the figure. To produce 20 vehicles an hour, the firm installs the plant with the short-run average total cost curve ATC_1. The average cost of producing a vehicle is \$20,000.

Producing 20 vehicles an hour doesn't use the plant at its lowest possible average total cost. If the firm could sell enough cars for it to produce 40 vehicles an hour, the firm could use its current plant and produce at an average cost of \$15,000 a vehicle.

But if the firm planned to produce 40 vehicles an hour, it would not stick with its current plant. The firm would install a bigger plant with the short-run average total cost curve ATC_2, and produce 40 vehicles an hour for \$10,000 a car.

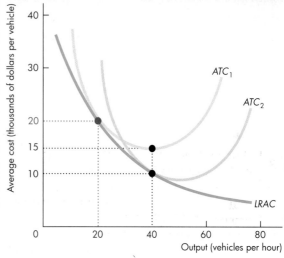

Automobile Plant Average Cost Curves

output more than doubles to 15 sweaters a day, so average cost decreases and Campus Sweaters experiences economies of scale. With 4 machines and 4 workers, total cost doubles again but output less than doubles to 26 sweaters a day, so average cost increases and the firm experiences diseconomies of scale.

Minimum Efficient Scale A firm's **minimum efficient scale** is the *smallest* output at which long-run average cost reaches its lowest level. At Campus Sweaters, the minimum efficient scale is 15 sweaters a day.

The minimum efficient scale plays a role in determining market structure. In a market in which the minimum efficient scale is small relative to market demand, the market has room for many firms, and the market is competitive. In a market in which the minimum efficient scale is large relative to market demand, only a small number of firms, and possibly only one firm, can make a profit and the market is either an oligopoly or monopoly. We will return to this idea in the next three chapters.

REVIEW QUIZ

1 What does a firm's production function show and how is it related to a total product curve?
2 Does the law of diminishing returns apply to capital as well as labor? Explain why or why not.
3 What does a firm's $LRAC$ curve show? How is it related to the firm's short-run ATC curves?
4 What are economies of scale and diseconomies of scale? How do they arise? What do they imply for the shape of the $LRAC$ curve?
5 What is a firm's minimum efficient scale?

Work these questions in Study Plan 11.4 and get instant feedback. Do a Key Terms Quiz.   MyEconLab

Economics in the News on pp. 264–265 applies what you've learned about a firm's cost curves. It looks at Starbucks' cost curves and explains how increasing plant size by adding stores can lower average total cost.

Expanding Capacity at Starbucks

Starbucks Canada to Open 150 New Outlets, Biggest Expansion Ever

Financial Post
February 8, 2013

Thanks in part to Target, Starbucks Canada will be undertaking the biggest expansion effort in its history this year, with plans to open more than 150 new locations across the country.

…

The subsidiary of Seattle-based Starbucks Corp. will open outlets inside many of the 124 Target locations opening in Canada in 2013 beginning next month—but the exact number is still a secret, Starbucks Canada president Annie Young-Scrivner said Friday.

The growth is also a response to company's successful bid to tap into the Canadian palate with its burgeoning Blonde roast coffee in a way that it had not before, bringing a host of new customers through its doors, she said in an interview on Friday. …

After the first nine months, Blonde grew to represent 12% of Starbucks Canada brewed coffee sales. Since the company began a sampling and marketing push last month in Canada, the lighter blend now accounts for 20% of those sales. Typically 38% of Starbucks Canada customers drink dark roast and 42% drink medium roast, she said. "Some people thought our roast was too dark before. We had a lot of customers who would come to us for their lattes, but would go somewhere else for their coffee. I think our mix will continue to shift more towards the Blonde roast." …

Copyright Financial Post. 2013 Reproduced with permission.

ESSENCE OF THE STORY

- Starbucks plans to open more than 150 new locations across Canada.

- Many of the new outlets will be inside Target stores.

- Starbucks has expanded its number of customers with a successful Blonde roast coffee variety.

- Canadians prefer lighter roasts, and Starbucks expects continued growth of business with ongoing shift towards the Blonde roast.

MyEconLab More Economics in the News

ECONOMIC ANALYSIS

- Starbucks can increase output by hiring more labor, or by increasing its plant size. Or it can both increase its plant size and hire more labor.

- Starbucks can increase its plant size by either replacing an existing café with a larger one, or expanding the number of cafés.

- The decision turns on comparing costs, and Starbucks has figured that it minimizes cost by expanding the number of cafés and hiring more labor.

- We don't know Starbucks' costs, but we can gain insight into the firm's decision with an example.

- The table shows an assumed total product schedule for a Starbucks café. It also shows Starbucks' total cost (TC), marginal cost (MC), and average total cost, (ATC).

- Figure 1 graphs the marginal cost and average total cost curves.

- If Starbucks wants to increase production in a café to above 1,000 coffees per day, marginal cost rises sharply.

- But if Starbucks opens a new café, a given quantity of labor can produce a greater output.

- With a bigger capacity, fixed cost increases, so at low output levels, average total cost also increases.

- But at higher output levels, because *average* fixed cost decreases, average total cost also decreases.

- Figure 2 shows Starbucks original ATC curve, ATC_0, and the new ATC curve, ATC_1, which shows average total cost when the firm has added one more café.

	Labor (workers per day)	Output (coffees per day)	Total cost (TC) (dollars per day)	Marginal cost (MC)	Average total cost (ATC)
				(dollars per coffee)	
A	0	0	1,000	—	
				..... 2.00	
B	10	400	1,800		4.50
				..... 1.33	
C	20	1,000	2,600		2.60
				..... 2.67	
D	30	1,300	3,400		2.62
				..... 4.00	
E	40	1,500	4,200		2.80
				..... 8.00	
F	50	1,600	5,000		3.13

- Increasing output with a larger plant size avoids the sharply rising marginal cost of the original café.

- In this example, Starbucks can now hire more labor to operate two cafés and average total cost falls as output increases above 1,000 coffees per day.

- Figure 2 also shows Starbucks long-run average cost curve ($LRAC$).

- If the firm wants to expand output yet further and avoid the rising costs along ATC_1, it can open additional cafés and move along its long-run average cost curve.

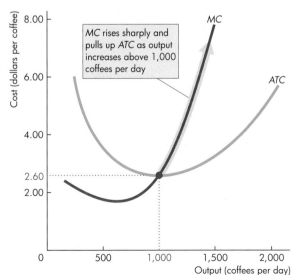

Figure 1 Starbucks' Short-Run Cost Curves

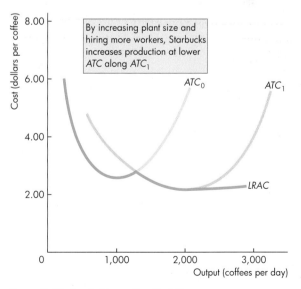

Figure 2 Starbucks' Long-Run Cost Curve

SUMMARY

Key Points

Decision Time Frames (p. 248)

- In the short run, the quantity of at least one factor of production is fixed and the quantities of the other factors of production can be varied.
- In the long run, the quantities of all factors of production can be varied.

Working Problem 1 will give you a better understanding of a firm's decision time frames.

Short-Run Technology Constraint (pp. 249–252)

- A total product curve shows the quantity a firm can produce with a given quantity of capital and different quantities of labor.
- Initially, the marginal product of labor increases as the quantity of labor increases, because of increased specialization and the division of labor.
- Eventually, marginal product diminishes because an increasing quantity of labor must share a fixed quantity of capital—the law of diminishing returns.
- Initially, average product increases as the quantity of labor increases, but eventually average product diminishes.

Working Problems 2 to 6 will give you a better understanding of a firm's short-run technology constraint.

Short-Run Cost (pp. 253–259)

- As output increases, total fixed cost is constant, and total variable cost and total cost increase.
- As output increases, average fixed cost decreases and average variable cost, average total cost, and marginal cost decrease at low outputs and increase at high outputs. These cost curves are U-shaped.

Working Problems 7 to 11 will give you a better understanding of a firm's short-run cost.

Long-Run Cost (pp. 260–263)

- A firm has a set of short-run cost curves for each different plant. For each output, the firm has one least-cost plant. The larger the output, the larger is the plant that will minimize average total cost.
- The long-run average cost curve traces out the lowest attainable average total cost at each output when both capital and labor inputs can be varied.
- With economies of scale, the long-run average cost curve slopes downward. With diseconomies of scale, the long-run average cost curve slopes upward.

Working Problems 12 to 14 will give you a better understanding of a firm's long-run cost.

Key Terms

MyEconLab Key Terms Quiz

Average fixed cost, 254
Average product, 249
Average total cost, 254
Average variable cost, 254
Constant returns to scale, 262
Diminishing marginal returns, 251
Diseconomies of scale, 262

Economies of scale, 262
Law of diminishing returns, 251
Long run, 248
Long-run average cost curve, 261
Marginal cost, 254
Marginal product, 249
Minimum efficient scale, 263

Short run, 248
Sunk cost, 248
Total cost, 253
Total fixed cost, 253
Total product, 249
Total variable cost, 253

WORKED PROBLEM

MyEconLab   You can work this problem in Chapter 11 Study Plan.

The table provides data about a firm's short-run cost. It shows the firm's total cost, TC, and marginal cost, MC, at five levels of output, including zero output.

Output	MC	TC	TFC	TVC	ATC	AFC	AVC
0		$12	?	?			
	$10						
1		?	?	?	?	?	?
	$2						
2		?	?	?	?	?	?
	$6						
3		?	?	?	?	?	?
	$22						
4		?	?	?	?	?	?

Questions

1. Fill in the cells marked "?" to record the firm's costs: TC, TFC, TVC, ATC, AFC, and AVC at each output.
2. Draw a graph of the total cost curves, and a graph of the average and marginal cost curves.

Solutions

1a. Begin by using the fact that marginal cost, MC, is the change in total cost, TC, when output increases by 1 unit. This fact means that TC at 1 unit equals TC at zero units plus MC of the first unit. TC is $12 at zero and MC of the first unit is $10, so TC at 1 unit equals $22. The rest of the TC column is calculated in the same way. For example, TC at 4 units is $52, which equals $30 + $22.

1b. TFC equals TC at zero output, so you can fill in the TFC column as $12 at each quantity of output.
1c. Because $TC = TFC + TVC$, you can fill in the TVC column as $TVC = TC - TFC$. For example, at 1 unit of output, $TVC = $22 - $12 = $10.
1d. Average cost equals $TC \div$ output, so to fill in the ATC, AFC, and AVC columns, divide the numbers for TC, TFC, and TVC by the output level. For example, ATC at 3 units of output is $30 \div 3 = $10.

Output	MC	TC	TFC	TVC	ATC	AFC	AVC
0		$12	$12	0			
	$10						
1		$22	$12	$10	$22	$12	$10
	$2						
2		$24	$12	$12	$12	$6	$6
	$6						
3		$30	$12	$18	$10	$4	$6
	$22						
4		$52	$12	$40	$13	$3	$10

Key Point: Given a firm's total cost at zero output and its marginal cost at each output, by using the relationships among the cost concepts, we can calculate the total costs and the average costs at each output.

2. The key figure (a) graphs the total cost curves and the key figure (b) graphs the marginal and average cost curves.

Key Point: The marginal cost curve intersects the average cost curves at their minimum points.

Key Figure

MyEconLab Interactive Animation

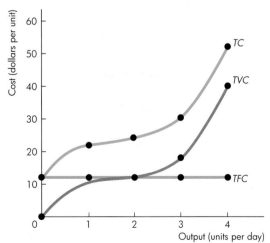

(a) Total Cost Curves

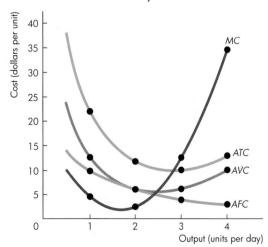

(b) Average and Marginal Cost Curves

STUDY PLAN PROBLEMS AND APPLICATIONS

MyEconLab   You can work Problems 1 to 14 in Chapter 11 Study Plan and get instant feedback.

Decision Time Frames (Study Plan 11.1)

1. Which of the following news items involves a short-run decision and which involves a long-run decision? Explain.

   January 31, 2008: Starbucks will open 75 more stores abroad than originally predicted, for a total of 975.

   February 25, 2008: For three hours on Tuesday, Starbucks will shut down every single one of its 7,100 stores so that baristas can receive a refresher course.

   June 2, 2008: Starbucks replaces baristas with vending machines.

   July 18, 2008: Starbucks is closing 616 stores by the end of March.

Short-Run Technology Constraint (Study Plan 11.2)

Use the following table to work Problems 2 to 6. The table sets out Sue's Surfboards' total product schedule.

Labor (workers per week)	Output (surfboards per week)
1	30
2	70
3	120
4	160
5	190
6	210
7	220

2. Draw the total product curve.
3. Calculate the average product of labor and draw the average product curve.
4. Calculate the marginal product of labor and draw the marginal product curve.
5. a. Over what output range does Sue's Surfboards enjoy the benefits of increased specialization and division of labor?

   b. Over what output range does the firm experience diminishing marginal product of labor?

   c. Over what output range does the firm experience an increasing average product of labor but a diminishing marginal product of labor?

6. Explain how it is possible for a firm to experience simultaneously an increasing *average* product but a diminishing *marginal* product.

Short-Run Cost (Study Plan 11.3)

Use the following data to work Problems 7 to 11. Sue's Surfboards, in Problem 2, hires workers at $500 a week and its total fixed cost is $1,000 a week.

7. Calculate total cost, total variable cost, and total fixed cost of each output in the table. Plot these points and sketch the short-run total cost curves.
8. Calculate average total cost, average fixed cost, average variable cost, and marginal cost of each output in the table. Plot these points and sketch the short-run average and marginal cost curves.
9. Illustrate the connection between Sue's *AP, MP, AVC,* and *MC* curves in graphs like those in Fig. 11.7.
10. Sue's Surfboards rents a factory. If the rent rises by $200 a week and other things remain the same, how do Sue's Surfboards' short-run average cost curves and marginal cost curve change?
11. Workers at Sue's Surfboards negotiate a wage increase of $100 a week per worker. If other things remain the same, explain how Sue's Surfboards' short-run average cost curves and marginal cost curve change.

Long-Run Cost (Study Plan 11.4)

Use the following data to work Problems 12 to 14. Jackie's Canoe Rides rents canoes at $100 per day and pays $50 per day for each canoe operator it hires. The table shows the firm's production function.

Labor (workers per day)	Output (rides per day)			
	Plant 1	Plant 2	Plant 3	Plant 4
10	20	40	55	65
20	40	60	75	85
30	65	75	90	100
40	75	85	100	110
Canoes	**10**	**20**	**30**	**40**

12. Graph the *ATC* curves for Plant 1 and Plant 2. Explain why these *ATC* curves differ.
13. Graph the *ATC* curves for Plant 3 and Plant 4. Explain why these *ATC* curves differ.
14. a. On Jackie's *LRAC* curve, what is the average cost of producing 40, 75, and 85 rides a week?

    b. What is Jackie's minimum efficient scale?

    c. Does Jackie's production function feature economies of scale or diseconomies of scale?

ADDITIONAL PROBLEMS AND APPLICATIONS

MyEconLab   You can work these problems in MyEconLab if assigned by your instructor.

Decision Time Frames

15. **A Bakery on the Rise**

    Some 500 customers a day line up to buy Avalon's breads, scones, muffins, and coffee. Staffing and management are worries. Avalon now employs 35 and plans to hire 15 more. Its payroll will climb by 30 percent to 40 percent. The new CEO has executed an ambitious agenda that includes the move to a larger space, which will increase the rent from $3,500 to $10,000 a month.

    Source: CNN, March 24, 2008

    a. Which of Avalon's decisions described in the news clip is a short-run decision and which is a long-run decision?

    b. Why is Avalon's long-run decision riskier than its short-run decision?

16. **The Sunk-Cost Fallacy**

    You have good tickets to a basketball game an hour's drive away. There's a blizzard raging outside, and the game is being televised. You can sit warm and safe at home and watch it on TV, or you can bundle up, dig out your car, and go to the game. What do you do?

    Source: *Slate*, September 9, 2005

    a. What type of cost is your expenditure on tickets?

    b. Why is the cost of the ticket irrelevant to your current decision about whether to stay at home or go to the game?

Short-Run Technology Constraint

17. Terri runs a rose farm. One worker produces 1,000 roses a week; hiring a second worker doubles her total product; hiring a third worker doubles her output again; hiring a fourth worker increased her total product but by only 1,000 roses. Construct Terri's marginal product and average product schedules. Over what range of workers do marginal returns increase?

Short-Run Cost

18. Use the events described in the news clip in Problem 15. By how much will Avalon's short-run decision increase its total variable cost? By how much will Avalon's long-run decision increase its monthly total fixed cost? Sketch Avalon's short-run *ATC* curve before and after the events described in the news clip.

19. Bill's Bakery has a fire and Bill loses some of his cost data. The bits of paper that he recovers after the fire provide the information in the following table (all the cost numbers are dollars).

TP	AFC	AVC	ATC	MC
10	120	100	220	
				80
20	*A*	*B*	150	
				90
30	40	90	130	
				130
40	30	*C*	*D*	
				E
50	24	108	132	

Bill asks you to come to his rescue and provide the missing data in the five spaces identified as *A*, *B*, *C*, *D*, and *E*.

Use the following table to work Problems 20 and 21. ProPainters hires students at $250 a week to paint houses. It leases equipment at $500 a week. The table sets out its total product schedule.

Labor (students)	Output (houses painted per week)
1	2
2	5
3	9
4	12
5	14
6	15

20. If ProPainters paints 12 houses a week, calculate its total cost, average total cost, and marginal cost. At what output is average total cost a minimum?

21. Explain why the gap between ProPainters' total cost and total variable cost is the same no matter how many houses are painted.

22. **For Pepsi, a Business Decision with Social Benefit**

    PepsiCo has done a deal with 300 small Mexican farmers close to their two factories to buy corn at a guaranteed price. PepsiCo saves transportation costs and the use of local farms assures it access to the type of corn best suited to its products and processes. "That gives us great leverage because corn prices don't fluctuate so much, but transportation costs do," said Pedro Padierna, president of PepsiCo in Mexico.

Source: *The New York Times*, February 21, 2011

a. How do fluctuations in the price of corn and in transportation costs influence PepsiCo's short-run cost curves?

b. How does the deal with the farmers to avoid fluctuations in costs benefit PepsiCo?

Long-Run Cost

Use the table in Problem 20 and the following information to work Problems 23 and 24.

If ProPainters doubles the number of students it hires and doubles the amount of equipment it leases, it experiences diseconomies of scale.

23. Explain how the *ATC* curve with one unit of equipment differs from that when ProPainters uses double the amount of equipment.

24. Explain what might be the source of the diseconomies of scale that ProPainters experiences.

Use the following information to work Problems 25 to 27.

The table shows the production function of Bonnie's Balloon Rides. Bonnie's pays $500 a day for each balloon it rents and $25 a day for each balloon operator it hires.

Labor (workers per day)	Output (rides per day)			
	Plant 1	Plant 2	Plant 3	Plant 4
10	6	10	13	15
20	10	15	18	20
30	13	18	22	24
40	15	20	24	26
50	16	21	25	27
Balloons (number)	1	2	3	4

25. Graph the *ATC* curves for Plant 1 and Plant 2. Explain why these *ATC* curves differ.

26. Graph the *ATC* curves for Plant 3 and Plant 4. Explain why these *ATC* curves differ.

27. a. On Bonnie's *LRAC* curve, what is the average cost of producing

    (i) 15 rides a day?

    (ii) 18 rides a day?

    b. Explain how Bonnie's uses its long-run average cost curve to decide how many balloons to rent.

Economics in the News

28. After you have studied *Economics in the News* on pp. 264–265, answer the following questions.

    a. Explain the distinction between the short run and the long run and identify when Starbucks would want to make each type of change.

    b. Explain economies of scale. Does Starbucks reap economies of scale in the example on p. 265?

    c. Draw a graph to illustrate Starbucks' cost curves as it opens more and more cafés in Target stores.

    d. Explain why Starbucks is opening cafés in Target stores rather than stand alone cafés.

29. **Starbucks Unit Brews Up Self-Serve Espresso Bars**

    Coinstar has installed automated, self-serve espresso kiosks in grocery stores. Kiosks cost just under $40,000 each and Coinstar provides maintenance. The self-serve kiosk removes the labor costs of having a barista serve Starbucks' coffee, and store personnel refill the machine.

    Source: MSNBC, June 1, 2008

    a. What is Coinstar's total fixed cost of operating one self-serve kiosk? What are its variable costs of providing coffee at a self-serve kiosk?

    b. Assume that a coffee machine operated by a barista costs less than $40,000. Explain how the fixed costs, variable costs, and total costs of barista-served and self-served coffee differ.

    c. Sketch the marginal cost and average cost curves implied by your answer to part (b).

Use the following news clip to work Problems 30 and 31.

Gap Will Focus on Smaller Scale Stores

Gap has too many stores that are 12,500 square feet. The target store size is 6,000 square feet to 10,000 square feet, so Gap plans to combine previously separate concept stores. Some Gap body, adult, maternity, baby and kids stores will be combined in one store.

Source: CNN, June 10, 2008

30. Thinking of a Gap store as a production plant, explain why Gap is making a decision to reduce the size of its stores. Is Gap's decision a long-run decision or a short-run decision?

31. How might Gap take advantage of economies of scale by combining concept stores into one store?

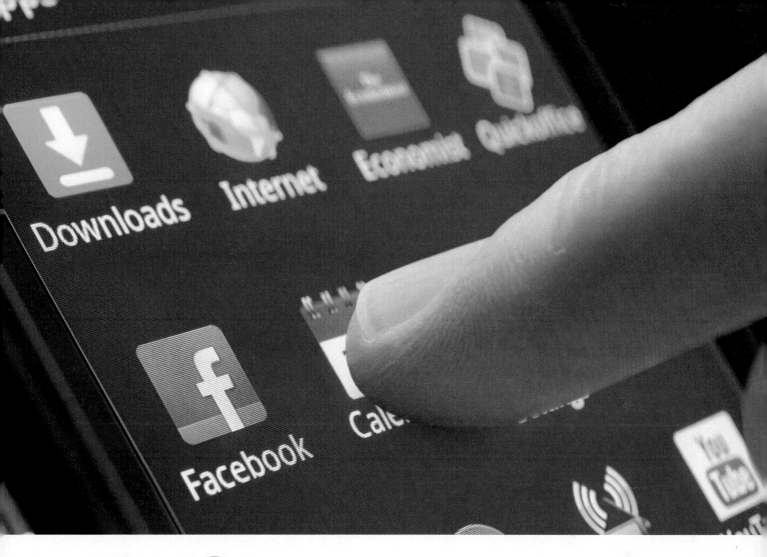

12

PERFECT COMPETITION

After studying this chapter, you will be able to:

◆ Define perfect competition

◆ Explain how a firm makes its output decision

◆ Explain how price and output are determined in perfect competition

◆ Explain why firms enter and leave a market

◆ Predict the effects of technological change in a competitive market

◆ Explain why perfect competition is efficient

A million "apps" have been created for smartphones and tablets. Most of these apps are the work of individuals in intense competition with each other. No single app writer can influence the price of an app, but each writer can and must decide how many hours to work and how many apps to produce.

In this chapter, we study producers who, like small app developers, are in intense competition—in *perfect competition*. At the end of the chapter, in *Economics in the News*, we apply the perfect competition model to the highly competitive market in apps.

◆ What Is Perfect Competition?

The firms that you study in this chapter face the force of raw competition. We call this extreme form of competition perfect competition. **Perfect competition** is a market in which

- Many firms sell identical products to many buyers.
- There are no restrictions on entry into the market.
- Established firms have no advantage over new ones.
- Sellers and buyers are well informed about prices.

Farming, fishing, wood pulping and paper milling, the manufacture of paper cups and shopping bags, grocery and fresh flower retailing, photo finishing, lawn services, plumbing, painting, dry cleaning, and laundry services are all examples of highly competitive industries.

How Perfect Competition Arises

Perfect competition arises if the minimum efficient scale of a single producer is small relative to the market demand for the good or service. In this situation, there is room in the market for many firms. A firm's *minimum efficient scale* is the smallest output at which long-run average cost reaches its lowest level. (See Chapter 11, p. 263.)

In perfect competition, each firm produces a good that has no unique characteristics, so consumers don't care which firm's good they buy.

Price Takers

Firms in perfect competition are price takers. A **price taker** is a firm that cannot influence the market price because its production is an insignificant part of the total market.

Imagine that you are a wheat farmer in Kansas. You have a thousand acres planted—which sounds like a lot. But compared to the millions of acres in Colorado, Oklahoma, Texas, Nebraska, and the Dakotas, as well as the millions more in Canada, Argentina, Australia, and Ukraine, your thousand acres are a drop in the ocean. Nothing makes your wheat any better than any other farmer's, and all the buyers of wheat know the price at which they can do business.

If the market price of wheat is $4 a bushel, then that is the highest price you can get for your wheat. Ask for $4.10 and no one will buy from you. Offer it for $3.90 and you'll be sold out in a flash and have given away 10¢ a bushel. You take the market price.

Economic Profit and Revenue

A firm's goal is to maximize *economic profit*, which is equal to total revenue minus total cost. Total cost is the *opportunity cost* of production, which includes *normal profit*. (See Chapter 10, p. 225.)

A firm's **total revenue** equals the price of its output multiplied by the number of units of output sold (price × quantity). **Marginal revenue** is the change in total revenue that results from a one-unit increase in the quantity sold. Marginal revenue is calculated by dividing the change in total revenue by the change in the quantity sold.

Figure 12.1 illustrates these revenue concepts. In part (a), the market demand curve, *D*, and market supply curve, *S*, determine the market price. The market price is $25 a sweater. Campus Sweaters is just one of many producers of sweaters, so the best it can do is to sell its sweaters for $25 each.

Total Revenue Total revenue is equal to the price multiplied by the quantity sold. In the table in Fig. 12.1, if Campus Sweaters sells 9 sweaters, its total revenue is $225 (9 × $25).

Figure 12.1(b) shows the firm's total revenue curve (*TR*), which graphs the relationship between total revenue and the quantity sold. At point *A* on the *TR* curve, the firm sells 9 sweaters and has a total revenue of $225. Because each additional sweater sold brings in a constant amount—$25—the total revenue curve is an upward-sloping straight line.

Marginal Revenue Marginal revenue is the change in total revenue that results from a one-unit increase in quantity sold. In the table in Fig. 12.1, when the quantity sold increases from 8 to 9 sweaters, total revenue increases from $200 to $225, so marginal revenue is $25 a sweater.

Because the firm in perfect competition is a price taker, the change in total revenue that results from a one-unit increase in the quantity sold equals the market price. *In perfect competition, the firm's marginal revenue equals the market price*. Figure 12.1(c) shows the firm's marginal revenue curve (*MR*) as the horizontal line at the market price.

Demand for the Firm's Product The firm can sell any quantity it chooses at the market price. So the demand curve for the firm's product is a horizontal line at the market price, the same as the firm's marginal revenue curve.

FIGURE 12.1   Demand, Price, and Revenue in Perfect Competition

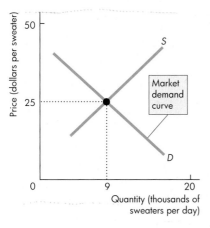

(a) Sweater market

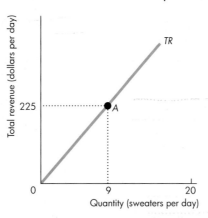

(b) Campus Sweaters' total revenue

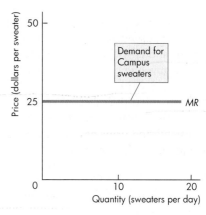

(c) Campus Sweaters' marginal revenue

Quantity sold (Q) (sweaters per day)	Price (P) (dollars per sweater)	Total revenue (TR = P × Q) (dollars)	Marginal revenue (MR = ∆TR/∆Q) (dollars per additional sweater)
8	25	200	
			 25
9	25	225	
			 25
10	25	250	

In part (a), market demand and market supply determine the market price (and quantity). Part (b) shows the firm's total revenue curve (*TR*). Point *A* corresponds to the second row of the table—Campus Sweaters sells 9 sweaters at $25 a sweater, so total revenue is $225. Part (c) shows the firm's marginal revenue curve (*MR*). This curve is also the demand curve for the firm's sweaters. The demand for sweaters from Campus Sweaters is perfectly elastic at the market price of $25 a sweater.

MyEconLab Animation

A horizontal demand curve illustrates a perfectly elastic demand, so the demand for the firm's product is perfectly elastic. A sweater from Campus Sweaters is a *perfect substitute* for a sweater from any other factory. But the *market* demand for sweaters is *not* perfectly elastic: Its elasticity depends on the substitutability of sweaters for other goods and services.

The Firm's Decisions

The goal of the competitive firm is to maximize economic profit, given the constraints it faces. To achieve its goal, a firm must decide

1. How to produce at minimum cost
2. What quantity to produce
3. Whether to enter or exit a market

You've already seen how a firm makes the first decision. It does so by operating with the plant that minimizes long-run average cost—by being on its long-run average cost curve. We'll now see how the firm makes the other two decisions. We start by looking at the firm's output decision.

◆ The Firm's Output Decision

A firm's cost curves (total cost, average cost, and marginal cost) describe the relationship between its output and costs (see Chapter 11, pp. 253–259). And a firm's revenue curves (total revenue and marginal revenue) describe the relationship between its output and revenue (pp. 272–273). From the firm's cost curves and revenue curves, we can find the output that maximizes the firm's economic profit.

Figure 12.2 shows how to do this for Campus Sweaters. The table lists the firm's total revenue and total cost at different outputs, and part (a) of the figure shows the firm's total revenue curve, *TR*, and total cost curve, *TC*. These curves are graphs of

numbers in the first three columns of the table.

Economic profit equals total revenue minus total cost. The fourth column of the table in Fig. 12.2 shows the economic profit made by Campus Sweaters, and part (b) of the figure graphs these numbers as its economic profit curve, *EP*.

Campus Sweaters maximizes its economic profit by producing 9 sweaters a day: Total revenue is $225, total cost is $183, and economic profit is $42. No other output rate achieves a larger profit.

At outputs of less than 4 sweaters and more than 12 sweaters a day, Campus Sweaters would incur an economic loss. At either 4 or 12 sweaters a day, Campus Sweaters would make zero economic profit, called a *break-even point*.

FIGURE 12.2   Total Revenue, Total Cost, and Economic Profit

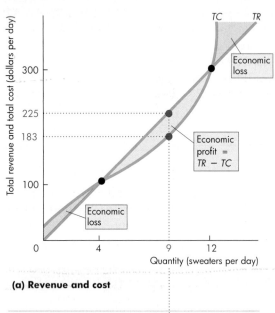

(a) Revenue and cost

(b) Economic profit and loss

Quantity (Q) (sweaters per day)	Total revenue (TR) (dollars)	Total cost (TC) (dollars)	Economic profit (TR − TC) (dollars)
0	0	22	−22
1	25	45	−20
2	50	66	−16
3	75	85	−10
4	100	100	0
5	125	114	11
6	150	126	24
7	175	141	34
8	200	160	40
9	**225**	**183**	**42**
10	250	210	40
11	275	245	30
12	300	300	0
13	325	360	−35

The table lists Campus Sweaters' total revenue, total cost, and economic profit. Part (a) graphs the total revenue and total cost curves, and part (b) graphs economic profit.

Campus Sweaters makes maximum economic profit, $42 a day ($225 − $183), when it produces 9 sweaters a day. At outputs of 4 sweaters and 12 sweaters a day, Campus Sweaters makes zero economic profit—these are break-even points. At an output less than 4 sweaters and greater than 12 sweaters a day, Campus Sweaters incurs an economic loss.

Marginal Analysis and the Supply Decision

Another way to find the profit-maximizing output is to use marginal analysis, which compares marginal revenue, *MR*, with marginal cost, *MC*. As output increases, the firm's marginal revenue is constant but its marginal cost eventually increases.

If marginal revenue exceeds marginal cost (*MR* > *MC*), then the revenue from selling one more unit exceeds the cost of producing it and an increase in output increases economic profit. If marginal revenue is less than marginal cost (*MR* < *MC*), then the revenue from selling one more unit is less than the cost of producing that unit and a *decrease* in output *increases* economic profit. If marginal revenue equals marginal cost (*MR* = *MC*), then the revenue from selling one more unit equals the cost incurred to produce that unit. Economic profit is maximized and either an increase or a decrease in output decreases economic profit.

Figure 12.3 illustrates these propositions. If Campus Sweaters increases its output from 8 sweaters to 9 sweaters a day, marginal revenue ($25) exceeds marginal cost ($23), so by producing the 9th sweater economic profit increases by $2 from $40 to $42 a day. The blue area in the figure shows the increase in economic profit when the firm increases production from 8 to 9 sweaters per day.

If Campus Sweaters increases its output from 9 sweaters to 10 sweaters a day, marginal revenue ($25) is less than marginal cost ($27), so by producing the 10th sweater, economic profit decreases. The last column of the table shows that economic profit decreases from $42 to $40 a day. The red area in the figure shows the economic loss that arises from increasing production from 9 to 10 sweaters a day.

Campus Sweaters maximizes economic profit by producing 9 sweaters a day, the quantity at which marginal revenue equals marginal cost.

A firm's profit-maximizing output is its quantity supplied at the market price. The quantity supplied at a price of $25 a sweater is 9 sweaters a day. If the price were higher than $25 a sweater, the firm would increase production. If the price were lower than $25 a sweater, the firm would decrease production. These profit-maximizing responses to different market prices are the foundation of the law of supply:

> Other things remaining the same, the higher the market price of a good, the greater is the quantity supplied of that good.

FIGURE 12.3 Profit-Maximizing Output

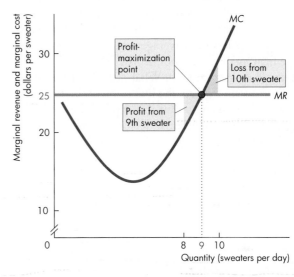

Quantity (Q) (sweaters per day)	Total revenue (TR) (dollars)	Marginal revenue (MR) (dollars per additional sweater)	Total cost (TC) (dollars)	Marginal cost (MC) (dollars per additional sweater)	Economic profit (TR − TC) (dollars)
7	175		141		34
		 25		 19	
8	200		160		40
		 25		 23	
9	225		183		42
		 25		 27	
10	250		210		40
		 25		 35	
11	275		245		30

The firm maximizes profit by producing the output at which marginal revenue equals marginal cost and marginal cost is increasing. The table and figure show that marginal cost equals marginal revenue and economic profit is maximized when Campus Sweaters produces 9 sweaters a day. The table shows that if Campus Sweaters increases output from 8 to 9 sweaters, marginal cost is $23, which is less than the marginal revenue of $25. If output increases from 9 to 10 sweaters, marginal cost is $27, which exceeds the marginal revenue of $25. If marginal revenue exceeds marginal cost, an increase in output increases economic profit. If marginal revenue is less than marginal cost, an increase in output decreases economic profit. If marginal revenue equals marginal cost, economic profit is maximized.

MyEconLab Animation and Draw Graph

Temporary Shutdown Decision

You've seen that a firm maximizes profit by producing the quantity at which marginal revenue (price) equals marginal cost. But suppose that at this quantity, price is less than average total cost. In this case, the firm incurs an economic loss. Maximum profit is a loss (a minimum loss). What does the firm do?

If the firm expects the loss to be permanent, it goes out of business. But if it expects the loss to be temporary, the firm must decide whether to shut down temporarily and produce no output, or to keep producing. To make this decision, the firm compares the loss from shutting down with the loss from producing and takes the action that minimizes its loss.

Loss Comparisons A firm's economic loss equals total fixed cost, *TFC*, plus total variable cost minus total revenue. Total variable cost equals average variable cost, *AVC*, multiplied by the quantity produced, *Q*, and total revenue equals price, *P*, multiplied by the quantity *Q*. So:

$$\text{Economic loss} = TFC + (AVC - P) \times Q.$$

If the firm shuts down, it produces no output ($Q = 0$). The firm has no variable costs and no revenue but it must pay its fixed costs, so its economic loss equals total fixed cost.

If the firm produces, then in addition to its fixed costs, it incurs variable costs. But it also receives revenue. Its economic loss equals total fixed cost—the loss when shut down—plus total variable cost minus total revenue. If total variable cost exceeds total revenue, this loss exceeds total fixed cost and the firm shuts down. Equivalently, if average variable cost *exceeds* price, this loss exceeds total fixed cost and the firm *shuts down*.

The Shutdown Point A firm's **shutdown point** is the price and quantity at which it is indifferent between producing and shutting down. The shutdown point occurs at the price and the quantity at which average variable cost is a minimum. At the shutdown point, the firm is minimizing its loss and its loss equals total fixed cost. If the price falls below minimum average variable cost, the firm shuts down temporarily and continues to incur a loss equal to total fixed cost. At prices above minimum average variable cost but below average total cost, the firm produces the loss-minimizing output and incurs a loss, but a loss that is less than total fixed cost.

Figure 12.4 illustrates the firm's shutdown decision and the shutdown point that we've just described for Campus Sweaters.

The firm's average variable cost curve is *AVC* and the marginal cost curve is *MC*. Average variable cost has a minimum of $17 a sweater when output is 7 sweaters a day. The *MC* curve intersects the *AVC* curve at its minimum. (We explained this relationship in Chapter 11; see pp. 254–255.)

The figure shows the marginal revenue curve *MR* when the price is $17 a sweater, a price equal to min-imum average variable cost. Marginal revenue equals marginal cost at 7 sweaters a day, so this quantity maximizes economic profit (minimizes economic loss). The *ATC* curve shows that the firm's average total cost of producing 7 sweaters a day is $20.14 a sweater. The firm incurs a loss equal to $3.14 a sweater on 7 sweaters a day, so its loss is $22 a day. The table in Fig. 12.2 shows that Campus Sweaters' loss equals its total fixed cost.

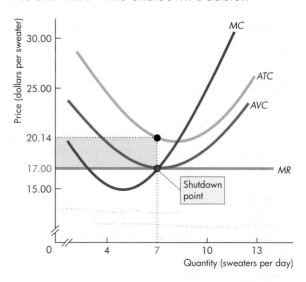

FIGURE 12.4   The Shutdown Decision

The shutdown point is at minimum average variable cost. At a price below minimum average variable cost, the firm shuts down and produces no output. At a price equal to minimum average variable cost, the firm is indifferent between shutting down and producing no output or producing the output at minimum average variable cost. Either way, the firm minimizes its economic loss and incurs a loss equal to total fixed cost.

MyEconLab Animation and Draw Graph

The Firm's Supply Curve

A perfectly competitive firm's supply curve shows how its profit-maximizing output varies as the market price varies, other things remaining the same. The supply curve is derived from the firm's marginal cost curve and average variable cost curves. Figure 12.5 illustrates the derivation of the supply curve.

When the price *exceeds* minimum average variable cost (more than $17), the firm maximizes profit by producing the output at which marginal cost equals price. If the price rises, the firm increases its output—it moves up along its marginal cost curve.

When the price is *less than* minimum average variable cost (less than $17 a sweater), the firm maximizes profit by temporarily shutting down and producing no output. The firm produces zero output at all prices below minimum average variable cost.

When the price *equals* minimum average variable cost, the firm maximizes profit *either* by temporarily shutting down and producing no output *or* by producing the output at which average variable cost is a minimum—the shutdown point, *T*. The firm never produces a quantity between zero and the quantity at the shutdown point *T* (a quantity greater than zero and less than 7 sweaters a day).

The firm's supply curve in Fig. 12.5(b) runs along the *y*-axis from a price of zero to a price equal to minimum average variable cost, jumps to point *T*, and then, as the price rises above minimum average variable cost, follows the marginal cost curve.

◆ REVIEW QUIZ

1 Why does a firm in perfect competition produce the quantity at which marginal cost equals price?

2 What is the lowest price at which a firm produces an output? Explain why.

3 What is the relationship between a firm's supply curve, its marginal cost curve, and its average variable cost curve?

Work these questions in Study Plan 12.2 and get instant feedback. Do a Key Terms Quiz.   MyEconLab

So far, we've studied a single firm in isolation. We've seen that the firm's profit-maximizing decision depends on the market price, which it takes as given. How is the market price determined? Let's find out.

FIGURE 12.5   A Firm's Supply Curve

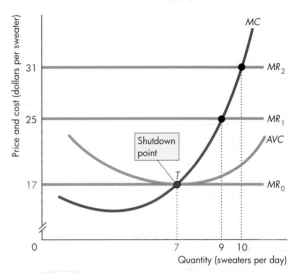

(a) Marginal cost and average variable cost

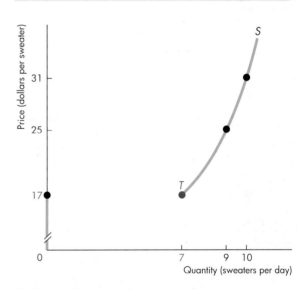

(b) Campus Sweaters' short-run supply curve

Part (a) shows the firm's profit-maximizing output at various market prices. At $25 a sweater, it produces 9 sweaters, and at $17 a sweater, it produces 7 sweaters. At all prices below $17 a sweater, Campus Sweaters produces nothing. Its shutdown point is *T*. Part (b) shows the firm's supply curve—the quantity of sweaters it produces at each price. Its supply curve is made up of the marginal cost curve at all prices above minimum average variable cost and the vertical axis at all prices below minimum average variable cost.

——— MyEconLab Animation and Draw Graph ———

◆ Output, Price, and Profit in the Short Run

To determine the price and quantity in a perfectly competitive market, we need to know how market demand and market supply interact. We start by studying a perfectly competitive market in the short run. The short run is a situation in which the number of firms is fixed.

Market Supply in the Short Run

The **short-run market supply curve** shows the quantity supplied by all the firms in the market at each price when each firm's plant and the number of firms remain the same.

You've seen how an individual firm's supply curve is determined. The market supply curve is derived from the individual supply curves. The quantity supplied by the market at a given price is the sum of the quantities supplied by all the firms in the market at that price.

Figure 12.6 shows the supply curve for the competitive sweater market. In this example, the market consists of 1,000 firms exactly like Campus Sweaters. At each price, the quantity supplied by the market is 1,000 times the quantity supplied by a single firm.

The table in Fig. 12.6 shows the firm's and the market's supply schedules and how the market supply curve is constructed. At prices below $17 a sweater, every firm in the market shuts down; the quantity supplied by the market is zero. At $17 a sweater, each firm is indifferent between shutting down and producing nothing or operating and producing 7 sweaters a day. Some firms will shut down, and others will supply 7 sweaters a day. The quantity supplied by each firm is *either* 0 or 7 sweaters, and the quantity supplied by the market is *between* 0 (all firms shut down) and 7,000 (all firms produce 7 sweaters a day each).

The market supply curve is a graph of the market supply schedules, and the points on the supply curve *A* through *D* represent the rows of the table.

To construct the market supply curve, we sum the quantities supplied by all the firms at each price. Each of the 1,000 firms in the market has a supply schedule like Campus Sweaters. At prices below $17 a sweater, the market supply curve runs along the *y*-axis. At $17 a sweater, the market supply curve is horizontal—supply is perfectly elastic. As the price

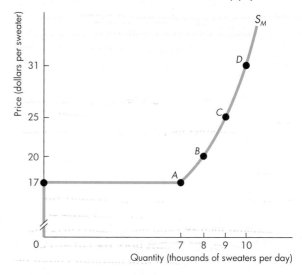

FIGURE 12.6   Short-Run Market Supply Curve

	Price (dollars per sweater)	Quantity supplied by Campus Sweaters (sweaters per day)	Quantity supplied by market (sweaters per day)
A	17	0 or 7	0 to 7,000
B	20	8	8,000
C	25	9	9,000
D	31	10	10,000

The market supply schedule is the sum of the supply schedules of all the individual firms. A market that consists of 1,000 identical firms has a supply schedule similar to that of one firm, but the quantity supplied by the market is 1,000 times as large as that of the one firm (see the table). The market supply curve is S_M. Points *A*, *B*, *C*, and *D* correspond to the rows of the table. At the shutdown price of $17 a sweater, each firm produces either 0 or 7 sweaters a day and the quantity supplied by the market is between 0 and 7,000 sweaters a day. The market supply is perfectly elastic at the shutdown price.

MyEconLab Animation

rises above $17 a sweater, each firm increases its quantity supplied and the quantity supplied by the market increases by 1,000 times that of one firm.

Short-Run Equilibrium

Market demand and short-run market supply determine the market price and market output. Figure 12.7(a) shows a short-run equilibrium. The short-run supply curve, S, is the same as S_M in Fig. 12.6. If the market demand curve is D_1, the market price is $20 a sweater. Each firm takes this price as given and produces its profit-maximizing output, which is 8 sweaters a day. Because the market has 1,000 identical firms, the market output is 8,000 sweaters a day.

A Change in Demand

Changes in demand bring changes to short-run market equilibrium. Figure 12.7(b) shows these changes.

If demand increases and the demand curve shifts rightward to D_2, the market price rises to $25 a sweater. At this price, each firm maximizes profit by increasing its output to 9 sweaters a day. The market output increases to 9,000 sweaters a day.

If demand decreases and the demand curve shifts leftward to D_3, the market price falls to $17. At this price, each firm maximizes profit by decreasing its output. If each firm produces 7 sweaters a day, the market output decreases to 7,000 sweaters a day.

If the demand curve shifts farther leftward than D_3, the market price remains at $17 a sweater because the market supply curve is horizontal at that price. Some firms continue to produce 7 sweaters a day, and others temporarily shut down. Firms are indifferent between these two activities, and whichever they choose, they incur an economic loss equal to total fixed cost. The number of firms continuing to produce is just enough to satisfy the market demand at a price of $17 a sweater.

Profits and Losses in the Short Run

In short-run equilibrium, although the firm produces the profit-maximizing output, it does not necessarily end up making an economic profit. It might do so, but it might alternatively break even or incur an economic loss. Economic profit (or loss) per sweater is price, P, minus average total cost, ATC. So economic profit (or loss) is $(P - ATC) \times Q$. If price

---

FIGURE 12.7   Short-Run Equilibrium

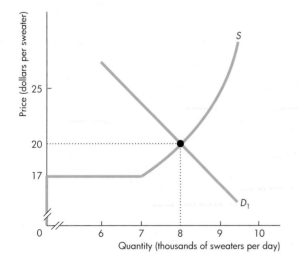

(a) Equilibrium

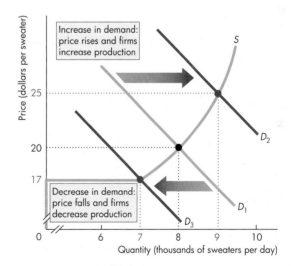

(b) Change in equilibrium

In part (a), the market supply curve is S and the market demand curve is D_1. The market price is $20 a sweater. At this price, each firm produces 8 sweaters a day and the market produces 8,000 sweaters a day.

In part (b), if the market demand increases to D_2, the

price rises to $25 a sweater. Each firm produces 9 sweaters a day and market output is 9,000 sweaters. If market demand decreases to D_3, the price falls to $17 a sweater and each firm decreases its output. If each firm produces 7 sweaters a day, the market output is 7,000 sweaters a day.

equals average total cost, a firm breaks even—the entrepreneur makes normal profit. If price exceeds average total cost, a firm makes an economic profit. If price is less than average total cost, a firm incurs an economic loss. Figure 12.8 shows these three possible short-run profit outcomes for Campus Sweaters. These outcomes correspond to the three different levels of market demand that we've just examined.

Three Possible Short-Run Outcomes

Figure 12.8(a) corresponds to the situation in Fig. 12.7(a) where the market demand is D_1. The equilibrium price of a sweater is $20 and the firm produces 8 sweaters a day. Average total cost is $20 a sweater. Price equals average total cost (ATC), so the firm breaks even (makes zero economic profit).

Figure 12.8(b) corresponds to the situation in Fig. 12.7(b) where the market demand is D_2. The equilibrium price of a sweater is $25 and the firm produces 9 sweaters a day. Here, price exceeds average total cost, so the firm makes an economic profit. Its economic profit is $42 a day, which equals $4.67 per sweater ($25.00 − $20.33) multiplied by 9, the

profit-maximizing number of sweaters produced. The blue rectangle shows this economic profit. The height of that rectangle is profit per sweater, $4.67, and the length is the quantity of sweaters produced, 9 a day. So the area of the rectangle is economic profit of $42 a day.

Figure 12.8(c) corresponds to the situation in Fig. 12.7(b) where the market demand is D_3. The equilibrium price of a sweater is $17. Here, the price is less than average total cost, so the firm incurs an economic loss. Price and marginal revenue are $17 a sweater, and the profit-maximizing (in this case, loss-minimizing) output is 7 sweaters a day. Total revenue is $119 a day (7 × $17). Average total cost is $20.14 a sweater, so the economic loss is $3.14 per sweater ($20.14 − $17.00). This loss per sweater multiplied by the number of sweaters is $22. The red rectangle shows this economic loss. The height of that rectangle is economic loss per sweater, $3.14, and the length is the quantity of sweaters produced, 7 a day. So the area of the rectangle is the firm's economic loss of $22 a day. If the price dips below $17 a sweater, the firm temporarily shuts down and incurs an economic loss equal to total fixed cost.

FIGURE 12.8   Three Short-Run Outcomes for the Firm

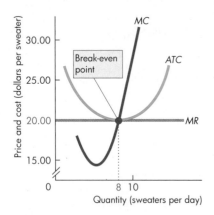

(a) Break even

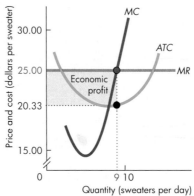

(b) Economic profit

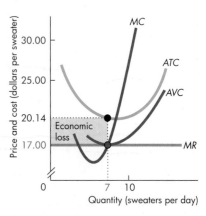

(c) Economic loss

In the short run, the firm might break even (make zero economic profit), make an economic profit, or incur an economic loss. In part (a), the price equals minimum average total cost. At the profit-maximizing output, the firm breaks even and makes zero economic profit. In part (b), the market price is $25 a sweater. At the profit-maximizing output,

the price exceeds average total cost and the firm makes an economic profit, which is equal to the area of the blue rectangle. In part (c), the market price is $17 a sweater. At the profit-maximizing output, the price is below minimum average total cost and the firm incurs an economic loss, which is equal to the area of the red rectangle.

MyEconLab Animation

ECONOMICS IN ACTION

Production Cutback and Temporary Shutdown

The high price of gasoline and anxiety about unemployment and future incomes brought a decrease in the demand for luxury goods including high-end motorcycles such as Harley-Davidsons.

Harley-Davidson's profit-maximizing response to the decrease in demand was to cut production and lay off workers. Some of the production cuts and lay-offs were temporary and some were permanent.

Harley-Davidson's bike production plant in York County, Pennsylvania, was temporarily shut down in the summer of 2008 because total revenue was insufficient to cover total variable cost.

The firm also permanently cut its workforce by 300 people. This permanent cut was like that at Campus Sweaters when the market demand for sweaters decreased from D_1 to D_3 in Fig. 12.7(b).

◆ REVIEW QUIZ

1 How do we derive the short-run market supply curve in perfect competition?
2 In perfect competition, when market demand increases, explain how the price of the good and the output and profit of each firm changes in the short run.
3 In perfect competition, when market demand decreases, explain how the price of the good and the output and profit of each firm changes in the short run.

Work these questions in Study Plan 12.3 and get instant feedback. Do a Key Terms Quiz.   MyEconLab

◆ Output, Price, and Profit in the Long Run

In short-run equilibrium, a firm might make an economic profit, incur an economic loss, or break even. Although each of these three situations is a short-run equilibrium, only one of them is a long-run equilibrium. The reason is that in the long run, firms can enter or exit the market.

Entry and Exit

Entry occurs in a market when new firms come into the market and the number of firms increases. Exit occurs when existing firms leave a market and the number of firms decreases.

Firms respond to economic profit and economic loss by either entering or exiting a market. New firms enter a market in which existing firms are making an economic profit. Firms exit a market in which they are incurring an economic loss. Temporary economic profit and temporary economic loss don't trigger entry and exit. It's the prospect of persistent economic profit or loss that triggers entry and exit.

Entry and exit change the market supply, which influences the market price, the quantity produced by each firm, and its economic profit (or loss).

If firms enter a market, supply increases and the market supply curve shifts rightward. The increase in supply lowers the market price and eventually eliminates economic profit. When economic profit reaches zero, entry stops.

If firms exit a market, supply decreases and the market supply curve shifts leftward. The market price rises and economic loss decreases. Eventually, economic loss is eliminated and exit stops.

To summarize:

- New firms enter a market in which existing firms are making an economic profit.
- As new firms enter a market, the market price falls and the economic profit of each firm decreases.
- Firms exit a market in which they are incurring an economic loss.
- As firms leave a market, the market price rises and the economic loss incurred by the remaining firms decreases.
- Entry and exit stop when firms make zero economic profit.

A Closer Look at Entry

The sweater market has 800 firms with cost curves like those in Fig. 12.9(a). The market demand curve is D, the market supply curve is S_1, and the price is $25 a sweater in Fig. 12.9(b). Each firm produces 9 sweaters a day and makes an economic profit.

This economic profit is a signal for new firms to enter the market. As entry takes place, supply increases and the market supply curve shifts rightward toward S^*. As supply increases with no change in demand, the market price gradually falls from $25 to $20 a sweater. At this lower price, each firm makes zero economic profit and entry stops.

Entry results in an increase in market output, but each firm's output *decreases*. Because the price falls, each firm moves down its supply curve and produces less. Because the number of firms increases, the market produces more.

A Closer Look at Exit

The sweater market has 1,200 firms with cost curves like those in Fig. 12.9(a). The market demand curve is D, the market supply curve is S_2, and the price is $17 a sweater in Fig. 12.9(b). Each firm produces 7 sweaters a day and incurs an economic loss.

This economic loss is a signal for firms to exit the market. As exit takes place, supply decreases and the market supply curve shifts leftward toward S^*. As supply decreases with no change in demand, the market price gradually rises from $17 to $20 a sweater. At this higher price, losses are eliminated, each firm makes zero economic profit, and exit stops.

Exit results in a decrease in market output, but each firm's output *increases*. Because the price rises, each firm moves up its supply curve and produces more. Because the number of firms decreases, the market produces less.

FIGURE 12.9   Entry, Exit, and Long-Run Equilibrium

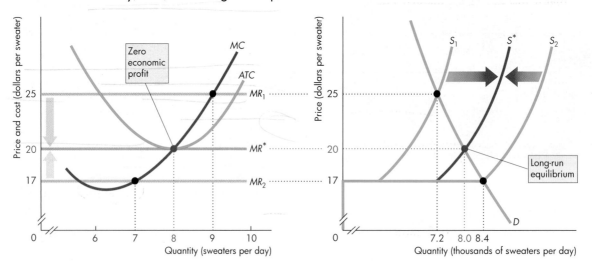

(a) Campus Sweaters

(b) The sweater market

Each firm has cost curves like those of Campus Sweaters in part (a). The market demand curve is D in part (b).

When the market supply curve in part (b) is S_1, the price is $25 a sweater. In part (a), each firm produces 9 sweaters a day and makes an economic profit. Profit triggers the entry of new firms and as new firms enter, the market supply curve shifts rightward, from S_1 toward S^*. The price falls from $25 to $20 a sweater, and the quantity produced increases from 7,200 to 8,000 sweaters. Each firm decreases its output to 8

sweaters a day and its economic profit falls to zero.

When the market supply curve is S_2, the price is $17 a sweater. In part (a), each firm produces 7 sweaters a day and incurs an economic loss. Loss triggers exit and as firms exit, the market supply curve shifts leftward, from S_2 toward S^*. The price rises from $17 to $20 a sweater, and the quantity produced decreases from 8,400 to 8,000 sweaters. Each firm increases its output from 7 to 8 sweaters a day and its economic profit rises to zero.

ECONOMICS IN ACTION

Entry and Exit

An example of entry and falling prices occurred during the 1980s and 1990s in the personal computer market. When IBM introduced its first PC in 1981, IBM had little competition. The price was $7,000 (about $16,850 in today's money) and IBM made a large economic profit selling the new machine.

Observing IBM's huge success, new firms such as Gateway, NEC, Dell, and a host of others entered the market with machines that were technologically identical to IBM's. In fact, they were so similar that they came to be called "clones." The massive wave of entry into the personal computer market increased the market supply and lowered the price. The economic profit for all firms decreased.

Today, a $400 computer is vastly more powerful than its 1981 ancestor that cost 42 times as much.

The same PC market that saw entry during the 1980s and 1990s has seen some exit more recently. In 2001, IBM, the firm that first launched the PC, announced that it was exiting the market. The intense competition from Gateway, NEC, Dell, and others that entered the market following IBM's lead has lowered the price and eliminated the economic profit. So IBM now concentrates on servers and other parts of the computer market.

IBM exited the PC market because it was incurring economic losses. Its exit decreased market supply and made it possible for the remaining firms in the market to make zero economic profit.

International Harvester, a manufacturer of farm equipment, provides another example of exit. For decades, people associated the name "International Harvester" with tractors, combines, and other farm machines. But International Harvester wasn't the only maker of farm equipment. The market became intensely competitive, and the firm began to incur economic losses. Now the firm has a new name, Navistar International, and it doesn't make tractors any more. After years of economic losses and shrinking revenues, it got out of the farm-machine business in 1985 and started to make trucks.

International Harvester exited because it was incurring an economic loss. Its exit decreased supply and made it possible for the remaining firms in the market to break even.

Long-Run Equilibrium

You've now seen how economic profit induces entry, which in turn eliminates the profit. You've also seen how economic loss induces exit, which in turn eliminates the loss.

When economic profit and economic loss have been eliminated and entry and exit have stopped, a competitive market is in *long-run equilibrium.*

You've seen how a competitive market adjusts toward its long-run equilibrium. But a competitive market is rarely *in* a state of long-run equilibrium. Instead, it is constantly and restlessly evolving toward long-run equilibrium. The reason is that the market is constantly bombarded with events that change the constraints that firms face.

Markets are constantly adjusting to keep up with changes in tastes, which change demand, and changes in technology, which change costs.

In the next sections, we're going to see how a competitive market reacts to changing tastes and technology and how the market guides resources to their highest-valued use.

◆ REVIEW QUIZ

1 What triggers entry in a competitive market? Describe the process that ends further entry.
2 What triggers exit in a competitive market? Describe the process that ends further exit.

Work these questions in Study Plan 12.4 and get instant feedback.   MyEconLab

◆ Changes in Demand and Supply as Technology Advances

The arrival of high-speed Internet service increased the demand for personal computers and the demand for music and movie downloads. At the same time, the arrival of these technologies decreased the demand for the retail services of record stores.

What happens in a competitive market when the demand for its product changes? The perfect competition model can answer this question.

An Increase in Demand

Producers of computer components are in long-run equilibrium making zero economic profit when the arrival of the high-speed Internet brings an increase in the demand for computers and the components from which they are built. The equilibrium price of a component rises and producers make economic profits. New firms start to enter the market. Supply

increases and the price stops rising and then begins to fall. Eventually, enough firms have entered for the supply and the increased demand to be in balance at a price that enables the firms in the market to return to zero economic profit—long-run equilibrium.

Figure 12.10 illustrates. In the market in part (a), demand is D_0, supply is S_0, price is P_0, and market output is Q_0. At the firm in part (b), profit is maximized with marginal revenue, MR_0, equal to marginal cost, MC, at output q_0. Economic profit is zero.

Market demand increases and the demand curve shifts rightward to D_1, in Fig. 12.10(a). The price rises to P_1, and the quantity supplied increases from Q_0 to Q_1 as the market moves up along its short-run supply curve S_0. In Fig. 12.10(b), the firm maximizes profit by producing q_1, where marginal revenue MR_1 equals MC. The market is now in short-run equilibrium in which each firm makes an economic profit.

The economic profit brings entry and short-run supply increases—the market supply curve starts to shift rightward. The increase in supply lowers the

---

FIGURE 12.10   An Increase in Demand

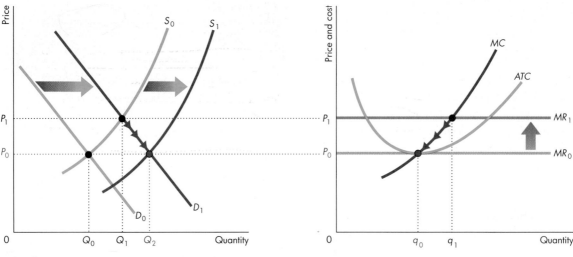

(a) Market

(b) Firm

A market starts out in long-run competitive equilibrium. Part (a) shows the market demand curve D_0, the market supply curve S_0, the market price P_0, and the equilibrium quantity Q_0. Each firm sells its output at the price P_0, so its marginal revenue curve is MR_0 in part (b). Each firm produces q_0 and makes zero economic profit.

Market demand increases from D_0 to D_1 in part (a) and the market price rises to P_1. Each firm maximizes profit by increasing its output to q_1 in part (b), and the market output

increases to Q_1 in part (a). Firms now make economic profits. New firms enter the market, and as they do so, the market supply curve gradually shifts rightward, from S_0 toward S_1. This shift gradually lowers the market price from P_1 back to P_0. While the price is above P_0, firms make economic profits, so new firms keep entering the market. Once the price has returned to P_0, each firm makes zero economic profit and there is no incentive for firms to enter. Each firm produces q_0, and the market output is Q_2.

price and firms decrease output—move down along their marginal cost or supply curve in Fig. 12.10(b).

Eventually, entry shifts the supply curve to S_1 in Fig. 12.10(a). The market price has returned to its original level, P_0. At this price, each firm produces q_0, the same as the quantity produced before the increase in demand. Market output is Q_2 in a long-run equilibrium.

The difference between the initial long-run equilibrium and the new long-run equilibrium is the number of firms in the market. An increase in demand has increased the number of firms. In the

process of moving from the initial equilibrium to the new one, each firm makes an economic profit.

A Decrease in Demand

A *decrease* in demand triggers a similar response to the one you've just studied but in the opposite direction. A decrease in demand brings a lower price, economic losses, and exit. Exit decreases supply, which raises the price to its original level and economic profit returns to zero in a new long-run equilibrium. *Economics in the News* below looks at an example.

ECONOMICS IN THE NEWS

Record Stores Exit

Iconic Central Texas Record Store Set to Close

Bobby Barnard opened Sundance Records & Tapes in San Marcos in 1977. But the customers stopped coming, so in 2012 this oldest continually operating music store in Central Texas closed its doors.

Source: Associated Press, March 28, 2012

THE PROBLEM

Provide a graphical analysis to explain why Sundance exited the market and the effects of exit on the market for record store services.

THE SOLUTION

■ With demand D_0 and supply S_0, Q_0 customers are served at a price P_0 in part (a) of Fig. 1.

■ With marginal revenue MR_0 and marginal cost MC, a record store serves q_0 customers in long-run equilibrium in part (b) of Fig. 1.

■ Demand decreases to D_1, the price falls to P_1, and marginal revenue falls to MR_1. Customers decrease to q_1 (and Q_1) and stores incur economic losses.

■ Faced with economic loss, Sundance and other stores exit and the market supply decreases to S_1.

■ The decrease in supply raises the price and firms remaining return to zero economic profit.

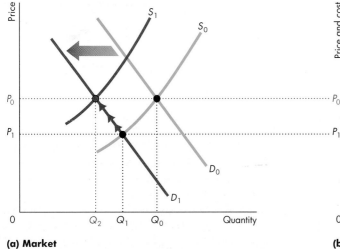

(a) Market

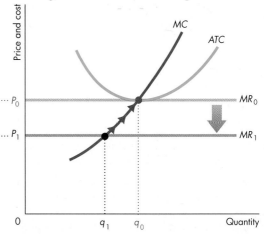

(b) Individual record store

Figure 1 The Market for Record Store Services

MyEconLab More Economics in the News

Technological Advances Change Supply

We've studied the effects of technological change on demand and to isolate those effects we've kept the individual firm's cost curves unchanged. But new technologies also lower production costs. We now study those effects of advancing technology.

Starting from a long-run equilibrium, when a new technology becomes available that lowers production costs, the first firms to use it make economic profit. But as more firms begin to use the new technology, market supply increases and the price falls. At first, new-technology firms continue to make positive economic profits, so more enter. But firms that continue to use the old technology incur economic losses. Why? Initially they were making zero economic profit and now with the lower price they incur economic losses. So old-technology firms exit.

Eventually, all the old-technology firms have exited and enough new-technology firms have entered to increase the market supply to a level that lowers the price to equal the minimum average total cost using the new technology. In this situation, all the firms, all of which are now new-technology firms, are making zero economic profit.

Figure 12.11 illustrates the process that we've just described. Part (a) shows the market demand and supply curves and market equilibrium. Part (b) shows the cost and revenue curves for a firm using the original old technology. Initially these are the only firms. Part (c) shows the cost and revenue curves for a firm using a new technology after it becomes available.

In part (a), the demand curve is D and initially the supply curve is S_0, so the price is P_0 and the equilibrium quantity is Q_0.

In part (b), marginal revenue is MR_0 and each firm produces q_0 where MR_0 equals MC_{Old}. Economic profit is zero and firms are producing at minimum average total cost on the curve ATC_{Old}.

When a new technology becomes available, average total cost and marginal cost of production fall, and firms that use the new technology produce with the average total cost curve ATC_{New} and marginal cost curve MC_{New} in part (c).

When one firm adopts the new technology, it is too small to influence supply, so the price remains at P_0 and the firm makes an economic profit. But economic profit brings entry of new-technology firms. Market supply increases and the price falls.

FIGURE 12.11   A Technological Advance Lowers Production Costs

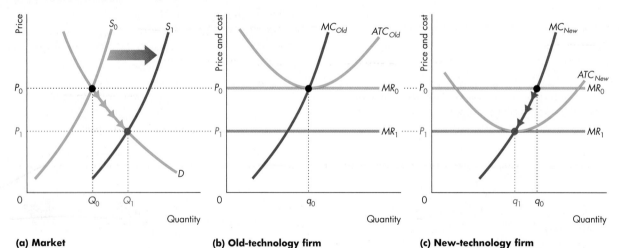

(a) Market   **(b) Old-technology firm**   **(c) New-technology firm**

In part (a), the demand curve is D and initially the supply curve is S_0. The price is P_0 and the equilibrium quantity is Q_0. In part (b), marginal revenue is MR_0 and each firm produces q_0 where MR_0 equals MC_{Old}. Economic profit is zero.

A new technology becomes available with lower costs of ATC_{New} and MC_{New} in part (c). A firm that uses this technology produces q_0 where MR_0 equals MC_{New}.

As more firms use this technology, market supply increases and the price falls. With price below P_0 and above P_1, old-technology firms incur economic losses and exit and new-technology firms make economic profits and new firms enter the market.

In the new long-run equilibrium, the old-technology firms have gone. New-technology firms increase the market supply to S_1. The price falls to P_1, marginal revenue is MR_1, and each firm produces q_1 where MR_1 equals MC_{New}.

ECONOMICS IN THE NEWS

The Falling Cost of Sequencing DNA

Company Announces Low-Cost DNA Decoding Machine

Life Technologies Corp. announced it has developed a $149,000 machine that can decode a person's DNA in a day, at a long-sought price goal of $1,000, making a person's genome useful for medical care.

Source: *USA Today*, January 11, 2012

SOME DATA

The graph shows how the cost of sequencing a person's entire genome has fallen. Life Technologies (in the news clip) is one of around 40 firms competing to develop a machine that can lower that cost from the current $5,000 to $1,000 or less. Many dozens of firms operate DNA sequencing machines and sell their services in a competitive market.

THE QUESTIONS

- What are the competitive markets in the news clip?
- Are any of these markets in long-run equilibrium?
- Are any firms in these markets likely to be making an economic profit?
- Are any of the firms in these markets likely to be incurring an economic loss?
- Are these markets likely to be experiencing entry, exit, or both? If both, which is likely to be greater?
- Who gains from the advances in DNA sequencing technology in the short run and in the long run: producers, or consumers, or both?

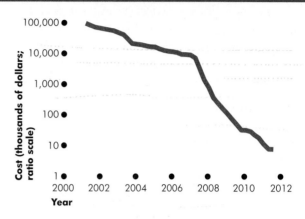

Figure 1 Cost per Genome

Source of data: National Human Genome Research Institute.

THE ANSWERS

- The markets are for DNA sequencing machines and for DNA sequencing services.
- With massive ongoing technological change, neither market is likely to be in long-run equilibrium.
- Firms using the latest technology are likely to be making economic profit.
- Firms using the older technology are likely to be incurring economic loss.
- New-technology firms are entering and old-technology firms are exiting, but with a falling price, there is more entry than exit.
- In the short run, firms gain from higher profit and consumers gain from the lower price. In the long run, economic profit will be zero but consumers will continue to gain from the low price.

MyEconLab More Economics in the News

With price below P_0, old-technology firms incur an economic loss and exit. With price above P_1, new-technology firms make an economic profit and enter. When a new long-run equilibrium is achieved, the old-technology firms have gone. The number of new-technology firms that have entered have shifted the supply curve to S_1. The price is P_1, marginal revenue is MR_1, and each firm in Fig. 12.11(c) produces q_1 using the new technology where MR_1 equals MC_{New}.

Technological change brings only temporary gains to producers. But the lower prices and better products that technological advances bring are permanent gains for consumers.

REVIEW QUIZ

Describe what happens to output, price, and economic profit in the short run and in the long run in a competitive market following

1 An increase in demand
2 A decrease in demand
3 The adoption of a new technology that lowers production costs.

Work these questions in Study Plan 12.5 and get instant feedback.   MyEconLab

◆ Competition and Efficiency

You've seen how firms in perfect competition decide the quantity to produce in the short run and in the long run. You've also seen how these individual decisions determine the market supply that interacts with market demand to determine the equilibrium price and quantity.

We're now going to use what you've learned to gain a deeper understanding of why competition achieves an efficient allocation of resources.

Efficient Use of Resources

Resource use is efficient when we produce the goods and services that people value most highly (see Chapter 2, pp. 35–37, and Chapter 5, p. 112). If it is possible to make someone better off without anyone else becoming worse off, resources are *not* being used efficiently. For example, suppose we produce a computer that no one wants and no one will ever use and, at the same time, some people are clamoring for more video games. If we produce fewer computers and reallocate the unused resources to produce more video games, some people will be better off and no one will be worse off. So the initial resource allocation was inefficient.

We can test whether resources are allocated efficiently by comparing marginal social benefit and marginal social cost. In the computer and video games example, the marginal social benefit of a video game exceeds its marginal social cost; the marginal social cost of a computer exceeds its marginal social benefit. So by producing fewer computers and more video games, we move resources toward a higher-valued use.

Choices, Equilibrium, and Efficiency

We can use what you have learned about the decisions of consumers and firms and equilibrium in a competitive market to describe an efficient use of resources.

Choices Consumers allocate their budgets to get the most value possible out of them. We derive a consumer's demand curve by finding how the best budget allocation changes as the price of a good changes. So consumers get the most value out of their resources at all points along their demand curves. If the people who consume a good or service are the

only ones who benefit from it, then the market demand curve measures the benefit to the entire society and is the marginal social benefit curve.

Competitive firms produce the quantity that maximizes profit. We derive the firm's supply curve by finding the profit-maximizing quantity at each price. So firms get the most value out of their resources at all points along their supply curves. If the firms that produce a good or service bear all the costs of producing it, then the market supply curve measures the marginal cost to the entire society and the market supply curve is the marginal social cost curve.

Equilibrium and Efficiency Resources are used efficiently when marginal social benefit equals marginal social cost. Competitive equilibrium achieves this efficient outcome because, with no externalities, price equals marginal social benefit for consumers, and price equals marginal social cost for producers.

The gains from trade are the sum of consumer surplus and producer surplus. The gains from trade for consumers are measured by *consumer surplus*, which is the area below the demand curve and above the price paid. (See Chapter 5, p. 109.) The gains from trade for producers are measured by *producer surplus*, which is the area above the supply curve and below the price received. (See Chapter 5, p. 111.) The total gains from trade equals *total surplus*—the sum of consumer surplus and producer surplus. When the market for a good or service is in equilibrium, the gains from trade are maximized.

Efficiency in the Sweater Market Figure 12.12 illustrates the efficiency of perfect competition in the sweater market. Part (a) shows the market, and part (b) shows Campus Sweaters.

In part (a), consumers get the most value from their budgets at all points on the market demand curve, $D = MSB$. Producers get the most value from their resources at all points on the market supply curve, $S = MSC$. At the equilibrium quantity and price, marginal social benefit equals marginal social cost, and resources are allocated efficiently. Consumer surplus is the green area, producer surplus is the blue area, and *total surplus* (the sum of producer surplus and consumer surplus) is maximized.

In part (b) Campus Sweaters (and every other firm) makes zero economic profit, and each firm has the plant that enables it to produce at the lowest possible average total cost. Consumers are as well off as

FIGURE 12.12   Efficiency of Perfect Competition

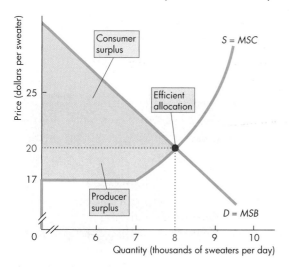

(a) The sweater market

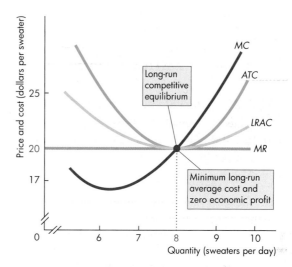

(b) Campus Sweaters

In part (a), market demand, *D*, and market supply, *S*, determine the equilibrium price and quantity. Consumers have made the best available choices on the demand curve, and firms are producing at least cost on the supply curve.

Marginal social benefit, *MSB*, equals marginal social cost, *MSC*, so resources are used efficiently. In part (b), Campus Sweaters produces at the lowest possible long-run average total cost and makes zero economic profit.

MyEconLab Animation and Draw Graph

possible because the good cannot be produced at a lower cost and the equilibrium price equals that least possible cost.

When firms in perfect competition are away from long-run equilibrium, either entry or exit moves the market toward the situation depicted in Fig. 12.12. During this process, the market is efficient because marginal social benefit equals marginal social cost. But it is only in long-run equilibrium that economic profit is driven to zero and consumers pay the lowest feasible price.

◆ You've now completed your study of perfect competition. *Economics in the News* on pp. 290–291 gives you an opportunity to use what you have learned to understand the market for smartphone and tablet computer "apps."

Although many markets approximate the model of perfect competition, many do not. In Chapter 13, we study markets at the opposite extreme of market power: monopoly. Then in the following chapters we'll study markets that lie between perfect competition

and monopoly. In Chapter 14, we study monopolistic competition and in Chapter 15, we study oligopoly. When you have completed this study, you'll have a tool kit that will enable you to understand the variety of real-world markets.

◆ REVIEW QUIZ

1 State the conditions that must be met for resources to be allocated efficiently.
2 Describe the choices that consumers make and explain why consumers are efficient on the market demand curve.
3 Describe the choices that producers make and explain why producers are efficient on the market supply curve.
4 Explain why resources are used efficiently in a competitive market.

Work these questions in Study Plan 12.6 and get instant feedback.   MyEconLab

Perfect Competition in Smart Phone Apps

From Zero to 75 Billion in Six Years

When Apple launched its App Store in July 2008, it had 10 million downloads in the first weekend. That number grew to 100 million in the first two months, 500 million in the first six months, and 1 billion in the first nine months. By mid-2014, downloads hit 75 billion and were growing at 800 apps per second.

At its launch, the store had just 552 apps, but within six months, that number had grown to 15,000 and the pace of growth accelerated. Total apps passed the million mark in October 2013 and hit 1.2 million by mid-2014 and continue to grow at a pace of 25,000 to 30,000 new apps a month.

As the app market grew, so did the number of app developers, which had reached 6.1 million by mid-2013 and 9 million by June 2014.

Developers began to see cash flowing in. Although Apple takes a 30 percent cut, it had paid developers $1 billion by June 2010, $10 billion by June 2013, and $13 billion by June 2014.

Google's app store opened three months later than Apples', but it grew even-more spectacularly to top 1.3 million apps in 2014.

Most apps (62 percent) are free, and of those that are not free the most common price is 99 cents. But one gaming app costs $999.99.

Games represent 18 percent of apps and education another 11 percent.

Sources of information: Sarah Perez, "iTunes App Store Now Has 1.2 Million Apps, Has Seen 75 Billion Downloads to Date," *TechCrunch* June 2, 2014; Chuck Jones, "Apples App Store About To Hit 1 Million Apps," *Forbes*, December 11 2013; apps-world.net, July 11, 2013; and statistica.com, August 28, 2014.

ESSENCE OF THE STORY

- Apple has 1.2 million apps, a number that is growing by 25,000 to 30,000 per month.

- 75 billion apps have been downloaded.

- Nine million people have registered as Apple app developers, up from 6.1 million a year earlier.

- Apple has paid $13 billion to app developers.

- App prices range from zero (for 62 percent of apps) to $999.99, and the most common price is 99 cents.

- Google (Android) apps are also growing and its store offers 1.3 million apps.

MyEconLab More Economics in the News

ECONOMIC ANALYSIS

- The iPhone, iPad, and Android smartphones and tablet computers have created a large demand for apps.

- Although apps are not like corn or sweaters and come in thousands of varieties, the market for apps is highly competitive and we can use the perfect competition model to explain what is happening in that market.

- The market began to operate in 2008, when the first app developers got to work using a software development kit made available by Apple.

- During 2009 through 2014, the number of iPhones and Android smartphones increased dramatically. By the end of 2013, 420 million iPhones and 750 million Android phones had been sold.

- The increase in the number of devices in use increased the demand for apps.

- Thousands of developers, most of them individuals, saw a profit opportunity and got to work creating apps. Their entry into the market increased the supply of apps.

- But the demand for apps kept growing and despite the entry of more developers, profit opportunities remained.

- Figure 1 illustrates the market for apps. In 2013, the demand for apps was D_0 and the supply was S_0. The equilibrium price was P_0 and the quantity was Q_0.

- Figure 2 illustrates the cost and revenue curves of an individual app developer. With marginal revenue MR and marginal cost MC, the developer maximizes profit by producing an app that sells q_0 units.

- Average total cost of an app (on the ATC curve) is less than the price, so the developer makes an economic profit.

- Economic profit brings entry, so in Fig. 1, supply increases in 2014 to S_1. But the demand for apps also keeps increasing and in 2014 the demand curve is D_1.

- The equilibrium quantity increases to Q_1, and this quantity is produced by an increased number of developers—each producing q_0 units and each continuing to make an economic profit.

- The developer's cost curves in Fig. 2 are unchanged, but as development tools improve, development costs will fall and the cost curves will shift downward, which will further increase supply.

- At some future date, market supply will increase by enough to eliminate economic profit and the market for apps will be in long-run equilibrium. That date is unknown but likely to be a long way off.

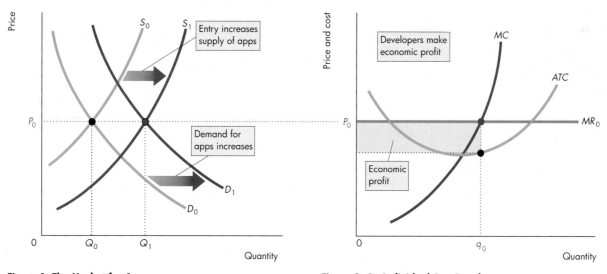

Figure 1 The Market for Apps

Figure 2 An Individual App Developer

SUMMARY

Key Points

What Is Perfect Competition? (pp. 272–273)

- In perfect competition, many firms sell identical products to many buyers; there are no restrictions on entry; sellers and buyers are well informed about prices.
- A perfectly competitive firm is a price taker.
- A perfectly competitive firm's marginal revenue always equals the market price.

Working Problem 1 will give you a better understanding of perfect competition.

The Firm's Output Decision (pp. 274–277)

- The firm produces the output at which marginal revenue (price) equals marginal cost.
- In short-run equilibrium, a firm can make an economic profit, incur an economic loss, or break even.
- If price is less than minimum average variable cost, the firm temporarily shuts down.
- At prices below minimum average variable cost, a firm's supply curve runs along the y-axis; at prices above minimum average variable cost, a firm's supply curve is its marginal cost curve.

Working Problems 2 to 5 will give you a better understanding of a firm's output decision.

Output, Price, and Profit in the Short Run (pp. 278–281)

- The market supply curve shows the sum of the quantities supplied by each firm at each price.
- Market demand and market supply determine price.
- A firm might make a positive economic profit, a zero economic profit, or incur an economic loss.

Working Problem 6 will give you a better understanding of output, price, and profit in the short run.

Output, Price, and Profit in the Long Run (pp. 281–283)

- Economic profit induces entry and economic loss induces exit.
- Entry increases supply and lowers price and profit. Exit decreases supply and raises price and profit.
- In long-run equilibrium, economic profit is zero. There is no entry or exit.

Working Problem 7 will give you a better understanding of output, price, and profit in the long run.

Changes in Demand and Supply as Technology Advances (pp. 284–287)

- A permanent increase in demand leads to a larger market output and a larger number of firms. A permanent decrease in demand leads to a smaller market output and a smaller number of firms.
- New technologies lower the cost of production, increase supply, and in the long run lower the price and increase the quantity.

Working Problem 8 will give you a better understanding of changes in demand and supply as technology advances.

Competition and Efficiency (pp. 288–289)

- Resources are used efficiently when we produce goods and services in the quantities that people value most highly.
- Perfect competition achieves an efficient allocation. In long-run equilibrium, consumers pay the lowest possible price and marginal social benefit equals marginal social cost.

Working Problem 9 will give you a better understanding of competition and efficiency.

Key Terms

MyEconLab Key Terms Quiz

Marginal revenue, 272
Perfect competition, 272
Price taker, 272

Short-run market supply curve, 278
Shutdown point, 276
Total revenue, 272

MyEconLab You can work this problem in Chapter 12 Study Plan.

The table provides data on a market demand schedule (top two rows) and a firm's average and marginal cost schedules (bottom four rows).

Price P ($)	24	20	16	12	8
Quantity	3,000	4,000	5,000	6,000	7,000

Firm's output	1	2	3	4	5
MC ($)	11.00	11.13	12.00	13.63	16.00
ATC ($)	13.50	12.25	12.00	12.19	12.70
AVC ($)	11.25	11.13	11.25	11.63	12.25

Questions

1. What is the firm's shutdown point?
2. If there are 1,000 identical firms in the market, what is the market price and quantity?
3. With 1,000 firms, will firms enter or exit?
4. What is the long-run equilibrium price, quantity, and number of firms?

Solutions

1. The firm will stop producing if the market price falls below minimum *AVC*. In the table, *AVC* is at a minimum of $11.13 when 2 units are produced, so that is the shutdown point.

Key Point: A firm shuts down if the market price is *less* than minimum *AVC*.

2. The first step is to find the market supply schedule. The firm supplies the quantity at which marginal cost equals market price and its supply

curve is its *MC* curve above the shutdown point. The market supply curve is the sum of the 1,000 firms' supply curves. For example, at a price (*MC*) of $12, the quantity supplied is 3,000 units—one point on the supply curve.

The second step is to find the price at which the quantity supplied by 1,000 firms equals quantity demanded. When the price (*MC*) is $16, each firm produces 5 units, so the quantity supplied by the market is 5,000 units. At $16, the quantity demanded is 5,000 units, so the market price is $16 and the quantity is 5,000 units.

Key Point: Each firm supplies the quantity at which marginal cost equals market price.

3. Firms will enter if the price exceeds *ATC* and exit if the price is below *ATC*. In the equilibrium above, *P* is $16 and *ATC* is $12.70, so firms enter.

Key Point: Firms enter when *P > ATC*.

4. In long-run equilibrium, economic profit is zero, so *P = ATC*. Firms maximize profit, so *P = MC*. This outcome occurs at minimum *ATC*. From the table, minimum *ATC* is $12 and the firm's output is 3 units. At $12, 6,000 units are demanded, so firms enter until this quantity is supplied. The number of firms increases to 2,000 (6,000 units divided by 3 units per firm).

Key Point: In long-run equilibrium, economic profit is zero and the market price equals minimum *ATC*.

Key Figure

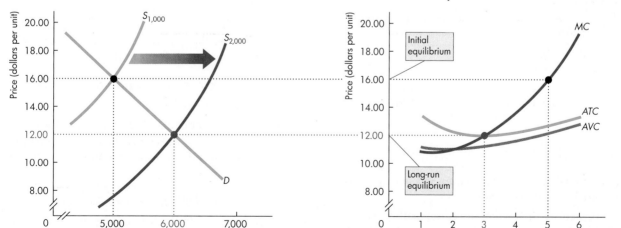

(a) Market

(b) Individual firm

MyEconLab Interactive Animation

STUDY PLAN PROBLEMS AND APPLICATIONS

MyEconLab   You can work Problems 1 to 9 in Chapter 12 Study Plan and get instant feedback.

What Is Perfect Competition? (Study Plan 12.1)

1. Lin's makes fortune cookies. Anyone can make and sell fortune cookies, so there are dozens of producers. All fortune cookies are the same and buyers and sellers know this fact. In what type of market does Lin's operate? What determines the price of fortune cookies? What determines Lin's marginal revenue?

The Firm's Output Decision (Study Plan 12.2)

Use the following table to work Problems 2 to 4. Pat's Pizza Kitchen is a price taker and the table shows its costs of production.

Output (pizzas per hour)	Total cost (dollars per hour)
0	10
1	21
2	30
3	41
4	54
5	69

2. Calculate Pat's profit-maximizing output and economic profit if the market price is (i) $14 a pizza, (ii) $12 a pizza, and (iii) $10 a pizza.

3. What is Pat's shutdown point and what is Pat's economic profit if it shuts down temporarily?

4. Derive Pat's supply curve.

5. The market for paper is perfectly competitive and 1,000 firms produce paper. The table sets out the market demand schedule for paper.

Price (dollars per box)	Quantity demanded (thousands of boxes per week)
3.65	500
5.20	450
6.80	400
8.40	350
10.00	300
11.60	250
13.20	200

The table in the next column sets out the costs of each producer of paper.

Calculate the market price, the market output, the quantity produced by each firm, and the firm's economic profit or loss.

Output (boxes per week)	Marginal cost (dollars per additional box)	Average variable cost	Average total cost
		(dollars per box)	
200	6.40	7.80	12.80
250	7.00	7.00	11.00
300	7.65	7.10	10.43
350	8.40	7.20	10.06
400	10.00	7.50	10.00
450	12.40	8.00	10.22
500	20.70	9.00	11.00

Output, Price, and Profit in the Short Run

(Study Plan 12.3)

6. In Problem 5, the market demand decreases and the demand schedule becomes:

Price (dollars per box)	Quantity demanded (thousands of boxes per week)
2.95	500
4.13	450
5.30	400
6.48	350
7.65	300
8.83	250
10.00	200
11.18	150

If firms have the same costs set out in Problem 5, what is the market price and the firm's economic profit or loss in the short run?

Output, Price, and Profit in the Long Run

(Study Plan 12.5)

7. In Problem 5, in the long run what is the market price and the quantity of paper produced? What is the number of firms in the market?

Changes in Demand and Supply as Technology Advances (Study Plan 12.5)

8. If the market demand for paper remains the same as in Problem 6, calculate the market price, market output, and the economic profit or loss of each firm.

Competition and Efficiency (Study Plan 12.6)

9. In perfect competition in long-run equilibrium, can consumer surplus or producers surplus be increased? Explain your answer.

ADDITIONAL PROBLEMS AND APPLICATIONS

MyEconLab   You can work these problems in MyEconLab if assigned by your instructor.

What Is Perfect Competition?

Use the following news clip to work Problems 10 to 12.

Money in the Tank

Two gas stations stand on opposite sides of the road: Rutter's Farm Store and Sheetz gas station. Rutter's doesn't even have to look across the highway to know when Sheetz changes its price for a gallon of gas. When Sheetz raises the price, Rutter's pumps are busy. When Sheetz lowers prices, there's not a car in sight. Both gas stations survive, but each has no control over the price.

Source: *The Mining Journal*, May 24, 2008

10. In what type of market do these gas stations operate? What determines the price of gasoline and the marginal revenue from gasoline?

11. Describe the elasticity of demand that each of these gas stations faces.

12. Why does each of these gas stations have so little control over the price of the gasoline it sells?

The Firm's Output Decision

13. The figure shows the costs of Quick Copy, one of many copy shops near campus.

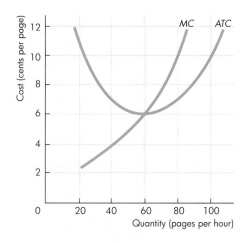

If the market price of copying is 10¢ a page, calculate Quick Copy's
a. Profit-maximizing output
b. Economic profit

14. The market for smoothies is perfectly competitive. The table in the next column sets out the market demand schedule.

Price (dollars per smoothie)	Quantity demanded (smoothies per hour)
1.90	1,000
2.00	950
2.20	800
2.91	700
4.25	550
5.25	400
5.50	300

Each of the 100 producers of smoothies has the following costs when it uses its least-cost plant:

Output (smoothies per hour)	Marginal cost (dollars per additional smoothie)	Average variable cost	Average total cost
		(dollars per smoothie)	
3	2.50	4.00	7.33
4	2.20	3.53	6.03
5	1.90	3.24	5.24
6	2.00	3.00	4.67
7	2.91	2.91	4.34
8	4.25	3.00	4.25
9	8.00	3.33	4.44

a. What is the market price of a smoothie?
b. What is the market quantity of smoothies?
c. How many smoothies does each firm sell?
d. What is the economic profit made or economic loss incurred by each firm?

15. **Chevy Volt Production Temporarily Shut Down**
GM will temporarily lay off 1,300 employees as the company stops production of the electric car, Chevy Volt, for five weeks. GM had hoped to sell 10,000 Volts last year, but ended up selling just 7,671. It plans to maintain inventory levels by adjusting production to match demand.

Source: *Politico*, March 2, 2012

a. Explain how the shutdown decision will affect GM Chevy Volt's *TFC, TVC,* and *TC.*
b. Under what conditions would this shutdown decision maximize Chevy Volt's economic profit (or minimize its loss)? Explain your answer.
c. Under what conditions will GM start producing the Chevy Volt again? Explain your answer.

Output, Price, and Profit in the Short Run

16. **Big Drops in Prices for Crops Make It Tough Down on the Farm**

    Grain prices have fallen roughly 50 percent from earlier this year. With better-than-expected crop yields, world grain production this year will rise 5 percent from 2007 to a record high.

    Source: *USA Today*, October 23, 2008

    Why did grain prices fall in 2008? Draw a graph to show that short-run effect on an individual farmer's economic profit.

Output, Price, and Profit in the Long Run

17. In Problem 14, do firms enter or exit the market for smoothies in the long run? What is the market price and the equilibrium quantity in the long run?

18. In Problem 15, under what conditions would GM stop producing the Chevy Volt and exit the market for electric cars? Explain your answer.

19. **Exxon Mobil Selling All Its Retail Gas Stations**

    Exxon Mobil is not alone among Big Oil exiting the retail gas business, a market where profits have gotten tougher as crude oil prices have risen. Gas station owners say they're struggling to turn a profit because while wholesale gasoline prices have risen sharply, they've been unable to raise pump prices fast enough to keep pace.

    Source: *Houston Chronicle*, June 12, 2008

    a. Is Exxon Mobil making a shutdown or exit decision in the retail gasoline market?

    b. Under what conditions will this decision maximize Exxon Mobil's economic profit?

    c. How might Exxon Mobil's decision affect the economic profit of other gasoline retailers?

Changes in Demand and Supply as Technology Advances

20. **Another DVD Format, but It's Cheaper**

    New Medium Enterprises claims that its new system, HD VMD, is equal to Blu-ray's but at $199 it's cheaper than the $300 Blu-ray player. The Blu-ray Disc Association says New Medium will fail because it believes that Blu-ray technology will always be more expensive. But mass production will cut the cost of a Blu-ray player to $90.

    Source: *The New York Times*, March 10, 2008

    a. Explain how technological change in Blu-ray production might support the prediction of lower prices in the long run. Illustrate your explanation with a graph.

    b. Even if Blu-ray prices do drop to $90 in the long run, why might the HD VMD still end up being less expensive at that time?

Competition and Efficiency

21. In a perfectly competitive market, each firm maximizes its profit by choosing only the quantity to produce. Regardless of whether the firm makes an economic profit or incurs an economic loss, the short-run equilibrium is efficient. Is the statement true? Explain why or why not.

Economics in the News

22. After you have studied *Economics in the News* on pp. 290–291, answer the following questions.

    a. What are the features of the market for apps that make it competitive?

    b. Does the information provided in the news article suggest that the app market is in long-run equilibrium? Explain why or why not.

    c. How would an advance in development technology that lowered a developer's costs change the market supply and the developer's marginal revenue, marginal cost, average total cost, and economic profit?

    d. Illustrate your answer to part (c) with an appropriate graphical analysis.

23. **Smartphones: 2.6 Billion and Rising**

    Smartphone subscriptions increased by 40 percent in 2013 to reach 2.6 billion. This number is expected to rise to 5.6 billion by 2019. Emerging markets, especially China and India, provide most of the growth as many people buy their first smartphone.

    Source: CNET News, November 11, 2013

    a. Explain the effects of the increase in global demand for smartphones on the market for smartphones and on an individual smartphone producer in the short run.

    b. Draw a graph to illustrate your explanation in part (a).

    c. Explain the long-run effects of the increase in global demand for smartphones on the market for smartphones.

13

MONOPOLY

After studying this chapter, you will be able to:

- ◆ Explain how monopoly arises
- ◆ Explain how a single-price monopoly determines its output and price
- ◆ Compare the performance and efficiency of single-price monopoly and competition
- ◆ Explain how price discrimination increases profit
- ◆ Explain how monopoly regulation influences output, price, economic profit, and efficiency

Google and Microsoft are big players in the markets for Web search and advertising and for computer operating systems, markets that are obviously not perfectly competitive.

In this chapter, we study markets dominated by one big firm. We call such a market monopoly. We study the performance and the efficiency of monopoly and compare it with perfect competition.

In *Economics in the News* at the end of the chapter, we look at the remarkable success of Google and ask whether Google is serving the social interest or violating U.S. and European antitrust laws.

◆ Monopoly and How It Arises

A **monopoly** is a market with a single firm that produces a good or service with no close substitutes and that is protected by a barrier that prevents other firms from entering that market.

How Monopoly Arises

Monopoly arises for two key reasons:

- No close substitutes
- Barrier to entry

No Close Substitutes If a good has a close substitute, even though only one firm produces it, that firm effectively faces competition from the producers of the substitute. A monopoly sells a good or service that has no good substitutes. Tap water and bottled water are close substitutes for drinking, but tap water has no effective substitutes for showering or washing a car and a local public utility that supplies tap water is a monopoly.

Barrier to Entry A constraint that protects a firm from potential competitors is called a **barrier to entry.** There are three types of barrier to entry:

- Natural
- Ownership
- Legal

Natural Barrier to Entry A natural barrier to entry creates a **natural monopoly**: a market in which economies of scale enable one firm to supply the entire market at the lowest possible cost. The firms that deliver gas, water, and electricity to our homes are examples of natural monopoly.

Figure 13.1 illustrates a natural monopoly. The market demand curve for electric power is *D*, and the long-run average cost curve is *LRAC*. Economies of scale prevail over the entire length of the *LRAC* curve. At a price of 5 cents per kilowatt-hour, the quantity demanded is 4 million kilowatt-hours and one firm can produce that quantity at a cost of 5 cents per kilowatt-hour. If two firms shared the market equally, it would cost each of them 10 cents per kilowatt-hour to produce a total of 4 million kilowatt-hours.

Ownership Barrier to Entry An ownership barrier to entry occurs if one firm owns a significant portion of a key resource. An example of this type of monopoly occurred during the last century when De Beers

FIGURE 13.1   Natural Monopoly

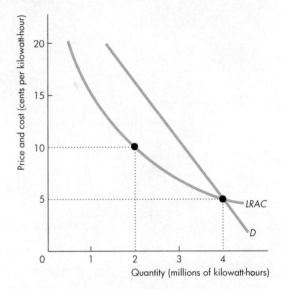

The market demand curve for electric power is *D*, and the long-run average cost curve is *LRAC*. Economies of scale exist over the entire *LRAC* curve. One firm can distribute 4 million kilowatt-hours at a cost of 5 cents a kilowatt-hour. This same total output costs 10 cents a kilowatt-hour with two firms. One firm can meet the market demand at a lower cost than two or more firms can. The market is a natural monopoly.

—— MyEconLab Animation ——

controlled up to 90 percent of the world's supply of diamonds. (Today, its share is only 65 percent.)

Legal Barrier to Entry A legal barrier to entry creates a **legal monopoly**: a market in which competition and entry are restricted by the granting of a public franchise, government license, patent, or copyright.

A *public franchise* is an exclusive right granted to a firm to supply a good or service. An example is the U.S. Postal Service, which has the exclusive right to carry first-class mail. A *government license* controls entry into particular occupations, professions, and industries. Examples of this type of barrier to entry occur in medicine, law, dentistry, schoolteaching, architecture, and many other professional services. Licensing does not always create a monopoly, but it does restrict competition.

A *patent* is an exclusive right granted to the inventor of a product or service. A *copyright* is an exclusive right granted to the author or composer of a literary, musical, dramatic, or artistic work. Patents and copyrights are valid for a limited time period that varies from country to country. In the United States, a patent is valid for 20 years. Patents encourage the *invention* of new products and production methods. They also stimulate *innovation*—the use of new inventions—by encouraging inventors to publicize their discoveries and offer them for use under license. Patents have stimulated innovations in areas as diverse as soybean seeds, pharmaceuticals, memory chips, and video games.

ECONOMICS IN ACTION

Information-Age Monopolies

Information-age technologies have created three big natural monopolies—firms with large plant costs but almost zero marginal cost, so they experience economies of scale.

These firms are Microsoft, Google, and Facebook. The operating system of 87 percent of personal computers is some version of Windows; Google performs 67 percent of Internet searches and 58 percent of Web browsing is done using Chrome; and Facebook has a 50 percent share of the social media market.

These same information-age technologies have also destroyed monopolies. FedEx, UPS, the fax machine, and e-mail have weakened the monopoly of the U.S. Postal Service; and the satellite dish has weakened cable television monopolies.

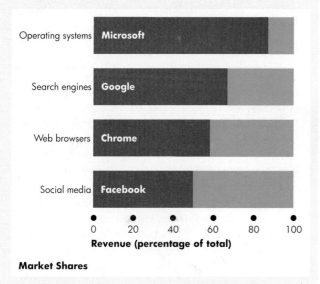

Market Shares

Monopoly Price-Setting Strategies

A major difference between monopoly and competition is that a monopoly sets its own price. In doing so, the monopoly faces a market constraint: To sell a larger quantity, the monopoly must set a lower price. There are two monopoly situations that create two pricing strategies:

- Single price
- Price discrimination

Single Price A **single-price monopoly** is a firm that must sell each unit of its output for the same price to all its customers. De Beers sells diamonds (of a given size and quality) for the same price to all its customers. If it tried to sell at a low price to some customers and at a higher price to others, only the low-price customers would buy from De Beers. Others would buy from De Beers' low-price customers. De Beers is a *single-price* monopoly.

Price Discrimination When a firm practices **price discrimination**, it sells different units of a good or service for different prices. Many firms price discriminate. Microsoft sells its Windows and Office software at different prices to different buyers. Computer manufacturers who install the software on new machines, students and teachers, governments, and businesses all pay different prices. Pizza producers offer a second pizza for a lower price than the first one. These are examples of *price discrimination*.

When a firm price discriminates, it looks as though it is doing its customers a favor. In fact, it is charging the highest possible price for each unit sold and making the largest possible profit.

◆ REVIEW QUIZ

1 How does monopoly arise?
2 How does a natural monopoly differ from a legal monopoly?
3 Distinguish between a price-discriminating monopoly and a single-price monopoly.

Work these questions in Study Plan 13.1 and get instant feedback. Do a Key Terms Quiz.   MyEconLab

We start with a single-price monopoly and see how it makes its decisions about the quantity to produce and the price to charge to maximize its profit.

◆ A Single-Price Monopoly's Output and Price Decision

To understand how a single-price monopoly makes its output and price decision, we must first study the link between price and marginal revenue.

Price and Marginal Revenue

Because in a monopoly there is only one firm, the demand curve facing the firm is the market demand curve. Let's look at Bobbie's Barbershop, the sole supplier of haircuts in Cairo, Nebraska. The table in Fig. 13.2 shows the market demand schedule. At a price of $20, Bobbie sells no haircuts. The lower the price, the more haircuts per hour she can sell. For example, at $12, consumers demand 4 haircuts per hour (row E).

Total revenue (TR) is the price (P) multiplied by the quantity sold (Q). For example, in row D, Bobbie sells 3 haircuts at $14 each, so total revenue is $42. Marginal revenue ($MR$) is the change in total revenue (ΔTR) resulting from a one-unit increase in the quantity sold. For example, if the price falls from $16 (row C) to $14 (row D), the quantity sold increases from 2 to 3 haircuts. Total revenue increases from $32 to $42, so the change in total revenue is $10. Because the quantity sold increases by 1 haircut, marginal revenue equals the change in total revenue and is $10. Marginal revenue is placed between the two rows to emphasize that marginal revenue relates to the *change* in the quantity sold.

Figure 13.2 shows the market demand curve and marginal revenue curve (MR) and also illustrates the calculation we've just made. Notice that at each level of output, marginal revenue is less than price—the marginal revenue curve lies *below* the demand curve.

Why is marginal revenue *less* than price? It is because when the price is lowered to sell one more unit, two opposing forces affect total revenue. The lower price results in a revenue loss on the original units sold and a revenue gain on the increased quantity sold. For example, at a price of $16 a haircut, Bobbie sells 2 haircuts (point C). If she lowers the price to $14, she sells 3 haircuts and has a revenue gain of $14 on the third haircut. But she now receives only $14 on each of the first 2 haircuts—$2 less than before. As a result, she loses $4 of revenue on the first 2 haircuts. To calculate marginal revenue, she must deduct this amount from the revenue gain of $14. So marginal revenue is $10, which is less than the price.

FIGURE 13.2   Demand and Marginal Revenue

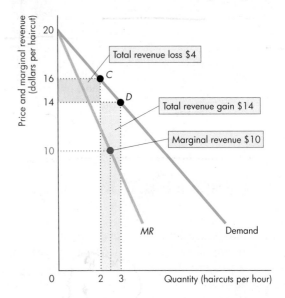

	Price (P) (dollars per haircut)	Quantity demanded (Q) (haircuts per hour)	Total revenue (TR = P × Q) (dollars)	Marginal revenue (MR = ΔTR/ΔQ) (dollars per haircut)
A	20	0	0	
				 18
B	18	1	18	
				 14
C	16	2	32	
				 10
D	14	3	42	
				 6
E	12	4	48	
				 2
F	10	5	50	

The table shows the demand schedule. Total revenue (*TR*) is price multiplied by quantity sold. For example, in row *C*, the price is $16 a haircut, Bobbie sells 2 haircuts, and total revenue is $32. Marginal revenue (*MR*) is the change in total revenue that results from a one-unit increase in the quantity sold. For example, when the price falls from $16 to $14 a haircut, the quantity sold increases from 2 to 3, an increase of 1 haircut, and total revenue increases by $10. Marginal revenue is $10. The demand curve and the marginal revenue curve, *MR*, are based on the numbers in the table and illustrate the calculation of marginal revenue when the price falls from $16 to $14 a haircut.

MyEconLab Animation and Draw Graph

Marginal Revenue and Elasticity

A single-price monopoly's marginal revenue is related to the *elasticity of demand* for its good. The demand for a good can be *elastic* (the elasticity is greater than 1), *inelastic* (the elasticity is less than 1), or *unit elastic* (the elasticity is equal to 1). Demand is *elastic* if a 1 percent fall in the price brings a greater than 1 percent increase in the quantity demanded. Demand is *inelastic* if a 1 percent fall in the price brings a less than 1 percent increase in the quantity demanded. Demand is *unit elastic* if a 1 percent fall in the price brings a 1 percent increase in the quantity demanded. (See Chapter 4, pp. 84–86.)

If demand is elastic, a fall in the price brings an increase in total revenue—the revenue gain from the increase in quantity sold outweighs the revenue loss from the lower price—and marginal revenue is *positive*. If demand is inelastic, a fall in the price brings a decrease in total revenue—the revenue gain from the increase in quantity sold is outweighed by the revenue loss from the lower price—and marginal revenue is *negative*. If demand is unit elastic, total revenue does not change—the revenue gain from the increase in the quantity sold offsets the revenue loss from the lower price—and marginal revenue is *zero*. (See Chapter 4, p. 88.)

Figure 13.3 illustrates the relationship between marginal revenue, total revenue, and elasticity. As the price gradually falls from $20 to $10 a haircut, the quantity demanded increases from 0 to 5 haircuts an hour. Over this output range, marginal revenue is positive in part (a), total revenue increases in part (b), and the demand for haircuts is elastic. As the price falls from $10 to $0 a haircut, the quantity of haircuts demanded increases from 5 to 10 an hour. Over this output range, marginal revenue is negative in part (a), total revenue decreases in part (b), and the demand for haircuts is inelastic. When the price is $10 a haircut, marginal revenue is zero in part (a), total revenue is at a maximum in part (b), and the demand for haircuts is unit elastic.

In Monopoly, Demand Is Always Elastic

The relationship between marginal revenue and elasticity of demand that you've just discovered implies that a profit-maximizing monopoly never produces an output in the inelastic range of the market demand curve. If it did so, it could charge a higher price, produce a smaller quantity, and increase its profit. Let's now look at a monopoly's price and output decision.

FIGURE 13.3   Marginal Revenue and Elasticity

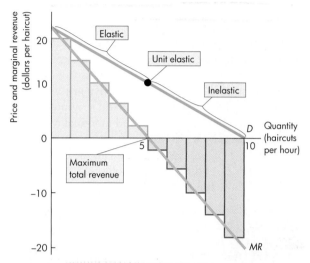

(a) Demand and marginal revenue curves

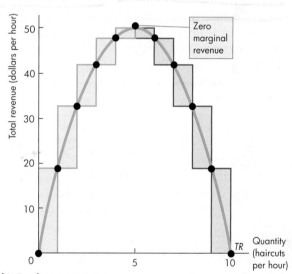

(b) Total revenue curve

In part (a), the demand curve is *D* and the marginal revenue curve is *MR*. In part (b), the total revenue curve is *TR*. Over the range 0 to 5 haircuts an hour, a price cut increases total revenue, so marginal revenue is positive—as shown by the blue bars. Demand is elastic. Over the range 5 to 10 haircuts an hour, a price cut decreases total revenue, so marginal revenue is negative—as shown by the red bars. Demand is inelastic. At 5 haircuts an hour, total revenue is maximized and marginal revenue is zero. Demand is unit elastic.

MyEconLab Animation

Price and Output Decision

A monopoly sets its price and output at the levels that maximize economic profit. To determine this price and output level, we need to study the behavior of both cost and revenue as output varies. A monopoly faces the same types of technology and cost constraints as a competitive firm, so its costs (total cost, average cost, and marginal cost) behave just like those of a firm in perfect competition. And a monopoly's revenues (total revenue, price, and marginal revenue) behave in the way we've just described.

Table 13.1 provides information about Bobbie's costs, revenues, and economic profit, and Fig. 13.4 shows the same information graphically.

Maximizing Economic Profit You can see in Table 13.1 and Fig. 13.4(a) that total cost (*TC*) and total revenue (*TR*) both rise as output increases, but *TC* rises at an increasing rate and *TR* rises at a decreasing rate. Economic profit, which equals *TR* minus *TC*, increases at small output levels, reaches a maximum, and then decreases. The maximum profit ($12) occurs when Bobbie sells 3 haircuts for $14 each. If she sells 2 haircuts for $16 each or 4 haircuts for $12 each, her economic profit will be only $8.

Marginal Revenue Equals Marginal Cost You can see Bobbie's marginal revenue (*MR*) and marginal cost (*MC*) in Table 13.1 and Fig. 13.4(b).

When Bobbie increases output from 2 to 3 haircuts, *MR* is $10 and *MC* is $6. *MR* exceeds *MC* by $4 and Bobbie's profit increases by that amount. If Bobbie increases output yet further, from 3 to 4 haircuts, *MR* is $6 and *MC* is $10. In this case, *MC* exceeds *MR* by $4, so profit decreases by that amount. When *MR* exceeds *MC*, profit increases if output increases. When *MC* exceeds *MR*, profit increases if output *decreases*. When *MC* equals *MR*, profit is maximized.

Figure 13.4(b) shows the maximum profit as price (on the demand curve *D*) minus average total cost (on the *ATC* curve) multiplied by the quantity produced—the blue rectangle.

Maximum Price the Market Will Bear Unlike a firm in perfect competition, a monopoly influences the price of what it sells. But a monopoly doesn't set the price at the maximum *possible* price. At the maximum possible price, the firm would be able to sell only one unit of output, which in general is less than the profit-maximizing quantity. Rather, a monopoly produces the profit-maximizing quantity and sells that quantity for the highest price it can get.

TABLE 13.1 A Monopoly's Output and Price Decision

Price (P) (dollars per haircut)	Quantity demanded (Q) (haircuts per hour)	Total revenue (TR = P × Q) (dollars)	Marginal revenue (MR = ΔTR/ΔQ) (dollars per haircut)	Total cost (TC) (dollars)	Marginal cost (MC = ΔTC/ΔQ) (dollars per haircut)	Profit (TR − TC) (dollars)
20	0	0		20		−20
			18		1	
18	1	18		21		−3
			14		3	
16	2	32		24		+8
			10		6	
14	3	42		30		+12
			6		10	
12	4	48		40		+8
			2		15	
10	5	50		55		−5

This table gives the information needed to find the profit-maximizing output and price. Total revenue (TR) equals price multiplied by the quantity sold. Profit equals total revenue minus total cost (TC). Profit is maximized when 3 haircuts are sold at a price of $14 each. Total revenue is $42, total cost is $30, and economic profit is $12 ($42 − $30).

FIGURE 13.4   A Monopoly's Output and Price

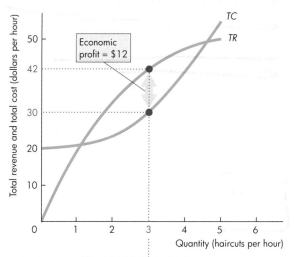

(a) Total revenue and total cost curves

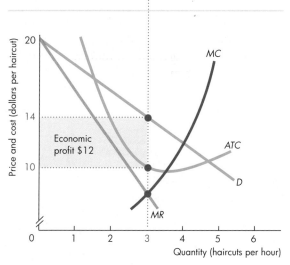

(b) Demand and marginal revenue and cost curves

In part (a), economic profit is the vertical distance equal to total revenue (*TR*) minus total cost (*TC*) and it is maximized at 3 haircuts an hour.

In part (b), economic profit is maximized when marginal cost (*MC*) equals marginal revenue (*MR*). The profit-maximizing output is 3 haircuts an hour. The price is determined by the demand curve (*D*) and is $14 a haircut. The average total cost of a haircut is $10, so economic profit, the blue rectangle, is $12—the profit per haircut ($4) multiplied by 3 haircuts.

MyEconLab *Animation and Draw Graph*

All firms maximize profit by producing the output at which marginal revenue equals marginal cost. For a competitive firm, price equals marginal revenue, so price also equals marginal cost. For a monopoly, price exceeds marginal revenue, so price also exceeds marginal cost.

A monopoly charges a price that exceeds marginal cost, but does it always make an economic profit? In Fig. 13.4(b), Bobbie produces 3 haircuts an hour. Her average total cost is $10 (on the *ATC* curve) and her price is $14 (on the *D* curve), so her profit per haircut is $4 ($14 minus $10). Bobbie's economic profit is shown by the area of the blue rectangle, which equals the profit per haircut ($4) multiplied by the number of haircuts (3), for a total of $12.

If firms in a perfectly competitive market make a positive economic profit, new firms enter. That does *not* happen in monopoly. Barriers to entry prevent new firms from entering the market, so a monopoly can make a positive economic profit and might continue to do so indefinitely. Sometimes that economic profit is large, as in the international diamond business.

Bobbie makes a positive economic profit. But suppose that Bobbie's landlord increases the rent on her salon. If Bobbie pays an additional $12 an hour for rent, her fixed cost increases by $12 an hour. Her marginal cost and marginal revenue don't change, so her profit-maximizing output remains at 3 haircuts an hour. Her profit decreases by $12 an hour to zero. If Bobbie's salon rent increases by more than $12 an hour, she incurs an economic loss. If this situation were permanent, Bobbie would go out of business.

◆ REVIEW QUIZ

1 What is the relationship between marginal cost and marginal revenue when a single-price monopoly maximizes profit?

2 How does a single-price monopoly determine the price it will charge its customers?

3 What is the relationship between price, marginal revenue, and marginal cost when a single-price monopoly is maximizing profit?

4 Why can a monopoly make a positive economic profit even in the long run?

Work these questions in Study Plan 13.2 and get instant feedback.   MyEconLab

◆ Single-Price Monopoly and Competition Compared

Imagine a market that is made up of many small firms operating in perfect competition. Then imagine that a single firm buys out all these small firms and creates a monopoly.

What will happen in this market? Will the price rise or fall? Will the quantity produced increase or decrease? Will economic profit increase or decrease? Will either the original competitive situation or the new monopoly situation be efficient?

These are the questions we're now going to answer. First, we look at the effects of monopoly on the price and quantity produced. Then we turn to the questions about efficiency.

Comparing Price and Output

Figure 13.5 shows the market we'll study. The market demand curve is D. The demand curve is the same regardless of how the industry is organized. But the supply side and the equilibrium are different in monopoly and competition. First, let's look at the case of perfect competition.

Perfect Competition Initially, with many small perfectly competitive firms in the market, the market supply curve is S. This supply curve is obtained by summing the supply curves of all the individual firms in the market.

In perfect competition, equilibrium occurs where the supply curve and the demand curve intersect. The price is P_C, and the quantity produced by the industry is Q_C. Each firm takes the price P_C and maximizes its profit by producing the output at which its own marginal cost equals the price. Because each firm is a small part of the total industry, there is no incentive for any firm to try to manipulate the price by varying its output.

Monopoly Now suppose that this industry is taken over by a single firm. Consumers do not change, so the market demand curve remains the same as in the case of perfect competition. But now the monopoly recognizes this demand curve as a constraint on the price at which it can sell its output. The monopoly's marginal revenue curve is MR.

The monopoly maximizes profit by producing the quantity at which marginal revenue equals marginal cost. To find the monopoly's marginal cost curve, first

recall that in perfect competition, the market supply curve is the sum of the supply curves of the firms in the industry. Also recall that each firm's supply curve is its marginal cost curve (see Chapter 12, p. 277). So when the market is taken over by a single firm, the competitive market's supply curve becomes the monopoly's marginal cost curve. To remind you of this fact, the supply curve is also labeled MC.

The output at which marginal revenue equals marginal cost is Q_M. This output is smaller than the competitive output Q_C. And the monopoly charges the price P_M, which is higher than P_C. We have established that

> Compared to a perfectly competitive market, a single-price monopoly produces a smaller output and charges a higher price.

We've seen how the output and price of a monopoly compare with those in a competitive market. Let's now compare the efficiency of the two types of market.

FIGURE 13.5 Monopoly's Smaller Output and Higher Price

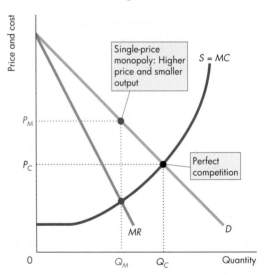

A competitive market produces the quantity Q_C at price P_C. A single-price monopoly produces the quantity Q_M at which marginal revenue equals marginal cost and sells that quantity for the price P_M. Compared to perfect competition, a single-price monopoly produces a smaller output and charges a higher price.

MyEconLab Animation

Efficiency Comparison

Perfect competition (with no externalities) is efficient. Figure 13.6(a) illustrates the efficiency of perfect competition and serves as a benchmark against which to measure the inefficiency of monopoly. Along the demand and marginal social benefit curve ($D = MSB$), consumers are efficient. Along the supply curve and marginal social cost curve ($S = MSC$), producers are efficient. In competitive equilibrium, the price is P_C, the quantity is Q_C, and marginal social benefit equals marginal social cost.

Consumer surplus is the green triangle under the demand curve and above the equilibrium price (see Chapter 5, p. 109). *Producer surplus* is the blue area above the supply curve and below the equilibrium price (see Chapter 5, p. 111). Total surplus (consumer surplus and producer surplus) is maximized.

Also, in long-run competitive equilibrium, entry and exit ensure that each firm produces its output at the minimum possible long-run average cost.

To summarize: At the competitive equilibrium, marginal social benefit equals marginal social cost; total surplus is maximized; firms produce at the lowest possible long-run average cost; and resource use is efficient.

Figure 13.6(b) illustrates the inefficiency of monopoly and the sources of that inefficiency. A monopoly produces Q_M and sells its output for P_M. The smaller output and higher price drive a wedge between marginal social benefit and marginal social cost and create a *deadweight loss*. The gray triangle shows the deadweight loss and its magnitude is a measure of the inefficiency of monopoly.

Consumer surplus shrinks for two reasons. First, consumers lose by having to pay more for the good. This loss to consumers is a gain for monopoly and increases the producer surplus. Second, consumers lose by getting less of the good, and this loss is part of the deadweight loss.

Although the monopoly gains from a higher price, it loses some producer surplus because it produces a smaller output. That loss is another part of the deadweight loss.

A monopoly produces a smaller output than perfect competition and faces no competition, so it does not produce at the lowest possible long-run average cost. As a result, monopoly damages the consumer interest in three ways: A monopoly produces less, increases the cost of production, and raises the price by more than the increased cost of production.

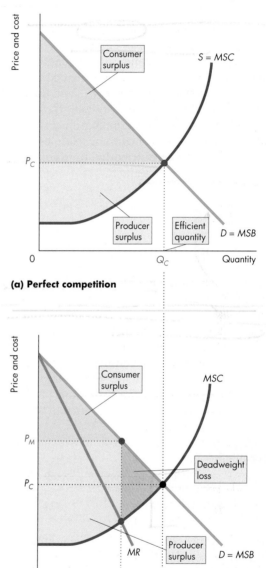

FIGURE 13.6   Inefficiency of Monopoly

(a) Perfect competition

(b) Monopoly

In perfect competition in part (a), output is Q_C and the price is P_C. Marginal social benefit (*MSB*) equals marginal social cost (*MSC*); total surplus, the sum of consumer surplus (the green triangle) and producer surplus (the blue area), is maximized; and in the long run, firms produce at the lowest possible average cost. Monopoly in part (b) produces Q_M and raises the price to P_M. Consumer surplus shrinks, the monopoly gains, and a deadweight loss (the gray triangle) arises.

MyEconLab Animation and Draw Graph

Redistribution of Surpluses

You've seen that monopoly is inefficient because marginal social benefit exceeds marginal social cost and there is deadweight loss—a social loss. But monopoly also brings a *redistribution* of surpluses.

Some of the lost consumer surplus goes to the monopoly. In Fig. 13.6, the monopoly takes the difference between the higher price, P_M, and the competitive price, P_C, on the quantity sold, Q_M. So the monopoly takes that part of the consumer surplus. This portion of the loss of consumer surplus is not a loss to society. It is a redistribution from consumers to the monopoly producer.

Rent Seeking

You've seen that monopoly creates a deadweight loss and is inefficient. But the social cost of monopoly can exceed the deadweight loss because of an activity called rent seeking. Any surplus—consumer surplus, producer surplus, or economic profit—is called **economic rent.** The pursuit of wealth by capturing economic rent is called **rent seeking.**

You've seen that a monopoly makes its economic profit by diverting part of consumer surplus to itself—by converting consumer surplus into economic profit. So the pursuit of economic profit by a monopoly is rent seeking. It is the attempt to capture consumer surplus.

Rent seekers pursue their goals in two main ways. They might

- Buy a monopoly
- Create a monopoly

Buy a Monopoly To rent seek by buying a monopoly, a person searches for a monopoly that is for sale at a lower price than the monopoly's economic profit. Trading of taxicab licenses is an example of this type of rent seeking. In some cities, taxicabs are regulated. The city restricts both the fares and the number of taxis that can operate so that operating a taxi results in economic profit. A person who wants to operate a taxi must buy a license from someone who already has one. People rationally devote time and effort to seeking out profitable monopoly businesses to buy. In the process, they use up scarce resources that could otherwise have been used to produce goods and services. The value of this lost production is part of the social cost of monopoly. The amount paid for a monopoly is not a social cost because the payment is just a transfer of an existing producer surplus from the buyer to the seller.

Create a Monopoly Rent seeking by creating a monopoly is mainly a political activity. It takes the form of lobbying and trying to influence the political process. Such influence might be sought by making campaign contributions in exchange for legislative support or by indirectly seeking to influence political outcomes through publicity in the media or more direct contacts with politicians and bureaucrats. An example of a monopoly created in this way is the government-imposed restrictions on the quantities of textiles that may be imported into the United States. Another is a regulation that limits the number of oranges that may be sold in the United States. These are regulations that restrict output and increase price.

This type of rent seeking is a costly activity that uses up scarce resources. Taken together, firms spend billions of dollars lobbying Congress, state legislators, and local officials in the pursuit of licenses and laws that create barriers to entry and establish a monopoly.

Rent-Seeking Equilibrium

Barriers to entry create monopoly. But there is no barrier to entry into rent seeking. Rent seeking is like perfect competition. If an economic profit is available, a new rent seeker will try to get some of it. And competition among rent seekers pushes up the price that must be paid for a monopoly, to the point at which the rent seeker makes zero economic profit by operating the monopoly. For example, competition for the right to operate a taxi in New York City leads to a price of more than $100,000 for a taxi license, which is sufficiently high to eliminate the economic profit made by a taxi operator.

Figure 13.7 shows a rent-seeking equilibrium. The cost of rent seeking is a fixed cost that must be added to a monopoly's other costs. Rent seeking and rent-seeking costs increase to the point at which no economic profit is made. The average total cost curve, which includes the fixed cost of rent seeking, shifts upward until it just touches the demand curve. Economic profit is zero. It has been lost in rent seeking.

Consumer surplus is unaffected, but the deadweight loss from monopoly is larger. The deadweight loss now includes the original deadweight loss triangle plus the lost producer surplus, shown by the enlarged gray area in Fig. 13.7.

FIGURE 13.7   Rent-Seeking Equilibrium

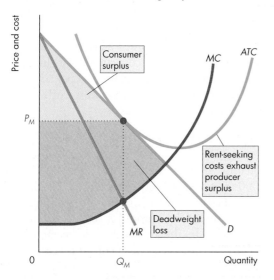

With competitive rent seeking, a single-price monopoly uses all its economic profit to maintain its monopoly. The firm's rent-seeking costs are fixed costs. They add to total fixed cost and to average total cost. The *ATC* curve shifts upward until, at the profit-maximizing price, the firm breaks even.

MyEconLab Animation

REVIEW QUIZ

1 Why does a single-price monopoly produce a smaller output and charge more than the price that would prevail if the market were perfectly competitive?

2 How does a monopoly transfer consumer surplus to itself?

3 Why is a single-price monopoly inefficient?

4 What is rent seeking and how does it influence the inefficiency of monopoly?

Work these questions in Study Plan 13.3 and get instant feedback. Do a Key Terms Quiz.   *MyEconLab*

So far, we've considered only a single-price monopoly. But many monopolies do not operate with a single price. Instead, they price discriminate. Let's now see how a price-discriminating monopoly works.

 Price Discrimination

You encounter *price discrimination*—selling a good or service at a number of different prices—when you travel, go to the movies, get your hair cut, visit an art museum or theme park, or buy pizza. These are all examples of firms with market power, setting the prices of an identical good or service at different levels for different customers.

Not all price *differences* are price *discrimination*: they reflect differences in production costs. For example, real-time meters for electricity enable power utilities to charge a different price at peak-load times than during the night. But it costs more per kilowatt-hour to generate electricity at peak-load times so this price difference reflects production cost differences and is not price discrimination.

At first sight, price discrimination appears to be inconsistent with profit maximization. Why would a movie theater allow children to see movies at a discount? Why would a hairdresser charge students and senior citizens less? Aren't these firms losing profit by being nice to their customers? The answer, as you are about to discover, is that price discrimination is profitable: It increases economic profit.

But to be able to price discriminate, the firm must sell a product that cannot be resold; and it must be possible to identify and separate different buyer types.

Two Ways of Price Discriminating

Firms price discriminate in two broad ways. They discriminate

■ Among groups of buyers
■ Among units of a good

Discriminating Among Groups of Buyers People differ in the value they place on a good—their marginal benefit and willingness to pay. Some of these differences are correlated with features such as age, employment status, and other easily distinguished characteristics. When such a correlation is present, firms can profit by price discriminating among the different groups of buyers.

For example, salespeople and other business travelers know that a face-to-face sales meeting with a customer might bring a large and profitable order. So for these travelers, the marginal benefit from a trip is large and the price that such a traveler is willing to pay for a trip is high. In contrast, for a leisure traveler, any of several different trips and even no trip at all are options. So for leisure travelers, the marginal benefit of a trip is small and the price that such a traveler is willing to pay for a trip is low. Because the price that business travelers are willing to pay exceeds what leisure travelers are willing to pay, it is possible for an airline to price discriminate between these two groups and increase its profit. We'll return to this example of price discrimination below.

Discriminating Among Units of a Good Everyone experiences diminishing marginal benefit, so if all the units of the good are sold for a single price, buyers end up with a consumer surplus equal to the value they get from each unit minus the price paid for it.

A firm that price discriminates by charging a buyer one price for a single item and a lower price for a second or third item can capture some of the consumer surplus. Buy one pizza and get a second one for a lower price is an example of this type of price discrimination.

Increasing Profit and Producer Surplus

By getting buyers to pay a price as close as possible to their maximum willingness to pay, a monopoly captures the consumer surplus and converts it into producer surplus. And more producer surplus means more economic profit.

To see why more producer surplus means more economic profit, recall some definitions. With total revenue TR and total cost TC,

$$\text{Economic profit} = TR - TC.$$

Producer surplus is total revenue minus the area under the marginal cost curve. But the area under the marginal cost curve is total *variable* cost, TVC. So producer surplus equals total revenue minus TVC, or

$$\text{Producer surplus} = TR - TVC.$$

You can see that the difference between economic profit and producer surplus is the same as the difference between TC and TVC. But TC minus TVC equals total *fixed* cost, TFC. So

$$\text{Economic profit} = \text{Producer surplus} - TFC.$$

For a given level of total fixed cost, anything that increases producer surplus also increases economic profit.

Let's now see how price discrimination works by looking at a price-discriminating airline.

A Price-Discriminating Airline

Inter-City Airlines has a monopoly on passenger flights between two cities. Figure 13.8 shows the market demand curve, D, for travel on this route. It also shows Inter-City Airline's marginal revenue curve, MR, and marginal cost curve, MC. Inter-City's marginal cost is a constant $40 per trip. (It is easier to see how price discrimination works for a firm with constant marginal cost.)

Single-Price Profit Maximization As a single-price monopoly, Inter-City maximizes profit by producing the quantity of trips at which MR equals MC, which is 8,000 trips a week, and charging $120 a trip. With a marginal cost of $40 a trip, producer surplus is $80 a trip, and Inter-City's producer surplus is $640,000 a week, shown by the area of the blue rectangle. Inter-City's customers enjoy a consumer surplus shown by the area of the green triangle.

FIGURE 13.8   A Single Price of Air Travel

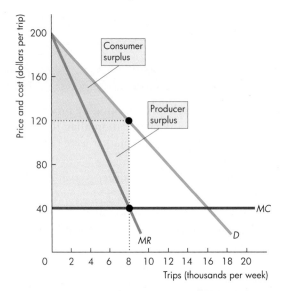

Inter-City Airlines has a monopoly on an air route with a market demand curve D. Inter-City's marginal cost, MC, is $40 per trip. As a single-price monopoly, Inter-City's marginal revenue curve is MR. Profit is maximized by selling 8,000 trips a week at $120 a trip. Producer surplus is $640,000 a week—the blue rectangle—and Inter-City's customers enjoy a consumer surplus—the green triangle.

MyEconLab Animation

Discrimination Between Two Types of Travelers

Inter-City surveys its customers and discovers that they are all business travelers. It also surveys people who are *not* its customers and discovers that they are mainly people who travel for leisure. These people travel by bus or car, but would travel by air at a low fare. Inter-City would like to attract some of these travelers and knows that to do so, it must offer a fare below the current $120 a trip. How can it do that?

Inter-City digs more deeply into its survey results and discovers that its current customers always plan their travel less than two weeks before departure. In contrast, the people who travel by bus or car know their travel plans at least two weeks ahead of time.

Inter-City sees that it can use what it has discovered about its current and potential new customers to separate the two types of travelers into two markets: one market for business travel and another for leisure travel.

Figure 13.9 shows Inter-City's two markets. Part (a), the market for business travel, is the same as Fig. 13.8. Part (b) shows the market for leisure travel. No leisure traveler is willing to pay the business fare of $120 a trip, so at that price, the quantity demanded in part (b) is zero. The demand curve D_L is the demand for travel on this route after satisfying the demand of business travelers. Inter-City's marginal cost remains at $40 a trip, so its marginal revenue curve is MR_L. Inter-City maximizes profit by setting the leisure fare at $80 a trip and attracting 4,000 leisure travelers a week. Inter-City's producer surplus increases by $160,000 a week—the area of the blue rectangle in Fig. 13.9(b)—and leisure travelers enjoy a consumer surplus—the area of the green triangle.

Inter-City announces its new fare schedule: no restrictions, $120 and 14-day advance purchase, $80. Inter-City increases its passenger count by 50 percent and increases its producer surplus by $160,000.

FIGURE 13.9   Price Discrimination

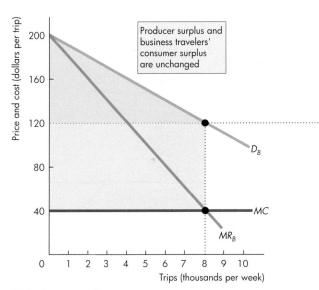

(a) Business travel

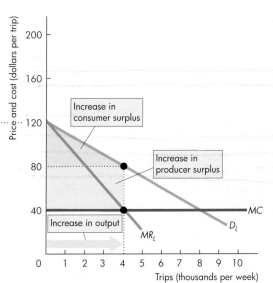

(b) Leisure travel

Inter-City separates its market into two types of travel: business travel with no restrictions in part (a) and leisure travel that requires a 14-day advance purchase in part (b). For business travel, the profit-maximizing price is $120 a trip with 8,000 trips a week. For leisure travel, the profit-maximizing price is $80 a trip with 4,000 trips a week.

Inter-City continues to make the same producer surplus on business travel as it did with a single price and business travelers continue to enjoy the same consumer surplus. But in part (b), Inter-City sells 4,000 trips to leisure travelers, which increases its producer surplus—the blue rectangle—and increases consumer surplus—the green triangle.

Discrimination Among Several Types of Travelers

Pleased with the success of its price discrimination between business and leisure travelers, Inter-City sees that it might be able to profit even more by dividing its customers into a larger number of types. So it does another customer survey, which reveals that some business travelers are willing to pay $160 for a fully-refundable, unrestricted ticket while others are willing to pay only $120 for a nonrefundable ticket. So applying the same principles as it used to discriminate between business and leisure travelers, Inter-City now discriminates between business travelers who want a refundable ticket and those who want a non-refundable ticket.

Another survey of leisure travelers reveals that they fall into two goups: those who are able to plan 14 days ahead and others who can plan 21 days ahead. So Inter-City discriminates between these two groups with two fares: an $80 and a $60 fare.

By offering travelers four different fares, the airline increases its producer surplus and increases its economic profit. But why only four fares? Why not keep looking for ever more traveler types and offer even more fares?

Perfect Price Discrimination

Firms try to capture an ever larger part of consumer surplus by devising a host of special conditions, each one of which appeals to a tiny segment of the market but at the same time excludes others from taking advantage of a lower price. The more consumer surplus a firm is able to capture, the closer it gets to the extreme case called **perfect price discrimination**, which occurs if a firm can sell each unit of output for the highest price someone is willing to pay for it. In this extreme (hypothetical) case consumer surplus is eliminated and captured as producer surplus.

With perfect price discrimination, something special happens to marginal revenue—the market demand curve becomes the marginal revenue curve. The reason is that when the monopoly cuts the price to sell a larger quantity, it sells only the marginal unit at the lower price. All the other units continue to be sold for the highest price that each buyer is willing to pay. So for the perfect price discriminator, marginal revenue *equals* price and the market demand curve becomes the monopoly's marginal revenue curve.

With marginal revenue equal to price, Inter-City can obtain even greater producer surplus by increasing output up to the point at which price (and marginal revenue) equals marginal cost.

So Inter-City seeks new travelers who will not pay as much as $60 a trip but who will pay more than $40, its marginal cost. Inter-City offers a variety of vacation specials at different low fares that appeal only to new travelers. Existing customers continue to pay the higher fares and some, with further perks and frills that have no effect on cost, are induced to pay fares going all the way up to $200 a trip.

With all these special conditions and fares, Inter-City increases its output to the quantity demanded at marginal cost, extracts the entire consumer surplus on that quantity, and maximizes economic profit.

Figure 13.10 shows the outcome with perfect price discrimination and compares it with the single-price monopoly outcome. The range of business-class fares extract the entire consumer surplus from this group. The new leisure-class fares going down to $40 a trip attract an additional 8,000 travelers and take the entire consumer surplus of leisure travelers. Inter-City makes the maximum possible economic profit.

FIGURE 13.10   Perfect Price Discrimination

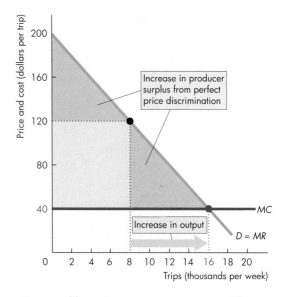

Dozens of fares discriminate among many different types of business travelers, and many new low fares with restrictions appeal to leisure travelers. With perfect price discrimination, the market demand curve becomes Inter-City's marginal revenue curve. Producer surplus is maximized when the lowest fare equals marginal cost. Inter-City sells 16,000 trips and makes the maximum possible economic profit.

MyEconLab Animation

*Would it bother you to hear how
little I paid for this flight?*

From William Hamilton, "Voodoo Economics," © 1992 by
The Chronicle Publishing Company, p. 3.
Reprinted with permission of Chronicle Books.

Efficiency and Rent Seeking with Price Discrimination

With perfect price discrimination, output increases to the point at which price equals marginal cost. This output is identical to that of perfect competition. Perfect price discrimination pushes consumer surplus to zero but increases the monopoly's producer surplus to equal the total surplus in perfect competition. With perfect price discrimination, no deadweight loss is created, so perfect price discrimination achieves efficiency.

> The more perfectly the monopoly can price discriminate, the closer its output is to the competitive output and the more efficient is the outcome.

But the outcomes of perfect competition and perfect price discrimination differ. First, the distribution of the total surplus is not the same. In perfect competition, total surplus is shared by consumers and producers, while with perfect price discrimination, the monopoly takes it all. Second, because the monopoly takes all the total surplus, rent seeking is profitable.

People use resources in pursuit of economic rent, and the bigger the rents, the more resources are used in pursuing them. With free entry into rent seeking, the long-run equilibrium outcome is that rent seekers use up the entire producer surplus.

Real-world airlines are as creative as Inter-City Airlines, as you can see in the cartoon! Disney Corporation is creative too in extracting consumer surplus, as *Economics in Action* shows.

We next study some key monopoly policy issues.

ECONOMICS IN ACTION
Attempting Perfect Price Discrimination

If you want to spend a day at Disney World, it will cost you $99. You can spend a second consecutive day for an extra $89. A third day will cost you $86. But for a fourth day, you'll pay only $20 and for more days all the way up to 10, you'll pay only $10 a day.

The Disney Corporation hopes that it has read your willingness to pay correctly and not left you with too much consumer surplus.

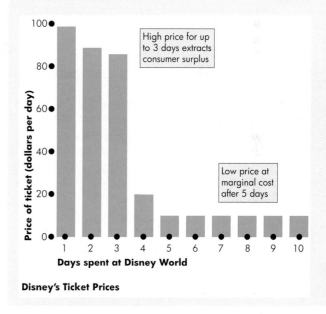

Disney's Ticket Prices

◆ REVIEW QUIZ

1 What is price discrimination and how is it used to increase a monopoly's profit?

2 Explain how consumer surplus changes when a monopoly price discriminates.

3 Explain how consumer surplus, economic profit, and output change when a monopoly perfectly price discriminates.

4 What are some of the ways that real-world airlines price discriminate?

Work these questions in Study Plan 13.4 and get instant feedback. Do a Key Terms Quiz.   MyEconLab

ECONOMICS IN THE NEWS

Microsoft Monopoly

Microsoft Windows 8 to Go on Sale in October

Microsoft announced that its Windows 8 operating system will be released in October 2012, three years after Windows 7 went public. Windows 8 will be available in 109 languages across 231 markets worldwide.

Source: Associated Press, July 9, 2012

SOME DATA

Microsoft Windows 8 Versions and U.S. Prices

Version	Price
Full from Microsoft	249.99
Upgrade from Microsoft	199.99
Full from Amazon	162.99
OEM	148.95
Student from Microsoft	69.99

Microsoft sold 180 million Windows 8 licenses at different prices in different national markets.

THE QUESTIONS

- Is Microsoft a monopoly?
- Is Microsoft a natural monopoly or a legal monopoly?
- Does Microsoft price discriminate or do the different prices of Windows reflect cost differences?
- Sketch a demand curve for Windows, Microsoft's marginal cost curve, and the distribution of the total surplus between consumers and Microsoft.

THE ANSWERS

- Microsoft controls 87 percent of the market for computer operating systems, and almost 100 percent of the non-Apple market, which makes it an effective monopoly.
- Microsoft is a natural monopoly. It has large fixed costs and almost zero marginal cost, so its long-run average cost curve (*LRAC*) slopes downward and economies of scale are achieved when the *LRAC* curve intersects the demand curve.
- Microsoft sells Windows for a number of different prices to different market segments and the marginal cost of a Windows license is the same for all market segments, so Microsoft is a price-discriminating monopoly.

- The figure illustrates the demand curve, *D*, and marginal cost curve, *MC*, for Windows licenses.
- Using the U.S. prices in the data table, the figure shows how Microsoft converts consumer surplus into producer surplus by price discriminating.
- Because Microsoft also price discriminates among its different national markets, it gains even more producer surplus than the figure illustrates.

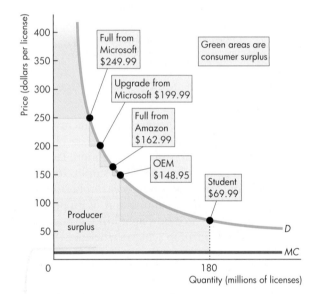

Microsoft Grabs Consumer Surplus

Windows 8 has 109 foreign language versions, which expands Microsoft's scope for price discrimination.

MyEconLab More Economics in the News

◆ Monopoly Regulation

Natural monopoly presents a dilemma. With economies of scale, it produces at the lowest possible cost. But with market power, it has an incentive to raise the price above the competitive price and produce too little—to operate in the self-interest of the monopolist and not in the social interest.

Regulation—rules administered by a government agency to influence prices, quantities, entry, and other aspects of economic activity in a firm or industry—is a possible solution to this dilemma.

To implement regulation, the government establishes agencies to oversee and enforce the rules. For example, the Surface Transportation Board regulates prices on interstate railroads, some trucking and bus lines, and water and oil pipelines. By the 1970s, almost a quarter of the nation's output was produced by regulated industries (far more than just natural monopolies) and a process of deregulation began.

Deregulation is the process of removing regulation of prices, quantities, entry, and other aspects of economic activity in a firm or industry. During the past 30 years, deregulation has occurred in domestic air transportation, telephone service, interstate trucking, and banking and financial services. Cable TV was deregulated in 1984, re-regulated in 1992, and deregulated again in 1996.

Regulation is a possible solution to the dilemma presented by natural monopoly but not a guaranteed solution. There are two theories about how regulation actually works: the *social interest theory* and the *capture theory*.

The **social interest theory** is that the political and regulatory process relentlessly seeks out inefficiency and introduces regulation that eliminates deadweight loss and allocates resources efficiently.

The **capture theory** is that regulation serves the self-interest of the producer, who captures the regulator and maximizes economic profit. Regulation that benefits the producer but creates a deadweight loss gets adopted because the producer's gain is large and visible while each individual consumer's loss is small and invisible. No individual consumer has an incentive to oppose the regulation, but the producer has a big incentive to lobby for it.

We're going to examine efficient regulation that serves the social interest and see why it is not a simple matter to design and implement such regulation.

Efficient Regulation of a Natural Monopoly

A cable TV company is a *natural monopoly*—it can supply the entire market at a lower price than two or more competing firms can. Cox Communications, based in Atlanta, provides cable TV to households in 20 states. The firm has invested heavily in satellite receiving dishes, cables, and control equipment and so has large fixed costs. These fixed costs are part of the firm's average total cost. Its average total cost decreases as the number of households served increases because the fixed cost is spread over a larger number of households.

Unregulated, Cox produces the quantity that maximizes profit. Like all single-price monopolies, the profit-maximizing quantity is less than the efficient quantity, and underproduction results in a deadweight loss.

How can Cox be regulated to produce the efficient quantity of cable TV service? The answer is by being regulated to set its price equal to marginal cost, known as the **marginal cost pricing rule.** The quantity demanded at a price equal to marginal cost is the efficient quantity—the quantity at which marginal benefit equals marginal cost.

Figure 13.11 illustrates the marginal cost pricing rule. The demand curve for cable TV is *D*. Cox's marginal cost curve is *MC*. That marginal cost curve is (assumed to be) horizontal at $10 per household per month—that is, the cost of providing each additional household with a month of cable programming is $10. The efficient outcome occurs if the price is regulated at $10 per household per month with 10 million households served.

But there is a problem: At the efficient output, average total cost exceeds marginal cost, so a firm that uses marginal cost pricing incurs an economic loss. A cable TV company that is required to use a marginal cost pricing rule will not stay in business for long. How can the firm cover its costs and, at the same time, obey a marginal cost pricing rule?

There are two possible ways of enabling the firm to cover its costs: price discrimination and a two-part price (called a *two-part tariff*).

For example, Verizon offers plans at a fixed monthly price that give access to the cellphone network and unlimited free calls. The price of a call (zero) equals Verizon's marginal cost of a call. Similarly, a cable TV operator can charge a one-time connection fee that covers its fixed cost and then charge a monthly fee equal to marginal cost.

FIGURE 13.11   Regulating a Natural Monopoly

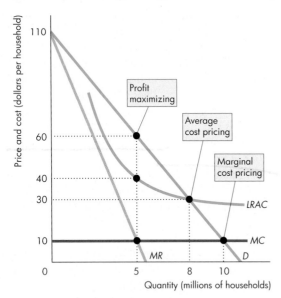

A natural monopoly cable TV supplier faces the demand curve *D*. The firm's marginal cost is constant at $10 per household per month, as shown by the curve labeled *MC*. The long-run average cost curve is *LRAC*.

Unregulated, as a profit-maximizer, the firm serves 5 million households at a price of $60 a month. An efficient marginal cost pricing rule sets the price at $10 a month. The monopoly serves 10 million households and incurs an economic loss. A second-best average cost pricing rule sets the price at $30 a month. The monopoly serves 8 million households and earns zero economic profit.

MyEconLab Animation

Second-Best Regulation of a Natural Monopoly

A natural monopoly cannot always be regulated to achieve an efficient outcome. There are two possible ways of enabling a regulated monopoly to avoid an economic loss:

- Average cost pricing
- Government subsidy

Average Cost Pricing The **average cost pricing rule** sets price equal to average total cost. With this rule the firm produces the quantity at which the average

total cost curve cuts the demand curve. This rule results in the firm making zero economic profit—breaking even. But because for a natural monopoly average total cost exceeds marginal cost, the quantity produced is less than the efficient quantity and a deadweight loss arises.

Figure 13.11 illustrates the average cost pricing rule. The price is $30 a month and 8 million households get cable TV.

Government Subsidy A government subsidy is a direct payment to the firm equal to its economic loss. To pay a subsidy, the government must raise the revenue by taxing some other activity. You saw in Chapter 6 that taxes themselves generate deadweight loss.

And the Second-Best Is ... Which is the better option, average cost pricing or marginal cost pricing with a government subsidy? The answer depends on the relative magnitudes of the two deadweight losses. Average cost pricing generates a deadweight loss in the market served by the natural monopoly. A subsidy generates deadweight losses in the markets for the items that are taxed to pay for the subsidy. The smaller deadweight loss is the second-best solution to regulating a natural monopoly. Making this calculation in practice is too difficult, so average cost pricing is generally preferred to a subsidy.

Implementing average cost pricing presents the regulator with a challenge because it is not possible to be sure what a firm's costs are. So regulators use one of two practical rules:

- Rate of return regulation
- Price cap regulation

Rate of Return Regulation Under **rate of return regulation,** a firm must justify its price by showing that its return on capital doesn't exceed a specified target rate. This type of regulation can end up serving the self-interest of the firm rather than the social interest. The firm's managers have an incentive to inflate costs by spending on items such as private jets, free baseball tickets (disguised as public relations expenses), and lavish entertainment. Managers also have an incentive to use more capital than the efficient amount. The rate of return on capital is regulated but not the total return on capital, and the greater the amount of capital, the greater is the total return.

Price Cap Regulation For the reason that we've just examined, rate of return regulation is increasingly being replaced by price cap regulation. A **price cap regulation** is a price ceiling—a rule that specifies the highest price the firm is permitted to set. This type of regulation gives a firm an incentive to operate efficiently and keep costs under control. Price cap regulation has become common for the electricity and telecommunications industries and is replacing rate of return regulation.

To see how a price cap works, let's suppose that the cable TV operator is subject to this type of regulation. Figure 13.12 shows that without regulation, the firm maximizes profit by serving 5 million households and charging a price of $60 a month. If a price cap is set at $30 a month, the firm is permitted to sell

any quantity it chooses at that price or at a lower price. At 5 million households, the firm now incurs an economic loss. It can decrease the loss by increasing output to 8 million households. To increase output above 8 million households, the firm would have to lower the price and again it would incur a loss. So the profit-maximizing quantity is 8 million households—the same as with average cost pricing.

Notice that a price cap lowers the price and increases output. This outcome is in sharp contrast to the effect of a price ceiling in a competitive market that you studied in Chapter 6 (pp. 128–130). The reason is that in a monopoly, the unregulated equilibrium output is less than the competitive equilibrium output, and the price cap regulation replicates the conditions of a competitive market.

In Fig. 13.12, the price cap delivers average cost pricing. In practice, the regulator might set the cap too high. For this reason, price cap regulation is often combined with *earnings sharing regulation*—a regulation that requires firms to make refunds to customers when profits rise above a target level.

FIGURE 13.12 Price Cap Regulation

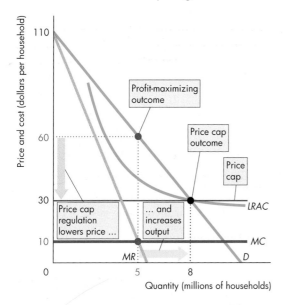

A natural monopoly cable TV supplier faces the demand curve *D*. The firm's marginal cost is constant at $10 per household per month, as shown by the curve labeled *MC*. The long-run average cost curve is *LRAC*.

Unregulated, the firm serves 5 million households at a price of $60 a month. A price cap sets the maximum price at $30 a month. The firm has an incentive to minimize cost and serve the quantity of households that demand service at the price cap. The price cap regulation lowers the price and increases the quantity.

MyEconLab Animation

REVIEW QUIZ

1 What is the pricing rule that achieves an efficient outcome for a regulated monopoly? What is the problem with this rule?

2 What is the average cost pricing rule? Why is it not an efficient way of regulating monopoly?

3 What is a price cap? Why might it be a more effective way of regulating monopoly than rate of return regulation?

4 Compare the consumer surplus, producer surplus, and deadweight loss that arise from average cost pricing with those that arise from profit-maximization pricing and marginal cost pricing.

Work these questions in Study Plan 13.5 and get instant feedback. Do a Key Terms Quiz.   MyEconLab

◆ You've now completed your study of monopoly. *Economics in the News* on pp. 316–317 looks at Google's dominant position in the market for Internet search advertising.

In the next chapter, we study markets that lie between the extremes of perfect competition and monopoly and that blend elements of the two.

Is Google Misusing Monopoly Power?

Google and E.U. Agree to Settle Search Row

The Financial Times
February 5, 2014

Google ended its three-year tangle with antitrust regulators on Wednesday, as it reached a deal with Brussels which critics claimed would cement its dominance of some of the most valuable commercial activity on the web.

Following the U.S. Federal Trade Commission closing a similar case last year, regulators on both sides of the Atlantic have now largely cleared Google's practice of overriding its own algorithmically chosen results to put paid-for links at the top of its pages.

The European Commission went further than U.S. regulators by extracting a concession that will require the internet group to give rival Internet services a showing alongside its own preferred results, provided they bid against each other for the space.

Rivals immediately panned the approach as "worse than nothing" as it gave Brussels' blessing to Google sucking traffic from other Internet sites for some of the most valuable searches on the web, such as users looking for digital cameras or hotels. ...

Joaquín Almunia, the E.U. competition chief, said ... "Google should not be prevented from trying to provide users with what they're looking for." ... "What Google should do is also give rivals a prominent space ... in a visual format which will attract users."...

Although it still faces an investigation in Canada, the deal effectively brings the curtain down on Google's first showdown with the world's leading antitrust regulators. Unlike Microsoft, which became embroiled in a 10-year battle with Brussels, it chose to settle rather than risk large fines or tying up senior management attention in a fight. ...

...

Alex Barker and Richard Waters, "Google and E.U. Agree to Settle Search Row," *Financial Times*, February 14, 2014.

MyEconLab More Economics in the News

ESSENCE OF THE STORY

- Google reached a settlement with the European Union antitrust regulators.

- It settled a similar case with the U.S. Federal Trade Commission 2013 but still faces an investigation in Canada.

- The European regulators require Google display rival Internet services alongside its preferred results, provided they bid against each other for the space.

- Competitors say the regulations are too weak and enable Google to capture traffic from other Internet sites for some of the most valuable searches.

ECONOMIC ANALYSIS

- Google gets its revenue by selling advertisements associated with search keywords.

- Google sells keywords based on a combination of willingness-to-pay and the number of clicks an advertisement receives, with bids starting at 5 cents per click.

- Google has steadily improved its search engine and refined and simplified its interface with both searchers and advertisers to make searches more powerful and advertising more effective.

- Figure 1 shows Google's extraordinary success in terms of its revenue, cost, and profit.

- Google could have provided a basic search engine with none of the features of today's Google.

- If Google had followed this strategy, people seeking information would have used other search engines and advertisers would have been willing to pay lower prices for Google ads.

- Google would have faced the market described in Fig. 2 and earned a small economic profit.

- Instead, Google improved its search engine and the effectiveness of advertising. The demand for Google ads increased.

- By selling keywords to the highest bidder, Google is able to achieve perfect price discrimination.

- Figure 3 shows the consequences of Google's successful strategy. With perfect price discrimination, Google's producer surplus is maximized. Google produces the efficient quantity of search and advertising by accepting ads at prices that exceed or equal marginal cost.

- Google does not appear to be acting against the social interest: There is no antitrust case to answer.

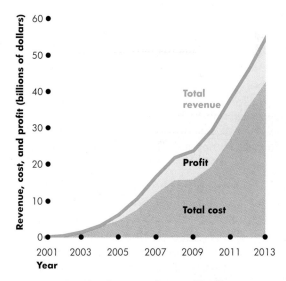

Figure 1 Google's Revenue, Cost, and Profit

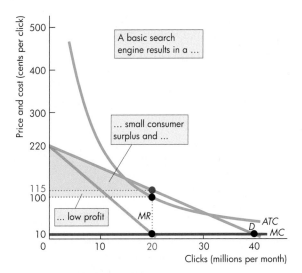

Figure 2 Basic Search Engine

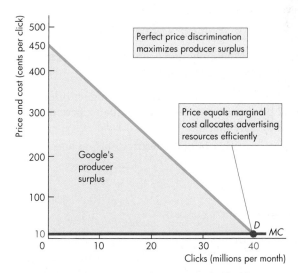

Figure 3 Google with AdWords and Other Features

317

SUMMARY

Key Points

Monopoly and How It Arises (pp. 298–299)

- A monopoly is a market with a single supplier of a good or service that has no close substitutes and in which barriers to entry prevent competition.
- Barriers to entry may be legal (public franchise, license, patent, or copyright), ownership (one firm controls a resource), or natural (created by economies of scale).
- A monopoly might be able to price discriminate when there is no resale possibility.
- Where resale is possible, a firm charges one price.

Working Problem 1 will give you a better understanding of monopoly and how it arises.

A Single-Price Monopoly's Output and Price Decision (pp. 300–303)

- A monopoly's demand curve is the market demand curve and a single-price monopoly's marginal revenue is less than price.
- A monopoly maximizes profit by producing the output at which marginal revenue equals marginal cost and by charging the maximum price that consumers are willing to pay for that output.

Working Problems 2 to 4 will give you a better understanding of a single-price monopoly's output and price decision.

Single-Price Monopoly and Competition Compared (pp. 304–307)

- A single-price monopoly charges a higher price and produces a smaller quantity than a perfectly competitive market.
- A single-price monopoly restricts output and creates a deadweight loss.

- The total loss that arises from monopoly equals the deadweight loss plus the cost of the resources devoted to rent seeking.

Working Problem 5 will give you a better understanding of the comparison of single-price monopoly and perfect competition.

Price Discrimination (pp. 307–312)

- Price discrimination converts consumer surplus into economic profit.
- Perfect price discrimination extracts the entire consumer surplus; each unit is sold for the maximum price that each consumer is willing to pay; the quantity produced is the efficient quantity.
- Rent seeking with perfect price discrimination might eliminate the entire consumer surplus and producer surplus.

Working Problem 6 will give you a better understanding of price discrimination.

Monopoly Regulation (pp. 313–315)

- Monopoly regulation might serve the social interest or the interest of the monopoly (the monopoly captures the regulator).
- Price equal to marginal cost achieves efficiency but results in economic loss.
- Price equal to average cost enables the firm to cover its cost but is inefficient.
- Rate of return regulation creates incentives for inefficient production and inflated cost.
- Price cap regulation with earnings sharing regulation can achieve a more efficient outcome than rate of return regulation.

Working Problems 7 to 9 will give you a better understanding of monopoly regulation.

Key Terms

MyEconLab Key Terms Quiz

Average cost pricing rule, 314
Barrier to entry, 298
Capture theory, 313
Deregulation, 313
Economic rent, 306
Legal monopoly, 298

Marginal cost pricing rule, 313
Monopoly, 298
Natural monopoly, 298
Perfect price discrimination, 310
Price cap regulation, 315
Price discrimination, 299

Rate of return regulation, 314
Regulation, 313
Rent seeking, 306
Single-price monopoly, 299
Social interest theory, 313

WORKED PROBLEM

MyEconLab   You can work this problem in Chapter 13 Study Plan.

Tanya's Tattoos is local monopoly. Columns 1 and 2 of the table set out the market demand schedule and columns 2 and 3 set out the total cost schedule.

Price (dollars per tattoo)	Quantity (tattoos per hour)	Total cost (dollars per hour)
60	0	30
50	1	50
40	2	70
30	3	90
20	4	110

Questions

1. If Tanya's Tattoos is a single-price monopoly, what is Tanya's profit-maximizing quantity? What price does Tanya's charge? What are its economic profit and producer surplus?
2. If Tanya's Tattoos perfectly price discriminates, what quantity does Tanya's produce? What are its economic profit and producer surplus?

Solutions

1. The profit-maximizing quantity is that at which marginal cost equals marginal revenue. Marginal cost—the increase in total cost when output increases by one unit—is $20 at all output levels. Marginal revenue—the change in total revenue when output increases by one unit—is calculated in the table at the top of the next column.

   Marginal revenue equals marginal cost of $20 at 2 tattoos per hour (midway between $30 and $10). So this quantity maximizes profit. The

Demand schedule		Total revenue (dollars per hour)	Marginal revenue (dollars per tattoo)
Price (dollars per tattoo)	Quantity (tattoos per hour)		
60	0	0	
			· · · · · · · 50
50	1	50	
			· · · · · · · 30
40	2	80	
			· · · · · · · 10
30	3	90	
			· · · · · · · −10
20	4	80	

highest price at which 2 tattoos an hour can be sold is $40 per tattoo, so total revenue is $80. Total cost is $70, so economic profit is $10. *TFC* (*TC* at zero output) is $30, so *TVC* is $40. Producer surplus (*TR − TVC*) is $40 an hour.

Key Point: Profit is maximized when marginal cost equals marginal revenue.

2. If Tanya can perfectly price discriminate, she produces 4 tattoos an hour and sells one for $50, one for $40, one for $30, and one for $20. Total revenue is $140 and total cost is $110, so economic profit is $30 an hour. Producer surplus (*TR − TVC*) = $140 − $80 = $60 an hour.

Key Point: With perfect price discrimination, a firm charges the highest price that each buyer is willing to pay and increases production to the quantity at which the lowest price equals marginal cost.

The key figure illustrates the two outcomes.

Key Figure

MyEconLab Interactive Animation

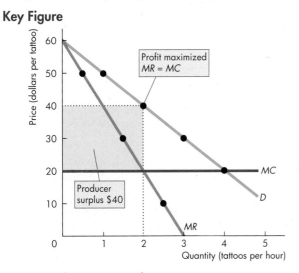

(a) Single-price monopoly

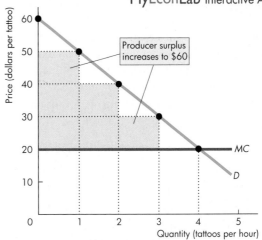

(b) Price-discriminating monopoly

STUDY PLAN PROBLEMS AND APPLICATIONS

MyEconLab   You can work problems 1 to 9 in Chapter 13 Study Plan and get instant feedback.

Monopoly and How It Arises (Study Plan 13.1)

1. The U.S. Postal Service has a monopoly on non-urgent First Class Mail. Pfizer Inc. makes LIPI-TOR, a prescription drug that lowers cholesterol. Cox Communications is the sole provider of cable television service in some parts of San Diego.

   Are any these firms protected by a barrier to entry? Do any of these firms produce a good or service that has a substitute? Might any of them be able to profit from price discrimination? Explain your answers.

A Single-Price Monopoly's Output and Price Decision

(Study Plan 13.2)

Use the following table to work Problems 2 to 4. Minnie's Mineral Springs is a single-price monopoly. Columns 1 and 2 of the table set out the market demand schedule for Minnie's water and columns 2 and 3 set out Minnie's total cost schedule.

Price (dollars per bottle)	Quantity (bottles per hour)	Total cost (dollars per hour)
10	0	1
8	1	3
6	2	7
4	3	13
2	4	21
0	5	31

2. Calculate Minnie's marginal revenue schedule and draw a graph of the market demand curve and Minnie's marginal revenue curve. Explain why Minnie's marginal revenue is less than the price.

3. At what price is Minnie's total revenue maximized and over what price range is the demand for water elastic? Why will Minnie not produce a quantity at which the market demand is inelastic?

4. Calculate Minnie's profit-maximizing output and price and economic profit.

Single-Price Monopoly and Competition Compared

(Study Plan 13.3)

5. Use the data in Problem 2 to work Problem 5.
   a. Use a graph to illustrate the producer surplus generated from Minnie's Mineral Springs' water production and consumption.

   b. Is Minnie's an efficient producer of water? Explain your answer.

   c. Suppose that new wells were discovered nearby to Minnie's and Minnie's faced competition from new producers. Explain what would happen to Minnie's output, price, and profit.

Price Discrimination (Study Plan 13.4)

6. La Bella Pizza can produce a pizza for a marginal cost of $2. Its price of a pizza is $15.
   a. Could La Bella Pizza make a larger economic profit by offering a second pizza for $5? Use a graph to illustrate your answer.
   b. How might La Bella Pizza make even more economic profit? Would it then be more efficient than when it charged $15 for each pizza?

Monopoly Regulation (Study Plan 13.5)

Use the following figure to work Problems 7 to 9. The figure shows Calypso, a U.S. natural gas distributor. It is a natural monopoly that cannot price discriminate.

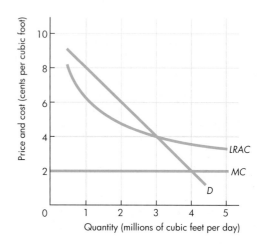

What quantity will Calypso produce, what price will it charge, and what will be the total surplus and deadweight loss if Calypso is

7. An unregulated profit-maximizing firm?
8. Regulated to make zero economic profit?
9. Regulated to be efficient?

ADDITIONAL PROBLEMS AND APPLICATIONS

MyEconLab   You can work these problems in MyEconLab if assigned by your instructor.

Monopoly and How It Arises

Use the following list, which gives some information about seven firms, to answer Problems 10 and 11.

- Coca-Cola cuts its price below that of Pepsi-Cola in an attempt to increase its market share.
- A single firm, protected by a barrier to entry, produces a personal service that has no close substitutes.
- A barrier to entry exists, but the good has some close substitutes.
- A firm offers discounts to students and seniors.
- A firm can sell any quantity it chooses at the going price.
- The government issues Nike an exclusive license to produce golf balls.
- A firm experiences economies of scale even when it produces the quantity that meets the entire market demand.

10. In which of the seven cases might monopoly arise?

11. Which of the seven cases are natural monopolies and which are legal monopolies? Which can price discriminate, which cannot, and why?

A Single-Price Monopoly's Output and Price Decision

Use the following information to work Problems 12 to 16.

Hot Air Balloon Rides is a single-price monopoly. Columns 1 and 2 of the table set out the market demand schedule and columns 2 and 3 set out the total cost schedule.

Price (dollars per ride)	Quantity (rides per month)	Total cost (dollars per month)
220	0	80
200	1	160
180	2	260
160	3	380
140	4	520
120	5	680

12. Construct Hot Air's total revenue and marginal revenue schedules.

13. Draw a graph of the market demand curve and Hot Air's marginal revenue curve.

14. Find Hot Air's profit-maximizing output and price and calculate the firm's economic profit.

15. If the government imposes a tax on Hot Air's profit, how do its output and price change?

16. If instead of taxing Hot Air's profit, the government imposes a sales tax on balloon rides of $30 a ride, what are the new profit-maximizing quantity, price, and economic profit?

17. The figure illustrates the situation facing the publisher of the only newspaper containing local news in an isolated community.

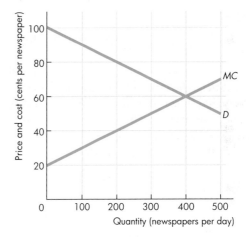

   a. On the graph, mark the profit-maximizing quantity and price and the publisher's total revenue per day.
   b. At the price charged, is the demand for this newspaper elastic or inelastic? Why?

Single-Price Monopoly and Competition Compared

18. Show on the graph in Problem 17 the consumer surplus from newspapers and the deadweight loss created by the monopoly. Explain why this market might encourage rent seeking.

19. If the newspaper market in Problem 17 were perfectly competitive, what would be the quantity, price, consumer surplus, and producer surplus? Mark each on the graph.

20. **What the Apple-Samsung Verdict Means for Your Smartphone**
   A California jury found Samsung guilty of violating the majority of the patents in question, including software features like double-tap zooming and scrolling. It recommended that Apple be awarded more than $1 billion in damages. This verdict

could significantly affect both smartphone users and producers.

> Source: CNN Money, August 26, 2012

a. If Apple became a monopoly in the smartphone market, who would benefit and who would lose?

b. Compared to a smartphone monopoly, who would benefit and who would lose if the smartphone market became perfectly competitive?

c. Explain which market would be efficient: a perfectly competitive one or a monopoly.

Price Discrimination

21. **AT&T Moves Away from Unlimited-Data Pricing**

AT&T said it will eliminate its $30 unlimited data plan as the crush of data use from the iPhone has hurt call quality. AT&T is introducing new plans costing $15 a month for 200 megabytes of data traffic or $25 a month for 2 gigabytes. AT&T says those who exceed 2 gigabytes of usage will pay $10 a month for each additional gigabyte. AT&T hopes that these plans will attract more customers.

> Source: *The Wall Street Journal*, June 2, 2010

a. Explain why AT&T's new plans might be price discrimination.

b. Draw a graph to illustrate the original plan and the new plans.

Monopoly Regulation

22. **iSurrender**

In 2008, getting your hands on the new iPhone meant signing a two-year AT&T contract. Some markets, because of the costs of being a player, tend toward either a single firm or a small number of firms. Everyone hoped the wireless market would be different. A telephone monopoly has been the norm for most of American telecommunication history, except for what may turn out to have been a brief experimental period from 1984 through 2012, or so. It may be that telephone monopolies in America are a national tradition.

> Source: *Slate*, June 10, 2008

a. How did AT&T, the exclusive provider of wireless service for the iPhone in 2008, influence the wireless telecommunication market?

b. Explain why the wireless market might "tend toward either a single firm or a small number of firms." Why might this justify allowing a regulated monopoly to exist in this market?

Economics in the News

23. After you have studied *Economics in the News* on pp. 316–317, answer the following questions.

a. Why did the European regulators say that Google was misusing its monopoly power? Do you agree? Explain why or why not.

b. Explain why it would be inefficient to regulate Google to make it charge the same price per keyword click to all advertisers.

c. Explain why selling keywords to the highest bidder can lead to an efficient allocation of advertising resources.

24. **F.C.C. Planning Rules to Open Cable Market**

The Federal Communications Commission (F.C.C.) is setting new regulations to open the cable television market to independent programmers and rival video services. The new rules will make it easier for small independent programmers to lease access to cable channels, and the size of the nation's largest cable companies will be capped at 30 percent of the market.

> Source: *The New York Times*, November 10, 2007

a. What barriers to entry exist in the cable television market?

b. Are high cable prices evidence of monopoly power?

c. Draw a graph to illustrate the effects of the F.C.C.'s new regulations on the price, quantity, total surplus, and deadweight loss.

25. **Antitrust Inquiry Launched into Intel**

Intel, the world's largest chipmaker, holds 80 percent of the microprocessor market. Advanced Micro Devices complains that Intel stifles competition, but Intel says that the 42.4 percent fall in prices between 2000 and 2007 shows that this industry is fiercely competitive.

> Source: *The Washington Post*, June 7, 2008

a. Is Intel a monopoly in the chip market?

b. Evaluate the argument made by Intel that the fall in prices "shows that this industry is fiercely competitive."

14 MONOPOLISTIC COMPETITION

After studying this chapter, you will be able to:

- ◆ Define and identify monopolistic competition
- ◆ Explain how a firm in monopolistic competition determines its price and output in the short run and the long run
- ◆ Explain why advertising costs are high and why firms in monopolistic competition use brand names

At tennis-warehouse.com, you have a choice of racquets made by 19 producers. The top five have 265 different racquets to choose among. Tennis racquet producers compete, but each has a monopoly on its own special kind of racquet—the market is an example of monopolistic competition.

The model of monopolistic competition helps us to understand the competition that we see every day. And in *Economics in the News*, at the end of the chapter, we apply the model to the market for tennis racquets.

What Is Monopolistic Competition?

You have studied perfect competition, in which a large number of firms produce at the lowest possible cost, make zero economic profit, and are efficient. You've also studied monopoly, in which a single firm restricts output, produces at a higher cost and price than in perfect competition, and is inefficient.

Most real-world markets are competitive but not perfectly competitive, because firms in these markets have some power to set their prices, as monopolies do. We call this type of market *monopolistic competition*.

Monopolistic competition is a market structure in which

- A large number of firms compete.
- Each firm produces a differentiated product.
- Firms compete on product quality, price, and marketing.
- Firms are free to enter and exit the industry.

Large Number of Firms

In monopolistic competition, as in perfect competition, the industry consists of a large number of firms. The presence of a large number of firms has three implications for the firms in the industry.

Small Market Share In monopolistic competition, each firm supplies a small part of the total industry output. Consequently, each firm has only limited power to influence the price of its product. Each firm's price can deviate from the average price of other firms by only a relatively small amount.

Ignore Other Firms A firm in monopolistic competition must be sensitive to the average market price of the product, but the firm does not pay attention to any one individual competitor. Because all the firms are relatively small, no one firm can dictate market conditions, and so no one firm's actions directly affect the actions of the other firms.

Collusion Impossible Firms in monopolistic competition would like to be able to conspire to fix a higher price—called *collusion*. But because the number of firms in monopolistic competition is large, coordination is difficult and collusion is not possible.

Product Differentiation

A firm practises **product differentiation** if it makes a product that is slightly different from the products of competing firms. A differentiated product is one that is a close substitute but not a perfect substitute for the products of the other firms. Some people are willing to pay more for one variety of the product, so when its price rises, the quantity demanded of that variety decreases, but it does not (necessarily) decrease to zero. For example, Adidas, Asics, Diadora, Etonic, Fila, New Balance, Nike, Puma, and Reebok all make differentiated running shoes. If the price of Adidas running shoes rises and the prices of the other shoes remain constant, Adidas sells fewer shoes and the other producers sell more. But Adidas shoes don't disappear unless the price rises by a large enough amount.

Competing on Quality, Price, and Marketing

Product differentiation enables a firm to compete with other firms in three areas: product quality, price, and marketing.

Quality The quality of a product is the physical attributes that make it different from the products of other firms. Quality includes design, reliability, the service provided to the buyer, and the buyer's ease of access to the product. Quality lies on a spectrum that runs from high to low. Some firms—such as Dell Computer Corp.—offer high-quality products. They are well designed and reliable, and the customer receives quick and efficient service. Other firms offer a lower-quality product that is poorly designed, that might not work perfectly, and that is not supported by effective customer service.

Price Because of product differentiation, a firm in monopolistic competition faces a downward-sloping demand curve. So, like a monopoly, the firm can set both its price and its output. But there is a tradeoff between the product's quality and price. A firm that makes a high-quality product can charge a higher price than a firm that makes a low-quality product.

Marketing Because of product differentiation, a firm in monopolistic competition must market its product. Marketing takes two main forms: advertising and packaging. A firm that produces a high-quality

ECONOMICS IN ACTION

Monopolistic Competition Today

These ten industries operate in monopolistic competition. The number of firms in the industry is shown in parentheses after the name of the industry. The red bars show the percentage of industry sales by the 4 largest firms. The green bars show the percentage of industry sales by the next 4 largest firms, and the blue bars show the percentage of industry sales by the next 12 largest firms. So the entire length of the combined red, green, and blue bars shows the percentage of industry sales by the 20 largest firms. The Herfindahl-Hirschman Index is shown on the right.

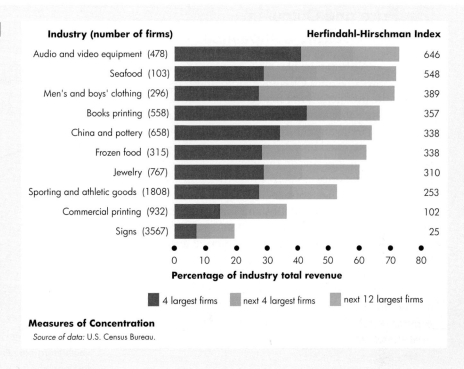

Measures of Concentration
Source of data: U.S. Census Bureau.

product wants to sell it for a suitably high price. To be able to do so, it must advertise and package its product in a way that convinces buyers that they are getting the higher quality for which they are paying a higher price. For example, pharmaceutical companies advertise and package their brand-name drugs to persuade buyers that these items are superior to the lower-priced generic alternatives. Similarly, a low-quality producer uses advertising and packaging to persuade buyers that although the quality is low, the low price more than compensates for this fact.

Entry and Exit

Monopolistic competition has no barriers to prevent new firms from entering the industry in the long run. Consequently, a firm in monopolistic competition cannot make an economic profit in the long run. When existing firms make an economic profit, new firms enter the industry. This entry lowers prices and eventually eliminates economic profit. When firms incur economic losses, some firms leave the industry in the long run. This exit increases prices and eventually eliminates the economic loss.

In long-run equilibrium, firms neither enter nor leave the industry and the firms in the industry make zero economic profit.

Examples of Monopolistic Competition

Economics in Action below shows 10 industries that are good examples of monopolistic competition. These industries have a large number of firms, which is shown in parentheses. In the market for audio and video equipment, the 4 largest firms produce only 41 percent of the industry's total sales and the 20 largest firms produce 72 percent of total sales. The number on the right is the Herfindahl-Hirschman Index (see Chapter 10, p. 234).

◆ REVIEW QUIZ

1 What are the distinguishing characteristics of monopolistic competition?

2 How do firms in monopolistic competition compete?

3 Provide some examples of industries near your school that operate in monopolistic competition (excluding those in the figure below).

Work these questions in Study Plan 14.1 and get instant feedback. Do a Key Terms Quiz.   MyEconLab

Price and Output in Monopolistic Competition

Suppose you've been hired by VF Corporation, the firm that owns Nautica Clothing Corporation, to manage the production and marketing of Nautica jackets. Think about the decisions that you must make at Nautica. First, you must decide on the design and quality of jackets and on your marketing program. Second, you must decide on the quantity of jackets to produce and the price at which to sell them.

We'll suppose that Nautica has already made its decisions about design, quality, and marketing and now we'll concentrate on the output and pricing decisions. We'll study quality and marketing decisions in the next section.

For a given quality of jackets and marketing activity, Nautica faces given costs and market conditions. Given its costs and the demand for its jackets, how does Nautica decide the quantity of jackets to produce and the price at which to sell them?

The Firm's Short-Run Output and Price Decision

In the short run, a firm in monopolistic competition makes its output and price decision just like a monopoly firm does. Figure 14.1 illustrates this decision for Nautica jackets.

The demand curve for Nautica jackets is *D*. This demand curve tells us the quantity of Nautica jackets demanded at each price, given the prices of other jackets. It is not the demand curve for jackets in general.

The *MR* curve shows the marginal revenue curve associated with the demand curve for Nautica jackets. It is derived just like the marginal revenue curve of a single-price monopoly that you studied in Chapter 13.

The *ATC* curve and the *MC* curve show the average total cost and the marginal cost of producing Nautica jackets.

Nautica's goal is to maximize its economic profit. To do so, it produces the output at which marginal revenue equals marginal cost. In Fig. 14.1, this output is 125 jackets a day. Nautica charges the price that buyers are willing to pay for this quantity, which is determined by the demand curve. This price is $75 per jacket. When Nautica produces 125 jackets a day, its average total cost is $25 per jacket and it makes an economic profit of $6,250 a day ($50 per jacket

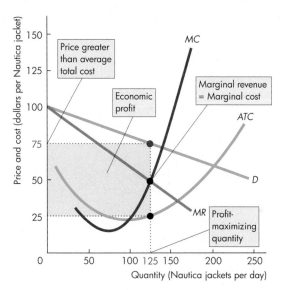

FIGURE 14.1 Economic Profit in the Short Run

Nautica maximizes profit by producing the quantity at which marginal revenue equals marginal cost, 125 jackets a day, and charging the price of $75 a jacket. This price exceeds the average total cost of $25 a jacket, so the firm makes an economic profit of $50 a jacket. The blue rectangle illustrates economic profit, which equals $6,250 a day ($50 a jacket multiplied by 125 jackets a day).

MyEconLab Animation and Draw Graph

multiplied by 125 jackets a day). The blue rectangle shows Nautica's economic profit.

Profit Maximizing Might Be Loss Minimizing

Figure 14.1 shows that Nautica is making a large economic profit. But such an outcome is not inevitable. A firm might face a level of demand for its product that is too low for it to make an economic profit.

Excite@Home was such a firm. Offering high-speed Internet service over the same cable that provides television, Excite@Home hoped to capture a large share of the Internet portal market in competition with AOL, MSN, and a host of other providers.

Figure 14.2 illustrates the situation facing Excite@Home in 2001. The demand curve for its portal service is *D*, the marginal revenue curve is *MR*, the average total cost curve is *ATC*, and the marginal cost curve is *MC*. Excite@Home maximized profit—

FIGURE 14.2   Economic Loss in the Short Run

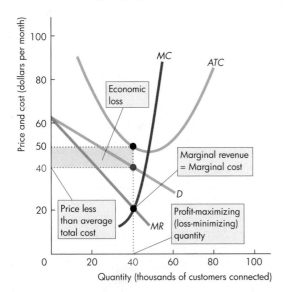

Profit is maximized where marginal revenue equals marginal cost. The loss-minimizing quantity is 40,000 customers. The price of $40 a month is less than the average total cost of $50 a month, so the firm incurs an economic loss of $10 a customer. The red rectangle illustrates economic loss, which equals $400,000 a month ($10 a customer multiplied by 40,000 customers).

—————— MyEconLab Animation ——————

equivalently, it minimized its loss—by producing the output at which marginal revenue equals marginal cost. In Fig. 14.2, this output is 40,000 customers. Excite@Home charged the price that buyers were willing to pay for this quantity, which was determined by the demand curve and which was $40 a month. With 40,000 customers, Excite@Home's average total cost was $50 per customer, so it incurred an economic loss of $400,000 a month ($10 a customer multiplied by 40,000 customers). The red rectangle shows Excite@Home's economic loss.

So far, the firm in monopolistic competition looks like a single-price monopoly. It produces the quantity at which marginal revenue equals marginal cost and then charges the price that buyers are willing to pay for that quantity, as determined by the demand curve. The key difference between monopoly and monopolistic competition lies in what happens next when firms either make an economic profit or incur an economic loss.

Long Run: Zero Economic Profit

A firm like Excite@Home is not going to incur an economic loss for long. Eventually, it goes out of business. Also, there is no restriction on entry into monopolistic competition, so if firms in an industry are making economic profit, other firms have an incentive to enter that industry.

As the Gap and other firms start to make jackets similar to those made by Nautica, the demand for Nautica jackets decreases. The demand curve for Nautica jackets and the marginal revenue curve shift leftward. As these curves shift leftward, the profit-maximizing quantity and price fall.

Figure 14.3 shows the long-run equilibrium. The demand curve for Nautica jackets and the marginal revenue curve have shifted leftward. The firm produces 75 jackets a day and sells them for $25 each. At this output level, average total cost is also $25 per jacket.

FIGURE 14.3   Output and Price in the Long Run

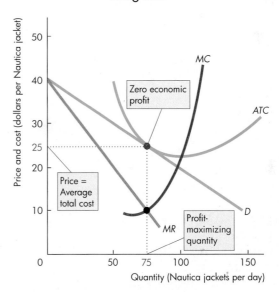

Economic profit encourages entry, which decreases the demand for each firm's product. When the demand curve touches the ATC curve at the quantity at which MR equals MC, the market is in long-run equilibrium. The output that maximizes profit is 75 jackets a day, and the price is $25 per jacket. Average total cost is also $25 per jacket, so economic profit is zero.

—————— MyEconLab Animation ——————

So Nautica is making zero economic profit on its jackets. When all the firms in the industry are making zero economic profit, there is no incentive for new firms to enter.

If demand is so low relative to costs that firms incur economic losses, exit will occur. As firms leave an industry, the demand for the products of the remaining firms increases and their demand curves shift rightward. The exit process ends when all the firms in the industry are making zero economic profit.

Monopolistic Competition and Perfect Competition

Figure 14.4 compares monopolistic competition and perfect competition and highlights two key differences between them:

- Excess capacity
- Markup

Excess Capacity A firm has **excess capacity** if it produces less than its **efficient scale**, which is the quantity at which average total cost is a minimum—the quantity at the bottom of the U-shaped *ATC* curve. In Fig. 14.4, the efficient scale is 100 jackets a day. Nautica in part (a) produces 75 Nautica jackets a day and has *excess capacity* of 25 jackets a day. But if all jackets are alike and are produced by firms in perfect competition, each firm in part (b) produces 100 jackets a day, which is the efficient scale. Average total cost is the lowest possible only in *perfect* competition.

You can see the excess capacity in monopolistic competition all around you. Family restaurants (except for the truly outstanding ones) almost always have some empty tables. You can always get a pizza delivered in less than 30 minutes. It is rare that every pump at a gas station is in use with customers waiting in line. Many real estate agents are ready to help you find or sell a home. These industries are examples of monopolistic competition. The firms have excess

---

FIGURE 14.4   Excess Capacity and Markup

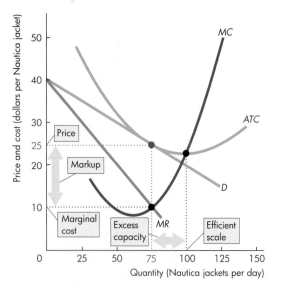

(a) Monopolistic competition

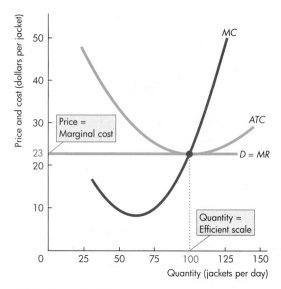

(b) Perfect competition

The efficient scale is 100 jackets a day. In monopolistic competition in the long run, because the firm faces a downward-sloping demand curve for its product, the quantity produced is less than the efficient scale and the firm has excess capacity. Price exceeds marginal cost by the amount of the markup.

In contrast, because in perfect competition the demand for each firm's product is perfectly elastic, the quantity produced in the long run equals the efficient scale and price equals marginal cost. The firm produces at the least possible cost and there is no markup.

MyEconLab Animation and Draw Graph

capacity. They could sell more by cutting their prices, but they would then incur losses.

Markup A firm's **markup** is the amount by which price exceeds marginal cost. Figure 14.4(a) shows Nautica's markup. In perfect competition, price always equals marginal cost and there is no markup. Figure 14.4(b) shows this case. In monopolistic competition, buyers pay a higher price than in perfect competition and also pay more than marginal cost.

Is Monopolistic Competition Efficient?

Resources are used efficiently when marginal social benefit equals marginal social cost. Price equals marginal social benefit and the firm's marginal cost equals marginal social cost (assuming there are no external benefits or costs). So if the price of a Nautica jacket exceeds the marginal cost of producing it, the quantity of Nautica jackets produced is less than the efficient quantity. And you've just seen that in long-run equilibrium in monopolistic competition, price *does* exceed marginal cost. So is the quantity produced in monopolistic competition less than the efficient quantity?

Making the Relevant Comparison Two economists meet in the street, and one asks the other, "How is your husband?" The quick reply is "Compared to what?" This bit of economic wit illustrates a key point: Before we can conclude that something needs fixing, we must check out the available alternatives.

The markup that drives a gap between price and marginal cost in monopolistic competition arises from product differentiation. It is because Nautica jackets are not quite the same as jackets from Banana Republic, CK, Diesel, DKNY, Earl Jackets, Gap, Levi's, Ralph Lauren, or any of the other dozens of producers of jackets that the demand for Nautica jackets is not perfectly elastic. The only way in which the demand for jackets from Nautica might be perfectly elastic is if there were only one kind of jacket and all firms made it. In this situation, Nautica jackets are indistinguishable from all other jackets. They don't even have identifying labels.

If there were only one kind of jacket, the total benefit of jackets would almost certainly be less than it is with variety. People value variety—not only because it enables each person to select what he or she likes best but also because it provides an external benefit. Most of us enjoy seeing variety in the choices of others. Contrast a scene from the China of the 1960s, when everyone wore a Mao tunic, with the China of today, where everyone wears the clothes of their own choosing. Or contrast a scene from the Germany of the 1930s, when almost everyone who could afford a car owned a first-generation Volkswagen Beetle, with the world of today with its enormous variety of styles and types of automobiles.

If people value variety, why don't we see infinite variety? The answer is that variety is costly. Each different variety of any product must be designed, and then customers must be informed about it. These initial costs of design and marketing—called setup costs—mean that some varieties that are too close to others already available are just not worth creating.

The Bottom Line Product variety is both valued and costly. The efficient degree of product variety is the one for which the marginal social benefit of product variety equals its marginal social cost. The loss that arises because the quantity produced is less than the efficient quantity is offset by the gain that arises from having a greater degree of product variety. So compared to the alternative—product uniformity—monopolistic competition might be efficient.

 REVIEW QUIZ

1 How does a firm in monopolistic competition decide how much to produce and at what price to offer its product for sale?

2 Why can a firm in monopolistic competition make an economic profit only in the short run?

3 Why do firms in monopolistic competition operate with excess capacity?

4 Why is there a price markup over marginal cost in monopolistic competition?

5 Is monopolistic competition efficient?

Work these questions in Study Plan 14.2 and get instant feedback. Do a Key Terms Quiz.   MyEconLab

You've seen how the firm in monopolistic competition determines its output and price in both the short run and the long run when it produces a given product and undertakes a *given* marketing effort. But how does the firm choose its product quality and marketing effort? We'll now study these decisions.

◆ Product Development and Marketing

When Nautica made its price and output decision that we've just studied, it had already made its product quality and marketing decisions. We'll now look at these decisions and see how they influence the firm's output, price, and economic profit.

Product Development

The prospect of new firms entering the industry keeps firms in monopolistic competition on their toes! To enjoy economic profits, they must continually seek ways of keeping one step ahead of imitators—other firms who imitate the success of profitable firms.

To maintain economic profit, a firm must either develop an entirely new product, or develop a significantly improved product that provides it with a competitive edge, even if only temporarily. A firm that introduces a new or improved and more differentiated product faces a demand that is less elastic and is able to increase its price and make an economic profit. Eventually, imitators will make close substitutes for the firm's new product and compete away the economic profit arising from an initial advantage. So to restore economic profit, the firm must develop another new or seriously improved product.

Profit-Maximizing Product Development The decision to develop a new or improved product is based on the same type of profit-maximizing calculation that you've already studied.

Product development is a costly activity, but it also brings in additional revenues. The firm must balance the cost and revenue at the margin.

The marginal dollar spent on developing a new or improved product is the marginal cost of product development. The marginal dollar that the new or improved product earns for the firm is the marginal revenue of product development. At a low level of product development, the marginal revenue from a better product exceeds the marginal cost. At a high level of product development, the marginal cost of a better product exceeds the marginal revenue.

When the marginal cost and marginal revenue of product development are equal, the firm is undertaking the profit-maximizing amount of product development.

Efficiency and Product Development Is the profit-maximizing amount of product development also the efficient amount? Efficiency is achieved if the marginal social benefit of a new and improved product equals its marginal social cost.

The marginal social benefit of an improved product is the increase in price that consumers are willing to pay for it. The marginal social cost is the amount that the firm must pay to make the improvement. Profit is maximized when marginal *revenue* equals marginal cost. But in monopolistic competition, marginal revenue is less than price, so product development is probably not pushed to its efficient level.

Monopolistic competition brings many product changes that cost little to implement and are purely cosmetic, such as improved packaging or a new scent in laundry powder. Even when there is a truly improved product, it is never as good as the consumer would like and for which the consumer is willing to pay a higher price. For example, "The Legend of Zelda: Skyward Sword" is regarded as an almost perfect and very cool game, but users complain that it isn't quite perfect. It is a game whose features generate a marginal revenue equal to the marginal cost of creating them.

Advertising

A firm with a differentiated product needs to ensure that its customers know how its product is different from the competition. A firm also might attempt to create a consumer perception that its product is different, even when that difference is small. Firms use advertising and packaging to achieve this goal.

Advertising Expenditures Firms in monopolistic competition incur huge costs to ensure that buyers appreciate and value the differences between their own products and those of their competitors. So a large proportion of the price that we pay for a good covers the cost of selling it, and this proportion is increasing. Advertising in newspapers and magazines and on radio, television, and the Internet is the main selling cost. But it is not the only one. Selling costs include the cost of shopping malls that look like movie sets, glossy catalogs and brochures, and the salaries, airfares, and hotel bills of salespeople.

Advertising expenditures affect the profits of firms in two ways: They increase costs, and they change demand. Let's look at these effects.

ECONOMICS IN ACTION
The Cost of Selling a Pair of Shoes

When you buy a pair of running shoes that cost you $70, you're paying $9 for the materials from which the shoes are made, $2.75 for the services of the Malaysian worker who made the shoes, and $5.25 for the production and transportation services of a manufacturing firm in Asia and a shipping company. These numbers total $17. You pay $3 to the U.S. government in import duty. So we've now accounted for a total of $20. Where did the other $50 go? It is the cost of advertising, retailing, and other sales and distribution services.

The selling costs associated with running shoes are not unusual. Almost everything that you buy includes a selling cost component that exceeds one half of the total cost. Your clothing, food, electronic items, DVDs, magazines, and even your textbooks cost more to sell than they cost to manufacture.

Advertising costs are only a part, and often a small part, of total selling costs. For example, Nike spends about $4 on advertising per pair of running shoes sold.

For the U.S. economy as a whole, there are some 20,000 advertising agencies, which employ more than 200,000 people and have sales of $45 billion. These numbers are only part of the total cost of advertising because firms have their own internal advertising departments, the costs of which we can only guess.

But the biggest part of selling costs is not the cost of advertising. It is the cost of retailing services. The retailer's selling costs (and economic profit) are often as much as 50 percent of the price you pay.

| Raw materials $9 | Production costs $8 | Import duty $3 | Selling costs $50 |

Selling Costs and Total Cost Selling costs are fixed costs and they increase the firm's total cost. So like the fixed cost of producing a good, advertising costs per unit decrease as the quantity produced increases.

Figure 14.5 shows how selling costs change a firm's average total cost. The blue curve shows the average total cost of production. The red curve shows the firm's average total cost of production plus advertising. The height of the red area between the two curves shows the average fixed cost of advertising. The *total* cost of advertising is fixed. But the *average* cost of advertising decreases as output increases.

Figure 14.5 shows that if advertising increases the quantity sold by a large enough amount, it can lower average total cost. For example, if the quantity sold increases from 25 jackets a day with no advertising to 100 jackets a day with advertising, average total cost falls from $60 to $40 a jacket. The reason is that although the *total* fixed cost has increased, the greater fixed cost is spread over a greater output, so average total cost decreases.

FIGURE 14.5   Selling Costs and Total Cost

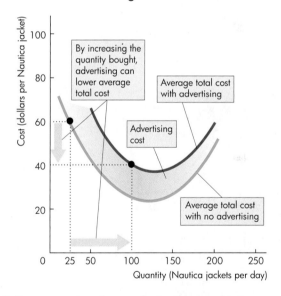

Selling costs such as the cost of advertising are fixed costs. When added to the average total cost of production, selling costs increase average total cost by a greater amount at small outputs than at large outputs. If advertising enables sales to increase from 25 jackets a day to 100 jackets a day, average total cost *falls* from $60 to $40 a jacket.

MyEconLab Animation

Selling Costs and Demand Advertising and other selling efforts change the demand for a firm's product. But how? Does demand increase or does it decrease? The most natural answer is that advertising increases demand. By informing people about the quality of its products or by persuading people to switch from the products of other firms, a firm might expect to increase the demand for its own products.

But all firms in monopolistic competition advertise, and all seek to persuade customers that they have the best deal. If advertising enables a firm to survive, the number of firms in the market might increase. And to the extent that the number of firms does increase, advertising *decreases* the demand faced by any one firm. It also makes the demand for any one firm's product more elastic. So advertising can end up not only lowering average total cost but also lowering the markup and the price.

Figure 14.6 illustrates this possible effect of advertising. In part (a), with no advertising, the demand for Nautica jackets is not very elastic. Profit is maximized at 75 jackets per day, and the markup is large. In part (b), advertising, which is a fixed cost, increases average total cost from ATC_0 to ATC_1 but leaves marginal cost unchanged at MC. Demand becomes much more elastic, the profit-maximizing quantity increases, and the markup shrinks.

Using Advertising to Signal Quality

Some advertising, like the Roger Federer Rolex watch ad in glossy magazines or the huge number of dollars that Coke and Pepsi spend, seems hard to understand. There doesn't seem to be any concrete information about a watch in a tennis player's smile. And surely everyone knows about Coke and Pepsi. What is the gain from pouring millions of dollars into advertising these well-known colas?

One answer is that advertising is a signal to the consumer of a high-quality product. A **signal** is an action taken by an informed person (or firm) to send a message to uninformed people. Think about two colas:

FIGURE 14.6   Advertising and the Markup

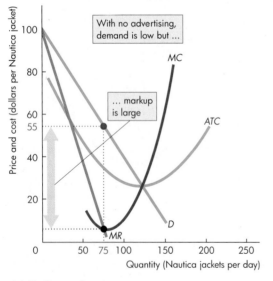

(a) No firms advertise

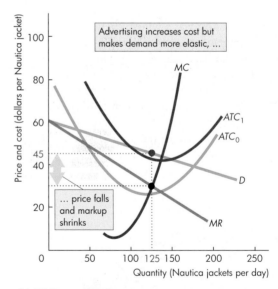

(b) All firms advertise

If no firms advertise, demand for each firm's product is low and not very elastic. The profit-maximizing output is small, the markup is large, and the price is high.

Advertising increases average total cost and shifts the *ATC* curve upward from ATC_0 to ATC_1. If all firms advertise, the demand for each firm's product becomes more elastic. Output increases, the price falls, and the markup shrinks.

MyEconLab Animation

Coke and Oke. Oke knows that its cola is not very good and that its taste varies a lot depending on which cheap batch of unsold cola it happens to buy each week. So Oke knows that while it could get a lot of people to try Oke by advertising, they would all quickly discover what a poor product it is and switch back to the cola they bought before. Coke, in contrast, knows that its product has a high-quality, consistent taste and that once consumers have tried it, there is a good chance they'll never drink anything else. On the basis of this reasoning, Oke doesn't advertise but Coke does. And Coke spends a lot of money to make a big splash.

Cola drinkers who see Coke's splashy ads know that the firm would not spend so much money advertising if its product were not truly good. So consumers reason that Coke is indeed a really good product. The flashy expensive ad has signaled that Coke is really good without saying anything about Coke.

Notice that if advertising is a signal, it doesn't need any specific product information. It just needs to be expensive and hard to miss. That's what a lot of advertising looks like. So the signaling theory of advertising predicts much of the advertising that we see.

Brand Names

Many firms create and spend a lot of money promoting a brand name. Why? What benefit does a brand name bring to justify the sometimes high cost of establishing it?

The basic answer is that a brand name provides information to consumers about the quality of a product, and is an incentive to the producer to achieve a high and consistent quality standard.

To see how a brand name helps the consumer, think about how you use brand names to get information about quality. You're on a road trip, and it is time to find a place to spend the night. You see roadside advertisements for Holiday Inn, Joe's Motel, and Annie's Driver's Stop. You know about Holiday Inn because you've stayed in it before. You've also seen their advertisements and know what to expect. You have no information at all about Joe's and Annie's. They might be better than the lodgings you do know about, but without that knowledge, you're not going to try them. You use the brand name as information and stay at Holiday Inn.

This same story explains why a brand name provides an incentive to achieve high and consistent quality. Because no one would know whether Joe's and Annie's were offering a high standard of service, they

have no incentive to do so. But equally, because everyone expects a given standard of service from Holiday Inn, a failure to meet a customer's expectation would almost surely lose that customer to a competitor. So Holiday Inn has a strong incentive to deliver what it promises in the advertising that creates its brand name.

Efficiency of Advertising and Brand Names

To the extent that advertising and brand names provide consumers with information about the precise nature of product differences and product quality, they benefit the consumer and enable a better product choice to be made. But the opportunity cost of the additional information must be weighed against the gain to the consumer.

The final verdict on the efficiency of monopolistic competition is ambiguous. In some cases, the gains from extra product variety offset the selling costs and the extra cost arising from excess capacity. The tremendous varieties of books, magazines, clothing, food, and drinks are examples of such gains. It is less easy to see the gains from being able to buy a brand-name drug with the identical chemical composition to that of a generic alternative, but many people willingly pay more for the brand-name alternative.

REVIEW QUIZ

1 How, other than by adjusting price, do firms in monopolistic competition compete?
2 Why might product development be efficient and why might it be inefficient?
3 Explain how selling costs influence a firm's cost curves and its average total cost.
4 Explain how advertising influences the demand for a firm's product.
5 Are advertising and brand names efficient?

Work these questions in Study Plan 14.3 and get instant feedback. Do a Key Terms Quiz.   MyEconLab

Monopolistic competition is one of the most common market structures that you encounter in your daily life. *Economics in the News* on pp. 334–335 applies the model of monopolistic competition to the market for tennis racquets and shows why you can expect continual improvement and the introduction of new racquets from Babolat, Wilson, Head, Prince, Dunlop, and other racquet producers.

Product Differentiation in Tennis Racquets

Big Serves, Big Data: The First Connected Tennis Racquet

Popular Mechanics
November 7, 2013

Tennis players know all about the feel of hitting the sweet spot in the strings. Now they can back up that feeling with facts. The first tennis racquet with an on/off switch is also the first racquet to track stroke data, including where the ball hits the string bed.

The Babolat Play Pure Drive Set will launch on Dec. 12. Babolat, a French racquet manufacturer founded in 1875, revealed the racquet to PopMech early, showing off the culmination of a 10-year project.

CEO Eric Babolat envisioned the connected racquet a decade ago, but it took time for sensor technology to shrink down and lighten up enough so that he wouldn't have to strap a backpack and wires to players. ...

Babolat teamed with French firm Movea, the company behind the Nintendo Wii remote, to build the digital guts. Inside the otherwise-hollow grip they placed an accelerometer and gyroscope along with a 6-hour battery, USB port, Bluetooth connectivity, and enough memory to hold 150 hours of play data. ...

The Babolat Play detects stroke type—forehand, backhand, smash, and first and second serves— measures spin and power, tracks rally length and play time, and maps out the location the ball strikes the string bed. The racquet saves all that data, which is available for download to an app via either Bluetooth to Android or Apple mobile devices, or USB to a computer. In two test sessions, the app distilled the information accurately. ...

The app saves training and match sessions, shares information in a community setting, and compares data head-to-head with friends or top players—so you can see how well you stack up against a champion like Nadal. ...

"The oldest company in tennis is making tennis cool," Eric Babolat says. All with an on/off switch.

Copyright Popular Mechanics 2013.

ESSENCE OF THE STORY

- Babolat, a French tennis recquet manufacturer, has created a tennis racquet that tracks and stores stroke data.

- Babolat started making tennis racquets in 1875.

- CEO Eric Babolat envisioned the racquet 10 years ago, but the technology needed was not then available.

- Babolat worked with the company behind the Nintendo Wii remote to create the new racquet.

- The oldest company in tennis is at the forefront of racquet technology.

MyEconLab More Economics in the News

ECONOMIC ANALYSIS

- The market for tennis racquets is an example of monopolistic competition.

- Nineteen firms compete in a market with up to 1,000 differentiated racquets.

- Although the racquets are differentiated, most of them are close substitutes for each other.

- Close substitutes have highly elastic demand, so markups are low and economic profit is competed away.

- To make an economic profit, a firm must keep innovating.

- The market for tennis racquets has seen a sequence of innovation: metal frame (Wilson, 1967), oversize frame (Prince, 1976), and graphite frame (Prince, 1980).

- Today's innovation is Babolat's Play Pure Drive electronic racquet described in the news article.

- By creating a substantially differentiated product, Babolat was able to bring to the market a product more clearly differentiated from its competitors.

- The monopolistic competition model explains what is now happening at Babolat and what the future holds.

- Figure 1 shows the market for Babolat's electronic racquet. (The numbers are assumptions.)

- Because Babolat's smart racquet differs from other racquets and has features that users value, the demand curve, D, and marginal revenue curve, MR, provide a large short-run profit opportunity.

- The marginal cost curve is MC and the average total cost curve is ATC. Babolat maximizes its economic profit by producing the quantity at which marginal revenue equals marginal cost.

- This quantity of racquets can be sold for $400 each.

- The blue rectangle shows Babolat's economic profit.

- Because Babolat makes an economic profit, entry will take place. Dunlop, Head, Prince, and Wilson will enter the smart racquet market.

- Figure 2 shows the consequences of entry for Babolat.

- The demand for the Babolat racquet decreases as the market is shared with the other racquets.

- Babolat's profit-maximizing price for the electronic racquet falls, and in the long run economic profit is eliminated.

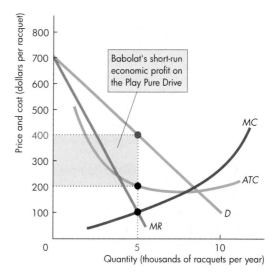

Figure 1 Economic Profit in the Short Run

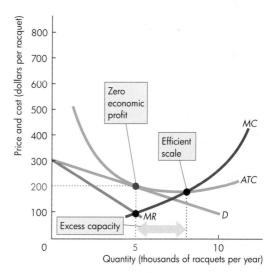

Figure 2 Zero Economic Profit in the Long Run

- With zero economic profit, Babolat (along with the other producers) has an incentive to develop an even better differentiated racquet and start the cycle described here again, making an economic profit with a new racquet in the short run.

335

SUMMARY

Key Points

What Is Monopolistic Competition? (pp. 324–325)

- Monopolistic competition occurs when a large number of firms compete with each other on product quality, price, and marketing.

Working Problems 1 and 2 will give you a better understanding of what monopolistic competition is.

Price and Output in Monopolistic Competition
(pp. 326–329)

- Each firm in monopolistic competition faces a downward-sloping demand curve and produces the profit-maximizing quantity.
- Entry and exit result in zero economic profit and excess capacity in long-run equilibrium.

Working Problems 3 to 8 will give you a better understanding of price and output in monopolistic competition.

Product Development and Marketing (pp. 330–333)

- Firms in monopolistic competition innovate and develop new products.
- Advertising expenditures increase total cost, but average total cost might fall if the quantity sold increases by enough.
- Advertising expenditures might increase demand, but demand might decrease if competition increases.
- Whether monopolistic competition is inefficient depends on the value we place on product variety.

Working Problem 9 will give you a better understanding of product development and marketing.

Key Terms   MyEconLab Key Terms Quiz

Efficient scale, 328   Markup, 329   Product differentiation, 324
Excess capacity, 328   Monopolistic competition, 324   Signal, 332

◆ WORKED PROBLEM

MyEconLab   You can work this problem in Chapter 14 Study Plan.

The table provides information about Prue's Personal Trainer Service, a firm that is in monopolistic competition with similar firms that offer slightly differentiated services.

Demand schedule		Production costs	
Price (dollars per session)	Quantity (sessions per hour)	MC (dollars per session)	ATC (dollars per session)
45	0		..
		········ 12	
40	1		33
		········ 5	
35	2		19
		········ 7	
30	3		15
		······· 27	
25	4		18

Questions

1. What is Prue's profit-maximizing quantity? What is Prue's price?
2. What is Prue's markup and does she have excess capacity?
3. Is Prue in a long-run equilibrium?

Solutions

1. The profit-maximizing quantity is that at which marginal cost equals marginal revenue. The table above provides the marginal cost data. For example, the marginal cost of the 4th session per hour is $27. The table below shows the calculation of marginal revenue. Mutliply quantity by price to find total revenue (third column) and then calculate the change in total revenue when the quantity increases by 1 session (fourth column).

Demand schedule		Total revenue (dollars per hour)	Marginal revenue (dollars per session)
Price (dollars per session)	Quantity (sessions per hour)		
45	0	0	
			······40
40	1	40	
			······30
35	2	70	
			······20
30	3	90	
			······10
25	4	100	

When the number of sessions increases from 2 to 3 an hour, marginal revenue ($20) exceeds marginal cost ($7), so profit increases. But when the number of sessions increases from 3 to 4 an hour, marginal cost ($27) exceeds marginal revenue ($10), so profit decreases. So 3 sessions an hour maximizes Prue's profit. The highest price at which 3 sessions an hour can be sold is $30 a session, which is the profit-maximizing price.

Key Point: To maximize profit, increase production if $MR > MC$ and decrease production if $MR < MC$.

2. To find Prue's markup, we compare price to marginal cost. Use the fact that $MC = ATC$ at minimum ATC and notice that minimum ATC is $15 a session at 3 sessions an hour. The price is $30 a session, so the markup is 100 percent. Prue is producing at minimum ATC, which is the efficient scale, so she has no excess capacity.

Key Point: Markup is the amount by which price exceeds marginal cost; and excess capacity is the gap between output and the efficient scale.

3. In the long run, entry decreases demand and drives economic profit to zero. Prue is making a profit of $45 an hour (price of $30 a session minus ATC of $15 a session, multiplied by 3 sessions an hour). So Prue is not in a long-run equilibrium.

Key Point: Entry decreases the demand for the firm's good or service and economic profit falls to zero. The key figure illustrates Prue's short-run equilibrium situation.

Key Figure   MyEconLab Interactive Animation

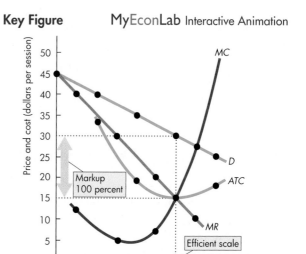

♦ STUDY PLAN PROBLEMS AND APPLICATIONS

MyEconLab   You can work Problems 1 to 9 in Chapter 14 Study Plan and get instant feedback.

What Is Monopolistic Competition? (Study Plan 14.1)

1. Which of the following items are sold by firms in monopolistic competition? Explain your selections.
   - Cable television service
   - Wheat
   - Athletic shoes
   - Soda
   - Toothbrushes
   - Ready-mix concrete

2. The four-firm concentration ratio for audio equipment makers is 30 and for electric lamp makers it is 89. The HHI for audio equipment makers is 415 and for electric lamp makers it is 2,850. Which of these markets is an example of monopolistic competition?

Price and Output in Monopolistic Competition

(Study Plan 14.2)

Use the following information to work Problems 3 and 4.

Sara is a dot.com entrepreneur who has established a Web site at which people can design and buy sweatshirts. Sara pays $1,000 a week for her Web server and Internet connection. The sweatshirts that her customers design are made to order by another firm, and Sara pays this firm $20 a sweatshirt. Sara has no other costs. The table sets out the demand schedule for Sara's sweatshirts.

Price (dollars per sweatshirt)	Quantity demanded (sweatshirts per week)
0	100
20	80
40	60
60	40
80	20
100	0

3. Calculate Sara's profit-maximizing output, price, and economic profit.

4. a. Do you expect other firms to enter the Web sweatshirt business and compete with Sara?

   b. What happens to the demand for Sara's sweatshirts in the long run? What happens to Sara's economic profit in the long run?

Use the following figure, which shows the situation facing Flight Inc., a producer of running shoes, to work Problems 5 to 8.

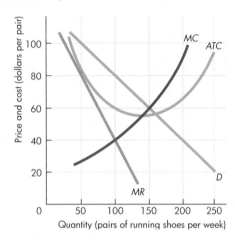

5. What quantity does Flight produce, what price does it charge, and what is its economic profit?

6. In the long run, how does Flight change its price and the quantity it produces? What happens to the market output of running shoes?

7. Does Flight have excess capacity in the long run? If it has excess capacity in the long run, why doesn't it decrease its capacity?

8. Is the market for running shoes efficient or inefficient in the long run? Explain your answer.

Product Development and Marketing (Study Plan 14.3)

9. Suppose that Tommy Hilfiger's marginal cost of a jacket is a constant $100 and the total fixed cost at one of its stores is $2,000 a day. This store sells 20 jackets a day, which is its profit-maximizing number of jackets. Then the stores nearby start to advertise their jackets. The Tommy Hilfiger store now spends $2,000 a day advertising its jackets, and its profit-maximizing number of jackets sold jumps to 50 a day.

   a. What is this store's average total cost of a jacket sold (i) before the advertising begins and (ii) after the advertising begins?

   b. Can you say what happens to the price of a Tommy Hilfiger jacket, Tommy's markup, and Tommy's economic profit? Why or why not?

ADDITIONAL PROBLEMS AND APPLICATIONS

 MyEconLab   You can work these problems in MyEconLab if assigned by your instructor

What Is Monopolistic Competition?

10. Which of the following items are sold by firms in monopolistic competition? Explain your selection.
    - Orange juice
    - Canned soup
    - PCs
    - Chewing gum
    - Breakfast cereals
    - Corn

11. The HHI for automobiles is 2,350, for sporting goods it is 161, for batteries it is 2,883, and for jewelry it is 81. Which of these markets is an example of monopolistic competition?

Price and Output in Monopolistic Competition

Use the following data to work Problems 12 and 13. Lorie teaches singing. Her fixed costs are $1,000 a month, and it costs her $50 of labor to give one class. The table shows the demand schedule for Lorie's singing lessons.

Price (dollars per lesson)	Quantity demanded (lessons per month)
0	250
50	200
100	150
150	100
200	50
250	0

12. Calculate Lorie's profit-maximizing output, price, and economic profit.

13. a. Do you expect other firms to enter the singing lesson business and compete with Lorie?

    b. What happens to the demand for Lorie's lessons in the long run? What happens to Lorie's economic profit in the long run?

Use the figure in the next column, which shows the situation facing Mike's Bikes, a producer of mountain bikes, to work Problems 14 to 18. The demand and costs of other mountain bike producers are similar to those of Mike's Bikes.

14. What quantity does the firm produce and what is its price? Calculate the firm's economic profit or economic loss.

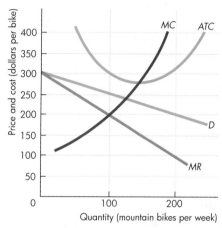

15. What will happen to the number of firms producing mountain bikes in the long run?

16. a. How will the price of a mountain bike and the number of bikes produced by Mike's Bikes change in the long run?

    b. How will the quantity of mountain bikes produced by all firms change in the long run?

17. Is there any way for Mike's Bikes to avoid having excess capacity in the long run?

18. Is the market for mountain bikes efficient or inefficient in the long run? Explain your answer.

Use the following news clip to work Problems 19 and 20.

Groceries for the Gourmet Palate

No food, it seems, is safe from being repackaged to look like an upscale product. Samuel Adams' $120 Utopias, in a ridiculous copper-covered 24-oz. bottle meant to resemble an old-fashioned brew kettle, is barely beer. It's not carbonated like a Bud, but aged in oak barrels like scotch. It has a vintage year, like a Bordeaux, is light, complex, and free of any alcohol sting, despite having six times as much alcohol content as a regular can of brew.

Source: *Time*, April 14, 2008

19. a. Explain how Samuel Adams has differentiated its Utopias to compete with other beer brands in terms of quality, price, and marketing.

    b. Predict whether Samuel Adams produces at, above, or below the efficient scale in the short run.

20. a. Predict whether the $120 price tag on the Utopias is at, above, or below marginal cost
      (i) In the short run   (ii) In the long run
    b. Do you think that Samuel Adams' Utopias makes the market for beer inefficient?

Use the following news clip to work Problems 21 and 22.

Swinging for Female Golfers

One of the hottest areas of innovation is in clubs for women, who now make up nearly a quarter of the 24 million golfers in the United States. Callaway and Nike, two of the leading golf-equipment manufacturers, recently released new clubs designed for women.

Source: *Time*, April 21, 2008

21. a. How are Callaway and Nike attempting to maintain economic profit?
    b. Draw a graph to illustrate the cost curves and revenue curves of Callaway or Nike in the market for golf clubs for women.
    c. Show on your graph in part (b) the short-run economic profit.

22. a. Explain why the economic profit that Callaway and Nike make on golf clubs for women is likely to be temporary.
    b. Draw a graph to illustrate the cost curves and revenue curves of Callaway or Nike in the market for golf clubs for women in the long run. Mark the firm's excess capacity.

Product Development and Marketing

Use the following data to work Problems 23 to 25. Bianca bakes delicious cookies. Her total fixed cost is $40 a day, and her average variable cost is $1 a bag. Few people know about Bianca's Cookies, and she is maximizing her profit by selling 10 bags a day for $5 a bag. Bianca thinks that if she spends $50 a day on advertising, she can increase her market share and sell 25 bags a day for $5 a bag.

23. If Bianca's advertising works as she expects, can she increase her economic profit by advertising?

24. If Bianca advertises, will her average total cost increase or decrease at the quantity produced?

25. If Bianca advertises, will she continue to sell her cookies for $5 a bag or will she change her price?

Use the following news clip to work Problems 26 and 27.

A Thirst for More Champagne

Champagne exports have tripled in the past 20 years. That poses a problem for northern France, where the bubbly hails from—not enough grapes. So French authorities have unveiled a plan to extend the official Champagne grape-growing zone to cover 40 new villages. This revision has provoked debate. The change will take several years to become effective. In the meantime the vineyard owners whose land values will jump markedly if the changes are finalized certainly have reason to raise a glass.

Source: *Fortune*, May 12, 2008

26. a. Why is France so strict about designating the vineyards that can use the Champagne label?
    b. Explain who most likely opposes this plan.

27. Assuming that vineyards in these 40 villages are producing the same quality of grapes with or without this plan, why will their land values "jump markedly" if this plan is approved?

28. **Under Armour's Big Step Up**
    Under Armour, the red-hot athletic-apparel brand, has joined Nike, Adidas, and New Balance as a major player in the market for athletic footwear. Under Armour plans to revive the long-dead cross-training category. But will young athletes really spend $100 for a cross training shoe to lift weights in?

    Source: *Time*, May 26, 2008

    What factors influence Under Armour's ability to make an economic profit in the cross-training shoe market?

Economics in the News

29. After you have studied *Economics in the News* on pp. 334–335, answer the following questions.
    a. Why do you think Babolat worked with the firm that helped Nintendo develop the Wii remote?
    b. How would Babolat's cost curves (*MC* and *ATC*) have been different if they had not worked with the Wii developer?
    c. How do you think the launch of Babolat's new-technology racquet has influenced the demand for other firms' racquets?
    d. Explain the effects of the introduction of the new-technology racquet on Prince and other firms in the market for tennis racquets.
    e. Draw a graph to illustrate your answer to part (c). Explain your answer.
    f. What do you predict will happen to the markup in the market for smart racquets?
    g. What do you predict will happen to excess capacity in the market for smart racquets? Explain your answer.

15 OLIGOPOLY

After studying this chapter, you will be able to:

◆ Define and identify oligopoly

◆ Use game theory to explain how price and output are determined in oligopoly

◆ Use game theory to explain other strategic decisions

◆ Describe the antitrust laws that regulate oligopoly

Chances are that your cellphone service provider is Verizon or AT&T. Two thirds of Americans have plans with these two firms. Similarly, the chip in your computer was made by either Intel or AMD; the battery in your TV remote by Duracell or Energizer; and the airplane that takes you on a long-distance trip by Boeing or the European firm Airbus.

How does a market work when only two or a handful of firms compete? To answer this question, we use the model of oligopoly.

At the end of the chapter, in *Economics in the News*, we'll look at the market for cellphone service and see how Verizon and AT&T battle to maximize profit.

What Is Oligopoly?

Oligopoly, like monopolistic competition, lies between perfect competition and monopoly. The firms in oligopoly might produce an identical product and compete only on price, or they might produce a differentiated product and compete on price, product quality, and marketing. **Oligopoly** is a market structure in which

- Natural or legal barriers prevent the entry of new firms.
- A small number of firms compete.

Barriers to Entry

Natural or legal barriers to entry can create oligopoly. You saw in Chapter 13 how economies of scale and demand form a natural barrier to entry that can create a *natural monopoly*. These same factors can create a *natural oligopoly*.

Figure 15.1 illustrates two natural oligopolies. The demand curve, D (in both parts of the figure), shows the demand for taxi rides in a town. If the average

total cost curve of a taxi company is ATC_1 in part (a), the market is a natural **duopoly**—an oligopoly market with two firms. You can probably see some examples of duopoly where you live. Some cities have only two taxi companies, two car rental firms, two copy centers, or two college bookstores.

The lowest price at which the firm would remain in business is $10 a ride. At that price, the quantity of rides demanded is 60 a day, the quantity that can be provided by just two firms. There is no room in this market for three firms. But if there were only one firm, it would make an economic profit and a second firm would enter to take some of the business and economic profit.

If the average total cost curve of a taxi company is ATC_2 in part (b), the efficient scale of one firm is 20 rides a day. This market is large enough for three firms.

A legal oligopoly arises when a legal barrier to entry protects the small number of firms in a market. A city might license two taxi firms or two bus companies, for example, even though the combination of demand and economies of scale leaves room for more than two firms.

FIGURE 15.1   Natural Oligopoly

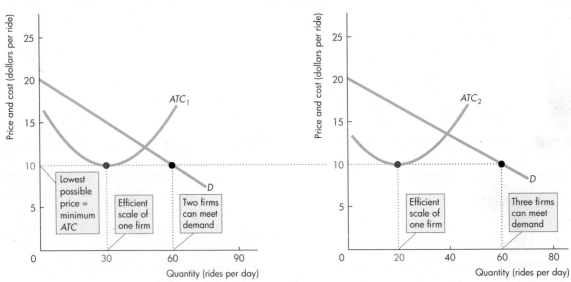

(a) Natural duopoly

(b) Natural oligopoly with three firms

The minimum average total cost of producing a ride is $10, so $10 a ride is the lowest possible price that a firm can charge. When a firm produces the efficient scale of 30 rides a day, two firms can satisfy the market demand. This market is

a natural oligopoly with two firms—a natural duopoly. When the efficient scale of one firm is 20 rides per day, three firms can satisfy the market demand at the lowest possible price. This natural oligopoly has three firms.

ECONOMICS IN ACTION
Oligopoly Today

These markets are oligopolies. Although in some of them the number of firms (in parentheses) is large, the share of the market held by the four largest firms (the red bars) is close to 100 percent.

The most concentrated markets—batteries, glass containers, breakfast cereals, computer hard drives, and light bulbs—are dominated by a handful of firms.

If you want to buy a battery for your TV remote or toothbrush, you'll find it hard to avoid buying a Duracell or an Energizer.

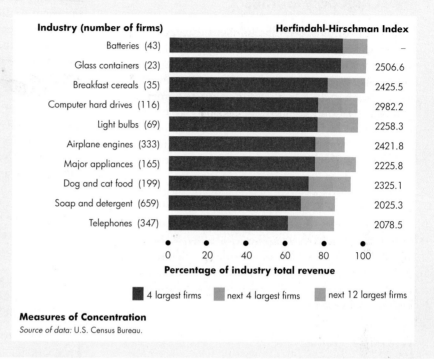

Measures of Concentration
Source of data: U.S. Census Bureau.

Small Number of Firms

Because barriers to entry exist, oligopoly consists of a small number of firms, each of which has a large share of the market. Such firms are interdependent, and they face a temptation to cooperate to increase their joint economic profit.

Interdependence With a small number of firms in a market, each firm's actions influence the profits of all the other firms. When Penny Stafford opened her coffee shop in Bellevue, Washington, a nearby Starbucks coffee shop took a hit. Within days, Starbucks began to attract Penny's customers with enticing offers and lower prices. Starbucks survived, but Penny eventually went out of business. Penny Stafford and Starbucks were interdependent.

Temptation to Cooperate When a small number of firms share a market, they can increase their profits by forming a cartel and acting like a monopoly. A **cartel** is a group of firms acting together—colluding—to limit output, raise price, and increase economic profit. Cartels are illegal, but they do operate in some markets. But for reasons that you'll discover in this chapter, cartels tend to break down.

Examples of Oligopoly

Economics in Action above shows some examples of oligopoly. The dividing line between oligopoly and monopolistic competition is hard to pin down. As a practical matter, we identify oligopoly by looking at concentration ratios, the Herfindahl-Hirschman Index, and information about the geographical scope of the market and barriers to entry. The HHI that divides oligopoly from monopolistic competition is generally taken to be 2,500. An HHI below 2,500 is usually an example of monopolistic competition, and a market in which the HHI exceeds 2,500 is usually an example of oligopoly.

◆ REVIEW QUIZ

1 What are the two distinguishing characteristics of oligopoly?
2 Why are firms in oligopoly interdependent?
3 Why do firms in oligopoly face a temptation to collude?
4 Can you think of some examples of oligopolies that you buy from?

Work these questions in Study Plan 15.1 and get instant feedback. Do a Key Terms Quiz.   MyEconLab

◆ Oligopoly Games

Economists think about oligopoly as a game between two or a few players, and to study oligopoly markets they use game theory. **Game theory** is a set of tools for studying *strategic behavior*—behavior that takes into account the expected behavior of others and the recognition of mutual interdependence. Game theory was invented by John von Neumann in 1937 and extended by von Neumann and Oskar Morgenstern in 1944 (p. 367). Today, it is one of the major research fields in economics.

Game theory seeks to understand oligopoly as well as other forms of economic, political, social, and even biological rivalries by using a method of analysis specifically designed to understand games of all types, including the familiar games of everyday life (see Talking with Thomas Hubbard on p. 368). To lay the foundation for studying oligopoly games, we first think about the features that all games share.

What Is a Game?

What is a game? At first thought, the question seems silly. After all, there are many different games. There are ball games and parlor games, games of chance and games of skill. But what is it about all these different activities that makes them games? What do all these games have in common? All games share four common features:

- Rules
- Strategies
- Payoffs
- Outcome

We're going to look at these features of games by playing a game called "the prisoners' dilemma." The prisoners' dilemma game displays the essential features of many games, including oligopoly games, and it gives a good illustration of how game theory works and generates predictions.

The Prisoners' Dilemma

Art and Bob have been caught red-handed stealing a car. Facing airtight cases, they will receive a sentence of two years each for their crime. During his interviews with the two prisoners, the district attorney begins to suspect that he has stumbled on the two people who were responsible for a multimillion-dollar bank robbery some months earlier. But this is just a suspicion. He has no evidence on which he can convict them of the greater crime unless he can get them to confess. But how can he extract a confession? The answer is by making the prisoners play a game. The district attorney makes the prisoners play the following game.

Rules Each prisoner (player) is placed in a separate room and cannot communicate with the other prisoner. Each is told that he is suspected of having carried out the bank robbery and that

If both of them confess to the larger crime, each will receive a sentence of 3 years for both crimes.

If he alone confesses and his accomplice does not, he will receive only a 1-year sentence while his accomplice will receive a 10-year sentence.

Strategies In game theory, **strategies** are all the possible actions of each player. Art and Bob each have two possible actions:

1. Confess to the bank robbery.
2. Deny having committed the bank robbery.

Because there are two players, each with two strategies, there are four possible outcomes:

1. Both confess.
2. Both deny.
3. Art confesses and Bob denies.
4. Bob confesses and Art denies.

Payoffs Each prisoner can work out his *payoff* in each of these situations, and we can tabulate the four possible payoffs for each of the prisoners in what is called a payoff matrix for the game. A **payoff matrix** is a table that shows the payoffs for every possible action by each player for every possible action by each other player.

Table 15.1 shows a payoff matrix for Art and Bob. The squares show the payoffs for each prisoner—the red triangle in each square shows Art's and the blue triangle shows Bob's. If both prisoners confess (top left), each gets a prison term of 3 years. If Bob confesses but Art denies (top right), Art gets a 10-year sentence and Bob gets a 1-year sentence. If Art confesses and Bob denies (bottom left), Art gets a 1-year sentence and Bob gets a 10-year sentence. Finally, if both of them deny (bottom right), neither can be convicted of the bank robbery charge but both are sentenced for the car theft—a 2-year sentence.

Outcome The choices of both players determine the outcome of the game. To predict that outcome, we use an equilibrium idea proposed by John Nash of Princeton University (who received the Nobel Prize for Economic Science in 1994 and was the subject of the 2001 movie *A Beautiful Mind*). In **Nash equilibrium**, player *A* takes the best possible action given the action of player *B* and player *B* takes the best possible action given the action of player *A*.

In the case of the prisoners' dilemma, the Nash equilibrium occurs when Art makes his best choice given Bob's choice and when Bob makes his best choice given Art's choice.

To find the Nash equilibrium, we compare all the possible outcomes associated with each choice and eliminate those that are dominated—that are not as good as some other choice. Let's find the Nash equilibrium for the prisoners' dilemma game.

Finding the Nash Equilibrium Look at the situation from Art's point of view. If Bob confesses (top row), Art's best action is to confess because in that case, he is sentenced to 3 years rather than 10 years. If Bob denies (bottom row), Art's best action is still to confess because in that case, he receives 1 year rather than 2 years. So Art's best action is to confess.

Now look at the situation from Bob's point of view. If Art confesses (left column), Bob's best action is to confess because in that case, he is sentenced to 3 years rather than 10 years. If Art denies (right column), Bob's best action is still to confess because in that case, he receives 1 year rather than 2 years. So Bob's best action is to confess.

Because each player's best action is to confess, each does confess, each goes to jail for 3 years, and the district attorney has solved the bank robbery. This is the Nash equilibrium of the game.

The Nash equilibrium for the prisoners' dilemma is called a **dominant-strategy equilibrium**, which is an equilibrium in which the best strategy of each player is to cheat (confess) *regardless of the strategy of the other player*.

The Dilemma The dilemma arises as each prisoner contemplates the consequences of his decision and puts himself in the place of his accomplice. Each knows that it would be best if both denied. But each also knows that if he denies it is in the best interest of the other to confess. So each considers whether to deny and rely on his accomplice to deny or to confess

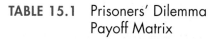

TABLE 15.1   Prisoners' Dilemma Payoff Matrix

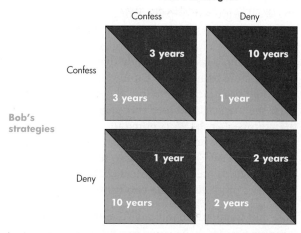

Each square shows the payoffs for the two players, Art and Bob, for each possible pair of actions. In each square, the red triangle shows Art's payoff and the blue triangle shows Bob's. For example, if both confess, the payoffs are in the top left square. The equilibrium of the game is for both players to confess and each gets a 3-year sentence.

———— MyEconLab Animation ————

hoping that his accomplice denies but expecting him to confess. The dilemma leads to the equilibrium of the game.

A Bad Outcome For the prisoners, the equilibrium of the game, with each confessing, is not the best outcome. If neither of them confesses, each gets only 2 years for the lesser crime. Isn't there some way in which this better outcome can be achieved? It seems that there is not, because the players cannot communicate with each other. Each player can put himself in the other player's place, and so each player can figure out that there is a best strategy for each of them. The prisoners are indeed in a dilemma. Each knows that he can serve 2 years *only* if he can trust the other to deny. But each prisoner also knows that it is *not* in the best interest of the other to deny. So each prisoner knows that he must confess, thereby delivering a bad outcome for both.

The firms in an oligopoly are in a similar situation to Art and Bob in the prisoners' dilemma game. Let's see how we can use this game to understand oligopoly.

An Oligopoly Price-Fixing Game

We can use game theory and a game like the prisoners' dilemma to understand price fixing, price wars, and other aspects of the behavior of firms in oligopoly. We'll begin with a price-fixing game.

To understand price fixing, we're going to study the special case of duopoly—an oligopoly with two firms. Duopoly is easier to study than oligopoly with three or more firms, and it captures the essence of all oligopoly situations. Somehow, the two firms must share the market. And how they share it depends on the actions of each. We're going to describe the costs of the two firms and the market demand for the item they produce. We're then going to see how game theory helps us to predict the prices charged and the quantities produced by the two firms in a duopoly.

Cost and Demand Conditions Two firms, Trick and Gear, produce switchgears. They have identical costs. Figure 15.2(a) shows their average total cost curve (*ATC*) and marginal cost curve (*MC*). Figure 15.2(b) shows the market demand curve for switchgears (*D*). The two firms produce identical switchgears, so one firm's switchgear is a perfect substitute for the other's, and the market price of each firm's product is identical. The quantity demanded depends on that price—the higher the price, the smaller is the quantity demanded.

This industry is a natural duopoly. Two firms can produce this good at a lower cost than either one firm or three firms can. For each firm, average total cost is at its minimum when production is 3,000 units a week. When price equals minimum average total cost, the total quantity demanded is 6,000 units a week, and two firms can just produce that quantity.

Collusion We'll suppose that Trick and Gear enter into a collusive agreement. A **collusive agreement** is an agreement between two (or more) producers to form a cartel to restrict output, raise the price, and increase profits. Such an agreement is illegal in the United States and is undertaken in secret. The firms in a cartel can pursue two startegies:

- Comply
- Cheat

A firm that complies carries out the agreement. A firm that cheats breaks the agreement to its own benefit and to the cost of the other firm.

Because each firm has two strategies, there are four possible combinations of actions for the firms:

1. Both firms comply.
2. Both firms cheat.
3. Trick complies and Gear cheats.
4. Gear complies and Trick cheats.

FIGURE 15.2 Costs and Demand

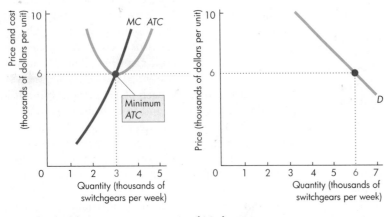

(a) Individual firm

(b) Industry

The average total cost curve for each firm is *ATC*, and the marginal cost curve is *MC* (part a). Minimum average total cost is $6,000 a unit, and it occurs at a production of 3,000 units a week.

Part (b) shows the market demand curve. At a price of $6,000, the quantity demanded is 6,000 units per week. The two firms can produce this output at the lowest possible average cost. If the market had one firm, it would be profitable for another to enter. If the market had three firms, one would exit. There is room for only two firms in this industry. It is a natural duopoly.

Colluding to Maximize Profits Let's work out the payoffs to the two firms if they collude to make the maximum profit for the cartel by acting like a monopoly. The calculations that the two firms perform are the same calculations that a monopoly performs. (You can refresh your memory of these calculations by looking at Chapter 13, pp. 302–303.) The only thing that the firms in duopoly must do beyond what a monopoly does is to agree on how much of the total output each of them will produce.

Figure 15.3 shows the price and quantity that maximize industry profit for the duopoly. Part (a) shows the situation for each firm, and part (b) shows the situation for the industry as a whole. The curve labeled MR is the industry marginal revenue curve. This marginal revenue curve is like that of a single-price monopoly (Chapter 13, p. 300). The curve labeled MC_I is the industry marginal cost curve if each firm produces the same quantity of output. This curve is constructed by adding together the outputs of the two firms at each level of marginal cost. Because the two firms are the same size, at each level of marginal cost the industry output is twice the output of one firm. The curve MC_I in part (b) is twice as far to the right as the curve MC in part (a).

To maximize industry profit, the firms in the duopoly agree to restrict output to the rate that makes the industry marginal cost and marginal revenue equal. That output rate, as shown in part (b), is 4,000 units a week. The demand curve shows that the highest price for which the 4,000 switchgears can be sold is $9,000 each. Trick and Gear agree to charge this price.

To hold the price at $9,000 a unit, production must be 4,000 units a week. So Trick and Gear must agree on output rates for each of them that total 4,000 units a week. Let's suppose that they agree to split the market equally so that each firm produces 2,000 switchgears a week. Because the firms are identical, this division is the most likely.

The average total cost (ATC) of producing 2,000 switchgears a week is $8,000, so the profit per unit is $1,000 and economic profit is $2 million (2,000 units × $1,000 per unit). The economic profit of each firm is represented by the blue rectangle in Fig. 15.3(a).

We have just described one possible outcome for a duopoly game: The two firms collude to produce the monopoly profit-maximizing output and divide that output equally between themselves. From the industry point of view, this solution is identical to a monopoly. A duopoly that operates in this way is indistinguishable from a monopoly. The economic profit that is made by a monopoly is the maximum total profit that can be made by the duopoly when the firms collude.

But with price greater than marginal cost, either firm might think of trying to increase profit by cheating on the agreement and producing more than the agreed amount. Let's see what happens if one of the firms does cheat in this way.

FIGURE 15.3   Colluding to Make Monopoly Profits

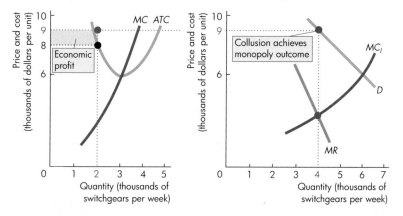

(a) Individual firm   **(b) Industry**

The industry marginal cost curve, MC_I in part (b), is the horizontal sum of the two firms' marginal cost curves, MC in part (a). The industry marginal revenue curve is MR. To maximize profit, the firms produce 4,000 units a week (the quantity at which marginal revenue equals marginal cost). They sell that output for $9,000 a unit. Each firm produces 2,000 units a week. Average total cost is $8,000 a unit, so each firm makes an economic profit of $2 million (blue rectangle)—2,000 units multiplied by $1,000 profit a unit.

One Firm Cheats on a Collusive Agreement To set the stage for cheating on their agreement, Trick convinces Gear that demand has decreased and that it cannot sell 2,000 units a week. Trick tells Gear that it plans to cut its price so that it can sell the agreed 2,000 units each week. Because the two firms produce an identical product, Gear matches Trick's price cut but still produces only 2,000 units a week.

In fact, there has been no decrease in demand. Trick plans to increase output, which it knows will lower the price, and Trick wants to ensure that Gear's output remains at the agreed level.

Figure 15.4 illustrates the consequences of Trick's cheating. Part (a) shows Gear (the complier); part (b) shows Trick (the cheat); and part (c) shows the industry as a whole. Suppose that Trick increases output to 3,000 units a week. If Gear sticks to the agreement to produce only 2,000 units a week, total output is now 5,000 a week, and given demand in part (c), the price falls to $7,500 a unit.

Gear continues to produce 2,000 units a week at a cost of $8,000 a unit and incurs a loss of $500 a unit, or $1 million a week. This economic loss is shown by the red rectangle in part (a). Trick produces 3,000 units a week at a cost of $6,000 a unit. With a price

of $7,500, Trick makes a profit of $1,500 a unit and therefore an economic profit of $4.5 million. This economic profit is the blue rectangle in part (b).

We've now described a second possible outcome for the duopoly game: One of the firms cheats on the collusive agreement. In this case, the industry output is larger than the monopoly output and the industry price is lower than the monopoly price. The total economic profit made by the industry is also smaller than the monopoly's economic profit. Trick (the cheat) makes an economic profit of $4.5 million, and Gear (the complier) incurs an economic loss of $1 million. The industry makes an economic profit of $3.5 million. This industry profit is $0.5 million less than the economic profit that a monopoly would make, but it is distributed unevenly. Trick makes a bigger economic profit than it would under the collusive agreement, while Gear incurs an economic loss.

A similar outcome would arise if Gear cheated and Trick complied with the agreement. The industry profit and price would be the same, but in this case, Gear (the cheat) would make an economic profit of $4.5 million and Trick (the complier) would incur an economic loss of $1 million.

Let's next see what happens if both firms cheat.

FIGURE 15.4 One Firm Cheats

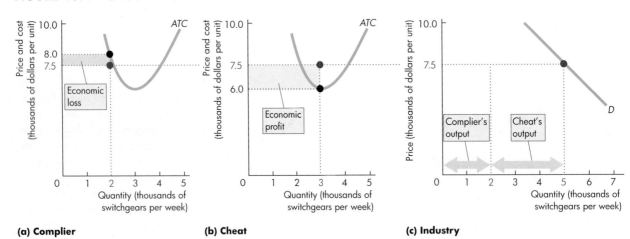

(a) Complier   **(b) Cheat**   **(c) Industry**

One firm, shown in part (a), complies with the agreement and produces 2,000 units. The other firm, shown in part (b), cheats on the agreement and increases its output to 3,000 units a week. Given the market demand curve, shown in part (c), and with a total production of 5,000 units a week,

the price falls to $7,500 a unit. At this price, the complier in part (a) incurs an economic loss of $1 million ($500 per unit × 2,000 units), shown by the red rectangle. In part (b), the cheat makes an economic profit of $4.5 million ($1,500 per unit × 3,000 units), shown by the blue rectangle.

MyEconLab Animation

Both Firms Cheat Suppose that both firms cheat and that each firm behaves like the cheating firm that we have just analyzed. Each tells the other that it is unable to sell its output at the going price and that it plans to cut its price. But because both firms cheat, each will propose a successively lower price. As long as price exceeds marginal cost, each firm has an incentive to increase its production—to cheat. Only when price equals marginal cost is there no further incentive to cheat. This situation arises when the price has reached $6,000. At this price, marginal cost equals price. Also, price equals minimum average total cost. At a price less than $6,000, each firm incurs an economic loss. At a price of $6,000, each firm covers all its costs and makes zero economic profit. Also, at a price of $6,000, each firm wants to produce 3,000 units a week, so the industry output is 6,000 units a week. Given the demand conditions, 6,000 units can be sold at a price of $6,000 each.

Figure 15.5 illustrates the situation just described. Each firm, in part (a), produces 3,000 units a week, and its average total is a minimum ($6,000 per unit). The market as a whole, in part (b), operates at the point at which the market demand curve (D) intersects the industry marginal cost curve (MC_I). Each firm has lowered its price and increased its output to try to gain an advantage over the other firm. Each has pushed this process as far as it can without incurring an economic loss.

We have now described a third possible outcome of this duopoly game: Both firms cheat. If both firms cheat on the collusive agreement, the output of each firm is 3,000 units a week and the price is $6,000 a unit. Each firm makes zero economic profit.

The Payoff Matrix Now that we have described the strategies and payoffs in the duopoly game, we can summarize the strategies and the payoffs in the form of the game's payoff matrix. Then we can find the Nash equilibrium.

Table 15.2 sets out the payoff matrix for this game. It is constructed in the same way as the payoff matrix for the prisoners' dilemma in Table 15.1. The squares show the payoffs for the two firms—Gear and Trick. In this case, the payoffs are profits. (For the prisoners' dilemma, the payoffs were losses.)

The table shows that if both firms cheat (top left), they achieve the perfectly competitive outcome—each firm makes zero economic profit. If both firms comply (bottom right), the industry makes the monopoly profit and each firm makes an economic profit of $2 million. The top right and bottom left squares show the payoff if one firm cheats while the other complies. The firm that cheats makes an economic profit of $4.5 million, and the one that complies incurs a loss of $1 million.

Nash Equilibrium in the Duopolists' Dilemma The duopolists have a dilemma like the prisoners' dilemma. Do they comply or cheat? To answer this question, we must find the Nash equilibrium.

FIGURE 15.5 Both Firms Cheat

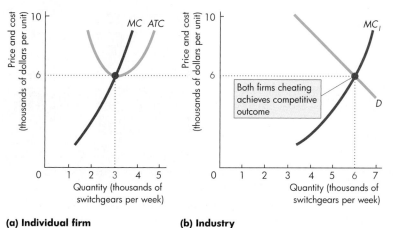

(a) Individual firm

(b) Industry

If both firms cheat by increasing production, the collusive agreement collapses. The limit to the collapse is the competitive equilibrium. Neither firm will cut its price below $6,000 (minimum average total cost) because to do so will result in losses. In part (a), each firm produces 3,000 units a week at an average total cost of $6,000. In part (b), with a total production of 6,000 units, the price falls to $6,000. Each firm now makes zero economic profit. This output and price are the ones that would prevail in a competitive industry.

TABLE 15.2   Duopoly Payoff Matrix

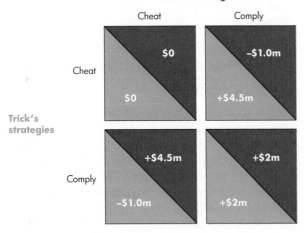

Gear's strategies

Each square shows the payoffs from a pair of actions. For example, if both firms comply with the collusive agreement, the payoffs are recorded in the bottom right square. The red triangle shows Gear's payoff, and the blue triangle shows Trick's. In Nash equilibrium, both firms cheat.

——— MyEconLab Animation ———

Look at things from Gear's point of view. Gear reasons as follows: Suppose that Trick cheats. If I comply, I will incur an economic loss of $1 million. If I also cheat, I will make zero economic profit. Zero is better than *minus* $1 million, so I'm better off if I cheat. Now suppose Trick complies. If I cheat, I will make an economic profit of $4.5 million, and if I comply, I will make an economic profit of $2 million. A $4.5 million profit is better than a $2 million profit, so I'm better off if I cheat. So regardless of whether Trick cheats or complies, it pays Gear to cheat. Cheating is Gear's best strategy.

Trick comes to the same conclusion as Gear because the two firms face an identical situation. So both firms cheat. The Nash equilibrium of the duopoly game is that both firms cheat. And although the industry has only two firms, they charge the same price and produce the same quantity as those in a competitive industry. Also, as in perfect competition, each firm makes zero economic profit.

Economics in Action (on this page) and *Economics in the News* (p. 353) look at some other prisoners' dilemma games. But not all games are prisoners' dilemmas, as you'll now see.

ECONOMICS IN ACTION

A Game in the Market for Tissues

Anti-Viral Kleenex and Puffs Plus Lotion didn't get developed because Kimberly-Clark (Kleenex) and P&G (Puffs) were thinking about helping you cope with a miserable cold. These new-style tissues and other innovations in the quality of facial tissues are the product of a costly research and development (R&D) game.

The table below illustrates the game (with hypothetical numbers). Each firm can spend either $25 million or nothing on R&D. If neither firm spends, Kimberly-Clark makes an economic profit of $70 million and P&G of $30 million (bottom right). If each firm spends on R&D, Kimberly-Clark's economic profit is $45 million and P&G's is $5 million (top left). The other parts of the matrix show the economic profits for each when one spends on R&D and the other doesn't.

Confronted with these payoffs, Kimberly-Clark sees that it gets a bigger profit if it spends on R&D regardless of what P&G does. P&G reaches the same conclusion: It, too, gets a bigger profit by spending on R&D regardless of what Kimberly-Clark does.

Because R&D is the best strategy for both players, it is the Nash equilibrium—a *dominant-strategy Nash equilibrium.*

The outcome of this game is that both firms conduct R&D. They make less profit than they would if they could collude to achieve the cooperative outcome of no R&D. But you get a better Kleenex or Puffs tissue.

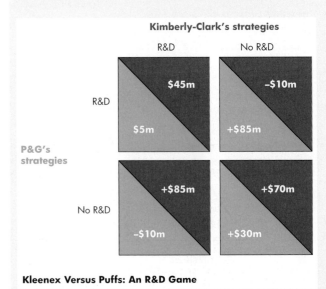

Kleenex Versus Puffs: An R&D Game

A Game of Chicken

The Nash equilibrium for the prisoners' dilemma is unique: both players cheat (confess). Not all games have a unique equilibrium, and one that doesn't is a game called "chicken."

An Example of the Game of Chicken A graphic, if disturbing, version of "chicken" has two cars racing toward each other. The first driver to swerve and avoid a crash is the "chicken." The payoffs are a big loss for both if no one "chickens out;" zero for both if both "chicken out;" and zero for the chicken and a gain for the one who stays the course. If player 1 swerves, player 2's best strategy is to stay the course; and if player 1 stays the course, player 2's best strategy is to swerve.

An Economic Example of Chicken An economic game of chicken can arise when research and development (R&D) creates a new technology that cannot be kept secret or patented, so both firms benefit from the R&D of either firm. The chicken in this case is the firm that does the R&D.

Suppose, for example, that either Apple or Nokia spends $9 million developing a new touch-screen technology that both would end up being able to use regardless of which of them developed it.

Table 15.3 illustrates a payoff matrix for the game that Apple and Nokia play. Each firm has two strategies: Do the R&D ("chicken out") or do not do the R&D. Each entry shows the additional profit (the profit from the new technology minus the cost of the research), given the strategies adopted.

If neither firm does the R&D, each makes zero additional profit. If both firms conduct the R&D, each firm makes an additional $5 million. If one of the firms does the R&D ("chickens out"), the chicken makes $1 million and the other firm makes $10 million. Confronted with these payoffs the two firms calculate their best strategies. Nokia is better off doing R&D if Apple does no R&D. Apple is better off doing R&D if Nokia does no R&D. There are two Nash equilibrium outcomes: Only one of them does the R&D, but we can't predict which one.

You can see that an outcome with no firm doing R&D isn't a Nash equilibrium because one firm would be better off doing it. Also both firms doing R&D isn't a Nash equilibrium because one firm would be better off *not* doing it. To decide *which* firm does the R&D, the firms might toss a coin, called a mixed strategy.

TABLE 15.3 An R&D Game of Chicken

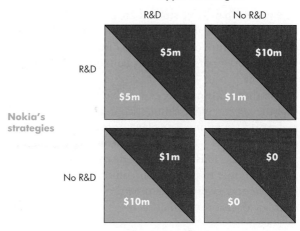

Apple's strategies

If neither firm does the R&D, their payoffs are in the bottom right square. When one firm "chickens out" and does the R&D while the other does no R&D, their payoffs are in the top right and bottom left squares. When both "chicken out" and do the R&D, the payoffs are in the top left square. The red triangle shows Apple's payoff, and the blue triangle shows Nokia's. The equilibrium for this R&D game of chicken is for only one firm to undertake the R&D. We cannot tell which firm will do the R&D and which will not.

◆ REVIEW QUIZ

1 What are the common features of all games?
2 Describe the prisoners' dilemma game and explain why the Nash equilibrium delivers a bad outcome for both players.
3 Why does a collusive agreement to restrict output and raise the price create a game like the prisoners' dilemma?
4 What creates an incentive for firms in a collusive agreement to cheat and increase output?
5 What is the equilibrium strategy for each firm in a duopolists' dilemma and why do the firms not succeed in colluding to raise the price and profits?
6 Describe the payoffs for an R&D game of chicken and contrast them with the payoffs in a prisoners' dilemma game.

Work these questions in Study Plan 15.2 and get instant feedback. Do a Key Terms Quiz.   MyEconLab

◆ Repeated Games and Sequential Games

The games that we've studied are played just once. In contrast, many real-world games are played repeatedly. This feature of games turns out to enable real-world duopolists to cooperate, collude, and make a monopoly profit.

Another feature of the games that we've studied is that the players move simultaneously. But in many real-world situations, one player moves first and then the other moves—the play is sequential rather than simultaneous. This feature of real-world games creates a large number of possible outcomes.

We're now going to examine these two aspects of strategic decision making.

A Repeated Duopoly Game

If two firms play a game repeatedly, one firm has the opportunity to penalize the other for previous "bad" behavior. If Gear cheats this week, perhaps Trick will cheat next week. Before Gear cheats this week, won't it consider the possibility that Trick will cheat next week? What is the equilibrium of this game?

Actually, there is more than one possibility. One is the Nash equilibrium that we have just analyzed. Both players cheat, and each makes zero economic profit forever. In such a situation, it will never pay one of the players to start complying unilaterally because to do so would result in a loss for that player and a profit for the other. But a **cooperative equilibrium** in which the players make and share the monopoly profit is possible.

A cooperative equilibrium might occur if cheating is punished. There are two extremes of punishment. The smallest penalty is called "tit for tat." A *tit-for-tat strategy* is one in which a player cooperates in the current period if the other player cooperated in the previous period, but cheats in the current period if the other player cheated in the previous period. The most severe form of punishment is called a trigger strategy. A *trigger strategy* is one in which a player cooperates if the other player cooperates but plays the Nash equilibrium strategy forever thereafter if the other player cheats.

In the duopoly game between Gear and Trick, a tit-for-tat strategy keeps both players cooperating and making monopoly profits. Let's see why with an example.

Table 15.4 shows the economic profit that Trick and Gear will make over a number of periods under two alternative sequences of events: colluding and cheating with a tit-for-tat response by the other firm.

If both firms stick to the collusive agreement in period 1, each makes an economic profit of $2 million. Suppose that Trick contemplates cheating in period 1. The cheating produces a quick $4.5 million economic profit and inflicts a $1 million economic loss on Gear. But a cheat in period 1 produces a response from Gear in period 2. If Trick wants to get back into a profit-making situation, it must return to the agreement in period 2 even though it knows that Gear will punish it for cheating in period 1. So in period 2, Gear punishes Trick and Trick cooperates. Gear now makes an economic profit of $4.5 million, and Trick incurs an economic loss of $1 million. Adding up the profits over two periods of play, Trick would have made more profit by cooperating—$4 million compared with $3.5 million.

What is true for Trick is also true for Gear. Because each firm makes a larger profit by sticking with the collusive agreement, both firms do so and the monopoly price, quantity, and profit prevail.

In reality, whether a cartel works like a one-play game or a repeated game depends primarily on the

---

TABLE 15.4 Cheating with Punishment

Period of play	Collude		Cheat with tit-for-tat	
	Trick's profit (millions of dollars)	Gear's profit (millions of dollars)	Trick's profit (millions of dollars)	Gear's profit (millions of dollars)
1	2	2	4.5	−1.0
2	2	2	−1.0	4.5
3	2	2	2.0	2.0
4	⋮	⋮	⋮	⋮

If duopolists repeatedly collude, each makes a profit of $2 million per period of play. If one player cheats in period 1, the other player plays a tit-for-tat strategy and cheats in period 2. The profit from cheating can be made for only one period and must be paid for in the next period by incurring a loss. Over two periods of play, the best that a duopolist can achieve by cheating is a profit of $3.5 million, compared to an economic profit of $4 million by colluding.

ECONOMICS IN THE NEWS

Airbus Versus Boeing

Boeing Strikes Back in Single-Aisle Market

Airbus and Boeing are in fierce competition in the narrow-body passenger jet market. Airbus got moving first with its A320neo for which it has 1,400 orders. Boeing responded with the 737 Max for which it had 549 orders in mid-2012 and an aim for 1,000 orders by the end of 2012.

Boeing rejected suggestions that it was in a price war with Airbus over the A320neo and 737 Max but confirmed it would woo some airline customers of its European rival.

Source: *Financial Times*, July 9, 2012

SOME DATA

Aircraft	List price
Airbus Neo	$96.7 million
Boeing Max	$96.0 million

ASSUMPTIONS

- Assume that the performance and operating costs of the A320neo and the Max are identical.
- At list prices, Airbus and Boeing can get another 200 orders each and make $2 billion each in economic profit.
- At discounted prices, Airbus and Boeing can get another 225 orders each and make $1 billion each in economic profit.
- If one of them holds the list price and the other discounts, the discounter can get 450 new orders and make $3 billion and the other will get no new orders.

THE QUESTIONS

- In what type of market are Airbus and Boeing competing?
- How did moving first benefit Airbus?
- Given the assumptions above, will the airplane producers discount their prices or stick to the list prices? To answer this question, set out the payoff matrix for the game that Airbus and Boeing are playing and find the Nash equilibrium.
- If the game could be played repeatedly, how might the strategies and equilibrium change?

THE ANSWERS

- Airbus and Boeing are a duopoly.
- By moving first, Airbus had a temporary monopoly and was able to grab a large market share.

- The table illustrates the payoff matrix for the game between Airbus and Boeing.
- The outcome is a dominant-strategy Nash equilibrium. Both firms discount their prices and get 225 new orders each. If one firm held the list price, the other would discount and take the 450 new orders.
- If the game could be played repeatedly, the discounter could be punished and a cooperative equilibrium would arise in which neither discounts.

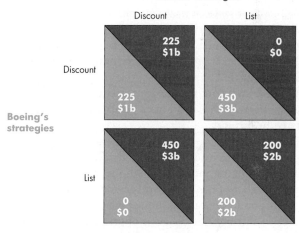

Duopoly Game: Market for Airplanes

Are the A320neo and Max in a price war?

MyEconLab More Economics in the News

number of players and the ease of detecting and punishing cheating. The larger the number of players, the harder it is to maintain a cartel.

Games and Price Wars A repeated duopoly game can help us understand real-world behavior and, in particular, price wars. Some price wars can be interpreted as the implementation of a tit-for-tat strategy. But the game is a bit more complicated than the one we've looked at because the players are uncertain about the demand for the product.

Playing a tit-for-tat strategy, firms have an incentive to stick to the monopoly price. But fluctuations in demand lead to fluctuations in the monopoly price, and sometimes, when the price changes, it might seem to one of the firms that the price has fallen because the other has cheated. In this case, a price war will break out. The price war will end only when each firm is satisfied that the other is ready to cooperate again. There will be cycles of price wars and the restoration of collusive agreements. Fluctuations in the world price of oil might be interpreted in this way.

Some price wars arise from the entry of a small number of firms into an industry that had previously been a monopoly. Although the industry has a small number of firms, the firms are in a prisoners' dilemma and they cannot impose effective penalties for price cutting. The behavior of prices and outputs in the computer chip industry during 1995 and 1996 can be explained in this way. Until 1995, the market for Pentium chips for IBM-compatible computers was dominated by one firm, Intel Corporation, which was able to make maximum economic profit by producing the quantity of chips at which marginal cost equaled marginal revenue. The price of Intel's chips was set to ensure that the quantity demanded equaled the quantity produced. Then in 1995 and 1996, with the entry of a small number of new firms, the industry became an oligopoly. If the firms had maintained Intel's price and shared the market, together they could have made economic profits equal to Intel's profit. But the firms were in a prisoners' dilemma, so prices fell toward the competitive level.

Let's now study a sequential game. There are many such games, and the one we'll examine is among the simplest. It has an interesting implication and it will give you the flavor of this type of game. The sequential game that we'll study is an entry game in a contestable market.

A Sequential Entry Game in a Contestable Market

If two firms play a sequential game, one firm makes a decision at the first stage of the game and the other makes a decision at the second stage.

We're going to study a sequential game in a **contestable market**—a market in which firms can enter and leave so easily that firms in the market face competition from *potential* entrants. Examples of contestable markets are routes served by airlines and by barge companies that operate on the major waterways. These markets are contestable because firms could enter if an opportunity for economic profit arose and could exit with no penalty if the opportunity for economic profit disappeared.

If the Herfindahl-Hirschman Index (p. 234) is used to determine the degree of competition, a contestable market appears to be uncompetitive. But a contestable market can behave as if it were perfectly competitive. To see why, let's look at an entry game for a contestable air route.

A Contestable Air Route Agile Air is the only firm operating on a particular route. Demand and cost conditions are such that there is room for only one airline to operate. Wanabe Inc. is another airline that could offer services on the route.

We describe the structure of a sequential game by using a *game tree* like that in Fig. 15.6. At the first stage, Agile Air must set a price. Once the price is set and advertised, Agile can't change it. That is, once set, Agile's price is fixed and Agile can't react to Wanabe's entry decision. Agile can set its price at either the monopoly level or the competitive level.

At the second stage, Wanabe must decide whether to enter or to stay out. Customers have no loyalty (there are no frequent-flyer programs) and they buy from the lowest-price firm. So if Wanabe enters, it sets a price just below Agile's and takes all the business.

Figure 15.6 shows the payoffs from the various decisions (Agile's in the red triangles and Wanabe's in the blue triangles).

To decide on its price, Agile's CEO reasons as follows: Suppose that Agile sets the monopoly price. If Wanabe enters, it earns 90 (think of all payoff numbers as thousands of dollars). If Wanabe stays out, it earns nothing. So Wanabe will enter. In this case Agile will lose 50.

Now suppose that Agile sets the competitive price. If Wanabe stays out, it earns nothing, and if it enters,

FIGURE 15.6   Agile Versus Wanabe: A Sequential Entry Game in a Contestable Market

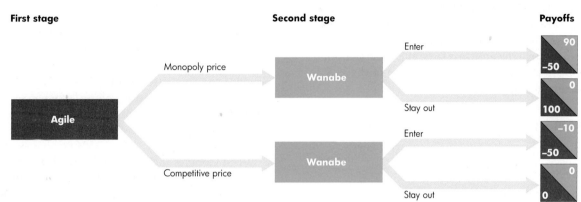

First stage	Second stage	Payoffs

If Agile sets the monopoly price, Wanabe makes 90 (thousand dollars) by entering and earns nothing by staying out. So if Agile sets the monopoly price, Wanabe enters.

If Agile sets the competitive price, Wanabe earns nothing if it stays out and incurs a loss if it enters. So if Agile sets the competitive price, Wanabe stays out.

MyEconLab Animation

it loses 10, so Wanabe will stay out. In this case, Agile will make zero economic profit.

Agile's best strategy is to set its price at the competitive level and make zero economic profit. The option of earning 100 by setting the monopoly price with Wanabe staying out is not available to Agile. If Agile sets the monopoly price, Wanabe enters, undercuts Agile, and takes all the business.

In this example, Agile sets its price at the competitive level and makes zero economic profit. A less costly strategy, called **limit pricing**, sets the price at the highest level that inflicts a loss on the entrant. Any loss is big enough to deter entry, so it is not always necessary to set the price as low as the competitive price. In the example of Agile and Wanabe, at the competitive price, Wanabe incurs a loss of 10 if it enters. A smaller loss would still keep Wanabe out.

This game is interesting because it points to the possibility of a monopoly behaving like a competitive industry and serving the social interest without regulation. But the result is not general and depends on one crucial feature of the setup of the game: At the second stage, Agile is locked in to the price set at the first stage.

If Agile could change its price in the second stage, it would want to set the monopoly price if Wanabe stayed out—100 with the monopoly price beats zero with the competitive price. But Wanabe can figure out what Agile would do, so the price set at the first stage

has no effect on Wanabe. Agile sets the monopoly price and Wanabe might either stay out or enter.

We've looked at two of the many possible repeated and sequential games, and you've seen how these types of games can provide insights into the complex forces that determine prices and profits.

◆ REVIEW QUIZ

1   If a prisoners' dilemma game is played repeatedly, what punishment strategies might the players employ and how does playing the game repeatedly change the equilibrium?

2   If a market is contestable, how does the equilibrium differ from that of a monopoly?

Work these questions in Study Plan 15.3 and get instant feedback. Do a Key Terms Quiz.   *MyEconLab*

So far, we've studied oligopoly with unregulated market power. Firms like Trick and Gear are free to collude to maximize their profit with no concern for the consumer or the law.

But when firms collude to achieve the monopoly outcome, they also have the same effects on efficiency and the social interest as monopoly. Profit is made at the expense of consumer surplus and a deadweight loss arises. Your next task is to see how U.S. antitrust law limits market power.

◆ Antitrust Law

Antitrust law is the law that regulates oligopolies and prevents them from becoming monopolies or behaving like monopolies. Two government agencies cooperate to enforce the antitrust laws: the Federal Trade Commission and the Antitrust Division of the U.S. Department of Justice.

The Antitrust Laws

The United States has two main antitrust laws:

- The Sherman Act, 1890
- The Clayton Act, 1914

The Sherman Act The Sherman Act made it a felony to create or attempt to create a monopoly or a cartel.

During the 1880s, lawmakers and the general public were outraged and disgusted by the practices of some of the big-name leaders of American business. The actions of J.P. Morgan, John D. Rockefeller, and W.H. Vanderbilt led to them being called the "robber barons." It turns out that the most lurid stories of the actions of these great American capitalists were not of their creation of monopoly power to exploit consumers but of their actions to damage each other.

Nevertheless, monopolies that damaged the consumer interest did emerge. For example, John D. Rockefeller had a virtual monopoly in the market for oil.

Table 15.5 summarizes the two main provisions of the Sherman Act. Section 1 of the act is precise:

TABLE 15.5   The Sherman Act of 1890

Section 1:

Every contract, combination in the form of trust or otherwise, or conspiracy, in restraint of trade or commerce among the several States, or with foreign nations, is hereby declared to be illegal.

Section 2:

Every person who shall monopolize, or attempt to monopolize, or combine or conspire with any other person or persons, to monopolize any part of the trade or commerce among the several States, or with foreign nations, shall be deemed guilty of a felony.

Conspiring with others to restrict competition is illegal. But Section 2 is general and imprecise. Just what is an "attempt to monopolize"?

The Clayton Act The Clayton Act, which was passed in response to a wave of mergers that occurred at the beginning of the twentieth century, provided the answer to the question left dangling by the Sherman Act: It defined the "attempt to monopolize." The Clayton Act supplemented the Sherman Act and strengthened and clarified the antitrust law.

When Congress passed the Clayton Act, it also established the Federal Trade Commission, the federal agency charged with the task of preventing monopoly practices that damage the consumer interest.

Two amendments to the Clayton Act—the Robinson-Patman Act of 1936 and the Celler-Kefauver Act of 1950—outlaw specific practices and provide even greater precision to the antitrust law. Table 15.6 describes these practices and summarizes the main provisions of these three acts.

TABLE 15.6   The Clayton Act and Its Amendments

Clayton Act	**1914**
Robinson-Patman Act	**1936**
Celler-Kefauver Act	**1950**

These acts prohibit the following practices *only if* they substantially lessen competition or create monopoly:

1. Price discrimination

2. Contracts that require other goods to be bought from the same firm (called *tying arrangements*)

3. Contracts that require a firm to buy all its requirements of a particular item from a single firm (called *requirements contracts*)

4. Contracts that prevent a firm from selling competing items (called *exclusive dealing*)

5. Contracts that prevent a buyer from reselling a product outside a specified area (called *territorial confinement*)

6. Acquiring a competitor's shares or assets

7. Becoming a director of a competing firm

Price Fixing Always Illegal

Colluding with competitors to fix the price is *always* a violation of the antitrust law. If the Justice Department can prove the existence of a price fixing cartel, also called a *horizontal price fixing agreement,* defendants can offer no acceptable excuse.

The predictions of the effects of price fixing that you saw in the previous sections of this chapter provide the reasons for the unqualified attitude toward price fixing. A duopoly cartel can maximize profit and behave like a monopoly. To achieve the monopoly outcome, the cartel restricts production and fixes the price at the monopoly level. The consumer suffers because consumer surplus shrinks. And the outcome is inefficient because a deadweight loss arises.

It is for these reasons that the law declares that all price fixing is illegal. No excuse can justify the practice.

Other practices raise antitrust concerns but are more controversial and generate debate among lawyers and economists. We'll examine three of these practices.

Three Antitrust Policy Debates

Some practices that engender antitrust policy debate are

- Resale price maintenance
- Tying arrangements
- Predatory pricing

Resale Price Maintenance Most manufacturers sell their products to the final consumer indirectly through a wholesale and retail distribution system. **Resale price maintenance** occurs when a distributor agrees with a manufacturer to resell a product *at or above a specified minimum price.*

A resale price maintenance agreement, also called a *vertical price fixing agreement,* is *not* illegal under the Sherman Act provided it is not anticompetitive. Nor is it illegal for a manufacturer to refuse to supply a retailer who doesn't accept guidance on what the minimum price should be.

In 2007, the Supreme Court ruled that a handbag manufacturer could impose a minimum retail price on a Dallas store, Kay's Kloset. Since that ruling, many manufacturers have imposed minimum retail prices. The practice is judged on a case-by-case basis.

Does resale price maintenance create an inefficient or efficient use of resources? Economists can be found on both sides of this question.

Inefficient Resale Price Maintenance Resale price maintenance is inefficient if it enables dealers to charge the monopoly price. By setting and enforcing the resale price, the manufacturer might be able to achieve the monopoly price.

Efficient Resale Price Maintenance Resale price maintenance might be efficient if it enables a manufacturer to induce dealers to provide the efficient standard of service. Suppose that SilkySkin wants shops to demonstrate the use of its new unbelievable moisturizing cream in an inviting space. With resale price maintenance, SilkySkin can offer all the retailers the same incentive and compensation. Without resale price maintenance, a cut-price drug store might offer SilkySkin products at a low price. Buyers would then have an incentive to visit a high-price shop for a product demonstration and then buy from the low-price shop. The low-price shop would be a free rider (like the consumer of a public good in Chapter 16, p. 374), and an inefficient level of service would be provided.

SilkySkin could pay a fee to retailers that provide good service and leave the resale price to be determined by the competitive forces of supply and demand. But it might be too costly for SilkySkin to monitor shops and ensure that they provide the desired level of service.

Tying Arrangements A **tying arrangement** is an agreement to sell one product only if the buyer agrees to buy another, different product. With tying, the only way the buyer can get the one product is to also buy the other product. Microsoft has been accused of tying Internet Explorer and Windows. Textbook publishers sometimes tie a Web site and a textbook and force students to buy both. (You can't buy the book you're now reading, new, without the Web site. But you can buy the Web site access without the book, so these products are not tied.)

Could textbook publishers make more money by tying a book and access to a Web site? The answer is sometimes but not always. Suppose that you and other students are willing to pay $80 for a book and $20 for access to a Web site. The publisher can sell these items separately for these prices or bundled for $100. The publisher does not gain from bundling.

But now suppose that you and only half of the students are willing to pay $80 for a book and $20 for a Web site and the other half of the students are willing to pay $80 for a Web site and $20 for a book. Now if the two items are sold separately, the publisher can charge $80 for the book and $80 for the Web site. Half the students buy the book but not the Web site, and the other half buy the Web site but not the book. But if the book and Web site are bundled for $100, everyone buys the bundle and the publisher makes an extra $20 per student. In this case, bundling has enabled the publisher to price discriminate.

There is no simple, clear-cut test of whether a firm is engaging in tying or whether, by doing so, it has increased its market power and profit and created inefficiency.

Predatory Pricing **Predatory pricing** is setting a low price to drive competitors out of business with the intention of setting a monopoly price when the competition has gone. John D. Rockefeller's Standard Oil Company was the first to be accused of this practice in the 1890s, and it has been claimed often in antitrust cases since then. Predatory pricing is an attempt to create a monopoly and as such it is illegal under Section 2 of the Sherman Act.

It is easy to see that predatory pricing is an idea, not a reality. Economists are skeptical that predatory pricing occurs. They point out that a firm that cuts its price below the profit-maximizing level loses during the low-price period. Even if it succeeds in driving its competitors out of business, new competitors will enter as soon as the price is increased, so any potential gain from a monopoly position is temporary. A high and certain loss is a poor exchange for a temporary and uncertain gain. No case of predatory pricing has been definitively found.

ECONOMICS IN ACTION

The United States Versus Microsoft

In 1998, the Antitrust Division of the U.S. Department of Justice along with the Departments of Justice of a number of states charged Microsoft, the world's largest producer of software for personal computers, with violations of both sections of the Sherman Act.

A 78-day trial followed that pitched two prominent MIT economics professors against each other, Franklin Fisher for the government and Richard Schmalensee for Microsoft.

The Case Against Microsoft The claims against Microsoft were that it

- Possessed monopoly power.
- Used predatory pricing and tying arrangements.
- Used other anticompetitive practices.

It was claimed that with 80 percent of the market for PC operating systems, Microsoft had excessive monopoly power. This monopoly power arose from two barriers to entry: economies of scale and network economies. Microsoft's average total cost falls as production increases (economies of scale) because the fixed cost of developing an operating system such as Windows is large while the marginal cost of producing one copy of Windows is small. Further, as the number of Windows users increases, the range of Windows applications expands (network economies), so a potential competitor would need to produce not only a competing operating system but also an entire range of supporting applications as well.

When Microsoft entered the Web browser market with its Internet Explorer, it offered the browser for a zero price. This price was viewed as predatory pricing. Microsoft integrated Internet Explorer with Windows so that anyone who uses this operating system would not need a separate browser such as Netscape Navigator. Microsoft's competitors claimed that this practice was an illegal tying arrangement.

Microsoft's Response Microsoft challenged all these claims. It said that Windows was vulnerable to competition from other operating systems such as Linux and Apple's Mac OS and that there was a permanent threat of competition from new entrants.

Microsoft claimed that integrating Internet Explorer with Windows provided a single, unified product of greater consumer value like a refrigerator with a chilled water dispenser or an automobile with a CD player.

The Outcome The court agreed that Microsoft was in violation of the Sherman Act and ordered that it be broken into two firms: an operating systems producer and an applications producer. Microsoft successfully appealed this order. In the final judgment, though, Microsoft was ordered to disclose to other software developers details of how its operating system works, so that they could compete effectively against Microsoft. In the summer of 2002, Microsoft began to comply with this order.

ECONOMICS IN ACTION

No Cellphone Service Merger

The FTC used its HHI guidelines (summarized in the figure) to block a proposed merger in the market for cellphone service. In 2011, AT&T wanted to buy T-Mobile from the German Deutsch Telecommunication. But the market for cellphone service is highly concentrated. Verizon is the largest service provider with close to 40 percent of the market share. AT&T has a 30 percent share and Sprint and T-Mobile about 12 percent each. Another 14 small firms share the remaining market. So the four largest firms in this market have a 94 percent market share. The HHI is around 2,800.

The figure shows how the HHI would have changed with the merger of AT&T and T-Mobile. It would have increased the HHI by around 700 points. With an HHI of 2,800 and an increase of 700, there was a presumption that the merger would give AT&T too much market power, so the FTC decided to block it.

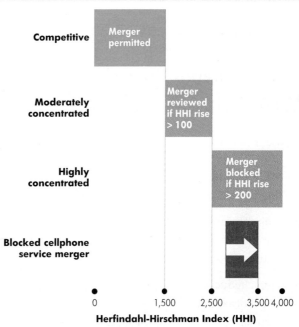

Figure 1 Merger Guidelines

Mergers and Acquisitions

Mergers, which occur when two or more firms agree to combine to create one larger firm, and *acquisitions*, which occur when one firm buys another firm, are common events. Mergers occurred when Chrysler and the German auto producer Daimler-Benz combined to form DaimlerChrysler and when the Belgian beer producer InBev bought the U.S. brewing giant Anheuser-Busch and created a new combined company, Anheuser-Busch InBev. An acquisition occurred when Rupert Murdoch's News Corp bought Myspace.

The mergers and acquisitions that occur don't create a monopoly. But two (or more) firms might be tempted to try to merge so that they can gain market power and operate like a monopoly. If such a situation arises, the Federal Trade Commission (FTC) takes an interest in the move and stands ready to block the merger. To determine which mergers it will examine and possibly block, the FTC uses guidelines, one of which is the Herfindahl-Hirschman Index (HHI) (see Chapter 10, pp. 234–235).

A market in which the HHI is less than 1,500 is regarded as competitive. An index between 1,500 and 2,500 indicates a moderately concentrated market, and a merger in this market that would increase the index by 100 points is challenged by the FTC. An index above 2,500 indicates a concentrated market, and a merger in this market that would increase the index by 200 points is generally blocked. You can see an application of these guidelines in *Economics in Action* above.

◆ REVIEW QUIZ

1 What are the two main antitrust laws and when were they enacted?
2 When is price fixing not a violation of the antitrust laws?
3 What is an attempt to monopolize an industry?
4 What are resale price maintenance, tying arrangements, and predatory pricing?
5 Under what circumstances is a merger unlikely to be approved?

Work these questions in Study Plan 15.4 and get instant feedback. Do a Key Terms Quiz. MyEconLab

◆ Oligopoly is a market structure that you often encounter in your daily life. *Economics in the News* on pp. 360–361 looks at a game played in the market for cellphone service.

Oligopoly Games in Cellphone Service

AT&T Extends Price Cuts in Battle With T-Mobile for Data Users

Bloomberg
March 8, 2014

AT&T is cutting mobile-phone subscription charges for the second time in two months, seeking to hold on to smartphone customers amid a price war with T-Mobile.

Starting tomorrow, AT&T customers can sign up for a Shared Value plan with 2 gigabytes of data for $65 a month, down from $80. Adding a second phone to the plan brings the price up to $90, down from $105. …

The price reduction comes a day after T-Mobile said it will double to 1 gigabyte the amount of data allotted to its $50-a-month Simple Choice package. AT&T cut its shared data plan for families by $40 last month as it seeks to keep pace with T-Mobile's aggressive pricing strategy. T-Mobile gained 2.1 million customers in the past three quarters, reversing its performance in 2012. The company offers a plan with 2.5 gigabytes of data for $60 a month for one phone or $90 a month for two phones.

Over the past year, Bellevue, Washington-based T-Mobile introduced a series of pricing changes to shake up the industry, becoming the first carrier to offer customers quicker phone upgrades, payment financing, and international data and text-messaging at no extra charge. It also started a $450 credit program for users who switch from other providers.

AT&T, based in Dallas, is the second-largest U.S. wireless carrier, trailing Verizon Communications Inc. T-Mobile is fourth, behind Sprint Corp. Competition between AT&T and T-Mobile, which abandoned a merger attempt in 2011, has intensified in part because they use similar technology, making it easier for customers to switch devices between their networks.

Scott Moritz, "AT&T Extends Price Cuts in Battle With T-Mobile for Data Users," *Bloomberg*, March 8, 2014"

MyEconLab More Economics in the News

ESSENCE OF THE STORY

- AT&T and T-Mobile use similar technology, which makes it easy for customers to switch devices between their networks.

- The two firms are in a smartphone-service price war.

- T-Mobile has gained 2.1 million customers by increasing the value of its plans without raising prices.

- AT&T has cut the prices of its plans.

ECONOMIC ANALYSIS

- The U.S. market in cellphone service is dominated by four firms: Verizon, AT&T Mobility, Sprint, and T-Mobile.

- Figure 1 shows the shares in this market. You can see that Verizon has 35 percent of the market; AT&T has 33 percent, Sprint has 16 percent; and T-Mobile has 14 percent. Another nine small firms share the remaining 2 percent.

- In 2013, T-Mobile and AT&T increased the intensity of their competition.

- T-Mobile increased the value and cost of production of its plans but held prices, and so decreased its profit.

- AT&T cut its prices, which decreased its profit.

- We can interpret this competition as a prisoners' dilemma game.

- Table 1 shows the payoff matrix (millions of dollars of profit) for the game played by T-Mobile and AT&T. (The numbers are hypothetical.)

- This game is a prisoners' dilemma like that on p. 345 and has a dominant-strategy Nash equilibrium.

- If T-Mobile offers an increased value of service, AT&T avoids a larger loss by cutting its price; and if T-Mobile does nothing different (no change), AT&T increases its profit by cutting its prices and gaining market share.

- So AT&T's best strategy is to cut prices.

- If AT&T cuts its prices, T-Mobile avoids a larger loss by incurring a higher cost of offering its customers greater value plans; and if AT&T doesn't cut its price (no change),

T-Mobile increases profit by offering its customers greater value plans.

- So T-Mobile's best strategy is to incur the higher cost of offering its customers greater value plans.

- Because the best strategy for AT&T is to cut price and for T-Mobile to incur the higher cost of offering its customers greater value plans, that is the equilibrium of the game.

- The firms are in a prisoners' dilemma because each would be better off avoiding the contest on quality of service and price.

- But each firm can see that if it doesn't take its best action, the other firm will gain and it will lose.

- The game we've just described is played only once, and both firms move at the same time.

- But in the game played by T-Mobile and AT&T, the firms move sequentially and repeatedly.

- If T-Mobile and AT&T adopt a tit-for-tat punishment strategy, it is possible that the current war between them will end and they will return to higher prices and larger profits.

- This market is one that affects everyone, and one that will expand as cellphones become ever smarter and used for more data-intensive activities.

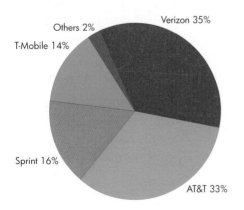

Figure 1 Market Shares in Cellphone Service

T-Mobile's strategies

	Increase value	No change
Cut price	–$1b / –$1b	–$2b / $2b
No change	$2b / –$2b	$0 / $0

AT&T's strategies

Table 1 T-Mobile and AT&T in a Prisoners' Dilemma

SUMMARY

Key Points

What Is Oligopoly? (pp. 342–343)

- Oligopoly is a market in which a small number of firms compete.

Working Problems 1 to 3 will give you a better understanding of what oligopoly is.

Oligopoly Games (pp. 344–351)

- Oligopoly is studied by using game theory, which is a method of analyzing strategic behavior.
- In a prisoners' dilemma game, two prisoners acting in their own self-interest harm their joint interest.
- An oligopoly (duopoly) price-fixing game is a prisoners' dilemma in which the firms might collude or cheat.
- In Nash equilibrium, both firms cheat and output and price are the same as in perfect competition.
- Firms' decisions about advertising and R&D can be studied by using game theory.

Working Problems 4 to 6 will give you a better understanding of oligopoly games.

Repeated Games and Sequential Games (pp. 352–355)

- In a repeated game, a punishment strategy can produce a cooperative equilibrium in which price and output are the same as in a monopoly.

- In a sequential contestable market game, a small number of firms can behave like firms in perfect competition.

Working Problem 7 will give you a better understanding of repeated and sequential games.

Antitrust Law (pp. 356–359)

- The first antitrust law, the Sherman Act, was passed in 1890, and the law was strengthened in 1914 when the Clayton Act was passed and the Federal Trade Commission was created.
- All price-fixing agreements are violations of the Sherman Act, and no acceptable excuse exists.
- Resale price maintenance might be efficient if it enables a producer to ensure the efficient level of service by distributors.
- Tying arrangements can enable a monopoly to price discriminate and increase profit, but in many cases, tying would not increase profit.
- Predatory pricing is unlikely to occur because it brings losses and only temporary potential gains.
- The Federal Trade Commission uses guidelines such as the Herfindahl-Hirschman Index to determine which mergers to investigate and possibly block.

Working Problem 8 will give you a better understanding of antitrust law.

Key Terms

MyEconLab Key Terms Quiz

Antitrust law, 356
Cartel, 343
Collusive agreement, 346
Contestable market, 354
Cooperative equilibrium, 352
Dominant-strategy equilibrium, 345

Duopoly, 342
Game theory, 344
Limit pricing, 355
Nash equilibrium, 345
Oligopoly, 342
Payoff matrix, 344

Predatory pricing, 358
Resale price maintenance, 357
Strategies, 344
Tying arrangement, 357

◆ WORKED PROBLEM

MyEconLab   You can work this problem in Chapter 15 Study Plan.

Black and White are the two and only producers of piano keys. The firms are identical. They have the same technologies and costs, and they produce the same quantities of piano keys. Their keys are identical too, so they sell for the same price regardless of whether Black or White produces them.

The firms are busy and operating at capacity output. But profit margins are thin and they are making zero economic profit.

Despite it being illegal, the two firms decide to collude: to restrict output and raise the price. The deal is that each of them cuts output to 50 percent of the current level and raises the price.

With the deal in place, the firms can earn the maximum monopoly profit and share it equally.

But each firm wants a bigger share of the market and to get back to the original output level. They each know, though, that if only one of them increases output, profit will increase for the one with larger output and the other will incur an economic loss. They also know that if both of them increase production, they will be back in the situation before the deal.

Questions

1. Describe the game played by Black and White.
2. Make up some profit numbers for Black and White that are consistent with the above account of their situation. Construct a payoff matrix for the game they are playing, and find the equilibrium of the game.

Solutions

1. The game played by Black and White is a duopoly prisoners' dilemma cartel game.

   Each player has two strategies: 1) keep the cartel agreement and 2) break the cartel agreement.

   The payoffs are symmetric.

   If both keep the agreement, they each earn 50 percent of the maximum attainable monopoly profit.

   If both break the agreement, they each earn zero economic profit.

   If one of them breaks the agreement, the breaker earns a profit that is larger than 50 percent of the monopoly profit and the other incurs a loss.

   The game is a prisoners' dilemma because each knows that the joint best outcome requires keeping the agreement and that the other has an incentive to break it.

   Key Point: A duopoly price-fixing game is a prisoners' dilemma in which the firms might keep or break an agreement to collude—might comply or cheat.

2. The table below shows a payoff matrix with profit (and loss) numbers that are consistent with the story about Black and White.

   If both break the agreement (top left), they earn zero economic profit ($0 in the table).

   If both keep the agreement (bottom right), they earn a monopoly profit and share it equally ($10m each in the table).

   If one keeps the agreement and the other breaks it (top right and bottom left), the keeper incurs a loss (−$5m in the table) and the breaker gets a profit larger than half the monopoly profit ($14m in the table).

   The Nash equilibrium is for both firms to break the agreement and make zero economic profit.

   For each firm, breaking the agreement is the best strategy regardless of the strategy of the other player.

   If the other firm keeps the agreement, then the firm that breaks it increases its profit by $4m.

   But if the other firm also breaks the agreement, then breaking the agreement avoids economic loss.

Key Point: The Nash equilibrium of a prisoners' dilemma is not the best joint outcome.

Key Table

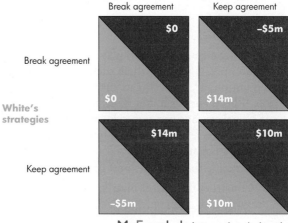

MyEconLab Interactive Animation

STUDY PLAN PROBLEMS AND APPLICATIONS

MyEconLab   You can work Problems 1 to 8 in Chapter 15 Study Plan and get instant feedback.

What Is Oligopoly? (Study Plan 15.1)

1. Intel and Advanced Micro Devices make most of the chips that power a PC. What makes the market for PC chips a duopoly? Sketch the market demand and cost curves that describe the situation in the market and that prevent firms from entering.

2. **Sparks Fly for Energizer**

   Energizer is gaining market share against competitor Duracell and its profit is rising despite the sharp rise in the price of zinc, a key battery ingredient.

   Source: www.businessweek.com, August 2007

   In what type of market are batteries sold? Explain your answer.

3. **Oil City**

   In the 1990s, Reliance spent $6 billion to build a world-class oil refinery at Jamnagar, India. Now Reliance's expansion will make it the world's biggest producer of gasoline—1.2 million gallons per day, or about 5% of global capacity. Reliance plans to sell the gasoline in the United States and Europe where it's too expensive and politically difficult to build new refineries. The bulked-up Jamnagar will be able to move the market and Singapore traders expect a drop in fuel prices as soon as it's going at full steam.

   Source: *Fortune*, April 28, 2008

   a. Explain why the news clip implies that the gasoline market is not perfectly competitive.

   b. What barriers to entry might limit competition and allow Reliance to influence the price?

Oligopoly Games (Study Plan 15.2)

4. Consider a game with two players who cannot communicate, and in which each player is asked a question. The players can answer honestly or lie. If both answer honestly, each receives $100. If one player answers honestly and the other lies, the liar receives $500 and the honest player gets nothing. If both lie, then each receives $50.
   a. Describe the strategies and the payoffs.
   b. Construct the payoff matrix.
   c. What is the equilibrium of this game?
   d. Compare this game to the prisoners' dilemma. Are the games similar or different? Explain.

5. Soapy Inc. and Suddies Inc., the only soap-powder producers, collude and agree to share the market equally. If neither firm cheats, each makes $1 million. If one firm cheats, it makes $1.5 million, while the complier incurs a loss of $0.5 million. If both cheat, they break even. Neither firm can monitor the other's actions.
   a. What are the strategies in this game? Construct the payoff matrix for this game.
   b. If the game is played only once what is the equilibrium? Is it a dominant-strategy equilibrium? Explain.

6. **The World's Largest Airline**

   United Airlines and Continental Airlines announced a $3 billion merger to create the world's biggest airline. The new airline will be able to better compete with low-cost domestic and foreign airlines. Travelers could face higher fares, although the merged airline has no such plans. But one rationale for any merger is to cut capacity.

   Source: *The New York Times*, June 7, 2010

   a. Explain how this airline merger might (i) increase air travel prices or (ii) lower air travel production costs.

   b. Explain how cost savings arising from a cut in capacity might be passed on to travelers or boost producers' profits. Which might happen from this airline merger and why?

Repeated Games and Sequential Games

(Study Plan 15.3)

7. If Soapy Inc. and Suddies Inc. play the game in Problem 5 repeatedly, on each round of play
   a. What strategies might each firm adopt?
   b. Can the firms adopt a strategy that gives the game a cooperative equilibrium?
   c. Would one firm still be tempted to cheat in a cooperative equilibrium? Explain your answer.

Antitrust Law (Study Plan 15.4)

8. AT&T offers iPhone users a $15 a month plan for 200 megabytes of data and a $25 a month plan for 2 gigabytes of data. It won't take Verizon Wireless long to begin offering data plans too.

   Source: Cnet News, June 3, 2010

   a. Is AT&T likely to be using predatory pricing?
   b. If a price war develops, who benefits most?

ADDITIONAL PROBLEMS AND APPLICATIONS

MyEconLab   You can work these problems in MyEconLab if assigned by your instructor.

What Is Oligopoly?

9. **An Energy Drink with a Monster of a Stock**

   The $5.7 billion energy-drink category, in which Monster holds the No. 2 position behind industry leader Red Bull, has slowed down as copycat brands jostle for shelf space. Over the past five years Red Bull's market share in dollar terms has gone from 91 percent to well under 50 percent and much of that loss has been Monster's gain.

   Source: *Fortune*, December 25, 2006

   a. Describe the structure of the energy-drink market. How has that structure changed over the past few years?

   b. If Monster and Red Bull formed a cartel, how would the price charged for energy drinks and the profits made change?

Oligopoly Games

Use the following data to work Problems 10 and 11. Bud and Wise are the only two producers of aniseed beer, a New Age product designed to displace root beer. Bud and Wise are trying to figure out how much of this new beer to produce. They know

   (i)   If they both produce 10,000 gallons a day, they will make the maximum attainable joint economic profit of $200,000 a day, or $100,000 a day each.

   (ii) If either firm produces 20,000 gallons a day while the other produces 10,000 gallons a day, the one that produces 20,000 gallons will make an economic profit of $150,000 and the other will incur an economic loss of $50,000.

   (iii) If both produce 20,000 gallons a day, each firm will make zero economic profit.

10. Construct a payoff matrix for the game that Bud and Wise must play.

11. Find the Nash equilibrium of the game that Bud and Wise play.

12. **Asian Rice Exporters to Discuss Cartel**

    The Asian rice-exporting nations planned to discuss a proposal that they form a cartel. Ahead of the meeting, the countries said that the purpose of the rice cartel would be to contribute to ensuring food stability, not just in an individual country but also to address food shortages in the region and the world. The cartel will not hoard rice and raise prices when there are shortages.

    The Philippines says that it is a bad idea. It will create an oligopoly, and the cartel could price the grain out of reach for millions of people.

    Source: CNN, May 6, 2008

    a. Assuming the rice-exporting nations become a profit-maximizing colluding oligopoly, explain how they would influence the global market for rice and the world price of rice.

    b. Assuming the rice-exporting nations become a profit-maximizing colluding oligopoly, draw a graph to illustrate their influence on the global market for rice.

    c. Even in the absence of international antitrust laws, why might it be difficult for this cartel to successfully collude? Use the ideas of game theory to explain.

13. Suppose that Mozilla and Microsoft each develop their own versions of an amazing new Web browser that allows advertisers to target consumers with great precision. Also, the new browser is easier and more fun to use than existing browsers. Each firm is trying to decide whether to sell the browser or to give it away. What are the likely benefits from each action? Which action is likely to occur?

14. Why do Coca-Cola and PepsiCo spend huge amounts on advertising? Do they benefit? Does the consumer benefit? Explain your answer by constructing a game to illustrate the choices Coca-Cola and PepsiCo make.

Use the following news clip to work Problems 15 and 16.

PS4 vs. Xbox One Battle Means Gamers Win, Sony Says

Microsoft's latest move in the PlayStation 4 vs. Xbox One battle was to lower the price of Xbox One to $399—the same price as the PS4.

   Source: *GameSpot*, July 1, 2014

15. a. Thinking about the competition between Sony and Microsoft in the market for game consoles as a game, describe the firms' strategies concerning design, marketing, and price.

    b. What, based on the information provided, turned out to be the equilibrium of the game?

16. Can you think of reasons why the two consoles are different?

Repeated Games and Sequential Games

17. If Bud and Wise in Problems 10 and 11 play the game repeatedly, what is the equilibrium of the game?

18. Agile Airlines' profit on a route on which it has a monopoly is $10 million a year. Wanabe Airlines is considering entering the market and operating on this route. Agile warns Wanabe to stay out and threatens to cut the price so that if Wanabe enters it will make no profit. Wanabe determines that the payoff matrix for the game in which it is engaged with Agile is shown in the table.

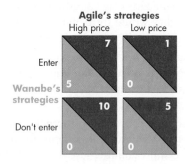

Does Wanabe believe Agile's assertion? Does Wanabe enter or not? Explain.

19. **Oil Trading Probe May Uncover Manipulation**

Amid soaring oil prices the Commodity Futures Trading Commission (CFTC) is looking into manipulation of the oil market—withholding oil in an attempt to drive prices higher. The CFTC has found such evidence in the past and it's likely it will find evidence again. But it is unlikely that a single player acting alone would be able to run the price up from $90 to $135.

Source: CNN, May 30, 2008

What type of market does the news clip imply best describes the U.S. oil market?

Antitrust Law

Use the following news clip to work Problems 20 and 21.

Gadgets for Sale ... or Not

How come the prices of some gadgets, like the iPod, are the same no matter where you shop? No, the answer isn't that Apple illegally manages prices. In reality, Apple uses an accepted retail strategy called minimum advertised price to discourage resellers from discounting. The minimum advertised price (MAP) is the absolute lowest price of a product that resellers can advertise. Marketing subsidies offered by a manufacturer to its resellers usually keep the price at

or above the MAP. Stable prices are important to the company that is both a manufacturer and a retailer. If Apple resellers advertised the iPod below cost, they could squeeze the Apple Stores out of their own markets. The downside to the price stability is that by limiting how low sellers can go, MAP keeps prices artificially high (or at least higher than they might otherwise be with unfettered price competition).

Source: *Slate*, December 22, 2006

20. a. Describe the practice of resale price maintenance that violates the Sherman Act.

 b. Describe the MAP strategy used by Apple and explain how it differs from a resale price maintenance agreement that would violate the Sherman Act.

21. Why might the MAP strategy be against the social interest and benefit only the producer?

Economics in the News

22. After you have studied *Economics in the News* on pp. 360–361, answer the following questions.

 a. What are the strategies of T-Mobile and AT&T in the market for cellphone service?

 b. Why, according to the news article, is it that AT&T and T-Mobile are in a fierce battle?

 c. Why wouldn't AT&T stick with its high price and leave T-Mobile to incur the cost of offering higher-valued plans?

 d. Could T-Mobile do something that would make it the market leader? Would that action maximize T-Mobile's profit?

23. **Boeing and Airbus Predict Asian Sales Surge**

Airlines in the Asia-Pacific region are emerging as the biggest customers for aircraft makers Boeing and Airbus. The two firms predict that over the next 20 years, more than 8,000 planes worth up to $1.2 trillion will be sold there.

Source: BBC News, February 3, 2010

 a. In what type of market are big airplanes sold?

 b. Thinking of competition between Boeing and Airbus as a game, what are the strategies and the payoffs?

 c. Set out a hypothetical payoff matrix for the game you've described in part (b). What is the equilibrium of the game?

 d. Do you think the market for big airplanes is efficient? Explain and illustrate your answer.

Managing Change and Limiting Market Power

Our economy is constantly changing. Every year, new goods appear and old ones disappear. New firms are born, and old ones die. This process of change is initiated and managed by firms operating in markets.

When a new product appears, just one or two firms sell it: Apple and IBM were the only producers of personal computers; Microsoft was (and almost still is) the only producer of the PC operating system; Intel was the only producer of the PC chip. These firms had enormous power to determine the quantity to produce and the price of their products.

In many markets, entry eventually brings competition. Even with just two rivals, the industry changes its face in a dramatic way. *Strategic interdependence* is capable of leading to an outcome like perfect competition.

With the continued arrival of new firms in an industry, the market becomes competitive. But in most markets, the competition isn't perfect: it becomes *monopolistic competition* with each firm selling its own differentiated product.

Often, an industry that is competitive becomes less so as the bigger and more successful firms in the industry begin to swallow up the smaller firms, either by driving them out of business or by acquiring their assets. Through this process, an industry might return to oligopoly or even monopoly. You can see such a movement in the auto and banking industries today.

By studying firms and markets, we gain a deeper understanding of the forces that allocate resources and begin to see the invisible hand at work.

John von Neumann *was one of the great minds of the twentieth century. Born in Budapest, Hungary, in 1903, Johnny, as he was known, showed early mathematical brilliance. He was 25 when he published the article that changed the social sciences and began a flood of research on* **game theory**—*a flood that has not subsided. In that article, von Neumann proved that in a zero-sum game (such as sharing a pie), there exists a best strategy for each player.*

Von Neumann did more than invent game theory: He also invented and built the first practical computer, and he worked on the Manhattan Project, which developed the atomic bomb during World War II.

Von Neumann believed that the social sciences would progress only if they used their own mathematical tools, not those of the physical sciences.

"Real life consists of bluffing, of little tactics of deception, of asking yourself what is the other man going to think I mean to do."

JOHN VON NEUMANN, told to Jacob Bronowski (in a London taxi) and reported in *The Ascent of Man.*

367

THOMAS HUBBARD is the John L. and Helen Kellogg Distinguished Professor of Management and Strategy at the Kellogg School of Management, Northwestern University and a research fellow at the National Bureau of Economic Research.

Professor Hubbard is an empirical economist. His work is driven by data. The central problems that unify much of his work are the limits to information and the fact that information is costly to obtain. Professor Hubbard studies the ways in which information problems influence the organization of firms; the extent to which firms make or buy what they sell; and the structure and performance of markets.

His work appears in the leading journals such as the *American Economic Review*, the *Quarterly Journal of Economics*, and the *Rand Journal of Economics*. He is a co-editor of the *Journal of Industrial Economics*.

Michael Parkin talked with Thomas Hubbard about his research and what we learn from it about the choices that firms make and their implications for market structure and performance.

Professor Hubbard, you have made important contributions to our understanding of outsourcing: whether a firm will make it or buy it. Can you summarize what economists know about this issue?

If there is one thing that Coase (Ronald Coase, see p. 417) taught us about the boundaries of the firm, it is that when thinking about whether to do something internally or to outsource it, a very useful starting point is to make the decision on a transaction-by-transaction basis.

The way I like to think about it is to boil it down to the theory of markets and incentives. Markets provide strong incentives but not necessarily good incentives. So when you outsource something, you rely on a market mechanism rather than on something within a firm that is less than a market mechanism. By outsourcing, you expose people to a strong market incentive. Now that can be good, and it is good most of the time. Strong market incentives get people to do things that the market rewards. Market rewards are generally quite valuable, but in some circumstances what the market rewards isn't

> **Markets provide strong incentives but not necessarily good incentives.**

what the buyer would want to reward. So there's a tradeoff. Strong incentives are sometimes good and sometimes bad. Therefore, keeping things inside the firm provides a weaker incentive. Sometimes that is good.

Can you provide an example?

Think about McDonald's. McDonald's is not one firm. It is many firms because a lot of the outlets are owned and managed by franchisees and some are owned and managed internally by McDonald's.

McDonald's thinks about whether to run one of its restaurants itself or to franchise it out.

One thing that it has in mind is that if it franchises it out, then the franchisee is going to be exposed to very strong market incentives. Now under some circumstances this is great. The franchisee treats the business as if he owns it. So the good part about it is the franchisee works hard to try to develop his business.

But a flip side to the franchisee's treating the business as his own is that it can be harmful for the McDonald's brand.

*Read the full interview with Thomas Hubbard in MyEconLab.

16

PUBLIC CHOICES, PUBLIC GOODS, AND HEALTHCARE

After studying this chapter, you will be able to:

◆ Explain why some choices are *public* choices and how they are made in a political marketplace

◆ Explain how the free-rider problem arises and how the quantity of public goods is determined

◆ Explain why governments provide healthcare and how our healthcare markets work

The George Washington Bridge that links New York and New Jersey is one of 607,380 road bridges in the United States built and maintained by governments. Healthcare along with a wide array of other goods and services are also provided by governments. But why governments? Why not private firms?

Are governments efficient in their provision of bridges, healthcare, and other goods and services?

These are the questions we study in this chapter. In *Economics in the News* at the end of the chapter, we return to bridges and look at the problem of keeping them safe.

◆ Public Choices

All economic choices are made by individuals, but some choices are *private* and some are *public*. A *private choice* is a decision that has consequences for the person making it. Your decision to buy a textbook or work at McDonald's is a private choice.

A **public choice** is a decision that has consequences for many people and perhaps for an entire society. The decision by members of Congress to pass the Affordable Care Act—Obamacare—and the decisions that created the enrollment website Healthcare.gov are examples of public choices.

Some of the things we care most about are decided by people making public choices, and very large quantities of scarce resources get used as a result of these choices. *Economics in Action* opposite provides a snapshot of what our federal, state, and local governments buy.

Why do governments allocate a large quantity of resources? The economic theory of government answers this question.

Why Governments?

Governments perform three economic functions: They establish and maintain property rights, provide nonmarket mechanisms for allocating scarce resources, and redistribute income and wealth.

Property rights and the legal system that enforces them are the foundation of the market economy, which, in many situations, functions well and allocates scarce resources efficiently. But sometimes the market fails (see Chapter 5, pp. 114–115).

When market failure occurs, choices made in the pursuit of self-interest have not served the social interest.

The market economy also delivers a distribution of income and wealth that most people regard as unfair. Equity requires some redistribution.

Replacing markets with government resource-allocation decisions is no simple matter. Just as there can be market failure, there can also be government failure. **Government failure** is a situation in which government actions lead to inefficiency—to either underprovision or overprovision.

Government failure can arise because government is made up of many individuals, each with their own economic objectives. Public choices are the outcome of the choices made by these individuals. To analyze these choices, economists have developed a public choice theory of the political marketplace.

ECONOMICS IN ACTION

The Goods and Services Provided by Governments

The U.S. federal government spent $2 trillion on goods and services in 2013. The state and local governments spent another $1.8 trillion. The total of $3.8 trillion is one quarter of all expenditure in the U.S. economy.

The figure shows what our governments buy. The biggest item is healthcare, with education not far behind. National defense comes next. The total spent on the nation's highways and bridges (transportation), police and fire services (protection), and government itself is about one fifth of government expenditure.

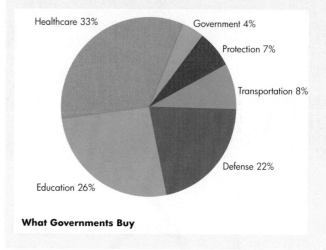

What Governments Buy

Public Choice and the Political Marketplace

The four groups of decision makers shown in Fig. 16.1 interact in the political marketplace. They are

- Voters
- Firms
- Politicians
- Bureaucrats

Voters Voters evaluate politicians' policy proposals, benefit from public goods and services, and pay some of the taxes. They support the politicians whose policy proposals make them better off and express their demand for public goods and services by voting, helping in political campaigns, lobbying, and making campaign contributions.

Firms Firms also evaluate politicians' policy proposals, benefit from public goods and services, and pay some of the taxes. Although firms don't vote, they

FIGURE 16.1   The Political Marketplace

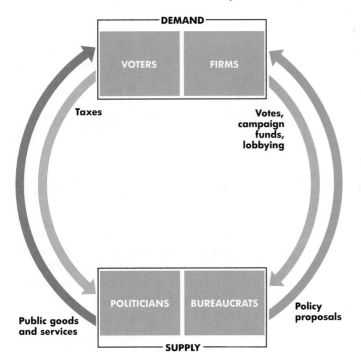

Voters and firms demand public goods and services and policies that serve their self-interest.

Voters support the policies they like with their votes. And voters and firms support policies they like with campaign contributions and by lobbying.

Politicians and bureaucrats supply public goods and services, set taxes, and make policy proposals that serve their self-interest.

Politicians want to attract enough votes to get them elected and keep them in office. Bureaucrats want to get the largest possible budget for their departments.

A political equilibrium balances all these public choices.

do make campaign contributions and are a major source of funds for political parties. Firms also engage in lobbying activity to persuade politicians to propose policies that benefit them.

Politicians   Politicians are the elected persons in the federal, state, and local governments. The goal of a politician is to get elected and to remain in office. Votes to a politician are like profit to a firm. Politicians also direct bureaucrats.

Bureaucrats   Bureaucrats are the public servants who work in government departments. They administer tax collection, the delivery of public goods and services, and the administration of rules and regulations.

The self-interest of a bureaucrat is served when the budget of her or his department is maximized. The bigger the budget of a department, the greater is the prestige of its chief and the greater are the opportunities for promotion for people farther down the bureaucratic ladder. This economic assumption implies that in doing what they perceive to be a good job in the public interest, they take care of their own self-interest too.

Political Equilibrium

Voters, firms, politicians, and bureaucrats make their economic choices in their own self-interest. Public choices, like private choices, are constrained by what is feasible. Each person's public choices are also constrained by the public choices of others.

The balance of forces in the political marketplace determines the outcome of all the public choices that people make. In a **political equilibrium** the choices of voters, firms, politicians, and bureaucrats are all compatible and no group can see a way of improving its position by making a different choice.

Ideally, the political equilibrium achieves allocative efficiency and serves the social interest, but this outcome is not guaranteed, as you'll see in this chapter.

We make public choices because some situations just don't permit private choices. The core of the reason we can't always make private choices is that some goods and services (and some factors of production) have a public nature—they are *public* goods and services.

Your next task is to see exactly what we mean by a *public* good or service.

What Is a Public Good?

To see what makes a good a *public* good, we distinguish between two features of all goods: the extent to which people can be *excluded* from consuming them and the extent to which one person's consumption *rivals* someone else's consumption.

Excludable A good is **excludable** if it is possible to prevent someone from enjoying its benefits. Brink's security services, East Point Seafood's fish, and a U2 concert are examples. People must pay to benefit from them.

A good is **nonexcludable** if it is impossible (or extremely costly) to prevent anyone from benefiting from it. The services of the LAPD, fish in the Pacific Ocean, and a concert on network television are examples. When an LAPD cruiser enforces the speed limit, everyone on the highway benefits; anyone with a boat can fish in the ocean; and anyone with a TV can watch a network broadcast.

Rival A good is **rival** if one person's use of it decreases the quantity available for someone else. A Brink's truck can't deliver cash to two banks at the same time. A fish can be consumed only once.

A good is **nonrival** if one person's use of it does not decrease the quantity available for someone else. The services of the LAPD and a concert on network television are nonrival. One person's benefit doesn't lower the benefit of others.

A Fourfold Classification

Figure 16.2 classifies goods, services, and resources into four types.

Private Goods A **private good** is both rival and excludable. A can of Coke and a fish on East Point Seafood's farm are examples of private goods.

Public Goods A **public good** is both nonrival and nonexcludable. A public good simultaneously benefits everyone, and no one can be excluded from its benefits. National defense is the best example of a public good.

Common Resources A **common resource** is rival and nonexcludable. A unit of a common resource can be used only once, but no one can be prevented from using what is available. Ocean fish are a common resource. They are rival because a fish taken by one person isn't available for anyone else, and they are nonexcludable because it is difficult to prevent people from catching them.

FIGURE 16.2 Fourfold Classification of Goods

	Private goods	Common resources
Rival	Food and drink Car House	Fish in ocean Atmosphere National parks
	Natural monopoly goods	**Public goods**
Nonrival	Internet Cable television Bridge or tunnel	National defense The law Air traffic control
	Excludable	**Nonexcludable**

A private good is rival and excludable: You must pay to get it and you alone enjoy it. A public good is nonrival and nonexcludable: You and everyone else enjoy it without paying for it. A common resource is rival but nonexcludable. And a good that is nonrival but excludable is produced by a natural monopoly.

MyEconLab Animation

Natural Monopoly Goods A **natural monopoly good** is nonrival but excludable. Potential consumers can be excluded if they don't pay but adding one more user doesn't rival other users, so marginal cost is zero. Examples of natural monopoly goods are the Internet, cable television, and an uncongested bridge or tunnel.

Why is a nonrival but excludable good a natural monopoly good? It is because there is a fixed cost of producing it. With a zero marginal cost, average total cost falls as output increases so economies of scale exist over the entire range of output for which there is a demand, and one firm can produce the good at a lower cost than can two or more firms (see p. 298).

The Things Our Governments Buy

Of the things that our governments buy, shown in *Economics in Action* on p. 370, national defense, protection, and constructing and maintaining the transportation infrastructure fit the definition of a public good. They are nonrival and nonexcludable. But what about healthcare and education, the two biggest items? They don't look like public goods. A person can be excluded from a hospital or college. And one person's use of a hospital bed or place in college rivals another's. So aren't healthcare and education private goods? Why do governments provide them?

ECONOMICS IN ACTION

Is a Lighthouse a Public Good?

Built on Little Brewster Island in 1716 to guide ships into and out of the Boston Harbor, Boston Lighthouse was the first light station in North America.

For two centuries, economists used the lighthouse as an example of a public good. No one can be prevented from seeing its warning light—*nonexcludable*—and one person seeing its light doesn't prevent someone else from doing so too—*nonrival*.

Ronald Coase, who won the 1991 Nobel Prize for ideas he first developed when he was an undergraduate at the London School of Economics, discovered that before the nineteenth century, lighthouses in England were built and operated by private corporations that earned profits by charging tolls on ships docking at nearby ports. A ship that refused to pay the lighthouse toll was *excluded* from the port.

So the benefit arising from the services of a lighthouse is *excludable*. Because the services provided by a lighthouse are nonrival but excludable, a lighthouse is an example of a natural monopoly good and not a public good.

Healthcare Healthcare is two goods: care supplied by doctors and other professionals, and insurance. Governments provide both healthcare services and health insurance because, left to the market alone, they would be inefficiently underprovided and unfairly distributed. For a majority of voters, it is unfair and unethical to allocate scarce healthcare resources only to those who can afford them—those who are willing and able to pay. Most people want the government to provide a single mother who is living in poverty with access to a doctor or hospital when she needs those services.

To work well, a market needs buyers and sellers who are well informed about the item being traded. In the case of healthcare services, doctors and healthcare professionals are better informed than patients about the service and treatment needed. And in the case of health insurance, the insured is better informed than the insurer about the risks faced.

Also, lacking the relevant information about risk, fit and healthy people often take too short a view and don't buy enough insurance.

Education Governments provide public education because it brings benefits that spill over to others—called *external benefits*. Everyone benefits from living in an educated society where friends and neighbors share a common heritage.

The rest of this chapter studies the public choices that must be made to avoid the underprovision of public goods and healthcare. Chapter 17 studies the ways of coping with externalities, including those arising from education, and the challenge of conserving common resources.

REVIEW QUIZ

1. List the economic functions of governments.
2. Describe the political marketplace: Who are the participants, what do they do, and what is a political equilibrium?
3. Distinguish among public goods, private goods, common resources, and natural monopoly goods.
4. Why are healthcare and education not public goods and why do governments play a large role in the markets for these services?

Work these questions in Study Plan 16.1 and get instant feedback. Do a Key Terms Quiz.   MyEconLab

◆ Providing Public Goods

Why do governments provide firefighting services? Why don't the people of California buy brush firefighting services from Firestorm, a private firm that competes for our dollars in the marketplace in the same way that McDonald's does? The answer is that firefighting is a public good. It is nonexcludable and nonrival and it has a free-rider problem.

The Free-Rider Problem

A free rider enjoys the benefits of a good or service without paying for it. Because a public good is provided for everyone to use and no one can be excluded from its benefits, no one has an incentive to pay his or her share of the cost. Everyone has an incentive to free ride. The **free-rider problem** is that the economy would provide an inefficiently small quantity of a public good. Marginal social benefit from the public good would exceed its marginal social cost and a deadweight loss would arise.

Let's look at the marginal social benefit and marginal social cost of a public good.

Marginal Social Benefit from a Public Good

Lisa and Max (the only people in a society) value fire-fighting airplanes. Figures 16.3(a) and 16.3(b) graph their marginal benefits from the airplanes as MB_L for Lisa and MB_M for Max. The marginal benefit from a public good (like that from a private good) diminishes as the quantity of the good increases.

Figure 16.3(c) shows the marginal *social* benefit curve, *MSB*. Because everyone gets the same quantity of a public good, its marginal social benefit is the sum of the marginal benefits of all the individuals at each *quantity*. So the marginal social benefit curve is the *vertical* sum of the individual marginal benefit curves. The curve *MSB* is the marginal social benefit curve for the economy made up of Lisa and Max. For each airplane, Lisa's marginal benefit is added to Max's marginal benefit.

Contrast the *MSB* curve for a public good with that of a private good. To obtain the economy's *MSB* curve for a private good, we sum the *quantities demanded* by all the individuals at each *price*—we sum the individual marginal benefit curves *horizontally* (see Chapter 5, pp. 108–109).

FIGURE 16.3   Benefits of a Public Good

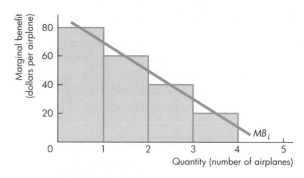

(a) Lisa's marginal benefit

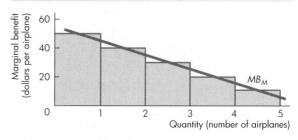

(b) Max's marginal benefit

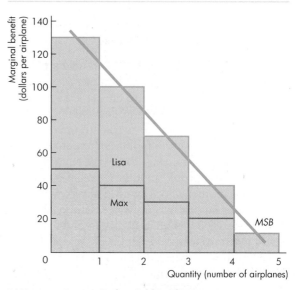

(c) Economy's marginal social benefit

The marginal social benefit at each quantity of the public good is the sum of the marginal benefits of all individuals. The marginal benefit curves are MB_L for Lisa and MB_M for Max. The economy's marginal social curve is *MSB*.

—— MyEconLab Animation ——

Marginal Social Cost of a Public Good

The marginal social cost of a public good is determined in exactly the same way as that of a private good—see Chapter 5, p. 110. The principle of increasing marginal cost applies to the marginal cost of a public good, so the marginal social cost increases as the quantity of the public good increases.

Efficient Quantity of a Public Good

To determine the efficient quantity of a public good, we use the principles that you learned in Chapter 5. The efficient quantity is that at which marginal social benefit equals marginal social cost.

Figure 16.4 shows the marginal social benefit curve, *MSB*, and the marginal social cost curve, *MSC*, for firefighting airplanes. (We'll now think of society as consisting of Lisa and Max and the other 39 million Californians.)

If marginal social benefit exceeds marginal social cost, as it does with 2 airplanes, resources can be used more efficiently by increasing the number of airplanes. The extra benefit exceeds the extra cost. If marginal social cost exceeds marginal social benefit, as it does with 4 airplanes, resources can be used more efficiently by decreasing the number of airplanes. The cost saving exceeds the loss of benefit.

If marginal social benefit equals marginal social cost, as it does with 3 airplanes, resources are allocated efficiently. Resources cannot be used more efficiently because to provide more than 3 airplanes increases cost by more than the extra benefit, and to provide fewer airplanes lowers the benefit by more than the cost saving.

Inefficient Private Provision

Could a private firm—Firestorm—deliver the efficient quantity of firefighting airplanes? Most likely it couldn't, because no one would have an incentive to buy his or her share of the airplanes. Everyone would reason as follows: The number of airplanes provided by Firestorm is not affected by my decision to pay my share or not. But my own private consumption will be greater if I free ride and do not pay my share of the cost of the airplanes. If I don't pay, I enjoy the same level of fire protection and I can buy more private goods. I will spend my money on private goods and free ride on fire

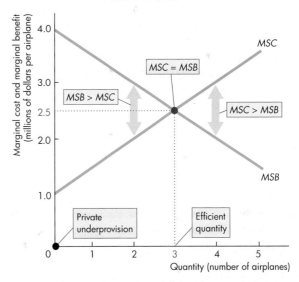

FIGURE 16.4   The Efficient Quantity of a Public Good

With fewer than 3 airplanes, marginal social benefit, *MSB*, exceeds marginal social cost, *MSC*. With more than 3 airplanes, *MSC* exceeds *MSB*. Only with 3 airplanes is *MSC* equal to *MSB* and the number of airplanes is efficient.

—————— MyEconLab Animation ——————

protection. Such reasoning is the free-rider problem. If everyone reasons the same way, Firestorm has no revenue and so provides no airplanes. Because the efficient number of airplanes is 3, private provision is inefficient.

Efficient Public Provision

The outcome of the political process might be efficient or inefficient. We look first at an efficient outcome. There are two political parties: Fears and Hopes. They agree on all issues except the number of firefighting airplanes: The Fears want 4, and the Hopes want 2. Both parties want to get elected, so they run a voter survey and discover the marginal social benefit curve of Fig. 16.5. They also consult with airplane producers to establish the marginal cost curve. The parties then do a "what-if" analysis. If the Fears propose 4 airplanes and the Hopes propose 2, the voters will be equally unhappy with both parties. Compared to the efficient quantity, the Hopes want an underprovision of 1 airplane and the Fears want an overprovision of 1 airplane. The deadweight losses are equal and the election would be too close to call.

Contemplating this outcome, the Fears realize that they are too fearful to get elected. They figure that, if they scale back to 3 airplanes, they will win the election if the Hopes stick with 2. The Hopes reason in a similar way and figure that, if they increase the number of airplanes to 3, they can win the election if the Fears propose 4.

So they both propose 3 airplanes. The voters are indifferent between the parties, and each party receives 50 percent of the vote. But regardless of which party wins the election, 3 airplanes are provided and this quantity is efficient. Competition in the political marketplace results in the efficient provision of a public good.

The Principle of Minimum Differentiation The **principle of minimum differentiation** is the tendency for competitors (including political parties) to make themselves similar to appeal to the maximum number of clients or voters. This principle describes the behavior of political parties. It also explains why fast-food restaurants cluster in the same block. For example, if Domino's opens a new pizza outlet, it is likely that Pizza Hut will soon open nearby.

FIGURE 16.5   An Efficient Political Outcome

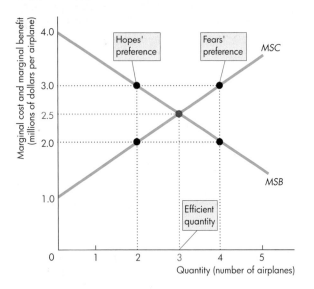

The Hopes would like to provide 2 airplanes and the Fears would like to provide 4 airplanes. The political outcome is 3 airplanes because unless each party proposes 3 airplanes, the other party will beat it in an election.

MyEconLab Animation

ECONOMICS IN ACTION
Fighting Colorado's Wildfires

The 2012 wildfire season was extreme. Colorado had its worst season in a decade with major fires that devastated communities in and around Colorado Springs. And across the Western states, close to half a million acres (780 square miles) of land were burned.

Wildfires are natural and vital for the ecosystem, but some fires are started by human action, and some both human-made and naturally occurring fires, like the 2012 fires in Colorado, burn close to where people live. So protection against wildfires is a vital *public good*.

But not all fire protection services are *produced* by government. *Private* wildfire service contractors supply around 40 percent of wildfire suppression services. So fighting wildfires is an example of a public good that is *provided* by government and paid for with tax revenues, but in part *produced* by private firms.

Firestorm Wildfire Suppression Inc. is one such firm. Operating from Chico, CA, Firestorm hires and trains firefighters and produces firefighting services to maximize its profit. To achieve this goal, the firm must produce firefighting services at the lowest possible cost.

But if Firestorm (and its competitors) tried to sell their services to each individual homeowner in the wildfire regions, they wouldn't get enough revenue to remain in business. There would be a free-rider problem. The free-rider problem is avoided because governments buy the services of Firestorm.

For the political process to deliver the efficient outcome, voters must be well informed, evaluate the alternatives, and vote in the election. Political parties must be well informed about voter preferences. As the next section shows, we can't expect to achieve this outcome.

Inefficient Public Overprovision

If competition between two political parties is to deliver the efficient quantity of a public good, bureaucrats must cooperate and help to achieve this outcome. But bureaucrats might have a different idea and end up frustrating rather than facilitating an efficient outcome. Their actions might bring *government failure.*

Objective of Bureaucrats Bureaucrats want to maximize their department's budget because a bigger budget brings greater status and more power. So the Emergency Services Department's objective is to maximize the budget for firefighting airplanes.

Figure 16.6 shows the outcome if the bureaucrats are successful in the pursuit of their goal. They might try to persuade the politicians that 3 airplanes cost more than the originally budgeted amount; or they might press their position more strongly and argue for more than 3 airplanes. In Fig. 16.6, the Emergency Services Department persuades the politicians to provide 4 airplanes.

Why don't the politicians block the bureaucrats? Won't overproviding airplanes cost future votes? It will if voters are well informed and know what is best for them. But voters might not be well informed, and well-informed interest groups might enable the bureaucrats to achieve their objective and overcome the objections of the politicians.

Rational Ignorance A principle of the economic analysis of public choices is that it is rational for a voter to be ignorant about an issue unless that issue has a perceptible effect on the voter's economic welfare. Each voter knows that he or she can make virtually no difference to the fire protection policy of the government of California and that it would take an enormous amount of time and effort to become even moderately well informed about alternative fire-protection technologies. Rationally uninformed voters enable bureaucrats and special interest groups to overprovide public goods.

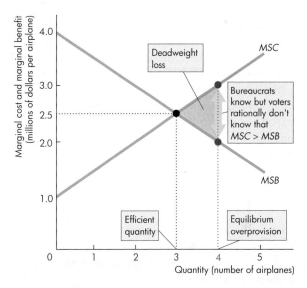

FIGURE 16.6 Bureaucratic Overprovision

Well-informed bureaucrats want to maximize their budget and rationally ignorant voters enable the bureaucrats to go some way toward achieving their goal. A public good might be inefficiently overprovided with a deadweight loss.

—— MyEconLab Animation ——

◆ REVIEW QUIZ

1 What is the free-rider problem? Why do free riders make the private provision of a public good inefficient?
2 Under what conditions will competition among politicians for votes result in an efficient provision of a public good?
3 How do rationally ignorant voters and budget-maximizing bureaucrats prevent the political marketplace from delivering the efficient quantity of a public good?
4 Explain why public choices might lead to the overprovision rather than the underprovision of a public good.

Work these questions in Study Plan 16.2 and get instant feedback. Do a Key Terms Quiz.   MyEconLab

You've seen how the political marketplace provides public goods and why it might *over*provide them. Your next task is to see how the political marketplace provides healthcare.

◆ The Economics of Healthcare

Governments spend more on healthcare than on any other item. (see *Economics in Action* on p. 370). The key reason why governments play a large role in healthcare is that it would be underprovided and unfairly distributed if left to the market alone.

You are now going to see how governments influence the provision of healthcare, how healthcare markets in the United States compare with those in some other countries, and how it might be possible to improve on our current healthcare programs.

We begin by seeing why the market would underprovide healthcare—why there would be a healthcare market failure.

Healthcare Market Failure

Healthcare consists of healthcare services (the services of physicians, specialists, nurses, other professionals, and hospitals) and health insurance. Both would be underprovided and unfairly distributed without some government action.

The *social* benefit of healthcare exceeds the benefit perceived by its consumers, which means that the *marginal social benefit* of healthcare exceeds the willingness and ability to pay for it.

Three problems make healthcare a special good: Consumers and potential consumers of healthcare

- Underestimate its benefit
- Underestimate their future needs
- Can't afford the care they need

Underestimate Benefit People don't have enough information to value the benefit of healthcare correctly. Most people lack the medical knowledge to determine their treatment needs. And many (especially healthy and young people) optimistically underestimate the health risks that they face. So they undervalue the insurance policies that can help them pay for healthcare; and they undervalue the healthcare resources that stand ready to help them when needed.

Underestimate Future Needs People take too short a view of the benefits of healthcare. The young and healthy know that they will become old and less healthy and will likely become big consumers of healthcare. But the time horizon over which they plan doesn't stretch that far into the future. The end result is that many people perceive too small a marginal benefit from health insurance, and are not willing to pay what it is actually worth to them.

Can't Afford For many people, the price of health insurance is beyond their ability to pay for it. Two groups of people are unable to afford adequate health insurance: those with a long-term health problem and the aged. But these are the people with the greatest need for healthcare.

Most people want to live in a society that treats these less healthy, older, and poorer people with compassion and ensure that they are provided with access to affordable healthcare. So there is an additional social benefit from healthcare for less healthy, older, and poorer people.

Because the marginal social benefit of healthcare exceeds the marginal benefit perceived by its consumers, a competitive market in healthcare would underprovide it. And this underprovision has two dimensions. It is

- Inefficient, and
- Unfair

Inefficient Figure 16.7 illustrates the inefficient underprovision of a competitive market in healthcare.

The curve $D = MB$ shows the demand for healthcare, which is determined by the willingness and ability to pay for it, which in turn is determined by its *perceived* marginal benefit, MB.

The curve $S = MSC$ shows the supply of healthcare. The supply curve is also the marginal cost curve, which we will assume correctly measures the marginal social cost, MSC.

The equilibrium quantity of healthcare is at the intersection of the demand curve, $D = MB$, and the supply curve, $S = MSC$. In Fig. 16.7, that quantity is 0.3 billion patients per year.

The curve MSB shows the marginal social benefit of healthcare, which, for the reasons explained above, exceeds the willingness and ability to pay.

The efficient quantity of healthcare is that at which $MSB = MSC$. In Fig. 16.7, that quantity is 0.7 billion patients per year.

Because the efficient quantity exceeds the market quantity, the market underprovides healthcare. The marginal social benefit that patients who fail to get care would generate exceeds the marginal social cost of providing care, so the underprovision creates the deadweight loss shown by the gray triangle.

Unfair Not only is there deadweight loss, but also there is an unfair distribution of the loss. The people who receive healthcare are the ones who are willing and able to pay for it. They are people who are normally fit and healthy and able to earn an average or

FIGURE 16.7 Healthcare Market Failure

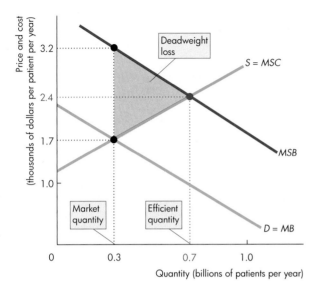

The demand curve, $D = MB$, shows the marginal benefit and willingness to pay for healthcare, and the supply curve, $S = MSC$, shows the marginal social cost of providing healthcare. A competitive market would provide care for 0.3 billion patients. The curve MSB shows the marginal social benefit of healthcare. The efficient quantity is that at which $MSB = MSC$ and is 0.7 billion patients. The gray triangle shows the deadweight loss from underprovision.

MyEconLab Animation Draw Graph

better than average income. The people who don't receive healthcare and who bear the deadweight loss are the long-term sick and the aged who can't afford the cost of healthcare.

Because the market would deliver an inefficient and unfair outcome, healthcare is provided by the *public* choices of governments. But there are alternative methods and scales of public provision, so governments must consider the effects of the alternatives in making their choices.

Alternative Public Choice Solutions

We're now going to examine the public choices that deliver healthcare services. You can see in *Economics in Action* on this page that there is a wide range of levels of public funding of healthcare. Public choices pay 83 percent of the healthcare bills in the United Kingdom, 70 percent in Canada, and 46 percent in the United States. But among these three countries, public expenditure per person is highest in the United States.

ECONOMICS IN ACTION

U.S. Healthcare Expenditures in Global Perspective

The best U.S. healthcare is the best in the world, but it is costly. Americans spend 18 percent of income—almost $9,000 per person per year—on healthcare. This amount is *more than double* the average spent in other rich countries. And this expenditure is projected to rise as the U.S. population ages and the "baby boom" generation retires.

The figure below compares U.S. healthcare costs with those of 13 other countries: some rich and some not so rich.

The figure shows that even rich countries such as Canada, Germany, and France spend barely a half as much, per person, on healthcare as do Americans. And health outcomes measured by life expectancy and quality of health are as good as or better in these other rich countries than those in the United States.

Another feature of U.S. healthcare expenditure is its very large public component (the blue bars in the figure). Government expenditure per person on healthcare in the United States is the second highest in the world, exceeded only by that of the Netherlands. It exceeds that in Canada, where selling private health insurance is illegal, and in Germany and France, where there is a greater acceptance of high taxes and big government than in the United States.

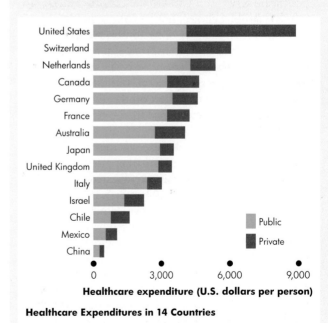

Healthcare Expenditures in 14 Countries

Different public choice solutions lead to these differences in healthcare expenditures. And the different solutions have implications for both the efficiency and the cost of healthcare.

We examine three approaches to supplementing or replacing the market: one used in Canada and the United Kingdom and two used in the United States. The three approaches are

- Universal coverage, single payer
- Private and government insurance
- Subsidized private insurance: Obamacare

Universal Coverage, Single Payer In Canada and the United Kingdom, healthcare is provided by a system with two key features: universal coverage and a single payer.

Universal coverage means that everyone is covered by health insurance, with no exceptions and no excluded preconditions.

Single payer means that the government alone pays the healthcare bills. The government pays the doctors, nurses, and hospitals, and it pays for prescription drugs.

In the United Kingdom, most of the doctors are employed by the government and most of the hospitals are government owned. In Canada, the doctors and hospitals are independent private agents, but they may not sell their services other than to the government.

Because the government is the sole buyer of healthcare services, it chooses the quantity of care to supply. A public choice, not a market equilibrium, determines the quantity of healthcare service.

Patients access healthcare services at a zero (or low) price, so the quantity demanded is that at which the marginal benefit is zero (or low). But the demand for healthcare has no direct effect on the quantity actually available, which is determined by the government's supply decision.

The quantity demanded exceeds the quantity supplied and in the absence of a market price to allocate the scarce resources, services are allocated on a first-come, first-served basis (see Chapter 5, pp. 106–107). The result is a long wait time for treatment.

Figure 16.8 shows how this system works. The $D = MB$, MSB, and $S = MSC$ curves are the same as in Fig. 16.7. The quantity supplied is fixed at a level that exceeds the market equilibrium but is less than the efficient quantity, so a deadweight loss arises.

The area of the gray triangle shows the smallest possible amount of deadweight loss, which would be the loss if patients were treated in the order of their

FIGURE 16.8   Public Production with Waiting

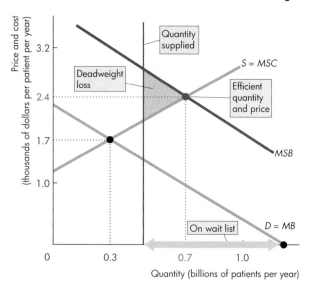

The government produces a fixed quantity of healthcare that exceeds the market quantity at the intersection of the $D = MB$ and $S = MSC$ curves but is less than the efficient quantity at the intersection of the MSB and $S = MSC$ curves. Patients face a zero price, so the quantity of healthcare demanded exceeds the quantity supplied. The available healthcare resources are allocated by doctors and patients wait for their treatment.

MyEconLab Animation

willingness to pay. But some people who are waiting in a long line are willing to pay more than the cost of the attention their health problem needs—their marginal benefit exceeds the marginal cost. Others get service even if their marginal benefit is less than the marginal cost. So the full deadweight loss exceeds the area of the gray triangle.

Defenders of this system say that inefficiencies are small and worth accepting because the outcome is fair as everyone has equal access to services. But it isn't exactly true that everyone has equal access. Some people are better at playing the system than others and are able to jump the line.

Private and Government Insurance In the United States, most healthcare services are produced by private doctors and hospitals that receive their incomes from three sources: private health insurance, governments, and patients. Private health insurance pays 41 percent of the bills, government Medicare, Medicaid, and other programs pay 46 percent, and the remaining 13 percent comes from patients. Patients' out-of-pocket payments arise because some

ECONOMICS IN ACTION

How We Pay for Our Healthcare Services

Total healthcare expenditure in the United States is around $3 trillion a year—18 percent of total income. Governments, both federal and state, spend 46 percent of the healthcare dollars. Private insurance companies pay 41 percent and the remaining 13 percent comes directly from the patient's pocket.

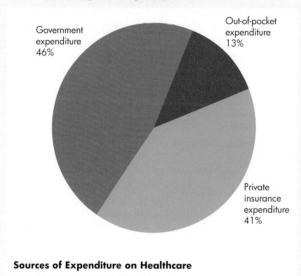

Sources of Expenditure on Healthcare

people are uninsured, and those who are insured face deductibles in their private insurance policies or co-payments for services provided under Medicare and Medicaid.

The scale of out-of-pocket costs combined with conditions set out in insurance plans and the demand for healthcare service determine the quantity of healthcare service provided. Measured by visits to a physician's office, that quantity is 1 billion patients per year. (The average number of physician visits is 3 per person per year.)

Inefficient Overproduction? We don't know whether private insurance together with Medicare and Medicaid provides the efficient quantity of healthcare. But relative to what is spent in other rich countries, the scale of expenditure on these programs suggests that they do overprovide. That is what we will assume in examining how the market works.

Figure 16.9 shows the market for healthcare services. Again, the $D = MB$, MSB, and $S = MSC$ curves are the same as those in Fig. 16.7.

The quantity provided is the quantity demanded by patients and supplied by doctors at the out-of-pocket cost to patients.

FIGURE 16.9 Private and Public Inefficient Overproduction and Uncontrolled Expenditure

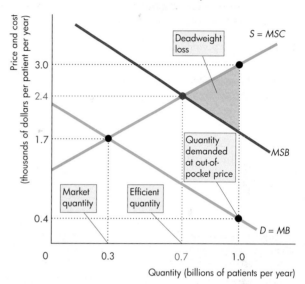

(a) Inefficiency

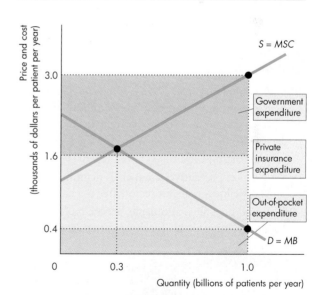

(b) Uncontrolled public expenditure

The quantity of healthcare service is determined by the quantity demanded at the out-of-pocket price. In both parts of the figure, this quantity is 1 billion patients per year.

In part (a), the quantity of healthcare service exceeds the efficient quantity and creates a deadweight loss. In part (b), out-of-pocket payments, private insurance, and government expenditure meet the cost of the quantity of care demanded of $3,000 per patient per year.

MyEconLab Animation

Doctors and hospitals negotiate fees with the government that equal marginal cost, which also equals marginal social cost. Marginal social cost of the quantity provided exceeds marginal benefit, so the over-provision creates the deadweight loss shown by the area of the gray triangle in Fig. 16.9(a).

Uncontrolled Expenditure Figure 16.9(b) illustrates the sources of expenditure: patients' out-of-pocket expenditure (red), expenditure by private insurers (blue), and government expenditure (purple).

Government expenditure is determined by the quantity of care demanded, not by a fixed budget. And without changes in the Medicare and Medicaid programs, this expenditure will grow as the aged population grows. *At Issue* below suggests a solution to this problem.

Obamacare The Patient Protection and Affordable Care Act, 2010 (Obamacare) has created a Health Insurance Marketplace to provide subsidized insurance.

On the supply side of the new marketplace are private insurers. On the demand side are the uninsured and those who want to find a better plan than their current one.

To qualify for subsidies, plans offered through the marketplace must cover pre-existing conditions, preventive services, and 10 essential health benefits.

The premium paid depends on family size and income. An example: A couple both aged 31 with two children and earning the median family income of $51,371 receive a subsidy (as a tax credit) of $5,534 leaving them to pay $3,562 for a $9,096 policy.

AT **ISSUE**

Is Obamacare the Solution to U.S. Healthcare Problems?

The *Patient Protection and Affordable Care Act, 2010* (Obamacare) has created a Health Insurance Marketplace to provide subsidized insurance. By the end of April 2014, 8 million families had signed up for Obamacare. The Act remains controversial, and alternative solutions to the healthcare problem have been proposed. So, *is* Obamacare the solution?

Yes

- A Whitehouse *Fact Sheet* says the *Affordable Care Act* keeps healthcare costs low, promotes prevention, and holds insurance companies accountable.

- It stops insurance companies denying coverage of pre-existing conditions.

- It makes preventive care such as mammograms and wellness visits for seniors free of charge.

- It makes quality, affordable, private health-insurance plans available for those currently uninsured.

The Healthcare Fix

Universal Insurance for All Americans

Laurence J. Kotlikoff

Professor Laurence J. Kotlikoff of Boston University; author of *The Healthcare Fix* and creator of *Medicare Part C for All.*

No

- Laurence Kotlikoff, an economics professor at Boston University, says Obamacare has no effective mechanism for containing costs.

- He proposes a universal private health-insurance Basic Plan that creates incentives to improve health and deliver healthcare services efficiently.

- Each year, each American gets a voucher to buy health insurance from a company of their choice.

- The voucher's value equals the expected cost of covering the person, which is determined by health indicators. (Example: An 80-year-old diabetic might get a $70,000 voucher while a healthy 14-year-old girl might get a $3,000 voucher.)

- The total value of vouchers does not exceed 10 percent of total U.S. income.

- Public expenditure on healthcare grows as income grows, and an Independent Panel adds procedures and technologies covered by the Basic Plan but at a slower pace than in the current system.

Families with no health insurance in 2014 are required to pay a monthly fee of $95 per adult and $47.50 per child or 1 percent of income, whichever is higher, with a maximum family fee of $285 ($3,420 a year).

Figure 16.10 illustrates how the Obamacare subsidy works. The demand and marginal benefit curve $D = MB$ and the supply and marginal social cost curve $S = MSC$ determine the market quantity of 2 million insured at a price of $6,000 per family.

A subsidy of $5,000 puts a gap between the price paid of $4,000 and the price received by the insurer, $9,000. The government pays the subsidy and the total payment, the blue rectangle, is the subsidy per family multiplied by the number of families receiving the subsidy.

The numbers in Fig. 16.10 are calibrated approximately to the actual premiums and subsidies in Obamacare. The median household receives a subsidy of about $5,000, and (in 2014) 8 million families signed up through the Obamacare marketplace. The total subsidy paid by the government is around $40 billion ($5,000 × 8 million = $40 billion).

To determine whether the outcome of the Obamacare subsidy achieves an efficient outcome, we would need to have an estimate of the extent to which the marginal social benefit of health insurance for the affected families exceeds their ability and willingness to pay. The subsidy might be too large, too small, or just right.

Vouchers a Better Solution?

The power of the market leads economists to seek a market solution to all resource allocation problems, and healthcare is no exception.

When a market failure arises because marginal social benefit exceeds the ability and willingness to pay, economists say that vouchers should be used. A **voucher** is a token that can be used to buy only the item that the voucher specifies. So a healthcare voucher could be used only to buy health insurance.

Laurence Kotlikoff (see *At Issue* on the previous page) suggests that every American be given a health care voucher, the value of which is tied to each individual's health profile.

The voucher program would replace Medicare, Medicaid, Obamacare, and some other smaller government programs. The total value of vouchers would be limited, and the government, not the consumer of healthcare services, would be in control of the healthcare budget.

The markets for health insurance and healthcare services would be free to work like any other competitive market to seek an efficient outcome.

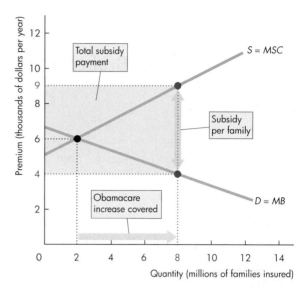

FIGURE 16.10 Subsidized Health Insurance

In the market for health insurance, the demand and marginal private benefit curve, $D = MB$, and the supply and marginal social cost curve, $S = MSC$, would deliver an equilibrium with too many people uninsured. A subsidy puts a gap between what the insured pays and the insurer receives and increases the number of families covered. The outcome is efficient if the subsidy brings marginal social benefit into equality with marginal social cost.

MyEconLab Animation

◆ REVIEW QUIZ

1 What is special about healthcare that makes it a good provided by government?

2 Why would the market economy produce too little healthcare?

3 How do Canada and the United Kingdom deliver healthcare and what is the problem left unresolved?

4 What are the problems with Medicare and Medicaid?

5 What is the problem that Obamacare seeks to solve and how does the solution work?

Work these questions in Study Plan 16.3 and get instant feedback. Do a Key Terms Quiz.   MyEconLab

 Economics in the News on pp. 384–385 returns to public goods and looks at the challenge of maintaining our transportation infrastructure.

Maintaining the Transportation Infrastructure

U.S. Infrastructure: Broken System

The Financial Times
April 24, 2014

"Thank you for shopping here" reads the sign on the old gas station at the corner of 10th Avenue and 24th Street in Manhattan. "Your custom is appreciated." But there was not sufficient custom to save the business. The plot is surrounded by wooden hoardings and is to be redeveloped as luxury apartments.

The station, most recently run by Russia's Lukoil, closed last year – one of thousands across the United States to have drawn down the shutters. A combination of increasing fuel efficiency and a steady reduction in the number of miles Americans drive each year has cut into the country's demand to fill up.

The declining fuel sales do not only threaten the narrow world of gas station owners and attendants. For every gallon pumped at the 10th Avenue station, the U.S. federal government received 18.4 cents toward its Highway Trust Fund, which disburses tens of billions of dollars annually to pay for the construction and upkeep of roads, bridges, and other infrastructure in U.S. states. The State of New York took another 69.6 cents. With fewer gallons being pumped, there is less revenue to keep the U.S. transportation system in good shape. ...

A barrier to mobilizing support for greater investment is that past scandals over the misuse of infrastructure funds are better remembered than tragedies resulting from underfunding. ...

The best-known tragedy is the collapse of a freeway bridge over the Mississippi in August 2007 in Minneapolis, which killed 13 people. ...

ESSENCE OF THE STORY

- Americans are driving fewer miles and in more fuel-efficient vehicles, so the quantity of gasoline consumed is falling.

- The federal and state governments get funds from the gas tax to maintain the highway system, and these funds are now too small to do the job required.

- Underfunding results in inadequate maintenance that sometimes leads to tragedy such as the collapse of a bridge in Minneapolis.

- Scandals over the misuse of infrastructure funds are a barrier to mobilizing support for greater investment.

MyEconLab More Economics in the News

ECONOMIC ANALYSIS

- The road transportation infrastructure of the United States consists of 4 million miles of roads, 47,000 miles of interstate highways, and 607,000 bridges.

- As the news article explains, the gas tax is the main source of funds for maintaining this vast stock of transportation capital, and declining gas use is decreasing these funds.

- The result is too little expenditure on maintaining the infrastructure.

- Bridge collapse is the most visible and worrying consequence of inadequate maintenance.

- The American Society of Civil Engineers says that one in nine (that's 67,487) bridges are structurally deficient.

- A spending increase of $8 billion annually is needed to bring the nation's bridges to a safe standard by 2028.

- You can explain the problem of bridge maintenance by using the tools you've learned in this chapter.

- In Fig. 1, the x-axis measures the number of bridges repaired per year and the y-axis measures the marginal benefit and cost of repairing a bridge.

- The MSC curve shows the marginal social cost of repairing a bridge and the MSB curve shows the marginal social benefit.

- The efficient use of resources occurs when 6,000 bridges per year are repaired at a cost of $3 million per bridge, with a total expenditure of $18 billion per year.

- Restricted funds block this efficient outcome. The actual number of bridges repaired is 4,000 per year at a cost of $2.5 million per bridge, with a total expenditure of $10 billion per year. (The numbers are in the region of the actual U.S. data but are assumptions.)

- Because the number of bridges repaired per year is less than the efficient quantity, there is a deadweight loss.

- If Fig. 1 is a correct description of the problem, a political party can propose a bridge repair and tax program that achieves an efficient outcome.

- The problem is that taxes are collected now and bridges are repaired later, so the political party must be able to credibly commit to doing the work after it has collected the funds.

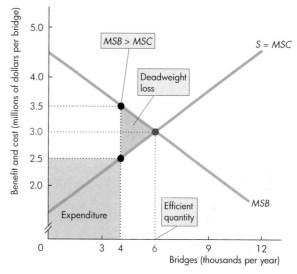

Figure 1 Underprovision of Infrastructure

The collapsed freeway bridge over the Mississippi in Minneapolis in August 2007.

SUMMARY

Key Points

Public Choices (pp. 370–373)

- Governments establish and maintain property rights, provide nonmarket mechanisms for allocating scarce resources, and redistribute income and wealth.
- Public choice theory explains how voters, firms, politicians, and bureaucrats interact in the political marketplace and why government failure might occur.
- A private good is a good or service that is rival and excludable.
- A public good is a good or service that is nonrival and nonexcludable.
- Healthcare and education are private goods that governments provide on the basis of need rather than on the ability and willingness to pay.

Working Problems 1 and 2 will give you a better understanding of public choices.

Providing Public Goods (pp. 374–377)

- Because a public good is a good or service that is *nonrival* and *nonexcludable*, it creates a *free-rider* problem: No one has an incentive to pay their share of the cost of providing a public good.
- The efficient level of provision of a public good is that at which marginal social benefit equals marginal social cost.

- Competition between political parties can lead to the efficient scale of provision of a public good.
- Bureaucrats who maximize their budgets and voters who are rationally ignorant can lead to the inefficient overprovision of a public good—government failure.

Working Problems 3 to 6 will give you a better understanding of providing public goods.

The Economics of Healthcare (pp. 378–383)

- Governments provide healthcare because people underestimate its value, don't plan far enough into the future, and many can't afford its cost.
- The marginal social benefit of healthcare exceeds the willingness and ability to pay for it.
- A competitive market would underprovide healthcare.
- In some countries, governments provide healthcare at a zero or low price and ration with wait times.
- U.S. private insurance, Medicare, and Medicaid possibly overprovide for those covered.
- Obamacare provides subsidized insurance and compels everyone to make a minimum contribution for health coverage.

Working Problems 7 to 10 will give you a better understanding of the economics of healthcare.

Key Terms

MyEconLab Key Terms Quiz

Common resource, 372	Nonexcludable, 372	Private good, 372
Excludable, 372	Nonrival, 372	Public choice, 370
Free-rider problem, 374	Political equilibrium, 371	Public good, 372
Government failure, 370	Principle of minimum	Rival, 372
Natural monopoly good, 372	differentiation, 376	Voucher, 383

WORKED PROBLEM

MyEconLab   You can work this problem in Chapter 16 Study Plan.

The table sets out the marginal benefits that Ann, Sue, and Zack receive from spraying their shared swamp to control mosquitos. The marginal social cost (*MSC*) is a constant $12 per spray.

Number of sprays per season	Marginal benefit		
	Ann	Sue	Zack
	(dollars per spray)		
0	5	10	15
1	4	8	12
2	3	6	9
3	2	4	6
4	1	2	3
5	0	0	0

Questions

1. What is the marginal social benefit from mosquito control at each quantity of sprays?
2. What is the efficient number of sprays per season?

Solutions

1. Mosquito control is a public good, so its marginal social benefit (*MSB*) is found by summing the marginal benefits of the three people at each quantity of sprays.

   The table below records the calculations. At 2 sprays per season, for example, marginal social benefit is $18 per spray, which is the sum of $3 (Ann), $6 (Sue), and $9 Zack). The other rows of the table show the marginal social benefit for other quantities of sprays.

   Figure 1 illustrates the calculation and constructs the *MSB* curve.

Number of sprays per season	Marginal benefit			Marginal social benefit
	Ann	Sue	Zack	
	(dollars per spray)			
0	5	10	15	30
1	4	8	12	24
2	3	6	9	18
3	2	4	6	12
4	1	2	3	6
5	0	0	0	0

Key Point: The marginal social benefit curve of a public good is the *vertical* sum of the individual marginal benefit curves.

2. To find the efficient number of sprays, we need to determine the number of sprays per season at which the *MSB* equals the *MSC* of $12 per spray.

   From the table above, *MSB* equals $12 per spray at 3 sprays per season, so that is the efficient quantity.

Key Point: The efficient quantity of a public good is that at which its marginal social benefit equals its marginal social cost.

Key Figures

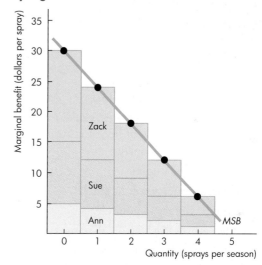

Figure 1 Marginal Social Benefit

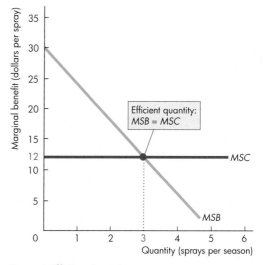

Figure 2 Efficient Quantity

MyEconLab Interactive Animation

STUDY PLAN PROBLEMS AND APPLICATIONS

MyEconLab   You can work Problems 1 to 10 in Chapter 16 Study Plan and get instant feedback.

Public Choices (Study Plan 16.1)

1. Classify each of the following items as excludable, nonexcludable, rival, or nonrival. Explain your answer.
   - A Big Mac
   - Brooklyn bridge
   - A view of the Statue of Liberty
   - A hurricane warning system

2. Classify each of the following items as a public good, a private good, a natural monopoly good, or a common resource. Explain your answer.
   - Highway patrol services
   - Internet service
   - Fish in the Atlantic ocean
   - UPS courier service

Providing Public Goods (Study Plan 16.2)

3. For each of the following goods, explain why a free-rider problem arises or how it is avoided.
   - July 4th fireworks display
   - Interstate 81 in Virginia
   - Wireless Internet access in hotels
   - The public library in your city

4. The table sets out the benefits that Terri and Sue receive from on-campus police at night:

Police officers on duty (number per night)	Marginal benefit	
	Terri	Sue
	(dollars per police officer)	
1	18	22
2	14	18
3	10	14
4	6	10
5	2	6

Suppose that Terri and Sue are the only students on campus at night. Draw a graph to show the marginal social benefit from the on-campus police at night.

Use the data on mosquito control in the table in the next column to work Problems 5 and 6.

5. What quantity of spraying would a private firm provide? What is the efficient quantity of spraying? In a single-issue election on mosquito control, what quantity would the winner provide?

Quantity (square miles sprayed per day)	Marginal social cost	Marginal social benefit
	(thousands of dollars per day)	
1	2	10
2	4	8
3	6	6
4	8	4
5	10	2

6. If the government appoints a bureaucrat to run the program, would mosquito spraying most likely be underprovided, overprovided, or provided at the efficient quantity?

The Economics of Healthcare (Study Plan 16.3)

Use the following figure, which shows the marginal benefit from health insurance and the willingness and ability to pay for it, to work Problems 7 to 10.

The marginal cost of insurance is a constant $6,000 per family per year. Marginal social benefit from insurance exceeds the willingness and ability to pay by a constant $4,000 per family per year.

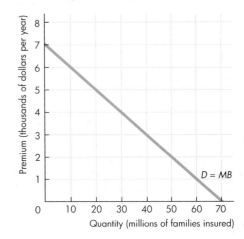

7. With no public health insurance market, how many families buy insurance, what is the premium, and is the coverage efficient?

8. If the government provides healthcare to achieve the efficient coverage, how many families are covered and how much must taxpayers pay?

9. If the government subsidizes private insurers, what subsidy will achieve the efficient coverage?

10. If the government gave coverage to everyone, what problems would arise in the related market for healthcare services?

ADDITIONAL PROBLEMS AND APPLICATIONS

MyEconLab   You can work these problems in MyEconLab if assigned by your instructor.

Public Choices

11. Classify each of the following items as excludable, nonexcludable, rival, or nonrival.
    - Homeland security
    - A Starbucks coffee
    - A view of the Liberty Bell
    - The Appalachian Trail
    - A Google search

12. Classify each of the following items as a public good, a private good, a natural monopoly good, or a common resource. Explain your answer.
    - Measles vaccinations
    - Tuna in the Pacific Ocean
    - Airline service in the United States
    - Local storm-water system

13. Classify each of the following goods as a private good, a public good, a natural monopoly good, or none of the above.
    - Chewing gum
    - Cable TV
    - The New York City subway
    - A skateboard
    - The Santa Monica beach

Providing Public Goods

14. The table sets out the marginal benefits that Sam and Nick receive from the town's street lighting:

Number of street lights	Marginal benefit	
	Sam	Nick
	(dollars per street light)	
1	10	12
2	8	9
3	6	6
4	4	3
5	2	0

   a. Is the town's street lighting a private good or a public good?
   b. Suppose that Sam and Nick are the only residents of the town. Draw a graph to show the marginal social benefit from the town's street lighting.

15. What is the principle of diminishing marginal benefit? In Problem 14, does Sam's, Nick's, or the society's marginal benefit diminish faster?

Use the following news clip to work Problems 16 and 17.

A Bridge Too Far Gone

The gas taxes paid for much of America's post-war freeway system. Now motorists pay about one-third in gas taxes to drive a mile as they did in the 1960s. Yet raising such taxes is politically tricky. This would matter less if private cash was flooding into infrastructure, or if new ways were being found to control demand. Neither is happening, and private companies building toll roads brings howls of outrage.

Source: *The Economist*, August 9, 2007

16. Why is it "politically tricky" to raise gas taxes to finance infrastructure?

17. What in the news clip points to the distinction between public *production* of a public good and public *provision*? Give examples of three public goods that are *produced* by private firms but *provided* by government and paid for with taxes.

18. **Vaccination Dodgers**

   Doctors struggle to eradicate polio worldwide, but one of the biggest problems is persuading parents to vaccinate their children. Since the discovery of the vaccine, polio has been eliminated from Europe and the law requires everyone to be vaccinated. People who refuse to be vaccinated are "free riders."

Source: *USA Today*, March 12, 2008

   a. Explain why someone in a rich country who has not opted out on medical or religious grounds and refuses to be vaccinated is a "free rider."
   b. Polio in poor countries such as Myanmar has reappeared in 2010 and is increasing. Are people who are too poor to afford the vaccination "free riders"? Should vaccinations be compulsory? Explain your answer.

The Economics of Healthcare

19. **Obamacare Hits Enrollment Goal**

   A last-minute enrollment surge enabled the White House to meet its 7 million sign-up target for the Affordable Care Act. President Barack Obama said on Tuesday that 7.1 million people had signed up on federal or state exchanges for coverage under the healthcare law.

Source: *CNN*, April 1, 2014

a. If the White House target was to enroll the efficient quantity of families in Obamacare, how would it have determined that target?

b. Draw a graph to illustrate the health-insurance market and illustrate how the Obamacare subsidy influences the number of families covered.

c. How would the demand for health insurance change if the penalty for not signing up for Obamacare were abolished? Draw a graph to illustrate the outcome

Use the following information and figure to work Problems 20 to 22.

The marginal cost of health insurance is a constant $8,000 a year and the figure shows the marginal benefit and willingness and ability to pay curve. Suppose that the marginal social benefit of insurance exceeds the willingness and ability to pay by a constant $2,000 per family per year.

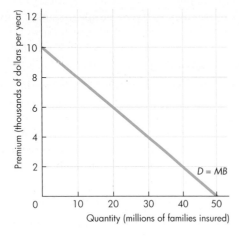

20. If all health insurance is private and the market for insurance is competitive, how many families are covered, what is the premium, and what is the deadweight loss created?

21. If the government decides to provide public health insurance (like Canada), what healthcare fee does it charge to achieve an efficient coverage? How much will taxpayers have to pay?

22. If the government decides to subsidize health insurance (like Obamacare), what subsidy will achieve the efficient coverage?

Economics in the News

23. After you have studied *Economics in the News* on pp. 384–385, answer the following questions.

a. What is the source of revenue for constructing and maintaining the transportation infrastructure?

b. Why has that revenue source not grown fast enough to deliver an efficient scale of infrastructure provision?

c. What other revenue sources can you suggest that could provide a solution to underprovision?

d. How would you expect population growth to influence the marginal social benefit of highways and bridges?

e. Illustrate your answer to (d) by drawing a version of the figure on p. 385 that shows the effect of an increase in the population.

24. **Who's Hiding Under Our Umbrella?**

Students of the Cold War learn that, to deter possible Soviet aggression, the United States placed a "strategic umbrella" over NATO Europe and Japan, with the United States providing most of their national security. Under President Ronald Reagan, the United States spent 6 percent of total income on defense, whereas the Europeans spent only 2 to 3 percent and the Japanese spent only 1 percent, although all faced a common enemy. Thus the U.S. taxpayer paid a disproportionate share of the overall defense spending, whereas NATO Europe and Japan spent more on consumer goods or saved.

Source: *International Herald Tribune*, January 30, 2008

a. Explain the free-rider problem described in this news clip.

b. Does the free-rider problem in international defense mean that the world has too little defense against aggression?

c. How do nations try to overcome the free-rider problem among nations?

17

EXTERNALITIES

After studying this chapter, you will be able to:

◆ Explain how externalities arise

◆ Explain why external costs bring market failure and overproduction and how property rights and public choices might achieve an efficient outcome

◆ Explain the tragedy of the commons and its possible solutions

◆ Explain why external benefits bring market failure and underproduction and public choices might achieve an efficient outcome

How can we use less coal to generate electricity and reduce carbon emissions that bring climate change? What can we do to conserve the ocean's fish stocks and save them from extinction? How can we ensure that we spend enough on our schools and colleges?

These are the questions we study in this chapter. They arise because some of our choices impose costs on or bring benefits to others that we don't think about when we make those choices.

In *Economics in the News* at the end of the chapter, we look at the Obama administration's ideas on how to counter carbon emissions and climate change.

◆ Externalities In Our Lives

An **externality** is a cost of or a benefit from an action that falls on someone other than the person or firm choosing the action. We call an externality that imposes a cost a **negative externality**; and we call an externality that provides a benefit a **positive externality**.

We identify externalities as four types:

- Negative production externalities
- Positive production externalities
- Negative consumption externalities
- Positive consumption externalities

Negative Production Externalities

Burning coal to generate electricity emits carbon dioxide that is warming the planet. Logging and the clearing of forests is destroying the habitat of wildlife and also adding carbon dioxide to the atmosphere. These activities are negative production externalities, the costs of which are borne by everyone, and even by future generations.

Noise is another negative production externality. When the U.S. Open tennis tournament is being played at Flushing Meadows, players, spectators, and television viewers around the world share a cost that New Yorkers experience every day: the noise of airplanes taking off from LaGuardia Airport. Aircraft noise imposes a cost on millions of people who live under the flight paths to airports in every major city.

Positive Production Externalities

To produce orange blossom honey, Honey Run Honey of Chico, California, locates beehives next to an orange orchard. The honeybees collect pollen and nectar from the orange blossoms to make the honey. At the same time, they transfer pollen between the blossoms, which helps to fertilize the blossoms. Two positive production externalities are present in this example. Honey Run Honey gets a positive production externality from the owner of the orange orchard; and the orange grower gets a positive production externality from Honey Run.

Negative Consumption Externalities

Negative consumption externalities are a source of irritation for most of us. Smoking tobacco in a confined space creates fumes that many people find unpleasant and that pose a health risk. So smoking in restaurants and on airplanes generates a negative externality. To avoid this negative externality, many restaurants and all airlines ban smoking. But while a smoking ban avoids a negative consumption externality for most people, it imposes a negative external cost on smokers who would prefer to enjoy the consumption of tobacco while dining or taking a plane trip.

Noisy parties and outdoor rock concerts are other examples of negative consumption externalities. They are also examples of the fact that a simple ban on an activity is not a solution. Banning noisy parties avoids the external cost on sleep-seeking neighbors, but it results in the sleepers imposing an external cost on the fun-seeking partygoers.

Permitting dandelions to grow in lawns, not picking up leaves in the fall, allowing a dog to bark loudly or to foul a neighbor's lawn, and letting a cellphone ring in class are other examples of negative consumption externalities.

Positive Consumption Externalities

When you get a flu vaccination, you lower your risk of being infected. If you avoid the flu, your neighbor, who didn't get vaccinated, has a better chance of remaining healthy. Flu vaccinations generate positive consumption externalities.

When the owner of a historic building restores it, everyone who sees the building gets pleasure from it. Similarly, when someone erects a spectacular home—such as those built by Frank Lloyd Wright during the 1920s and 1930s—or other exciting building—such as the Chrysler and Empire State Buildings in New York or the Walt Disney Concert Hall in Los Angeles—an external consumption benefit flows to everyone who has an opportunity to view it.

Education, which we examine in more detail in this chapter, is a major example of this type of externality.

◆ REVIEW QUIZ

1 What are the four types of externality?
2 Provide an example of each type of externality that is different from the ones described above.

Work these questions in Study Plan 17.1 and get instant feedback. Do a Key Terms Quiz.   MyEconLab

We're now going to examine the market failure that arises from an externality and the ways in which it can be avoided. We begin by looking at the negative production externality, pollution.

ECONOMICS IN ACTION

Opposing Trends: Success and Failure

The trends in local U.S. air quality and global greenhouse gas concentrations are starkly opposing. The concentrations of air pollutants in U.S. cities is decreasing, as it has done so for the past 32 years. In contrast, the concentration of greenhouse gases (mainly carbon dioxide) in the global atmosphere is increasing and posing an ever more urgent problem.

Air Pollution Trends Figure 1 shows the trends in the concentrations of the six main pollutants of the air in the United States between 1980 and 2012. The concentrations of all these pollutants decreased.

The Clean Air Act has brought regulations that almost eliminated lead and cut emissions of carbon monoxide, sulfur dioxide, and nitrogen dioxide to below 40 percent and ozone to 80 percent of their 1980 levels, and particulate matter to 64 percent of its 2000 level. And economic actions that you will learn about in this chapter have almost eliminated lead from highway vehicles and industrial processes.

These reductions in air pollution are even more impressive seen against the trends in economic activity. Between 1980 and 2012, total production in the United States increased by 145 percent, vehicle miles traveled increased by 95 percent, and the population increased by 40 percent.

Global CO_2 and Temperature Trends Figure 2 shows the global trends in carbon dioxide (CO_2) concentration and temperature.

Both trends are starkly upward. CO_2 concentration has increased by almost 40 percent since 1850, and global temperature has been rising for more than 100 years.

Scientists agree that the scale on which we burn fossil fuels is the major source of the rising CO_2 trend. There is more uncertainty about the effect of the increase in CO_2 on global temperature, but the consensus is that the effect is significant.

Stopping the rising CO_2 trend requires joint action by the governments of every nation. But a binding agreement among nations to reduce greenhouse gas emissions, the *Kyoto Protocol*, excluded the major developing countries and the United States refused to ratify it. You will see in this chapter why global warming is a much harder problem to solve than reducing air pollution in the United States.

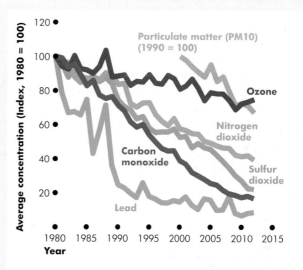

Figure 1 U.S. Air Pollution Trends
Source of data: United States Environmental Protection Agency.

Los Angeles still has a smoggy dawn on some days

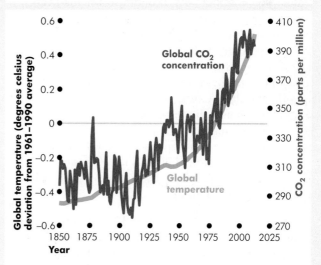

Figure 2 Global Warming Trends
Sources of data: Temperature: Met Office Hadley Centre (combined land and oceans); CO_2: Scripps Institution of Oceanography, Mauna Loa Observatory, Hawaii, data since 1960 and ice-core estimates before 1960.

◆ Negative Externality: Pollution

To see the effects and possible remedies for a negative production externality, we'll look at the example of production activities that pollute. We begin by distinguishing among three costs: private, external, and social.

Private, External, and Social Cost

A *private cost* of production is a cost that is borne by the producer of a good or service. *Marginal cost* is the cost of producing an *additional unit* of a good or service. So **marginal private cost** (*MC*) is the cost of producing an additional unit of a good or service that is borne by its producer.

An *external cost* is a cost of producing a good or service that is *not* borne by the producer but borne by other people. A **marginal external cost** is the cost of producing an additional unit of a good or service that falls on people other than the producer.

Marginal social cost (*MSC*) is the marginal cost incurred by the producer and by everyone else on whom the cost falls—by society. It is the sum of marginal private cost and marginal external cost. That is,

$$MSC = MC + \text{Marginal external cost.}$$

We express costs in dollars, but we must always remember that a cost is an opportunity cost—something real, such as clean air or a clean river, is given up to get something.

Valuing an External Cost Economists use market prices to put a dollar value on the external cost of pollution. For example, suppose that there are two similar rivers, one polluted and the other clean. Ten identical homes are built along the side of each river. The homes on the clean river rent for $2,000 per month, and those on the polluted river rent for $1,500 per month. If the pollution is the only detectable difference between the two rivers and the two locations, the rent difference of $500 per month is the pollution cost per home. With 10 homes on the side of a polluted river, the external cost of pollution is $5,000 per month.

External Cost and Output Figure 17.1 shows an example of the relationship between output and cost in a paint industry that pollutes rivers. The marginal cost curve, *MC*, describes the marginal private cost borne by the paint producers, which increases as the quantity of paint produced increases.

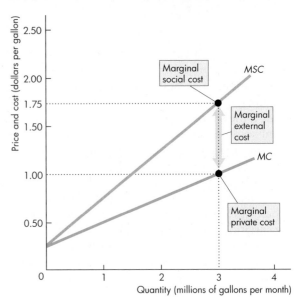

FIGURE 17.1   An External Cost

The *MC* curve shows the marginal private cost borne by the factories that produce paint. The *MSC* curve shows the sum of marginal private cost and marginal external cost. When output is 3 million gallons of paint per month, marginal private cost is $1.00 per gallon, marginal external cost is 75¢ per gallon, and marginal social cost is $1.75 per gallon.

— MyEconLab Animation —

If a firm pollutes a river, it imposes an external cost borne by other users of the river. Pollution and its marginal external cost increase with the amount of paint produced.

The marginal social cost curve, *MSC*, is found by adding marginal external cost to marginal private cost. So a point on the *MSC* curve shows the sum of the marginal private cost and marginal external cost at a given level of output.

For example, if 3 million gallons of paint per month are produced, marginal private cost is $1.00 per gallon, marginal external cost is 75¢ per gallon, and marginal social cost is $1.75 per gallon.

Let's now see how much paint gets produced and how much pollution gets created.

Equilibrium and Amount of Pollution Equilibrium in the market for paint determines the amount of pollution. Figure 17.2 has the same *MC* and *MSC* curves as Fig. 17.1 and also has a market demand and marginal social benefit curve, *D = MSB*. Equilibrium occurs at a price of $1.00 per gallon and 3 million

FIGURE 17.2   Inefficiency with an External Cost

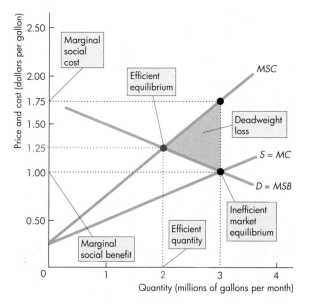

The factories' marginal private cost curve is the market supply curve, $S = MC$. The market demand curve is the marginal social benefit curve, $D = MSB$. The market equilibrium occurs at a price of $1.00 per gallon and 3 million gallons per month. This outcome is inefficient because marginal social cost exceeds marginal social benefit. The efficient quantity of paint is 2 million gallons per month. The gray triangle shows the deadweight loss created by the pollution.

—————— MyEconLab Animation and Draw Graph ——————

gallons per month. This equilibrium is one with *inefficient overproduction* (Chapter 5, p. 114) because marginal social cost at $1.75 per gallon exceeds marginal social benefit at $1.00 per gallon.

The efficient equilibrium occurs where marginal social benefit *equals* marginal social cost at 2 million gallons of paint per month. Too much paint is produced, too much pollution is created, and the area of the deadweight loss triangle measures the society's loss.

The deadweight loss arises because the paint factories only take their private cost into account when making their production decision. If some method can be found to get paint factories to create less pollution and eliminate the deadweight loss, everyone—the owners of paint factories and the residents of the riverside homes—can gain. So, what can be done to fix the inefficiency that arises from an external

cost? Three approaches are available and we will examine each of them. They are

- Establish property rights
- Mandate clean technology
- Tax or price pollution

Establish Property Rights

Property rights are legally established titles to the ownership, use, and disposal of factors of production and goods and services that are enforceable in the courts. Property rights are a foundation stone of the market economy. But they don't apply to all property. Establishing property rights can confront producers with the costs of their actions and provide the incentives that allocate resources efficiently.

To see how property rights work, suppose that the paint producers have property rights on a river and the homes alongside it—they *own* the river and the homes. The rental income that the paint producers are able to make on the homes depends on the amount of pollution they create. Using the earlier example, people are willing to pay a rent of $2,000 a month to live alongside a pollution-free river but only $1,500 a month to live with the pollution created by producing 3 million gallons of paint per month.

The forgone rental income from homes alongside a polluted river is an opportunity cost of producing paint. The paint producers must now decide how to respond to this cost. There are two possible responses:

- Use an abatement technology
- Produce less and pollute less

Use an Abatement Technology An **abatement technology** is a production technology that reduces or prevents pollution. The catalytic converter in every U.S. car is an example of an abatement technology. Its widespread adoption (with lead-free gasoline) has dramatically reduced pollution from highway vehicles and helped to achieve the trends in U.S. air quality shown on p. 393.

Abatement technologies exist to eliminate or reduce pollution from electricity generation and many industrial processes, including the manufacture of paint.

Produce Less and Pollute Less An alternative to incurring the cost of using an abatement technology is to use the polluting technology but cut production, reduce pollution, and get a higher income from renting homes by the river. The decision turns on cost: Firms will choose the least-cost alternative.

Efficient Market Equilibrium Figure 17.3 illustrates the efficient market outcome. With property rights in place, the paint producers face the pollution costs or the abatement costs, whichever is lower. The *MSC* curve includes the cost of producing paint plus *either* the cost of abatement *or* the cost of pollution (forgone rent), whichever is lower. This curve, labeled $S = MC = MSC$, is now the market supply curve.

Market equilibrium occurs at a price of $1.25 per gallon and 2 million gallons of paint per month. This outcome is efficient.

If the forgone rent is less than the abatement cost, the factories will still create some pollution, but it will be the efficient quantity. If the abatement cost is lower than the forgone rent, the factories will stop polluting. But they will produce the efficient quantity because marginal cost includes the abatement cost.

The Coase Theorem Does it matter whether the polluter or the victim of the pollution owns the resource that might be polluted? Until 1960, everyone thought that it did matter. But in 1960, Ronald Coase (see p. 417) had a remarkable insight that we now call the Coase theorem.

The **Coase theorem** is the proposition that if property rights exist and the transactions costs of enforcing them are low, then private transactions are efficient and it doesn't matter who has the property rights.

Application of the Coase Theorem Suppose that instead of the paint factories owning the homes, the residents own their homes and the river. Now the factories must pay a fee to the homeowners for the right to dump their waste. The greater the quantity of waste dumped into the river, the more the factories must pay. So again, the factories face the opportunity cost of the pollution they create. The quantity of paint produced and the amount of waste dumped are the same whoever owns the homes and the river. If the factories own them, they bear the cost of pollution because they receive a lower income from home rents. If the residents own the homes and the river, the factories bear the cost of pollution because they must pay a fee to the homeowners. In both cases, the factories bear the cost of their pollution and dump the efficient amount of waste into the river.

The Coase solution works only when transactions costs are low. **Transactions costs** are the opportunity costs of conducting a transaction. For example, when you buy a house, you pay an agent to help you find the best place and a lawyer to run checks that assure you that the seller owns the property and that after you've paid for it, the ownership has been properly transferred to you. These costs are transactions costs.

In the example of the homes alongside a river, the transactions costs that are incurred by a small number of paint factories and a few homeowners might be low enough to enable them to negotiate the deals that produce an efficient outcome. But in many situations, transactions costs are so high that it would be inefficient to incur them. In these situations, the Coase solution is not available.

Mandate Clean Technology

When property rights are too difficult to define and enforce, public choices are made. Regulation is a government's most likely response.

FIGURE 17.3   Property Rights Achieve an Efficient Outcome

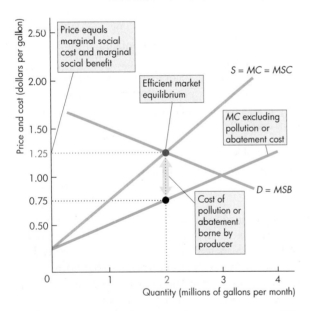

With property rights, the marginal cost curve that excludes pollution and abatement costs shows only part of the producers' marginal cost. The marginal cost of producing paint now includes the cost of pollution—the external cost—or the cost of abatement. So the market supply curve is $S = MC = MSC$. Market equilibrium occurs at a price of $1.25 per gallon and 2 million gallons of paint per month. Marginal social cost equals marginal social benefit, so the outcome is efficient.

MyEconLab Animation

Most countries regulate what may be dumped in rivers and lakes and emitted into the atmosphere. The environmental resources of the United States are heavily regulated.

An example of environmental regulation is the Clean Air Act of 1970 and its later amendments, which give the Environmental Protection Agency (EPA) the authority to issue regulations that limit emissions and achieve defined air quality standards.

The EPA has issued thousands of regulations that require chemical plants, utilities, and steel mills to adopt best-practice pollution abatement technologies and limit their emissions of specified air pollutants. Other regulations have been issued that govern road vehicle emission limits, which must be met by the vehicle manufacturers.

In 2007, the Supreme Court ruled that the EPA has authority to regulate greenhouse gas emissions.

Although direct regulation can and has reduced emissions and improved air quality, economists are generally skeptical about this approach. Abatement is not always the least-cost solution. Also, government agencies are not well placed to find the cost-minimizing solution to a pollution problem. Individual firms seeking to minimize cost and maximize profit and responding to price signals are more likely to achieve an efficient outcome. We'll now examine these other approaches to pollution.

Tax or Cap and Price Pollution

Governments use two main methods of confronting polluters with the costs of their decisions:

- Taxes
- Cap-and-trade

Taxes Governments can use taxes as an incentive for producers to cut back the pollution they create. Taxes used in this way are called **Pigovian taxes**, in honor of Arthur Cecil Pigou, the British economist who first worked out this method of dealing with external costs during the 1920s.

By setting the tax equal to the marginal external cost (or marginal abatement cost if it is lower), firms can be made to behave in the same way as they would if they bore the cost of the externality directly.

To see how government actions can change the outcome in a market with external costs, let's return to the example of paint factories and the river. Assume that the government has assessed the marginal external cost of pollution accurately and

imposes a tax on the factories that exactly equals this cost. The producers are now confronted with the social cost of their actions. The market equilibrium is one in which price equals marginal social cost—an efficient outcome.

Figure 17.4 illustrates the effects of a Pigovian tax on paint factory pollution. The curve $D = MSB$ is the market demand and the marginal social benefit curve. The curve MC is the marginal cost curve. The tax equals the marginal external cost of the pollution. We add this tax to the marginal private cost to find the market supply curve, the curve labeled $S = MC + tax = MSC$. This curve is the market supply curve because it tells us the quantity supplied at each price, given the factories' marginal cost and the tax they must pay. This curve is also the marginal social cost curve because the pollution tax has been set equal to the marginal external cost.

FIGURE 17.4 A Pollution Tax to Achieve an Efficient Outcome

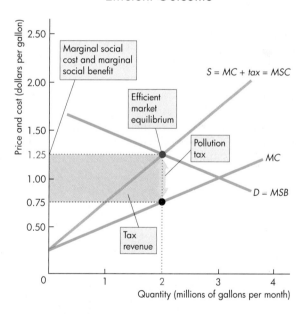

When the government imposes a pollution tax equal to the marginal external cost of pollution, the market supply curve becomes the marginal private cost curve, MC, plus the tax—the curve $S = MC + tax$. Market equilibrium occurs at a price of $1.25 per gallon and a quantity of 2 million gallons of paint per month. This equilibrium is efficient because marginal social cost equals marginal social benefit. The purple rectangle shows the government's tax revenue.

—— MyEconLab Animation and Draw Graph ——

ECONOMICS IN ACTION
Taxing Carbon Emissions

British Columbia, Ireland, and the United Kingdom are making their carbon footprints smaller.

British Columbia's Carbon Tax Introduced in 2008 at $10 per metric ton of carbon emitted, British Columbia's tax increased each year to its final rate of $30 per metric ton in 2012. The tax applies to all forms of carbon emission from coal, oil, and natural gas. The tax is revenue-neutral, which means that other taxes, personal and corporate income taxes, are cut by the amount raised by the carbon tax. Between 2008 and 2012, carbon emissions fell by 17 percent.

Ireland's Carbon Tax Since 2010, Ireland has taxed kerosene, gas oil, liquid petroleum gas, fuel oil, natural gas, and solid fuels. The tax rate in 2013 was 10 euros ($13) per metric ton of CO_2 emitted and 20 euros ($26) per ton in 2014. Emissions have fallen since the tax was introduced, but recession as well as the carbon tax brought this fall.

U.K. Tax on Gasoline The United Kingdom doesn't call its gasoline tax a carbon tax, but it has the same effect on drivers. The figure shows the U.K. price of gasoline compared with that in three other countries. The enormous differences arise almost entirely from tax differences. An effect of these price differences is that cars in the United Kingdom get an average of 38 miles per gallon while in the United States, the average is 23 miles per gallon. A high gas tax cuts carbon emissions by inducing people to drive smaller cars and to drive less.

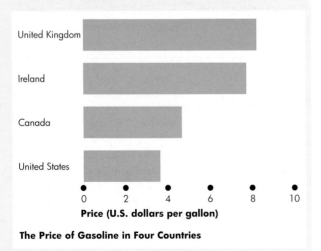

The Price of Gasoline in Four Countries

Demand and supply now determine the market equilibrium price at $1.25 per gallon and a quantity of 2 million gallons of paint a month. At this quantity of paint production, the marginal social cost is $1.25 and the marginal social benefit is $1.25, so the market outcome is efficient. The factories incur a marginal private cost of 75¢ per gallon and pay a pollution tax of 50¢ per gallon. The government collects tax revenue of $1 million per month.

Cap-and-Trade A cap is an upper limit. You met the idea of a government imposing an upper limit when you learned about production quotas (Chapter 6, p. 139) and import quotas (Chapter 7, p. 160). A cap is a quota—a pollution quota.

A government that uses this method must first estimate the efficient quantity of pollution and set the overall cap at that level.

Just like a production or import quota, a pollution quota or cap must somehow be allocated to individual firms (and possibly even households). In an efficient allocation of pollution quotas, each firm has the same marginal social cost. So to make an efficient allocation of the cap across firms, the government would need to know each firm's marginal production cost and marginal abatement cost.

A Pigovian tax achieves an efficient allocation of pollution across firms because each firm chooses how much to produce and pollute taking the tax into account, and produces the quantity at which marginal social cost equals price. Because all firms face the same market price, they also incur the same marginal social cost.

The government solves the allocation problem by making an initial distribution of the cap across firms and allowing them to trade in a market for pollution permits. Firms that have a low marginal abatement cost sell permits and make big cuts in pollution. Firms that have a high marginal abatement cost buy permits and make smaller cuts or perhaps even no cuts in pollution.

The market in permits determines the equilibrium price of pollution and each firm, confronted with that price, maximizes profit by setting its marginal pollution cost or marginal abatement cost, whichever is lower, equal to the market price of a permit.

By confronting polluters with a price of pollution, trade in pollution permits can achieve the same efficient outcome as a Pigovian tax.

◆ AT **ISSUE**

Should We be Doing More to Reduce Carbon Emissions?

Economists agree that tackling the global-warming problem requires changes in the incentives that people face. The cost of carbon-emitting activities must rise and the cost of clean-energy technologies must fall.

Disagreement centers on *how* to change incentives. Should more countries set targets for cutting carbon emissions at a faster rate? Should they introduce a carbon tax, emissions charges, or cap-and-trade to cut emissions? Should clean energy research and development be subsidized?

Yes: *The Stern Review*

- Confronting emitters with a tax or price on carbon imposes low present costs for high future benefits.
- The cost of reducing greenhouse gas emissions to safe levels can be kept to 1 percent of global income each year.
- The future benefits are incomes at least 5 percent and possibly 20 percent higher than they will be with inaction every year forever.
- Climate change is a global problem that requires an international coordinated response.
- Unlike most taxes, which bring deadweight loss, a carbon tax eliminates (or reduces) deadweight loss.
- Strong, deliberate policy action is required to change the incentives that emitters face.
- Policy actions should include:
  1. Emissions limits and emissions trading
  2. Increased subsidies for energy research and development, including the development of low-cost clean technology for generating electricity
  3. Reduced deforestation and research into new drought and flood-resilient crop varieties

No: **The Copenhagen Consensus**

- Confronting emitters with a tax or price on carbon imposes high present costs and low future benefits.
- Unless the entire world signs on to an emissions reduction program, free riders will increase their emissions and carbon leakage will occur.
- A global emissions reduction program and carbon tax would lower living standards in the rich countries and slow the growth rate of living standards in developing countries.
- Technology is already advancing and the cost of cleaner energy is falling.
- Fracking technology has vastly expanded the natural gas deposits that can be profitably exploited and replacing coal with gas halves the carbon emissions from electricity generation.
- Free-market price signals will allocate resources to the development of new technologies that stop and eventually reverse the upward trend in greenhouse gasses.

Economist Nicholas Stern, principal author of *The Stern Review on the Economics of Climate Change.* Greenhouse gas emission is "the greatest market failure the world has ever seen."

To avoid the risk of catastrophic climate change, the upward CO_2 trend must be stopped.

Bjørn Lomborg, President of the Copenhagen Consensus and author of *The Skeptical Environmentalist.* "For little environmental benefit, we could end up sacrificing growth, jobs, and opportunities for the big majority, especially in the developing world."

ECONOMICS IN ACTION
A Global Prisoners' Dilemma

China, the United States, and the European Union create 52 percent of global carbon emissions. Another six large countries create a further 21 percent (see Fig. 1).

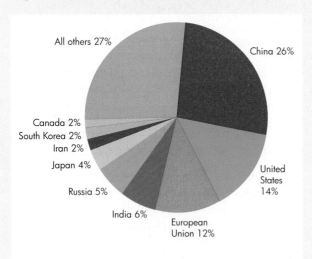

Figure 1 The Global Distribution of CO_2 Emissions

Cutting global carbon emissions is a *prisoners' dilemma* (see pp. 344–345). The payoff matrix illustrates the dilemma. The strategies for the United States and other countries are to keep increasing carbon emissions or to cut them.

Cutting emissions requires using production technologies with higher private costs. But higher private costs make the nation's exporters less competitive in world markets. By letting others cut their emissions and continuing to use low-cost carbon emitting technologies, a nation can gain a competitive advantage.

In the payoff matrix below, China is better off increasing emissions regardless of what others do; and the others are better off increasing their emissions regardless of what China does. The *Nash equilibrium* (see p. 345) is for all countries to keep increasing their emissions. But the world is better off if all cut.

The challenge is to find a cooperative outcome that avoids this prisoners' dilemma.

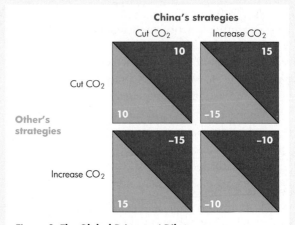

Figure 2 The Global Prisoners' Dilemma

Coping with Global Externalities

The United States has cut the emissions of local air pollutants and made its own air cleaner by adopting the measures you've just seen. But one country, even a big country such as the United States that accounts for 20 percent of the value of global production and 14 percent of carbon emissions, can't solve the problem of global warming and climate change alone. Coping with this problem requires public choices at a *global* level, choices by all governments, which are much harder to make and coordinate.

A lower CO_2 concentration in the world's atmosphere is a global *public good*. And like all public goods, it brings a *free-rider problem* (see Chapter 16, p. 374). Without a mechanism to ensure participation in a global carbon reduction program, countries are in a *prisoners' dilemma* (see *Economics in Action* above).

◆ REVIEW QUIZ

1 What is the distinction between private cost and social cost?
2 How do external costs prevent a competitive market from allocating resources efficiently?
3 How can external costs be eliminated by assigning property rights?
4 How do taxes, pollution charges, and cap-and-trade work to reduce emissions?

Work these questions in Study Plan 17.2 and get instant feedback. Do a Key Terms Quiz.   MyEconLab

Your next task is to study another negative production externality, the tragedy of the commons, and the arrangements that can achieve the efficient use of common resources.

◆ Negative Externality: The Tragedy of the Commons

Overgrazing the pastures around a village in Middle Ages England, and overfishing the Southern Bluefin tuna, Pacific Yellowfin tuna, Atlantic cod, and Minke whales during the recent past are tragedies of the commons. Other current tragedies are the destruction of tropical rainforests in Africa and the Amazon basin of South America.

The **tragedy of the commons** is the overuse of a common resource that arises when its users have no incentive to conserve it and use it sustainably and efficiently.

To study the tragedy of the commons and its possible remedies, we'll focus on one of the recent and current tragedies – overfishing and depleting the stock of tuna. You're about to discover that there are two problems that give rise to the tragedy of the commons:

- Unsustainable use of a common resource
- Inefficient use of a common resource

Unsustainable Use of a Common Resource

Many common resources are renewable—they replenish themselves by the birth and growth of new members of the population. Fish, trees, and the fertile soil are all examples of this type of resource. At any given time, there is a stock of the resource and a rate at which it is being used.

A common resource is being used *unsustainably* if its rate of use persistently decreases its stock. A common resource is being used *sustainably* if its rate of use is less than or equal to its rate of renewal so that the stock available either grows or remains constant.

Focusing on the example of fish, a species is being used unsustainably if the catch persistently decreases the stock and it is being used sustainably if the catch is less than or equal to the rate of renewal of the fish population.

The sustainable catch depends on the stock of fish and in the way illustrated by the sustainable catch curve, *SCC*, in Fig. 17.5.

Along the *SCC* curve, with a small stock of fish the quantity of new fish born is also small, so the sustainable catch is small.

With a large stock of fish many fish are born but they must compete with each other for food, so only a few survive to reproduce and to grow large enough to catch, and again the sustainable catch is small.

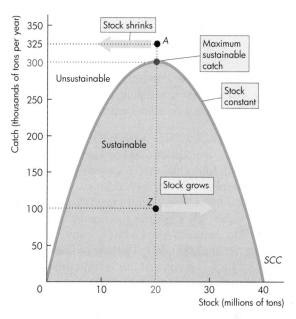

FIGURE 17.5   Sustainable Catch

As the fish stock increases (on the x-axis), the sustainable catch (on the y-axis) increases to a maximum. As the stock increases further, the fish must compete for food and the sustainable catch falls. If the catch exceeds the sustainable catch, such as at point A, the fish stock diminishes. If the catch is less than the sustainable catch, such as at point Z, the fish stock increases.

MyEconLab Animation

Between a small and a large stock is a stock of fish that maximizes the sustainable catch. In Fig. 17.5, this stock is 20 million tons and the maximum sustainable catch is 300,000 tons per year.

The maximum sustainable catch arises from a balancing of the birth of new fish from the stock and the availability of food to sustain the fish population. If the quantity of fish caught is less than the sustainable catch, at a point such as Z, the fish stock grows. If the quantity caught equals the sustainable catch, at any point on the *SCC*, the fish stock remains constant and is available for future generations of fishers in the same quantity that is available today.

But if the quantity caught exceeds the sustainable catch, at a point such as *A*, the fish stock shrinks and, unchecked, eventually falls to zero.

You now understand the problem of using a common renewable natural resource sustainably. But another problem is using it efficiently.

Inefficient Use of a Common Resource

In an unregulated market, even if the catch is sustainable, it will be bigger than the efficient catch: overfishing occurs. And most likely, the catch will not be sustainable. Why does overfishing occur? The answer is that fishers face only their own private cost and don't face the cost they impose on others—the external cost. The social cost of fishing combines the private cost and the external cost. Let's examine these costs.

Marginal Private Cost The *marginal private cost* of catching fish is the cost incurred by keeping a boat and crew at sea for long enough to increase the catch by one ton. Keeping a fishing boat at sea eventually runs into *diminishing marginal returns* (see Chapter 11, p. 251). As the crew gets tired, the storage facilities get overfull, and the boat's speed is cut to conserve fuel, the catch per hour decreases. The cost of keeping the boat at sea for an additional hour is constant, so the marginal cost of catching fish increases as the quantity caught increases.

You've just seen that the *principle of increasing marginal cost* applies to catching fish just as it applies to other production activities: Marginal private cost increases as the quantity of fish caught increases.

The marginal private cost of catching fish determines an indiviual fisher's supply of fish. A profit-maximizing fisher is willing to supply the quantity at which the market price of fish covers the marginal private cost. And the market supply is the sum of the quantities supplied by each individual fisher.

Marginal External Cost The marginal external cost of catching fish is the cost per additional ton that one fisher's production imposes on all other fishers. This additional cost arises because one fisher's catch decreases the remaining stock, which in turn decreases the renewal rate of the stock and makes it harder for others to find and catch fish.

Marginal external cost also increases as the quantity of fish caught increases. If the quantity of fish caught is so large that it drives the species to near extinction, the marginal external cost becomes infinitely large.

Marginal Social Cost The *marginal social cost* of catching fish is the marginal private cost plus the marginal external cost. Because both components of marginal social cost increase as the quantity caught increases, marginal social cost also increases with the quantity of fish caught.

Marginal Social Benefit and Demand The marginal social benefit from fish is the price that consumers are willing to pay for an additional pound of fish. Marginal social benefit decreases as the quantity of fish consumed increases, so the market demand curve, which is also the marginal social benefit curve, slopes downward.

Overfishing Equilibrium Figure 17.6 illustrates overfishing and how it arises. The market demand curve for fish is the marginal social benefit curve, *MSB*. The market supply curve is the marginal *private* cost curve, *MC*. Market equilibrium occurs at the intersection point of these two curves. The equilibrium quantity is 800,000 tons of fish per year and the equilibrium price is $10 per pound. At this market equilibrium, overfishing occurs.

FIGURE 17.6   Why Overfishing Occurs

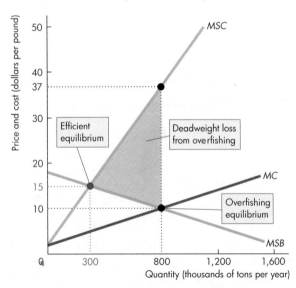

The market supply curve is the marginal private cost curve, *MC*. The market demand curve is the marginal social benefit curve, *MSB*. Market equilibrium occurs at a quantity of 800,000 tons per year and a price of $10 per pound.

The marginal social cost curve is *MSC* and at the market equilibrium there is overfishing—marginal social cost exceeds marginal social benefit.

The quantity at which *MSC* equals *MSB* is the efficient quantity, 300,000 tons per year. The area of the gray triangle measures the deadweight loss from overfishing.

Figure 17.6 illustrates why overfishing occurs. At the market equilibrium quantity, marginal social benefit (and willingness to pay) is $10 per pound, but the marginal social cost ($37 per pound) exceeds this amount. The marginal external cost is the cost of running down the fish stock.

Efficient Equilibrium What is the efficient use of a common resource? It is the use of the resource that makes the marginal social benefit from the resource equal to the marginal social cost of using it.

In Fig. 17.6, the efficient quantity of fish is 300,000 tons per year—the quantity that makes marginal social cost (on the *MSC* curve) equal to marginal social benefit (on the *MSB* curve). At this quantity, the marginal catch of each individual fisher costs society what people are willing to pay for it.

Deadweight Loss from Overfishing Deadweight loss measures the cost of overfishing. The area of the gray triangle in Fig. 17.6 illustrates this loss. It is the marginal social cost minus the marginal social benefit from all the fish caught in excess of the efficient quantity.

ECONOMICS IN ACTION

The Original Tragedy of the Commons

The term "tragedy of the commons" comes from 14th-century England, where areas of rough grassland surrounding villages were overgrazed and the quantity of cows and sheep that they could feed kept falling.

During the 16th century, the price of wool increased, sheep farming became profitable, and sheep owners wanted to control the land they used. So the commons were gradually privatized and land use became more efficient.

One of Today's Tragedies of the Commons

Before 1970, Atlantic cod was abundant, despite the fact that it had been fished for many centuries and was a major food source for the first European settlers in North America. By 1620, there were more than 1,000 fishing boats catching large quantities of cod in the northwest Atlantic off the coast of what is now New England and Newfoundland. Most of the fishing during these years was done using lines and productivity was low. But low productivity limited the catch and enabled cod to be caught sustainably over hundreds of years.

The situation changed dramatically during the 1960s with the introduction of huge nets, sonar technology to find fish concentrations, and large ships with efficient processing and storage facilities. These technological advances brought soaring cod harvests and cod landings almost tripled in a decade.

This volume of cod could not be taken without a serious collapse in the remaining stock and by the 1980s it became vital to regulate cod fishing. But regulation was of limited success and stocks continued to decline. In 1992, a total ban on cod fishing in the North Atlantic stabilized the population but at a very low level. Two decades of ban have enabled the species to repopulate, and it is now hoped that one day cod fishing will return but at a low and sustainable rate.

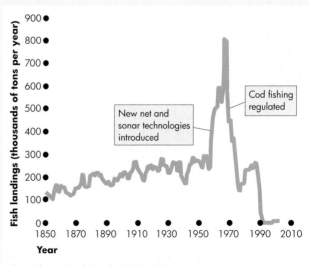

The Atlantic Cod Catch: 1850–2005

Achieving an Efficient Outcome

Defining the conditions under which a common resource is used efficiently is easier than delivering those conditions. To use a common resource efficiently, it is necessary to design an incentive mechanism that confronts the users of the resource with the marginal *social* consequences of their actions. The same principles apply to common resources as those that you met earlier in this chapter when you studied the external cost of pollution.

The three main methods that might be used to achieve the efficient use of a common resource are

- Property rights
- Production quotas
- Individual transferable quotas (ITQs)

Property Rights A common resource that no one owns and that anyone is free to use contrasts with *private property*, which is a resource that *someone* owns and has an incentive to use in the way that maximizes its value. One way of overcoming the tragedy of the commons is to convert a common resource to private property. By assigning private property rights to what was previously a common resource, its owner faces the same conditions as society faces. It doesn't matter who owns the resource. The users of the resource will be confronted with the full cost of using it because they either own it or pay a fee to the owner for permission to use it.

When private property rights over a resource are established and enforced, the *MSC* curve becomes the marginal *private* cost curve, and the use of the resource is efficient.

Figure 17.3, which illustrates an efficient outcome with property rights when confronted with pollution, also applies to the over-fishing problem. The supply curve $S = MC = MSC$ and the demand curve $D = MSB$ determine the equilibrium price and quantity. The price equals both marginal social benefit and marginal social cost and the fish catch is efficient.

The private property solution to the tragedy of the commons *is* available in some cases. It was the solution to the original tragedy of the commons in England's Middle Ages. It is also a solution that has been used to prevent overuse of the airwaves that carry cellphone services. The right to use this space (called the frequency spectrum) has been auctioned by governments to the highest bidders. The owner of each part of the spectrum is the only one permitted to use it (or to license someone else to use it).

But assigning private property rights is not always feasible. It would be difficult to assign private property rights to the oceans because the cost of enforcing them would be too high. In the absence of property rights, some form of government intervention is used. One such intervention is a production quota.

Production Quotas A *production quota* is an upper limit to the quantity of a good that may be produced in a specified period. Each individual producer is allocated a quota.

You studied the effects of a production quota in Chapter 6 (pp. 139–140) and learned that a quota can drive a wedge between marginal social benefit and marginal social cost and create deadweight loss. In that earlier example, the market was efficient without a quota. But in the case of common resources, the market overuses the resource and produces an inefficient quantity. A production quota in this market brings a move toward a more efficient outcome. But implementing a production quota has two problems.

First, it is in every fisher's self-interest to catch more fish than the quantity permitted under the quota. The reason is that price exceeds marginal private cost, so by catching more fish, a fisher gets a higher income. If enough fishers break the quota, overfishing and the tragedy of the commons remain.

Second, marginal cost is not, in general, the same for all producers—as we're assuming here. Efficiency requires that the quota be allocated to the producers with the lowest marginal cost. But bureaucrats who allocate quotas do not have information about the marginal cost of individual producers. Even if they tried to get this information, producers would have an incentive to lie about their costs so as to get a bigger quota.

So where producers are difficult, or very costly, to monitor or where marginal cost varies across producers, a production quota cannot achieve an efficient outcome.

Individual Transferable Quotas Where producers are difficult to monitor or where marginal cost varies across producers, a more sophisticated quota system can be effective. It is an **individual transferable quota (ITQ)**, which is a production limit that is assigned to an individual who is then free to transfer (sell) the quota to someone else. A market in ITQs emerges and ITQs are traded at their market price. (Cap-and-trade to limit pollution is an ITQ for pollution).

The market price of an ITQ is the highest price that someone is willing to pay for one. That price is marginal social benefit minus marginal cost. The price of an ITQ will rise to this level because fishers who don't have a quota would be willing to pay this amount to get one.

A fisher with an ITQ could sell it for the market price, so by not selling the ITQ the fisher incurs an opportunity cost. The marginal cost of fishing, which now includes the opportunity cost of the ITQ, equals the marginal social benefit from the efficient quantity.

Figure 17.7 illustrates how ITQs work. Each fisher receives an allocation of ITQs and the total catch permitted by the ITQs is 300,000 tons per year. Fishers trade ITQs: Those with low marginal cost buy ITQs from those with high marginal cost, and the market price of an ITQ settles at $10 per pound of fish. The marginal private cost of fishing now becomes the original marginal private cost, *MC*, plus the cost of the ITQ. The marginal private cost curve shifts upward from *MC* to *MC + price of ITQ* and each fisher is confronted with the marginal *social* cost of fishing. No one has an incentive to exceed the quota because to do so would send marginal cost above price and result in a loss on the marginal catch. The outcome is efficient.

FIGURE 17.7   ITQs to Use a Common
                   Resource Efficiently

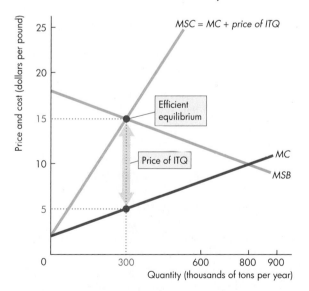

ITQs are issued on a scale that keeps output at the efficient level. The market price of an ITQ equals the marginal social benefit minus marginal cost. Because each user of the common resource faces the opportunity cost of using the resource, self-interest achieves the social interest.

MyEconLab Animation

ECONOMICS IN ACTION
ITQs Work

Iceland introduced the first ITQs in 1984 to conserve its stocks of lobster. In 1986, New Zealand and a bit later Australia introduced ITQs to conserve fish stocks in the South Pacific and Southern Oceans. And this system was introduced in Alaska to manage halibut stocks during the 1990s.

The evidence from these cases suggests that ITQs work well when they are properly enforced.

ITQs help maintain fish stocks, but they also reduce the size of the fishing industry. This consequence of ITQs puts them against the self-interest of fishers. In all countries, the fishing industry opposes restrictions on its activities, but in Iceland, Australia, New Zealand, and Alaska the opposition is not strong enough to block ITQs.

In the United States, other than Alaska, the opposition has been harder to overcome, and in 1996 Congress passed the Sustainable Fishing Act that put a moratorium on ITQs. This moratorium was lifted in 2004 and since then, ITQs have been applied to 28 fisheries from the Gulf of Alaska to the Gulf of Mexico.

Economists have studied the effects of ITQs extensively and agree that in most cases they work and offer an effective tool for achieving an efficient use of the stock of ocean fish.

But in some situations, ITQs have been unsuccessful. The main reasons for failure of an ITQ system are that the total permitted catch might be set too large; some fish species migrate and get overfished outside the regions covered by the ITQs; and sometimes the monitoring and enforcement of quotas is inadequate.

◆ REVIEW QUIZ

1 What is the tragedy of the commons? Give two examples, including one from your state.
2 Describe the conditions under which a common resource is used efficiently.
3 Review three methods that might achieve the efficient use of a common resource and explain the obstacles to efficiency.

Work these questions in Study Plan 17.3 and get instant feedback. Do a Key Terms Quiz.   MyEconLab

◆ Positive Externality: Knowledge

Knowledge comes from education and research. And both bring external benefits. To keep the explanation of the problems that arise from external benefits and the possible solutions to those problems as clear as possible, we will focus on just one aspect of the production of knowledge, the provision of college education.

We begin by distinguishing between private benefits and social benefits.

Private Benefits and Social Benefits

A *private benefit* is a benefit that the consumer of a good or service receives. For example, expanded job opportunities and a higher income are private benefits of a college education.

Marginal benefit is the benefit from an *additional unit* of a good or service. So **marginal private benefit** (*MB*) is the benefit that the consumer of a good or service receives from an additional unit of it. When one additional student attends college, the benefit that student receives is the marginal private benefit from college education.

The *external benefit* from a good or service is the benefit that someone other than the consumer of the good or service receives. College graduates generate many external benefits. On average, they are better citizens, have lower crime rates, and are more tolerant of the views of others. They enable the success of high-quality newspapers and television broadcasts, music, theater, and other organized social activities that bring benefits to many other people.

A **marginal external benefit** is the benefit from an additional unit of a good or service that people *other than its consumer* enjoy. The benefit that your friends and neighbors get from your college education is the marginal external benefit of your college education.

Marginal social benefit (*MSB*) is the marginal benefit enjoyed by society—by the consumer of a good or service (marginal private benefit) and by others (the marginal external benefit). That is,

$$MSB = MB + \text{Marginal external benefit}.$$

Figure 17.8 shows an example of the relationship between marginal private benefit, marginal external benefit, and marginal social benefit. The marginal benefit curve, *MB*, describes the marginal private benefit enjoyed by the people who receive a college education. Marginal private benefit decreases as the number of students enrolled in college increases.

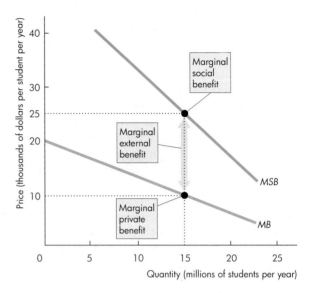

FIGURE 17.8   An External Benefit

The *MB* curve shows the marginal private benefit enjoyed by the people who receive a college education. The *MSB* curve shows the sum of marginal private benefit and marginal external benefit. When 15 million students attend college, the marginal private benefit is $10,000 per student, the marginal external benefit is $15,000 per student, and the marginal social benefit is $25,000 per student.

MyEconLab Animation

In the example in Fig. 17.8, when 15 million students enroll in college, the marginal external benefit is $15,000 per student per year. The marginal social benefit curve, *MSB*, is the sum of marginal private benefit and marginal external benefit at each number of students. For example, when 15 million students a year enroll in college, the marginal private benefit is $10,000 per student and the marginal external benefit is $15,000 per student, so the marginal social benefit is $25,000 per student.

When people make schooling decisions, they ignore its external benefits and consider only its private benefits. So if education were provided by private schools that charged full-cost tuition, there would be too few college graduates.

Figure 17.9 illustrates this private underprovision. The supply curve is the marginal social cost curve, *S = MSC*. The demand curve is the marginal *private* benefit curve, *D = MB*. Market equilibrium occurs at a tuition of $15,000 per student per year and

7.5 million students per year. At this equilibrium, the marginal social benefit of $38,000 per student exceeds the marginal social cost by $23,000 per student. Too few students are enrolled in college. The efficient number is 15 million per year, where marginal social benefit equals marginal social cost. The gray triangle shows the deadweight loss created.

To get closer to producing the efficient quantity of a good with an external benefit, we make public choices, through governments, to modify the market outcome.

Government Actions in the Market with External Benefits

To encourage more students to enroll in college—to achieve an efficient quantity of college education—students must be confronted with a lower market price and the taxpayer must somehow pay for the costs not covered by what the student pays.

FIGURE 17.9   Inefficiency with an External Benefit

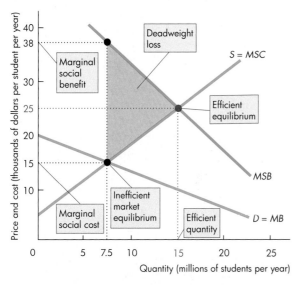

The market demand curve is the marginal private benefit curve, $D = MB$. The supply curve is the marginal social cost curve, $S = MSC$. Market equilibrium at a tuition of $15,000 a year and 7.5 million students is inefficient because marginal social benefit exceeds marginal social cost. The efficient quantity is 15 million students. A deadweight loss arises (gray triangle) because too few students enroll in college.

—— MyEconLab Animation and Draw Graph ——

Three devices that governments can use to achieve a more efficient allocation of resources in the presence of external benefits are

- Public production
- Private subsidies
- Vouchers

Public Production With **public production**, a good or service is produced by a public authority that receives its revenue from the government. The education services produced by state universities and colleges and public schools are examples of public production.

Private Subsidies A **subsidy** is a payment that the government makes to private producers. By making the subsidy depend on the level of output, the government can induce private decision makers to consider external benefits when they make their choices.

Vouchers A **voucher** is a token that the government provides to households, which they can use to buy specified goods or services. Food stamps are examples of vouchers. The vouchers (food stamps) can be spent only on food and are designed to improve the diet and health of extremely poor families.

School vouchers have been advocated as a means of improving the quality of education and are used in Washington, D.C. A school voucher allows parents to choose the school their children will attend and to use the voucher to pay part of the cost. The school cashes the vouchers to pay its bills. A voucher could be provided to a college student in a similar way, and although technically not a voucher, a federal Pell Grant has a similar effect.

Because vouchers can be spent only on a specified item, they increase the willingness to pay for that item and so increase the demand for it.

Illustrating an Efficient Outcome

Figure 17.10 illustrates an efficient outcome. With marginal social cost curve *MSC* and marginal social benefit curve *MSB*, the efficient number of college students is 15,000. The marginal *private* benefit curve *MB* tells us that 15,000 students will enroll only if the tuition is $10,000 per year. But the marginal social cost of 15,000 students is $25,000 per year. To enable the marginal social cost to be paid, taxpayers must pay the balance of $15,000 per student per year.

To achieve the efficient outcome with public production, public colleges receive funds from government equal to $15,000 per student per year, charge tuition of $10,000 per student per year, and enroll 15 million students.

To achieve the efficient outcome with private provision, private colleges receive a government subsidy of $15,000 per student per year. This subsidy reduces the colleges' costs and would make their marginal cost equal to $10,000 per student at the efficient quantity. Tuition of $10,000 covers this cost, and the subsidy of $15,000 per student covers the balance of the cost.

To achieve an efficient outcome with vouchers, government provides a voucher to each student with a value equal to the marginal external benefit at the efficient number of students. In Fig. 17.10, the efficient number of students is 15 million and the voucher is valued at $15,000 per student. Each student pays $10,000 tuition and gives the college a $15,000 voucher. The colleges receive $25,000 per student, which equals their marginal cost.

Bureaucratic Inefficiency and Government Failure

You've seen three government actions that achieve an efficient provision of a good with an external benefit. In each case, if the government estimates the marginal external benefit correctly and makes marginal social benefit equal to marginal social cost, the outcome is efficient.

Does the comparison that we've just made mean that pubic provision, subsidized private provision, and vouchers are equivalent? It does not. And the reason lies in something that you've already encountered in your study of public goods in Chapter 16—the behavior of bureaucrats combined with rational ignorance that leads to government failure.

Problems with Public Production Public colleges and schools are operated by a bureaucracy and are subject to the same problems as the provision of public goods. Bureaucrats seek to maximize their budgets, which brings inefficient overspending.

In the case of colleges and schools, overspending doesn't mean *overprovision*. Just the opposite: People complain about *underprovision*. The overspending is budget padding and waste.

Education bureaucrats incur costs that exceed the minimum efficient cost. They might hire more assistants than the number needed to do their work efficiently; give themselves sumptuous offices; get generous expense allowances; build schools in the wrong places where land costs are too high.

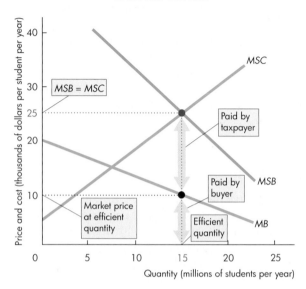

FIGURE 17.10   An Efficient Outcome with an External Benefit

The efficient number of college students is 15 million, where marginal social benefit equals marginal social cost. With the demand and marginal private benefit curve, $D = MB$, the price at which the efficient number will enroll is $10,000 per year. If students pay this price, the taxpayer must somehow pay the rest, which equals the marginal external benefit at the efficient quantity—$15,000 per student per year.

MyEconLab Animation and Draw Graph

Economists have compared the costs of private and public schools and have found that the costs per student of public schools are on the order of *three times* the costs of comparable private schools (see Talking with Carolyn Hoxby on p. 418.)

But bureaucracy can be limited and public production made more efficient. Charter schools (see *Economics in Action* on p. 409) are showing one way of cutting costs even while improving quality.

Problems with Private Subsidies Subsidizing private producers might overcome some of the problems created by public production. A private producer has an incentive to produce at minimum cost and avoid the budget padding of a bureaucratic producer. But two problems arise with private subsidies.

First, the subsidy budget must be allocated by a bureau. A national, state, or local department of education must lobby for its own budget and allocate this budget between school subsidies and its own administration costs. To the extent that the bureau-crats succeed in maximizing their own adminstration budget, they siphon off resources from schools and a problem similar to that of public production arises.

Second, it is in the self-interest of subsidized pro-ducers to maximize their subsidy. These producers might even spend some of the subsidy they receive lobbying for an even bigger one.

So subsidized private provision is unlikely to achieve an efficient allocation of resources. What about the third method: vouchers?

Are Vouchers the Solution? Vouchers have four advantages over the other two approaches:

1. Vouchers can be used with public production, private provision, or competition between the two.
2. Governments can set the value of vouchers and the total voucher budget to overcome bureau-cratic overprovision and budget padding.
3. Vouchers spread the public contribution thinly across millions of consumers, so no one con-sumer has an interest in wasting part of the value received in lobbying for overprovision.
4. By giving the buying power to the final con-sumer, producers must compete for business and provide a high standard of service at the lowest attainable cost.

For these four reasons, vouchers are popular with economists. But they are controversial and opposed by most education administrators and teachers.

In *The Economics of School Choice,* a book edited by Caroline M. Hoxby, economists study the effect of school choice on student achievement and school productivity and show how vouchers can be designed to achieve their goals while avoiding their potential pitfalls. Caroline Hoxby is confident that she can design a voucher that best achieves any educational and school performance objective.

◆ *Economics in the News* on pp. 410–411 looks at the economics of President Obama's proposals for lowering carbon emissions.

The next two chapters examine the third big ques-tion of economics: For whom are goods and services produced? We examine the markets for factors of production and discover how factor incomes and the distribution of income are determined.

ECONOMICS IN ACTION
Education Quality and Cost: Charter Schools

A *charter school* is a public school, so it is funded like a regular public school but is free to make its own educa-tion policy. Around 4,000 charter schools in 40 states, teaching more than 1 million students, are in opera-tion today. When the demand for places in a charter school exceeds the supply, students are chosen by lot-tery. This method of selection provides rich data for testing the performance of charter schools.

Are charter schools succeeding? Success has two dimensions: educational standards attained and cost per student. Charter schools perform well on both di-mensions. They achieve higher standards and cost less. Charter school students achieve better test scores in math and reading than equivalent students who apply to but randomly don't get into a charter school.

Charter schools also achieve this higher standard at lower cost. For example, in Detroit, cost per student in charter schools is 25 percent less than in regular public schools in equivalent areas.

Children in an inner-city Detroit charter school

◆ REVIEW QUIZ

1 Why would the market economy produce too little education?
2 How might governments achieve an efficient provision of education?
3 What are the key differences among public pro-duction, private subsidies, and vouchers?
4 Why do economists generally favor vouchers to achieve an efficient outcome?

Work these questions in Study Plan 17.4 and get instant feedback. Do a Key Terms Quiz.   MyEconLab

A Carbon Reduction Plan

Obama Proposes Biggest Ever U.S. Push for Carbon Cuts

The Financial Times
June 2, 2014

The Obama administration has launched the most ambitious plan to combat climate change in U.S. history by proposing to … cut carbon dioxide emissions from power stations by 30 percent by 2030 from 2005 levels. …

The Environmental Protection Agency, the regulator that drew up the plan, said it would create tens of thousands of jobs and lead to lower household electricity bills because of improvements in energy efficiency.

But business groups, with representatives of the coal industry in the forefront, warned that the plans would raise bills, cause job losses, and increase the risk of blackouts. …

Under the plan, each U.S. state is given a different target for cutting carbon emissions from its power sector. They will decide how to achieve the cuts by switching to cleaner energy sources such as natural gas, nuclear, or wind power, by improving grid efficiency or by reducing electricity consumption. …

When burnt for power generation, coal creates roughly twice as much CO_2 as gas, and coal miners and power plants would be hurt the most by the administration's plan.

The EPA said its proposals could cut demand for coal by up to 27 percent and prices by up to 17 percent.

Despite Republican accusations that Mr. Obama is waging a "war on coal," the administration said it still expected 30 percent of U.S. electricity to come from coal by 2030.

The proposals would benefit other sources of generation, including gas, renewables, and nuclear power. …

MyEconLab More Economics in the News

ESSENCE OF THE STORY

- The Environmental Protection Agency (EPA) has a plan that cuts carbon dioxide emissions from power stations to 30 percent below their 2005 levels by 2030.

- Using coal to generate electricity creates twice as much CO_2 as using gas, and states will hit targets by switching from coal to natural gas, nuclear, and wind power, or by cutting electricity consumption.

- The EPA says the plan creates jobs and cuts electricity bills because of improvements in energy efficiency.

- Business groups say the plan raises electricity bills, destroys jobs, and increases the risk of blackouts.

- The EPA says its plan cuts coal use by up to 27 percent and lowers the price of coal by up to 17 percent

ECONOMIC ANALYSIS

- Because coal used to generate electricity creates twice as much CO_2 as gas, by converting from coal to gas, CO_2 emissions can be cut without lowering the amount of electricity consumed.

- A switch from coal to gas can be achieved by mandating power utilities or by confronting them with a price for carbon emissions that makes a switch in their self-interest.

- Regardless of the method used, a switch from coal to gas decreases the demand for coal and increases the demand for gas. The price of coal falls and the price of gas rises.

- The inefficiency arising from carbon emissions is measured by the deadweight loss it creates. Switching from coal to gas decreases the deadweight loss from using coal, increases the deadweight loss from using gas, and decreases the overall deadweight loss.

- But deadweight loss remains unless the consumption of electricity is cut to the point at which its marginal benefit and price equals its marginal *social* cost.

- The figures illustrate what will happen if the EPA plan is achieved.

- In Fig. 1, the demand for and marginal social benefit of electricity generated using coal is $D = MSB$. The supply of coal and the marginal private cost curve is $S = MC$, and the marginal social benefit curve is MSC. The efficient quantity of coal-generated electricity is 1.2 terawatt-hours per year. But the equilibrium quantity is 1.6 terawatt-hours per year, so overproduction brings a deadweight loss as shown by the area of the gray triangle.

- The EPA plan decreases the use of coal. In Fig. 1, the EPA target for coal generators is the efficient quantity, so the deadweight loss is eliminated.

- Figure 2 illustrates the effects of the switch from coal to gas. Gas generators are a bit more costly to operate than coal generators, so the marginal cost of producing electricity increases from MC_0 to MC_1 when gas generators replace coal generators.

- But gas is cleaner than coal, so emissions decrease and the marginal external cost falls. The marginal social cost falls from MSC_0 to MSC_1.

- Because the marginal cost of generating electricity increases, supply of electricity decreases, the price rises, and the equilibrium quantity decreases.

- The deadweight loss from generating electricity decreases from the area of the light gray triangle to the area of the dark gray triangle.

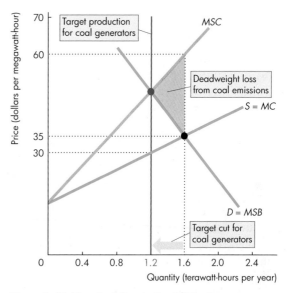

Figure 1 **Making Coal Generation Efficient**

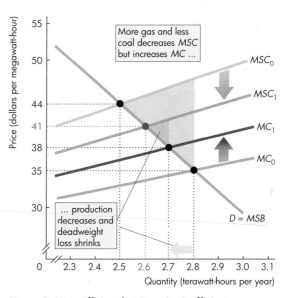

Figure 2 **More Efficient but Remains Inefficient**

- The success of this plan to lower carbon emissions will depend on the ways in which incentives are changed. The cost of using coal must rise to induce power utilities to find the most efficient substitutes for coal.

- The planned changes in the quantity and price of electricity leave a large amount of carbon emissions in place.

411

SUMMARY

Key Points

Externalities in Our Lives (pp. 392–393)

- An externality can arise from either a production activity or a consumption activity.
- A negative externality imposes an external cost. A positive externality provides an external benefit.

Working Problems 1 and 2 will give you a better understanding of the externalities in our lives.

Negative Externality: Pollution (pp. 394–400)

- A competitive market would produce too much of a good that has external production costs.
- External costs are costs of production that fall on people other than the producer of a good or service. Marginal social cost equals marginal private cost plus marginal external cost.
- Producers take account only of marginal private cost and produce more than the efficient quantity when there is a marginal external cost.
- Sometimes it is possible to overcome a negative externality by assigning a property right.
- When property rights cannot be assigned, governments might overcome externalities by using taxes or cap-and-trade.

Working Problems 3 and 4 will give you a better understanding of the external costs of pollution.

Negative Externality: The Tragedy of the Commons (pp. 401–405)

- Common resources create a problem that is called the tragedy of the commons—no one has a private incentive to conserve the resources and use them at an efficient rate.
- A common resource is used to the point at which the marginal private benefit equals the marginal cost.
- A common resource might be used efficiently by creating a private property right, setting a quota, or issuing individual transferable quotas.

Working Problems 5 and 6 will give you a better understanding of the tragedy of the commons.

Positive Externality: Knowledge (pp. 406–409)

- External benefits are benefits that are received by people other than the consumer of a good or service. Marginal social benefit equals marginal private benefit plus marginal external benefit.
- External benefits from education arise because better-educated people tend to be better citizens, commit fewer crimes, and support social activities.
- Vouchers or subsidies to schools or the provision of public education below cost can achieve a more efficient provision of education.

Working Problems 7 to 9 will give you a better understanding of the external benefit from knowledge.

Key Terms

MyEconLab Key Terms Quiz

Abatement technology, 395	Marginal privavte benefit, 406	Property rights, 395
Coase theorem, 396	Marginal private cost, 394	Public production, 407
Externality, 392	Marginal social benefit, 406	Subsidy, 407
Individual transferable quota (ITQ), 404	Marginal social cost, 394	Tragedy of the commons, 401
Marginal external benefit, 406	Negative externality, 392	Transactions costs, 396
Marginal external cost, 394	Pigovian taxes, 397	Voucher, 407
	Positive externality, 392	

WORKED PROBLEM

MyEconLab   You can work this problem in Chapter 17 Study Plan.

The first two columns of the table show the demand schedule for fitness sessions with independent coaches; the second and third columns show the coaches' marginal cost. Fitness creates an external benefit and the marginal external benefit is $10 per session. The market for fitness sessions is competitive.

Price (dollars per session)	Quantity (sessions per month)	Marginal cost (dollars per session)
10	800	30
15	600	25
20	400	20
25	200	15
30	0	10

Questions

1. What is the market-determined quantity of fitness sessions per month and what is the price of a session?
2. Calculate the marginal social benefit from fitness sessions at each quantity of sessions.
3. What is the efficient number of fitness sessions per month?

Solutions

1. In the market for fitness sessions the supply schedule is the same as the marginal cost schedule. The quantity of sessions is that at which marginal private benefit equals marginal cost. Marginal private benefit is the same as price, so the number of sessions per month is 400 and the price of a session is $20.

Key Point: The market outcome is determined by marginal private benefit and marginal cost.

2. Marginal social benefit (MSB) equals the sum of marginal private benefit (MB), which equals price, and the marginal external benefit of $10 per session.

The table below shows the calculations.

Quantity (sessions per month)	MB (dollars per session)	MSB (dollars per session)
800	10	20
600	15	25
400	20	30
200	25	35
0	-	-

For example, the marginal social benefit from 600 sessions per month equals the marginal private benefit of $15 per session plus the marginal external benefit of $10 per session, which equals $25 per session.

Key Point: The marginal social benefit from a service that creates a positive externality is the sum of the marginal private benefit and the marginal external benefit.

3. To find the efficient number of sessions, we need to determine the number of sessions per month at which the marginal social benefit (MSB) equals marginal cost (MC).

The table below combines the data from the other two tables.

Quantity (sessions per month)	MSB (dollars per session)	MC (dollars per session)
800	20	30
600	25	25
400	30	20
200	35	15
0	-	10

By inspecting the table above, you can see that MSB equals MC at 600 sessions per month, so that is the efficient quantity.

Key Point: The efficient quantity of a service that creates a positive externality is the quantity at which marginal social benefit from the service equals the marginal cost of producing the service.

Key Figure

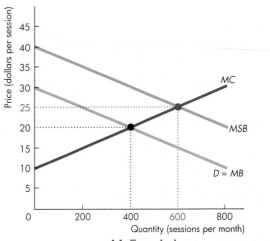

MyEconLab Interactive Animation

STUDY PLAN PROBLEMS AND APPLICATIONS

MyEconLab   You can work Problems 1 to 9 in Chapter 17 Study Plan and get instant feedback.

Externalities in Our Lives (Study Plan 17.1)

1. Describe three consumption activities that create external costs.

2. Describe three production activities that create external benefits.

Negative Externality: Pollution (Study Plan 17.2)

Use the following figure, which illustrates the market for cotton, to work Problems 3 and 4.

Suppose that the cotton growers use a chemical to control insects and waste flows into the town's river. The marginal social cost of producing the cotton is double the marginal private cost.

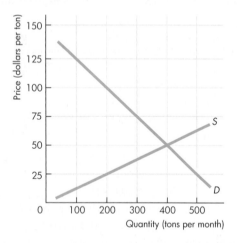

3. If no one owns the river and the town takes no action to control the waste, what is the quantity of cotton and the deadweight loss created?

4. If the town owns the river and taxes cotton growers so that the efficient quantity is grown, how much tax revenue does the town receive? Is the quantity of waste zero? Explain your answer.

Negative Externality: Tragedy of the Commons
(Study Plan 17.3)

Use the figure in the next column to work Problems 5 and 6.

The figure illustrates the market for North Atlantic tuna.

5. a. What is the quantity of tuna that fishers catch and the price of tuna? Is the tuna stock being used efficiently? Explain why or why not.

   b. What would be the price of tuna, if the stock of tuna were used efficiently?

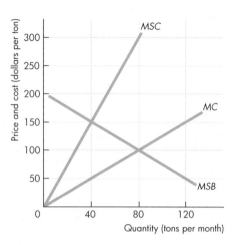

6. With a quota of 40 tons a month for the tuna fishing industry, what is the price of tuna and the quantity caught? Does overfishing occur?

Positive Externality: Knowledge (Study Plan 17.4)

Use the following figure, which shows the demand for college education, to work Problems 7 to 9.

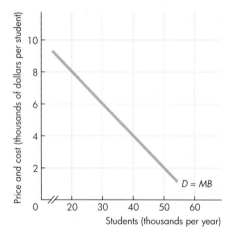

The marginal cost is a constant $6,000 per student per year. The marginal external benefit from a college education is a constant $4,000 per student per year.

7. What is the efficient number of students? If all colleges are private, how many people enroll in college and what is the tuition?

8. If the government provides public colleges, what tuition will achieve the efficient number of students? How much will taxpayers have to pay?

9. If the government offers students vouchers, what is the value of the voucher that will achieve the efficient number of students?

ADDITIONAL PROBLEMS AND APPLICATIONS

MyEconLab   You can work these problems in MyEconLab if assigned by your instructor.

Externalities in Our Lives

10. What externalities arise from smoking tobacco products and how do we deal with them?

11. What externalities arise from beautiful and ugly buildings and how do we deal with them?

Negative Externality: Pollution

12. Betty and Anna work at the same office in Philadelphia and they have to attend a meeting in Pittsburgh. They decide to drive to the out-of-town meeting together. Betty is a cigarette smoker and her marginal benefit from smoking a pack of cigarettes a day is $40. Cigarettes are $6 a pack. Anna dislikes cigarette smoke, and her marginal benefit from a smoke-free environment is $50 a day. What is the outcome if

    a. Betty drives her car with Anna as a passenger?

    b. Anna drives her car with Betty as a passenger?

Use the following data and the figure, which illustrates the market for a pesticide with no government intervention, to work Problems 13 to 16.

When factories produce pesticide, they also create waste, which they dump into a lake on the outskirts of the town. The marginal external cost of the waste is equal to the marginal private cost of producing the pesticide (that is, the marginal social cost of producing the pesticide is double the marginal private cost).

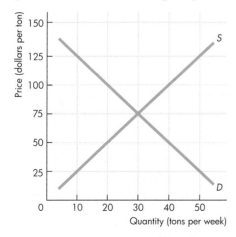

13. What is the quantity of pesticide produced if no one owns the lake and what is the efficient quantity of pesticide?

14. If the town owns the lake, what is the quantity of pesticide produced and how much does the town charge the factories to dump waste?

15. If the pesticide factories own the lake, how much pesticide is produced?

16. If no one owns the lake and the government levies a pollution tax, what is the tax that achieves the efficient outcome?

Use the following table to work Problems 17 to 19. The first two columns of the table show the demand schedule for electricity from a coal burning utility; the second and third columns show the utility's cost of producing electricity. The marginal external cost of the pollution created equals the marginal cost.

Price (cents per kilowatt)	Quantity (kilowatts per day)	Marginal cost (cents per kilowatt)
4	500	10
8	400	8
12	300	6
16	200	4
20	100	2

17. With no government action to control pollution, what is the quantity of electricity produced, the price of electricity, and the marginal external cost of the pollution generated?

18. With no government action to control pollution, what is the marginal social cost of the electricity generated and the deadweight loss created?

19. If the government levies a pollution tax such that the utility produces the efficient quantity, what is the price of electricity, the tax levied, and the government's tax revenue per day?

Negative Externality: The Tragedy of the Commons

20. **Polar Ice Cap Shrinks Further and Thins**
    With the warming of the planet, the polar ice cap is shrinking and the Arctic Sea is expanding. As the ice cap shrinks further, more and more underwater mineral resources will become accessible. Many countries are staking out territorial claims to parts of the polar region.
        Source: *The Wall Street Journal*, April 7, 2009

    Explain how ownership of these mineral resources will influence the amount of damage done to the Arctic Sea and its wildlife.

Use the following figure to work Problems 21 to 23.

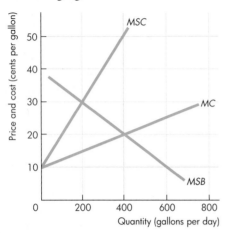

A spring runs under a village. Everyone can sink a well on her or his land and take water from the spring. The figure shows the marginal social benefit from and the marginal cost of taking water.

21. What is the quantity of water taken and what is the private cost of the water taken?

22. What is the efficient quantity of water taken and the marginal social cost at the efficient quantity?

23. If the village council sets a quota on the total amount of water such that the spring is used efficiently, what would be the quota and the market value of the water taken per day?

24. If hikers and other visitors were required to pay a fee to use the Appalachian Trail,
    a. Would the use of this common resource be more efficient?
    b. Would it be even more efficient if the most popular spots along the trail had the highest prices?
    c. Why do you think we don't see more market solutions to the tragedy of the commons?

Positive Externality: Knowledge

Use the following data to work Problems 25 to 28. The table shows the demand for college education. The marginal cost of educating a student is a

Price (dollars per student)	Quantity (students per year)
6,000	10,000
5,000	20,000
4,000	30,000
3,000	40,000
2,000	50,000

constant $4,000 a year and education creates an external benefit of a constant $2,000 per student per year.

25. If all colleges are private and the market for education is competitive, calculate the number of students, the tuition, and the deadweight loss.

26. If all colleges are public colleges, calculate the tuition that will achieve the efficient number of students. How much will taxpayers have to pay?

27. If the government decides to subsidize private colleges, what subsidy will achieve the efficient number of college students?

28. If all colleges are private and the government offers vouchers to those who enroll at a college, calculate the value of the voucher that will achieve the efficient number of students.

Economics in the News

29. After you have studied *Economics in the News* on pp. 410–411, answer the following questions.
    a. What are the marginal private costs of and marginal private benefits from using gas rather than coal to generate electricity?
    b. What are the marginal social costs of and marginal social benefits from using gas rather than coal to generate electricity?
    c. How will the EPA's plan for power utilities to switch from coal to gas change the price that households pay for electricity?
    d. How will the EPA's plan for utilities to switch from coal to gas change the efficiency of electricity production?

30. **Where the Tuna Roam**
    To the first settlers, the Great Plains posed the same problem as the oceans today: a vast, open area where there seemed to be no way to protect animals. But animals thrived once the settlers divvied up the land and devised ways to protect their livestock. Today, the oceans are much like an open range. Fishers catch as much as they can, even if they are overfishing. They figure any fish they don't take for themselves will just be taken by someone else.
    Source: *The New York Times*, November 4, 2006

    a. What are the similarities between the problems faced by the earliest settlers in the West and today's fishers?
    b. Can the tragedy of the commons in the oceans be eliminated in the same manner used by the early settlers on the plains?
    c. How can ITQs change the short-term outlook of fishers to a long-term outlook?

We, the People, …

UNDERSTANDING MARKET FAILURE AND GOVERNMENT

Thomas Jefferson knew that creating a government of the people, by the people, and for the people was a huge enterprise and one that could easily go wrong. Creating a constitution that made despotic and tyrannical rule impossible was relatively easy. The founding fathers did their best to practice sound economics. They designed a sophisticated system of incentives—of carrots and sticks—to make the government responsive to public opinion and to limit the ability of individual self-interests to gain at the expense of the majority. But they were not able to create a constitution that effectively blocks the ability of special interest groups to capture the consumer and producer surpluses that result from specialization and exchange.

We have created a system of government to deal with four market failures: (1) monopoly; (2) externalities; (3) public goods; and (4) common resources.

Government might help cope with these market failures, but as the founding fathers knew well, government does not eliminate the pursuit of self-interest. Voters, politicians, and bureaucrats pursue their self-interest, sometimes at the expense of the social interest, and instead of market failure, we get government failure.

Many economists have thought long and hard about the problems discussed in this part. But none has had as profound an effect on our ideas in this area as Ronald Coase.

Ronald Coase *(1910–2013) was born in England and educated at the London School of Economics, where he was deeply influenced by his teacher, Arnold Plant, and by the issues of his youth: communist central planning versus free markets.*

Professor Coase lived in the United States from 1951 until his dealth in 2013. He first visited America as a 20-year-old on a traveling scholarship during the depths of the Great Depression. It was on this visit, and before he had completed his bachelor's degree, that he conceived the ideas that 60 years later were to earn him the 1991 Nobel Prize for Economic Science.

Ronald Coase discovered and clarified the significance of transactions costs and property rights for the functioning of the economy. He revolutionized the way we think about property rights and externalities and opened up the growing field of law and economics.

"The question to be decided is: Is the value of fish lost greater or less than the value of the product which contamination of the stream makes possible?"

RONALD H. COASE
The Problem of Social Cost

CAROLINE M. HOXBY is the Allie S. Freed Professor of Economics at Harvard University. Born in Cleveland, Ohio, she was an undergraduate at Harvard and a graduate student at Oxford and MIT.

Professor Hoxby is a leading scholar of the economics of education. She has written many articles on this topic and has published books entitled *The Economics of School Choice* and *College Choices* (both University of Chicago Press, 2003 and 2004, respectively). She is Program Director of the Economics of Education Program at the National Bureau of Economic Research, serves on several other national boards that study education issues, and has advised or provided testimony to several state legislatures and the United States Congress.

Michael Parkin talked with Caroline Hoxby about her work and the progress that economists have made in understanding how the financing and the provision of education influence the quality of education and the equality of access to it.

Why did you decide to become an economist?

I've wanted to be an economist from about the age of 13. That was when I took my first class in economics (an interesting story in itself) and discovered that all of the thoughts swimming around in my head belonged to a "science" and there was an entire body of people who understood this science—a lot better than I did, anyway. I can still recall reading *The Wealth of Nations* for the first time; it was a revelation.

What drew you to study the economics of education?

We all care about education, perhaps because it is the key means by which opportunity is (or should be) extended to all in the United States. Also, nearly everyone now acknowledges that highly developed countries like the United States rely increasingly on education as the engine of economic growth. Thus, one reason I was drawn to education is its importance. However, what primarily drew me was that education issues were so clearly begging for economic analysis and that there was so little of it. I try hard to understand educational institutions and problems, but I insist on bringing economic logic to bear on educational issues.

What can economists say about the alternative methods of financing education? Is there a voucher solution that could work?

There is definitely a voucher solution that could work because vouchers are inherently an extremely flexible policy. ...

> **Economists should say to policy makers: "Tell me your goals; I'll design you a voucher."**

Any well-designed voucher system will give schools an incentive to compete. However, when designing vouchers, we can also build in remedies for a variety of educational problems. Vouchers can be used to ensure that disabled children get the funding they need and the program choices they need.

Compared to current school finance programs, vouchers can do a better job of ensuring that low-income families have sufficient funds to invest in the child's education. Well-designed vouchers can encourage schools to make their student bodies socio-economically diverse.

Economists should say to policy makers: "Tell me your goals; I'll design you a voucher."

*Read the full interview with Caroline Hoxby in MyEconLab.

18 MARKETS FOR FACTORS OF PRODUCTION

After studying this chapter, you will be able to:

◆ Describe the anatomy of factor markets
◆ Explain how the value of marginal product determines the demand for a factor of production
◆ Explain how wage rates and employment are determined and how labor unions influence labor markets
◆ Explain how capital and land rental rates and natural resource prices are determined

A teacher in a public school earns much more than an equally good teacher in a charter school, and your college basketball coach earns much more than your economics professor. Why? What determines the wages that people earn? Wages are important, but finding a job is important too. Why are so many manufacturing jobs disappearing and what new jobs are being created?

In this chapter, we study labor markets as well as markets for capital and natural resources. In *Economics in the News* at the end of the chapter we answer the question about teachers' pay.

419

◆ The Anatomy of Factor Markets

The four factors of production are

- Labor
- Capital
- Land (natural resources)
- Entrepreneurship

Let's take a brief look at the anatomy of the markets in which these factors of production are traded.

Markets for Labor Services

Labor services are the physical and mental work effort that people supply to produce goods and services. A labor market is a collection of people and firms who trade labor services. The price of labor services is the wage rate.

Some labor services are traded day by day. These services are called *casual labor*. People who pick fruit and vegetables often just show up at a farm and take whatever work is available that day. But most labor services are traded on a job contract.

Most labor markets have many buyers and many sellers and are competitive. In these markets, supply and demand determine the wage rate and quantity of labor employed. Jobs expand when demand increases and jobs disappear when demand decreases.

In some labor markets, a labor union operates like a monopoly on the supply-side of the labor market. In this type of labor market, a bargaining process between the union and the employer determines the wage rate.

We'll study both competitive labor markets and labor unions in this chapter.

Markets for Capital Services

Capital consists of the tools, instruments, machines, buildings, and other constructions that have been produced in the past and that businesses now use to produce goods and services. These physical objects are themselves goods—capital goods. Capital goods are traded in goods markets, just as bottled water and toothpaste are. The price of a dump truck, a capital good, is determined by supply and demand in the market for dump trucks. This market is not a market for capital services.

A market for *capital services* is a *rental market*—a market in which the services of capital are hired.

An example of a market for capital services is the vehicle rental market in which Avis, Budget, Hertz,

U-Haul, and many other firms offer automobiles and trucks for hire. The price in a capital services market is a *rental rate*.

Most capital services are not traded in a market. Instead, a firm buys capital and uses it itself. The services of the capital that a firm owns and operates have an implicit price that arises from depreciation and interest costs (see Chapter 10, pp. 224–225). You can think of this price as the implicit rental rate of capital. Firms that buy capital and use it themselves are *implicitly* renting the capital to themselves.

Markets for Land Services and Natural Resources

Land consists of all the gifts of nature—natural resources. The market for land as a factor of production is the market for the *services of land*—the use of land. The price of the services of land is a rental rate.

Most natural resources, such as farm land, can be used repeatedly. But a few natural resources are nonrenewable. **Nonrenewable natural resources** are resources that can be used only once. Examples are oil, natural gas, and coal. The prices of nonrenewable natural resources are determined in global *commodity markets* and are called *commodity prices*.

Entrepreneurship

Entrepreneurial services are not traded in markets. Entrepreneurs receive the profit or bear the loss that results from their business decisions.

◆ REVIEW QUIZ

1 What are the factors of production and their prices?
2 What is the distinction between capital and the services of capital?
3 What is the distinction between the price of capital equipment and the rental rate of capital?

Work these questions in Study Plan 18.1 and get instant feedback. Do a Key Term Quiz.   MyEconLab

The rest of this chapter explores the influences on the demand and supply of factors of production. We begin by studying the demand for a factor of production.

The Demand for a Factor of Production

The demand for a factor of production is a **derived demand**—it is derived from the demand for the goods and services that the labor produces. You've seen, in Chapters 10 through 15, how a firm determines its profit-maximizing output. The quantities of factors of production demanded are a consequence of the firm's output decision. A firm hires the quantities of factors of production that produce the firm's profit-maximizing output.

To decide the quantity of a factor of production to hire, a firm compares the cost of hiring an additional unit of the factor with its value to the firm. The cost of hiring an additional unit of a factor of production is the factor price. The value to the firm of hiring one more unit of a factor of production is called the factor's **value of marginal product.** We calculate the value of marginal product as the price of a unit of output multiplied by the marginal product of the factor of production.

To study the demand for a factor of production, we'll use labor as the example. But what you learn here about the demand for labor applies to the demand for all factors of production.

Value of Marginal Product

Table 18.1 shows you how to calculate the value of marginal product of labor at Angelo's Bakery.

The first two columns show Angelo's total product schedule—the number of loaves per hour that each quantity of labor can produce. The third column shows the marginal product of labor—the change in total product that results from a one-unit increase in the quantity of labor employed. (See Chapter 11, pp. 249–252 for a refresher on product schedules.)

Angelo can sell bread at the going market price of $2 a loaf. Given this information, we can calculate the value of marginal product (fourth column). It equals price multiplied by marginal product. For example, the marginal product of hiring the second worker is 6 loaves. Each loaf sold brings in $2, so the value of marginal product of the second worker is $12 (6 loaves at $2 each).

A Firm's Demand for Labor

The value of marginal product of labor tells us what an additional worker is worth to a firm. It tells us the revenue that the firm earns by hiring one more worker. The wage rate tells us what an additional worker costs a firm.

The value of marginal product of labor and the wage rate together determine the quantity of labor demanded by a firm. Because the value of marginal product decreases as the quantity of labor employed increases, there is a simple rule for maximizing profit: Hire the quantity of labor at which the value of marginal product equals the wage rate.

If the value of marginal product of labor exceeds the wage rate, a firm can increase its profit by hiring

---

TABLE 18.1   Value of Marginal Product at Angelo's Bakery

	Quantity of labor (L) (workers)	Total product (TP) (loaves per hour)	Marginal product ($MP = \Delta TP/\Delta L$) (loaves per worker)	Value of marginal product ($VMP = MP \times P$) (dollars per worker)
A	0	0		
			7	14
B	1	7		
			6	**12**
C	**2**	13		
			5	10
D	3	18		
			4	8
E	4	22		
			3	6
F	5	25		

The value of marginal product of labor equals the price of the product multiplied by marginal product of labor. If Angelo's hires 2 workers, the marginal product of the second worker is 6 loaves (in the third column). The price of a loaf is $2, so the value of marginal product of the second worker is $2 a loaf multiplied by 6 loaves, which is $12 (in fourth column).

one more worker. If the wage rate exceeds the value of marginal product of labor, a firm can increase its profit by firing one worker. But if the wage rate equals the value of marginal product of labor, the firm cannot increase its profit by changing the number of workers it employs. The firm is making the maximum possible profit. So

> The quantity of labor demanded by a firm is the quantity at which the value of marginal product of labor equals the wage rate.

A Firm's Demand for Labor Curve

A firm's demand for labor curve is derived from its value of marginal product curve. Figure 18.1 shows these two curves. Figure 18.1(a) shows the value of marginal product curve at Angelo's Bakery. The blue bars graph the numbers in Table 18.1. The curve labeled *VMP* is Angelo's value of marginal product curve.

If the wage rate falls and other things remain the same, a firm hires more workers. Figure 18.1(b) shows Angelo's demand for labor curve.

Suppose the wage rate is $10 an hour. You can see in Fig.18.1(a) that if Angelo hires 2 workers, the value of the marginal product of labor is $12 an hour. At a wage rate of $10 an hour, Angelo makes a profit of $2 an hour on the second worker. If Angelo hires a third worker, the value of marginal product of that worker is $10 an hour. So on this third worker, Angelo breaks even.

If Angelo hired 4 workers, his profit would fall. The fourth worker generates a value of marginal product of only $8 an hour but costs $10 an hour, so Angelo does not hire the fourth worker. When the wage rate is $10 an hour, the quantity of labor demanded by Angelo is 3 workers.

Figure 18.1(b) shows Angelo's demand for labor curve, *D*. At $10 an hour, the quantity of labor demanded by Angelo is 3 workers. If the wage rate increased to $12 an hour, Angelo would decrease the quantity of labor demanded to 2 workers. If the wage rate decreased to $8 an hour, Angelo would increase the quantity of labor demanded to 4 workers.

A change in the wage rate brings a change in the quantity of labor demanded and a movement along the demand for labor curve.

A change in any other influence on a firm's labor-hiring plans changes the demand for labor and shifts the demand for labor curve.

FIGURE 18.1 The Demand for Labor at Angelo's Bakery

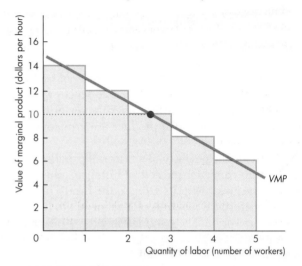

(a) Value of marginal product

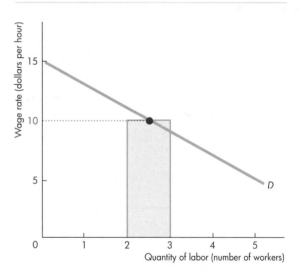

(b) Demand for labor

Angelo's Bakery can sell any quantity of bread at $2 a loaf. The blue bars in part (a) represent the firm's value of marginal product of labor (based on Table 18.1). The line labeled *VMP* is the firm's value of marginal product curve. Part (b) shows Angelo's demand for labor curve. Angelo hires the quantity of labor that makes the value of marginal product equal to the wage rate. The demand for labor curve slopes downward because the value of marginal product diminishes as the quantity of labor employed increases.

MyEconLab Animation and Draw Graph

Changes in a Firm's Demand for Labor

A firm's demand for labor depends on

- The price of the firm's output
- The prices of other factors of production
- Technology

The Price of the Firm's Output The higher the price of a firm's output, the greater is the firm's demand for labor. The price of output affects the demand for labor through its influence on the value of marginal product of labor. A higher price for the firm's output increases the value of marginal product of labor. A change in the price of a firm's output leads to a shift in the firm's demand for labor curve. If the price of the firm's output increases, the demand for labor increases and the demand for labor curve shifts rightward.

For example, if the price of bread increased to $3 a loaf, the value of marginal product of Angelo's fourth worker would increase from $8 an hour to $12 an hour. At a wage rate of $10 an hour, Angelo would now hire 4 workers instead of 3.

The Prices of Other Factors of Production If the price of using capital decreases relative to the wage rate, a firm substitutes capital for labor and increases the quantity of capital it uses. Usually, the demand for labor will decrease when the price of using capital falls. For example, if the price of a bread-making machine falls, Angelo might decide to install one machine and lay off a worker. But the demand for labor could increase if the lower price of capital led to a sufficiently large increase in the scale of production. For example, with cheaper machines available, Angelo might install a machine and hire more labor to operate it. This type of factor substitution occurs in the long run when the firm can change the size of its plant.

Technology New technologies decrease the demand for some types of labor and increase the demand for other types. For example, if a new automated bread-making machine becomes available, Angelo might install one of these machines and fire most of his workforce—a decrease in the demand for bakery workers. But the firms that manufacture and service automated bread-making machines hire more labor, so there is an increase in the demand for this type of labor. An event similar to this one occurred during the 1990s when the introduction of electronic telephone exchanges decreased the demand for telephone operators and increased the demand for computer programmers and electronics engineers.

Table 18.2 summarizes the influences on a firm's demand for labor.

TABLE 18.2 A Firm's Demand for Labor

The Law of Demand

(Movements along the demand curve for labor)

The quantity of labor demanded by a firm

Decreases if:	Increases if:
■ The wage rate increases	■ The wage rate decreases

Changes in Demand

(Shifts in the demand curve for labor)

A firm's demand for labor

Decreases if:	Increases if:
■ The price of the firm's output decreases	■ The price of the firm's output increases
■ The price of a substitute for labor falls	■ The price of a substitute for labor rises
■ The price of a complement of labor rises	■ The price of a complement of labor falls
■ A new technology or new capital decreases the marginal product of labor	■ A new technology or new capital increases the marginal product of labor

◆ REVIEW QUIZ

1 What is the value of marginal product of labor?
2 What is the relationship between the value of marginal product of labor and the marginal product of labor?
3 How is the demand for labor derived from the value of marginal product of labor?
4 What are the influences on the demand for labor?

Work these questions in Study Plan 18.2 and get instant feedback. Do a Key Terms Quiz.   MyEconLab

◆ Labor Markets

Labor services are traded in many different labor markets. Examples are markets for bakery workers, van drivers, crane operators, computer support specialists, air traffic controllers, surgeons, and economists. Some of these markets, such as the market for bakery workers, are local. They operate in a given neighborhood or town. Some labor markets, such as the market for air traffic controllers, are national. Firms and workers search across the nation for the right match of worker and job. And some labor markets are global, such as the market for superstar hockey, basketball, baseball, and soccer players.

We'll look at a local market for bakery workers as an example. First, we'll look at a *competitive* labor market. Then, we'll see how monopoly elements can influence a labor market.

A Competitive Labor Market

A competitive labor market is one in which many firms demand labor and many households supply labor.

Market Demand for Labor Earlier in the chapter, you saw how an individual firm decides how much labor to hire. The market demand for labor is derived from the demand for labor by individual firms. We determine the market demand for labor by adding together the quantities of labor demanded by all the firms in the market at each wage rate. (The market demand for a good or service is derived in a similar way—see Chapter 5, pp. 108–109.)

Because each firm's demand for labor curve slopes downward, the market demand for labor curve also slopes downward.

The Market Supply of Labor The market supply of labor is derived from the supply of labor decisions made by individual households.

Individual's Labor Supply Decision People can allocate their time to two broad activities: labor supply and leisure. (Leisure is a catch-all term. It includes all activities other than supplying labor.) For most people, leisure is more fun than work so to induce them to work they must be offered a wage.

Think about the labor supply decision of Jill, one of the workers at Angelo's Bakery. Let's see how the wage rate influences the quantity of labor she is willing to supply.

Reservation Wage Rate Jill enjoys her leisure time, and she would be pleased if she didn't have to spend her time working at Angelo's Bakery. But Jill wants to earn an income, and as long as she can earn a wage rate of at least $5 an hour, she's willing to work. This wage is called her *reservation wage*. At any wage rate above her reservation wage, Jill supplies some labor.

The wage rate at Angelo's is $10 an hour, and at that wage rate, Jill chooses to work 30 hours a week. At a wage rate of $10 an hour, Jill regards this use of her time as the best available. Figure 18.2 illustrates.

Backward-Bending Labor Supply Curve If Jill were offered a wage rate between $5 and $10 an hour, she would want to work fewer hours. If she were offered a wage rate above $10 an hour, she would want to work more hours, but only up to a point. If Jill could

FIGURE 18.2   Jill's Labor Supply Curve

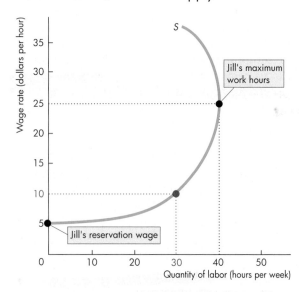

Jill's labor supply curve is S. Jill supplies no labor at wage rates below her reservation wage of $5 an hour. As the wage rate rises above $5 an hour, the quantity of labor that Jill supplies increases to a maximum of 40 hours a week at a wage rate of $25 an hour. As the wage rate rises above $25 an hour, Jill supplies a decreasing quantity of labor: her labor supply curve bends backward. The income effect on the demand for leisure dominates the substitution effect.

MyEconLab Animation

earn $25 an hour, she would be willing to work 40 hours a week (and earn $1,000 a week). But at a wage rate above $25 an hour, with the goods and services that Jill can buy for $1,000, her priority would be a bit more leisure time. So if the wage rate increased above $25 an hour, Jill would cut back on her work hours and take more leisure. Jill's labor supply curve eventually bends backward.

Jill's labor supply decisions are influenced by a substitution effect and an income effect.

Substitution Effect At wage rates below $25 an hour, the higher the wage rate Jill is offered, the greater is the quantity of labor that she supplies. Jill's wage rate is her *opportunity cost of leisure*. If she quits work an hour early to catch a movie, the cost of that extra hour of leisure is the wage rate that Jill forgoes. The higher the wage rate, the less willing Jill is to forgo the income and take the extra leisure time. This tendency for a higher wage rate to induce Jill to work longer hours is a *substitution effect*.

Income Effect The higher Jill's wage rate, the higher is her income. A higher income, other things remaining the same, induces Jill to increase her demand for most goods and services. Leisure is one of those goods. Because an increase in income creates an increase in the demand for leisure, it also creates a decrease in the quantity of labor supplied.

Market Supply Curve The market supply curve shows the quantity of labor supplied by all households in a particular job market. It is found by adding together the quantities of labor supplied by all households to a given job market at each wage rate, so the greater the number of households (the greater is the working-age population), the greater is the market supply of labor.

Despite the fact that an individual's labor supply curve eventually bends backward, the market supply curve of labor slopes upward. The higher the wage rate for bakery workers, the greater is the quantity of bakery workers supplied in that labor market.

One reason why the market supply curve doesn't bend backward is that different households have different reservation wage rates and different wage rates at which their labor supply curves bend backward.

Also, along a supply curve in a particular job market, the wage rates available in other job markets remain the same. For example, along the supply curve of bakers, the wage rates of salespeople and all other types of labor are constant.

Let's now look at labor market equilibrium.

Competitive Labor Market Equilibrium Labor market equilibrium determines the wage rate and employment. In Fig. 18.3, the market demand curve for bakery workers is D and the market supply curve of bakery workers is S. The equilibrium wage rate is $10 an hour, and the equilibrium quantity is 300 bakery workers. If the wage rate exceeded $10 an hour, there would be a surplus of bakery workers. More people would be looking for jobs in bakeries than firms were willing to hire. In such a situation, the wage rate would fall as firms found it easy to hire people at a lower wage rate. If the wage rate were less than $10 an hour, there would be a shortage of bakery workers. Firms would not be able to fill all the positions they had available. In this situation, the wage rate would rise as firms found it necessary to offer higher wages to attract labor. Only at a wage rate of $10 an hour are there no forces operating to change the wage rate.

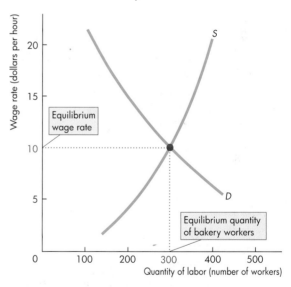

FIGURE 18.3 The Market for Bakery Workers

A competitive labor market coordinates firms' and households' plans. The market is in equilibrium—the quantity of labor demanded equals the quantity supplied at a wage rate of $10 an hour when 300 workers are employed. If the wage rate exceeds $10 an hour, the quantity supplied exceeds the quantity demanded and the wage rate will fall. If the wage rate is below $10 an hour, the quantity demanded exceeds the quantity supplied and the wage rate will rise.

MyEconLab Animation

ECONOMICS IN ACTION

Wage Rates in the United States

In 2013, the average weekly wage in the United States was $776. The figure shows the *median weekly wage rates* for 20 jobs selected from the more than 700 jobs for which the Bureau of Labor Statistics reports wage rate data.

You can see that a chief executive, on average, earns more than 5 times as much per week as a fast-food worker and twice as much as a high-school teacher. Remember that these numbers are medians. Some chief executives earn much more and some earn less than the median.

Many more occupations earn a wage rate below the national average than above it. Most of the occupations that earn more than the national average require a college degree and postgraduate training.

Earning differences are explained by differences in the value of the marginal product of the skills in the various occupations and in market power.

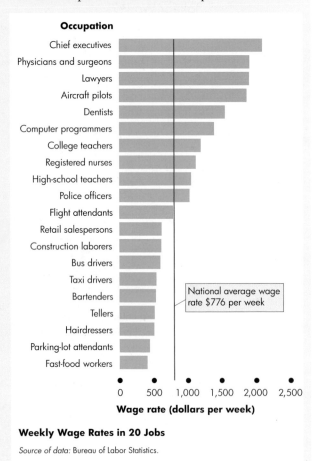

Occupation

Weekly Wage Rates in 20 Jobs

Source of data: Bureau of Labor Statistics.

Differences and Trends in Wage Rates

You can use what you've learned about labor markets to explain some of the differences in wage rates across occupations and the trends in wage rates.

Wage rates are unequal, and *Economics in Action* on this page shows a sample of the inequality in wages in 2013. The differences in wage rates across occupations—including college professors and basketball coaches—are driven by differences in demand and supply in labor markets. The highest wage rates are earned in occupations where the value of marginal product is highest and where few people have the ability and training to perform the job.

Rising Wage Rates Wage rates increase over time and trend upward. The reason is that the value of marginal product of labor also increases over time. Technological change and the new types of capital that it brings make workers more productive. With greater labor productivity, the demand for labor increases, which increases the wage rate. Even jobs in which physical productivity doesn't increase experience increases in the *value* of marginal product. Child care is an example. A child-care worker can't care for an increasing number of children, but an increasing number of parents who earn high wages are willing to hire child-care workers. The *value* of marginal product of these workers increases, so the demand for their services increases, and so does their wage rate.

Increased Wage Inequality In recent years wage inequality has increased. High wage rates have increased more rapidly than the low ones, and some low wage rates have stagnated or even fallen. The reasons are complex and not fully understood, but the best explanation is that there is an interaction between technology and education.

The new information technologies of the 1990s and 2000s made well-educated, skilled workers more productive, so it raised their wage rates. For example, the computer created the jobs and increased the wage rates of computer programmers and electronic engineers.

These same technologies destroyed some low-skilled jobs. For example, the ATM took the jobs and lowered the wage rate of bank tellers, and automatic telephones took the jobs of telephone operators.

Another reason for increased inequality is that globalization has brought increased competition for low-skilled workers and at the same time opened global markets for high-skilled workers.

ECONOMICS IN THE NEWS

College Major and Job Prospects

The Most Valuable College Major

Which college major is most likely to land you a well-paying job right out of school? Katie Bardaro, an economist at PayScale, a compensation research firm, says biomedical engineering is your best bet. The median salary starts at $53,800 and by mid-career reaches $84,700 and keeps rising. The median salary for all biomedical engineers in 2012 was $88,000.

Some other science and engineering jobs pay more but don't have as good an outlook for jobs growth. The Bureau of Labor Statistics projects that the number of jobs for biomedical engineers will increase from today's 20,000 to 32,000 in 2020—an increase of more than 60 percent. In contrast, the working-age population will increase by only 8 percent by 2020.

Sources: The Bureau of Labor Statistics and
Forbes, May 15, 2012

THE QUESTIONS

- Why is the number of jobs for biomedical engineering graduates increasing?
- What determines the demand for biomedical engineers and why might it be increasing?
- What determines the supply of biomedical engineers and why might it be increasing?
- What determines whether the wage rate of biomedical engineers will rise?
- Provide a graphical illustration of the market for biomedical engineers in 2012 and 2020.

Biomedical engineers design and build replacement parts for the human body.

MyEconLab More Economics in the News

THE ANSWERS

- The number of jobs for biomedical engineers is growing because *both* demand for and supply of biomedical engineers are increasing.
- The demand for biomedical engineers is *derived* from the demand for biomedical products. The demand for replacement parts for the human body is increasing because technological advances are creating new and improved products.
- The supply of biomedical engineers is determined by the working-age population and the number of people who decide to major in the subject. The supply is increasing because the working-age population is increasing and good job prospects are attracting a larger percentage of people to study biomedical engineering.
- The wage rate of biomedical engineers will rise if the demand for their services increases faster than supply.
- The figure illustrates the market for biomedical engineers in 2012 and in 2020.
- Demand is expected to increase from D_{12} to D_{20}.
- Supply is expected to increase from S_{12} to S_{20}.
- The increase in demand is much greater than the increase in supply.
- The equilibrium quantity (the number of jobs) increases from 20,000 in 2012 to 32,000 in 2020.
- Because demand increases by more than supply, the equilibrium wage rate rises. (The 2020 wage rate is an assumption.)

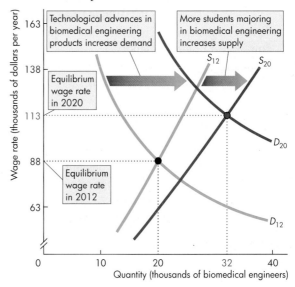

The Market for Biomedical Engineers in 2012 and 2020

A Labor Market with a Union

A **labor union** is an organized group of workers that aims to increase the wage rate and influence other job conditions. Let's see what happens when a union enters a competitive labor market.

Influences on Labor Supply One way of raising the wage rate is to decrease the supply of labor. In some labor markets, a union can restrict supply by controlling entry into apprenticeship programs or by influencing job qualification standards. Markets for skilled workers, doctors, dentists, and lawyers are the easiest ones to control in this way.

If there is an abundant supply of nonunion labor, a union can't decrease supply. For example, in the market for farm labor in southern California, the flow of nonunion labor from Mexico makes it difficult for a union to control the supply.

On the demand side of the labor market, the union faces a tradeoff: The demand for labor curve slopes downward, so restricting supply to raise the wage rate costs jobs. For this reason, unions also try to influence the demand for union labor.

Influences on Labor Demand A union tries to increase the demand for the labor of its members in four main ways:

1. Increasing the value of marginal product of its members by organizing and sponsoring training schemes and apprenticeship programs, and by professional certification.
2. Lobbying for import restrictions and encouraging people to buy goods made by unionized workers.
3. Supporting minimum wage laws, which increase the cost of employing low-skilled labor and lead firms to substitute high-skilled union labor for low-skilled nonunion labor.
4. Lobbying for restrictive immigration laws to decrease the supply of foreign workers.

Labor Market Equilibrium with a Union Figure 18.4 illustrates what happens to the wage rate and employment when a union successfully enters a competitive labor market. With no union, the demand curve is D_C, the supply curve is S_C, the wage rate is $10 an hour, and 300 workers have jobs.

Now a union enters this labor market. First, look at what happens if the union has sufficient control over the supply of labor to be able to restrict supply

FIGURE 18.4 A Union Enters a Competitive Labor Market

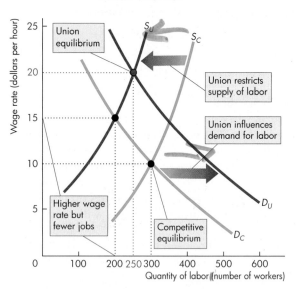

In a competitive labor market, the demand curve is D_C and the supply curve is S_C. The wage rate is $10 an hour and 300 workers are employed. If a union decreases the supply of labor and the supply of labor curve shifts to S_U, the wage rate rises to $15 an hour and employment decreases to 200 workers. If the union can also increase the demand for labor and shift the demand for labor curve to D_U, the wage rate rises to $20 an hour and 250 workers are employed.

MyEconLab Animation and Draw Graph

below its competitive level—to S_U. If that is all the union is able to do, employment falls to 200 workers and the wage rate rises to $15 an hour.

Suppose now that the union is also able to increase the demand for labor to D_U. The union can get an even bigger increase in the wage rate and with a smaller fall in employment. By maintaining the restricted labor supply at S_U, the union increases the wage rate to $20 an hour and achieves an employment level of 250 workers.

Because a union restricts the supply of labor in the market in which it operates, the union's actions spill over into nonunion markets. Workers who can't get union jobs must look elsewhere for work. This action increases the supply of labor in nonunion markets and lowers the wage rate in those markets. This spillover effect further widens the gap between union and nonunion wages.

Monopsony in the Labor Market Not all labor markets in which unions operate are competitive. Rather, some are labor markets in which the employer possesses market power and the union enters to try to counteract that power.

A market in which there is a single buyer is called a **monopsony**. A monopsony labor market has one employer. In some parts of the country, managed healthcare organizations are the major employer of healthcare professionals. In some communities, Wal-Mart is the main employer of salespeople. These firms have monopsony power.

A monopsony acts on the buying side of a market in a similar way to a monopoly on the selling side. The firm maximizes profit by hiring the quantity of labor that makes the marginal cost of labor equal to the value of marginal product of labor and by paying the lowest wage rate at which it can attract this quantity of labor.

Figure 18.5 illustrates a monopsony labor market. Like all firms, a monopsony faces a downward-sloping value of marginal product curve, *VMP*, which is its demand for labor curve, *D*—the curve labeled *VMP = D* in the figure.

What is special about monopsony is the marginal cost of labor. For a firm in a competitive labor market, the marginal cost of labor is the wage rate. For a monopsony, the marginal cost of labor exceeds the wage rate. The reason is that being the only buyer in the market, the firm faces an upward-sloping supply of labor curve—the curve *S* in the figure.

To attract one more worker, the monopsony must offer a higher wage rate. But it must pay this higher wage rate to all its workers, so the marginal cost of a worker is the wage rate plus the increased wage bill that arises from paying all the workers the higher wage rate.

The supply curve is now the average cost of labor curve and the relationship between the supply curve and the marginal cost of labor curve, *MCL*, is similar to that between a monopoly's demand curve and marginal revenue curve (see p. 300). The relationship between the supply curve and the *MCL* curve is also similar to that between a firm's average cost curve and marginal cost curve (see pp. 258–259).

To find the profit-maximizing quantity of labor to hire, the monopsony sets the marginal cost of labor equal to the value of marginal product of labor. In Fig. 18.5, this outcome occurs when the firm employs 100 workers.

To hire 100 workers, the firm must pay $10 an hour (on the supply of labor curve). Each worker is paid $10 an hour, but the value of marginal product of labor is $20 an hour, so the firm makes an economic profit of $10 an hour on the marginal worker.

If the labor market in Fig. 18.5 were competitive, the equilibrium wage rate and employment would be determined by the demand and supply curves. The wage rate would be $15 an hour, and 150 workers would be employed. So compared with a competitive labor market, a monopsony pays a lower wage rate and employs fewer workers.

A Union and a Monopsony A union is like a monopoly. If the union (monopoly seller) faces a monopsony buyer, the situation is called **bilateral monopoly**. An example of bilateral monopoly is the Writers Guild of America that represents film, television, and radio

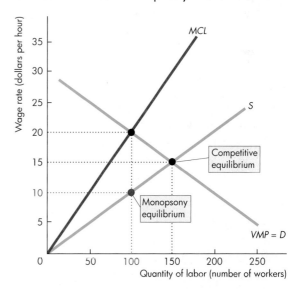

FIGURE 18.5 A Monopsony Labor Market

A monopsony is a market structure in which there is a single buyer. A monopsony in the labor market has a value of marginal product curve *VMP = D*, and faces a labor supply curve *S*. The marginal cost of labor curve is *MCL*. Making the marginal cost of labor equal to the value of marginal product of labor maximizes profit. The monopsony hires 100 hours of labor and pays the lowest wage rate for which that quantity of labor will work—$10 an hour.

MyEconLab Animation

AT **ISSUE**

Monopoly Power for Evil or Good?

The standard view of economists is that monopoly is bad. It prevents resources from being used efficiently, and on any criterion of fairness or equity, monopoly is unfair. It fails to serve the social interest.

We normally think of a monopoly as a big firm that gouges its customers. But a surprising monopoly (and monopsony) has attracted attention—the National Collegiate Athletic Association (NCAA).

Does the NCAA do a good job at efficiently allocating the talents of college athletes and providing those athletes with a fair return for their efforts?

The standard economist's view is that the NCAA doesn't serve the social interest. But there is an opposing view.

Let's look at both sides of this argument.

The **Standard View**

Robert Barro expresses the standard economist view. While acknowledging that the NCAA has boosted the productivity of college sports programs, he says that the NCAA monopoly

- Suppresses financial competition in college sports.

- Restricts scholarships and other payments to college athletes.

- Prevents college basketball players who come from poor families from accumulating wealth during a college career.

- Keeps poor students poor.

Despite doing these bad things, the NCAA manages to convince most people that the bad guys are the colleges that violate NCAA rules by attempting to pay their athletes competitive wages.

An **Opposing View**

Richard B. McKenzie of the University of California, Irvine, and Dwight R. Lee of the University of Georgia, in their book, *In Defense of Monopoly: How Market Power Fosters Creative Production* (University of Michigan Press, 2008), say the NCAA

- Helps its members to cooperate to everyone's benefit.
- Has enabled healthy growth of college athletics over the past 50 years.
- Has generated economic profits for member schools.
- Does not lower student athletes' wages.
- Has stimulated the demand for student athletes and increased their wages and employment opportunities.

Permitting NCAA colleges to pay athletes competitive wages is misguided.

The contenders for best monopoly in America include the Post Office, Microsoft, and the NCAA. And the winner is ... the NCAA.

Robert Barro, "The Best Little Monopoly in America," *BusinessWeek*, December 9, 2002

The Connecticut Huskies celebrate their victory at the 2014 NCAA National Championship

writers, and an employers' alliance that represents CBS, MGM, NBC, and other entertainment companies. Every three years, the Writers Guild and the employers' alliance negotiate a pay deal.

In bilateral monopoly, the outcome is determined by bargaining, which depends on the costs that each party can inflict on the other. The firm can shut down temporarily and lock out its workers, and the workers can shut down the firm by striking. Each party estimates the other's strength and what it will lose if it does not agree to the other's demands.

Usually, an agreement is reached without a strike or a lockout. The threat is usually enough to bring the bargaining parties to an agreement. When a strike or lockout does occur, it is because one party has misjudged the costs each party can inflict on the other. Such an event occurred in November 2007 when the writers and entertainment producers failed to agree on a compensation deal. A 100-day strike followed that ended up costing the entertainment industry an estimated $2 billion.

In the example in Fig. 18.5, if the union and employer are equally strong, and each party knows the strength of the other, they will agree to split the gap between $10 (the wage rate on the supply curve) and $20 (the wage rate on the demand curve) and agree to a wage rate of $15 an hour.

You've now seen that in a monopsony, a union can bargain for a higher wage rate without sacrificing jobs. A similar outcome can arise in a monopsony labor market when a minimum wage law is enforced. Let's look at the effect of a minimum wage.

Monopsony and the Minimum Wage In a competitive labor market, a minimum wage that exceeds the equilibrium wage decreases employment (see Chapter 6, pp. 131–132). In a monopsony labor market, a minimum wage can increase both the wage rate and employment. Let's see how.

Figure 18.6 shows a monopsony labor market without a union. The wage rate is $10 an hour and 100 workers are employed.

A minimum wage law is passed that requires employers to pay at least $15 an hour. The monopsony now faces a perfectly elastic supply of labor at $15 an hour up to 150 workers (along the minimum wage line). To hire more than 150 workers, a wage rate above $15 an hour must be paid (along the supply curve). Because the wage rate is $15 an hour up to 150 workers, so is the marginal cost of labor $15 an hour up to 150 workers. To maximize profit, the monopsony sets the marginal cost of labor equal to the value of marginal product of

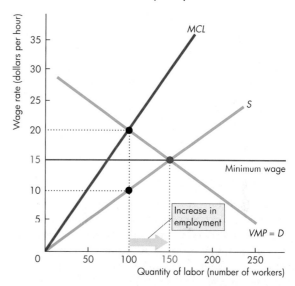

FIGURE 18.6 Minimum Wage Law in Monopsony

In a monopsony labor market, the wage rate is $10 an hour and 100 workers are hired. If a minimum wage law increases the wage rate to $15 an hour, the wage rate rises to this level and employment increases to 150 workers.

MyEconLab Animation and Draw Graph

labor (on the demand curve). That is, the monopsony hires 150 workers and pays $15 an hour. The minimum wage law has succeeded in raising the wage rate and increasing the number of workers employed.

REVIEW QUIZ

1 What determines the amount of labor that households plan to supply?
2 How are the wage rate and employment determined in a competitive labor market?
3 How do labor unions influence wage rates?
4 What is a monopsony and why is a monopsony able to pay a lower wage rate than a firm in a competitive labor market?
5 How is the wage rate determined when a union faces a monopsony?
6 What is the effect of a minimum wage law in a monopsony labor market?

Work these questions in Study Plan 18.3 and get instant feedback. Do a Key Terms Quiz. **MyEconLab**

◆ Capital and Natural Resource Markets

The markets for capital and land can be understood by using the same basic ideas that you've seen when studying a competitive labor market. But markets for nonrenewable natural resources are different. We'll now examine three groups of factor markets:

- Capital rental markets
- Land rental markets
- Nonrenewable natural resource markets

Capital Rental Markets

The demand for capital is derived from the *value of marginal product of capital*. Profit-maximizing firms hire the quantity of capital services that makes the value of marginal product of capital equal to the *rental rate of capital*. The *lower* the rental rate of capital, other things remaining the same, the *greater* is the quantity of capital demanded. The supply of capital responds in the opposite way to the rental rate. The *higher* the rental rate, other things remaining the same, the *greater* is the quantity of capital supplied. The equilibrium rental rate makes the quantity of capital demanded equal to the quantity supplied.

Figure 18.7 illustrates the rental market for tower cranes—capital used to construct high-rise buildings. The value of marginal product and the demand curve is $VMP = D$. The supply curve is S. The equilibrium rental rate is $1,000 per day and 100 tower cranes are rented.

Rent-Versus-Buy Decision Some capital services are obtained in a rental market like the market for tower cranes. And as with tower cranes, many of the world's large airlines rent their airplanes. But not all capital services are obtained in a rental market. Instead, firms buy the capital equipment that they use. You saw in Chapter 10 (pp. 224–225) that the cost of the services of the capital that a firm owns and operates itself is an implicit rental rate that arises from depreciation and interest costs. Firms that buy capital *implicitly* rent the capital to themselves.

The decision to obtain capital services in a rental market rather than buy capital and rent it implicitly is made to minimize cost. The firm compares the cost of explicitly renting the capital and the cost of buying and implicitly renting it. This decision is the same as

FIGURE 18.7   A Rental Market for Capital

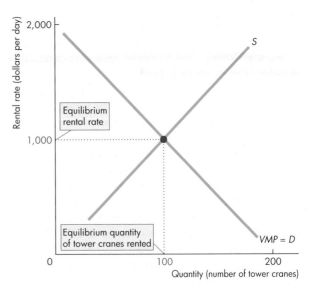

The value of marginal product of tower cranes, *VMP*, determines the demand, *D*, for tower crane rentals. With the supply curve *S*, the equilibrium rental rate is $1,000 a day and 100 cranes are rented.

MyEconLab Animation

the one that a household makes in deciding whether to rent or buy a home.

To make a rent-versus-buy decision, a firm must compare a cost incurred in the *present* with a stream of rental costs incurred over some *future* period. The Mathematical Note (pp. 438–439) explains how to make this comparison by calculating the *present value* of a future amount of money. If the *present value* of the future rental payments of an item of capital equipment exceeds the cost of buying the capital, the firm will buy the equipment. If the *present value* of the future rental payments of an item of capital equipment is less than the cost of buying the capital, the firm will rent (or lease) the equipment.

Land Rental Markets

The demand for land is based on the same factors as the demand for labor and the demand for capital— the *value of marginal product of land*. Profit-maximizing firms rent the quantity of land at which the value of marginal product of land is equal to the *rental rate of land.* The *lower* the rental rate, other things remaining the same, the *greater* is the quantity of land demanded.

But the supply of land is special: Its quantity is fixed, so the quantity supplied cannot be changed by people's decisions. The supply of each particular block of land is perfectly inelastic.

The equilibrium rental rate makes the quantity of land demanded equal to the quantity available. Figure 18.8 illustrates the market for a 10-acre block of land on 42nd Street in New York City. The quantity supplied is fixed and the supply curve is *S*. The value of marginal product and the demand curve is *VMP = D*. The equilibrium rental rate is $1,000 an acre per day.

The rental rate of land is high in New York because the willingness to pay for the services produced by that land is high, which in turn makes the *VMP* of land high. A Big Mac costs more at McDonald's on 42nd Street, New York, than at McDonald's on Jefferson Avenue, St. Louis, but not because the rental rate of land is higher in New York. The rental rate of land is higher in New York because of the greater willingness to pay for a Big Mac (and other goods and services) in New York.

FIGURE 18.8 A Rental Market for Land

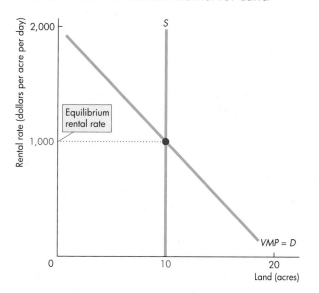

The value of marginal product of a 10-acre block, *VMP*, determines the rental demand, *D*, for this land. With the supply curve *S*, this block rents for $1,000 per acre per day.

————— MyEconLab Animation —————

Nonrenewable Natural Resource Markets

The nonrenewable natural resources are oil, gas, and coal. Burning one of these fuels converts it to energy and other by-products, and the used resource cannot be re-used. The natural resources that we use to make metals are also nonrenewable, but they can be used again, at some cost, by recycling them.

Oil, gas, and coal are traded in global commodity markets. The price of a given grade of crude oil is the same in New York, London, and Singapore. Traders, linked by telephone and the Internet, operate these markets around the clock every day of the year.

Demand and supply determine the prices and the quantities traded in these commodity markets. We'll look at the influences on demand and supply by considering the global market for crude oil.

The Demand for Oil The two key influences on the demand for oil are

1. The *value of marginal product* of oil
2. The expected future price of oil

The value of marginal product of oil is the *fundamental* influence on demand. It works in exactly the same way for a nonrenewable resource as it does for any other factor of production. The greater the quantity of oil used, the smaller is the value of marginal product of oil. Diminishing value of marginal product makes the demand curve slope downward. The lower the price, the greater is the quantity demanded.

The higher the expected future price of oil, the greater is the present demand for oil. The expected future price is a *speculative* influence on demand. Oil in the ground and oil in storage tanks are inventories that can be held or sold. A trader might plan to buy oil to hold now and to sell it later for a profit. Instead of buying oil to hold and sell later, the trader could buy a bond and earn interest. The interest forgone is the opportunity cost of holding the oil. If the price of oil is expected to rise by a bigger percentage than the interest rate, a trader will hold oil and incur the opportunity cost. In this case, the return from holding oil exceeds the return from holding bonds.

The Supply of Oil The three key influences on the supply of oil are

1. The known oil reserves
2. The scale of current oil production facilities
3. The expected future price of oil

Known oil reserves are the oil that has been discovered and can be extracted with today's technology. This quantity increases over time because advances in technology enable ever-less accessible sources to be discovered. The greater the size of known reserves, the greater is the supply of oil. But this influence on supply is small and indirect. It operates by changing the expected distant future price of oil. Even a major new discovery of oil would have a negligible effect on current supply of oil.

The scale of current oil production facilities is the *fundamental* influence on the supply of oil. Producing oil is like any production activity: It is subject to increasing marginal cost. The increasing marginal cost of extracting oil means that the supply curve of oil slopes upward. The higher the price of oil, the greater is the quantity supplied. When new oil wells are sunk or when new faster pumps are installed, the supply of oil increases. When existing wells run dry, the supply of oil decreases. Over time, the factors that increase supply are more powerful than those that decrease supply, so changes in the scale of current oil production facilities increase the supply of oil.

Speculative forces based on expectations about the future price also influence the supply of oil. The *higher* the expected future price of oil, the *smaller* is the present supply of oil. A trader with an oil inventory might plan to sell now or to hold and sell later. You've seen that interest forgone is the opportunity cost of holding the oil. If the price of oil is expected to rise by a bigger percentage than the interest rate, it is profitable to incur the opportunity cost of holding oil rather than selling it immediately.

The Equilibrium Price of Oil

The demand for oil and the supply of oil determine the equilibrium price and quantity traded. Figure 18.9 illustrates the market equilibrium.

The value of marginal product of oil, *VMP*, is the *fundamental determinant of demand*, and the marginal cost of extraction, *MC*, is the *fundamental determinant of supply*. Together, they determine the *market fundamentals price*.

If expectations about the future price are also based on fundamentals, the equilibrium price is the market fundamentals price. But if expectations about the future price of oil depart from what the market fundamentals imply, *speculation* can drive a wedge between the equilibrium price and the market fundamentals price.

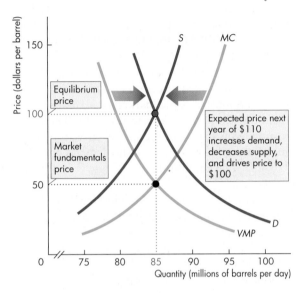

FIGURE 18.9   A Nonrenewable Natural Resource Market

The value of marginal product of a natural resource, *VMP*, and the marginal cost of extraction, *MC*, determine the *market fundamentals* price. Demand, *D*, and supply, *S*, which determine the equilibrium price, are influenced by the expected future price. Speculation can bring a gap between the market fundamentals price and the equilibrium price.

MyEconLab Animation

The Hotelling Principle   Harold Hotelling, an economist at Columbia University, had an incredible idea: Traders expect the price of a nonrenewable natural resource to rise at a rate equal to the interest rate. We call this idea the **Hotelling principle**. Let's see why it is correct.

You've seen that the interest rate is the opportunity cost of holding an oil inventory. If the price of oil is expected to rise at a rate that exceeds the interest rate, it is profitable to hold a bigger inventory. Demand increases, supply decreases, and the price rises. If the interest rate exceeds the rate at which the price of oil is expected to rise, it is not profitable to hold an oil inventory. Demand decreases, supply increases, and the price falls. But if the price of oil is expected to rise at a rate equal to the interest rate, holding an inventory of oil is just as good as holding bonds. Demand and supply don't change and the price does not change. Only when the price of oil is expected to rise at a rate equal to the interest rate is the price at its equilibrium.

ECONOMICS IN ACTION
The World and U.S. Markets for Oil

The world produced 85 million barrels of oil per day in 2013 and the price was steady at around $110 a barrel.

Although the United States imports oil from other countries, most of it comes from close to home and domestic production has increased in recent years. Figure 1 provides the details: Only 12 percent of the U.S. oil supply comes from the Middle East and one third comes from Canada, Mexico, and other Western Hemisphere countries.

Even if the United States produced all its own oil, it would still face a fluctuating global price. U.S. producers would not willingly sell to U.S. buyers for a price below the world price. So energy independence doesn't mean an independent oil price.

The Hotelling principle tells us that we must expect the price of oil to rise at a rate equal to the interest rate. But expecting the price to rise at a rate equal to the interest rate doesn't mean that the price will rise at this rate. As you can see in Fig. 2, the price of oil over the past 50 or so years has not followed the path predicted by the Hotelling principle.

The forces that influence expectations are not well understood. The expected future price of oil depends on its expected future rate of use and the rate of discovery of new sources of supply. One person's expectation about a future price also depends on guesses about other people's expectations. These guesses can change abruptly and become self-reinforcing. When the expected future price of oil changes for whatever

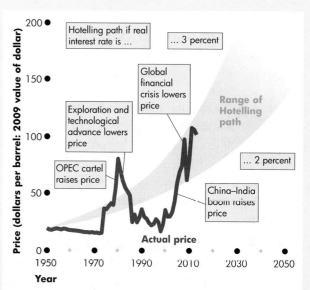

Figure 2 The Price of Oil and Its Hotelling Path
Source of data: U.S. Energy Information Administration.

reason, demand and supply change, and so does the price. Prices in speculative markets are always volatile.

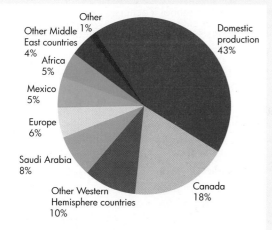

Figure 1 Our Diverse Sources of Oil
Source of data: U.S. Energy Information Administration.

◆ REVIEW QUIZ

1 What determines demand and supply in rental markets for capital and land?
2 What determines the demand for a nonrenewable natural resource?
3 What determines the supply of a nonrenewable natural resource?
4 What is the market fundamentals price and how might it differ from the equilibrium price?
5 Explain the Hotelling principle.

Work these questions in Study Plan 18.4 and get instant feedback. Do a Key Terms Quiz.   MyEconLab

◆ *Economics in the News* on pp. 436–437 contrasts the outcomes in competitive and union labor markets for teachers.

The next chapter looks more closely at the distribution of income and its trends. The chapter also looks at the efforts by governments to redistribute income and modify the market outcome.

Labor Markets in Action

Comparing Teacher Salaries by School Type

Illinois Network of Charter Schools, National Center on School Choice, Vanderbilt University, and journalgazette.net

Reported on the Illinois Network of Charter Schools' web site (http://incschools.org/), charter school teachers in Illinois with 1 to 3 years experience earn $44,500 on average. That is $9,500 less than the average salary for similarly experienced traditional public school teachers. And the difference grows. For teachers with 10 to 12 years experience, a charter school teacher earns an average of $56,600 per year while a traditional public school teacher earns $81,800 per year—a difference of $25,200 per year or 45 percent of a charter school teacher's pay.

Research by David Stuit and Thomas M. Smith of the National Center on School Choice at Vanderbilt Univer sity shows that teacher turnover rates at charter schools substantially exceed those at traditional public schools. Stuit and Smith found that the odds of a charter school teacher leaving to take a job outside teaching were 130 percent greater than those of a traditional public school teacher. And the odds of a charter school teacher leaving to take a job in another school were 76 percent greater.

Because charter school teachers are more likely to quit than are traditional public school teachers, the average years of teaching experience is less in charter schools than in public schools.

Charter school leaders interviewed by journalgazette.net (of Fort Wayne, Indiana) say that while restricted budgets make it impossible to match traditional public school salaries, there is a supply of teachers "drawn to charters out of an appreciation of their mission, a love for the kids they serve, and a desire for autonomy not granted in tra-ditional public school environments."

Most charter schools hire non-union teachers and are free from many of the restrictions arising from teachers' unions and regulation.

MyEconLab More Economics in the News

ESSENCE OF THE STORY

- In Illinois, experienced charter school teachers earn an average of $56,600 per year and traditional public school teachers earn an aver-age of $81,800 per year, a gap of $25,200 per year.

- Charter schools have substantially higher teacher turnover rates than traditional public schools.

- Charter schools have smaller budgets than traditional public schools.

- Charter school teachers have less experience than public school teachers.

- Charter school teachers value greater autonomy.

- Most charter schools do not have teachers' unions.

ECONOMIC ANALYSIS

- Teachers in charter schools are paid much lower salaries (wage rates), on average, than teachers in traditional public schools for three main reasons:
  1. Charter school teachers are less experienced.
  2. Charter schools have tighter budgets than traditional public schools.
  3. Charter school teachers are not (usually) unionized.

- Charter school teachers are, on average, less experienced than public school teachers, so their marginal product is less than that of traditional public school teachers, which means that their *VMP* is lower and the demand for their services is reduced.

- Because charter schools have tighter budgets than public schools, the market values the services of charter school teachers at a lower (implicit) price, which further lowers their *VMP* and reduces the charter schools' demand for teachers.

- Some teachers say that they value the freedom and autonomy that a charter school gives them. This preference for working in a charter school increases the supply of charter school teachers (relative to what it would be without the autonomy.)

- The combination of a reduced demand and greater supply lowers the equilibrium wage rate of charter school teachers. Figure 1 illustrates.

- If teachers in charter schools had the same experience as those in traditional public schools and if charter school budgets were as big as traditional public school budgets, the charter schools' demand curve for teachers would be D_P.

- If charter school teachers didn't have the autonomy they enjoy, the supply curve of charter school teachers would be S_P. The equilibrium wage rate would be $70,000 per year. (This wage rate is an assumption.)

- The factors discussed above decrease demand to D_C, increase supply to S_C, and lower the equilibrium wage rate to $60,000 per year.

- The fact that traditional public school teachers are unionized and most charter school teachers are not makes the wage gap even bigger.

- In Fig. 2, the teachers' union at traditional public schools boosts the demand for teachers by lobbying for bigger school budgets and the union restricts the supply of teachers by raising qualification requirements.

- The demand for public school teachers increases from its competitive level, D_P, to D_U and the supply decreases

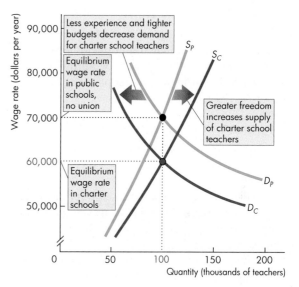

Figure 1 The Market for Charter School Teachers

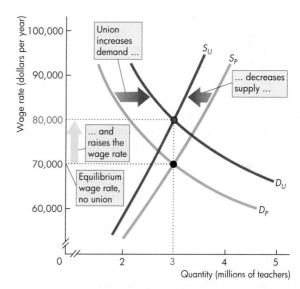

Figure 2 The Market for Unionized Public School Teachers

from its competitive level, S_P, to S_U. The equilibrium wage rate rises to $80,000 per year.

- When a traditional public school is replaced by a charter school, the teachers who remain in the charter school take a very large wage cut.

- The wage cut explains the higher teacher turnover rate of charter schools. The wage cut is too big for some teachers, so they search for an alternative better paying job and quit teaching.

437

MATHEMATICAL NOTE
Present Value and Discounting

Rent-Versus-Buy Decision

To decide whether to rent an item of capital equipment or to buy the capital and implicitly rent it, a firm must compare the present expenditure on the capital with the future rental cost of the capital.

Comparing Current and Future Dollars

To compare a present expenditure with a future expenditure, we convert the future expenditure to its "present value."

The present value of a future amount of money is the amount that, if invested today, will grow to be as large as that future amount when the interest that it will earn is taken into account.

So the present value of a future amount of money is smaller than the future amount. The calculation that we use to convert a future amount of money to its present value is called discounting.

The easiest way to understand discounting and present value is to first consider its opposite: How a present value grows to a future amount of money because of *compound interest*.

Compound Interest

Compound interest is the interest on an initial investment plus the interest on the interest that the investment has previously earned. Because of compound interest, a present amount of money (a present value) grows into a larger future amount. The future amount is equal to the present amount (present value) plus the interest it will earn in the future. That is,

Future amount = Present value + Interest income.

The interest in the first year is equal to the present value multiplied by the interest rate, r, so

Amount after 1 year = Present value + (r × Present value).

or

Amount after 1 year = Present value × $(1 + r)$.

If you invest $100 today and the interest rate is 10 percent a year ($r = 0.1$), 1 year from today you will have $110—the original $100 plus $10 interest.

Check that the above formula delivers that answer:

$$\$100 \times 1.1 = \$110.$$

If you leave this $110 invested to earn 10 percent during a second year, at the end of that year you will have

Amount after 2 years = Present value × $(1 + r)^2$.

With the numbers of the previous example, you invest $100 today at an interest rate of 10 percent a year ($r = 0.1$). After 1 year, you will have $110—the original $100 plus $10 interest. And after 2 years, you will have $121. In the second year, you earned $10 on your initial $100 plus $1 on the $10 interest that you earned in the first year.

Check that the above formula delivers that answer:

$$\$100 \times (1.1)^2 = \$100 \times 1.21 = \$121.$$

If you leave your $100 invested for n years, it will grow to

Amount after n years = Present value × $(1 + r)^n$.

With an interest rate of 10 percent a year, your $100 will grow to $195 after 7 years ($n = 7$)—almost double the present value of $100.

Discounting a Future Amount

We have just calculated future amounts 1 year, 2 years, and n years in the future, knowing the present value and the interest rate. To calculate the present value of these future amounts, we just work backward.

To find the present value of an amount 1 year in the future, we divide the future amount by $(1 + r)$.

That is,

$$\text{Present value} = \frac{\text{Amount of money one year in future}}{(1 + r)}.$$

Let's check that we can use the present value formula by calculating the present value of $110 1 year from now when the interest rate is 10 percent a year.

You'll be able to guess that the answer is $100 because we just calculated that $100 invested today at 10 percent a year becomes $110 in one year. So the present value of $110 to be received 1 year from today is $100. But let's use the formula. Putting the numbers into the above formula, we have

$$\text{Present value} = \frac{\$110}{(1 + 0.1)}$$
$$= \frac{\$110}{1.1} = \$100.$$

To calculate the present value of an amount of money 2 years in the future, we use the formula:

$$\text{Present value} = \frac{\text{Amount of money two years in future}}{(1 + r)^2}$$

Use this formula to calculate the present value of $121 to be received 2 years from now at an interest rate of 10 percent a year. With these numbers, the formula gives

$$\text{Present value} = \frac{\$121}{(1 + 0.1)^2}$$
$$= \frac{\$121}{(1.1)^2}$$
$$= \frac{\$121}{1.21}$$
$$= \$100.$$

We can calculate the present value of an amount of money n years in the future by using the general formula

$$\text{Present value} = \frac{\text{Amount of money } n \text{ years in future}}{(1 + r)^n}$$

For example, if the interest rate is 10 percent a year, $100 to be received 10 years from now has a present value of $38.55. That is, if $38.55 is invested today at 10 percent a year it will accumulate to $100 in 10 years.

Present Value of a Sequence of Future Amounts

You've seen how to calculate the present value of an amount of money to be received 1 year, 2 years, and n years in the future. Most practical applications of present value calculate the present value of a sequence of future amounts of money that are spread over several years. An airline's payment of rent for the lease of airplanes is an example.

To calculate the present value of a sequence of amounts over several years, we use the formula you have learned and apply it to each year. We then sum the present values for all the years to find the present value of the sequence of amounts.

For example, suppose that a firm expects to pay $100 a year for each of the next 5 years and the interest rate is 10 percent a year ($r = 0.1$). The present value (PV) of these five payments of $100 each is calculated by using the following formula:

$$PV = \frac{\$100}{1.1} + \frac{\$100}{1.1^2} + \frac{\$100}{1.1^3} + \frac{\$100}{1.1^4} + \frac{\$100}{1.1^5},$$

which equals

$$PV = \$90.91 + \$82.64 + \$75.13 + \$68.30 + \$62.09$$
$$= \$379.07.$$

You can see that the firm pays $500 over 5 years. But because the money is paid in the future, it is not worth $500 today. Its present value is only $379.07. And the farther in the future the money is paid, the smaller is its present value. The $100 paid 1 year in the future is worth $90.91 today, but the $100 paid 5 years in the future is worth only $62.09 today.

The Decision

If this firm could lease a machine for 5 years at $100 a year or buy the machine for $500, it would jump at leasing. Only if the firm could buy the machine for less than $379.07 would it want to buy.

Many personal and business decisions turn on calculations like the one you've just made. A decision to buy or rent an apartment, to buy or lease a car, and to pay off a student loan or let the loan run another year can all be made using the above calculation.

SUMMARY

Key Points

The Anatomy of Factor Markets (p. 420)

■ The factor markets are job markets for labor; rental markets (often implicit rental markets) for capital and land; and global commodity markets for nonrenewable natural resources.

■ The services of entrepreneurs are not traded on a factor market.

Working Problem 1 will give you a better understanding of the anatomy of factor markets.

The Demand for a Factor of Production (pp. 421–423)

■ The value of marginal product determines the demand for a factor of production.

■ The value of marginal product decreases as the quantity of the factor employed increases.

■ The firm employs the quantity of each factor of production that makes the value of marginal product equal to the factor price.

Working Problems 2 to 6 will give you a better understanding of the demand for a factor of production.

Labor Markets (pp. 424–431)

■ The value of marginal product of labor determines the demand for labor. A rise in the wage rate brings a decrease in the quantity demanded.

■ The quantity of labor supplied depends on the wage rate. At low wage rates, a rise in the wage rate increases the quantity supplied. Beyond a high enough wage rate, a rise in the wage rate decreases the quantity supplied—the supply curve eventually bends backward.

■ Demand and supply determine the wage rate in a competitive labor market.

■ A labor union can raise the wage rate by restricting the supply or increasing the demand for labor.

■ A monopsony can lower the wage rate below the competitive level.

■ A union or a minimum wage in a monopsony labor market can raise the wage rate without a fall in employment.

Working Problems 7 to 9 will give you a better understanding of labor markets.

Capital and Natural Resource Markets (pp. 432–435)

■ The value of marginal product of capital (and land) determines the demand for capital (and land).

■ Firms make a rent-versus-buy decision by choosing the option that minimizes cost.

■ The supply of land is inelastic and the demand for land determines the rental rate.

■ The demand for a nonrenewable natural resource depends on the value of marginal product and on the expected future price.

■ The supply of a nonrenewable natural resource depends on the known reserves, the cost of extraction, and the expected future price.

■ The price of nonrenewable natural resources can differ from the market fundamentals price because of speculation based on expectations about the future price.

■ The price of a nonrenewable natural resource is expected to rise at a rate equal to the interest rate.

Working Problem 10 will give you a better understanding of capital and natural resource markets.

Key Terms

MyEconLab Key Terms Quiz

Bilateral monopoly, 429
Derived demand, 421
Hotelling principle, 434

Labor union, 428
Monopsony, 429

Nonrenewable natural
    resources, 420
Value of marginal product, 421

WORKED PROBLEM

MyEconLab   You can work this Problem in Chapter 18 Study Plan.

Tom hires workers to pack the tomatoes he grows. The market for tomatoes is perfectly competitive, and the price of tomatoes is $2 a box. The labor market is competitive, and the market wage rate is $16 an hour. The table shows the workers' total product schedule.

Number of workers	Quantity produced (boxes packed per hour)
1	14
2	26
3	36
4	44
5	50

Questions

1. Calculate the marginal product of the third worker hired and that worker's value of marginal product.
2. How many workers will Tom hire to maximize profit and what will the workers produce?
3. If the market wage rate rises to $20 an hour, how many workers will Tom hire?

Solutions

1. Marginal product (*MP*) of the 3rd worker equals the total product (*TP*) of 3 workers (36 boxes) minus the *TP* of 2 workers (26 boxes), so the *MP* of the 3rd worker is 10 boxes of tomatoes.

   The 3rd worker's value of marginal product (*VMP*) equals the 3rd worker's *MP* (10 boxes of tomatoes an hour) multiplied by the price of a box of tomatoes ($2), so the *VMP* of the 3rd worker equals $20 an hour.

   The figure shows the *VMP* of each worker.

Key Point: The value of marginal product of labor is the marginal product of labor multiplied by the market price of the good produced by the labor.

2. Tom maximizes profit by hiring the number of workers at which *VMP* equals the market wage rate. The table in the next column shows the calculations.

   The market wage rate is $16 an hour, so Tom hires the number of workers at which the *VMP* equals $16 an hour. You can see in the table that *VMP* equal $16 an hour when Tom hires the 4th worker. So Tom maximizes profit when he hires

Number of workers	TP (boxes per hour)	MP (boxes per worker)	VMP (dollars per hour)
1	14		
		……12	24
2	26		
		……10	20
3	36		
		…… 8	16
4	44		
		…… 6	12
5	50		

4 workers who produce 44 boxes of tomatoes. Tom sells the tomatoes for $88 and pays the wages of $64, so his profit is $24 an hour. The figure shows this equality.

Key Point: The firm maximizes profit by hiring the quantity of labor at which the value of marginal product of labor equals the market wage rate.

3. If the market wage rate rises to $20 an hour, the *VMP* of labor does not change and remains the same as in the table above. But now with a market wage rate of $20 an hour, Tom hires fewer workers. *VMP* equals $20 an hour when Tom hire the 3rd worker. So Tom cuts the number of workers to 3.

Key Point: When the market wage rate rises, the firm maximizes profit by hiring fewer workers.

Key Figure

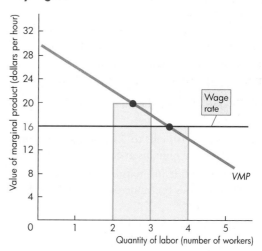

MyEconLab Interactive Animation

STUDY PLAN PROBLEMS AND APPLICATIONS

MyEconLab   You can work Problems 1 to 10 in Chapter 18 Study Plan and get instant feedback.

The Anatomy of Factor Markets (Study Plan 18.1)

1. Tim is opening a new online store. He plans to hire two workers at $10 an hour. Tim is also considering buying or leasing some new computers. The purchase price of a computer is $900 and after three years it is worthless. The annual cost of leasing a computer is $450.
   a. In which factor markets does Tim operate?
   b. What is the price of the capital equipment and the rental rate of capital?

The Demand for a Factor of Production

(Study Plan 18.2)

Use the following data to work Problems 2 to 6. Wanda's is a fish store that hires students to pack the fish. Students can pack the following amounts of fish:

Number of students	Quantity of fish packed (pounds)
1	20
2	50
3	90
4	120
5	145
6	165
7	180
8	190

The fish market is competitive and the price of fish is 50¢ a pound. The market for packers is competitive and their market wage rate is $7.50 an hour.

2. Calculate the value of marginal product of labor and draw the value of marginal product curve.
3. a. Find Wanda's demand for labor curve.
   b. How many students does Wanda's employ?

Use the following additional data to work Problems 4 and 5.

The market price of fish falls to 33.33¢ a pound, but the packers' wage rate remains at $7.50 an hour.

4. How does the students' marginal product change? How does the value of marginal product of labor change?
5. How does Wanda's demand for labor change? What happens to the number of students that Wanda employs?

6. At Wanda's fish store, packers' wages increase to $10 an hour, but the price of fish remains at 50¢ a pound.
   a. What happens to the value of marginal product of labor?
   b. What happens to Wanda's demand for labor curve?
   c. How many students does Wanda's employ?

Labor Markets (Study Plan 18.3)

Use the following news clip to work Problems 7 to 9.

In Modern Rarity, Workers Form Union at Small Chain

In New York's low-income neighborhoods, labor unions have virtually no presence. But after a year-long struggle, 95 workers at a chain of 10 sneaker stores have formed a union. After months of negotiations, the two sides signed a three-year contract that sets the wage rate at $7.25 an hour.
    Source: *The New York Times*, February 5, 2006
7. Why are labor unions scarce in New York's low-income neighborhoods?
8. Who wins from this union contract? Who loses?
9. How can this union try to change the demand for labor?

Capital and Natural Resource Markets

(Study Plan 18.4)

10. **Land Prices Reflect High Commodity Prices**
    As their family grows, the Steens are finding it more difficult for the next generation to stay in ranching. "The problem is they don't create any more land," Steen said. As the prices for cattle, corn, and other commodities climb, so does the value of land in South Dakota.
        Source: *Rapid City Journal*, January 30, 2012
    a. Why does the price of land in South Dakota keep rising? In your answer include a discussion of the demand for and supply of land.
    b. Use a graph to show why the price of land in South Dakota increased over the past decade.
    c. Is the supply of land in South Dakota perfectly inelastic?

◆ ADDITIONAL PROBLEMS AND APPLICATIONS

MyEconLab   You can work these problems in MyEconLab if assigned by your instructor.

The Anatomy of Factor Markets

11. Venus is opening a tennis school. She plans to hire a marketing graduate to promote and manage the school at $20 an hour. Venus is also considering buying or leasing a new tennis ball machine. The purchase price of the machine is $1,000 and after three years it is worthless. The annual cost of leasing the machine is $500.
    a. In which factor markets does Venus operate?
    b. What is the price of the capital equipment and the rental rate of capital?

The Demand for a Factor of Production

Use the following data to work Problems 12 to 15. Kaiser's Ice Cream Parlor hires workers to produce milk shakes. The market for milk shakes is perfectly competitive, and the price of a milk shake is $4. The labor market is competitive, and the wage rate is $40 a day. The table shows the workers' total product schedule.

Number of workers	Quantity produced (milk shakes per day)
1	7
2	21
3	33
4	43
5	51
6	55

12. Calculate the marginal product of hiring the fourth worker and the fourth worker's value of marginal product.

13. How many workers will Kaiser's hire to maximize its profit and how many milk shakes a day will Kaiser's produce?

14. If the price of a milk shake rises to $5, how many workers will Kaiser's hire?

15. Kaiser's installs a new machine for making milk shakes that increases the productivity of workers by 50 percent. If the price of a milk shake remains at $4 and the wage rises to $48 a day, how many workers does Kaiser's hire?

16. **Detroit Oil Refinery Expansion Approved**
    Marathon Oil Saturday started work on a $1.9 billion expansion of its gasoline refinery in Detroit. Marathon will employ 800 construction workers and add 135 permanent jobs to the existing 480 workers at the refinery.
    Source: *United Press International*, June 21, 2008
    a. Explain how rising gasoline prices influence the market for refinery labor.
    b. Draw a graph to illustrate the effects of rising gasoline prices on the market for refinery labor.

Labor Markets

Use the following news clip to work Problems 17 and 18.

Miner Sacks 17,000 Workers Over Pay Dispute
Impala Platinum has sacked 17,000 South African miners at its Rustenburg mine because they took part in an illegal strike. The miners refused to have their union negotiate in the two-week pay dispute with the world's second largest platinum producer. Mining provides a quarter of all jobs in Rustenburg.
Source: abc.com.au, February 3, 2012

17. How would the wage rate and employment for the Rustenburg miners be determined in a competitive market?

18. a. Explain how it is possible that the mine workers were being paid less than the wage that would be paid in a competitive labor market.
    b. What would be the effect of a minimum wage law in the market for miners?

Use the following news clip to work Problems 19 to 22.

The New War over Wal-Mart
Today, Wal-Mart employs more people—1.7 million—than any other private employer in the world. With size comes power: Wal-Mart's prices are lower and United Food and Commercial Workers International Union argues that Wal-Mart's wages are also lower than its competitors. Last year, the workers at a Canadian outlet joined the union and Wal-Mart immediately closed the outlet. But does Wal-Mart behave any worse than its competitors? When it comes to payroll, Wal-Mart's median hourly wage tracks the national median wage for general retail jobs.
Source: *The Atlantic*, June 2006

19. a. Assuming that Wal-Mart has market power in a labor market, explain how the firm could use that market power in setting wages.

b. Draw a graph to illustrate how Wal-Mart might use labor market power to set wages.

20. a. Explain how a union of Wal-Mart's employees would attempt to counteract Wal-Mart's wage offers (a bilateral monopoly).

b. Explain the response by the Canadian Wal-Mart to the unionization of employees.

21. Based upon evidence presented in this article, does Wal-Mart function as a monopsony in labor markets, or is the market for retail labor more competitive? Explain.

22. If the market for retail labor is competitive, explain the potential effect of a union on the wage rates. Draw a graph to illustrate your answer.

Capital and Natural Resource Markets

23. New technology has allowed oil to be pumped from much deeper offshore oil fields than before. For example, 28 deep ocean rigs operate in the deep waters of the Gulf of Mexico.

a. What effect do you think deep ocean sources have had on the world oil price?

b. Who will benefit from drilling for oil in the Gulf of Mexico? Explain your answer.

24. Water is a natural resource that is plentiful in Canada but not plentiful in Arizona.

a. If Canadians start to export bulk water to Arizona, what do you predict will be the effect on the price of bulk water?

b. Will Canada eventually run out of water?

c. Do you think the Hotelling principle applies to Canada's water? Explain why or why not.

25. **Gas Prices Create Land Rush**

There is a land rush going on across Pennsylvania, but buyers aren't interested in the land itself. Buyers are interested in what lies beneath the earth's surface—mineral rights to natural gas deposits. Record high natural gas prices have pushed up drilling activity across the state, but drilling companies have discovered a new technology that will enable deep gas-bearing shale to be exploited. Development companies, drilling companies, and speculators have been trying to lease mineral rights from landowners. The new drilling techniques might recover about 10 percent of those reserves, and that would ring up at a value of $1 trillion.

Source: *Erie Times-News*, June 15, 2008

a. Explain why the demand for land in Pennsylvania has increased.

b. If companies are responding to the higher prices for natural gas by drilling right now wherever they can, what does that imply about their assumptions about the future price of natural gas in relation to current interest rates?

c. What could cause the price of natural gas to fall in the future?

Economics in the News

26. After you have studied *Economics in the News* on pp. 436–437, answer the following questions.

a. Is the average difference in the salaries of charter school and regular public school teachers greater or smaller than the difference at the top end of the pay scales?

b. What are the influences on the demand for the highest-paid teachers that explain their high wage rates?

c. What are the influences on the supply of the highest-paid teachers that explain their high wage rates?

d. Draw a graph of the market for the highest-paid teachers.

e. If all charter school teachers became unionized, how would the market for these teachers change? Illustrate your answer with a graph.

f. How would you expect unionization of charter school teachers to influence the unionized market for regular public school teachers?

g. If the public school systems were able to break the teachers' union, how would the market for regular public school teachers change? Illustrate your answer with a graph.

Mathematical Note

27. Keshia is opening a new bookkeeping service. She is considering buying or leasing some new laptop computers. The purchase price of a laptop is $1,500 and after three years it is worthless. The annual lease rate is $550 per laptop. The value of marginal product of one laptop is $700 a year. The value of marginal product of a second laptop is $625 a year. The value of marginal product of a third laptop is $575 a year. And the value of marginal product of a fourth laptop is $500 a year.

a. How many laptops will Keshia lease or buy?

b. If the interest rate is 4 percent a year, will Keshia lease or buy her laptops?

c. If the interest rate is 6 percent a year, will Keshia lease or buy her laptops?

19 ECONOMIC INEQUALITY

After studying this chapter, you will be able to:

◆ Describe the distributions of income and wealth and the trends in economic inequality in the United States

◆ Describe the distribution of income and the trends in inequality in selected countries and the world

◆ Explain the sources of economic inequality and its trends

◆ Describe the scale of government income redistribution in the United States

When Apple hired Angela Ahrendts to manage its retail stores, it paid her a signing bonus worth $67 million. Other top-earning women include Marissa Mayer at Yahoo! and Sheryl Sandberg at Facebook. At the other end of the pay scale are the thousands of fast-food workers calling for a rise in the minimum wage. Why do a few people get enormous incomes, while most struggle to get by on a few dollars an hour? In this chapter, we study economic inequality—its extent, its sources, and the things governments do to make it less extreme. In *Economics in the News* at the end of the chapter, we return to Angela Ahrendts and see why Apple thinks she is worth so much.

445

◆ Economic Inequality in the United States

The most commonly used measure of economic inequality is the distribution of annual income. The Census Bureau defines income as **money income**, which equals *market income* plus cash payments to households by government. **Market income** equals wages, interest, rent, and profit earned in factor markets, before paying income taxes.

The Distribution of Income

Figure 19.1 shows the distribution of annual income across the 122 million households in the United States in 2012. Note that the *x*-axis measures household money income and the *y*-axis measures the percentage of households.

The most common household income is called the *mode* income. In 2012, almost 6 percent of the households had incomes of between $15,000 and $20,000. The value of $15,000 marked on the figure is an estimate.

The middle level of household income in 2012, called the *median* income, was $51,017. Fifty percent of households have an income that exceeds the median and fifty percent have an income below the median.

The average household money income in 2012, called the *mean* income, was $71,274. This number equals total household income, about $8.7 trillion, divided by the 122 million households. You can see in Fig. 19.1 that the mode is less than the median and that the median is less than the mean. This feature of the distribution of income tells us that there are more households with low incomes than with high incomes. It also tells us that some of the high incomes are very high.

The income distribution in Fig. 19.1 is called a *positively skewed* distribution, which means that it has a long tail of high values. This distribution contrasts with the bell that describes the distribution of people's heights. In a bell-shaped distribution, the mean, median, and mode are all equal.

Another way of looking at the distribution of income is to measure the percentage of total income received by each given percentage of households. Data are reported for five groups—called *quintiles* or fifth shares—each consisting of 20 percent of households.

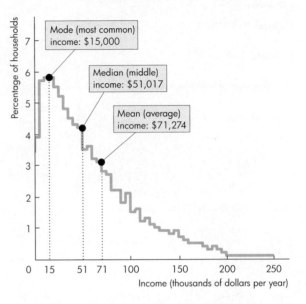

FIGURE 19.1   The Distribution of Income in the United States in 2012

The distribution of income is positively skewed. The mode (most common) income is less than the median (middle) income, which in turn is less than the mean (average) income. The distribution shown here ends at $250,000 because data above that level are not available, but the distribution goes up to several million dollars a year.

Source of data: DeNavas-Walt, Carmen, Bernadette D. Proctor, and Jessica C. Smith, U.S. Census Bureau, Current Population Reports, P60–245, Income, Poverty, and Health Insurance Coverage in the United States: 2012, U.S. Government Printing Office, Washington, DC, 2013.

——— MyEconLab Animation ———

Figure 19.2 shows the distribution based on these shares in 2012. The poorest 20 percent of households received 3.2 percent of total income; the second poorest 20 percent received 8.3 percent of total income; the middle 20 percent received 14.4 percent of total income; the next highest 20 percent received 23.0 percent of total income; and the highest 20 percent received 51.1 percent of total income.

The distribution of income in Fig. 19.1 and the quintile shares in Fig. 19.2 tell us that income is distributed unequally. But we need a way of comparing the distribution of income in different periods and using different measures. A clever graphical tool called the *Lorenz curve* enables us to make such comparisons.

FIGURE 19.2   U.S. Quintile Shares in 2012

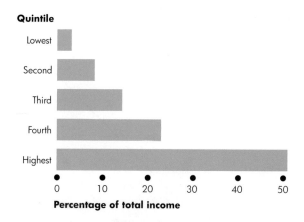

Households (quintile)	Income (percentage of total income)
Lowest	3.2
Second	8.3
Third	14.4
Fourth	23.0
Highest	51.1

In 2012, the lowest quintile of households received 3.2 percent of total income; the second quintile received 8.3 percent; the third quintile received 14.4 percent; the fourth quintile received 23.0 percent; and the highest quintile received 51.1 percent.

Source of data: See Fig. 19.1.

———— MyEconLab Animation ————

The Income Lorenz Curve

The income **Lorenz curve** graphs the cumulative percentage of income against the cumulative percentage of households. Figure 19.3 shows the income Lorenz curve using the quintile shares from Fig. 19.2. The table shows the percentage of income of each quintile group. For example, row *A* tells us that the lowest quintile of households receives 3.2 percent of total income. The table also shows the *cumulative* percentages of households and income. For example, row *B* tells us that the lowest two quintiles (lowest 40 percent) of households receive 11.5 percent of total income (3.2 percent for the lowest quintile plus 8.3 percent for the next lowest).

FIGURE 19.3   The Income Lorenz Curve in 2012

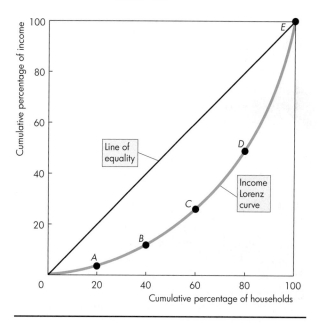

	Households		Income	
Quintile		Cumulative percentage	Percentage	Cumulative percentage
A	Lowest	20	3.2	3.2
B	Second	40	8.3	11.5
C	Third	60	14.4	25.9
D	Fourth	80	23.0	48.9
E	Highest	100	51.1	100.0

The cumulative percentage of income is graphed against the cumulative percentage of households. Points *A* through *E* on the Lorenz curve correspond to the rows of the table. If incomes were distributed equally, each quintile of households would receive 20 percent of total income and the Lorenz curve would fall along the line of equality. The Lorenz curve shows that income is unequally distributed.

Source of data: See Fig. 19.1.

———— MyEconLab Animation and Draw Graph ————

The Lorenz curve provides a direct visual clue about the degree of income inequality by comparing it with the line of equality. This line, identified in Fig. 19.3, shows what the Lorenz curve would be if everyone had the same level of income.

If income were distributed equally across all the households, each quintile would receive 20 percent of total income and the cumulative percentages of income received would equal the cumulative percentages of households, so the Lorenz curve would be the straight line labeled "Line of equality."

The actual distribution of income shown by the curve labeled "Income Lorenz curve" can be compared with the line of equality. The closer the Lorenz curve is to the line of equality, the more equal is the distribution of income.

The Distribution of Wealth

The distribution of wealth provides another way of measuring economic inequality. A household's **wealth** is the value of the things that it owns at a *point in time*. In contrast, income is the amount that the household receives over a given *period of time*.

Figure 19.4 shows the Lorenz curve for wealth in the United States in 2010 (the most recent year for which we have wealth distribution data). The median household wealth in 2010 was $77,300. Wealth is extremely unequally distributed, and for this reason, the data are grouped by five unequal groups of households. The poorest 25 percent of households have no wealth and the next poorest 25 percent own only 1.1 percent of total wealth (row B' in the table in Fig. 19.4). Even the third richest 25 percent own only 8.5 percent of total wealth. The richest 25 percent of households own 90.4 percent of wealth, and within this wealthiest group the richest 10 percent of households own 74.5 percent of total wealth.

Figure 19.4 shows the income Lorenz curve (from Fig. 19.3) alongside the wealth Lorenz curve. You can see that the Lorenz curve for wealth is much farther away from the line of equality than is the Lorenz curve for income, which means that the distribution of wealth is much more unequal than the distribution of income.

Wealth or Income?

We've seen that wealth is much more unequally distributed than is income. Which distribution provides the better description of the degree of inequality? To answer this question, we need to think about the connection between wealth and income.

Wealth is a stock of assets, and income is the flow of earnings that results from the stock of wealth. Suppose that a person owns assets worth

FIGURE 19.4   Lorenz Curves for Income and Wealth

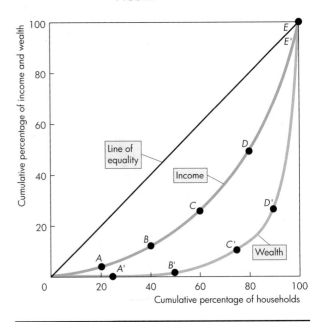

Households			Wealth		
	Percentage	Cumulative percentage		Percentage	Cumulative percentage
A'	Lowest 25	25		0.0	0.0
B'	Next 25	50		1.1	1.1
C'	Next 25	75		8.5	9.6
D'	Next 15	90		15.9	25.5
E'	Highest 10	100		74.5	100.0

The cumulative percentage of wealth is graphed against the cumulative percentage of households. Points A' through E' on the Lorenz curve for wealth correspond to the rows of the table. By comparing the Lorenz curves for income and wealth, we can see that wealth is distributed much more unequally than is income.

Sources of data: For the income distribution data, see Fig. 19.1. The wealth distribution data are calculated from the Federal Reserve Board's Survey of Consumer Finances for 2010, reported in Jesse Bricker, Arthur B. Kennickell, Kevin B. Moore, and John Sabelhaus, with assistance from Samuel Ackerman, Robert Argento, Gerhard Fries, and Richard A. Windle, "Changes in U.S. Family Finances from 2007 to 2010: Evidence from the Survey of Consumer Finances," *Federal Reserve Bulletin*, June 2012, Vol. 98, No. 2.

MyEconLab Animation

$1 million—has a wealth of $1 million. If the rate of return on assets is 5 percent a year, then this person receives an income of $50,000 a year from those assets. We can describe this person's economic condition by using either the wealth of $1 million or the income of $50,000. When the rate of return is 5 percent a year, $1 million of wealth equals $50,000 of income in perpetuity. Wealth and income are just different ways of looking at the same thing.

But in Fig. 19.4, the distribution of wealth is more unequal than the distribution of income. Why? It is because the wealth data do not include the value of human capital, while the income data measure income from all wealth, including human capital.

Think about Lee and Peter, two people with equal income and equal wealth. Lee's wealth is human capital and his entire income is from employment. Peter's wealth is in the form of investments in stocks and bonds and his entire income is from these investments.

When a Census Bureau agent interviews Lee and Peter in a national income and wealth survey, their incomes are recorded as being equal, but Lee's wealth is recorded as zero, while Peter's wealth is recorded as the value of his investments. Peter looks vastly more wealthy than Lee in the survey data.

Because the national survey of wealth excludes human capital, the income distribution is a more accurate measure of economic inequality than the wealth distribution.

Annual or Lifetime Income and Wealth?

A typical household's income changes over its life cycle. Income starts out low, grows to a peak when the household's workers reach retirement age, and then falls after retirement. Also, a typical household's wealth changes over time. Like income, it starts out low, grows to a peak at the point of retirement, and falls after retirement.

Think about three households with identical lifetime incomes, one young, one middle-aged, and one retired. The middle-aged household has the highest income and wealth, the retired household has the lowest, and the young household falls in the middle. The distributions of annual income and wealth in a given year are unequal, but the distributions of lifetime income and wealth are equal.

The data on inequality share the bias that you've just seen. Inequality in annual income and wealth data overstates lifetime inequality because households are at different stages in their life cycles.

Trends in Inequality

To see trends in the income distribution, we use a measure called the Gini ratio. The **Gini ratio** equals the area between the Lorenz curve and the line of equality divided by the entire area beneath the line of equality. The more the Lorenz curve bows away from the line of equality, the larger is the Gini ratio. And the larger the Gini ratio, the greater is the degree of income inequality. If income is equally distributed, the Lorenz curve is the same as the line of equality, so the Gini ratio is zero. If most people have an income close to zero and a few people have very large incomes, the Gini ratio is close to 1.

Figure 19.5 shows the U.S. Gini ratio from 1972 to 2012. You can see that the Gini ratio has steadily increased, which means that incomes have become less equal.

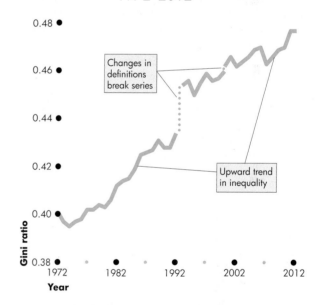

FIGURE 19.5   The U.S. Gini Ratio: 1972–2012

Measured by the Gini ratio, the distribution of income in the United States became more unequal from 1972 to 2012. The percentage of income earned by the richest households increased through these years. Changes in definitions make the numbers before and after 1992 and before and after 2000 not comparable. Despite the breaks in the data, the trends are still visible.

Source of data: See Fig. 19.1.

MyEconLab Animation

ECONOMICS IN ACTION

The Rich Get Richer, but School Still Pays

American incomes have been getting steadily more unequal, and 67 percent of Americans told the Gallup poll that they think incomes in 2012 are too unequal. Twenty-one years earlier, in 1991, only 21 percent of Americans thought there were too many people who were too rich.

A key feature of rising inequality is the trend in the incomes of the super rich. Emmanuel Saez of the University of California, Berkeley, used tax returns data to get the numbers graphed in Fig. 1.

After decades of a falling share, starting in 1981, the share of income received by the richest one percent began a steady climb. By 2012 (the latest year in the database), the richest one percent were earning 19.3 percent of the nation's income.

The bottom quintile gets 3.2 percent of total income, so an average household in the top one percent receives more than 120 times the average income of a household in the lowest quintile.

Movie stars, sports stars, and the CEOs of large corporations are among the super rich. People who scratch out a living doing seasonal work on farms earn the lowest incomes. Aside from these extremes, what are the characteristics of the people who earn high

incomes and the people who earn low incomes? Figure 2 below answers this question. (The data are for 2012, but the patterns are persistent).

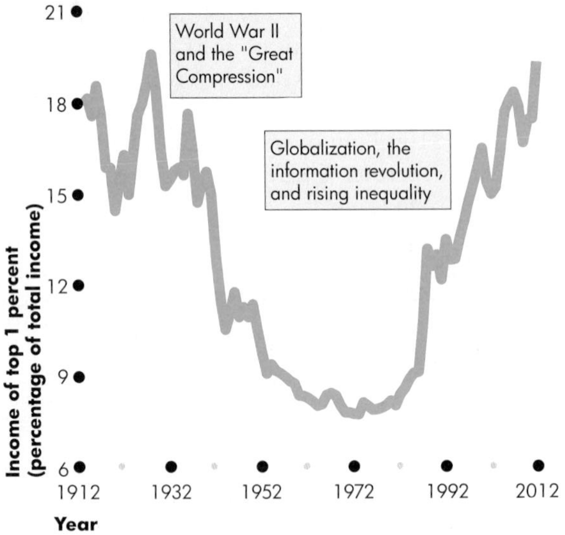

Figure 1 The Income Shares of the Top One Percent

Source of data: Alvaredo, Facundo, Anthony B. Atkinson, Thomas Piketty, and Emmanuel Saez, The World Top Incomes Database, http://g-mond.parisschoolofeconomics.eu/topincomes, 12/08/2012.

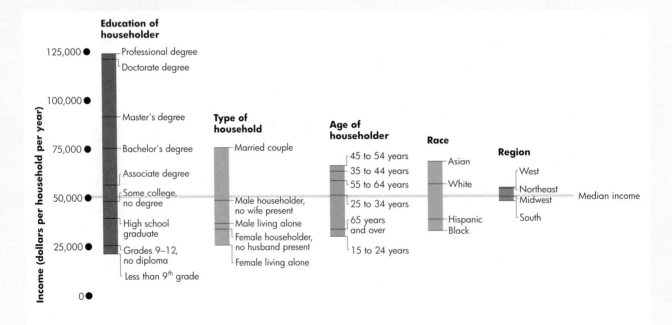

Figure 2 The Distribution of Income by Selected Household Characteristics

Source of data: See Fig. 19.1.

Education A postgraduate education is the main source of a high income. A person with a professional degree (such as a medical or law degree) earns, on average, $121,000—more than double the median income. Just completing high school raises a person's income by more than $12,000 a year; and getting a bachelor's degree adds another $30,000 a year. The average income of people who have not completed 9th grade is $22,000—less than half the median income.

Type of Household Married couples earn more, on average, than people who live alone. A married couple earns about $76,000. In contrast, men who live alone earn about $37,000, and women who live alone earn only $26,000.

Age of Householder Households with the oldest and youngest householders have lower incomes than do those with middle-aged householders. When the householder is aged between 45 and 54, household income averages $66,000. And when the householder is aged between 35 and 44, household income averages $64,000. When the householder is aged between 15 and 24, average household income is $31,000. And for householders over 65, the average household income is $34,000.

Race and Ethnicity White Americans have an average income of $57,000, while black Americans have an average income of $33,000. People of Hispanic origin are a bit better off, with an average income of $39,000. Asians are best off with an average income of $69,000.

Region People who live in the West and Northeast earn more, on average, than people who live in the Midwest and the South. While the region does make a difference, its magnitude is small compared to the dominating effect of education.

The bottom line: School pays and so does marriage.

Poverty

Households at the bottom of the income distribution are so poor that they are considered to be living in poverty. **Poverty** is a situation in which a household's income is too low to be able to buy the quantities of food, shelter, and clothing that are deemed necessary. This concept of poverty is relative: People are poor compared to what is regarded as normal or average, and so poor that their situation is regarded as a problem that needs attention.

A different poverty concept is *absolute poverty*—poverty so extreme that it challenges survival. For millions of people living in Africa and Asia, poverty is absolute. The poorest struggle to survive on incomes of less than $400 a year.

Official U.S. Poverty Measure In the United States, the poverty level is calculated each year by the Social Security Administration. In 2012, the poverty level for a four-person household was an income of $23,492. Other income levels apply to households of different sizes.

Amount of Poverty About 46 million Americans—15 percent of the population—live in households that have incomes below the poverty level. The incidence of poverty varies by race, age, work experience, physical ability, and household status.

We'll look at each of these influences on poverty.

Race The poverty rate among white Americans is 13 percent compared to 26 percent for Hispanic-origin Americans and 27 percent of black Americans.

But the absolute number of white Americans in poverty, 31 million, is greater than the number of minority households—11 million black and 14 million Hispanic.

Age Poverty rates are 22 percent for children, 14 percent for people aged 18 to 64, and 9 percent for seniors aged 65 and over.

Work Experience Americans with a job, either full time or part time, are much less likely to be living in poverty than those without a job. The poverty rate for those with jobs is 7 percent and for those without jobs is 33 percent.

Physical Ability The poverty rate among people with disabilities is very high—29 percent. These people often have no jobs and no easy access to care.

Household Status More than 28 percent of households in which the householder is a female with no husband present have incomes below the poverty level.

The overall poverty rate and the averages for the groups we've just examined have increased during the past few years following a major economic recession. But aside from this recent upturn in the poverty rate, it has been remarkably constant.

ECONOMICS IN ACTION

Is the American Dream Still Alive?

The "American Dream" is that with hard work and fair play, everyone can expect to be rewarded with a better and a rising standard of living. Is this idea alive and well today?

Of the several ways in which we might test whether the dream is still alive, the one that we'll examine here is the mobility that occurs up and down the income distribution. Can households in the third,

downward movement to about a quarter of households, even moved all the way to the lowest quintile.

Part (b) shows that a majority of households remained in the same quintile, and at both extremes more remained than moved. A majority of the third quintile moved, but in roughly equal numbers in both directions.

So what do these data say about the dream? It is alive for some: It is possible to move up the income ladder. But it is also possible to move down. There is two-way mobility for American households.

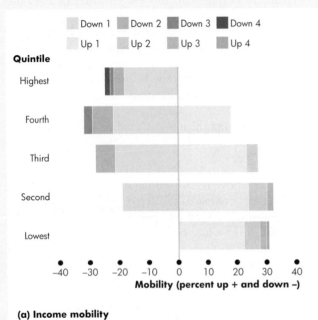

(a) Income mobility
Income Mobility and Immobility 2007–2009

Sources of data: See Fig. 19.4.

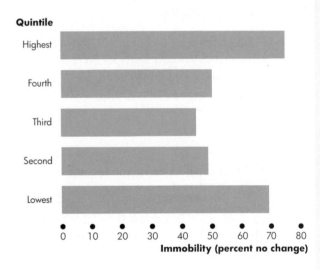

(b) Income immobility

second, and lowest quintiles move up to a higher quintile?

The graphs, which show data for 2007 to 2009, provide an answer to this question. Part (a) shows that about a quarter of the households in the third quintile moved up one quintile and a few moved up two quintiles to the highest. Some households in the second and lowest quintiles also moved up two, three, and even four quintiles.

But by the definition of an income distribution, for all the movements up there must be some movements down. Households in the highest quintile don't have a permanent right to be at the top. And as you can see in the graph, close to one fifth of the highest quintile moved down one quintile and a few, bringing the total

REVIEW QUIZ

1 Which is distributed more unequally, income or wealth? Why? Which is the better measure?
2 How has the distribution of income changed in the past few decades?
3 What are the main characteristics of high-income and low-income households?
4 What is poverty and how does its incidence vary across the races?
5 How much mobility has there been through the income quintiles since 2007?

Work these questions in Study Plan 19.1 and get instant feedback. Do a Key Terms Quiz.   MyEconLab

Inequality in the World Economy

Which countries have the greatest economic inequality and which have the least and the greatest equality? Where does the United States rank? Is it one of the most equal or most unequal, or is it somewhere in the middle? And how much inequality is there in the world as a whole when we consider the entire world as a single global economy?

We'll answer these questions by first looking at the income distribution in a selection of countries and then by examining features of the global distribution of income.

Income Distributions in Selected Countries

By inspecting the income distribution data for every country, we can compare the degree of income inequality and identify the countries with the most inequality and those with the least inequality.

Figure 19.6 summarizes some extremes and shows where the United States lies in the range of degrees of income inequality.

Look first at the numbers in the table. They tell us that in Brazil and South Africa, the lowest quintile of households receive only 2 percent of total income while the highest quintile receive 65 percent of total income. An average person in the highest quintile receives 32.5 times the income of an average person in the lowest quintile.

Contrast these numbers with those for Finland and Sweden. In these countries, the lowest quintile receives 8 percent of total income and the highest quintile receives 35 percent. So an average person in the highest quintile receives 4.4 times the income of an average person in the lowest quintile.

The numbers for the United States lie between these extremes with an average person in the highest quintile receiving just under 10 times the amount received by an average person in the lowest quintile.

Brazil and South Africa are extremes not matched in any other major country or region. Inequality is large in these countries because they have a relatively small but rich European population and a large and relatively poor indigenous population.

Finland and Sweden are extremes, but they are not unusual. Income distributions similar to these are found in many European countries in which governments pursue aggressive income redistribution policies.

We look next at the global income distribution.

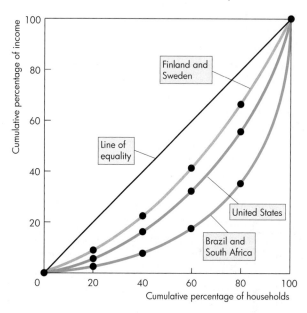

FIGURE 19.6   Lorenz Curves Compared

Households (quintile)	Percentage of total income[1]		
	Brazil and South Africa	United States	Finland and Sweden
Lowest	2	5	8
Second	5	11	14
Third	10	16	20
Fourth	18	24	23
Highest	65	44	35

The table shows the percentages of total income received by each quintile. The figure shows the cumulative percentage of income graphed against the cumulative percentage of households. The data and the Lorenz curves show that income is distributed most unequally in Brazil and South Africa and least unequally in Finland and Sweden. The degree of income inequality in the United States lies between these extremes.

Sources of data: Brazil, South Africa, Finland, and Sweden, Klaus W. Deininger and Lyn Squire, Measuring Income Inequality Database, World Bank, http://go.worldbank.org/. United States, see Fig. 19.1.

[1]The data are based on income *after* redistribution. See pp. 459–461 for an account of income redistribution in the United States.

MyEconLab Animation

Global Inequality and Its Trends

The global distribution of income is much more unequal than the distribution within any one country. The reason is that many countries, especially in Africa and Asia, are in a pre-industrial stage of economic development and are poor, while industrial countries such as the United States are rich. When we look at the distribution of income across the entire world population that goes from the low income of the poorest African to the high income of the richest American, we observe a very large degree of inequality.

To put some raw numbers on this inequality, start with the poorest. Measured in the value of the U.S. dollar in 2005, a total of 3 billion people or 50 percent of the world population live on $2.50 a day or less. Another 2 billion people or 30 percent of the world population live on more than $2.50 but less than $10 a day. So 5 billion people or 80 percent of the world population live on $10 a day or less.

In contrast, in the rich United States, the *average* person has an income of $115 per day and an average person in the highest income quintile has an income of $460 a day.

So the average American earns 46 times the income of one of the world's 3 billion poorest people and more than 11.5 times the income of 80 percent of the people who live in developing economies. An American with the average income in the highest quintile earns 184 times that of the world's poorest people but only 16 times that of an average bottom quintile American.

World Gini Ratio   We can compare world inequality with U.S. inequality by comparing Gini ratios. You saw that the U.S. Gini ratio in 2012 was about 0.47. The world Gini ratio is about 0.61. Recalling the interpretation of the Gini ratio in terms of the Lorenz curve, the world Lorenz curve lies much farther from the line of equality than does the U.S. Lorenz curve.

World Trend   You saw (in Fig. 19.5 on p. 449) that incomes have become more unequal in the United States—the Gini ratio has increased. The same trends are found in most economies. Increased income inequality is a big issue in two of the world's largest and poor nations, China and India. In these two economies, urban middle classes are getting richer at a faster pace than the rural farmers.

Despite greater inequality within countries, the world is becoming *less* unequal. Figure 19.7 shows

FIGURE 19.7   The World Gini Ratio: 1970–2005

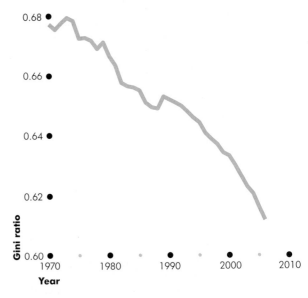

Measured by the Gini ratio, the distribution of income in the entire world became more equal between 1970 and 2005.

Source of data: Xavier Sala-i-Martin and Maxim Pinkovskiy, "Parametric estimations of the world distribution of income," 22 January 2010, http://www.voxeu.org/article/parametric-estimations-world-distribution-income.

MyEconLab Animation

this trend toward less inequality as measured by the world Gini ratio. How can the world income distribution become less unequal while individual countries become more unequal? The answer is that average incomes in poorer countries are rising much faster than average incomes in rich countries. While the gap between rich and poor is widening within countries, it is narrowing across countries.

◆ REVIEW QUIZ

1   In which countries are incomes distributed most unequally and least unequally?
2   Which income distribution is more unequal and why: the income distribution in the United States or in the entire world?
3   How can incomes become *more* unequally distributed within countries and *less* unequally distributed across countries?

Work these questions in Study Plan 19.2 and get instant feedback.   MyEconLab

The Sources of Economic Inequality

We've described some key facts about economic inequality and its trends and our task now is to explain those facts. We began this task in Chapter 18 by learning about the forces that influence demand and supply in the markets for labor, capital, and land. We're now going to deepen our understanding of these forces.

Inequality arises from unequal labor market outcomes and from unequal ownership of capital. We'll begin by looking at labor markets and three features of them that contribute to differences in income:

- Human capital
- Discrimination
- Contests among superstars

Human Capital

A clerk in a law firm earns less than a tenth of the amount earned by the attorney he assists. An operating room assistant earns less than a tenth of the amount earned by the surgeon with whom she works. A bank teller earns less than a tenth of the amount earned by the bank's CEO. Some of the differences in these earnings arise from differences in human capital.

To see the influence of human capital on labor incomes, consider the example of a law clerk and the attorney he assists. (The same reasoning can be applied to an operating room assistant and surgeon, or a bank teller and bank CEO.)

Demand, Supply, and Wage Rates

An attorney performs many tasks that a law clerk cannot perform. Imagine an untrained law clerk cross-examining a witness in a complicated trial. The tasks that the attorney performs are valued highly by her clients who willingly pay for her services. Using a term that you learned in Chapter 18, an attorney has a *high value of marginal product*, and a higher value of marginal product than law clerk. But you also learned in Chapter 18 that the value of marginal product of labor determines (is the same as) the demand for labor. So, because an attorney has a higher value of marginal product, the demand for attorney services is greater than the demand for law-clerk services.

To become an attorney, a person must acquire human capital. But human capital is costly to acquire. This cost—an opportunity cost—includes expenditures on tuition and textbooks. It also includes forgone earnings during the years spent in college and law school. It might also include low earnings doing on-the-job training in a law office during the summer.

Because the human capital needed to supply attorney services is costly to acquire, a person's willingness to supply these services reflects this cost. The supply of attorney services is smaller than the supply of law-clerk services.

The demand for and supply of each type of labor determine the wage rate that each type of labor earns. Attorneys earn a higher wage rate than law clerks because the demand for attorneys is greater and the supply of attorneys is smaller. The gap between the wage rates reflects the higher value of marginal product of an attorney (demand) and the cost of acquiring human capital (supply).

Trends in Wage Inequality

You've seen that high-income households have earned an increasing share of total income while low-income households have earned a decreasing share: The distribution of income in the United States has become more unequal. Technological change and globalization are two possible sources of this increased inequality.

Technological Change

Information technologies such as computers and laser scanners are *substitutes in production* for low-skilled labor: They perform tasks that previously were performed by low-skilled labor. The introduction of these technologies has lowered the marginal product and the demand for low-skilled labor. These same technologies require high-skilled labor to design, program, and run them. High-skilled labor and the information technologies are *complements in production*. So these new technologies have increased the marginal product and demand for high-skilled labor.

Figure 19.8 illustrates the effects of information technologies on wages and employment. The supply of low-skilled labor in part (a) and that of high-skilled labor in part (b) are S, and initially, the demand in each market is D_0. The low-skill wage rate is $5 an hour, and the high-skill wage rate is $10 an hour. The demand for low-skilled labor decreases to D_1 in part (a) and the demand for high-skilled labor increases to D_1 in part (b). The low-skill wage rate falls to $4 an hour and the high-skill wage rate rises to $15 an hour.

Globalization

The entry of China and other developing countries into the global economy has

FIGURE 19.8   Explaining the Trend in Income
                   Distribution

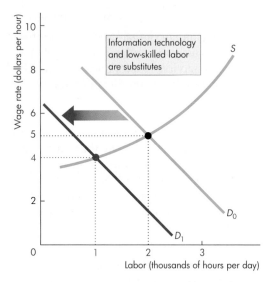

Information technology
and low-skilled labor
are substitutes

(a) A decrease in demand for low-skilled labor

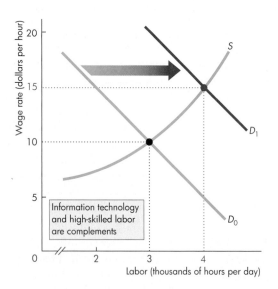

Information technology
and high-skilled labor
are complements

(b) An increase in demand for high-skilled labor

Low-skilled labor and information technologies are substitutes in production. In part (a), advances in information technology decrease the demand for low-skilled labor and lower its wage rate. High-skilled labor and information technologies are complements in production. In part (b), advances in information technology increase the demand for high-skilled labor and raise its wage rate.

MyEconLab Animation

lowered the prices of many manufactured goods. Lower prices for the firm's output lowers the value of marginal product of the firm's workers and decreases the demand for their labor. A situation like that in Fig. 19.8(a) occurs. The wage rate falls, and employment shrinks.

At the same time, the growing global economy increases the demand for services that employ high-skilled workers, and the value of marginal product and the demand for high-skilled labor increases. A situation like that in Fig. 19.8(b) occurs. The wage rate rises, and employment opportunities for high-skilled workers expand.

Discrimination

Human capital differences can explain some of the economic inequality that we observe. Discrimination is another possible source of inequality.

Suppose that black females and white males have identical abilities as investment advisors. If everyone is free of race and sex prejudice, the market determines the same wage rate for both groups. But if customers are prejudiced against women and minorities, this prejudice is reflected in the wage rates—white men earn more than black women.

Counteracting Forces Economists disagree about whether prejudice actually causes wage differentials, and one line of reasoning implies that it does not. In the above example, customers who buy from white men pay a higher service charge for investment advice than do the customers who buy from black women. This price difference acts as an incentive to encourage people who are prejudiced to buy from the people against whom they are prejudiced. This force could be strong enough to eliminate the effects of discrimination altogether. Suppose, as is true in manufacturing, that a firm's customers never meet its workers. If such a firm discriminates against women or minorities, it can't compete with firms who hire these groups because its costs are higher than those of the nonprejudiced firms. Only firms that do not discriminate survive in a competitive industry.

Whether because of discrimination or from some other source, women and visible minorities do earn lower incomes than white males. Another possible source of lower wage rates of women arises from differences in the relative degree of specialization of women and men.

Differences in the Degree of Specialization Couples must choose how to allocate their time between working for a wage and doing jobs in the home, such as cooking, cleaning, shopping, organizing vacations, and, most important, bearing and raising children. Let's look at the choices of Bob and Sue.

Bob might specialize in earning an income and Sue in taking care of the home. Or Sue might specialize in earning an income and Bob in taking care of the home. Or both of them might earn an income and share home production jobs.

The allocation they choose depends on their preferences and on their earning potential. The choice of an increasing number of households is for each person to diversify between earning an income and doing some household chores. But in most households, Bob will specialize in earning an income and Sue will both earn an income and bear a larger share of the task of running the home. With this allocation, Bob will probably earn more than Sue. If Sue devotes time and effort to ensuring Bob's mental and physical well-being, the quality of Bob's market labor will be higher than it would be if he were diversified. If the roles were reversed, Sue would be able to supply market labor that earns more than Bob's.

To test whether the degree of specialization accounts for earnings differences between the sexes, economists have compared the incomes of never-married men and women. They have found that, on the average, with equal amounts of human capital, the wages of these two groups are the same.

Contests Among Superstars

The differences in income that arise from differences in human capital are important and affect a large proportion of the population. But human capital differences can't account for some of the really large income differences.

The super rich—those in the top one percent of the income distribution whose income share has been rising—earn vastly more than can be explained by human capital differences. What makes a person super rich?

A clue to the answer is provided by thinking about the super rich in tennis and golf. What makes tennis players and golfers special is that their earnings depend on where they finish in a tournament. When Rafael Nadal won the U.S. Open Tennis Championship in 2013, he received $2,600,000. The runner-up in this event, Novak Djokovic,

received $1,300,000. So Rafa earned double the amount earned by Novak. And he earned 81 times the amount received by the players who lost in the first round of the tournament.

It is true that Rafael Nadal has a lot of human capital. He practices hard and long and is a remarkable athlete. But anyone who is good enough to get into a tennis Grand Slam tournament is similarly well equipped with human capital and has spent a similar number of long hours in training and practice. It isn't human capital that explains the differences in earnings. It is the tournament and the prize differences that accounts for the large differences in earnings.

Three questions jump out: First, why do we reward superstar tennis players (and golfers) with prizes for winning a contest? Second, why are the prizes so different? And third, do the principles that apply on the tennis court (and golf course) apply more generally to corporations?

Why Prizes for a Contest? The answer to this question (which was noted in Chapter 5, p. 106) is that contests with prizes do a good job of allocating scarce resources efficiently when the efforts of the participants are hard to monitor and reward directly. There is only one winner, but many people work hard in an attempt to be that person. So a great deal of diligent effort is induced by a contest.

Why Are Prizes So Different? The prizes need to be substantially different to induce enough effort. If the winner received 10 percent more than the runner up, the gain from being the winner would be insufficient to encourage anyone to work hard enough. Someone would win but no one would put in much effort. Tennis matches would be boring, golf scores would be high, and no one would be willing to pay to see these sports. Big differences are necessary to induce a big enough effort to generate the quality of performance that people are willing to pay to see.

Does the Principle Apply More Generally? Winner-takes-all isn't confined to tennis and golf. Movie stars; superstars in baseball, basketball, football, and ice hockey; and top corporate executives can all be viewed as participants in contests that decide the winners. The prize for the winner is an income at least double that of the runner up and many multiples of the incomes of those who drop out earlier in the tournament.

Do Contests Among Superstars Explain the Trend?
Contests among superstars can explain large differences in incomes. But can contests explain the trend toward greater inequality with an increasing share of total income going to the super rich as shown on p. 450?

An idea first suggested by University of Chicago economist Sherwin Rosen suggests that a winner-takes-all contest can explain the trend. The key is that globalization has increased the market reach of the winner and increased the spread between the winner and the runners-up.

Global television audiences now watch all the world's major sporting events and the total revenue generated by advertising spots during these events has increased. Competition among networks and cable and satellite television distributors has increased the fees that event organizers receive. And to attract the top star performers, prize money has increased and the winner gets the biggest share of the prize pot.

So the prizes in sports have become bigger and the share of income going to the "winner" has increased.

A similar story can be told about superstars and the super rich in business. As the cost of doing business on a global scale has fallen, more and more corporations have become global in their reach. Not only are large multinational corporations sourcing their inputs from far afield and selling in every country, they are also recruiting their top executives from a global talent pool. With a larger source of talent, and a larger total revenue, firms must make the "prize"—the reward for the top job—more attractive to compete for the best managers.

We've examined some sources of inequality in the labor market. Let's now look at the way inequality arises from unequal ownership of capital.

Unequal Wealth

You've seen that wealth inequality—excluding human capital—is much greater than income inequality. This greater wealth inequality arises from two sources: life-cycle saving patterns and transfers of wealth from one generation to the next.

Life-Cycle Saving Patterns Over a family's life cycle, wealth starts out at zero or perhaps less than zero. A student who has financed education all the way through graduate school might have lots of human capital and an outstanding student loan of $60,000. This person has negative wealth. Gradually loans get paid off and a retirement fund is accumulated. At the point of retiring from full-time work, the family has maximum wealth. Then, during its retirement years, the family spends its wealth. This life-cycle pattern means that much of the wealth is owned by people in their sixties.

Intergenerational Transfers Some households inherit wealth from the previous generation. Some save more than enough on which to live during retirement and transfer wealth to the next generation. But these intergenerational transfers of wealth do not always increase wealth inequality. If a generation that has a high income saves a large part of that income and leaves wealth to a succeeding generation that has a lower income, this transfer decreases the degree of inequality. But one feature of intergenerational transfers of wealth leads to increased inequality: wealth concentration through marriage.

Marriage and Wealth Concentration People tend to marry within their own socioeconomic class—a phenomenon called *assortative mating*. In everyday language, "like attracts like." Although there is a good deal of folklore that "opposites attract," perhaps such Cinderella tales appeal to us because they are so rare in reality. Wealthy people seek wealthy partners.

Because of assortative mating, wealth becomes more concentrated in a small number of families and the distribution of wealth becomes more unequal.

REVIEW QUIZ

1 What role does human capital play in accounting for income inequality?
2 What role might discrimination play in accounting for income inequality?
3 What role might contests among superstars play in accounting for income inequality?
4 How might technological change and globalization explain trends in the distribution of income?
5 Does inherited wealth make the distribution of income less equal or more equal?

Work these questions in Study Plan 19.3 and get instant feedback. MyEconLab

Next, we're going to see how U.S. taxes and government programs redistribute income and decrease the degree of economic inequality.

◆ Income Redistribution

The three main ways in which governments in the United States redistribute income are

- Income taxes
- Income maintenance programs
- Subsidized services

Income Taxes

Income taxes may be progressive, regressive, or proportional. A **progressive income tax** is one that taxes income at an average rate that increases as income increases. A **regressive income tax** is one that taxes income at an average rate that decreases as income increases. A **proportional income tax** (also called a *flat-rate income tax*) is one that taxes income at a constant rate, regardless of the level of income.

The income tax rates that apply in the United States are composed of two parts: federal and state taxes. Some cities, such as New York City, also have an income tax. There is variety in the detailed tax arrangements in the individual states, but the tax system, at both the federal and state levels, is progressive. The poorest working households receive money from the government through an earned income tax credit. Successively higher-income households pay 10 percent, 15 percent, 25 percent, 28 percent, 33 percent, and 35 percent of each additional dollar earned.

Income Maintenance Programs

Three main types of programs redistribute income by making direct payments (in cash, services, or vouchers) to people in the lower part of the income distribution. They are

- Social Security programs
- Unemployment compensation
- Welfare programs

Social Security Programs The main Social Security program is OASDHI—Old Age, Survivors, Disability, and Health Insurance. Monthly cash payments to retired or disabled workers or their surviving spouses and children are paid for by compulsory payroll taxes on both employers and employees.

In 2013, total Social Security expenditure was budgeted at $1.3 trillion, and the average monthly Social Security check was $1,230 or $14,760 per year.

The other component of Social Security is Medicare, which provides hospital and health insurance for the elderly and disabled.

Unemployment Compensation To provide an income to unemployed workers, every state has established an unemployment compensation program. Under these programs, a tax is paid that is based on the income of each covered worker and such a worker receives a benefit when he or she becomes unemployed. The details of the benefits vary from state to state.

Welfare Programs The purpose of welfare is to provide incomes for people who do not qualify for Social Security or unemployment compensation. They are

1. Supplementary Security Income (SSI) program, designed to help the neediest elderly, disabled, and blind people
2. Temporary Assistance for Needy Households (TANF) program, designed to help households that have inadequate financial resources
3. Food Stamp program, designed to help the poorest households obtain a basic diet
4. Medicaid, designed to cover the costs of medical care for households receiving help under the SSI and TANF programs

Subsidized Services

A great deal of redistribution takes place in the United States through the provision of subsidized services—services provided by the government at prices below the cost of production. The taxpayers who consume these goods and services receive a transfer in kind from the taxpayers who do not consume them. The two most important areas in which this form of redistribution takes place are healthcare and education—both kindergarten through grade 12 and college and university.

In 2013–2014, students enrolled in the University of California system paid annual tuition and fees of $13,200. The cost of providing a year's education at the University of California was probably about $40,000. So a household with just one member enrolled in one of these institutions received a benefit from the government of $26,800 a year.

ECONOMICS IN ACTION

Income Redistribution: Only the Richest Pay

A household's *market income* tells us what a household earns in the absence of government redistribution. You've seen that market income is *not* the official basis for measuring the distribution of income that we've used in this chapter. The Census Bureau's measure is *money income* (market income plus cash transfers from the government). But market income is the correct starting point for measuring the scale of income redistribution.

We begin with market income and then subtract taxes and add the amounts received in benefits. The result is the distribution of income after taxes and benefits. The data available on benefits exclude the value of subsidized services such as college, so the resulting distribution might understate the total amount of redistribution from the rich to the poor.

The figures show the scale of redistribution in 2001, the most recent year for which the Census Bureau has provided these data. In Fig. 1, the blue Lorenz curve describes the market distribution of income and the green Lorenz curve shows the distribution of income after all taxes and benefits, including Medicaid and Medicare benefits. (The Lorenz curve based on money income in Fig. 19.3 lies between these two curves.)

The distribution after taxes and benefits is less unequal than is the market distribution. The lowest quintile of households received only 0.7 percent of market income but 4.6 percent of income after taxes and benefits. The highest quintile of households received 54 percent of market income, but only 44.4 percent of income after taxes and benefits.

Figure 2 highlights the percentage of total income redistributed among the five groups. The share of total income received by the lowest 60 percent of households increased. The share received by the fourth quintile barely changed, but the share received by the highest quintile fell by 9.6 percent.

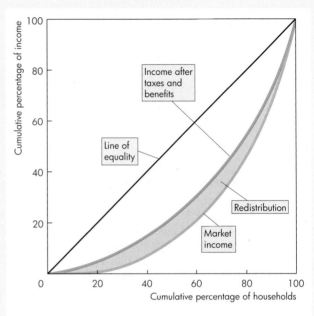

Figure 1 Income Distribution Before and After Redistribution

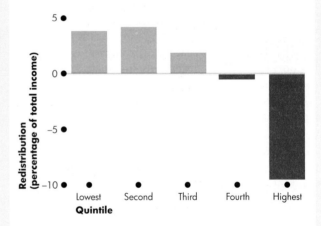

Figure 2 The Scale of Redistribution

Source of data: U.S. Bureau of the Census, Current Population Survey Annual Social and Economic Supplement, Effect of Benefits and Taxes on Income and Poverty, Table 1 Income Distribution Measures, by Definition of Income: 2009.

Government provision of healthcare services has grown to the scale of private provision. Programs such as Medicaid and Medicare bring high-quality and high-cost healthcare to millions of people who earn too little to buy such services themselves.

The Big Tradeoff

The redistribution of income creates what has been called the **big tradeoff**, a tradeoff between equity and efficiency. The big tradeoff arises because redistribution uses scarce resources and weakens incentives.

A dollar collected from a rich person does not translate into a dollar received by a poor person. Some of it gets used up in the process of redistribution. Tax-collecting agencies such as the Internal Revenue Service and welfare-administering agencies (as well as tax accountants and lawyers) use skilled labor, computers, and other scarce resources to do their work. The bigger the scale of redistribution, the greater is the opportunity cost of administering it.

But the cost of collecting taxes and making welfare payments is a small part of the total cost of redistribution. A bigger cost arises from the inefficiency (deadweight loss) of taxes and benefits. Greater equality can be achieved only by taxing productive activities such as work and saving. Taxing people's income from their work and saving lowers the after-tax income they receive. This lower after-tax income makes them work and save less, which in turn results in smaller output and less consumption not only for the rich who pay the taxes but also for the poor who receive the benefits.

It is not only taxpayers who face weaker incentives to work. Benefit recipients also face weaker incentives. In fact, under the welfare arrangements that prevailed before the 1996 reforms, households that benefited from welfare faced the weakest incentives to work. When a welfare recipient got a job, benefits were withdrawn and eligibility for programs such as Medicaid ended, so the household in effect paid a tax of more than 100 percent on its earnings. This arrangement locked poor households in a welfare trap.

So the agencies that determine the scale and methods of income redistribution must pay close attention to the incentive effects of taxes and benefits. Let's close this chapter by looking at one way in which lawmakers are tackling the big tradeoff today.

A Major Welfare Challenge

Young women who have not completed high school, have a child (or children), live without a partner, and more likely are black or Hispanic are among the poorest people in the United States today. They and their children present a major welfare challenge.

First, their numbers are large. In 2012, there were 15.5 million single-mother families, 5 million of which were in poverty. In 2009 (the most recent year with census data), single mothers were owed $35 billion in child support and 30 percent of the women received no support from their children's fathers.

The long-term solution to the problem these women face is education and job training—acquiring human capital. The short-term solutions are enforcing child support payments by absent fathers and former spouses and providing welfare.

Welfare must be designed to minimize the disincentive to pursue the long-term goal of becoming self-supporting. The current welfare program in the United States tries to walk this fine line.

Passed in 1996, the Personal Responsibility and Work Opportunities Reconciliation Act strengthened the Office of Child Support Enforcement and increased the penalties for nonpayment of support. The act also created the Temporary Assistance for Needy Households (TANF) program. TANF is a block grant paid to the states, which administer payments to individuals. It is not an open-ended entitlement program. An adult member of a household that is receiving assistance must either work or perform community service, and there is a five-year limit for assistance.

REVIEW QUIZ

1 How do governments in the United States redistribute income?
2 Describe the scale of redistribution in the United States.
3 What is one of the major welfare challenges today and how is it being tackled in the United States?

Work these questions in Study Plan 19.4 and get instant feedback. Do a Key Terms Quiz.   MyEconLab

We've examined economic inequality in the United States. We've seen how inequality arises and that inequality has been increasing. *Economics in the News* on pp. 462–463 looks at the increasing inequality that began during the early 1980s and continues today.

The next chapter focuses on some problems for the market economy that arise from uncertainty and incomplete information. But unlike the cases we studied in Chapters 16 and 17, this time the market does a good job of coping with the problems.

Trends in Incomes of the Super Rich

Apple Gives Ex-Burberry CEO Potential $67M Signing Bonus as She Takes Reins as Retail Boss

New York Daily News
May 7, 2014

Now that's some golden apple.

Apple is handing over a whopping signing bonus potentially worth as much as $67 million to its new retail boss, Angela Ahrendts, according to a regulatory filing.

The massive payday, in the form of restricted stock, makes the ex-Burberry CEO the highest-paid female exec at a public U.S. company and among the best paid in the country, according to compensation research firm Equilar.

"If you put her on a list of the highest-paid executives of public traded companies in 2013, she is likely in the top five," Aaron Boyd, director of governance research at Equilar, told the *Daily News*.

Ahrendts' payday is even bigger than the $60 million package handed to Marissa Mayer to lure her to the top spot at Yahoo!. …

Apple is known for handing out generous pay packages to its execs. Ahrendts is the only female on Apple's 10-person executive team. She reports to Apple CEO Tim Cook. The computer giant was willing to pay up for a seasoned retail vet who can potentially give its 400-plus stores a lift.

Ahrendts took the helm at Burberry in 2006 and is widely credited with sprucing up the fabled British brand and taking it more upscale.

Apple's new retail boss will be tasked with boosting its retail stores.

During her tenure, sales more than doubled and Burberry's stock price tripled. She won props for using social media to tout the fashion house. …

MyEconLab More Economics in the News

ESSENCE OF THE STORY

- Angela Ahrendts, Apple's retail boss, got a signing bonus that could be worth $67 million.

- Ahrendts' task is to increase sales in Apple's retail stores.

- Her previous job was CEO at Burberry, an upscale British brand.

- During her tenure at Burberry, the firm's sales more than doubled and its stock price tripled.

- Ahrendts is in the top five highest-paid executives at a public U.S. company and the top female.

ECONOMIC ANALYSIS

- The news article reports the extremely high incomes received by two top female executives. These high incomes are not rare today and have been getting less rare.

- Economists Thomas Piketty of l'Ecole d'économie de Paris—Paris School of Economics and Emmanuel Saez of U.C. Berkeley examined the tax returns of the super rich and found the trend shown in Fig. 1.

- Figure 1 shows the income share (percentage of total income) received by the top 0.01 percent of the population.

- The top 0.01 percent includes the top corporate executives and in 2008 was made up of 15,246 families with incomes that exceeded $9,141,000.

- The average family in the top 0.01 percent received 296 times the income of the average family in the bottom quintile. This ratio was 27 in 1965. These ratios are in line with the trend reported in the news article.

- Why are executives like Angela Ahrendts paid so much? And why have top incomes risen so much? Isn't there an abundance of talent around? Could not and should not these people be paid much less?

- It is true that there is an abundance of talent. Globalization has made the entire world the talent pool that large corporations tap for their top executive spots.

- But it is because of the abundance of talent that executive pay has become so high.

- You saw on p. 457 that we can view top executives as the winners of a contest among potential superstars.

- Contests induce high effort and productivity from managers at all levels as they compete for the top job.

- How hard people compete (how productive they are) depends on the size of the prize and the probability of winning it.

- You can think of the contest in terms of the pyramids in Fig. 2. The talent pool is the base of the pyramid and the contest delivers a winner who gets to the top.

- When the talent pool is small, as it was in 1965, the chance of being the winner is large enough for a moderate prize to induce enough effort.

- When the talent pool is large, as it is today, the chance of being the winner is very small, so to induce the same amount of effort, the prize is very large.

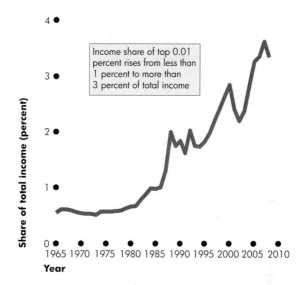

> Income share of top 0.01 percent rises from less than 1 percent to more than 3 percent of total income

Figure 1   Income Share of the Top 0.01 Percent

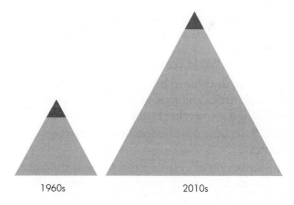

Figure 2   Bigger Pyramid Means Bigger Prizes for Getting to Top

Source of data: Figure 1, Emmanuel Saez, "Striking it Richer: The Evolution of Top Incomes in the United States," *Pathways*, Winter 2008 issue.

- This superstar contest idea explains the direction of change—why top executives' earnings have increased relative to the average wage.

- It also explains why Angela Ahrendts and Marissa Mayer earn such enormous incomes.

SUMMARY

Key Points

Economic Inequality in the United States (pp. 446–452)

- In 2012, the mode money income was between $15,000 and $20,000 a year, the median money income was $51,017, and the mean money income was $71,274.
- The income distribution is positively skewed.
- In 2012, the poorest 20 percent of households received 3.2 percent of total income and the wealthiest 20 percent received 51.1 percent of total income.
- Wealth is distributed more unequally than money income because the wealth data exclude the value of human capital.
- Since 1972, the distribution of income has become more unequal.
- Education, type of household, age of householder, and race all influence household income.

Working Problems 1 and 2 will give you a better understanding of economic inequality in the United States.

Inequality in the World Economy (pp. 453–454)

- Incomes are distributed most unequally in Brazil and South Africa and least unequally in Finland, Sweden, and some other European economies.
- The U.S. income distribution lies between the extremes.
- The distribution of income across individuals in the global economy is much more unequal than in the United States.
- The global income distribution has been getting less unequal as rapid income growth in China and India has lifted millions from poverty.

Working Problems 3 to 5 will give you a better understanding of economic inequality in the world economy.

The Sources of Economic Inequality (pp. 455–458)

- Inequality arises from differences in human capital and from contests among superstars.
- Trends in the distribution of human capital and in the rewards to superstars that arise from technological change and globalization can explain some of the trend in increased inequality.
- Inequality might arise from discrimination.
- Inequality between men and women might arise from differences in the degree of specialization.
- Intergenerational transfers of wealth lead to increased inequality because people can't inherit debts and assortative mating tends to concentrate wealth.

Working Problem 6 will give you a better understanding of the sources of economic inequality.

Income Redistribution (pp. 459–461)

- Governments redistribute income through progressive income taxes, income maintenance programs, and subsidized services.
- Redistribution increases the share of total income received by the lowest 60 percent of households and decreases the share of total income received by the highest quintile. The share of the fourth quintile barely changes.
- Because the redistribution of income weakens incentives, it creates a tradeoff between equity and efficiency.
- Effective redistribution seeks to support the long-term solution to low income, which is education and job training—acquiring human capital.

Working Problems 7 and 8 will give you a better understanding of income redistribution.

Key Terms   MyEconLab Key Terms Quiz

Big tradeoff, 460   Money income, 446   Regressive income tax, 459
Gini ratio, 449   Poverty, 451   Wealth, 448
Lorenz curve, 447   Progressive income tax, 459
Market income, 446   Proportional income tax, 459

WORKED PROBLEM

MyEconLab   You can work this problem in Chapter 19 Study Plan.

The table shows the quintile shares of income in South Africa and Norway

Households (quintile)	Norway	South Africa
	(percentage of total income)	
Lowest	10	3
Second	16	5
Third	19	8
Fourth	22	16
Highest	33	68

Questions

1. Make a table to show the cumulative percentage of income against the cumulative percentage of households in Norway and find five points on the Lorenz curve for Norway.

2. Is income in Norway distributed more equally or less equally than in South Africa? Explain.

3. If the government of South Africa redistributed income so that its distribution matched that of Norway, which quintiles would see their incomes increase and which would decrease?

Solutions

1. To make a cumulative distribution table (below), start with the lowest quintile (20 percent of households) who receive 10 percent of income. Now add the income share of the second quintile to show that the lowest 40 percent of households receive $10 + 16 = 26$ percent of income. Repeating: the lowest 60 percent households receive $26 + 19 = 45$ percent of income, the lowest 80 percent receive $45 + 22 = 67$ percent of income, and 100 percent receive $67 + 33 = 100$ percent of income.

	Households		Income	
Quintile	Cumulative percentage	Percentage		Cumulative percentage
Lowest	20	10		10
Second	40	16		26
Third	60	19		45
Fourth	80	22		67
Highest	100	33		100

The Lorenz curve shows the percentages of total income received by the cumulative percentages of

households. The rows of the following table shows the five points.

Households (percentage)	Cumulative percentage
Lowest 20	10
Lowest 40	26
Lowest 60	45
Lowest 80	67
All 100	100

Key Point: To calculate the cumulative distribution, start with the lowest quintile's share and gradually add the next higher quintile's share.

2. Each quintile in Norway except the highest one receives a larger percentage of total income than does the corresponding quintile in South Africa. So income in Norway is more equally distributed than in South Africa. Compare the Lorenz curves in the figure.

3. To make the South African distribution match Norway's, the lowest quintile would have to receive and additional 7 percent. The second quintile would have to receive an additional 11 percent, the third quintile and additional 11 percent and the fourth quintile and additional 6 percent.

   The second and third quintiles would receive the biggest increase and only the highest quintile would have a smaller share of income.

Key Point: To make the distribution more equal, redistribute income from higher to lower quintiles.

Key Figure   MyEconLab Interactive Animation

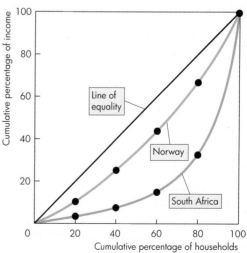

STUDY PLAN PROBLEMS AND APPLICATIONS

MyEconLab   You can work Problems 1 to 8 in Chapter 19 Study Plan and get instant feedback.

Economic Inequality in the United States

(Study Plan 19.1)

1. What is money income? Describe the U.S. distribution of money income in 2012.

2. The table shows money income shares in the United States in 2001.

Households (quintile)	Money income (percentage of total)
Lowest	3.5
Second	8.8
Third	14.5
Fourth	23.1
Highest	50.1

   Draw a U.S. Lorenz curve in 2001. Was the U.S. distribution of income more equal in 2001 than in 2012 (see p. 447)? Explain your answer.

Inequality in the World Economy (Study Plan 19.2)

3. Incomes in China and India are a small fraction of U.S. income, but incomes in China and India are growing at more than twice the rate of U.S. incomes.
   a. Explain how economic inequality in China and India is changing relative to that in the United States.
   b. How is the world Lorenz curve and world Gini ratio changing?

Use the following table to work Problems 4 and 5. The table shows the income shares in the United States, Canada, and the United Kingdom in 2009.

Households (quintile)	United States	Canada	United Kingdom
	(percentage of total income)		
Lowest	3	7	3
Second	8	13	5
Third	15	18	14
Fourth	24	25	25
Highest	50	37	53

4. Draw the Lorenz curves for the United States and Canada. In which country was money income less equally distributed in 2009?

5. Draw the Lorenz curves for the United States and the United Kingdom. In which country was income less equally distributed in 2009?

The Sources of Economic Inequality (Study Plan 19.3)

6. The following figure shows the market for low-skilled labor.

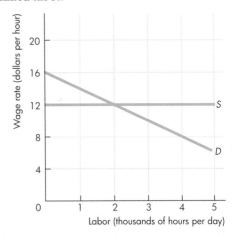

   The value of marginal product of high-skilled workers is $16 an hour greater than that of low-skilled workers at each quantity of labor. The cost of acquiring human capital adds $12 an hour to the wage that must be offered to attract high-skilled labor.

   Compare the equilibrium wage rates of low-skilled labor and high-skilled labor. Explain why the difference between these wage rates equals the cost of acquiring human capital.

Income Redistribution (Study Plan 19.4)

Use the following table to work Problems 7 and 8. The table shows three redistribution schemes.

Before-tax income (dollars)	Plan A tax (dollars)	Plan B tax (dollars)	Plan C tax (dollars)
10,000	1,000	1,000	2,000
20,000	2,000	4,000	2,000
30,000	3,000	9,000	2,000

7. Which scheme has
   (i) a proportional tax?
   (ii) a regressive tax?
   (iii) a progressive tax?

8. Which scheme will
   (i) increase economic inequality?
   (ii) reduce economic inequality?
   (iii) have no effect on economic inequality?

ADDITIONAL PROBLEMS AND APPLICATIONS

MyEconLab   You can work these problems in MyEconLab if assigned by your instructor.

Economic Inequality in the United States

Use the following table to work Problems 9 and 10. The table shows the distribution of market income in the United States in 2007.

Households (quintile)	Market income (percentage of total)
Lowest	1.1
Second	7.1
Third	13.9
Fourth	22.8
Highest	55.1

9. a. What is the definition of market income?

   b. Draw the Lorenz curve for the distribution of market income.

10. Compare the distribution of market income with the distribution of money income shown in Fig. 19.3 on p. 447. Which distribution is more unequal and why?

Inequality in the World Economy

Use the following table to work Problems 11 to 13. The table shows shares of income in Australia.

Households (quintile)	Income share (percentage of total)
Lowest	7
Second	13
Third	18
Foourth	24
Highest	38

11. Draw the Lorenz curves for the income distribution in Australia and in Brazil and South Africa (use the data in Fig. 19.6 on p. 453). Is income distributed more equally or less equally in Brazil and South Africa than in Australia?

12. Is the Gini ratio for Australia larger or smaller than that for Brazil and South Africa? Explain your answer.

13. What are some reasons for the differences in the distribution of income in Australia and in Brazil and South Africa?

The Sources of Economic Inequality

14. The figure shows the market for a group of workers who are discriminated against. Suppose

that other workers in the same industry are not discriminated against and their value of marginal product is perceived to be twice that of the workers who are discriminated against. Suppose also that the supply of these other workers is 2,000 hours per day less at each wage rate.

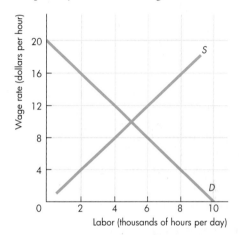

a. What is the wage rate of the workers who are discriminated against?

b. For workers who are discriminated against, what quantity of labor is employed?

c. What is the wage rate of the workers who do not face discrimination?

d. For workers who do not face discrimination, what quantity of labor is employed?

15. **Where Women's Pay Trumps Men's**

Men work more than women on the job, at least in terms of overall hours. That's just one reason why in most fields, men's earnings exceed women's earnings. But Warren Farrell found 39 occupations in which women's median earnings exceeded men's earnings by at least 5 percent and in some cases by as much as 43 percent. In fields like engineering, a company may get one woman and seven men applying for a job. If the company wants to hire the woman, it might have to pay a premium to get her. Also, where women can combine technical expertise with people skills—such as those required in sales and where customers prefer dealing with a woman—that's likely to contribute to a premium in pay.

Source: CNN, March 2, 2006

a. Draw a graph to illustrate why discrimination

could result in female workers getting paid more than male workers for some jobs.

b. Explain how market competition could potentially eliminate this wage differential.

c. If customers "prefer dealing with a woman" in some markets, how might that lead to a persistent wage differential between men and women?

Use the following data to work Problems 16 and 17.

In 2010, 828,000 Americans had full-time management jobs that paid an average of $96,450 a year while 4.3 million Americans had full-time retail sales jobs that paid an average of $20,670 a year.

Managers require a high school certificate while retail sales people don't but they undergo training.

Source: Bureau of Labor Statistics

16. Explain why managers are paid more than retail salespeople.

17. If the online shopping trend continues, how do you think the market for salespeople will change in coming years?

Income Redistribution

18. Use the information provided in Problem 9 and in Fig. 19.3 on p. 447.
    a. What is the percentage of total income that is redistributed from the highest income group?
    b. What percentages of total income are redistributed to the lower income groups?

19. Describe the effects of increasing the amount of income redistribution in the United States to the point at which the lowest income group receives 15 percent of total income and the highest income group receives 30 percent of total income.

Use the following news clip to work Problems 20 and 21.

The Tax Debate We Should be Having

A shrinking number of Americans are bearing an even bigger share of the nation's income tax burden. In 2005, the bottom 40 percent of Americans by income had an effective tax rate that's negative: Their households received more money through the income tax system than they paid. The top 50% of taxpayers pay 97% of total income tax and the top 10% of taxpayers pay 70%. The top 1% paid almost 40% of all income tax, a proportion that has jumped dramatically since 1986.

Given the U.S. tax system, any tax cut must benefit the rich, but in terms of the change in effective tax rates: The bottom 50% got a much bigger tax cut under the Bush tax cut than the top 1%. Did the dollar value of Bush's tax cuts go mostly to the wealthy? Absolutely.

Source: *Fortune*, April 14, 2008

20. Explain why tax cuts in a progressive income tax system are consistently criticized for favoring the wealthy.

21. How might the benefits of tax cuts "trickle down" to others whose taxes are not cut?

Economics in the News

22. After you have studied *Economics in the News* on pp. 462–463, answer the following questions.
    a. What is the trend in top executive pay?
    b. How can the idea of a contest among potential top executives explain their high pay?
    c. How can the idea of a contest among potential top executives explain the trend in their pay?
    d. If the contest among potential top executives is the correct explanation for their high pay, what would be the effects of a cap on top executive pay?

23. **The Best and Worst College Degrees by Salary**
    Business administration is always a strong contender for honors as the most popular college major. This is no surprise since students think business is the way to make big bucks. But is business administration really as lucrative as students and their parents believe? Nope.

    In a new survey by PayScale, Inc. of salaries by college degree, business administration didn't even break into the list of the top 10 or 20 most lucrative college degrees. A variety of engineering majors claim eight of the top 10 salary spots with chemical engineering ($65,700) winning best for starting salaries. Out of 75 undergrad college majors, business administration ($42,900) came in 35th, behind such degrees as occupational therapy ($61,300), information technology ($49,400), and economics ($48,800).

    Source: moneywatch.com, July 21, 2009

    a. Why do college graduates with different majors have drastically different starting salaries?
    b. Draw a graph of the labor markets for economics majors and business administration majors to illustrate your explanation of the differences in the starting salaries of these two groups.

20

UNCERTAINTY AND INFORMATION

After studying this chapter, you will be able to:

◆ Explain how people make decisions when they are uncertain about the consequences

◆ Explain how markets enable people to buy and sell risk

◆ Explain how markets cope when buyers and sellers have private information

◆ Explain how uncertainty and incomplete information influence the efficiency of markets

You want an A in your economics course and you want to graduate with a high GPA. But what if grades are inflated and you along with everyone else gets an A? What happens in the job market for college graduates? And how do accurate grades help the market work?

The job market for college graduates is an example of a market with uncertainty and incomplete information. Can this market achieve an efficient outcome? This chapter answers these questions. In *Economics in the News* at the end of the chapter, you will see why grade inflation is not in your best interest.

◆ Decisions in the Face of Uncertainty

Tania, a student, is trying to decide which of two summer jobs to take. She can work as a house painter and earn enough to save $2,000 by the end of the summer. There is no uncertainty about the income from this job. If Tania takes it, she will definitely have $2,000 in her bank account at the end of the summer. The other job, working as a telemarketer selling subscriptions to a magazine, is risky. If Tania takes this job, her bank balance at the end of the summer will depend on her success at selling. She will earn enough to save $5,000 if she is successful but only $1,000 if she turns out to be a poor salesperson. Tania has never tried selling, so she doesn't know how successful she'll be. But some of her friends have done this job, and 50 percent of them do well and 50 percent do poorly. Basing her expectations on this experience, Tania thinks there is a 50 percent chance that she will earn $5,000 and a 50 percent chance that she will earn $1,000.

Tania is equally as happy to paint as she is to make phone calls. She cares only about the money. Which job does she prefer: the one that provides her with $2,000 for sure or the one that offers her a 50 percent chance of making $5,000 but a 50 percent risk of making only $1,000?

To answer this question, we need a way of comparing the two outcomes. One comparison is the expected wealth that each job creates.

Expected Wealth

Expected wealth is the money value of what a person expects to own at a given point in time. An expectation is an average calculated by using a formula that weights each possible outcome with the probability (chance) that it will occur.

For Tania, the probability that she will have $5,000 is 0.5 (a 50 percent chance). The probability that she will have $1,000 is also 0.5. Notice that the probabilities sum to 1. Using these numbers, we can calculate Tania's expected wealth, EW, which is

$$EW = (\$5,000 \times 0.5) + (\$1,000 \times 0.5) = \$3,000.$$

Notice that expected wealth decreases if the risk of a poor outcome increases. For example, if Tania has a

20 percent chance of success (and 80 percent chance of failure), her expected wealth falls to $1,800—

$$(\$5,000 \times 0.2) + (\$1,000 \times 0.8) = \$1,800.$$

Tania can now compare the expected wealth from each job—$3,000 for the risky job and $2,000 for the non-risky job.

So does Tania prefer the risky job because it gives her a greater expected wealth? The answer is we don't know because we don't know how much Tania dislikes risk.

Risk Aversion

Risk aversion is the dislike of risk. Almost everyone is risk averse but some more than others. In football, running is less risky than passing. Coach John Harbaugh of the Baltimore Ravens, who favors a cautious running game, is risk averse. Denver quarterback Peyton Manning, who favors a risky passing game, is less risk averse. But almost everyone is risk averse to some degree.

We can measure the degree of risk aversion by the compensation needed to make a given amount of risk acceptable. Returning to Tania: If she needs to be paid more than $1,000 to take on the risk arising from the telemarketing job, she will choose the safe painting job and take the $2,000 non-risky income. But if she thinks that the extra $1,000 of expected income is enough to compensate her for the risk, she will take the risky job.

To make this idea concrete, we need a way of thinking about how a person values different levels of wealth. The concept that we use is *utility*. We apply the same idea that explains how people make expenditure decisions (see Chapter 8) to explain risk aversion and decisions in the face of risk.

Utility of Wealth

Wealth (money in the bank and other assets of value) is like all good things. It yields utility. The more wealth a person has, the greater is that person's total utility. But each additional dollar of wealth brings a diminishing increment in total utility—the marginal utility of wealth diminishes as wealth increases.

Diminishing marginal utility of wealth means that the gain in utility from an increase in wealth is smaller than the loss in utility from an equal decrease in wealth. Stated differently, *the pain from a loss is greater than the pleasure from a gain of equal size.*

Figure 20.1 illustrates Tania's utility of wealth. Each point *A* through *F* on Tania's utility of wealth curve corresponds to the value identified by the same letter in the table. For example, at point *C*, Tania's wealth is $2,000, and her total utility is 70 units. As Tania's wealth increases, her total utility increases and her marginal utility decreases. Her marginal utility is 25 units when wealth increases from $1,000 to $2,000, but only 13 units when wealth increases from $2,000 to $3,000.

We can use a person's utility of wealth curve to calculate expected utility and the cost of risk.

Expected Utility

Expected utility is the utility value of what a person expects to own at a given point in time. Like expected wealth, it is calculated by using a formula that weights each possible outcome with the probability that it will occur. But it is the utility outcome, not the money outcome, that is used to calculate expected utility.

Figure 20.2 illustrates the calculation for Tania. Wealth of $5,000 gives 95 units of utility and wealth of $1,000 gives 45 units of utility. Each outcome has a probability of 0.5 (a 50 percent chance). Using these numbers, we can calculate Tania's expected utility, *EU*, which is

$$EU = (95 \times 0.5) + (45 \times 0.5) = 70.$$

FIGURE 20.1   The Utility of Wealth

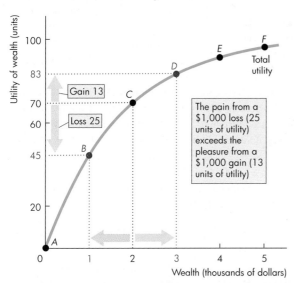

	Wealth (dollars)	Total utility (units)	Marginal utility (units)
A	0	0	
			45
B	1,000	45	
			25
C	2,000	70	
			13
D	3,000	83	
			8
E	4,000	91	
			4
F	5,000	95	

The table shows Tania's utility of wealth schedule, and the figure shows her utility of wealth curve. Utility increases as wealth increases, but the marginal utility of wealth diminishes.

MyEconLab Animation

FIGURE 20.2   Expected Utility

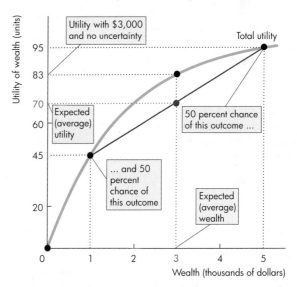

Tania has a 50 percent chance of having $5,000 of wealth and a total utility of 95 units. She also has a 50 percent chance of having $1,000 of wealth and a total utility of 45 units. Tania's expected wealth is $3,000 (the average of $5,000 and $1,000) and her expected utility is 70 units (the average of 95 and 45). With a wealth of $3,000 and no uncertainty, Tania's total utility is 83 units. For a given expected wealth, the greater the range of uncertainty, the smaller is expected utility.

MyEconLab Animation

Expected utility decreases if the risk of a poor outcome increases. For example, if Tania has a 20 percent chance of success (and an 80 percent chance of failure), her expected utility is 55 units—

$$(95 \times 0.2) + (45 \times 0.8) = 55.$$

Notice how the range of uncertainty affects expected utility. Figure 20.2 shows that with $3,000 of wealth and no uncertainty, total utility is 83 units. But with the same expected wealth and Tania's uncertainty—a 50 percent chance of having $5,000 and a 50 percent chance of having $1,000—expected utility is only 70 units. Tania's uncertainty lowers her expected utility by 13 units.

Expected utility combines expected wealth and risk into a single index.

Making a Choice with Uncertainty

Faced with uncertainty, a person chooses the action that maximizes expected utility. To select the job that gives her the maximum expected utility, Tania must:

1. Calculate the expected utility from the risky telemarketing job
2. Calculate the expected utility from the safe painting job
3. Compare the two expected utilities

Figure 20.3 illustrates the calculations. You've just seen that the risky telemarketing job gives Tania an expected utility of 70 units. The safe painting job also gives Tania a utility of 70. That is, the total utility of $2,000 with no risk is 70 units. So with either job, Tania has an expected utility of 70 units. She is indifferent between these two jobs.

If Tania had only a 20 percent chance of success and an 80 percent chance of failure in the telemarketing job, her expected utility would be 55 (calculated above). In this case, she would take the painting job and get 70 units of utility. But if the probabilities were reversed and she had an 80 percent chance of success and only a 20 percent chance of failure in the telemarketing job, her expected utility would be 85 units—$(95 \times 0.8) + (45 \times 0.2) = 85$. In this case, she would take the risky telemarketing job.

We can calculate the cost of risk by comparing the expected wealth in a given risky situation with the wealth that gives the same total utility but no risk. Using this principle, we can find Tania's cost of bearing the risk that arises from the telemarketing job. That cost, highlighted in Fig. 20.3, is $1,000.

FIGURE 20.3   Choice Under Uncertainty

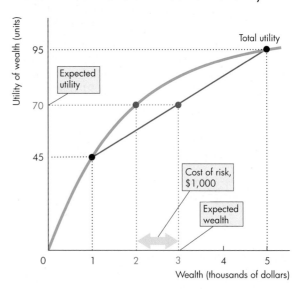

With a 50 percent chance of having $5,000 of wealth and a 50 percent chance of having $1,000 of wealth, Tania's expected wealth is $3,000 and her expected utility is 70 units. Tania would have the same 70 units of total utility with wealth of $2,000 and no risk, so Tania's cost of bearing this risk is $1,000. Tania is indifferent between the job that pays $2,000 with no risk and the job that offers an equal chance of $5,000 and $1,000.

——— MyEconLab Animation and Draw Graph ———

◆ REVIEW QUIZ

1 What is the distinction between expected wealth and expected utility?
2 How does the concept of utility of wealth capture the idea that pain of loss exceeds the pleasure of gain?
3 What do people try to achieve when they make a decision under uncertainty?
4 How is the cost of the risk calculated when making a decision with an uncertain outcome?

Work these questions in Study Plan 20.1 and get instant feedback. Do a Key Terms Quiz.   MyEconLab

You've now seen how a person makes a risky decision. In the next section, we'll see how markets enable people to reduce the risks they face.

◆ Buying and Selling Risk

You've seen at many points in your study of markets how both buyers and sellers gain from trade. Buyers gain because they value what they buy more highly than the price they must pay—they receive a *consumer surplus*. And sellers gain because they face costs that are less than the price at which they can sell—they receive a *producer surplus*.

Just as buyers and sellers gain from trading goods and services, so they can also gain by trading risk. But risk is a bad, not a good. The good that is traded is risk avoidance. A buyer of risk avoidance can gain because the value of avoiding risk is greater than the price that must be paid to someone else to get them to bear the risk. The seller of risk avoidance faces a lower cost of risk than the price that people are willing to pay to avoid the risk.

We're going to put some flesh on the bare bones of this brief account of how people can gain from trading risk by looking at insurance markets.

Insurance Markets

Insurance plays a huge role in our economic lives. We'll explain

- How insurance reduces risk
- Why people buy insurance
- How insurance companies earn a profit

How Insurance Reduces Risk Insurance reduces the risk that people face by sharing or pooling the risks. When people buy insurance against the risk of an unwanted event, they pay an insurance company a *premium*. If the unwanted event occurs, the insurance company pays out the amount of the insured loss.

Think about auto collision insurance. The probability that any one person will have a serious auto accident is small. But a person who does have an auto accident incurs a large loss. For a large population, the probability of one person having an accident is the proportion of the population that has an accident. But this proportion is known, so the probability of an accident occurring and the total cost of accidents can be predicted. An insurance company can pool the risks of a large population and enable everyone to share the costs. It does so by collecting premiums from everyone and paying out benefits to those who suffer a loss. An insurance company that remains in business collects at least as much in premiums as it pays out in benefits.

Why People Buy Insurance People buy insurance and insurance companies earn a profit by selling insurance because people are risk averse. To see why people buy insurance and why it is profitable, let's consider an example. Dan owns a car worth $10,000, and that is his only wealth. There is a 10 percent chance that Dan will have a serious accident that makes his car worth nothing. So there is a 90 percent chance that Dan's wealth will remain at $10,000 and a 10 percent chance that his wealth will be zero. Dan's expected wealth is $9,000—($10,000 × 0.9) + ($0 × 0.1).

Dan is risk averse (just like Tania in the previous example). Because Dan is risk averse, he will be better off by buying insurance to avoid the risk that he faces, if the insurance premium isn't too high.

Without knowing some details about just how risk averse Dan is, we don't know the most that he would be willing to pay to avoid this risk. But we do know that he would pay more than $1,000. If Dan did pay $1,000 to avoid the risk, he would have $9,000 of wealth and face no uncertainty about his wealth. If he does not have an accident, his wealth is the $10,000 value of his car minus the $1,000 he pays the insurance company. If he does lose his car, the insurance company pays him $10,000, so he still has $9,000. Being risk averse, Dan's expected utility from $9,000 with no risk is greater than his expected utility from an expected $9,000 with risk. So Dan would be willing to pay more than $1,000 to avoid this risk.

How Insurance Companies Earn a Profit For the insurance company, $1,000 is the minimum amount at which it would be willing to insure Dan and other people like him. With say 50,000 customers all like Dan, 5,000 customers (50,000 × 0.1) lose their cars and 45,000 don't. Premiums of $1,000 give the insurance company a total revenue of $50,000,000. With 5,000 claims of $10,000, the insurance company pays out $50,000,000. So a premium of $1,000 enables the insurance company to break even (make zero economic profit) on this business.

But Dan (and everyone else) is willing to pay more than $1,000, so insurance is a profitable business and there is a gain from trading risk.

The gain from trading risk is shared by Dan (and the other people who buy insurance) and the insurance company. The exact share of the gain depends on the state of competition in the market for insurance.

If the insurance market is a monopoly, the insurance company can take all the gains from trading risk. But if the insurance market is competitive, economic profit will induce entry and profits will be competed away. In this case, Dan (and the other buyers of insurance) gets the gain.

A Graphical Analysis of Insurance

We can illustrate the gains from insurance by using a graph of Dan's utility of wealth curve. We begin, in Fig. 20.4, with the situation if Dan doesn't buy insurance and decides to bear the risk he faces.

Risk-Taking Without Insurance With no accident, Dan's wealth is $10,000 and his total utility is 100 units. If Dan has an accident, his car is worthless: he has no wealth and no utility. Because the chance of an accident is 10 percent (or 0.1), the chance of not having an accident is 90 percent (or 0.9). Dan's expected wealth is $9,000—($10,000 × 0.9) + ($0 × 0.1)—and his expected utility is 90 units—(100 × 0.9) + (0 × 0.1).

You've just seen that without insurance, Dan gets 90 units of utility. But Dan also gets 90 units of utility if he faces no uncertainty with a smaller amount of wealth.

We're now going to see how much Dan will pay to avoid uncertainty.

The Value and Cost of Insurance Figure 20.5 shows the situation when Dan buys insurance. You can see that for Dan, having $7,000 with no risk is just as good as facing a 90 percent chance of having $10,000 and a 10 percent chance of having no wealth. So if Dan pays $3,000 for insurance, he has $7,000 of wealth, faces no uncertainty, and gets 90 units of utility. The amount of $3,000 is the maximum that Dan is willing to pay for insurance. It is the value of insurance to Dan.

Figure 20.5 also shows the cost of insurance. With a large number of customers each of whom has a 10 percent chance of making a $10,000 claim for the loss of a vehicle, the insurance company can provide insurance at a cost of $1,000 (10 percent of $10,000). If Dan pays only $1,000 for insurance, his

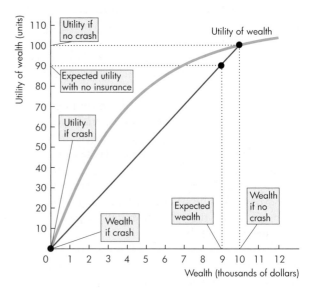

FIGURE 20.4   Taking a Risk Without Insurance

Dan's wealth (the value of his car) is $10,000, which gives him 100 units of utility.

With no insurance, if Dan has a crash, he has no wealth and no utility.

With a 10 percent chance of a crash, Dan's expected wealth is $9,000 and his expected utility is 90 units.

— MyEconLab Animation —

wealth is $9,000 (the $10,000 value of his car minus the $1,000 he pays for insurance), and his utility from $9,000 of wealth with no uncertainty is about 98 units.

Gains from Trade Because Dan is willing to pay up to $3,000 for insurance that costs the insurance company $1,000, there is a gain from trading risk of $2,000 per insured person. How the gains are shared depends on the nature of the market. If the insurance market is competitive, entry will increase supply and lower the price to $1,000 (plus normal profit and operating costs). Dan (and the other buyers of insurance) enjoys a consumer surplus. If the insurance market is a monopoly, the insurance company takes the $2,000 per insured person as economic profit.

FIGURE 20.5 The Gains from Insurance

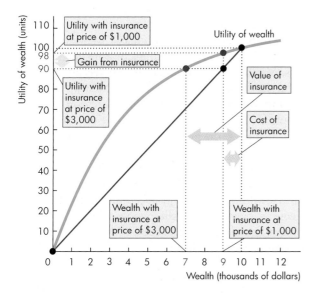

If Dan pays $3,000 for insurance, his wealth is $7,000 and his utility is 90 units—the same utility as with no insurance—so $3,000 is the value of insurance for Dan.

If Dan pays $1,000 for insurance, which is the insurance company's cost of providing insurance, his wealth is $9,000 and his utility is about 98 units.

Dan and the insurance company share the gain from insurance.

──── MyEconLab Animation ────

Risk That Can't Be Insured

The gains from auto collision insurance that we've studied here apply to all types of insurance. Examples are property and casualty insurance, life insurance, and healthcare insurance. One person's risks associated with driving, life, and health are independent of other persons'. That's why insurance is possible. The risks are spread across a population.

But not all risks can be insured. To be insurable, risks must be independent. If an event causes everyone to be a loser, it isn't possible to spread and pool the risks. For example, flood insurance is often not available for people who live on a floodplain because if one person incurs a loss, most likely all do.

Also, to be insurable, a risky event must be observable to both the buyer and seller of insurance. But much of the uncertainty that we face arises

ECONOMICS IN ACTION

Insurance in the United States

We spend 7 percent of our income on private insurance. That's more than we spend on cars or food. The figure shows the relative sizes of the four main types of private insurance. More than 80 percent of Americans have life insurance, and most have private health insurance.

In addition, we buy Medicare, Medicaid, Social Security, and unemployment insurance through our taxes.

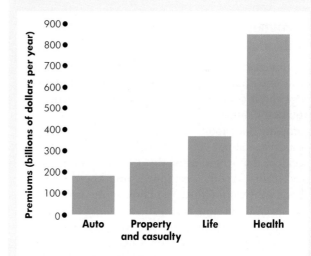

The U.S. Insurance Industry

Sources of data: U.S. Bureau of the Census, National Institute for Healthcare Management, and the American Council of Life Insurers.

◆ REVIEW QUIZ

1 How does insurance reduce risk?
2 How do we determine the value (willingness to pay) for insurance?
3 How can an insurance company offer people a deal worth taking? Why do both the buyers and the sellers of insurance gain?
4 What kinds of risks can't be insured?

Work these questions in Study Plan 20.2 and get instant feedback.   MyEconLab

because we know less (or more) than others with whom we do business. In the next section, we look at the way markets cope when buyers and sellers have different information.

◆ Private Information

In all the markets that you've studied so far, the buyers and the sellers are well informed about the good, service, or factor of production being traded. But in some markets, either the buyers or the sellers—usually the sellers—are better informed about the value of the item being traded than the person on the other side of the market. Information about the value of the item being traded that is possessed by only buyers or sellers is called **private information**. And a market in which the buyers or sellers have private information has **asymmetric information**.

Asymmetric Information: Examples and Problems

Asymmetric information affects many of your own economic transactions. One example is your knowledge about your driving skills and temperament. You know much more than your auto insurance company does about how carefully and defensively you drive—about your personal risk of having an accident that would cause the insurance company to pay a claim. Another example is your knowledge about your work effort. You know more than your employer about how hard you are willing to work. Yet another example is your knowledge about the quality of your car. You know whether it's a lemon, but the person to whom you are about to sell it does not know and can't find out until after he or she has bought it.

Asymmetric information creates two problems:

- Adverse selection
- Moral hazard

Adverse Selection **Adverse selection** is the tendency for people to *enter into agreements* in which they can use their private information to their own advantage and to the disadvantage of the uninformed party.

For example, if Jackie offers her salespeople a fixed wage, she will attract lazy salespeople. Hardworking salespeople will prefer not to work for Jackie because they can earn more by working for someone who pays by results. The fixed-wage contract adversely selects those with private information (knowledge about their work habits) who can use that knowledge to their own advantage and to the disadvantage of the other party.

Moral Hazard **Moral hazard** is the tendency for people with private information, *after entering into an agreement*, to use that information for their own benefit and at the cost of the less-informed party. For example, Jackie hires Mitch as a salesperson and pays him a fixed wage regardless of how much he sells. Mitch faces a moral hazard. He has an incentive to put in the least possible effort, benefiting himself and lowering Jackie's profits. For this reason, salespeople are usually paid by a formula that makes their income higher, the greater is the volume (or value) of their sales.

A variety of devices have evolved that enable markets to function in the face of moral hazard and adverse selection. We've just seen one, the use of incentive payments for salespeople. We're going to look at how three markets cope with adverse selection and moral hazard. They are

- The market for used cars
- The market for loans
- The market for insurance

The Market for Used Cars

When a person buys a car, it might turn out to be a lemon. If the car is a lemon, it is worth less to the buyer than if it has no defects. Does the used car market have two prices reflecting these two values—a low price for lemons and a higher price for cars without defects? It turns out that it does. But it needs some help to do so and to overcome what is called the **lemons problem**—the problem that in a market in which it is not possible to distinguish reliable products from lemons, there are too many lemons and too few reliable products traded.

To see how the used car market overcomes the lemons problem, we'll first look at a used car market that has a lemons problem.

The Lemons Problem in a Used Car Market
To explain the lemons problem as clearly as possible, we'll assume that there are only two kinds of cars: defective cars—lemons—and cars without defects that we'll call good cars. Whether or not a car is a lemon is private information that is available only to the current owner. The buyer of a used car can't tell whether he is buying a lemon until after he has bought the car and learned as much about it as its current owner knows.

Some people with low incomes and the time and ability to fix cars are willing to buy lemons as long as they know what they're buying and pay an appropriately low price. Suppose that a lemon is worth $5,000 to a buyer. More people want to buy a good car and we'll assume that a good car is worth $25,000 to a buyer.

But the buyer can't tell the difference between a lemon and a good car. Only the seller has this information. And telling the buyer that a car is not a lemon does not help. The seller has no incentive to tell the truth.

So the most that the buyer knows is the probability of buying a lemon. If half of the used cars sold turn out to be lemons, the buyer knows that he has a 50 percent chance of getting a good car and a 50 percent chance of getting a lemon.

The price that a buyer is willing to pay for a car of unknown quality is more than the value of a lemon because the car might be a good one. But the price is less than the value of a good car because it might turn out to be a lemon.

Now think about the sellers of used cars, who know the quality of their cars. Someone who owns a good car is going to be offered a price that is less than the value of that car to the buyer. Many owners will

be reluctant to sell for such a low price. So the quantity of good used cars supplied will not be as large as it would be if people paid the price they are worth.

In contrast, someone who owns a lemon is going to be offered a price that is greater than the value of that car to the buyer. So owners of lemons will be eager to sell and the quantity of lemons supplied will be greater than it would be if people paid the price that a lemon is worth.

Figure 20.6 illustrates the used car market that we've just described. Part (a) shows the demand for used cars, D, and the supply of used cars, S. The market equilibrium occurs at a price of $10,000 per car with 400 cars traded each month.

Some cars are good ones and some are lemons, but buyers can't tell the difference until it is too late to influence their decision to buy. But buyers do know what a good car and a lemon are worth to them, and sellers know the quality of the cars they are offering for sale. Figure 20.6(b) shows the demand curve for good cars, D_G, and the supply curve of good cars, S_G. Figure 20.6(c) shows the demand curve for lemons, D_L, and the supply curve of lemons, S_L.

At the market price of $10,000 per car, owners of good cars supply 200 cars a month for sale. Owners

FIGURE 20.6   The Lemons Problem

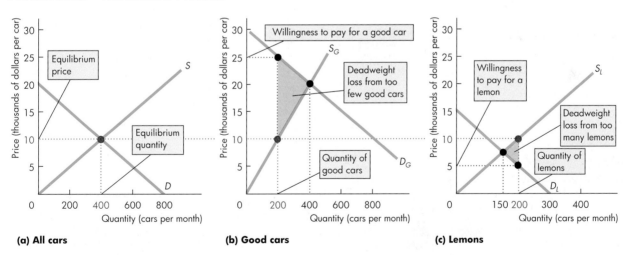

(a) All cars

(b) Good cars

(c) Lemons

Buyers can't tell a good used car from a lemon. Demand and supply determine the price and quantity of used cars traded in part (a). In part (b), D_G is the demand curve for good used cars and S_G is the supply curve. At the market price, too few

good cars are available, which brings a deadweight loss. In part (c), D_L is the demand curve for lemons and S_L is the supply curve. At the market price, too many lemons are available, which brings a deadweight loss.

MyEconLab Animation

of lemons also supply 200 cars a month for sale. The used car market is inefficient because there are too many lemons and not enough good cars. Figure 20.6 makes this inefficiency clear by using the concept of deadweight loss (see Chapter 5, pp. 114–115).

At the quantity of good cars supplied, buyers are willing to pay $25,000 for a good car. They are willing to pay more than a good car is worth to its current owner for all good cars up to 400 cars a month. The gray triangle shows the deadweight loss that results from there being too few good used cars.

At the quantity of lemons supplied, buyers are willing to pay $5,000 for a lemon. They are willing to pay less than a lemon is worth to its current owner for all lemons above 150 cars a month. The gray triangle shows the deadweight loss that results from there being too many lemons.

You can see *adverse selection* in this used car market because there is a greater incentive to offer a lemon for sale. You can see *moral hazard* because the owner of a lemon has little incentive to take good care of it. The market for used cars is not working well. Too many lemons and too few good cars are traded.

A Used Car Market with Dealers' Warranties

How can used car dealers convince buyers that a car isn't a lemon? The answer is by giving a guarantee in the form of a warranty. By providing warranties only on good cars, dealers signal which cars are good ones and which are lemons.

Signaling occurs when an informed person takes actions that send information to uninformed persons. The grades and degrees that a university awards students are signals. They inform potential (uninformed) employers about the ability of the people they are considering hiring.

In the market for used cars, dealers send signals by giving warranties on the used cars they offer for sale. The message in the signal is that the dealer agrees to pay the costs of repairing the car if it turns out to have a defect.

Buyers believe the signal because the cost of sending a false signal is high. A dealer who gives a warranty on a lemon ends up bearing a high cost of repairs—and gains a bad reputation. A dealer who gives a warranty only on good cars has no repair costs and a reputation that gets better and better. It pays

FIGURE 20.7   Warranties Make the Used Car Market Efficient

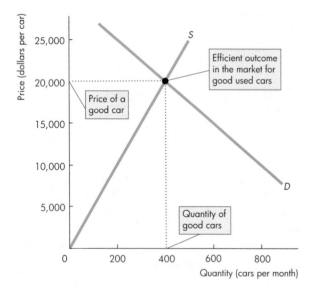

(a) Good cars

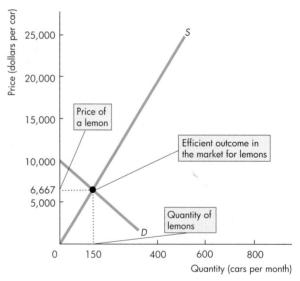

(b) Lemons

With dealers' warranties as signals, the equilibrium price of a good used car is $20,000 and 400 cars are traded. The market for good used cars is efficient. Because the signal

enables buyers to spot a lemon, the price of a lemon is $6,667 and 150 lemons are traded. The market for lemons is efficient.

MyEconLab Animation

dealers to send an accurate signal, and it is rational for buyers to believe the signal.

So a car with a warranty is a good car; a car without a warranty is a lemon. Warranties solve the lemons problem and enable the used car market to function efficiently with two prices: one for lemons and one for good cars.

Figure 20.7 illustrates this outcome. In part (a) the demand for and supply of good cars determine the price of a good car. In part (b), the demand for and supply of lemons determine the price of a lemon. Both markets are efficient.

Pooling Equilibrium and Separating Equilibrium

You've seen two outcomes in the market for used cars. Without warranties, there is only one message visible to the buyer: All cars look the same. So there is one price regardless of whether the car is a good car or a lemon. We call the equilibrium in a market when only one message is available and an uninformed person cannot determine quality a **pooling equilibrium.**

But in a used car market with warranties, there are two messages: Good cars have warranties and lemons don't. So there are two car prices for the two types of cars. We call the equilibrium in a market when signaling provides full information to a previously uninformed person a **separating equilibrium.**

The Market for Loans

When you buy a tank of gasoline and swipe your credit card, you are taking a loan from the bank that issued your card. You demand and your bank supplies a loan. Have you noticed the interest rate on an unpaid credit card balance? In 2014, it ranged between 7 percent a year and 36 percent a year. Why are these interest rates so high? And why is there such a huge range?

The answer is that when banks make loans, they face the risk that the loan will not be repaid. The risk that a borrower, also known as a creditor, might not repay a loan is called **credit risk** or **default risk.** For credit card borrowing, the credit risk is high and it varies among borrowers. The highest-risk borrowers pay the highest interest rate.

Interest rates and the price of credit risk are determined in the market for loans. The lower the interest rate, the greater is the quantity of loans demanded and for a given level of credit risk, the higher the interest rate, the greater is the quantity of loans supplied. Demand and supply determine the interest rate and the price of credit risk.

If lenders were unable to charge different interest rates to reflect different degrees of credit risk, there would be a pooling equilibrium and an inefficient loans market.

Inefficient Pooling Equilibrium To see why a pooling equilibrium would be inefficient, suppose that banks can't identify the individual credit risk of their borrowers: they have no way of knowing how likely it is that a given loan will be repaid. In this situation, every borrower pays the same interest rate and the market is in a pooling equilibrium.

If all borrowers pay the same interest rate, the market for loans has the same problem as the used car market. Low-risk customers borrow less than they would if they were offered the low interest rate appropriate for their low credit risk. High-risk customers borrow more than they would if they faced the high interest rate appropriate for their high credit risk. So banks face an *adverse selection* problem. Too many borrowers are high risk and too few are low risk.

Signaling and Screening in the Market for Loans Lenders don't know how likely it is that a given loan will be repaid, but the borrower does know. Low-risk borrowers have an incentive to signal their risk by providing lenders with relevant information. Signals might include information about the length of time a person has been in the current job or has lived at the current address, home ownership, marital status, age, and business record.

High-risk borrowers might be identified simply as those who have failed to signal low risk. These borrowers have an incentive to mislead lenders; and lenders have an incentive to induce high-risk borrowers to reveal their risk level. Inducing an informed party to reveal relevant private information is called **screening.**

By not lending to people who refuse to reveal relevant information, banks are able to screen as well as receive signals that help them to separate their borrowers into a number of credit-risk categories. If lenders succeed, the market for loans comes to a separating equilibrium with a high interest rate for high-risk borrowers and a low interest rate for low-risk borrowers. Signaling and screening in the market for loans act like warranties in the used car market and work to avoid the deadweight loss of a pooling equilibrium.

ECONOMICS IN ACTION
The Sub-Prime Credit Crisis

A sub-prime mortgage is a loan to a homebuyer who has a high risk of default. Figure 1 shows that between 2001 and 2005, the price of risk was low. Figure 2 shows why: The supply of credit, S_0, was large and so was the amount of risk taking. In 2007, the supply of credit decreased to S_1. The price of risk jumped and, faced with a higher interest rate, many sub-prime borrowers defaulted. Defaults in the sub-prime mortgage market spread to other markets that supplied the funds that financed mortgages.

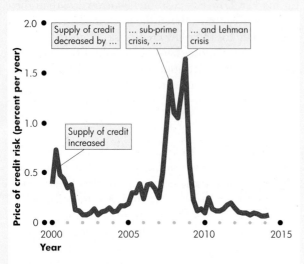

Figure 1 The Price of Commercial Credit Risk

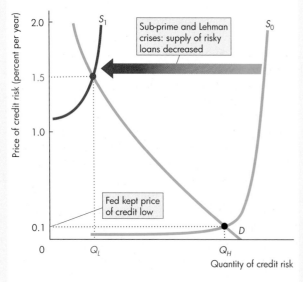

Figure 2 The Market for Risky Loans

The Market for Insurance

People who buy insurance face moral hazard, and insurance companies face adverse selection. *Moral hazard* arises because a person with insurance against a loss has less incentive than an uninsured person to avoid the loss. For example, a business with fire insurance has less incentive to install a fire alarm or sprinkler system than a business with no fire insurance does. *Adverse selection* arises because people who create greater risks are more likely to buy insurance. For example, a person with a history of driving infringements is more likely to buy collision insurance than is a person with a history of good driving.

Insurance companies have an incentive to find ways around the moral hazard and adverse selection problems. By doing so, they can lower premiums for low-risk people and raise premiums for high-risk people.

One way in which auto insurance companies separate high-risk and low-risk customers is with a *no-claim bonus*. A driver accumulates a no-claim bonus by driving safely and avoiding accidents. The greater the bonus, the greater is the incentive to drive carefully. Insurance companies also use a *deductible*. A deductible is the amount of a loss that the insured person agrees to bear. The premium is smaller, the larger is the deductible, and the decrease in the premium is more than proportionate to the increase in the deductible. By offering insurance with full coverage—no deductible—on terms that are attractive only to the high-risk people and by offering coverage with a deductible on more favorable terms that are attractive to low-risk people, insurance companies can do profitable business with everyone. High-risk people choose policies with a low deductible and a high premium; low-risk people choose policies with a high deductible and a low premium.

◆ REVIEW QUIZ

1 How does private information create adverse selection and moral hazard?
2 How do markets for cars use warranties to cope with private information?
3 How do markets for loans use signaling and screening to cope with private information?
4 How do markets for insurance use no-claim bonuses to cope with private information?

Work these questions in Study Plan 20.3 and get instant feedback. Do a Key Terms Quiz.   MyEconLab

Uncertainty, Information, and the Invisible Hand

A recurring theme throughout microeconomics is the big question: When do choices made in the pursuit of *self-interest* also promote the *social interest?* When does the invisible hand work well and when does it fail us? You've learned about the concept of efficiency, a major component of what we mean by the social interest. And you've seen that while competitive markets generally do a good job in helping to achieve efficiency, impediments such as monopoly and the absence of well-defined property rights can prevent the attainment of an efficient use of resources.

How do uncertainty and incomplete information affect the ability of self-interested choices to lead to a social interest outcome? Are these features of economic life another reason why markets fail and why some type of government intervention is required to achieve efficiency?

These are hard questions, and there are no definitive answers. But there are some useful things that we can say about the effects of uncertainty and a lack of complete information on the efficiency of resource use. We'll begin our brief review of this issue by thinking about information as just another good.

Information as a Good

More information is generally useful, and less uncertainty about the future is generally useful. Think about information as one of the goods that we want more of.

The most basic lesson about efficiency that you learned in Chapter 2 can be applied to information. Along our production possibilities frontier, we face a tradeoff between information and all other goods and services. Information, like everything else, can be produced at an increasing opportunity cost—an increasing marginal cost. For example, we could get more accurate weather forecasts, but only at increasing marginal cost, as we increased the amount of information that we gather from the atmosphere and the amount of money that we spend on supercomputers to process the data.

The principle of decreasing marginal benefit also applies to information. More information is valuable, but the more you know, the less you value another increment of information. For example, knowing that it will rain tomorrow is valuable information.

Knowing the amount of rain to within an inch is even more useful. But knowing the amount of rain to within a millimeter probably isn't worth much more.

Because the marginal cost of information is increasing and the marginal benefit is decreasing, there is an efficient amount of information. It would be inefficient to be overinformed.

In principle, competitive markets in information might deliver this efficient quantity. Whether they actually do so is hard to determine.

Monopoly in Markets that Cope with Uncertainty

There are probably large economies of scale in providing services that cope with uncertainty and incomplete information. The insurance industry, for example, is highly concentrated. Where monopoly elements exist, exactly the same inefficiency issues arise as occur in markets where uncertainty and incomplete information are not big issues. So it is likely that in some information markets, including insurance markets, there is underproduction arising from the attempt to maximize monopoly profit.

◆ REVIEW QUIZ

1 Thinking about information as a good, what determines the information that people are willing to pay for?
2 Why is it inefficient to be overinformed?
3 Why are some of the markets that provide information likely to be dominated by monopolies?

Work these questions in Study Plan 20.4 and get instant feedback.   MyEconLab

---

◆ You've seen how people make decisions when faced with uncertainty and how markets work when there is asymmetric information. *Economics in the News* on pp. 482–483 looks at the way markets in human capital and labor use grades as signals that sort students by ability so that employers can hire the type of labor they seek. You'll see why grade deflation can be efficient and grade inflation is inefficient. Discriminating grades are in the social interest and in the self-interest of universities and students.

Grades as Signals

Dean Says Median Grade at Harvard College Is A-, Most Common Grade Is A

The Crimson
December 4, 2013

The median grade at Harvard College is an A-, and the most frequently awarded mark is an A, Dean of Undergraduate Education Jay M. Harris said on Tuesday afternoon, supporting suspicions that the College employs a softer grading standard than many of its peer institutions. ...

"A little bird has told me that the most frequently given grade at Harvard College right now is an A-," Mansfield said during the meeting's question period. "If this is true or nearly true, it represents a failure on the part of this faculty and its leadership to maintain our academic standards."...

...Classics Department chair Mark J. Schiefsky, ... said he was surprised by how high the median grade was.

"I don't know what should be done about it, but it seems to me troubling," Schicfsky said. "One has a range of grades to give and one would presumably expect a wider distribution."...

The issue of grade inflation has taken center stage at some of Harvard's peer institutions as well. In 2004, Princeton substantially restructured its grading system, instructing professors to award grades in the A-range to no more than 35 percent of their students in undergraduate coursework and no more than 55 percent of students in junior and senior year independent study. ...

Yale has initiated its own discussion about grading policies in the last year, forming an ad hoc committee on the subject. In a review last spring, that committee found that 62 percent of grades awarded at Yale College from 2010 to 2012 were in the A-range.

Copyright © 2014 The Harvard Crimson, Inc.

Matthew Q. Clarida and Nicholas P. Fandos "Substantiating Fears of Grade Inflation, Dean Says Median Grade at Harvard College Is A-, Most Common Grade Is A". The Harvard Crimson. 2 December 2013.

ESSENCE OF THE STORY

- The median grade at Harvard is an A-.

- The most frequently awarded grade is an A.

- Harvard's Dean of Undergraduate Education Jay suspects the College employs a softer grading standard than many similar institutions.

- Harvard's Classics Department Chair Mark J. Schiefsky says the high grades are troubling and he would "expect a wider distribution."

- Princeton has set guidelines that limit the percentage of grades in the A-range.

- At Yale, 62 percent of grades between 2010 and 2012 were in the A-range and the school has created a committee to review the matter.

MyEconLab More Economics in the News

ECONOMIC ANALYSIS

- Accurate grades provide valuable information to students and potential employers about a student's ability.

- Harvard, Princeton, and Yale (and most schools) want to provide accurate information and avoid grade inflation—awarding a high grade to most students.

- The labor market for new college graduates works badly with grade inflation and works well with accurate grading.

- Figure 1 shows a labor market for new college graduates when there is grade inflation.

- Students with high ability are not distinguished from other students, and the supply curve represents the supply of students of all ability levels.

- The demand curve shows the employers' willingness to hire new workers without knowledge of their true ability.

- Students get hired for a low wage rate. Eventually, they get sorted by ability as employers discover the true ability of their workers from on-the-job performance.

- Figures 2 and 3 show the outcome with accurate grading.

- In Fig. 2, students with high grades get high-wage jobs and in Fig. 3, students with low grades get low-wage jobs.

- The outcomes in Figs. 2 and 3 that arise immediately with accurate grading occur eventually with grade inflation as employers accumulate information about the abilities of the workers.

- But the cost to the student and the employer of discovering true ability is greater with grade inflation than with accurate grading.

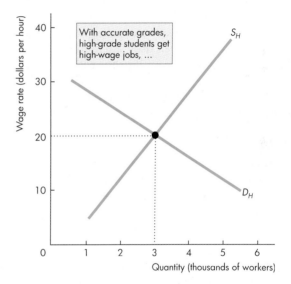

Figure 2 The Market for A Students

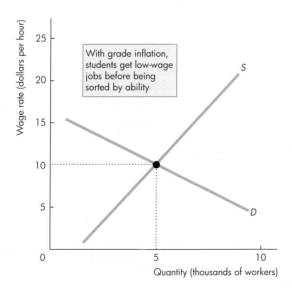

Figure 1   Market with Grade Inflation

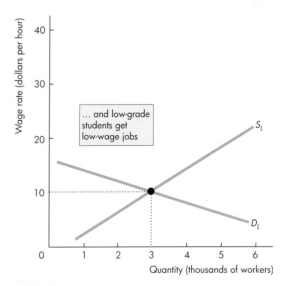

Figure 3 The Market for D Students

483

SUMMARY

Key Points

Decisions in the Face of Uncertainty (pp. 470–472)

- To make a rational choice under uncertainty, people choose the action that maximizes the expected utility of wealth.
- A decreasing marginal utility of wealth makes people risk averse. A sure outcome with a given expected wealth is preferred to a risky outcome with the same expected wealth—risk is costly.
- The cost of risk is found by comparing the expected wealth in a given risky situation with the wealth that gives the same utility but with no risk.

Working Problem 1 will give you a better understanding of decisions in the face of uncertainty.

Buying and Selling Risk (pp. 473–475)

- People trade risk in markets for insurance.
- By pooling risks, insurance companies can reduce the risks people face (from insured activities) at a lower cost than the value placed on the lower risk.

Working Problems 2 and 3 will give you a better understanding of buying and selling risk.

Private Information (pp. 476–480)

- Asymmetric information creates adverse selection and moral hazard problems.

- When it is not possible to distinguish good-quality products from lemons, too many lemons and too few good-quality products are traded in a pooling equilibrium.
- Signaling can overcome the lemons problem.
- In the market for used cars, warranties signal good cars and an efficient separating equilibrium occurs.
- Private information about credit risk is overcome by using signals and screening based on personal characteristics.
- Private information about risk in insurance markets is overcome by using the no-claim bonus and deductibles.

Working Problems 4 and 5 will give you a better understanding of private information.

Uncertainty, Information, and the Invisible Hand (p. 481)

- Less uncertainty and more information can be viewed as a good that has increasing marginal cost and decreasing marginal benefit.
- Competitive information markets might be efficient, but economies of scale might bring inefficient underproduction of information and insurance.

Working Problem 6 will give you a better understanding of uncertainty, information, and the invisible hand.

Key Terms

MyEconLab Key Terms Quiz

Adverse selection, 476
Asymmetric information, 476
Credit risk or default risk, 479
Expected utility, 471
Expected wealth, 470

Lemons problem, 476
Moral hazard, 476
Pooling equilibrium, 479
Private information, 476
Risk aversion, 470

Screening, 479
Separating equilibrium, 479
Signaling, 478

◆ WORKED PROBLEM

MyEconLab   You can work this problem in Chapter 20 Study Plan.

Lou is offered a risky summer lawn-mowing job. If he takes this job, there is a 50 percent chance that at the end of the summer he will have $5,000 and a 50 percent chance that he will have only $1,000. The table shows Lou's utility from his end-of-summer wealth.

Wealth (dollars)	Utility (units)
0	0
1,000	8
2,000	14
3,000	17
4,000	19
5,000	20
6,000	21

Questions

1. What is Lou's expected end-of-summer wealth from taking this job?

2. What is Lou's expected utility from taking this job?

3. Another firm offers Lou a job with no risk. How much end-of-summer wealth would Lou need from that job for him to take it in preference to the risky lawn-mowing job?

4. What is Lou's cost of risk?

Solutions

1. With a 50 percent chance of having $5,000 and a 50 percent chance of having $1,000, Lou's expected wealth equals (5,000 × 0.5) + (1,000 × 0.5), which equals $3,000.

Key Point: Expected wealth is the average wealth calculated by using a formula that weights each possible outcome with the probablity (chance) that it will occur.

2. Lou's expected utility from taking this job depends on his utility from the two outcomes. Lou's utility from $5,000 is 20 units and his utility from $1,000 is 8 units. Each possibility occurs with a probability of 0.5, so his expected utility equals (20 × 0.5) + (8 × 0.5) = 14 units.

Key Point: Expected utility is the average utility calculated by using a formula that weights the utility from each outcome with the probablity (chance) that it will occur.

3. For Lou to take the no-risk job rather than the risky lawn-mowing job, he would need to get an end-of-summer utility that exceeds his expected utility of 14 units from the risky lawn-mowing job.

    From the data in the table, for Lou to have the same utility at the end of the summer as he'd get from the risky job, he would need the no-risk job to give him $2,000 of wealth.

Key Point: A risky outcome must have a larger expected wealth than a no-risk outcome to give the same expected utility.

4. Lou's cost of risk from taking the lawn-mowing job equals his expected wealth from taking the risky job ($3,000) minus the wealth from the no-risk job that gives him the same utility ($2,000) as the risky job. So for Lou, the cost of risk is $1,000.

Key Point: The cost of risk equals the amount that a person would have to be offered to create the incentive to bear the risk.

Key Figure

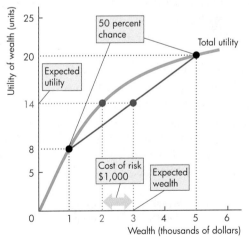

MyEconLab Interactive Animation

STUDY PLAN PROBLEMS AND APPLICATIONS

MyEconLab   You can work Problems 1 to 6 in Chapter 20 Study Plan and get instant feedback.

Decisions in the Face of Uncertainty (Study Plan 20.1)

1. The figure shows Lee's utility of wealth curve.

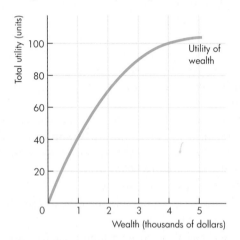

Lee is offered a job as a salesperson in which there is a 50 percent chance that she will make $4,000 a month and a 50 percent chance that she will make nothing.

a. What is Lee's expected income from taking this job?

b. What is Lee's expected utility from taking this job?

c. How much would another firm have to offer Lee with certainty to persuade her not to take the risky sales job?

d. What is Lee's cost of risk?

Buying and Selling Risk (Study Plan 20.2)

Use the following data to work Problems 2 and 3.
Larry lives in a neighborhood in which 20 percent of the cars are stolen every year. Larry's car, which he parks on the street overnight, is worth $20,000. (This is Larry's only wealth.) The table shows Larry's utility of wealth schedule.

Wealth (dollars)	Utility (units)
20,000	400
16,000	350
12,000	280
8,000	200
4,000	110
0	0

2. If Larry cannot buy auto theft insurance, what is his expected wealth and his expected utility?

3. High-Crime Auto Theft, an insurance company, offers to sell Larry insurance at $8,000 a year and promises to provide Larry with a replacement car worth $20,000 if his car is stolen. Is Larry willing to buy this insurance? If not, is he willing to pay $4,000 a year for such insurance?

Private Information (Study Plan 20.3)

4. Suppose that there are three national soccer leagues: Time League, Goal Difference League, and Bonus for Win League. The leagues are of equal quality, but the players are paid differently. Players in the Time League are paid by the hour for time spent practicing and playing. Players in the Goal Difference League are paid an amount that depends on the goals scored by the team minus the goals scored against it. Players in the Bonus for Win League are paid one wage for a loss, a higher wage for a tie, and the highest wage of all for a win.

a. Describe the predicted differences in the quality of the games played by each of the leagues.

b. Which league is the most attractive to players?

c. Which league will generate the largest profits?

5. You can't buy insurance against the risk of being sold a lemon. Why isn't there such a market? How does the market provide a buyer with some protection against being sold a lemon? What are the main ways in which markets overcome the lemons problem?

Uncertainty, Information, and the Invisible Hand
(Study Plan 20.4)

6. **Show Us Our Money**
I have no clue what my colleagues make and I consider my salary my own business. It turns out that could be a huge mistake. What if employers made all employee salaries known? If you think about it, who is served by all the secrecy? Knowing what other workers make might be more ammunition to gun for a raise.

Source: *Time*, May 12, 2008

Explain why a worker might be willing to pay for the salary information of other workers.

ADDITIONAL PROBLEMS AND APPLICATIONS

MyEconLab   You can work these problems in MyEconLab if assigned by your instructor.

Decisions in the Face of Uncertainty

Use the following table, which shows Jimmy's and Zenda's utility of wealth schedules, to work Problems 7 to 9.

Wealth	Jimmy's utility	Zenda's utility
0	0	0
100	200	512
200	300	640
300	350	672
400	375	678
500	387	681
600	393	683
700	396	684

7. What are Jimmy's and Zenda's expected utilities from a bet that gives them a 50 percent chance of having a wealth of $600 and a 50 percent chance of having nothing?

8. a. Calculate Jimmy's and Zenda's marginal utility of wealth schedules.

   b. Who is more risk averse, Jimmy or Zenda? How do you know?

9. Suppose that Jimmy and Zenda each have $400 and are offered a business investment opportunity that involves committing the entire $400 to the project. The project could return $600 (a profit of $200) with a probability of 0.85 or $200 (a loss of $200) with a probability of 0.15. Who goes for the project and who hangs on to the initial $400?

Use the following information to work Problems 10 to 12.

Two students, Jim and Kim, are offered summer jobs managing a student house-painting business. There is a 50 percent chance that either of them will be successful and end up with $21,000 of wealth to get them through the next school year. But there is also a 50 percent chance that either will end up with only $3,000 of wealth. Each could take a completely safe but back-breaking job picking fruit that would leave them with a guaranteed $9,000 at the end of the summer. The table in the next column shows Jim's and Kim's utility of wealth schedules.

Wealth	Jim's utility	Kim's utility
0	0	0
3,000	100	200
6,000	200	350
9,000	298	475
12,000	391	560
15,000	482	620
18,000	572	660
21,000	660	680

10. Does anyone take the painting job? If so, who takes it and why? Does anyone take the job picking fruit? If so, who takes it and why?

11. In Problem 10, what is each student's maximized expected utility? Who has the larger expected wealth? Who ends up with the larger wealth at the end of the summer?

12. In Problem 10, if one of the students takes the risky job, how much more would the fruit-picking job have needed to pay to attract that student?

Buying and Selling Risk

Use the following table, which shows Chris's utility of wealth schedule, to work Problems 13 and 14.

Chris's wealth is $5,000 and it consists entirely of her share in a risky ice cream business. If the summer is cold, the business will fail, and she will have no wealth. Where Chris lives there is a 50 percent chance each year that the summer will be cold.

Wealth (dollars)	Utility (units)
5,000	150
4,000	140
3,000	120
2,000	90
1,000	50
0	0

13. If Chris cannot buy cold-summer insurance, what is her expected wealth and what is her expected utility?

14. Business Loss Recovery, an insurance company, is willing to sell Chris cold-summer insurance at a price of $3,000 a year and promises to pay her

$5,000 if the summer is cold and the business fails. Is Chris willing to buy this loss insurance? If she is, is she willing to pay $4,000 a year for it?

Private Information

Use the following information to work Problems 15 to 17.

Larry has a good car that he wants to sell; Harry has a lemon that he wants to sell. Each knows what type of car he is selling. You are looking at used cars and plan to buy one.

15. If both Larry and Harry are offering their cars for sale at the same price, from whom would you most want to buy, Larry or Harry, and why?

16. If you made an offer of the same price to Larry and Harry, who would sell to you and why? Describe the adverse selection problem that arises if you offer the same price to Larry and Harry.

17. How can Larry signal that he is selling a good car so that you are willing to pay Larry the price that he knows his car is worth, and a higher price than what you are willing to offer Harry?

18. Pam is a safe driver and Fran is a reckless driver. Each knows what type of driver she is, but no one else knows. What might an automobile insurance company do to get Pam to signal that she is a safe driver so that it can offer her insurance at a lower premium than it offers to Fran?

19. Why do you think it is not possible to buy insurance against having to put up with a low-paying, miserable job? Explain why a market in insurance of this type would be valuable to workers but unprofitable for an insurance provider and so would not work.

Uncertainty, Information, and the Invisible Hand

Use the following news clip to work Problems 20 and 21.

Why We Worry About the Things We Shouldn't … and Ignore the Things We Should

We pride ourselves on being the only species that understands the concept of risk, yet we have a confounding habit of worrying about mere possibilities while ignoring probabilities, building barricades against perceived dangers while leaving ourselves exposed to real ones: 20% of all adults still smoke; nearly 20% of drivers and more than 30% of back-seat passengers don't use seat belts; two thirds of us

are overweight or obese. We dash across the street against the light and build our homes in hurricane-prone areas—and when they're demolished by a storm, we rebuild in the same spot.

Source: *Time*, December 4, 2006

20. Explain how "worrying about mere possibilities while ignoring probabilities" can result in people making decisions that not only fail to satisfy social interest, but also fail to satisfy self-interest.

21. How can information be used to improve people's decision making?

Economics in the News

22. After you have studied *Economics in the News* on pp. 482–483, answer the following questions.
    a. What information do accurate grades provide that grade inflation hides?
    b. If grade inflation became widespread in high schools, colleges, and universities, what new arrangements do you predict would emerge to provide better information about student ability?
    c. Do you think grade inflation is in anyone's self-interest? Explain who benefits and how they benefit from grade inflation.
    d. How do you think grade inflation might be controlled?

23. **Are You Paid What You're Worth?**
    How do you know if your pay adequately reflects your contributions to your employer's profits? In many instances, you don't. Your employer has more and better information than you do about how your salary and bonus compare to others in your field, to others in your office, and relative to the company's profits in any given year. You can narrow the information gap a bit if you're willing to buy salary reports from compensation sources. For example, at $200, a quick-call salary report from Economic Research Institute will offer you compensation data for your position based on your years of experience, your industry and the place where your company is located.

    Source: CNN, April 3, 2006

    a. Explain the role that asymmetric information can play in worker wages.
    b. What adverse selection problem exists if a firm offers lower wages to current workers?
    c. What will determine how much a worker should actually pay for a detailed salary report?

For Whom?

During the past 35 years, the gap between the richest and the poorest in America has widened. But millions in Asia have been lifted from poverty and are now enjoying a high and rapidly rising standard of living. What are the forces that generate these trends? The answer to this question is the forces of demand and supply in factor markets. These forces determine wages, interest rates, rents, and the prices of natural resources. These forces also determine people's incomes.

In America, human capital and entrepreneurship are the most prized resources, and their incomes have grown most rapidly. In Asia, labor has seen its wage rates transformed. And in all regions rich in oil, incomes have risen on the back of high and fast-rising energy prices.

Many outstanding economists have advanced our understanding of factor markets and the role they play in helping to resolve the conflict between the demands of humans and the resources available. One of them is Thomas Robert Malthus.

Another is Harold Hotelling, whose prediction of an ever-rising price of nonrenewable natural resources implies an ever-falling rate of their use and an intensifying search for substitutes.

Yet another is Julian Simon, who challenged both the Malthusian gloom and the Hotelling Principle. He believed that people are the "ultimate resource" and predicted that a rising population lessens the pressure on natural resources. A bigger population provides a larger number of resourceful people who can discover more efficient ways of using scarce resources.

Thomas Robert Malthus *(1766–1834), an English clergyman and economist, was an extremely influential social scientist. In his best-selling* Essay on the Principle of Population, *published in 1798, he predicted that population growth would outstrip food production and said that wars, famine, and disease were inevitable unless population growth was held in check by marrying at a late age and living a celibate life. (He married at 38 a wife of 27, marriage ages that he recommended for others.)*

Malthus had a profound influence on Charles Darwin, who got the key idea that led him to the theory of natural selection from the Essay on the Principle of Population. *But it was also Malthus's gloomy predictions that made economics the "dismal science."*

"The passion between the sexes has appeared in every age to be so nearly the same, that it may always be considered, in algebraic language, as a given quantity."

THOMAS ROBERT MALTHUS
An Essay on the Principle of Population

RAJ CHETTY is the William Henry Bloomberg Professor of Economics, at Harvard University, where he was also an undergraduate, earning his BA summa cum laude in 2000, and graduate student, completing his PhD in 2003.

Professor Chetty is also Director of Harvard's Lab for Economic Applications and Policy, Co-Director of the Public Economics Program or the National Bureau of Economic Research, a member of the Congressional Budget Office Panel of Economic Advisers, and editor of the Journal of Public Economics.

His list of honors is extraordinarily long and includes the 2013 John Bates Clark Medal of the American Economic Association, awarded to the best economist under 40 years of age, the National Tax Association Best Dissertation Prize in 2003, and the Harris, Hoopes, and Williams Prizes for the best thesis and undergraduate in economics at Harvard, in 2000.

He has published more than 20 papers in leading journals on a wide range of policy issues and come up with interesting answers, some of which he describes here.

Michael Parkin talked with Raj Chetty about his research and what we learn from it about how to design more effective government economic policies.

Every economics student learns that tax incidence and deadweight loss depend on the elasticities of supply and demand, and that one of the most crucial elasticities is that of the supply of labor. What does your work tell us about this elasticity? Is labor supply elastic or inelastic?

It is true that the labor supply elasticity is a key determinant of the deadweight loss from income taxation. If people are very responsive in how much they work, that is, if labor supply is very elastic with respect to tax rates, then having high tax rates will generate a lot of inefficiency.

My work has shown that the picture is actually quite a bit more complicated than that because there are many other factors that affect how people respond to tax changes beyond what we have in standard economic models.

> ... labor supply might be somewhat elastic in the long run ... [but in the short run] may not be very elastic.

To take one example, we usually assume that people perfectly understand and pay attention to the complicated income tax system that we face in the United States today. But we have a number of studies showing that in fact many people aren't aware of tax rates they face, don't really pay attention to tax changes, and may not, at least in the short run, respond by changing the amount they work when the tax code is changed in complicated ways.

The bottom line is that labor supply might be somewhat elastic in the long run if you've got very high tax rates, say, as in European economies for 50 years consistently. People might start to think "Oh, I don't get to keep so much of my paycheck, maybe it doesn't pay to work." With a short-run tax increase of 5 or 10 percent, our growing sense is that people may not respond as much, and labor supply may not be very elastic.

*Read the full interview with Raj Chetty in MyEconLab.

21

MEASURING GDP AND ECONOMIC GROWTH

After studying this chapter, you will be able to:

- ◆ Define GDP and explain why GDP equals aggregate expenditure and aggregate income
- ◆ Explain how the Bureau of Economic Analysis measures U.S. GDP and real GDP
- ◆ Explain the uses and limitations of real GDP as a measure of economic well-being

Will our economy start to expand more rapidly in 2015 or will growth remain slow? Or worse, will the economy slip into recession? U.S. businesses, both small and large, want to know the answers to these questions. To assess the state of the economy and to make big decisions about business expansion, firms such as Google and Amazon use forecasts of GDP. What is GDP and what does it tell us about the state of the economy?

In this chapter, you will find out how economic statisticians at the Bureau of Economic Analysis measure GDP and its rate of growth. You will also learn about the uses and the limitations of these measures. In *Economics in the News* at the end of the chapter, you can see what GDP tells us about the state of the U.S. economy today.

491

◆ Gross Domestic Product

What exactly is GDP, how is it calculated, what does it mean, and why do we care about it? You are going to discover the answers to these questions in this chapter. First, what *is* GDP?

GDP Defined

GDP, or **gross domestic product**, is the market value of the final goods and services produced within a country in a given time period. This definition has four parts:

- Market value
- Final goods and services
- Produced within a country
- In a given time period

We'll examine each in turn.

Market Value To measure total production, we must add together the production of apples and oranges, computers and popcorn. Just counting the items doesn't get us very far. For example, which is the greater total production: 100 apples and 50 oranges or 50 apples and 100 oranges?

GDP answers this question by valuing items at their *market values*—the prices at which items are traded in markets. If the price of an apple is 10 cents, then the market value of 50 apples is $5. If the price of an orange is 20 cents, then the market value of 100 oranges is $20. By using market prices to value production, we can add the apples and oranges together. The market value of 50 apples and 100 oranges is $5 plus $20, or $25.

Final Goods and Services To calculate GDP, we value the *final goods and services* produced. A **final good** (or service) is an item that is bought by its final user during a specified time period. It contrasts with an **intermediate good** (or service), which is an item that is produced by one firm, bought by another firm, and used as a component of a final good or service.

For example, a Ford truck is a final good, but a Firestone tire on the truck is an intermediate good. An iPad is a final good, but an Apple A5X chip inside it is an intermediate good.

If we were to add the value of intermediate goods and services produced to the value of final goods and services, we would count the same thing many times—a problem called *double counting*. The value of a truck already includes the value of the tires, and the value of an iPad already includes the value of the chip inside it.

Some goods can be an intermediate good in some situations and a final good in other situations. For example, the ice cream that you buy on a hot summer day is a final good, but the ice cream that a restaurant buys and uses to make sundaes is an intermediate good. The sundae is the final good. So whether a good is an intermediate good or a final good depends on what it is used for, not what it is.

The purchase of a secondhand good—for example, a used car or existing home—isn't part of GDP. It was part of GDP in the year in which it was produced.

Produced Within a Country Only goods and services that are produced *within a country* count as part of that country's GDP. Nike Corporation, a U.S. firm, produces sneakers in Vietnam, and the market value of those shoes is part of Vietnam's GDP, not part of U.S. GDP. Toyota, a Japanese firm, produces automobiles in Georgetown, Kentucky, and the value of this production is part of U.S. GDP, not part of Japan's GDP.

In a Given Time Period GDP measures the value of production *in a given time period*—normally either a quarter of a year—called the quarterly GDP data—or a year—called the annual GDP data.

GDP and the Circular Flow of Expenditure and Income

GDP is a measure of the value of total production. We can measure this value either by the total income earned producing GDP or the total expenditure on GDP. The equality between the value of total production and total income is important because it shows the direct link between productivity and living standards. Our standard of living rises when our incomes rise and we can afford to buy more goods and services. But we must produce more goods and services if we are to be able to buy more goods and services.

Rising incomes and a rising value of production go together. They are two aspects of the same phenomenon. You're now going to see why.

The Circular Flow Model Figure 21.1 illustrates the circular flow model. The economy consists of households, firms, governments, and the rest of the world (the rectangles), which trade in factor markets and goods (and services) markets. We focus first on households and firms.

Households and Firms Households sell and firms buy the services of labor, capital, and land in factor markets. For these factor services, firms pay income to households: wages for labor services, interest for the use of capital, and rent for the use of land. A fourth factor of production, entrepreneurship, receives profit.

Firms' retained earnings—profits that are not distributed to households—are part of the household sector's income. You can think of retained earnings as being income that households save and lend back to firms. Figure 21.1 shows the total income—*aggregate*

income—received by households, including retained earnings, as the blue flow labeled *Y*.

Firms sell and households buy consumer goods and services in goods markets. The total payment for these goods and services is **consumption expenditure**, shown by the red flow labeled *C*.

Firms buy and sell new capital equipment—such as computer systems, airplanes, trucks, and assembly line equipment—in goods markets. Some of what firms produce is not sold but is added to inventory. For example, if GM produces 1,000 cars and sells 950 of them, the other 50 cars remain in GM's inventory of unsold cars, which increases by 50 cars. When a firm adds unsold output to inventory, we can think of the firm as buying goods from itself. The purchase of new plant, equipment, and buildings and the additions to inventories are **investment**, shown by the red flow labeled *I*.

FIGURE 21.1 The Circular Flow of Expenditure and Income

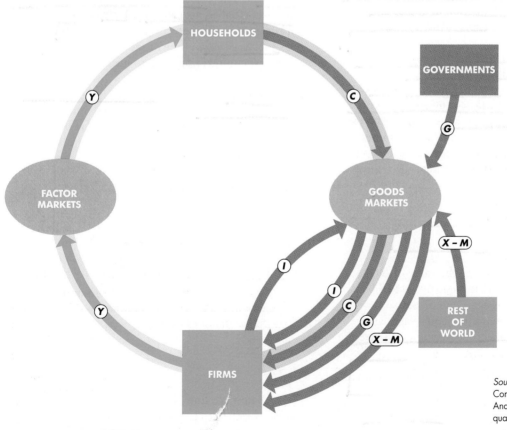

Households make consumption expenditures (*C*); firms make investments (*I*); governments buy goods and services (*G*); and the rest of the world buys net exports (*X − M*). Firms pay incomes (*Y*) to households. Aggregate income equals aggregate expenditure.

Billions of dollars in 2014

C =	11,729
I =	2,714
G =	3,139
X − M =	−538
Y =	17,044

Source of data: U.S. Department of Commerce, Bureau of Economic Analysis. (The data are for the first quarter of 2014 annual rate.)

MyEconLab Animation and Draw Graph

Governments Governments buy goods and services from firms—**government expenditure.** In Fig. 21.1, government expenditure is shown as the red flow *G*.

Governments finance their expenditure with taxes and make financial transfers to households, such as Social Security benefits and unemployment benefits, and pay subsidies to firms. But taxes and financial transfers are not part of the circular flow of expenditure and income.

Rest of the World Firms in the United States sell goods and services to the rest of the world—**exports**—and buy goods and services from the rest of the world—**imports.** The value of exports (*X*) minus the value of imports (*M*) is called **net exports**, the red flow *X − M* in Fig 21.1. If net exports are positive, the net flow is from U.S. firms to the rest of the world. If net exports are negative, the net flow is from the rest of the world to U.S. firms.

GDP Equals Expenditure Equals Income Gross domestic product can be measured in two ways: By the total expenditure on goods and services or by the total income earned producing goods and services.

The total expenditure—*aggregate expenditure*—is the sum of the red flows in Fig. 21.1. Aggregate expenditure equals consumption expenditure plus investment plus government expenditure plus net exports.

Aggregate income is equal to the total amount paid for the services of the factors of production used to produce final goods and services—wages, interest, rent, and profit. The blue flow in Fig. 21.1 shows aggregate income. Because firms pay out as incomes (including retained profits) everything they receive from the sale of their output, aggregate income (the blue flow) equals aggregate expenditure (the sum of the red flows). That is,

$$Y = C + I + G + X - M.$$

The table in Fig. 21.1 shows the value of each expenditure in 2014 and that their sum is $17,044 billion, which also equals aggregate income.

Because aggregate expenditure equals aggregate income, the two methods of measuring GDP give the same answer. So

> GDP equals aggregate expenditure and equals aggregate income.

The circular flow model is the foundation on which the national economic accounts are built.

Why "Domestic" and Why "Gross"?

What do the words "domestic" and "gross" mean in the term gross domestic product?

Domestic *Domestic* product is production *within a country*. It contrasts with a related concept, *national* product, which is the value of goods and services produced anywhere in the world by the residents of a nation. For example, Nike's income from shoe factories that it owns in Vietnam is part of U.S. national product. But it is part of Vietnam's domestic product. Gross national product, GNP, equals GDP plus net income from factors of production owned in other countries.

Gross *Gross* means before subtracting the depreciation of capital. The opposite of gross is *net*, which means after subtracting the depreciation of capital.

Depreciation is the decrease in the value of a firm's capital that results from wear and tear and obsolescence. The total amount spent both buying new capital and replacing depreciated capital is called **gross investment.** The amount by which the value of capital increases is called **net investment.** Net investment equals gross investment minus depreciation.

Gross investment is one of the expenditures included in the expenditure approach to measuring GDP. So the resulting value of total product is a gross measure.

Gross profit, which is a firm's profit before subtracting depreciation, is one of the incomes included in the income approach to measuring GDP. So again, the resulting value of total product is a gross measure.

◆ REVIEW QUIZ

1 Define GDP and distinguish between a final good and an intermediate good. Provide examples.
2 Why does GDP equal aggregate income and also equal aggregate expenditure?
3 What are the distinctions between domestic and national, and gross and net?

Work these questions in Study Plan 21.1 and get instant feedback. Do a Key Terms Quiz.   MyEconLab

Let's now see how the ideas that you've just studied are used in practice. We'll see how GDP and its components are measured in the United States today.

◆ Measuring U.S. GDP

The Bureau of Economic Analysis (BEA) uses the concepts in the circular flow model to measure GDP and its components in the *National Income and Product Accounts*. Because the value of aggregate production equals aggregate expenditure and aggregate income, there are two approaches available for measuring GDP, and both are used. They are

- The expenditure approach
- The income approach

The Expenditure Approach

The *expenditure approach* measures GDP as the sum of consumption expenditure (C), investment (I), government expenditure on goods and services (G), and net exports of goods and services ($X - M$). These expenditures correspond to the red flows through the goods markets in the circular flow model in Fig. 21.1 and Fig. 21.2. Table 21.1 shows these expenditures and GDP for 2014.

Personal consumption expenditures (the red flow C in Fig. 21.2) are the expenditures by U.S. households on goods and services produced in the United States and in the rest of the world. They include goods such as soda and books and services such as banking and legal advice. They also include the purchase of consumer durable goods such as TVs and microwave ovens.

FIGURE 21.2 Aggregate Expenditure

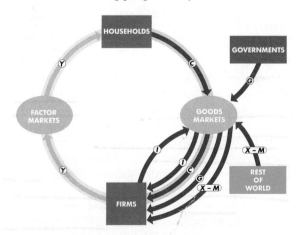

Aggregate expenditure is the sum of the red flows.

MyEconLab Animation

TABLE 21.1   GDP: The Expenditure Approach

Item	Symbol	Amount in 2014 (billions of dollars)	Percentage of GDP
Personal consumption expenditures	C	11,729	68.8
Gross private domestic investment	I	2,714	15.9
Government expenditure on goods and services	G	3,139	18.4
Net exports of goods and services	X–M	–538	–3.2
Gross domestic product	**Y**	**17,044**	**100.0**

The expenditure approach measures GDP as the sum of personal consumption expenditures, C, gross private domestic investment, I, government expenditure on goods and services, G, and net exports, X – M. In 2014, GDP measured by the expenditure approach was $17,044 billion. Expenditure on personal consumption goods and services is more than two thirds of aggregate expenditure.

Source of data: U.S. Department of Commerce, Bureau of Economic Analysis. The data are for the first quarter of 2014 at an annual rate.

But they do *not* include the purchase of new homes, which the BEA counts as part of investment.

Gross private domestic investment (the red flow I in Fig. 21.2) is expenditure on capital equipment and buildings by firms and the additions to business inventories. It also includes expenditure on new homes by households.

Government expenditure on goods and services (the red flow G in Fig. 21.2) is the expenditure by all levels of government on goods and services such as national defense and garbage collection. It does *not* include *transfer payments*, such as unemployment benefits, because they are not expenditures on goods and services.

Net exports of goods and services (the red flow $X - M$ in Fig. 21.2) are the value of exports minus the value of imports. This item includes the value of airplanes that Boeing sells to British Airways (a U.S. export), and the value of Japanese DVD players that Best Buy purchases from Sony (a U.S. import).

The Income Approach

The *income approach* measures GDP by summing the incomes that firms pay households for the services of the factors of production they hire—wages for labor, interest for capital, rent for land, and profit for entrepreneurship. These incomes correspond to the blue flows through the factor markets in the circular flow model in Fig. 21.1 and Fig. 21.3. Table 21.2 shows these incomes and GDP for 2014.

Compensation of employees (the blue flow *W* in Fig. 21.3) is the payment for labor services. It includes net wages and salaries (called "take-home pay") that workers receive plus taxes withheld on earnings plus fringe benefits such as Social Security and pension fund contributions. This item is more than 50 percent of total income.

Net interest, rental income, corporate profits, and proprietors' income are earned by capital and land. These other factor incomes are in the blue flow *OFI* in Fig. 21.3.

The factor incomes sum to *net domestic income at factor cost*, which is the cost of the factors of production used to produce final goods. The *expenditures* on final goods are valued at *market prices*, which differ from factor cost because of indirect taxes and subsidies.

An *indirect tax* is a tax such as a sales tax or a tax on gasoline. Market price includes indirect taxes, so exceeds factor cost. A *subsidy* is a payment, such as a farm subsidy, by the government to a producer. Subsidies make market price less than factor cost.

TABLE 21.2   GDP: The Income Approach

Item	Amount in 2014 (billions of dollars)	Percentage of GDP
Compensation of employees	9,109	53.4
Net interest	685	4.0
Rental income	623	3.7
Corporate profits	1,514	8.9
Proprietors' income	1,351	7.9
Net domestic income at factor cost	13,282	77.9
Indirect taxes *less* subsidies	1,244	7.3
Net domestic income at market prices	14,526	85.2
Depreciation	2,699	15.8
GDP (income approach)	**17,225**	**101.1**
Statistical discrepancy	−181	−1.1
GDP (expenditure approach)	**17,044**	**100.0**

The sum of factor incomes equals *net domestic income at factor cost*. GDP equals net domestic income at factor cost plus indirect taxes minus subsidies plus depreciation.

In 2014, GDP measured by the income approach was $17,225 billion. This amount is $181 billion more than GDP measured by the expenditure approach—a statistical discrepancy of $181 billion or 1.1 percent of GDP.

Compensation of employees—labor income—is by far the largest component of aggregate income.

Source of data: U.S. Department of Commerce, Bureau of Economic Analysis. The data are for the first quarter of 2014 at annual rate.

FIGURE 21.3   Aggregate Income

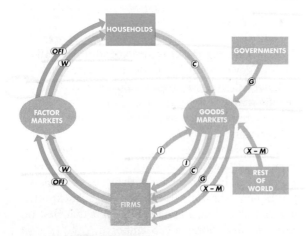

Aggregate income is the sum of the blue flows.

MyEconLab Animation

To get from factor cost to market price, we add indirect taxes and subtract subsidies and get *net domestic income at market prices*. We still must get from a *net* to a *gross* measure.

Total expenditure is a *gross* number because it includes *gross* investment. Net domestic income at market prices is a net income measure because corporate profits are measured *after deducting depreciation*. They are a *net* income measure. To get from net income to gross income, we must *add depreciation*.

We've now arrived at GDP using the income approach. This number is not exactly the same as GDP using the expenditure approach because all the numbers are estimates. The gap between the two measures of GDP, called the *statistical discrepancy*, is never large. In 2014, it was 1.1 percent of GDP.

Nominal GDP and Real GDP

Often, we want to *compare* GDP in two periods, say 2000 and 2014. In 2000, GDP was $10,285 billion and in 2014, it was $17,044 billion—66 percent higher than in 2000. This increase in GDP is a combination of an increase in production and a rise in prices. To isolate the increase in production from the rise in prices, we distinguish between *real* GDP and *nominal* GDP.

Real GDP is the value of final goods and services produced in a given year when *valued at the prices of a reference base year*. By comparing the value of production in the two years at the same prices, we reveal the change in production.

Currently, the reference base year is 2009 and we describe real GDP as measured in 2009 dollars—in terms of what the dollar would buy in 2009.

Nominal GDP is the value of final goods and services produced in a given year when valued at the prices of that year. Nominal GDP is just a more precise name for GDP.

Economists at the Bureau of Economic Analysis calculate real GDP using the method described in the Mathematical Note on pp. 508–509. Here, we'll explain the basic idea but not the technical details.

Calculating Real GDP

We'll calculate real GDP for an economy that produces one consumption good, one capital good, and one government service. Net exports are zero.

Table 21.3 shows the quantities produced and the prices in 2009 (the base year) and in 2014. In part (a), we calculate nominal GDP in 2009. For each item, we multiply the quantity produced in 2009 by its price in 2009 to find the total expenditure on the item. We sum the expenditures to find nominal GDP, which in 2009 is $100 million. Because 2009 is the base year, both real GDP and nominal GDP equal $100 million.

In Table 21.3(b), we calculate nominal GDP in 2014, which is $300 million. Nominal GDP in 2014 is three times its value in 2009. But by how much has production increased? Real GDP will tell us.

In Table 21.3(c), we calculate real GDP in 2014. The quantities of the goods and services produced are those of 2014, as in part (b). The prices are those in the reference base year—2009, as in part (a).

For each item, we multiply the quantity produced in 2014 by its price in 2009. We then sum these expenditures to find real GDP in 2014, which is $160 million. This number is what total expenditure

TABLE 21.3 Calculating Nominal GDP and Real GDP

	Item	Quantity (millions)	Price (dollars)	Expenditure (millions of dollars)
(a) In 2009				
C	T-shirts	10	5	50
I	Computer chips	3	10	30
G	Security services	1	20	20
Y	Real GDP in 2009			100
(b) In 2014				
C	T-shirts	4	5	20
I	Computer chips	2	20	40
G	Security services	6	40	240
Y	Nominal GDP in 2014			300
(c) Quantities of 2014 valued at prices of 2009				
C	T-shirts	4	5	20
I	Computer chips	2	10	20
G	Security services	6	20	120
Y	Real GDP in 2014			160

In 2009, the reference base year, real GDP equals nominal GDP and was $100 million. In 2014, nominal GDP increased to $300 million, but real GDP, which is calculated by using the quantities in 2014 in part (b) and the prices in 2009 in part (a), was only $160 million—a 60 percent increase from 2009.

would have been in 2014 if prices had remained the same as they were in 2009.

Nominal GDP in 2014 is three times its value in 2009, but real GDP in 2014 is only 1.6 times its 2009 value—a 60 percent increase in production.

◆ REVIEW QUIZ

1 What is the expenditure approach to measuring GDP?
2 What is the income approach to measuring GDP?
3 What adjustments must be made to total income to make it equal GDP?
4 What is the distinction between nominal GDP and real GDP?
5 How is real GDP calculated?

Work these questions in Study Plan 21.2 and get instant feedback. Do a Key Terms Quiz.   MyEconLab

◆ The Uses and Limitations of Real GDP

Economists use estimates of real GDP for two main purposes:

- To compare the standard of living over time
- To compare the standard of living across countries

The Standard of Living Over Time

One method of comparing the standard of living over time is to calculate real GDP per person in different years. **Real GDP per person** is real GDP divided by the population. Real GDP per person tells us the value of goods and services that the average person can enjoy. By using *real* GDP, we remove any influence that rising prices and a rising cost of living might have had on our comparison.

We're interested in both the long-term trends and the shorter-term cycles in the standard of living.

Long-Term Trend A handy way of comparing real GDP per person over time is to express it as a ratio of some reference year. For example, in 1960, real GDP per person was $17,210 and in 2013, it was $49,658. So real GDP per person in 2013 was almost 3 times its 1960 level ($49,658 ÷ $17,210 = 2.9). To the extent that real GDP per person measures the standard of living, people were 2.9 times as well off in 2013 as their grandparents had been in 1960.

Figure 21.4 shows the path of U.S. real GDP per person for the 53 years from 1960 to 2013 and highlights two features of our expanding living standard:

- The growth of potential GDP per person
- Fluctuations of real GDP per person

The Growth of Potential GDP **Potential GDP** is the maximum level of real GDP that can be produced while avoiding shortages of labor, capital, land, and entrepreneurial ability that would bring rising inflation. Potential GDP per person, the smoother black line in Fig. 21.4, grows at a steady pace because the quantities of the factors of production and their productivities grow at a steady pace.

But potential GDP per person doesn't grow at a *constant* pace. During the 1960s, it grew at 2.8 percent per year but slowed to only 2.3 percent per year during the 1970s. This slowdown might seem small, but it had big consequences, as you'll soon see.

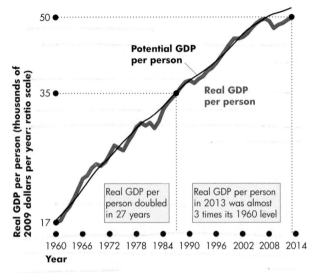

FIGURE 21.4 Rising Standard of Living in the United States

Real GDP per person in the United States doubled between 1960 and 1987 and almost tripled between 1960 and 2013. Real GDP per person, the red line, fluctuates around potential GDP per person, the black line. (The y-axis is a ratio scale—see the Appendix, pp. 506–507.)

Sources of data: U.S. Department of Commerce Bureau of Economic Analysis and Congressional Budget Office.

MyEconLab Real-time data

Fluctuations of Real GDP You can see that real GDP shown by the red line in Fig. 21.4 fluctuates around potential GDP, and sometimes real GDP shrinks.

Let's take a closer look at the two features of our expanding living standard that we've just outlined.

Productivity Growth Slowdown How costly was the slowdown in productivity growth after 1970? The answer is provided by the *Lucas wedge*, which is the dollar value of the accumulated gap between what real GDP per person would have been if the 1960s growth rate had persisted and what real GDP per person turned out to be. (Nobel Laureate Robert E. Lucas Jr. drew attention to this gap.)

Figure 21.5 illustrates the Lucas wedge. The wedge started out small during the 1970s, but by 2013 real GDP per person was $31,000 per year lower than it would have been with no growth slowdown, and the accumulated gap was an astonishing $400,000 per person.

FIGURE 21.5   The Cost of Slower Growth: The Lucas Wedge

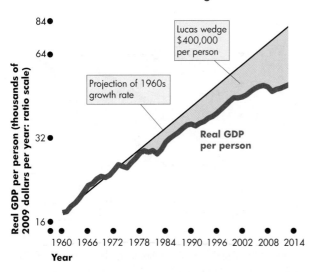

The black line projects the 1960s growth rate of real GDP per person to 2013. The Lucas wedge arises from the slow-down of productivity growth that began during the 1970s. The cost of the slowdown is $400,000 per person.

Sources of data: U.S. Department of Commerce Bureau of Economic Analysis, Congressional Budget Office, and author's calculations.

MyEconLab Real-time data

Real GDP Fluctuations—The Business Cycle We call the fluctuations in the pace of expansion of real GDP the business cycle. The **business cycle** is a periodic but irregular up-and-down movement of total production and other measures of economic activity. The business cycle isn't a regular predictable cycle like the phases of the moon, but every cycle has two phases:

1. Expansion
2. Recession

and two turning points:

1. Peak
2. Trough

Figure 21.6 shows these features of the most recent U.S. business cycle.

An **expansion** is a period during which real GDP increases. In the early stage of an expansion, real GDP returns to potential GDP; and as the expansion progresses, potential GDP grows and real GDP eventually exceeds potential GDP.

A common definition of **recession** is a period during which real GDP decreases—its growth rate is negative—for at least two successive quarters. The definition used by the National Bureau of Economic Research, which dates the U.S. business cycle phases and turning points, is "a period of significant decline in total output, income, employment, and trade, usually lasting from six months to a year, and marked by contractions in many sectors of the economy."

An expansion ends and recession begins at a business cycle *peak*, which is the highest level that real GDP has attained up to that time. A recession ends at a *trough*, when real GDP reaches a temporary low point and from which the next expansion begins.

In 2008, the U.S. economy went into an unusually severe recession. Starting from a long way below potential GDP, a new expansion began in mid-2009. Estimates of the exact depth of the recession have changed with revisions of the real GDP data.

FIGURE 21.6   The Most Recent U.S. Business Cycle

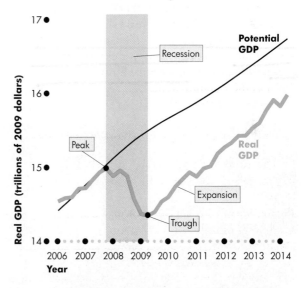

A recession began at a peak in the fourth quarter of 2007 and ended at a trough in the second quarter of 2009. A slow expansion then began, but real GDP has remained below potential GDP for more than five years.

Sources of data: U.S. Department of Commerce Bureau of Economic Analysis, Congressional Budget Office, and National Bureau of Economic Research.

MyEconLab Real-time data

The Standard of Living Across Countries

Two problems arise in using real GDP to compare living standards across countries. First, the real GDP of one country must be converted into the same currency units as the real GDP of the other country. Second, the goods and services in both countries must be valued at the same prices. Comparing the United States and China provides a striking example of these two problems.

China and the United States in U.S. Dollars In 2013, nominal GDP per person in the United States was $53,000 and in China it was 42,000 yuan. The yuan is the currency of China and the price at which the dollar and the yuan exchanged, the *market exchange rate*, was 6.2 yuan per $1 U.S. Using this exchange rate, 42,000 yuan converts to $6,775. On these numbers, GDP per person in the United States in 2013 was 7.9 times that in China.

The red line in Fig. 21.7 shows *real* GDP per person in China from 1980 to 2013 when the market exchange rate is used to convert yuan to U.S. dollars.

China and the United States at PPP Figure 21.7 shows a second estimate of China's real GDP per person that values China's production on the same terms as U.S. production. It uses *purchasing power parity* or *PPP* prices, which are the *same prices* for both countries.

In July 2014, a Big Mac cost $4.80 in Chicago and 16.93 yuan or $2.73 in Shanghai. To compare real GDP in China and the United States, we must value China's Big Macs at the $4.80 U.S. price—the PPP price.

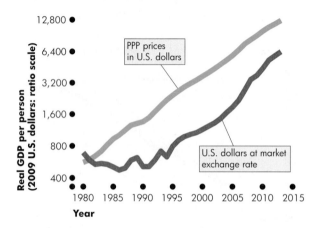

FIGURE 21.7   Two Views of Real GDP in China

Real GDP per person in China has grown rapidly. But how rapidly it has grown and to what level depends on how real GDP is valued. When GDP in 2013 is valued at the market exchange rate, U.S. income per person is 7.9 times that in China. China looks like a poor developing country. But this comparison is misleading. When GDP is valued at purchasing power parity prices (PPP), U.S. income per person is only 5.4 times that in China.

Source of data: International Monetary Fund, *World Economic Outlook database*, April 2014.

MyEconLab Animation

The prices of some goods are higher in the United States than in China, so these items get a smaller weight in the calculation of China's real GDP than they get in U.S. real GDP. An example is a Big Mac that costs $4.80 in Chicago. In Shanghai, a Big Mac costs 16.93 yuan which is the equivalent of $2.73. So in China's real GDP, a Big Mac gets about half the weight that it gets in U.S. real GDP.

Some prices in China are higher than in the United States but more prices are lower, so Chinese prices put a lower value on China's production than do U.S. prices.

According to the PPP comparisons (same prices in both countries), real GDP per person in the United States in 2013 was 5.4 times that of China, not 7.9 times.

You've seen how real GDP is used to make standard of living comparisons over time and across countries. But real GDP isn't a perfect measure of the standard of living and we'll now examine its limitations.

Limitations of Real GDP

Real GDP measures the value of goods and services that are bought in markets. Some of the factors that influence the standard of living and that are not part of GDP are

- Household production
- Underground economic activity
- Leisure time
- Environmental quality

Household Production   Preparing meals, changing a light bulb, cutting grass, and caring for a child are all examples of household production. Because these productive activities are not traded in markets, they are not included in GDP.

The omission of household production from GDP means that GDP *underestimates* total production. But it also means that the growth rate of GDP *overestimates* the growth rate of total production. The reason is that some of the growth rate of market production (included in GDP) is a replacement for home production. So part of the increase in GDP arises from a decrease in home production.

Underground Economic Activity   The *underground economy* is the part of the economy that is purposely hidden from the view of the government to avoid taxes and regulations or because the goods and services being produced are illegal. Because underground economic activity is unreported, it is omitted from GDP. The underground economy in the United States ranges between 9 and 30 percent of GDP ($1,500 billion to $5,000 billion).

Leisure Time   Leisure time is an economic good that adds to our economic well-being and the standard of living. Other things remaining the same, the more leisure we have, the better off we are. Our working time is valued as part of GDP, but our leisure time is not. Yet that leisure time must be at least as valuable to us as the wage that we earn for the last hour worked. If it were not, we would work instead of taking leisure. Over the years, leisure time has steadily increased. The workweek has become shorter, more people take early retirement, and the number of vacation days has increased. These improvements in economic well-being are not reflected in real GDP.

Environmental Quality   Economic activity directly influences the quality of the environment. Burning oil and coal brings global warming and climate change. Depleting nonrenewable resources, clearing forests, and polluting lakes and rivers are other environmental consequences of industrial production.

Resources used to protect the environment are valued as part of GDP. For example, the value of catalytic converters that help to protect the atmosphere from automobile emissions is part of GDP. But the cost of pollution is not subtracted from GDP.

An industrial society possibly produces more atmospheric pollution than an agricultural society does. But pollution does not always increase as we become wealthier. Wealthy people value a clean environment and are willing to pay for one. Compare the pollution in China today with pollution in the United States. China, a poor country, pollutes its rivers, lakes, and atmosphere in a way that is unimaginable in the United States.

Whose production is more valuable: the chef's whose work gets counted in GDP ...

... or the busy mother's whose dinner preparation and child minding don't get counted?

AT **ISSUE**

Should GNNP Replace GDP?

The standard view of economists is that despite its limitations, GDP is a useful measure of the value of production and the overall level of economic activity in a country or region.

But a prominent economist, Joseph Stiglitz, has argued that GDP is dangerously misleading and needs to be replaced by a measure that he calls Green Net National Product (or GNNP).

Let's look at both sides of this issue.

Joe **Stiglitz** says ...

- GDP has passed its use-by date.

- A *gross* measure is wrong because it ignores the depreciation of assets.

- A *domestic* measure is wrong because it ignores the incomes paid to foreigners who exploit a nation's resources.

- A *green* measure is needed to take account of the environmental damage that arises from production.

- GNNP subtracts from GDP incomes paid to foreigners, depreciation, the value of depleted natural resources, and the cost of a degraded environment.

- The existence of a market price for carbon emissions makes it possible to measure the cost of these emissions and subtract them from GDP.

- A bad accounting framework is likely to lead to bad decisions.

- America's "drain America first" energy policy is an example of a bad decision. It increases GDP but decreases GNNP and makes us poorer.

The **Mainstream View**

- As a measure of the value of market production in an economy, GDP does a good job.

- GDP is used to track the ups and downs of economic activity and it is a useful indicator for making macroeconomic stabilization policy decisions.

- GDP is *not* used to measure net national economic well-being nor to guide microeconomic resource allocation decisions.

- There is no disagreement that a *net national* measure is appropriate for measuring national economic well-being.

- There is no disagreement that "negative externalities" arising from carbon emissions and other pollution detract from economic well-being.

- The omissions from GDP of household production and underground production are *bigger* problems than those emphasized by Stiglitz.

- It isn't clear that depleting oil and coal resources is costly and misguided because advances in green energy technology will eventually make oil and coal of little value. The stone-age didn't end because we ran out of stone, and the carbon-age won't end because we run out of oil and coal!

Bad accounting frameworks are likely to lead to bad decisions. A government focused on GDP might be encouraged to give away mining or oil concessions; a focus on green NNP might make it realize that the country risks being worse off.

Joseph Stiglitz,
"Good Numbers Gone Bad,"
Fortune, September 25, 2006

When Anglo-Australian company BHP Billiton mines copper in Papua New Guinea, the country's GDP rises, but profits go abroad and 40,000 who live by a polluted river lose their means of earning a living. GNNP measures that loss.

ECONOMICS IN ACTION

A Broader Indicator of Economic Well-Being

The limitations of real GDP reviewed in this chapter affect the standard of living and general well-being of every country. So to make international comparisons of the general state of economic well-being, we must look at real GDP and other indicators.

The United Nations has constructed a broader measure called the Human Development Index (HDI), which combines real GDP, life expectancy and health, and education. Real GDP per person (measured on the PPP basis) is a major component of the HDI so, as you can see in the figure, the two are strongly correlated.

The figure shows the data for 2012. In that year, Norway had the highest HDI and Australia had the second highest, but Qatar had the highest real GDP per person. The United States had the fifth highest HDI.

The HDI of the United States is lower than that of Norway and Australia because the people of those countries live longer and have better access to healthcare and education than do Americans.

African nations have the lowest levels of economic well-being. The figure shows that Niger had the lowest

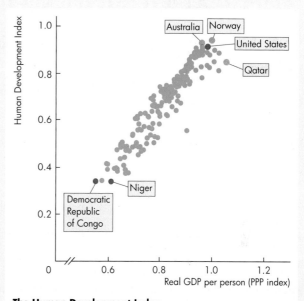

The Human Development Index

Source of data: United Nations hdr.undp.org/en/statistics/data.

HDI and the Democratic Republic of Congo had the lowest real GDP per person.

The Bottom Line Do we get the wrong message about the level and growth in economic well-being and the standard of living by looking at the growth of real GDP? The influences that are omitted from real GDP are probably large. Developing countries have a larger amount of household production than do developed countries, so the gap between their living standards is exaggerated. Also, as real GDP grows, part of the growth is a switch from home production to market production. This switch overstates the growth in economic well-being and the improvement in the standard of living.

It is possible to construct broader measures that combine the many influences that contribute to human happiness. The United Nations' Human Development Index or HDI (above), and Green Net National Product or GNNP (previous page) are two examples of dozens of other measures that have been proposed.

Despite all the alternatives, real GDP per person remains the most widely used indicator of economic well-being.

REVIEW QUIZ

1 Distinguish between real GDP and potential GDP and describe how each grows over time.
2 How does the growth rate of real GDP contribute to an improved standard of living?
3 What is a business cycle and what are its phases and turning points?
4 What is PPP and how does it help us to make valid international comparisons of real GDP?
5 Explain why real GDP might be an unreliable indicator of the standard of living.

Work these questions in Study Plan 21.3 and get instant feedback. Do a Key Terms Quiz.   MyEconLab

◆ You now know how economists measure GDP and what the GDP data tell us. *Economics in the News* on pp. 504–505 uses GDP to describe some possible future paths as we emerge from recession.

The Expansion Continues

U.S. Economy Roars Back with 4% Growth in the Second Quarter

Financial Times
July 30, 2014

The U.S. economy roared ahead with annualized growth of 4 percent in the second quarter, confirming that weakness early this year was an aberration and the recovery is back on track.

Growth easily beat expectations of 3.1 percent, with the strength of the rebound demonstrating that robust jobs data in recent months was not a fluke, and the world's largest economy is picking up speed. ...

The second quarter strength comes after a dismal 2.9 percent annualized fall in the first quarter—which was revised to a 2.1 percent decline with this release. The rebound confirms there was no fundamental weakness in the first quarter. Most analysts blame the poor performance on bad weather, inventory rundowns, and difficulty estimating healthcare spending following the introduction of Obamacare.

"Some of the past quarter's growth performance reflects a catch-up from the dismal first quarter performance," said Gad Levanon, director of macroeconomic research at the Conference Board. "But this stellar growth figure also suggests that the economy has gained some momentum and could hold on to this newfound dynamism through the second half of 2014."

The details of the second quarter release were less positive than the headline figure. Of the 4 percent increase, 1.7 percentage points came from an inventory build-up, which reversed a big decline in the first quarter but is not sustainable. ...

Consumption contributed 1.7 percentage points to growth, business investment added 0.7 percentage points and government spending contributed 0.3 percentage points. Net trade remained a drag, knocking off 0.6 percentage points in total, because of a large rise in imports. ...

The Financial Times Limited, July 30, 2014.

MyEconLab More Economics in the News

ESSENCE OF THE STORY

- U.S. real GDP grew at an annualized rate of 4 percent in the second quarter of 2014.

- The expected growth rate was 3.1 percent.

- U.S. real GDP shrank at an annualized rate of 2.9 percent in the first quarter of 2014.

- Of the 4 percent increase, 1.7 percentage points came from an increase in business inventories, 1.7 percentage points from consumption, 0.7 percentage points from investment, and 0.3 percentage points from government spending.

- A rise in imports decreased net exports and lowered real GDP by 0.6 percentage points.

ECONOMIC ANALYSIS

- The news article reports the first estimates of real GDP and its expenditure components for the second quarter of 2014.

- A news article on this topic appears every three months.

- In the second quarter of 2014, real GDP increased by $154 billion from $15,832 billion to $15,986 billion.

- The increase in real GDP during the second quarter was a bit less than 1 percent ($154 is 0.97 percent of $15,832).

- If this growth rate is maintained for a full year, real GDP will be 4 percent higher at the end of the year. That is what the news article means when it reports that real GDP grew at an annualized rate of 4 percent.

- The growth in the second quarter of 2014 came after a quarter in which real GDP shrank, so some of the second quarter growth was returning to the level at the end of 2013.

- Figure 1 shows the increases in real GDP and the expenditure components for the second quarter of 2014 as the blue bars and for the full year from the second quarter of 2013 as the red bars.

- Year-over-year, the red bars in Fig. 1, real GDP increased by $379 billion and consumption expenditure increased most.

- In the second quarter of 2014, as reported in the news article and shown by the blue bars in Fig.1, business inventories (shown separately from business fixed investment) and consumption contributed most to the expansion. Government expenditure barely changed, and net exports decreased aggregate expenditure (were "a drag" says the news report).

- The news article says that a big contributor to expansion came from a business "inventory build-up, which reversed a big decline in the first quarter but is not sustainable."

- Figure 2 shows whether the news article is correct.

- It is correct that an increase in business inventories were a large component of the second quarter expansion. They increased by $93 billion, which is 60 percent of the increase in real GDP.

- But the news article is not correct that inventories decreased in the first quarter. They increased by $35 billion despite a fall in real GDP.

- The news article might also be wrong about sustainability. Figure 2 shows that in almost every quarter (except

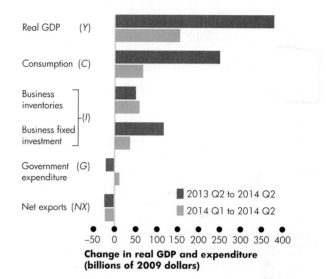

Figure 1 Aggregate Expenditure Changes

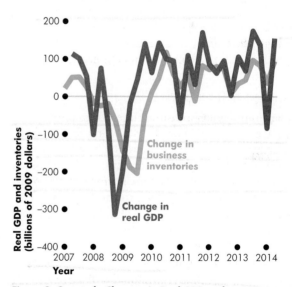

Figure 2 Quarterly Changes in Real GDP and Business Inventories

one) since 2010 the change in business inventories has been positive—business inventories have increased.

- Figure 2 also shows that business inventories and real GDP generally change in the same direction but that inventories sometimes lag the change in real GDP.

APPENDIX

Graphs in Macroeconomics

After studying this appendix, you will be able to:

◆ Make and interpret a time-series graph

◆ Make and interpret a graph that uses a ratio scale

◆ The Time-Series Graph

In macroeconomics we study the fluctuations and trends in the key variables that describe macroeconomic performance and policy. These variables include GDP and its expenditure and income components that you've learned about in this chapter. They also include variables that describe the labor market and consumer prices that you study in Chapter 22.

Regardless of the variable of interest, we want to be able to compare its value today with that in the past; and we want to describe how the variable has changed over time. The most effective way to do these things is to make a time-series graph.

Making a Time-Series Graph

A **time-series graph** measures time (for example, years, quarters, or months) on the *x*-axis and the variable or variables in which we are interested on the *y*-axis. Figure A21.1 is an example of a time-series graph. It provides some information about unemployment in the United States since 1994. In this figure, we measure time in years starting in 1994. We measure the unemployment rate (the variable that we are interested in) on the *y*-axis.

A time-series graph enables us to visualize how a variable has changed over time and how its value in one period relates to its value in another period. It conveys an enormous amount of information quickly and easily.

Let's see how to "read" a time-series graph.

Reading a Time-Series Graph

To practice reading a time-series graph, take a close look at Fig. A21.1. The graph shows the level, change, and speed of change of the variable.

FIGURE A21.1   A Time-Series Graph

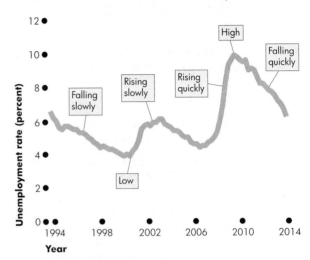

A time-series graph plots the level of a variable on the *y*-axis against time (here measured in years) on the *x*-axis. This graph shows the unemployment rate each year from 1994 to 2014. The graph shows when unemployment was high, when it was low, when it increased, when it decreased, and when it changed quickly and slowly.

MyEconLab Animation

■ The *level* of the variable: It tells us when unemployment is *high* and *low*. When the line is a long distance above the *x*-axis, the unemployment rate is high, as it was, for example, in 2009. When the line is close to the *x*-axis, the unemployment rate is low, as it was, for example, in 2001.

■ The *change* in the variable: It tells us how unemployment *changes*—whether it *increases* or *decreases*. When the line slopes upward, as it did in 2008 and 2009, the unemployment rate is rising. When the line slopes downward, as it did in 1997, the unemployment rate is falling.

■ The *speed of change* in the variable: It tells us whether the unemployment rate is rising or falling *quickly* or *slowly*. If the line is very steep, then the unemployment rate increases or decreases quickly. If the line is not steep, the unemployment rate increases or decreases slowly. For example, the unemployment rate rose quickly in 2008 and slowly in 2003 and it fell quickly in 2012 and slowly in 1997.

Ratio Scale Reveals Trend

A time-series graph also reveals whether a variable has a **cycle**, which is a tendency for a variable to alternate between upward and downward movements, or a **trend**, which is a tendency for a variable to move in one general direction.

The unemployment rate in Fig. A21.1 has a cycle but no trend. When a trend is present, a special kind of time-series graph, one that uses a ratio scale on the *y*-axis, reveals the trend.

A Time-Series with a Trend

Many macroeconomic variables, among them GDP and the average level of prices, have an upward trend. Figure A21.2 shows an example of such a variable: the average prices paid by consumers.

In Fig. A21.2(a), consumer prices since 1974 are graphed on a normal scale. In 1974 the level is 100. In other years, the average level of prices is measured as a percentage of the 1974 level.

The graph clearly shows the upward trend of prices. But it doesn't tell us when prices were rising fastest or whether there was any change in the trend. Just looking at the upward-sloping line in Fig. A21.2(a) gives the impression that the pace of growth of consumer prices was constant.

Using a Ratio Scale

On a graph axis with a normal scale, the gap between 1 and 2 is the same as that between 3 and 4. On a graph axis with a ratio scale, the gap between 1 and 2 is the same as that between 2 and 4. The ratio 2 to 1 equals the ratio 4 to 2. By using a ratio scale, we can "see" when the growth rate (the percentage change per unit of time) changes.

Figure A21.2(b) shows an example of a ratio scale. Notice that the values on the *y*-axis get closer together but the gap between 400 and 200 equals the gap between 200 and 100: The ratio gaps are equal.

Graphing the data on a ratio scale reveals the trends. In the case of consumer prices, the trend is much steeper during the 1970s and early 1980s than in the later years. The steeper the line in the ratio-scale graph in part (b), the faster are prices rising. Prices rose rapidly during the 1970s and early 1980s and more slowly in the later 1980s and 1990s. The ratio-scale graph reveals this fact. We use ratio-scale graphs extensively in macroeconomics.

FIGURE A21.2   Ratio Scale Reveals Trend

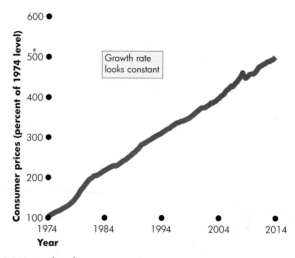

(a) Normal scale

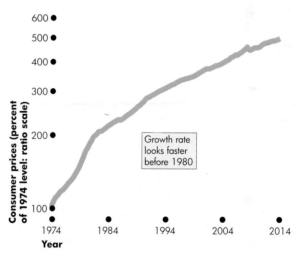

(b) Ratio scale

The graph shows the average of consumer prices from 1974 to 2014. The level is 100 in 1974, and the values for the other years are percentages of the 1974 level. Consumer prices normally rise each year, so the line slopes upward. In part (a), where the *y*-axis scale is normal, the rate of increase appears to be constant.

In part (b), where the *y*-axis is a ratio scale (the ratio of 400 to 200 equals the ratio 200 to 100), prices rose faster during the 1970s and early 1980s and slower in the later years. The ratio scale reveals this trend.

MyEconLab Animation

MATHEMATICAL NOTE

Chained-Dollar Real GDP

In the real GDP calculation on p. 497, real GDP in 2014 is 1.6 times its value in 2009. But suppose that we use 2014 as the reference base year and value real GDP in 2009 at 2014 prices. If you do the math, you will see that real GDP in 2009 is $150 million at 2014 prices. GDP in 2014 is $300 million (in 2014 prices), so now the numbers say that real GDP has doubled. Which is correct: Did real GDP increase 1.6 times or double? Should we use the prices of 2009 or 2014? The answer is that we need to use *both* sets of prices.

The Bureau of Economic Analysis uses a measure of real GDP called *chained-dollar real GDP*. Three steps are needed to calculate this measure:

- Value production in the prices of adjacent years
- Find the average of two percentage changes
- Link (chain) back to the reference base year

Value Production in Prices of Adjacent Years

The first step is to value production in *adjacent* years at the prices of *both* years. We'll make these calculations for 2014 and its preceding year, 2013.

Table 1 shows the quantities produced and prices in the two years. Part (a) shows the nominal GDP calculation for 2013—the quantities produced in 2013 valued at the prices of 2013. Nominal GDP in 2013 is $145 million. Part (b) shows the nominal GDP calculation for 2014—the quantities produced in 2014 valued at the prices of 2014. Nominal GDP in 2014 is $300 million. Part (c) shows the value of the quantities produced in 2014 at the prices of 2013. This total is $160 million. Finally, part (d) shows the value of the quantities produced in 2013 at the prices of 2014. This total is $275 million.

Find the Average of Two Percentage Changes

The second step is to find the percentage change in the value of production based on the prices in the two adjacent years. Table 2 summarizes these calculations.

Part (a) shows that, valued at the prices of 2013, production increased from $145 million in 2013 to $160 million in 2014, an increase of 10.3 percent.

TABLE 1   Real GDP Calculation Step 1: Value Production in Adjacent Years at Prices of Both Years

Item		Quantity (millions)	Price (dollars)	Expenditure (millions of dollars)
(a) In 2013				
C	T-shirts	3	5	15
I	Computer chips	3	10	30
G	Security services	5	20	100
Y	Nominal GDP in 2013			**145**
(b) In 2014				
C	T-shirts	4	5	20
I	Computer chips	2	20	40
G	Security services	6	40	240
Y	Nominal GDP in 2014			**300**
(c) Quantities of 2014 valued at prices of 2013				
C	T-shirts	4	5	20
I	Computer chips	2	10	20
G	Security services	6	20	120
Y	2014 production at 2013 prices			**160**
(d) Quantities of 2013 valued at prices of 2014				
C	T-shirts	3	5	15
I	Computer chips	3	20	60
G	Security services	5	40	200
Y	2013 production at 2014 prices			**275**

Step 1 is to value the production of adjacent years at the prices of both years. Here, we value the production of 2013 and 2014 at the prices of both 2013 and 2014. The value of 2013 production at 2013 prices, in part (a), is nominal GDP in 2013. The value of 2014 production at 2014 prices, in part (b), is nominal GDP in 2014. Part (c) calculates the value of 2014 production at 2013 prices, and part (d) calculates the value of 2013 production at 2014 prices. We use these numbers in Step 2.

Part (b) shows that, valued at the prices of 2014, production increased from $275 million in 2013 to $300 million in 2014, an increase of 9.1 percent. Part (c) shows that the average of these two percentage changes in the value of production is 9.7. That is, $(10.3 + 9.1) \div 2 = 9.7$.

This average percentage change is the *growth rate* of real GDP in 2014. This growth rate depends only on production and prices in 2013 and 2014.

The final step is to find the *level* of real GDP.

TABLE 2   Real GDP Calculation Step 2: Find Average of Two Percentage Changes

Value of Production	Millions of dollars	
(a) At 2013 prices		
Nominal GDP in 2013	145	
2014 production at 2013 prices	160	
Percentage change in production at 2013 prices		10.3
(b) At 2014 prices		
2013 production at 2014 prices	275	
Nominal GDP in 2014	300	
Percentage change in production at 2014 prices		9.1
(c) Average percentage change in 2014		**9.7**

Using the numbers calculated in Step 1, the change in production from 2013 to 2014 valued at 2013 prices is 10.3 percent, in part (a). The change in production from 2013 to 2014 valued at 2014 prices is 9.1 percent, in part (b). The average of these two percentage changes is 9.7 percent in part (c).

Link (Chain) to the Base Year

The *level* of real GDP depends on the choice of a *base year*. To see how, we'll first suppose that the base year is 2013.

By definition, real GDP and nominal GDP are equal in the base year. So real GDP in 2013 (in 2013 dollars) is $145 million (in Table 1).

In 2014, real GDP grew by 9.7 percent, so real GDP in 2014 (in 2013 dollars) is 9.7 percent greater than $145 million, which equals $159 million. (Check the calculation: Real GDP increased by $14 million, which is 9.7 percent of $145 million.)

Today, the base year is 2009 and to find the level of real GDP in other years, both before and after 2009, more calculations are needed.

The BEA must calculate the percentage change in real GDP for *each* pair of years from the base year to the most recent year. And to find real GDP for years before the base year, the BEA must calculate the growth rates for each pair of years back to the earliest one for which it has data.

Finally, using the percentage changes it has calculated, the BEA finds the levels of real GDP in 2009 prices by linking them to the value of real GDP in 2009.

To illustrate this third step, we'll assume that the

BEA has used the method we've described to calculate the percentage changes of real GDP for the years 2006 through 2014. Figure 1 shows these percentage changes and illustrates the chain-link calculations.

In the reference base year, 2009, real GDP equals nominal GDP, which we'll assume is $125 million. The growth rate in 2009 was 6 percent, so real GDP in 2009 is 6 percent higher than it was in 2008, which means that real GDP in 2008 is $118 million ($118 \times 1.06 = 125$).

The growth rate in 2010 was 4 percent, so real GDP in 2010 is 4 percent higher than it was in 2009, which means that real GDP in 2010 is $130 million ($125 \times 1.04 = 130$).

By repeating these calculations for each year, we obtain the *chained-dollar real GDP* in 2009 dollars for each year.

For 2013, the *chained-dollar real GDP* in 2009 dollars is $159 million. So the 9.7 percent growth rate in 2014 that we calculated in Table 2 means that real GDP in 2014 is $174 million ($159 \times 1.097 = 174$).

Notice that the growth rates are independent of the reference base year, so changing the reference base year does not change the growth rates.

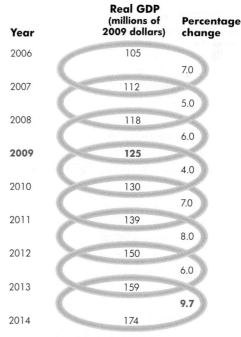

Year	Real GDP (millions of 2009 dollars)	Percentage change
2006	105	
		7.0
2007	112	
		5.0
2008	118	
		6.0
2009	**125**	
		4.0
2010	130	
		7.0
2011	139	
		8.0
2012	150	
		6.0
2013	159	
		9.7
2014	174	

Figure 1 Real GDP Calculation Step 3: Link (Chain) to Base Year

SUMMARY

Key Points

Gross Domestic Product (pp. 492–494)

- GDP, or gross domestic product, is the market value of all the final goods and services produced in a country during a given period.
- A final good is an item that is bought by its final user, and it contrasts with an intermediate good, which is a component of a final good.
- GDP is calculated by using either the expenditure or income totals in the circular flow model.
- Aggregate expenditure on goods and services equals aggregate income and GDP.

Working Problems 1 to 3 will give you a better understanding of gross domestic product.

Measuring U.S. GDP (pp. 495–497)

- Because aggregate expenditure, aggregate income, and the value of aggregate production are equal, we can measure GDP by using the expenditure approach or the income approach.
- The expenditure approach sums consumption expenditure, investment, government expenditure on goods and services, and net exports.
- The income approach sums wages, interest, rent, and profit (plus indirect taxes less subsidies plus depreciation).

- Real GDP is measured using a common set of prices to remove the effects of inflation from GDP.

Working Problems 4 to 6 will give you a better understanding of measuring U.S. GDP.

The Uses and Limitations of Real GDP (pp. 498–503)

- Real GDP is used to compare the standard of living over time and across countries.
- Real GDP per person grows and fluctuates around the more smoothly growing potential GDP.
- A slowing of the growth rate of real GDP per person during the 1970s has lowered incomes by a large amount.
- International real GDP comparisons use PPP prices.
- Real GDP is not a perfect measure of the standard of living because it excludes household production, the underground economy, leisure time, and environmental quality.

Working Problem 7 will give you a better understanding of the uses and limitations of real GDP.

Key Terms

MyEconLab Key Terms Quiz

Business cycle, 499
Consumption expenditure, 493
Cycle, 507
Depreciation, 494
Expansion, 499
Exports, 494
Final good, 492
Government expenditure, 494

Gross domestic product (GDP), 492
Gross investment, 494
Imports, 494
Intermediate good, 492
Investment, 493
Net exports, 494
Net investment, 494
Nominal GDP, 497

Potential GDP, 498
Real GDP, 497
Real GDP per person, 498
Recession, 499
Time-series graph, 506
Trend, 507

◆ WORKED PROBLEM

MyEconLab   You can work this problem in Chapter 21 Study Plan.

Items in Dreamland's national accounts include

- Government expenditure on goods and services: $600
- Consumption expenditure: $1,950
- Rent and interest: $400
- Indirect taxes less subsidies: $350
- Investment: $550
- Wages: $1,600
- Profit: $500
- Net exports: $200
- Depreciation: $450

Questions

1. Use the expenditure approach to calculate GDP.
2. Calculate net domestic income at factor cost.
3. Calculate net domestic income at market prices.
4. Use the income approach to calculate GDP.

Solutions

1. The expenditure approach sums the expenditure on final goods and services. That is, GDP is the sum of consumption expenditure, investment, government expenditure, and net exports. That is, GDP = $1,950 + $550 + $600 + $200 = $3,300.

Key Point: GDP equals the sum of consumption expenditure, investment, government expenditure on goods and services, and net exports. See the figure.

2. Net domestic income at factor cost is the income paid to factors of production: wages, rent, interest, and profit. Net domestic income at factor cost

equals $1,600 + $400 + $500 = $2,500.

Key Point: The incomes earned by the factors of production (labor, land, capital, and entrepreneurship) sum to net domestic income at factor cost. See the figure.

3. Expenditure on goods and services equals the quantity bought multiplied by the market price. Incomes are total factor costs. The market price of a good or service equals the cost of the factors of production used to produce it if production is not subsidized and sale of the good is not taxed.

If the producer of a good receives a subsidy, then the market price of the good is less than the cost of producing it. If a tax is imposed on the sale of the good, then the market price exceeds the cost of producing it. So

Market price = Factor cost + Indirect taxes less subsidies.

Net domestic income at factor cost is $2,500, so net domestic income at market prices equals $2,500 + $350 = $2,850.

Key Point: To convert from factor cost to market prices add indirect taxes less subsidies. See the figure.

4. GDP is a gross measure of total production at market prices while net domestic income at market prices is a net measure. So using the income approach to measuring GDP, depreciation must be added to net domestic income at market prices to convert it to GDP. That is, using the income approach, GDP = $2,850 + $450 = $3,300.

Key Point: To convert net domestic income at market prices into GDP add depreciation. See the figure.

Key Figure

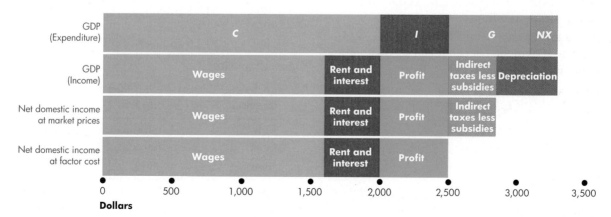

◆ STUDY PLAN PROBLEMS AND APPLICATIONS

MyEconLab   You can work Problems 1 to 8 in Chapter 21 Study Plan and get instant feedback.
Problems marked update with real-time data.

Gross Domestic Product (Study Plan 21.1)

1. Classify the following items as a final good or
   service or an intermediate good or service and
   identify each item as a component of consump-
   tion expenditure, investment, or government
   expenditure on goods and services:
   - Airline ticket bought by a student.
   - New airplanes bought by Southwest Airlines.
   - Cheese bought by Domino's.
   - Your purchase of a new iPhone.
   - New house bought by Bill Gates.

2. The following figure illustrates the circular flow
   model.

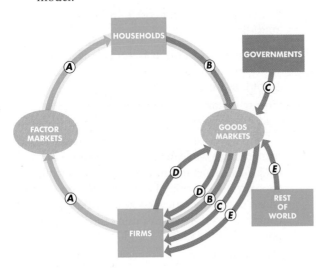

During 2014, flow *A* was $13.0 trillion, flow *B*
was $9.1 trillion, flow *D* was $3.3 trillion, and
flow *E* was −$0.8 trillion. Calculate (i) GDP and
(ii) Government expenditure.

3. Use the following data to calculate aggregate
   expenditure and imports of goods and services.
   - Government expenditure: $20 billion
   - Aggregate income: $100 billion
   - Consumption expenditure: $67 billion
   - Investment: $21 billion
   - Exports of goods and services: $30 billion

Measuring U.S. GDP (Study Plan 21.2)

4. The table in the next column lists some national
   accounts data for the United States in 2008.
   a. Calculate U.S. GDP in 2008.

Item	Billions of dollars
Wages	8,000
Consumption expenditure	10,000
Other factor incomes	3,200
Investment	2,000
Government expenditure	2,800
Net exports	−700
Depreciation	1,800

   b. Explain the approach (expenditure or income)
      you used to calculate GDP.

Use the following data to work Problems 5 and 6.
Tropical Republic produces only bananas and
coconuts. The base year is 2013, and the table gives
the quantities produced and the market prices.

Quantities	2013	2014
Bananas	800 bunches	900 bunches
Coconuts	400 bunches	500 bunches

Prices	2013	2014
Bananas	$2 a bunch	$4 a bunch
Coconuts	$10 a bunch	$5 a bunch

5. Calculate nominal GDP in 2013 and 2014.

6. Calculate real GDP in 2014 expressed in base-
   year prices.

The Uses and Limitations of Real GDP (Study Plan 21.3)

7. Use the following table to work out in which
   year the U.S. standard of living (i) increases and
   (ii) decreases. Explain your answer.

Year	Real GDP	Population
2006	$13.0 trillion	300 million
2007	$13.2 trillion	302 million
2008	$13.2 trillion	304 million
2009	$12.8 trillion	307 million

Mathematical Note

8. An island economy produces only fish and crabs.

Quantities	2013	2014
Fish	1,000 tons	1,100 tons
Crabs	500 tons	525 tons

Prices	2013	2014
Fish	$20 a ton	$30 a ton
Crabs	$10 a ton	$8 a ton

Calculate the island's chained-dollar real
GDP in 2014 expressed in 2013 dollars.

ADDITIONAL PROBLEMS AND APPLICATIONS

MyEconLab You can work these problems in MyEconLab if assigned by your instructor. Problems marked 🌐 update with real-time data.

Gross Domestic Product

9. Classify each of the following items as a final good or service or an intermediate good or service and identify which is a component of consumption expenditure, investment, or government expenditure on goods and services:
   - Banking services bought by Google.
   - Security system bought by the New York Stock Exchange.
   - Coffee beans bought by Starbucks.
   - New coffee grinders bought by Starbucks.
   - Starbuck's grande mocha frappuccino bought by a student.
   - New battle ship bought by the U.S. Navy.

Use the figure in Problem 2 to work Problems 10 and 11.

10. In 2013, flow A was $1,000 billion, flow C was $250 billion, flow B was $650 billion, and flow E was $50 billion. Calculate investment.

11. In 2014, flow D was $2 trillion, flow E was −$1 trillion, flow A was $10 trillion, and flow C was $4 trillion. Calculate consumption expenditure.

Use the following information to work Problems 12 and 13.

Mitsubishi Heavy Industries makes the wings of the new Boeing 787 Dreamliner in Japan. Toyota assembles cars for the U.S. market in Kentucky.

12. Explain where these activities appear in the U.S. National Income and Product Accounts.

13. Explain where these activities appear in Japan's National Income and Product Accounts.

Use the following news clip to work Problems 14 and 15, and use the circular flow model to illustrate your answers.

Boeing Bets the House

Boeing is producing some components of its new 787 Dreamliner in Japan and is assembling it in the United States. Much of the first year's production will be sold to ANA (All Nippon Airways), a Japanese airline.

Source: *The New York Times*, May 7, 2006

14. Explain how Boeing's activities and its transactions affect U.S. and Japanese GDP.

15. Explain how ANA's activities and its transactions affect U.S. and Japanese GDP.

Measuring U.S. GDP

Use the following data to work Problems 16 and 17. The table lists some macroeconomic data for the United States in 2009.

Item	Billions of dollars
Wages	8,000
Consumption expenditure	10,000
Other factor incomes	3,400
Investment	1,500
Government expenditure	2,900
Net exports	−340

🌐 16. Calculate U.S. GDP in 2009.

17. Explain the approach (expenditure or income) that you used to calculate GDP.

Use the following data to work Problems 18 and 19. An economy produces only apples and oranges. The base year is 2012, and the table gives the quantities produced and the prices.

Quantities	2012	2013
Apples	60	160
Oranges	80	220
Prices	**2012**	**2013**
Apples	$0.50	$1.00
Oranges	$0.25	$2.00

18. Calculate nominal GDP in 2012 and 2013.

19. Calculate real GDP in 2012 and 2013 expressed in base-year prices.

20. **GDP Expands 11.4 Percent, Fastest in 13 Years**
   China's gross domestic product grew 11.4 percent last year and marked a fifth year of double-digit growth. The increase was especially remarkable given that the United States is experiencing a slowdown due to the sub-prime crisis and housing slump. Citigroup estimates that each 1 percent drop in the U.S. economy will shave 1.3 percent off China's growth, because Americans are heavy users of Chinese products. In spite of the uncertainties, China is expected to post its sixth year of double-digit growth next year.

   Source: *The China Daily*, January 24, 2008

   Use the expenditure approach for calculating China's GDP to explain why "each 1 percent drop in the U.S. economy will shave 1.3 percent off China's growth."

The Uses and Limitations of Real GDP

21. The United Nations' Human Development Index (HDI) is based on real GDP per person, life expectancy at birth, and indicators of the quality and quantity of education.

    a. Explain why the HDI might be better than real GDP as a measure of economic welfare.

    b. Which items in the HDI are part of real GDP and which items are not in real GDP?

    c. Do you think the HDI should be expanded to include items such as pollution, resource depletion, and political freedom? Explain.

    d. What other items should be included in a comprehensive measure of economic welfare?

22. **U.K. Living Standards Outstrip U.S.**

    Oxford analysts report that living standards in Britain are set to rise above those in America for the first time since the nineteenth century. Real GDP per person in Britain will be £23,500 this year, compared with £23,250 in America. But the Oxford analysts also point out that Americans benefit from lower prices than those in Britain.

    Source: *The Sunday Times*, January 6, 2008

    If real GDP per person is greater in the United Kingdom than in the United States but Americans pay lower prices, does this comparison of real GDP per person really tell us which country has the higher standard of living?

23. Use the news clip in Problem 20.

    a. Why might China's recent GDP growth rates overstate the actual increase in the level of production taking place in China?

    b. Explain the complications involved with attempting to compare the economic welfare in China and the United States by using the GDP for each country.

24. **Poor India Makes Millionaires at Fastest Pace**

    India, with the world's largest population of poor people, created millionaires at the fastest pace in the world in 2007. India added another 23,000 more millionaires in 2007 to its 2006 tally of 100,000 millionaires measured in dollars. That is 1 millionaire for about 7,000 people living on less than $2 a day.

    Source: *The Times of India*, June 25, 2008

    a. Why might real GDP per person misrepresent the standard of living of the average Indian?

    b. Why might $2 a day underestimate the standard of living of the poorest Indians?

Economics in the News

25. After you have studied *Economics in the News* on pp. 504–505, answer the following questions.

    a. By what percentage did real GDP grow from the second quarter of 2013 to the second quarter of 2014? (You can find the data you need to calculate this percentage change on p. 505.)

    b. Comparing the increase in the second quarter with the year-on-year increase, what can you say about the change in the real GDP growth rate? Is it slowing or speeding up?

    c. Describe the relationship between the fluctuations in the change in real GDP and business inventory investment. Why might inventory changes sometimes lag real GDP changes?

26. **Totally Gross**

    GDP has proved useful in tracking both short-term fluctuations and long-run growth. Which isn't to say GDP doesn't miss some things. Amartya Sen, at Harvard, helped create the United Nations' Human Development Index, which combines health and education data with per capita GDP to give a better measure of the wealth of nations. Joseph Stiglitz, at Columbia, advocates a "green net national product" that takes into account the depletion of natural resources. Others want to include happiness in the measure. These alternative benchmarks have merit but can they be measured with anything like the frequency, reliability, and impartiality of GDP?

    Source: *Time*, April 21, 2008

    a. Explain the factors that the news clip identifies as limiting the usefulness of GDP as a measure of economic welfare.

    b. What are the challenges involved in trying to incorporate measurements of those factors in an effort to better measure economic welfare?

    c. What does the ranking of the United States in the Human Development Index imply about the levels of health and education relative to other nations?

Mathematical Note

27. Use the information in Problem 18 to calculate the chained-dollar real GDP in 2013 expressed in 2012 dollars.

Rise To Meet
Your Potential

Career Opportunities:
• Engineering
• Sales
• Finance/Accounting
• MBA
• Purchasing
• Marketing

22 MONITORING JOBS AND INFLATION

After studying this chapter, you will be able to:

◆ Explain why unemployment is a problem and how we measure the unemployment rate and other labor market indicators

◆ Explain why unemployment occurs and why it is present even at full employment

◆ Explain why inflation is a problem and how we measure the inflation rate

Each month, we chart the course of unemployment and inflation as measures of U.S. economic health. How do we measure the unemployment rate and the inflation rate and are they reliable vital signs for the economy?

As the U.S. economy slowly expanded after a recession in 2008 and 2009, job growth was weak and questions about the health of the labor market became of vital importance to millions of American families. *Economics in the News*, at the end of this chapter, puts the spotlight on the labor market through recession and a weak 2010–2014 expansion.

◆ Employment and Unemployment

What kind of job market will you enter when you graduate? Will there be plenty of good jobs to choose among, or will jobs be so hard to find that you end up taking one that doesn't use your education and pays a low wage? The answer depends, to a large degree, on the total number of jobs available and on the number of people competing for them.

The class of 2014 had a tough time in the jobs market. In July 2014, four years after a recession, 10 million Americans wanted a job but couldn't find one, and another 8 million had either given up the search for a job or had reluctantly settled for a part-time job.

Despite the high unemployment, the U.S. economy is an incredible job-creating machine. Even in 2009 at the depths of recession, 139 million people had jobs—22 million more than in 1989. But in recent years, population growth has outstripped jobs growth, so unemployment is a serious problem.

Why Unemployment Is a Problem

Unemployment is a serious personal and social economic problem for two main reasons. It results in

- Lost incomes and production
- Lost human capital

Lost Incomes and Production The loss of a job brings a loss of income and lost production. These losses are devastating for the people who bear them and they make unemployment a frightening prospect for everyone. Unemployment benefits create a safety net, but they don't fully replace lost earnings.

Lost production means lower consumption and a lower investment in capital, which lowers the living standard in both the present and the future.

Lost Human Capital Prolonged unemployment permanently damages a person's job prospects by destroying human capital.

ECONOMICS IN ACTION

What Kept Ben Bernanke Awake at Night

The Great Depression began in October 1929, when the U.S. stock market crashed. It reached its deepest point in 1933, when 25 percent of the labor force was unemployed, and lasted until 1941, when the United States entered World War II. The depression quickly spread globally to envelop most nations.

The 1930s were and remain the longest and worst period of high unemployment in history. Failed banks, shops, farms, and factories left millions of Americans without jobs, homes, and food. Without the support of government and charities, millions would have starved.

The Great Depression was an enormous political event: It fostered the rise of the German and Japanese militarism that were to bring the most devastating war humans have ever fought. It also led to President Franklin D. Roosevelt's "New Deal," which enhanced the role of government in economic life and made government intervention in markets popular and the market economy unpopular.

The Great Depression also brought a revolution in economics. British economist John Maynard Keynes published his *General Theory of Employment, Interest, and Money* and created what we now call macroeconomics.

Many economists have studied the Great Depression and tried to determine why what started out as an ordinary recession became so devastating. Among them is Ben Bernanke, the former Chairman of the Federal Reserve.

One of the reasons the Fed was so aggressive in cutting interest rates and saving banks from going under is that Ben Bernanke is so vividly aware of the horrors of total economic collapse and was determined to avoid any risk of a repeat of the Great Depression.

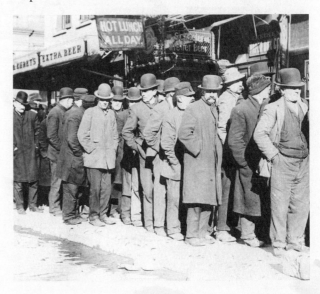

Think about a manager who loses his job when his employer downsizes. The only work he can find is driving a taxi. After a year in this work, he discovers that he can't compete with new MBA graduates. Eventually, he gets hired as a manager but in a small firm and at a lower wage than before. He has lost some of his human capital.

The cost of unemployment is spread unequally, which makes it a highly charged political problem as well as a serious economic problem.

Governments make strenuous efforts to measure unemployment accurately and to adopt policies to moderate its level and ease its pain. Here, we'll learn how the U.S. government monitors unemployment.

Current Population Survey

Every month, the U.S. Census Bureau surveys 60,000 households and asks a series of questions about the age and job market status of the members of each household. This survey is called the Current Population Survey (or CPS). The Census Bureau uses the answers to chart the course of the labor force.

Figure 22.1 shows the population categories used by the Census Bureau and the relationships among the categories.

The population divides into two broad groups: the working-age population and others who are too young to work or who live in institutions and are unable to work. The **working-age population** is the total number of people aged 16 years and over who are not in jail, hospital, or some other form of institutional care.

The Census Bureau divides the working-age population into two groups: those in the labor force and those not in the labor force. It also divides the labor force into two groups: the employed and the unemployed. So the **labor force** is the sum of the employed and the unemployed.

To be counted as employed in the Current Population Survey, a person must have either a full-time job or a part-time job. To be counted as *un*employed, a person must be available for work and must be in one of three categories:

1. Without work but has made specific efforts to find a job within the previous four weeks

2. Waiting to be called back to a job from which he or she has been laid off

3. Waiting to start a new job within 30 days

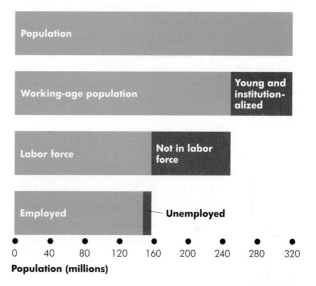

FIGURE 22.1 Population Labor Force Categories

The total population is divided into the working-age population and the young and institutionalized. The working-age population is divided into those in the labor force and those not in the labor force. The labor force is divided into the employed and the unemployed.

Source of data: Bureau of Labor Statistics.

MyEconLab Animation

Anyone surveyed who satisfies one of these three criteria is counted as unemployed. People in the working-age population who are neither employed nor unemployed are classified as *not in the labor force*.

In June 2014, the population of the United States was 318 million; the working-age population was 248 million. Of this number, 92 million were not in the labor force. Most of these people were in school full time or had retired from work. The remaining 156 million people made up the U.S. labor force. Of these, 146.3 million were employed and 9.7 million were unemployed.

Three Labor Market Indicators

The Census Bureau calculates three indicators of the state of the labor market. They are

- The unemployment rate
- The employment-to-population ratio
- The labor force participation rate

The Unemployment Rate The amount of unemployment is an indicator of the extent to which people who want jobs can't find them. The **unemployment rate** is the percentage of the people in the labor force who are unemployed. That is,

$$\text{Unemployment rate} = \frac{\text{Number of people unemployed}}{\text{Labor force}} \times 100$$

and

$$\text{Labor force} = \text{Number of people employed} + \text{Number of people unemployed}.$$

In June 2014, the number of people employed was 146.3 million and the number unemployed was 9.7 million. By using the above equations, you can verify that the labor force was 156 million (146.3 million plus 9.7 million) and the unemployment rate was 6.2 percent (9.7 million divided by 156.0 million, multiplied by 100).

Figure 22.2 shows the unemployment rate from 1980 to 2014. The average unemployment rate during this period is 6.5 percent—equivalent to 10.1 million people being unemployed in 2014

The unemployment rate fluctuates over the business cycle and reaches a peak value after a recession ends.

Each peak unemployment rate in the recessions of 1982, 1990–1991, and 2001 was lower than the previous one. But the recession of 2008–2009 ended the downward trend.

The Employment-to-Population Ratio The number of people of working age who have jobs is an indicator of both the availability of jobs and the degree of match between people's skills and jobs. The **employment-to-population ratio** is the percentage of people of working age who have jobs. That is,

$$\text{Employment to population ratio} = \frac{\text{Number of people employed}}{\text{Working-age population}} \times 100.$$

In June 2014, the number of people employed was 146.3 million and the working-age population was 248 million. By using the above equation, you can verify that the employment-to-population ratio was 59 percent (146.3 million divided by 248 million, multiplied by 100).

Figure 22.3 shows the employment-to-population ratio. This indicator followed an upward trend before 2000 and then a downward trend. The increase before 2000 means that the U.S. economy created

---

FIGURE 22.2   The Unemployment Rate: 1980–2014

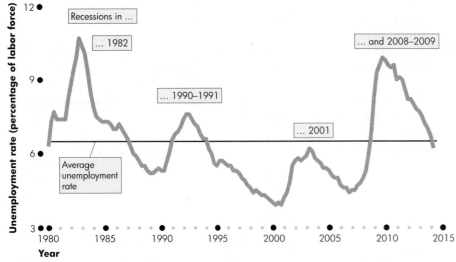

The average unemployment rate from 1980 to 2014 was 6.5 percent. The unemployment rate increases in a recession, peaks after the recession ends, and decreases in an expansion. The peak unemployment rate during a recession was on a downward trend before the 2008–2009 recession, with each successive recession having a lower unemployment rate. The severe recession of 2008–2009 broke this trend.

Source of data: Bureau of Labor Statistics.

FIGURE 22.3   Labor Force Participation and Employment: 1980–2014

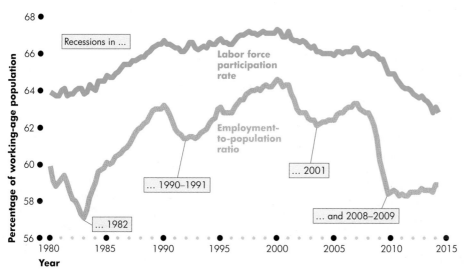

The trend in the labor force participation rate and the employment-to-population ratio is upward before 2000 and downward after 2000.

The employment-to-population ratio fluctuates more than the labor force participation rate over the business cycle and reflects cyclical fluctuations in the unemployment rate.

The fall in both measures was steep during 2008 and 2009.

Source of data: Bureau of Labor Statistics.

MyEconLab Real-time data

jobs at a faster rate than the working-age population grew. This indicator also fluctuates: It falls during a recession and increases during an expansion.

The Labor Force Participation Rate The number of people in the labor force is an indicator of the willingness of people of working age to take jobs. The **labor force participation rate** is the percentage of the working-age population who are members of the labor force. That is,

$$\text{Labor force participation rate} = \frac{\text{Labor force}}{\text{Working-age population}} \times 100.$$

In June 2014, the labor force was 156.0 million and the working-age population was 248.0 million. By using the above equation, you can verify that the labor force participation rate was 62.9 percent (156.0 million divided by 248.0 million, multiplied by 100).

Figure 22.3 shows the labor force participation rate. Like the employment-to-population ratio, this indicator has an upward trend before 2000 and then a downward trend. It also has mild fluctuations around the trend but a steep decrease in 2008 and 2009. Unsuccessful job seekers left the labor force during the recession and didn't reenter during the weak expansion that began in 2010.

Other Definitions of Unemployment

Do fluctuations in the labor force participation rate over the business cycle mean that people who leave the labor force during a recession should be counted as unemployed? Or are they correctly counted as being not in the labor force?

The Bureau of Labor Statistics believes that the official unemployment definition gives the correct measure. But it provides data on two types of *underemployed* labor excluded from the official measure. They are

- Marginally attached workers
- Part-time workers who want full-time jobs

Marginally Attached Workers A **marginally attached worker** is a person who currently is neither working nor looking for work but has indicated that he or she wants and is available for a job and has looked for work sometime in the recent past. A marginally attached worker who has stopped looking for a job because of repeated failure to find one is called a **discouraged worker.**

The official unemployment measure excludes marginally attached workers because they haven't made specific efforts to find a job within the past four weeks. In all other respects, they are unemployed.

Part-Time Workers Who Want Full-Time Jobs Many part-time workers want to work part time. This arrangement fits in with the other demands on their time. But some part-time workers would like full-time jobs and can't find them. In the official statistics, these workers are called economic part-time workers and they are partly unemployed.

Most Costly Unemployment

All unemployment is costly, but the most costly is long-term unemployment that results from job loss.

People who are unemployed for a few weeks and then find another job bear some costs of unemployment. But these costs are low compared to the costs borne by people who remain unemployed for many weeks.

Also, people who are unemployed because they voluntarily quit their jobs to find better ones or because they have just entered or reentered the labor market bear some costs of unemployment. But these costs are lower than those borne by people who lose their job and are forced back into the job market.

The unemployment rate doesn't distinguish among these different categories of unemployment. If most of the unemployed are long-term job losers, the situation is much worse than if most are short-term voluntary job searchers.

Alternative Measures of Unemployment

To provide information about the aspects of unemployment that we've just discussed, the Bureau of Labor Statistics reports six alternative measures of the unemployment rate: two that are narrower than the official measure and three that are broader. The narrower measures focus on the personal cost of unemployment and the broader measures focus on assessing the full amount of underemployed labor resources.

Figure 22.4 shows these measures from 1994 (the first year for which all six are available) to 2014. U–3 is the official unemployment rate. Long-term unemployment (U–1) and unemployed job losers (U–2) are about 40 percent of the unemployed on average but 60 percent in a deep recession. Adding discouraged workers (U–4) makes very little difference to the unemployment rate, but adding all other marginally attached workers (U–5) adds one percentage point. A big difference is made by adding the economic part-time workers (U–6). In June 2014, after adding these workers the *underemployment rate* was 12 percent.

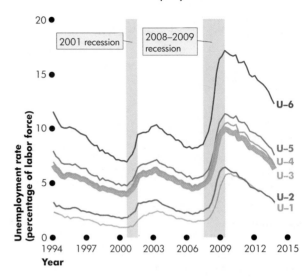

FIGURE 22.4   Six Alternative Measures of Unemployment

U–1 are those unemployed for 15 weeks or more, and U–2 are job losers. U–3 is the official unemployment rate. U–4 adds discouraged workers, and U–5 adds all other marginally attached workers. The broadest measure, U–6, adds part-time workers who want full-time jobs. Fluctuations in all the alternative measures are similar to those in the official measure, U–3.

Source of data: Bureau of Labor Statistics.

MyEconLab Real-time data

◆ REVIEW QUIZ

1 What determines if a person is in the labor force?
2 What distinguishes an unemployed person from one who is not in the labor force?
3 Describe the trends and fluctuations in the U.S. unemployment rate from 1980 to 2014.
4 Describe the trends and fluctuations in the U.S. employment-to-population ratio and labor force participation rate from 1980 to 2014.
5 Describe the alternative measures of unemployment.

Work these questions in Study Plan 22.1 and get instant feedback. Do a Key Terms Quiz.   MyEconLab

You've seen how we measure employment and unemployment. Your next task is to see what we mean by full employment and how unemployment and real GDP fluctuate over the business cycle.

Unemployment and Full Employment

There is always someone without a job who is searching for one, so there is always some unemployment. The key reason is that the economy is a complex mechanism that is always changing—it experiences frictions, structural change, and cycles.

Frictional Unemployment

There is an unending flow of people into and out of the labor force as people move through the stages of life—from being in school to finding a job, to working, perhaps to becoming unhappy with a job and looking for a new one, and finally, to retiring from full-time work.

There is also an unending process of job creation and job destruction as new firms are born, firms expand or contract, and some firms fail and go out of business.

The flows into and out of the labor force and the processes of job creation and job destruction create the need for people to search for jobs and for businesses to search for workers. Businesses don't usually hire the first person who applies for a job, and unemployed people don't usually take the first job that comes their way. Instead, both firms and workers spend time searching for what they believe will be the best available match. By this process of search, people can match their own skills and interests with the available jobs and find a satisfying job and a good income.

The unemployment that arises from the normal labor turnover we've just described—from people entering and leaving the labor force and from the ongoing creation and destruction of jobs—is called **frictional unemployment.** Frictional unemployment is a permanent and healthy phenomenon in a dynamic, growing economy.

Structural Unemployment

The unemployment that arises when changes in technology or international competition change the skills needed to perform jobs or change the locations of jobs is called **structural unemployment.** Structural unemployment usually lasts longer than frictional unemployment because workers must retrain and possibly relocate to find a job. When a steel plant in Gary, Indiana, is automated, some jobs in that city disappear. Meanwhile, new jobs for security guards, retail clerks, and life-insurance salespeople are created in Chicago and Indianapolis. The unemployed former steelworkers remain unemployed for several months until they move, retrain, and get one of these jobs. Structural unemployment is painful, especially for older workers for whom the best available option might be to retire early or take a lower-skilled, lower-paying job.

Cyclical Unemployment

The higher than normal unemployment at a business cycle trough and the lower than normal unemployment at a business cycle peak is called **cyclical unemployment.** A worker who is laid off because the economy is in a recession and who gets rehired some months later when the expansion begins has experienced cyclical unemployment.

"Natural" Unemployment

Natural unemployment is the unemployment that arises from frictions and structural change when there is no cyclical unemployment—when all the unemployment is frictional and structural. Natural unemployment as a percentage of the labor force is called the **natural unemployment rate.**

Full employment is defined as a situation in which the unemployment rate equals the natural unemployment rate.

What determines the natural unemployment rate? Is it constant or does it change over time?

The natural unemployment rate is influenced by many factors but the most important ones are

- The age distribution of the population
- The scale of structural change
- The real wage rate
- Unemployment benefits

The Age Distribution of the Population An economy with a young population has a large number of new job seekers every year and has a high level of frictional unemployment. An economy with an aging population has fewer new job seekers and a low level of frictional unemployment.

The Scale of Structural Change The scale of structural change is sometimes small. The same jobs using the same machines remain in place for many years. But sometimes there is a technological upheaval. The old ways are swept aside and millions of jobs are lost and the skill to perform them loses value. The amount of structural unemployment fluctuates with the pace and volume of technological change and the change driven by fierce international competition, especially from fast-changing Asian economies. A high level of structural unemployment is present in many parts of the United States today (as you can see in *Economics in Action* below).

The Real Wage Rate The natural unemployment rate is influenced by the level of the real wage rate. Real wage rates that bring unemployment are a *minimum wage* and an *efficiency wage*. Chapter 6 (see pp. 131–133) explains how the minimum wage creates unemployment. An *efficiency wage* is a wage set above the going market wage to enable firms to attract the most productive workers, get them to work hard, and discourage them from quitting.

Unemployment Benefits Unemployment benefits increase the natural unemployment rate by lowering the opportunity cost of job search. European countries have more generous unemployment benefits and higher natural unemployment rates than the United States. Extending unemployment benefits increases the natural unemployment rate.

There is no controversy about the existence of a natural unemployment rate. Nor is there disagreement that the natural unemployment rate changes. But economists don't know its exact size or the extent to which it fluctuates. The Congressional Budget Office estimates the natural unemployment rate and its estimate for 2012 was 6 percent—about 70 percent of the unemployment in that year.

Real GDP and Unemployment Over the Cycle

The quantity of real GDP at full employment is *potential GDP* (Chapter 21, p. 498). Over the business cycle, real GDP fluctuates around potential GDP. The gap between real GDP and potential GDP is called the **output gap.** As the output gap fluctuates over the business cycle, the unemployment rate fluctuates around the natural unemployment rate.

ECONOMICS IN ACTION

Structural and Cyclical Unemployment in Michigan

In 2010, 13.6 percent of Michigan's labor force was unemployed—the nation's highest official unemployment rate—and when marginally attached workers and part-time workers who want full-time jobs are added, almost 22 percent of the state's labor force was unemployed or underemployed. And 8.4 percent of Michigan's labor force were unemployed for long spells.

One of Michigan's problems was structural—a collapse of manufacturing jobs centered on the auto industry. These jobs had been disappearing steadily as robot technologies spread to do ever more of the tasks in the assembly of automobiles. The 2008–2009 recession accelerated this rate of job loss.

But by 2014, Michigan's unemployment rate had fallen to 7.5 percent, a fall larger than the fall in the U.S. average.

Around 11,000 businesses in Michigan produce high-tech scientific instruments and components for defense equipment, energy plants, and medical equipment. In 2010, these businesses employed around 400,000 people, which was more than 10 percent of the state's labor force and two thirds of all manufacturing jobs. Although the recession hit these firms, they cut employment by only 10 percent, compared with a 24 percent cut in manufacturing jobs in the rest of the Michigan economy. And these businesses and some new ones together with Michigan's traditional auto industry added jobs at a rapid pace after 2010. By mid-2014, more than 100,000 new manufacturing jobs had been created in Michigan.

FIGURE 22.5 The Output Gap and the Unemployment Rate

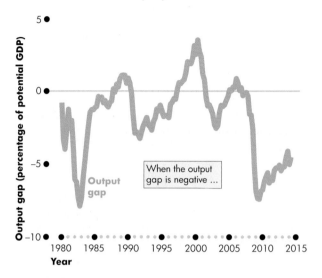

(a) Output gap

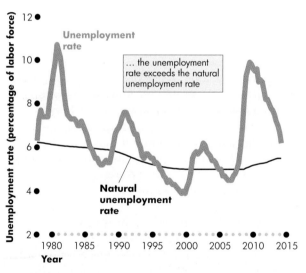

(b) Unemployment rate

As real GDP fluctuates around potential GDP in part (a), the unemployment rate fluctuates around the natural unemployment rate in part (b). In recessions, cyclical unemployment increases and the output gap becomes negative. At business cycle peaks, the unemployment rate falls below the natural rate and the output gap becomes positive. The natural unemployment rate decreased during the 1980s and 1990s.

Sources of data: Bureau of Economic Analysis, Bureau of Labor Statistics, and Congressional Budget Office.

MyEconLab   Real-time data

Figure 22.5 illustrates these fluctuations in the United States between 1980 and 2014—the output gap in part (a) and the unemployment rate and natural unemployment rate in part (b).

When the economy is at full employment, the unemployment rate equals the natural unemployment rate and real GDP equals potential GDP so the output gap is zero. When the unemployment rate is less than the natural unemployment rate, real GDP is greater than potential GDP and the output gap is positive. And when the unemployment rate is greater than the natural unemployment rate, real GDP is less than potential GDP and the output gap is negative.

Figure 22.5(b) shows the natural unemployment rate estimated by the Congressional Budget Office. This estimate puts the natural unemployment rate at 6.2 percent in 1980 and falling steadily through the 1980s and 1990s to 5.0 percent by the early 2000s and rising in the most recent recession to 6 percent.

◆ REVIEW QUIZ

1 Why does unemployment arise and what makes some unemployment unavoidable?
2 Define frictional unemployment, structural unemployment, and cyclical unemployment. Give examples of each type of unemployment.
3 What is the natural unemployment rate?
4 How does the natural unemployment rate change and what factors might make it change?
5 Why is the unemployment rate never zero, even at full employment?
6 What is the output gap? How does it change when the economy goes into recession?
7 How does the unemployment rate fluctuate over the business cycle?

Work these questions in Study Plan 22.2 and get instant feedback. Do a Key Terms Quiz.   MyEconLab

Your next task is to see how we monitor the price level and the inflation rate. You will learn about the Consumer Price Index (CPI), which is monitored every month. You will also learn about other measures of the price level and the inflation rate.

◆ The Price Level, Inflation, and Deflation

What will it *really* cost you to pay off your student loan? What will your parents' life savings buy when they retire? The answers depend on what happens to the **price level,** the average level of prices, and the value of money. A persistently rising price level is called **inflation;** a persistently falling price level is called **deflation.**

We are interested in the price level, inflation, and deflation for two main reasons. First, we want to measure the annual percentage change of the price level—the inflation rate or deflation rate. Second, we want to distinguish between the money values and real values of economic variables such as your student loan and your parents' savings.

We begin by explaining why inflation and deflation are problems. Then we'll look at how we measure the price level and the inflation rate. Finally, we'll return to the task of distinguishing real values from money values.

Why Inflation and Deflation Are Problems

Low, steady, and anticipated inflation or deflation isn't a problem, but an unexpected burst of inflation or period of deflation brings big problems and costs. An unexpected inflation or deflation

- Redistributes income
- Redistributes wealth
- Lowers real GDP and employment
- Diverts resources from production

Redistributes Income Workers and employers sign wage contracts that last for a year or more. An unexpected burst of inflation raises prices but doesn't immediately raise the wages. Workers are worse off because their wages buy less than they bargained for and employers are better off because their profits rise.

An unexpected period of deflation has the opposite effect. Wage rates don't fall but the prices fall. Workers are better off because their fixed wages buy more than they bargained for and employers are worse off with lower profits.

Redistributes Wealth People enter into loan contracts that are fixed in money terms and that pay an interest rate agreed as a percentage of the money borrowed and lent. With an unexpected burst of inflation, the

money that the borrower repays to the lender buys less than the money originally loaned. The borrower wins and the lender loses. The interest paid on the loan doesn't compensate the lender for the loss in the value of the money loaned. With an unexpected deflation, the money that the borrower repays to the lender buys *more* than the money originally loaned. The borrower loses and the lender wins.

Lowers Real GDP and Employment Unexpected inflation that raises firms' profits brings a rise in investment and a boom in production and employment. Real GDP rises above potential GDP and the unemployment rate falls below the natural rate. But this situation is *temporary*. Profitable investment dries up, spending falls, real GDP falls below potential GDP and the unemployment rate rises. Avoiding these swings in production and jobs means avoiding unexpected swings in the inflation rate.

An unexpected deflation has even greater consequences for real GDP and jobs. Businesses and households that are in debt (borrowers) are worse off and they cut their spending. A fall in total spending brings a recession and rising unemployment.

Diverts Resources from Production Unpredictable inflation or deflation turns the economy into a casino and diverts resources from productive activities to forecasting inflation. It can become more profitable to forecast the inflation rate or deflation rate correctly than to invent a new product. Doctors, lawyers, accountants, farmers—just about everyone—can make themselves better off, not by specializing in the profession for which they have been trained but by spending more of their time dabbling as amateur economists and inflation forecasters and managing their investments.

From a social perspective, the diversion of talent that results from unpredictable inflation is like throwing scarce resources onto a pile of garbage. This waste of resources is a cost of inflation.

At its worst, inflation becomes **hyperinflation**—an inflation rate of 50 percent a month or higher that grinds the economy to a halt and causes a society to collapse. Hyperinflation is rare, but Zimbabwe in recent years and several European and Latin American countries have experienced it.

We pay close attention to the inflation rate, even when its rate is low, to avoid its consequences. We monitor the price level every month and devote considerable resources to measuring it accurately. You're now going to see how we do this.

The Consumer Price Index

Every month, the Bureau of Labor Statistics (BLS) measures the price level by calculating the **Consumer Price Index (CPI),** which is a measure of the average of the prices paid by urban consumers for a fixed basket of consumer goods and services. What you learn here will help you to make sense of the CPI and relate it to your own economic life. The CPI tells you about the *value* of the money in your pocket.

Reading the CPI Numbers

The CPI is defined to equal 100 for a period called the *reference base period.* Currently, the reference base period is 1982–1984. That is, for the average of the 36 months from January 1982 through December 1984, the CPI equals 100.

In June 2014, the CPI was 237.7. This number tells us that the average of the prices paid by urban consumers for a fixed market basket of consumer goods and services was 137.7 percent *higher* in June 2014 than it was on average during 1982–1984.

Constructing the CPI

Constructing the CPI involves three stages:

- Selecting the CPI basket
- Conducting the monthly price survey
- Calculating the CPI

The CPI Basket The first stage in constructing the CPI is to select what is called the *CPI basket.* This basket contains the goods and services represented in the index, each weighted by its relative importance. The idea is to make the relative importance of the items in the CPI basket the same as that in the budget of an average urban household. For example, because people spend more on housing than on bus rides, the CPI places more weight on the price of housing than on the price of a bus ride.

To determine the CPI basket, the BLS conducts a Consumer Expenditure Survey. Today's CPI basket is based on data gathered in the Consumer Expenditure Survey of 2012–2013.

Figure 22.6 shows the CPI basket. As you look at the relative importance of the items in the CPI basket, remember that it applies to the *average* household. *Individual* households' baskets are spread around the average. Think about what you buy and compare your basket with the CPI basket.

FIGURE 22.6 The CPI Basket

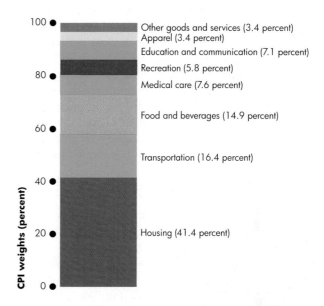

The CPI basket consists of the items that an average urban household buys. It consists mainly of housing (41.4 percent), transportation (16.4 percent), and food and beverages (14.9 percent). All other items sum to 27.3 percent of the total.

MyEconLab Animation

The Monthly Price Survey Each month, BLS employees check the prices of the 80,000 goods and services in the CPI basket in 30 metropolitan areas. Because the CPI aims to measure price *changes*, it is important that the prices recorded each month refer to exactly the same item. For example, suppose the price of a box of jelly beans has increased but a box now contains more beans. Has the price of jelly beans increased? The BLS employee must record the details of changes in quality or packaging so that price changes can be isolated from other changes.

Once the raw price data are in hand, the next task is to calculate the CPI.

Calculating the CPI To calculate the CPI, we

1. Find the cost of the CPI basket at base-period prices.
2. Find the cost of the CPI basket at current-period prices.
3. Calculate the CPI for the base period and the current period.

We'll work through these three steps for the simple artificial economy in Table 22.1, which shows the quantities in the CPI basket and the prices in the base period (2014) and current period (2015).

Part (a) contains the data for the base period. In that period, consumers bought 10 oranges at $1 each and 5 haircuts at $8 each. To find the cost of the CPI basket in the base-period prices, multiply the quantities in the CPI basket by the base-period prices. The cost of oranges is $10 (10 at $1 each), and the cost of haircuts is $40 (5 at $8 each). So the total cost of the CPI basket in the base period at base-period prices is $50 ($10 + $40).

Part (b) contains the price data for the current period. The price of an orange increased from $1 to $2, which is a 100 percent increase—($1 ÷ $1) × 100 = 100. The price of a haircut increased from $8 to $10, which is a 25 percent increase—($2 ÷ $8) × 100 = 25.

The CPI provides a way of averaging these price increases by comparing the cost of the basket rather than the price of each item. To find the cost of the CPI basket in the current period, 2015, multiply the quantities in the basket by their 2015 prices. The cost of

oranges is $20 (10 at $2 each), and the cost of haircuts is $50 (5 at $10 each). So total cost of the fixed CPI basket at current-period prices is $70 ($20 + $50).

You've now taken the first two steps toward calculating the CPI: calculating the cost of the CPI basket in the base period and the current period. The third step uses the numbers you've just calculated to find the CPI for 2014 and 2015.

The formula for the CPI is

$$\text{CPI} = \frac{\text{Cost of CPI basket at current prices}}{\text{Cost of CPI basket at base-period prices}} \times 100.$$

In Table 22.1, you established that in 2014 (the base period), the cost of the CPI basket was $50 and in 2015, it was $70. If we use these numbers in the CPI formula, we can find the CPI for 2014 and 2015. For 2014, the CPI is

$$\text{CPI in 2014} = \frac{\$50}{\$50} \times 100 = 100.$$

For 2015, the CPI is

$$\text{CPI in 2015} = \frac{\$70}{\$50} \times 100 = 140.$$

The principles that you've applied in this simplified CPI calculation apply to the more complex calculations performed every month by the BLS.

Measuring the Inflation Rate

A major purpose of the CPI is to measure changes in the cost of living and in the value of money. To measure these changes, we calculate the *inflation rate* as the annual percentage change in the CPI. To calculate the inflation rate, we use the formula:

$$\text{Inflation rate} = \frac{\text{CPI this year} - \text{CPI last year}}{\text{CPI last year}} \times 100.$$

We can use this formula to calculate the inflation rate in 2014. The CPI in June 2014 was 237.7, and the CPI in June 2013 was 232.9. So the inflation rate during the 12 months to June 2014 was

$$\text{Inflation rate} = \frac{(237.7 - 232.9)}{232.9} \times 100 = 2.1\%.$$

TABLE 22.1   The CPI:
A Simplified Calculation

(a) The cost of the CPI basket at base-period prices: 2014

| | CPI basket | | Cost of |
Item	Quantity	Price	CPI Basket
Oranges	10	$1.00	$10
Haircuts	5	$8.00	$40
Cost of CPI basket at base-period prices			$50

(b) The cost of the CPI basket at current-period prices: 2015

| | CPI basket | | Cost of |
Item	Quantity	Price	CPI Basket
Oranges	10	$2.00	$20
Haircuts	5	$10.00	$50
Cost of CPI basket at current-period prices			$70

Distinguishing High Inflation from a High Price Level

Figure 22.7 shows the CPI and the inflation rate in the United States between 1970 and 2014. The two parts of the figure are related and emphasize the distinction between high inflation and high prices.

When the price level in part (a) *rises rapidly*, (1970 through 1982), the inflation rate in part (b) is *high*. When the price level in part (a) *rises slowly*, (after 1982), the inflation rate in part (b) is *low*.

A high inflation rate means that the price level is rising rapidly. A high price level means that there has been a sustained period of rising prices.

When the price level in part (a) *falls* (2009), the inflation rate in part (b) is negative—deflation.

The CPI is not a perfect measure of the price level and changes in the CPI probably overstate the inflation rate. Let's look at the sources of bias.

The Biased CPI

The main sources of bias in the CPI are

- New goods bias
- Quality change bias
- Commodity substitution bias
- Outlet substitution bias

New Goods Bias If you want to compare the price level in 2014 with that in 1970, you must somehow compare the price of a computer today with that of a typewriter in 1970. Because a PC is more expensive than a typewriter was, the arrival of the PC puts an upward bias into the CPI and its inflation rate.

Quality Change Bias Cars and many other goods get better every year. Part of the rise in the prices of these goods is a payment for improved quality and is not inflation. But the CPI counts the entire price rise as inflation and so overstates inflation.

Commodity Substitution Bias Changes in relative prices lead consumers to change the items they buy. For example, if the price of beef rises and the price of chicken remains unchanged, people buy more chicken and less beef. This switch from beef to chicken might provide the same amount of meat and the same enjoyment as before and expenditure is the same as before. The price of meat has not changed. But because the CPI ignores the substitution of chicken for beef, it says the price of meat has increased.

FIGURE 22.7   The CPI and the Inflation Rate

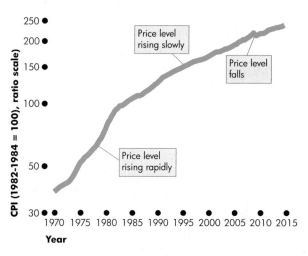

(a) CPI

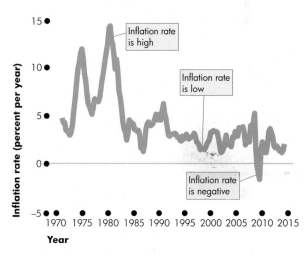

(b) Inflation rate

When the price level rises rapidly, the inflation rate is high; when the price level rises slowly, the inflation rate is low. When the price level falls, the inflation rate is negative.

From 1970 through 1982, the price level increased rapidly in part (a) and the inflation rate was high in part (b). After 1982, the price level rose slowly in part (a) and the inflation rate was low in part (b). In 2009, the price level fell and the inflation rate was negative—there was deflation.

Source of data: Bureau of Labor Statistics.

—— MyEconLab Real-time data ——

Outlet Substitution Bias When confronted with higher prices, people use discount stores more frequently and convenience stores less frequently. This phenomenon is called *outlet substitution*. The CPI surveys do not monitor outlet substitutions.

The Magnitude of the Bias

You've reviewed the sources of bias in the CPI. But how big is the bias? This question was tackled in 1996 by a Congressional Advisory Commission on the Consumer Price Index chaired by Michael Boskin, an economics professor at Stanford University. This commission said that the CPI overstates inflation by 1.1 percentage points a year. That is, if the CPI reports that inflation is 3.1 percent a year, most likely inflation is actually 2 percent a year.

Some Consequences of the Bias

The bias in the CPI distorts private contracts and increases government outlays. Many private agreements, such as wage contracts, are linked to the CPI. For example, a firm and its workers might agree to a three-year wage deal that increases the wage rate by 2 percent a year *plus* the percentage increase in the CPI. Such a deal ends up giving the workers more real income than the firm intended.

Close to a third of federal government outlays, including Social Security checks, are linked directly to the CPI. And while a bias of 1 percent a year seems small, accumulated over a decade it adds up to almost a trillion dollars of additional expenditures.

Alternative Price Indexes

The CPI is just one of many alternative price level index numbers and because of the bias in the CPI, other measures are used for some purposes. We'll describe three alternatives to the CPI and explain when and why they might be preferred to the CPI. The alternatives are

- Chained CPI
- Personal consumption expenditure deflator
- GDP deflator

Chained CPI The *chained CPI* is a price index that is calculated using a similar method to that used to calculate *chained-dollar real GDP* described in Chapter 21 (see pp. 508–509).

The *chained* CPI overcomes the sources of bias in the CPI. It incorporates substitutions and new goods bias by using current and previous period quantities rather than fixed quantities from an earlier period.

The chained CPI measures a lower inflation rate, on average, than the standard CPI. Between 2000 and 2014, the average inflation rate as measured by the chained CPI is only 0.7 percentage points lower than the standard CPI—1.7 percent versus 2.4 percent per year.

Personal Consumption Expenditure Deflator The *personal consumption expenditure deflator* (or *PCE deflator*) is calculated from data in the national income accounts that you studied in Chapter 21. When the Bureau of Economic Analysis calculates *real GDP*, it also calculates the real values of its expenditure components: real consumption expenditure, real investment, real government expenditure, and real net exports. These calculations are done in the same way as that for real GDP described in simplified terms on p. 497 and more technically on pp. 508–509 in Chapter 21.

To calculate the PCE deflator, we use the formula:

$$\text{PCE deflator} = (\text{Nominal } C \div \text{Real } C) \times 100,$$

where C is personal consumption expenditure.

The basket of goods and services included in the PCE deflator is broader than that in the CPI because it includes all consumption expenditure, not only the items bought by a typical urban family.

The difference between the PCE deflator and the CPI is small. Since 2000, the inflation rate measured by the PCE deflator is 1.9 percent per year, 0.5 percentage points lower than the CPI inflation rate.

GDP Deflator The *GDP deflator* is a bit like the PCE deflator except that it includes all the goods and services that are counted as part of GDP. So it is an index of the prices of the items in consumption, investment, government expenditure, and net exports.

$$\frac{\text{GDP}}{\text{deflator}} = (\text{Nominal GDP} \div \text{Real GDP}) \times 100.$$

This broader price index is appropriate for macroeconomics because it is a comprehensive measure of the cost of the real GDP basket of goods and services.

Since 2000, the GDP deflator has increased at an average rate of 2.0 percent per year, 0.4 percentage points below the CPI inflation rate.

Core Inflation

No matter whether we calculate the inflation rate using the CPI, the chained CPI, the PCE deflator, or the GDP deflator, the number bounces around a good deal from month to month or quarter to quarter. To determine the trend in the inflation rate, we need to strip the raw numbers of their volatility. The **core inflation rate** is a measure of the inflation rate that excludes volatile prices in an attempt to reveal the underlying inflation trend. (The inflation rate that *includes* all prices is called the *headline* inflation rate.)

As a practical matter, the core inflation rate is calculated as the percentage change in a price index excluding the prices of food and fuel. The prices of these two items are among the most volatile.

While the core PCE inflation rate removes the volatile elements in inflation, it can give a misleading view of the true underlying inflation rate. If the relative prices of the excluded items are changing, the core PCE inflation rate will give a biased measure of the true underlying inflation rate.

Such a misleading account was given during the years between 2003 and 2008 when the relative prices of food and fuel were rising. The result was a core inflation rate that was systematically below the headline inflation rate.

Figure 22.8 graphs the core and headline inflation rates since 2000 and shows how core inflation removes the extreme swings in the headline rate.

The Real Variables in Macroeconomics

You saw in Chapter 21 how we measure real GDP. And you've seen in this chapter how we can use nominal GDP and real GDP to provide another measure of the price level—the GDP deflator. But viewing real GDP as nominal GDP deflated, opens up the idea of other real variables. By using the GDP deflator, we can deflate other nominal variables to find their real values. For example, the *real wage rate* is the nominal wage rate divided by the GDP deflator.

We can adjust any nominal quantity or price variable for inflation by deflating it—by dividing it by the price level.

There is one variable that is a bit different—an interest rate. A real interest rate is *not* a nominal interest rate divided by the price level. You'll learn how to adjust the nominal interest rate for inflation to find the real interest rate in Chapter 24. But all the other real variables of macroeconomics are calculated by dividing a nominal variable by the price level.

FIGURE 22.8   Core Inflation

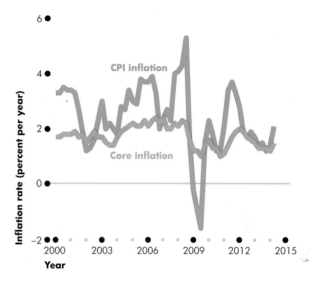

The core inflation rate excludes volatile price changes of food and fuel. Since 2003, the core inflation rate has mostly been below the CPI inflation rate because the relative prices of food and fuel have been rising.

Source of data: Bureau of Labor Statistics.

MyEconLab Real-time data

◆ REVIEW QUIZ

1 What is the price level?
2 What is the CPI and how is it calculated?
3 How do we calculate the inflation rate and what is its relationship with the CPI?
4 What are the four main ways in which the CPI is an upward-biased measure of the price level?
5 What problems arise from the CPI bias?
6 What are the alternative measures of the price level and how do they address the problem of bias in the CPI?

Work these questions in Study Plan 22.3 and get instant feedback. Do a Key Terms Quiz.   MyEconLab

◆ You've now completed your study of the measurement of macroeconomic performance. Your next task is to learn what determines that performance and how policy actions might improve it. But first, take a close-up look at the weak 2010–2014 expansion in *Economics in the News* on pp. 530–531.

Jobs Growth in Recovery

United States Adds 209,000 Jobs as Hiring Slows

The Financial Times
August 1, 2014

The United States added 209,000 jobs in July—below expectations of 233,000—indicating a slowdown in the pace of hiring since June but steady growth in the labor market overall.

The unemployment rate rose to 6.2 percent when it was expected to hold steady at 6.1 percent, reflecting the slight rise in the labor force participation rate at 62.9 percent in July.

While employment growth was not as strong as in June, when the United States added 298,000 jobs, July's figures reflected the sixth consecutive month of growth above 200,000. …

The jobs market in June was more robust than initially reported, with the government revising figures to add an additional 10,000 positions. The May numbers were also changed from 224,000 to 229,000.

"This encouraging trend in the labor market is consistent with other recent economic indicators, including the strong second-quarter [gross domestic product] growth reported on Wednesday," said Jason Furman, chairman of the White House's Council of Economic Advisers. …

Almost all of the jobs growth came from the private services sector, with business services adding 47,000 positions. Healthcare and the leisure sector remained static, with no meaningful change from June. Construction added 22,000 jobs and manufacturing put on 28,000. …

Earlier this week, the U.S. government reported that the economy enjoyed annualized growth of 4 percent in the second quarter, showing the recovery is back on track. GDP growth had fallen to a disappointing 2.1 percent in the first quarter, leading to questions about the strength of the economy.

MyEconLab More Economics in the News

ESSENCE OF THE STORY

- The United States added 209,000 jobs in July 2014 compared with 298,000 in June.

- The unemployment rate rose to 6.2 percent and the labor force participation rate rose to 62.9 percent.

- Private services created most of the jobs; 28,000 were in manufacturing and 22,000 in construction.

- The labor market trend is consistent with the annualized 4 percent second-quarter growth rate of real GDP.

ECONOMIC ANALYSIS

- This news article reports and comments on some labor market data for July 2014.

- The 209,000 jobs added during July 2014 are measured by a survey of payroll jobs at business establishments, called the *Current Employment Survey* (CES).

- The CES measures the change in the number of non-farm jobs.

- The CES is different from the *Current Population Survey* (CPS), a survey of households described on p. 517, which measures the number of people with a job—the number employed.

- In July 2014, the CPS reported that employment increased by 131,000.

- Although the two surveys can give a conflicting account in a single month, as they did in July 2014, over a longer period, they give the same message.

- To lower unemployment and to increase the labor force participation rate, the number of jobs must increase by more than the increase in population, which for the population (aged 16 and over) is about 200,000 per month.

- Figure 1 shows the change in the number of jobs (the blue curve) and the change in the population (the red curve) over the year from July 2013 to July 2014.

- You can see that in most months, the number of jobs created exeeded the increase in population.

- Figure 2 shows how job creation has changed the unemployment rate. With the exceptions of February and July 2014, the unemployment rate has fallen every month from 7.3 percent in July 2013 to 6.2 percent in July 2014.

- Figure 3 shows how job creation has changed the labor force participation rate, which fell from July to November 2013, but then increased through March 2014 before falling again.

- Look closely at the numbers on the *y*-axis of Fig. 3. The labor force participation rate changed by a very small amount from 63.4 percent in July 2013 to 62.9 percent in July 2014.

- To create enough jobs to employ the growing labor force plus the unemployed and the underemployed and to bring others back into the labor force, the pace of job creation will need to increase to beyond its level during 2014.

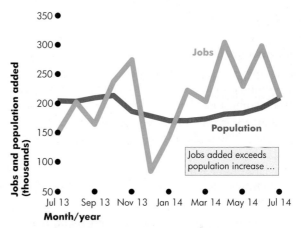

Figure 1 Jobs Created

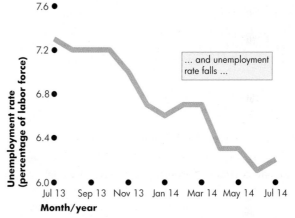

Figure 2 Unemployment Rate

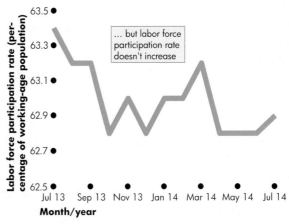

Figure 3 Labor Force Participation Rate

SUMMARY

Key Points

Employment and Unemployment (pp. 516–520)

- Unemployment is a serious personal, social, and economic problem because it results in lost output and income and a loss of human capital.
- The unemployment rate averaged 6.5 percent between 1980 and 2014. It increases in recessions and decreases in expansions.
- The labor force participation rate and the employment-to-population ratio have an upward trend and fluctuate with the business cycle.
- Two alternative measures of unemployment, narrower than the official measure, count the long-term unemployed and unemployed job losers.
- Three alternative measures of unemployment, broader than the official measure, count discouraged workers, other marginally attached workers, and part-time workers who want full-time jobs.

Working Problems 1 to 5 will give you a better understanding of employment and unemployment.

Unemployment and Full Employment (pp. 521–523)

- Some unemployment is unavoidable because people are constantly entering and leaving the labor force and losing or quitting jobs; also firms that create jobs are constantly being born, expanding, contracting, and dying.
- Unemployment can be frictional, structural, or cyclical.
- When all unemployment is frictional and structural, the unemployment rate equals the natural unemployment rate, the economy is at full employment, and real GDP equals potential GDP.

- Over the business cycle, real GDP fluctuates around potential GDP and the unemployment rate fluctuates around the natural unemployment rate.

Working Problems 6 and 7 will give you a better understanding of unemployment and full employment.

The Price Level, Inflation, and Deflation (pp. 524–529)

- Inflation and deflation that are unexpected redistribute income and wealth and divert resources from production.
- The Consumer Price Index (CPI) is a measure of the average of the prices paid by urban consumers for a fixed basket of consumer goods and services.
- The CPI is defined to equal 100 for a reference base period—currently 1982–1984.
- The inflation rate is the percentage change in the CPI from one period to the next.
- Changes in the CPI probably overstate the inflation rate because of the bias that arises from new goods, quality changes, commodity substitution, and outlet substitution.
- The bias in the CPI distorts private contracts and increases government outlays.
- Alternative price level measures such as the PCE deflator and GDP deflator avoid the bias of the CPI but do not make a large difference to the measured inflation rate.
- Real economic variables are calculated by dividing nominal variables by the price level.

Working Problems 8 to 11 will give you a better understanding of the price level, inflation, and deflation.

Key Terms   MyEconLab Key Terms Quiz

Consumer Price Index (CPI), 525
Core inflation rate, 529
Cyclical unemployment, 521
Deflation, 524
Discouraged worker, 519
Employment-to-population ratio, 518
Frictional unemployment, 521

Full employment, 521
Hyperinflation, 524
Inflation, 524
Labor force, 517
Labor force participation rate, 519
Marginally attached worker, 519
Natural unemployment rate, 521

Output gap, 522
Price level, 524
Structural unemployment, 521
Unemployment rate, 518
Working-age population, 517

WORKED PROBLEM

MyEconLab   You can work this problem in Chapter 22 Study Plan.

The Current Population Survey reported the following situations in July 2014:

- Sarah works 10 hours a week at McDonald's. She is available to work more hours but hasn't looked for extra work.
- Kevin spent the first six months of 2014 actively searching for a job but he didn't get hired. He believes there are no jobs, so he has given up looking.
- Pat quit the job he had for the past two years and is actively looking for a better paying job. He is available to work and is still searching for a job.
- Mary is a new graduate who was hired while she was a student to start a job in August.
- Johnnie quit his band in June, has no job in July, and is not looking for work.

Questions

1. Who does the BLS classify as being unemployed, a part-time worker, an employed person, a discouraged worker, and not in the labor force? Explain your classification.
2. How will the labor force change if Sarah starts a second job, Pat finds a good job and is hired, and Mary takes a job at McDonald's while she waits to start her new job?
3. How will the unemployment rate change if Sarah quits and starts to search for a full-time job?
4. How will the labor force participation rate change if Kevin starts creating football apps in his garage and they turn out to be very popular?

Solutions

1. Sarah is a part-time worker. As a part-time worker, BLS classifies Sarah as employed. She does not need to be looking for extra work.

   Kevin is a discouraged worker. He spent time looking for work but could not find a job, so he has given up the search. He is not unemployed because he didn't look for work, was not laid off, and is not waiting to start a job. The labor force includes those employed and those unemployed, so Kevin is not in the labor force. He is a marginally attached worker.

   Pat is unemployed. He doesn't have a job but is available and looked for a job during July.

   Mary doesn't have a job, but she is available for

work. Because she will start a job within 30 days, she is classified as unemployed.

Johnnie is a marginally attached worker. When he played in the band he was employed. But now he is not unemployed because he is not looking, not laid off, and not waiting to start a new job.

Key Point: To be in the labor force a person must be either employed or unemployed. To be counted as employed, a person must have a job or be starting one within 30 days. To be counted as unemployed, a person must have looked for a job in the last 30 days and be available for work.

2. The labor force consists of the people who are counted by the BLS survey as employed or unemployed.

   Sarah is already counted as employed, so when she starts a second job the labor force does not change.

   Pat is currently unemployed, so when he is hired he transfers from being unemployed to being employed. So his change of status does not change the labor force.

   Mary is currently counted as employed, so taking on a part-time job at McDonald's while she waits to start the new job does not change the labor force.

Key Point: The labor force increases if working-age people who are not currently in the labor force start to look for work and become unemployed or start a job and become employed.

3. The unemployment rate is the percentage of the labor force who are classified as unemployed. If Sarah quits her job and searches for a full-time job, she becomes unemployed. The labor force doesn't change, so the unemplyment rate rises.

Key Point: The unemployment rate rises as people quit or are laid off and start searching for a new job.

4. The labor force participation rate is the percentage of the working-age population who are in the labor force. Kevin is currently not in the labor force because he is a discouraged worker. When Kevin starts creating football apps in his garage and they turn out to be very popular, Kevin becomes employed. He is now in the labor force, so the labor force participation rate rises.

Key Point: The labor force participation rate changes as working-age people enter and exit the labor force.

◆ STUDY PLAN PROBLEMS AND APPLICATIONS

MyEconLab You can work Problems 1 to 11 in Chapter 22 Study Plan and get instant feedback. Problems marked update with real-time data.

Employment and Unemployment (Study Plan 22.1)

1. The BLS reported the following data for 2010:

   Labor force: 153.7 million
   Employment: 139.1 million
   Working-age population: 237.9 million

   Calculate the

   a. Unemployment rate.

   b. Labor force participation rate.

   c. Employment-to-population ratio.

2. In July 2014, in the economy of Sandy Island, 10,000 people were employed, 1,000 were unemployed, and 5,000 were not in the labor force. During August 2014, 80 people lost their jobs and didn't look for new ones, 20 people quit their jobs and retired, 150 unemployed people were hired, 50 people quit the labor force, and 40 people entered the labor force to look for work. Calculate for July 2014

   a. The unemployment rate.

   b. The employment-to-population ratio.

   And calculate for the end of August 2014

   c. The number of people unemployed.

   d. The number of people employed.

   e. The unemployment rate.

 Use the following data to work Problems 3 and 4. In October 2009, the U.S. unemployment rate was 10.0 percent. In October 2011, the unemployment rate was 8.9 percent. Predict what happened to

3. Unemployment between October 2009 and October 2011, if the labor force was constant.

4. The labor force between October 2009 and October 2011, if unemployment was constant.

5. **Shrinking U.S. Labor Force Keeps Unemployment Rate From Rising**

   An exodus of discouraged workers from the job market kept the unemployment rate from climbing above 10 percent. Had the labor force not decreased by 661,000, the unemployment rate would have been 10.4 percent. The number of discouraged workers rose to 929,000 last month.

   Source: Bloomberg, January 9, 2010

   What is a discouraged worker? Explain how an increase in discouraged workers influences the official unemployment rate and U–4.

Unemployment and Full Employment (Study Plan 22.2)

Use the following news clip to work Problems 6 and 7.

Some Firms Struggle to Hire Despite High Unemployment

Matching people with available jobs is always difficult after a recession as the economy remakes itself, but the disconnect is particularly acute this time. Since the recovery began in mid-2009, the number of job openings has risen more than twice as fast as actual hires. If the job market were working normally, openings would be getting filled as they appear. Some 5 million more would be employed and the unemployment rate would be 6.8%, instead of 9.5%.

Source: *The Wall Street Journal*, August 9, 2010

6. If the labor market is working properly, why would there be any unemployment at all?

7. Are the 5 million workers who cannot find jobs because of mismatching in the labor market counted as part of the economy's structural unemployment or part of cyclical unemployment?

The Price Level, Inflation, and Deflation

(Study Plan 22.3)

Use the following data to work Problems 8 and 9. The people on Coral Island buy only juice and cloth. The CPI basket contains the quantities bought in 2013. The average household spent $60 on juice and $30 on cloth in 2013 when juice was $2 a bottle and cloth was $5 a yard. In 2014, juice is $4 a bottle and cloth is $6 a yard.

8. Calculate the CPI basket and the percentage of the household's budget spent on juice in 2013.

9. Calculate the CPI and the inflation rate in 2014.

 Use the following data to work Problems 10 and 11. The BLS reported the following CPI data:

June 2008	217.3
June 2009	214.6
June 2010	216.9

10. Calculate the inflation rates for the years ended June 2009 and June 2010. How did the inflation rate change in 2010?

11. Why might these CPI numbers be biased? How can alternative price indexes avoid this bias?

ADDITIONAL PROBLEMS AND APPLICATIONS

 MyEconLab   You can work these problems in MyEconLab if assigned by your instructor.
Problems marked ⓦ update with real-time data.

Employment and Unemployment

12. What is the unemployment rate supposed to measure and why is it an imperfect measure?

ⓦ 13. The BLS reported the following data for July 2012:
Labor force participation rate: 63.7 percent
Working-age population: 243.4 million
Employment-to-population ratio: 58.4

Calculate the
a. Labor force.
b. Employment.
c. Unemployment rate.

14. **Jobs Report: Hiring Up, Unemployment Down**
The Labor Department reported that hiring accelerated in November, and the unemployment rate fell to 8.6 percent from 9 percent in October. Two reasons for the fall are that more Americans got jobs, but even more people gave up on their job searches altogether.
Source: CNNMoney, December 2, 2011

a. If the only change was that all the newly hired people had been unemployed in October, explain how the labor force and unemployment would have changed.

b. If the only change was that people gave up on their job searches, explain how the labor force and unemployment would have changed.

ⓦ 15. The BLS reported that in July 2012, employment decreased by 195,000 to 142,220,000 and the unemployment rate increased from 8.2 percent to 8.3 percent. About 3.4 million people were marginally attached workers and 0.9 million of them were discouraged.
a. Calculate the change in unemployment in July 2012.
b. With 3.4 million marginally attached workers and 0.9 million of them discouraged workers, what are the characteristics of the other 2.5 million marginally attached workers?

16. A high unemployment rate tells us that a large percentage of the labor force is unemployed but not why the unemployment rate is high. What unemployment measure tells us if (i) people are searching longer than usual to find a job, (ii) more people are economic part-time workers, or (iii) more unemployed people are job losers?

17. **Some Firms Struggle to Hire Despite High Unemployment**
With about 15 million Americans looking for work, some employers are swamped with job applicants, but many employers can't hire enough workers. The U.S. jobs market has changed. During the recession, millions of middle-skill, middle-wage jobs disappeared. Now with the recovery, these people can't find the skilled jobs that they seek and have a hard time adjusting to lower-skilled work with less pay.
Source: *The Wall Street Journal*, August 9, 2010

If the government extends the period over which it pays unemployment benefits to 99 weeks, how will the cost of being unemployed change?

18. Why might the unemployment rate underestimate the underutilization of labor resources?

Unemployment and Full Employment

Use the following data to work Problems 19 to 21.
The IMF *World Economic Outlook* reports the following unemployment rates:

Region	2010	2011
United States	9.6	9.0
Euro area	10.1	10.9
Japan	5.1	4.5

19. What do these numbers tell you about the phase of the business cycle in the three regions in 2011?

20. What do these numbers tell us about the relative size of their natural unemployment rates?

21. Do these numbers tell us anything about the relative size of their labor force participation rates and employment-to-population ratios?

22. **A Half-Year of Job Losses**
For the first six months of 2008, the U.S. economy lost 438,000 jobs. The job losses in June were concentrated in manufacturing and construction, two sectors that have been badly battered in the recession.
Source: CNN, July 3, 2008

a. Based on the news clip, what might be the main source of increased unemployment?
b. Based on the news clip, what might be the main type of increased unemployment?

23. **Governor Plans to Boost Economy with Eco-friendly Jobs**

    Oregon's 5.6 percent unemployment rate hovers close to the national average of 5.5 percent. A few years ago, Oregon had one of the highest unemployment rates in the nation. To avoid rising unemployment, Oregon Governor Kulongoski introduced a plan that provides public schools and universities with enough state funds to meet growing demand for skilled workers. Also Kulongoski wants to use state and federal money for bridges, roads, and buildings to stimulate more construction jobs.

    Source: *The Oregonian*, July 8, 2008

    a. What is the main type of unemployment that Governor Kulongoski is using policies to avoid? Explain.

    b. How might these policies impact Oregon's natural unemployment rate? Explain.

The Price Level, Inflation, and Deflation

24. A typical family on Sandy Island consumes only juice and cloth. Last year, which was the base year, the family spent $40 on juice and $25 on cloth. In the base year, juice was $4 a bottle and cloth was $5 a length. This year, juice is $4 a bottle and cloth is $6 a length. Calculate

    a. The CPI basket.

    b. The CPI in the current year.

    c. The inflation rate in the current year.

25. Amazon.com agreed to pay its workers $20 an hour in 1999 and $22 an hour in 2001. The price level for these years was 166 in 1999 and 180 in 2001. Calculate the real wage rate in each year. Did these workers really get a pay raise between 1999 and 2001?

26. **News release**

    In May 2012, real personal consumption expenditure (PCE) was $9,588 billion and the PCE deflator was 115.4. In June 2012, real personal consumption expenditure was $9,576 billion and personal consumption expenditure was $11,062 billion.

    Source: BEA, July 30, 2012

    Calculate personal consumption expenditure in May 2012 and the PCE deflator in June 2012. Was the percentage increase in real personal consumption expenditure greater or smaller than that in personal consumption expenditure?

27. **Hardworking Americans Should Not Be Living in Poverty**

    The federal minimum wage has remained frozen for the past three years at $7.25 an hour, while the prices of gas and milk have risen steadily. Over this three-year period, the real value of the minimum wage has fallen to $6.77 per hour.

    Source: CNN, July 25, 2012

    By what percentage did the CPI increase over these three years?

Economics in the News

28. After you have studied *Economics in the News* on pp. 530–531, answer the following questions.

    a. How many jobs must be created each month to keep pace with a growing population?

    b. What normally happens to the unemployment rate when the pace of job creation exceeds the increase in population?

    c. Why might the unemployment rate sometimes increase, when the pace of job creation exceeds the increase in population?

    d. How would you expect the labor force participation rate to respond to job creation in excess of population growth?

    e. How would you expect an increase in the growth rate of real GDP (see last paragraph of news article) to affect jobs and unemployment?

29. **Out of a Job and Out of Luck at 54**

    Too young to retire, too old to get a new job. That's how many older workers feel after getting the pink slip and spending time on the unemployment line. Many lack the skills to craft resumes and search online, experts say. Older workers took an average of 21.1 weeks to land a new job in 2007, about 5 weeks longer than younger people. "Older workers will be more adversely affected because of the time it takes to transition into another job," said Deborah Russell, AARP's director of workforce issues.

    Source: CNN, May 21, 2008

    a. What type of unemployment might older workers be more prone to experience?

    b. Explain how the unemployment rate of older workers is influenced by the business cycle.

    c. Why might older unemployed workers become marginally attached or discouraged workers during a recession?

The Big Picture

Macroeconomics is a large and controversial subject that is interlaced with political ideological disputes. And it is a field in which charlatans as well as serious thinkers have much to say.

You have just learned in Chapters 21 and 22 how we monitor and measure the main macroeconomic variables. We use real GDP to calculate the rate of economic growth and business cycle fluctuations. And we use the CPI and other measures of the price level to calculate the inflation rate and to "deflate" nominal values to find *real* values.

In the chapters that lie ahead, you will learn the theories that economists have developed to explain economic growth, fluctuations, and inflation.

First, in Chapters 23 through 26, you will study the long-term trends. This material is central to the oldest question in macroeconomics that Adam Smith tried to answer: What are the causes of the wealth of nations? You will also study three other old questions that Adam Smith's contemporary and friend David Hume first addressed: What causes inflation? What causes international deficits and surpluses? And why do exchange rates fluctuate?

In Chapters 27 through 29, you will study macroeconomic fluctuations.

Finally, in Chapters 30 and 31, you will study the policies that the federal government and Federal Reserve might adopt to make the economy perform well.

David Hume, *a Scot who lived from 1711 to 1776, did not call himself an economist. "Philosophy and general learning" is how he described the subject of his life's work. Hume was an extraordinary thinker and writer. Published in 1742, his* Essays, Moral and Political, *range across economics, political science, moral philosophy, history, literature, ethics, and religion and explore such topics as love, marriage, divorce, suicide, death, and the immortality of the soul!*

His economic essays provide astonishing insights into the forces that cause inflation, business cycle fluctuations, balance of payments deficits, and interest rate fluctuations; and they explain the effects of taxes and government deficits and debts.

Data were scarce in Hume's day, so he was not able to draw on detailed evidence to support his analysis. But he was empirical. He repeatedly appealed to experience and observation as the ultimate judge of the validity of an argument. Hume's fundamentally empirical approach dominates macroeconomics today.

"... in every kingdom into which money begins to flow in greater abundance than formerly, everything takes a new face: labor and industry gain life; the merchant becomes more enterprising, the manufacturer more diligent and skillful, and even the farmer follows his plow with greater alacrity and attention."

DAVID HUME
Essays, Moral and Political

The U.S. economy was hit in 2007 and 2008 by four significant negative shocks ... [three to aggregate demand and one to aggregate supply.]

RICHARD H. CLARIDA is the C. Lowell Harriss Professor of Economics at Columbia University, where he has taught since 1988. He graduated with highest honors from the University of Illinois at Urbana in 1979 and received his masters and Ph.D. in Economics from Harvard University in 1983, writing his dissertation under the supervision of Benjamin Friedman.

Professor Clarida has taught at Yale University and held public service positions as Senior Staff Economist with the President's Council of Economic Advisers in President Ronald Reagan's Administration and most recently as Assistant Secretary of the Treasury for Economic Policy in the Administration of President George W. Bush. He has also been a visiting scholar at the International Monetary Fund and at many central banks around the world, including the Federal Reserve, the European Central Bank, the Bank of Canada, the Deutsche Bundesbank, the Bank of Italy, and the Bank of England.

Professor Clarida has published a large number of important articles in leading academic journals and books on monetary policy, exchange rates, interest rates, and international capital flows.

Michael Parkin talked with Richard Clarida about his research and some of the macroeconomic policy challenges facing the United States and the world today.

Looking at the state of the U.S. economy today (fall 2012), why is the recovery so slow and unemployment so stubbornly high?

The U.S. economy was hit in 2007 and 2008 by four significant negative shocks: The bursting of the housing bubble, a major global dislocation in financial markets, a credit crunch as banks suffered losses and tightened lending standards, and record oil and gasoline prices.

The collapse of the housing market was a significant shock to aggregate demand. The dislocation in financial markets and the credit crunch were also negative shocks to aggregate demand. They decreased aggregate demand because tighter lending standards and higher credit spreads made it more expensive for firms and households to borrow for any given level of

the interest rate set by the Fed, so spending plans were scaled back.

These three shocks shifted the aggregate demand curve leftward (see Chapter 27, pp. 652–655).

Higher oil and commodity prices were a negative supply shock, which shifted the aggregate supply curve leftward (see Chapter 27, pp. 648–651).

Since 2009, the U.S. economy has been in recovery but has been growing at a disappointing pace. The fall in the unemployment rate has been welcome but slow. Real GDP growth has been slow because the private sector has increased its saving rate to pay off an excess of debt incurred during the credit bubble. U.S. growth has also been slow because a weak economy in Europe and a slowdown in China have slowed global economic growth and lowered the demand for U.S. exports.

*Read the full interview with Richard Clarida in MyEconLab.

23 ECONOMIC GROWTH

After studying this chapter, you will be able to:

◆ Define and calculate the economic growth rate and explain the implications of sustained growth

◆ Describe the economic growth trends in the United States and other countries and regions

◆ Explain what makes potential GDP grow

◆ Explain the sources of labor productivity growth

◆ Explain the theories of economic growth and policies to increase its rate

U.S. real GDP per person and the standard of living tripled between 1964 and 2014. We see even more dramatic change in China, where incomes have tripled not in 50 years but in the 14 years since 2000. Incomes are also growing rapidly in some African economies, one of which is the small but dynamic Botswana.

In this chapter, we study the forces that make real GDP grow; and in *Economics in the News* at the end of the chapter, we look at lessons we can learn from the slow growth of South Africa and its fast growing neighbor, Botswana.

◆ The Basics of Economic Growth

Economic growth is the expansion of production possibilities. A rapid pace of economic growth maintained over a number of years can transform a poor nation into a rich one. Such have been the stories of Hong Kong, South Korea, and some other Asian economies. Slow economic growth or the absence of growth can condemn a nation to devastating poverty. Such has been the fate of Sierra Leone, Somalia, Zambia, and much of the rest of Africa.

The goal of this chapter is to help you to understand why some economies expand rapidly and others stagnate. We'll begin by learning how to calculate a growth rate, by distinguishing between economic growth and a business cycle expansion, and by discovering the magic of sustained growth.

Calculating Growth Rates

We express a **growth rate** as the annual percentage change of a variable—the change in the level expressed as a percentage of the initial level. The growth rate of real GDP, for example, is calculated as:

$$\text{Real GDP growth rate} = \frac{\text{Real GDP in current year} - \text{Real GDP in previous year}}{\text{Real GDP in previous year}} \times 100.$$

Using some numbers, if real GDP in the current year is $11 trillion and if real GDP in the previous year was $10 trillion, then the economic growth rate is 10 percent.

The growth rate of real GDP tells us how rapidly the *total* economy is expanding. This measure is useful for telling us about potential changes in the balance of economic power among nations. But it does not tell us about changes in the standard of living.

The standard of living depends on **real GDP per person** (also called *per capita* real GDP), which is real GDP divided by the population. So the contribution of real GDP growth to the change in the standard of living depends on the growth rate of real GDP per person. We use the above formula to calculate this growth rate, replacing real GDP with real GDP per person.

Suppose, for example, that in the current year, when real GDP is $11 trillion, the population is 202 million. Then real GDP per person is $11 trillion divided by 202 million, which equals $54,455. And

suppose that in the previous year, when real GDP was $10 trillion, the population was 200 million. Then real GDP per person in that year was $10 trillion divided by 200 million, which equals $50,000.

Use these two values of real GDP per person with the growth formula above to calculate the growth rate of real GDP per person. That is,

$$\text{Real GDP per person growth rate} = \frac{\$54,455 - \$50,000}{\$50,000} \times 100 = 8.9 \text{ percent.}$$

The growth rate of real GDP per person can also be calculated (approximately) by subtracting the population growth rate from the real GDP growth rate. In the example you've just worked through, the growth rate of real GDP is 10 percent. The population changes from 200 million to 202 million, so the population growth rate is 1 percent. The growth rate of real GDP per person is approximately equal to 10 percent minus 1 percent, which equals 9 percent.

Real GDP per person grows only if real GDP grows faster than the population grows. If the growth rate of the population exceeds the growth rate of real GDP, then real GDP per person falls.

Economic Growth Versus Business Cycle Expansion

Real GDP can increase for two distinct reasons: The economy might be returning to full employment in an expansion phase of the business cycle or *potential GDP* might be increasing.

The return to full employment in an expansion phase of the business cycle isn't economic growth. It is just taking up the slack that resulted from the previous recession. The expansion of potential GDP is economic growth.

Figure 23.1 illustrates this distinction using the production possibilities frontier (the *PPF* that you studied in Chapter 2). A return to full employment in a business cycle expansion is a movement from inside the *PPF* at a point such as *A* to a point on the *PPF* such as *B*.

Economic growth is the expansion of production possibilities. It is an outward movement of the *PPF* such as the shift from PPF_0 to PPF_1 and the movement from point *B* on PPF_0 to point *C* on PPF_1.

The growth rate of potential GDP measures the pace of expansion of production possibilities and smoothes out the business cycle fluctuations in the growth rate of real GDP.

FIGURE 23.1 Economic Growth and a
Business Cycle Expansion

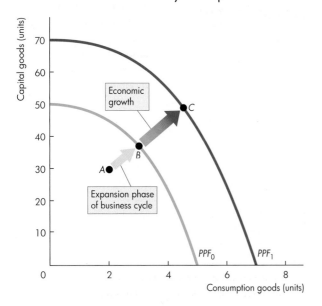

The increase in aggregate production in the move from point *A* inside PPF_0 to point *B* on PPF_0 is an expansion phase of the business cycle and it occurs with no change in production possibilities. Such an expansion is not economic growth. The increase in aggregate production in the move from point *B* on PPF_0 to point *C* on PPF_1 is economic growth—an expansion of production possibilities shown by an outward shift of the *PPF*.

—— MyEconLab Animation ——

FIGURE 23.2 Growth Rates of Real GDP
and Potential GDP

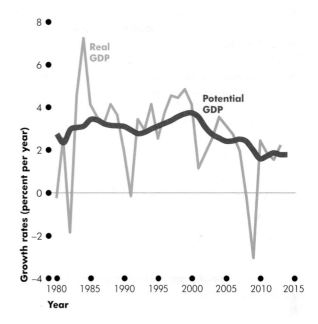

The annual growth rate of real GDP fluctuates widely over the business cycle and masks changes in the underlying trend growth rate. The annual growth rate of potential GDP provides information about changes in the trend growth rate. Both the growth rate of potential GDP and the trend growth rate of real GDP have fallen since 2000.

Sources of data: Real GDP: Bureau of Economic Analysis; Potential GDP: Congressional Budget Office.

—— MyEconLab Real-time data ——

Figure 23.2 shows how the growth rate of potential GDP (red curve) smoothes the more erratic fluctuations in the growth rate of real GDP. Business cycle fluctuations in the real GDP growth rate mask the underlying *trend* growth rate revealed by the growth rate of *potential* GDP.

The Magic of Sustained Growth

Sustained growth of real GDP per person can transform a poor society into a wealthy one. The reason is that economic growth is like compound interest.

Compound Interest Suppose that you put $100 in the bank and earn 5 percent a year interest on it. After one year, you have $105. If you leave that $105

in the bank for another year, you earn 5 percent interest on the original $100 *and on the $5 interest that you earned last year*. You are now earning interest on interest! The next year, things get even better. Then you earn 5 percent on the original $100 and on the interest earned in the first year and the second year. You are even earning interest on the interest that you earned on the interest of the first year.

Your money in the bank is growing at a rate of 5 percent a year. Before too many years have passed, your initial deposit of $100 will have grown to $200. But after how many years?

The answer is provided by a formula called the **Rule of 70**, which states that the number of years it takes for the level of any variable to double is approximately

FIGURE 23.3   The Rule of 70

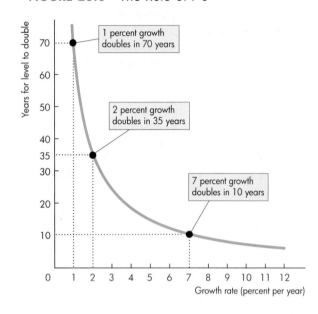

Growth rate (percent per year)	Years for level to double
1	70.0
2	35.0
3	23.3
4	17.5
5	14.0
6	11.7
7	10.0
8	8.8
9	7.8
10	7.0
11	6.4
12	5.8

The number of years it takes for the level of a variable to double is approximately 70 divided by the annual percentage growth rate of the variable.

MyEconLab Animation

70 divided by the annual percentage growth rate of the variable. Using the Rule of 70, you can now calculate how many years it takes your $100 to become $200. It is 70 divided by 5, which is 14 years.

Applying the Rule of 70

The Rule of 70 applies to any variable, so it applies to real GDP per person. Figure 23.3 shows the doubling time for growth rates of 1 percent per year to 12 percent per year.

You can see that real GDP per person doubles in 70 years (70 divided by 1)—an average human life span—if the growth rate is 1 percent a year. It doubles in 35 years if the growth rate is 2 percent a year and in just 10 years if the growth rate is 7 percent a year.

We can use the Rule of 70 to answer other questions about economic growth. For example, in 2010, U.S. real GDP per person was approximately 4 times that of China. China's recent growth rate of real GDP per person was 10 percent a year. If this growth rate were maintained, how long would it take China's real GDP per person to reach that of the United States in 2010? The answer, provided by the Rule of 70, is 14 years. China's real GDP per person doubles in 7 years

(70 divided by 10). It doubles again to 4 times its 2010 level in another 7 years. So after 14 years of growth at 10 percent a year, China's real GDP per person is 4 times its 2010 level and equals that of the United States in 2010.

Of course, after 14 years, U.S. real GDP per person would have increased, so China would still not have caught up to the United States. But at these growth rates, China's real GDP per person would equal that of the United States in 2010 by 2024.

◆ REVIEW QUIZ

1 What is economic growth and how do we calculate its rate?
2 What is the relationship between the growth rate of real GDP and the growth rate of real GDP per person?
3 Use the Rule of 70 to calculate the growth rate that leads to a doubling of real GDP per person in 20 years.

Work these questions in Study Plan 23.1 and get instant feedback. Do a Key Terms Quiz.   *MyEconLab*

◆ Long-Term Growth Trends

You have just seen the power of economic growth to increase incomes. At a 1 percent growth rate, it takes a human life span to double the standard of living. But at a 7 percent growth rate, the standard of living doubles every decade. How fast has our economy grown over the long term? How fast are other economies growing? Are poor countries catching up to rich ones, or do the gaps between the rich and poor persist or even widen?

Long-Term Growth in the U.S. Economy

Figure 23.4 shows real GDP per person in the United States for the hundred years from 1914 to 2014. The red line is actual real GDP and the black line (that starts in 1949) is potential GDP. The trend in potential GDP tells us about economic growth. Fluctuations around potential GDP tell us about the business cycle.

Two extraordinary events dominate the graph: the Great Depression of the 1930s, when growth stopped for a decade, and World War II of the 1940s, when growth briefly exploded.

For the century as a whole, the average growth rate was 2 percent a year. But the growth rate has not remained constant. From 1910 to the onset of the Great Depression in 1929, the average growth rate was a bit lower than the century average at 1.8 percent a year. Between 1930 and 1950, averaging out the Great Depression and World War II, the growth rate was 2.4 percent a year. After World War II, the growth rate started out at 2 percent a year. It then increased and growth averaged 3 percent a year during the 1960s. In 1973, and lasting for a decade, the growth rate slowed. Growth picked up somewhat during the 1980s and even more during the 1990s dot.com expansion. But the growth rate never returned to the pace achieved during the fast-growing 1960s.

A major goal of this chapter is to explain why our economy grows and why the growth rate changes. Another goal is to explain variations in the economic growth rate across countries. Let's now look at some other countries' growth rates.

FIGURE 23.4   A Hundred Years of Economic Growth in the United States

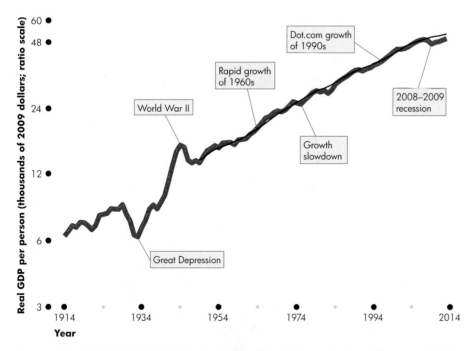

During the 100 years from 1914 to 2014, real GDP per person in the United States grew by 2 percent a year, on average. The growth rate was greater after World War II than it was before the Great Depression. Growth was most rapid during the 1960s. It slowed during the 1970s and speeded up again during the 1980s and 1990s, but it never returned to its rapid rate of the 1960s.

Sources of data: GDP (GNP) 1912–1928, Christina D. Romer, "World War I and the Postwar Depression: A Reinterpretation Based on Alternative Estimates of GNP," *Journal of Monetary Economics,* 22, 1988; 1929–2012, Bureau of Economic Analysis. Population data, Census Bureau.

MyEconLab Real-time data

Real GDP Growth in the World Economy

Figure 23.5 shows real GDP per person in the United States and in other countries between 1960 and 2010. Part (a) looks at the seven richest countries—known as the G7 nations. Among these nations, the United States has the highest real GDP per person. In 2010, Canada had the second-highest real GDP per person, ahead of Japan and France, Germany, Italy, and the United Kingdom (collectively the Europe Big 4).

During the fifty years shown here, the gaps between the United States, Canada, and the Europe Big 4 have been almost constant. But starting from a long way below, Japan grew fastest. It caught up to Europe in 1970 and to Canada in 1990. But during the 1990s, Japan's economy stagnated.

Many other countries are growing more slowly than, and falling farther behind, the United States. Figure 23.5(b) looks at some of these countries.

Real GDP per person in Central and South America was 28 percent of the U.S. level in 1960. It grew more quickly than the United States and reached 30 percent of the U.S. level by 1980, but then growth slowed and by 2010, real GDP per person in these countries was 23 percent of the U.S. level.

In Eastern Europe, real GDP per person has grown more slowly than anywhere except Africa, and fell from 32 percent of the U.S. level in 1980 to 19 percent in 2003 and then increased again to 22 percent in 2010.

Real GDP per person in Africa, the world's poorest continent, fell from 10 percent of the U.S. level in 1960 to 5 percent in 2007 and then increased slightly to 6 percent in 2010.

FIGURE 23.5   Economic Growth Around the World: Catch-Up or Not?

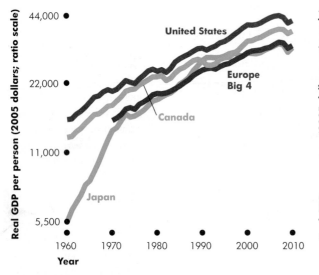

(a) Catch-up?

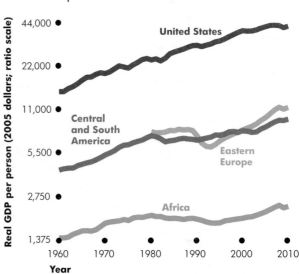

(b) No catch-up?

Real GDP per person has grown throughout the world. Among the rich industrial countries in part (a), real GDP per person has grown slightly faster in the United States than in Canada and the four big countries of Europe (France, Germany, Italy, and the United Kingdom). Japan had the fastest growth rate before 1973 but then growth slowed and Japan's economy stagnated during the 1990s.

Among a wider range of countries shown in part (b), growth rates have been lower than that of the United States. The gaps between the real GDP per person in the United States and in these countries have widened. The gap between the real GDP per person in the United States and Africa has widened by a large amount.

Sources of data: Alan Heston, Robert Summers, and Bettina Aten, Penn World Table Version 7.1, Center for International Comparisons of Production, Income, and Prices at the University of Pennsylvania, July 2012.

ECONOMICS IN ACTION

Fast Trains on the Same Track

Five Asian economies, Hong Kong, Korea, Singapore, Taiwan, and China, have experienced spectacular growth, which you can see in the figure. During the 1960s, real GDP per person in these economies ranged from 3 to 28 percent of that in the United States. But by 2010, real GDP per person in Singapore and Hong Kong had surpassed that of the United States.

The figure also shows that China is catching up rapidly but from a long way behind. China's real GDP per person increased from 3 percent of the U.S. level in 1960 to 26 percent in 2010.

The Asian economies shown here are like fast trains running on the same track at similar speeds and with a roughly constant gap between them. Singapore and Hong Kong are hooked together as the lead train, which runs about 20 years in front of Taiwan and Korea and 40 years in front of China.

Real GDP per person in Korea in 2010 was similar to that in Hong Kong in 1988, and real GDP in China in 2010 was similar to that of Hong Kong in 1976. Between 1976 and 2010, Hong Kong transformed itself from a poor developing economy into one of the richest economies in the world.

The rest of China is now doing what Hong Kong has done. China has a population 200 times that of Hong Kong and more than 4 times that of the United States. So if China continues its rapid growth, the world economy will change dramatically.

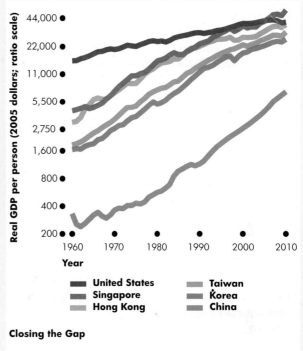

Closing the Gap

Sources of data: Alan Heston, Robert Summers, and Bettina Aten, Penn World Table Version 7.1, Center for International Comparisons of Production, Income, and Prices at the University of Pennsylvania, July 2012.

As these fast-growing Asian economies catch up with the United States, we can expect their growth rates to slow. But it will be surprising if China's growth rate slows much before it has closed the gap on the United States.

Even modest differences in economic growth rates sustained over a number of years bring enormous differences in the standard of living. And some of the differences that you've just seen are enormous. So the facts about economic growth in the United States and around the world raise some big questions.

What are the preconditions for economic growth? What sustains economic growth once it gets going? How can we identify the sources of economic growth and measure the contribution that each source makes? What can we do to increase the sustainable rate of economic growth?

We're now going to address these questions and discover the causes of economic growth. We start by seeing how potential GDP is determined and what makes it grow. You will see that labor productivity growth is the key to rising living standards and go on to explore the sources of this growth.

◆ REVIEW QUIZ

1   What has been the average growth rate of U.S. real GDP per person over the past 100 years? In which periods was growth most rapid and in which periods was it slowest?

2   Describe the gaps between real GDP per person in the United States and in other countries. For which countries is the gap narrowing? For which is it widening? For which is it the same?

3   Compare the growth rates in Hong Kong, Korea, Singapore, Taiwan, China, and the United States. In terms of real GDP per person, how far is China behind these others?

Work these questions in Study Plan 23.2 and get instant feedback.   MyEconLab

How Potential GDP Grows

Economic growth occurs when real GDP increases. But a one-shot rise in real GDP or a recovery from recession isn't economic growth. Economic growth is a sustained, year-after-year increase in *potential GDP*.

So what determines potential GDP and what are the forces that make it grow?

What Determines Potential GDP?

Labor, capital, land, and entrepreneurship produce real GDP, and the productivity of the factors of production determines the quantity of real GDP that can be produced.

The quantity of land is fixed and on any given day, the quantities of entrepreneurial ability and capital are also fixed and their productivities are given. The quantity of labor employed is the only *variable* factor of production. Potential GDP is the level of real GDP when the quantity of labor employed is the full-employment quantity.

To determine potential GDP, we use a model with two components:

- An aggregate production function
- An aggregate labor market

Aggregate Production Function When you studied the limits to production in Chapter 2 (see p. 32), you learned that the *production possibilities frontier* is the boundary between the combinations of goods and services that can be produced and those that cannot. We're now going to think about the production possibilities frontier for two special "goods": real GDP and the quantity of leisure time.

Think of real GDP as a number of big shopping carts. Each cart contains some of each kind of different goods and services produced, and one cartload of items costs $1 trillion. To say that real GDP is $13 trillion means that it is 13 very big shopping carts of goods and services.

The quantity of leisure time is the number of hours spent not working. Each leisure hour could be spent working. If we spent all our time taking leisure, we would do no work and produce nothing. Real GDP would be zero. The more leisure we forgo, the greater is the quantity of labor we supply and the greater is the quantity of real GDP produced.

But labor hours are not all equally productive. We use our most productive hours first, and as more

hours are worked, these hours are increasingly less productive. So for each additional hour of leisure forgone (each additional hour of labor), real GDP increases but by successively smaller amounts.

The **aggregate production function** is the relationship that tells us how real GDP changes as the quantity of labor changes when all other influences on production remain the same. Figure 23.6 shows this relationship—the curve labeled *PF*. An increase in the quantity of labor (and a corresponding decrease in leisure hours) brings a movement along the production function and an increase in real GDP.

Aggregate Labor Market In macroeconomics, we pretend that there is one large labor market that determines the quantity of labor employed and the quantity of real GDP produced. To see how this aggregate labor market works, we study the demand for labor, the supply of labor, and labor market equilibrium.

The Demand for Labor The *demand for labor* is the relationship between the quantity of labor demanded and the real wage rate. The quantity of labor demanded is the number of labor hours hired by all the firms in the economy during a given period. This

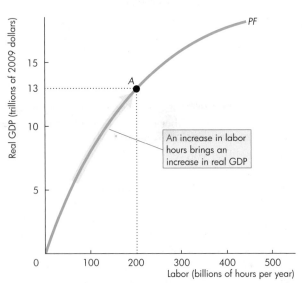

FIGURE 23.6   The Aggregate
Production Function

At point *A* on the aggregate production function *PF*, 200 billion hours of labor produce $13 trillion of real GDP.

MyEconLab Animation

quantity depends on the price of labor, which is the real wage rate.

The **real wage rate** is the money wage rate divided by the price level. The real wage rate is the quantity of goods and services that an hour of labor earns. It contrasts with the money wage rate, which is the number of dollars that an hour of labor earns.

The *real* wage rate influences the quantity of labor demanded because what matters to firms is not the number of dollars they pay (money wage rate) but how much output they must sell to earn those dollars.

The quantity of labor demanded *increases* as the real wage rate *decreases*—the demand for labor curve slopes downward. Why? The answer lies in the shape of the production function.

You've seen that along the production function, each additional hour of labor increases real GDP by successively smaller amounts. This tendency has a name: the *law of diminishing returns*. Because of diminishing returns, firms will hire more labor only if the real wage rate falls to match the fall in the extra output produced by that labor.

The Supply of Labor   The *supply of labor* is the relationship between the quantity of labor supplied and the real wage rate. The quantity of labor supplied is the number of labor hours that all the households in the economy plan to work during a given period. This quantity depends on the real wage rate.

The *real* wage rate influences the quantity of labor supplied because what matters to households is not the number of dollars they earn (money wage rate) but what they can buy with those dollars.

The quantity of labor supplied *increases* as the real wage rate *increases*—the supply of labor curve slopes upward. At a higher real wage rate, more people choose to work and more people choose to work longer hours if they can earn more per hour.

Labor Market Equilibrium   The price of labor is the real wage rate. The forces of supply and demand operate in labor markets just as they do in the markets for goods and services to eliminate a shortage or a surplus. But a shortage or a surplus of labor brings only a gradual change in the real wage rate. If there is a shortage of labor, the real wage rate rises to eliminate it; and if there is a surplus of labor, the real wage rate eventually falls to eliminate it. When there is neither a shortage nor a surplus, the labor market is in equilibrium—a full-employment equilibrium.

FIGURE 23.7   Labor Market Equilibrium

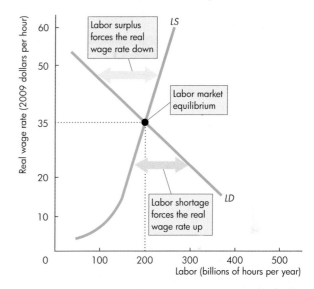

Labor market equilibrium occurs when the quantity of labor demanded equals the quantity of labor supplied. The equilibrium real wage rate is $35 an hour, and equilibrium employment is 200 billion hours per year.

At a wage rate above $35 an hour, there is a surplus of labor and the real wage rate falls to eliminate the surplus. At a wage rate below $35 an hour, there is a shortage of labor and the real wage rate rises to eliminate the shortage.

MyEconLab Animation

Figure 23.7 illustrates labor market equilibrium. The demand for labor curve is *LD* and the supply of labor curve is *LS*. This labor market is in equilibrium at a real wage rate of $35 an hour and 200 billion hours a year are employed.

If the real wage rate exceeds $35 an hour, the quantity of labor supplied exceeds the quantity demanded and there is a surplus of labor. When there is a surplus of labor, the real wage rate falls toward the equilibrium real wage rate where the surplus is eliminated.

If the real wage rate is less than $35 an hour, the quantity of labor demanded exceeds the quantity supplied and there is a shortage of labor. When there is a shortage of labor, the real wage rate rises toward the equilibrium real wage rate where the shortage is eliminated.

If the real wage rate is $35 an hour, the quantity of labor demanded equals the quantity supplied and there is neither a shortage nor a surplus of labor. In this situation, there is no pressure in either direction on the real wage rate. So the real wage rate remains constant and the market is in equilibrium. At this equilibrium real wage rate and level of employment, the economy is at *full employment*.

Potential GDP You've seen that the production function tells us the quantity of real GDP that a given amount of labor can produce—see Fig. 23.6. The quantity of real GDP produced increases as the quantity of labor increases. At the equilibrium quantity of labor, the economy is at full employment, and the quantity of real GDP at full employment is potential GDP. So the full-employment quantity of labor produces potential GDP.

Figure 23.8 illustrates the determination of potential GDP. Part (a) shows labor market equilibrium. At the equilibrium real wage rate, equilibrium employment is 200 billion hours. Part (b) shows the production function. With 200 billion hours of labor, the economy can produce a real GDP of $13 trillion. This amount is potential GDP.

What Makes Potential GDP Grow?

We can divide all the forces that make potential GDP grow into two categories:

- Growth of the supply of labor
- Growth of labor productivity

Growth of the Supply of Labor When the supply of labor grows, the supply of labor curve shifts rightward. The quantity of labor at a given real wage rate increases.

The quantity of labor is the number of workers employed multiplied by average hours per worker. The number employed equals the employment-to-population ratio multiplied by the working-age population, divided by 100 (see Chapter 22, p. 518). So the quantity of labor changes as a result of changes in

1. Average hours per worker
2. The employment-to-population ratio
3. The working-age population

Average hours per worker have decreased as the workweek has become shorter, and the employment-to-population ratio has increased as more women have entered the labor force. The combined effect of

FIGURE 23.8   The Labor Market and Potential GDP

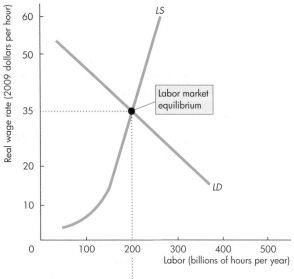

(a) The labor market

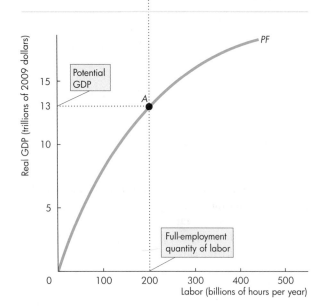

(b) Potential GDP

The economy is at full employment when the quantity of labor demanded equals the quantity of labor supplied, in part (a). The real wage rate is $35 an hour, and employment is 200 billion hours a year. Part (b) shows potential GDP. It is the quantity of real GDP determined by the production function at the full-employment quantity of labor.

MyEconLab Animation and Draw Graph

these two factors has kept the average hours per working-age person (approximately) constant.

Growth in the supply of labor has come from growth in the working-age population. In the long run, the working-age population grows at the same rate as the total population.

The Effects of Population Growth Population growth brings growth in the supply of labor, but it does not change the demand for labor or the production function. The economy can produce more output by using more labor, but there is no change in the quantity of real GDP that a given quantity of labor can produce.

With an increase in the supply of labor and no change in the demand for labor, the real wage rate falls and the equilibrium quantity of labor increases. The increased quantity of labor produces more output and potential GDP increases.

Illustrating the Effects of Population Growth Figure 23.9 illustrates the effects of an increase in the population. In Fig. 23.9(a), the demand for labor curve is *LD* and initially the supply of labor curve is LS_0. The equilibrium real wage rate is $35 an hour and the quantity of labor is 200 billion hours a year. In Fig. 23.9(b), the production function (*PF*) shows that with 200 billion hours of labor employed, potential GDP is $13 trillion at point *A*.

An increase in the population increases the supply of labor and the supply of labor curve shifts rightward to LS_1. At a real wage rate of $35 an hour, there is now a surplus of labor. So the real wage rate falls. In this example, the real wage rate will fall until it reaches $25 an hour. At $25 an hour, the quantity of labor demanded equals the quantity of labor supplied. The equilibrium quantity of labor increases to 300 billion a year.

Figure 23.9(b) shows the effect on real GDP. As the equilibrium quantity of labor increases from 200 billion to 300 billion hours, potential GDP increases along the production function from $13 trillion to $16 trillion at point *B*.

So an increase in the population increases the full-employment quantity of labor, increases potential GDP, and lowers the real wage rate. But the population increase *decreases* potential GDP per hour of labor. Initially, it was $65 ($13 trillion divided by 200 billion). With the population increase, potential GDP per hour of labor is $53.33 ($16 trillion divided by 300 billion). Diminishing returns are the source of the decrease in potential GDP per hour of labor.

FIGURE 23.9   The Effects of an Increase in Population

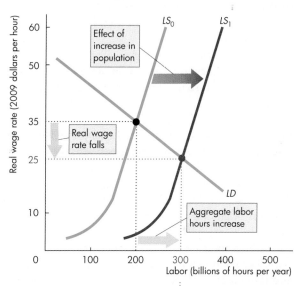

(a) The labor market

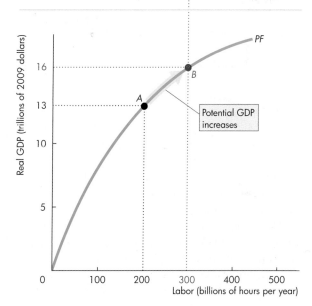

(b) Potential GDP

An increase in the population increases the supply of labor. In part (a), the supply of labor curve shifts rightward. The real wage rate falls and aggregate labor hours increase. In part (b), the increase in aggregate labor hours brings an increase in potential GDP. But diminishing returns bring a decrease in potential GDP per hour of labor.

MyEconLab Animation

Growth of Labor Productivity

Labor productivity is the quantity of real GDP produced by an hour of labor. It is calculated by dividing real GDP by aggregate labor hours. For example, if real GDP is $13 trillion and aggregate hours are 200 billion, labor productivity is $65 per hour.

When labor productivity grows, real GDP per person grows and brings a rising standard of living. Let's see how an increase in labor productivity changes potential GDP.

Effects of an Increase in Labor Productivity

If labor productivity increases, production possibilities expand. The quantity of real GDP that any given quantity of labor can produce increases. If labor is more productive, firms are willing to pay more for a given number of hours of labor so the demand for labor also increases.

With an increase in the demand for labor and *no change in the supply of labor*, the real wage rate rises and the quantity of labor supplied increases. The equilibrium quantity of labor also increases.

So an increase in labor productivity increases potential GDP for two reasons: Labor is more productive and more labor is employed.

Illustrating the Effects of an Increase in Labor Productivity

Figure 23.10 illustrates the effects of an increase in labor productivity.

In part (a), the production function initially is PF_0. With 200 billion hours of labor employed, potential GDP is $13 trillion at point A.

In part (b), the demand for labor curve is LD_0 and the supply of labor curve is LS. The real wage rate is $35 an hour, and the equilibrium quantity of labor is 200 billion hours a year.

Now labor productivity increases. In Fig. 23.10(a), the increase in labor productivity shifts the production function upward to PF_1. At each quantity of labor, more real GDP can be produced. For example, at 200 billion hours, the economy can now produce $18 trillion of real GDP at point B.

In Fig. 23.10(b), the increase in labor productivity increases the demand for labor and the demand for labor curve shifts rightward to LD_1. At the initial real wage rate of $35 an hour, there is now a shortage of labor. The real wage rate rises. In this example, the real wage rate will rise until it reaches $45 an hour. At $45 an hour, the quantity of labor demanded equals the quantity of labor supplied and the equilibrium quantity of labor is 225 billion hours a year.

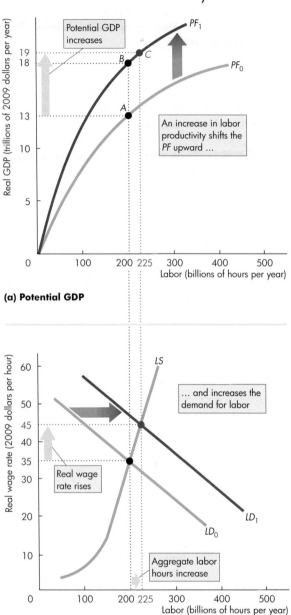

FIGURE 23.10   The Effects of an Increase in Labor Productivity

(a) Potential GDP

(b) The labor market

An increase in labor productivity shifts the production function upward from PF_0 to PF_1 in part (a) and shifts the demand for labor curve rightward from LD_0 to LD_1 in part (b). The real wage rate rises to $45 an hour, and aggregate labor hours increase from 200 billion to 225 billion. Potential GDP increases from $13 trillion to $19 trillion.

MyEconLab Animation and Draw Graph

Figure 23.10(a) shows the effects of the increase in labor productivity on potential GDP. There are two effects. At the initial quantity of labor, real GDP increases to point *B* on the new production function. But as the equilibrium quantity of labor increases from 200 billion to 225 billion hours, potential GDP increases to $19 trillion at point *C*.

Potential GDP per hour of labor also increases. Initially, it was $65 ($13 trillion divided by 200 billion). With the increase in labor productivity, potential GDP per hour of labor is $84.44 ($19 trillion divided by 225 billion).

The increase in aggregate labor hours that you have just seen is a consequence of an increase in labor productivity. This increase in aggregate labor hours and labor productivity is an example of the interaction effects that economists seek to identify in their search for the ultimate *causes* of economic growth. In the case that we've just studied, aggregate labor hours increase but that increase is a *consequence*, not a cause, of the growth of potential GDP. The source of the increase in potential GDP is an increase in labor productivity.

Labor productivity is the key to increasing output per hour of labor and rising living standards. But what brings an increase in labor productivity? The next section answers this question.

◆ REVIEW QUIZ

1 What is the aggregate production function?
2 What determines the demand for labor, the supply of labor, and labor market equilibrium?
3 What determines potential GDP?
4 What are the two broad sources of potential GDP growth?
5 What are the effects of an increase in the population on potential GDP, the quantity of labor, the real wage rate, and potential GDP per hour of labor?
6 What are the effects of an increase in labor productivity on potential GDP, the quantity of labor, the real wage rate, and potential GDP per hour of labor?

Work these questions in Study Plan 23.3 and get instant feedback. Do a Key Terms Quiz.   MyEconLab

◆ Why Labor Productivity Grows

You've seen that labor productivity growth makes potential GDP grow; and you've seen that labor productivity growth is essential if real GDP per person and the standard of living are to grow. But why does labor productivity grow? What are the preconditions that make labor productivity growth possible and what are the forces that make it grow? Why does labor productivity grow faster at some times and in some places than others?

Preconditions for Labor Productivity Growth

The fundamental precondition for labor productivity growth is the *incentive* system created by firms, markets, property rights, and money. These four social institutions are the same as those described in Chapter 2 (see pp. 44–45) that enable people to gain by specializing and trading.

It was the presence of secure property rights in Britain in the middle 1700s that got the Industrial Revolution going (see *Economics in Action* on p. 553). And it is their absence in some parts of Africa today that is keeping labor productivity stagnant.

With the preconditions for labor productivity growth in place, three things influence its pace:

■ Physical capital growth
■ Human capital growth
■ Technological advances

Physical Capital Growth

As the amount of capital per worker increases, labor productivity also increases. Production processes that use hand tools can create beautiful objects, but production methods that use large amounts of capital per worker are much more productive. The accumulation of capital on farms, in textile factories, in iron foundries and steel mills, in coal mines, on building sites, in chemical plants, in auto plants, in banks and insurance companies, and in shopping malls has added incredibly to the labor productivity of our economy. The next time you see a movie that is set in the Old West or colonial times, look carefully at the small amount of capital around. Try to imagine how productive you would be in such circumstances compared with your productivity today.

ECONOMICS IN ACTION
Women Are the Better Borrowers

Economic growth is driven by the decisions of billions of individuals to save and invest, and to borrow and lend. In developing countries, most people are too poor to save and too big a risk to be able to borrow from a bank. But they can get a *microloan* to start a business, employ a few people, and earn an income. And many of the most successful microloan borrowers are women.

Microloans originated in Bangladesh and have spread throughout the developing world. Kiva.org and MicroPlace.com (owned by eBay) are Web sites that enable people to lend money that is used to make microloans in developing economies.

Microloans are helping many women to feed and clothe their families and to grow their businesses. But not all microloan-financed businesses succeed. And the evidence from controlled experiments conducted by Esther Duflo* and her colleagues in the Abdul Latif Jameel Poverty Action Lab is that gains in consumption are temporary. A few years after getting a microloan, borrowers are no better off on average than they were before taking a loan. Making poor people less poor requires more than access to microloans.

This woman was able to set up her seamstress business with a microloan.

Human Capital Growth

Human capital—the accumulated skill and knowledge of human beings—is the fundamental source of labor productivity growth. Human capital grows when a new discovery is made and it grows as more and more people learn how to use past discoveries.

*See Talking with Esther Duflo on p. 54.

The development of one of the most basic human skills—writing—was the source of some of the earliest major gains in productivity. The ability to keep written records made it possible to reap ever-larger gains from specialization and trade. Imagine how hard it would be to do any kind of business if all the accounts, invoices, and agreements existed only in people's memories.

Later, the development of mathematics laid the foundation for the eventual extension of knowledge about physical forces and chemical and biological processes. This base of scientific knowledge was the foundation for the technological advances of the Industrial Revolution and of today's information revolution.

But a lot of human capital that is extremely productive is much more humble. It takes the form of millions of individuals learning and becoming remarkably more productive by repetitively doing simple production tasks. One much-studied example of this type of human capital growth occurred in World War II. With no change in physical capital, thousands of workers and managers in U.S. shipyards learned from experience and accumulated human capital that more than doubled their productivity in less than two years.

Technological Advances

The accumulation of physical capital and human capital have made a large contribution to labor productivity growth. But technological change—the discovery and the application of new technologies—has made an even greater contribution.

Labor is many times more productive today than it was a hundred years ago but not because we have more steam engines and more horse-drawn carriages per person. Rather, it is because we have transportation equipment that uses technologies that were unknown a hundred years ago and that are more productive than the old technologies were.

Technological advance arises from formal research and development programs and from informal trial and error, and it involves discovering new ways of getting more out of our resources.

To reap the benefits of technological change, capital must increase. Some of the most powerful and far-reaching fundamental technologies are embodied in human capital—for example, language, writing, and mathematics. But most technologies are embodied in physical capital. For example, to reap the benefits of the internal combustion engine, millions of horse-drawn carriages had to be replaced with automobiles; and to reap the benefits of digital music, millions of Discmans had to be replaced by iPods.

ECONOMICS IN ACTION

Intellectual Property Rights Propel Growth

In 1760, when the states that 16 years later would become the United States of America were developing agricultural economies, England was on the cusp of an economic revolution, the *Industrial Revolution.*

For 70 dazzling years, technological advances in the use of steam power, the manufacture of cotton, wool, iron, and steel, and in transportation, accompanied by massive capital investment associated with these technologies, transformed the economy of England. Incomes rose and brought an explosion in an increasingly urbanized population.

By 1825, advances in steam technology had reached a level of sophistication that enabled Robert Stevenson to build the world's first steam-powered rail engine (the Rocket, pictured here in the Science Museum, London) and the birth of the world's first railroad.

Why did the Industrial Revolution happen? Why did it start in 1760? And why in England?

Economic historians say that intellectual property rights—England's patent system—provides the answer.

England's patent system began with the Statute of Monopolies of 1624, which gave inventors a monopoly to use their idea for a term of 14 years. For about 100 years, the system was used to reward friends of the

royal court rather than true inventors. But from around 1720 onward, the system started to work well. To be granted a 14-year monopoly, an inventor only had to pay the required £100 fee (about $22,000 in today's money) and register his or her invention. The inventor was not required to describe the invention in too much detail, so registering and getting a patent didn't mean sharing the invention with competitors.

This patent system, which is essentially the same as today's, aligned the self-interest of entrepreneurial inventors with the social interest and unleashed a flood of inventions, the most transformative of which was steam power and, by 1825, the steam locomotive.

FIGURE 23.11   The Sources of Economic Growth

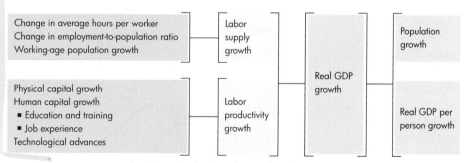

Labor supply growth and labor productivity growth combine to determine real GDP growth. Real GDP per person growth depends on real GDP growth and population growth.

MyEconLab Animation

Figure 23.11 summarizes the sources of labor productivity growth and more broadly, of real GDP growth. The figure also emphasizes that for real GDP per person to grow, real GDP must grow faster than the population.

Economics in the News on the next page provides an example of today's labor productivity growth arising from the spread of robot technologies.

REVIEW QUIZ

1 What are the preconditions for labor productivity growth?
2 Explain the influences on the pace of labor productivity growth.

You can work these questions in Study Plan 23.4 and get instant feedback.   MyEconLab

ECONOMICS IN THE NEWS

Robots as Skilled Workers

Skilled Work, Without the Worker

A new wave of robots, far more adept than those now commonly used by automakers and other heavy goods manufacturers, are replacing workers around the world in both manufacturing and distribution.

Source: *The New York Times*, August 18, 2012

SOME FACTS

"The Robot Report" (www.therobotreport.com) agrees with the news clip. The auto industry has been the main customer for industrial robots but the scene is changing. Robot manufacturers are creating equipment tailored to the requirements of producers of a wide range of items, just a few of which are metals, food and drink, glass, pharmaceuticals, medical devices, and solar panels.

Around 200 established firms worldwide specialize in the design and production of robots and more than 147 start-up companies have entered this industry in the past year. Almost 2,000 firms have some connection with industrial robots.

THE QUESTIONS

- How will the adoption of industrial robots change employment, the real wage rate, and potential GDP?
- Do robots kill jobs and create unemployment?

THE ANSWERS

- Robots make workers more productive. One person working with a robot can produce as much as hundreds of workers with non-robot technology.
- Robots replace some workers but create a demand for other workers to design, produce, install, and maintain robots.
- In aggregate, robots increase the productivity of labor. The production function shifts upward and the demand for labor curve shifts rightward.
- The equilibrium real wage rate rises, employment increases, and potential GDP increases.
- As robot production technologies spread, many jobs will disappear but many new jobs will be created.
- Some displaced workers will take new jobs with lower wages. Others will take jobs as skilled robot technicians and producers with higher wages. Average wages will rise.

MyEconLab More Economics in the News

A robot arm seals a box of Lego building toys for shipping.

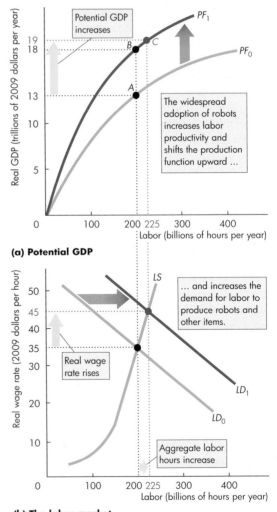

(a) Potential GDP

(b) The labor market

The Effects of Robots on Employment and GDP

◆ Is Economic Growth Sustainable? Theories, Evidence, and Policies

You've seen how population growth and labor productivity growth make potential GDP grow. You've also seen that the growth of physical capital and human capital and technological advances make labor productivity grow. But what *causes* economic growth? Why do growth rates vary? How do population growth, capital accumulation, and technological change interact to determine the economic growth rate? What can we say about the future of economic growth? Is growth sustainable? Will the rich economies and the economies of the developing world keep growing, or will growth end to be followed by stagnation or even a falling standard of living?

Economists have wrestled with these questions for the past 250 years and made progress in answering them. We're now going to look at the evolution of ideas about the sustainability of economic growth and the policies that might achieve faster growth.

We start by studying the three main theories about the process of economic growth:

- Classical growth theory
- Neoclassical growth theory
- New growth theory

Classical Growth Theory

Classical growth theory is the view that the growth of real GDP per person is temporary and that when it rises above the subsistence level, a population explosion eventually brings it back to the subsistence level. Adam Smith, Thomas Robert Malthus, and David Ricardo—the leading economists of the late eighteenth and early nineteenth centuries—proposed this theory, but the view is most closely associated with the name of Malthus and is sometimes called the *Malthusian theory*. Charles Darwin's ideas about evolution by natural selection were inspired by the insights of Malthus.

Modern-Day Malthusians Many people today are Malthusians. They say that if today's global population of 7.2 billion explodes to 11 billion by 2050 and perhaps 35 billion by 2300, we will run out of resources, real GDP per person will decline, and we will return to a primitive standard of living. We must, say Malthusians, contain population growth.

Modern-day Malthusians also point to global warming and climate change as reasons to believe that, eventually, real GDP per person will decrease.

Neoclassical Growth Theory

Neoclassical growth theory is the proposition that real GDP per person grows because technological change induces saving and investment that make capital per hour of labor grow. Growth ends if technological change stops because of diminishing marginal returns to both labor and capital. Robert Solow of MIT suggested the most popular version of this growth theory in the 1950s.

Neoclassical growth theory's big break with its classical predecessor is its view about population growth.

Neoclassical Theory of Population Growth The population explosion of eighteenth century Europe that created the classical theory of population growth eventually ended. The birth rate fell, and while the population continued to increase, its rate of increase moderated.

The key economic influence that slowed the population growth rate is the opportunity cost of a woman's time. As women's wage rates increase and their job opportunities expand, the opportunity cost of having children increases. Faced with a higher opportunity cost, families choose to have fewer children and the birth rate falls.

Technological advances that bring higher incomes also bring advances in healthcare that extend lives. So as incomes increase, both the birth rate and the death rate decrease. These opposing forces offset each other and result in a slowly rising population.

This modern view of population growth and the historical trends that support it contradict the views of the classical economists. They also call into question the modern doomsday view that the planet will be swamped with more people than it can support.

Technological Change and Diminishing Returns In neoclassical growth theory, the pace of technological change influences the economic growth rate but economic growth does not influence the pace of technological change. Neoclassical growth theory assumes that technological change results from chance. When we're lucky, we have rapid technological change, and when bad luck strikes, the pace of technological advance slows.

To understand neoclassical growth theory, imagine the world of the mid-1950s, when Robert Solow is explaining his idea. Income per person is around $12,000 a year in today's money. The population is growing at about 1 percent a year. Saving and investment are about 20 percent of GDP, which is enough to keep the quantity of capital per hour of labor constant. Income per person is growing but not very quickly.

Then technology begins to advance at a more rapid pace across a range of activities. The transistor revolutionizes an emerging electronics industry. New plastics revolutionize the manufacture of household appliances. The interstate highway system revolutionizes road transportation. Jet airliners start to replace piston-engine airplanes and speed air transportation.

These technological advances bring new profit opportunities. Businesses expand, and new businesses are created to exploit the newly available profitable technologies. Investment and saving increase. The economy enjoys new levels of prosperity and growth. But will the prosperity last? And will the growth last? Neoclassical growth theory says that the *prosperity* will last but the *growth* will not last unless technology keeps advancing.

According to neoclassical growth theory, the prosperity will persist because there is no classical population growth to induce the wage rate to fall. So the gains in income per person are permanent.

But growth will eventually stop if technology stops advancing because of diminishing marginal returns to capital. The high profit rates that result from technological change bring increased saving and capital accumulation. But as more capital is accumulated, more and more projects are undertaken that have lower rates of return—diminishing marginal returns. As the return on capital falls, the incentive to keep investing weakens. With weaker incentives to save and invest, saving decreases and the rate of capital accumulation slows. Eventually, the pace of capital accumulation slows so that it is only keeping up with population growth. Capital per worker remains constant.

A Problem with Neoclassical Growth Theory

All economies have access to the same technologies, and capital is free to roam the globe, seeking the highest available real interest rate. Capital will flow across regions until rates of return are equal, and rates of return will be equal when capital per hour of labor is equal. Real GDP growth rates and income levels per person around the world will converge. Figure 23.5 on p. 544 shows that while there is some sign of convergence among the rich countries in part (a), convergence is slow, and part (b) shows that it does not appear to be imminent for all countries. New growth theory overcomes this shortcoming of neoclassical growth theory. It also explains what determines the pace of technological change.

New Growth Theory

New growth theory holds that real GDP per person grows because of the choices people make in the pursuit of profit and that growth will persist indefinitely. Paul Romer of Stanford University developed this theory during the 1980s, based on ideas of Joseph Schumpeter during the 1930s and 1940s.

According to the new growth theory, the pace at which new discoveries are made—and at which technology advances—is not determined by chance. It depends on how many people are looking for a new technology and how intensively they are looking. The search for new technologies is driven by incentives.

Profit is the spur to technological change. The forces of competition squeeze profits, so to increase profit, people constantly seek either lower-cost methods of production or new and better products for which people are willing to pay a higher price. Inventors can maintain a profit for several years by taking out a patent or a copyright, but eventually, a new discovery is copied, and profits disappear. So more research and development is undertaken in the hope of creating a new burst of profitable investment and growth.

Two facts about discoveries and technological knowledge play a key role in the new growth theory: Discoveries are (at least eventually) a public capital good; and knowledge is capital that is not subject to diminishing marginal returns.

Economists call a good a *public good* when no one can be excluded from using it and when one person's use does not prevent others from using it. National defense is the classic example of a public good. The programming language used to write apps for the iPhone is another.

Because knowledge is a public good, as the benefits of a new discovery spread, free resources become available. Nothing is given up when they are used: They have a zero opportunity cost. When a student in Austin writes a new iPhone app, his use of the programming language doesn't prevent another student in Seattle from using it.

Knowledge is even more special because it is *not* subject to diminishing returns. But increasing the stock of knowledge makes both labor and machines more productive. Knowledge capital does not bring diminishing returns. Biotech knowledge illustrates this idea well. Biologists have spent a lot of time developing DNA sequencing technology. As more has been discovered, the productivity of this knowledge capital has relentlessly increased. In 1990, it cost about $50 to sequence one DNA base pair. That cost had fallen to $1 by 2000 and to 1/10,000th of a penny by 2010.

The implication of this simple and appealing observation is astonishing. Unlike the other two theories, new growth theory has no growth-stopping mechanism. As physical capital accumulates, the return to capital—the real interest rate—falls. But the incentive to innovate and earn a higher profit becomes stronger. So innovation occurs, capital becomes more productive, the demand for capital increases, and the real interest rate rises again.

Labor productivity grows indefinitely as people discover new technologies that yield a higher real interest rate. The growth rate depends only on people's incentives and ability to innovate.

A Perpetual Motion Economy New growth theory sees the economy as a perpetual motion machine, which Fig. 23.12 illustrates.

No matter how rich we become, our wants exceed our ability to satisfy them. We always want a higher standard of living. In the pursuit of a higher standard of living, human societies have developed incentive systems—markets, property rights, and money—that enable people to profit from innovation. Innovation leads to the development of new and better techniques of production and new and better products. To take advantage of new techniques and to produce new products, new firms start up and old firms go out of business—firms are born and die. As old firms die and new firms are born, some jobs are destroyed and others are created. The new jobs created are better than the old ones and they pay higher real wage rates. Also, with higher wage rates and more productive techniques, leisure increases. New and better jobs and new and better products lead to more consumption goods and services and, combined with increased leisure, bring a higher standard of living.

But our insatiable wants are still there, so the process continues: Wants and incentives create innovation, new and better products, and a yet higher standard of living.

FIGURE 23.12   A Perpetual Motion Machine

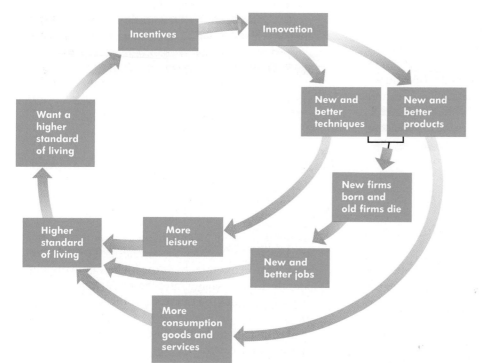

People want a higher standard of living and are spurred by profit incentives to make the innovations that lead to new and better techniques and new and better products.

These new and better techniques and products, in turn, lead to the birth of new firms and the death of some old firms, new and better jobs, and more leisure and more consumption goods and services.

The result is a higher standard of living, but people want a still higher standard of living, and the growth process continues.

Source: Based on a similar figure in *These Are the Good Old Days: A Report on U.S. Living Standards,* Federal Reserve Bank of Dallas 1993 Annual Report.

New Growth Theory Versus Malthusian Theory

The contrast between the Malthusian theory and new growth theory couldn't be more sharp. Malthusians see the end of prosperity as we know it today and new growth theorists see unending plenty. The contrast becomes clearest by thinking about the differing views about population growth.

To a Malthusian, population growth is part of the problem. To a new growth theorist, population growth is part of the solution. People are the ultimate economic resource. A larger population brings forth more wants, but it also brings a greater amount of scientific discovery and technological advance. So rather than being the source of falling real GDP per person, population growth generates faster labor productivity growth and rising real GDP per person. Resources are limited, but the human imagination and ability to increase productivity are unlimited.

Sorting Out the Theories

Which theory is correct? None of them tells us the whole story, but each teaches us something of value.

Classical growth theory reminds us that our physical resources are limited and that without advances in technology, we must eventually hit diminishing returns.

Neoclassical growth theory reaches the same conclusion but not because of a population explosion. Instead, it emphasizes diminishing returns to capital and reminds us that we cannot keep growth going just by accumulating physical capital. We must also advance technology and accumulate human capital. We must become more creative in our use of scarce resources.

New growth theory emphasizes the capacity of human resources to innovate at a pace that offsets diminishing returns. New growth theory fits the facts of today's world more closely than do either of the other two theories.

The Empirical Evidence on the Causes of Economic Growth

Economics makes progress by the interplay between theory and empirical evidence. A theory makes predictions about what we will observe if the theory is correct. Empirical evidence, the data generated by history and the natural experiments that it performs, provides the data for testing the theory.

Economists have done an enormous amount of research confronting theories of growth with the empirical evidence. The way in which this research has been conducted has changed over the years.

In 1776, when Adam Smith wrote about "the nature and causes of the Wealth of Nations" in his celebrated book, empirical evidence took the form of carefully selected facts described in words and stories. Today, large databases, sophisticated statistical methods, and fast computers provide numerical measurements of the causes of economic growth.

Economists have looked at the growth rate data for more than 100 countries for the period since 1960 and explored the correlations between the growth rate and more than 60 possible influences on it. The conclusion of this data crunching is that most of these possible influences have variable and unpredictable effects, but a few of them have strong and clear effects. Table 23.1 summarizes these more robust influences. They are arranged in order of difficulty (or in the case of region, impossibility) of changing. Political and economic systems are hard to change, but market distortions, investment, and openness to international trade are features of a nation's economy that can be influenced by policy.

Let's now look at growth policies.

Policies for Achieving Faster Growth

Growth theory supported by empirical evidence tells us that to achieve faster economic growth, we must increase the growth rate of physical capital, the pace of technological advance, or the growth rate of human capital and openness to international trade.

The main suggestions for achieving these objectives are

- Stimulate saving
- Stimulate research and development
- Improve the quality of education
- Provide international aid to developing nations
- Encourage international trade

Stimulate Saving Saving finances investment so stimulating saving increases economic growth. The East Asian economies have the highest growth rates and the highest saving rates. Some African economies have the lowest growth rates and the lowest saving rates.

Tax incentives can increase saving. Individual Retirement Accounts (IRAs) are a tax incentive to save. Economists claim that a tax on consumption rather than income provides the best saving incentive.

TABLE 23.1   The Influences on Economic Growth

Influence	Good for Economic Growth	Bad for Economic Growth
Region	■ Far from equator	■ Sub-Saharan Africa
Politics	■ Rule of law	■ Revolutions
	■ Civil liberties	■ Military coups
		■ Wars
Economic system	■ Capitalist	
Market distortions		■ Exchange rate distortions
		■ Price controls and black markets
Investment	■ Human capital	
	■ Physical capital	
International trade	■ Open to trade	

Source of data: Xavier Sala-i-Martin, "I Just Ran Two Million Regressions," *The American Economic Review*, Vol. 87, No. 2, (May 1997), pp. 178–183.

Stimulate Research and Development Everyone can use the fruits of *basic* research and development efforts. For example, all biotechnology firms can use advances in gene-splicing technology. Because basic inventions can be copied, the inventor's profit is limited and the market allocates too few resources to this activity. Governments can direct public funds toward financing basic research, but this solution is not foolproof. It requires a mechanism for allocating the public funds to their highest-valued use.

Improve the Quality of Education The free market produces too little education because it brings benefits beyond those valued by the people who receive the education. By funding basic education and by ensuring high standards in basic skills such as language, mathematics, and science, governments can contribute to a nation's growth potential. Education can also be stimulated and improved by using tax incentives to encourage improved private provision.

Provide International Aid to Developing Nations It seems obvious that if rich countries give financial aid to developing countries, investment and growth will increase in the recipient countries. Unfortunately, the obvious does not routinely happen. A large amount of data-driven research on the effects of aid on growth has turned up a zero and even negative effect. Aid often gets diverted and spent on consumption.

Encourage International Trade Trade, not aid, stimulates economic growth. It works by extracting the available gains from specialization and trade. The fastest-growing nations are those most open to trade. If the rich nations truly want to aid economic development, they will lower their trade barriers against developing nations, especially in farm products. The World Trade Organization's efforts to achieve more open trade are being resisted by the richer nations.

◆ **REVIEW QUIZ**

1 What is the key idea of classical growth theory that leads to the dismal outcome?

2 What, according to neoclassical growth theory, is the fundamental cause of economic growth?

3 What is the key proposition of new growth theory that makes economic growth persist?

Work these questions in Study Plan 23.5 and get instant feedback. Do a Key Terms Quiz.   MyEconLab

◆ To complete your study of economic growth, take a look at *Economics in the News* on pp. 560–561, which compares the contrasting growth performance of two African nations.

Making an Economy Grow

How to Make South Africa's Economy Roar

The Financial Times
July 27, 2012

It is clear South Africa needs a radical change in direction. This weekend the opposition Democratic Alliance aims to show how this is possible, launching a strategy to accelerate annual growth to 8 percent. In particular, it proposes tough reforms to labor laws by removing the automatic extension of collective bargaining agreements across sectors; establishing "jobs zones" featuring special exemptions from restrictive regulations; and lifting administrative requirements for small businesses.

These changes will reduce barriers to entry, encourage flexibility, and stimulate productivity in … mining, manufacturing, and agriculture. Combined with focused employment incentives such as a youth wage subsidy and market-driven skills development programs, the plan provides a radical overhaul of the country's labor market. …

Our plan contains … policies to distribute shares in state-owned companies; introduce tax deductions to incentivize employee shared-ownership schemes; promote a joint ownership model in the agricultural sector; and lower the cost barriers facing first-time homeowners.

These measures are essential for facilitating broad-based participation in the economy. …

Although international rankings such as the World Economic Forum's Global Competitiveness report praise the country's sophisticated financial sector and sound legal environment, South Africa falls short when it comes to the ease of doing business, and the barriers caused by excessive regulation and state inefficiency. My party's proposals in this area will cut the tax and regulatory burdens inhibiting new business growth.

Seven of the 10 fastest-growing economies in the world are in Africa. … High growth is resulting in rapidly declining poverty and unemployment in the developing world. With the right policies in place, South Africa can be part of this story.

ESSENCE OF THE STORY

- South Africa's opposition Democratic Alliance wants to accelerate real GDP growth to 8 percent per year.

- Labor market reforms would limit union agreements, establish "jobs zones" with exemptions from restrictive regulations, subsidize youth wages, and develop market-driven skills.

- Capital market reforms would ease small-business regulation, cut taxes, distribute shares in state-owned companies, provide tax incentives for employee shared-ownership, and make homeownership easier.

- The reforms aim to reduce barriers to entry and boost labor productivity in all parts of the economy.

MyEconLab More Economics in the News

ECONOMIC ANALYSIS

- South Africa's economic growth rate has not been spectacular.

- Before 1994, South Africa's economy was hit by sanctions aimed at ending apartheid and real GDP per person decreased.

- Since 1995, real GDP per person has increased but at a rate of 3.4 percent per year.

- South Africa's growth compares unfavorably with that of some other African nations, one of which is its neighbor Botswana, that are growing more rapidly.

- Figure 1 shows real GDP per person in South Africa and Botswana from 1980 to 2012. You can see that real GDP per person in Botswana has grown much more quickly than in South Africa.

- A key reason Botswana's real GDP per person has grown more rapidly than South Africa's is the pace of investment in new capital.

- Figure 2 shows that Botswana invests double the percentage of GDP invested by South Africa.

- The growth of physical capital and human capital and technological change are proceeding at a rapid pace in Botswana and bringing rapid growth in real GDP per person.

- Figure 3 illustrates how the production function is changing in these economies. It is shifting upward at a more rapid pace in Botswana than in South Africa.

- Why is Botswana more successful than South Africa and are the policies proposed in the news article enough to raise South Africa's growth rate to the desired 8 percent per year?

- Economists Daron Acemoglu, Simon Johnson, and James Robinson say that Botswana had the right institutions for growth—well defined and widely respected private property right*.

- The proposals in the news article don't directly address strengthening private property rights, but they do have that effect.

- The labor market reforms described in the article would increase human capital and labor productivity.

- The labor market and capital market reforms together would make capital accumulation and technological change more profitable and further contribute to labor productivity growth.

- The specific target of 8 percent growth is probably too ambitious.

*Daron Acemoglu, Simon Johnson, and James Robinson, "An African Success Story: Botswana," in *In Search of Prosperity: Analytic Narratives on Economic Growth* edited by Dani Rodrik, Princeton University Press, 2003, pp. 80–122.

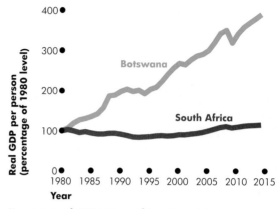

Figure 1 Real GDP in Two African Economies

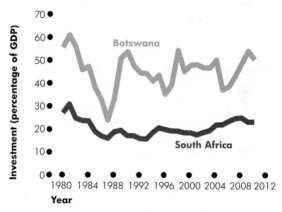

Figure 2 Investment in Two African Economies

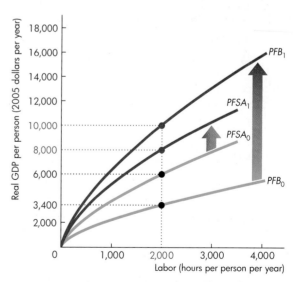

Figure 3 Labor Productivity Growth in Two African Economies

Sources of data: (1980–2010) Alan Heston, Robert Summers, and Bettina Aten, Penn World Table Version 7.1, Center for International Comparisons of Production, Income, and Prices at the University of Pennsylvania, July 2012; and (2011–2012) International Monetary Fund, *World Economic Outlook*, April 2012.

SUMMARY

Key Points

The Basics of Economic Growth (pp. 540–542)

- Economic growth is the sustained expansion of production possibilities and is measured as the annual percentage rate of change of real GDP.
- The Rule of 70 tells us the number of years in which real GDP doubles—70 divided by the annual percentage growth rate.

Working Problems 1 and 2 will give you a better understanding of the basics of economic growth.

Long-Term Growth Trends (pp. 543–545)

- Real GDP per person in the United States grows at an average rate of 2 percent a year. Growth was most rapid during the 1960s and the 1990s.
- The gap in real GDP per person between the United States and Central and South America has persisted. The gaps between the United States and Hong Kong, Korea, and China have narrowed. The gap between the United States and Africa has widened.

Working Problem 3 will give you a better understanding of long-term growth trends.

How Potential GDP Grows (pp. 546–551)

- The aggregate production function and equilibrium in the aggregate labor market determine potential GDP.
- Potential GDP grows if the labor supply grows or if labor productivity grows.

- Only labor productivity growth makes real GDP per person and the standard of living grow.

Working Problems 4 to 6 will give you a better understanding of how potential GDP grows.

Why Labor Productivity Grows (pp. 551–554)

- Labor productivity growth requires an incentive system created by firms, markets, property rights, and money.
- The sources of labor productivity growth are growth of physical capital and human capital and advances in technology.

Working Problem 7 will give you a better understanding of why labor productivity grows.

Is Economic Growth Sustainable? Theories, Evidence, and Policies (pp. 555–559)

- In classical theory, real GDP per person keeps returning to the subsistence level.
- In neoclassical growth theory, diminishing returns to capital limit economic growth.
- In new growth theory, economic growth persists indefinitely at a rate determined by decisions that lead to innovation and technological change.
- Policies for achieving faster growth include stimulating saving and research and development, encouraging international trade, and improving the quality of education.

Working Problem 8 will give you a better understanding of growth theories, evidence, and policies.

Key Terms

MyEconLab Key Terms Quiz

Aggregate production function, 546
Classical growth theory, 555
Economic growth, 540
Growth rate, 540

Labor productivity, 550
Neoclassical growth theory, 555
New growth theory, 556
Real GDP per person, 540

Real wage rate, 547
Rule of 70, 541

WORKED PROBLEM

MyEconLab   You can work this problem in Chapter 23 Study Plan.

The *World Economic Outlook* reports the following information:

- China's real GDP was 17.9 trillion yuan in 2012 and 19.3 trillion yuan in 2013.
- China's population was 1,361 million in 2012 and 1,368 million in 2013.

Questions

1. Calculate China's real GDP growth rate and its population growth rate during 2013.
2. Calculate the growth rate of China's standard of living during 2013.
3. If the growth rate of China's standard of living during 2013 is maintained, how many years will it take to double?

Solutions

1. The growth of a variable equals the change in the value from 2012 to 2013 calculated as a percentage of the value in 2012.

   China's growth rate of real GDP during 2013 equals (19.3 trillion yuan − 17.9 trillion yuan) divided by 17.9 trillion yuan, multiplied by 100. That is,

   Real GDP growth rate = (1.4 ÷ 17.9) × 100 = 7.8 percent.

   China's population growth rate equals (1,368 million − 1,361 million) divided by 1,361 million, multiplied by 100. That is,

   Population growth rate = (7 ÷ 1,361) × 100 = 0.5 percent.

Key Point: The growth rate of a variable equals the annual percentage change in the value of the variable.

2. Real GDP per person measures the standard of living.

   In 2012, real GDP per person was 17.9 trillion yuan divided by 1,361 million, which equals 13,152 yuan.

   In 2013, real GDP per person was 19.3 trillion yuan divided by 1,368 million, which equals 14,108 yuan.

The growth rate of real GDP per person equals (14,108 yuan − 13,152 yuan) ÷ 13,152 yuan, multiplied by 100.

The growth rate of real GDP per person equals (956 ÷ 13,152) × 100, which is 7.3 percent.

So during 2013, China's standard of living increased by 7.3 percent.

An alternative way of calculating the growth rate of the standard of living is to compare the growth rates of real GDP and the population.

Notice that a higher real GDP growth rate increases the growth rate of real GDP per person, but a higher population growth rate lowers the growth rate of real GDP per person.

So when real GDP grows by 7.8 percent and the population doesn't change, the standard of living grows by 7.8 percent.

When the population grows by 0.5 percent and real GDP doesn't change, the standard of living falls by 0.5 percent.

That is, the growth rate of China's standard of living during 2013 is approximately equal to the growth rate of real GDP minus the population growth rate, which equals 7.8 percent minus 0.5 percent, or 7.3 percent.

Key Point: The growth rate of the standard of living equals the growth rate of real GDP minus the growth rate of the population.

3. The number of years it will take for the standard of living to double its 2013 level is given by the Rule of 70.

   China's standard of living is growing at 7.3 percent a year. The Rule of 70 says that if this growth rate is sustained, China's standard of living will double in 70 years divided by 7.3, which equals 9.6 years.

   China's standard of living will be twice what it was in 2013 sometime during 2023.

Key Point: The time it takes for the standard of living to double equals 70 years divided by the sustained growth rate of the standard of living.

STUDY PLAN PROBLEMS AND APPLICATIONS

MyEconLab   You can work Problems 1 to 8 in Chapter 23 Study Plan and get instant feedback.

The Basics of Economic Growth (Study Plan 23.1)

1. Brazil's real GDP was 1,180 trillion reais in 2013 and 1,202 trillion reais in 2014. Brazil's population was 198 million in 2013 and 200 million in 2014. Calculate
   a. The growth rate of real GDP.
   b. The growth rate of real GDP per person.
   c. The approximate number of years it takes for real GDP per person in Brazil to double if the 2014 growth rate of real GDP and the population growth rate are maintained.

2. The IMF projects that China's real GDP per person will be 15,040 yuan in 2015 and 16,010 yuan in 2016 and that India's real GDP per person will be 54,085 rupees in 2015 and 56,840 rupees in 2016. By maintaining their current growth rates, which country will be first to double its standard of living?

Long-Term Growth Trends (Study Plan 23.2)

3. China was the largest economy for centuries because everyone had the same type of economy—subsistence—and so the country with the most people would be economically biggest. Then the Industrial Revolution sent the West on a more prosperous path. Now the world is returning to a common economy, this time technology- and information-based, so once again population triumphs.
   a. Why was China the world's largest economy until 1890?
   b. Why did the United States surpass China in 1890 to become the world's largest economy?

How Potential GDP Grows (Study Plan 23.3)

Use the following tables to work Problems 4 to 6. The tables describe an economy's labor market and its production function in 2014.

Real wage rate (dollars per hour)	Labor hours supplied	Labor hours demanded
80	45	5
70	40	10
60	35	15
50	30	20
40	25	25
30	20	30
20	15	35

Labor (hours)	Real GDP (2009 dollars)
5	425
10	800
15	1,125
20	1,400
25	1,625
30	1,800
35	1,925
40	2,000

4. What are the equilibrium real wage rate, the quantity of labor employed in 2014, labor productivity, and potential GDP in 2014?

5. In 2015, the population increases and labor hours supplied increase by 10 at each real wage rate. What are the equilibrium real wage rate, labor productivity, and potential GDP in 2015?

6. In 2015, the population increases and labor hours supplied increase by 10 at each real wage rate. Does the standard of living in this economy increase in 2015? Explain why or why not.

Why Labor Productivity Grows (Study Plan 23.4)

7. **Labor Productivity on the Rise**
   The BLS reported the following data for the year ended June 2009: In the nonfarm sector, output fell 5.5 percent as labor productivity increased 1.9 percent—the largest increase since 2003—but in the manufacturing sector, output fell 9.8 percent as labor productivity increased by 4.9 percent—the largest increase since the first quarter of 2005.
   Source: bls.gov/news.release, August 11, 2009

   In both sectors, output fell while labor productivity increased. Did the quantity of labor (aggregate hours) increase or decrease? In which sector was the change in the quantity of labor larger?

Is Economic Growth Sustainable? Theories, Evidence, and Policies (Study Plan 23.5)

8. Explain the processes that will bring the growth of real GDP per person to a stop according to
   a. Classical growth theory.
   b. Neoclassical growth theory.
   c. New growth theory.

ADDITIONAL PROBLEMS AND APPLICATIONS

MyEconLab   You can work these problems in MyEconLab if assigned by your instructor.

The Basics of Economic Growth

9. In 2014 China's real GDP is growing at 7 percent a year and its population is growing at 0.5 percent a year. If these growth rates continue, in what year will China's real GDP per person be twice what it is in 2014?

10. Mexico's real GDP was 13,405 trillion pesos in 2013 and 13,805 trillion pesos in 2014. Mexico's population was 118.4 million in 2013 and 119.5 million in 2014. Calculate
    a. The growth rate of real GDP.
    b. The growth rate of real GDP per person.
    c. The approximate number of years it takes for real GDP per person in Mexico to double if the 2014 growth rate of real GDP and the population growth rate are maintained.

11. South Africa's real GDP was 1,900 billion rand in 2011 and 1,970 billion rand in 2012. South Africa's population was 50.5 million in 2011 and 51.0 million in 2012. Calculate
    a. The growth rate of real GDP.
    b. The growth rate of real GDP per person.
    c. The approximate number of years it will take for real GDP per person in South Africa to double if the current growth rate of real GDP is maintained.

Long-Term Growth Trends

12. **The New World Order**

    While gross domestic product growth is picking up a bit in emerging market economies, it is picking up even more in the advanced economies. Real GDP in the emerging market economies is forecasted to grow at 5.4% in 2015 up from 4.9% in 2012. In the advanced economies, real GDP is expected to grow at 2.3% in 2015 up from 1.4% in 2012. The difference in growth rates means that the large spread between emerging market economies and advanced economies of the past 40 years will continue for many more years.

    Source: *World Economic Outlook*, January, 2014

    Do growth rates over the past few decades indicate that gaps in real GDP per person around the world are shrinking, growing, or staying the same? Explain.

How Potential GDP Grows

13. If a large increase in investment increases labor productivity, explain what happens to
    a. Potential GDP.
    b. Employment.
    c. The real wage rate.

14. If a severe drought decreases labor productivity, explain what happens to
    a. Potential GDP.
    b. Employment.
    c. The real wage rate.

Use the following tables to work Problems 15 to 17. The first table describes an economy's labor market in 2014 and the second table describes its production function in 2014.

Real wage rate (dollars per hour)	Labor hours supplied	Labor hours demanded
80	55	15
70	50	20
60	45	25
50	40	30
40	35	35
30	30	40
20	25	45

Labor (hours)	Real GDP (2009 dollars)
15	1,425
20	1,800
25	2,125
30	2,400
35	2,625
40	2,800
45	2,925
50	3,000

15. What are the equilibrium real wage rate and the quantity of labor employed in 2014?

16. What are labor productivity and potential GDP in 2014?

17. Suppose that labor productivity increases in 2014. What effect does the increased labor productivity have on the demand for labor, the supply of labor, potential GDP, and real GDP per person?

Why Labor Productivity Grows

18. **India's Economy Hits the Wall**

    Just six months ago, India was looking good. Annual growth was 9%, consumer demand was huge, and foreign investment was growing. But now most economic forecasts expect growth to slow to 7%—a big drop for a country that needs to accelerate growth. India needs urgently to upgrade its infrastructure and education and healthcare facilities. Agriculture is unproductive and needs better technology. The legal system needs to be strengthened with more judges and courtrooms.

    Source: *BusinessWeek*, July 1, 2008

    Explain five potential sources for faster economic growth in India suggested in this news clip.

Is Economic Growth Sustainable? Theories, Evidence, and Policies

19. **The Productivity Watch**

    According to former Federal Reserve chairman Alan Greenspan, IT investments in the 1990s boosted productivity, which boosted corporate profits, which led to more IT investments, and so on, leading to a nirvana of high growth.

    Source: *Fortune*, September 4, 2006

    Which of the growth theories that you've studied in this chapter best corresponds to the explanation given by Mr. Greenspan?

20. Is faster economic growth always a good thing? Argue the case for faster growth and the case for slower growth. Then reach a conclusion on whether growth should be increased or slowed.

21. **Why Canada's Industry Leaders Need to Embrace the Technology Mindset**

    We are at a tipping point where technology—from software to hardware and everything in between—is weaving its way into all that we do and is about to touch every industry. Every day, we are reminded how quickly things are changing from connected cars, to wearable devices, to manufacturing. Just look at the rapid advance in China's economy and standard of living driven in large part by an innovative spirit unleashed in the late 1990s.

    Source: *Financial Post*, July 11, 2014

    Explain which growth theory best describes the news clip.

Economics in the News

22. After you have studied *Economics in the News* on pp. 560–561, answer the following questions.

    a. How do economic growth rates of South Africa and Botswana compare?

    b. For South Africa to grow faster, how would the percentage of GDP invested in new capital need to change?

    c. If South Africa is able to achieve a growth rate of 8 percent per year, in how many years will real GDP have doubled?

    d. Describe the policies proposed by the author of the news article and explain how they might change labor productivity.

    e. What is the source of Botswana's growth success story and what must South Africa do to replicate that success?

    f. Draw a *PPF* graph to show what has happened in Botswana and South Africa since 1980.

23. **Make Way for India—The Next China**

    China grows at around 9 percent a year, but its one-child policy will start to reduce the size of China's working-age population within the next 10 years. India, by contrast, will have an increasing working-age population for another generation at least.

    Source: *The Independent*, March 1, 2006

    a. Given the expected population changes, do you think China or India will have the greater economic growth rate? Why?

    b. Would China's growth rate remain at 9 percent a year without the restriction on its population growth rate?

    c. India's population growth rate is 1.6 percent a year, and in 2005 its economic growth rate was 8 percent a year. China's population growth rate is 0.6 percent a year, and in 2005 its economic growth rate was 9 percent a year. In what year will real GDP per person double in each country?

ABN·AMRO

24

FINANCE, SAVING, AND INVESTMENT

After studying this chapter, you will be able to:

◆ Describe the flows of funds in financial markets

◆ Explain how saving and investment decisions interact in financial markets

◆ Explain how governments influence financial markets

Interest rates fell during 2014, and by mid-year the U.S. government could borrow at 2.5 percent per year. In 2012, when the economy was still feeling the effects of a financial meltdown in which billions of dollars had been lost, interest rates were even lower.

Behind the drama and headlines that interest rates create, financial markets play a crucial, unseen role funneling funds from savers and lenders to investors and borrowers. This chapter explains how financial markets work, and *Economics in the News* at the end of the chapter looks at the forces at work during 2014 that led to lower interest rates.

◆ Financial Institutions and Financial Markets

The financial institutions and markets that we study in this chapter provide the channels through which saving flows to finance the investment in new capital that makes the economy grow. In studying financial institutions and markets, we distinguish between

- Finance and money
- Capital and financial capital

Finance and Money

We use the term *finance* to describe the activity of providing the funds that finance expenditures on capital. The study of finance looks at how households and firms obtain and use financial resources and how they cope with the risks that arise in this activity.

Money is what we use to pay for goods and services and factors of production and to make financial transactions. The study of money looks at how households and firms use it, how much of it they hold, how banks create and manage it, and how its quantity influences the economy.

Finance and money are closely interrelated and some of the main financial institutions, such as banks, provide both financial services and monetary services. Nevertheless, by distinguishing between *finance* and *money* and studying them separately, we will better understand our financial and monetary markets and institutions.

For the rest of this chapter, we study finance. Money is the topic of the next chapter.

Capital and Financial Capital

Economists distinguish between capital and financial capital. Capital consists of physical capital—tools, instruments, machines, buildings, and inventories—and *human capital*. When economists use the term capital, they mean physical capital.

Financial capital consists of the funds that firms use to buy physical capital and that households use to buy a home or to invest in human capital.

You're going to see, in this chapter, how investment, saving, borrowing, and lending decisions influence the quantity of capital and make it grow and, as a consequence, make real GDP grow.

We begin by describing the links between capital and investment and between wealth and saving.

Capital and Investment

The quantity of capital changes because of investment and depreciation. *Investment* increases the quantity of capital and *depreciation* decreases it (see Chapter 21, p. 494). The total amount spent on new capital is called **gross investment**. The change in the value of capital is called **net investment**. Net investment equals gross investment minus depreciation.

Figure 24.1 illustrates these terms. On January 1, 2014, Ace Bottling Inc. had machines worth $30,000—Ace's initial capital. During 2014, the market value of Ace's machines fell by 67 percent—$20,000. After this depreciation, Ace's machines were valued at $10,000. During 2014, Ace spent $30,000 on new machines. This amount is Ace's gross investment. By December 31, 2014, Ace Bottling had capital valued at $40,000, so its capital had increased by $10,000. This amount is Ace's net investment. Ace's net investment equals its gross investment of $30,000 minus depreciation of its initial capital of $20,000.

Wealth and Saving

Wealth is the value of the things that people *own*. It contrasts with *income*, which is what people *earn* during a given time period from supplying the services of the resources they own. **Saving** is the amount of income that is not paid in taxes or spent on consumption goods and services. Saving increases wealth. Wealth also increases when the market value of assets rises—called *capital gains*—and decreases when the market value of assets falls—called *capital losses*.

For example, if at the end of the school year you have $250 in the bank and a coin collection worth $300, then your wealth is $550. During the summer, suppose that you earn $5,000 (net of taxes) and spend $1,000 on consumption goods and services, so your saving is $4,000. Your bank account increases to $4,250 and your wealth becomes $4,550. The $4,000 increase in wealth equals saving. If coins rise in value and your coin collection is now worth $500, you have a capital gain of $200, which is also added to your wealth.

National wealth and national saving work like this personal example. The wealth of a nation at the end of a year equals its wealth at the start of the year plus its saving during the year, which equals income minus consumption expenditure.

FIGURE 24.1   Capital and Investment

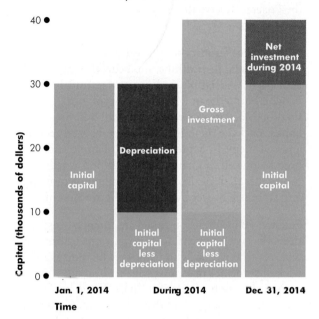

On January 1, 2014, Ace Bottling had capital worth $30,000. During the year, the value of Ace's capital fell by $20,000—depreciation—and Ace spent $30,000 on new capital—gross investment. Ace's net investment was $10,000 ($30,000 gross investment minus $20,000 depreciation) so that at the end of 2014, Ace had capital worth $40,000.

MyEconLab Animation

To make real GDP grow, saving and wealth must be transformed into investment and capital. This transformation takes place in the markets for financial capital and through the activities of financial institutions. We're now going to describe these markets and institutions.

Financial Capital Markets

Saving is the source of the funds that are used to finance investment, and these funds are supplied and demanded in three types of financial markets:

- Loan markets
- Bond markets
- Stock markets

Loan Markets Businesses often want short-term finance to buy inventories or to extend credit to their customers. Sometimes they get this finance in the form of a loan from a bank. Households often want finance to purchase big ticket items, such as automobiles or household furnishings and appliances. They get this finance as bank loans, often in the form of outstanding credit card balances.

Households also get finance to buy new homes. (Expenditure on new homes is counted as part of investment.) These funds are usually obtained as a loan that is secured by a **mortgage**—a legal contract that gives ownership of a home to the lender in the event that the borrower fails to meet the agreed loan payments (repayments and interest).

All of these types of financing take place in loan markets.

Bond Markets When Wal-Mart expands its business and opens new stores, it gets the finance it needs by selling bonds. Governments—federal, state, and municipal—also raise finance by issuing bonds.

A **bond** is a promise to make specified payments on specified dates. For example, you can buy a Wal-Mart bond that promises to pay $5.00 every year until 2024 and then to make a final payment of $100 in 2025.

The buyer of a bond from Wal-Mart makes a loan to the company and is entitled to the payments promised by the bond. When a person buys a newly issued bond, he or she may hold the bond until the borrower has repaid the amount borrowed or sell it to someone else. Bonds issued by firms and governments are traded in the **bond market**.

The term of a bond might be long (decades) or short (just a month or two). Firms often issue very short-term bonds as a way of getting paid for their sales before the buyer is able to pay. For example, when GM sells $100 million of railroad locomotives to Union Pacific, GM wants to be paid when the items are shipped. But Union Pacific doesn't want to pay until the locomotives are earning an income. In this situation, Union Pacific might promise to pay GM $101 million three months in the future. A bank would be willing to buy this promise for (say) $100 million. GM gets $100 million immediately and the bank gets $101 million in three months when Union Pacific honors its promise. The U.S. Treasury issues promises of this type, called Treasury bills.

Another type of bond is a **mortgage-backed security**, which entitles its holder to the income from a package of mortgages. Mortgage lenders create mortgage-backed securities. They make mortgage loans to homebuyers and then create securities that they sell to obtain more funds to make more mortgage loans. The holder of a mortgage-backed security is entitled to receive payments that derive from the payments received by the mortgage lender from the home-buyer–borrower.

Mortgage-backed securities were at the center of the storm in the financial markets in 2007–2008.

Stock Markets When Boeing wants finance to expand its airplane building business, it issues stock. A **stock** is a certificate of ownership and claim to the firm's profits. Boeing has issued about 900 million shares of its stock. So if you owned 900 Boeing shares, you would own one millionth of Boeing and be entitled to receive one millionth of its profits.

Unlike a stockholder, a bondholder does not own part of the firm that issued the bond.

A **stock market** is a financial market in which shares of stocks of corporations are traded. The New York Stock Exchange, the London Stock Exchange (in England), the Tokyo Stock Exchange (in Japan), and the Frankfurt Stock Exchange (in Germany) are all examples of stock markets.

Financial Institutions

Financial markets are highly competitive because of the role played by financial institutions in those markets. A **financial institution** is a firm that operates on both sides of the markets for financial capital. A financial institution is a borrower in one market and a lender in another.

Financial institutions also stand ready to trade so that households with funds to lend and firms or households seeking funds can always find someone on the other side of the market with whom to trade. The key financial institutions are

- Commercial banks
- Government-sponsored mortgage lenders
- Pension funds
- Insurance companies
- The Federal Reserve

Commercial Banks Commercial banks are financial institutions that accept deposits, provide payment services, and make loans to firms and households. The bank that you use for your own banking services and that issues your credit card is a commercial bank.

These institutions play a central role in the monetary system. We study commerical banks, along with the Federal Reserve that regulates them, in detail in Chapter 25.

Government-Sponsored Mortgage Lenders Two large financial institutions, the Federal National Mortgage Association, or Fannie Mae, and the Federal Home Loan Mortgage Corporation, or Freddie Mac, are enterprises that buy mortgages from banks, package them into mortgage-backed securities, and sell them. In September 2008, Fannie and Freddie owned or guaranteed $6 trillion worth of mortgages (half of the U.S. $12 trillion of mortgages) and were taken over by the federal government.

Pension Funds Pension funds are financial institutions that use the pension contributions of firms and workers to buy bonds and stocks. The mortgage-backed securities of Fannie Mae and Freddie Mac are among the assets of pension funds. Some pension funds are very large, and they play an active role in the firms whose stock they hold.

Insurance Companies Insurance companies enable households and firms to cope with risks such

ECONOMICS IN ACTION
The Financial Crisis and the Fix

Bear Stearns: absorbed by JPMorgan Chase with help from the Federal Reserve. Lehman Brothers: gone. Fannie Mae and Freddie Mac: taken into government oversight. Merrill Lynch: absorbed by Bank of America. AIG: given an $85 billion lifeline by the Federal Reserve and sold off in parcels to financial institutions around the world. Wachovia: taken over by Wells Fargo. Washington Mutual: taken over by JPMorgan Chase. Morgan Stanley: 20 percent bought by Mitsubishi, a large Japanese bank. These are some of the events in the financial crisis of 2008. What was going on and how can a replay be avoided?

What Was Going On?

Between 2002 and 2006, mortgage borrowing to buy a home exploded and home prices rocketed. You can see the rise in mortgage borrowing in Fig. 1. Mortgages increased from 65 percent of income in 2000 to more than 100 percent in 2006. And you can see the rocketing home prices in Fig. 2. Between 2000 and 2006, home prices doubled. Then, in 2007 they crashed.

Banks and other financial institutions that had made

mortgage loans to home buyers sold the loans to Fannie Mae, Freddie Mac, and other large banks that bundled these loans into *mortgage-backed securities* and sold them to eager buyers around the world.

When home prices began to fall in 2007, many home owners found themselves with a mortage that was bigger than the value of their home. The mortage default rate jumped and the prices of mortage-backed securities, and more widely of other assets, fell sharply. Financial institutions took big losses. Some losses were too big to bear and some big-name institutions failed.

Avoiding a Replay

In the hope of avoiding a replay, Congress enacted the *Dodd-Frank Wall Street Reform and Consumer Protection Act of 2010.* The main points of the Act are

- A Consumer Financial Protection Bureau to enforce consumer-oriented regulation, ensure that the fine print on financial services contracts is clear and accurate, and maintain a toll-free hotline for consumers to report alleged deception.

- A Financial Stability Oversight Council to anticipate financial market weakness.

- Authority for the Federal Deposit Insurance Corporation to seize, liquidate, and reconstruct troubled financial firms.

- Tight restrictions to stop banks gambling for their own profit and limit their risky investments.

- Mortgage reforms that require lenders to review the income and credit histories of applicants and ensure that they can afford payments.

- A requirement that the firms that create mortgage-backed securities keep at least 5 percent of them.

The 2010 Act does nothing to solve the problem that arises from government oversight of Fannie Mae and Freddie Mac. Many people believe that the measures are too timid and leave the financial system fragile.

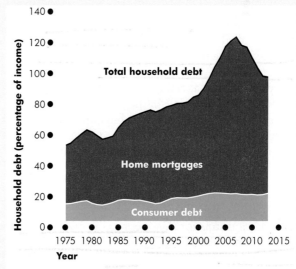

Figure 1 Household Debt

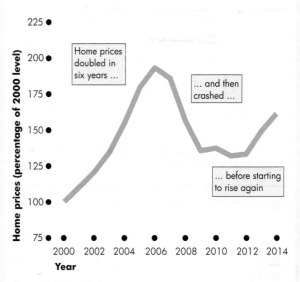

Figure 2 Home Prices

as accident, theft, fire, ill-health, and a host of other misfortunes. They receive premiums from their customers and pay claims. Insurance companies use the funds they have received but not paid out as claims to buy bonds and stocks on which they earn interest income.

In normal times, insurance companies have a steady flow of funds coming in from premiums and interest on the financial assets they hold and a steady, but smaller, flow of funds paying claims. Their profit is the gap between the two flows. But in unusual times, when large and widespread losses are being incurred, insurance companies can run into difficulty in meeting their obligations. Such a situation arose in 2008 for one of the biggest insurers, AIG, and the firm was taken into public ownership.

The Federal Reserve The **Federal Reserve *System*** (usually called the **Fed**) is the central bank of the United States, a public authority whose main role is the regulation of banks and money. In recent years, in reponse to a financial crisis in 2007 and 2008, the Fed has played a big role in the markets for bonds and mortgage-backed securities buying these items in large quantities. We study the Fed in detail in Chapter 25 but you need to keep in mind its presence in financial markets.

Insolvency and Illiquidity

A financial institution's **net worth** is the market value of what it has lent minus the market value of what it has borrowed. If net worth is positive, the institution is *solvent*. But if net worth is negative, the institution is *insolvent* and must go out of business. The owners of an insolvent financial institution—usually its stockholders—bear the loss.

A financial institution both borrows and lends, so it is exposed to the risk that its net worth might become negative. To limit that risk, financial institutions are regulated and a minimum amount of their lending must be backed by their net worth.

Sometimes, a financial institution is solvent but illiquid. A firm is *illiquid* if it has made long-term loans with borrowed funds and is faced with a sudden demand to repay more of what it has borrowed than its available cash. In normal times, a financial institution that is illiquid can borrow from another institution. But if all the financial institutions are short of cash, the market for loans among financial institutions dries up.

Both insolvency and illiquidity were at the core of the financial meltdown of 2007–2008.

Interest Rates and Asset Prices

Stocks, bonds, short-term securities, and loans are collectively called *financial assets*. The interest rate on a financial asset is the interest received expressed as a percentage of the price of the asset.

Because the interest rate is a percentage of the price of an asset, if the asset price rises, other things remaining the same, the interest rate falls. Conversely, if the asset price falls, other things remaining the same, the interest rate rises.

To see this inverse relationship between an asset price and the interest rate, let's look at an example. We'll consider a bond that promises to pay its holder $5 a year forever. What is the rate of return—the interest rate—on this bond? The answer depends on the price of the bond. If you could buy this bond for $50, the interest rate would be 10 percent per year:

Interest rate = ($5 ÷ $50) × 100 = 10 percent.

But if the price of this bond increased to $200, its rate of return or interest rate would be only 2.5 percent per year. That is,

Interest rate = ($5 ÷ $200) × 100 = 2.5 percent.

This relationship means that the price of an asset and the interest rate on that asset are determined simultaneously—one implies the other.

This relationship also means that if the interest rate on the asset rises, the price of the asset falls, debts become harder to pay, and the net worth of the financial institution falls. Insolvency can arise from a previously unexpected large rise in the interest rate.

In the next part of this chapter, we learn how interest rates and asset prices are determined in the financial markets.

◆ REVIEW QUIZ

1 Distinguish between physical capital and financial capital and give two examples of each.
2 What is the distinction between gross investment and net investment?
3 What are the three main types of markets for financial capital?
4 Explain the connection between the price of a financial asset and its interest rate.

Work these questions in Study Plan 24.1 and get instant feedback. Do a Key Terms Quiz.   MyEconLab

◆ The Loanable Funds Market

In macroeconomics, we group all the financial markets that we described in the previous section into a single loanable funds market. The **loanable funds market** is the aggregate of all the individual financial markets.

The circular flow model of Chapter 21 (see p. 493) can be extended to include flows in the loanable funds market that finance investment.

Funds that Finance Investment

Figure 24.2 shows the flows of funds that finance investment. They come from three sources:

1. Household saving
2. Government budget surplus
3. Borrowing from the rest of the world

Households' income, Y, is spent on consumption goods and services, C, saved, S, or paid in net taxes, T. **Net taxes** are the taxes paid to governments minus the cash transfers received from governments (such as Social Security and unemployment benefits). So income is equal to the sum of consumption expenditure, saving, and net taxes:

$$Y = C + S + T.$$

You saw in Chapter 21 (p. 494) that Y also equals the sum of the items of aggregate expenditure: consumption expenditure, C, investment, I, government expenditure, G, and exports, X, minus imports, M. That is:

$$Y = C + I + G + X - M.$$

By using these two equations, you can see that

$$I + G + X = M + S + T.$$

Subtract G and X from both sides of the last equation to obtain

$$I = S + (T - G) + (M - X).$$

This equation tells us that investment, I, is financed by household saving, S, the government budget surplus, $(T - G)$, and borrowing from the rest of the world, $(M - X)$.

The sum of private saving, S, and government saving, $(T - G)$, is called **national saving**. National saving

---

FIGURE 24.2   Financial Flows and the Circular Flow of Expenditure and Income

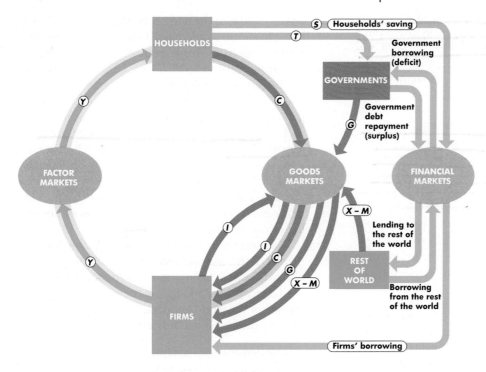

Households use their income for consumption expenditure (C), saving (S), and net taxes (T). Firms borrow to finance their investment expenditure. Governments borrow to finance a budget deficit or repay debt if they have a budget surplus. The rest of the world borrows to finance its deficit or lends its surplus.

and foreign borrowing finance investment.

In 2014, U.S. investment was $2.8 trillion. Governments (federal, state, and local combined) had a deficit of $0.8 trillion. This total of $3.6 trillion was financed by private saving of $3.0 trillion and borrowing from the rest of the world (negative net exports) of $0.6 trillion.

In the rest of this chapter, we focus on the influences on national saving and the effects of a government budget deficit (or surplus) in the loanable funds market. We broaden our view to examine the influences on and the effects of borrowing from the rest of the world in Chapter 26. You can think of this chapter as an account of the U.S. loanable funds market when exports equal imports, ($X = M$) or as an account of the global loanable funds market.

You're going to see how investment and saving and the flows of loanable funds—all measured in constant 2009 dollars—are determined. The price in the loanable funds market that achieves equilibrium is an interest rate, which we also measure in real terms as the *real* interest rate. In the loanable funds market, there is just one interest rate, which is an average of the interest rates on all the different types of financial securities that we described earlier. Let's see what we mean by the real interest rate.

The Real Interest Rate

The **nominal interest rate** is the number of dollars that a borrower pays and a lender receives in interest in a year expressed as a percentage of the number of dollars borrowed and lent. For example, if the annual interest paid on a $500 loan is $25, the nominal interest rate is 5 percent per year: $25 ÷ $500 × 100 or 5 percent.

The **real interest rate** is the nominal interest rate adjusted to remove the effects of inflation on the buying power of money. The real interest rate is approximately equal to the nominal interest rate minus the inflation rate.

You can see why if you suppose that you have put $500 in a savings account that earns 5 percent a year. At the end of a year, you have $525 in your savings account. Suppose that the inflation rate is 2 percent per year—during the year, all prices increased by 2

---

[1]The *exact* real interest rate formula, which allows for the change in the purchasing power of both the interest and the loan is:
Real interest rate = (Nominal interest rate − Inflation rate) ÷ (1 + Inflation rate/100). If the nominal interest rate is 5 percent a year and the inflation rate is 2 percent a year, the real interest rate is (5 − 2) ÷ (1 + 0.02) = 2.94 percent a year.

ECONOMICS IN ACTION
Nominal and Real Interest Rates

Nominal and real interest rates were extremely high during the 1970s and 1980s. They have trended downward for the past 30 years. Where will they go next? See *Economics in the News* on pp. 582–583.

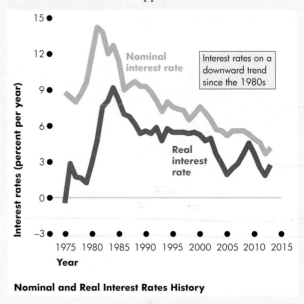

Nominal and Real Interest Rates History

percent. Now, at the end of the year, it costs $510 to buy what $500 would have bought one year ago. Your money in the bank has really only increased by $15, from $510 to $525. That $15 is equivalent to a real interest rate of 3 percent a year on your original $500. So the real interest rate is the 5 percent nominal interest rate minus the 2 percent inflation rate[1].

The real interest rate is the opportunity cost of loanable funds. The real interest *paid* on borrowed funds is the opportunity cost of borrowing. And the real interest rate *forgone* when funds are used either to buy consumption goods and services or to invest in new capital goods is the opportunity cost of not saving or not lending those funds.

We're now going to see how the loanable funds market determines the real interest rate, the quantity of funds loaned, saving, and investment. In the rest of this section, we will ignore the government and the rest of the world and focus on households and firms in the loanable funds market. We will study

- The demand for loanable funds
- The supply of loanable funds
- Equilibrium in the loanable funds market

ECONOMICS IN ACTION
The Total Quantities Supplied and Demanded

Around $80 trillion of loanable funds have been supplied and demanded. The figure shows who supplies the funds and who demands them. Almost one third of the funds are supplied to banks and similar financial institutions.

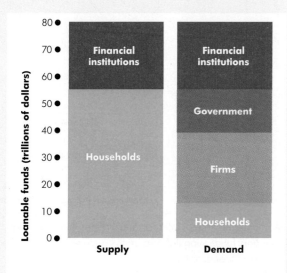

Supply and Demand in the Loanable Funds Market

The Demand for Loanable Funds

The *quantity of loanable funds demanded* is the total quantity of funds demanded to finance investment, the government budget deficit, and international investment or lending during a given period. Our focus here is on investment. We'll bring the government budget deficit into the picture later in this chapter.

What determines investment and the demand for loanable funds to finance it? Many details influence this decision, but we can summarize them in two factors:

1. The real interest rate
2. Expected profit

Firms invest in capital only if they expect to earn a profit and fewer projects are profitable at a high real interest rate than at a low real interest rate, so

> Other things remaining the same, the higher the real interest rate, the smaller is the quantity of loanable funds demanded; and the lower the real interest rate, the greater the quantity of loanable funds demanded.

FIGURE 24.3   The Demand for Loanable Funds

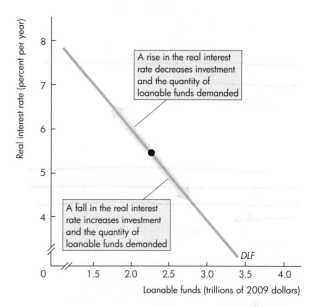

A change in the real interest rate changes the quantity of loanable funds demanded and brings a movement along the demand for loanable funds curve.

MyEconLab Animation

Demand for Loanable Funds Curve The **demand for loanable funds** is the relationship between the quantity of loanable funds demanded and the real interest rate, when all other influences on borrowing plans remain the same. The demand curve *DLF* in Fig. 24.3 is a demand for loanable funds curve.

To understand the demand for loanable funds, think about Amazon.com's decision to borrow $100 million to build some new warehouses. If Amazon expects to get a return of $5 million a year from this investment before paying interest costs and the interest rate is less than 5 percent a year, Amazon would make a profit, so it builds the warehouses. But if the interest rate is more than 5 percent a year, Amazon would incur a loss, so it doesn't build the warehouses. The quantity of loanable funds demanded is greater the lower is the real interest rate.

Changes in the Demand for Loanable Funds When the expected profit changes, the demand for loanable funds changes. Other things remaining the same, the greater the expected profit from new capital, the greater is the amount of investment and the greater the demand for loanable funds.

Expected profit rises during a business cycle expansion and falls during a recession; rises when technological change creates profitable new products; rises as a growing population brings increased demand for goods and services; and fluctuates with contagious swings of optimism and pessimism, called "animal spirits" by Keynes and "irrational exuberance" by Alan Greenspan.

When expected profit changes, the demand for loanable funds curve shifts.

The Supply of Loanable Funds

The *quantity of loanable funds supplied* is the total funds available from private saving, the government budget surplus, and supplied by the Fed, during a given period. Our focus here is on saving. We'll bring the government budget and the Fed into the picture in the next part of the chapter.

How do you decide how much of your income to save and supply in the loanable funds market? Your decision is influenced by many factors, but chief among them are

1. The real interest rate
2. Disposable income
3. Expected future income
4. Wealth
5. Default risk

We begin by focusing on the real interest rate.

> Other things remaining the same, the higher the real interest rate, the greater is the quantity of loanable funds supplied; and the lower the real interest rate, the smaller is the quantity of loanable funds supplied.

The Supply of Loanable Funds Curve The **supply of loanable funds** is the relationship between the quantity of loanable funds supplied and the real interest rate when all other influences on lending plans remain the same. The curve *SLF* in Fig. 24.4 is a supply of loanable funds curve.

Think about a student's decision to save some of what she earns from her summer job. With a real interest rate of 2 percent a year, she decides that it is not worth saving much—better to spend the income and take a student loan if funds run out during the semester. But if the real interest rate jumped to 10 percent a year, the payoff from saving would be high enough to encourage her to cut back on spending and increase the amount she saves.

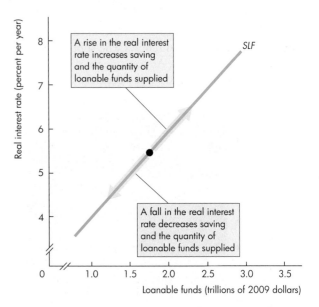

FIGURE 24.4   The Supply of Loanable Funds

A rise in the real interest rate increases saving and the quantity of loanable funds supplied

A fall in the real interest rate decreases saving and the quantity of loanable funds supplied

A change in the real interest rate changes the quantity of loanable funds supplied and brings a movement along the supply of loanable funds curve.

—— MyEconLab Animation ——

Changes in the Supply of Loanable Funds A change in disposable income, expected future income, wealth, or default risk changes the supply of loanable funds.

Disposable Income A household's *disposable income* is the income earned minus net taxes. When disposable income increases, other things remaining the same, consumption expenditure increases but by less than the increase in income. Some of the increase in income is saved. So the greater a household's disposable income, other things remaining the same, the greater is its saving.

Expected Future Income The higher a household's expected future income, other things remaining the same, the smaller is its saving today.

Wealth The higher a household's wealth, other things remaining the same, the smaller is its saving. If a person's wealth increases because of a capital gain, the person sees less need to save. For example, from 2002 through 2006, when house prices were rising rapidly, wealth increased despite the fact that personal saving dropped close to zero.

Default Risk The risk that a loan will not be repaid is called **default risk**. The greater that risk, the higher is the interest rate needed to induce a person to lend and the smaller is the supply of loanable funds.

Shifts of the Supply of Loanable Funds Curve

When any of the four influences on the supply of loanable funds changes, the supply of loanable funds changes and the supply curve shifts. An increase in disposable income, a decrease in expected future income, a decrease in wealth, or a fall in default risk increases saving and increases the supply of loanable funds.

Equilibrium in the Loanable Funds Market

You've seen that other things remaining the same, the higher the real interest rate, the greater is the quantity of loanable funds supplied and the smaller is the quantity of loanable funds demanded. There is one real interest rate at which the quantities of loanable funds demanded and supplied are equal, and that interest rate is the equilibrium real interest rate.

Figure 24.5 shows how the demand for and supply of loanable funds determine the real interest rate. The *DLF* curve is the demand curve and the *SLF* curve is the supply curve. If the real interest rate exceeds 6 percent a year, the quantity of loanable funds supplied exceeds the quantity demanded—a surplus of funds. Borrowers find it easy to get funds, but lenders are unable to lend all the funds they have available. The real interest rate falls and continues to fall until the quantity of funds supplied equals the quantity of funds demanded.

If the real interest rate is less than 6 percent a year, the quantity of loanable funds supplied is less than the quantity demanded—a shortage of funds. Borrowers can't get the funds they want, but lenders are able to lend all the funds they have. So the real interest rate rises and continues to rise until the quantity of funds supplied equals the quantity demanded.

Regardless of whether there is a surplus or a shortage of loanable funds, the real interest rate changes and is pulled toward an equilibrium level. In Fig. 24.5, the equilibrium real interest rate is 6 percent a year. At this interest rate, there is neither a surplus nor a shortage of loanable funds. Borrowers can get the funds they want, and lenders can lend all the funds they have available. The investment plans of borrowers and the saving plans of lenders are consistent with each other.

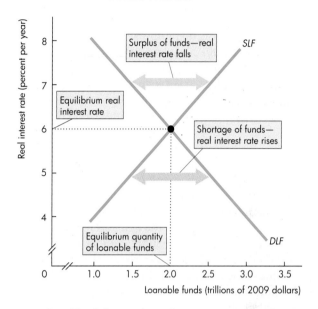

FIGURE 24.5 Equilibrium in the Loanable Funds Market

A surplus of funds lowers the real interest rate and a shortage of funds raises it. At an interest rate of 6 percent a year, the quantity of funds demanded equals the quantity supplied and the market is in equilibrium.

—————— MyEconLab Animation and Draw Graph ——————

Changes in Demand and Supply

Financial markets are highly volatile in the short run but remarkably stable in the long run. Volatility in the market comes from fluctuations in either the demand for loanable funds or the supply of loanable funds. These fluctuations bring fluctuations in the real interest rate and in the equilibrium quantity of funds lent and borrowed. They also bring fluctuations in asset prices.

Here we'll illustrate the effects of *increases* in demand and supply in the loanable funds market.

An Increase in Demand If the profits that firms expect to earn increase, they increase their planned investment and increase their demand for loanable funds to finance that investment. With an increase in the demand for loanable funds, but no change in the supply of loanable funds, there is a shortage of funds. As borrowers compete for funds, the interest rate rises and lenders increase the quantity of funds supplied.

Figure 24.6(a) illustrates these changes. An increase in the demand for loanable funds shifts the demand curve rightward from DLF_0 to DLF_1. With

ECONOMICS IN ACTION

Loanable Funds Fuel Home Price Bubble

The financial crisis that gripped the U.S. and global economies in 2007 and cascaded through the financial markets in 2008 had its origins much earlier in events taking place in the loanable funds market.

Between 2001 and 2005, a massive injection of loanable funds occurred. Some funds came from the rest of the world, but that source of supply has been stable. The Federal Reserve provided funds to keep interest rates low and that was a major source of the increase in the supply of funds. (The next chapter explains how the Fed does this.)

Figure 1 illustrates the loanable funds market starting in 2001. In that year, the demand for loanable funds was DLF_{01} and the supply of loanable funds was SLF_{01}. The equilibrium real interest rate was 4 percent a year and the equilibrium quantity of loanable funds was $29 trillion (in 2009 dollars).

During the ensuing four years, a massive increase in the supply of loanable funds shifted the supply curve rightward to SLF_{05}. A smaller increase in demand shifted the demand for loanable funds curve to DLF_{05}. The real interest rate fell to 1 percent a year and the quantity of loanable funds increased to $36 trillion—a 24 percent increase in just four years.

With this large increase in available funds, much of it in the form of mortgage loans to home buyers, the demand for homes increased by more than the increase in the supply of homes. Home prices rose and the expectation of further increases fueled the demand for loanable funds.

By 2006, the expectation of continued rapidly rising home prices brought a very large increase in the demand for loanable funds. At the same time, the Federal Reserve began to tighten credit. (Again, you'll learn how this is done in the next chapter). The result of the Fed's tighter credit policy was a slowdown in the pace of increase in the supply of loanable funds.

Figure 2 illustrates these events. In 2006, the demand for loanable funds increased from DLF_{05} to DLF_{06} and the supply of loanable funds increased by a smaller amount from SLF_{05} to SLF_{06}. The real interest rate increased to 3 percent a year.

The rise in the real interest rate (and a much higher rise in the nominal interest rate) put many homeowners in financial difficulty. Mortgage payments increased and some borrowers stopped repaying their loans.

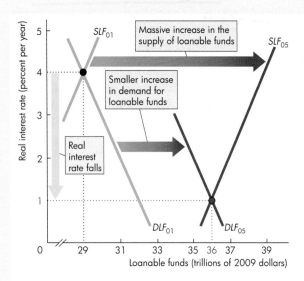

Figure 1 The Foundation of the Crisis: 2001–2005

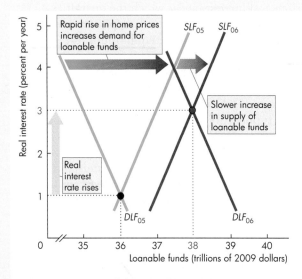

Figure 2 The Start of the Crisis: 2005–2006

By August 2007, the damage from mortgage default and foreclosure was so large that the credit market began to dry up. A large decrease in both demand and supply kept interest rates roughly constant but decreased the quantity of new business.

The total quantity of loanable funds didn't decrease, but the rate of increase slowed to a snail's pace and financial institutions most exposed to the bad mortgage debts and the securities that they backed (described on pp. 569–570) began to fail.

These events illustrate the crucial role played by the loanable funds market in our economy.

FIGURE 24.6 Changes in Demand and Supply

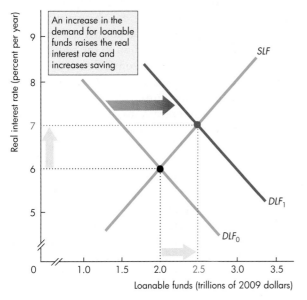

An increase in the demand for loanable funds raises the real interest rate and increases saving

(a) An increase in demand

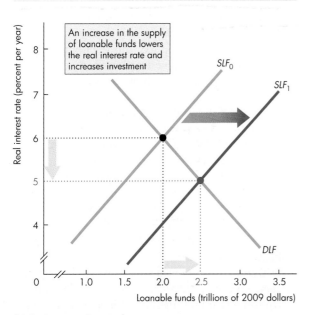

An increase in the supply of loanable funds lowers the real interest rate and increases investment

(b) An increase in supply

In part (a), the demand for loanable funds increases and supply doesn't change. The real interest rate rises (financial asset prices fall) and the quantity of funds increases.
In part (b), the supply of loanable funds increases and demand doesn't change. The real interest rate falls (financial asset prices rise) and the quantity of funds increases.

— MyEconLab Animation —

no change in the supply of loanable funds, there is a shortage of funds at a real interest rate of 6 percent a year. The real interest rate rises until it is 7 percent a year. Equilibrium is restored and the equilibrium quantity of funds has increased.

An Increase in Supply If one of the influences on saving plans changes and increases saving, the supply of loanable funds increases. With no change in the demand for loanable funds, the market is flush with loanable funds. Borrowers find bargains and lenders find themselves accepting a lower interest rate. At the lower interest rate, borrowers find additional investment projects profitable and increase the quantity of loanable funds that they borrow.

Figure 24.6(b) illustrates these changes. An increase in supply shifts the supply curve rightward from SLF_0 to SLF_1. With no change in demand, there is a surplus of funds at a real interest rate of 6 percent a year. The real interest rate falls until it is 5 percent a year. Equilibrium is restored and the equilibrium quantity of funds has increased.

Long-Run Growth of Demand and Supply Over time, both demand and supply in the loanable funds market fluctuate and the real interest rate rises and falls. Both the supply of loanable funds and the demand for loanable funds tend to increase over time. On the average, they increase at a similar pace, so although demand and supply trend upward, the real interest rate has no trend. It fluctuates around a constant average level.

◆ REVIEW QUIZ

1 What is the loanable funds market?
2 Explain why the real interest rate is the opportunity cost of loanable funds.
3 How do firms make investment decisions?
4 What determines the demand for loanable funds and what makes it change?
5 How do households make saving decisions?
6 What determines the supply of loanable funds and what makes it change?
7 How do changes in the demand for and supply of loanable funds change the real interest rate and quantity of loanable funds?

Work these questions in Study Plan 24.2 and get instant feedback. Do a Key Terms Quiz.   MyEconLab

Government in the Loanable Funds Market

Government enters the loanable funds market when it has a budget surplus or budget deficit. A budget surplus increases the supply of loanable funds and contributes to financing investment; a budget deficit increases the demand for loanable funds and competes with businesses for funds.

Let's study the effects of government on the loanable funds market.

A Government Budget Surplus

A government budget surplus increases the supply of loanable funds. The real interest rate falls, which decreases household saving and decreases the quantity of private funds supplied. The lower real interest rate increases the quantity of loanable funds demanded, and increases investment.

FIGURE 24.7   A Government Budget Surplus

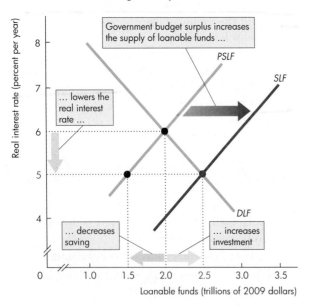

A government budget surplus of $1 trillion adds to private saving and the private supply of loanable funds curve, PSLF, to determine the supply of loanable funds curve, SLF. The real interest rate falls to 5 percent a year. Private saving decreases to $1.5 trillion, but investment increases to $2.5 trillion.

MyEconLab Animation

Figure 24.7 shows these effects of a government budget surplus. The private supply of loanable funds curve is PSLF. The supply of loanable funds curve, SLF, shows the sum of private supply and the government budget surplus. Here, the government budget surplus is $1 trillion, so at each real interest rate the SLF curve lies $1 trillion to the right of the PSLF curve. That is, the horizontal distance between the PSLF curve and the SLF curve equals the government budget surplus.

With no government surplus, the real interest rate is 6 percent a year, the quantity of loanable funds is $2 trillion a year, and investment is $2 trillion a year. But with the government surplus of $1 trillion a year, the equilibrium real interest rate falls to 5 percent a year and the equilibrium quantity of loanable funds increases to $2.5 trillion a year.

The fall in the interest rate decreases private saving to $1.5 trillion, but investment increases to $2.5 trillion, which is financed by private saving plus the government budget surplus (government saving).

A Government Budget Deficit

A government budget deficit increases the demand for loanable funds. The real interest rate rises, which increases household saving and increases the quantity of private funds supplied. But the higher real interest rate decreases investment and the quantity of loanable funds demanded by firms to finance investment.

Figure 24.8 shows these effects of a government budget deficit. The private demand for loanable funds curve is PDLF. The demand for loanable funds curve, DLF, shows the sum of private demand and the government budget deficit. Here, the government budget deficit is $1 trillion, so at each real interest rate the DLF curve lies $1 trillion to the right of the PDLF curve. That is, the horizontal distance between the PDLF curve and the DLF curve equals the government budget deficit.

With no government deficit, the real interest rate is 6 percent a year, the quantity of loanable funds is $2 trillion a year and investment is $2 trillion a year. But with the government budget deficit of $1 trillion a year, the equilibrium real interest rate rises to 7 percent a year and the equilibrium quantity of loanable funds increases to $2.5 trillion a year.

The rise in the real interest rate increases private saving to $2.5 trillion, but investment decreases to $1.5 trillion because $1 trillion of private saving must finance the government budget deficit.

FIGURE 24.8   A Government Budget Deficit

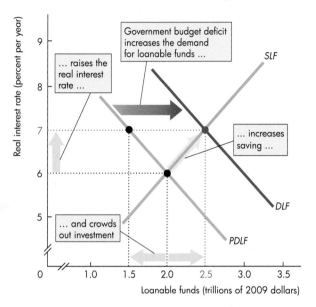

A government budget deficit adds to the private demand for loanable funds curve, *PDLF*, to determine the demand for loanable funds curve, *DLF*. The real interest rate rises, saving increases, but investment decreases—a crowding-out effect.

MyEconLab Animation and Draw Graph

FIGURE 24.9   The Ricardo-Barro Effect

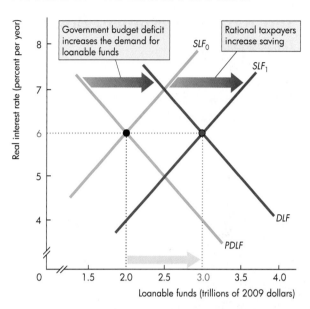

A budget deficit increases the demand for loanable funds. Rational taxpayers increase saving, which shifts the supply of loanable funds curve from SLF_0 to SLF_1. Crowding out is avoided: Increased saving finances the budget deficit.

MyEconLab Animation

The Crowding-Out Effect The tendency for a government budget deficit to raise the real interest rate and decrease investment is called the **crowding-out effect.** The crowding-out effect does not decrease investment by the full amount of the government budget deficit because a higher real interest rate induces an increase in private saving that partly contributes toward financing the deficit.

The Ricardo-Barro Effect First suggested by the English economist David Ricardo in the eighteenth century and refined by Robert J. Barro of Harvard University, the Ricardo-Barro effect holds that both of the effects we've just shown are wrong and the government budget has no effect on either the real interest rate or investment.

Barro says that taxpayers are rational and can see that a budget deficit today means that future taxes must be higher and future disposable incomes smaller. With smaller expected future disposable incomes, saving increases today. The private supply of loanable funds increases to match the quantity of loanable funds demanded by the government. So the budget deficit has no effect on either the real interest

rate or investment. Figure 24.9 shows this outcome.

Most economists regard the Ricardo-Barro view as extreme. But there might be some change in private saving that goes in the direction suggested by the Ricardo-Barro effect that lessens the crowding-out effect.

◆ REVIEW QUIZ

1 How does a government budget surplus or deficit influence the loanable funds market?
2 What is the crowding-out effect and how does it work?
3 What is the Ricardo-Barro effect and how does it modify the crowding-out effect?

Work these questions in Study Plan 24.3 and get instant feedback. Do a Key Terms Quiz.   MyEconLab

◆ To complete your study of financial markets, take a look at *Economics in the News* on pp. 582–583 and see how you can use the model of the loanable funds market to understand why interest rates fell in 2014.

Interest Rates Low but Fall

Top-Rated Government Bonds Defy Gravity

The Financial Times,
June 20, 2014

When you hit rock bottom, the only way is up. One day that might apply to yields on the world's safest and most liquid government bonds—U.S. Treasuries, U.K. gilts, German Bunds, and Japanese government bonds.

One day—but maybe not yet. Ten-year yields on core government bonds, which move inversely with prices, have edged lower in 2014—defying a near-universal start-of-the-year consensus that the only way was up.

German Bund 10-year yields this week hit a record low of just 1.12 percent. Ten-year U.S. Treasuries yields rose back above 2.5 percent on Wednesday on strong economic data but were 3 percent at the start of 2014.

Such historically meagre rates worry some investors. Low yields can already translate into negative real interest rates after taking account of inflation. If prices are in bubble territory, a correction could inflict heavy capital losses on bond portfolios.

Yields have already risen this year on two-year U.S. Treasuries and U.K. gilts, which track closely expectations about central bank interest rate moves.

Among strategists and analysts, it is hard to sense a bubble about to burst, however. "For there to be a bubble, there has to be irrational behavior," says Steven Major, global head of fixed income research at HSBC. "I don't see people borrowing to buy bonds—and I don't think values are far from fundamentals."

Instead, core government bonds offer havens in still-uncertain times—Russia's tensions with the west are escalating—while yields are held in check by ultra-loose central bank monetary policies and a global glut in savings.

Low yields also reflect global economic prospects. From Japan to the eurozone, growth remains weak. While U.K. gilts in particular may be vulnerable to sudden changes in interest rate expectations, it is arguably too early to claim the U.S. and U.K. recoveries will be sustained.

"We are unlikely to see U.S. bond yields rise in isolation; we should expect a synchronised move higher once the global economy is fully recovering," says Zach Pandl, portfolio manager at Columbia Management. ...

ESSENCE OF THE STORY

- Interest rates on government bonds fell during the first half of 2014.

- The interest rate on a German government 10-year bond was at a record low of 1.12 percent and the rate on a 10-year U.S. government bond fell from 3 percent to 2.5 percent during the first half of 2014.

- Real interest rates could become negative.

- When interest rates rise, bond prices will fall.

- Economic growth is weak in Japan and Europe, and it is uncertain whether the U.S. and U.K. expansions will be sustained.

MyEconLab More Economics in the News

ECONOMIC ANALYSIS

- The news article reports that the interest rates on government bonds fell during 2014 from an already low level and bond prices increased.

- Government bonds, called Treasuries in the United States, gilts in the United Kingdom, and bunds in Germany, are the safest securities in the loanable funds market.

- They are also easily traded, so they can be sold at a moment's notice, which makes them highly liquid.

- Because they are safe and liquid, government bonds have a lower interest rate than corporate bonds—bonds issued by corporations.

- Although the level of an interest rate depends on the safety and liquidity of the security, interest rates, on average, move up and down together and are influenced by common forces that change the supply of and demand for loanable funds.

- Figure 1 shows the interest rate on U.S. government 10-year bonds from 2010 to mid-2014 (both the nominal rate and the real rate.)

- The striking feature of this graph is that although the interest rate was low in 2014, it was not as low as it had been in 2012, when the real interest rate was close to zero for two years and briefly negative at the end of 2012.

- The news article says that the falling rate in 2014 risks making the real rate negative again, but that would require a full 1 percentage point fall in the nominal interest rate or a 1 percentage point rise in the inflation rate.

- The news article says that the interest rate on U.S. government bonds fell from 3 percent to 2.5 percent per year. With inflation constant at 1.4 percent per year, these numbers translate to a fall in the real interest rate from 1.6 percent to 1.1 percent per year.

- Figure 2 illustrates why the real interest rate fell. In January 2014, the demand for loanable funds was DLF_{Jan} and the supply of loanable funds was SLF_{Jan}. The equilibrium interest rate was 1.6 percent per year.

- During 2014, the factors described in the news article increased the supply of loanable funds to SLF_{Jun}.

- A key influence on the interest rate is missing from the news article: In 2014, the German, U.S., and U.K. government budget deficits shrank, which decreased the demand for loanable funds to DLF_{Jun}.

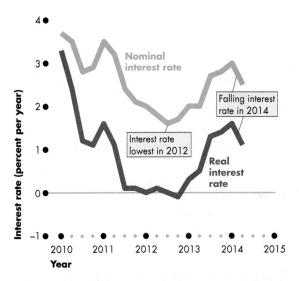

Figure 1 Interest Rates 2010 to 2014

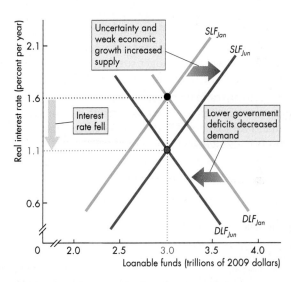

Figure 2 The Loanable Funds Market in 2014

- With an increase in supply and a decrease in demand, the equilibrium real interest rate fell from 1.6 percent to 1.1 percent per year.

- The news article speculates that bond prices will fall and interest rates will rise as economic expansion increases the demand for loanable funds.

583

SUMMARY

Key Points

Financial Institutions and Financial Markets

(pp. 568–572)

- Capital (*physical* and *human capital*) is a real productive resource; financial capital is the funds used to buy capital.
- Gross investment increases the quantity of capital and depreciation decreases it. Saving increases wealth.
- The markets for financial capital are the markets for loans, bonds, and stocks.
- Financial institutions ensure that borrowers and lenders can always find someone with whom to trade.

Working Problems 1 to 4 will give you a better understanding of financial institutions and financial markets.

The Loanable Funds Market (pp. 573–579)

- Investment in capital is financed by household saving, a government budget surplus, and funds from the rest of the world.
- The quantity of loanable funds demanded depends negatively on the real interest rate and the demand for loanable funds changes when profit expectations change.

- The quantity of loanable funds supplied depends positively on the real interest rate and the supply of loanable funds changes when disposable income, expected future income, wealth, and default risk change.
- Equilibrium in the loanable funds market determines the real interest rate and quantity of funds.

Working Problems 5 to 7 will give you a better understanding of the loanable funds market.

Government in the Loanable Funds Market

(pp. 580–581)

- A government budget surplus increases the supply of loanable funds, lowers the real interest rate, and increases investment and the equilibrium quantity of loanable funds.
- A government budget deficit increases the demand for loanable funds, raises the real interest rate, and increases the equilibrium quantity of loanable funds, but decreases investment in a crowding-out effect.
- The Ricardo-Barro effect is the response of rational taxpayers to a budget deficit: private saving increases to finance the budget deficit. The real interest rate remains constant and the crowding-out effect is avoided.

Working Problems 8 to 11 will give you a better understanding of government in the loanable funds market.

Key Terms

MyEconLab Key Terms Quiz

Bond, 569
Bond market, 569
Crowding-out effect, 581
Default risk, 577
Demand for loanable funds, 575
Federal Reserve System, 572
Financial capital, 568
Financial institution, 570

Gross investment, 568
Loanable funds market, 573
Mortgage, 569
Mortgage-backed security, 569
National saving, 573
Net investment, 568
Net taxes, 573
Net worth, 572

Nominal interest rate, 574
Real interest rate, 574
Saving, 568
Stock, 570
Stock market, 570
Supply of loanable funds, 576
Wealth, 568

WORKED PROBLEM

MyEconLab   You can work this problem in Chapter 24 Study Plan.

The following items are (approximate) facts about the U.S. economy:

- In 2005, the nominal interest rate on bonds was 5 percent a year and the real interest rate was 2 percent a year. Investment was $2.7 trillion and the government budget deficit was $0.5 trillion.
- By 2009, the real interest rate had increased to 5 percent a year, but the nominal interest rate was unchanged at 5 percent a year. Investment had crashed to $1.8 trillion and the government budget deficit had climbed to $1.8 trillion.

Assume that the private demand for and private supply of loanable funds did not change between 2005 and 2009.

Questions

1. What was the inflation rate in 2005 and 2009? How do you know?
2. What happened to the price of a bond between 2005 and 2009? How do you know?
3. What happened to the demand for loanable funds between 2005 and 2009? How do you know?
4. Did the change in the government budget deficit crowd out some investment?
5. What happened to the quantity of saving and investment?

Solutions

1. The real interest rate equals the nominal interest rate minus the inflation rate. So the inflation rate equals the nominal interest rate minus the real interest rate. In 2005, the inflation rate was 3 percent a year and in 2009 the inflation rate was zero.

Key Point: The nominal interest rate minus the real interest rate equals the inflation rate.

2. The price of a bond is inversely related to the nominal interest rate. Between 2005 and 2009, the nominal interest rate did not change—it remained at 5 percent a year. With the nominal interest rate unchanged, the price of a bond was also unchanged.

Key Point: The price of a bond is inversely related to the nominal interest rate.

3. The demand for loanable funds is the relationship between the quantity of loanable funds demanded and the real interest rate.

An increase in the government budget deficit increases the demand for loanable funds.

Between 2005 and 2009, the government budget deficit increased from $0.5 trillion to $1.8 trillion, so the demand for loanable funds increased.

Key Point: An increase in the government budget deficit increases the demand for loanable funds.

4. The increase in the government budget deficit increased the demand for loanable funds. With no change in the supply of loanable funds, the real interest rate increases.

Between 2005 and 2009, the real interest rate increased from 2 percent a year to 5 percent a year. As the real interest rate increased, the quantity of loanable funds demanded by firms decreased from $2.7 trillion to $1.8 trillion. Crowding out occurred.

Key Point: With no change in the supply of loanable funds, an increase in the government budget deficit increases the real interest rate and crowds out investment.

5. Saving and investment plans depend on the real interest rate. Between 2005 and 2009, the real interest rate increased, which increased saving and decreased investment. The increase in saving increased the quantity supplied of loanable funds. The decrease in investment decreased the quantity demanded of loanable funds.

Key Point: A change in the real interest rate does not change the supply of or demand for loanable funds: It changes the quantities supplied and demanded.

Key Figure

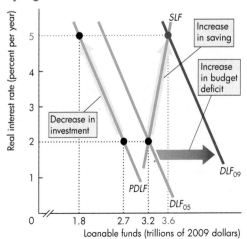

MyEconLab Interactive Animation

STUDY PLAN PROBLEMS AND APPLICATIONS

MyEconLab   You can work Problems 1 to 11 in Chapter 24 Study Plan and get instant feedback.

Financial Institutions and Financial Markets

(Study Plan 24.1)

Use the following data to work Problems 1 and 2.

Michael is an Internet service provider. On December 31, 2014, he bought an existing business with servers and a building worth $400,000. During 2015, his business grew and he bought new servers for $500,000. The market value of some of his older servers fell by $100,000.

1. What was Michael's gross investment, depreciation, and net investment during 2015?

2. What is the value of Michael's capital at the end of 2015?

3. Lori is a student who teaches golf on Saturdays. In a year, she earns $20,000 after paying her taxes. At the beginning of 2014, Lori owned $1,000 worth of books, DVDs, and golf clubs and she had $5,000 in a savings account at the bank. During 2014, the interest on her savings account was $300 and she spent a total of $15,300 on consumption goods and services. There was no change in the market values of her books, DVDs, and golf clubs.
   a. How much did Lori save in 2014?
   b. What was her wealth at the end of 2014?

4. **Treasury Yields Fall to Two-Week Low**
   Treasury bond prices rose on Monday, pushing interest rates down. The interest rate on 10-year bonds fell 4 basis points to 1.65%.
   Source: *The Wall Street Journal*, August 27, 2012

   What is the relationship between the price of a treasury bond and its interest rate? Why does the interest rate move inversely to price?

The Loanable Funds Market (Study Plan 24.2)

Use the following data to work Problems 5 and 6.

First Call, Inc., a smartphone company, plans to build an assembly plant that costs $10 million if the real interest rate is 6 percent a year or a larger plant that costs $12 million if the real interest rate is 5 percent a year or a smaller plant that costs $8 million if the real interest rate is 7 percent a year.

5. Draw a graph of First Call's demand for loanable funds curve.

6. First Call expects its profit to double next year.

Explain how this increase in expected profit influences First Call's demand for loanable funds.

7. The table sets out the data for an economy when the government's budget is balanced.

Real interest rate (percent per year)	Loanable funds demanded	Loanable funds supplied
	(trillions of 2009 dollars)	
4	8.5	5.5
5	8.0	6.0
6	7.5	6.5
7	7.0	7.0
8	6.5	7.5
9	6.0	8.0
10	5.5	8.5

   a. Calculate the equilibrium real interest rate, investment, and private saving.
   b. If planned saving increases by $0.5 trillion at each real interest rate, explain the change in the real interest rate.
   c. If planned investment increases by $1 trillion at each real interest rate, explain the change in saving and the real interest rate.

Government in the Loanable Funds Market

(Study Plan 24.3)

Use the data in Problem 7 to work Problems 8 and 9.

8. If the government's budget becomes a deficit of $1 trillion, what are the real interest rate and investment? Does crowding out occur?

9. If the government's budget becomes a deficit of $1 trillion and the Ricardo-Barro effect occurs, what are the real interest rate and investment?

Use the table in Problem 7 and the following data to work Problems 10 and 11.

Suppose that the quantity of loanable funds demanded increases by $1 trillion at each real interest rate and the quantity of loanable funds supplied increases by $2 trillion at each interest rate.

10. If the government budget remains balanced, what are the real interest rate, investment, and private saving? Does any crowding out occur?

11. If the government's budget becomes a deficit of $1 trillion, what are the real interest rate, investment, and private saving? Does any crowding out occur?

◆ ADDITIONAL PROBLEMS AND APPLICATIONS

MyEconLab   You can work these problems in MyEconLab if assigned by your instructor.

Financial Institutions and Financial Markets

12. On January 1, 2014, Terry's Towing Service owned 4 tow trucks valued at $300,000. During 2014, Terry's bought 2 new trucks for a total of $180,000. At the end of 2014, the market value of all of the firm's trucks was $400,000. What was Terry's gross investment? Calculate Terry's depreciation and net investment.

Use the following information to work Problems 13 and 14.

The Bureau of Economic Analysis reported that the U.S. capital stock was $46.3 trillion at the end of 2010, $46.6 trillion at the end of 2011, and $47.0 trillion at the end of 2012. Depreciation in 2011 was $2.4 trillion, and gross investment during 2012 was $2.8 trillion (all in 2009 dollars).

13. Calculate U.S. net investment and gross investment during 2011.

14. Calculate U.S. depreciation and net investment during 2012.

15. Annie runs a fitness center. On December 31, 2014, she bought an existing business with exercise equipment and a building worth $300,000. During 2015, business improved and she bought some new equipment for $50,000. At the end of 2015, her equipment and buildings were worth $325,000. Calculate Annie's gross investment, depreciation, and net investment during 2015.

16. Karrie is a golf pro, and after she paid taxes, her income from golf and interest from financial assets was $1,500,000 in 2013. At the beginning of 2013, she owned $900,000 worth of financial assets. At the end of 2013, Karrie's financial assets were worth $1,900,000.
    a. How much did Karrie save during 2013?
    b. How much did she spend on consumption goods and services?

17. In a speech at the CFA Society of Nebraska in February 2007, William Poole (former Chairman of the St. Louis Federal Reserve Bank) said:
    Over most of the post-World War II period, the personal saving rate averaged about 6 percent, with some higher rates from the mid-1970s to mid-1980s. The negative trend in the saving rate started in the mid-1990s, about the same time the stock market boom started. Thus it is hard to dismiss the hypothesis that the decline in the measured saving rate in the late 1990s reflected the response of consumption to large capital gains from corporate equity [stock]. Evidence from panel data of households also supports the conclusion that the decline in the personal saving rate since 1984 is largely a consequence of capital gains on corporate equities.
    a. Is the purchase of corporate equities part of household consumption or saving? Explain your answer.
    b. Equities reap a capital gain in the same way that houses reap a capital gain. Does this mean that the purchase of equities is investment? If not, explain why it is not.

The Loanable Funds Market

18. Draw a graph to illustrate the effect of an increase in the demand for loanable funds and an even larger increase in the supply of loanable funds on the real interest rate and the equilibrium quantity of loanable funds.

19. Draw a graph to illustrate how an increase in the supply of loanable funds and a decrease in the demand for loanable funds can lower the real interest rate and leave the equilibrium quantity of loanable funds unchanged.

Use the following data to work Problems 20 and 21.

In 2012, the Lee family had disposable income of $80,000, wealth of $140,000, and an expected future income of $80,000 a year. At a real interest rate of 4 percent a year, the Lee family saves $15,000 a year; at a real interest rate of 6 percent a year, they save $20,000 a year; and at a real interest rate of 8 percent, they save $25,000 a year.

20. Draw a graph of the Lee family's supply of loanable funds curve.

21. In 2013, suppose that the stock market crashes and the default risk increases. Explain how this increase in default risk influences the Lee family's supply of loanable funds curve.

22. **Keystone Pipeline Clears a Hurdle**
    A judge in Lamar County, Texas, ruled that TransCanada has permission to build its Keystone XL pipeline from Cushing, Okla. to Port Arthur, Texas. TransCanada has said it will start building as soon as possible.
    Source: CNN, August 23, 2012

Show on a graph the effect of TransCanada going to the loanable funds market to finance the building of its pipeline. Explain the effect on the real interest rate, private saving, and investment.

23. The table sets out the data for an economy when the government's budget is balanced.

Real interest rate (percent per year)	Loanable funds demanded	Loanable funds supplied
	(trillions of 2009 dollars)	
2	8.0	4.0
3	7.0	5.0
4	6.0	6.0
5	5.0	7.0
6	4.0	8.0
7	3.0	9.0
8	2.0	10.0

a. Calculate the equilibrium real interest rate, investment, and private saving.

b. If planned saving decreases by $1 trillion at each real interest rate, explain the change in the real interest rate and investment.

c. If planned investment decreases by $1 trillion at each real interest rate, explain the change in saving and the real interest rate.

Government in the Loanable Funds Market

Use the following information to work Problems 24 and 25.

India's Economy Hits the Wall

At the start of 2008, India had an annual growth of 9 percent, huge consumer demand, and increasing investment. But by July 2008, India had large government deficits and rising interest rates. Economic growth is expected to fall to 7 percent by the end of 2008. A Goldman Sachs report suggests that India needs to lower the government's deficit and raise educational achievement.

Source: *BusinessWeek*, July 1, 2008

24. If the Indian government reduces its deficit and returns to a balanced budget, how will the demand for or supply of loanable funds in India change?

25. With economic growth forecasted to slow, future incomes are expected to fall. If other things remain the same, how will the demand or supply of loanable funds in India change?

26. **Federal Deficit Surges to $1.38 trillion through August**

House Republican Leader John Boehner of Ohio asks: When will the White House tackle these jaw-dropping deficits that pile more and more debt on future generations while it massively increases federal spending?

Source: *USA Today*, September 11, 2009

Explain the effect of the federal deficit and the mounting debt on U.S. economic growth.

Economics in the News

27. After you have studied *Economics in the News* on pp. 582–583, answer the following questions.

a. Why does the news article say that bond prices and interest rates move in opposite directions? Is it correct? Explain.

b. How does a government budget deficit influence the loanable funds market and why does a decrease in the deficit lower the real interest rate?

c. When an economic expansion gets going, what happens to the demand for loanable funds and the real interest rate?

d. If an expanding economy increases government tax revenue, how will that affect the loanable funds market and the real interest rate?

e. Looking at Fig. 1 on p. 583, what must have happened to either the demand for or the supply of loanable funds during 2011, 2012, and 2013?

28. **Investors Help the Rich Pay off Student Loans**

Innovative financial institutions are buying student loans, bundling the loans into securities, and selling the securities to people looking for a higher interest rate.

Source: CNN Money, July 28, 2014

a. How does the financial innovation described in the news clip influence the supply of and demand for loanable funds and the equilibrium real interest rate?

b. If the securitization of student loans lowers the real interest rate faced by students, how would you expect it to influence the demand for human capital and the equilibrium quantity of human capital?

25

MONEY, THE PRICE LEVEL, AND INFLATION

After studying this chapter,
you will be able to:

◆ Define money and describe its functions

◆ Explain the economic functions of banks

◆ Describe the structure and functions of the
Federal Reserve System (the Fed)

◆ Explain how the banking system creates money

◆ Explain what determines the quantity of money
and the nominal interest rate

◆ Explain how the quantity of money influences
the price level and the inflation rate

Money, like fire and the wheel, has been around for
a long time, and it has taken many forms. It was beads
made from shells for North American Indians and tobacco for early American colonists. Today, we use dollar bills or swipe a card or, in some places, tap a cell
phone. Are all these things money?

In this chapter, we study money, its functions, how
it gets created, how the Federal Reserve regulates its
quantity, and what happens when its quantity changes.
In *Economics in the News* at the end of the chapter,
we look at the extraordinary increase in the quantity of
money in recent years and the prospect it will begin to
shrink.

◆ What Is Money?

What do wampum, tobacco, and nickels and dimes have in common? They are all examples of **money**, which is defined as any commodity or token that is generally acceptable as a means of payment. A **means of payment** is a method of settling a debt. When a payment has been made, there is no remaining obligation between the parties to a transaction. So what wampum, tobacco, and nickels and dimes have in common is that they have served (or still do serve) as the means of payment. Money serves three other functions:

- Medium of exchange
- Unit of account
- Store of value

Medium of Exchange

A *medium of exchange* is any object that is generally accepted in exchange for goods and services. Without a medium of exchange, goods and services must be exchanged directly for other goods and services—an exchange called *barter*. Barter requires a *double coincidence of wants*, a situation that rarely occurs. For example, if you want a hamburger, you might offer a CD in exchange for it. But you must find someone who is selling hamburgers and wants your CD.

A medium of exchange overcomes the need for a double coincidence of wants. Money acts as a medium of exchange because people with something to sell will always accept money in exchange for it. But money isn't the only medium of exchange. You can buy with a credit card, but a credit card isn't money. It doesn't make a final payment, and the debt it creates must eventually be settled by using money.

Unit of Account

A *unit of account* is an agreed measure for stating the prices of goods and services. To get the most out of your budget, you have to figure out whether seeing one more movie is worth its opportunity cost. But that cost is not dollars and cents. It is the number of ice-cream cones, sodas, or cups of coffee that you must give up. It's easy to do such calculations when all these goods have prices in terms of dollars and cents (see Table 25.1). If the price of a movie is $8 and the price of a cappuccino is $4, you know right away that seeing one movie costs you 2 cappuccinos.

TABLE 25.1 The Unit of Account Function of Money Simplifies Price Comparisons

Good	Price in money units	Price in units of another good
Movie	$8.00 each	2 cappuccinos
Cappuccino	$4.00 each	2 ice-cream cones
Ice cream	$2.00 per cone	2 packs of jelly beans
Jelly beans	$1.00 per pack	2 sticks of gum
Gum	$0.50 per stick	

Money as a unit of account: The price of a movie is $8 and the price of a stick of gum is 50¢, so the opportunity cost of a movie is 16 sticks of gum ($8.00 ÷ 50¢ = 16).

No unit of account: You go to a movie theater and learn that the cost of seeing a movie is 2 cappuccinos. You go to a grocery store and learn that a pack of jelly beans costs 2 sticks of gum. But how many sticks of gum does seeing a movie cost you? To answer that question, you go to the coffee shop and find that a cappuccino costs 2 ice-cream cones. Now you head for the ice-cream shop, where an ice-cream cone costs 2 packs of jelly beans. Now you get out your pocket calculator: 1 movie costs 2 cappuccinos, or 4 ice-cream cones, or 8 packs of jelly beans, or 16 sticks of gum!

If jelly beans are $1 a pack, one movie costs 8 packs of jelly beans. You need only one calculation to figure out the opportunity cost of any pair of goods and services.

Imagine how troublesome it would be if your local movie theater posted its price as 2 cappuccinos, the coffee shop posted the price of a cappuccino as 2 ice-cream cones, the ice-cream shop posted the price of an ice-cream cone as 2 packs of jelly beans, and the grocery store priced a pack of jelly beans as 2 sticks of gum! Now how much running around and calculating will you have to do to find out how much that movie is going to cost you in terms of the cappuccinos, ice-cream cones, jelly beans, or gum that you must give up to see it? You get the answer for cappuccinos right away from the sign posted on the movie theater. But for all the other goods, you're going to have to visit many different stores to establish the price of each good in terms of another and then calculate the prices in units that are relevant for your own decision. The hassle of doing all this research might be enough to make a person swear off movies! You can see how much simpler it is if all the prices are expressed in dollars and cents.

Store of Value

Money is a *store of value* in the sense that it can be held and exchanged later for goods and services. If money were not a store of value, it could not serve as a means of payment.

Money is not alone in acting as a store of value. A house, a car, and a work of art are other examples.

The more stable the value of a commodity or token, the better it can act as a store of value and the more useful it is as money. No store of value has a completely stable value. The value of a house, a car, or a work of art fluctuates over time. The values of the commodities and tokens that are used as money also fluctuate over time.

Inflation lowers the value of money and the values of other commodities and tokens that are used as money. To make money as useful as possible as a store of value, a low inflation rate is needed.

Money in the United States Today

In the United States today, money consists of

- Currency
- Deposits at banks and other depository institutions

Currency The notes and coins held by individuals and businesses are known as **currency**. Notes are money because the government declares them so with the words "This note is legal tender for all debts, public and private." You can see these words on every dollar bill. Notes and coins *inside* banks are not counted as currency because they are not held by individuals and businesses.

Deposits Deposits of individuals and businesses at banks and other depository institutions, such as savings and loan associations, are also counted as money. Deposits are money because the owners of the deposits can use them to make payments.

Official Measures of Money Two official measures of money in the United States today are known as M1

and M2. **M1** consists of currency and traveler's checks plus checking deposits owned by individuals and businesses. M1 does *not* include currency held by banks, and it does not include currency and checking deposits owned by the U.S. government. **M2** consists of M1 plus time deposits, savings deposits, and money market mutual funds and other deposits.

ECONOMICS IN ACTION
Official Measures of U.S. Money

The figure shows the relative magnitudes of the items that make up M1 and M2. Notice that M2 is almost five times as large as M1 and that currency is a small part of our money.

	$ billion in June 2014
M2	11,423
Money market mutual funds and other deposits	631
Savings deposits	7,406
Time deposits	530
M1	2,857
Checking deposits	1,635
Currency and traveler's checks	1,222

Two Measures of Money

M1
- Currency and traveler's checks
- Checking deposits at commercial banks, savings and loan associations, savings banks, and credit unions

M2
- M1
- Time deposits
- Savings deposits
- Money market mutual funds and other deposits

Source of data: The Federal Reserve Board. The data are for June 2014.

Are M1 and M2 Really Money? Money is the means of payment. So the test of whether an asset is money is whether it serves as a means of payment. Currency passes the test. But what about deposits? Checking deposits are money because they can be transferred from one person to another by writing a check or using a debit card. Such a transfer of ownership is equivalent to handing over currency. Because M1 consists of currency plus checking deposits and each of these is a means of payment, *M1 is money.*

But what about M2? Some of the savings deposits in M2 are just as much a means of payment as the checking deposits in M1. You can use an ATM to get funds from your savings account to pay for your purchase at the grocery store or the gas station. But some savings deposits are not means of payment. These deposits are known as liquid assets. *Liquidity* is the property of being easily convertible into a means of payment without loss in value. Because the deposits in M2 that are not means of payment are quickly and easily converted into a means of payment—currency or checking deposits—they are counted as money.

Deposits Are Money but Checks Are Not In defining money, we include, along with currency, deposits at banks and other depository institutions. But we do not count the checks that people write as money. Why are deposits money and checks not?

To see why deposits are money but checks are not, think about what happens when Colleen buys some roller-blades for $100 from Rocky's Rollers. When Colleen goes to Rocky's shop, she has $500 in her deposit account at the Laser Bank. Rocky has $1,000 in his deposit account—at the same bank, as it happens. The deposits of these two people total $1,500. Colleen writes a check for $100. Rocky takes the check to the bank right away and deposits it. Rocky's bank balance rises from $1,000 to $1,100, and Colleen's balance falls from $500 to $400. The deposits of Colleen and Rocky still total $1,500. Rocky now has $100 more than before, and Colleen has $100 less.

This transaction has transferred money from Colleen to Rocky, but the check itself was never money. There wasn't an extra $100 of money while the check was in circulation. The check instructs the bank to transfer money from Colleen to Rocky.

If Colleen and Rocky use different banks, there is an extra step. Rocky's bank credits $100 to Rocky's account and then takes the check to a check-clearing center. The check is then sent to Colleen's bank, which pays Rocky's bank $100 and then debits Colleen's account $100. This process can take a few days, but the principles are the same as when two people use the same bank.

Credit Cards Are Not Money You've just seen that checks are not money, but what about credit cards? Isn't having a credit card in your wallet and presenting the card to pay for your roller-blades the same thing as using money? Why aren't credit cards somehow valued and counted as part of the quantity of money?

When you pay by check, you are frequently asked to prove your identity by showing your driver's license. It would never occur to you to think of your driver's license as money. It's just an ID card. A credit card is also an ID card, but one that lets you take out a loan at the instant you buy something. When you sign a credit card sales slip, you are saying, "I agree to pay for these goods when the credit card company bills me." Once you get your statement from the credit card company, you must make at least the minimum payment due. To make that payment, you need money—you need to have currency or a checking deposit to pay the credit card company. So although you use a credit card when you buy something, the credit card is not the *means of payment* and it is not money.

> **REVIEW QUIZ**

1 What makes something money? What functions does money perform? Why do you think packs of chewing gum don't serve as money?
2 What are the problems that arise when a commodity is used as money?
3 What are the main components of money in the United States today?
4 What are the official measures of money? Are all the measures really money?
5 Why are checks and credit cards not money?

Work these questions in Study Plan 25.1 and get instant feedback. Do a Key Terms Quiz.   MyEconLab

We've seen that the main component of money in the United States is deposits at banks and other depository institutions. Let's take a closer look at these institutions.

◆ Depository Institutions

A **depository institution** is a financial firm that takes deposits from households and firms. These deposits are components of M1 and M2. You will learn what these institutions are, what they do, the economic benefits they bring, how they are regulated, and how they have innovated to create new financial products.

Types of Depository Institutions

The deposits of three types of financial firms make up the nation's money. They are

- Commercial banks
- Thrift institutions
- Money market mutual funds

Commercial Banks A *commercial bank* is a firm that is licensed to receive deposits and make loans. In 2014, about 6,800 commercial banks operated in the United States but mergers make this number fall each year as small banks disappear and big banks expand.

A few very large commercial banks offer a wide range of banking services and have extensive international operations. The largest of these banks are JPMorgan Chase, Bank of America, Wells Fargo, and Citigroup. Most commercial banks are small and serve their regional and local communities.

The deposits of commercial banks represent 50 percent of M1 and 71 percent of M2.

Thrift Institutions Savings and loan associations, savings banks, and credit unions are *thrift institutions*.

Savings and Loan Association A *savings and loan association* (S&L) is a depository institution that receives deposits and makes personal, commercial, and home-purchase loans.

Savings Bank A *savings bank* is a depository institution that accepts savings deposits and makes mostly home-purchase loans.

Credit Union A *credit union* is a depository institution owned by a social or economic group, such as a firm's employees, that accepts savings deposits and makes mostly personal loans.

The deposits of the thrift institutions represent 8 percent of M1 and 13 percent of M2.

Money Market Mutual Funds A *money market mutual fund* is a fund operated by a financial institution that sells shares in the fund and holds assets such as U.S. Treasury bills and short-term commercial bills.

Money market mutual fund shares act like bank deposits. Shareholders can write checks on their money market mutual fund accounts, but there are restrictions on most of these accounts. For example, the minimum deposit accepted might be $2,500, and the smallest check a depositor is permitted to write might be $500.

Money market mutual funds do not feature in M1 and represent 6 percent of M2.

What Depository Institutions Do

Depository institutions provide services such as check clearing, account management, and credit cards, all of which provide an income from service fees.

But depository institutions earn most of their income by using the funds they receive from depositors to buy securities and make loans that earn a higher interest rate than that paid to depositors. In this activity, a depository institution must perform a balancing act weighing return against risk. To see this balancing act, we'll focus on the commercial banks.

A commercial bank puts the funds it receives from depositors and other funds that it borrows into three types of assets:

- Cash assets
- Securities
- Loans

Cash Assets A bank's cash assets consist of notes and coins in the bank's vault (called *vault cash*), a deposit account at the Federal Reserve (the Fed), and loans to other banks. The first two items, vault cash and deposits at the Fed, are the bank's **reserves**. Loans to other banks earn interest and the interest rate on these loans is called the **federal funds rate** and the Fed sets a target for this interest rate to influence the economy. We explain how and why on pp. 760–761.

A bank holds cash assets as a first line of funds to ensure that it is always able to meet depositors' currency withdrawals and make payments to other banks. In normal times, a bank kept about a half of one percent of deposits as cash assets. But today, these assets earn interest and their quantity has swollen to 28 percent of total deposits.

Securities A bank holds U.S. government Treasury bills and commercial bills that earn a low but risk-free return, and U.S. government bonds and mortgage-backed securities that earn a higher but riskier return. Securities would be sold and converted into cash assets if a bank ran short of reserves.

Loans A loan is an advance of funds for a specified period of time to businesses to finance investment and to households to finance the purchase of homes, cars, and other durable goods. The outstanding balances on credit card accounts are also bank loans. Loans are a bank's riskiest and highest-earning assets: They can't be converted into cash assets until they are due to be repaid, and some borrowers default and never repay. To spread the risk on loans, some get converted to securities.

Table 25.2 provides a snapshot of the sources and uses of funds of the commercial banks in June 2014 and serves as a summary of what they do.

Economic Benefits Provided by Depository Institutions

You've seen that a depository institution earns part of its profit because it pays a lower interest rate on deposits than what it earns on loans. What benefits do these institutions provide that make depositors willing to put up with a low interest rate and borrowers willing to pay a higher one?

Depository institutions provide four benefits:

- Create liquidity
- Pool risk
- Lower the cost of borrowing
- Lower the cost of monitoring borrowers

Create Liquidity Depository institutions create liquidity by *borrowing short and lending long*—taking deposits and standing ready to repay them on short notice or on demand and making loan commitments that run for terms of many years.

Pool Risk A loan might not be repaid—a default. If you lend to one person who defaults, you lose the entire amount loaned. If you lend to 1,000 people (through a bank) and one person defaults, you lose almost nothing. Depository institutions pool risk.

Lower the Cost of Borrowing Imagine there are no depository institutions and a firm is looking for $1 million to buy a new factory. It hunts around for several dozen people from whom to borrow the funds. Depository institutions lower the cost of this search. The firm gets its $1 million from a single institution that gets deposits from a large number of people but spreads the cost of this activity over many borrowers.

Lower the Cost of Monitoring Borrowers By monitoring borrowers, a lender can encourage good decisions that prevent defaults. But this activity is costly. Imagine how costly it would be if each household that lent money to a firm incurred the costs of monitoring that firm directly. Depository institutions can perform this task at a much lower cost.

How Depository Institutions Are Regulated

Depository institutions are engaged in a risky business, and a failure, especially of a large bank, would have damaging effects on the entire financial system and the economy. To make the risk of failure small, depository institutions are required to hold levels of reserves and owners' capital that equal or surpass ratios laid down by regulation. If a depository institution fails, its deposits are guaranteed up to $250,000 per depositor per bank by the *Federal Deposit Insurance Corporation* or FDIC. The FDIC can take over management of a bank that appears to be heading toward failure.

TABLE 25.2   Commercial Banks: Sources and Uses of Funds

	Funds (billions of dollars)	Percentage of deposits
Total funds	14,662	144.3
Sources		
Deposits	10,161	100.0
Borrowing	1,698	16.7
Own capital and other sources (net)	2,803	27.6
Uses		
Cash Assets	2,850	28.0
Securities	2,809	27.6
Loans	7,666	75.4
Other assets	1,337	13.2

Commercial banks get most of their funds from depositors and use most of them to make loans. In normal times, banks hold less than 1 percent of deposits as cash assets. But in 2014, cash assets were 28 percent of deposits, most of which were at the Fed earning a low interest rate.

Source of data: The Federal Reserve Board. The data are for June 2014.

◆ AT **ISSUE**

Fractional-Reserve Banking Versus 100 Percent Reserve Banking

Fractional-reserve banking, a system in which banks keep a fraction of their depositors' funds as a cash reserve and lend the rest, was invented by goldsmiths in sixteenth century Europe and is the only system in use today.

This system contrasts with **100 percent reserve banking**, a system in which banks keep the full amount of their depositors' funds as a cash reserve.

The 2008 global financial crisis raises the question: Should banks be required to keep 100 percent cash reserves to prevent them from failing and bringing recession?

Yes

- The most unrelenting advocates of 100 percent reserve banking are a group of economists known as the *Austrian School*, who say that fractional-reserve banking violates property rights.

- Because a deposit is owned by the depositor and not the bank, the bank has no legal right to lend the deposit to someone else.

- Mainstream economists Irving Fisher in the 1930s and Milton Friedman in the 1950s supported 100 percent reserve banking.

- They said it enables the central bank to exercise more precise control over the quantity of money as well as eliminating the risk of a bank running out of cash.

Irving Fisher of Yale University supported 100 percent reserve banking.

No

- The requirement to hold 100 percent reserves would prevent the banks making loans and lower their profits.

- Lower bank profits weaken rather than strengthen the banks.

- The demand for loans would be met by a supply from unregulated institutions, and they might be riskier than the current fractional-reserve banks.

- Nonetheless, banks do need to be regulated.

- The Financial Stability Board, based in Basel, Switzerland, has drawn up rules, called Basel III, which are designed to eliminate the risk that a major bank will fail.

- Mark Carney, Chairman of the Financial Stability Board and Governor of the Bank of England, wants all banks to adopt the Basel III principles, which increase the amount of a bank's own capital that must be held as a buffer against a fall in asset values.

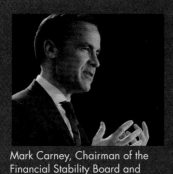

Mark Carney, Chairman of the Financial Stability Board and Governor of the Bank of England.

["Our destination should be one where financial institutions and markets play critical—and complementary— roles to support long-term economic prosperity. This requires institutions that are adequately capitalized, with sufficient liquidity buffers to manage shocks."
Mark Carney, remarks at the Institute of International Finance, Washington, D.C., September 25, 2011]

ECONOMICS IN ACTION

Commercial Banks Flush with Reserves

When Lehman Brothers (a New York investment bank) failed in October 2008, panic spread through financial markets. Banks that are normally happy to lend to each other overnight for an interest rate barely above the rate they can earn on safe Treasury bills lost confidence and the interest rate in this market shot up to 3 percentage points above the Treasury bill rate. Banks wanted to be safe and to hold cash and the Fed injected $1.5 trillion or 17.5 percent of deposits into the banks.

From 2009 through 2014, bank reserves grew to $3 trillion. The Fed pays interest on reserve balances, so the banks willingly hold these very large quantities of reserves.

The figure compares the commercial banks' sources and uses of funds (sources are liabilities and uses are assets) in 2008 with those in 2014.

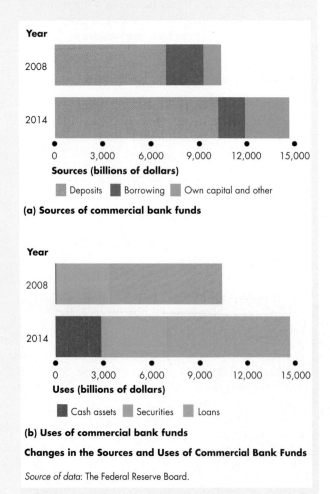

(a) Sources of commercial bank funds

(b) Uses of commercial bank funds

Changes in the Sources and Uses of Commercial Bank Funds

Source of data: The Federal Reserve Board.

Financial Innovation

In the pursuit of larger profit, depository institutions are constantly seeking ways to improve their products in a process called *financial innovation*.

During the late 1970s, a high inflation rate sent the interest rate on home-purchase loans to 15 percent a year. Traditional fixed interest rate mortgages became unprofitable and variable interest rate mortgages were introduced.

During the 2000s, when interest rates were low and depository institutions were flush with funds, sub-prime mortgages were developed. To avoid the risk of carrying these mortgages, mortgage-backed securities were developed. The original lending institution sold these securities, lowered their own exposure to risk, and obtained funds to make more loans.

The development of low-cost computing and communication brought financial innovations such as credit cards and daily interest deposit accounts.

Financial innovation has brought changes in the composition of money. Checking deposits at thrift institutions have become an increasing percentage of M1 while checking deposits at commercial banks have become a decreasing percentage. Savings deposits have decreased as a percentage of M2, while time deposits and money market mutual funds have expanded. Surprisingly, the use of currency has not fallen much.

◆ REVIEW QUIZ

1 What are depository institutions?
2 What are the functions of depository institutions?
3 How do depository institutions balance risk and return?
4 How do depository institutions create liquidity, pool risks, and lower the cost of borrowing?
5 How have depository institutions made innovations that have influenced the composition of money?

Work these questions in Study Plan 25.2 and get instant feedback. Do a Key Terms Quiz.   MyEconLab

You now know what money is. Your next task is to learn about the Federal Reserve System and the ways in which it can influence the quantity of money.

◆ The Federal Reserve System

The **Federal Reserve System** (usually called the **Fed**) is the central bank of the United States. A **central bank** is a bank's bank and a public authority that regulates a nation's depository institutions and conducts *monetary policy*, which means that it adjusts the quantity of money in circulation and influences interest rates.

We begin by describing the structure of the Fed.

The Structure of the Fed

Three key elements of the Fed's structure are

- The Board of Governors
- The regional Federal Reserve banks
- The Federal Open Market Committee

The Board of Governors A seven-member board appointed by the President of the United States and confirmed by the Senate governs the Fed. Members have 14-year (staggered) terms and one seat on the board becomes vacant every two years. The President appoints one board member as chairman for a 4-year renewable term—currently Janet Yellen, a former economics professor at UC Berkeley.

The Federal Reserve Banks The nation is divided into 12 Federal Reserve districts (shown in Fig. 25.1). Each district has a Federal Reserve Bank that provides check-clearing services to commercial banks and issues bank notes.

The Federal Reserve Bank of New York (known as the New York Fed) occupies a special place in the Federal Reserve System because it implements the Fed's policy decisions in the financial markets.

The Federal Open Market Committee The **Federal Open Market Committee** (FOMC) is the main policy-making organ of the Federal Reserve System. The FOMC consists of the following voting members:

- The chairman and the other six members of the Board of Governors
- The president of the Federal Reserve Bank of New York
- The presidents of the other regional Federal Reserve banks (of whom, on a yearly rotating basis, only four vote)

The FOMC meets approximately every six weeks to review the state of the economy and to decide the actions to be carried out by the New York Fed.

FIGURE 25.1   The Federal Reserve System

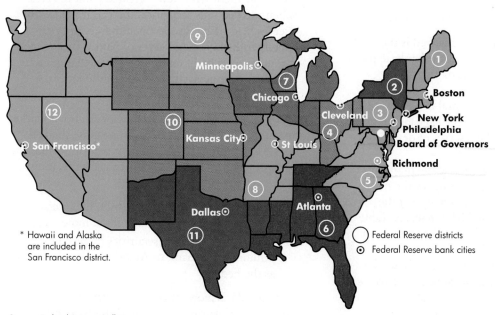

The nation is divided into 12 Federal Reserve districts, each having a Federal Reserve bank. (Some of the larger districts also have branch banks.) The Board of Governors of the Federal Reserve System is located in Washington, D.C.

* Hawaii and Alaska are included in the San Francisco district.

○ Federal Reserve districts
◉ Federal Reserve bank cities

Source: Federal Reserve Bulletin.

The Fed's Balance Sheet

The Fed influences the economy through the size and composition of its balance sheet—the assets that the Fed owns and the liabilities that it owes.

The Fed's Assets   The Fed has two main assets:

1. U.S. government securities
2. Mortgage-backed securities

U.S. Government Securities   The U.S. government securities held by the Fed are Treasury bonds. The Fed buys and sells these bonds in the *loanable funds market* (see pp. 573–574). The Fed does not buy bonds directly from the U.S. government.

Mortgage-Backed Securities   Traditionally, the Fed held only U.S. government securities. But in recent years, the Fed has purchased large quantities of mortgage-backed securities to increase the supply of *loanable funds* (see pp. 576–579).

The Fed's Liabilities   The Fed has two liabilities:

1. Currency
2. Reserves of depository institutions

Currency   Currency is the dollar bills that we use in our daily transactions. Some currency is in circulation and is a component of M1, and some is in banks and other depository institutions in their vaults and cash machines and is *vault cash*. (Coins are not a liability of the Fed. They are issued by the U.S. Mint.)

Reserves of Depository Institutions   The Fed is the banker for the banks and the reserves that the banks deposit at the Fed are a liability of the Fed.

The Monetary Base   The Fed's total liabilities make up the monetary base. That is, the **monetary base** is the sum of currency and the reserves of depository institutions.

The Fed's assets are the sources of the monetary base. They are also called the backing for the monetary base. The Fed's liabilities are the uses of the monetary base as currency and bank reserves. Table 25.3 provides a snapshot of the sources and uses of the monetary base in June 2014.

When the Fed changes the monetary base, the quantity of money and interest rate change. You're going to see how these changes come about later in this chapter. First, we'll look at the Fed's tools that enable it to influence money and interest rates.

TABLE 25.3   The Sources and Uses of the Monetary Base

Sources (billions of dollars)		Uses (billions of dollars)	
U.S. government securities	2,330	Currency	1,280
Mortgage-backed securities	1,618	Reserves of depository institutions	2,668
Monetary base	3,948	Monetary base	3,948

Source of data: The Federal Reserve Board. The data are for June 2014.

The Fed's Policy Tools

The Fed influences the quantity of money and interest rates by adjusting the quantity of reserves available to the banks and the reserves the banks must hold. To do this, the Fed manipulates three tools:

- Open market operations
- Last resort loans
- Required reserve ratio

Open Market Operations   An **open market operation** is the purchase or sale of securities by the Fed in the *loanable funds market*. When the Fed buys securities, it pays for them with newly created bank reserves. When the Fed sells securities, the Fed is paid with reserves held by banks. So open market operations directly influence the reserves of banks. By changing the quantity of bank reserves, the Fed changes the quantity of monetary base, which influences the quantity of money.

An Open Market Purchase   To see how an open market operation changes bank reserves, suppose the Fed buys $100 million of government securities from the Bank of America. When the Fed makes this transaction, two things happen:

1. The Bank of America has $100 million less securities, and the Fed has $100 million more securities.
2. The Fed pays for the securities by placing $100 million in the Bank of America's deposit account at the Fed.

Figure 25.2 shows the effects of these actions on the balance sheets of the Fed and the Bank of America. Ownership of the securities passes from the

FIGURE 25.2   The Fed Buys Securities in the Open Market

Federal Reserve Bank of New York

Assets (millions)		Liabilities (millions)
Securities +$100	Reserves of Bank of America	+$100
The Federal Reserve Bank of New York buys securities from a bank ...	... and pays for the securities by increasing the reserves of the bank	

Bank of America

Assets (millions)		Liabilities (millions)
Securities −$100		
Reserves +$100		

When the Fed buys securities in the open market, it creates bank reserves. The Fed's assets and liabilities increase, and the Bank of America exchanges securities for reserves.

————— MyEconLab Animation —————

Bank of America to the Fed, so the Bank of America's assets decrease by $100 million and the Fed's assets increase by $100 million, as shown by the blue arrow running from the Bank of America to the Fed.

The Fed pays for the securities by placing $100 million in the Bank of America's reserve account at the Fed, as shown by the green arrow running from the Fed to the Bank of America.

The Fed's assets and liabilities increase by $100 million. The Bank of America's total assets are unchanged: It sold securities to increase its reserves.

An Open Market Sale If the Fed sells $100 million of government securities to the Bank of America in the open market,

1. The Bank of America has $100 million ~~more~~ securities, and the Fed has $100 million less securities.
2. The Bank of America pays for the securities by using $100 million of its reserve deposit at the Fed.

You can follow the effects of these actions on the balance sheets of the Fed and the Bank of America by reversing the arrows and the plus and minus signs in Fig. 25.2. Ownership of the securities passes from the Fed to the Bank of America, so the Fed's assets decrease by $100 million and the Bank of America's assets increase by $100 million.

ECONOMICS IN ACTION
The Fed's Balance Sheet Explodes

The Fed's balance sheet underwent some remarkable changes following the financial crisis of 2007–2008 and the recession that the crisis triggered. The figure shows the effects of these changes on the size and composition of the monetary base by comparing the situation in 2014 with that before the financial crisis began in late 2007.

In a normal year, 2007, the Fed's holding of U.S. government securities is almost as large as the monetary base and the monetary base is composed of almost all currency.

But between 2007 and 2014 the Fed more than quadrupled the monetary base. Almost all of this increase was composed of bank reserves.

When, and how quickly, to unwind the large increase in the monetary base and bank reserves is an ongoing source of challenge for the Fed.

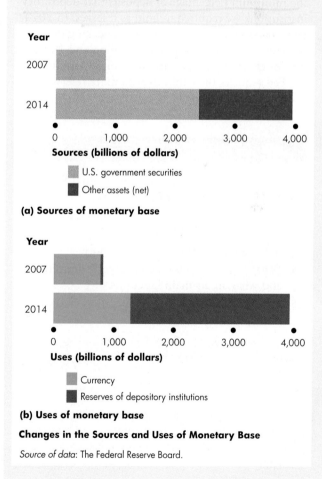

(a) Sources of monetary base

(b) Uses of monetary base

Changes in the Sources and Uses of Monetary Base

Source of data: The Federal Reserve Board.

The Bank of America uses $100 million of its reserves to pay for the securities.

Both the Fed's assets and liabilities decrease by $100 million. The Bank of America's total assets are unchanged: It has used reserves to buy securities.

The New York Fed conducts these open-market transactions on directions from the FOMC.

Last Resort Loans The Fed is the **lender of last resort**, which means that if a bank is short of reserves, it can borrow from the Fed. But the Fed sets the interest rate on last resort loans and this interest rate is called the *discount rate*.

During the period since August 2007 when the first effects of the financial crisis started to be felt, the Fed has been especially active as lender of last resort and, with the U.S. Treasury, has created a number of new lending facilities and initiatives to prevent banks from failing.

Required Reserve Ratio The **required reserve ratio** is the minimum percentage of deposits that depository institutions are required to hold as reserves. In 2014, required reserves were 3 percent of checking deposits between $13.3 million and $89 million and 10 percent of checking deposits in excess of $89 million. If the Fed requires the banks to hold more reserves, they must cut their lending.

◆ REVIEW QUIZ

1 What is the central bank of the United States and what functions does it perform?
2 What is the monetary base and how does it relate to the Fed's balance sheet?
3 What are the Fed's three policy tools?
4 What is the Federal Open Market Committee and what are its main functions?
5 How does an open market operation change the monetary base?

Work these questions in Study Plan 25.3 and get instant feedback. Do a Key Terms Quiz. MyEconLab

Next, we're going to see how the banking system—the banks and the Fed—creates money and how the quantity of money changes when the Fed changes the monetary base.

◆ How Banks Create Money

Banks create money. But this doesn't mean that they have smoke-filled back rooms in which counterfeiters are busily working. Remember, money is both currency and bank deposits. What banks create is deposits, and they do so by making loans.

Creating Deposits by Making Loans

The easiest way to see that banks create deposits is to think about what happens when Andy, who has a Visa card issued by Citibank, uses his card to buy a tank of gas from Chevron. When Andy swipes his card, two financial transactions occur. First, Andy takes a loan from Citibank and obligates himself to repay the loan at a later date. Second, a message is transmitted to Chevron's bank and the bank credits Chevron's account with the amount of Andy's purchase (minus the bank's commission).

For now, let's assume that Chevron, like Andy, banks at Citibank so that the two transactions we've just described both occur at the one bank.

You can see that these transactions have created a bank deposit and a loan. Andy has increased the size of his loan (his credit card balance), and Chevron has increased the size of its bank deposit. Because bank deposits are money, Citibank has created money.

If, as we've just assumed, Andy and Chevron use the same bank, no further transactions take place. But if two banks are involved, there is another transaction. To see this additional transaction and its effects, assume that Chevron's bank is Bank of America. To fully settle the payment for Andy's gas purchase, Citibank must pay Bank of America.

To make this payment, Citibank uses its reserves. Citibank's reserves decrease by the amount of its loan to Andy; Bank of America's reserves increase by the amount that Chevron's deposit increases. Payments like this one between the banks are made at the end of the business day. So, at the end of the business day the banking system as a whole has an increase in loans and deposits but no change in reserves.

Three factors limit the quantity of loans and deposits that the banking system can create through transactions like Andy's. They are

- The monetary base
- Desired reserves
- Desired currency holding

The Monetary Base You've seen that the *monetary base* is the sum of Federal Reserve notes, coins, and banks' deposits at the Fed. The size of the monetary base limits the total quantity of money that the banking system can create. The reason is that banks have a desired level of reserves, households and firms have a desired holding of currency, and both of these desired holdings of the monetary base depend on the quantity of deposits.

Desired Reserves A bank's *desired reserves* are the reserves that it *plans* to hold. They contrast with a bank's *required reserves*, which is the minimum quantity of reserves that a bank *must* hold.

The quantity of desired reserves depends on the level of deposits and is determined by the **desired reserve ratio**—the ratio of reserves to deposits that the banks *plan* to hold. The *desired* reserve ratio exceeds the *required* reserve ratio by an amount that the banks determine to be prudent on the basis of their daily business requirements and in the light of the current outlook in financial markets.

Desired Currency Holding The proportions of money held as currency and bank deposits—the ratio of currency to deposits—depend on how households and firms choose to make payments: Whether they plan to use currency or debit cards and checks.

Choices about how to make payments change slowly so the ratio of desired currency to deposits also changes slowly, and at any given time this ratio is fixed. If bank deposits increase, desired currency holding also increases. For this reason, when banks make loans that increase deposits, some currency leaves the banks—the banking system leaks reserves. We call the leakage of bank reserves into currency the *currency drain*, and we call the ratio of currency to deposits the **currency drain ratio**.

We've sketched the way that a loan creates a deposit and described the three factors that limit the amount of loans and deposits that can be created. We're now going to examine the money creation process more closely and discover a money multiplier.

The Money Creation Process

The money creation process begins with an increase in the monetary base, which occurs if the Fed conducts an open market operation in which it buys securities from banks and other institutions. The Fed pays for the securities it buys with newly created bank reserves.

When the Fed buys securities from a bank, the bank's reserves increase but its deposits don't change. So the bank has excess reserves. A bank's **excess reserves** are its actual reserves minus its desired reserves.

When a bank has excess reserves, it makes loans and creates deposits. When the entire banking system has excess reserves, total loans and deposits increase and the quantity of money increases.

One bank can make a loan and get rid of excess reserves. But the banking system as a whole can't get rid of excess reserves so easily. When the banks make loans and create deposits, the extra deposits lower excess reserves for two reasons. First, the increase in deposits increases desired reserves. Second, a currency drain decreases total reserves. But excess reserves don't completely disappear. So the banks lend some more and the process repeats.

As the process of making loans and increasing deposits repeats, desired reserves increase, total reserves decrease through the currency drain, and eventually enough new deposits have been created to use all the new monetary base.

Figure 25.3 summarizes one round in the process we've just described. The sequence has the following eight steps:

1. Banks have excess reserves.
2. Banks lend excess reserves.
3. The quantity of money increases.
4. New money is used to make payments.
5. Some of the new money remains on deposit.
6. Some of the new money is a *currency drain*.
7. Desired reserves increase because deposits have increased.
8. Excess reserves decrease.

If the Fed *sells* securities in an open market operation, then banks have negative excess reserves—they are short of reserves. When the banks are short of reserves, loans and deposits decrease and the process we've described above works in a downward direction until desired reserves plus desired currency holding has decreased by an amount equal to the decrease in monetary base.

A money multiplier determines the change in the quantity of money that results from a change in the monetary base.

FIGURE 25.3 How the Banking System Creates Money by Making Loans

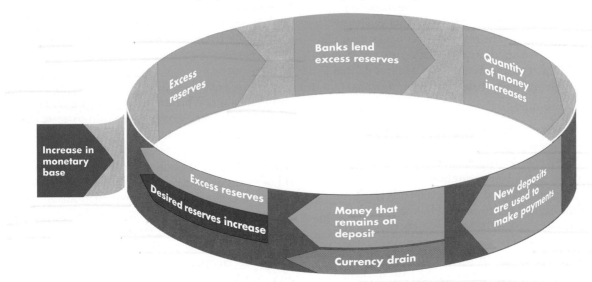

The Federal Reserve increases the monetary base, which increases bank reserves and creates excess reserves. Banks lend the excess reserves, which creates new deposits. The quantity of money increases. New deposits are used to make payments. Some of the new money remains on deposit at banks and some leaves the banks in a currency drain. The increase in bank deposits increases banks' desired reserves. But the banks still have excess reserves, though less than before. The process repeats until excess reserves have been eliminated.

MyEconLab Animation

ECONOMICS IN ACTION

The Variable Money Multipliers

We can measure the money multiplier, other things remaining the same, as the ratio of the quantity of money (M1 or M2) to the monetary base. In normal times, these ratios (and the money multipliers) change slowly.

In the early 1990s, the M1 multiplier—the ratio of M1 to the monetary base—was about 3 and the M2 multiplier—the ratio of M2 to the monetary base—was about 12. Through the 1990s and 2000s, the currency drain ratio gradually increased and the money multipliers decreased. By 2007, the M1 multiplier was 2 and the M2 multiplier was 9.

Since 2008, the unprecedented increase in the monetary base has been willingly held by banks as reserves. In an environment of uncertainty, desired reserves increased by a similar amount to the increase in actual reserves. The quantity of money changed by much less than the change in monetary base.

The Money Multiplier

The **money multiplier** is the ratio of the change in the quantity of money to the change in monetary base. For example, if a $1 million increase in the monetary base increases the quantity of money by $2.5 million, then the money multiplier is 2.5.

The smaller the banks' desired reserve ratio and the smaller the currency drain ratio, the larger is the money multiplier. (See the Mathematical Note on pp. 612–613 for details on the money multiplier).

◆ REVIEW QUIZ

1 How do banks create money?
2 What limits the quantity of money that the banking system can create?
3 A bank manager tells you that she doesn't create money. She just lends the money that people deposit. Explain why she's wrong.

Work these questions in Study Plan 25.4 and get instant feedback. Do a Key Terms Quiz. MyEconLab

ECONOMICS IN THE NEWS

A Massive Open Market Operation

QE2 Is No Silver Bullet

The Federal Reserve's $600 billion bond-buying pro-
gram initiated last year, known as the second round
of quantitative easing or QE2, will end on schedule
this month with a mixed legacy, having proved to be
neither the economy's needed elixir nor the scourge
that critics describe.

Source: *The Wall Street Journal*, June 22, 2011

THE QUESTIONS

- What is *quantitative easing*? What transactions does
  the Fed undertake in a period of quantitative easing?

- How did QE2 affect the quantity of reserves,
  loans, and deposits of the commercial banks?

- Why was QE2 neither "elixir" nor "scourge"?

THE ANSWERS

- *Quantitative easing* or QE is an open market purchase of securities by the Fed. QE2 was the purchase of $600 billion of long-term securities from
  businesses, pension funds, and other holders.

- The purchase was an open market operation similar to that described in Fig. 25.2 on p. 599 but
  with one more step because the Fed buys the securities from holders who are not banks.

- The figure illustrates the QE2 open market operation and the extra step in the chain of transactions.

- When the Fed buys securities, its assets increase.
  Its liabilities also increase because it creates monetary base to pay for the securities.

- For the businesses that sell bonds, their assets
  change: Securities decrease and bank deposits
  increase.

- For the commercial banks, deposit liabilities
  increase and reserves, an asset, also increase.

- You saw on p. 596 that the commercial banks are
  flush with reserves. They held on to the increase in
  reserves created by QE2. There was no multiplier
  effect on loans and deposits.

- QE2 would have been an "elixir" if it had resulted
  in a boost to bank lending, business investment,
  and economic expansion. It didn't have these
  effects mainly because the banks held on to the
  newly created reserves.

The New York Fed building where open market operations
are conducted.

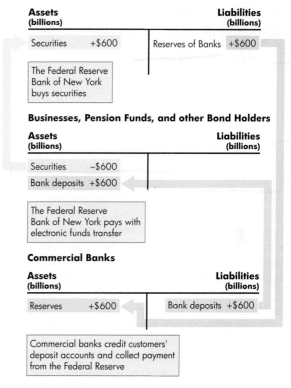

The QE2 Transactions

- QE2 would have been a "scourge" if it had caused
  inflation. That didn't happen.

- *Economics in the News* on pp. 610–611 looks at some
  other effects of QE2.

MyEconLab More Economics in the News

◆ The Money Market

There is no limit to the amount of money we would like to *receive* in payment for our labor or as interest on our savings. But there *is* a limit to how big an inventory of money we would like to *hold* and neither spend nor use to buy assets that generate an income. The *quantity of money demanded* is the inventory of money that people plan to hold on any given day. It is the quantity of money in our wallets and in our deposit accounts at banks. The quantity of money held must equal the quantity supplied, and the forces that bring about this equality in the money market have powerful effects on the economy, as you will see in the rest of this chapter.

But first, we need to explain what determines the amount of money that people plan to hold.

The Influences on Money Holding

The quantity of money that people plan to hold depends on four main factors:

- The price level
- The *nominal* interest rate
- Real GDP
- Financial innovation

The Price Level The quantity of money measured in dollars is *nominal money*. The quantity of nominal money demanded is proportional to the price level, other things remaining the same. If the price level rises by 10 percent, people hold 10 percent more nominal money than before, other things remaining the same. If you hold $20 to buy your weekly movies and soda, you will increase your money holding to $22 if the prices of movies and soda—and your wage rate—increase by 10 percent.

The quantity of money measured in constant dollars (for example, in 2009 dollars) is real money. *Real money* is equal to nominal money divided by the price level and is the quantity of money measured in terms of what it will buy. In the above example, when the price level rises by 10 percent and you increase your money holding by 10 percent, your *real* money holding is constant. Your $22 at the new price level buys the same quantity of goods and is the same quantity of *real money* as your $20 at the original price level. The quantity of real money demanded is independent of the price level.

The *Nominal* Interest Rate A fundamental principle of economics is that as the opportunity cost of something increases, people try to find substitutes for it. Money is no exception. The higher the opportunity cost of holding money, other things remaining the same, the smaller is the quantity of real money demanded. The nominal interest rate on other assets minus the nominal interest rate on money is the opportunity cost of holding money.

The interest rate that you earn on currency and checking deposits is zero. So the opportunity cost of holding these items is the nominal interest rate on other assets such as a savings bond or Treasury bill. By holding money instead, you forgo the interest that you otherwise would have received.

Money loses value because of inflation, so why isn't the inflation rate part of the cost of holding money? It is. Other things remaining the same, the higher the expected inflation rate, the higher is the nominal interest rate.

Real GDP The quantity of money that households and firms plan to hold depends on the amount they are spending. The quantity of money demanded in the economy as a whole depends on aggregate expenditure—real GDP.

Again, suppose that you hold an average of $20 to finance your weekly purchases of movies and soda. Now imagine that the prices of these goods and of all other goods remain constant but that your income increases. As a consequence, you now buy more goods and services and you also keep a larger amount of money on hand to finance your higher volume of expenditure.

Financial Innovation Technological change and the arrival of new financial products influence the quantity of money held. Financial innovations include

1. Daily interest checking deposits
2. Automatic transfers between checking and saving deposits
3. Automatic teller machines
4. Credit cards and debit cards
5. Internet banking and bill paying

These innovations have occurred because of the development of computing power that has lowered the cost of calculations and record keeping.

We summarize the effects of the influences on money holding by using a demand for money curve.

The Demand for Money

The **demand for money** is the relationship between the quantity of real money demanded and the nominal interest rate when all other influences on the amount of money that people wish to hold remain the same.

Figure 25.4 shows a demand for money curve, *MD*. When the interest rate rises, other things remaining the same, the opportunity cost of holding money rises and the quantity of real money demanded decreases—there is a movement up along the demand for money curve. Similarly, when the interest rate falls, the opportunity cost of holding money falls, and the quantity of real money demanded increases—there is a movement down along the demand for money curve.

When any influence on money holding other than the interest rate changes, there is a change in the demand for money and the demand for money curve shifts. Let's study these shifts.

Shifts in the Demand for Money Curve

A change in real GDP or financial innovation changes the demand for money and shifts the demand for money curve.

Figure 25.5 illustrates the change in the demand for money. A decrease in real GDP decreases the demand for money and shifts the demand for money curve leftward from MD_0 to MD_1. An increase in real GDP has the opposite effect: It increases the demand for money and shifts the demand for money curve rightward from MD_0 to MD_2.

The influence of financial innovation on the demand for money curve is more complicated. It decreases the demand for currency and might increase the demand for some types of deposits and decrease the demand for others. But generally, financial innovation decreases the demand for money.

Changes in real GDP and financial innovation have brought large shifts in the demand for money in the United States.

FIGURE 25.4   The Demand for Money

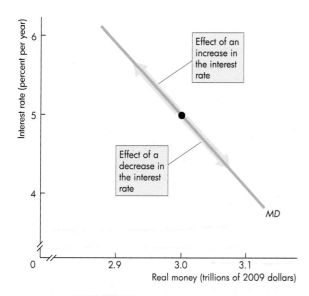

The demand for money curve, *MD*, shows the relationship between the quantity of real money that people plan to hold and the nominal interest rate, other things remaining the same. The interest rate is the opportunity cost of holding money. A change in the interest rate brings a movement along the demand for money curve.

MyEconLab Animation

FIGURE 25.5   Changes in the Demand for Money

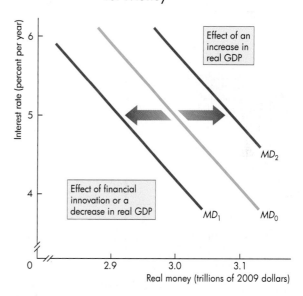

A decrease in real GDP decreases the demand for money. The demand for money curve shifts leftward from MD_0 to MD_1. An increase in real GDP increases the demand for money. The demand for money curve shifts rightward from MD_0 to MD_2. Financial innovation generally decreases the demand for money.

MyEconLab Animation

Money Market Equilibrium

You now know what determines the demand for money, and you've seen how the banking system creates money. Let's now see how the money market reaches an equilibrium.

Money market equilibrium occurs when the quantity of money demanded equals the quantity of money supplied. The adjustments that occur to bring money market equilibrium are fundamentally different in the short run and the long run.

Short-Run Equilibrium The quantity of money supplied is determined by the actions of the banks and the Fed. As the Fed adjusts the quantity of money, the interest rate changes.

In Fig. 25.6, the Fed uses open market operations to make the quantity of real money supplied equal to $3.0 trillion and the supply of money curve MS. With demand for money curve MD, the equilibrium interest rate is 5 percent a year.

If the interest rate were 4 percent a year, people would want to hold more money than is available.

FIGURE 25.6   Money Market Equilibrium

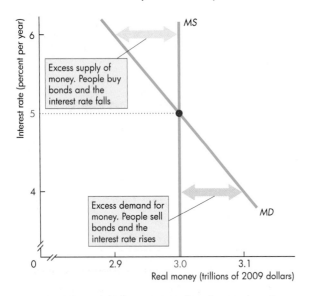

Money market equilibrium occurs when the quantity of money demanded equals the quantity supplied. In the short run, real GDP determines the demand for money curve, MD, and the Fed determines the quantity of real money supplied and the supply of money curve, MS. The interest rate adjusts to achieve equilibrium, here 5 percent a year.

———— MyEconLab Animation and Draw Graph ————

They would sell bonds, bid down their price, and the interest rate would rise. If the interest rate were 6 percent a year, people would want to hold less money than is available. They would buy bonds, bid up their price, and the interest rate would fall.

The Short-Run Effect of a Change in the Quantity of Money Starting from a short-run equilibrium, if the Fed increases the quantity of money, people find themselves holding more money than the quantity demanded. With a surplus of money holding, people enter the loanable funds market and buy bonds. The increase in demand for bonds raises the price of a bond and lowers the interest rate (refresh your memory by looking at Chapter 24, p. 572).

If the Fed decreases the quantity of money, people find themselves holding less money than the quantity demanded. They now enter the loanable funds market to sell bonds. The decrease in the demand for bonds lowers their price and raises the interest rate.

Figure 25.7 illustrates the effects of the changes in the quantity of money that we've just described. When the supply of money curve shifts rightward from MS_0 to MS_1, the interest rate falls to 4 percent a year; when the supply of money curve shifts leftward to MS_2, the interest rate rises to 6 percent a year.

Long-Run Equilibrium You've just seen how the nominal interest rate is determined in the money market at the level that makes the quantity of money demanded equal the quantity supplied by the Fed. You learned in Chapter 24 (on p. 577) that the real interest rate is determined in the loanable funds market at the level that makes the quantity of loanable funds demanded equal the quantity of loanable funds supplied. You also learned in Chapter 24 (on p. 574) that the real interest rate equals the nominal interest rate minus the inflation rate.

When the inflation rate equals the expected (or forecasted) inflation rate and when real GDP equals potential GDP, the money market, the loanable funds market, the goods market, and the labor market are in long-run equilibrium—the economy is in long-run equilibrium.

If in long-run equilibrium, the Fed increases the quantity of money, eventually a new long-run equilibrium is reached in which nothing real has changed. Real GDP, employment, the real quantity of money, and the real interest rate all return to their original levels. But something does change the price level. The price level rises by the same percentage as the rise

FIGURE 25.7   A Change in the Quantity of Money

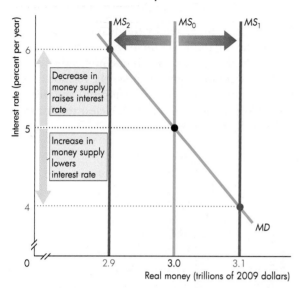

An increase in the quantity of money increases the supply of money. The supply of money curve shifts from MS_0 to MS_1 and the interest rate falls. A decrease in the quantity of money decreases the supply of money. The supply of money curve shifts from MS_0 to MS_2 and the interest rate rises.

MyEconLab Animation and Draw Graph

in the quantity of money. Why does this outcome occur in the long run?

The reason is that real GDP and employment are determined by the demand for labor, the supply of labor, and the production function—the real forces described in Chapter 23 (pp. 546–548); and the real interest rate is determined by the demand for and supply of (real) loanable funds—the real forces described in Chapter 24 (pp. 575–577). The only variable that is free to respond to a change in the supply of money in the long run is the price level. The price level adjusts to make the quantity of real money supplied equal to the quantity demanded.

So when the Fed changes the nominal quantity of money, in the long run the price level changes by a percentage equal to the percentage change in the quantity of nominal money. In the long run, the change in the price level is proportional to the change in the quantity of money.

The Transition from the Short Run to the Long Run

How does the economy move from the first short-run response to an increase in the quantity of money to the long-run response?

The adjustment process is lengthy and complex. Here, we'll only provide a sketch of the process. A more thorough account must wait until you've studied Chapter 27.

We start out in long-run equilibrium and the Fed increases the quantity of money by 10 percent. Here are the steps in what happens next.

First, the nominal interest rate falls (just like you saw on p. 606 and in Fig. 25.6). The real interest rate falls too, as people try to get rid of their excess money holdings and buy bonds.

With a lower real interest rate, people want to borrow and spend more. Firms want to borrow to invest and households want to borrow to invest in bigger homes or to buy more consumer goods.

The increase in the demand for goods cannot be met by an increase in supply because the economy is already at full employment. So there is a general shortage of all kinds of goods and services.

The shortage of goods and services forces the price level to rise.

As the price level rises, the real quantity of money decreases. The decrease in the quantity of real money raises the nominal interest rate and the real interest rate. As the interest rate rises, spending plans are cut back, and eventually the original full-employment equilibrium is restored. At the new long-run equilibrium, the price level has risen by 10 percent and nothing real has changed.

◆ REVIEW QUIZ

1 What are the main influences on the quantity of real money that people and businesses plan to hold?

2 Show the effects of a change in the nominal interest rate and a change in real GDP using the demand for money curve.

3 How is money market equilibrium determined in the short run?

4 How does a change in the quantity of money change the interest rate in the short run?

5 How does a change in the quantity of money change the interest rate in the long run?

Work these questions in Study Plan 25.5 and get instant feedback. Do a Key Terms Quiz.   MyEconLab

Let's explore the long-run link between money and the price level a bit further.

◆ The Quantity Theory of Money

In the long run, the price level adjusts to make the quantity of real money demanded equal the quantity supplied. A special theory of the price level and inflation—the quantity theory of money—explains this long-run adjustment of the price level.

The **quantity theory of money** is the proposition that in the long run, an increase in the quantity of money brings an equal percentage increase in the price level. To explain the quantity theory of money, we first need to define *the velocity of circulation*.

The **velocity of circulation** is the average number of times a dollar of money is used annually to buy the goods and services that make up GDP. But GDP equals the price level (P) multiplied by *real* GDP (Y). That is,

$$GDP = PY.$$

Call the quantity of money M. The velocity of circulation, V, is determined by the equation

$$V = PY/M.$$

For example, if GDP is $1,000 billion ($PY = $1,000 billion) and the quantity of money is $250 billion, then the velocity of circulation is 4.

From the definition of the velocity of circulation, the *equation of exchange* tells us how M, V, P, and Y are connected. This equation is

$$MV = PY.$$

Given the definition of the velocity of circulation, the equation of exchange is always true—it is true by definition. It becomes the quantity theory of money if the quantity of money does not influence the velocity of circulation or real GDP. In this case, the equation of exchange tells us that in the long run, the price level is determined by the quantity of money. That is,

$$P = M(V/Y),$$

where (V/Y) is independent of M. So a change in M brings a proportional change in P.

We can also express the equation of exchange in growth rates,[1] in which form it states that

| Money growth rate | + | Rate of velocity change | = | Inflation rate | + | Real GDP growth rate |

ECONOMICS IN ACTION

Does the Quantity Theory Work?

On average, as predicted by the quantity theory of money, the inflation rate fluctuates in line with fluctuations in the money growth rate minus the real GDP growth rate. Figure 1 shows the relationship between money growth (M2 definition) and inflation in the United States. You can see a clear relationship between the two variables.

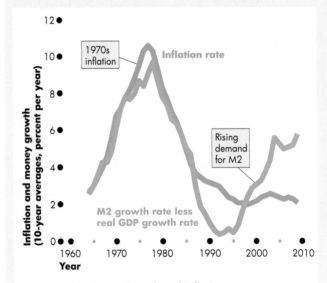

Figure 1 U.S. Money Growth and Inflation
Sources of data: Federal Reserve and Bureau of Labor Statistics.

Solving this equation for the inflation rate gives

| Inflation rate | = | Money growth rate | + | Rate of velocity change | − | Real GDP growth rate |

In the long run, the rate of velocity change is not influenced by the money growth rate. More strongly, in the long run, the rate of velocity change is

---

[1]To obtain this equation, begin with

$$MV = PY.$$

Then changes in these variables are related by the equation

$$V\Delta M + M\Delta V = Y\Delta P + P\Delta Y.$$

Divide this equation by the equation of exchange to obtain

$$\Delta M/M + \Delta V/V = \Delta P/P + \Delta Y/Y.$$

The term $\Delta M/M$ is the money growth rate, $\Delta V/V$ is the rate of velocity change, $\Delta P/P$ is the inflation rate, and $\Delta Y/Y$ is the real GDP growth rate.

International data also support the quantity theory. Figure 2 shows a scatter diagram of the inflation rate and the money growth rate in 134 countries and Fig. 3 shows the inflation rate and money growth rate in countries with inflation rates below 20 percent a year. You can see a general tendency for money growth and inflation to be correlated, but the quantity theory (the red line) does not predict inflation precisely.

The correlation between money growth and inflation isn't perfect, and the correlation does not tell us that money growth *causes* inflation. Money growth might cause inflation; inflation might cause money growth; or some third variable might cause both inflation and money growth. Other evidence does confirm, though, that causation runs from money growth to inflation.

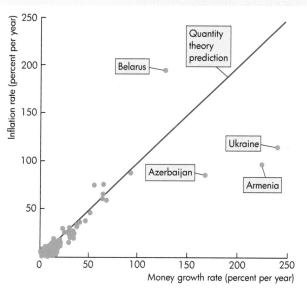

Figure 2 134 Countries: 1990–2005

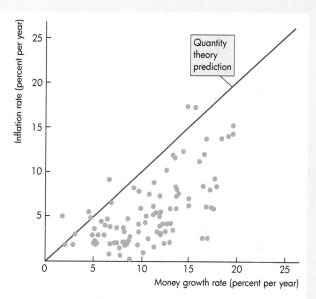

Figure 3 Lower-Inflation Countries: 1990–2005

Sources of data: International Financial Statistics Yearbook, 2008, and International Monetary Fund, World Economic Outlook, October 2008.

approximately zero. With this assumption, the inflation rate in the long run is determined as

$$\text{Inflation rate} = \text{Money growth rate} - \text{Real GDP growth rate}.$$

In the long run, fluctuations in the money growth rate minus the real GDP growth rate bring equal fluctuations in the inflation rate.

Also, in the long run, with the economy at full employment, real GDP equals potential GDP, so the real GDP growth rate equals the potential GDP growth rate. This growth rate might be influenced by inflation, but the influence is most likely small and the quantity theory assumes that it is zero. So the real GDP growth rate is given and doesn't change when the money growth rate changes—inflation is correlated with money growth.

◆ REVIEW QUIZ

1 What is the quantity theory of money?
2 How is the velocity of circulation calculated?
3 What is the equation of exchange?
4 Does the quantity theory correctly predict the effects of money growth on inflation?

Work these questions in Study Plan 25.6 and get instant feedback. Do a Key Terms Quiz. MyEconLab

◆ You now know what money is, how the banks create it, and how the quantity of money influences the nominal interest rate in the short run and the price level in the long run. *Economics in the News* on pp. 610–611 looks at what will happen to the quantity of money when interest rates begin to rise.

Money and the Interest Rate

U.S. Banks Braced for Large Deposit Outflows

The Financial Times
July 30, 2014

U.S. banks are steeling themselves for the possibility of losing as much as $1trillion in deposits as the Federal Reserve reverses its emergency economic policies and raises interest rates.

JPMorgan Chase, the biggest U.S. bank by deposits, has estimated that money funds may withdraw $100 billion in deposits in the second half of next year as the Fed uses a new tool to help wind down its asset purchase program and normalize rates.

Other banks including Citigroup, Bank of New York Mellon, and PNC Financial Services have also said they are trying to gauge the potential effect of the Fed's exit on institutional or retail depositors who might choose to switch to higher interest accounts or investments. ...

An outflow of deposits would be a reversal of a five-year trend that has seen significant amounts of extra cash poured into banks, thanks to the Fed flooding the financial system with liquidity. These deposits, which act as a cheaper source of funding, have helped banks weather the aftermath of the financial crisis.

Now the worry is that such deposit funding may prove fleeting as the Fed retreats. Banks might have to pay higher rates on deposits to retain customers—potentially hitting their profits and sparking a price war for client funds. ...

JPMorgan's $100 billion in projected outflows is roughly 7.8 percent of its deposit base as of the first quarter, according to SNL Financial. ...

MyEconLab More Economics in the News

ESSENCE OF THE STORY

- When the Fed starts to raise interest rates, U.S. bank deposits might decrease by $1 trillion.

- JPMorgan Chase estimates that its deposits will fall by $100 billion (7.8 percent of deposits) in the second half of 2015 if interest rates return to normal.

- A decrease in deposits would be a reversal of a five-year trend.

- Banks might have to pay higher interest rates on deposits.

ECONOMIC ANALYSIS

- A global financial crisis started quietly in the summer of 2007.

- In 2006, on the eve of the crisis, the interest rate on U.S. Treasury bills was 4.7 percent and the quantity of M2 money was a bit more than $7 trillion.

- Between 2006 and 2009, the interest rate fell to almost zero and it remained near zero through 2014 (see Fig. 1).

- Between 2006 and 2014, the quantity of M2 money increased by $2.8 trillion, an annual average growth rate of 6.6 percent (see Fig. 2).

- Of the $2.8 trillion increase in M2, bank deposits increased by $2.4 trillion and currency in circulation increased by $0.4 trillion.

- You've learned in this chapter that the quantity of money demanded depends inversely on the interest rate. So it is to be expected that a falling interest rate would bring an increasing quantity of money.

- Figure 3 shows this inverse relationship in the past 20 years (1993–2013). The demand for money is influenced by GDP, so the graph removes the influence of GDP by measuring the quantity of real M2 as a percentage of GDP.

- In Fig. 3, each red dot represents the quantity of money and the interest rate in a given year and the blue curve is the demand for M2 curve.

- Figure 3 highlights the bankers' concerns discussed in the news article, which reports that the banks expect deposits to decrease by $1 trillion if interest rates return to normal.

- The news article does not tell us what the bankers regard as normal. We can use the demand for M2 curve in Fig. 3 to find the quantity of money that will be held at different possible normal interest rates.

- At an interest rate of 1 percent per year the quantity of M2 demanded in Fig. 3 is 52.5 percent of GDP or $8.2 trillion.

- At an interest rate of zero, the quantity of M2 demanded is 64 percent of GDP, which is $10 trillion.

- So, based on the demand for M2 curve in Fig. 3, the quantity of M2 demanded will decrease by $1.8 trillion if the interest rate rises to 1 percent per year.

- Most of the decrease in the quantity of M2 demanded will be a decrease in bank deposits.

- The outcome for which the bankers are bracing themselves looks optimistic!

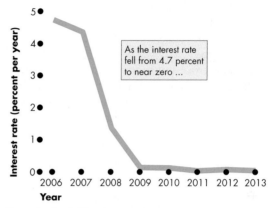

Figure 1 The Falling Interest Rate

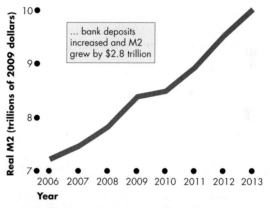

Figure 2 The Increasing Quantity of M2

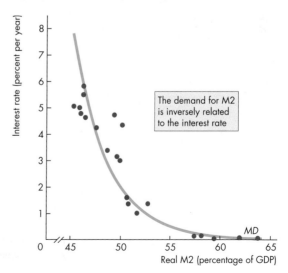

Figure 3 The Demand for M2

611

MATHEMATICAL NOTE
The Money Multiplier

This note explains the basic math of the money multiplier and shows how the value of the multiplier depends on the banks' desired reserve ratio and the currency drain ratio.

To make the process of money creation concrete, we work through an example for a banking system in which each bank has a desired reserve ratio of 10 percent of deposits and the currency drain ratio is 50 percent of deposits. (Although these ratios are larger than the ones in the U.S. economy, they make the process end more quickly and enable you to see more clearly the principles at work.)

The figure keeps track of the numbers. Before the process begins, all the banks have no excess reserves. Then the monetary base increases by $100,000 and one bank has excess reserves of this amount.

The bank lends the $100,000 of excess reserves. When this loan is made, new money increases by $100,000.

Some of the new money will be held as currency and some as deposits. With a currency drain ratio of 50 percent of deposits, one third of the new money will be held as currency and two thirds will be held as deposits. That is, $33,333 drains out of the banks as currency and $66,667 remains in the banks as deposits. The increase in the quantity of money of $100,000 equals the increase in deposits plus the increase in currency holdings.

The increased bank deposits of $66,667 generate an increase in desired reserves of 10 percent of that amount, which is $6,667. Actual reserves have increased by the same amount as the increase in deposits: $66,667. So the banks now have excess reserves of $60,000.

The process we've just described repeats but begins with excess reserves of $60,000. The figure shows the next two rounds. At the end of the process, the quantity of money has increased by a multiple of the increase in the monetary base. In this case, the increase is $250,000, which is 2.5 times the increase in the monetary base.

The sequence in the figure shows the first stages of the process that finally reaches the total shown in the final row of the "money" column.

To calculate what happens at the later stages in the process and the final increase in the quantity of

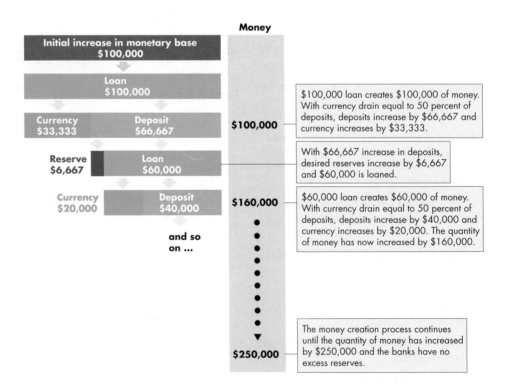

Figure 1 The Money Creation Process

money, look closely at the numbers in the figure. The initial increase in reserves is \$100,000 (call it A). At each stage, the loan is 60 percent (0.6) of the previous loan and the quantity of money increases by 0.6 of the previous increase. Call that proportion L ($L = 0.6$). We can write down the complete sequence for the increase in the quantity of money as

$$A + AL + AL^2 + AL^3 + AL^4 + AL^5 + \ldots .$$

Remember, L is a fraction, so at each stage in this sequence, the amount of new loans and new money gets smaller. The total value of loans made and money created at the end of the process is the sum of the sequence, which is[1]

$$A/(1 - L).$$

If we use the numbers from the example, the total increase in the quantity of money is

$$\$100,000 + 60,000 + 36,000 + \ldots$$

$$= \$100,000 \, (1 + 0.6 + 0.36 + \ldots)$$

$$= \$100,000 \, (1 + 0.6 + 0.6^2 + \ldots)$$

$$= \$100,000 \times 1/(1 - 0.6)$$

$$= \$100,000 \times 1/(0.4)$$

$$= \$100,000 \times 2.5$$

$$= \$250,000.$$

The magnitude of the money multiplier depends on the desired reserve ratio and the currency drain ratio. Let's explore this relationship

The money multiplier is the ratio of money to the monetary base. Call the money multiplier mm, the quantity of money M, and the monetary base MB.

---

[1]The sequence of values is called a convergent geometric series. To find the sum of a series such as this, begin by calling the sum S. Then write the sum as

$$S = A + AL + AL^2 + AL^3 + AL^4 + AL^5 + \ldots .$$

Multiply by L to get

$$LS = AL + AL^2 + AL^3 + AL^4 + AL^5 + \ldots$$

and then subtract the second equation from the first to get

$$S(1 - L) = A$$

or

$$S = A/(1 - L).$$

Then

$$mm = M/MB.$$

Next recall that money, M, is the sum of deposits and currency. Call deposits D and currency C. Then

$$M = D + C.$$

Finally, recall that the monetary base, MB, is the sum of banks' reserves and currency. Call banks' reserves R. Then

$$MB = R + C.$$

Use the equations for M and MB in the mm equation to give:

$$mm = M/MB = (D + C)/(R + C).$$

Now divide all the variables on the right side of the equation by D to give:

$$mm = M/MB = (1 + C/D)/(R/D + C/D).$$

In this equation, C/D is the currency drain ratio and R/D is the banks' reserve ratio. If we use the values in the example on the previous page, C/D is 0.5 and R/D is 0.1, and

$$mm = (1 + 0.5)/(0.1 + 0.5).$$

$$= 1.5/0.6 = 2.5.$$

The U.S. Money Multiplier

The money multiplier in the United States can be found by using the formula above along with the values of C/D and R/D in the U.S. economy.

Because we have two definitions of money, M1 and M2, we have two money multipliers. Call the M1 deposits $D1$ and call the M2 deposits $D2$.

The numbers for M1 in 2014 are $C/D1 = 0.81$ and $R/D1 = 1.69$. So

$$\text{M1 multiplier} = (1 + 0.81)/(1.69 + 0.81) = 0.72.$$

The numbers for M2 in 2014 are $C/D2 = 0.13$ and $R/D2 = 0.26$, so

$$\text{M2 multiplier} = (1 + 0.13)/(0.26 + 0.13) = 2.90.$$

SUMMARY

Key Points

What Is Money? (pp. 590–592)

- Money is the means of payment. It functions as a medium of exchange, a unit of account, and a store of value.
- Today, money consists of currency and deposits.

Working Problems 1 and 2 will give you a better understanding of what money is.

Depository Institutions (pp. 593–596)

- Commercial banks, S&Ls, savings banks, credit unions, and money market mutual funds are depository institutions whose deposits are money.
- Depository institutions provide four main economic services: They create liquidity, minimize the cost of obtaining funds, minimize the cost of monitoring borrowers, and pool risks.

Working Problem 3 will give you a better understanding of depository institutions.

The Federal Reserve System (pp. 597–600)

- The Federal Reserve System is the central bank of the United States.
- The Fed influences the quantity of money by setting the required reserve ratio, making last resort loans, and by conducting open market operations.
- When the Fed buys securities in an open market operation, the monetary base increases; when the Fed sells securities, the monetary base decreases.

Working Problem 4 will give you a better understanding of the Federal Reserve System.

How Banks Create Money (pp. 600–603)

- Banks create money by making loans.
- The total quantity of money that can be created depends on the monetary base, the desired reserve ratio, and the currency drain ratio.

Working Problems 5 and 6 will give you a better understanding of how banks create money.

The Money Market (pp. 604–607)

- The quantity of money demanded is the amount of money that people plan to hold.
- The quantity of real money equals the quantity of nominal money divided by the price level.
- The quantity of real money demanded depends on the nominal interest rate, real GDP, and financial innovation.
- The nominal interest rate makes the quantity of money demanded equal the quantity supplied.
- When the Fed increases the quantity of money, the nominal interest rate falls (the short-run effect).
- In the long run, when the Fed increases the quantity of money, the price level rises and the nominal interest rate returns to its initial level.

Working Problem 7 will give you a better understanding of the money market.

The Quantity Theory of Money (pp. 608–609)

- The quantity theory of money is the proposition that money growth and inflation move up and down together in the long run.

Working Problem 8 will give you a better understanding of the quantity theory of money.

Key Terms

Central bank, 597
Currency, 591
Currency drain ratio, 601
Demand for money, 605
Depository institution, 593
Desired reserve ratio, 601
Excess reserves, 601
Federal funds rate, 593

Federal Open Market
   Committee, 597
Federal Reserve System
   (the Fed), 597
Lender of last resort, 600
M1, 591
M2, 591
Means of payment, 590

Monetary base, 598
Money, 590
Money multiplier, 602
Open market operation, 598
Quantity theory of money, 608
Required reserve ratio, 600
Reserves, 593
Velocity of circulation, 608

◆ WORKED PROBLEM

MyEconLab   You can work this problem in Chapter 25 Study Plan.

In June 2014, individuals and businesses held

- $50 billion in currency and no traveler's checks
- $1,000 billion in checkable deposits
- $5,000 billion in savings deposits
- $500 billion in time deposits
- $250 billion in money market funds and other deposits.

In June 2014, banks held

- $450 billion in currency
- $100 billion in reserves at the central bank
- $800 billion in loans to households and businesses

Questions

1. Calculate the M1 and M2 measures of money.
2. Calculate the monetary base.
3. What are the currency drain ratio and the banks' reserve ratio?
4. What are the M1 and M2 money multipliers?
5. How is the money multiplier influenced by the banks' reserve ratio?

Solutions

1. M1 is the quantity of money held by individuals and businesses in the form of checkable deposits and currency.
   M1 = $1,000 billion + $50 billion = $1,050 billion.
   M2 is M1 plus other types of deposits and money market mutual funds held by individuals and businesses.
   M2 = $1,050 billion + $5,000 billion + $500 billion + $250 billion = $6,800 billion.

Key Point: M1 is a narrow measure of money that consists of checkable deposits and currency held by individuals and businesses.

M2 is a broad measure of money that consists of M1 plus other deposits and money market mutual funds of individuals and businesses.

2. Monetary base is the sum of bank reserves held at the central bank and currency issued by the central bank.
   Currency issued by the central bank is the currency held by individuals, businesses, and banks.

Monetary base = $100 billion + $450 billion + $50 billion = $600 billion

Key Point: Monetary base equals the central bank's liabilities—bank reserves held at the central bank and currency issued by the central bank.

3. Currency drain ratio = (Currency held by individuals and businesses ÷ Checkable deposits) × 100.
   Currency drain ratio = ($50 billion ÷ $1,000 billion) × 100 = 5 percent.
   Banks' reserve ratio = (Bank reserves ÷ Checkable deposits) × 100.
   Bank reserves = Currency held by banks + reserves at the central bank.
   Bank reserves = $450 billion + $100 billion = $550 billion.
   Banks' reserve ratio = ($550 billion ÷ $1,000 billion) × 100 = 55 percent.

Key Point: Currency drain ratio is the ratio of currency to checkable deposits held by individuals and businesses, expressed as a percentage.

Banks' reserve ratio is ratio of bank reserves to bank deposits, expressed as a percentage.

4. M1 money multiplier = M1 ÷ Monetary base = $1,050 billion ÷ $600 billion = 1.75.
   M2 money multiplier = M2 ÷ Monetary base = $6,800 billion ÷ $600 billion = 11.33.

Key Point: The money multiplier is the number by which the monetary base is multiplied to equal the quantity of money.

5. Money M is the sum of deposits D and currency C held by individuals and businesses.
   Monetary base MB is the sum of reserves R and currency C.
   Money multiplier = $(D + C) \div (R + C)$
   An increase in the banks' reserves R with no change in D increases the banks' reserve ratio and decreases the money multiplier.

Key Point: The money multiplier equals $(1 + C/D) \div (R/D + C/D)$, where C/D is the currency drain ratio and R/D is the banks' reserve ratio. An increase in the banks' reserve ratio decreases the money multiplier.

STUDY PLAN PROBLEMS AND APPLICATIONS

MyEconLab   You can work Problems 1 to 9 in Chapter 25 Study Plan and get instant feedback.
Problems marked update with real-time data.

What Is Money? (Study Plan 25.1)

1. Money in the United States today includes which of the following items? Cash in Citibank's cash machines; U.S. dollar bills in your wallet; your Visa card; your loan to pay for school fees.

2. In June 2013, currency held by individuals and businesses was $1,124 billion; traveler's checks were $4 billion; checkable deposits owned by individuals and businesses were $1,402 billion; savings deposits were $6,884 billion; time deposits were $583 billion; and money market funds and other deposits were $647 billion. Calculate M1 and M2 in June 2013.

Depository Institutions (Study Plan 25.2)

3. **Europe's Banks Must Be Forced to Recapitalize**
   E.U. banks must hold more capital. Where private funding is not forthcoming, recapitalization must be imposed by E.U. governments.
   Source: *The Financial Times*, November 24, 2011

   What is the "capital" referred to in the news clip? How might the requirement to hold more capital make banks safer?

The Federal Reserve System (Study Plan 25.3)

4. The FOMC sells $20 million of securities to Wells Fargo. Enter the transactions that take place to show the changes in the following balance sheets.

   Federal Reserve Bank of New York

Assets (millions)	Liabilities (millions)

   Wells Fargo

Assets (millions)	Liabilities (millions)

How Banks Create Money (Study Plan 25.4)

5. In the economy of Nocoin, bank deposits are $300 billion. Bank reserves are $15 billion, of which two thirds are deposits with the central bank. Households and firms hold $30 billion in bank notes. There are no coins. Calculate
   a. The monetary base and quantity of money.
   b. The banks' desired reserve ratio and the currency drain ratio (as percentages).

6. **China Cuts Banks' Reserve Ratios**
   The People's Bank of China announces it will cut the required reserve ratio.
   Source: *The Financial Times*, February 19, 2012

   Explain how lowering the required reserve ratio will impact banks' money creation process.

The Money Market (Study Plan 25.5)

7. The spreadsheet provides data about the demand for money in Minland. Columns A and B show the demand for money schedule when real GDP (Y_0) is $10 billion and Columns A and C show the demand for money schedule when real GDP (Y_1) is $20 billion. The quantity of money is $3 billion.

	A	B	C
1	r	Y_0	Y_1
2	7	1.0	1.5
3	6	1.5	2.0
4	5	2.0	2.5
5	4	2.5	3.0
6	3	3.0	3.5
7	2	3.5	4.0
8	1	4.0	4.5

   What is the interest rate when real GDP is $10 billion? Explain what happens in the money market in the short run if real GDP increases to $20 billion.

The Quantity Theory of Money (Study Plan 25.6)

8. In year 1, the economy is at full employment and real GDP is $400 million, the GDP deflator is 200 (the price level is 2), and the velocity of circulation is 20. In year 2, the quantity of money increases by 20 percent. If the quantity theory of money holds, calculate the quantity of money, the GDP deflator, real GDP, and the velocity of circulation in year 2.

Mathematical Note (Study Plan 25.MN)

9. In Problem 5, the banks have no excess reserves. Suppose that the central bank in Nocoin increases bank reserves by $0.5 billion.
   a. Explain what happens to the quantity of money and why the change in the quantity of money is not equal to the change in the monetary base.
   b. Calculate the money multiplier.

ADDITIONAL PROBLEMS AND APPLICATIONS

MyEconLab   You can work these problems in MyEconLab if assigned by your instructor.

What Is Money?

10. Sara withdraws $1,000 from her savings account at the Lucky S&L, keeps $50 in cash, and deposits the balance in her checking account at the Bank of Illinois. What is the immediate change in M1 and M2?

11. Rapid inflation in Brazil in the early 1990s caused the cruzeiro to lose its ability to function as money. Which of the following commodities would most likely have taken the place of the cruzeiro in the Brazilian economy? Explain why.
    a. Tractor parts
    b. Packs of cigarettes
    c. Loaves of bread
    d. Impressionist paintings
    e. Baseball trading cards

12. **Are You Ready to Pay by smartphone?**
    Starbucks customers can now pay for their coffee using their smartphone. Does this mean the move to electronic payments is finally coming?
    Source: *The Wall Street Journal*, January 20, 2011

    If people can use their smartphone to make payments, will currency disappear? How will the components of M1 change?

Depository Institutions

Use the following news clip to work Problems 13 and 14.

U.S. Bank Earnings Up 21% As Loan Losses Decline, FDIC Says

For the 12th straight quarter, U.S. bank profits increased. At $34.5 billion, they were 21 percent higher than a year earlier, and, according to the Federal Deposit Insurance Corporation (FDIC), balance sheets were less risky. FDIC Acting Chairman Martin Gruenberg said "Levels of troubled assets and troubled institutions remain high, but they are continuing to improve." The number of institutions on FDIC's list of banks deemed to be at greater risk of collapse fell for a fifth straight quarter. By August, 40 banks had failed in 2012. The FDIC's deposit insurance fund, which protects customer accounts up to $250,000 against bank failure, increased.

www.bloomberg.com
August 29, 2012

13. Explain how the pursuit of profits can sometimes lead to bank failures.

14. How does FDIC insurance help minimize the cost of bank failure? Does it bring more stability to the banking system?

The Federal Reserve System

15. Explain the distinction between a central bank and a commercial bank.

16. If the Fed makes an open market sale of $1 million of securities to a bank, what initial changes occur in the economy?

17. Set out the transactions that the Fed undertakes to increase the quantity of money.

18. Describe the Fed's assets and liabilities. What is the monetary base and how does it relate to the Fed's balance sheet?

19. **Fed Minutes Show Active Discussion of QE3**
    The FOMC discussed "a new large-scale asset purchase program" commonly called "QE3." Some FOMC members said such a program could help the economy by lowering long-term interest rates and making financial conditions more broadly easier. They discussed whether a new program should snap up more Treasury bonds or buy mortgage-backed securities issued by the likes of Fannie Mae and Freddie Mac.
    Source: *The Wall Street Journal*, August 22, 2012

    What would the Fed do to implement QE3, how would the monetary base change, and how would bank reserves change?

How Banks Create Money

20. Banks in New Transylvania have a desired reserve ratio of 10 percent of deposits and no excess reserves. The currency drain ratio is 50 percent of deposits. Now suppose that the central bank increases the monetary base by $1,200 billion.
    a. How much do the banks lend in the first round of the money creation process?
    b. How much of the initial amount lent flows back to the banking system as new deposits?
    c. How much of the initial amount lent does not return to the banks but is held as currency?
    d. Why does a second round of lending occur?

The Money Market

21. Explain the change in the nominal interest rate in the short run if
    a. Real GDP increases.
    b. The money supply increases.
    c. The price level rises.

22. The figure shows the demand for money curve.

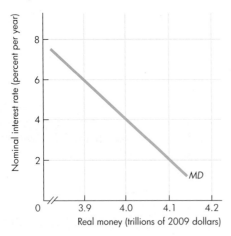

    If the Fed decreases the quantity of real money from $4 trillion to $3.9 trillion, explain how the price of a bond will change.

23. Use the data in Problem 7 to work this problem. The interest rate is 4 percent a year. Suppose that real GDP decreases from $20 billion to $10 billion and the quantity of money remains unchanged. Do people buy bonds or sell bonds? Explain how the interest rate changes.

The Quantity Theory of Money

24. The table provides some data for the United States in the first decade following the Civil War.

	1869	1879
Quantity of money	$1.3 billion	$1.7 billion
Real GDP (1929 dollars)	$7.4 billion	Z
Price level (1929 = 100)	X	54
Velocity of circulation	4.50	4.61

Source of data: Milton Friedman and Anna J. Schwartz, A Monetary History of the United States 1867–1960

    a. Calculate the value of X in 1869.
    b. Calculate the value of Z in 1879.
    c. Are the data consistent with the quantity theory of money? Explain your answer.

Economics in the News

25. After you have studied *Economics in the News* on pp. 610–611, answer the following questions.
    a. What changes in the interest rate and the quantity of M2 occurred between 2007 and 2014?
    b. Why is the outcome feared by bankers optimistic?
    c. By how much would the quantity of M2 demanded decrease if the interest rate rose to 2 percent, or 3 percent, or 4 percent? (Express your answer as a percentage of GDP.)
    d. What could the banks do to prevent deposits from decreasing by as much as predicted by the demand for M2 curve in Fig. 3 on p. 611?
    e. What would you expect to happen to the monetary base if interest rates rise? Why?

26. **Fed at Odds with ECB over Value of Policy Tool**

    Financial innovation and the spread of U.S. currency throughout the world has broken down relationships between money, inflation, and output growth, making monetary gauges a less useful tool for policy makers, the U.S. Federal Reserve chairman, Ben Bernanke, said. Many other central banks use monetary aggregates as a guide to policy decisions, but Bernanke believes reliance on monetary aggregates would be unwise. "There are differences between the United States and Europe in terms of the stability of money demand," Bernanke said.

    Source: *International Herald Tribune*, November 10, 2006

    a. Explain how the debate surrounding the quantity theory of money could make "monetary gauges a less useful tool for policy makers."
    b. What do Ben Bernanke's statements reveal about his view on the accuracy of the quantity theory of money?

Mathematical Note

27. In the United Kingdom, the currency drain ratio is 38 percent of deposits and the reserve ratio is 2 percent of deposits. In Australia, the quantity of money is $150 billion, the currency drain ratio is 33 percent of deposits, and the reserve ratio is 8 percent of deposits.
    a. Calculate the U.K. money multiplier.
    b. Calculate the monetary base in Australia.

26

THE EXCHANGE RATE AND THE BALANCE OF PAYMENTS

After studying this chapter, you will be able to:

◆ Explain how the exchange rate is determined

◆ Explain interest rate parity and purchasing power parity

◆ Describe the alternative exchange rate policies and explain their effects

◆ Describe the balance of payments accounts and explain what causes an international deficit

The dollar ($), the euro (€), and the yen (¥) are three of the world's monies and most international payments are made using one of them. But the world has more than 100 different monies. What determines the value of the dollar in terms of other kinds of money?

For almost thirty years, foreign entrepreneurs have roamed the United States with giant, virtual shopping carts buying U.S. businesses. Why?

In this chapter, you're going to discover the answers to these questions. In *Economics in the News* at the end of the chapter, we'll look at the rising dollar in the summer of 2014.

◆ The Foreign Exchange Market

When Wal-Mart imports Blu-ray players from Japan, it pays for them using Japanese yen. And when Japan Airlines buys an airplane from Boeing, it pays using U.S. dollars. When you take a European holiday, you pay for the holiday with euros. Whenever people buy things from another country, they use the currency of that country to make the transaction. It doesn't make any difference what the item is that is being traded internationally. It might be a Blu-ray player, an airplane, an international holiday, insurance or banking services, real estate, the stocks and bonds of a government or corporation, or even an entire business.

Foreign money is just like U.S. money. It consists of notes and coins issued by a central bank and mint and deposits in banks and other depository institutions. When we described U.S. money in Chapter 25, we distinguished between currency (notes and coins) and deposits. But when we talk about foreign money, we refer to it as foreign currency. **Foreign currency** is the money of other countries regardless of whether that money is in the form of notes, coins, or bank deposits.

We buy these foreign currencies and foreigners buy U.S. dollars in the foreign exchange market.

Trading Currencies

The currency of one country is exchanged for the currency of another in the **foreign exchange market.** The foreign exchange market is not a place like a downtown flea market or a fruit and vegetable market. The foreign exchange market is made up of thousands of people—importers and exporters, banks, international investors and speculators, international travelers, and specialist traders called *foreign exchange brokers*.

The foreign exchange market opens on Monday morning in Sydney, Australia, and Hong Kong, which is still Sunday evening in New York. As the day advances, markets open in Singapore, Tokyo, Bahrain, Frankfurt, London, New York, Chicago, and San Francisco. As the West Coast markets close, Sydney is only an hour away from opening for the next day of business. The sun barely sets in the foreign exchange market. Dealers around the world are in continual Internet contact, and on a typical day in 2014, $5.3 trillion (of all currencies) were traded in the foreign exchange market—that's $6 million every second.

Exchange Rates

An **exchange rate** is the price at which one currency exchanges for another currency in the foreign exchange market. For example, on August 25, 2014, $1 would buy 104 Japanese yen or 76 euro cents. So the exchange rate was 104 yen per dollar or, equivalently, 76 euro cents per dollar.

The exchange rate fluctuates. Sometimes it rises and sometimes it falls. A rise in the exchange rate is called an *appreciation* of the dollar, and a fall in the exchange rate is called a *depreciation* of the dollar. For example, when the exchange rate rises from 104 yen to 110 yen per dollar, the dollar appreciates against the yen; when the exchange rate falls from 110 yen to 104 yen per dollar, the dollar depreciates against the yen.

Economics in Action on p. 621 shows the fluctuations of the U.S. dollar against three currencies from 2000 to 2014.

Questions About the U.S. Dollar Exchange Rate

The performance of the U.S. dollar in the foreign exchange market raises a number of questions that we address in this chapter.

First, how is the exchange rate determined? Why does the U.S. dollar sometimes appreciate and at other times depreciate?

Second, how do the Fed and other central banks operate in the foreign exchange market? In particular, how was the exchange rate between the U.S. dollar and the Chinese yuan fixed and why did it remain constant for many years?

Third, how do exchange rate fluctuations influence our international trade and international payments? In particular, could we eliminate, or at least decrease, our international deficit by changing the exchange rate? Would an appreciation of the yuan change the balance of trade and payments between the United States and China?

We begin by learning how trading in the foreign exchange market determines the exchange rate.

An Exchange Rate Is a Price

An exchange rate is a price—the price of one currency in terms of another. And like all prices, an exchange rate is determined in a market—the *foreign exchange market*.

The U.S. dollar trades in the foreign exchange market and is supplied and demanded by tens of

ECONOMICS IN ACTION

The U.S. Dollar: More Down than Up

The figure shows the U.S. dollar exchange rate against the three currencies that feature prominently in U.S. imports—the Chinese yuan, the European euro, and the Japanese yen—between 2000 and 2014.

Against the yuan, the dollar was constant before 2005 and since then it has depreciated. Against the yen and the euro, the dollar appreciated before 2002. Since then, the dollar depreciated against the yen through 2012 and then appreciated. Against the euro, the dollar depreciated from 2002 through 2008 and then appreciated.

Notice the high-frequency fluctuations (rapid brief up and down movements) of the dollar against the euro and the yen compared to the smooth changes against the yuan. Think about why that might be, and we'll check your answer later in this chapter.

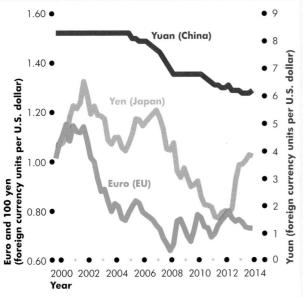

The U.S. Dollar Against Three Currencies

Source of data: Pacific Exchange Rate Service.

thousands of traders every hour of every business day. Because it has many traders and no restrictions on who may trade, the foreign exchange market is a *competitive market.*

In a competitive market, demand and supply determine the price. So to understand the forces that determine the exchange rate, we need to study the factors that influence demand and supply in the foreign exchange market. But there is a feature of the foreign exchange market that makes it special.

The Demand for One Money Is the Supply of Another Money

When people who are holding the money of some other country want to exchange it for U.S. dollars, they demand U.S. dollars and supply that other country's money. And when people who are holding U.S. dollars want to exchange them for the money of some other country, they supply U.S. dollars and demand that other country's money.

So the factors that influence the demand for U.S. dollars also influence the supply of European euros, or Japanese yen, or Chinese yuan. And the factors that influence the demand for that other country's money also influence the supply of U.S. dollars.

We'll first look at the influences on the demand for U.S. dollars in the foreign exchange market.

Demand in the Foreign Exchange Market

People buy U.S. dollars in the foreign exchange market so that they can buy U.S.-produced goods and services—U.S. exports. They also buy U.S. dollars so that they can buy U.S. assets such as bonds, stocks, businesses, and real estate or so that they can keep part of their money holding in a U.S. dollar bank account.

The quantity of U.S. dollars demanded in the foreign exchange market is the amount that traders plan to buy during a given time period at a given exchange rate. This quantity depends on many factors, but the main ones are

1. The exchange rate
2. World demand for U.S. exports
3. Interest rates in the United States and other countries
4. The expected future exchange rate

We look first at the relationship between the quantity of U.S. dollars demanded in the foreign exchange market and the exchange rate when the other three influences remain the same.

The Law of Demand for Foreign Exchange The law of demand applies to U.S. dollars just as it does to anything else that people value. Other things remaining the same, the higher the exchange rate, the smaller is the quantity of U.S. dollars demanded in the foreign exchange market. For example, if the market price of the U.S. dollar rises from 100 yen to 120 yen but nothing else changes, the quantity of U.S. dollars that people plan to buy in the foreign exchange market decreases. The exchange rate influences the quantity of U.S. dollars demanded for two reasons:

- Exports effect
- Expected profit effect

Exports Effect The larger the value of U.S. exports, the larger is the quantity of U.S. dollars demanded by the buyers of U.S. exports in the foreign exchange market. But the value of U.S. exports depends on the prices of U.S.-produced goods and services *expressed in the currency of the foreign buyer*. And these prices depend on the exchange rate. The lower the exchange rate, other things remaining the same, the lower are the prices of U.S.-produced goods and services to foreigners and the greater is the volume of U.S. exports. So if the exchange rate falls (and other influences remain the same), the quantity of U.S. dollars demanded in the foreign exchange market increases.

To see the exports effect at work, think about orders for Boeing's new 787 Dreamliner. If the price of this airplane is $100 million and the exchange rate is 90 euro cents per U.S. dollar, its price to KLM, a European airline, is €90 million. KLM decides that this price is too high, so it doesn't buy a Dreamliner. If the exchange rate falls to 80 euro cents per U.S. dollar and other things remain the same, the price of a Dreamliner falls to €80 million, so KLM decides to buy one and enters the foreign exchange market to buy 100 million U.S. dollars.

Expected Profit Effect The larger the expected profit from holding U.S. dollars, the greater is the quantity of U.S. dollars demanded in the foreign exchange market. But expected profit depends on the exchange rate. For a given expected future exchange rate, the lower the exchange rate today, the larger is the expected profit from buying U.S. dollars today and holding them, so the greater is the quantity of U.S. dollars demanded in the foreign exchange market today. Let's look at an example.

Suppose that Mitsubishi Bank, a Japanese bank, expects the exchange rate to be 120 yen per U.S. dollar at the end of the year. If today's exchange rate is also 120 yen per U.S. dollar, Mitsubishi Bank expects no profit from buying U.S. dollars and holding them until the end of the year. But if today's exchange rate is 100 yen per U.S. dollar and Mitsubishi Bank buys

U.S. dollars, it expects to sell those dollars at the end of the year for 120 yen per dollar and make a profit of 20 yen on each U.S. dollar bought.

The lower the exchange rate today, other things remaining the same, the greater is the expected profit from holding U.S. dollars, so the greater is the quantity of U.S. dollars demanded in the foreign exchange market today.

Demand Curve for U.S. Dollars

Figure 26.1 shows the demand curve for U.S. dollars in the foreign exchange market. A change in the exchange rate, other things remaining the same, brings a change in the quantity of U.S. dollars demanded and a movement along the demand curve. The arrows show such movements.

We will look at the factors that *change* demand in the next section of this chapter. Before doing that, let's see what determines the supply of U.S. dollars.

FIGURE 26.1   The Demand for U.S. Dollars

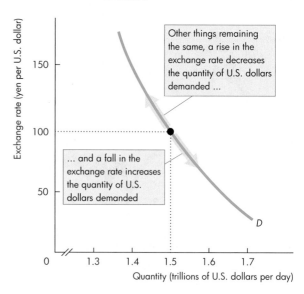

The quantity of U.S. dollars demanded depends on the exchange rate. Other things remaining the same, if the exchange rate rises, the quantity of U.S. dollars demanded decreases and there is a movement up along the demand curve for U.S. dollars. If the exchange rate falls, the quantity of U.S. dollars demanded increases and there is a movement down along the demand curve for U.S. dollars.

MyEconLab Animation

Supply in the Foreign Exchange Market

People and businesses sell U.S. dollars and buy other currencies so that they can buy foreign-produced goods and services—U.S. imports. They also sell U.S. dollars and buy foreign currencies so that they can buy foreign assets such as bonds, stocks, businesses, and real estate or so that they can hold part of their money in bank deposits denominated in a foreign currency.

The quantity of U.S. dollars supplied in the foreign exchange market is the amount that traders plan to sell during a given time period at a given exchange rate. This quantity depends on many factors, but the main ones are

1. The exchange rate
2. U.S. demand for imports
3. Interest rates in the United States and other countries
4. The expected future exchange rate

Let's look at the law of supply in the foreign exchange market—the relationship between the quantity of U.S. dollars supplied in the foreign exchange market and the exchange rate when the other three influences remain the same.

The Law of Supply of Foreign Exchange Other things remaining the same, the higher the exchange rate, the greater is the quantity of U.S. dollars supplied in the foreign exchange market. For example, if the exchange rate rises from 100 yen to 120 yen per U.S. dollar and other things remain the same, the quantity of U.S. dollars that people plan to sell in the foreign exchange market increases.

The exchange rate influences the quantity of dollars supplied for two reasons:

- Imports effect
- Expected profit effect

Imports Effect The larger the value of U.S. imports, the larger is the quantity of U.S. dollars supplied in the foreign exchange market. But the value of U.S. imports depends on the prices of foreign-produced goods and services *expressed in U.S. dollars*. These prices depend on the exchange rate. The higher the exchange rate, other things remaining the same, the lower are the prices of foreign-produced goods and services to Americans and the greater is the volume of U.S. imports. So if the exchange rate rises (and other influences remain the same), the quantity of

U.S. dollars supplied in the foreign exchange market increases.

Expected Profit Effect This effect works just like that on the demand for the U.S. dollar but in the opposite direction. The higher the exchange rate today, other things remaining the same, the larger is the expected profit from selling U.S. dollars today and holding foreign currencies, so the greater is the quantity of U.S. dollars supplied in the foreign exchange market.

Supply Curve for U.S. Dollars

Figure 26.2 shows the supply curve of U.S. dollars in the foreign exchange market. A change in the exchange rate, other things remaining the same, brings a change in the quantity of U.S. dollars supplied and a movement along the supply curve. The arrows show such movements.

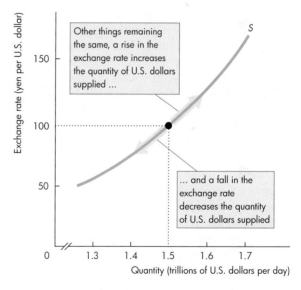

FIGURE 26.2 The Supply of U.S. Dollars

Other things remaining the same, a rise in the exchange rate increases the quantity of U.S. dollars supplied ...

... and a fall in the exchange rate decreases the quantity of U.S. dollars supplied

The quantity of U.S. dollars supplied depends on the exchange rate. Other things remaining the same, if the exchange rate rises, the quantity of U.S. dollars supplied increases and there is a movement up along the supply curve of U.S. dollars. If the exchange rate falls, the quantity of U.S. dollars supplied decreases and there is a movement down along the supply curve of U.S. dollars.

MyEconLab Animation

Market Equilibrium

Equilibrium in the foreign exchange market depends on how the Federal Reserve and other central banks operate. Here, we will study equilibrium when central banks keep out of the foreign exchange market and examine the effects of alternative central bank actions later (on pp. 631–633).

Figure 26.3 shows the demand curve for U.S. dollars, D, from Fig. 26.1, the supply curve of U.S. dollars, S, from Fig. 26.2, and the equilibrium exchange rate. The exchange rate acts as a regulator of the quantities demanded and supplied. If the exchange rate is too high, there is a surplus of dollars. For example, in Fig. 26.3, if the exchange rate is 150 yen per U.S. dollar, there is a surplus of U.S. dollars. If the exchange rate is too low, there is a shortage of dollars. For example, if the exchange rate is 50 yen per U.S. dollar, there is a shortage of U.S. dollars.

At the equilibrium exchange rate, there is neither a shortage nor a surplus—the quantity supplied equals the quantity demanded. In Fig. 26.3, the equilibrium exchange rate is 100 yen per U.S. dollar. At this exchange rate, the quantity demanded and the quantity supplied are each $1.5 trillion a day.

The foreign exchange market is constantly pulled to its equilibrium by foreign exchange traders who are constantly looking for the best price they can get. If they are selling, they want the highest price available. If they are buying, they want the lowest price available. Information flows from trader to trader through a worldwide computer network, and the price adjusts minute by minute to keep the exchange rate at its equilibrium.

But as you've seen (in *Economics in Action* on p. 621), the U.S. dollar fluctuates a lot against other currencies. Changes in the demand for U.S. dollars or the supply of U.S. dollars bring these exchange rate fluctuations. We'll now look at the factors that make demand and supply change, starting with the demand side of the market.

Changes in the Demand for U.S. Dollars

The demand for U.S. dollars in the foreign exchange market changes when there is a change in

- World demand for U.S. exports
- U.S. interest rate relative to the foreign interest rate
- The expected future exchange rate

FIGURE 26.3   Equilibrium Exchange Rate

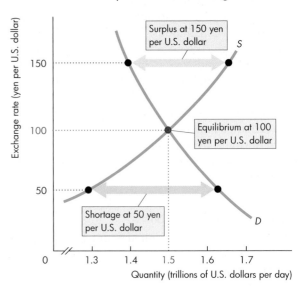

The demand curve for U.S. dollars is D, and the supply curve of U.S. dollars is S. If the exchange rate is 150 yen per U.S. dollar, there is a surplus of U.S. dollars and the exchange rate falls. If the exchange rate is 50 yen per U.S. dollar, there is a shortage of U.S. dollars and the exchange rate rises. If the exchange rate is 100 yen per U.S. dollar, there is neither a shortage nor a surplus of U.S. dollars and the exchange rate remains constant. The foreign exchange market is in equilibrium.

—— MyEconLab Animation and Draw Graph ——

World Demand for U.S. Exports An increase in world demand for U.S. exports increases the demand for U.S. dollars. To see this effect, think about Boeing's airplane sales. An increase in demand for air travel in Australia sends that country's airlines on a global shopping spree. They decide that the 787 is the ideal product, so they order 50 airplanes from Boeing. The demand for U.S. dollars now increases.

U.S. Interest Rate Relative to the Foreign Interest Rate People and businesses buy financial assets to make a return. The higher the interest rate that people can make on U.S. assets compared with foreign assets, the more U.S. assets they buy.

What matters is not the *level* of the U.S. interest rate, but the U.S. interest rate relative to the foreign interest rate—the U.S. interest rate minus the foreign interest rate, which is called the **U.S. interest rate differential**. If the U.S. interest rate rises and the foreign interest rate remains constant, the U.S. interest rate differential increases. The larger the U.S. interest rate differential, the greater is the demand for U.S. assets and the greater is the demand for U.S. dollars in the foreign exchange market.

The Expected Future Exchange Rate For a given current exchange rate, other things remaining the same, a rise in the expected future exchange rate increases the profit that people expect to make by holding U.S. dollars and the demand for U.S. dollars increases today.

Figure 26.4 summarizes the influences on the demand for U.S. dollars. An increase in the demand for U.S. exports, a rise in the U.S. interest rate differential, or a rise in the expected future exchange rate increases the demand for U.S. dollars today and shifts the demand curve rightward from D_0 to D_1. A decrease in the demand for U.S. exports, a fall in the U.S. interest rate differential, or a fall in the expected future exchange rate decreases the demand for U.S. dollars today and shifts the demand curve leftward from D_0 to D_2.

Changes in the Supply of U.S. Dollars

The supply of U.S. dollars in the foreign exchange market changes when there is a change in

- U.S. demand for imports
- U.S. interest rate relative to the foreign interest rate
- The expected future exchange rate

U.S. Demand for Imports An increase in the U.S. demand for imports increases the supply of U.S. dollars in the foreign exchange market. To see why, think about Wal-Mart's purchase of Blu-ray players. An increase in the demand for Blu-ray players sends Wal-Mart out on a global shopping spree. Wal-Mart decides that Panasonic Blu-ray players produced in Japan are the best buy, so Wal-Mart increases its purchases of these players. The supply of U.S. dollars now increases as Wal-Mart goes to the foreign exchange market for Japanese yen to pay Panasonic.

U.S. Interest Rate Relative to the Foreign Interest Rate The effect of the U.S. interest rate differential on the supply of U.S. dollars is the opposite of its

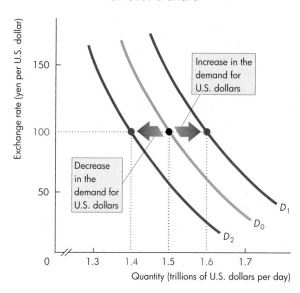

FIGURE 26.4 Changes in the Demand for U.S. Dollars

A change in any influence on the quantity of U.S. dollars that people plan to buy, other than the exchange rate, brings a change in the demand for U.S. dollars.

The demand for U.S. dollars

Increases if:	*Decreases if:*
■ World demand for U.S. exports increases	■ World demand for U.S. exports decreases
■ The U.S. interest rate differential rises	■ The U.S. interest rate differential falls
■ The expected future exchange rate rises	■ The expected future exchange rate falls

MyEconLab Animation

effect on the demand for U.S. dollars. The larger the U.S. interest rate differential, the *smaller* is the supply of U.S. dollars in the foreign exchange market.

With a higher U.S. interest rate differential, people decide to keep more of their funds in U.S. dollar assets and less in foreign currency assets. They buy a smaller quantity of foreign currency and sell a smaller quantity of dollars in the foreign exchange market.

So, a rise in the U.S. interest rate, other things remaining the same, decreases the supply of U.S. dollars in the foreign exchange market.

The Expected Future Exchange Rate For a given current exchange rate, other things remaining the same, a fall in the expected future exchange rate decreases the profit that can be made by holding U.S. dollars and decreases the quantity of U.S. dollars that people and businesses want to hold. To reduce their holdings of U.S. dollar assets, people and businesses must sell U.S. dollars. When they do so, the supply of U.S. dollars in the foreign exchange market increases.

Figure 26.5 summarizes the influences on the supply of U.S. dollars. If the supply of U.S. dollars increases, the supply curve shifts rightward from S_0 to

S_1. And if the supply of U.S. dollars decreases, the supply curve shifts leftward from S_0 to S_2.

Changes in the Exchange Rate

The exchange rate changes when either the demand for dollars or the supply of dollars changes.

If the demand for U.S. dollars increases and the supply does not change, the exchange rate rises. If the demand for U.S. dollars decreases and the supply does not change, the exchange rate falls.

Similarly, if the supply of U.S. dollars decreases and the demand does not change, the exchange rate rises. If the supply of U.S. dollars increases and the demand does not change, the exchange rate falls.

These predictions are exactly the same as those for any other market. Two episodes in the life of the U.S. dollar (next page) illustrate these predictions.

Two of the influences on demand and supply—the U.S. interest rate differential and the expected future exchange rate—change both sides of the foreign exchange market simultaneously. A rise in the U.S. interest rate differential or a rise in the expected future exchange rate increases demand, decreases supply, and raises the exchange rate. Similarly, a fall in the U.S. interest rate differential or a fall in the expected future exchange rate decreases demand, increases supply, and lowers the exchange rate.

We take a closer look at the interest rate differential and expectations in the next section.

FIGURE 26.5   Changes in the Supply of U.S. Dollars

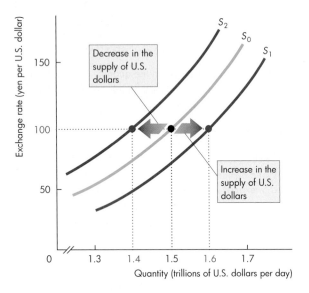

A change in any influence on the quantity of U.S. dollars that people plan to sell, other than the exchange rate, brings a change in the supply of dollars.

The supply of U.S. dollars

Increases if:

- U.S. import demand increases
- The U.S. interest rate differential falls
- The expected future exchange rate falls

Decreases if:

- U.S. import demand decreases
- The U.S. interest rate differential rises
- The expected future exchange rate rises

MyEconLab Animation

◆ REVIEW QUIZ

1 What are the influences on the demand for U.S. dollars in the foreign exchange market?
2 What are the influences on the supply of U.S. dollars in the foreign exchange market?
3 How is the equilibrium exchange rate determined?
4 What happens if there is a shortage or a surplus of U.S. dollars in the foreign exchange market?
5 What makes the demand for U.S. dollars change?
6 What makes the supply of U.S. dollars change?
7 What makes the U.S. dollar exchange rate fluctuate?

Work these questions in Study Plan 26.1 and get instant feedback. Do a Key Terms Quiz.   MyEconLab

ECONOMICS IN ACTION

The Dollar on a Roller Coaster

The foreign exchange market is a striking example of a competitive market. The expectations of thousands of traders around the world influence this market minute-by-minute throughout the 24-hour global trading day.

Demand and supply rarely stand still and their fluctuations bring a fluctuating exchange rate. Two episodes in the life of the dollar illustrate these fluctuations: 2007–2012, when the dollar depreciated and 2012–2014, when the dollar appreciated.

A Depreciating U.S. Dollar: 2007–2012 Between July 2007 and August 2012, the U.S. dollar depreciated against the yen. It fell from 120 yen to 77 yen per U.S. dollar. Part (a) of the figure provides a possible explanation for this depreciation.

In 2007, the demand and supply curves were those labeled D_{07} and S_{07}. The exchange rate was 120 yen per U.S. dollar.

During the last quarter of 2007 and the first three quarters of 2008, the U.S. economy entered a severe credit crisis. The Federal Reserve cut the interest rate in the United States, but the Bank of Japan kept the interest rate unchanged in Japan. With a narrowing of the U.S. interest rate differential, funds flowed out of the United States. Also, currency traders expected the U.S.

dollar to depreciate against the yen. The demand for U.S. dollars decreased and the supply of U.S. dollars increased.

In part (a) of the figure, the demand curve shifted leftward from D_{07} to D_{12}, the supply curve shifted rightward from S_{07} to S_{12}, and the exchange rate fell to 77 yen per U.S. dollar.

An Appreciating U.S. Dollar: 2012–2014 Between January 2012 and June 2014, the U.S. dollar appreciated against the yen. It rose from 77 yen to 102 yen per U.S. dollar. Part (b) of the figure provides an explanation for this appreciation. The demand and supply curves labeled D_{12} and S_{12} are the same as in part (a).

During 2013 and 2014, the Federal Reserve kept the U.S. interest rate low, but traders began to expect a future interest rate rise. Interest rates in Japan were even lower than in the United States, and the Bank of Japan, the central bank, embarked on a policy of expanding the Japanese money supply. With an expected future increase in U.S. interest rates and a lessened prospect of a rise in Japanese interest rates, the U.S. interest rate differential was expected to increase, so the dollar was expected to appreciate. The demand for U.S. dollars increased, and the supply of U.S. dollars decreased.

In the figure, the demand curve shifted rightward from D_{12} to D_{14}, the supply curve shifted leftward from S_{12} to S_{14}, and the exchange rate rose to 102 yen per U.S. dollar

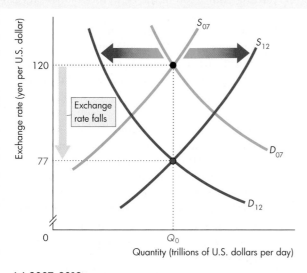

(a) 2007–2012

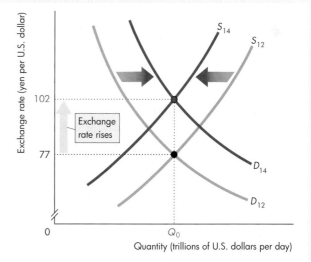

(b) 2012–2014

The Falling and Rising U.S. Dollar

◆ Arbitrage, Speculation, and Market Fundamentals

You've just seen how an exchange rate is determined. In our example, we used the U.S. dollar–Japanese yen exchange rate, but exchange rates between the U.S. dollar and all other currencies are determined in a similar way. So are the exchange rates *among* the other currencies such as that of the European euro and U.K. pound. Exchange rates are kept in alignment with each other by a process called *arbitrage*.

Arbitrage

Arbitrage is the practice of seeking to profit by buying in one market and selling for a higher price in another related market. Arbitrage in the foreign exchange market and international loans markets and goods markets achieves three outcomes:

- The law of one price
- No round-trip profit
- Interest rate parity
- Purchasing power parity

The Law of One Price The *law of one price* states that if an item is traded in more than one place, the price will be the same in all locations. An example of this law is that the exchange rate between the U.S. dollar and the U.K. pound is the same in New York as it is in London.

You can see why arbitrage brings about this outcome by imagining that the exchange rate in London is 0.60 U.K. pounds per dollar and the price in New York is 0.61 U.K. pounds per dollar. In this imaginary sitiuation, a trader who buys dollars in London and sells them in New York makes a profit of 0.01 U.K. pounds on every dollar traded. A trade of 1 million dollars brings a profit of 10,000 U.K. pounds.

Within a few seconds, the demand for U.K. pounds increases in London and the supply of U.K. pounds increases in New York. These changes in demand and supply raise the exchange rate in London and lower it in New York and make it equal in both markets—removing the profit opportunity.

No Round-Trip Profit A round trip is using currency *A* to buy currency *B*, and then using *B* to buy *A*. A round trip might involve more stages, using *B* to buy *C* and then using *C* to buy *A*.

Arbitrage removes profit from all transactions of this type. Any fleeting profit is taken, and the changes in supply and demand induced by the momentarily available profit snap the exchange rates back to levels that remove the profit.

Interest Rate Parity Borrowers and lenders must choose the currency in which to denominate their assets and debts. **Interest rate parity**, which means equal rates of return across currencies, means that for risk-free transactions, there is no gain from choosing one currency over another.

To see why interest rate parity always prevails, suppose a Brazilian real bank deposit in Rio de Janeiro earns 10 percent a year and a U.S. dollar bank deposit in New York earns 1 percent a year. Why wouldn't people move their funds from New York to Rio?

The answer begins with the fact that to earn 10 percent in Rio, funds must be converted from U.S. dollars to reals at the beginning of the year and from reals back to dollars at the end of the year. This transaction can be done without risk by selling reals for U.S. dollars today for delivery one year from today at an exchange rate agreed today. Such a transaction is called a *future* or *forward* transaction and it takes place at the *one-year forward exchange rate*.

Suppose that today's exchange rate is 2.30 reals per dollar, and you convert $100 to 230 reals. In one year, you will have 253 reals—your deposit of 230 reals plus interest of 23 reals. If the one-year forward exchange rate is 2.50 reals per U.S. dollar, you can contract today to sell 253 reals for $101 for delivery in one year. But that is exactly the amount you can earn by putting your $100 in the New York bank and earning 1 percent a year.

If for a few seconds, interest rate parity did not hold and it was possible to profit from buying and holding Brazilian reals, traders would flock to the profit opportunity, supply dollars and demand reals, and drive the exchange rate to its interest rate parity level.

Purchasing Power Parity Suppose a camera costs 10,000 yen in Tokyo and $100 in New York. If the exchange rate is 100 yen per dollar, the two monies have the same value. You can buy the camera in either Tokyo or New York for the same price. You can express that price as either 10,000 yen or $100, but the price is the same in the two currencies.

The situation we've just described is called **purchasing power parity** (or PPP), which means *equal value of money*. PPP is an example of the law of one price, and if it does not prevail, arbitrage forces go to work. To see these forces, suppose that the price of the camera in New York is $120, but in Tokyo it remains at 10,000 yen and the exchange rate remains at 100 yen per dollar. In this case, the camera in Tokyo still costs 10,000 yen or $100, but in New York, it costs $120 or 12,000 yen. Money buys more in Japan than in the United States. Money is *not* of equal value in the two countries.

Arbitrage now kicks in. With the camera cheaper in Toyko than in New York, the demand for cameras increases in Tokyo and the supply of cameras increases in New York. The New York price falls and the Tokyo price rises to eliminate the price difference and restore purchasing power parity.

If most goods and services cost more in one country than another, the currency of the first country is said to be *overvalued*: a depreciation of the currency would restore PPP. Similarly, the currency of the country with the lower prices is said to be *undervalued*: an appreciation of that currency would restore PPP. When goods and services cost the same in two countries, their currencies are said to be at their PPP levels.

Determining whether a currency is overvalued or undervalued based on PPP is not easy, and testing PPP by looking at individual prices requires care to ensure that the goods compared are identical. What is identical isn't always immediately obvious (see *Economics in Action* below).

Speculation

Speculation is trading on the *expectation* of making a profit. Speculation contrasts with arbitrage, which is trading on the certainty of making a profit. Most foreign exchange transactions are based on speculation, which explains why the expected future exchange rate plays such a central role in the foreign exchange market.

The expected future exchange rate influences both supply and demand, so it influences the current equilibrium exchange rate. But what determines the expected future exchange rate?

The Expected Future Exchange Rate An expectation is a forecast. Exchange rate forecasts, like weather forecasts, are made over horizons that run from a few hours to many months and perhaps years. Also, like weather forecasters, exchange rate forecasters use scientific models and data to make their predictions.

But exchange rate forecasting differs from weather forecasting in three ways. First, exchange rate forecasts are hedged with a lot of uncertainty; second, there are many divergent forecasts; and third, the forecasts influence the outcome.

The dependence of today's exchange rate on forecasts of tomorrow's exchange rate can give rise to exchange rate volatility in the short run.

ECONOMICS IN ACTION

A Big Mac Index

Because a Big Mac is the same in Chicago as in Beijing, *The Economist* magazine wondered if its price in these cities might tell us how far China's yuan is from its PPP level. In July 2014, the price of a Big Mac was $4.80 in America and 16.93 yuan or $2.73 in China. Does this dollar price difference mean that the yuan is undervalued?

The Big Mac price comparison doesn't answer this question. A Big Mac *looks* the same in all places but most of its value is in its *service*, not its *appearance*.

The figure shows the price of a Big Mac as a percentage of the U.S. price averaged over 2000, 2007, and 2014. It shows that the price is persistently above the U.S. price in a few rich countries and persistently below the U.S. price in lower-income countries.

The persistent differences arise from different relative prices of services, not from over- or under-valued currencies.

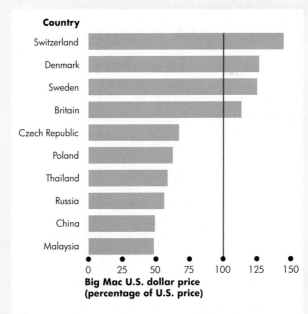

The U.S. Dollar Price of a Big Mac in 10 Countries

Source of data: *The Economist*, April 2000, June 2007, and July 2014.

Exchange Rate Volatility An exchange rate might rise one day and fall the next, as news about the influences on the exchange rate change the expected future exchange rate. For example, news that the Fed is going to start to raise U.S. interest rates next month brings an immediate increase in the demand for U.S. dollars, decrease in the supply of U.S. dollars, and appreciation of the U.S. dollar. As the news is digested and its expected consequences revised, expectations are revised, sometimes upward and sometimes downward, bringing further changes in the exchange rate.

The influences of expectations and the constant arrival of news about the influences on supply and demand, make day-to-day and week-to-week changes in the exchange rate impossible to predict. But trends around which the exchange rate fluctuates are predictable and depend on market fundamentals.

Market Fundamentals

The demand for U.S. dollars depends on world demand for U.S. exports, the supply of U.S. dollars depends on U.S. demand for imports, and both demand and supply depend on the U.S. interest rate differential. These are the market fundamentals that influence the exchange rate. But how they influence the exchange rate is different in the short run and the long run. The short-run influences are those described in the previous section of this chapter. To understand the long-run, we need to define and understand the role played by the real exchange rate.

The Real Exchange Rate The **real exchange rate** is the relative price of U.S.-produced goods and services to foreign-produced goods and services. It is a measure of the quantity of the real GDP of other countries that a unit of U.S. real GDP buys. For example, the real Japanese yen exchange rate, *RER*, is

$$RER = (E \times P) \div P^*,$$

where E is the exchange rate (yen per U.S. dollar), P is the U.S. price level, and P^* is the Japanese price level.

To understand the real exchange rate, suppose that the exchange rate E is 100 yen per dollar. The United States produces only computer chips priced at \$150 each, so P equals \$150 and $E \times P$ equals 15,000 yen. Japan produces only iPods priced at 5,000 yen each, so P^* equals 5,000 yen. Then the real Japanese yen exchange rate is

$$RER = (100 \times 150) \div 5,000 = 3 \text{ iPods per chip.}$$

If Japan and the United States produced identical goods, the real exchange rate would equal 1 unit of U.S. real GDP per unit of Japanese real GDP.

In reality, U.S. real GDP is a different bundle of goods and services from Japanese real GDP. So the real exchange rate is not 1 and it changes over time. The forces of demand and supply in the markets for the millions of goods and services that make up real GDP determine the relative price of Japanese and U.S. real GDP and the real exchange rate.

Price Levels and Money We can turn the real exchange rate equation around and determine the exchange rate as

$$E = RER \times P^* \div P.$$

This equation says that the exchange rate equals the real exchange rate multiplied by the foreign price level, divided by the domestic price level.

In the long run, the quantity of money determines the price level. But the quantity theory of money applies to all countries, so the quantity of money in Japan determines the price level in Japan, and the quantity of money in the United States determines the price level in the United States.

For a given real exchange rate, a change in the quantity of money brings a change in the price level *and* a change in the exchange rate.

The market fundamentals that determine the exchange rate in the long run are the real exchange rate and the quantities of money in each economy.

◆ REVIEW QUIZ

1 What is arbitrage and what are its effects in the foreign exchange market?
2 What is interest rate parity and what happens when this condition doesn't hold?
3 What makes an exchange rate hard to predict?
4 What is purchasing power parity and what happens when this condition doesn't hold?
5 What determines the real exchange rate and the nominal exchange rate in the short run?
6 What determines the real exchange rate and the nominal exchange rate in the long run?

Work these questions in Study Plan 26.2 and get instant feedback. Do a Key Terrms Quiz.   MyEconLab

Exchange Rate Policy

Because the exchange rate is the price of a country's money in terms of another country's money, governments and central banks must have a policy toward the exchange rate. Three possible exchange rate policies are

- Flexible exchange rate
- Fixed exchange rate
- Crawling peg

Flexible Exchange Rate

A **flexible exchange rate** is an exchange rate that is determined by demand and supply in the foreign exchange market with no direct intervention by the central bank.

Most countries, including the United States, operate a flexible exchange rate, and the foreign exchange market that we have studied so far in this chapter is an example of a flexible exchange rate regime.

But even a flexible exchange rate is influenced by central bank actions. If the Fed raises the U.S. interest rate and other countries keep their interest rates unchanged, the demand for U.S. dollars increases, the supply of U.S. dollars decreases, and the exchange rate rises. (Similarly, if the Fed lowers the U.S. interest rate, the demand for U.S. dollars decreases, the supply increases, and the exchange rate falls.)

In a flexible exchange rate regime, when the central bank changes the interest rate, its purpose is not usually to influence the exchange rate, but to achieve some other monetary policy objective. (We return to this topic at length in Chapter 31.)

Fixed Exchange Rate

A **fixed exchange rate** is an exchange rate that is determined by a decision of the government or the central bank and is achieved by central bank intervention in the foreign exchange market to block the unregulated forces of demand and supply.

The world economy operated a fixed exchange rate regime from the end of World War II to the early 1970s. China had a fixed exchange rate until recently. Hong Kong has had a fixed exchange rate for many years and continues with that policy today.

Active intervention in the foreign exchange market is required to achieve a fixed exchange rate.

If the Fed wanted to fix the U.S. dollar exchange rate against the Japanese yen, the Fed would have to sell U.S. dollars to prevent the exchange rate from rising above the target value and buy U.S. dollars to prevent the exchange rate from falling below the target value.

There is no limit to the quantity of U.S. dollars that the Fed can *sell*. The Fed creates U.S. dollars and can create any quantity it chooses. But there is a limit to the quantity of U.S. dollars the Fed can *buy*. That limit is set by U.S. official foreign currency reserves because to buy U.S. dollars the Fed must sell foreign currency. Intervention to buy U.S. dollars stops when U.S. official foreign currency reserves run out.

Let's look at the foreign exchange interventions that the Fed can make.

Suppose the Fed wants the exchange rate to be steady at 100 yen per U.S. dollar. If the exchange rate rises above 100 yen, the Fed sells dollars. If the exchange rate falls below 100 yen, the Fed buys dollars. By these actions, the Fed keeps the exchange rate close to its target rate of 100 yen per U.S. dollar.

Figure 26.6 shows the Fed's intervention in the foreign exchange market. The supply of dollars is S and initially the demand for dollars is D_0. The equilibrium exchange rate is 100 yen per dollar. This exchange rate is also the Fed's target exchange rate, shown by the horizontal red line.

When the demand for U.S. dollars increases and the demand curve shifts rightward to D_1, the Fed sells $100 billion. This action prevents the exchange rate from rising. When the demand for U.S. dollars decreases and the demand curve shifts leftward to D_2, the Fed buys $100 billion. This action prevents the exchange rate from falling.

If the demand for U.S. dollars fluctuates between D_1 and D_2 and on average is D_0, the Fed can repeatedly intervene in the way we've just seen. Sometimes the Fed buys and sometimes it sells but, on average, it neither buys nor sells.

But suppose the demand for U.S. dollars *increases permanently* from D_0 to D_1. To maintain the exchange rate at 100 yen per U.S. dollar, the Fed must sell dollars and buy foreign currency, so U.S. official foreign currency reserves would be increasing. At some point, the Fed would abandon the exchange rate of 100 yen per U.S. dollar and stop piling up foreign currency reserves.

Now suppose the demand for U.S. dollars *decreases permanently* from D_0 to D_2. In this situation, the Fed

FIGURE 26.6   Foreign Exchange
Market Intervention

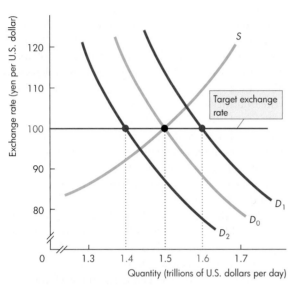

Initially, the demand for U.S. dollars is D_0, the supply of U.S. dollars is S, and the exchange rate is 100 yen per U.S. dollar. The Fed can intervene in the foreign exchange market to keep the exchange rate close to its target rate (100 yen in this example). If the demand for U.S. dollars increases and the demand curve shifts from D_0 to D_1, the Fed sells dollars. If the demand for U.S. dollars decreases and the demand curve shifts from D_0 to D_2, the Fed buys dollars. Persistent intervention on one side of the market cannot be sustained.

MyEconLab Animation

cannot maintain the exchange rate at 100 yen per U.S. dollar indefinitely. To hold the exchange rate at 100 yen, the Fed must *buy* U.S. dollars. When the Fed buys U.S. dollars in the foreign exchange market, it uses U.S. official foreign currency reserves. So the Fed's action decreases its foreign currency reserves. Eventually, the Fed would run out of foreign currency and would then have to abandon the target exchange rate of 100 yen per U.S. dollar.

Crawling Peg

A **crawling peg** is an exchange rate that follows a path determined by a decision of the government or the central bank and is achieved in a similar way to a fixed exchange rate by central bank intervention in the foreign exchange market. A crawling peg works like a fixed exchange rate except that the target value

ECONOMICS IN ACTION

The People's Bank of China in the Foreign Exchange Market

You saw in the figure on p. 621 that the exchange rate between the U.S. dollar and the Chinese yuan was constant for several years. The reason for this constant exchange rate is that China's central bank, the People's Bank of China, intervened to operate a *fixed exchange rate policy*. From 1997 until 2005, the yuan was pegged at 8.28 yuan per U.S. dollar. Since 2005, the yuan has appreciated slightly, but it has not been permitted to fluctuate freely. Since 2005, the yuan has been on a crawling peg.

Why Does China Manage Its Exchange Rate? The popular story is that China manages its exchange rate to keep its export prices low and to make it easier to compete in world markets. You've seen that this story is correct *only in the short run*. With prices in China unchanged, a lower yuan–U.S. dollar exchange rate brings lower U.S. dollar prices for China's exports. But the yuan–U.S. dollar exchange rate was fixed for almost 10 years and has been managed for five more years. This long period of a fixed exchange rate has long-run, not short-run, effects. In the long run, the exchange rate has no effect on competitiveness. The reason is that prices adjust to reflect the exchange rate and the real exchange rate is unaffected by the nominal exchange rate.

So why does China fix its exchange rate? The most convincing answer is that China sees a fixed exchange rate as a way of controlling its inflation rate. By making the yuan crawl against the U.S. dollar, China's inflation rate is anchored to the U.S. inflation rate and will depart from U.S. inflation by an amount determined by the speed of the crawl.

changes. The target might change at fixed intervals (daily, weekly, monthly) or at random intervals.

The Fed has never operated a crawling peg, but some prominent countries do use this system. When China abandoned its fixed exchange rate, it replaced it with a crawling peg. Developing countries might use a crawling peg as a method of trying to control inflation—of keeping the inflation rate close to target.

The ideal crawling peg sets a target for the exchange rate equal to the equilibrium exchange rate

The bottom line is that in the long run, exchange rate policy is monetary policy, not foreign trade policy. To change its exports and imports, a country must change its comparative advantage (Chapter 2).

How Does China Manage Its Exchange Rate? The People's Bank manages the exchange rate between the yuan and the U.S. dollar by intervening in the foreign exchange market and buying U.S. dollars. But to do so, it must pile up U.S. dollars.

Part (a) of the figure shows the scale of China's increase in official foreign currency reserves, some of which are euros and yen but most of which are U.S. dollars. You can see that China's reserves increased by more than $400 billion a year in 2007 through 2010.

The demand and supply curves in part (b) of the figure illustrate what is happening in the market for U.S. dollars priced in terms of the yuan and explains why China's reserves have increased. The demand curve D and supply curve S intersect at 5 yuan per U.S. dollar. If the People's Bank of China takes no actions in the market, this exchange rate is the equilibrium rate (an assumed value).

The consequence of the fixed (and crawling peg) yuan exchange rate is that China has piled up U.S. dollar reserves on a huge scale. By mid-2006, China's official foreign currency reserves approached $1 trillion and by 2014, they had reached $4 trillion!

If the People's Bank stopped buying U.S. dollars, the U.S. dollar would depreciate and the yuan would appreciate—the yuan–U.S. dollar exchange rate would fall—and China would stop piling up U.S. dollar reserves.

In the example in the figure, the dollar would depreciate to 5 yuan per dollar.

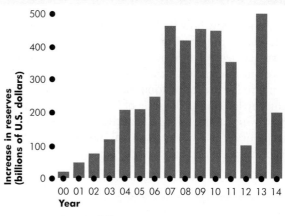

(a) Increase in U.S. dollar reserves

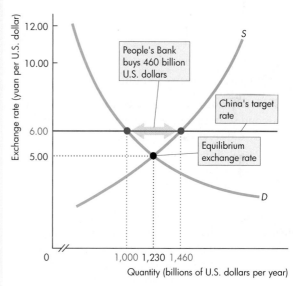

(b) Pegging the yuan

China's Foreign Exchange Market Intervention

Source of data: The People's Bank of China.

on average. The peg seeks only to prevent large swings in the expected future exchange rate that change demand and supply and make the exchange rate fluctuate too wildly.

A crawling peg departs from the ideal if, as often happens with a fixed exchange rate, the target rate departs from the equilibrium exchange rate for too long. When this happens, the country either runs out of reserves or piles up reserves.

In the final part of this chapter, we explain how the balance of international payments is determined.

◆ REVIEW QUIZ

1 What is a flexible exchange rate and how does it work?

2 What is a fixed exchange rate and how is its value fixed?

3 What is a crawling peg and how does it work?

4 How has China operated in the foreign exchange market, why, and with what effect?

Work these questions in Study Plan 26.3 and get instant feedback. Do a Key Terms Quiz.   MyEconLab

◆ Financing International Trade

You now know how the exchange rate is determined, but what is the effect of the exchange rate? How does currency depreciation or currency appreciation influence our international trade and payments? We're going to lay the foundation for addressing these questions by looking at the scale of international trading, borrowing, and lending and at the way in which we keep our records of international transactions. These records are called the *balance of payments accounts*.

Balance of Payments Accounts

A country's **balance of payments accounts** records its international trading, borrowing, and lending in three accounts:

1. Current account
2. Capital and financial account
3. Official settlements account

The **current account** records receipts from exports of goods and services sold abroad, payments for imports of goods and services from abroad, net interest income paid abroad, and net transfers abroad (such as foreign aid payments). The *current account balance* equals the sum of exports minus imports, net interest income, and net transfers.

The **capital and financial account** records foreign investment in the United States minus U.S. investment abroad. (This account also has a statistical discrepancy that arises from errors and omissions in measuring international capital transactions.)

The **official settlements account** records the change in **U.S. official reserves**, which are the government's holdings of foreign currency. If U.S. official reserves *increase*, the official settlements account balance is *negative*. The reason is that holding foreign money is like investing abroad. U.S. investment abroad is a minus item in the capital and financial account and in the official settlements account.

The sum of the balances on the three accounts *always* equals zero. That is, to pay for our current account deficit, we must either borrow more from abroad than we lend abroad or use our official reserves to cover the shortfall.

Table 26.1 shows the U.S. balance of payments accounts in 2013. Items in the current account and the capital and financial account that provide foreign

currency to the United States have a plus sign; items that cost the United States foreign currency have a minus sign. The table shows that in 2013, U.S. imports exceeded U.S. exports and the current account had a deficit of $400 billion. How do we pay for imports that exceed the value of our exports? That is, how do we pay for our current account deficit?

We pay by borrowing from the rest of the world. The capital account tells us by how much. We borrowed $1,017 billion (foreign investment in the United States) but made loans of $650 billion (U.S. investment abroad). Our *net* foreign borrowing was $1,017 billion minus $650 billion, which equals $367 billion. There is almost always a statistical discrepancy between capital and financial account and current account transactions, and in 2013, the discrepancy was $30 billion. Combining the discrepancy with the measured net foreign borrowing gives a capital and financial account balance of $397 billion.

TABLE 26.1   U.S. Balance of Payments Accounts in 2013

Current account	Billions of dollars
Exports of goods and services	+2,280
Imports of goods and services	–2,757
Net interest income	+209
Net transfers	–132
Current account balance	–400

Capital and financial account	
Foreign investment in the United States	+1,017
U.S. investment abroad	–650
Statistical discrepancy	+30
Capital and financial account balance	+397

Official settlements account	
Official settlements account balance	3

Source of data: Bureau of Economic Analysis.

The capital and financial account balance plus the current account balance equals the change in U.S. official reserves. In 2013, the capital and financial account balance of $397 billion plus the current account balance of –$400 billion equaled –$3 billion. Official reserves *decreased* in 2013 by $3 billion. Holding less foreign reserves is like borrowing from the rest of the world, so this amount appears in the official settlements account in Table 26.1 as +$3 billion. The sum of the balances on the three balance of payments accounts equals zero.

To see more clearly what the nation's balance of payments accounts mean, think about your own balance of payments accounts. They are similar to the nation's accounts.

An Individual's Balance of Payments Accounts An individual's current account records the income from supplying the services of factors of production and the expenditure on goods and services. Consider Jackie, for example. She worked in 2014 and earned an income of $25,000. Jackie has $10,000 worth of investments that earned her an interest income of $1,000. Jackie's current account shows an income of $26,000. Jackie spent $18,000 buying consumption goods and services. She also bought a new house, which cost her $60,000. So Jackie's total expenditure was $78,000. Jackie's expenditure minus her income is $52,000 ($78,000 minus $26,000). This amount is Jackie's current account deficit.

ECONOMICS IN ACTION
Three Decades of Deficits

The numbers that you reviewed in Table 26.1 give a snapshot of the balance of payments accounts in 2013. The figure below puts that snapshot into perspective by showing the balance of payments between 1980 and the first half of 2014.

Because the economy grows and the price level rises, changes in the dollar value of the balance of payments do not convey much information. To remove the influences of economic growth and inflation, the figure shows the balance of payments expressed as a percentage of nominal GDP.

As you can see, a large current account deficit emerged during the 1980s but declined from 1987 to 1991. The current account deficit then increased through 2006, decreased again through 2009, and then remained steady.

The capital and financial account balance is almost a mirror image of the current account balance. The official settlements balance is very small in comparison with the balances on the other two accounts.

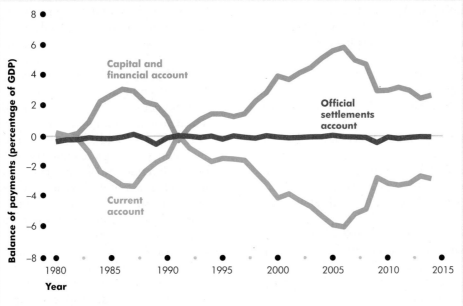

The U.S. Balance of Payments

Source of data: Bureau of Economic Analysis.

To pay for expenditure of $52,000 in excess of her income, Jackie must either use the money that she has in the bank or take out a loan. Suppose that Jackie took out a loan of $50,000 to help buy her house and that this loan was the only borrowing that she did. Borrowing is an *inflow* in the capital account, so Jackie's capital account *surplus* was $50,000. With a current account deficit of $52,000 and a capital account surplus of $50,000, Jackie was still $2,000 short. She got that $2,000 from her own bank account. Her cash holdings decreased by $2,000.

Jackie's income from her work is like a country's income from its exports. Her income from her investments is like a country's interest income from foreigners. Her purchases of goods and services, including her purchase of a house, are like a country's imports. Jackie's loan—borrowing from someone else—is like a country's borrowing from the rest of the world. The change in Jackie's bank account is like the change in the country's official reserves.

Borrowers and Lenders

A country that is borrowing more from the rest of the world than it is lending to the rest of the world is called a **net borrower**. Similarly, a **net lender** is a country that is lending more to the rest of the world than it is borrowing from the rest of the world.

The United States is a net borrower, but it has not always been in this situation. Throughout the 1960s and most of the 1970s, the United States was a net lender to the rest of the world—the United States had a current account surplus and a capital account deficit. But from the early 1980s, with the exception of only a single year, 1991, the United States has been a net borrower from the rest of the world. And during the years since 1992, the scale of U.S. borrowing has mushroomed.

Most countries are net borrowers like the United States. But a few countries, including China, Japan, and oil-rich Saudi Arabia, are net lenders. In 2014, when the United States borrowed more than $397 billion from the rest of the world, China alone lent more than $200 billion.

International borrowing and lending takes place in the global market for loanable funds. You studied the loanable funds market in Chapter 24, but there, we didn't take explicit account of the effects of the balance of payments and international borrowing and lending on the market. That's what we will now do.

The Global Loanable Funds Market

Figure 26.7(a) illustrates the demand for loanable funds, DLF_W, and the supply of loanable funds, SLF_W, in the global loanable funds market. The world equilibrium real interest rate makes the quantity of funds supplied in the world as a whole equal to the quantity demanded. In this example, the equilibrium real interest rate is 5 percent a year and the quantity of funds is $10 trillion.

An International Borrower Figure 26.7(b) shows the loanable funds market in a country that borrows from the rest of the world. The country's demand for loanable funds, DLF, is part of the world demand in Fig. 26.7(a). The country's supply of loanable funds, SLF_D, is part of the world supply.

If this country were isolated from the global market, the real interest rate would be 6 percent a year (where the DLF and SLF_D curves intersect). But if the country is integrated into the global economy, with an interest rate of 6 percent a year, funds would *flood into* it. With a real interest rate of 5 percent a year in the global market, suppliers of loanable funds would seek the higher return in this country. In effect, the country faces the supply of loanable funds curve, SLF, which is horizontal at the world equilibrium real interest rate.

The country's demand for loanable funds and the world interest rate determine the equilibrium quantity of loanable funds—$2.5 billion in Fig. 26.7(b).

An International Lender Figure 26.7(c) shows the situation in a country that lends to the rest of the world. As before, the country's demand for loanable funds, DLF, is part of the world demand and the country's supply of loanable funds, SLF_D, is part of the world supply in Fig. 26.7(a).

If this country were isolated from the global market, the real interest rate would be 4 percent a year (where the DLF and SLF_D curves intersect). But if this country is integrated into the global economy, with an interest rate of 4 percent a year, funds would quickly *flow out* of it. With a real interest rate of 5 percent a year in the rest of the world, domestic suppliers of loanable funds would seek the higher return in other countries. Again, the country faces the supply of loanable funds curve, SLF, which is horizontal at the world equilibrium real interest rate.

The country's demand for loanable funds and the world interest rate determine the equilibrium quantity of loanable funds—$1.5 billion in Fig. 26.7(c).

FIGURE 26.7 Borrowing and Lending in the Global Loanable Funds Market

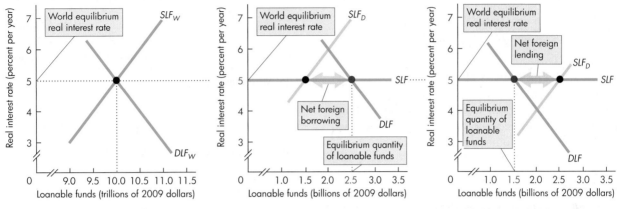

(a) The global market   **(b) An international borrower**   **(c) An international lender**

In the global loanable funds market in part (a), the demand for loanable funds curve, DLF_W, and the supply of funds curve, SLF_W, determine the world real interest rate. Each country can get funds at the world real interest rate and faces the (horizontal) supply curve SLF in parts (b) and (c).

At the world real interest rate, borrowers in part (b)

want more funds than the quantity supplied by domestic lenders, $1.5 million on the domestic supply curve SLF_D. The shortage is made up by net foreign borrowing.

Domestic suppliers of funds in part (c) want to lend more than domestic borrowers demand. The excess quantity supplied goes to foreign borrowers.

MyEconLab Animation

Debtors and Creditors

A net borrower might be decreasing its net assets held in the rest of the world, or it might be going deeper into debt. A nation's total stock of foreign investment determines whether it is a debtor or a creditor. A **debtor nation** is a country that during its entire history has borrowed more from the rest of the world than it has lent to it. It has a stock of outstanding debt to the rest of the world that exceeds the stock of its own claims on the rest of the world. A **creditor nation** is a country that during its entire history has invested more in the rest of the world than other countries have invested in it.

The United States was a debtor nation through the nineteenth century as we borrowed from Europe to finance our westward expansion, railroads, and industrialization. We paid off our debt and became a creditor nation for most of the twentieth century. But following a string of current account deficits, we became a debtor nation again in 1986.

Since 1986, the total stock of U.S. borrowing from the rest of the world has exceeded U.S. lending to the rest of the world. The largest debtor nations are the capital-hungry developing countries (such as the United States was during the nineteenth century).

The international debt of these countries grew from less than a third to more than a half of their gross domestic product during the 1980s and created what was called the "Third World debt crisis."

Should we be concerned that the United States is a net borrower and a debtor? The answer depends on whether the borrowing is financing investment that in turn is generating economic growth and higher income, or financing consumption expenditure. If the borrowed money is used to finance consumption, it will eventually have to be reduced, and the longer it goes on, the greater is the reduction in consumption that will eventually be necessary.

Is U.S. Borrowing for Consumption?

In 2014, the United States borrowed $397 billion from abroad. In that year, private investment in buildings, plant, and equipment was $2,829 billion and government investment in defense equipment and social projects was $588 billion. All this investment added to the nation's capital and increased productivity. Government also spends on education and healthcare services, which increase *human capital*. U.S. international borrowing is financing private and public investment, not consumption.

Current Account Balance

What determines a country's current account balance and net foreign borrowing? You've seen that net exports (*NX*) is the main item in the current account. We can define the current account balance (*CAB*) as

$$CAB = NX + \text{Net interest income} + \text{Net transfers}.$$

We can study the current account balance by looking at what determines net exports because the other two items are small and do not fluctuate much.

Net Exports

Net exports are determined by the government budget and private saving and investment. To see how net exports are determined, we need to recall some of the things that we learned in Chapter 24 about the flows of funds that finance investment. Table 26.2 refreshes your memory and summarizes some calculations.

Part (a) lists the national income variables that are needed, with their symbols. Part (b) defines three balances: net exports, the government sector balance, and the private sector balance.

Net exports is exports of goods and services minus imports of goods and services.

The **government sector balance** is equal to net taxes minus government expenditure on goods and services. If that number is positive, a government sector surplus is lent to other sectors; if that number is negative, a government deficit must be financed by borrowing from other sectors. The government sector deficit is the sum of the deficits of the federal, state, and local governments.

The **private sector balance** is saving minus investment. If saving exceeds investment, a private sector surplus is lent to other sectors. If investment exceeds saving, a private sector deficit is financed by borrowing from other sectors.

Part (b) also shows the values of these balances for the United States in 2014. As you can see, net exports were –$564 billion, a deficit of $564 billion. The government sector's revenue from *net* taxes was $2,362 billion and its expenditure was $3,162 billion, so the government sector balance was –$800 billion—a deficit of $800 billion. The private sector saved $3,065 billion and invested $2,829 billion, so its balance was $236 billion—a surplus of $236 billion.

Part (c) shows the relationship among the three balances. From the *National Income and Product*

TABLE 26.2 Net Exports, the Government Budget, Saving, and Investment

	Symbols and equations	United States in 2014 (billions of dollars)
(a) Variables		
Exports*	X	2,335
Imports*	M	2,899
Government expenditure	G	3,162
Net taxes	T	2,362
Investment	I	2,829
Saving	S	3,065
(b) Balances		
Net exports	X – M	2,335 – 2,899 = –564
Government sector	T – G	2,362 – 3,162 = –800
Private sector	S – I	3,065 – 2,829 = +236
(c) Relationship among balances		
National accounts	$Y = C + I + G + X - M$	
	$= C + S + T$	
Rearranging:	$X - M = S - I + T - G$	
Net exports	X – M	–564
equals:		
Government sector	T – G	–800
plus		
Private sector	S – I	+236

Source of data: Bureau of Economic Analysis. The data are for 2014, second quarter, seasonally adjusted at annual rate.

*The *National Income and Product Accounts* measures of exports and imports are slightly different from the balance of payments accounts measures in Table 26.1 on p. 634.

Accounts, we know that real GDP, *Y*, is the sum of consumption expenditure (*C*), investment, government expenditure, and net exports. Real GDP also equals the sum of consumption expenditure, saving, and net taxes. Rearranging these equations tells us that net exports is the sum of the government sector balance and the private sector balance. In the United States in 2014, the government sector balance was

ECONOMICS IN ACTION

The Three Sector Balances

You've seen that net exports equal the sum of the government sector balance and the private sector balance. How do these three sector balances fluctuate over time?

The figure answers this question. It shows the government sector balance (the red line), net exports (the blue line), and the private sector balance (the green line).

The private sector balance and the government sector balance move in opposite directions. When the government sector deficit increased during the late 1980s and early 1990s, the private sector surplus increased. And when the government sector deficit decreased and became a surplus during the late 1990s and early 2000s, the private sector's surplus decreased and became a deficit. And when the government deficit increased yet again from 2007 to 2009, the private sector deficit shrank and became a surplus.

Sometimes, when the government sector deficit increases, as it did during the first half of the 1980s, net exports become more negative. But after the early 1990s, net exports did not follow the government sector balance closely. Rather, net exports respond to the *sum* of the government sector and private sector

balances. When both the private sector and the government sector have a deficit, net exports are negative and the combined private and government deficit is financed by borrowing from the rest of the world. But the dominant trend in net exports is negative.

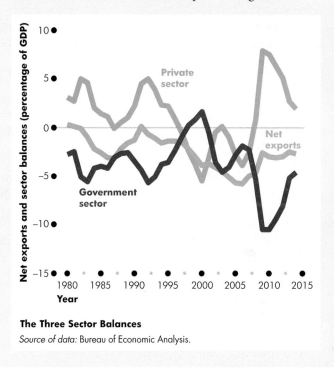

The Three Sector Balances

Source of data: Bureau of Economic Analysis.

−$800 billion and the private sector balance was $236 billion. The government sector balance plus the private sector balance equaled net exports of −$564 billion.

Where Is the Exchange Rate?

We haven't mentioned the exchange rate while discussing the balance of payments. Doesn't it play a role? The answer is that in the short run it does but in the long run it doesn't.

In the short run, a fall in the dollar lowers the real exchange rate, which makes U.S. imports more costly and U.S. exports more competitive. A higher price of imported consumption goods and services might induce a decrease in consumption expenditure and an increase in saving. A higher price of imported capital goods might induce a decrease in investment. Other things remaining the same, an increase in saving or a decrease in investment decreases the private sector deficit and decreases the current account deficit.

But in the long run, a change in the nominal exchange rate leaves the real exchange rate unchanged and plays no role in influencing the current account balance.

◆ REVIEW QUIZ

1 What are the transactions that the balance of payments accounts record?
2 Is the United States a net borrower or a net lender? Is it a debtor or a creditor nation?
3 How are net exports and the government sector balance linked?

Work these questions in Study Plan 26.4 and get instant feedback. Do a Key Terms Quiz.   MyEconLab

◆ *Economics in the News* on pp. 640–641 looks at the foreign exchange market as the U.S. dollar rose against the euro in the summer of 2014.

The Rising Dollar

Fed Minutes Lift U.S. Bond Yields and Dollar

The Financial Times
August 20, 2014

… [The] dollar extended its recent advance as the markets took a hawkish view of the minutes of the Federal Reserve's July policy meeting. …

Analysts said the minutes indicated that the Fed's Open Market Committee had moved closer toward raising interest rates. …

Paul Dales at Capital Economics said the minutes made it very clear that any change in officials' expectations of when the first rate hike would take place depended on incoming economic data. …

"Overall, a lot still depends on whether or not wage growth accelerates as the labor market continues to improve. Nonetheless, the minutes provide some support to our view that rates will first rise in March and will then increase by more than widely expected."…

But the bond and currency markets moved to price in an earlier tightening. The dollar index—a measure of the U.S. currency's value against a basket of its peers—was up 0.5 percent at its highest level in 11 months. The euro was down 0.4 percent at $1.3262—its first break below $1.33 since November—while the dollar was up 0.9 percent versus the yen at a four-month high of ¥103.75. …

This rekindled the prospect of an early U.K. rate rise and drove sterling as high as $1.6678 against the dollar—although it later eased back to $1.6593, down 0.1 percent on the day, as the dollar rose broadly. …

Recent data showing a drop in the annual rate of U.K inflation last month—and stagnant wage growth—had persuaded some in the markets to push back their expectations of the timing of a rate rise. …

©2014 The Financial Times. Printed with permission. Further reproduction prohibited.

MyEconLab More Economics in the News

ESSENCE OF THE STORY

- The minutes of the Federal Reserve's July FOMC meeting indicated a movement toward raising interest rates.
- When the first increase occurs will depend on wage and employment growth.
- Paul Dales of Capital Economics predicts that interest rates will first rise in March 2015 and then increase by more than most expect.
- Anticipating an earlier interest rate rise, the dollar strengthened against other currencies.

ECONOMIC ANALYSIS

- The news article says the dollar rose against "a basket" of other currencies when the Fed published the minutes of the July meeting of the FOMC on August 20, 2014.

- The main currencies in the "basket" are the Japanese yen, the European euro, and the U.K. pound.

- Figure 1 shows how the dollar exchange rate changed against these three currencies from July 2 to August 27, 2014.

- You can see that the dollar increased against all three currencies. It increased most against the European euro and the U.K. pound and least against the Japanese yen.

- The Fed's July meeting minutes indicated that the Fed was moving closer to being ready to raise interest rates, and the news article attributes the stronger dollar to this news.

- But as you can see in Fig. 1, although the foreign exchange value of the dollar did rise immediately after the July minutes were released, it had been rising for almost two months.

- Also, after August 21, the dollar rose only against the euro. Against the yen and the pound, the dollar remained approximately constant.

- These facts about the timing of changes in the exchange rate and the different behavior of the dollar against the euro from the other two currencies suggests that other forces are at work.

- The summer of 2014 was a time of global tension arising from the political situation in Ukraine. Currency traders sold the Russian ruble and the Ukrainian hryvinia and bought the U.S. dollar rather than the euro or pound.

- The Russia-Ukraine situation and the added effect of the expectation of a U.S. interest rate rise changed the demand for and supply of U.S. dollars in the foreign exchange market.

- The political tensions and predicted future rise in the U.S. interest rate increased the expected future exchange rate.

- With a higher expected future exchange rate, the demand for dollars increases and the supply of dollars decreases, and these changes in demand and supply bring an immediate appreciation of the dollar.

- Figure 2 shows these changes in supply and demand and their effects on the U.S. dollar–euro exchange rate.

- On July 2, demand was D_0 and supply was S_0. The equilibrium exchange rate was 0.732 euros per dollar. (The equilibrium quantity of dollars traded is an assumption.)

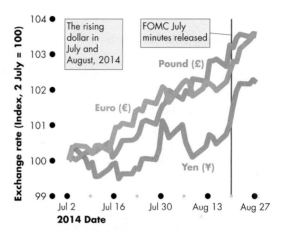

Figure 1 The U.S. Dollar Exchange Rate in July and August 2014

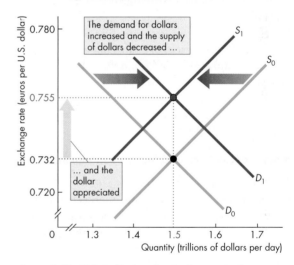

Figure 2 The U.S. Dollar Foreign Exchange Market

- On August 22, demand had increased to D_1 and supply had decreased to S_1. The equilibrium exchange rate had risen to 0.755 euros per dollar—an appreciation of the dollar (and a depreciation of the euro).

- Although we can explain past changes in the exchange rate, we can't predict the future exchange rate because we can't predict the course of the factors that influence it.

641

SUMMARY

Key Points

The Foreign Exchange Market (pp. 620–627)

- Foreign currency is obtained in exchange for domestic currency in the foreign exchange market.
- Demand and supply in the foreign exchange market determine the exchange rate.
- The higher the exchange rate, the smaller is the quantity of U.S. dollars demanded and the greater is the quantity of U.S. dollars supplied.
- The equilibrium exchange rate makes the quantity of U.S. dollars demanded equal the quantity of U.S. dollars supplied.
- Changes in the demand for U.S. exports change the demand for U.S. dollars and changes in the U.S. demand for imports change the supply of U.S. dollars .
- Changes in the U.S. interest rate differential or the expected future exchange rate change *both* the demand for and supply of U.S. dollars, but in opposite directions.

Working Problems 1 to 5 will give you a better understanding of the foreign exchange market.

Arbitrage, Speculation, and Market Fundamentals (pp. 628–630)

- Arbitrage in the foreign exchange market achieves interest rate parity and purchasing power parity.
- Speculation in the foreign exchange market can bring excess volatility to the exchange rate.
- In the long run, the exchange rate is determined by the real exchange rate and the relative quantities of money.

Working Problems 6 to 8 will give you a better understanding of arbitrage, speculation, and market fundamentals.

Exchange Rate Policy (pp. 631–633)

- An exchange rate can be flexible, fixed, or a crawling peg.
- To achieve a fixed or a crawling exchange rate, a central bank must either buy or sell foreign currency in the foreign exchange market.

Working Problem 9 will give you a better understanding of exchange rate policy.

Financing International Trade (pp. 634–639)

- A country's international transactions are recorded in its current account, capital account, and official settlements account.
- The current account balance is similar to net exports and is determined by the government sector balance plus the private sector balance.
- International borrowing and lending take place in the global loanable funds market.

Working Problem 10 will give you a better understanding of financing international trade.

Key Terms

MyEconLab Key Terms Quiz

Arbitrage, 628
Balance of payments accounts, 634
Capital and financial account, 634
Crawling peg, 632
Creditor nation, 637
Current account, 634
Debtor nation, 637
Exchange rate, 620

Fixed exchange rate, 631
Flexible exchange rate, 631
Foreign currency, 620
Foreign exchange market, 620
Government sector balance, 638
Interest rate parity, 628
Net borrower, 636
Net exports, 638

Net lender, 636
Official settlements account, 634
Private sector balance, 638
Purchasing power parity, 628
Real exchange rate, 630
U.S. interest rate differential, 625
U.S. official reserves, 634

WORKED PROBLEM

MyEconLab   You can work this problem in Chapter 26 Study Plan.

On June 1, 2015, the exchange rate was 101 yen per U.S. dollar. During that day, the Fed made a surprise announcement that it would raise the interest rate next month by 1 percentage point. At the same moment, the Bank of Japan announced that it would lower the interest rate next month.

On June 2, 2015, the exchange rate was 99 yen per U.S. dollar.

Questions

1. Explain the effect of the Fed's announcement on the demand for and supply of U.S. dollars.
2. Explain the effect of the Bank of Japan's announcement on the demand for and supply of U.S. dollars.
3. Explain the effect of the two announcements on the U.S. dollar–yen exchange rate: Would the U.S. dollar appreciate or depreciate?
4. Could the change in the exchange rate on June 2 have resulted from the two announcements or must some other influence have changed too? If so, what might that influence have been?

Solutions

1. The Fed's announcement of a 1 percentage point rise in the U.S. interest rate next month means that, other interest rates remaining the same, the U.S. interest rate differential will increase next month.

    An increase in the U.S. interest rate differential next month will increase the demand for U.S. dollars and decrease the supply of U.S. dollars next month. The exchange rate next month will increase.

    With the increase in the exchange rate expected next month, the demand for U.S. dollars will increase and the supply of U.S. dollars will decrease on June 2.

Key Point: An expected *future* rise in the interest rate differential increases the demand for U.S. dollars and decreases the supply of U.S. dollars immediately through its effect on the expected future exchange rate.

2. The Bank of Japan's announcement that it will lower the interest rate in Japan next month has the same effect on the U.S. interest rate differential as a rise in the U.S. interest rate.

So the effect of a Japanese interest rate cut reinforces that of a U.S. interest rate increase.

The even-larger increase in the interest rate differential next month will bring a larger increase in the demand for U.S. dollars and decrease in the supply of U.S. dollars next month, and a larger increase in the exchange rate next month.

The larger increase in the exchange rate expected next month will bring a larger increase in the demand for U.S. dollars and decrease the supply of U.S. dollars on June 2.

Key Point: A fall in the foreign interest rate has the same effects on the demand for and supply of U.S. dollars as a rise in the U.S. interest rate.

3. The two interest rate announcements have the same effects: They increase the demand for U.S. dollars and decrease the supply of U.S. dollars.

    An increase in the demand for U.S. dollars raises the exchange rate and a decrease in the supply of U.S. dollars raises the exchange rate, so the announcements would make the dollar appreciate.

Key Point: An increase in demand and a decrease in supply have the same effect on price: They raise the price. The exchange rate is a price.

4. When the U.S. dollar fell from 101 yen on June 1 to 99 yen on June 2, the U.S. dollar depreciated.

    Other things remaining the same, the two central bank announcements would have appreciated the U.S. dollar.

    Because the exchange rate fell—the dollar depreciated—either the demand for U.S. dollars must have decreased or the supply of U.S. dollars must have increased.

    The influences on demand and supply that might have changed are U.S. exports or U.S. imports.

    A decrease in U.S. exports would have decreased the demand for U.S. dollars.

    An increase in U.S. imports would have increased the supply of U.S. dollars.

Key Point: When the exchange rate falls, either the demand for U.S. dollars has decreased or the supply of U.S. dollars has increased or both have occurred.

STUDY PLAN PROBLEMS AND APPLICATIONS

MyEconLab   You can work Problems 1 to 10 in Chapter 26 Study Plan and get instant feedback. Problems marked update with real-time data.

The Foreign Exchange Market (Study Plan 26.1)

Use the following data to work Problems 1 to 3.

The U.S. dollar exchange rate increased from $0.96 Canadian in June 2011 to $1.03 Canadian in June 2012, and it decreased from 81 Japanese yen in June 2011 to 78 yen in June 2012.

1. Did the U.S. dollar appreciate or depreciate against the Canadian dollar? Did the U.S. dollar appreciate or depreciate against the yen?

2. What was the value of the Canadian dollar in terms of U.S. dollars in June 2011 and June 2012? Did the Canadian dollar appreciate or depreciate against the U.S. dollar over the year June 2011 to June 2012?

3. What was the value of 100 yen in terms of U.S. dollars in June 2011 and June 2012? Did the yen appreciate or depreciate against the U.S. dollar over the year June 2011 to June 2012?

4. On March 30, 2012, the U.S. dollar was trading at 82 yen per U.S. dollar on the foreign exchange market. On August 30, 2012, the U.S. dollar was trading at 79 yen per U.S. dollar.
   a. What events in the foreign exchange market could have brought this fall in the value of the U.S. dollar?
   b. Did the events you've described change the demand for U.S. dollars, the supply of U.S. dollars, or both demand and supply in the foreign exchange market?

5. Colombia is the world's biggest producer of roses. The global demand for roses increases and at the same time Columbia's central bank increases the interest rate. In the foreign exchange market for Colombian pesos, what happens to
   a. The demand for pesos?
   b. The supply of pesos?
   c. The quantity of pesos demanded?
   d. The quantity of pesos supplied?
   e. The peso–U.S. dollar exchange rate?

Arbitrage, Speculation, and Market Fundamentals
(Study Plan 26.2)

6. If a euro deposit in a bank in France earns interest of 4 percent a year and a yen deposit in Japan earns 0.5 percent a year, other things remaining the same and adjusted for risk, what is the exchange rate expectation of the Japanese yen?

7. The U.K. pound is trading at 1.50 U.S. dollars per U.K. pound and purchasing power parity holds. The U.S. interest rate is 1 percent a year and the U.K. interest rate is 3 percent a year.
   a. Calculate the U.S. interest rate differential.
   b. What is the U.K. pound expected to be worth in terms of U.S. dollars one year from now?
   c. Which country more likely has the lower inflation rate? How can you tell?

8. The U.S. price level is 115, the Japanese price level is 92, and the real exchange rate is 98.75 Japanese real GDP per unit of U.S. real GDP. What is the nominal exchange rate?

Exchange Rate Policy (Study Plan 26.3)

9. With the strengthening of the yen against the U.S. dollar in 2012, Japan's central bank did not take any action. A Japanese politician called on the central bank to take actions to weaken the yen, saying it will help exporters in the short run and have no long-run effects.
   a. What is Japan's current exchange rate policy?
   b. What does the politician want the exchange rate policy to be in the short run? Why would such a policy have no effect on the exchange rate in the long run?

Financing International Trade (Study Plan 26.4)

10. The table gives some information about the U.S. international transactions.

Item	Billions of U.S. dollars
Imports of goods and services	2,215
Foreign investment in the United States	1,408
Exports of goods and services	1,754
U.S. investment abroad	1,200
Net interest income	167
Net transfers	−142
Statistical discrepancy	231

   a. Calculate the balance on the three balance of payments accounts.
   b. Was the United States a net borrower or a net lender? Explain your answer.

◆ ADDITIONAL PROBLEMS AND APPLICATIONS

MyEconLab   You can work these problems in MyEconLab if assigned by your instructor.
Problems marked update with real-time data.

The Foreign Exchange Market

11. Suppose that yesterday, the U.S. dollar was trading on the foreign exchange market at 0.75 euros per U.S. dollar and today the U.S. dollar is trading at 0.80 euros per U.S. dollar. Which of the two currencies (the U.S. dollar or the euro) has appreciated and which has depreciated today?

12. Suppose that the exchange rate fell from 80 yen per U.S. dollar to 70 yen per U.S. dollar. What is the effect of this change on the quantity of U.S. dollars that people plan to buy in the foreign exchange market?

13. Suppose that the exchange rate rose from 80 yen per U.S. dollar to 90 yen per U.S. dollar. What is the effect of this change on the quantity of U.S. dollars that people plan to sell in the foreign exchange market?

14. Today's exchange rate between the yuan and the U.S. dollar is 6.40 yuan per dollar and the central bank of China is buying U.S. dollars in the foreign exchange market. If the central bank of China did not purchase U.S. dollars would there be excess demand or excess supply of U.S. dollars in the foreign exchange market? Would the exchange rate remain at 6.40 yuan per U.S. dollar? If not, which currency would appreciate?

15. Yesterday, the current exchange rate was $1.05 Canadian per U.S. dollar and traders expected the exchange rate to remain unchanged for the next month. Today, with new information, traders now expect the exchange rate next month to fall to $1 Canadian per U.S. dollar. Explain how the revised expected future exchange rate influences the demand for U.S. dollars, or the supply of U.S. dollars, or both in the foreign exchange market.

16. In 2011, the exchange rate changed from 94 yen per U.S. dollar in January to 84 yen per U.S. dollar in June, and back to 94 yen per dollar in December. What information would you need to determine the factors that caused these changes in the exchange rate? Which factors would change *both* demand and supply?

17. Australia produces natural resources (coal, iron ore, natural gas, and others), the demand for which has increased rapidly as China and other emerging economies expand.

a. Explain how growth in the demand for Australia's natural resources would affect the demand for Australian dollars in the foreign exchange market.

b. Explain how the supply of Australian dollars would change.

c. Explain how the value of the Australian dollar would change.

d. Illustrate your answer with a graphical analysis.

Arbitrage, Speculation, and Market Fundamentals

Use the following news clip to work Problems 18 and 19.

Indian Entrepreneur Seeks Opportunities

Rahul Reddy, an Indian real estate entrepreneur, believes that "The United States is good for speculative higher-risk investments." He profited from earlier investment in Australia and a strong Australian dollar provided him with the funds to enter the U.S. real estate market at prices that he believed "we will probably not see for a long time." He said, "The United States is an economic powerhouse that I think will recover, and if the exchange rate goes back to what it was a few years ago, we will benefit."

Based on an article in *Forbes*, July 10, 2008

18. Explain why Mr. Reddy is investing in the U.S. real estate market.

19. Explain what would happen if the speculation made by Mr. Reddy became widespread. Would expectations become self-fulfilling?

Use the following information to work Problems 20 and 21.

Brazil's Overvalued Real

The Brazilian real has appreciated 33 percent against the U.S. dollar and has pushed up the price of a Big Mac in Sao Paulo to $4.60, higher than the New York price of $3.99. Despite Brazil's interest rate being at 8.75 percent a year compared to the U.S. interest rate at near zero, foreign funds flowing into Brazil surged in October.

Source: Bloomberg News, October 27, 2009

20. Does purchasing power parity hold? If not, does PPP predict that the Brazilian real will appreciate or depreciate against the U.S. dollar? Explain.

21. Does interest rate parity hold? If not, why not?

Will the Brazilian real appreciate further or depreciate against the U.S. dollar if the Fed raises the interest rate while the Brazilian interest rate remains at 8.75 percent a year?

22. **When the Chips Are Down**

The *Economist* magazine uses the price of a Big Mac to determine whether a currency is undervalued or overvalued. In July 2012, the price of a Big Mac was $4.33 in New York, 15.65 yuan in Beijing, and 6.50 Swiss francs in Geneva. The exchange rates were 6.37 yuan per U.S. dollar and 0.98 Swiss francs per U.S. dollar.

Source: *The Economist*, July 25, 2012

a. Was the yuan undervalued or overvalued relative to purchasing power parity?

b. Was the Swiss franc undervalued or overvalued relative to purchasing power parity?

c. Do you think the price of a Big Mac in different countries provides a valid test of purchasing power parity?

Exchange Rate Policy

Use the following news clip to work Problems 23 to 25.

U.S. Declines to Cite China as Currency Manipulator

In 2007, the U.S. trade deficit with China hit an all-time high of $256.3 billion, the largest deficit ever recorded with a single country. Chinese currency, the yuan, has risen in value by 18.4 percent against the U.S. dollar since the Chinese government loosened its currency system in July 2005. However, U.S. manufacturers contend the yuan is still undervalued by as much as 40 percent, making Chinese goods more competitive in this country and U.S. goods more expensive in China. China buys U.S. dollar-denominated securities to maintain the value of the yuan in terms of the U.S. dollar.

Source: MSN, May 15, 2008

23. What was the exchange rate policy adopted by China until July 2005? Explain how it worked. Draw a graph to illustrate your answer.

24. What was the exchange rate policy adopted by China after July 2005? Explain how it works.

25. Explain how fixed and crawling peg exchange rates can be used to manipulate trade balances in the short run, but not the long run.

26. **Aussie Dollar Hit by Interest Rate Talk**

The Australian dollar fell against the U.S. dollar to its lowest value in the past two weeks. The

CPI inflation rate was reported to be generally as expected but not high enough to justify previous expectations for an aggressive interest rate rise by Australia's central bank next week.

Source: Reuters, October 28, 2009

a. What is Australia's exchange rate policy? Explain why expectations about the Australian interest rate lowered the value of the Australian dollar against the U.S. dollar.

b. To avoid the fall in the value of the Australian dollar against the U.S. dollar, what action could the central bank of Australia have taken? Would such an action signal a change in Australia's exchange rate policy?

Financing International Trade

Use the following table to work Problems 27 and 28. The table gives some data about the U.K. economy:

Item	Billions of U.K. pounds
Consumption expenditure	721
Exports of goods and services	277
Government expenditures	230
Net taxes	217
Investment	181
Saving	162

27. Calculate the private sector and government sector balances.

28. What is the relationship between the government sector balance and net exports?

Economics in the News

29. After you have studied *Economics in the News* on pp. 640–641 answer the following questions.

a. What happened to the foreign exchange value of the U.S. dollar in July and August 2014?

b. What could the Fed have done to stop the rise in the dollar?

c. What could the European Central Bank have done that might have stopped the fall in the euro?

d. What can you infer about the changes in U.K. pound–euro exchange rate during July and August 2014? Can you think of a reason for the behavior of that exchange rate?

e. If the dollar continues its upward path against the euro, what do you predict will be the consequences for U.S. and European relative inflation rates?

Expanding the Frontier

UNDERSTANDING MACROECONOMIC TRENDS

Economics is about how we cope with scarcity. We cope as individuals by making choices that balance marginal benefits and marginal costs so that we use our scarce resources efficiently. We cope as societies by creating incentive systems and social institutions that encourage specialization and exchange.

These choices and the incentive systems that guide them determine what we specialize in; how much work we do; how hard we work at school to learn the mental skills that form our human capital and that determine the kinds of jobs we get and the incomes we earn; how much we save for future big-ticket expenditures; how much businesses and governments spend on new capital—on auto assembly lines, computers and fiber cables for improved Internet services, shopping malls, highways, bridges, and tunnels; how intensively existing capital and natural resources are used and how quickly they wear out or are used up; and the problems that scientists, engineers, and other inventors work on to develop new technologies.

All the choices we've just described combine to determine the standard of living and the rate at which it improves—the economic growth rate.

Money that makes specialization and exchange in markets possible is a huge contributor to economic growth. But too much money brings a rising cost of living with no improvement in the standard of living.

Joseph Schumpeter, *the son of a textile factory owner, was born in Austria in 1883. He moved from Austria to Germany during the tumultuous 1920s when those two countries experienced hyperinflation. In 1932, in the depths of the Great Depression, he came to the United States and became a professor of economics at Harvard University.*

This creative economic thinker wrote about economic growth and development, business cycles, political systems, and economic biography. He was a person of strong opinions who expressed them forcefully and delighted in verbal battles.

Schumpeter saw the development and diffusion of new technologies by profit-seeking entrepreneurs as the source of economic progress. But he saw economic progress as a process of creative destruction—the creation of new profit opportunities and the destruction of currently profitable businesses. For Schumpeter, economic growth and the business cycle were a single phenomenon.

"Economic progress, in capitalist society, means turmoil."

JOSEPH SCHUMPETER
Capitalism, Socialism, and Democracy
Routledge, 1976

XAVIER SALA-I-MARTIN is Professor of Economics at Columbia University. He is also a Research Associate at the National Bureau of Economic Research, Senior Economic Advisor to the World Economic Forum, Associate Editor of the *Journal of Economic Growth,* founder and CEO of Umbele Foundation: A Future for Africa, and President of the Economic Commission of the Barcelona Football Club.

Professor Sala-i-Martin was an undergraduate at Universitat Autonoma de Barcelona and a graduate student at Harvard University, where he obtained his Ph.D. in 1990.

In 2004, he was awarded the Premio Juan Carlos I de Economía, a biannual prize given by the Bank of Spain to the best economist in Spain and Latin America. With Robert Barro, he is the author of *Economic Growth* Second Edition (MIT Press, 2003), the definitive graduate level text on this topic.

Michael Parkin talked with Xavier Sala-i-Martin about his work and the progress that economists have made in understanding economic growth.

How did economic growth become your major field of research?

I studied economics. I liked it. I studied mathematical economics. I liked it too, and I went to graduate school. In my second year at Harvard, Jeffrey Sachs hired me to go to Bolivia. I saw poor people for the first time in my life. I was shocked. I decided I should try to answer the question "Why are these people so poor and why are we so rich, and what can we do to turn their state into our state?" We live in a bubble world in the United States and Europe, and we don't realize how poor people really are. When you see poverty at first hand, it is very hard to think about something else. So I decided to study economic growth. Coincidentally, when I returned from Bolivia, I was assigned to be Robert Barro's teaching assistant. He was teaching economic growth, so I studied with him and eventually wrote books and articles with him.

> If there's no investment, there's no growth. ... Incentives are important.

What do we know today about the nature and causes of the wealth of nations that Adam Smith didn't know?

Actually, even though over the last two hundred years some of the best minds have looked at the question, we know surprisingly little. We have some general principles that are not very easy to apply in practice. We know, for example, that markets are good. We know that for the economy to work, we need property rights to be guaranteed. If there are thieves—government or private thieves—that can steal the proceeds of the investment, there's no investment and there's no growth. We know that the incentives are very important.

These are general principles. Because we know these principles we should ask: How come Africa is still poor? The answer is, it is very hard to translate "Markets are good" and "Property rights work" into practical actions. We know that Zimbabwe has to guarantee property rights. With the government it has, that's not going to work. The U.S. constitution works in the United States. If you try to copy the constitution and impose the system in Zimbabwe, it's not going to work.

*You can read the full interview with Xavier Sala-i-Martin in MyEconLab.

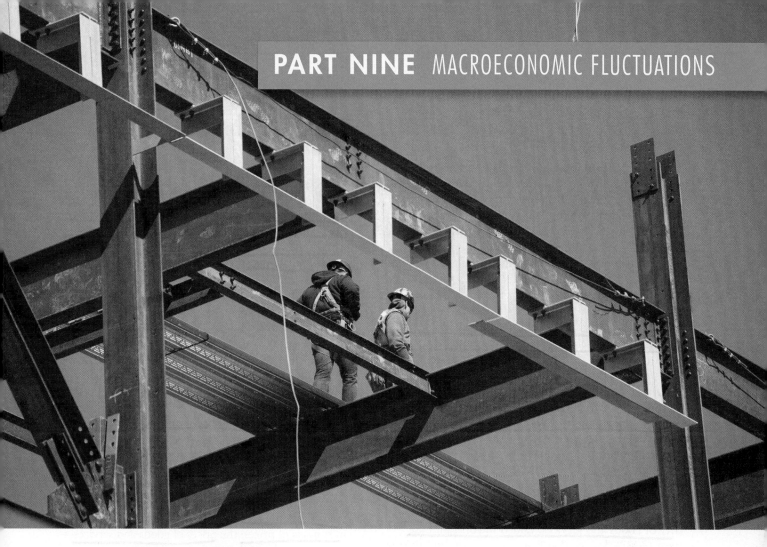

27

AGGREGATE SUPPLY AND AGGREGATE DEMAND

After studying this chapter, you will be able to:

◆ Explain what determines aggregate supply in the long run and in the short run

◆ Explain what determines aggregate demand

◆ Explain how real GDP and the price level are determined and what causes growth, inflation, and cycles

◆ Describe the main schools of thought in macroeconomics today

Real GDP grew by 4.2 percent in the second quarter of 2014 after shrinking in the first quarter. The inflation rate also edged upward in 2014. Why do real GDP and inflation fluctuate?

This chapter explains the economic fluctuations that we call the business cycle. You will study the *aggregate supply–aggregate demand model* or *AS-AD model*—a model of real GDP and the price level. And in *Economics in the News* at the end of the chapter, you will use that model to interpret and explain the state of the U.S. economy in 2014.

649

◆ Aggregate Supply

The purpose of the aggregate supply–aggregate demand model that you study in this chapter is to explain how real GDP and the price level are determined and how they interact. The model uses similar ideas to those that you encountered in Chapter 3 when you learned how the quantity and price in a competitive market are determined. But the *aggregate supply–aggregate* demand model (*AS-AD* model) isn't just an application of the competitive market model. Some differences arise because the *AS-AD* model is a model of an imaginary market for the total of all the final goods and services that make up real GDP. The quantity in this "market" is real GDP and the price is the price level measured by the GDP deflator.

One thing that the *AS-AD* model shares with the competitive market model is that both distinguish between *supply* and the *quantity supplied*. We begin by explaining what we mean by the quantity of real GDP supplied.

Quantity Supplied and Supply

The *quantity of real GDP supplied* is the total quantity of goods and services, valued in constant base-year (2009) dollars, that firms plan to produce during a given period. This quantity depends on the quantity of labor employed, the quantity of physical and human capital, and the state of technology.

At any given time, the quantity of capital and the state of technology are fixed. They depend on decisions that were made in the past. The population is also fixed. But the quantity of labor is not fixed. It depends on decisions made by households and firms about the supply of and demand for labor.

The labor market can be in any one of three states: at full employment, above full employment, or below full employment. At full employment, the quantity of real GDP supplied is *potential GDP*, which depends on the full-employment quantity of labor (see Chapter 23, pp. 546–548). Over the business cycle, employment fluctuates around full employment and the quantity of real GDP supplied fluctuates around potential GDP.

Aggregate supply is the relationship between the quantity of real GDP supplied and the price level. This relationship is different in the long run than in the short run and to study aggregate supply, we distinguish between two time frames:

- Long-run aggregate supply
- Short-run aggregate supply

Long-Run Aggregate Supply

Long-run aggregate supply is the relationship between the quantity of real GDP supplied and the price level when the money wage rate changes in step with the price level to maintain full employment. The quantity of real GDP supplied at full employment equals potential GDP and this quantity is the same regardless of the price level.

The long-run aggregate supply curve in Fig. 27.1 illustrates long-run aggregate supply as the vertical line at potential GDP labeled *LAS*. Along the long-run aggregate supply curve, as the price level changes, the money wage rate also changes so the real wage rate remains at the full-employment equilibrium level and real GDP remains at potential GDP. The long-run aggregate supply curve is always vertical and is always located at potential GDP.

The long-run aggregate supply curve is vertical because potential GDP is independent of the price level. The reason for this independence is that a movement along the *LAS* curve is accompanied by a change in *two* sets of prices: the prices of goods and services—the price level—and the prices of the factors of production, most notably, the money wage rate. A 10 percent increase in the prices of goods and services is matched by a 10 percent increase in the money wage rate. Because the price level and the money wage rate change by the same percentage, the *real wage rate* remains unchanged at its full-employment equilibrium level. So when the price level changes and the real wage rate remains constant, employment remains constant and real GDP remains constant at potential GDP.

Production at a Pepsi Plant You can see more clearly why real GDP is unchanged when all prices change by the same percentage by thinking about production decisions at a Pepsi bottling plant. How does the quantity of Pepsi supplied change if the price of Pepsi changes and the wage rate of the workers and prices of all the other resources used vary by the same percentage? The answer is that the quantity supplied doesn't change. The firm produces the quantity that maximizes profit. That quantity depends on the price of Pepsi relative to the cost of producing it. With no change in price *relative to cost*, production doesn't change.

Short-Run Aggregate Supply

Short-run aggregate supply is the relationship between the quantity of real GDP supplied and the price level when the money wage rate, the prices of other resources, and potential GDP remain constant. Figure 27.1 illustrates this relationship as the short-run aggregate supply curve *SAS* and the short-run aggregate supply schedule. Each point on the *SAS* curve corresponds to a row of the short-run aggregate supply schedule. For example, point *A* on the *SAS* curve and row *A* of the schedule tell us that if the price level is 100, the quantity of real GDP supplied is $15 trillion. In the short run, a rise in the price level brings an increase in the quantity of real GDP supplied. The short-run aggregate supply curve slopes upward.

With a given money wage rate, there is one price level at which the real wage rate is at its full-employment equilibrium level. At this price level, the quantity of real GDP supplied equals potential GDP and the *SAS* curve intersects the *LAS* curve. In this example, that price level is 110. If the price level rises above 110, the quantity of real GDP supplied increases along the *SAS* curve and exceeds potential GDP; if the price level falls below 110, the quantity of real GDP supplied decreases along the *SAS* curve and is less than potential GDP.

Back at the Pepsi Plant You can see why the short-run aggregate supply curve slopes upward by returning to the Pepsi bottling plant. If production increases, marginal cost rises and if production decreases, marginal cost falls (see Chapter 2, p. 35).

If the price of Pepsi rises with no change in the money wage rate and other costs, Pepsi can increase profit by increasing production. Pepsi is in business to maximize its profit, so it increases production.

Similarly, if the price of Pepsi falls while the money wage rate and other costs remain constant, Pepsi can avoid a loss by decreasing production. The lower price weakens the incentive to produce, so Pepsi decreases production.

What's true for Pepsi bottlers is true for the producers of all goods and services. When all prices rise, the *price level rises*. If the price level rises and the money wage rate and other factor prices remain constant, all firms increase production and the quantity of real GDP supplied increases. A fall in the price level has the opposite effect and decreases the quantity of real GDP supplied.

FIGURE 27.1   Long-Run and Short-Run Aggregate Supply

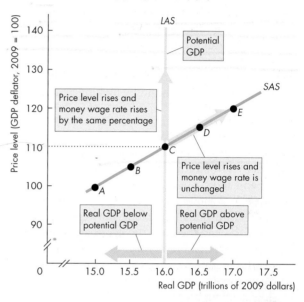

	Price level (GDP deflator)	Real GDP supplied (trillions of 2009 dollars)
A	100	15.0
B	105	15.5
C	**110**	**16.0**
D	115	16.5
E	120	17.0

In the long run, the quantity of real GDP supplied is potential GDP and the *LAS* curve is vertical at potential GDP. In the short run, the quantity of real GDP supplied increases if the price level rises, while all other influences on supply plans remain the same.

The short-run aggregate supply curve, *SAS*, slopes upward. The short-run aggregate supply curve is based on the aggregate supply schedule in the table. Each point *A* through *E* on the curve corresponds to the row in the table identified by the same letter.

When the price level is 110, the quantity of real GDP supplied is $16 trillion, which is potential GDP. If the price level rises above 110, the quantity of real GDP supplied increases and exceeds potential GDP; if the price level falls below 110, the quantity of real GDP supplied decreases below potential GDP.

MyEconLab Animation and Draw Graph

Changes in Aggregate Supply

A change in the price level changes the quantity of real GDP supplied, which is illustrated by a movement along the short-run aggregate supply curve. It does not change aggregate supply. Aggregate supply changes when an influence on production plans other than the price level changes. These other influences include changes in potential GDP and changes in the money wage rate. Let's begin by looking at a change in potential GDP.

Changes in Potential GDP When potential GDP changes, aggregate supply changes. An increase in potential GDP increases both long-run aggregate supply and short-run aggregate supply.

Figure 27.2 shows the effects of an increase in potential GDP. Initially, the long-run aggregate supply curve is LAS_0 and the short-run aggregate supply curve is SAS_0. If potential GDP increases to $17 trillion, long-run aggregate supply increases and the long-run aggregate supply curve shifts rightward to LAS_1. Short-run aggregate supply also increases, and the short-run aggregate supply curve shifts rightward to SAS_1. The two supply curves shift by the same amount only if the full-employment price level remains constant, which we will assume to be the case.

Potential GDP can increase for any of three reasons:

- An increase in the full-employment quantity of labor
- An increase in the quantity of capital
- An advance in technology

Let's look at these influences on potential GDP and the aggregate supply curves.

An Increase in the Full-Employment Quantity of Labor A Pepsi bottling plant that employs 100 workers bottles more Pepsi than does an otherwise identical plant that employs 10 workers. The same is true for the economy as a whole. The larger the quantity of labor employed, the greater is real GDP.

Over time, potential GDP increases because the labor force increases. But (with constant capital and technology) *potential* GDP increases only if the full-employment quantity of labor increases. Fluctuations in employment over the business cycle bring fluctuations in real GDP. But these changes in real GDP are fluctuations around potential GDP. They are not changes in potential GDP and long-run aggregate supply.

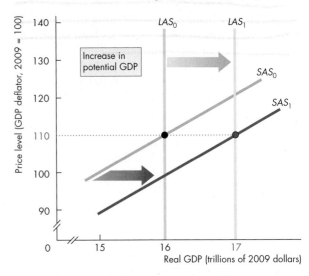

FIGURE 27.2   A Change in Potential GDP

An increase in potential GDP increases both long-run aggregate supply and short-run aggregate supply. The long-run aggregate supply curve shifts rightward from LAS_0 to LAS_1 and the short-run aggregate supply curve shifts from SAS_0 to SAS_1.

MyEconLab Animation

An Increase in the Quantity of Capital A Pepsi bottling plant with two production lines bottles more Pepsi than does an otherwise identical plant that has only one production line. For the economy, the larger the quantity of capital, the more productive is the labor force and the greater is its potential GDP. Potential GDP per person in the capital-rich United States is vastly greater than that in capital-poor China or Russia.

Capital includes *human capital*. One Pepsi plant is managed by an economics major with an MBA and has a labor force with an average of 10 years of experience. This plant produces a larger output than does an otherwise identical plant that is managed by someone with no business training or experience and that has a young labor force that is new to bottling. The first plant has a greater amount of human capital than the second. For the economy as a whole, the larger the quantity of *human capital*—the skills that people have acquired in school and through on-the-job training—the greater is potential GDP.

An Advance in Technology A Pepsi plant that has pre-computer age machines produces less than one that uses the latest robot technology. Technological change enables firms to produce more from any given amount of factors of production. So even with fixed quantities of labor and capital, improvements in technology increase potential GDP.

Technological advances are by far the most important source of increased production over the past two centuries. As a result of technological advances, one farmer in the United States today can feed 100 people and in a year one autoworker can produce almost 14 cars and trucks.

Let's now look at the effects of changes in the money wage rate.

Changes in the Money Wage Rate

When the money wage rate (or the money price of any other factor of production such as oil) changes, short-run aggregate supply changes but long-run aggregate supply does not change.

Figure 27.3 shows the effect of an increase in the money wage rate. Initially, the short-run aggregate supply curve is SAS_0. A rise in the money wage rate *decreases* short-run aggregate supply and shifts the short-run aggregate supply curve leftward to SAS_2.

A rise in the money wage rate decreases short-run aggregate supply because it increases firms' costs. With increased costs, the quantity that firms are willing to supply at each price level decreases, which is shown by a leftward shift of the SAS curve.

A change in the money wage rate does not change long-run aggregate supply because on the LAS curve, the change in the money wage rate is accompanied by an equal percentage change in the price level. With no change in *relative* prices, firms have no incentive to change production and real GDP remains constant at potential GDP. With no change in potential GDP, the long-run aggregate supply curve LAS does not shift.

What Makes the Money Wage Rate Change?

The money wage rate can change for two reasons: departures from full employment and expectations about inflation. Unemployment above the natural rate puts downward pressure on the money wage rate, and unemployment below the natural rate puts upward pressure on it. An expected rise in the inflation rate makes the money wage rate rise faster, and an expected fall in the inflation rate slows the rate at which the money wage rate rises.

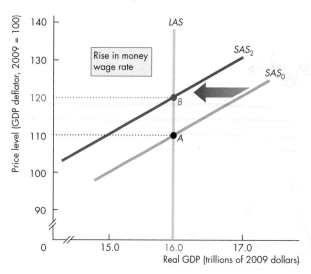

FIGURE 27.3   A Change in the Money Wage Rate

A rise in the money wage rate decreases short-run aggregate supply and shifts the short-run aggregate supply curve leftward from SAS_0 to SAS_2. A rise in the money wage rate does not change potential GDP, so the long-run aggregate supply curve does not shift.

MyEconLab Animation

◆ REVIEW QUIZ

1 If the price level and the money wage rate rise by the same percentage, what happens to the quantity of real GDP supplied? Along which aggregate supply curve does the economy move?

2 If the price level rises and the money wage rate remains constant, what happens to the quantity of real GDP supplied? Along which aggregate supply curve does the economy move?

3 If potential GDP increases, what happens to aggregate supply? Does the LAS curve shift or is there a movement along the LAS curve? Does the SAS curve shift or is there a movement along the SAS curve?

4 If the money wage rate rises and potential GDP remains the same, does the LAS curve or the SAS curve shift or is there a movement along the LAS curve or the SAS curve?

Work these questions in Study Plan 27.1 and get instant feedback. Do a Key Terms Quiz.   *MyEconLab*

◆ Aggregate Demand

The quantity of real GDP demanded (Y) is the sum of real consumption expenditure (C), investment (I), government expenditure (G), and exports (X) minus imports (M). That is,

real GDP → $Y = C + I + G + X - M.$

The *quantity of real GDP demanded* is the total amount of final goods and services produced in the United States that people, businesses, governments, and foreigners plan to buy.

These buying plans depend on many factors. Some of the main ones are

buying plans {
1. The price level
2. Expectations
3. Fiscal policy and monetary policy
4. The world economy

We first focus on the relationship between the quantity of real GDP demanded and the price level. To study this relationship, we keep all other influences on buying plans the same and ask: How does the quantity of real GDP demanded vary as the price level varies?

The Aggregate Demand Curve

Other things remaining the same, the higher the price level, the smaller is the quantity of real GDP demanded. This relationship between the quantity of real GDP demanded and the price level is called **aggregate demand**. Aggregate demand is described by an *aggregate demand schedule* and an *aggregate demand curve*.

Figure 27.4 shows an aggregate demand curve (AD) and an aggregate demand schedule. Each point on the AD curve corresponds to a row of the schedule. For example, point C' on the AD curve and row C' of the schedule tell us that if the price level is 110, the quantity of real GDP demanded is $16 trillion.

The aggregate demand curve slopes downward for two reasons:

{
- Wealth effect
- Substitution effects

Wealth Effect   When the price level rises but other things remain the same, *real* wealth decreases. Real

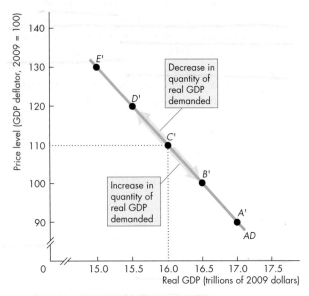

FIGURE 27.4   Aggregate Demand

	Price level (GDP deflator)	Real GDP demanded (trillions of 2009 dollars)
A'	90	17.0
B'	100	16.5
C'	**110**	**16.0**
D'	120	15.5
E'	130	15.0

The aggregate demand curve (*AD*) shows the relationship between the quantity of real GDP demanded and the price level. The aggregate demand curve is based on the aggregate demand schedule in the table. Each point *A'* through *E'* on the curve corresponds to the row in the table identified by the same letter. When the price level is 110, the quantity of real GDP demanded is $16 trillion, as shown by point *C'* in the figure. A change in the price level, when all other influences on aggregate buying plans remain the same, brings a change in the quantity of real GDP demanded and a movement along the *AD* curve.

MyEconLab Animation

wealth is the amount of money in the bank, bonds, stocks, and other assets that people own, measured not in dollars but in terms of the goods and services that the money, bonds, and stocks will buy.

People save and hold money, bonds, and stocks for many reasons. One reason is to build up funds for education expenses. Another reason is to build up enough funds to meet possible medical expenses or other big bills. But the biggest reason is to build up enough funds to provide a retirement income.

If the price level rises, real wealth decreases. People then try to restore their wealth. To do so, they must increase saving and, equivalently, decrease current consumption. Such a decrease in consumption is a decrease in aggregate demand.

Maria's Wealth Effect You can see how the wealth effect works by thinking about Maria's buying plans. Maria lives in Moscow, Russia. She has worked hard all summer and saved 20,000 rubles (the ruble is the currency of Russia), which she plans to spend attending graduate school when she has finished her economics degree. So Maria's wealth is 20,000 rubles. Maria has a part-time job, and her income from this job pays her current expenses. The price level in Russia rises by 100 percent, and now Maria needs 40,000 rubles to buy what 20,000 once bought. To try to make up some of the fall in value of her savings, Maria saves even more and cuts her current spending to the bare minimum.

Substitution Effects When the price level rises and other things remain the same, interest rates rise. The reason is related to the wealth effect that you've just studied. A rise in the price level decreases the real value of the money in people's pockets and bank accounts. With a smaller amount of real money around, banks and other lenders can get a higher interest rate on loans. But faced with a higher interest rate, people and businesses delay plans to buy new capital and consumer durable goods and cut back on spending.

This substitution effect involves changing the timing of purchases of capital and consumer durable goods and is called an *intertemporal* substitution effect—a substitution across time. Saving increases to increase future consumption.

To see this intertemporal substitution effect more clearly, think about your own plan to buy a new computer. At an interest rate of 5 percent a year, you might borrow $1,000 and buy the new computer. But at an interest rate of 10 percent a year, you might decide that the payments would be too high. You don't abandon your plan to buy the computer, but you decide to delay your purchase.

A second substitution effect works through international prices. When the U.S. price level rises and other things remain the same, U.S.-made goods and services become more expensive relative to foreign-made goods and services. This change in *relative prices* encourages people to spend less on U.S.-made items and more on foreign-made items. For example, if the U.S. price level rises relative to the Japanese price level, Japanese buy fewer U.S.-made cars (U.S. exports decrease) and Americans buy more Japanese-made cars (U.S. imports increase). U.S. GDP decreases.

Maria's Substitution Effects In Moscow, Russia, Maria makes some substitutions. She was planning to trade in her old motor scooter and get a new one. But with a higher price level and a higher interest rate, she decides to make her old scooter last one more year. Also, with the prices of Russian goods sharply increasing, Maria substitutes a low-cost dress made in Malaysia for the Russian-made dress she had originally planned to buy.

Changes in the Quantity of Real GDP Demanded

When the price level rises and other things remain the same, the quantity of real GDP demanded decreases—a movement up along the *AD* curve as shown by the arrow in Fig. 27.4. When the price level falls and other things remain the same, the quantity of real GDP demanded increases—a movement down along the *AD* curve.

We've now seen how the quantity of real GDP demanded changes when the price level changes. How do other influences on buying plans affect aggregate demand?

Changes in Aggregate Demand

A change in any factor that influences buying plans other than the price level brings a change in aggregate demand. The main factors are

- Expectations
- Fiscal policy and monetary policy
- The world economy

Expectations An increase in expected future income increases the amount of consumption goods (especially big-ticket items such as cars) that people plan to buy today and increases aggregate demand.

An increase in the expected future inflation rate increases aggregate demand today because people decide to buy more goods and services at today's relatively lower prices.

An increase in expected future profits increases the investment that firms plan to undertake today and increases aggregate demand.

Fiscal Policy and Monetary Policy The government's attempt to influence the economy by setting and changing taxes, making transfer payments, and purchasing goods and services is called **fiscal policy**. A tax cut or an increase in transfer payments—for example, unemployment benefits or welfare payments—increases aggregate demand. Both of these influences operate by increasing households' *disposable* income. **Disposable income** is aggregate income minus taxes plus transfer payments. The greater the disposable income, the greater is the quantity of consumption goods and services that households plan to buy and the greater is aggregate demand.

Government expenditure on goods and services is one component of aggregate demand. So if the government spends more on spy satellites, schools, and highways, aggregate demand increases.

The Federal Reserve's (Fed's) attempt to influence the economy by changing interest rates and the quantity of money is called **monetary policy**. The Fed influences the quantity of money and interest rates by using the tools and methods described in Chapter 25.

An increase in the quantity of money increases aggregate demand through two main channels: It lowers interest rates and makes it easier to get a loan.

With lower interest rates, businesses plan a greater level of investment in new capital and households plan greater expenditure on new homes, on home improvements, on automobiles, and a host of other consumer durable goods. Banks and others eager to lend lower their standards for making loans and more people are able to get home loans and other consumer loans.

A decrease in the quantity of money has the opposite effects and lowers aggregate demand.

The World Economy Two main influences that the world economy has on aggregate demand are the exchange rate and foreign income. The *exchange rate* is the amount of a foreign currency that you can buy with a U.S. dollar. Other things remaining the same, a rise in the exchange rate decreases aggregate

ECONOMICS IN ACTION
World Economy Headwinds

As the U.S. economy expanded in 2014, it faced strong headwinds from the global economy.

Although the U.S. economy is the world's largest economy and it can generate much of its growth from consumer and business investment spending, the United States gets help from the other large economies, China, the European Union, and Japan.

In 2014, real GDP growth in the euro area ground to a halt, real GDP shrank in Japan, and growth slowed in China.

Additionally, in 2014, the U.S. dollar appreciated making U.S. exporters and producers of import-competing goods and services less competitive.

A weak world economy and a strong dollar slows U.S. exports growth and leaves a recessionary gap with spare capacity at ports like that at Long Beach, California.

European Central Bank, Frankfurt, Germany

Port of Long Beach, California

FIGURE 27.5 Changes in Aggregate Demand

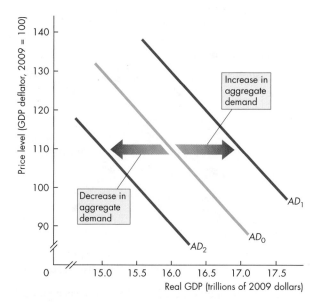

Aggregate demand

Decreases if:

- Expected future income, inflation, or profit decreases
- Fiscal policy decreases government expenditure, increases taxes, or decreases transfer payments
- Monetary policy decreases the quantity of money and increases interest rates
- The exchange rate increases or foreign income decreases

Increases if:

- Expected future income, inflation, or profit increases
- Fiscal policy increases government expenditure, decreases taxes, or increases transfer payments
- Monetary policy increases the quantity of money and decreases interest rates
- The exchange rate decreases or foreign income increases

MyEconLab Animation

demand. To see how the exchange rate influences aggregate demand, suppose that the exchange rate is 1.20 euros per U.S. dollar. An Airbus plane made in France costs 120 million euros, and an equivalent Boeing airplane made in the United States costs $110 million. In U.S. dollars, the Airbus plane costs

$100 million, so airlines both in the United States and around the world buy the cheaper airplane from France. Now suppose the exchange rate falls to 1 euro per U.S. dollar. The Airbus airplane now costs $120 million and is more expensive than the Boeing airplane. Airlines will switch from Airbus to Boeing. U.S. exports will increase and U.S. imports will decrease, so U.S. aggregate demand will increase.

An increase in foreign income increases U.S. exports and increases U.S. aggregate demand. For example, an increase in income in Japan and Germany increases Japanese and German consumers' and producers' planned expenditures on U.S.-produced goods and services.

Shifts of the Aggregate Demand Curve When aggregate demand changes, the aggregate demand curve shifts. Figure 27.5 shows two changes in aggregate demand and summarizes the factors that bring about such changes.

Aggregate demand increases and the *AD* curve shifts rightward from AD_0 to AD_1 when expected future income, inflation, or profit increases; government expenditure on goods and services increases; taxes are cut; transfer payments increase; the quantity of money increases and the interest rate falls; the exchange rate falls; or foreign income increases.

Aggregate demand decreases and the *AD* curve shifts leftward from AD_0 to AD_2 when expected future income, inflation, or profit decreases; government expenditure on goods and services decreases; taxes increase; transfer payments decrease; the quantity of money decreases and the interest rate rises; the exchange rate rises; or foreign income decreases.

◆ REVIEW QUIZ

1 What does the aggregate demand curve show? What factors change and what factors remain the same when there is a movement along the aggregate demand curve?

2 Why does the aggregate demand curve slope downward?

3 How do changes in expectations, fiscal policy and monetary policy, and the world economy change aggregate demand and the aggregate demand curve?

Work these questions in Study Plan 27.2 and get instant feedback. Do a Key Terms quiz.   MyEconLab

Explaining Macroeconomic Trends and Fluctuations

The purpose of the *AS-AD* model is to explain changes in real GDP and the price level. The model's main purpose is to explain business cycle fluctuations in these variables. But the model also aids our understanding of economic growth and inflation trends. We begin by combining aggregate supply and aggregate demand to determine real GDP and the price level in equilibrium. Just as there are two time frames for aggregate supply, there are two time frames for macroeconomic equilibrium: a long-run equilibrium and a short-run equilibrium. We'll first look at short-run equilibrium.

Short-Run Macroeconomic Equilibrium

The aggregate demand curve tells us the quantity of real GDP demanded at each price level, and the short-run aggregate supply curve tells us the quantity of real GDP supplied at each price level. **Short-run macroeconomic equilibrium** occurs when the quantity of real GDP demanded equals the quantity of real GDP supplied. That is, short-run macroeconomic equilibrium occurs at the point of intersection of the *AD* curve and the *SAS* curve.

Figure 27.6 shows such an equilibrium at a price level of 110 and real GDP of $16 trillion (points *C* and *C'*).

To see why this position is the equilibrium, think about what happens if the price level is something other than 110. Suppose, for example, that the price level is 120 and that real GDP is $17 trillion (at point *E* on the *SAS* curve). The quantity of real GDP demanded is less than $17 trillion, so firms are unable to sell all their output. Unwanted inventories pile up, and firms cut both production and prices. Production and prices are cut until firms can sell all their output. This situation occurs only when real GDP is $16 trillion and the price level is 110.

Now suppose the price level is 100 and real GDP is $15 trillion (at point *A* on the *SAS* curve). The quantity of real GDP demanded exceeds $15 trillion, so firms are unable to meet the demand for their output. Inventories decrease, and customers clamor for goods and services, so firms increase production and raise prices. Production and prices increase until firms can meet the demand for their

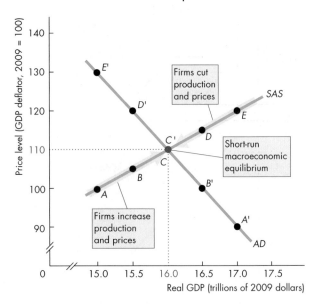

FIGURE 27.6   Short-Run Equilibrium

Short-run macroeconomic equilibrium occurs when real GDP demanded equals real GDP supplied—at the intersection of the aggregate demand curve (*AD*) and the short-run aggregate supply curve (*SAS*).

MyEconLab Animation and Draw Graph

output. This situation occurs only when real GDP is $16 trillion and the price level is 110.

In the short run, the money wage rate is fixed. It does not adjust to move the economy to full employment. So in the short run, real GDP can be greater than or less than potential GDP. But in the long run, the money wage rate adjusts and real GDP moves toward potential GDP. Let's look at the long-run equilibrium and see how we get there.

Long-Run Macroeconomic Equilibrium

Long-run macroeconomic equilibrium occurs when real GDP equals potential GDP—equivalently, when the economy is on its *LAS* curve.

When the economy is away from long-run equilibrium, the money wage rate adjusts. If the money wage rate is too high, short-run equilibrium is below potential GDP and the unemployment rate is above the natural rate. With an excess supply of labor, the money wage rate falls. If the money wage rate is too low, short-run equilibrium is above potential GDP and the unemployment rate is below the natural rate.

With an excess demand for labor, the money wage rate rises.

Figure 27.7 shows the long-run equilibrium and how it comes about. If the short-run aggregate supply curve is SAS_1, the money wage rate is too high to achieve full employment. A fall in the money wage rate shifts the SAS curve to SAS^* and brings full employment. If the short-run aggregate supply curve is SAS_2, the money wage rate is too low to achieve full employment. Now, a rise in the money wage rate shifts the SAS curve to SAS^* and brings full employment.

In long-run equilibrium, potential GDP determines real GDP, and potential GDP and aggregate demand together determine the price level. The money wage rate adjusts until the SAS curve passes through the long-run equilibrium point.

Let's now see how the AS-AD model helps us to understand economic growth and inflation.

Economic Growth and Inflation in the *AS-AD* Model

Economic growth results from a growing labor force and increasing labor productivity, which together make potential GDP grow (Chapter 23, pp. 548–551). Inflation results from a growing quantity of money that outpaces the growth of potential GDP (Chapter 25, pp. 608–609).

The *AS-AD* model explains and illustrates economic growth and inflation. It explains economic growth as increasing long-run aggregate supply and it explains inflation as a persistent increase in aggregate demand at a faster pace than that of the increase in potential GDP.

FIGURE 27.7   Long-Run Equilibrium

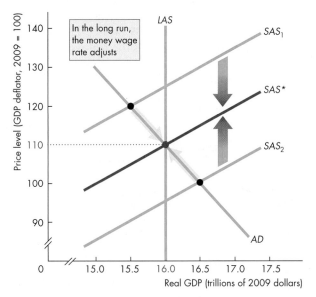

In long-run macroeconomic equilibrium, real GDP equals potential GDP. So long-run equilibrium occurs where the aggregate demand curve, *AD*, intersects the long-run aggregate supply curve, *LAS*. In the long run, aggregate demand determines the price level and has no effect on real GDP. The money wage rate adjusts in the long run, so that the *SAS* curve intersects the *LAS* curve at the long-run equilibrium price level.

MyEconLab Animation and Draw Graph

ECONOMICS IN ACTION

U.S. Economic Growth and Inflation

The figure is a *scatter diagram* of U.S. real GDP and the price level. The graph has the same axes as those of the *AS-AD* model. Each dot represents a year between 1960 and 2014. The red dots are recession years. The pattern formed by the dots shows the combination of economic growth and inflation. Economic growth was fastest during the 1960s; inflation was fastest during the 1970s.

The *AS-AD* model interprets each dot as being at the intersection of the *SAS* and *AD* curves.

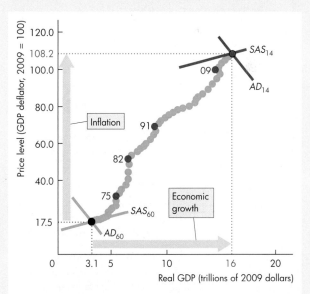

The Path of Real GDP and the Price Level
Source of data: Bureau of Economic Analysis.

Figure 27.8 illustrates this explanation in terms of the shifting *LAS* and *AD* curves.

When the *LAS* curve shifts rightward from LAS_0 to LAS_1, potential GDP grows from $16 trillion to $17 trillion. And in long-run equilibrium, real GDP also grows to $17 trillion.

When the *AD* curve shifts rightward from AD_0 to AD_1 and the growth of aggregate demand outpaces the growth of potential GDP, the price level rises from 110 to 120.

If aggregate demand were to increase at the same pace as long-run aggregate supply, real GDP would grow with no inflation.

Our economy experiences periods of growth and inflation, like those shown in Fig. 27.8, but it does not experience *steady* growth and *steady* inflation. Real GDP fluctuates around potential GDP in a business cycle. When we study the business cycle, we ignore economic growth and focus on the fluctuations around the trend growth rate. By doing so, we see the business cycle more clearly. Let's now see how the *AS-AD* model explains the business cycle.

The Business Cycle in the *AS-AD* Model

The business cycle occurs because aggregate demand and short-run aggregate supply fluctuate but the money wage rate does not adjust quickly enough to keep real GDP at potential GDP. Figure 27.9 shows three types of short-run equilibrium.

Figure 27.9(a) shows an above full-employment equilibrium. An **above full-employment equilibrium** is an equilibrium in which real GDP exceeds potential GDP. The gap between real GDP and potential GDP is the **output gap**. When real GDP exceeds potential GDP, the output gap is called an **inflationary gap**.

The above full-employment equilibrium shown in Fig. 27.9(a) occurs where the aggregate demand curve AD_0 intersects the short-run aggregate supply curve SAS_0 at a real GDP of $16.2 trillion. There is an inflationary gap of $0.2 trillion.

ECONOMICS IN ACTION

The U.S. Business Cycle

The U.S. economy had an inflationary gap in 2000 (at *A* in the figure), full employment in 2007 (at *B*), and a recessionary gap in 2009 (at *C*). The fluctuating output gap in the figure is the real-world version of Fig. 27.9(d) and is generated by fluctuations in aggregate demand and short-run aggregate supply.

FIGURE 27.8   Economic Growth and Inflation

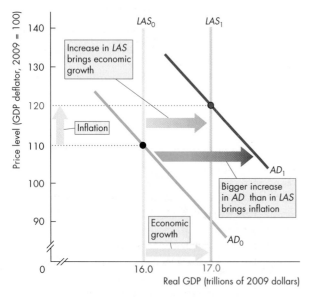

Economic growth results from a persistent increase in potential GDP—a rightward shift of the *LAS* curve. Inflation results from persistent growth in the quantity of money that shifts the *AD* curve rightward at a faster pace than the real GDP growth rate.

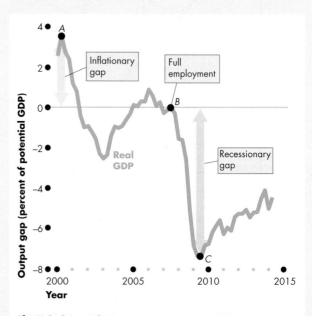

The U.S. Output Gap

Sources of data: Bureau of Economic Analysis and Congressional Budget Office.

In Fig. 27.9(b), real GDP equals potential GDP and there is a **full-employment equilibrium**. In this example, the equilibrium occurs where the aggregate demand curve AD_1 intersects the short-run aggregate supply curve SAS_1 at a real GDP and potential GDP of $16 trillion.

In part (c), there is a below full-employment equilibrium. A **below full-employment equilibrium** is an equilibrium in which potential GDP exceeds real GDP. When potential GDP exceeds real GDP, the output gap is called a **recessionary gap**.

The below full-employment equilibrium shown in

Fig. 27.9(c) occurs where the aggregate demand curve AD_2 intersects the short-run aggregate supply curve SAS_2 at a real GDP of $15.8 trillion. Potential GDP is $16 trillion, so the recessionary gap is $0.2 trillion.

The economy moves from one type of macroeconomic equilibrium to another as a result of fluctuations in aggregate demand and in short-run aggregate supply. These fluctuations produce fluctuations in real GDP. Figure 27.9(d) shows how real GDP fluctuates around potential GDP.

Let's now look at some of the sources of these fluctuations around potential GDP.

FIGURE 27.9 The Business Cycle

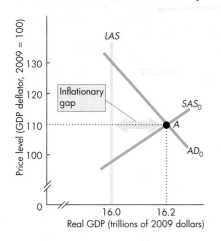

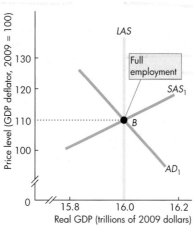

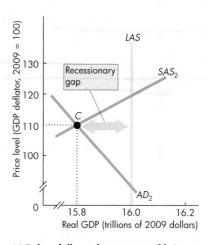

(a) Above full-employment equilibrium   (b) Full-employment equilibrium   (c) Below full-employment equilibrium

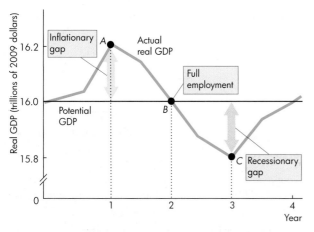

(d) Fluctuations in real GDP

Part (a) shows an above full-employment equilibrium in year 1; part (b) shows a full-employment equilibrium in year 2; and part (c) shows a below full-employment equilibrium in year 3. Part (d) shows how real GDP fluctuates around potential GDP in a business cycle during year 1, year 2, and year 3.

In year 1, an inflationary gap exists and the economy is at point A in parts (a) and (d). In year 2, the economy is at full employment and the economy is at point B in parts (b) and (d). In year 3, a recessionary gap exists and the economy is at point C in parts (c) and (d).

Fluctuations in Aggregate Demand

One reason real GDP fluctuates around potential GDP is that aggregate demand fluctuates. Let's see what happens when aggregate demand increases.

Figure 27.10(a) shows an economy at full employment. The aggregate demand curve is AD_0, the short-run aggregate supply curve is SAS_0, and the long-run aggregate supply curve is LAS. Real GDP equals potential GDP at \$16 trillion, and the price level is 110.

Now suppose that the world economy expands and that the demand for U.S.-produced goods increases in Asia and Europe. The increase in U.S. exports increases aggregate demand in the United States, and the aggregate demand curve shifts rightward from AD_0 to AD_1 in Fig. 27.10(a).

Faced with an increase in demand, firms increase production and raise prices. Real GDP increases to \$16.5 trillion, and the price level rises to 115. The economy is now in an above full-employment equilibrium. Real GDP exceeds potential GDP, and there is an inflationary gap.

The increase in aggregate demand has increased the prices of all goods and services. Faced with higher prices, firms increased their output rates. At this stage, prices of goods and services have increased but the money wage rate has not changed. (Recall that as we move along the SAS curve, the money wage rate is constant.)

The economy cannot produce in excess of potential GDP forever. Why not? What are the forces at work that bring real GDP back to potential GDP?

Because the price level has increased and the money wage rate is unchanged, workers have experienced a fall in the buying power of their wages and firms' profits have increased. Under these circumstances, workers demand higher wages and firms, anxious to maintain their employment and output levels, meet those demands. If firms do not raise the money wage rate, they will either lose workers or have to hire less productive ones.

As the money wage rate rises, the short-run aggregate supply begins to decrease. In Fig. 27.10(b), the short-run aggregate supply curve begins to shift from

---

FIGURE 27.10   An Increase in Aggregate Demand

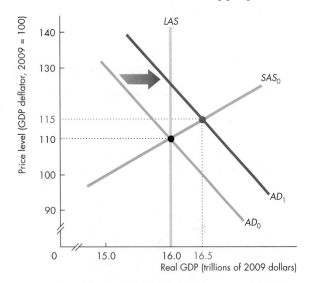

(a) Short-run effect

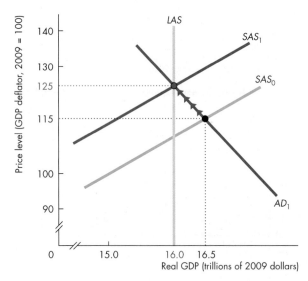

(b) Long-run effect

An increase in aggregate demand shifts the aggregate demand curve from AD_0 to AD_1. In short-run equilibrium, real GDP increases to \$16.5 trillion and the price level rises to 115. In this situation, an inflationary gap exists. In the long run in part (b), the money wage rate starts to rise and short-run

aggregate supply starts to decrease. The SAS curve gradually shifts from SAS_0 toward SAS_1, intersecting the aggregate demand curve AD_1 at higher price levels and real GDP decreases. Eventually, the price level has risen to 125 and real GDP has decreased to \$16 trillion—potential GDP.

MyEconLab Animation

SAS_0 toward SAS_1. The rise in the money wage rate and the shift in the *SAS* curve produce a sequence of new equilibrium positions. Along the adjustment path, real GDP decreases and the price level rises. The economy moves up along its aggregate demand curve as shown by the arrows in the figure.

Eventually, the money wage rate rises by the same percentage as the price level. At this time, the aggregate demand curve AD_1 intersects SAS_1 at a new full-employment equilibrium. The price level has risen to 125, and real GDP is back where it started, at potential GDP.

A decrease in aggregate demand has effects similar but opposite to those of an increase in aggregate demand. That is, a decrease in aggregate demand shifts the aggregate demand curve leftward. Real GDP decreases to less than potential GDP, and a recessionary gap emerges. Firms cut prices. The lower price level increases the purchasing power of wages and increases firms' costs relative to their output prices because the money wage rate is unchanged. Eventually, the money wage rate falls and the short-run aggregate supply increases.

Let's now work out how real GDP and the price level change when aggregate supply changes.

Fluctuations in Aggregate Supply

Fluctuations in short-run aggregate supply can bring fluctuations in real GDP around potential GDP. Suppose that initially real GDP equals potential GDP. Then there is a large but temporary rise in the price of oil. What happens to real GDP and the price level?

Figure 27.11 answers this question. The aggregate demand curve is AD_0, the short-run aggregate supply curve is SAS_0, and the long-run aggregate supply curve is *LAS*. Real GDP is $16 trillion, which equals potential GDP, and the price level is 110. Then the price of oil rises. Faced with higher energy and transportation costs, firms decrease production. Short-run aggregate supply decreases, and the short-run aggregate supply curve shifts leftward to SAS_1. The price level rises to 120, and real GDP decreases to $15.5 trillion. Because real GDP decreases, the economy experiences recession. Because the price level increases, the economy experiences inflation. A combination of recession and inflation is called **stagflation**. The United States experienced stagflation in the mid-1970s and early 1980s, but events like this are not common.

When the price of oil returns to its original level, the economy returns to full employment.

FIGURE 27.11 A Decrease in Aggregate Supply

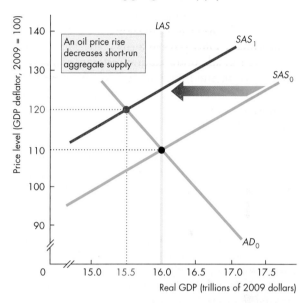

An increase in the price of oil decreases short-run aggregate supply and shifts the short-run aggregate supply curve from SAS_0 to SAS_1. Real GDP decreases from $16 trillion to $15.5 trillion, and the price level rises from 110 to 120. The economy experiences stagflation.

MyEconLab Animation

REVIEW QUIZ

1 Does economic growth result from increases in aggregate demand, short-run aggregate supply, or long-run aggregate supply?
2 Does inflation result from increases in aggregate demand, short-run aggregate supply, or long-run aggregate supply?
3 Describe three types of short-run macroeconomic equilibrium.
4 How do fluctuations in aggregate demand and short-run aggregate supply bring fluctuations in real GDP around potential GDP?

Work these questions in Study Plan 27.3 and get instant feedback. Do a Key Terms Quiz.   MyEconLab

We can use the *AS-AD* model to explain and illustrate the views of the alternative schools of thought in macroeconomics. That is your next task.

Macroeconomic Schools of Thought

Macroeconomics is an active field of research, and much remains to be learned about the forces that make our economy grow and fluctuate. There is a greater degree of consensus and certainty about economic growth and inflation—the longer-term trends in real GDP and the price level—than there is about the business cycle—the short-term fluctuations in these variables. Here, we'll look only at differences of view about short-term fluctuations.

The *AS-AD* model that you've studied in this chapter provides a good foundation for understanding the range of views that macroeconomists hold about this topic. But what you will learn here is just a first glimpse at the scientific controversy and debate. We'll return to these issues at various points later in the text and deepen your appreciation of the alternative views.

Classification usually requires simplification, and classifying macroeconomists is no exception to this general rule. The classification that we'll use here is simple, but it is not misleading. We're going to divide macroeconomists into three broad schools of thought and examine the views of each group in turn. The groups are

- Classical
- Keynesian
- Monetarist

The Classical View

A **classical** macroeconomist believes that the economy is self-regulating and always at full employment. The term "classical" derives from the name of the founding school of economics that includes Adam Smith, David Ricardo, and John Stuart Mill.

A **new classical** view is that business cycle fluctuations are the efficient responses of a well-functioning market economy that is bombarded by shocks that arise from the uneven pace of technological change.

The classical view can be understood in terms of beliefs about aggregate demand and aggregate supply.

Aggregate Demand Fluctuations In the classical view, technological change is the most significant influence on both aggregate demand and aggregate

supply. For this reason, classical macroeconomists don't use the *AS-AD* framework. But their views can be interpreted in this framework. A technological change that increases the productivity of capital brings an increase in aggregate demand because firms increase their expenditure on new plant and equipment. A technological change that lengthens the useful life of existing capital decreases the demand for new capital, which decreases aggregate demand.

Aggregate Supply Response In the classical view, the money wage rate that lies behind the short-run aggregate supply curve is instantly and completely flexible. The money wage rate adjusts so quickly to maintain equilibrium in the labor market that real GDP always adjusts to equal potential GDP.

Potential GDP itself fluctuates for the same reasons that aggregate demand fluctuates: technological change. When the pace of technological change is rapid, potential GDP increases quickly and so does real GDP. And when the pace of technological change slows, so does the growth rate of potential GDP.

Classical Policy The classical view of policy emphasizes the potential for taxes to stunt incentives and create inefficiency. Minimizing the disincentive effects of taxes will allow employment, investment, and technological advance to be at their efficient levels and the economy to expand at an appropriate and rapid pace.

The Keynesian View

A **Keynesian** macroeconomist believes that left alone, the economy would rarely operate at full employment and that to achieve and maintain full employment, active help from fiscal policy and monetary policy is required.

The term "Keynesian" derives from the name of one of the twentieth century's most famous economists, John Maynard Keynes (see p. 727).

The Keynesian view is based on beliefs about the forces that determine aggregate demand and short-run aggregate supply.

Aggregate Demand Fluctuations In the Keynesian view, *expectations* are the most significant influence on aggregate demand. Those expectations are based on herd instinct, or what Keynes himself called "animal spirits." A wave of pessimism about future profit prospects can lead to a fall in aggregate demand and plunge the economy into recession.

Aggregate Supply Response In the Keynesian view, the money wage rate that lies behind the short-run aggregate supply curve is extremely sticky in the downward direction. Basically, the money wage rate doesn't fall. So if there is a recessionary gap, there is no automatic mechanism for getting rid of it. If it were to happen, a fall in the money wage rate would increase short-run aggregate supply and restore full employment. But the money wage rate doesn't fall, so the economy remains stuck in recession.

A modern version of the Keynesian view, known as the **new Keynesian** view, holds not only that the money wage rate is sticky but also that prices of goods and services are sticky. With a sticky price level, the short-run aggregate supply curve is horizontal at a fixed price level.

Policy Response Needed The Keynesian view calls for fiscal policy and monetary policy to actively offset changes in aggregate demand that bring recession.

By stimulating aggregate demand in a recession, full employment can be restored.

The Monetarist View

A **monetarist** is a macroeconomist who believes that the economy is self-regulating and that it will normally operate at full employment, provided that monetary policy is not erratic and that the pace of money growth is kept steady.

The term "monetarist" was coined by an outstanding twentieth-century economist, Karl Brunner, to describe his own views and those of Milton Friedman (see p. 783).

The monetarist view can be interpreted in terms of beliefs about the forces that determine aggregate demand and short-run aggregate supply.

Aggregate Demand Fluctuations In the monetarist view, *the quantity of money* is the most significant influence on aggregate demand. The quantity of money is determined by the Federal Reserve (the Fed). If the Fed keeps money growing at a steady pace, aggregate demand fluctuations will be minimized and the economy will operate close to full employment. But if the Fed decreases the quantity of money or even just slows its growth rate too abruptly, the economy will go into recession. In the monetarist view, all recessions result from inappropriate monetary policy.

Aggregate Supply Response The monetarist view of short-run aggregate supply is the same as the Keynesian view: the money wage rate is sticky. If the economy is in recession, it will take an unnecessarily long time for it to return unaided to full employment.

Monetarist Policy The monetarist view of policy is the same as the classical view on fiscal policy. Taxes should be kept low to avoid disincentive effects that decrease potential GDP. Provided that the quantity of money is kept on a steady growth path, no active stabilization is needed to offset changes in aggregate demand.

The Way Ahead

In the chapters that follow, you're going to encounter Keynesian, classical, and monetarist views again. In the next chapter, we study the original Keynesian model of aggregate demand. This model remains useful today because it explains how expenditure fluctuations are magnified and bring changes in aggregate demand that are larger than the changes in expenditure. We then go on to apply the *AS-AD* model to a deeper look at the business cycle, inflation, and deflation.

Our attention then turns to macroeconomic policy—the fiscal policy of the Administration and Congress and the monetary policy of the Fed.

◆ REVIEW QUIZ

1 What are the defining features of classical macroeconomics and what policies do classical macroeconomists recommend?

2 What are the defining features of Keynesian macroeconomics and what policies do Keynesian macroeconomists recommend?

3 What are the defining features of monetarist macroeconomics and what policies do monetarist macroeconomists recommend?

Work these questions in Study Plan 27.4 and get instant feedback. Do a Key Terms Quiz.   MyEconLab

◆ To complete your study of the *AS-AD* model, *Economics in the News* on pp. 666–667 looks at the U.S. economy in 2014 through the eyes of this model.

Aggregate Supply and Aggregate Demand in Action

U.S. Rebound Stronger than First Thought

The Financial Times
August 28, 2014

The U.S. economy's second-quarter bounce was stronger than previously thought, with the official annualized growth estimate increased from 4 percent to 4.2 percent.

The revision is more evidence of robust underlying growth in the world's biggest economy as it swung back from a weather-affected 2.1 percent fall in the first quarter.

It will encourage U.S. Federal Reserve policy makers to view the first quarter as an anomaly, increasing their confidence that the economy can grow well from here. ...

The revision was more substantial than it first appeared because as well as the slight increase in the headline figure, there was a significant improvement in the quality of the growth.

The initial report was strongly boosted by an inventory build-up but the revision knocked 0.3 percentage points off growth from stockpiles and added 0.3 percentage points from business investment plus 0.2 percentage points from net trade. ...

That suggests more sustainable growth: Final sales of domestic product, which excludes inventories, were revised up from an annualized 2.3 percent to 2.8 percent. ...

The report contained an estimate for corporate profits in the second quarter, showing that they bounced back near to the record levels seen in 2013, rising 8 percent from the first quarter. ...

But most economists think profits will soon hit a wall as the labor market picks up and firms have to pay more in wages. ...

MyEconLab More Economics in the News

ESSENCE OF THE STORY

- U.S. real GDP grew at an annual rate of 4.2 percent during the second quarter of 2014 to $13.56 trillion.

- This growth rate is a revision of the initial estimate of 4.0 percent.

- The growth of business fixed investment was revised upward and the growth of inventories revised downward.

- Corporate profits grew, but economists expect them to stabilize when wages begin to rise.

- The strong rebound will signal to the Federal Reserve that growth can be sustained.

ECONOMIC ANALYSIS

- U.S. real GDP grew at an annual rate of 4.2 percent during the second quarter of 2014—a faster than average growth rate and slightly higher than the original estimate a month earlier.

- In the second quarter of 2014, real GDP was estimated to be $16.0 trillion. The price level was 108 (up 8 percent since 2009).

- A year earlier, in the second quarter of 2013, real GDP was $15.6 trillion and the price level was 106.

- Figure 1 illustrates the situation in the second quarter of 2013. The aggregate demand curve was AD_{13} and the short-run aggregate supply curve was SAS_{13}. Real GDP ($15.6 trillion) and the price level (106) are at the intersection of these curves.

- The Congressional Budget Office (CBO) estimated that *potential* GDP in the second quarter of 2013 was $16.5 trillion, so the long-run aggregate supply curve in 2013 was LAS_{13} in Fig. 1.

- Figure 1 shows the output gap in 2013, which was a recessionary gap of $0.9 trillion—about 5.5 percent of potential GDP.

- During the year from June 2013 to June 2014, the labor force increased, the capital stock increased, and labor productivity increased. Potential GDP increased to an estimated $16.7 trillion.

- In Fig. 2, the LAS curve shifted rightward to LAS_{14}.

- Also during the year from June 2013 to June 2014, a combination of fiscal and monetary policy stimulus and an increase in demand from a slowly expanding world economy increased aggregate demand.

- The increase in aggregate demand exceeded the increase in long-run aggregate supply, and the AD curve shifted rightward to AD_{14}.

- Two forces act on short-run aggregate supply: The increase in potential GDP shifts the SAS curve rightward and a rise in the money wage rate and other factor prices shifts the SAS curve leftward.

- Because potential GDP didn't increase by much, short-run aggregate supply probably didn't change by much, and here we assume it didn't change at all. The SAS curve in 2014, SAS_{14}, was the same as SAS_{13}.

- Real GDP increased to $16.0 trillion and the price level increased to 108.

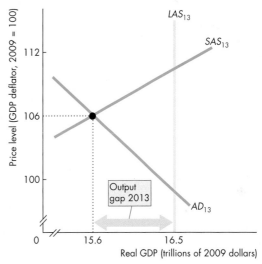

Figure 1 *AS-AD in Second Quarter of 2013*

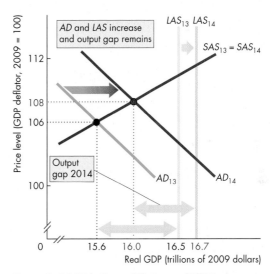

Figure 2 *AS-AD in Second Quarter of 2014*

- The output gap narrowed slightly to $0.7 trillion or 4.4 percent of potential GDP.

- If real GDP continues to grow at 4 percent a year for the rest of 2014, the output gap will shrink further.

- If real GDP maintains an annual growth rate of 4 percent, and if the CBO estimates of potential GDP are correct, the output gap will be zero and full employment will be restored in the fourth quarter of 2016.

SUMMARY

Key Points

Aggregate Supply (pp. 650–653)

- In the long run, the quantity of real GDP supplied is potential GDP.
- In the short run, a rise in the price level increases the quantity of real GDP supplied.
- A change in potential GDP changes long-run and short-run aggregate supply. A change in the money wage rate changes only short-run aggregate supply.

Working Problems 1 and 2 will give you a better understanding of aggregate supply.

Aggregate Demand (pp. 654–657)

- A rise in the price level decreases the quantity of real GDP demanded.
- Changes in expected future income, inflation, and profits; in fiscal policy and monetary policy; and in foreign income and the exchange rate change aggregate demand.

Working Problems 3 to 5 will give you a better understanding of aggregate demand.

Explaining Macroeconomic Trends and Fluctuations (pp. 658–663)

- Aggregate demand and short-run aggregate supply determine real GDP and the price level.
- In the long run, real GDP equals potential GDP and aggregate demand determines the price level.
- The business cycle occurs because aggregate demand and aggregate supply fluctuate.

Working Problems 6 to 8 will give you a better understanding of macroeconomic trends and fluctuations.

Macroeconomic Schools of Thought (pp. 664–665)

- Classical economists believe that the economy is self-regulating and always at full employment.
- Keynesian economists believe that full employment can be achieved only with active policy.
- Monetarist economists believe that recessions result from inappropriate monetary policy.

Working Problem 9 will give you a better understanding of the macroeconomic schools of thought.

Key Terms

MyEconLab Key Terms Quiz

Above full-employment equilibrium, 660
Aggregate demand, 654
Below full-employment equilibrium, 661
Classical, 664
Disposable income, 656
Fiscal policy, 656

Full-employment equilibrium, 661
Inflationary gap, 660
Keynesian, 664
Long-run aggregate supply, 650
Long-run macroeconomic equilibrium, 658
Monetarist, 665
Monetary policy, 656

New classical, 664
New Keynesian, 665
Output gap, 660
Recessionary gap, 661
Short-run aggregate supply, 651
Short-run macroeconomic equilibrium, 658
Stagflation, 663

WORKED PROBLEM

MyEconLab You can work this problem in Chapter 27 Study Plan.

The table shows the aggregate demand and short-run aggregate supply schedules of Lizard Island in which potential GDP is $600 billion.

Price level	Real GDP demanded	Real GDP supplied in the short run
	(billions of 2009 dollars)	
100	600	550
110	575	575
120	550	600
130	525	625

Questions

1. Calculate the short-run equilibrium real GDP and price level.
2. Does the country have an inflationary gap or a recessionary gap and what is its magnitude?
3. If aggregate demand increases by $50 billion, what is the new short-run macroeconomic equilibrium and the output gap?

Solutions

1. Short-run macroeconomic equilibrium occurs at the price level at which the quantity of real GDP demanded equals the quantity of real GDP supplied.

   At a price level of 110, the quantity of real GDP demanded is $575 billion and the quantity of real GDP supplied is $575 billion, so equilibrium real GDP is $575 billion and the price level is 110. See the equilibrium in the figure.

Key Point: Aggregate demand and aggregate supply determine the short-run macroeconomic equilibrium.

2. The output gap is the gap between equilibrium real GDP and potential GDP. Equilibrium real GDP is $575 billion and potential GDP is $600 billion, so the output gap is $25 billion. Because potential GDP exceeds equilibrium real GDP, the economy is in a below full-employment equilibrium and the output gap is a recessionary gap.

Key Point: A recessionary gap occurs when the economy is in a below full-employment equilibrium. When the economy is in an above full-employment equilibrium, the output gap is an inflationary gap.

3. The table below shows the new aggregate demand schedule when aggregate demand increases by $50 billion.

Price level	Real GDP demanded	Real GDP supplied in the short run
	(billions of 2009 dollars)	
100	650	550
110	625	575
120	600	600
130	575	675

At a price level of 110, the quantity of real GDP demanded ($625 billion) exceeds the quantity of real GDP supplied ($575 billion). Firms are unable to meet the demand for their output, so inventories start to decline. As people clamor for goods and services, firms increase production and start to raise their prices. Production and prices will continue to increase until a new short-run equilibrium is reached.

At the new equilibrium, real GDP is $600 billion and the price level is 120. Because equilibrium real GDP equals potential GDP of $600 billion, the economy is at full employment and there is no output gap. See the new short-run equilibrium in the figure.

Key Point: An increase in aggregate demand with no change in aggregate supply increases the price level and increases equilibrium real GDP.

Key Figure   MyEconLab Interactive Animation

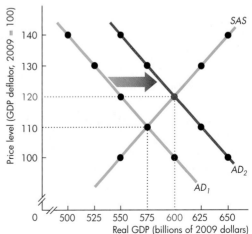

STUDY PLAN PROBLEMS AND APPLICATIONS

MyEconLab   You can work Problems 1 to 9 in Chapter 27 Study Plan and get instant feedback.

Aggregate Supply (Study Plan 27.1)

1. Explain the influence of each of the following events on the quantity of real GDP supplied and aggregate supply in India and use a graph to illustrate.
   - U.S. firms move their call handling, IT, and data functions to India.
   - Fuel prices rise.
   - Wal-Mart and Starbucks open in India.
   - Universities in India increase the number of engineering graduates.
   - The money wage rate rises.
   - The price level in India increases.

2. Labor productivity is rising at a rapid rate in China and wages are rising at a similar rate. Explain how a rise in labor productivity and wages in China will influence the quantity of real GDP supplied and aggregate supply in China.

Aggregate Demand (Study Plan 27.2)

3. Canada trades with the United States. Explain the effect of each of the following events on Canada's aggregate demand.
   - The government of Canada cuts income taxes.
   - The United States experiences strong economic growth.
   - Canada sets new environmental standards that require power utilities to upgrade their production facilities.

4. The Fed cuts the quantity of money and all other things remain the same. Explain the effect of the cut in the quantity of money on aggregate demand in the short run.

5. **Gross Domestic Product for the Second Quarter of 2012**

   The increase in real GDP in the second quarter primarily reflected increases in personal consumption expenditures, exports, and investment. Government spending decreased.

   Source: Bureau of Economic Analysis, August 29, 2012

   Explain how the items in the news clip influence U.S. aggregate demand.

Explaining Macroeconomic Trends and Fluctuations (Study Plan 27.3)

Use the following graph to work Problems 6 to 8. Initially, the short-run aggregate supply curve is SAS_0 and the aggregate demand curve is AD_0.

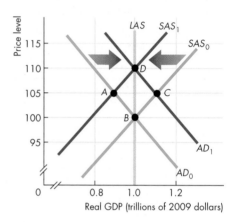

6. Some events change aggregate demand from AD_0 to AD_1. Describe two events that could have created this change in aggregate demand. What is the equilibrium after aggregate demand changed? If potential GDP is $1 trillion, the economy is at what type of macroeconomic equilibrium?

7. Some events change aggregate supply from SAS_0 to SAS_1. Describe two events that could have created this change in aggregate supply. What is the equilibrium after aggregate supply changed? If potential GDP is $1 trillion, does the economy have an inflationary gap, a recessionary gap, or no output gap?

8. Some events change aggregate demand from AD_0 to AD_1 and aggregate supply from SAS_0 to SAS_1. What is the new macroeconomic equilibrium?

Macroeconomic Schools of Thought (Study Plan 27.4)

9. Describe the policy change that a classical macroeconomist, a Keynesian, and a monetarist would recommend for U.S. policymakers to adopt in response to each of the following events:
   a. Growth in the world economy slows.
   b. The world price of oil rises.
   c. U.S. labor productivity declines.

ADDITIONAL PROBLEMS AND APPLICATIONS

MyEconLab   You can work these problems in MyEconLab if assigned by your instructor.

Aggregate Supply

10. Explain for each event whether it changes the quantity of real GDP supplied, short-run aggregate supply, long-run aggregate supply, or a combination of them.
    - Automotive firms in the United States switch to a new technology that raises productivity.
    - Toyota and Honda build additional plants in the United States.
    - The prices of auto parts imported from China rise.
    - Autoworkers agree to a lower money wage rate.
    - The U.S. price level rises.

Aggregate Demand

11. Explain for each event whether it changes the quantity of real GDP demanded or aggregate demand in the United States.
    - U.S. exports to the European Union boom.
    - U.S. firms build new gas-fuel utilities.
    - U.S. inflation rate is expected to rise next year.
    - The U.S. price level rises.

12. **Inventory Investment Decreases**
    When real GDP increased in the second quarter of 2012, consumption expenditure, exports, and fixed investment increased but business inventory investment fell.

    Source: Bureau of Economic Analysis, August 29, 2012

    Explain how a fall in inventories influences aggregate demand.

13. **Exports and Imports Increase**
    Real exports of goods and services increased 6.0 percent in the second quarter, compared with an increase of 4.4 percent in the first. Real imports of goods and services increased 2.9 percent, compared with an increase of 3.1 percent.

    Source: Bureau of Economic Analysis, August 29, 2012

    Explain how the changes in exports and imports reported here influence the quantity of real GDP demanded and aggregate demand. In which of the two quarters reported did exports and imports make the greater contribution to aggregate demand growth?

Explaining Macroeconomic Trends and Fluctuations

Use the following information to work Problems 14 to 16.
The following events have occurred at times in the history of the United States:
- The world economy goes into an expansion.
- U.S. businesses expect future profits to rise.
- The government increases its expenditure on goods and services in a time of war or increased international tension.

14. Explain for each event whether it changes short-run aggregate supply, long-run aggregate supply, aggregate demand, or some combination of them.

15. Explain the separate effects of each event on U.S. real GDP and the price level, starting from a position of long-run equilibrium.

16. Explain the combined effects of these events on U.S. real GDP and the price level, starting from a position of long-run equilibrium.

Use the following information to work Problems 17 and 18.

In Japan, potential GDP is 600 trillion yen and the table shows the aggregate demand and short-run aggregate supply schedules.

Price level	Real GDP demanded	Real GDP supplied in the short run
	(trillions of 2009 yen)	
75	600	400
85	550	450
95	500	500
105	450	550
115	400	600
125	350	650
135	300	700

17. a. Draw a graph of the aggregate demand curve and the short-run aggregate supply curve.
    b. What is the short-run equilibrium real GDP and price level?

18. Does Japan have an inflationary gap or a recessionary gap and what is its magnitude?

Use the following news clip to work Problems 19 and 20.

Spending by Women Jumps

The magazine *Women of China* reported that Chinese women in big cities spent 63% of their income on consumer goods last year, up from 26% in 2007. Clothing accounted for the biggest chunk of that spending, at nearly 30%, followed by digital products such as cellphones (11%) and travel (10%). Chinese consumption as a whole grew faster than the overall economy and is expected to reach 42% of GDP by 2020, up from the current 36%.

Source: *The Wall Street Journal*,
August 27, 2010

19. Explain the effect of a rise in consumption expenditure on real GDP and the price level in the short run.

20. If the economy had been operating at a full-employment equilibrium,
    a. Describe the macroeconomic equilibrium after the rise in consumer spending.
    b. Explain and draw a graph to illustrate how the economy can adjust in the long run to restore a full-employment equilibrium.

21. Suppose that the E.U. economy goes into an expansion. Explain the effect of the expansion on U.S. real GDP and unemployment in the short run.

22. Explain why changes in consumer spending and business investment play a large role in the business cycle.

23. **How to Avoid Recession? Let the Fed Do Its Work**

    Greg Mankiw wrote in 2007 on the eve of the Global Financial Crisis, "Congress made its most important contribution to taming the business cycle back in 1913, when it created the Federal Reserve System. Today, the Fed remains the first line of defense against recession."

    Source: *The New York Times*, December 23, 2007

    a. Describe the process by which the Fed's action in times of recession flows through the economy.
    b. Draw a graph to illustrate the Fed's action and its effect.

Macroeconomic Schools of Thought

24. **Cut Taxes and Boost Spending? Raise Taxes and Cut Spending? Cut Taxes and Cut Spending?**

    This headline expresses three views about what to do to get the U.S. economy growing more rapidly and contribute to closing the recessionary gap.

    Economists from which macroeconomic school of thought would recommend pursuing policies described by each of these views?

Economics in the News

25. After you have studied *Economics in the News* on pp. 666–667, answer the following questions.
    a. What are the main features of the U.S. economy in the second quarter of 2014?
    b. Did the United States have a recessionary gap or an inflationary gap in 2014? How do you know?
    c. Use the *AS-AD* model to show the changes in aggregate demand and aggregate supply that occurred in 2013 and 2014 that brought the economy to its situation in mid-2014.
    d. Use the *AS-AD* model to show the changes in aggregate demand and aggregate supply that will have occurred when full employment is restored.
    e. Use the *AS-AD* model to show the changes in aggregate demand and aggregate supply that would occur if the federal government increased its expenditure on goods and services or cut taxes by enough to restore full employment.
    f. Use the *AS-AD* model to show the changes in aggregate demand and aggregate supply that would occur if the economy moved into an inflationary gap. Show the short-run and the long-run effects.

26. **Brazil Falls into Recession**

    A decade ago Brazil had rapid growth, but now its economy is experiencing a slowdown with investment falling and inventories increasing. Potential GDP growth rate has slowed. Business and consumer confidence has fallen.

    Source: BBC News, August 29, 2014

    a. Explain the effect of a decrease in investment on real GDP and potential GDP.
    b. Explain how business and consumer confidence influences aggregate expenditure.

28 EXPENDITURE MULTIPLIERS

After studying this chapter, you will be able to:

◆ Explain how expenditure plans are determined when the price level is fixed

◆ Explain how real GDP is determined when the price level is fixed

◆ Explain the expenditure multiplier

◆ Explain the relationship between aggregate expenditure and aggregate demand

Investment and inventories fluctuate like the volume of a rock singer's voice and the uneven surface of a New York City street. How does the economy react to those fluctuations? Does it behave like an amplifier, blowing up the fluctuations and spreading them out to affect the many millions of participants in an economic rock concert? Or does it react like a limousine, absorbing the shocks and providing a smooth ride for the economy's passengers?

   You will explore these questions in this chapter and in *Economics in the News* at the end of the chapter you will see the role played by inventory investment during 2014 as the economy expanded.

Fixed Prices and Expenditure Plans

In the model that we study in this chapter, all the firms are like your grocery store: They set their prices and sell the quantities their customers are willing to buy. If they persistently sell more than they plan to and keep running out of inventory, they eventually raise their prices. And if they persistently sell less than they plan to and have inventories piling up, they eventually cut their prices. But on any given day, their prices are fixed and the quantities they sell depend on demand, not supply.

Because each firm's prices are fixed, for the economy as a whole

1. The *price level* is fixed, and
2. *Aggregate demand* determines real GDP.

We call this model the *Keynesian model* because it was first suggested by John Maynard Keynes (see p. 727) as a model of persistent depression.

We begin by identifying the forces that determine expenditure plans.

Expenditure Plans

Aggregate expenditure has four components: consumption expenditure, investment, government expenditure on goods and services, and net exports (exports *minus* imports). These four components sum to real GDP (see Chapter 21, pp. 493–494).

Aggregate planned expenditure is equal to the sum of the *planned* levels of consumption expenditure, investment, government expenditure on goods and services, and exports minus imports. Two of these components of planned expenditure, consumption expenditure and imports, change when income changes and so they depend on real GDP.

A Two-Way Link Between Aggregate Expenditure and Real GDP
There is a two-way link between aggregate expenditure and real GDP. Other things remaining the same,

- An increase in real GDP increases aggregate expenditure, and
- An increase in aggregate expenditure increases real GDP.

You are now going to study this two-way link.

Consumption and Saving Plans

Several factors influence consumption expenditure and saving plans. The more important ones are

1. Disposable income
2. Real interest rate
3. Wealth
4. Expected future income

Disposable income is aggregate income minus taxes plus transfer payments. Aggregate income equals real GDP, so disposable income depends on real GDP. To explore the two-way link between real GDP and planned consumption expenditure, we focus on the relationship between consumption expenditure and disposable income when the other three factors listed above are constant.

Consumption Expenditure and Saving The table in Fig. 28.1 lists the consumption expenditure and the saving that people plan at each level of disposable income. Households can only spend their disposable income on consumption or save it, so planned consumption expenditure plus planned saving *always* equals disposable income.

The relationship between consumption expenditure and disposable income, other things remaining the same, is called the **consumption function**. The relationship between saving and disposable income, other things remaining the same, is called the **saving function**.

Consumption Function Figure 28.1(a) shows a consumption function. The *y*-axis measures consumption expenditure, and the *x*-axis measures disposable income. Along the consumption function, the points labeled *A* through *F* correspond to the rows of the table. For example, point *E* shows that when disposable income is $8 trillion, consumption expenditure is $7.5 trillion. As disposable income increases, consumption expenditure also increases.

At point *A* on the consumption function, consumption expenditure is $1.5 trillion even though disposable income is zero. This consumption expenditure is called *autonomous consumption*, and it is the amount of consumption expenditure that would take place in the short run even if people had no current income. Consumption expenditure in excess of this amount is called *induced consumption*, which is the consumption expenditure that is induced by an increase in disposable income.

45° Line Figure 28.1(a) also contains a 45° line, the height of which measures disposable income. At each point on this line, consumption expenditure equals disposable income. Between points *A* and *D*, consumption expenditure exceeds disposable income, between points *D* and *F* consumption expenditure is less than disposable income, and at point *D*, consumption expenditure equals disposable income.

Saving Function Figure 28.1(b) shows a saving function. Again, the points *A* through *F* correspond to the rows of the table. For example, point *E* shows that when disposable income is $8 trillion, saving is $0.5 trillion. As disposable income increases, saving increases. Notice that when consumption expenditure exceeds disposable income in part (a), saving is negative, called *dissaving,* in part (b).

FIGURE 28.1   Consumption Function and Saving Function

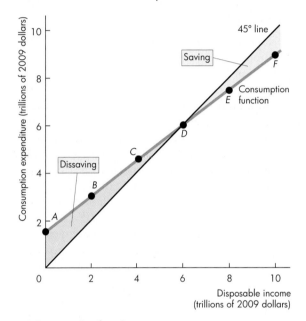

(a) Consumption function

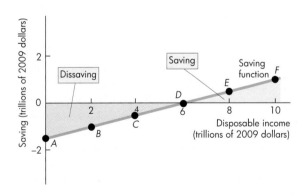

(b) Saving function

	Disposable income	Planned consumption expenditure	Planned saving
		(trillions of 2009 dollars)	
A	0	1.5	−1.5
B	2	3.0	−1.0
C	4	4.5	−0.5
D	6	6.0	0
E	8	7.5	0.5
F	10	9.0	1.0

The table shows consumption expenditure and saving plans at various levels of disposable income. Part (a) of the figure shows the relationship between consumption expenditure and disposable income (the consumption function). The height of the consumption function measures consumption expenditure at each level of disposable income. Part (b) shows the relationship between saving and disposable income (the saving function). The height of the saving function measures saving at each level of disposable income. Points *A* through *F* on the consumption and saving functions correspond to the rows in the table.

The height of the 45° line in part (a) measures disposable income. So along the 45° line, consumption expenditure equals disposable income. Consumption expenditure plus saving equals disposable income. When the consumption function is above the 45° line, saving is negative (dissaving occurs). When the consumption function is below the 45° line, saving is positive. At the point where the consumption function intersects the 45° line, all disposable income is spent on consumption and saving is zero.

MyEconLab Animation

Marginal Propensities to Consume and Save

The **marginal propensity to consume** (*MPC*) is the fraction of a *change* in disposable income that is spent on consumption. It is calculated as the *change* in consumption expenditure (ΔC) divided by the *change* in disposable income (ΔYD). The formula is

$$MPC = \frac{\Delta C}{\Delta YD}.$$

In the table in Fig. 28.1, when disposable income increases by $2 trillion, consumption expenditure increases by $1.5 trillion. The *MPC* is $1.5 trillion divided by $2 trillion, which equals 0.75.

The **marginal propensity to save** (*MPS*) is the fraction of a *change* in disposable income that is saved. It is calculated as the *change* in saving (ΔS) divided by the *change* in disposable income (ΔYD). The formula is

$$MPS = \frac{\Delta S}{\Delta YD}.$$

In the table in Fig. 28.1, when disposable income increases by $2 trillion, saving increases by $0.5 trillion. The *MPS* is $0.5 trillion divided by $2 trillion, which equals 0.25.

Because an increase in disposable income is either spent on consumption or saved, the marginal propensity to consume plus the marginal propensity to save equals 1. You can see why by using the equation:

$$\Delta C + \Delta S = \Delta YD.$$

Divide both sides of the equation by the change in disposable income to obtain

$$\frac{\Delta C}{\Delta YD} + \frac{\Delta S}{\Delta YD} = 1.$$

$\Delta C/\Delta YD$ is the marginal propensity to consume (*MPC*), and $\Delta S/\Delta YD$ is the marginal propensity to save (*MPS*), so

$$MPC + MPS = 1.$$

Slopes and Marginal Propensities

The slope of the consumption function is the marginal propensity to consume, and the slope of the saving function is the marginal propensity to save.

Figure 28.2(a) shows the *MPC* as the slope of the consumption function. An increase in disposable income of $2 trillion is the base of the red triangle. The increase in consumption expenditure that results from this increase in disposable income is $1.5 trillion and is the height of the triangle. The slope of the consumption function is given by the formula "slope equals rise over run" and is $1.5 trillion divided by $2 trillion, which equals 0.75—the *MPC*.

Figure 28.2(b) shows the *MPS* as the slope of the saving function. An increase in disposable income of $2 trillion (the base of the red triangle) increases saving by $0.5 trillion (the height of the triangle). The slope of the saving function is $0.5 trillion divided by $2 trillion, which equals 0.25—the *MPS*.

FIGURE 28.2   The Marginal Propensities to Consume and Save

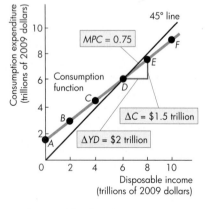

(a) Consumption function

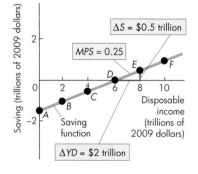

(b) Saving function

The marginal propensity to consume, *MPC*, is equal to the change in consumption expenditure divided by the change in disposable income, other things remaining the same. It is measured by the slope of the consumption function. In part (a), the *MPC* is 0.75.

The marginal propensity to save, *MPS*, is equal to the change in saving divided by the change in disposable income, other things remaining the same. It is measured by the slope of the saving function. In part (b), the *MPS* is 0.25.

MyEconLab Animation

ECONOMICS IN ACTION

The U.S. Consumption Function

The figure shows the U.S. consumption function. Each point identified by a blue dot represents consumption expenditure and disposable income for a particular year. (The dots are for the years 1980 to 2014, and the dots for five of those years are identified in the figure.)

The U.S. consumption function is CF_0 in 1980 and CF_1 in 2014.

The slope of the consumption function in the figure is 0.9, which means that a $1 increase in disposable income increases consumption expenditure by 90 cents. This slope, which is an estimate of the marginal propensity to consume, is an assumption that is at the upper end of the range of values that economists have estimated for the marginal propensity to consume.

The consumption function shifts upward over time as other influences on consumption expenditure change. Of these other influences, the real interest rate and wealth fluctuate and so bring upward and downward shifts in the consumption function.

But increasing wealth and increasing expected future income bring a steady upward shift in the consumption function. As the consumption function shifts upward, autonomous consumption increases.

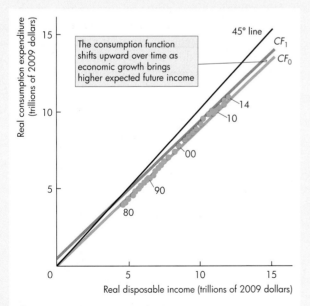

The U.S. Consumption Function

Source of data: Bureau of Economic Aanalysis.

Consumption as a Function of Real GDP

Consumption expenditure changes when disposable income changes and disposable income changes when real GDP changes. So consumption expenditure depends not only on disposable income but also on real GDP. We use this link between consumption expenditure and real GDP to determine equilibrium expenditure. But before we do so, we need to look at one further component of aggregate expenditure: imports. Like consumption expenditure, imports are influenced by real GDP.

Import Function

Of the many influences on U.S. imports in the short run, U.S. real GDP is the main influence. Other things remaining the same, an increase in U.S. real GDP increases the quantity of U.S. imports.

The relationship between imports and real GDP is determined by the **marginal propensity to import**, which is the fraction of an increase in real GDP that is spent on imports. It is calculated as the change in imports divided by the change in real GDP, other things remaining the same. For example, if an increase in real GDP of $1 trillion increases imports by $0.25 trillion, the marginal propensity to import is 0.25.

⬥ **REVIEW QUIZ**

1 Which components of aggregate expenditure are influenced by real GDP?
2 Define and explain how we calculate the marginal propensity to consume and the marginal propensity to save.
3 How do we calculate the effects of real GDP on consumption expenditure and imports by using the marginal propensity to consume and the marginal propensity to import?

Work these questions in Study Plan 28.1 and get instant feedback. Do a Key terms Quiz.   MyEconLab

Real GDP influences consumption expenditure and imports, which in turn influence real GDP. Your next task is to study this second piece of the two-way link between aggregate expenditure and real GDP and see how all the components of aggregate planned expenditure interact to determine real GDP.

Real GDP with a Fixed Price Level

You are now going to see how, at a given price level, aggregate expenditure plans determine real GDP. We start by looking at the relationship between aggregate planned expenditure and real GDP. This relationship can be described by an aggregate expenditure schedule or an aggregate expenditure curve. The *aggregate expenditure schedule* lists aggregate planned expenditure generated at each level of real GDP. The *aggregate expenditure curve* is a graph of the aggregate expenditure schedule.

Aggregate Planned Expenditure

The table in Fig. 28.3 sets out an aggregate expenditure schedule. To calculate aggregate planned expenditure at a given real GDP, we add the expenditure components together. The first column of the table shows real GDP, and the second column shows the planned consumption at each level of real GDP. A $1 trillion increase in real GDP increases consumption expenditure by $0.7 trillion—the *MPC* is 0.7.

The next two columns show investment and government expenditure on goods and services, both of which are independent of the level of real GDP. Investment depends on the real interest rate and the expected profit (see Chapter 24, p. 575). At a given point in time, these factors generate a given level of investment. Suppose this level of investment is $2.5 trillion. Also, suppose that government expenditure is $3.5 trillion.

The next two columns show exports and imports. Exports are influenced by events in the rest of the world, prices of foreign-produced goods and services relative to the prices of similar U.S.-produced goods and services, and exchange rates. But they are not directly affected by U.S. real GDP. Exports are a constant $2.0 trillion. Imports increase as U.S. real GDP increases. A $1 trillion increase in U.S. real GDP generates a $0.2 trillion increase in imports—the marginal propensity to import is 0.2.

The final column shows aggregate planned expenditure—the sum of planned consumption expenditure, investment, government expenditure on goods and services, and exports minus imports.

Figure 28.3 plots an aggregate expenditure curve. Real GDP is shown on the *x*-axis, and aggregate planned expenditure is shown on the *y*-axis. The aggregate expenditure curve is the red line *AE*. Points

A through *F* on that curve correspond to the rows of the table. The *AE* curve is a graph of aggregate planned expenditure (the last column) plotted against real GDP (the first column).

Figure 28.3 also shows the components of aggregate expenditure. The constant components—investment (I), government expenditure on goods and services (G), and exports (X)—are shown by the horizontal lines in the figure. Consumption expenditure (C) is the vertical gap between the lines labeled $I + G + X$ and $I + G + X + C$.

To construct the *AE* curve, subtract imports (M) from the $I + G + X + C$ line. Aggregate expenditure is expenditure on U.S.-produced goods and services. But the components of aggregate expenditure—C, I, and G—include expenditure on imported goods and services. For example, if you buy a new cellphone, your expenditure is part of consumption expenditure. But if the cellphone is a Nokia made in Finland, your expenditure on it must be subtracted from consumption expenditure to find out how much is spent on goods and services produced in the United States—on U.S. real GDP. Money paid to Nokia for cellphone imports from Finland does not add to aggregate expenditure in the United States.

Because imports are only a part of aggregate expenditure, when we subtract imports from the other components of aggregate expenditure, aggregate planned expenditure still increases as real GDP increases, as you can see in Fig. 28.3.

Consumption expenditure minus imports, which varies with real GDP, is called **induced expenditure**. The sum of investment, government expenditure, and exports, which does not vary with real GDP, is called **autonomous expenditure**. Consumption expenditure and imports can also have an autonomous component—a component that does not vary with real GDP. Another way of thinking about autonomous expenditure is that it would be the level of aggregate planned expenditure if real GDP were zero.

In Fig. 28.3, autonomous expenditure is $8 trillion—aggregate planned expenditure when real GDP is zero (point *A*). For each $1 trillion increase in real GDP, induced expenditure increases by $0.5 trillion.

The aggregate expenditure curve summarizes the relationship between aggregate *planned* expenditure and real GDP. But what determines the point on the aggregate expenditure curve at which the economy operates? What determines *actual* aggregate expenditure?

FIGURE 28.3   Aggregate Planned Expenditure: The *AE* Curve

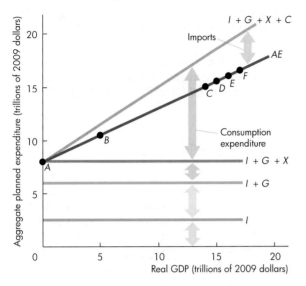

Aggregate planned expenditure is the sum of planned consumption expenditure, investment, government expenditure on goods and services, and exports minus imports. For example, in row *C* of the table, when real GDP is $14 trillion, planned consumption expenditure is $9.8 trillion, planned investment is $2.5 trillion, planned government expenditure is $3.5 trillion, planned exports are $2.0 trillion, and planned imports are $2.8 trillion. So when real GDP is $14 trillion, aggregate planned expenditure is $15 trillion ($9.8 + $2.5 + $3.5 + $2.0 − $2.8).

The schedule shows that aggregate planned expenditure increases as real GDP increases. This relationship is graphed as the aggregate expenditure curve *AE*. The components of aggregate expenditure that increase with real GDP are consumption expenditure and imports. The other components—investment, government expenditure, and exports—do not vary with real GDP.

	Real GDP (Y)	Consumption expenditure (C)	Investment (I)	Government expenditure (G)	Exports (X)	Imports (M)	Aggregate planned expenditure (AE = C + I + G + X − M)
				(trillions of 2009 dollars)			
A	0	0	2.5	3.5	2.0	0.0	8.0
B	5	3.5	2.5	3.5	2.0	1.0	10.5
C	14	9.8	2.5	3.5	2.0	2.8	15.0
D	15	10.5	2.5	3.5	2.0	3.0	15.5
E	16	11.2	2.5	3.5	2.0	3.2	16.0
F	17	11.9	2.5	3.5	2.0	3.4	16.5

MyEconLab Animation

Actual Expenditure, Planned Expenditure, and Real GDP

Actual aggregate expenditure is always equal to real GDP, as we saw in Chapter 21 (p. 494). But aggregate *planned* expenditure is not always equal to actual aggregate expenditure and therefore is not always equal to real GDP. How can actual expenditure and planned expenditure differ? The answer is that firms can end up with inventories that are greater or smaller than planned. People carry out their consumption

expenditure plans, the government implements its planned expenditure on goods and services, and net exports are as planned. Firms carry out their plans to purchase new buildings, plant, and equipment. But one component of investment is the change in firms' inventories. If aggregate planned expenditure is less than real GDP, firms sell less than they planned to sell and end up with unplanned inventories. If aggregate planned expenditure exceeds real GDP, firms sell more than they planned to sell and end up with inventories being too low.

Equilibrium Expenditure

Equilibrium expenditure is the level of aggregate expenditure that occurs when aggregate *planned* expenditure equals real GDP. Equilibrium expenditure is a level of aggregate expenditure and real GDP at which spending plans are fulfilled. At a given price level, equilibrium expenditure determines real GDP. When aggregate planned expenditure and actual aggregate expenditure are unequal, a process of convergence toward equilibrium expenditure occurs. Throughout this process, real GDP adjusts. Let's examine equilibrium expenditure and the process that brings it about.

Figure 28.4(a) illustrates equilibrium expenditure. The table sets out aggregate planned expenditure at various levels of real GDP. These values are plotted as

FIGURE 28.4   Equilibrium Expenditure

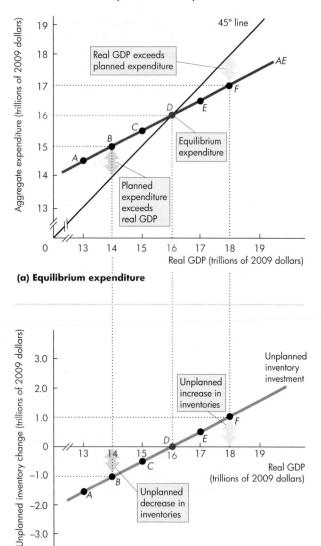

(a) Equilibrium expenditure

(b) Unplanned inventory changes

	Real GDP (Y)	Aggregate planned expenditure (AE)	Unplanned inventory change (Y − AE)
		(trillions of 2009 dollars)	
A	13	14.5	−1.5
B	14	15.0	−1.0
C	15	15.5	−0.5
D	**16**	**16.0**	**0**
E	17	16.5	0.5
F	18	17.0	1.0

The table shows expenditure plans at different levels of real GDP. When real GDP is $16 trillion, aggregate planned expenditure equals real GDP.

Part (a) of the figure illustrates equilibrium expenditure, which occurs when aggregate planned expenditure equals real GDP at the intersection of the 45° line and the AE curve. Part (b) of the figure shows the forces that bring about equilibrium expenditure.

When aggregate planned expenditure exceeds real GDP, inventories decrease—for example, at point B in both parts of the figure. So, firms increase production, and real GDP increases.

When aggregate planned expenditure is less than real GDP, inventories increase—for example, at point F in both parts of the figure. So, firms cut production, and real GDP decreases.

When aggregate planned expenditure equals real GDP, there are no unplanned inventory changes and real GDP remains constant at equilibrium expenditure.

MyEconLab Animation and Draw Graph

points *A* through *F* along the *AE* curve. The 45° line shows all the points at which aggregate planned expenditure equals real GDP. So where the *AE* curve lies above the 45° line, aggregate planned expenditure exceeds real GDP; where the *AE* curve lies below the 45° line, aggregate planned expenditure is less than real GDP; and where the *AE* curve intersects the 45° line, aggregate planned expenditure equals real GDP. Point *D* illustrates equilibrium expenditure. At this point, real GDP is $16 trillion.

Convergence to Equilibrium

What are the forces that move aggregate expenditure toward its equilibrium level? To answer this question, we must look at a situation in which aggregate expenditure is away from its equilibrium level.

From Below Equilibrium   Suppose that in Fig. 28.4, real GDP is $14 trillion. With real GDP at $14 trillion, actual aggregate expenditure is also $14 trillion. But aggregate *planned* expenditure is $15 trillion, point *B* in Fig. 28.4(a). Aggregate planned expenditure exceeds *actual* expenditure. When people spend $15 trillion and firms produce goods and services worth $14 trillion, firms' inventories fall by $1 trillion, point *B* in Fig. 28.4(b). Because the change in inventories is part of investment, *actual* investment is $1 trillion less than *planned* investment.

Real GDP doesn't remain at $14 trillion for very long. Firms have inventory targets based on their sales. When inventories fall below target, firms increase production to restore inventories to the target level.

To increase inventories, firms hire additional labor and increase production. Suppose that they increase production in the next period by $1 trillion. Real GDP increases by $1.0 trillion to $15.0 trillion. But again, aggregate planned expenditure exceeds real GDP. When real GDP is $15.0 trillion, aggregate planned expenditure is $15.5 trillion, point *C* in Fig. 28.4(a). Again, inventories decrease, but this time by less than before. With real GDP of $15.0 trillion and aggregate planned expenditure of $15.5 trillion, inventories decrease by $0.5 trillion, point *C* in Fig. 28.4(b). Again, firms hire additional labor and production increases; real GDP increases yet further.

The process that we've just described—planned expenditure exceeds real GDP, inventories decrease, and production increases to restore inventories—ends when real GDP has reached $16 trillion. At this real GDP, there is equilibrium. Unplanned inventory changes are zero. Firms do not change their production.

From Above Equilibrium   If in Fig. 28.4, real GDP is $18 trillion, the process that we've just described works in reverse. With real GDP at $18 trillion, actual aggregate expenditure is also $18 trillion. But aggregate planned expenditure is $17 trillion, point *F* in Fig. 28.4(a). Actual expenditure exceeds planned expenditure. When people spend $17 trillion and firms produce goods and services worth $18 trillion, firms' inventories rise by $1 trillion, point *F* in Fig. 28.4(b). Now, real GDP begins to decrease. As long as actual expenditure exceeds planned expenditure, inventories rise, and production decreases. Again, the process ends when real GDP has reached $16 trillion, the equilibrium at which unplanned inventory changes are zero and firms do not change their production.

◆ **REVIEW QUIZ**

1   What is the relationship between aggregate planned expenditure and real GDP at equilibrium expenditure?

2   How does equilibrium expenditure come about? What adjusts to achieve equilibrium?

3   If real GDP and aggregate expenditure are less than equilibrium expenditure, what happens to firms' inventories? How do firms change their production? And what happens to real GDP?

4   If real GDP and aggregate expenditure are greater than equilibrium expenditure, what happens to firms' inventories? How do firms change their production? And what happens to real GDP?

Work these questions in Study Plan 28.2 and get instant feedback. Do a Key Terms Quiz.   MyEconLab

We've learned that when the price level is fixed, real GDP is determined by equilibrium expenditure. And we have seen how unplanned changes in inventories and the production response they generate bring a convergence toward equilibrium expenditure. We're now going to study *changes* in equilibrium expenditure and discover an economic amplifier called the *multiplier*.

◆ The Multiplier

Investment and exports can change for many reasons. A fall in the real interest rate might induce firms to increase their planned investment. A wave of innovation, such as occurred with the spread of multimedia computers in the 1990s, might increase expected future profits and lead firms to increase their planned investment. An economic boom in Western Europe and Japan might lead to a large increase in their expenditure on U.S.-produced goods and services—on U.S. exports. These are all examples of increases in autonomous expenditure.

When autonomous expenditure increases, aggregate expenditure increases and so does equilibrium expenditure and real GDP. But the increase in real GDP is *larger* than the change in autonomous expenditure. The **multiplier** is the amount by which a change in autonomous expenditure is magnified or multiplied to determine the change in equilibrium expenditure and real GDP.

To get the basic idea of the multiplier, we'll work with an example economy in which there are no income taxes and no imports. So we'll first assume that these factors are absent. Then, when you understand the basic idea, we'll bring these factors back into play and see what difference they make to the multiplier.

The Basic Idea of the Multiplier

Suppose that investment increases. The additional expenditure by businesses means that aggregate expenditure and real GDP increase. The increase in real GDP increases disposable income, and with no income taxes, real GDP and disposable income increase by the same amount. The increase in disposable income brings an increase in consumption expenditure. And the increased consumption expenditure adds even more to aggregate expenditure. Real GDP and disposable income increase further, and so does consumption expenditure. The initial increase in investment brings an even bigger increase in aggregate expenditure because it induces an increase in consumption expenditure. The magnitude of the increase in aggregate expenditure that results from an increase in autonomous expenditure is determined by the *multiplier*.

The table in Fig. 28.5 sets out an aggregate planned expenditure schedule. Initially, when real GDP is $15 trillion, aggregate planned expenditure is $15.25 trillion. For each $1 trillion increase in real GDP, aggregate planned expenditure increases by $0.75 trillion. This aggregate expenditure schedule is shown in the figure as the aggregate expenditure curve AE_0. Initially, equilibrium expenditure is $16 trillion. You can see this equilibrium in row B of the table and in the figure where the curve AE_0 intersects the 45° line at the point marked B.

Now suppose that autonomous expenditure increases by $0.5 trillion. What happens to equilibrium expenditure? You can see the answer in Fig. 28.5. When this increase in autonomous expenditure is added to the original aggregate planned expenditure, aggregate planned expenditure increases by $0.5 trillion at each level of real GDP. The new aggregate expenditure curve is AE_1. The new equilibrium expenditure, highlighted in the table (row D'), occurs where AE_1 intersects the 45° line and is $18 trillion (point D'). At this real GDP, aggregate planned expenditure equals real GDP.

The Multiplier Effect

In Fig. 28.5, the increase in autonomous expenditure of $0.5 trillion increases equilibrium expenditure by $2 trillion. That is, the change in autonomous expenditure leads, like a rock singer's electronic equipment, to an amplified change in equilibrium expenditure. This amplified change is the *multiplier effect*—equilibrium expenditure increases by *more than* the increase in autonomous expenditure. The multiplier is greater than 1.

Initially, when autonomous expenditure increases, aggregate planned expenditure exceeds real GDP. As a result, inventories decrease. Firms respond by increasing production so as to restore their inventories to the target level. As production increases, so does real GDP. With a higher level of real GDP, *induced expenditure* increases. Equilibrium expenditure increases by the sum of the initial increase in autonomous expenditure and the increase in induced expenditure. In this example, equilibrium expenditure increases by $2 trillion following the increase in autonomous expenditure of $0.5 trillion, so induced expenditure increases by $1.5 trillion.

Although we have just analyzed the effects of an *increase* in autonomous expenditure, this analysis also applies to a decrease in autonomous expenditure. If initially the aggregate expenditure curve is AE_1, equilibrium expenditure and real GDP are $18 trillion. A decrease in autonomous expenditure of $0.5 trillion shifts the aggregate expenditure curve downward by

FIGURE 28.5   The Multiplier

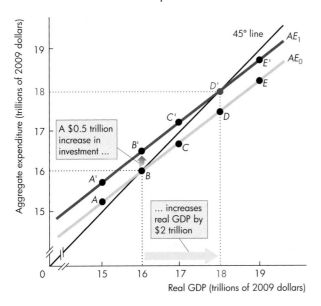

Real GDP (Y)	Aggregate planned expenditure			
	Original (AE₀)		New (AE₁)	
	(trillions of 2009 dollars)			
15	A	15.25	A'	15.75
16	**B**	**16.00**	B'	16.50
17	C	16.75	C'	17.25
18	**D**	**17.50**	**D'**	**18.00**
19	E	18.25	E'	18.75

A $0.5 trillion increase in autonomous expenditure shifts the AE curve upward by $0.5 trillion from AE_0 to AE_1. Equilibrium expenditure increases by $2 trillion from $16 trillion to $18 trillion. The increase in equilibrium expenditure is 4 times the increase in autonomous expenditure, so the multiplier is 4.

——— MyEconLab Animation and Draw Graph ———

$0.5 trillion to AE_0. Equilibrium expenditure decreases from $18 trillion to $16 trillion. The decrease in equilibrium expenditure ($2 trillion) is larger than the decrease in autonomous expenditure that brought it about ($0.5 trillion).

Why Is the Multiplier Greater Than 1?

We've seen that equilibrium expenditure increases by more than the increase in autonomous expenditure. This makes the multiplier greater than 1. How come? Why does equilibrium expenditure increase by more than the increase in autonomous expenditure?

The multiplier is greater than 1 because induced expenditure increases—an increase in autonomous expenditure *induces* further increases in expenditure. The NASA space program costs about $18 billion a year. This expenditure adds $18 billion a year directly to real GDP. But that is not the end of the story. Astronauts and engineers now have more income, and they spend part of the extra income on goods and services. Real GDP now rises by the initial $18 billion plus the extra consumption expenditure induced by the $18 billion increase in income. The producers of cars, TVs, vacation cruises, and other goods and services now have increased incomes, and they, in turn, spend part of the increase in their incomes on consumption goods and services. Additional income induces additional expenditure, which creates additional income.

How big is the multiplier effect?

The Size of the Multiplier

Suppose that the economy is in a recession. Profit prospects start to look better, and firms are planning a large increase in investment. The world economy is also heading toward expansion. The question on everyone's lips is: How strong will the expansion be? This is a hard question to answer, but an important ingredient in the answer is the size of the multiplier.

The *multiplier* is the amount by which a change in autonomous expenditure is multiplied to determine the change in equilibrium expenditure that it generates. To calculate the multiplier, we divide the change in equilibrium expenditure by the change in autonomous expenditure.

Let's calculate the multiplier for the example in Fig. 28.5. Initially, equilibrium expenditure is $16 trillion. Then autonomous expenditure increases by $0.5 trillion, and equilibrium expenditure increases by $2 trillion, to $18 trillion. Then

$$\text{Multiplier} = \frac{\text{Change in equilibrium expenditure}}{\text{Change in autonomous expenditure}}$$

$$\text{Multiplier} = \frac{\$2 \text{ trillion}}{\$0.5 \text{ trillion}} = 4.$$

The Multiplier and the Slope of the *AE* Curve

The magnitude of the multiplier depends on the slope of the *AE* curve. In Fig. 28.6, the *AE* curve in part (a) is steeper than the *AE* curve in part (b), and the multiplier is larger in part (a) than in part (b). To see why, let's do a calculation.

Aggregate expenditure and real GDP change because induced expenditure and autonomous expenditure change. The change in real GDP (ΔY) equals the change in induced expenditure (ΔN) plus the change in autonomous expenditure (ΔA). That is,

$$\Delta Y = \Delta N + \Delta A.$$

But the change in induced expenditure is determined by the change in real GDP and the slope of the *AE* curve. To see why, begin with the fact that the slope of the *AE* curve equals the "rise," ΔN, divided by the "run," ΔY. That is,

$$\text{Slope of } AE \text{ curve} = \Delta N \div \Delta Y.$$

So

$$\Delta N = \text{Slope of } AE \text{ curve} \times \Delta Y.$$

Now, use this equation to replace ΔN in the first equation above to give

$$\Delta Y = \text{Slope of } AE \text{ curve} \times \Delta Y + \Delta A.$$

Now, solve for ΔY as

$$(1 - \text{Slope of } AE \text{ curve}) \times \Delta Y = \Delta A$$

Now rearrange the equation to give

$$\Delta Y = \frac{\Delta A}{1 - \text{Slope of } AE \text{ curve}}.$$

Finally, divide both sides of this equation by ΔA to give

$$\text{Multiplier} = \frac{\Delta Y}{\Delta A} = \frac{1}{1 - \text{Slope of } AE \text{ curve}}.$$

If we use the example in Fig. 28.5, the slope of the *AE* curve is 0.75, so

$$\text{Multiplier} = \frac{1}{1 - 0.75} = \frac{1}{0.25} = 4.$$

Where there are no income taxes and no imports, the slope of the *AE* curve equals the marginal propensity to consume (*MPC*). So

$$\text{Multiplier} = \frac{1}{1 - MPC}.$$

But $(1 - MPC)$ equals *MPS*. So another formula is

$$\text{Multiplier} = \frac{1}{MPS}.$$

Again using the numbers in Fig. 28.5, we have

$$\text{Multiplier} = \frac{1}{0.25} = 4.$$

Because the marginal propensity to save (*MPS*) is a fraction—a number between 0 and 1—the multiplier is greater than 1.

FIGURE 28.6   The Multiplier and the Slope of the *AE* Curve

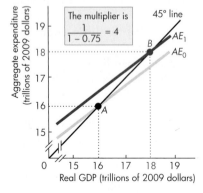

(a) Multiplier is 4

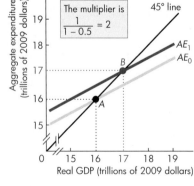

(b) Multiplier is 2

Imports and income taxes make the *AE* curve less steep and reduce the value of the multiplier. In part (a), with no imports and no income taxes, the slope of the *AE* curve is 0.75 (the marginal propensity to consume) and the multiplier is 4. But with imports and income taxes, the slope of the *AE* curve is less than the marginal propensity to consume. In part (b), the slope of the *AE* curve is 0.5. In this case, the multiplier is 2.

MyEconLab Animation

Imports and Income Taxes

Imports and income taxes influence the size of the multiplier and make it smaller than it otherwise would be.

To see why imports make the multiplier smaller, think about what happens following an increase in investment. The increase in investment increases real GDP, which in turn increases consumption expenditure. But part of the increase in expenditure is on imported goods and services. Only expenditure on U.S.-produced goods and services increases U.S. real GDP. The larger the marginal propensity to import, the smaller is the change in U.S. real GDP. The Mathematical Note on pp. 694–697 shows the effects of imports and income taxes on the multiplier.

Income taxes also make the multiplier smaller than it otherwise would be. Again, think about what happens following an increase in investment. The increase in investment increases real GDP. Income tax payments increase so disposable income increases by less than the increase in real GDP and consumption expenditure increases by less than it would if taxes had not changed. The larger the income tax rate, the smaller is the change in real GDP.

The marginal propensity to import and the income tax rate together with the marginal propensity to consume determine the multiplier. And their combined influence determines the slope of the *AE* curve.

Over time, the value of the multiplier changes as tax rates change and as the marginal propensity to consume and the marginal propensity to import change. These ongoing changes make the multiplier hard to predict. But they do not change the fundamental fact that an initial change in autonomous expenditure leads to a magnified change in aggregate expenditure and real GDP.

The Multiplier Process

The multiplier effect isn't a one-shot event. It is a process that plays out over a few months. Figure 28.7 illustrates the multiplier process. Autonomous expenditure increases by $0.5 trillion and real GDP increases by $0.5 trillion (the green bar in round 1). This increase in real GDP increases induced expenditure in round 2. With the slope of the *AE* curve equal to 0.75, induced expenditure increases by 0.75 times the increase in real GDP, so the increase in real GDP of $0.5 trillion induces a further increase in expenditure of $0.375 trillion. This

change in induced expenditure (the green bar in round 2) when added to the previous increase in expenditure (the blue bar in round 2) increases real GDP by $0.875 trillion. The round 2 increase in real GDP induces a round 3 increase in induced expenditure. The process repeats through successive rounds. Each increase in real GDP is 0.75 times the previous increase and eventually real GDP increases by $2 trillion.

FIGURE 28.7   The Multiplier Process

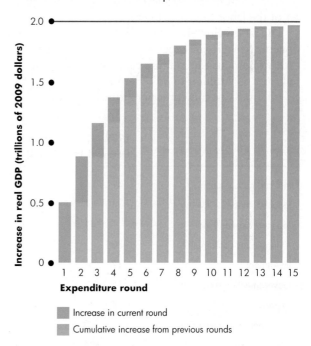

Increase in real GDP (trillions of 2009 dollars) vs. Expenditure round

■ Increase in current round
■ Cumulative increase from previous rounds

Autonomous expenditure increases by $0.5 trillion. In round 1, real GDP increases by the same amount. With the slope of the *AE* curve equal to 0.75, each additional dollar of real GDP induces an additional 0.75 of a dollar of induced expenditure. The round 1 increase in real GDP brings an increase in induced expenditure of $0.375 trillion in round 2.

At the end of round 2, real GDP has increased by $0.875 trillion. The extra $0.375 trillion of real GDP in round 2 brings a further increase in induced expenditure of $0.281 trillion in round 3.

At the end of round 3, real GDP has increased by $1.156 trillion. This process continues with real GDP increasing by ever-smaller amounts. When the process comes to an end, real GDP has increased by a total of $2 trillion.

MyEconLab Animation

ECONOMICS IN ACTION

The Multiplier in the Great Depression

The aggregate expenditure model and its multiplier were developed during the 1930s by John Maynard Keynes to understand the most traumatic event in economic history, the *Great Depression.*

In 1929, the U.S. and global economies were booming. U.S. real GDP and real GDP per person had never been higher. By 1933, real GDP had fallen to 73 percent of its 1929 level and more than a quarter of the labor force was unemployed.

The table below shows the GDP numbers and components of aggregate expenditure in 1929 and 1933.

Autonomous expenditure collapsed as investment fell from $17 billion to $3 billion and exports fell by $3 billion. Government expenditure held steady.

	1929	1933
	(billions of 1929 dollars)	
Induced consumption	47	34
Induced imports	−6	−4
Induced expenditure	41	30
Autonomous consumption	30	30
Investment	17	3
Government expenditure	10	10
Exports	6	3
Autonomous expenditure	63	46
GDP	**104**	**76**

Source of data: Bureau of Economic Analysis.

The figure uses the *AE* model to illustrate the Great Depression. In 1929, with autonomous expenditure of $63 billion, the *AE* curve was AE_{29}. Equilibrium expenditure and real GDP were $104 billion.

By 1933, autonomous expenditure had fallen by $17 billion to $46 billion and the *AE* curve had shifted downward to AE_{33}. Equilibrium expenditure and real GDP had fallen to $76 billion.

The decrease in autonomous expenditure of $17 billion brought a decrease in real GDP of $28 billion. The multiplier was $28/$17 = 1.6. The slope of the *AE* curve is 0.39—the fall in induced expenditure, $11 billion, divided by the fall in real GDP, $28 billion. The multiplier formula, 1/(1 − Slope of *AE* curve), delivers a multiplier equal to 1.6.

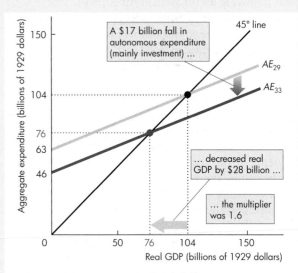

Aggregate Expenditure in the Great Depression

Business Cycle Turning Points

At business cycle turning points, the economy moves from expansion to recession or from recession to expansion. Economists understand these turning points as seismologists understand earthquakes. They know quite a lot about the forces and mechanisms that produce them, but they can't predict them. The forces that bring business cycle turning points are the swings in autonomous expenditure, such as investment and exports. The multiplier that you've just studied is the mechanism that gives momentum to the economy's new direction.

◆ **REVIEW QUIZ**

1   What is the multiplier? What does it determine? Why does it matter?

2   How do the marginal propensity to consume, the marginal propensity to import, and the income tax rate influence the multiplier?

3   How do fluctuations in autonomous expenditure influence real GDP?

Work these questions in Study Plan 28.3 and get instant feedback. Do a Key Terms Quiz.   MyEconLab

◆ The Multiplier and the Price Level

We have just considered adjustments in spending that occur in the very short run when the price level is fixed. In this time frame, the economy's cobblestones, which are changes in investment and exports, are not smoothed by shock absorbers like those on a limousine. Instead, they are amplified like a rock singer's voice. But these outcomes occur only when the price level is fixed. We now investigate what happens after a long enough time lapse for the price level to change.

Adjusting Quantities and Prices

When firms can't keep up with sales and their inventories fall below target, they increase production, but at some point, they raise their prices. Similarly, when firms find unwanted inventories piling up, they decrease production, but eventually they cut their prices. So far, we've studied the macroeconomic consequences of firms changing their production levels when their sales change, but we haven't looked at the effects of price changes. When individual firms change their prices, the economy's price level changes.

To study the simultaneous determination of real GDP and the price level, we use the *AS-AD model*, which is explained in Chapter 27. But to understand how aggregate demand adjusts, we need to work out the connection between the *AS-AD* model and the aggregate expenditure model that we've used in this chapter. The key to understanding the relationship between these two models is the distinction between the aggregate *expenditure* and aggregate *demand* and the related distinction between the aggregate *expenditure curve* and the aggregate *demand curve*.

Aggregate Expenditure and Aggregate Demand

The aggregate expenditure curve is the relationship between the aggregate planned expenditure and real GDP, all other influences on aggregate planned expenditure remaining the same. The aggregate demand curve is the relationship between the aggregate quantity of goods and services demanded and the price level, all other influences on aggregate

demand remaining the same. Let's explore the links between these two relationships.

Deriving the Aggregate Demand Curve

When the price level changes, aggregate planned expenditure changes and the quantity of real GDP demanded changes. The aggregate demand curve slopes downward. Why? There are two main reasons:

- Wealth effect
- Substitution effects

Wealth Effect Other things remaining the same, the higher the price level, the smaller is the purchasing power of wealth. For example, suppose you have $100 in the bank and the price level is 105. If the price level rises to 125, your $100 buys fewer goods and services. You are less wealthy. With less wealth, you will probably want to try to spend a bit less and save a bit more. The higher the price level, other things remaining the same, the lower is aggregate planned expenditure.

Substitution Effects For a given expected future price level, a rise in the price level today makes current goods and services more expensive relative to future goods and services and results in a delay in purchases—an *intertemporal substitution*. A rise in the U.S. price level, other things remaining the same, makes U.S.-produced goods and services more expensive relative to foreign-produced goods and services. As a result, U.S. imports increase and U.S. exports decrease—an *international substitution*.

When the price level rises, each of these effects reduces aggregate planned expenditure at each level of real GDP. As a result, when the price level *rises*, the aggregate expenditure curve shifts *downward*. A fall in the price level has the opposite effect. When the price level *falls*, the aggregate expenditure curve shifts *upward*.

Figure 28.8(a) shows the shifts of the *AE* curve. When the price level is 110, the aggregate expenditure curve is AE_0, which intersects the 45° line at point *B*. Equilibrium expenditure is $16 trillion. If the price level rises to 130, the aggregate expenditure curve shifts *downward* to AE_1, which intersects the 45° line at point *A*. Equilibrium expenditure decreases to $15 trillion. If the price level falls to 90, the aggregate expenditure curve shifts *upward* to AE_2, which intersects the 45° line at point C. Equilibrium expenditure increases to $17 trillion.

We've just seen that when the price level changes, other things remaining the same, the aggregate expenditure curve *shifts* and the equilibrium expenditure changes. But when the price level changes and other things remain the same, there is a *movement along* the aggregate demand curve.

Figure 28.8(b) shows the movements along the aggregate demand curve. At a price level of 110, the aggregate quantity of goods and services demanded is $16 trillion—point B on the AD curve. If the price level rises to 130, the aggregate quantity of goods and services demanded decreases to $15 trillion and there is a movement up along the aggregate demand curve to point A. If the price level falls to 90, the aggregate quantity of goods and services demanded increases to $17 trillion and there is a movement down along the aggregate demand curve to point C.

Each point on the aggregate demand curve corresponds to a point of equilibrium expenditure. The equilibrium expenditure points A, B, and C in Fig. 28.8(a) correspond to the points A, B, and C on the aggregate demand curve in Fig. 28.8(b).

Changes in Aggregate Expenditure and Aggregate Demand

When any influence on aggregate planned expenditure other than the price level changes, both the aggregate expenditure curve and the aggregate demand curve shift. For example, an increase in investment or exports increases both aggregate planned expenditure and aggregate demand and shifts both the AE curve and the AD curve. Figure 28.9 illustrates the effect of such an increase.

Initially, the aggregate expenditure curve is AE_0 in part (a) and the aggregate demand curve is AD_0 in part (b). The price level is 110, real GDP is $16 trillion, and the economy is at point A in both parts of Fig. 28.9. Now suppose that investment increases by $1 trillion. At a constant price level of 110, the aggregate expenditure curve shifts upward to AE_1. This curve intersects the 45° line at an equilibrium expenditure of $18 trillion (point B). This equilibrium expenditure of $18 trillion is the aggregate quantity of goods and services demanded at a price level of 110, as shown by point B in part (b). Point B lies

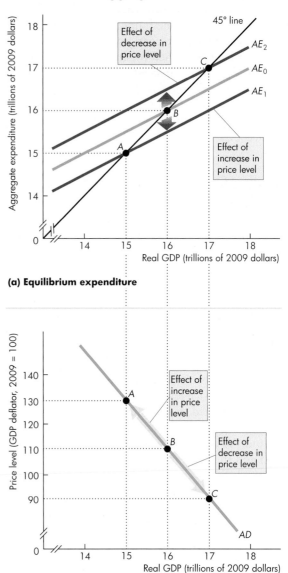

FIGURE 28.8 Equilibrium Expenditure and Aggregate Demand

(a) Equilibrium expenditure

(b) Aggregate demand

A change in the price level *shifts* the AE curve and results in a *movement along* the AD curve. When the price level is 110, the AE curve is AE_0 and equilibrium expenditure is $16 trillion at point B. A rise in the price level to 130 shifts the AE curve downward to AE_1. Equilibrium expenditure decreases to $15 trillion at point A. A fall in the price level from 110 to 90 shifts the AE curve upward to AE_2. Equilibrium expenditure increases to $17 trillion at point C. Points A, B, and C on the AD curve in part (b) correspond to the equilibrium expenditure points A, B, and C in part (a).

MyEconLab Animation and Draw Graph

FIGURE 28.9   A Change in Aggregate Demand

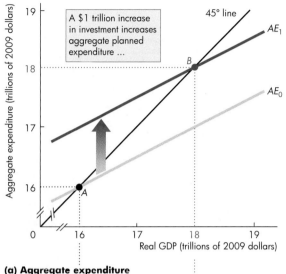

A $1 trillion increase in investment increases aggregate planned expenditure ...

(a) Aggregate expenditure

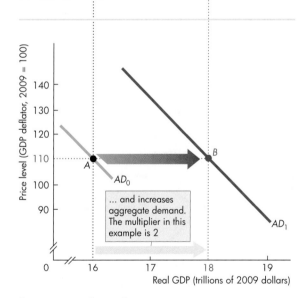

... and increases aggregate demand. The multiplier in this example is 2

(b) Aggregate demand

An increase in autonomous expenditure increases aggregate demand. The price level is 110. When the aggregate expenditure curve is AE_0 in part (a), the aggregate demand curve is AD_0 in part (b). The economy is at point A in both parts of the figure. An increase in autonomous expenditure shifts the AE curve upward to AE_1. The new equilibrium expenditure is $18 trillion at point B in part (a). Because the quantity of real GDP demanded at a price level of 110 increases from $16 trillion to $18 trillion, the AD curve shifts rightward to AD_1.

MyEconLab Animation

on a new aggregate demand curve. The aggregate demand curve has shifted rightward to AD_1 to pass through point B.

But how do we know by how much the AD curve shifts? The multiplier determines the answer. The larger the multiplier, the larger is the shift in the aggregate demand curve that results from a given change in autonomous expenditure. In this example, the multiplier is 2. A $1 trillion increase in investment produces a $2 trillion increase in the aggregate quantity of goods and services demanded at each price level. That is, a $1 trillion increase in autonomous expenditure shifts the aggregate demand curve rightward by $2 trillion.

A decrease in autonomous expenditure shifts the aggregate expenditure curve downward and shifts the aggregate demand curve leftward. You can see these effects by reversing the change that we've just described. If the economy is initially at point B on the aggregate expenditure curve AE_1 and on the aggregate demand curve AD_1, a decrease in autonomous expenditure shifts the aggregate expenditure curve downward to AE_0. The aggregate quantity of goods and services demanded decreases from $18 trillion to $16 trillion, and the aggregate demand curve shifts leftward to AD_0.

Let's summarize what we have just discovered:

> If some factor other than a change in the price level increases autonomous expenditure, then the AE curve shifts upward and the AD curve shifts rightward. The size of the AD curve shift equals the change in autonomous expenditure multiplied by the multiplier.

Equilibrium Real GDP and the Price Level

In Chapter 27, we learned that aggregate demand and short-run aggregate supply determine equilibrium real GDP and the price level. We've now put aggregate demand under a more powerful microscope and have discovered that a change in investment (or in any component of autonomous expenditure) changes aggregate demand and shifts the aggregate demand curve. The magnitude of the shift depends on the multiplier. But whether a change in autonomous expenditure results ultimately in a change in real GDP, a change in the price level, or a combination of the two depends on aggregate supply. There are two time frames to consider: the short run and the long run. First we'll see what happens in the short run.

An Increase in Aggregate Demand in the Short Run
Figure 28.10 describes the economy. Initially, in part (a), the aggregate expenditure curve is AE_0 and equilibrium expenditure is $16 trillion—point A. In part (b), aggregate demand is AD_0 and the short-run aggregate supply curve is SAS. (Chapter 27, pp. 651–653, explains the SAS curve.) Equilibrium is at point A in part (b), where the aggregate demand and short-run aggregate supply curves intersect. The price level is 110, and real GDP is $16 trillion.

Now suppose that investment increases by $1 trillion. With the price level fixed at 110, the aggregate expenditure curve shifts upward to AE_1. Equilibrium expenditure increases to $18 trillion—point B in part (a). In part (b), the aggregate demand curve shifts rightward by $2 trillion, from AD_0 to AD_1. How far the aggregate demand curve shifts is determined by the multiplier when the price level is fixed.

But with this new aggregate demand curve, the price level does *not* remain fixed. The price level rises, and as it does, the aggregate expenditure curve shifts downward. The short-run equilibrium occurs when the aggregate expenditure curve has shifted downward to AE_2 and the new aggregate demand curve, AD_1, intersects the short-run aggregate supply curve at point C in both part (a) and part (b). Real GDP is $17.3 trillion, and the price level is 123.

When price level effects are taken into account, the increase in investment still has a multiplier effect on real GDP, but the multiplier is smaller than it would be if the price level were fixed. The steeper the slope of the short-run aggregate supply curve, the larger is the increase in the price level and the smaller is the multiplier effect on real GDP.

An Increase in Aggregate Demand in the Long Run
Figure 28.11 illustrates the long-run effect of an increase in aggregate demand. In the long run, real GDP equals potential GDP and there is full employment. Potential GDP is $16 trillion, and the long-run aggregate supply curve is LAS. Initially, the economy is at point A in parts (a) and (b).

Investment increases by $1 trillion. In Fig. 28.11, the aggregate expenditure curve shifts to AE_1 and the aggregate demand curve shifts to AD_1. With no change in the price level, the economy would move to point B and real GDP would increase to $18 trillion. But in the short run, the price level rises to 123 and real GDP increases to only $17.3 trillion. With the higher price level, the AE curve shifts from AE_1 to

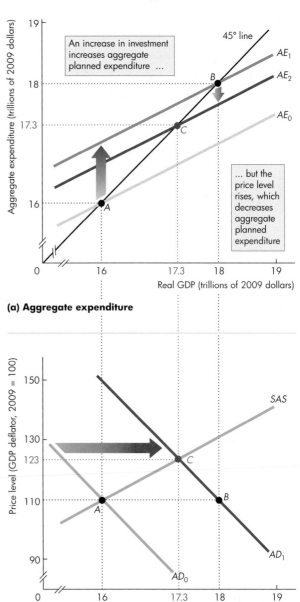

FIGURE 28.10   The Multiplier in the Short Run

An increase in investment increases aggregate planned expenditure ...

45° line

... but the price level rises, which decreases aggregate planned expenditure

(a) Aggregate expenditure

(b) Aggregate demand

An increase in investment shifts the AE curve from AE_0 to AE_1 and the AD curve from AD_0 to AD_1. The price level rises, and the higher price level shifts the AE curve downward from AE_1 to AE_2. The economy moves to point C in both parts. In the short run, when prices are flexible, the multiplier effect is smaller than when the price level is fixed.

MyEconLab Animation

FIGURE 28.11   The Multiplier in the Long Run

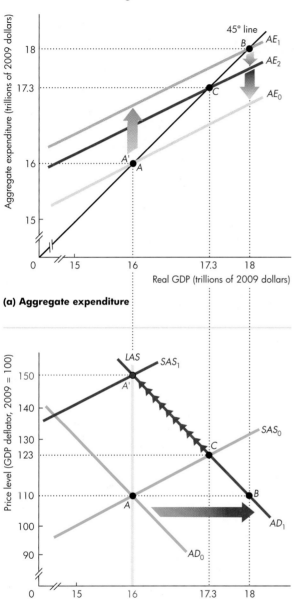

(a) Aggregate expenditure

(b) Aggregate demand

Starting from point A, an increase in investment shifts the AE curve to AE_1 and the AD curve to AD_1. In the short run at point C the economy is in an above full-employment equilibrium. In the long run, the money wage rate rises and the SAS curve shifts to SAS_1. As the price level rises, the AE curve shifts down to AE_0 and the economy moves to point A'. In the long run, the multiplier is zero.

— MyEconLab Animation —

AE_2. The economy is now in a short-run equilibrium at point C in both part (a) and part (b).

Real GDP now exceeds potential GDP. The labor force is more than fully employed, and in the long run, shortages of labor increase the money wage rate. The higher money wage rate increases firms' costs, which decreases short-run aggregate supply and shifts the SAS curve leftward to SAS_1. The price level rises above 123 and real GDP decreases. There is a movement along AD_1, and the AE curve shifts downward from AE_2 toward AE_0. When the money wage rate and the price level have increased by the same percentage, real GDP is again equal to potential GDP and the economy is at point A'. In the long run, the multiplier is zero.

◆ REVIEW QUIZ

1 How does a change in the price level influence the AE curve and the AD curve?

2 If autonomous expenditure increases with no change in the price level, what happens to the AE curve and the AD curve? Which curve shifts by an amount that is determined by the multiplier and why?

3 How does an increase in autonomous expenditure change real GDP in the short run? Does real GDP change by the same amount as the change in aggregate demand? Why or why not?

4 How does real GDP change in the long run when autonomous expenditure increases? Does real GDP change by the same amount as the change in aggregate demand? Why or why not?

Work these questions in Study Plan 28.4 and get instant feedback.   MyEconLab

◆ You are now ready to build on what you've learned about aggregate expenditure fluctuations. We'll study the business cycle and the roles of fiscal policy and monetary policy in smoothing the cycle while achieving price stability and sustained economic growth. In Chapter 29 we study the U.S. business cycle and inflation, and in Chapters 30 and 31 we study fiscal policy and monetary policy, respectively. But before you leave the current topic, look at *Economics in the News* on pp. 692–693 and see the aggregate expenditure model in action in the U.S. economy during 2014.

Expenditure Changes in the 2014 Expansion

Gross Domestic Product Up in 2014 Second Quarter

Bureau of Economic Analysis News Release
August 28, 2014

Real gross domestic product (GDP) increased at an annual rate of 4.2 percent in the second quarter of 2014, according to the "second" estimate released by the Bureau of Economic Analysis on August 28.

All the components of aggregate expenditure contributed to the increase in real GDP in the second quarter. Personal consumption expenditure, private inventory investment, exports, nonresidential fixed investment, state and local government spending, and residential fixed investment all increased. Imports, which is a subtraction from aggregate expenditure, also increased.

The detailed changes in the components of aggregate expenditure (all measured in 2009 chained dollars and percentages at annual rates) are

Personal consumption expenditure up 2.5 percent;

Nonresidential fixed investment up 8.4 percent;

Investment in nonresidential structures up 9.4 percent;

Investment in equipment up 10.7 percent;

Investment in intellectual property products up 4.4 percent;

Residential fixed investment up 7.2 percent;

Exports of goods and services up 10.1 percent;

Imports of goods and services up 11.0 percent; and

Private business inventories up $83.9 billion.

Real gross domestic income (GDI), which measures the output of the economy as the costs incurred and the incomes earned in the production of GDP, increased 4.7 percent. For a given quarter, the estimates of GDP and GDI may differ because they come from different and independent data sources, but over longer time spans the estimates of GDP and GDI tend to follow similar patterns of change.

Source of information: Bureau of Economic Analysis, 2014.

ESSENCE OF THE STORY

- U.S. real GDP grew at an annual rate of 4.2 percent during the second quarter of 2014.

- Exports and investment increased most.

- Business inventories increased.

- The expenditure and income estimates of real GDP were similar but estimated income grew a bit faster than estimated expenditure.

MyEconLab More Economics in the News

ECONOMIC ANALYSIS

- The BEA news release reports that real GDP increased in the second quarter of 2014 and identifies exports and investment as two sources of expansion. Business inventories also inreased.

- Table 1 shows the real GDP and aggregate expenditure numbers for the first two quarters of 2014 along with the change in the second quarter.

- Figure 1 shows the changes in inventories and real GDP. The two variables fluctuate together but real GDP has larger swings than inventories.

- Figure 2 interprets the data for 2014 using the Keynesian model of equilibrium expenditure.

- In 2014 Q1, the AE curve was AE_0 and real GDP was $15.83 trillion, which we assume to be an expenditure equilibrium.

- The slope of the AE curve is 0.5 (an assumption).

- In Fig. 2(a), an increase in autonomous expenditure shifted the AE curve upward to AE_1 and aggregate planned expenditure temporarily exceeded real GDP.

- In Fig. 2(b), an unplanned decrease in inventories occurred as real GDP increased toward its second quarter equilibrium.

- When real GDP reached its second quarter equilibrium, unplanned inventory changes had returned to zero.

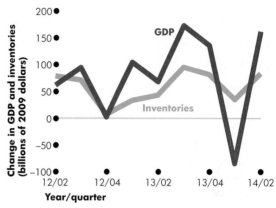

Figure 1 Inventories and the Change in Real GDP

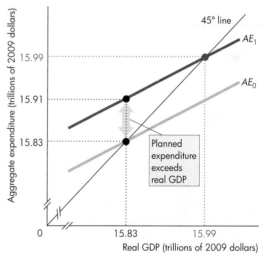

(a) Convergence to equilibrium expenditure in 2014

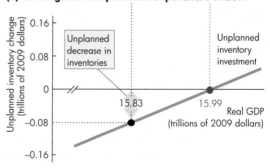

(b) Unplanned inventory change in 2014

Figure 2 Equilibrium Expenditure in 2014

Table 1   The Components of Aggregate Expenditure

Item	2014 Q1	2014 Q2	Change
	(billions of 2009 dollars)		
Consumption expenditure	10,844	10,910	66
Investment	2,588	2,695	107
Government expenditure	2,869	2,879	10
Exports	2,027	2,076	49
Imports	2,474	2,540	66
Real GDP*	**15,832**	**15,994**	**163**
Change in inventories	35	84	49

*Chained-dollar real variables are calculated for each expenditure component independently of chained-dollar real GDP and the components don't exactly sum to real GDP.

MATHEMATICAL NOTE

The Algebra of the Keynesian Model

This mathematical note derives formulas for equilibrium expenditure and the multipliers when the price level is fixed. The variables are

- Aggregate planned expenditure, AE
- Real GDP, Y
- Consumption expenditure, C
- Disposable income, YD
- Investment, I
- Government expenditure, G
- Exports, X
- Imports, M
- Net taxes, T
- Autonomous consumption expenditure, a
- Autonomous taxes, T_a
- Marginal propensity to consume, b
- Marginal propensity to import, m
- Marginal tax rate, t
- Autonomous expenditure, A

Aggregate Expenditure

Aggregate planned expenditure (AE) is the sum of the planned amounts of consumption expenditure (C), investment (I), government expenditure (G), and exports (X) minus the planned amount of imports (M).

$$AE = C + I + G + X - M.$$

Consumption Function Consumption expenditure (C) depends on disposable income (YD), and we write the consumption function as

$$C = a + bYD.$$

Disposable income (YD) equals real GDP minus net taxes ($Y - T$). So if we replace YD with ($Y - T$), the consumption function becomes

$$C = a + b(Y - T).$$

Net taxes, T, equal autonomous taxes (that are independent of income), T_a, plus induced taxes (that vary with income), tY.

So we can write net taxes as

$$T = T_a + tY.$$

Use this last equation to replace T in the consumption function. The consumption function becomes

$$C = a - bT_a + b(1 - t)Y.$$

This equation describes consumption expenditure as a function of real GDP.

Import Function Imports depend on real GDP, and the import function is

$$M = mY.$$

Aggregate Expenditure Curve Use the consumption function and the import function to replace C and M in the AE equation. That is,

$$AE = a - bT_a + b(1 - t)Y + I + G + X - mY.$$

Collect the terms that involve Y on the right side of the equation to obtain

$$AE = (a - bT_a + I + G + X) + [b(1 - t) - m]Y.$$

Autonomous expenditure (A) is $(a - bT_a + I + G + X)$, and the slope of the AE curve is $[b(1 - t) - m]$. So the equation for the AE curve, which is shown in Fig. 1, is

$$AE = A + [b(1 - t) - m]Y.$$

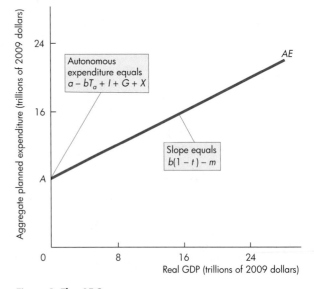

Figure 1 The AE Curve

Equilibrium Expenditure

Equilibrium expenditure occurs when aggregate planned expenditure (AE) equals real GDP (Y). That is,

$$AE = Y.$$

In Fig. 2, the scales of the x-axis (real GDP) and the y-axis (aggregate planned expenditure) are identical, so the 45° line shows the points at which aggregate planned expenditure equals real GDP.

Figure 2 shows the point of equilibrium expenditure at the intersection of the AE curve and the 45° line.

To calculate equilibrium expenditure, solve the equations for the AE curve and the 45° line for the two unknown quantities AE and Y. So starting with

$$AE = A + [b(1 - t) - m]Y$$

$$AE = Y,$$

replace AE with Y in the AE equation to obtain

$$Y = A + [b(1 - t) - m]Y.$$

The solution for Y is

$$Y = \frac{1}{1 - [b(1 - t) - m]} A.$$

The Multiplier

The *multiplier* equals the change in equilibrium expenditure and real GDP (Y) that results from a change in autonomous expenditure (A) divided by the change in autonomous expenditure.

A change in autonomous expenditure (ΔA) changes equilibrium expenditure and real GDP by

$$\Delta Y = \frac{1}{1 - [b(1 - t) - m]} \Delta A.$$

$$\text{Multiplier} = \frac{1}{1 - [b(1 - t) - m]}.$$

The size of the multiplier depends on the slope of the AE curve, $b(1 - t) - m$. The larger the slope, the larger is the multiplier. So the multiplier is larger,

- The greater the marginal propensity to consume (b)
- The smaller the marginal tax rate (t)
- The smaller the marginal propensity to import (m)

An economy with no imports and no income taxes has $m = 0$ and $t = 0$. In this special case, the multiplier equals $1/(1 - b)$. If b is 0.75, then the multiplier is 4, as shown in Fig. 3.

In an economy with imports and income taxes, if $b = 0.75$, $t = 0.2$, and $m = 0.1$, the multiplier equals 1 divided by $[1 - 0.75(1 - 0.2) - 0.1]$, which equals 2. Make up some more examples to show the effects of b, t, and m on the multiplier.

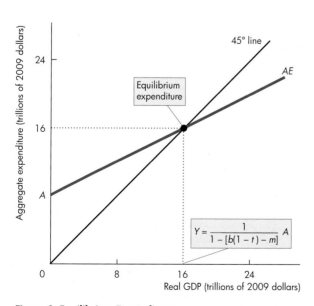

Figure 2 Equilibrium Expenditure

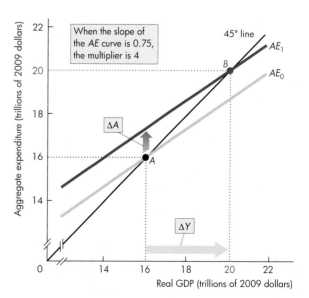

Figure 3 The Multiplier

Government Expenditure Multiplier

The **government expenditure multiplier** equals the change in equilibrium expenditure and real GDP (Y) that results from a change in government expenditure (G) divided by the change in government expenditure. Because autonomous expenditure is equal to

$$A = a - bT_a + I + G + X,$$

the change in autonomous expenditure equals the change in government expenditure. That is,

$$\Delta A = \Delta G.$$

You can see from the solution for equilibrium expenditure Y that

$$\Delta Y = \frac{1}{1 - [b(1 - t) - m]} \Delta G.$$

The government expenditure multiplier equals

$$\frac{1}{1 - [b(1 - t) - m]}.$$

In an economy in which $t = 0$ and $m = 0$, the government expenditure multiplier is $1/(1 - b)$. With $b = 0.75$, the government expenditure multiplier is 4, as Fig. 4 shows. Make up some examples and use the above formula to show how b, m, and t influence the government expenditure multiplier.

Autonomous Tax Multiplier

The **autonomous tax multiplier** equals the change in equilibrium expenditure and real GDP (Y) that results from a change in autonomous taxes (T_a) divided by the change in autonomous taxes. Because autonomous expenditure is equal to

$$A = a - bT_a + I + G + X,$$

the change in autonomous expenditure equals *minus* b multiplied by the change in autonomous taxes. That is,

$$\Delta A = - b\Delta T_a.$$

You can see from the solution for equilibrium expenditure Y that

$$\Delta Y = \frac{-b}{1 - [b(1 - t) - m]} \Delta T_a.$$

The autonomous tax multiplier equals

$$\frac{-b}{1 - [b(1 - t) - m]}.$$

In an economy in which $t = 0$ and $m = 0$, the autonomous tax multiplier is $-b/(1 - b)$. In this special case, with $b = 0.75$, the autonomous tax multiplier equals -3, as Fig. 5 shows. Make up some examples and use the above formula to show how b, m, and t influence the autonomous tax multiplier.

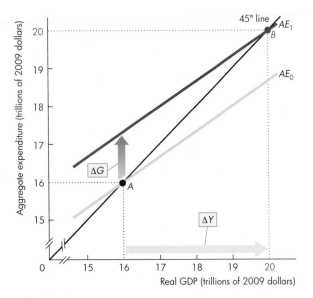

Figure 4 Government Expenditure Multiplier

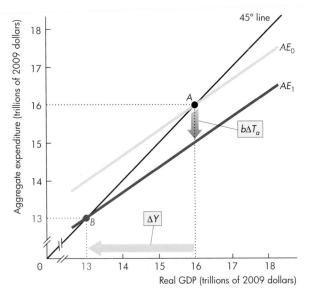

Figure 5 Autonomous Tax Multiplier

Balanced Budget Multiplier

The **balanced budget multiplier** equals the change in equilibrium expenditure and real GDP (Y) that results from equal changes in government expenditure and lump-sum taxes divided by the change in government expenditure. Because government expenditure and autonomous taxes change by the same amount, the budget balance does not change.

The change in equilibrium expenditure that results from the change in government expenditure is

$$\Delta Y = \frac{1}{1 - [b(1 - t) - m]} \Delta G.$$

And the change in equilibrium expenditure that results from the change in autonomous taxes is

$$\Delta Y = \frac{-b}{1 - [b(1 - t) - m]} \Delta T_a.$$

So the change in equilibrium expenditure resulting from the changes in government expenditure and autonomous taxes is

$$\Delta Y = \frac{1}{1 - [b(1 - t) - m]} \Delta G +$$

$$\frac{-b}{1 - [b(1 - t) - m]} \Delta T_a.$$

Notice that

$$\frac{1}{1 - [b(1 - t) - m]}$$

is common to both terms on the right side. So we can rewrite the equation as

$$\Delta Y = \frac{1}{1 - [b(1 - t) - m]} (\Delta G - b\Delta T_a).$$

The AE curve shifts upward by $\Delta G - b\Delta T_a$ as shown in Fig. 6.

But the change in government expenditure equals the change in autonomous taxes. That is,

$$\Delta G = \Delta T_a.$$

So we can write the equation as

$$\Delta Y = \frac{1 - b}{1 - [b(1 - t) - m]} \Delta G.$$

The balanced budget multiplier equals

$$\frac{1 - b}{1 - [b(1 - t) - m]}.$$

In an economy in which $t = 0$ and $m = 0$, the balanced budget multiplier is $(1 - b)/(1 - b)$, which equals 1, as Fig. 6 shows. Make up some examples and use the above formula to show how b, m, and t influence the balanced budget multiplier.

Exercise

In an economy, autonomous consumption expenditure is $50 billion, investment is $200 billion, and government expenditure is $250 billion. The marginal propensity to consume is 0.7 and net taxes are $250 billion. Exports are $500 billion and imports are $450 billion. Assume that net taxes and imports are autonomous and the price level is fixed.

a. What is the consumption function?
b. What is the equation of the AE curve?
c. Calculate equilibrium expenditure.
d. Calculate the multiplier.
e. If investment decreases to $150 billion, what is the change in equilibrium expenditure?
f. Describe the process in part (e) that moves the economy to its new equilibrium expenditure.

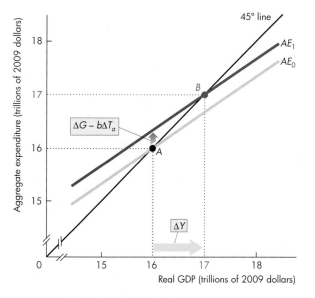

Figure 6 Balanced Budget Multiplier

SUMMARY

Key Points

Fixed Prices and Expenditure Plans (pp. 674–677)

- When the price level is fixed, expenditure plans determine real GDP.
- Consumption expenditure is determined by disposable income, and the marginal propensity to consume (*MPC*) determines the change in consumption expenditure brought about by a change in disposable income. Real GDP determines disposable income.
- Imports are determined by real GDP, and the marginal propensity to import determines the change in imports brought about by a change in real GDP.

Working Problem 1 will give you a better understanding of fixed prices and expenditure plans.

Real GDP with a Fixed Price Level (pp. 678–681)

- Aggregate *planned* expenditure depends on real GDP.
- Equilibrium expenditure occurs when aggregate planned expenditure equals actual expenditure and real GDP.

Working Problems 2 to 5 will give you a better understanding of real GDP with a fixed price level.

The Multiplier (pp. 682–686)

- The multiplier is the magnified effect of a change in autonomous expenditure on equilibrium expenditure and real GDP.

- The multiplier is determined by the slope of the *AE* curve.
- The slope of the *AE* curve is influenced by the marginal propensity to consume, the marginal propensity to import, and the income tax rate.

Working Problems 6 to 8 will give you a better understanding of the multiplier.

The Multiplier and the Price Level (pp. 687–691)

- The *AD* curve is the relationship between the quantity of real GDP demanded and the price level, other things remaining the same.
- The *AE* curve is the relationship between aggregate planned expenditure and real GDP, other things remaining the same.
- At a given price level, there is a given *AE* curve. A change in the price level changes aggregate planned expenditure and shifts the *AE* curve. A change in the price level also creates a movement along the *AD* curve.
- A change in autonomous expenditure that is not caused by a change in the price level shifts the *AE* curve and shifts the *AD* curve. The magnitude of the shift of the *AD* curve depends on the multiplier and on the change in autonomous expenditure.
- The multiplier decreases as the price level changes, and the long-run multiplier is zero.

Working Problems 9 to 13 will give you a better understanding of the multiplier and the price level.

Key Terms

MyEconLab Key Terms Quiz

Aggregate planned expenditure, 674
Autonomous expenditure, 678
Autonomous tax multiplier, 696
Balanced budget multiplier, 697

Consumption function, 674
Disposable income, 674
Equilibrium expenditure, 680
Government expenditure multiplier, 696
Induced expenditure, 678

Marginal propensity to consume, 676
Marginal propensity to import, 677
Marginal propensity to save, 676
Multiplier, 682
Saving function, 674

WORKED PROBLEM

MyEconLab   You can work this problem in Chapter 28 Study Plan.

You are given the following data about an economy that has a fixed price level, no imports, and no taxes.

Disposable income	Consumption expenditure
(billions of dollars per year)	
0	5
100	80
200	155
300	230
400	305

Questions

1. Calculate the marginal propensity to consume.
2. Calculate autonomous consumption expenditure.
3. Calculate saving at each level of disposable income and the marginal propensity to save.
4. Calculate the multiplier.
5. Calculate the increase in real GDP when autonomous spending increases by $5 billion. Why does real GDP increase by more than $5 billion?

Solutions

1. The marginal propensity to consume equals the fraction of an increase in disposable income that is spent on consumption.

   When disposable income increases from $100 billion to $200 billion, consumption expenditure increases from $80 billion to $155 billion. The increase in disposable income of $100 billion increases consumption expenditure by $75 billion. The marginal propensity to consume equals $75 billion ÷ $100 billion, which equals 0.75.

   Key Point: The marginal propensity to consume is the fraction of an increase in disposable income that is spent on consumption.

2. Autonomous consumption expenditure is the amount of consumption expenditure when disposabale income is zero. From the table, autonomous consumption expenditure is $5 billion.

   Key Point: Autonomous consumption expenditure is the amount of consumption expenditure that depends on things other than disposable income.

3. Disposable income is spent on consumption or saved.

   Saving = Disposable income − Consumption expenditure.

For example, when disposable income is $100 billion, consumption expenditure is $80 billion, so saving is $20 billion.

The table below sets out saving at each level of disposable income.

Disposable income	Saving
(billions of dollars per year)	
0	−5
100	20
200	45
300	70
400	95

The marginal propensity to save equals the fraction of an increase in disposable income that is saved. When disposable income increases by $100 billion, saving increases by $25 billion, so the marginal propensity to save equals 0.25.

Key Point: The marginal propensity to consume plus the marginal propensity to save equals 1.

4. When the price level is fixed, the multiplier equals 1/(1 − Slope of the *AE* curve). With no income taxes, the slope of the *AE* curve equals the marginal propensity to consume (*MPC*), which is 0.75.

   The multiplier = 1/(1 − 0.75) = 1/0.25 = 4.

   Because (1 − *MPC*) = *MPS*, the multiplier also equals 1/*MPS*.

Key Point: With a fixed price level, the multiplier equals 1/(1 − *MPC*) or 1/*MPS*.

5. The increase in real GDP when the price level is fixed equals the change in autonomous spending multiplied by the multiplier. That is,

   Change in real GDP = Change in autonomous spending × Multiplier

   Change in real GDP = $5 billion × 4

                      = $20 billion.

   An increase in autonomous spending increases income, which increases induced consumption, which in turn increases income. The quantity of real GDP demanded increases.

Key Point: With a fixed price level, real GDP increases by more than the increase in autonomous spending because induced consumption expenditure increases.

STUDY PLAN PROBLEMS AND APPLICATIONS

MyEconLab   You can work Problems 1 to 14 in Chapter 28 Study Plan and get instant feedback.

Fixed Prices and Expenditure Plans (Study Plan 28.1)

1. In an economy, when income increases from $400 billion to $500 billion, consumption expenditure changes from $420 billion to $500 billion. Calculate the marginal propensity to consume, the change in saving, and the marginal propensity to save.

Real GDP with a Fixed Price Level (Study Plan 28.2)

Use the following figure to work Problems 2 and 3.
The figure illustrates the components of aggregate planned expenditure on Turtle Island. Turtle Island has no imports or exports, no incomes taxes, and the price level is fixed.

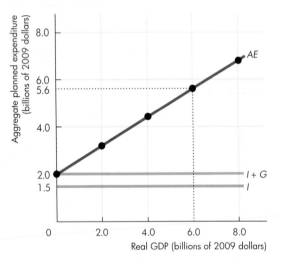

2. Calculate autonomous expenditure and the marginal propensity to consume.
3. a. What is aggregate planned expenditure when real GDP is $6 billion?
    b. If real GDP is $4 billion, what is happening to inventories?
    c. If real GDP is $6 billion, what is happening to inventories?
4. Explain the difference between induced consumption expenditure and autonomous consumption expenditure. Why isn't all consumption expenditure induced expenditure?
5. Explain how an increase in business investment at a constant price level changes equilibrium expenditure.

The Multiplier (Study Plan 28.3)

Use the following data to work Problems 6 and 7.
An economy has a fixed price level, no imports, and no income taxes. *MPC* is 0.80, and real GDP is $150 billion. Businesses increase investment by $5 billion.

6. Calculate the multiplier and the change in real GDP.
7. Calculate the new real GDP and explain why real GDP increases by more than $5 billion.
8. An economy has a fixed price level, no imports, and no income taxes. An increase in autonomous expenditure of $2 trillion increases equilibrium expenditure by $8 trillion. Calculate the multiplier and explain what happens to the multiplier if an income tax is introduced.

The Multiplier and the Price Level (Study Plan 28.4)

Use the following data to work Problems 9 to 13.
Suppose that the economy is at full employment, the price level is 100, and the multiplier is 2. Investment increases by $100 billion.

9. What is the change in equilibrium expenditure if the price level remains at 100?
10. a. What is the immediate change in the quantity of real GDP demanded?
    b. In the short run, does real GDP increase by more than, less than, or the same amount as the immediate change in the quantity of real GDP demanded?
11. In the short run, does the price level remain at 100? Explain why or why not.
12. a. In the long run, does real GDP increase by more than, less than, or the same amount as the immediate increase in the quantity of real GDP demanded?
    b. Explain how the price level changes in the long run.
13. Are the values of the multipliers in the short run and the long run larger or smaller than 2?

Mathematical Note (Study Plan 28.MN)

14. Use the data in the Worked Problem on p. 699. Calculate the change in equilibrium expenditure when investment decreases by $150 billion.

ADDITIONAL PROBLEMS AND APPLICATIONS

MyEconLab   You can work these problems in MyEconLab if assigned by your instructor.

Fixed Prices and Expenditure Plans

Use the following data to work Problems 15 and 16. You are given the following information about the economy of Australia.

Disposable income	Saving
(billions of dollars per year)	
0	0
100	25
200	50
300	75
400	100

15. Calculate the marginal propensity to save.
16. Calculate consumption at each level of disposable income. Calculate the marginal propensity to consume.

Use the following news clip to work Problems 17 to 19.

Americans $2.4 Trillion Poorer

The Federal Reserve reported that household wealth decreased by $2.4 trillion or $21,000 per household in the third quarter of 2011. This drop is the steepest since 2008 and the second consecutive quarterly drop. Foreclosures lowered household debt slightly but credit card debt increased. Many households are struggling to buy the essentials and spending on food has decreased. Separately, the Bureau of Economic Analysis reported that consumption expenditure increased by $39 billion in the third quarter of 2011.

Sources: *The New American*, December 11, 2011, and the Bureau of Economic Analysis

17. Explain and draw a graph to illustrate how a fall in household wealth would be expected to influence the consumption function and saving function.
18. What factors might explain the actual changes in consumption expenditure and wealth that occured in the third quarter of 2011?
19. Draw a graph of a consumption function. Mark the actual points at which consumers were in the second and third quarters. Make any necessary assumptions and explain your answer.

Real GDP with a Fixed Price Level

Use the spreadsheet in the next column to work Problems 20 and 21. The spreadsheet lists real GDP (Y) and the components of aggregate planned expenditure in billions of dollars.

	A	B	C	D	E	F	G
1		Y	C	I	G	X	M
2	A	100	110	50	60	60	15
3	B	200	170	50	60	60	30
4	C	300	230	50	60	60	45
5	D	400	290	50	60	60	60
6	E	500	350	50	60	60	75
7	F	600	410	50	60	60	90

20. Calculate autonomous expenditure. Calculate the marginal propensity to consume.
21. a. What is aggregate planned expenditure when real GDP is $200 billion?
    b. If real GDP is $200 billion, explain the process that moves the economy toward equilibrium expenditure.
    c. If real GDP is $500 billion, explain the process that moves the economy toward equilibrium expenditure.

22. **Wholesale Inventories Decline, Sales Rise**

    The Commerce Department reported that wholesale inventories fell 1.3 percent in August for a record 12th consecutive month, evidence that companies are trimming orders to factories, which helped depress economic output during the recession. Economists hope that the rising sales will encourage businesses to begin restocking their inventories, which would boost factory production and help bolster broad economic growth in coming months.

    Source: *The New York Times*, October 8, 2009

    Explain why a fall in inventories is associated with recession and a restocking of inventories might bolster economic growth.

The Multiplier

23. **Obama's New Stimulus**

    The Obama recovery plan announced on Monday includes proposed spending of $50 billion to rebuild 150,000 miles of roads, construct and maintain 4,000 miles of rail, and fix or rebuild 150 miles of runways.

    Source: *USA Today*, September 10, 2010

    If the slope of the *AE* curve is 0.7, calculate the immediate change in aggregate planned expenditure and the change in real GDP in the short run if the price level remains unchanged.

24. **Obama's Economic Recovery Plan**

President Obama's proposal to jolt a listless recovery with $180 billion worth of tax breaks and transportation projects left economists largely unimpressed Tuesday.

Source: *USA Today*, September 10, 2010

If taxes fall by $90 billion and the spending on transport projects increases by $90 billion, which component of Obama's recovery plan would have the larger effect on equilibrium expenditure, other things remaining the same?

The Multiplier and the Price Level

Use the following news item to work Problems 25 to 27.

The BEA reported that in the third quarter of 2014 U.S. exports increased by $40 billion.

25. Explain and draw a graph to illustrate the effect of an increase in exports on equilibrium expenditure in the short run.

26. Explain and draw a graph to illustrate the effect of an increase in exports on equilibrium real GDP in the short run.

27. Explain and draw a graph to illustrate the effect of an increase in exports on equilibrium real GDP in the long run.

28. Compare the multiplier in the short run and the long run and explain why they are not identical.

Use the following news clip to work Problems 29 to 31.

Consumer Sentiment in U.S. Rose to Three-Month High

Consumer sentiment was up in August helped by merchant discounts, especially from auto dealerships who received incentives from automakers Honda, General Motors, and Toyota to lower prices.

But consumers are worried about the future. They are worried about tax changes and government budget cuts that are on the horizon. Capital spending fell somewhat.

Source: Bloomberg, September 1, 2012

29. For each of the expenditures listed in the news clip say which is part of induced expenditure and which is part of autonomous expenditure?

30. Which of the events reported in the news clip would change aggregate demand and which would change the quantity of real GDP demanded? Provide a graphical illustration of the distinction.

31. Explain and draw a graph to illustrate how increasing consumer confidence influences aggregate expenditure and aggregate demand.

32. **Japan Slides Into Recession**

In Japan, consumer prices slid at a faster pace in July and industrial production unexpectedly slumped.

Source: Bloomberg, September 1, 2012

Contrast what the news clip says is happening in Japan with what is happening in the United States in Problem 29 and provide a graphical analysis of the differences.

Economics in the News

33. After you have studied *Economics in the News* on pp. 692–693, answer the following questions.

   a. If the 2014 changes in inventories were mainly *planned* changes, what role did they play in shifting the *AE* curve and changing equilibrium expenditure? Use a two-part figure (similar to that on p. 680) to answer this question.

   b. The BEA news release reports that exports of goods and services were up 10.1 percent and imports of goods and services were up 11.0 percent. Were these increases in expenditure increases in autonomous expenditure or increases in induced expenditure, and how do they influence the magnitude of the multiplier?

   c. Using the assumptions made in Fig. 2 on p. 693, what is the value of the autonomous expenditure multiplier?

Mathematical Note

34. In an economy with a fixed price level, autonomous spending is $20 trillion and the slope of the *AE* curve is 0.6.

   a. What is the equation of the *AE* curve?

   b. Calculate equilibrium expenditure.

   c. Calculate the multiplier.

   d. Calculate the shift of the aggregate demand curve if investment increases by $1 billion.

29 THE BUSINESS CYCLE, INFLATION, AND DEFLATION

After studying this chapter, you will be able to:

◆ Explain how aggregate demand shocks and aggregate supply shocks create the business cycle

◆ Explain how demand-pull and cost-push forces bring cycles in inflation and output

◆ Explain the causes and consequences of deflation

◆ Explain the short-run and long-run tradeoff between inflation and unemployment

We fear deflation because it brings stagnant incomes and high unemployment. And we worry about inflation because it raises our cost of living. We want low inflation, low unemployment, and rapid income growth. But can we have all these things at the same time? Or do we face a tradeoff among them? As this chapter explains, we face a tradeoff in the short run but not in the long run.

At the end of the chapter, in *Economics in the News*, we examine a stagnating European economy and the lessons it holds for the United States and other countries.

◆ The Business Cycle

The business cycle is easy to describe but hard to explain and the next peak or trough is impossible to predict. We'll look at two approaches to understanding the business cycle:

- Mainstream business cycle theory
- Real business cycle theory

Mainstream Business Cycle Theory

The mainstream business cycle theory is that potential GDP grows at a steady rate while aggregate demand grows at a fluctuating rate. Because the money wage rate is sticky, if aggregate demand grows faster than potential GDP, real GDP moves above potential GDP and an inflationary gap emerges. And if aggregate demand grows slower than potential GDP, real GDP moves below potential GDP and a recessionary gap emerges. If aggregate demand decreases, real GDP also decreases in a recession.

Figure 29.1 illustrates this business cycle theory. Initially, potential GDP is $13 trillion. The long-run aggregate supply curve is LAS_0, the aggregate demand curve is AD_0, and the price level is 100. The economy is at full employment at point A.

An expansion occurs when potential GDP increases and the LAS curve shifts rightward to LAS_1. During an expansion, aggregate demand also increases, and usually by more than potential GDP, so the price level rises. Assume that in the current expansion, the price level is expected to rise to 110 and the money wage rate has been set based on that expectation. The short-run aggregate supply curve is SAS_1.

If aggregate demand increases to AD_1, real GDP increases from $13 trillion to $16 trillion, the new level of potential GDP, and the price level rises, as expected, to 110. The economy remains at full employment but now at point B.

If aggregate demand increases more slowly to AD_2, real GDP grows by less than potential GDP and the economy moves to point C, with real GDP at $15.5 trillion and the price level at 107. Real GDP growth is slower and inflation is lower than expected.

If aggregate demand increases more quickly to AD_3, real GDP grows by more than potential GDP and the economy moves to point D, with real GDP at $16.5 trillion and the price level at 113. Real GDP growth is faster and inflation is higher than expected.

Growth, inflation, and the business cycle arise from the relentless increases in potential GDP, faster (on average) increases in aggregate demand, and fluctuations in the pace of aggregate demand growth.

FIGURE 29.1   The Mainstream Business Cycle Theory

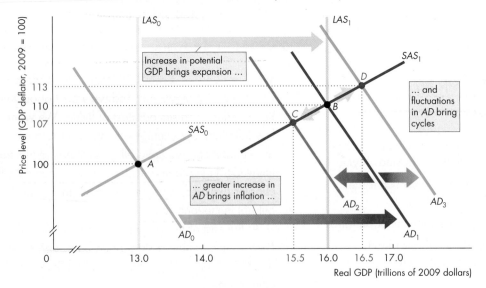

In a business cycle expansion, potential GDP increases and the LAS curve shifts rightward from LAS_0 to LAS_1. A greater than expected increase in aggregate demand brings inflation.

If the aggregate demand curve shifts to AD_1, the economy remains at full employment. If the aggregate demand curve shifts to AD_2, a recessionary gap arises. If the aggregate demand curve shifts to AD_3, an inflationary gap arises.

This mainstream theory comes in a number of special forms that differ regarding the source of fluctuations in aggregate demand growth and the source of money wage stickiness.

Keynesian Cycle Theory In **Keynesian cycle theory**, fluctuations in investment driven by fluctuations in business confidence—summarized by the phrase "animal spirits"—are the main source of fluctuations in aggregate demand.

Monetarist Cycle Theory In **monetarist cycle theory**, fluctuations in both investment and consumption expenditure, driven by fluctuations in the growth rate of the quantity of money, are the main source of fluctuations in aggregate demand.

Both the Keynesian and monetarist cycle theories simply assume that the money wage rate is rigid and don't explain that rigidity.

Two newer theories seek to explain money wage rate rigidity and to be more careful about working out its consequences.

New Classical Cycle Theory In **new classical cycle theory**, the rational expectation of the price level, which is determined by potential GDP and *expected* aggregate demand, determines the money wage rate and the position of the *SAS* curve. In this theory, only *unexpected* fluctuations in aggregate demand bring fluctuations in real GDP around potential GDP.

New Keynesian Cycle Theory The **new Keynesian cycle theory** emphasizes the fact that today's money wage rates were negotiated at many past dates, which means that *past* rational expectations of the current price level influence the money wage rate and the position of the *SAS* curve. In this theory, both unexpected and currently expected fluctuations in aggregate demand bring fluctuations in real GDP around potential GDP.

The mainstream cycle theories don't rule out the possibility that aggregate supply shocks might occur. An oil price rise, a widespread drought, a major hurricane, or another natural disaster, could, for example, bring a recession. But supply shocks are not the normal source of fluctuations in the mainstream theories. In contrast, real business cycle theory puts supply shocks at center stage.

Real Business Cycle Theory

The newest theory of the business cycle, known as **real business cycle theory** (or RBC theory), regards random fluctuations in productivity as the main source of economic fluctuations. These productivity fluctuations are assumed to result mainly from fluctuations in the pace of technological change, but they might also have other sources, such as international disturbances, climate fluctuations, or natural disasters. The origins of RBC theory can be traced to the rational expectations revolution set off by Robert E. Lucas, Jr., but the first demonstrations of the power of this theory were given by Edward Prescott and Finn Kydland and by John Long and Charles Plosser. Today, RBC theory is part of a broad research agenda called dynamic general equilibrium analysis, and hundreds of young macroeconomists do research on this topic.

We'll explore RBC theory by looking first at its impulse and then at the mechanism that converts that impulse into a cycle in real GDP.

The RBC Impulse The impulse in RBC theory is the growth rate of productivity that results from technological change. RBC theorists believe this impulse to be generated mainly by the process of research and development that leads to the creation and use of new technologies (see *Economics in Action*).

The pace of technological change and productivity growth is not constant. Sometimes productivity growth speeds up, sometimes it slows, and occasionally it even *falls*—labor and capital become less productive, on average. A period of rapid productivity growth brings a business cycle expansion, and a slowdown or fall in productivity triggers a recession.

It is easy to understand why technological change brings productivity growth. But how does it *decrease* productivity? All technological change eventually increases productivity. But if initially, technological change makes a sufficient amount of existing capital—especially human capital—obsolete, productivity can temporarily fall. At such a time, more jobs are destroyed than created and more businesses fail than start up.

The RBC Mechanism Two effects follow from a change in productivity that sparks an expansion or a contraction: Investment demand changes and the demand for labor changes. We'll study these effects and their consequences during a recession. In an

ECONOMICS IN ACTION
The Real Business Cycle Impulse

To isolate the RBC impulse, economists measure the change in the combined productivity of capital and labor—called *total factor productivity*. The figure shows the RBC impulse for the United States from 1963 through 2013.

You can see that the productivity growth rate fluctuations are not directly correlated with real GDP fluctuations. Their influence on real GDP growth is spread out over time.

You can also see that the fluctuations in real GDP growth have wider swings than those of productivity growth.

Real business cycle theory explains these facts.

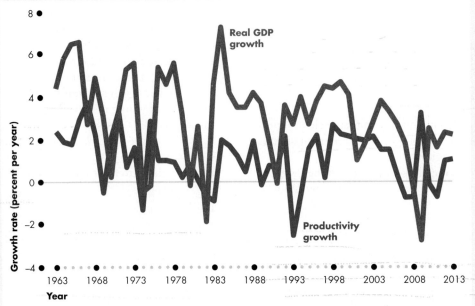

Sources of data: Real GDP, Bureau of Economic Analysis; Productivity growth, Federal Reserve Bank of San Francisco.

expansion, they work in the direction opposite to what is described here.

Technological change makes some existing capital obsolete and temporarily decreases productivity. Firms expect the future profits to fall and see their labor productivity falling. With lower profit expectations, they cut back their purchases of new capital, and with lower labor productivity, they plan to lay off some workers. So the initial effect of a temporary fall in productivity is a decrease in investment demand and a decrease in the demand for labor.

Figure 29.2 illustrates these two initial effects of a decrease in productivity. Part (a) shows the effects of a decrease in investment demand in the loanable funds market. The demand for loanable funds curve is *DLF* and the supply of loanable funds curve is *SLF* (both of which are explained in Chapter 24, pp. 575–577). Initially, the demand for loanable funds curve is DLF_0 and the equilibrium quantity of funds is $2 trillion at a real interest rate of 6 percent a year.

A decrease in productivity decreases investment demand, and the demand for loanable funds curve shifts leftward from DLF_0 to DLF_1. The real interest rate falls to 4 percent a year, and the equilibrium quantity of loanable funds decreases to $1.7 trillion.

Figure 29.2(b) shows the demand for labor and supply of labor (which are explained in Chapter 23, pp. 546–547). Initially, the demand for labor curve is LD_0, the supply of labor curve is LS_0, and equilibrium employment is 200 billion hours a year at a real wage rate of $35 an hour. The decrease in productivity decreases the demand for labor, and the demand for labor curve shifts leftward from LD_0 to LD_1.

Before we can determine the new level of employment and real wage rate, we need to look at a ripple effect—the key effect in RBC theory.

The Key Decision: When to Work? According to RBC theory, people decide *when* to work by doing a cost-benefit calculation. They compare the return

FIGURE 29.2   Loanable Funds and Labor Markets in a Real Business Cycle

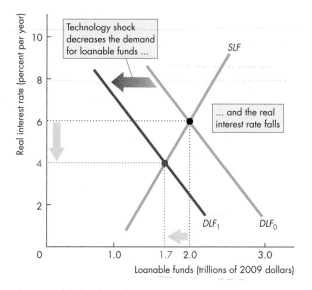

(a) Loanable funds and interest rate

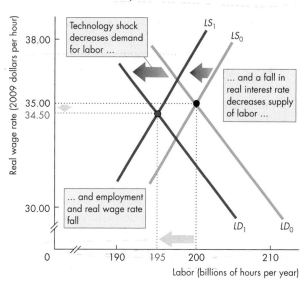

(b) Labor and wage rate

In part (a), the supply of loanable funds *SLF* and the initial demand for loanable funds DLF_0 determine the real interest rate at 6 percent a year. In part (b), the initial demand for labor LD_0 and the supply of labor LS_0 determine the real wage rate at $35 an hour and employment at 200 billion hours. A technological change temporarily decreases productivity, and both the demand for loanable funds and the

demand for labor decrease. The two demand curves shift leftward to DLF_1 and LD_1. In part (a), the real interest rate falls to 4 percent a year. In part (b), the fall in the real interest rate decreases the supply of labor (the when-to-work decision) and the supply of labor curve shifts leftward to LS_1. Employment decreases to 195 billion hours, and the real wage rate falls to $34.50 an hour. A recession is under way.

from working in the current period with the *expected* return from working in a later period. You make such a comparison every day in school. Suppose your goal in this course is to get an A. To achieve this goal, you work hard most of the time. But during the few days before the midterm and final exams, you work especially hard. Why? Because you believe that the return from studying close to the exam is greater than the return from studying when the exam is a long time away. So during the term, you take time off for the movies and other leisure pursuits, but at exam time, you study every evening and weekend.

RBC theory says that workers behave like you. They work fewer hours, sometimes zero hours, when the real wage rate is temporarily low, and they work more hours when the real wage rate is temporarily high. But to properly compare the current wage rate with the expected future wage rate, workers must use

the real interest rate. If the real interest rate is 6 percent a year, a real wage of $1 an hour earned this week will become $1.06 a year from now. If the real wage rate is expected to be $1.05 an hour next year, today's real wage of $1 looks good. By working longer hours now and shorter hours a year from now, a person can get a 1 percent higher real wage. But suppose the real interest rate is 4 percent a year. In this case, $1 earned now is worth $1.04 next year. Working fewer hours now and more next year is the way to get a 1 percent higher real wage.

So the when-to-work decision depends on the real interest rate. The lower the real interest rate, other things remaining the same, the smaller is the supply of labor today. Many economists believe this *intertemporal substitution* effect to be of negligible size. RBC theorists believe that the effect is large, and it is the key feature of the RBC mechanism.

You saw in Fig. 29.2(a) that the decrease in the demand for loanable funds lowers the real interest rate. This fall in the real interest rate lowers the return to current work and decreases the supply of labor.

In Fig. 29.2(b), the labor supply curve shifts leftward to LS_1. The effect of the decrease in productivity on the demand for labor is larger than the effect of the fall in the real interest rate on the supply of labor. That is, the demand curve shifts farther leftward than does the supply curve. As a result, the real wage rate falls to $34.50 an hour and employment decreases to 195 billion hours. A recession has begun and is intensifying.

What Happened to Money? The name *real* business cycle theory is no accident. It reflects the central prediction of the theory. Real things, not nominal or monetary things, cause the business cycle. If the quantity of money changes, aggregate demand changes. But if there is no real change—with no change in the use of resources and no change in potential GDP—the change in the quantity of money changes only the price level. In RBC theory, this outcome occurs because the aggregate supply curve is the *LAS* curve, which pins real GDP down at potential GDP, so when aggregate demand changes, only the price level changes.

Cycles and Growth The shock that drives the business cycle of RBC theory is the same as the force that generates economic growth: technological change. On average, as technology advances, productivity grows; but as you saw in *Economics in Action* on p. 706, it grows at an uneven pace. Economic growth arises from the upward trend in productivity growth and, according to RBC theory, the mostly positive but occasionally negative higher frequency shocks to productivity bring the business cycle.

Criticisms and Defenses of RBC Theory The three main criticisms of RBC theory are that

1. The money wage rate *is* sticky, and to assume otherwise is at odds with a clear fact.
2. Intertemporal substitution is too weak a force to account for large fluctuations in labor supply and employment with small real wage rate changes.
3. Productivity shocks are as likely to be caused by *changes in aggregate demand* as by technological change.

If aggregate demand fluctuations cause the fluctuations in productivity, then the traditional aggregate demand theories are needed to explain them. Fluctuations in productivity do not cause the business cycle but are caused by it!

Building on this theme, the critics point out that the so-called productivity fluctuations that growth accounting measures are correlated with changes in the growth rate of money and other indicators of changes in aggregate demand.

The defenders of RBC theory claim that the theory explains the macroeconomic facts about the business cycle and is consistent with the facts about economic growth. In effect, a single theory explains *both growth and the business cycle*. The growth accounting exercise that explains slowly changing trends also explains the more frequent business cycle swings. Its defenders also claim that RBC theory is consistent with a wide range of *micro*economic evidence about labor supply decisions, labor demand and investment demand decisions, and information on the distribution of income between labor and capital.

◆ REVIEW QUIZ

1 Explain the mainstream theory of the business cycle.
2 What are the four special forms of the mainstream theory of the business cycle and how do they differ?
3 According to RBC theory, what is the source of the business cycle? What is the role of fluctuations in the rate of technological change?
4 According to RBC theory, how does a fall in productivity growth influence investment demand, the market for loanable funds, the real interest rate, the demand for labor, the supply of labor, employment, and the real wage rate?
5 What are the main criticisms of RBC theory and how do its supporters defend it?

Work these questions in Study Plan 29.1 and get instant feedback. Do a Key Terms Quiz. MyEconLab

In this first section, we've focussed on the cycles in real GDP and the loanable funds and labor markets. Next, we're going to look at the causes and effects of cycles in the inflation rate.

◆ Inflation Cycles

In the long run, inflation is a monetary phenomenon. It occurs if the quantity of money grows faster than potential GDP. But in the short run, many factors can start an inflation, and real GDP and the price level interact. To study these interactions, we distinguish between two sources of inflation:

- Demand-pull inflation
- Cost-push inflation

Demand-Pull Inflation

An inflation that starts because aggregate demand increases is called **demand-pull inflation**. Demand-pull inflation can be kicked off by *any* of the factors that change aggregate demand. Examples are a cut in the interest rate, an increase in the quantity of money, an increase in government expenditure, a tax cut, an increase in exports, or an increase in investment stimulated by an increase in expected future profits.

Initial Effect of an Increase in Aggregate Demand

Suppose that last year the price level was 110 and real GDP was \$16 trillion. Potential GDP was also \$16 trillion. Figure 29.3(a) illustrates this situation. The aggregate demand curve is AD_0, the short-run aggregate supply curve is SAS_0, and the long-run aggregate supply curve is LAS.

Now suppose that the Fed cuts the interest rate. The quantity of money increases and the aggregate demand curve shifts from AD_0 to AD_1. With no change in potential GDP and no change in the money wage rate, the long-run aggregate supply curve and the short-run aggregate supply curve remain at LAS and SAS_0, respectively.

The price level and real GDP are determined at the point where the aggregate demand curve AD_1 intersects the short-run aggregate supply curve. The price level rises to 113, and real GDP increases above potential GDP to \$16.5 trillion. Unemployment falls below its natural rate. The economy is at an above full-employment equilibrium and there is an inflationary gap. The next step in the unfolding story is a rise in the money wage rate.

FIGURE 29.3 A Demand-Pull Rise in the Price Level

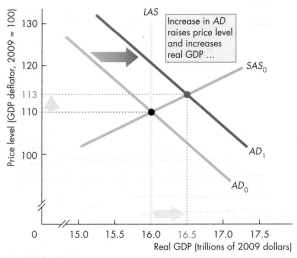

(a) Initial effect

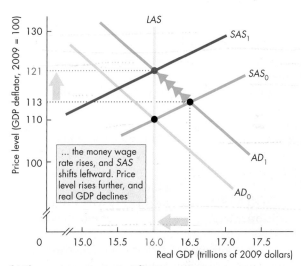

(b) The money wage rate adjusts

In part (a), the aggregate demand curve is AD_0, the short-run aggregate supply curve is SAS_0, and the long-run aggregate supply curve is LAS. The price level is 110, and real GDP is \$16 trillion, which equals potential GDP. Aggregate demand increases to AD_1. The price level rises to 113, and real GDP increases to \$16.5 trillion.

In part (b), starting from the above full-employment equilibrium, the money wage rate begins to rise and the short-run aggregate supply curve shifts leftward toward SAS_1. The price level rises further, and real GDP returns to potential GDP.

Money Wage Rate Response Real GDP cannot remain above potential GDP forever. With unemployment below its natural rate, there is a shortage of labor. In this situation, the money wage rate begins to rise. As it does so, short-run aggregate supply decreases and the *SAS* curve starts to shift leftward. The price level rises further, and real GDP begins to decrease.

With no further change in aggregate demand—that is, the aggregate demand curve remains at AD_1—this process ends when the short-run aggregate supply curve has shifted to SAS_1 in Fig. 29.3(b). At this time, the price level has increased to 121 and real GDP has returned to potential GDP of $16 trillion, the level at which it started.

A Demand-Pull Inflation Process The events that we've just described bring a *one-time rise in the price level*, not an inflation. For inflation to proceed, aggregate demand must *persistently* increase.

The only way in which aggregate demand can persistently increase is if the quantity of money persistently increases. Suppose the government has a budget deficit that it finances by selling bonds. Also suppose that the Fed buys some of these bonds. When the Fed buys bonds, it creates more money. In this situation, aggregate demand increases year after year. The aggregate demand curve keeps shifting rightward. This persistent increase in aggregate demand puts continual upward pressure on the price level. The economy now experiences demand-pull inflation.

Figure 29.4 illustrates the process of demand-pull inflation. The starting point is the same as that shown in Fig. 29.3. The aggregate demand curve is AD_0, the short-run aggregate supply curve is SAS_0, and the long-run aggregate supply curve is *LAS*. Real GDP is $16 trillion, and the price is 110. Aggregate demand increases, shifting the aggregate demand curve to AD_1. Real GDP increases to $16.5 trillion, and the price level rises to 113. The economy is at an above full-employment equilibrium. There is a shortage of labor, and the money wage rate rises. The short-run aggregate supply curve shifts to SAS_1. The price level rises to 121, and real GDP returns to potential GDP.

But the Fed increases the quantity of money again, and aggregate demand continues to increase. The aggregate demand curve shifts rightward to AD_2. The price level rises further to 125, and real GDP again exceeds potential GDP at $16.5 trillion. Yet again,

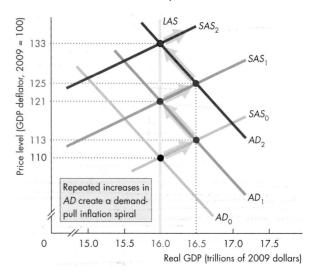

FIGURE 29.4 A Demand-Pull Inflation Spiral

Each time the quantity of money increases, aggregate demand increases and the aggregate demand curve shifts rightward from AD_0 to AD_1 to AD_2, and so on. Each time real GDP increases above potential GDP, the money wage rate rises and the short-run aggregate supply curve shifts leftward from SAS_0 to SAS_1 to SAS_2, and so on. The price level rises from 110 to 113, 121, 125, 133, and so on. There is a demand-pull inflation spiral. Real GDP fluctuates between $16 trillion and $16.5 trillion.

—— MyEconLab Animation and Draw Graph ——

the money wage rate rises and decreases short-run aggregate supply. The *SAS* curve shifts to SAS_2, and the price level rises further, to 133. As the quantity of money continues to grow, aggregate demand increases and the price level rises in an ongoing demand-pull inflation process.

The process you have just studied generates inflation—a persistently rising price level.

Demand-Pull Inflation in Kalamazoo You may better understand the inflation process that we've just described by considering what is going on in an individual part of the economy, such as a Kalamazoo soda-bottling plant. Initially, when aggregate demand increases, the demand for soda increases and the price of soda rises. Faced with a higher price, the soda plant works overtime and increases production. Conditions are good for workers in Kalamazoo, and the soda factory finds it hard to hang on to its best people. To do so, it offers a higher money wage rate. As the wage rate rises, so do the soda factory's costs.

What happens next depends on aggregate demand. If aggregate demand remains constant, the firm's costs increase but the price of soda does not increase as quickly as its costs. In this case, the firm cuts production. Eventually, the money wage rate and costs increase by the same percentage as the rise in the price of soda. In real terms, the soda factory is in the same situation as it was initially. It produces the same amount of soda and employs the same amount of labor as before the increase in demand.

But if aggregate demand continues to increase, so does the demand for soda and the price of soda rises at the same rate as wages. The soda factory continues to operate at above full employment and there is a persistent shortage of labor. Prices and wages chase each other upward in a demand-pull inflation spiral.

Demand-Pull Inflation in the United States A demand-pull inflation like the one you've just studied occurred in the United States during the late 1960s. In 1960, inflation was a moderate 2 percent a year, but its rate increased slowly to 3 percent by 1966. Then, in 1967, a large increase in government expenditure on the Vietnam War and an increase in spending on social programs, together with an increase in the growth rate of the quantity of money, increased aggregate demand more quickly. Consequently, the rightward shift of the aggregate demand curve accelerated and the price level increased more quickly. Real GDP moved above potential GDP, and the unemployment rate fell below its natural rate.

With unemployment below its natural rate, the money wage rate started to rise more quickly and the short-run aggregate supply curve shifted leftward. The Fed responded with a further increase in the money growth rate, and a demand-pull inflation spiral unfolded. By 1970, the inflation rate had reached 5 percent a year.

For the next few years, aggregate demand grew even more quickly and the inflation rate kept rising. By 1974, the inflation rate had reached 11 percent a year.

Next, let's see how shocks to aggregate supply can create cost-push inflation.

Cost-Push Inflation

An inflation that is kicked off by an increase in costs is called **cost-push inflation**. The two main sources of cost increases are

1. An increase in the money wage rate
2. An increase in the money prices of raw materials

At a given price level, the higher the cost of production, the smaller is the amount that firms are willing to produce. So if the money wage rate rises or if the prices of raw materials (for example, oil) rise, firms decrease their supply of goods and services. Aggregate supply decreases, and the short-run aggregate supply curve shifts leftward.[1] Let's trace the effects of such a decrease in short-run aggregate supply on the price level and real GDP.

Initial Effect of a Decrease in Aggregate Supply Suppose that last year the price level was 110 and real GDP was $16 trillion. Potential real GDP was also $16 trillion. Figure 29.5(a) illustrates this situation. The aggregate demand curve was AD_0, the short-run aggregate supply curve was SAS_0, and the long-run aggregate supply curve was LAS. In the current year, the world's oil producers form a price-fixing organization that strengthens their market power and increases the relative price of oil. They raise the price of oil, and this action decreases short-run aggregate supply. The short-run aggregate supply curve shifts leftward to SAS_1. The price level rises to 117, and real GDP decreases to $15.5 trillion. The economy is at a below full-employment equilibrium and there is a recessionary gap.

This event is a *one-time rise in the price level*. It is not inflation. In fact, a supply shock on its own cannot cause inflation. Something more must happen to enable a one-time supply shock, which causes a one-time rise in the price level, to be converted into a process of ongoing inflation. The quantity of money must persistently increase. Sometimes it does increase, as you will now see.

---

[1] Some cost-push forces, such as an increase in the price of oil accompanied by a decrease in the availability of oil, can also decrease long-run aggregate supply. We'll ignore such effects here and examine cost-push factors that change only short-run aggregate supply. Later in the chapter, we study the effects of shocks to long-run aggregate supply.

FIGURE 29.5   A Cost-Push Rise in the Price Level

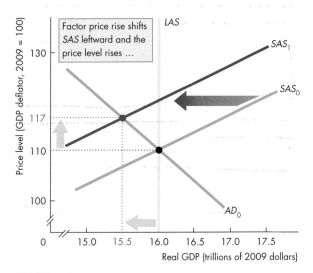

(a) Initial cost push

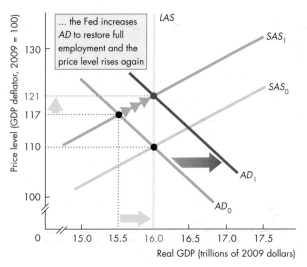

(b) The Fed responds

Initially, the aggregate demand curve is AD_0, the short-run aggregate supply curve is SAS_0; and the long-run aggregate supply curve is LAS. A decrease in aggregate supply (for example, resulting from a rise in the world price of oil) shifts the short-run aggregate supply curve to SAS_1. The economy moves to the point where the short-run aggregate supply curve SAS_1 intersects the aggregate demand curve

AD_0. The price level rises to 117, and real GDP decreases to $15.5 trillion.

In part (b), if the Fed responds by increasing aggregate demand to restore full employment, the aggregate demand curve shifts rightward to AD_1. The economy returns to full employment, but the price level rises further to 121.

Aggregate Demand Response When real GDP decreases, unemployment rises above its natural rate. In such a situation, there is often an outcry of concern and a call for action to restore full employment. Suppose that the Fed cuts the interest rate and increases the quantity of money. Aggregate demand increases. In Fig. 29.5(b), the aggregate demand curve shifts rightward to AD_1 and full employment is restored. But the price level rises further to 121.

A Cost-Push Inflation Process The oil producers now see the prices of everything they buy increasing, so oil producers increase the price of oil again to restore its new high relative price. Figure 29.6 continues the story. The short-run aggregate supply curve now shifts to SAS_2. The price level rises and real GDP decreases.

The price level rises further, to 129, and real GDP decreases to $15.5 trillion. Unemployment

increases above its natural rate. If the Fed responds yet again with an increase in the quantity of money, aggregate demand increases and the aggregate demand curve shifts to AD_2. The price level rises even higher—to 133—and full employment is again restored. A cost-push inflation spiral results. The combination of a rising price level and decreasing real GDP is called **stagflation**.

You can see that the Fed has a dilemma. If it does not respond when producers raise the oil price, the economy remains below full employment. If the Fed increases the quantity of money to restore full employment, it invites another oil price hike that will call forth yet a further increase in the quantity of money.

If the Fed responds to each oil price hike by increasing the quantity of money, inflation will rage along at a rate decided by oil producers. But if the Fed keeps the lid on money growth, the economy remains below full employment.

FIGURE 29.6   A Cost-Push Inflation Spiral

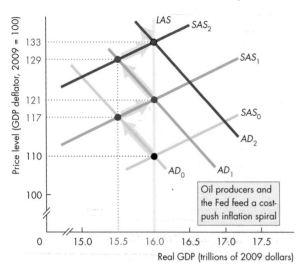

Each time a cost increase occurs, the short-run aggregate supply curve shifts leftward from SAS_0 to SAS_1 to SAS_2, and so on. Each time real GDP decreases below potential GDP, the Fed increases the quantity of money and the aggregate demand curve shifts rightward from AD_0 to AD_1 to AD_2, and so on. The price level rises from 110 to 117, 121, 129, 133, and so on. There is a cost-push inflation spiral. Real GDP fluctuates between $16 trillion and $15.5 trillion.

MyEconLab Animation and Draw Graph

Cost-Push Inflation in Kalamazoo What is going on in the Kalamazoo soda-bottling plant when the economy is experiencing cost-push inflation?

When the oil price increases, so do the costs of bottling soda. These higher costs decrease the supply of soda, increasing its price and decreasing the quantity produced. The soda plant lays off some workers.

This situation persists until either the Fed increases aggregate demand or the price of oil falls. If the Fed increases aggregate demand, the demand for soda increases and so does its price. The higher price of soda brings higher profits, and the bottling plant increases its production. The soda factory rehires the laid-off workers.

Cost-Push Inflation in the United States A cost-push inflation like the one you've just studied occurred in the United States during the 1970s. It began in 1974

when the Organization of the Petroleum Exporting Countries (OPEC) raised the price of oil fourfold. The higher oil price decreased aggregate supply, which caused the price level to rise more quickly and real GDP to shrink. The Fed then faced a dilemma: Would it increase the quantity of money and accommodate the cost-push forces, or would it keep aggregate demand growth in check by limiting money growth? In 1975, 1976, and 1977, the Fed repeatedly allowed the quantity of money to grow quickly and inflation proceeded at a rapid rate. In 1979 and 1980, OPEC was again able to push oil prices higher. On that occasion, the Fed decided not to respond to the oil price hike with an increase in the quantity of money. The result was a recession but also, eventually, a fall in inflation.

Expected Inflation

If inflation is expected, the fluctuations in real GDP that accompany demand-pull and cost-push inflation that you've just studied don't occur. Instead, inflation proceeds as it does in the long run, with real GDP equal to potential GDP and unemployment at its natural rate. Figure 29.7 explains why.

Suppose that last year the aggregate demand curve was AD_0, the aggregate supply curve was SAS_0, and the long-run aggregate supply curve was LAS. The price level was 110, and real GDP was $16 trillion, which is also potential GDP.

To keep things as simple as possible, suppose that potential GDP does not change, so the LAS curve doesn't shift. Also suppose that aggregate demand is expected to increase to AD_1.

In anticipation of this increase in aggregate demand, the money wage rate rises and the short-run aggregate supply curve shifts leftward. If the money wage rate rises by the same percentage as the price level is expected to rise, the short-run aggregate supply curve for next year is SAS_1.

If aggregate demand turns out to be the same as expected, the aggregate demand curve is AD_1. The short-run aggregate supply curve, SAS_1, and AD_1 determine the actual price level at 121. Between last year and this year, the price level increased from 110 to 121 and the economy experienced an inflation rate equal to that expected. If this inflation is ongoing, aggregate demand increases (as expected) in the following year and the aggregate demand curve shifts to AD_2. The money wage rate rises to reflect the expected inflation, and the short-run aggregate

FIGURE 29.7   Expected Inflation

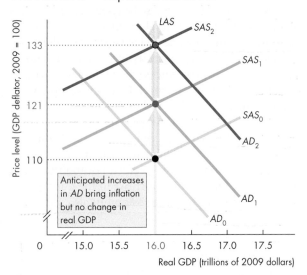

Potential real GDP is $16 trillion. Last year, aggregate demand was AD_0 and the short-run aggregate supply curve was SAS_0. The actual price level was the same as the expected price level: 110. This year, aggregate demand is expected to increase to AD_1 and the price level is expected to rise from 110 to 121. As a result, the money wage rate rises and the short-run aggregate supply curve shifts to SAS_1. If aggregate demand actually increases as expected, the actual aggregate demand curve AD_1 is the same as the expected aggregate demand curve. Real GDP is $16 trillion, and the actual price level rises to 121. The inflation is expected. Next year, the process continues with aggregate demand increasing as expected to AD_2 and the money wage rate rising to shift the short-run aggregate supply curve to SAS_2. Again, real GDP remains at $16 trillion, and the price level rises, as expected, to 133.

MyEconLab Animation and Draw Graph

supply curve shifts to SAS_2. The price level rises, as expected, to 133.

What caused this inflation? The immediate answer is that because people expected inflation, the money wage rate increased and the price level increased. But the expectation was correct. Aggregate demand was expected to increase, and it did increase. It is the actual and expected increase in aggregate demand that caused the inflation.

An expected inflation at full employment is exactly the process that the quantity theory of money predicts. To review the quantity theory of money, see Chapter 25, pp. 608–609.

This broader account of the inflation process and its short-run effects shows why the quantity theory of money doesn't explain the *fluctuations* in inflation. The economy follows the course described in Fig. 29.7, but as predicted by the quantity theory, only if aggregate demand growth is forecasted correctly.

Forecasting Inflation

To anticipate inflation, people must forecast it. Some economists who work for macroeconomic forecasting agencies, banks, insurance companies, labor unions, and large corporations specialize in inflation forecasting. The best forecast available is one that is based on all the relevant information and is called a **rational expectation**. A rational expectation is not necessarily a correct forecast. It is simply the best forecast with the information available. It will often turn out to be wrong, but no other forecast that could have been made with the information available could do better.

Inflation and the Business Cycle

When the inflation forecast is correct, the economy operates at full employment. If aggregate demand grows faster than expected, real GDP rises above potential GDP, the inflation rate exceeds its expected rate, and the economy behaves like it does in a demand-pull inflation. If aggregate demand grows more slowly than expected, real GDP falls below potential GDP and the inflation rate slows.

Deflation

An economy experiences *deflation* when it has a persistently *falling* price level. Equivalently, during a period of deflation, the inflation rate is negative.

In most economies and for most of the time, the inflation rate is positive—the price level is rising—and deflation is rare. But deflation does happen, and most recently it was present in Japan (see *Economics in Action* on p. 716).

We're going to answer three questions about deflation:

- What causes deflation?
- What are the consequences of deflation?
- How can deflation be ended?

What Causes Deflation?

The starting point for understanding the cause of deflation is to distinguish between a one-time fall in the price level and a persistently falling price level. A one-time *fall* in the price level is not deflation. Deflation is a persistent and ongoing *falling* price level.

A One-Time Fall in the Price Level The price level can fall either because aggregate demand decreases or because short-run aggregate supply increases. So any of the influences on aggregate demand and short-run aggregate supply that you studied in Chapter 27 can bring a one-time fall in the price level.

Some examples on the demand side are a fall in global demand for a country's exports, or a fall in profit expectations that lowers business investment. Some examples on the supply side are an increase in capital or advance in technology that increases potential GDP, or (unlikely but possible) a fall in the money wage rate.

But none of these sources of a decrease in aggregate demand or increase in aggregate supply can bring a persistently falling price level.

A Persistently Falling Price Level The price level falls persistently if aggregate demand increases at a persistently slower rate than aggregate supply. The trend rate of increase in aggregate supply is determined by the forces that make potential GDP grow. These forces are the growth rates of the labor force and capital stock and the growth rate of productivity that results from technological change. Notice that all these variables are real, not monetary, and they have trends that change slowly.

In contrast, the forces that drive aggregate demand include the quantity of money. And this quantity can grow as quickly or as slowly as the central bank chooses.

In most situations, the central bank doesn't have a target for the money stock or its growth rate and instead sets the interest rate. But the money stock is under central bank control, and its growth rate has a powerful effect on the growth rate of aggregate demand. To see the effect of growth in the money stock in the long term, we need to return to the quantity theory of money.

The Quantity Theory and Deflation The quantity theory of money explains the trends in inflation by focusing on the trend influences on aggregate supply and aggregate demand.

The foundation of the quantity theory is the *equation of exchange* (see Chapter 25, p. 608), which in its growth rate version and solved for the inflation rate states

$$\text{Inflation rate} = \text{Money growth rate} + \text{Rate of velocity change} - \text{Real GDP growth rate}$$

This equation, true by definition, derives from the fact that the amount of money spent on real GDP, *MV*, equals the money value of GDP, *PY*. (*M* is the money stock, *V* is its velocity of circulation, *P* is the price level, and *Y* is real GDP.)

The quantity theory adds to the equation of exchange two propositons. First, the trend rate of change in the velocity of circulation does not depend on the money growth rate and is determined by decisions about the quantity of money to hold and to spend. Second, the trend growth rate of real GDP equals the growth rate of potential GDP and, again, is independent of the money growth rate.

With these two assumptions, the equation of exchange becomes the quantity theory of money and predicts that a change in the money growth rate brings an equal change in the inflaton rate.

For example, suppose velocity increases by 2 percent per year and potential GDP grows by 3 percent per year. Then the quantity theory predicts that the trend inflation rate equals the money growth rate minus 1 percent. If the central bank makes the quantity of money grow by 1 percent, the inflation rate will be zero. If money grows at a rate faster than 1 percent, the economy will experience inflation. And if money grows at a slower rate than 1 percent, the economy will experience deflation.

ECONOMICS IN ACTION

Fifteen Years of Deflation in Japan

Japan experienced deflation for the 15 years from 1998 to 2013.

Japan's Deflation Rate

Figure 1 shows the inflation rate in Japan from 1990 to 2013. The inflation rate fluctuated between −1 percent and −2 percent per year and accumulated to a 17 percent fall in the price level.

Cause of Japan's Deflation

Deflation, like its opposite, inflation, is primarily a monetary phenomenon. Japan's money stock grew too slowly during the deflation years.

Figure 2 shows the facts about inflation and money growth in Japan from 1995 to 2013. The relevant money growth rate that brings inflation or deflation is that of money itself *plus* the trend rate of change in the velocity of circulaton *minus* the growth rate of potential GDP. That is the money growth rate shown in Fig. 2 and except for one year, 1997, it is negative, which means that Japan's money stock did not grow fast enough to accommodate the growth of potential GDP and a trend rise in velocity.

Consequences of Japan's Deflation

At first, Japan's deflation was unexpected and loan and wage contracts had been entered into that anticipated an ongoing low but positive inflation rate. So when the price level started to fall, the real value of debt increased and the real wage rate increased.

With higher real debt and wages, businesses cut back on both investment and hiring labor and cut production. Real GDP fell and the recessionary gap increased.

Because investment decreased, the capital stock increased more slowly and the growth rate of potential GDP slowed. From being one of the world's most dynamic rich economies, Japan became the world's most sluggish.

Figure 3 tells the story. The 1960s saw Japan doubling its real GDP in seven years. The growth rate slowed in the 1970s and 1980s but remained one of the world's fastest. Then, during the deflation years, the growth rate dropped to 1.5 percent (in the 1990s) and 0.5 percent (in the 2000s).

Japan's inflation rate turned positive in 2014, and real GDP growth picked up, but money growth rate remained too low. Without a sustained increase in money growth, deflation cannot end.

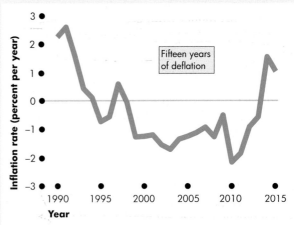

Figure 1 Japan's Long Deflation

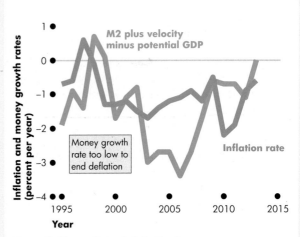

Figure 2 Money Growth Rate Too Low

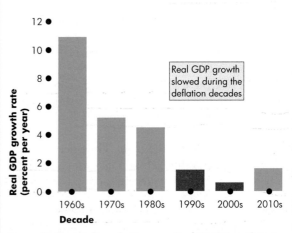

Figure 3 Japan's Decade Average Real GDP Growth Rates

Sources of data: *Financial Statistics* and *World Economic Outlook*, International Monetary Fund, Washington, DC.

Japan Example In the example of Japan during the 1990s and 2000s (see *Economics in Action* on previous page), the money (M2) growth rate during the 15 years 1998–2013 was 2.5 percent per year. The velocity growth rate was negative and it *decreased* at a rate of 3 percent per year. Potential GDP grew at an average rate of 0.8 percent per year. Combining these numbers, the quantity theory predicts an inflation rate equal to –1.3 percent per year:

$$+2.5 + (-3) - 0.8 = -1.3.$$

In fact, the average inflation rate was –1.2 percent per year. So the quantity theory prediction is not exactly correct, but it is close. Its prediction of the deflation rate of 1.3 percent per year is off by only 0.1.

You now know what causes deflation. Let's turn to its consequences.

What are the Consequences of Deflation?

Chapter 22 (p. 524) discusses why deflation and inflation are problems. But with what you now know about aggregate supply and aggregate demand and the determinants of potential GDP and its growth rate, you can gain deeper insight into the costs of deflation (and the related costs of inflation.)

The effects of deflation (like those of inflation) depend on whether it is anticipated or unanticipated. But because inflation is normal and deflation is rare, when deflation occurs, it is usually unanticipated.

Unanticipated deflation redistributes income and wealth, lowers real GDP and employment, and diverts resources from production.

Workers with long-term wage contracts find their real wages rising. But on the other side of the labor market, employers respond to a higher and rising real wage by hiring fewer workers. So the level of employment and output falls.

With lower output and profits, firms re-evaluate their investment plans and cut back on projects that they now see as unprofitable. This fall in investment slows the pace of capital accumulation and slows the growth rate of potential GDP.

Another consequence of deflation is a low nominal interest rate, which, in turn, brings an increase in the quantity of money that people plan to hold and a decrease in the velocity of circulation. A lower velocity adds to the deflationary forces and, if unattended to, lowers the inflation rate yet further.

So, what is the cure for deflation?

How Can Deflation be Ended?

Deflation can be ended by removing its cause: The quantity of money is growing too slowly. If the central bank ensures that the quantity of money grows at the target inflation rate *plus* the growth rate of potential GDP *minus* the growth rate of the velocity of circulation, then, on average, the inflation rate will turn out to be close to target.

In the example of Japan, if the Bank of Japan, the central bank, wanted to get a 2 percent inflation rate, and other things remaining the same, it would have needed to make the quantity of money grow at an annual average rate of 5.8 percent. (Money growth 5.8 *plus* velocity growth of –3 *minus* potential GDP growth of 0.8 equals target inflation of 2 percent.) If raising the inflation rate brought faster potential GDP growth, a yet higher money growth rate would be needed to sustain the higher inflation rate.

Money Growth, Not Quantity Notice that it is an increase in the *growth rate* of the money stock, not a one-time increase in the quantity of money, that is required to end deflation. Central banks sometimes increase the quantity of money and fail to increase its growth rate. An increase in the *level* with no change in the *growth rate* brings a temporary inflation as the price level adjusts but not ongoing inflation, so it does not end deflation.

◆ REVIEW QUIZ

1 What is deflation?
2 What is the distinction between deflation and a one-time fall in the price level?
3 What causes deflation?
4 How does the quantity theory of money help us to understand the process of deflation?
5 What are the consequences of deflation?
6 How can deflation be ended?

Work these questions in Study Plan 29.3 and get instant feedback.   MyEconLab

In the final section of this chapter, we're going to look at an alternative model of short-run fluctuations and one that focuses on inflation and unemployment.

◆ The Phillips Curve

The *Phillips curve* is a relationship between inflation and unemployment. It is so named because it was first suggested by New Zealand economist A.W. (Bill) Phillips. We distinguish between two time frames for the Phillips curve (similar to the two aggregate supply time frames). We study

- The short-run Phillips curve
- The long-run Phillips curve

The Short-Run Phillips Curve

The **short-run Phillips curve** is the relationship between inflation and unemployment, holding constant

1. The expected inflation rate
2. The natural unemployment rate

You've seen what determines the expected inflation rate earlier in this chapter (see p. 714) and the influences on the natural unemployment rate were explained in Chapter 22 (pp. 521–522).

Figure 29.8 shows a short-run Phillips curve, *SRPC*. Suppose that the expected inflation rate is 10 percent a year and the natural unemployment rate is 6 percent, point *A* in the figure. A short-run Phillips curve passes through this point. If inflation rises above its expected rate, unemployment falls below its natural rate in a movement up along the short-run Phillips curve from point *A* to point *B*. Similarly, if inflation falls below its expected rate, unemployment rises above its natural rate in a movement down along the short-run Phillips curve from point *A* to point *C*.

The Long-Run Phillips Curve

The **long-run Phillips curve** is the relationship between inflation and unemployment when the actual inflation rate equals the expected inflation rate. The long-run Phillips curve is vertical at the natural unemployment rate because, in the long run, any expected inflation rate is possible. In Fig. 29.9(a), the long-run Phillips curve is the vertical line *LRPC*.

Change in Expected Inflation A change in the expected inflation rate shifts the short-run Phillips curve, but it does not shift the long-run Phillips curve. In Fig. 29.9(a), if the expected inflation rate is 10 percent a year, the short-run Phillips curve is $SRPC_0$. If the expected inflation rate falls to 6 percent a year, the short-run Phillips curve shifts downward to

FIGURE 29.8 A Short-Run Phillips Curve

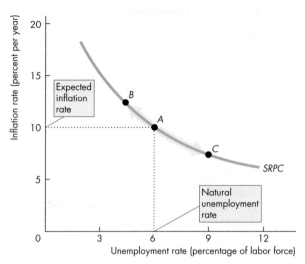

The short-run Phillips curve, *SRPC*, is the relationship between inflation and unemployment at a given expected inflation rate and a given natural unemployment rate. Here, the expected inflation rate is 10 percent a year and the natural unemployment rate is 6 percent at point *A*.

A change in the actual inflation rate brings a movement along the short-run Phillips curve from *A* to *B* or from *A* to *C*.

MyEconLab Animation

$SRPC_1$. The vertical distance by which the short-run Phillips curve shifts from point *A* to point *D* is equal to the change in the expected inflation rate. If the actual inflation rate also falls from 10 percent to 6 percent, there is a movement down the long-run Phillips curve from *A* to *D*. An increase in the expected inflation rate has the opposite effect to that shown in Fig. 29.9(a).

The other source of a shift in the Phillips curve is a change in the natural unemployment rate.

Change in Natural Unemployment Rate A change in the natural unemployment rate shifts both the short-run and long-run Phillips curves. Figure 29.9(b) illustrates such shifts.

If the natural unemployment rate increases from 6 percent to 9 percent, the long-run Phillips curve shifts from $LRPC_0$ to $LRPC_1$, and if expected inflation is constant at 10 percent a year, the short-run Phillips curve shifts from $SRPC_0$ to $SRPC_1$. Because the expected inflation rate is constant, $SRPC_1$ intersects the long-run curve $LRPC_1$ (point *E*) at the same inflation rate at which $SRPC_0$ intersects the long-run curve $LRPC_0$ (point *A*).

FIGURE 29.9   Short-Run and Long-Run Phillips Curves

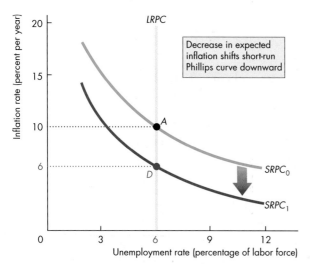

(a) A change in expected inflation

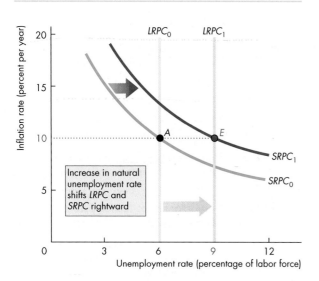

(b) A change in natural unemployment

In part (a), the long-run Phillips curve is *LRPC*. A fall in expected inflation shifts the short-run Phillips curve downward from *SRPC*$_0$ to *SRPC*$_1$. The long-run Phillips curve does not shift. In part (b), a change in the natural unemployment rate shifts both the short-run and long-run Phillips curves.

MyEconLab Animation

Economics in Action above looks at the U.S. Phillips curve from 2001 to 2013, a period through which the expected inflation rate and the natural unemployment rate didn't change much. Over longer periods, big changes in the expected inflation rate have shifted the U.S. Phillips curve.

ECONOMICS IN ACTION
The U.S. Phillips Curve

The figure below is a scatter diagram of the U.S. inflation rate (measured by the GDP deflator) and the unemployment rate since 2001. *LRPC* is at a natural unemployment rate of 5.5 percent and *SRPC* at an expected inflation rate of 2 percent. The dots for each year (five of which are identified) show that the *SRPC* jumps around as inflation expectations change.

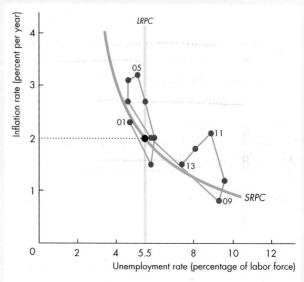

The U.S. Phillips Curve in the 2000s

Sources of data: Bureau of Labor Statistics and Bureau of Economic Analysis.

◆ REVIEW QUIZ

1 How would you use the Phillips curve to illustrate an unexpected change in inflation?
2 If the expected inflation rate increases by 10 percentage points, how do the short-run Phillips curve and the long-run Phillips curve change?
3 If the natural unemployment rate increases, what happens to the short-run Phillips curve and the long-run Phillips curve?
4 Does the United States have a stable short-run Phillips curve? Explain why or why not.

Work these questions in Study Plan 29.4 and get instant feedback. Do a Key Terms Quiz.   *MyEconLab*

◆ *Economics in the News* on pp. 720–721 looks at the stagnating economy of Europe and the plans of the European Central Bank to revive it.

The Stagnating Eurozone

Draghi Launches His Counter Attack

The Financial Times
September 4, 2014

When Mario Draghi departed from his script at the central bankers' gathering at Jackson Hole last month, the world took note.

The president of the European Central Bank did not quite promise to do "whatever it takes" to stave off deflation in the eurozone. But he said enough for investors to believe the Frankfurt-based institution had finally woken up to the threat of stagnation.

Mr. Draghi yesterday threw more troops into his counter-offensive. Admitting that eurozone inflation would fall short of expectations in each of the next three years, he committed the ECB to a series of measures designed to sustain flagging demand.

Mr. Draghi drew a final line under conventional monetary measures as he announced a cut in the repo rate from 0.15 percent to 0.05 percent and increased the amount the ECB would charge lenders for deposits to 0.2 percent.

More importantly, he said the ECB would launch purchases of asset-backed securities.

While this is not the full-scale quantitative easing which many market observers were looking for, it has merits in a world in which eurozone banks have yet to restore their balance sheets. Reducing sovereign yields in such circumstances may do little to increase the propensity of financial institutions to lend.

Mr. Draghi's plans are not without their difficulties. Purchases of asset-backed securities will only make a difference if the pool of underlying assets is large enough and if loans are genuinely taken off strained bank balance sheets, freeing space for new lending. ...

MyEconLab More Economics in the News

ESSENCE OF THE STORY

- Mario Draghi, the president of the European Central Bank (ECB), is fighting stagnation.

- Eurozone inflation is forecast to be lower than desired for the next three years.

- The ECB lowered its policy interest rate from 0.15 percent to 0.05 percent per year.

- The ECB also increased the interest rate it makes banks pay on reserves to 0.2 percent per year.

- The ECB also planned to launch purchases of asset-backed securities.

- ECB purchases of asset-backed securities need to be large enough to take bad assets from the banks and free them to increase loans.

ECONOMIC ANALYSIS

- The Eurozone is the group of 18 European countries that use the euro as their money and for which the European Central Bank (ECB) makes monetary policy decisions.

- The Eurozone economy is stagnating and has a high unemployment rate.

- Figure 1 shows the Eurozone unemployment rate compared with that of the United States.

- The Eurozone unemployment rate has been persistently higher than that of the United States and the average difference is structural, not cyclical.

- A high structural unemployment rate in the Eurozone results from high minimum wages, generous unemployment benefits and welfare payments, and extensive regulation of the labor market.

- ECB monetary policy can do nothing to lower the structural unemployment rate. But it can act to lower the cyclical unemployment rate.

- Eurozone also has a low inflation rate that is below the ECB target rate of 2 percent per year.

- Figure 2 shows the Eurozone inflation rate compared with that of the United States. Both economies had inflation rates below 2 percent per year in 2013, but in the Eurozone inflation had been below 2 percent for 6 years.

- The high unemployment and stagnating real GDP result from real structural problems that make the Eurozone natural unemployment rate high and from high cyclical unemployment and below-target inflation that result from insufficient aggregate demand.

- The aggregate demand problem arises from the fact that the ECB has not expanded the money stock quickly enough.

- Figure 3 shows the growth rate of money plus the growth rate of velocity minus the growth rate of potential GDP.

- The growth rate of money plus the growth rate of velocity minus the growth rate of potential GDP equals the inflation rate that can be sustained at full employment.

- To lower cyclical unemployment, the growth rate of money plus the growth rate of velocity minus the growth rate of potential GDP must *exceed* the target and expected inflation rate.

- If, as in 2009 and 2010, the growth rate of money plus the growth rate of velocity minus the growth rate of potential GDP decreases, cyclical unemployment will increase and inflation will decrease.

- To end stagnation, the ECB must buy assets and increase the growth rate of money. A big one-off asset purchase will not do the job required.

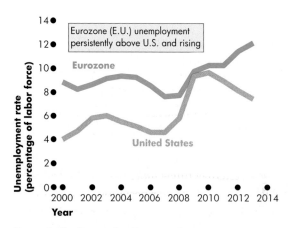

Figure 1 The Stagnating Eurozone Economy

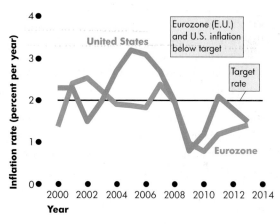

Figure 2 Inflation Rates Miss Targets

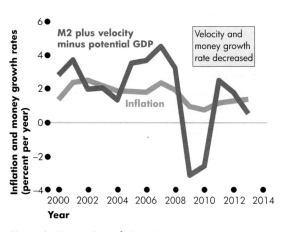

Figure 3 Money Growth Rate Too Low

721

SUMMARY

Key Points

The Business Cycle (pp. 704–708)

- The mainstream business cycle theory explains the business cycle as fluctuations of real GDP around potential GDP and as arising from a steady expansion of potential GDP combined with an expansion of aggregate demand at a fluctuating rate.
- Real business cycle theory explains the business cycle as fluctuations of potential GDP, which arise from fluctuations in the influence of technological change on productivity growth.

Working Problem 1 will give you a better understanding of the business cycle.

Inflation Cycles (pp. 709–714)

- Demand-pull inflation is triggered by an increase in aggregate demand and fueled by ongoing money growth. Real GDP cycles above full employment.
- Cost-push inflation is triggered by an increase in the money wage rate or raw material prices and is fueled by ongoing money growth. Real GDP cycles below full employment in a stagflation.
- When the forecast of inflation is correct, real GDP remains at potential GDP.

Working Problems 2 to 5 will give you a better understanding of inflation cycles.

Deflation (pp. 715–717)

- Deflation is a falling price level or negative inflation rate.
- Deflation is caused by a money growth rate that is too low to accommodate the growth of potential GDP and changes in the velocity of circulation.
- Unanticipated deflation brings stagnation.
- Deflation can be ended by increasing the money growth rate to a rate that accommodates the growth of potential GDP and changes in the velocity of circulation.

Working Problem 6 will give you a better understanding of deflation.

The Phillips Curve (pp. 718–719)

- The short-run Phillips curve shows the tradeoff between inflation and unemployment when the expected inflation rate and the natural unemployment rate are constant.
- The long-run Phillips curve, which is vertical, shows that when the actual inflation rate equals the expected inflation rate, the unemployment rate equals the natural unemployment rate.

Working Problems 7 and 8 will give you a better understanding of the Phillips curve.

Key Terms

MyEconLab Key Terms Quiz

Cost-push inflation, 711
Demand-pull inflation, 709
Keynesian cycle theory, 705
Long-run Phillips curve, 718

Monetarist cycle theory, 705
New classical cycle theory, 705
New Keynesian cycle theory, 705
Rational expectation, 714

Real business cycle theory, 705
Short-run Phillips curve, 718
Stagflation, 712

◆ WORKED PROBLEM

MyEconLab   You can work this problem in Chapter 29 Study Plan.

The table shows the aggregate demand and short-run aggregate supply schedules of Shell Island in which potential GDP is $600 billion. The economy is at full-employment.

Price level	Real GDP demanded	Real GDP supplied in the short run
	(billions of 2009 dollars)	
100	650	550
110	625	575
120	600	600
130	575	625
140	550	650

Questions

1. An unexpected increase in exports increases aggregate demand by $50 billion. What happens to the price level and real GDP? Has Shell Island experienced inflation or deflation and what type of output gap does it now have?

2. The price of oil falls unexpectedly and aggregate supply increases by $50 billion. What type of output gap appears? If the central bank responds to close the output gap, does Shell Island experience inflation or deflation?

3. The government of Shell Island announces an increase in spending of $50 billion a year and the central bank will increase the quantity of money to pay for the spending. Does the economy go into a boom? Will there be inflation?

Solutions

1. When aggregate demand increases by $50 billion, the price level rises from 120 to 130 and real GDP increases from $600 billion to $625 billion. The economy is at an above full-employment equilibrium.

   Shell Island experiences a one-time change in the price level and *not* inflation. The output gap is an inflationary gap, but it was unexpected. Demand-pull inflation does not take off until businesses respond to the labor shortage by raising the money wage rate.

Key Point: For an increase in aggregate demand to create demand-pull inflation, the shortage of labor must put pressure on the money wage rate to rise to close the inflationary gap.

2. When the price of oil falls unexpectedly, aggregate supply increases. The price level falls from 120 to 110 and real GDP increases from $600 billion to $625 billion. The economy is at an above full-employment equilibrium. An inflationary gap arises. Shell Island experiences a one-time change in the price level and not inflation.

   If the central bank responds to close the output gap, it cuts the quantity of money. Aggregate demand shifts leftward and a cost-push deflation is created. See the figure.

Key Point: Cost-push deflation is created if the central bank responds to a fall in costs by decreasing the quantity of money.

3. When the government announces an increase in spending of $50 billion a year, aggregate demand increases and the increase in aggregate demand is anticipated. Because the central bank increases the quantity of money, businesses anticipate the rise in the price level, so the money wage rises. Aggregate supply decreases.

   Real GDP remains at $600 billion and no output gap is created, but an anticipated inflation occurs.

Key Point: An anticipated increase in aggregate demand accompanied by an increase in the quantity of money creates an anticipated inflation spiral with the economy at full employment.

Key Figure

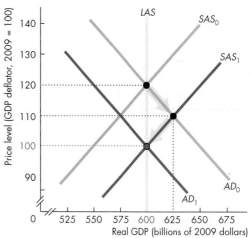

MyEconLab Interactive Animation

STUDY PLAN PROBLEMS AND APPLICATIONS

MyEconLab   You can work Problems 1 to 8 in Chapter 29 Study Plan and get instant feedback.

The Business Cycle (Study Plan 29.1)

1. **Debate on Causes of Joblessness Grows**
   What is the cause of the high unemployment rate? One side says there is not enough government spending. The other says it's a structural problem—people who can't move to take new jobs because they are tied down to burdensome mortgages or firms that can't find workers with the requisite skills to fill job openings.
   Source: *The Wall Street Journal*, September 4, 2010

   Which business cycle theory would say that most of the unemployment is cyclical? Which would say it is an increase in the natural rate? Why?

Inflation Cycles (Study Plan 29.2)

2. **High Food and Energy Prices Here to Stay**
   On top of rising energy prices, a severe drought, bad harvests, and a poor monsoon season in Asia have sent grain prices soaring. Globally, this is the third major food price shock in five years.
   Source: *The Telegraph*, August 29, 2012

   Explain what type of inflation the news clip is describing and provide a graphical analysis of it.

Use the following figure to work Problems 3 to 5.

The economy starts out on the curves labeled AD_0 and SAS_0.

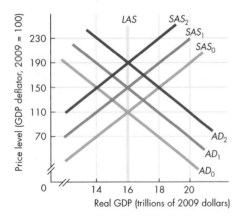

3. Some events occur and the economy experiences a demand-pull inflation. What might those events have been? Describe their initial effects and explain how a demand-pull inflation spiral results.

4. Some events occur and the economy experiences a cost-push inflation. What might those events have been? Describe their initial effects and explain how a cost-push inflation spiral develops.

5. Some events occur and the economy is expected to experience inflation. What might those events have been? Describe their initial effects and what happens as an expected inflation proceeds.

Deflation (Study Plan 29.3)

6. Suppose that the velocity of circulation of money is constant and real GDP is growing at 3 percent a year.
   a. To achieve an inflation target of 2 percent a year, at what rate would the central bank grow the quantity of money?
   b. At what growth rate of the quantity of money would deflation be created?

The Phillips Curve (Study Plan 29.4)

7. **Eurozone Unemployment Hits Record High As Inflation Rises Unexpectedly**
   Eurozone unemployment rose to 10.7 percent. At the same time, eurozone inflation unexpectedly rose to 2.7 percent a year, up from the previous month's 2.6 percent a year.
   Source: *Huffington Post*, March 1, 2012

   a. How does the Phillips curve model account for a very high unemployment rate?
   b. Explain the change in unemployment and inflation in the eurozone in terms of what is happening to the short-run and long-run Phillips curves.

8. **From the Fed's Minutes**
   Members expected real GDP growth to be moderate over coming quarters and then to pick up very gradually, with the unemployment rate declining only slowly. With longer-term inflation expectations stable, members anticipated that inflation over the medium run would be at or below 2 percent a year.
   Source: FOMC Minutes, June 2012

   Are FOMC members predicting that the U.S. economy will move along a short-run Phillips curve or that the short-run Phillips curve will shift through 2012 and 2013? Explain.

ADDITIONAL PROBLEMS AND APPLICATIONS

MyEconLab   You can work these problems in MyEconLab if assigned by your instructor.

The Business Cycle

Use the following information to work Problems 9 to 11.

Suppose that the business cycle in the United States is best described by RBC theory and that a new technology increases productivity.

9. Draw a graph to show the effect of the new technology in the market for loanable funds.
10. Draw a graph to show the effect of the new technology in the labor market.
11. Explain the when-to-work decision when technology advances.
12. **Real Wages Fail to Match a Rise in Productivity**

    For most of the last century, wages and productivity—the key measure of the economy's efficiency—have risen together, increasing rapidly through the 1950s and '60s and far more slowly in the 1970s and '80s. But in recent years, the productivity gains have continued while the pay increases have not kept up.

    Source: *The New York Times*, August 28, 2006

    Explain the relationship between wages and productivity in this news clip in terms of real business cycle theory.

Inflation Cycles

Use the following news clip to work Problems 13 and 14.

Inflation Should Be Feared

The Fed is trying as hard as it can to spur growth, and to create some inflation. But the Fed must be careful. Inflation remains a danger because U.S. debt is skyrocketing, with no visible plan to pay it back. For the moment, foreigners are buying that debt. But they are buying out of fear that their governments are worse. They are short-term investors, waiting out the storm, not long-term investors confident that the United States will pay back its debts. If their fear passes, or they decide some other haven is safer, watch out. Inflation will come with a vengeance. It's not happening yet: Interest rates are low now. But if inflation takes off, it will happen with little warning, the Fed will be powerless to stop it, and it will bring stagnation rather than prosperity.

Source: John H. Cochrane, *The New York Times*, August 22, 2012

13. What type of inflation process does John Cochrane warn could happen? Explain the role that inflation expectations would play if the outbreak of inflation were to "happen with little warning."
14. Explain why the inflation that John Cochrane fears would "bring stagnation rather than prosperity."

Deflation

15. **Europe's Deflation Risk**

    The United States is planning to push Europe toward new and more aggressive efforts to boost aggregate demand given a renewed risk of deflation in the euro zone.

    Source: Reuters, September 12, 2014

    a. Explain the process by which deflation occurs.
    b. How might Europe boost its aggregate demand? Might the boost to aggregate demand create demand-pull inflation?

The Phillips Curve

Use the following data to work Problems 16 and 17.

An economy has an unemployment rate of 4 percent and an inflation rate of 5 percent a year at point A in the figure. Then some events occur that move the economy from A to B to D to C and back to A.

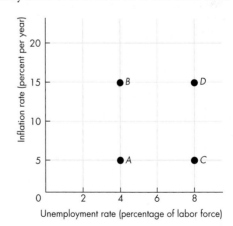

16. Describe the events that could create this sequence. Has the economy experienced demand-pull inflation, cost-push inflation, expected inflation, or none of these?
17. Draw in the figure the sequence of the economy's short-run and long-run Phillips curves.

Use the following information to work Problems 18 and 19.

The Reserve Bank of New Zealand signed an agreement with the New Zealand government in which the Bank agreed to maintain inflation inside a low target range. Failure to achieve the target would result in the governor of the Bank (the equivalent of the chairman of the Fed) losing his job.

18. Explain how this arrangement might have influenced New Zealand's short-run Phillips curve.

19. Explain how this arrangement might have influenced New Zealand's long-run Phillips curve.

20. **Fed Pause Promises Financial Disaster**

    The indication is that inflationary expectations have become entrenched and strongly rooted in world markets. As a result, the risk of global stagflation has become significant. A drawn-out inflationary process always precedes stagflation. Following the attritional effect of inflation, the economy starts to grow below its potential. It experiences a persistent output gap, rising unemployment, and increasingly entrenched inflationary expectations.

    Source: *Asia Times Online*, May 20, 2008

    Evaluate the claim that if "inflationary expectations" become strongly "entrenched" an economy will experience "a persistent output gap."

Use the following information to work Problems 21 and 22.

Because the Fed doubled the monetary base in 2008 and the government spent billions of dollars bailing out troubled banks, insurance companies, and auto producers, some people are concerned that a serious upturn in the inflation rate will occur, not immediately but in a few years' time. At the same time, massive changes in the global economy might bring the need for structural change in the United States.

21. Explain how the Fed's doubling of the monetary base and government bailouts might influence the short-run and long-run Phillips curves. Will the influence come from changes in the expected inflation rate, the natural unemployment rate, or both?

22. Explain how large-scale structural change might influence the short-run and long-run Phillips curves. Will the influence come from changes in the expected inflation rate, the natural unemployment rate, or both?

Economics in the News

23. After you have studied *Economics in the News* on pp. 720–721, answer the following questions.

    a. What are the macroeconomic problems in the Eurozone economy that the ECB is seeking to address?

    b. Is the European unemployment problem structural, cyclical, or both and how can we determine its type?

    c. Explain which type of unemployment the ECB can help with.

    d. Use the *AS-AD* model to show the changes in aggregate demand and/or aggregate supply that created the Eurozone's macroeconomic problems.

    e. Use the *AS-AD* model to show the changes in aggregate demand and/or aggregate supply that the ECB must bring about to achieve its goal.

24. **Germany Leads Slowdown in Eurozone**

    The pace of German economic growth has weakened "markedly," but the reason is the weaker global prospects. Although German policymakers worry about the country's exposure to a fall in demand for its export goods, evidence is growing that the recovery is broadening with real wage rates rising and unemployment falling, which will lead into stronger consumer spending.

    Source: *The Financial Times*, September 23, 2010

    a. How does "exposure to a fall in demand for its export goods" influence Germany's aggregate demand, aggregate supply, unemployment, and inflation?

    b. Use the *AS-AD* model to illustrate your answer to part (a).

    c. Use the Phillips curve model to illustrate your answer to part (a).

    d. What do you think the news clip means by "the recovery is broadening with real wage rates rising and unemployment falling, which will lead into stronger consumer spending"?

    e. Use the *AS-AD* model to illustrate your answer to part (d).

    f. Use the Phillips curve model to illustrate your answer to part (d).

Boom and Bust

UNDERSTANDING MACROECONOMIC FLUCTUATIONS

To cure a disease, doctors must first understand how the disease responds to different treatments. It helps to understand the mechanisms that operate to cause the disease, but sometimes a workable cure can be found even before the full story of the causes has been told.

Curing economic ills is similar to curing our medical ills. We need to understand how the economy responds to the treatments we might prescribe for it. And sometimes, we want to try a cure even though we don't fully understand the reasons for the problem we're trying to control.

You've seen how the pace of capital accumulation and technological change determine the long-term growth trend. You've learned how fluctuations around the long-term trend can be generated by changes in aggregate demand and aggregate supply. And you've learned about the key sources of fluctuations in aggregate demand and aggregate supply.

The *AS-AD* model explains the forces that determine real GDP and the price level in the short run. The model also enables us to see the big picture or grand vision of the different schools of macroeconomic thought concerning the sources of aggregate fluctuations. The Keynesian aggregate expenditure model provides an account of the factors that determine aggregate demand and make it fluctuate.

An alternative real business cycle theory puts all the emphasis on fluctuations in long-run aggregate supply. According to this theory, money changes aggregate demand and the price level but leaves the real economy untouched. The events of 2008 and 2009 will provide a powerful test of this theory.

John Maynard Keynes, *born in England in 1883, was one of the outstanding minds of the twentieth century. He represented Britain at the Versailles peace conference at the end of World War I, was a master speculator on international financial markets (an activity he conducted from bed every morning and which made and lost him several fortunes), and played a prominent role in creating the International Monetary Fund.*

He was a member of the Bloomsbury Group, a circle of outstanding artists and writers that included E. M. Forster, Bertrand Russell, and Virginia Woolf.

Keynes was a controversial and quick-witted figure. A critic once complained that Keynes had changed his opinion on some matter, to which Keynes retorted: "When I discover I am wrong, I change my mind. What do you do?"

Keynes' book, The General Theory of Employment, Interest and Money, *written during the Great Depression and published in 1936, revolutionized macroeconomics.*

"The ideas of economists and political philosophers, both when they are right and when they are wrong, are more powerful than is commonly understood. Indeed the world is ruled by little else."

JOHN MAYNARD KEYNES
The General Theory of Employment, Interest and Money

RICARDO J. CABALLERO is Ford Professor of International Economics at MIT. He has received many honors, the most notable of which are the Frisch Medal of the Econometric Society (2002) and being named Chile's Economist of the Year (2001). A highly regarded teacher, he is much sought as a special lecturer and in 2005 gave the prestigious Yrjo Jahnsson Lecture at the University of Helsinki.

Professor Caballero earned his B.S. degree in 1982 and M.A. in 1983 at Pontificia Universidad Católica de Chile. He then moved to the United States and obtained his Ph.D. at MIT in 1988.

Michael Parkin talked with Ricardo Caballero about his work and the progress that economists have made in understanding economic fluctuations.

Professor Caballero, why did you decide to become an economist?

Did I decide? I'm convinced that one is either born an economist or not. I began studying business, but as soon as I took the first course in economics, I was captivated by the simple but elegant logic of (good) economic reasoning. Given the complexity of the real world, economic analysis is necessarily abstract. But at the same time, economics is mostly about concrete and important issues that affect the lives of millions of people. Abstraction and relevance—this is a wonderful but strange combination. Not everybody feels comfortable with it, but if you do, economics is for you.

Most of your work has been on business cycles and other high-frequency phenomena. Can we begin by reviewing the costs of recessions? Robert Lucas says that postwar U.S. recessions have cost very little. Do you agree?

No … but I'm not sure Robert Lucas was really trying to say that. My sense is that he was trying to push the profession to focus a bit more on long-run growth issues. Putting down the costs of recessions was a useful debating device to make his important point.

I believe that the statement that recessions are not costly is incorrect.

First, I think his calculation of this magnitude reflects some fundamental flaw in the way the workhorse models we use in economics fail to account for the costs of risk and volatility. This flaw shows up in many different puzzles in economics, including the well-known equity premium puzzle. Economic models underestimate, by an order of magnitude, how unhappy agents are about facing uncertainty.

> Recessions are costly because they waste enormous resources [and] affect physical and human investment decisions.

Second, it is highly unlikely that recessions and medium-term growth are completely separable. In particular, the ongoing process of restructuring, which is central to productivity growth, is severely hampered by deep recessions.

Recessions are costly because they waste enormous resources, affect physical and human investment decisions, have large negative distributional consequences, influence political outcomes, and so on.

*You can read the full interview with Ricardo J. Caballero in MyEconLab.

30 FISCAL POLICY

After studying this chapter, you will be able to:

- ◆ Describe the federal budget process and the recent history of outlays, receipts, deficits, and debt
- ◆ Explain the supply-side effects of fiscal policy
- ◆ Explain how fiscal policy choices redistribute benefits and costs across generations
- ◆ Explain how fiscal stimulus is used to fight a recession

Most governments have a budget deficit and debt, but Japan's tops them all and might be a warning to the United States and others about dangers that lie ahead.

How do government deficits and debt influence the economy? Do they create jobs, or do they destroy them? Do they slow economic growth? Do they impose a burden on future generations?

This chapter studies these fiscal policy questions in the U.S. economy today. In *Economics in the News* at the end of the chapter, we look at the extreme fiscal policy challenges facing Japan and the lesson they hold for the United States.

◆ The Federal Budget

The **federal budget** is an annual statement of the outlays and receipts of the government of the United States together with the laws and regulations that approve and support them. The federal budget has two purposes:

1. To finance federal government programs and activities, and
2. To achieve macroeconomic objectives

The first purpose of the federal budget was its only purpose before the Great Depression of the 1930s. The second purpose arose as a reaction to the Great Depression and the rise of the ideas of economist John Maynard Keynes. The use of the federal budget to achieve macroeconomic objectives such as full employment, sustained economic growth, and price level stability is called **fiscal policy.** It is this aspect of the budget that is the focus of this chapter.

The Institutions and Laws

Fiscal policy is made by the president and Congress on an annual timeline that is shown in Fig. 30.1 for the 2015 budget.

The Roles of the President and Congress The president *proposes* a budget to Congress each February. Congress debates the proposed budget and passes the budget acts in September. The president either signs those acts into law or vetoes the *entire* budget bill. The president does not have the veto power to eliminate specific items in a budget bill and approve others—known as a *line-item veto*. Many state governors have long had line-item veto authority. Congress attempted to grant these powers to the president of the United States in 1996, but in a 1998 Supreme Court ruling, the line-item veto for the president was declared unconstitutional. Although the president proposes and ultimately approves the budget, the task of making the tough decisions on spending and taxes rests with Congress.

Congress begins its work on the budget with the president's proposal. The House of Representatives and the Senate develop their own budget ideas in their respective House and Senate Budget Committees. Formal conferences between the two houses eventually resolve differences of view, and a series of spending

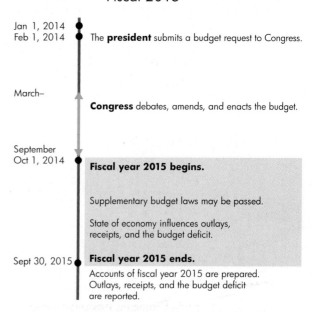

FIGURE 30.1   The Federal Budget Timeline in Fiscal 2015

Jan 1, 2014
Feb 1, 2014   The **president** submits a budget request to Congress.

March–

Congress debates, amends, and enacts the budget.

September
Oct 1, 2014   **Fiscal year 2015 begins.**

Supplementary budget laws may be passed.

State of economy influences outlays, receipts, and the budget deficit.

Sept 30, 2015   **Fiscal year 2015 ends.**
Accounts of fiscal year 2015 are prepared. Outlays, receipts, and the budget deficit are reported.

The federal budget process begins with the president's request in February. Congress debates and amends the request and enacts a budget before the start of the fiscal year on October 1. The president signs the budget acts into law or vetoes the entire budget bill. Throughout the fiscal year, Congress might pass supplementary budget laws. The budget outcome is calculated after the end of the fiscal year.

——— MyEconLab Animation ———

acts and an overall budget act are usually passed by both houses before the start of the fiscal year. A *fiscal year* is a year that runs from October 1 to September 30 in the next calendar year. *Fiscal* 2015 is the fiscal year that *begins* on October 1, 2014.

During a fiscal year, Congress often passes supplementary budget laws, and the budget outcome is influenced by the evolving state of the economy. For example, if a recession begins, tax revenues fall and welfare payments increase.

The Employment Act of 1946 Fiscal policy operates within the framework of the landmark *Employment Act of 1946* in which Congress declared that

> … it is the continuing policy and responsibility of the Federal Government to use all practicable means … to coordinate and utilize all its plans, functions, and resources … to promote maximum employment, production, and purchasing power.

This act recognized a role for government actions to keep unemployment low, the economy expanding, and inflation in check. The *Full Employment and Balanced Growth Act of 1978*, more commonly known as the *Humphrey-Hawkins Act*, went farther than the Employment Act of 1946 and set a specific target of 4 percent for the unemployment rate. But this target has never been treated as an unwavering policy goal. Under the 1946 act, the president must describe the current economic situation and the policies he believes are needed in the annual *Economic Report of the President*, which the Council of Economic Advisers writes.

The Council of Economic Advisers The president's Council of Economic Advisers was established in the Employment Act of 1946. The Council consists of a chairperson and two other members, all of whom are economists on a one- or two-year leave from their regular university or public service jobs. In 2014, the chair of President Obama's Council of Economic Advisers was Jason Furman formerly at the Brookings Institution. The **Council of Economic Advisers** monitors the economy and keeps the President and the public informed about the current state of the economy and the best available forecasts of where it is heading. This economic intelligence activity is one source of data that informs the budget-making process.

Let's look at the most recent federal budget.

Highlights of the 2015 Budget

Table 30.1 shows the main items in the federal budget proposed by President Obama for 2015. The numbers are projected amounts for the fiscal year beginning on October 1, 2014—Fiscal 2015. Notice the three main parts of the table: *Receipts* are the government's tax revenues, *outlays* are the government's payments, and the *deficit* is the amount by which the government's outlays exceed its receipts.

Receipts Receipts were projected to be $3,514 billion in Fiscal 2015. These receipts come from four sources:

1. Personal income taxes
2. Social Security taxes
3. Corporate income taxes
4. Indirect taxes and other receipts

The largest source of receipts is *personal income taxes*, which in 2015 are expected to be $1,505 billion.

These taxes are paid by individuals on their incomes. The second largest source is *Social Security taxes*. These taxes are paid by workers and their employers to finance the government's Social Security programs. Third in size are *corporate income taxes*. These taxes are paid by companies on their profits. Finally, the smallest source of federal receipts is what are called *indirect taxes*. These taxes are on the sale of gasoline, alcoholic beverages, and a few other items.

Outlays Outlays are classified into three categories:

1. Transfer payments
2. Expenditure on goods and services
3. Debt interest

The largest item of outlays, *transfer payments*, is the payment to individuals, businesses, other levels of government, and the rest of the world. In 2015, this item is expected to be $2,649 billion. It includes Social Security benefits, Medicare and Medicaid, unemployment checks, welfare payments, farm subsidies, grants to state and local governments, and payments to international agencies. It also includes capital transfers to bail out failing financial institutions. Transfer payments, especially those for Medicare and Medicaid, are sources of persistent growth in

TABLE 30.1 Federal Budget in Fiscal 2015

Item	Projections (billions of dollars)
Receipts	**3,514**
Personal income taxes	1,505
Social Security taxes	1,176
Corporate income taxes	537
Indirect taxes and other receipts	296
Outlays	**4,158**
Transfer payments	2,649
Expenditure on goods and services	1,030
Debt interest	479
Deficit	**644**

Source of data: Budget of the United States Government, Fiscal Year 2015, Table 14.1.

government expenditures and are a major source of concern and political debate.

Expenditure on goods and services is the expenditure on final goods and services, and in 2015 it is expected to total $1,030 billion. This expenditure, which includes that on national defense, homeland security, research on cures for AIDS, computers for the Internal Revenue Service, government cars and trucks, and federal highways, has decreased in recent years. This component of the federal budget is the *government expenditure on goods and services* that appears in the circular flow of expenditure and income and in the National Income and Product Accounts (see Chapter 21, pp. 493–494).

Debt interest is the interest on the government debt. In 2015, this item is expected to be $479 billion—almost 12 percent of total expenditure. This interest payment is large because the government has a debt of almost $13 trillion, which has arisen from many years of budget deficits during the 1970s, 1980s, 1990s, and 2000s.

Surplus or Deficit The government's budget balance is equal to receipts minus outlays.

$$\text{Budget balance} = \text{Receipts} - \text{Outlays}.$$

If receipts exceed outlays, the government has a **budget surplus**. If outlays exceed receipts, the government has

a **budget deficit**. If receipts equal outlays, the government has a **balanced budget**. For Fiscal 2015, with projected outlays of $4,158 billion and receipts of $3,514 billion, the government projected a budget deficit of $644 billion.

Big numbers like these are hard to visualize and hard to compare over time. To get a better sense of the magnitude of receipts, outlays, and the deficit, we often express them as percentages of GDP. Expressing them in this way lets us see how large government is relative to the size of the economy, and it also helps us to study *changes* in the scale of government over time.

How typical is the federal budget of Fiscal 2015? Let's look at the recent history of the budget.

The Budget in Historical Perspective

Figure 30.2 shows the government's receipts, outlays, and budget surplus or deficit since 1990. You can see that except for the four years around 2000, the budget has been in persistent deficit.

You can also see that after 2008, the deficit was extraordinarily large, peaking in 2010 at more than 10 percent of GDP and remaining close to 10 percent for three years.

An earlier large deficit in 1992 gradually shrank through the 1990s expansion and in 1998 the first

FIGURE 30.2   The Budget Surplus and Deficit

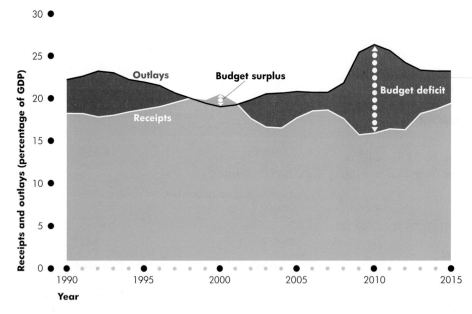

The figure records the federal government's outlays, receipts, and budget balance from 1990 to 2015. Except for the four years 1998 through 2001, the budget has been in deficit. The deficit after 2008 reached a new all-time high and occurred because outlays increased. Receipts have fluctuated but have displayed no trend (as a percentage of GDP).

Source of data: Budget of the United States Government, Fiscal Year 2015, Table 14.2.

budget surplus since 1969 emerged. But by 2002, the budget was again in deficit and during the 2008–2009 recession, the deficit reached a new all-time high.

Why did the budget deficit grow during the early 1990s, vanish in the late 1990s, and re-emerge in the 2000s? Did outlays increase, or did receipts shrink, and which components of outlays and receipts changed most to swell and then shrink the deficit? Let's look at receipts and outlays in a bit more detail.

Receipts Figure 30.3(a) shows the components of government receipts as percentages of GDP from 1990 to 2015. Total receipts fluctuate because personal income taxes and corporate income taxes fluctuate. Other receipts (Social Security taxes and indirect taxes) are a near-constant percentage of GDP.

Personal and corporate income tax receipts trended upward during the 1990s, downward during the 2000s, and then upward again after 2010.

FIGURE 30.3   Federal Government Receipts and Outlays

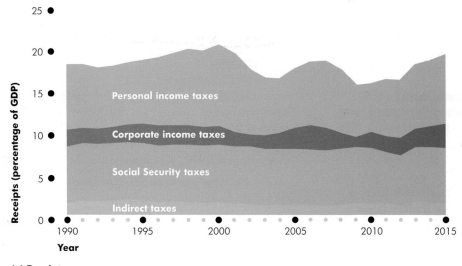

(a) Receipts

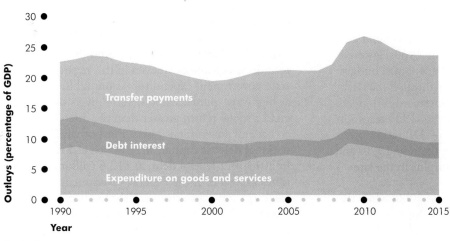

(b) Outlays

In part (a), receipts from personal and corporate income taxes (as a percentage of GDP) increased during the 1990s, and fluctuated wildly during the 2000s. The other components of receipts remained steady. Over the entire period, receipts fell slightly.

In part (b), expenditure on goods and services as a percentage of GDP decreased through 2001 but then increased because expenditure on security-related goods and services increased sharply after 2001.

Transfer payments increased through the 1990s and exploded to a new all-time high percentage of GDP by 2010, before shrinking slightly.

Debt interest decreased during the 1990s and early 2000s, helped by a shrinking budget deficit during the 1990s and low interest rates after 2008.

Source of data: Budget of the United States Government, Fiscal Year 2015, Table 14.2.

Outlays Figure 30.3(b) shows the components of government outlays as percentages of GDP from 1990 to 2015. Two features of government outlays stand out. First, expenditure on goods and services decreased from 1990 through 2000 and then increased. The increase after 2000 was mainly on security-related goods and services in the wake of the attacks that occurred on September 11, 2001, and defense expenditure. Second, transfer payments increased over the entire period and exploded after 2008 when the government tried to stimulate economic activity.

You've seen that the U.S. government budget deficit is large. But how does it compare to the deficits of other countries? The answer: It is one of the largest as *Economics in Action* (p. 736) shows. Of the major economies, only Japan has a larger deficit as a percentage of GDP.

Deficits bring debts, as you will now see.

Budget Balance and Debt

When the government has a budget deficit it borrows, and when it has a budget surplus it makes loan repayments. **Government debt** is the total amount that the government has borrowed. It is the sum of past budget deficits minus the sum of past budget surpluses. A government budget deficit increases government debt. A persistent budget deficit feeds itself: It leads to increased borrowing, which leads to larger interest payments, which in turn lead to a larger deficit. That is the story of an increasing budget deficit during the 1970s and 1980s and again today.

Figure 30.4 shows government debt since 1940, measured as a percentage of GDP—the debt-to-GDP ratio. The government debt-to-GDP ratio was at an all-time high at the end of World War II when it exceeded 110 percent. Budget surpluses and rapid economic growth, especially during the 1960s, lowered the debt-to-GDP ratio through 1974. Small budget deficits increased the ratio slightly through the 1970s, and large budget deficits increased it dramatically during the 1980s and the 1990–1991 recession.

The growth rate of the debt-to-GDP ratio slowed as the economy expanded during the mid-1990s and fell when the budget went into surplus in the late 1990s and early 2000s.

After the global financial crisis of 2008, when the budget deficit reached a record high for peacetime, and real GDP stopped growing, the debt-to-GDP ratio climbed again, and steeply.

FIGURE 30.4   The Federal Government Debt

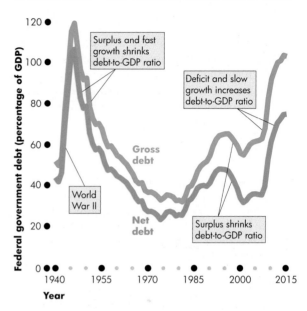

Government debt (the accumulation of past budget deficits minus past budget surpluses) was at its highest at the end of World War II. Debt as a percentage of GDP fell through 1974 but then started to increase. After a further brief decline during the 1990s, it exploded during the 2010s.

Source of data: Budget of the United States Government, Fiscal Year 2015, Table 7.1.

MyEconLab Real-time data

Debt and Capital Businesses and individuals incur debts to buy capital—assets that yield a return. In fact, the main point of debt is to enable people to buy assets that will earn a return that exceeds the interest paid on the debt. The government is similar to individuals and businesses in this regard. Much state government expenditure is on public assets such as highways, public schools, and universities, that yield a social return greater than the interest rate.

Federal government assets, most of which are national defense capital, were valued at $1.8 trillion in 2013. But federal debt, at $12.6 trillion, is seven times the value of the Federal government's capital stock. So some government debt has been incurred to finance public consumption expenditure and transfer payments, which do not have a social return. Future generations bear the cost of this debt.

AT ISSUE

How, Whether, and When to Balance the Federal Budget

The details change from year to year but the central issue remains: Should fiscal policy focus on stimulating demand to achieve full employment and redistribute income from the richest Americans to the middle class and the poor? Or should the focus be on strengthening the incentives to work, save, and invest and on lowering the ratio of federal debt to GDP to increase potential GDP and speed economic growth?

Both sides argue that their approach benefits the middle class and poorer Americans. Let's look at the competing proposals.

The Obama Budget Plan

- The President's budget plan envisions an ongoing deficit and growing debt.

- In Fiscal 2015, spending increases by less than tax revenues and the deficit shrinks by $85 billion from 3.7 percent of GDP to 3.1 percent.

- The budget plan for 2015 through 2024 keeps the dollar value of the deficit at an average of $500 billion a year but lowers the deficit as a percentage of GDP to 1.6 percent by 2025.

- Government debt (net of financial assets held by government) grows from $11.5 trillion in 2014 to $16.5 trillion in 2024, but the debt-to-GDP ratio shrinks from 75 percent to 69 percent.

- Spending cuts through 2024 arising from health savings, immigration reform, and debt interest will save $750 billion over the decade.

- Additional spending on education, innovation, infrastructure, and security will add $140 billion over the decade.

- Reforms in the way businesses are taxed are expected to increase tax revenues by $150 billion over the decade.

Paul Ryan's Budget Plan

- Paul Ryan's (House Republican) budget plan seeks to balance the budget by 2023 and thereafter run a surplus that gradually lowers government debt.

- Ryan's proposed deficit slashing begins with a bang in Fiscal 2015: a cut of $433 billion in spending and an increase of $370 billion in tax revenues.

- The budget plan for 2015 through 2024 keeps the dollar value of the deficit at an average of less than $100 billion a year and holds the deficit as a percentage of GDP to less than 0.5 percent.

- Government debt (net of financial assets held by government) grows only slightly and the debt-to-GDP ratio shrinks to less than 60 percent.

- Ryan get all of his savings from spending cuts. His revenue plan brings in the same number of dollars as in the President's plan.

- Healthcare is the item that takes the greatest hit, with Ryan proposing to cut Medicaid and end Obamacare, lowering spending by almost $300 billion per year.

"What I offer in this budget is a set of concrete, practical proposals to speed up growth, strengthen the middle class, and build new ladders of opportunity into the middle class—all while continuing to improve the Nation's long-run fiscal position."

Budget Message of the President, Fiscal 2015

"Unless we change course, we will have a debt crisis. Pressed for cash, the government will take the easy way out: It will crank up the printing presses. The final stage of this intergenerational theft will be the debasement of our currency."

The Path to Prosperity: A Responsible, Balanced Budget
www.budget.house.gov

ECONOMICS IN ACTION

The U.S. Government Budget in Global Perspective

How does the U.S. government budget deficit compare with those of other major economies?

Comparing Like with Like

To compare the budget deficits of governments across economies, we must take into account the fact that some countries, and the United States is one of them, have large state and local governments, while others, and the United Kingdom is one, have a large central government and small local governments. These differences make the international comparison more valid at the level of total government.

Deficits Almost Everywhere

The figure shows the budget balances of all levels of government in eight economies in 2014. Fiscal stimulus to fight the global recession of 2008 resulted in deficits almost everywhere. Of the countries shown here, only Germany had a budget surplus in 2014.

Japan had the largest deficit and the United States had the second largest. The United Kingdom and some other European countries also had large deficits.

Italy and other advanced economies as a group, which includes the newly industrialized economies of Asia (Hong Kong, South Korea, Singapore, and Taiwan) had the smallest deficits.

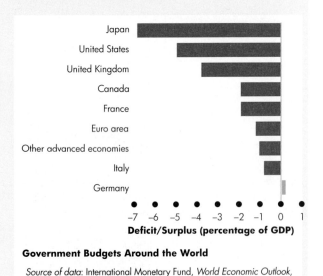

Government Budgets Around the World

Source of data: International Monetary Fund, *World Economic Outlook*, April 2014.

State and Local Budgets

The *total government* sector of the United States includes state and local governments as well as the federal government. In Fiscal 2015, when federal government outlays were $4,158 billion, state and local outlays were a further $2,700 billion. Most of these expenditures were on public schools, colleges, and universities ($550 billion); local police and fire services; and roads.

It is the combination of federal, state, and local government receipts, outlays, and budget deficits that influences the economy. But state and local budgets are not designed to stabilize the aggregate economy. So sometimes, when the federal government cuts taxes or outlays, state and local governments do the reverse and, to a degree, cancel out the effects of the federal actions. For example, since 2000, federal taxes have decreased as a percentage of GDP, but state and local taxes and total government taxes have increased.

◆ REVIEW QUIZ

1 What is fiscal policy, who makes it, and what is it designed to influence?
2 What special role does the president play in creating fiscal policy?
3 What special roles do the Budget Committees of the House of Representatives and the Senate play in creating fiscal policy?
4 What is the timeline for the U.S. federal budget each year? When does a fiscal year begin and end?
5 Is the federal government budget today in surplus or deficit?

Work these questions in Study Plan 30.1 and get instant feedback. Do a Key Terms Quiz.   MyEconLab

---

Now that you know what the federal budget is and what the main components of receipts and outlays are, it is time to study the *effects* of fiscal policy. We begin by learning about the effects of taxes on employment, aggregate supply, and potential GDP. Then we see how fiscal policy brings redistribution across generations. Finally, we look at fiscal stimulus and see how it might be used to speed recovery from recession and stabilize the business cycle.

Supply-Side Effects of Fiscal Policy

How do taxes on personal and corporate income affect real GDP and employment? The answer to these questions is controversial. Some economists, known as *supply-siders*, believe these effects to be large and an accumulating body of evidence suggests that they are correct. To see why these effects might be large, we'll begin with a refresher on how full employment and potential GDP are determined in the absence of taxes. Then we'll introduce an income tax and see how it changes the economic outcome.

Full Employment and Potential GDP

You learned in Chapter 23 (pp. 546–548) how the full-employment quantity of labor and potential GDP are determined. At full employment, the real wage rate adjusts to make the quantity of labor demanded equal the quantity of labor supplied. Potential GDP is the real GDP that the full-employment quantity of labor produces.

Figure 30.5 illustrates a full-employment situation. In part (a), the demand for labor curve is *LD* and the supply of labor curve is *LS*. At a real wage rate of $30 an hour, 250 billion hours of labor a year are employed and the economy is at full employment.

In Fig. 30.5(b), the production function is *PF*. When 250 billion hours of labor are employed, real GDP—which is also potential GDP—is $16 trillion.

Let's now see how an income tax changes potential GDP.

The Effects of the Income Tax

The tax on labor income influences potential GDP and aggregate supply by changing the full-employment quantity of labor. The income tax weakens the incentive to work and drives a wedge between the take-home wage of workers and the cost of labor to businesses. The result is a smaller quantity of labor and a smaller potential GDP.

Figure 30.5 shows this outcome. In the labor market, the income tax has no effect on the demand for labor, which remains at *LD*. The reason is that the quantity of labor that businesses plan to hire depends only on how productive labor is and what it costs—its real wage rate.

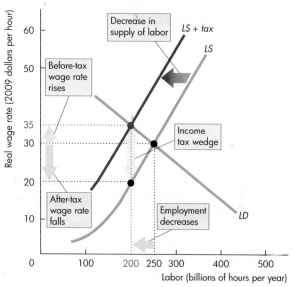

FIGURE 30.5 The Effects of the Income Tax on Aggregate Supply

(a) Income tax and the labor market

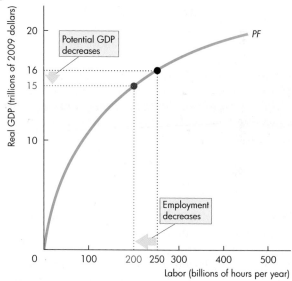

(b) Income tax and potential GDP

In part (a), with no income tax, the real wage rate is $30 an hour and employment is 250 billion hours. In part (b), potential GDP is $16 trillion. An income tax shifts the supply of labor curve leftward to *LS* + *tax*. The before-tax wage rate rises to $35 an hour, the after-tax wage rate falls to $20 an hour, and the quantity of labor employed decreases to 200 billion hours. With less labor, potential GDP decreases.

MyEconLab Animation and Draw Graph

But the supply of labor *does* change. With no income tax, the real wage rate is $30 an hour and 250 billion hours of labor a year are employed. An income tax weakens the incentive to work and decreases the supply of labor. The reason is that for each dollar of before-tax earnings, workers must pay the government an amount determined by the income tax code. So workers look at the after-tax wage rate when they decide how much labor to supply. An income tax shifts the supply curve leftward to *LS + tax*. The vertical distance between the *LS* curve and the *LS + tax* curve measures the amount of income tax. With the smaller supply of labor, the *before-tax* wage rate rises to $35 an hour but the *after-tax* wage rate falls to $20 an hour. The gap created between the before-tax and after-tax wage rates is called the **tax wedge**.

The new equilibrium quantity of labor employed is 200 billion hours a year—less than in the no-tax case. Because the full-employment quantity of labor decreases, so does potential GDP. And a decrease in potential GDP decreases aggregate supply.

In this example, the tax rate is high—$15 tax on a $35 wage rate is a tax rate of about 43 percent. A lower tax rate would have a smaller effect on employment and potential GDP.

An increase in the tax rate to above 43 percent would decrease the supply of labor by more than the decrease shown in Fig. 30.5. Equilibrium employment and potential GDP would also decrease still further. A tax cut would increase the supply of labor, increase equilibrium employment, and increase potential GDP.

Taxes on Expenditure and the Tax Wedge

The tax wedge that we've just considered is only a part of the wedge that affects labor-supply decisions. Taxes on consumption expenditure add to the wedge. The reason is that a tax on consumption raises the prices paid for consumption goods and services and is equivalent to a cut in the real wage rate.

The incentive to supply labor depends on the goods and services that an hour of labor can buy. The higher the taxes on goods and services and the lower the after-tax wage rate, the less is the incentive to supply labor. If the income tax rate is 25 percent and the tax rate on consumption expenditure is 10 percent, a dollar earned buys only 65 cents worth of goods and services. The tax wedge is 35 percent.

ECONOMICS IN ACTION
Some Real-World Tax Wedges

Edward C. Prescott of Arizona State University, who shared the 2004 Nobel Prize for Economic Science, has estimated the tax wedges for a number of countries, among them the United States, the United Kingdom, and France.

The U.S. tax wedge is a combination of 13 percent tax on consumption and 32 percent tax on incomes. The income tax component of the U.S. tax wedge includes Social Security taxes and is the *marginal* tax rate—the tax rate paid on the marginal dollar earned.

Prescott estimates that in France, tax rates on consumption are 33 percent and on incomes are 49 percent.

The estimates for the United Kingdom fall between those for the United States and France. The figure shows these components of the tax wedges in the three countries.

Does the Tax Wedge Matter?

According to Prescott's estimates, the tax wedge has a powerful effect on employment and potential GDP. Potential GDP in France is 30 percent below that of the United States (per person), and the entire difference can be attributed to the difference in the tax wedge in the two countries.

Potential GDP in the United Kingdom is 28 percent below that of the United States (per person), and about a third of the difference arises from the different tax wedges. (The rest is due to different productivities.)

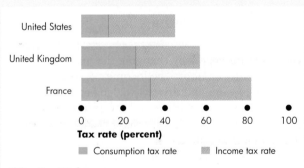

Three Tax Wedges

Source of data: Edward C. Prescott, "Prosperity and Depression," *The American Economic Review*, Vol. 92, No. 2, Papers and Proceedings (May, 2002), pp. 1–15.

Taxes and the Incentive to Save and Invest

A tax on interest income weakens the incentive to save and drives a wedge between the after-tax interest rate earned by savers and the interest rate paid by firms. These effects are analogous to those of a tax on labor income. But they are more serious for two reasons.

First, a tax on labor income lowers the quantity of labor employed and lowers potential GDP, while a tax on capital income lowers the quantity of saving and investment and *slows the growth rate of real GDP*.

Second, the true tax rate on interest income is much higher than that on labor income because of the way in which inflation and taxes on interest income interact. Let's examine this interaction.

Effect of Tax Rate on Real Interest Rate The interest rate that influences investment and saving plans is the *real after-tax interest rate*. The real *after-tax* interest rate subtracts the income tax rate paid on interest income from the real interest rate. But the taxes depend on the nominal interest rate, not the real interest rate. So the higher the inflation rate, the higher is the true tax rate on interest income. Here is an example. Suppose the real interest rate is 4 percent a year and the tax rate is 40 percent.

If there is no inflation, the nominal interest rate equals the real interest rate. The tax on 4 percent interest is 1.6 percent (40 percent of 4 percent), so the real after-tax interest rate is 4 percent minus 1.6 percent, which equals 2.4 percent.

If the inflation rate is 6 percent a year, the nominal interest rate is 10 percent. The tax on 10 percent interest is 4 percent (40 percent of 10 percent), so the real after-tax interest rate is 4 percent minus 4 percent, which equals zero. The true tax rate in this case is not 40 percent but 100 percent!

Effect of Income Tax on Saving and Investment In Fig. 30.6, initially there are no taxes. Also, the government has a balanced budget. The demand for loanable funds curve, which is also the investment demand curve, is *DLF*. The supply of loanable funds curve, which is also the saving supply curve, is *SLF*. The equilibrium interest rate is 3 percent a year, and the quantity of funds borrowed and lent is $2 trillion a year.

A tax on interest income has no effect on the demand for loanable funds. The quantity of investment and borrowing that firms plan to undertake depends only on how productive capital is and what it costs—its

FIGURE 30.6 The Effects of a Tax on Capital Income

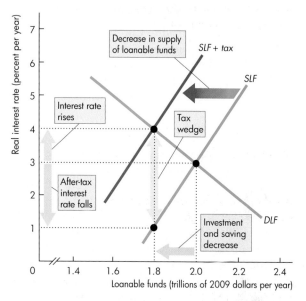

The demand for loanable funds and investment demand curve is *DLF*, and the supply of loanable funds and saving supply curve is *SLF*. With no income tax, the real interest rate is 3 percent a year and investment is $2 trillion. An income tax shifts the supply curve leftward to *SLF + tax*. The interest rate rises to 4 percent a year, the after-tax interest rate falls to 1 percent a year, and investment decreases to $1.8 trillion. With less investment, the real GDP growth rate decreases.

MyEconLab Animation and Draw Graph

real interest rate. But a tax on interest income weakens the incentive to save and lend and decreases the supply of loanable funds. For each dollar of before-tax interest, savers must pay the government an amount determined by the tax code. So savers look at the after-tax real interest rate when they decide how much to save.

When a tax is imposed, saving decreases and the supply of loanable funds curve shifts leftward to *SLF + tax*. The amount of tax payable is measured by the vertical distance between the *SLF* curve and the *SLF + tax* curve. With this smaller supply of loanable funds, the interest rate rises to 4 percent a year but the *after-tax* interest rate falls to 1 percent a year. A tax wedge is driven between the interest rate and the after-tax interest rate, and the equilibrium quantity of loanable funds decreases. Saving and investment also decrease.

ECONOMICS IN THE NEWS

Taxes and the Global Location of Business

U.S. Firms Move Abroad to Cut Taxes

More big U.S. companies are moving abroad. Tax bills are their main reason and some are moving because they worry that U.S. taxes will rise in the future as the tax code changes to shrink the federal budget deficit.

Source: *The Wall Street Journal*, August 28, 2012

SOME FACTS ABOUT CORPORATE INCOME TAXES

- The U.S. corporate income tax rate is among the world's highest.
- Figure 1 shows the corporation income tax rates in a selection of countries.

THE QUESTIONS

- On which factor incomes does the corporate income tax fall?
- How does the U.S. corporate income tax influence investment, potential GDP, and the growth rate?
- How does the U.S. corporate income tax rate influence employment?

THE ANSWERS

- The corporate income tax is a tax on interest earned by capital and profit earned by entrepreneurs.
- The corporate income tax rate influences investment and the level and growth rate of potential GDP by driving a wedge between the interest paid by borrowers and the interest earned by lenders.
- Figure 2 illustrates the corporate income tax wedge in the market for loanable funds.
- The demand for loanable funds is *DLF* and with no corporate income tax, the supply of loanable funds is *SLF*. The equilibrium real interest rate is 3.4 percent a year and this quantity of loanable funds finances saving and investment of $2.5 trillion. (The numbers are assumed but realistic.)
- With the tax wedge from the U.S. 40 percent corporate tax rate, the supply of loanable funds curve is *SLF + U.S. tax*. The real interest rate is 4 percent and investment and saving are only $2 trillion.
- With the smaller tax wedge from Canada's 26 percent corporate tax rate, the supply of loanable funds curve is *SLF + Canada tax*. The real interest rate is lower at 3.8 percent a year and investment

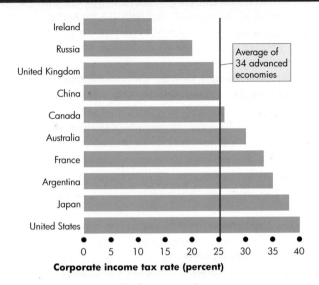

Figure 1 International Comparison of Corporate Income Tax Rates

and saving are higher at $2.2 trillion.

- A smaller amount of saving and investment means a smaller capital stock, smaller potential GDP, and a slower growth rate of potential GDP.
- A smaller capital stock means that labor is less productive, the demand for labor is lower, and the quantity of labor employed is smaller.
- The high U.S. corporate income tax rate lowers incomes and costs jobs.

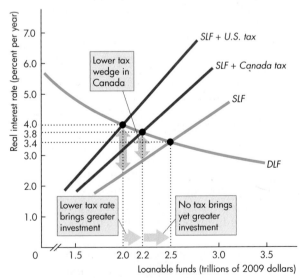

Figure 2 How the Corporate Tax Rate Changes Saving and Investment

MyEconLab More Economics in the News

Tax Revenues and the Laffer Curve

An interesting consequence of the effect of taxes on employment and saving is that a higher tax *rate* does not always bring greater tax *revenue*. A higher tax rate brings in more revenue per dollar earned. But because a higher tax rate decreases the number of dollars earned, two forces operate in opposite directions on the tax revenue collected.

The relationship between the tax rate and the amount of tax revenue collected is called the **Laffer curve**. The curve is so named because Arthur B. Laffer, a member of President Reagan's Economic Policy Advisory Board, drew such a curve on a table napkin and launched the idea that tax *cuts* could *increase* tax revenue.

Figure 30.7 shows a Laffer curve. The tax *rate* is on the *x*-axis, and total tax *revenue* is on the *y*-axis. For tax rates below T^*, an increase in the tax rate increases tax revenue; at T^*, tax revenue is maximized; and a tax rate increase above T^* decreases tax revenue.

Most people think that the United States is on the upward-sloping part of the Laffer curve; so is the United Kingdom. But France might be close to the maximum point or perhaps even beyond it.

The Supply-Side Debate

Before 1980, few economists paid attention to the supply-side effects of taxes on employment and potential GDP. Then, when Ronald Reagan took office as president, a group of supply-siders began to argue the virtues of cutting taxes. Arthur Laffer was one of them. Laffer and his supporters were not held in high esteem among mainstream economists, but they were influential for a period. They correctly argued that tax cuts would increase employment and increase output. But they incorrectly argued that tax cuts would increase tax revenues and decrease the budget deficit. For this prediction to be correct, the United States would have had to be on the "wrong" side of the Laffer curve. Given that U.S. tax rates are among the lowest in the industrial world, it is unlikely that this condition was met. And when the Reagan administration did cut taxes, the budget deficit increased, a fact that reinforces this view.

Supply-side economics became tarnished because of its association with Laffer and came to be called "voodoo economics." But mainstream economists, including Martin Feldstein, a Harvard professor who was Reagan's chief economic adviser, recognized the

power of tax cuts as incentives but took the standard view that tax cuts without spending cuts would swell the budget deficit and bring further serious problems. This view is now widely accepted by economists of all political persuasions.

FIGURE 30.7   A Laffer Curve

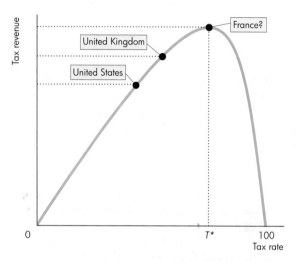

A Laffer curve shows the relationship between the tax rate and tax revenues. For tax rates below T^*, an increase in the tax rate increases tax revenue. At the tax rate T^*, tax revenue is maximized. For tax rates above T^*, an increase in the tax rate decreases tax revenue.

MyEconLab Animation

REVIEW QUIZ

1 How does a tax on labor income influence the equilibrium quantity of employment?
2 How does the tax wedge influence potential GDP?
3 Why are consumption taxes relevant for measuring the tax wedge?
4 Why are income taxes on capital income more powerful than those on labor income?
5 What is the Laffer curve and why is it unlikely that the United States is on the "wrong" side of it?

Work these questions in Study Plan 30.2 and get instant feedback. Do a Key Terms Quiz.   *MyEconLab*

You now know how taxes influence potential GDP and saving and investment. Next we look at the intergenerational effects of fiscal policy.

◆ Generational Effects of Fiscal Policy

Is a budget deficit a burden on future generations? If it is, how will the burden be borne? And is the budget deficit the only burden on future generations? What about the deficit in the Social Security fund? Does it matter who owns the bonds that the government sells to finance its deficit? What about the bonds owned by foreigners? Won't repaying those bonds impose a bigger burden than repaying bonds owned by Americans?

To answer questions like these, we use a tool called **generational accounting**—an accounting system that measures the lifetime tax burden and benefits of each generation. This accounting system was developed by Alan Auerbach of the University of Pennsylvania and Laurence Kotlikoff of Boston University. Generational accounts for the United States have been prepared by Jagadeesh Gokhale of the Cato Institute and Kent Smetters of the Wharton School at the University of Pennsylvania.

Generational Accounting and Present Value

Income taxes and Social Security taxes are paid by people who have jobs. Social Security benefits are paid to people after they retire. So to compare taxes and benefits, we must compare the value of taxes paid by people during their working years with the benefits received in their retirement years. To compare the value of an amount of money at one date with that at a later date, we use the concept of present value. A *present value* is an amount of money that, if invested today, will grow to equal a given future amount when the interest that it earns is taken into account. We can compare dollars today with dollars in 2065 or any other future year by using present values.

For example, if the interest rate is 5 percent a year, $1,000 invested today will grow, with interest, to $11,467 after 50 years. So the present value (in 2015) of $11,467 in 2065 is $1,000.

By using present values, we can assess the magnitude of the government's debts to older Americans in the form of pensions and medical benefits.

But the assumed interest rate and growth rate of taxes and benefits critically influence the answers we get. For example, at an interest rate of 3 percent a year, the present value (in 2015) of $11,467 in 2065

is $2,616. The lower the interest rate, the greater is the present value of a given future amount.

Because there is uncertainty about the proper interest rate to use to calculate present values, plausible alternative numbers are used to estimate a range of present values.

Using generational accounting and present values, economists have studied the situation facing the federal government arising from its Social Security obligations, and they have found a time bomb!

The Social Security Time Bomb

When Social Security was introduced in the New Deal of the 1930s, today's demographic situation was not foreseen. The age distribution of the U.S. population today is dominated by the surge in the birth rate after World War II that created what is called the "baby boom generation." There are 77 million "baby boomers."

The first of the baby boomers started collecting Social Security pensions in 2008 and in 2011 they became eligible for Medicare benefits. By 2030, all the baby boomers will have reached retirement age and the population supported by Social Security and Medicare benefits will have doubled.

Under the existing laws, the federal government has an obligation to this increasing number of citizens to pay pensions and Medicare benefits on an already declared scale. These obligations are a debt owed by the government and are just as real as the bonds that the government issues to finance its current budget deficit.

To assess the full extent of the government's obligations, economists use the concept of fiscal imbalance. **Fiscal imbalance** is the present value of the government's commitments to pay benefits minus the present value of its tax revenues. Fiscal imbalance is an attempt to measure the scale of the government's true liabilities.

In an update, Gokhale estimates that the Social Security and Medicare fiscal imbalance was $68 trillion in 2014. To put the $68 trillion in perspective, note that U.S. GDP in 2014 was $17 trillion. So the fiscal imbalance was 4 times the value of one year's production. Furthermore, the fiscal imbalance grows every year by an amount that in 2014 was approaching $2 trillion.

These are enormous numbers and point to a catastrophic future. How can the federal government meet its Social Security obligations? Gokhale and

Smetters consider four alternatives. They are

- Raise income taxes
- Raise Social Security taxes
- Cut Social Security benefits
- Cut federal government discretionary spending

Gokhale and Smetters estimate that if we had started in 2003 and made only one of these changes, income taxes would need to be raised by 69 percent, or Social Security taxes raised by 95 percent, or Social Security benefits cut by 56 percent. Even if the government stopped all its discretionary spending, including that on national defense, it would not be able to pay its bills. By combining the four measures, the pain from each could be lessened, but the pain would still be severe.

A further way of meeting these obligations is to pay by printing money. As you learned in Chapter 25 (see pp. 608–609), the consequence of this solution would be a seriously high inflation rate.

Generational Imbalance

A fiscal imbalance must eventually be corrected and when it is, people either pay higher taxes or receive lower benefits. The concept of generational imbalance tells us who will pay. **Generational imbalance** is the division of the fiscal imbalance between the current and future generations, assuming that the current generation will enjoy the existing levels of taxes and benefits.

Figure 30.8 shows an estimate of how the fiscal imbalance is distributed across the current generation (those born before 1988) and the future generation (those born in or after 1988). The generational imbalance also shows that the major source of the imbalance is Medicare. Social Security pension benefits create a fiscal imbalance, but these benefits will be more than fully paid for by the current generation. But the current generation will not pay for all its Medicare costs, and the balance will fall on future generations. If we sum all the items, the current generation will pay 83 percent and future generations will pay 17 percent of the fiscal imbalance.

Because the estimated fiscal imbalance is so large, it is not possible to predict how it will be resolved. But we can predict that the outcome will involve both lower benefits and higher taxes, or paying bills with new money and creating inflation.

The Fed would have to cooperate if inflation were to be used to deal with the imbalance, and this cooperation might be hard to obtain.

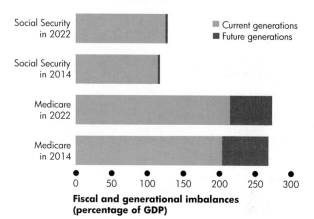

FIGURE 30.8 Fiscal and Generational Imbalances

The bars show the scale of the fiscal imbalance. The largest component at more than 250 percent of GDP is Medicare benefits. These benefits are also the main component of the generational imbalance. Social Security pensions are paid for entirely by the current generation.

Source of data: Jagadeesh Gokhale, *The Government Debt Iceberg*, The Institute of Economic Affairs, London, 2014.

—— MyEconLab Animation ——

International Debt

So far in our discussion of government deficits and debts, we've ignored the role played by the rest of the world. We'll conclude this discussion by considering the role and magnitude of international debt.

You've seen that borrowing from the rest of the world is one source of loanable funds. And you've also seen that this source of funds became larger during the late 1990s and 2000s.

How large is the contribution of the rest of the world? How much business investment have we paid for by borrowing from the rest of the world? And how much U.S. government debt is held abroad?

Table 30.2 answers these questions. In June 2014, the United States had a net debt to the rest of the world of $11.7 trillion. Of that debt, $5.8 trillion was U.S. government borrowing—about 48 percent of total U.S. government debt. U.S. corporations had used $8.6 trillion of foreign funds (in bonds and equities).

The international debt of the United States is important because, when that debt is repaid, the United States will transfer real resources to the rest of

TABLE 30.2   What the United States Owed
the Rest of the World in
June 2014

	$ trillions
(a) U.S. liabilities	
Deposits in U.S. banks	1.2
U.S. government securities	5.8
U.S. corporate bonds and equities	8.6
Other items (net)	−3.9
Total	**11.7**
(b) U.S. government securities	
Held by rest of world	5.8
Held in the United States	6.2
Total	**12.0**

Source of data: Federal Reserve Board.

the world. Instead of running a large net exports deficit, the United States will need a surplus of exports over imports. To make a surplus possible, U.S. saving must increase and consumption must decrease. Some tough choices lie ahead.

 REVIEW QUIZ

1 What is a present value?
2 Distinguish between fiscal imbalance and generational imbalance.
3 How large was the estimated U.S. fiscal imbalance in 2014 and how did it divide between current and future generations?
4 What is the source of the U.S. fiscal imbalance and what are the painful choices that we face?
5 How much of U.S. government debt is held by the rest of the world?

Work these questions in Study Plan 30.3 and get instant feedback. Do a Key Terms Quiz.   MyEconLab

You now know how the supply-side effects of fiscal policy work and you've seen the shocking scale of fiscal imbalance. We conclude this chapter by looking at fiscal policy as a tool for fighting a recession.

◆ Fiscal Stimulus

The 2008–2009 recession brought Keynesian macroeconomic ideas (see Chapter 27, pp. 664–665) back into fashion and put a spotlight on **fiscal stimulus**—the use of fiscal policy to increase production and employment. But whether fiscal policy is truly stimulating, and if so, how stimulating, are questions that generate much discussion and disagreement. You're now going to explore these questions.

Fiscal stimulus can be either *automatic* or *discretionary.* A fiscal policy action that is triggered by the state of the economy with no action by government is called **automatic fiscal policy.** The increase in total unemployment benefits triggered by the massive rise in the unemployment rate through 2009 is an example of automatic fiscal policy.

A fiscal policy action initiated by an act of Congress is called **discretionary fiscal policy.** It requires a change in a spending program or in a tax law. A fiscal stimulus act passed by Congress in 2009 (see *Economics in Action* on p. 746) is an example of discretionary fiscal policy.

Whether automatic or discretionary, an increase in government outlays or a decrease in government receipts can stimulate production and jobs. An increase in expenditure on goods and services directly increases aggregate expenditure. And an increase in transfer payments (such as unemployment benefits) or a decrease in tax revenues increases disposable income, which enables people to increase consumption expenditure. Lower taxes also strengthen the incentives to work and invest.

We'll begin by looking at automatic fiscal policy and the interaction between the business cycle and the budget balance.

Automatic Fiscal Policy and Cyclical and Structural Budget Balances

Two items in the government budget change automatically in response to the state of the economy. They are *tax revenues* and *needs-tested spending.*

Automatic Changes in Tax Revenues The tax laws that Congress enacts don't legislate the number of tax *dollars* the government will raise. Rather they define the tax *rates* that people must pay. Tax dollars paid depend on tax rates and incomes. But incomes vary with real GDP, so tax revenues depend on real GDP. When real GDP increases in a business cycle expansion, wages and profits rise, so tax revenues from these incomes rise. When real GDP decreases in a recession, wages and profits fall, so tax revenues fall.

Needs-Tested Spending The government creates programs that pay benefits to qualified people and businesses. The spending on these programs results in transfer payments that depend on the economic state of individual citizens and businesses. When the economy expands, unemployment falls, the number of people experiencing economic hardship decreases, so needs-tested spending decreases. When the economy is in a recession, unemployment is high and the number of people experiencing economic hardship increases, so needs-tested spending on unemployment benefits and food stamps increases.

Automatic Stimulus Because government receipts fall and outlays increase in a recession, the budget provides automatic stimulus that helps to shrink the recessionary gap. Similarly, because receipts rise and outlays decrease in a boom, the budget provides automatic restraint to shrink an inflationary gap.

Cyclical and Structural Budget Balances To identify the government budget deficit that arises from the business cycle, we distinguish between the **structural surplus or deficit**, which is the budget balance that would occur if the economy were at full employment, and the **cyclical surplus or deficit**, which is the actual surplus or deficit *minus* the structural surplus or deficit.

Figure 30.9 illustrates these concepts. Outlays *decrease* as real GDP *increases*, so the outlays curve slopes downward; and receipts *increase* as real GDP *increases*, so the receipts curve slopes upward.

In Fig. 30.9(a), potential GDP is $17 trillion and if real GDP equals potential GDP, the government has a *balanced budget*. There is no structural surplus or deficit. But there might be a cyclical surplus or deficit. If real GDP is less than potential GDP at $16 trillion, outlays exceed receipts and there is a *cyclical deficit*. If real GDP is greater than potential GDP at $18 trillion, outlays are less than receipts and there is a *cyclical surplus*.

In Fig. 30.9(b), if potential GDP equals $17 trillion (line *B*), the *structural balance is zero*. But if potential GDP is $16 trillion (line *A*), the government budget has a *structural deficit*. And if potential GDP is $18 trillion (line *C*), the government budget has a *structural surplus*.

FIGURE 30.9 Cyclical and Structural Surpluses and Deficits

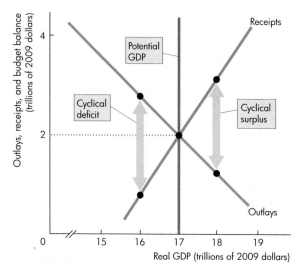

(a) Cyclical deficit and cyclical surplus

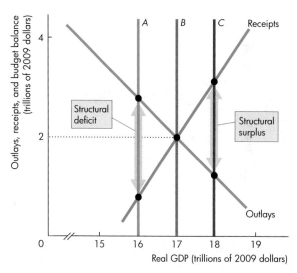

(b) Structural deficit and structural surplus

In part (a), potential GDP is $17 trillion. When real GDP is less than potential GDP, the budget is in deficit and it is a *cyclical deficit*. When real GDP exceeds potential GDP, the budget is in surplus and it is a *cyclical surplus*. The government has a *balanced budget* when real GDP equals potential GDP.

In part (b), if potential GDP is $16 trillion, the deficit is a *structural deficit* and if potential GDP is $18 trillion, the surplus is a *structural surplus*. If potential GDP is $17 trillion, the budget is in structural balance.

MyEconLab Animation

U.S. Structural Budget Balance in 2014 The U.S. federal budget in 2014 was in deficit at $0.64 trillion and the recessionary gap (the gap between real GDP and potential GDP) was $0.7 trillion. With a large recessionary gap, you would expect some of the deficit to be cyclical. But how much of the 2014 deficit was cyclical and how much was structural?

The Congressional Budget Office (CBO) answers this question by analyzing the detailed items in the budget. According to the CBO, the cyclical deficit in 2014 was $0.18 trillion and the structural deficit was $0.46 trillion. Figure 30.10 shows the cyclical and structural deficit between 1990 and 2015.

You can see that the structural deficit was small in 2007, increased in 2008, and exploded in 2009. The 2009 fiscal stimulus package (see *Economics in Action*) created most of this structural deficit.

When full employment returns, which the CBO says will be in 2018, the cyclical deficit will vanish. But the structural deficit must be addressed by further acts of Congress. No one knows the discretionary measures that will be taken to reduce the structural deficit and this awkward fact creates enormous uncertainty.

FIGURE 30.10   U.S. Cyclical and Structural Budget Balance

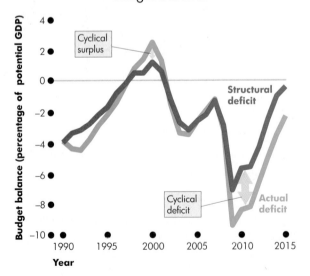

As real GDP shrank in the 2008–2009 recession, receipts fell, outlays increased, and the budget deficit increased. But the cyclical deficit is small compared to the actual deficit.

Source of data: Congressional Budget Office.

————— MyEconLab Animation —————

ECONOMICS IN ACTION
The 2009 Fiscal Stimulus Package

Congress passed the *American Recovery and Reinvestment Act of 2009* (the 2009 Fiscal Stimulus Act) in February 2009, and President Obama signed it into law at an economic forum he hosted in Denver. This act was the third and most ambitious in a series of stimulus packages and its purpose was to increase investment and consumer expenditure and lead to the creation of jobs.

The total package added $862 billion to the federal government's budget deficit: $288 billion from tax cuts and the rest from increased spending. The spending increases included payments to state and local governments ($144 billion), spending on infrastructure and science projects ($111 billion), and programs in healthcare ($59 billion), education and training ($53 billion), and energy ($43 billion).

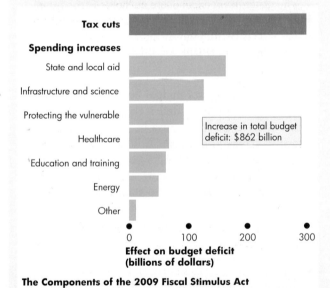

The Components of the 2009 Fiscal Stimulus Act

The president signs the 2009 fiscal stimulus act.

Discretionary Fiscal Stimulus

Most discussion of *discretionary* fiscal stimulus focuses on its effects on aggregate demand. But you've seen (on pp. 737–739) that taxes influence aggregate supply and that the balance of taxes and spending—the government budget deficit—can crowd out investment and slow the pace of economic growth. So discretionary fiscal stimulus has both supply-side and demand-side effects that end up determining its overall effectiveness.

We're going to begin our examination of discretionary fiscal stimulus by looking at its effects on aggregate demand.

Fiscal Stimulus and Aggregate Demand

Changes in government expenditure and changes in taxes change aggregate demand by their influence on spending plans, and they also have multiplier effects.

Let's look at the two main fiscal policy multipliers: the government expenditure and tax multipliers.

The **government expenditure multiplier** is the quantitative effect of a change in government expenditure on real GDP. Because government expenditure is a component of aggregate expenditure, an increase in government spending increases aggregate expenditure and real GDP. But does a $1 billion increase in government expenditure increase real GDP by $1 billion, or more than $1 billion, or less than $1 billion?

When an increase in government expenditure increases real GDP, incomes rise and the higher incomes bring an increase in consumption expenditure. If this were the only consequence of increased government expenditure, the government expenditure multiplier would be greater than 1.

But an increase in government expenditure increases government borrowing (or decreases government lending if there is a budget surplus) and raises the real interest rate. With a higher cost of borrowing, investment decreases, which partly offsets the increase in government spending. If this were the only consequence of increased government expenditure, the multiplier would be less than 1.

The actual multiplier depends on which of the above effects is stronger and the consensus is that the crowding-out effect is strong enough to make the government expenditure multiplier less than 1.

The **tax multiplier** is the quantitative effect of a change in taxes on real GDP. The demand-side effects of a tax cut are likely to be smaller than an equivalent increase in government expenditure. The reason is that a tax cut influences aggregate demand by increasing

disposable income, only part of which gets spent. So the initial injection of expenditure from a $1 billion tax cut is less than $1 billion.

A tax cut has similar crowding-out consequences to a spending increase. It increases government borrowing (or decreases government lending), raises the real interest rate, and cuts investment.

The tax multiplier effect on aggregate demand depends on these two opposing effects and is probably quite small.

Graphical Illustration of Fiscal Stimulus

Figure 30.11 shows how fiscal stimulus is supposed to work if it is perfectly executed and has its desired effects.

Potential GDP is $17 trillion and real GDP is below potential at $16 trillion so the economy has a recessionary gap of $1 trillion.

To restore full employment, the government passes a fiscal stimulus package. An increase in

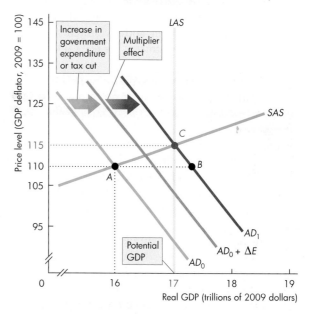

FIGURE 30.11   Expansionary Fiscal Policy

Potential GDP is $17 trillion, real GDP is $16 trillion, and there is a $1 trillion recessionary gap. An increase in government expenditure and a tax cut increase aggregate expenditure by ΔE. The multiplier increases consumption expenditure. The AD curve shifts rightward to AD_1, the price level rises to 115, real GDP increases to $17 trillion, and the recessionary gap is eliminated.

government expenditure and a tax cut increase aggregate expenditure by ΔE. If this were the only change in spending plans, the AD curve would shift rightward to become the curve labeled $AD_0 + \Delta E$ in Fig. 30.11. But if fiscal stimulus sets off a multiplier process that increases consumption expenditure, and does not crowd out much investment expenditure, aggregate demand increases further and the AD curve shifts to AD_1.

With no change in the price level, the economy would move from point A to point B on AD_1. But the increase in aggregate demand brings a rise in the price level along the upward-sloping SAS curve and the economy moves to point C.

At point C, the economy returns to full employment and the recessionary gap is eliminated.

Fiscal Stimulus and Aggregate Supply You've seen earlier in this chapter that taxes influence aggregate supply. A tax on labor income (on wages) drives a wedge between the cost of labor and the take-home pay of workers and lowers employment and output (p. 738). A tax on capital income (on interest) drives a wedge between the cost of borrowing and the return to lending and lowers saving and investment (p. 739). With less saving and investment, the real GDP growth rate slows.

These negative effects of taxes on real GDP and its growth rate and on employment mean that a tax *cut* increases real GDP and its growth rate and increases employment.

These supply-side effects of a tax cut occur along with the demand-side effects and are probably much larger than the demand-side effects and make the overall tax multiplier much larger than the government expenditure multiplier—see *Economics in Action.*

An increase in government expenditure financed by borrowing increases the demand for loanable funds and raises the real interest rate, which in turn lowers investment and private saving. This cut in investment is the main reason why the government expenditure multiplier is so small and why a deficit-financed increase in government spending ends up making only a small contribution to job creation. And because government expenditure crowds out investment, it lowers future real GDP.

So a fiscal stimulus package that is heavy on tax cuts and light on government spending works. But an increase in government expenditure alone is not an effective way to stimulate production and create jobs.

The description of the effects of discretionary fiscal stimulus and its graphical illustration in Fig. 30.11 make it look easy: Calculate the recessionary gap and the multipliers, change government expenditure and taxes, and eliminate the gap. In reality, things are not that easy.

Getting the magnitude and the timing right is difficult, and we'll now examine this challenge.

Magnitude of Stimulus Economists have diverging views about the size of the government spending and tax multipliers because there is insufficient empirical evidence on which to pin their size with accuracy. This fact makes it impossible for Congress to determine the amount of stimulus needed to close a given

ECONOMICS IN ACTION
How Big Are the Fiscal Stimulus Multipliers?

When the 2009 fiscal stimulus package cut taxes by $300 billion and increased government spending by a little over $500 billion, by how much did aggregate expenditure and real GDP change? How big were the fiscal policy multipliers? Was the government expenditure multiplier larger than the tax multiplier? These questions are about the multiplier effects on *equilibrium real GDP*, not just on aggregate demand.

President Obama's chief economic adviser in 2009, Christina Romer, a University of California, Berkeley, professor, expected the government expenditure multiplier to be about 1.5. So she was expecting the spending increase of $500 billion to go a long way toward closing the $1 trillion output gap by some time in 2010.

Robert Barro, a professor at Harvard University, says this multiplier number is not in line with previous experience. Based on his calculations, an additional $500 billion of government spending would increase aggregate expenditure by only $250 billion because it would lower private spending in a crowding-out effect by $250 billion—the multiplier is 0.5.

Harald Uhlig, a professor at the University of Chicago, says that the government expenditure multiplier on real GDP is even smaller and lies between 0.3 and 0.4, so that a $500 billion increase in government spending increases aggregate expenditure by between $150 billion and $200 billion.

output gap. Further, the actual output gap is not known and can only be estimated with error. For these two reasons, discretionary fiscal policy is risky.

Time Lags Discretionary fiscal stimulus actions are also seriously hampered by three time lags:

- Recognition lag
- Law-making lag
- Impact lag

Recognition Lag The recognition lag is the time it takes to figure out that fiscal policy actions are needed. This process involves assessing the current state of the economy and forecasting its future state.

Law-Making Lag The *law-making lag* is the time it takes Congress to pass the laws needed to change taxes or spending. This process takes time because each member of Congress has a different idea about what is the best tax or spending program to change, so long debates and committee meetings are needed to reconcile conflicting views. The economy might benefit from fiscal stimulation today, but by the time Congress acts, a different fiscal medicine might be needed.

Impact Lag The *impact lag* is the time it takes from passing a tax or spending change to its effects on real GDP being felt. This lag depends partly on the speed with which government agencies can act and partly on the timing of changes in spending plans by households and businesses. These changes are spread out over a number of quarters and possibly a number of years.

Economic forecasting is steadily improving, but it remains inexact and subject to error. The range of uncertainty about the magnitudes of the spending and tax multipliers make discretionary fiscal stimulus an imprecise tool for boosting production and jobs and the crowding out consequences raise serious questions about its effects on long-term economic growth.

There is greater agreement about tax multipliers. Because tax cuts strengthen the incentive to work and to invest, they increase aggregate supply as well as aggregate demand.

These multipliers get bigger as more time elapses. Harald Uhlig says that after one year, the tax multiplier is 0.5 so that the $300 billion tax cut would increase real GDP by about $150 billion by early 2010. But with two years of time to respond, real GDP would be $600 billion higher—a multiplier of 2. And after three years, the tax multiplier builds up to more than 6.

The implications of the work of Barro and Uhlig are that tax cuts are a powerful way to stimulate real GDP and employment but spending increases are not effective.

Christina Romer agrees that the economy hasn't performed in line with a multiplier of 1.5 but says other factors deteriorated and without the fiscal stimulus, the outcome would have been even worse.

Christina Romer: 1.5

Robert Barro: 0.5

Harald Uhlig: 0.4

◆ REVIEW QUIZ

1 What is the distinction between automatic and discretionary fiscal policy?
2 How do taxes and needs-tested spending programs work as automatic fiscal policy to dampen the business cycle?
3 How do we tell whether a budget deficit needs discretionary action to remove it?
4 How can the federal government use discretionary fiscal policy to stimulate the economy?
5 Why might fiscal stimulus crowd out investment?

Work these questions in Study Plan 30.4 and get instant feedback. Do a Key Terms Quiz.   MyEconLab

◆ You've now seen the effects of fiscal policy, and *Economics in the News* on pp. 750–751 applies what you've learned to examine Japan's extreme situation and the fiscal policy challenge it faces.

A Fiscal Policy Challenge

Japanese Debt: Still Climbing

The Financial Times
March 24, 2014

Last summer Takeshi Fujimaki ran for parliament on a platform of economic Armageddon. Japan's debt was out of control, he told voters, and it was only a matter of time before everyone dumped government bonds, sending yields soaring, and the yen skittering all the way to 1,000 against the dollar. ...

Mr. Fujimaki is not a lone crank. Although few share his sense of abject despair, no one disputes that Japan's debt is worryingly high. The International Monetary Fund and OECD both warn that deep cuts to spending must be made, beyond the government's basic pledge to balance its books—excluding debt-servicing costs—by 2020. ...

Last ... week the Diet waved through its biggest budget for the fiscal year ahead. Gross debt issuance comes to a record Y182tn ($1.78tn), about the same size as the economy of India. ...

Mr. Abe is going all-out for growth because he has to. Barring the type of scenario outlined by Mr. Fujimaki, only growth can fix its debt problem. ...

State finances have deteriorated partly because of demography. Social Security payments to a fast-ageing population have nearly tripled since 1990 to Y31tn—about a third of the total budget—in the fiscal year beginning in April. ...

But the real problem is that as the economy languished, Japan collected less and less tax, forcing the state to borrow to plug gaps between income and expenditure. ...

MyEconLab More Economics in the News

ESSENCE OF THE STORY

- Since 1990, slow real GDP growth has lowered tax revenues, a fast-ageing population has nearly tripled Social Security payments, and Japan's government debt has soared.

- Only faster real GDP growth or inflation can fix Japan's debt problem.

- The government has pledged to have no deficit—excluding debt interest—by 2020.

- The IMF and OECD say even deeper government spending cuts must be made.

- In March 2014, the Diet (parliament) passed its biggest budget ever, borrowing 182 trillion yen ($1.78 trillion).

ECONOMIC ANALYSIS

- Japan's fiscal policy challenge described in the news article is finding a way to stop and then reverse an ever rising government debt ratio—government debt as a percentage of GDP.

- Figure 1 shows the scale and upward direction of the problem. Gross debt was 250 percent of GDP in 2014, up from about 70 percent in 1990.

- The news article says that only faster growth or inflation can fix the debt problem. The debt ratio = Debt ÷ GDP. And GDP = PY, where P is the price level and Y is real GDP, so the debt ratio = Debt ÷ PY. Faster growth increases Y faster and inflation increases P faster, either of which lowers the debt ratio.

- There is a third way to fix the debt problem: Cut government spending. And that is the only effective way. The reason is that high government spending crowds out investment and without an increase in investment, real GDP cannot grow faster.

- Figure 2 shows how government spending has crowded out investment. In 1990, investment at 34 percent of GDP was larger than government spending (expenditure on goods and services and transfer payments) at 30 percent. By 2014, investment had shrunk to 20 percent and government spending had increased to 40 percent of GDP.

- The problem with cutting government spending is that in the short run, it decreases aggregate demand and widens the output gap.

- Figure 3 illustrates this short-run consequence of a government spending cut.

- In 2013, Japan's potential GDP was 537 trillion yen, shown by the long-run aggregate supply curve, LAS. The short-run aggregate supply curve was SAS.

- With the 2013 aggregate demand curve AD_0, real GDP was 525 trillion yen and the price level was 91 (91 percent of its 2009 level).

- Japan was experiencing stagnation and deflation.

- A fiscal policy aimed at cutting government expenditure and lowering the budget deficit by also increasing taxes would decrease aggregate demand.

- If aggregate demand decreased to AD_1, real GDP would decrease to 500 trillion yen and the recessionary gap would widen.

- Monetary policy might be used alongside fiscal policy to avoid this outcome and prevent real GDP from falling.

- Japan's government budget and debt is an extreme version of the United States'.

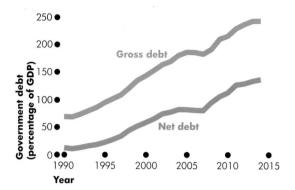

Figure 1 Japan's Government Debt

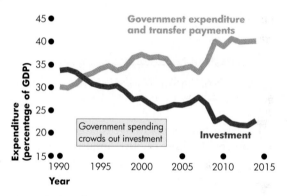

Figure 2 Crowding Out

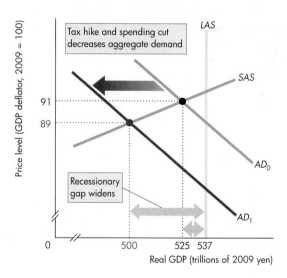

Figure 3 Short-Run Effects of Budget Cuts

- Like Japan, the United States has an aging population that will bring persistently increasing government expenditure on healthcare and Social Security.

- The United States' challenge is to contain these expenditures and avoid crowding out investment and stopping growth.

SUMMARY

Key Points

The Federal Budget (pp. 730–736)

- The federal budget is used to achieve macroeconomic objectives.
- Tax revenues can exceed, equal, or fall short of outlays—the budget can be in surplus, balanced, or in deficit.
- Budget deficits create government debt.

Working Problems 1 and 2 will give you a better understanding of the federal budget.

Supply-Side Effects of Fiscal Policy (pp. 737–741)

- Fiscal policy has supply-side effects because taxes weaken the incentive to work and decrease employment and potential GDP.
- The U.S. labor market tax wedge is large, but it is small compared to those of other industrialized countries.
- Fiscal policy has supply-side effects because taxes weaken the incentive to save and invest, which lowers the growth rate of real GDP.
- The Laffer curve shows the relationship between the tax rate and the amount of tax revenue collected.

Working Problems 3 to 5 will give you a better understanding of the supply-side effects of fiscal policy.

Generational Effects of Fiscal Policy (pp. 742–744)

- Generational accounting measures the lifetime tax burden and benefits of each generation.
- A major study estimated the U.S. fiscal imbalance to be $68 trillion—4 times the value of one year's production.
- Future generations will pay for 17 percent of the benefits of the current generation.
- About 48 percent of U.S. government debt is held by the rest of the world.

Working Problem 6 will give you a better understanding of the generational effects of fiscal policy.

Fiscal Stimulus (pp. 744–749)

- Fiscal policy can be automatic or discretionary.
- Automatic fiscal policy might moderate the business cycle by stimulating demand in recession and restraining demand in a boom.
- Discretionary fiscal stimulus influences aggregate demand *and* aggregate supply.
- Discretionary changes in government expenditure or taxes have multiplier effects of uncertain magnitude but the tax multiplier is likely the larger one.
- Fiscal stimulus policies are hampered by uncertainty about the multipliers and by time lags (law-making lags and the difficulty of correctly diagnosing and forecasting the state of the economy).

Working Problems 7 to 11 will give you a better understanding of fiscal stimulus.

Key Terms

MyEconLab Key Terms Quiz

Automatic fiscal policy, 744
Balanced budget, 732
Budget deficit, 732
Budget surplus, 732
Council of Economic Advisers, 731
Cyclical surplus or deficit, 745

Discretionary fiscal policy, 744
Federal budget, 730
Fiscal imbalance, 742
Fiscal policy, 730
Fiscal stimulus, 744
Generational accounting, 742
Generational imbalance, 743

Government debt, 734
Government expenditure multiplier, 747
Laffer curve, 741
Structural surplus or deficit, 745
Tax multiplier, 747
Tax wedge, 738

WORKED PROBLEM

MyEconLab   You can work this problem in Chapter 30 Study Plan.

The economy is at full employment, the inflation rate is 2 percent a year, and the federal budget deficit is 3.5 percent of GDP. Congress wants to make real GDP grow faster and is debating whether to spend more on infrastructure or to cut income taxes.

Questions

1. What would be the short-run effects of new infrastructure expenditure?
2. What would be the long-run effects of new infrastructure expenditure?
3. How would lower income taxes change the macroeconomic variables?
4. Which policy would increase the economic growth rate?

Solutions

1. With no change in government receipts, the infrastructure expenditure will increase government outlays and the budget deficit. To fund the infrastructure work the government goes to the loanable funds market. The demand for loanable funds increases and, with no change in the supply of loanable funds, the real interest rate rises. A higher real interest rate increases private saving and decreases private investment. The increased government expenditure crowds out some private investment.

    Aggregate demand increases by an amount equal to the infrastructure expenditure minus the crowded-out private investment plus the induced increase in consumption expenditure. With no change in aggregate supply, real GDP increases to above full employment and creates an inflationary gap.

    Key Point: In the short run, a change in government expenditure changes the budget balance, the real interest rate, the quantities of private saving and private investment, aggregate demand, real GDP, and the output gap.

2. Two further things change in the long run. (1) An inflationary gap makes the money wage rate rise, and (2) the increase in infrastructure capital increases potential GDP.

    The higher money wage rate decreases short-run aggregate supply and the increase in potential GDP lessens that decrease. The price level rises, and real GDP decreases to its new, higher, full-employment level.

    Key Point: An output gap brings changes in the labor market and the goods market, and increased capital increases potential GDP. In the long run, real GDP is at a higher full-employment equilibrium.

3. A cut in the tax rate on wage income increases the supply of labor, increases the quantity of labor employed, and increases potential GDP. A cut in the tax rate on interest income increases saving and investment, increases the quantity of capital, and increases potential GDP.

    Lower tax receipts increase the budget deficit, which sends the government to the loanable funds market. The demand for loanable funds increases, which lessens the effect of the cut in the tax on interest income.

    In the short run, the tax cut increases aggregate demand and brings an inflationary gap, which increases the money wage rate and decreases short-run aggregate supply.

    In the long run, the economy returns to full-employment equilibrium, but one in which more people are employed and real GDP is larger.

    Key Point: A change in the income tax rate changes the labor market equilibrium and the loanable funds market equilibrium. Employment, private investment, and potential GDP change.

4. A change in the real GDP growth rate is a long-run effect.

    In the long run, an increase in infrastructure capital increases potential GDP and crowds out private investment, which decreases potential GDP. If the crowding out is incomplete, a larger capital stock increases potential GDP. To make real GDP grow faster, capital must keep increasing at a faster pace. A one-shot expenditure on new infrastructure does not have this effect.

    A lower tax rate on interest income increases private investment, which increases the rate of capital accumulation and increases the growth rate of real GDP.

    Key Point: A one-shot investment in infrastructure increases real GDP but not economic growth. A cut in the tax rate on interest income increases investment, which increases the rate of capital accumulation and the real GDP growth rate.

◆ STUDY PLAN PROBLEMS AND APPLICATIONS

MyEconLab   You can work Problems 1 to 11 in Chapter 30 Study Plan and get instant feedback.

The Federal Budget (Study Plan 30.1)

Use the following news clip to work Problems 1 and 2.

Economy Needs Treatment

It's the debt, stupid! Only when the government sets out a credible business plan will confidence and hiring rebound.

> Source: *The Wall Street Journal*, October 7, 2010

1. How has the U.S. government debt changed since 2008? What are the sources of the change in U.S. government debt?

2. What would be a "credible business plan" for the government to adopt?

Supply-Side Effects of Fiscal Policy (Study Plan 30.2)

3. The government is considering raising the tax rate on labor income. Explain the supply-side effects of such an action and use appropriate graphs to show the *directions* of change, not exact magnitudes. What will happen to
   a. The supply of labor and why?
   b. The demand for labor and why?
   c. Equilibrium employment and why?
   d. The equilibrium before-tax wage rate and why?
   e. The equilibrium after-tax wage rate and why?
   f. Potential GDP?

4. What fiscal policy action might increase investment and speed economic growth? Explain how the policy action would work.

5. Suppose that instead of taxing *nominal* capital income, the government taxed *real* capital income. Use appropriate graphs to explain and illustrate the effect that this change would have on
   a. The tax rate on capital income.
   b. The supply of and demand for loanable funds.
   c. Investment and the real interest rate.

Generational Effects of Fiscal Policy (Study Plan 30.3)

6. Under current policies, a plausible projection is that U.S. public debt will reach 250 percent of GDP in 30 years and 500 percent in 50 years.
   a. What is a fiscal imbalance? How might the U.S. government reduce the fiscal imbalance?
   b. How would your answer to part (a) influence the generational imbalance?

Fiscal Stimulus (Study Plan 30.4)

7. The economy is in a recession, and the recessionary gap is large.
   a. Describe the discretionary and automatic fiscal policy actions that might occur.
   b. Describe a discretionary fiscal stimulus package that could be used that would *not* bring an increase in the budget deficit.
   c. Explain the risks of discretionary fiscal policy in this situation.

8. An economy is in a recession with a large recessionary gap and a government budget deficit.
   a. Is the government budget deficit a structural deficit or a cyclical deficit? Explain.
   b. Explain how automatic fiscal policy is changing the output gap.
   c. If the government increases its discretionary expenditure, explain how the structural deficit might change.

Use the following news clip and fact to work Problems 9 to 11.

Senate Approves Obama Tax Cut Plan

The U.S. Senate has passed legislation to extend the Bush-era tax cuts for high-income earners to middle-class Americans earning up to $250,000 per year.

> Source: *Financial Times*, July 26, 2012

Fact: Middle and low-income earners spend almost all their disposable incomes. High-income earners save a significant part of their disposable incomes.

9. a. Explain the intended effect of extending tax cuts to middle-class Americans but not for high-income families. Draw a graph to illustrate the intended effect.
   b. Explain why the effect of tax cuts depends on who receives them.

10. What would have a larger effect on aggregate demand: extending the Bush-era tax cuts to everyone; extending them to the middle-class only; or extending them for high-income earners only? How would each alternative compare with no tax cuts but an equivalent increase in government expenditure?

11. Compare the impact on equilibrium real GDP of a same-sized decrease in taxes and increase in government expenditure on goods and services.

ADDITIONAL PROBLEMS AND APPLICATIONS

MyEconLab   You can work these problems in MyEconLab if assigned by your instructor.

The Federal Budget

12. **2012 Deficit: Smaller, But Still Big**

    The Congressional Budget Office said the budget deficit was about $1.1 trillion in fiscal year 2012. That is about $200 billion smaller than in 2011, but still ranks as the fourth-largest deficit since World War II.

    > Source: The Congressional Budget Office, October 5, 2012

    Of the components of government outlays and receipts, which have changed most to contribute to the huge budget deficits in 2011 and 2012?

Supply-Side Effects of Fiscal Policy

Use the following information to work Problems 13 and 14.

Suppose that investment is $1,600 billion, saving is $1,400 billion, government expenditure on goods and services is $1,500 billion, exports are $2,000 billion, and imports are $2,500 billion.

13. Calculate the amount of tax revenue and the government budget balance.

14. a. Explain the impact of the government budget balance on investment.

    b. What fiscal policy action might increase investment and speed economic growth? Explain how the policy action would work.

15. Suppose that capital income taxes are based (as they are in the United States) on nominal interest rates. If the inflation rate increases by 5 percent a year, explain and use appropriate graphs to illustrate the effect of the rise in inflation on

    a. The tax rate on capital income.

    b. The supply of loanable funds.

    c. The demand for loanable funds.

    d. Equilibrium investment.

    e. The equilibrium real interest rate.

Use the following data to work Problems 16 and 17.

Policy Changes Scheduled to Take Effect in 2013

A host of significant provisions of the Job Creation Act of 2010 are set to expire on January 1, 2013, including the emergency unemployment benefits and a temporary reduction of 2 percentage points in the Social Security payroll tax.

> Source: The Congressional Budget Office, October 5, 2012

16. Explain the supply-side effects of allowing unemployment benefits and the Social Security payroll tax cut to expire.

17. a. Explain the potential demand-side effects of extending unemployment benefits and not increasing the Social Security payroll tax.

    b. Explain the potential supply-side effects of the fiscal policy actions in part (a).

    c. Draw a graph to illustrate the combined demand-side and supply-side effect of the fiscal policy actions in part (a).

Use the following news clip to work Problems 18 and 19.

Paul Ryan's Roadmap Business Tax

Paul Ryan has proposed replacing the corporate income tax, which is among the highest in the industrialized world, with what he calls a business consumption tax but what is in effect a tax of a firm's value added. He proposes that this tax be set at 8.5 percent, which is half that of the value-added taxes in the rest of the industrialized world.

> Source: *A Roadmap for America's Future*
> http://roadmap.republicans.budget.house.gov/

18. Explain the potential supply-side effects of Paul Ryan's tax plan.

19. Where on the Laffer curve do you think Paul Ryan believes the U.S. economy lies? Explain your answer.

Generational Effects of Fiscal Policy

20. **Mandatory Spending Is Hard to Contain**

    In Fiscal 2012, spending on the big three entitlement programs—Social Security, Medicare, and Medicaid—was $2.1 trillion. The CBO baseline projection sees this expenditure rising by 70 percent to $3.55 trillion by 2022. Over that same period, discretionary expenditure, mainly national defense, is projected to grow by only 17 percent from $1.2 trillion to $1.4 trillion. The deficit is projected to fall from $1 trillion to $200 billion.

    > Source: Congressional Budget Office, 2012

    If politicians continue to avoid debating the projected increases in the three big entitlement programs, how do you think the fiscal imbalance will change? If Congress introduced changes that slowed the growth of expenditure on the three entitlement programs, who would benefit and who would pay?

Fiscal Stimulus

21. The economy is in a boom and the inflationary gap is large.
    a. Describe the discretionary and automatic fiscal policy actions that might occur.
    b. Describe a discretionary fiscal restraint package that could be used that would not produce serious negative supply-side effects.
    c. Explain the risks of discretionary fiscal policy in this situation.

22. The economy is growing slowly, the inflationary gap is large, and there is a budget deficit.
    a. Do we know whether the budget deficit is structural or cyclical? Explain your answer.
    b. Do we know whether automatic fiscal policy is increasing or decreasing aggregate demand? Explain your answer.
    c. If a discretionary decrease in government expenditure occurs, what happens to the structural budget balance? Explain your answer.

Use the following news clip to work Problems 23 to 25.

Is Fiscal Stimulus Necessary?

China's economy is slowing from its normal 9 percent or higher rate to just below 9 percent. The source of the slowdown is the global economic slowdown that is restricting exports growth and the government's deliberate decision to discourage unproductive investment. The situation now is not like that in 2008 when real GDP growth dropped from 9 percent to 6.8 percent and fiscal stimulus does not appear to be urgently needed.

Source: *China Daily*, June 8, 2012

23. Explain why fiscal stimulus was needed in 2008 but not in 2012.
24. Would you expect automatic fiscal policy to be having an effect in 2012 and if so, what effects might it have?
25. Why might a stimulus come too late? What are the potential consequences of a stimulus coming too late?

Economics in the News

26. After you have studied *Economics in the News* on pp. 750–751, answer the following questions.
    a. What was the state of the Japanese economy in 2013?
    b. Explain the effects of Japan's high level of government spending and debt on the level of employment and potential GDP.
    c. Explain how inflation and faster growth might lower Japan's government debt ratio and why neither is an attractive option.
    d. Explain how monetary policy might be used to offset a fiscal-policy induced decrease in aggregate demand and draw a graph to illustrate your answer.

27. **More Fiscal Stimulus Needed?**
    In *New York Times* articles and in blogs, economists Paul Krugman and Joseph Stiglitz say there is a need for more fiscal stimulus in both the United States and Europe despite the large federal budget deficit and large deficits in some European countries.
    a. Do you agree with Krugman and Stiglitz? Why?
    b. What are the dangers of not engaging in further fiscal stimulus?
    c. What are the dangers of embarking on further fiscal stimulus when the budget is in deficit?

28. **Payroll Tax Cut Is Unlikely to Survive Into Next Year**
    The payroll tax holiday in 2012 reduced workers' tax by $700 for an income of $35,000 a year and by $2,202 for incomes of $110,100 and over. If the tax holiday ends, the Economic Policy Institute recommends replacing the payroll tax cut with infrastructure spending.

    Source: *The New York Times*, September 30, 2012

    a. Explain how a payroll tax affects the before-tax and after-tax wage rate and employment and unemployment.
    b. Explain the effects of an increase in infrastructure spending on employment and unemployment.
    c. Explain which fiscal policy action would have the bigger effect on employment: continuing the payroll tax cut or new infrastructure spending.

31

MONETARY POLICY

After studying this chapter, you will be able to:

- ◆ Describe the objectives of U.S. monetary policy and the framework for setting and achieving them

- ◆ Explain how the Federal Reserve makes its interest rate decision and achieves its interest rate target

- ◆ Explain the transmission channels through which the Federal Reserve influences real GDP, jobs, and inflation

- ◆ Explain the Fed's extraordinary policy actions

At eight regularly scheduled meetings a year and in an emergency between regular meetings, the Federal Reserve decides whether to change its interest rate target. How does the Fed make its interest rate decision? Can the Fed speed up economic growth by lowering the interest rate and can it keep inflation in check by raising the interest rate? What special measures can the Fed take in a financial crisis like the one that engulfed the U.S. and global economies in 2008?

This chapter answers these questions and *Economics in the News* at the end of the chapter looks at the Fed's attempt to restore full employment.

◆ Monetary Policy Objectives and Framework

A nation's monetary policy objectives and the framework for setting and achieving those objectives stem from the relationship between the central bank and the government.

We'll describe the objectives of U.S. monetary policy and the framework and assignment of responsibility for achieving those objectives.

Monetary Policy Objectives

The objectives of U.S. monetary policy are set out in the mandate of the Board of Governors of the Federal Reserve System, which is defined by the Federal Reserve Act of 1913 and its subsequent amendments, the most recent of which was passed in 2000.

Federal Reserve Act The Fed's mandate was most recently clarified in amendments to the Federal Reserve Act passed by Congress in 2000. The 2000 law states that mandate in the following words:

> The Board of Governors of the Federal Reserve System and the Federal Open Market Committee shall maintain long-run growth of the monetary and credit aggregates commensurate with the economy's long-run potential to increase production, so as to promote effectively the goals of maximum employment, stable prices, and moderate long-term interest rates.

Goals and Means This description of the Fed's monetary policy objectives has two distinct parts: a statement of the goals, or ultimate objectives, and a prescription of the means by which the Fed should pursue its goals.

Goals of Monetary Policy The goals are "maximum employment, stable prices, and moderate long-term interest rates." In the long run, these goals are in harmony and reinforce each other. But in the short run, these goals might come into conflict. Let's examine these goals a bit more closely.

Achieving the goal of "maximum employment" means attaining the maximum sustainable growth rate of potential GDP and keeping real GDP close to potential GDP. It also means keeping the unemployment rate close to the natural unemployment rate.

Achieving the goal of "stable prices" means keeping the inflation rate low (and perhaps close to zero).

Achieving the goal of "moderate long-term interest rates" means keeping long-term *nominal* interest rates close to (or even equal to) long-term *real* interest rates.

Price stability is the key goal. It is the source of maximum employment and moderate long-term interest rates. Price stability provides the best available environment for households and firms to make the saving and investment decisions that bring economic growth. So price stability encourages the maximum sustainable growth rate of potential GDP.

Price stability delivers moderate long-term interest rates because the nominal interest rate reflects the inflation rate. The nominal interest rate equals the real interest rate plus the inflation rate. With stable prices, the nominal interest rate is close to the real interest rate, and most of the time, this rate is likely to be moderate.

In the short run, the Fed faces a tradeoff between inflation and interest rates and between inflation and real GDP, employment, and unemployment. Taking an action that is designed to lower the inflation rate and achieve stable prices might mean raising interest rates, which lowers employment and real GDP and increases the unemployment rate in the short run.

Means for Achieving the Goals The 2000 law instructs the Fed to pursue its goals by "maintain[ing] long-run growth of the monetary and credit aggregates commensurate with the economy's long-run potential to increase production." You perhaps recognize this statement as being consistent with the quantity theory of money that you studied in Chapter 25 (see pp. 608–609). The "economy's long-run potential to increase production" is the growth rate of potential GDP. The "monetary and credit aggregates" are the quantities of money and loans. By keeping the growth rate of the quantity of money in line with the growth rate of potential GDP, the Fed is expected to be able to maintain full employment and keep the price level stable.

To pursue the goals of monetary policy, the Fed must make the general concepts of price stability and maximum employment precise and operational.

Operational "Stable Prices" Goal

The Fed pays attention to two measures of inflation: the Consumer Price Index (CPI) and the personal consumption expenditure (PCE) deflator. But the *core PCE deflator*, which excludes food and fuel prices, is the Fed's operational guide and the Fed defines the rate of increase in the core PCE deflator as the **core inflation rate.**

The Fed focuses on the core inflation rate because it is less volatile than the total CPI inflation rate and the Fed believes that it provides a better indication of whether price stability is being achieved.

The Fed has not defined price stability, but it almost certainly doesn't regard it as meaning a core inflation rate equal to zero.

A former Fed Chairman, Alan Greenspan, suggested that "price stability is best thought of as an environment in which inflation is so low and stable over time that it does not materially enter into the decisions of households and firms." He also believes that a "specific numerical inflation target would represent an unhelpful and false precision."[1]

Ben Bernanke, Alan Greenspan's successor, was more precise and suggested that a core inflation rate of between 1 and 2 percent a year is the equivalent of price stability. This inflation range came to be known as the Fed's "comfort zone."

Figure 31.1 shows the core inflation rate since 2000 along with the Fed's comfort zone. You can see that most of the time, the Fed has kept the core inflation rate inside its comfort zone. But between 2004 and 2008, a period during which a major financial crisis occured, inflation was above its comfort zone.

Operational "Maximum Employment" Goal

The Fed regards stable prices (a core inflation rate of 1 to 2 percent a year) as the primary goal of monetary policy and as a means to achieving the other two goals. But the Fed also pays attention to the business cycle and tries to steer a steady course between inflation and recession. To gauge the state of output and employment relative to full employment, the Fed looks at a large number of indicators that include the labor force participation rate, the unemployment rate, measures of capacity utilization, activity in the

[1]Alan Greenspan, "Transparency in Monetary Policy," *Federal Reserve of St. Louis Review*, 84(4), 5–6, July/August 2002.

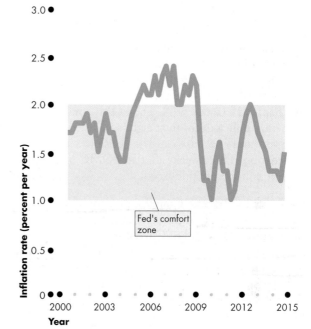

FIGURE 31.1 Operational Price Stability Goal: Core Inflation

The core inflation rate—based on the core PCE deflator— was inside the Fed's comfort zone between 2000 and 2004 and after 2008 but above the comfort zone upper limit between 2004 and 2008.

Sources of data: Bureau of Labor Statistics and Bureau of Economic Analysis.

MyEconLab Real-time data

housing market, the stock market, and regional information gathered by the regional Federal Reserve Banks. All these data that describe the current state of the economy are summarized in the Fed's **Beige Book**.

While the Fed considers a vast range of data, one number stands out as a summary of the overall state of aggregate demand relative to potential GDP. That number is the *output gap*—the percentage deviation of real GDP from potential GDP.

When the output gap is positive, it is an inflationary gap that brings an increase in the inflation rate. And when the output gap is negative, it is a recessionary gap that results in lost output and in employment being below its full-employment equilibrium level. So the Fed tries to minimize the output gap.

Responsibility for Monetary Policy

Who is responsible for monetary policy in the United States? What are the roles of the Fed, Congress, and the president?

The Role of the Fed The Federal Reserve Act makes the Board of Governors of the Federal Reserve System and the Federal Open Market Committee (FOMC) responsible for the conduct of monetary policy. We described the composition of the FOMC in Chapter 25 (see p. 597). The FOMC makes a monetary policy decision at eight scheduled meetings each year and communicates its decision with a brief explanation. Three weeks after an FOMC meeting, the full minutes are published.

The Role of Congress Congress plays no role in making monetary policy decisions but the Federal Reserve Act requires the Board of Governors to report on monetary policy to Congress. The Fed makes two reports each year, one in February and another in July. These reports and the Fed chairman's testimony before Congress along with the minutes of the FOMC communicate the Fed's thinking on monetary policy to lawmakers and the public.

The Role of the President The formal role of the president of the United States is limited to appointing the members and the chairman of the Board of Governors. But some presidents—Richard Nixon was one—have tried to influence Fed decisions.

You now know the objectives of monetary policy and can describe the framework and assignment of responsibility for achieving those objectives. Your next task is to see how the Federal Reserve conducts its monetary policy.

◆ REVIEW QUIZ

1 What are the objectives of monetary policy?
2 Are the goals of monetary policy in harmony or in conflict (a) in the long run and (b) in the short run?
3 What is the core inflation rate and how does it differ from the overall CPI inflation rate?
4 Who is responsible for U.S. monetary policy?

Work these questions in Study Plan 31.1 and get instant feedback. Do a Key Terms Quiz. MyEconLab

◆ The Conduct of Monetary Policy

How does the Fed conduct its monetary policy? This question has two parts:

- What is the monetary policy instrument?
- How does the Fed make its policy decisions?

The Monetary Policy Instrument

A **monetary policy instrument** is a variable that the Fed can directly control or at least very closely target. The Fed has two possible instruments: the monetary base or the interest rate at which banks borrow and lend monetary base overnight.

The Fed's choice of monetary policy instrument is the interest rate at which the banks make overnight loans to each other. The market in which the banks borrow and lend overnight is called the *federal funds market* and the interest rate in that market is called the **federal funds rate**.

Figure 31.2 shows the federal funds rate from 2000 to 2014. You can see that the federal funds rate ranges between a high of 6.8 percent a year and a low of 0.2 percent a year. In 2000 and 2006, when the federal funds rate was high, the Fed's actions were aimed at lowering the inflation rate.

Between 2002 and 2004 and again in and since 2008, the federal funds rate was set at historically low levels. During these years, inflation was well anchored at close to or below 2 percent a year, and the Fed was less concerned about inflation than it was about recession and high unemployment. So the Fed set a low interest rate to fight recession.

Although the Fed can change the federal funds rate by any (reasonable) amount that it chooses, it normally changes the federal funds rate by only a quarter of a percentage point.[2]

Having decided the appropriate level for the federal funds rate, how does the Fed move the rate to its target level? The answer is by using open-market operations (see Chapter 25, pp. 598–600) to adjust the quantity of monetary base.

To see how an open market operation changes the federal funds rate, we need to examine the federal funds market and the market for bank reserves.

In the federal funds market, the higher the federal funds rate, the greater is the quantity of overnight

---

[2]A quarter of a percentage point is also called 25 *basis points*. A basis point is one hundredth of one percentage point.

FIGURE 31.2 The Federal Funds Rate

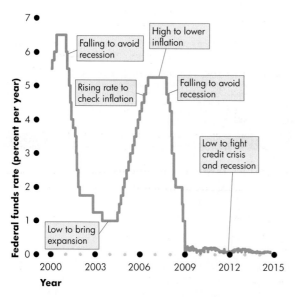

The Fed sets a target for the federal funds rate and then takes actions to keep the rate close to its target. When the Fed wants to slow inflation, it takes actions that raise the federal funds rate. When inflation is low and the Fed wants to avoid recession, it takes actions that lower the federal funds rate.

Source of data: Board of Governors of the Federal Reserve System.

MyEconLab Real-time data

FIGURE 31.3 The Market for Reserves

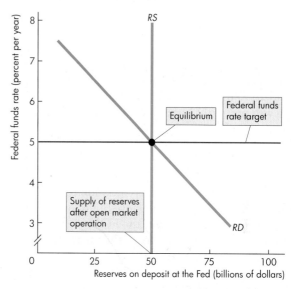

The demand curve for reserves is *RD*. The quantity of reserves demanded decreases as the federal funds rate rises because the federal funds rate is the opportunity cost of holding reserves. The supply curve of reserves is *RS*. The Fed uses open market operations to make the quantity of reserves supplied equal the quantity of reserves demanded ($50 billion in this case) at the federal funds rate target (5 percent a year in this case).

MyEconLab Animation

loans supplied and the smaller is the quantity of overnight loans demanded. The equilibrium federal funds rate balances the quantities demanded and supplied.

An equivalent way of looking at the forces that determine the federal funds rate is to consider the demand for and supply of bank reserves. Banks hold reserves to meet the required reserve ratio and so that they can make payments. But reserves are costly to hold because they can be loaned in the federal funds market and earn the federal funds rate. So the higher the federal funds rate, the smaller is the quantity of reserves demanded.

Figure 31.3 illustrates the demand for bank reserves. The *x*-axis measures the quantity of reserves that banks hold on deposit at the Fed, and the *y*-axis measures the federal funds rate. The demand for reserves is the curve labeled *RD*.

The Fed's open market operations determine the supply of reserves, which is shown by the supply

curve *RS*. Equilibrium in the market for bank reserves determines the federal funds rate where the quantity of reserves demanded by the banks equals the quantity of reserves supplied by the Fed. By using open market operations, the Fed adjusts the supply of reserves to keep the federal funds rate on target.

Next, we see how the Fed makes its policy decisions.

The Fed's Decision-Making Strategy

The Fed's decision making begins with the *Beige Book* exercise described in *Economics in Action* on the next page. The Fed then turns to forecasting three key variables: the inflation rate, the unemployment rate, and the output gap.

Inflation Rate The Fed's forecasts of the inflation rate are a crucial ingredient in its interest rate decision. If inflation is above or is expected to move above the top of the comfort zone, the Fed considers raising the

ECONOMICS IN ACTION

FOMC Decision Making

The Fed's decision making begins with an intensive assessment of the current state of the economy, which is conducted by the Federal Reserve districts and summarized in the *Beige Book*. Today, the Beige Book is a web posting at http://www.federalreserve.gov/monetarypolicy/beigebook/default.htm (see the screenshot).

The FOMC then turns its attention to the likely near-future evolution of the economy and the interest rate change that will keep inflation in check and the economy expanding at close to full employment. In making this assessment, the FOMC pays close attention to the inflation rate, the unemployment rate, and the output gap.

Balancing the signals that it gets from monitoring the three main features of macroeconomic performance, the FOMC meets in its imposing room (see the photo) and makes a decision on whether to change its federal funds rate target and if so, what the new target should be.

Having decided on the appropriate target for the federal funds rate, the FOMC instructs the New York Fed to conduct open market operations aimed at hitting the federal funds rate target.

If the goal is to raise the federal funds rate, the New York Fed sells securities in the open market. If the goal is to lower the federal funds rate, the New York Fed buys securities in the open market.

Beige Book

Summary of Commentary on Current Economic Conditions by Federal Reserve District

Commonly known as the Beige Book, this report is published eight times per year. Each Federal Reserve Bank gathers anecdotal information on current economic conditions in its District through reports from Bank and Branch directors and interviews with key business contacts, economists, market experts, and other sources. The Beige Book summarizes this information by District and sector. An overall summary of the twelve district reports is prepared by a designated Federal Reserve Bank on a rotating basis.

2014		
January	15	HTML	PDF
March	05	HTML	PDF
April	16	HTML	PDF
June	04	HTML	PDF
July	16	HTML	PDF
September	03	HTML	PDF
October	15	
December	03	

federal funds rate target; and if inflation is below or is expected to move below the bottom of the comfort zone, it considers lowering the interest rate.

Unemployment Rate The Fed monitors and forecasts the unemployment rate and its relation to the natural unemployment rate (see Chapter 22, pp. 521–523). If the unemployment rate is below the natural rate, a labor shortage might put upward pressure on wage rates, which might feed through to increase the inflation rate. So a higher interest rate might be called for. If the unemployment rate is above the natural rate, a lower inflation rate is expected, which indicates the need for a lower interest rate.

Output Gap The Fed monitors and forecasts real GDP and potential GDP and the gap between them, the *output gap* (see Chapter 27, pp. 660–661). If the output gap is positive, an *inflationary gap*, the inflation rate will most likely accelerate, so a higher interest rate might be required. If the output gap is negative, a *recessionary gap*, inflation might ease, which indicates room to lower the interest rate.

We next look at the transmission of monetary policy and see how it achieves its goals.

◆ REVIEW QUIZ

1 What is the Fed's monetary policy instrument?
2 How is the federal funds rate determined in the market for reserves?
3 What are the main influences on the FOMC federal funds rate decision?

Work these questions in Study Plan 31.2 and get instant feedback. Do a Key Terms Quiz.   MyEconLab

Monetary Policy Transmission

You've seen that the Fed's goal is to keep the price level stable (keep the inflation rate around 2 percent a year) and to achieve maximum employment (keep the output gap close to zero). And you've seen how the Fed can use its power to set the federal funds rate at its desired level. We're now going to trace the events that follow a change in the federal funds rate and see how those events lead to the ultimate policy goal. We'll begin with a quick overview of the transmission process and then look at each step a bit more closely.

Quick Overview

When the Fed lowers the federal funds rate, the Fed securities in an open market operation and other short-term interest rates and the exchange rate also fall. The quantity of money and the supply of loanable funds increase. The long-term real interest rate falls. The lower real interest rate increases consumption expenditure and investment. And the lower exchange rate makes U.S. exports cheaper and imports more costly, so net exports increase. Easier bank loans reinforce the effect of lower interest rates on aggregate expenditure. Aggregate demand increases, which increases real GDP and the price level relative to what they would have been had the Fed not lowered the federal funds rate. Real GDP growth and inflation speed up.

When the Fed raises the federal funds rate, the Fed sells securities in an open market operation and as the sequence of events that we've just reviewed plays out, the effects are in the opposite directions.

Figure 31.4 provides a schematic summary of these ripple effects for both a cut and a rise in the federal funds rate.

These ripple effects stretch out over a period of between one and two years. The interest rate and exchange rate effects are immediate. The effects on money and bank loans follow in a few weeks and run for a few months. Real long-term interest rates change quickly and often in anticipation of the short-term interest rate changes. Spending plans change and real GDP growth changes after about one year. The inflation rate changes between one year and two years after the change in the federal funds rate. But these time lags are not entirely predictable and can be longer or shorter.

We're going to look at each stage in the transmission process, starting with the interest rate effects.

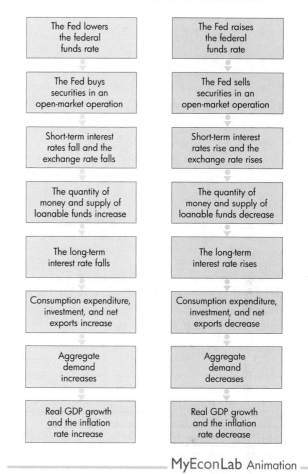

FIGURE 31.4   The Ripple Effects of a Change in the Federal Funds Rate

The Fed lowers the federal funds rate	The Fed raises the federal funds rate
The Fed buys securities in an open-market operation	The Fed sells securities in an open-market operation
Short-term interest rates fall and the exchange rate falls	Short-term interest rates rise and the exchange rate rises
The quantity of money and supply of loanable funds increase	The quantity of money and supply of loanable funds decrease
The long-term interest rate falls	The long-term interest rate rises
Consumption expenditure, investment, and net exports increase	Consumption expenditure, investment, and net exports decrease
Aggregate demand increases	Aggregate demand decreases
Real GDP growth and the inflation rate increase	Real GDP growth and the inflation rate decrease

MyEconLab Animation

Interest Rate Changes

The first effect of a monetary policy decision by the FOMC is a change in the federal funds rate. To achieve that, the Fed conducts an open market operation. Other interest rates then change. These interest rate effects occur quickly and relatively predictably.

Figure 31.5 shows the fluctuations in three interest rates: the federal funds rate, the 3-month Treasury bill rate, and the long-term bond rate.

Federal Funds Rate As soon as the FOMC announces a new setting for the federal funds rate, the New York Fed undertakes the necessary open market operations to hit the target. There is no doubt about where the interest rate changes shown in Fig. 31.5 are generated. They are driven by the Fed's monetary policy.

FIGURE 31.5   Three Interest Rates

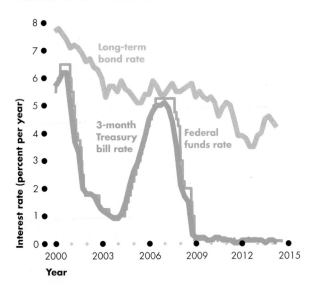

The short-term interest rates—the federal funds rate and the 3-month Treasury bill rate—move closely together. The long-term bond rate is higher than the short-term rates, and it fluctuates less than the short-term rates.

Source of data: Board of Governors of the Federal Reserve System.

MyEconLab Real-time data

Short-Term Bill Rate The short-term bill rate is the interest rate paid by the U.S. government on 3-month Treasury bills. It is similar to the interest rate paid by U.S. businesses on short-term loans. Notice how closely the 3-month Treasury bill rate follows the federal funds rate. The two rates are almost identical.

A powerful substitution effect keeps these two interest rates close. Commercial banks have a choice about how to hold their short-term liquid assets, and an overnight loan to another bank is a close substitute for short-term securities such as Treasury bills. If the interest rate on Treasury bills is higher than the federal funds rate, the quantity of overnight loans supplied decreases and the demand for Treasury bills increases. The price of Treasury bills rises and the interest rate falls.

Similarly, if the interest rate on Treasury bills is lower than the federal funds rate, the quantity of overnight loans supplied increases and the demand for Treasury bills decreases. The price of Treasury bills falls, and the interest rate rises.

When the interest rate on Treasury bills is close to the federal funds rate, there is no incentive for a bank to switch between making an overnight loan and buying Treasury bills. Both the Treasury bill market and the federal funds market are in equilibrium.

The Long-Term Bond Rate The long-term bond rate is the interest rate paid on bonds issued by large corporations. It is this interest rate that businesses pay on the loans that finance their purchase of new capital and that influences their investment decisions.

Two features of the long-term bond rate stand out: It is higher than the short-term rates, and it fluctuates less than the short-term rates.

The long-term interest rate is higher than the two short-term rates because long-term loans are riskier than short-term loans. To provide the incentive that brings forth a supply of long-term loans, lenders must be compensated for the additional risk. Without compensation for the additional risk, only short-term loans would be supplied.

The long-term interest rate fluctuates less than the short-term rates because it is influenced by expectations about future short-term interest rates as well as current short-term interest rates. The alternative to borrowing or lending long term is to borrow or lend using a sequence of short-term securities. If the long-term interest rate exceeds the expected average of future short-term interest rates, people will lend long term and borrow short term. The long-term interest rate will fall. And if the long-term interest rate is below the expected average of future short-term interest rates, people will borrow long term and lend short term. The long-term interest rate will rise.

These market forces keep the long-term interest rate close to the expected average of future short-term interest rates (plus a premium for the extra risk associated with long-term loans). The expected average future short-term interest rate fluctuates less than the current short-term interest rate.

Exchange Rate Fluctuations

The exchange rate responds to changes in the interest rate in the United States relative to the interest rates in other countries—*the U.S. interest rate differential*. We explain this influence in Chapter 26 (see p. 625).

When the Fed raises the federal funds rate, the U.S. interest rate differential rises and, other things remaining the same, the U.S. dollar appreciates, and when the Fed lowers the federal funds rate, the U.S. interest rate differential falls and, other things remaining the same, the U.S. dollar depreciates.

Many factors other than the U.S. interest rate differential influence the exchange rate, so when the Fed changes the federal funds rate, the exchange rate does not usually change in exactly the way it would with other things remaining the same. So while monetary policy influences the exchange rate, many other factors also make the exchange rate change.

Money and Bank Loans

The quantity of money and bank loans change when the Fed changes the federal funds rate target. A rise in the federal funds rate decreases the quantity of money and bank loans, and a fall in the federal funds rate increases the quantity of money and bank loans. These changes occur for two reasons: The quantity of deposits and loans created by the banking system changes and the quantity of money demanded changes.

You've seen that to change the federal funds rate, the Fed must change the quantity of bank reserves. A change in the quantity of bank reserves changes the monetary base, which in turn changes the quantity of deposits and loans that the banking system can create. A rise in the federal funds rate decreases reserves and decreases the quantity of deposits and bank loans created; and a fall in the federal funds rate increases reserves and increases the quantity of deposits and bank loans created.

The quantity of money created by the banking system must be held by households and firms. The change in the interest rate changes the quantity of money demanded. A fall in the interest rate increases the quantity of money demanded, and a rise in the interest rate decreases the quantity of money demanded.

A change in the quantity of money and the supply of bank loans directly affects consumption and investment plans. With more money and easier access to loans, consumers and firms spend more. With less money and loans harder to get, consumers and firms spend less.

The Long-Term Real Interest Rate

Demand and supply in the market for loanable funds determine the long-term *real interest rate*, which

equals the long-term *nominal* interest rate minus the expected inflation rate. The long-term real interest rate influences expenditure decisions.

In the long run, demand and supply in the loanable funds market depend only on real forces—on saving and investment decisions. But in the short run, when the price level is not fully flexible, the supply of loanable funds is influenced by the supply of bank loans. Changes in the federal funds rate change the supply of bank loans, which changes the supply of loanable funds and changes the interest rate in the loanable funds market.

A fall in the federal funds rate that increases the supply of bank loans increases the supply of loanable funds and lowers the equilibrium real interest rate. A rise in the federal funds rate that decreases the supply of bank loans decreases the supply of loanable funds and raises the equilibrium real interest rate.

These changes in the real interest rate, along with the other factors we've just described, change expenditure plans.

Expenditure Plans

The ripple effects that follow a change in the federal funds rate change three components of aggregate expenditure:

- Consumption expenditure
- Investment
- Net exports

Consumption Expenditure Other things remaining the same, the lower the real interest rate, the greater is the amount of consumption expenditure and the smaller is the amount of saving.

Investment Other things remaining the same, the lower the real interest rate, the greater is the amount of investment.

Net Exports Other things remaining the same, the lower the interest rate, the lower is the exchange rate and the greater are exports and the smaller are imports.

So eventually, a cut in the federal funds rate increases aggregate expenditure and a rise in the federal funds rate curtails aggregate expenditure. These changes in aggregate expenditure plans change aggregate demand, real GDP, and the price level.

The Change in Aggregate Demand, Real GDP, and the Price Level

The final link in the transmission chain is a change in aggregate demand and a resulting change in real GDP and the price level. By changing real GDP and the price level relative to what they would have been without a change in the federal funds rate, the Fed influences its ultimate goals: the inflation rate and the output gap.

The Fed Fights Recession

If inflation is low and real GDP is below potential GDP, the Fed takes actions that are designed to restore full employment. Figure 31.6 shows the effects of the Fed's actions, starting in the market for bank reserves and ending in the market for real GDP.

Market for Bank Reserves In Fig. 31.6(a), which shows the market for bank reserves, the FOMC lowers the target federal funds rate from 5 percent to 4

percent a year. To achieve the new target, the New York Fed buys securities and increases the supply of reserves of the banking system from RS_0 to RS_1.

Money Market With increased reserves, the banks create deposits by making loans and the supply of money increases. The short-term interest rate falls and the quantity of money demanded increases. In Fig. 31.6(b), the supply of money increases from MS_0 to MS_1, the interest rate falls from 5 percent to 4 percent a year, and the quantity of money increases from $3 trillion to $3.1 trillion. The interest rate in the money market and the federal funds rate are kept close to each other by the powerful substitution effect described on p. 764.

Loanable Funds Market Banks create money by making loans. In the long run, an increase in the supply of bank loans is matched by a rise in the price level and the quantity of *real* loans is unchanged. But in the short run, with a sticky price level, an increase in the supply of bank loans increases the supply of (real) loanable funds.

FIGURE 31.6   The Fed Fights Recession

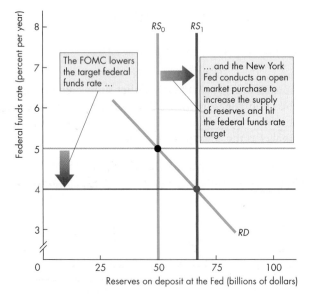

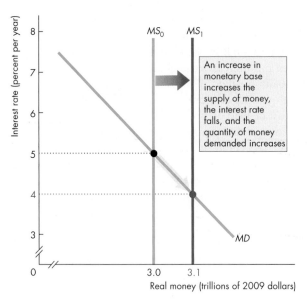

(a) The market for bank reserves

(b) Money market

In part (a), the FOMC lowers the federal funds rate target from 5 percent to 4 percent. The New York Fed buys securities in an open market operation and increases the supply of reserves from RS_0 to RS_1 to hit the new federal funds rate target.

In part (b), the supply of money increases from MS_0 to MS_1, the short-term interest rate falls, and the quantity of money demanded increases. The short-term interest rate and the federal funds rate change by similar amounts.

In Fig. 31.6(c), the supply of loanable funds curve shifts rightward from SLF_0 to SLF_1. With the demand for loanable funds at DLF, the real interest rate falls from 6 percent to 5.5 percent a year. (We're assuming a zero inflation rate so that the real interest rate equals the nominal interest rate.) The long-term interest rate changes by a smaller amount than the change in the short-term interest rate for the reason explained on p. 764.

The Market for Real GDP Figure 31.6(d) shows aggregate demand and aggregate supply—the demand for and supply of real GDP. Potential GDP is $16 trillion, where LAS is located. The short-run aggregate supply curve is SAS, and initially, the aggregate demand curve is AD_0. Real GDP is $15.8 trillion, which is less than potential GDP, so there is a recessionary gap. The Fed is reacting to this recessionary gap.

The increase in the supply of loans and the decrease in the real interest rate increase aggregate planned expenditure. (Not shown in the figure, a fall in the interest rate lowers the exchange rate, which increases net exports and aggregate planned expenditure.) The increase in aggregate expenditure, ΔE, increases aggregate demand and shifts the aggregate demand curve rightward to $AD_0 + \Delta E$. A multiplier process begins. The increase in expenditure increases income, which induces an increase in consumption expenditure. Aggregate demand increases further, and the aggregate demand curve eventually shifts rightward to AD_1.

The new equilibrium is at full employment. Real GDP is equal to potential GDP. The price level rises to 110 and then becomes stable at that level. So after a one-time adjustment, there is price stability.

In this example, we have given the Fed a perfect hit at achieving full employment and keeping the price level stable. It is unlikely that the Fed would be able to achieve the precision of this example. If the Fed stimulated demand by too little and too late, the economy would experience a recession. And if the Fed hit the gas pedal too hard, it would push the economy from recession to inflation.

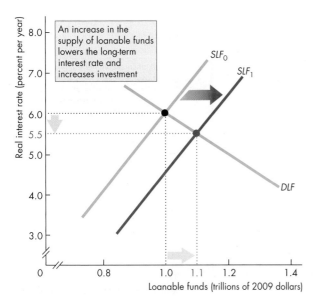

(c) The market for loanable funds

In part (c), the increase in the quantity of money increases the supply of bank loans. The supply of loanable funds increases and shifts the supply curve from SLF_0 to SLF_1. The real interest rate falls and investment increases.

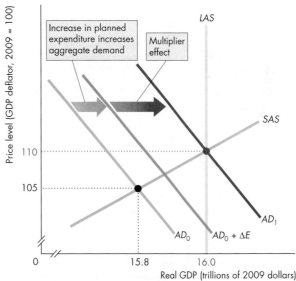

(d) Real GDP and the price level

In part (d), the increase in investment increases aggregate planned expenditure. The aggregate demand curve shifts to $AD_0 + \Delta E$ and eventually it shifts rightward to AD_1. Real GDP increases to potential GDP, and the price level rises.

MyEconLab Animation

The Fed Fights Inflation

If the inflation rate is too high and real GDP is above potential GDP, the Fed takes actions that are designed to lower the inflation rate and restore price stability. Figure 31.7 shows the effects of the Fed's actions starting in the market for reserves and ending in the market for real GDP.

Market for Bank Reserves In Fig. 31.7(a), which shows the market for bank reserves, the FOMC raises the target federal funds rate from 5 percent to 6 percent a year. To achieve the new target, the New York Fed sells securities and decreases the supply of reserves of the banking system from RS_0 to RS_1.

Money Market With decreased reserves, the banks shrink deposits by decreasing loans and the supply of money decreases. The short-term interest rate rises and the quantity of money demanded decreases. In Fig. 31.7(b), the supply of money decreases from MS_0 to MS_1, the interest rate rises from 5 percent to

6 percent a year, and the quantity of money decreases from $3 trillion to $2.9 trillion.

Loanable Funds Market With a decrease in reserves, banks must decrease the supply of loans. The supply of (real) loanable funds decreases, and the supply of loanable funds curve shifts leftward in Fig. 31.7(c) from SLF_0 to SLF_1. With the demand for loanable funds at DLF, the real interest rate rises from 6 percent to 6.5 percent a year. (Again, we're assuming a zero inflation rate so that the real interest rate equals the nominal interest rate.)

The Market for Real GDP Figure 31.7(d) shows aggregate demand and aggregate supply in the market for real GDP. Potential GDP is $16 trillion where LAS is located. The short-run aggregate supply curve is SAS and initially the aggregate demand is AD_0. Now, real GDP is $16.2 trillion, which is greater than potential GDP, so there is an inflationary gap. The Fed is reacting to this inflationary gap.

FIGURE 31.7   The Fed Fights Inflation

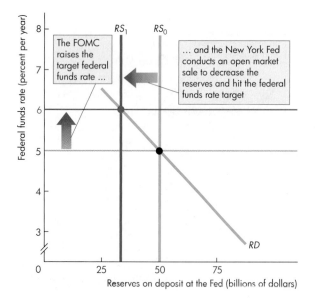

(a) The market for bank reserves

In part (a), the FOMC raises the federal funds rate from 5 percent to 6 percent. The New York Fed sells securities in an open market operation to decrease the supply of reserves from RS_0 to RS_1 and hit the new federal funds rate target.

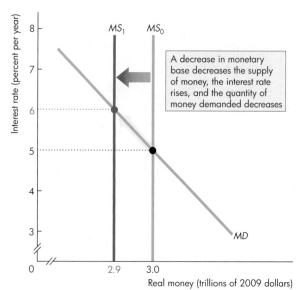

(b) Money market

In part (b), the supply of money decreases from MS_0 to MS_1, the short-term interest rate rises, and the quantity of money demanded decreases. The short-term interest rate and the federal funds rate change by similar amounts.

The increase in the short-term interest rate, the decrease in the supply of bank loans, and the increase in the real interest rate decrease aggregate planned expenditure. (Not shown in the figures, a rise in the interest rate raises the exchange rate, which decreases net exports and aggregate planned expenditure.)

The decrease in aggregate expenditure, ΔE, decreases aggregate demand and shifts the aggregate demand curve to $AD_0 - \Delta E$. A multiplier process begins. The decrease in expenditure decreases income, which induces a decrease in consumption expenditure. Aggregate demand decreases further, and the aggregate demand curve eventually shifts leftward to AD_1.

The economy returns to full employment. Real GDP is equal to potential GDP. The price level falls to 110 and then becomes stable at that level. So after a one-time adjustment, there is price stability.

Again, in this example, we have given the Fed a perfect hit at achieving full employment and keeping the price level stable. If the Fed decreased aggregate demand by too little and too late, the economy would have remained with an inflationary gap and the inflation rate would have moved above the rate that is consistent with price stability. And if the Fed hit the brakes too hard, it would push the economy from inflation to recession.

Loose Links and Long and Variable Lags

The ripple effects of monetary policy that we've just analyzed with the precision of an economic model are, in reality, very hard to predict and anticipate.

To achieve price stability and full employment, the Fed needs a combination of good judgment and good luck. Too large an interest rate cut in an underemployed economy can bring inflation, as it did during the 1970s. And too large an interest rate rise in an inflationary economy can create unemployment, as it did in 1981 and 1991. Loose links between the federal funds rate and the ultimate policy goals make unwanted outcomes inevitable and long and variable time lags add to the Fed's challenges.

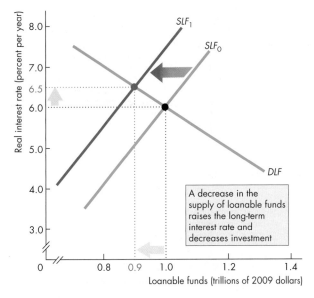

(c) The market for loanable funds

In part (c), the decrease in the quantity of money decreases the supply of bank loans. The supply of loanable funds decreases and the supply curve shifts from SLF_0 to SLF_1. The real interest rate rises and investment decreases.

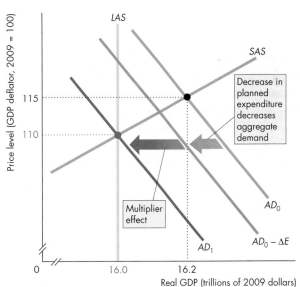

(d) Real GDP and the price level

In part (d), the decrease in investment decreases aggregate planned expenditure. Aggregate demand decreases and the AD curve shifts leftward from AD_0 to AD_1. Real GDP decreases to potential GDP, and the price level falls.

MyEconLab Animation

◆ ECONOMICS IN THE NEWS

Monetary Stimulus Not Stimulating

Why GDP Has Been Weak Despite Aggressive Fed Policy

The U.S economy has been struggling since the crisis of 2008. The Federal Reserve countered with an unprecedented amount of monetary stimulus. Despite this, GDP remains weak.

Source: *Forbes*, July 30, 2014

SOME FACTS

- Figure 31.2 (p. 761) shows the changes in the fed eral funds rate.
- Figure 1 shows the effects of the Fed's open market operations on the monetary base.
- Figure 31.5 (p. 764) shows how interest rates have changed.
- Consumption expenditure *plus* investment *plus* exports increased by only 11 percent in six years.

THE QUESTIONS

- What are the ripple effects of a change in the federal funds rate and massive open market operations?
- At which stage in the ripple effects did monetary stimulus since 2008 become weak?

THE ANSWERS

- Figure 2 shows the stages in the transmission of monetary stimulus.
- The notes in the right column indicate what happened at each stage since the start of monetary stimulus in 2008.
- The first five steps unfolded as expected although the fifth step—a fall in the long-term interest rate—did not happen until a year after short-term interest rates had fallen.
- The ripple effects weakened with the expenditure response. Consumption expenditure, investment, and exports increased by a small amount in response to lower interest rates. Consequently, real GDP didn't grow faster and the inflation rate didn't increase.
- The Fed believes that its stimulus policy worked and that without it, consumption expenditure and investment would have fallen to bring a very deep recession or depression.

MyEconLab More Economics in the News

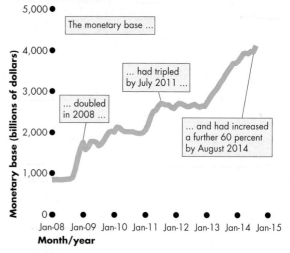

Figure 1   The Monetary Base

Source of data: Federal Reserve Board of Governors of the Federal Reserve System.

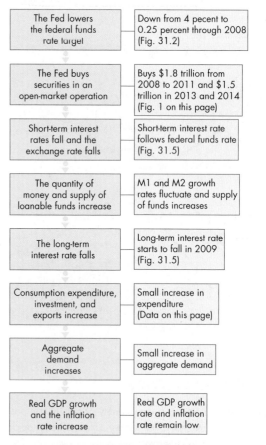

The Fed lowers the federal funds rate target	Down from 4 pecent to 0.25 percent through 2008 (Fig. 31.2)
The Fed buys securities in an open-market operation	Buys $1.8 trillion from 2008 to 2011 and $1.5 trillion in 2013 and 2014 (Fig. 1 on this page)
Short-term interest rates fall and the exchange rate falls	Short-term interest rate follows federal funds rate (Fig. 31.5)
The quantity of money and supply of loanable funds increase	M1 and M2 growth rates fluctuate and supply of funds increases
The long-term interest rate falls	Long-term interest rate starts to fall in 2009 (Fig. 31.5)
Consumption expenditure, investment, and exports increase	Small increase in expenditure (Data on this page)
Aggregate demand increases	Small increase in aggregate demand
Real GDP growth and the inflation rate increase	Real GDP growth rate and inflation rate remain low

Figure 2   Where the Ripples Weakened

ECONOMICS IN ACTION

A View of the Long and Variable Lag

You've studied the theory of monetary policy. Does it really work in the way we've described? It does, and the figure opposite provides some evidence to support this claim.

The blue line in the figure is the federal funds rate that the Fed targets *minus* the long-term bond rate. (When the long-term bond rate exceeds the federal funds rate, this gap is negative.)

We can view the gap between the federal funds rate and the long-term bond rate as a measure of how hard the Fed is trying to steer a change in the economy's course.

When the Fed is more concerned about recession than inflation and is trying to stimulate real GDP growth, it cuts the federal funds rate target and the gap between the long-term bond rate and the federal funds rate widens.

When the Fed is more concerned about inflation than recession and is trying to restrain real GDP growth, it raises the federal funds rate target and the gap between the long-term bond rate and the federal funds rate narrows.

The red line in the figure is the real GDP growth rate *two years later*. You can see that when the FOMC raises the federal funds rate, the real GDP growth rate slows two years later. And when the Fed lowers

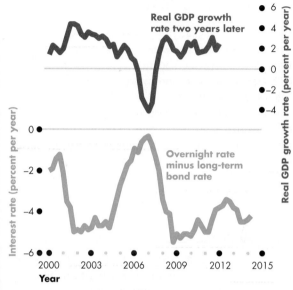

Interest Rates and Real GDP Growth

Sources of data: Interest rates, see Fig. 31.5; real GDP growth rate, Bureau of Economic Analysis.

the federal funds rate, the real GDP growth rate speeds up two years later.

Not shown in the figure, the inflation rate increases and decreases corresponding to the fluctuations in the real GDP growth rate. But the effects on the inflation rate take even longer and are not as strong as the effects on the real GDP growth rate.

Loose Link from Federal Funds Rate to Spending

The real long-term interest rate that influences spending plans is linked only loosely to the federal funds rate. Also, the response of the *real* long-term interest rate to a change in the nominal interest rate depends on how inflation expectations change. And the response of expenditure plans to changes in the real interest rate depend on many factors that make the response hard to predict.

Time Lags in the Adjustment Process

The Fed is especially handicapped by the fact that the monetary policy transmission process is long and drawn out. Also, the economy does not always respond in exactly the same way to a policy change. Further, many factors other than policy are constantly changing and bringing new situations to which policy must respond.

◆ REVIEW QUIZ

1 Describe the channels by which monetary policy ripples through the economy and explain how each channel operates.
2 Do interest rates fluctuate in response to the Fed's actions?
3 How do the Fed's actions change the exchange rate?
4 How do the Fed's actions influence real GDP and how long does it take for real GDP to respond to the Fed's policy changes?
5 How do the Fed's actions influence the inflation rate and how long does it take for inflation to respond to the Fed's policy changes?

Work these questions in Study Plan 31.3 and get instant feedback.   MyEconLab

Extraordinary Monetary Stimulus

During the financial crisis and recession of 2008–2009, the Fed lowered the federal funds rate target to the floor. The rate can't go below zero, so what can the Fed do to stimulate the economy when it can't lower the interest rate any further?

The Fed has answered this question with some extraordinary policy actions. To understand those actions, we need to dig a bit into the anatomy of the financial crisis to which the Fed is responding. That's what we'll now do. We'll look at the key elements in the financial crisis and then look at the Fed's response.

The Key Elements of the Crisis

We can describe the crisis by identifying the events that changed the values of the assets and liabilities of banks and other financial institutions.

Figure 31.8 shows the stylized balance sheet of a bank: deposits plus equity equals reserves plus loans and securities (see Chapter 25, p. 594). Deposits and own capital —equity—are the bank's sources of funds (other borrowing by banks is ignored here). Deposits are the funds loaned to the bank by households and firms. Equity is the capital provided by the bank's stockholders and includes the bank's undistributed profits (and losses). The bank's reserves are currency and its deposit at the Fed. The bank's loans and securities are the loans made by the bank and government bonds, private bonds, asset-backed bonds, and other securities that the bank holds.

Three main events can put a bank under stress:

1. Widespread fall in asset prices
2. A significant currency drain
3. A run on the bank

Figure 31.8 summarizes the problems that each event presents to a bank. A widespread fall in asset prices means that the bank suffers a *capital loss*. It must write down the value of its assets and the value of the bank's equity decreases by the same amount as the fall in the value of its securities. If the fall in asset prices is large enough, the bank's equity might fall to zero, in which case the bank is insolvent. It fails.

A significant currency drain means that depositors withdraw funds and the bank loses reserves. This event puts the bank in a liquidity crisis. It is short of cash reserves.

A run on the bank occurs when depositors lose confidence in the bank and massive withdrawals of deposits occur. The bank loses reserves and must call in loans and sell off securities at unfavorable prices. Its equity shrinks.

The red arrows in Fig. 31.8 summarize the effects of these events and the problems they brought in the 2007–2008 financial crisis. A widespread fall in asset prices was triggered by the bursting of a house-price bubble that saw house prices switch from rapidly rising to falling. With falling house prices, sub-prime mortgage defaults occurred and the prices of mortgage-backed securities and derivatives whose values are based on these securities began to fall.

People with money market mutual fund deposits began to withdraw them, which created a fear of a massive withdrawal of these funds analagous to a run on a bank. In the United Kingdom, one bank, Northern Rock, experienced a bank run.

With low reserves and even lower equity, banks turned their attention to securing their balance sheets and called in loans. The loanable funds market and money market dried up.

Because the loanable funds market is global, the same problems quickly spread to other economies, and foreign exchange markets became highly volatile.

Hard-to-get loans, market volatility, and increased uncertainty transmitted the financial and monetary crisis to real expenditure decisions.

FIGURE 31.8   The Ingredients of a Financial and Banking Crisis

Event	Deposits	+ Equity	= Reserves	+ Loans and securities	Problem
Widespread fall in asset prices		▼		▼	Solvency
Currency drain	▼		▼		Liquidity
Run on bank	▼	▼	▼	▼	Liquidity and solvency

MyEconLab Animation

The Policy Actions

Policy actions in response to the financial crisis dribbled out over a period of more than a year. But by November 2008, eight groups of policies designed to contain the crisis and minimize its impact on the real economy were in place. Figure 31.9 summarizes them, describes their effects on a bank's balance sheet (red and blue arrows), and identifies the problem that each action sought to address.

An open market operation is the classic policy (see Chapter 25, pp. 598–600) for providing liquidity and enabling the Fed to hit its interest rate target. With substantial interest rate cuts, open market operations were used on a massive scale to keep the banks well supplied with reserves. This action lowered bank holdings of securities and increased their reserves.

By extending deposit insurance (see Chapter 25, p. 594), the FDIC gave depositors greater security and less incentive to withdraw their bank deposits. This action increased both deposits and reserves.

Three actions by the Fed provided additional liquidity in exchange for troubled assets. Term auction credit, primary dealer and broker credit, and the asset-backed commercial paper money market mutual fund liquidity facility enabled institutions to swap troubled assets for reserves or safer assets. All of these actions decreased bank holdings of securities and increased reserves.

The Troubled Asset Relief Program (TARP) was an action by the U.S. Treasury, so technically it isn't a monetary policy action, but it had a direct impact on banks and other financial institutions. The program was funded by $700 billion of national debt.

The original intent (we'll call it TARP 1) was for the U.S. Treasury to buy troubled assets from banks and other holders and replace them with U.S. government securities. Implementing this program proved more difficult than initially anticipated and the benefits of the action came to be questioned.

So instead of buying troubled assets, the Treasury decided to buy equity stakes in troubled institutions (we'll call it TARP 2). This action directly increased the institutions' reserves and equity.

The final action was neither monetary policy nor fiscal policy but a change in accounting standards. It relaxed the requirement for institutions to value their assets at current market value—called "mark-to-market"—and permitted them, in rare conditions, to use a model to assess "fair market value."

Taken as a whole, a huge amount of relief was thrown at the financial crisis but the economy continued to perform poorly through 2009 and 2010.

Persistently Slow Recovery

Despite extraordinary monetary (and fiscal) stimulus, at the end of 2010, the U.S. economy remained stuck with slow real GDP growth and an unemployment rate close to 10 percent. Why?

No one knows for sure, but the Fed's critics say that the Fed itself contributed to the problem more than to the solution. That problem is extreme uncertainty about the future that is keeping business investment low. Critics emphasize the need for greater clarity about monetary policy *strategy*. We'll conclude this review of monetary policy by looking at two suggested policy strategies.

FIGURE 31.9   Policy Actions in a Financial and Banking Crisis

Action	Deposits	+ Equity	= Reserves	+ Loans and securities	Problem addressed
Open market operation			▲	▼	Liquidity
Extension of deposit insurance	▲		▲		Liquidity
Term auction credit			▲	▼	Liquidity
Primary dealer and other broker credit			▲	▼	Liquidity
Asset-backed commercial paper money market mutual fund liquidity facility			▲	▼	Liquidity
Troubled Asset Relief Program (TARP 1)			▲	▼	Liquidity
Troubled Asset Relief Program (TARP 2)		▲	▲		Solvency
Fair value accounting		▲		▲	Solvency

MyEconLab Animation

AT **ISSUE**

Support for and Opposition to Keeping Interest Rates Low for a "Considerable Time"

At an FOMC meeting held on September 16-17, 2014, the FOMC decided to cut its purchases of mortgage-backed securities from $10 billion to $5 billion per month. And as it had done at several earlier meetings, the committee renewed its pledge to maintain a very low interest rate of between zero and 0.25 percent for a "considerable time."

Fifteen FOMC members supported these announcements and two members voted against the low interest rate committment.

Let's look at both sides of this issue.

Janet **Yellen** and FOMC **Majority** say ...

- The Fed's mandate is to foster maximum employment and price stability.

- In the conditions of September 2014, inflation was unlikely, so price stability was not in danger.

- But continued weak growth made it likely that unemployment would remain high.

- Further risks to growth were coming from the global economy.

- Because prices were stable and unemployment high, monetary stimulus was still needed.

- The federal funds rate was already at its lowest possible level.

- Maximum downward pressure on long-term interest rates was still needed.

- By committing to low interest rates for a "considerable time," the Fed could avoid putting a calendar date on its interest rate move and at the same time put needed additional downward pressure on long-term interest rates to boost demand.

FOMC **Minority** say...

- Richard Fisher, President of the Dallas Fed, has been a longstanding opponent of the Fed's stimulus and in 2012 said "the engine room is already flush" when opposing the large-scale purchase of mortgage-backed securities.

- In September 2014, Fisher believed that the time was fast approaching to raise interest rates.

- Charles Plosser, President of the Philadelphia Fed, says further monetary stimulus is inappropriate to tackle high unemployment and it won't work.

- Plosser says the unemployment rate is high for structural reasons and the economy is much closer to full employment than the majority assume.

- He also dislikes the fact that the words "considerable time" make it appear that interest rates are set by the calendar rather than economic conditions.

- And he believes those economic conditions will soon call for higher interest rates.

The FOMC has done enough already, says Richard Fisher of the Dallas Fed.

With a commitment to keep interest rates low for a "considerable time," the Fed can lower long-term interest rates and increase household and business spending, believes Janet Yellen, Chair of the Fed.

Monetary policy can't cure structural unemployment, says Charles Plosser of the Philadelphia Fed.

Policy Strategies and Clarity

Two alternative approaches to monetary policy have been suggested and one of them has been used in other countries. They are

- Inflation rate targeting
- Taylor rule

Inflation Rate Targeting A monetary policy strategy in which the central bank makes a public commitment to achieve an explicit inflation target and explain how its policy actions will achieve it is called **inflation rate targeting**. Australia, Canada, New Zealand, Sweden, the United Kingdom, and the European Union have been targeting inflation since the 1990s.

Inflation targeting focuses the public debate on what monetary policy can achieve and the best contribution it can make to attaining full employment and sustained growth. The central fact is that monetary policy is about managing inflation expectations. An explicit inflation target that is taken seriously and toward which policy actions are aimed and explained is a sensible way to manage those expectations.

It is when the going gets tough that inflation targeting has the greatest benefit. It is difficult to imagine a serious inflation-targeting central bank permitting inflation to take off in the way that it did during the 1970s. And it is difficult to imagine deflation and ongoing recession such as Japan has endured for the past 10 years if monetary policy is guided by an explicit inflation target.

Taylor Rule One way to pursue an inflation target is to set the policy interest rate (for the Fed, the federal funds rate) by using a rule or formula. The most famous and most studied interest rate rule is the *Taylor rule* described in *Economics in Action*.

Supporters of the Taylor rule argue that in computer simulations, the rule works well and limits fluctuations in inflation and output. By using such a rule, monetary policy contributes toward lessening uncertainty—the opposite of current monetary policy. In financial markets, labor markets, and markets for goods and services, people make long-term commitments. So markets work best when plans are based on correctly anticipated inflation. A well-understood monetary policy helps to create an environment in which inflation is easier to forecast and manage.

The debates on inflation targeting and the Taylor rule will continue!

ECONOMICS IN ACTION
The Taylor Rule

The *Taylor rule* is a formula for setting the federal funds rate. Calling the federal funds rate *FFR*, the inflation rate *INF*, and the output gap *GAP* (all percentages), the Taylor rule formula is

$$FFR = 2 + INF + 0.5(INF - 2) + 0.5GAP.$$

In words, the Taylor rule sets the federal funds rate at 2 percent a year plus the inflation rate plus one half of the deviation of inflation from 2 percent a year, plus one half of the output gap.

Stanford University economist John B. Taylor, who devised this rule, says inflation and real GDP would fluctuate much less if the FOMC were to use it—the Taylor rule beats the FOMC's historical performance.

The Taylor rule implies that the Fed caused the boom and bust of the past decade. The federal funds rate was 1.5 percentage points (on average) too low from 2001 through 2005, which fuelled the boom; and the rate was 0.5 percentage points (on average) too high in 2006 and 2007, which triggered the bust.

In the conditions of 2009, the Taylor rule delivered a negative interest rate, a situation that wouldn't have arisen if the Taylor rule had been followed.

REVIEW QUIZ

1 What are the three ingredients of a financial and banking crisis?
2 What are the policy actions taken by the Fed and the U.S. Treasury in response to the financial crisis?
3 Why was the recovery from the 2008–2009 recession so slow?
4 How might inflation targeting improve the Fed's monetary policy?
5 How might using the Taylor rule improve the Fed's monetary policy?

Work these questions in Study Plan 31.4 and get instant feedback. Do a Key Terms Quiz.   MyEconLab

To complete your study of monetary policy, take a look at *Economics in the News* on pp. 776–777, which examines the Fed's challenge in 2014.

The Fed Keeps Stimulating

Fed Renews Pledge on Low Rates

The Financial Times
September 17, 2014

The U.S. Federal Reserve maintained its commitment to keeping rates low for a "considerable time" after it stops buying assets in October, but forecast a faster pace of rate rises in 2015 and 2016.

The statement, which noted the unemployment rate was "little changed," suggests Fed chairwoman Janet Yellen has prioritized support for the economic recovery over the concerns of officials who believe that interest rates may need to rise early next year.

But the FOMC's new forecasts, which pointed to a faster pace of rate rises, showed the building pressure for a change of guidance. Instead of an interest rate of 1 percent to 1.25 percent at the end of 2015, the FOMC now expects a rate of 1.25 percent to 1.5 percent. …

The statement prompted dissent from two officials, compared with one at the previous meeting. Richard Fisher of Dallas joined Charles Plosser of Philadelphia in voting against. The final vote was 8-2.

In her press conference, Ms. Yellen said that while "considerable time" was still appropriate, markets should not take it as meaning the Fed would not raise rates early if the economic data were strong.

"I know 'considerable time' sounds like it's a calendar concept, but it is highly conditional and it's linked to the committee's assessment of the economy," said Ms. Yellen. "There is no mechanical interpretation of what the term 'considerable time' means." …

By the end of 2016, the FOMC now expects an interest rate of 2.75-3 percent. That implies a further six rate rises during 2016—a fairly rapid pace of tightening. …

MyEconLab More Economics in the News

ESSENCE OF THE STORY

- The Fed maintained its view that interest rates would be low for a "considerable time."
- Janet Yellen said that "considerable time" is not a calendar concept but conditional on economic data.
- The FOMC forecasts an interest rate of 1.25 to 1.5 percent by the end of 2015 and 2.75 to 3 percent by the end of 2016.
- Two officials voted against the majority and want to see greater flexibility to start raising the interest rate earlier.

ECONOMIC ANALYSIS

- The recovery from the 2008–2009 recession has been slow, and a high unemployment rate and a recessionary gap have persisted.

- In September 2014, the Fed was sufficiently concerned about the slow pace of the recovery to maintain its "forward guidance" on interest rates by continuing its pledge to keep a very low interest rate for a "considerable time."

- Everyone agreed that in 2014 unemployment remained a problem but inflation was well inside the comfort zone.

- But not everyone agreed with the Fed's assessment of the situation and some wanted a more flexible approach and a willingness to raise interest rates earlier.

- The Fed's commitment to ongoing stimulus from a near zero interest rate was based on a view that the output gap remained large.

- But there is great uncertainty about the size of the output gap.

- Figure 1 shows two views of the gap. CBO is the official view of the Congressional Budget Office and most likely the view of the FOMC majority. SF is an estimate by economists at the San Francisco Fed and most likely the view of the two FOMC dissenters.

- While there is disagreement about when to start raising interest rates, there is no disagreement that they are going up in 2015, 2016, and 2017.

- Figure 2 shows the forecasts of the 8 FOMC members and 9 other Fed board members and regional Fed presidents. (The data behind Fig. 2 are published in the FOMC minutes for its July 2014 meeting.)

- Whether the Fed will get the economy back to full employment without triggering a new outburst of inflation depends on the true size of the output gap and the speed with which a future rise in interest rates keeps aggregate demand at a non-inflationary level.

- Figure 3 illustrates the Fed's challenge. In mid-2014, real GDP was \$16 trillion and the price level was 108 at the intersection of AD_0 and SAS.

- The CBO says potential GDP was \$16.7 trillion, with a recessionary gap of \$0.7 trillion on LAS_{CBO}. The San Francisco Fed says potential GDP was \$16.1 trillion, with a recessionary gap of \$0.1 trillion on LAS_{SF}.

- If continued low interest rates into 2015 increases aggregate demand to AD_1, real GDP will increase to \$16.7 trillion and the price level will rise to 110 (a low inflation rate).

- What happens next depends on who is correct about potential GDP. If the CBO is correct, full employment is restored and inflation remains subdued.

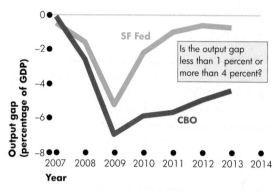

Figure 1 Two Views of the Output Gap

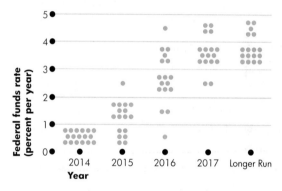

Figure 2 Seventeen Views on the Interest Rate

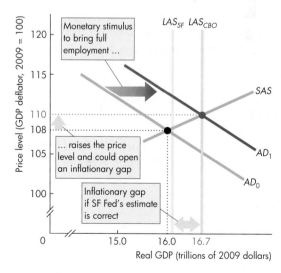

Figure 3 Two Possible Outcomes

- If the San Francisco Fed economists' view is correct, an inflationary gap will open and a demand-pull inflation will begin.

777

SUMMARY

Key Points

Monetary Policy Objectives and Framework

(pp. 758–760)

- The Federal Reserve Act requires the Fed to use monetary policy to achieve maximum employment, stable prices, and moderate long-term interest rates.
- The goal of stable prices delivers maximum employment and low interest rates in the long run but can conflict with the other goals in the short run.
- The Fed translates the goal of stable prices as an inflation rate of between 1 and 2 percent per year.
- The FOMC has the responsibility for the conduct of monetary policy, but the Fed reports to the public and to Congress.

Working Problems 1 to 3 will give you a better understanding of monetary policy objectives and framework.

The Conduct of Monetary Policy

(pp. 760–762)

- The Fed's monetary policy instrument is the federal funds rate.
- The Fed sets the federal funds rate target and announces changes on eight dates each year.
- To decide on the appropriate level of the federal funds rate target, the Fed monitors the inflation rate, the unemployment rate, and real GDP.
- A rise in the interest rate is indicated when inflation is above 2 percent, unemployment is below the natural rate, and real GDP is above potential GDP.
- A fall in the interest rate is indicated when inflation is below 1 percent, unemployment is above the natural rate, and real GDP is below potential GDP.

- The Fed hits its federal funds rate target by using open market operations.
- By buying or selling government securities in the open market, the Fed is able to change bank reserves and change the federal funds rate.

Working Problems 4 to 8 will give you a better understanding of the conduct of monetary policy.

Monetary Policy Transmission

(pp. 763–771)

- A change in the federal funds rate changes other interest rates, the exchange rate, the quantity of money and loans, aggregate demand, and eventually real GDP and the price level.
- Changes in the federal funds rate change real GDP about one year later and change the inflation rate with an even longer time lag.

Working Problems 9 to 14 will give you a better understanding of monetary policy transmission.

Extraordinary Monetary Stimulus

(pp. 772–775)

- A financial crisis has three ingredients: a widespread fall in asset prices, a currency drain, and a run on banks.
- The Fed and U.S. Treasury responded to the financial crisis with classic open market operations on a massive scale and by several other unconventional measures.
- Inflation targeting and the Taylor rule are monetary policy strategies designed to enable the central bank to manage inflation expectations and reduce uncertainty.

Working Problem 15 will give you a better understanding of extraordinary monetary stimulus.

Key Terms

MyEconLab Key Terms Quiz

Beige Book, 759
Core inflation rate, 759
Federal funds rate, 760

Inflation rate targeting, 775
Monetary policy instrument, 760

WORKED PROBLEM

MyEconLab   You can work this problem in Chapter 31 Study Plan.

The U.S. economy is at full employment, the inflation rate is 2 percent a year, and the federal funds rate is at 4 percent a year. But real GDP is growing more slowly than average, so the Fed decides to lower interest rates.

Questions

1. Which macroeconomic variables change immediately and in which direction?
2. Which macroeconomic variables change over the next few weeks or months and in which direction?
3. Which macroeconomic variables change over the next year or two and in which direction?
4. Does the economic growth rate increase?

Solutions

1. The Fed lowers its federal funds rate target and the New York Fed buys securities on the open market. An increase in the monetary base creates excess reserves and the interest rate at which banks lend and borrow reserves—the federal funds rate—falls.

   The banks buy short-term bills, the price of which rises and the interest rate on which falls. The lower interest rate makes the U.S. dollar depreciate on the foreign exchange market.

Key Point: A change in the federal funds rate flows immediately into the inter-bank loans market, the short-term securities market, and the foreign exchange market, changing the short-term interest rate and the U.S. dollar exchange rate.

2. Over the next weeks and months, the banks increase loans. The quantity of money increases and the supply of loans increases. In the loanable funds market, an increase in supply lowers the real interest rate, and saving starts to decrease and investment starts to increase.

   The lower dollar on the foreign exchange market increases exports and decreases imports.

Key Point: A few weeks and months after the Fed changes the interest rate, ripples reach the loanable funds market and a change in the real interest rate starts to change saving and investment.

Net exports begin to respond to the changed exchange rate.

3. Over the next year, the lower real interest rate continues to decrease saving and increase consumption expenditure and business investment. And the lower dollar continues to increase net exports. With all the components of aggregate expenditure rising, U.S. aggregate demand increases and real GDP increases.

   The increase in real GDP is also an increase in income, which induces a further increase in consumption expenditure—an expenditure multiplier process.

   If aggregate demand increases before investment in new capital and new technology changes aggregate supply, the economy moves above full employment and an inflationary gap appears. Businesses face a shortage of labor. As time goes on, wage rates and prices start to rise and after about two years the inflation rate rises.

Key Point: A change in the real interest rate influences the goods market. Aggregate demand changes and, with no change in aggregate supply, real GDP increases. But the inflation rate changes about two years after the Fed lowers the interest rate target.

4. The increase in aggregate demand increases real GDP, but will the economic growth rate be higher? With no change in aggregate supply, real GDP will eventually return to its initial level and a short burst of growth will have occurred. But in the long run, the U.S. economy will be back to its initial full-employment situation with no faster growth rate and a higher inflation rate.

   For the growth rate to increase, investment in new capital and new technologies must increase the rate of productivity growth to speed the growth rate of aggregate supply. Changing the interest rate will work its way through the economy to increase real GDP in the short term but not create economic growth.

Key Point: When the Fed changes the interest rate, changes ripple through all markets. The money market, the loanable funds market, the labor market, and the goods market all respond to the interest rate change one after the other, but unless the pace of productivity growth increases, the economic growth rate will not increase. Monetary policy cannot be used to increase the economic growth rate.

STUDY PLAN PROBLEMS AND APPLICATIONS

MyEconLab   You can work Problems 1 to 15 in Chapter 31 Study Plan and get instant feedback.

Monetary Policy Objectives and Framework

(Study Plan 31.1)

1. "Unemployment is a more serious economic problem than inflation and it should be the focus of the Fed's monetary policy." Evaluate this statement and explain why the Fed's primary policy goal is price stability.

2. "Monetary policy is too important to be left to the Fed. The President should be responsible for it." How is responsibility for monetary policy allocated among the Fed, the Congress, and the President?

3. **Fed's Easing Has Little Impact So Far**

   The Federal Reserve's latest easing program may be nicknamed "QE Infinity" on Wall Street, but it's having a limited effect on the economy so far.

   Source: cnbc.com, October 3, 2012

   a. What does the Federal Reserve Act of 2000 say about the Fed's control of the quantity of money?

   b. How can the massive increase in the monetary base resulting from "quantitative easing" or QE be reconciled with the Federal Reserve Act of 2000?

The Conduct of Monetary Policy (Study Plan 31.2)

4. What are the two possible monetary policy instruments, which one does the Fed use, and how has its value behaved since 2000?

5. How does the Fed hit its federal funds rate target? Illustrate your answer with an appropriate graph.

6. What does the Fed do to determine whether the federal funds rate should be raised, lowered, or left unchanged?

Use the following news clip to work Problems 7 and 8.

Fed Sees Unemployment and Inflation Rising

It is May 2008 and the Fed is confronted with a rising unemployment rate and rising inflation.

Source: CNN, May 21, 2008

7. Explain the dilemma faced by the Fed in May 2008.

8. a. Why might the Fed decide to cut the interest rate in the months after May 2008?

   b. Why might the Fed decide to raise the interest rate in the months after May 2008?

Monetary Policy Transmission (Study Plan 31.3)

Use the following data to work Problems 9 to 11.

The Bureau of Economic Analysis reported that business investment in the second quarter of 2012 was $1,483 billion, $97 billion less than in 2008.

9. Explain the effects of the Fed's low interest rates on business investment and use a graph to illustrate your explanation.

10. Explain the effects of business investment on aggregate demand. Would you expect it to have a multiplier effect? Why or why not?

11. What actions might the Fed take to stimulate business investment further?

Use the following news clip to work Problems 12 to 14.

IMF Warns Global Economic Slowdown Deepens, Prods U.S., Europe

The IMF said the global economic slowdown is worsening and warned U.S. and European policymakers that failure to fix their economic ills would prolong the slump.

Source: Reuters, October 9, 2012

12. If the IMF forecasts turn out to be correct, what would most likely happen to the output gap and unemployment in 2013?

13. a. What actions taken by the Fed in 2011 and 2012 would you expect to have influenced real GDP growth in 2013? Explain how those policy actions would transmit to real GDP.

    b. Draw a graph of aggregate demand and aggregate supply to illustrate your answer to part (a).

14. What further actions might the Fed take in 2013 to influence the real GDP growth in 2014? (Remember the time lags in the operation of monetary policy.)

Extraordinary Monetary Stimulus (Study Plan 31.4)

15. **Prospects Rise for Fed Easing Policy**

    William Dudley, president of the New York Fed, raised the prospect of the Fed becoming more explicit about its inflation goal to "help anchor inflation expectations at the desired rate."

    Source: ft.com, October 1, 2010

    What monetary policy strategy is Mr. Dudley raising? How does inflation rate targeting work and why might it "help anchor inflation expectations at the desired rate"?

ADDITIONAL PROBLEMS AND APPLICATIONS

MyEconLab You can work these problems in MyEconLab if assigned by your instructor.

Monetary Policy Objectives and Framework

Use the following information to work Problems 16 to 18.

The Fed's mandated policy goals are "maximum employment, stable prices, and moderate long-term interest rates."

16. Explain the harmony among these goals in the long run.

17. Explain the conflict among these goals in the short run.

18. Based on the performance of U.S. inflation and unemployment, which of the Fed's goals appears to have taken priority since 2000?

19. What is the core inflation rate and why does the Fed regard it as a better measure on which to focus than the CPI?

20. Suppose Congress decided to strip the Fed of its monetary policy independence and legislate interest rate changes. How would you expect the policy choices to change? Which arrangement would most likely provide price stability?

Use the following CBO report to work Problems 21 to 23.

Fiscal 2012 Deficit: Smaller, But Still Big

The budget deficit was about $1.1 trillion in fiscal year 2012, CBO estimates. That is about $200 billion smaller than in 2011, but still ranks as the fourth-largest deficit since World War II.

Source: Congressional Budget Office

21. How does the federal government get funds to cover its budget deficit? How does financing the budget deficit affect the Fed's monetary policy?

22. How was the budget deficit of 2012 influenced by the Fed's low interest rate policy?

23. a. How would the budget deficit change in 2013 and 2014 if the Fed moved interest rates up?

   b. How would the budget deficit change in 2013 and 2014 if the Fed's monetary policy led to a rapid depreciation of the dollar?

24. The Federal Reserve Act of 2000 instructs the Fed to pursue its goals by "maintain[ing] long-run growth of the monetary and credit aggregates commensurate with the economy's long-run potential to increase production."

   a. Has the Fed followed this instruction?

   b. Why might the Fed increase money by more than the potential to increase production?

The Conduct of Monetary Policy

25. Looking at the federal funds rate since 2000, identify periods during which, with the benefit of hindsight, the rate might have been kept too low. Identify periods during which it might have been too high.

26. Now that the Fed has created $3 trillion of bank reserves, how would you expect a further open market purchase of securities to influence the federal funds rate? Why? Illustrate your answer with an appropriate graph.

27. What is the Beige Book and what role does it play in the Fed's monetary policy decision-making process?

To work Problems 28 to 30, use the information that during 2012 the inflation rate increased but remained in the "comfort zone" and the unemployment rate remained high.

28. Explain the dilemma that rising inflation and high unemployment poses for the Fed.

29. Why might the Fed decide to try to lower interest rates (or stimulate in other ways) in this situation?

30. Why might the Fed decide to raise interest rates in this situation?

Monetary Policy Transmission

Use the following information to work Problems 31 to 33.

From 2009 through 2012, the long-term *real* interest rate paid by the safest U.S. corporations fell from 4 percent a year to 2 percent a year. During that same period, the federal funds rate was roughly constant at 0.25 percent a year.

31. What role does the long-term real interest rate play in the monetary policy transmission process?

32. How does the federal funds rate influence the long-term real interest rate?

33. What do you think happened to inflation expectations between 2009 and 2012 and why?

34. **Dollar Reaches New Low vs. Yen**

    Traders continued to make bets in favor of the yen, sending the dollar to a record low against the Japanese currency.

    Source: *The Wall Street Journal*, August 20, 2011

    a. How do "bets in favor of the yen" influence the exchange rate?

    b. How does the Fed's monetary policy influence the exchange rate?

Use the following news clip to work Problems 35 and 36.

Top Economist Says America Could Plunge into Recession

Robert Shiller, Professor of Economics at Yale University, predicted that there was a very real possibility that the United States would be plunged into a Japan-style slump, with house prices declining for years.

Source: timesonline.co.uk, December 31, 2007

35. If the Fed had agreed with Robert Shiller in December 2007, what actions might it have taken differently from those it did take? How could monetary policy prevent house prices from falling?

36. Describe the time lags in the response of output and inflation to the policy actions you have prescribed.

Extraordinary Monetary Stimulus

37. **Philly Fed's Plosser Opposes QE3**

    Federal Reserve Bank of Philadelphia president Charles Plosser does not think that monetary policy can "do much to speed up the slow progress" in the labor market and opposes the Fed's latest round of stimulus, known as QE3, saying he does not think it prudent to risk the Fed's hard-won credibility.

    Source: *Philadelphia Inquirer*, September 25, 2012

    a. Describe the QE3 asset purchases that are causing Charles Plosser concern.

    b. How might asset purchases damage the Fed's credibility?

38. Suppose that the Reserve Bank of New Zealand is following the Taylor rule. In 2012, it sets the official cash rate (its equivalent of the federal funds rate) at 4 percent a year. If the inflation rate in New Zealand is 2 percent a year, what is its output gap?

Use the following news clip to work Problems 39 and 40.

Bernanke on Inflation Targeting

Inflation targeting promotes well-anchored inflation expectations, which facilitate more effective stabilization of output and employment. Thus inflation targeting can deliver good results with respect to output and employment as well as inflation.

Source: Federal Reserve Board, remarks by Ben Bernanke to the National Association of Business Economists, March 25, 2003

39. What is inflation targeting and how do "well-anchored inflation expectations" help to achieve more stable output as well as low inflation?

40. Explain how inflation targeting as described by Ben Bernanke is consistent with the Fed's dual mandate.

Economics in the News

41. After you have studied *Economics in the News* on pp. 776–777, answer the following questions.

    a. What was the state of the U.S. economy in the fall of 2014 when the Fed made the decision to commit to keeping interest rates low for a "considerable time"?

    b. What was the FOMC majority expectation about future employment, real GDP, and inflation in September 2014?

    c. How would an earlier and faster rise in interest rates influence aggregate demand?

    d. If the San Francisco Fed view of the output gap is correct, where will interest rates be in 2016 and 2017? Why?

42. **Fed's Evans: Offers Full Support for New Stimulus**

    Federal Reserve Bank of Chicago President Charles Evans expressed strong support for the new stimulus provided by the central bank saying, "This was the time to act" and adding, "I am optimistic that we can achieve better outcomes through more monetary policy accommodation."

    Source: *The Wall Street Journal*, September 18, 2012

    a. Why, in the economic conditions of September 2012, was Charles Evans happy to see the Fed stimulating the economy?

    b. What would be the effects of the Fed's QE3 and other stimulative actions? Explain the immediate effects and the ripple effects.

    c. What are the risks arising from greater monetary stimulus?

Tradeoffs and Free Lunches

A policy tradeoff arises if, in taking an action to achieve one goal, some other goal must be forgone. The Fed wants to avoid a rise in the inflation rate and a rise in the unemployment rate. But if the Fed raises the interest rate to curb inflation, it might lower expenditure and increase unemployment. The Fed faces a short-run tradeoff between inflation and unemployment.

A policy free lunch arises if in taking actions to pursue one goal, some other (intended or unintended) goal is also achieved. The Fed wants to keep inflation in check and, at the same time, to boost the economic growth rate. If lower inflation brings greater certainty about the future and stimulates saving and investment, the Fed gets both lower inflation and faster real GDP growth. It enjoys a free lunch.

The two chapters in this part have described the institutional framework in which fiscal policy (Chapter 30) and monetary policy (Chapter 31) are made, described the instruments of policy, and analyzed the effects of policy. This exploration of economic policy draws on almost everything that you learned in previous chapters.

These policy chapters serve as a capstone on your knowledge of macroeconomics and draw together all the strands in your study of the previous chapters.

Milton Friedman, whom you meet below, has profoundly influenced our understanding of macroeconomic policy, especially monetary policy.

Milton Friedman *was born into a poor immigrant family in New York City in 1912. He was an undergraduate at Rutgers and a graduate student at Columbia University during the Great Depression. From 1977 until his death in 2006, Professor Friedman was a Senior Fellow at the Hoover Institution at Stanford University. But his reputation was built between 1946 and 1983, when he was a leading member of the "Chicago School," an approach to economics developed at the University of Chicago and based on the views that free markets allocate resources efficiently and that stable and low money supply growth delivers macroeconomic stability.*

Friedman has advanced our understanding of the forces that determine macroeconomic performance and clarified the effects of the quantity of money. For this work, he was awarded the 1977 Nobel Prize for Economic Science.

By reasoning from basic economic principles, Friedman (along with Edmund S. Phelps, the 2006 Economics

"Inflation is always and everywhere a monetary phenomenon."

MILTON FRIEDMAN
The Counter-Revolution in Monetary Theory

Nobel Laureate) predicted that persistent demand stimulation would not increase output but would cause inflation.

When output growth slowed and inflation broke out in the 1970s, Friedman seemed like a prophet, and for a time, his policy prescription, known as monetarism, *was embraced around the world.*

STEPHANIE SCHMITT-GROHÉ is Professor of Economics at Columbia University. Born in Germany, she received her first economics degree at Westfälische Wilhelms-Universität Münster in 1987, her M.B.A in Finance at Baruch College, City University of New York in 1989, and her Ph.D. in economics at the University of Chicago in 1994.

Professor Schmitt-Grohé's research covers a wide range of fiscal policy and monetary policy issues that are especially relevant in today's economy as the consequences of the 2007 mortgage crisis play out.

Working with her husband, Martin Uribe, also a Professor of Economics at Columbia University, she has published papers in leading economics journals on how best to conduct monetary policy and fiscal policy and how to avoid problems that might arise from the inappropriate use of a simple policy rule for setting the federal funds rate. She has also contributed to the debate on inflation targeting.

In 2004, Professor Schmitt-Grohé was awarded the Bernácer Prize, awarded annually to a European economist under the age of 40 who has made outstanding contributions in the fields of macroeconomics and finance.

Michael Parkin talked with Stephanie Schmitt-Grohé about her work and the challenges of conducting stabilization policy.

...the optimal inflation rate is well below the two percent or more that we observe.

Only a few years out of graduate school, you and your economist husband Martin Uribe accepted a challenge to contribute to an assessment of "dollarization" for Mexico. First, would you explain what dollarization is?

When a country dollarizes, the U.S. dollar becomes legal tender, replacing the domestic currency. Ecuador, for example, is dollarized. In the case of Mexico in 1999, there were proposals, mainly coming from the business community, to replace the peso with the U.S. dollar.

Why might dollarization be a good idea?

Such proposals are typically motivated by the desire to avoid excessive inflation and excessive exchange rate volatility. Dollarization also makes inflationary finance of the Treasury Department impossible.

You've done some recent research with Martin on the optimal or best inflation rate. What is the optimal rate?

Many central banks have an inflation target. In developed economies it is about 2 percent per year and in emerging market economies it is about 4 percent per year. Martin and I are trying to answer the seemingly simple and innocent question: Which level of the inflation rate should a central bank target? Is it the observed values of 2 percent and 4 percent? Or should it be zero, or 6 percent, or why not aim for a negative inflation rate—a falling price level? ...

In a realistic model of the economy that incorporates all the costs and benefits of inflation, the best inflation rate is at most half a percent per year. So the optimal inflation rate is well below the two percent or more that we observe.

*Read the full interview with Stephanie Schmitt-Grohé in MyEconLab.

Abatement technology A production technology that reduces or prevents pollution. (p. 395)

Above full-employment equilibrium A macroeconomic equilibrium in which real GDP exceeds potential GDP. (p. 660)

Absolute advantage A person has an absolute advantage if that person is more productive than another person. (p. 40)

Adverse selection The tendency for people to *enter into agreements* in which they can use their private information to their own advantage and to the disadvantage of the uninformed party. (p. 476)

Aggregate demand The relationship between the quantity of real GDP demanded and the price level. (p. 654)

Aggregate planned expenditure The sum of planned consumption expenditure, planned investment, planned government expenditure on goods and services, and planned exports minus planned imports. (p. 674)

Aggregate production function The relationship between real GDP and the quantity of labor when all other influences on production remain the same. (p. 546)

Allocative efficiency A situation in which goods and services are produced at the lowest possible cost and in the quantities that provide the greatest possible benefit. We cannot produce more of any good without giving up some of another good that we *value more highly*. (p. 35)

Antitrust law A law that regulates oligopolies and prevents them from becoming monopolies or behaving like monopolies. (p. 356)

Arbitrage The practice of seeking to profit by buying in one market and selling for a higher price in another related market. (p. 628)

Asymmetric information A market in which buyers or sellers have private information. (p. 476)

Automatic fiscal policy A fiscal policy action that is triggered by the state of the economy with no action by the government. (p. 744)

Autonomous expenditure The sum of those components of aggregate planned expenditure that are not influenced by real GDP. Autonomous expenditure equals the sum of investment, government expenditure, exports, and the autonomous parts of consumption expenditure and imports. (p. 678)

Autonomous tax multiplier The change in equilibrium expenditure and real GDP that results from a change in autonomous taxes divided by the change in autonomous taxes. (p. 696)

Average cost pricing rule A rule that sets price to cover cost including normal profit, which means setting the price equal to average total cost. (p. 314)

Average fixed cost Total fixed cost per unit of output. (p. 254)

Average product The average product of a factor of production. It equals total product divided by the quantity of the factor employed. (p. 249)

Average total cost Total cost per unit of output. (p. 254)

Average variable cost Total variable cost per unit of output. (p. 254)

Balanced budget A government budget in which receipts and outlays are equal. (p. 732)

Balanced budget multiplier The change in equilibrium expenditure and real GDP that results from equal changes in government expenditure and lump-sum taxes divided by the change in government expenditure. (p. 697)

Balance of payments accounts A country's record of international trading, borrowing, and lending. (p. 634)

Barrier to entry A natural or legal constraint that protects a firm from potential competitors. (p. 298)

Behavioral economics A study of the ways in which limits on the human brain's ability to compute and implement rational decisions influences economic behavior—both the decisions that people make and the consequences of those decisions for the way markets work. (p. 192)

Beige Book The Fed's publication that summarizes all the data that it gathers and that describes the current state of the economy. (p. 759)

Below full-employment equilibrium A macroeconomic equilibrium in which potential GDP exceeds real GDP. (p. 661)

Benefit The benefit of something is the gain or pleasure that it brings and is determined by preferences. (p. 9)

Big tradeoff The tradeoff between efficiency and fairness. (pp. 117, 460)

Bilateral monopoly A situation in which a monopoly seller faces a monopsony buyer. (p. 429)

Black market An illegal market in which the equilibrium price exceeds the legally imposed price ceiling. (p. 128)

Bond A promise to make specified payments on specified dates. (p. 569)

Bond market The market in which bonds issued by firms and governments are traded. (p. 569)

Budget deficit A government's budget balance that is negative—outlays exceed receipts. (p. 732)

Budget line The limit to a household's consumption choices. It marks the boundary between those combinations of goods and services that a household can afford to buy and those that it cannot afford. (pp. 178, 202)

Budget surplus A government's budget balance that is positive—receipts exceed outlays. (p. 732)

Business cycle The periodic but irregular up-and-down movement of total production and other measures of economic activity. (p. 499)

Capital The tools, equipment, buildings, and other constructions that businesses use to produce goods and services. (p. 4)

Capital accumulation The growth of capital resources, including *human capital*. (p. 38)

Capital and financial account A record of foreign investment in a country minus its investment abroad. (p. 634)

Capture theory A theory that regulation serves the self-interest of the producer, who captures the regulator and maximizes economic profit. (p. 313)

Cartel A group of firms acting together—colluding— to limit output, raise the price, and increase economic profit. (p. 343)

Central bank A bank's bank and a public authority that regulates the nation's depository institutions and conducts *monetary policy*, which means it adjusts the quantity of money in circulation and influences interest rates. (p. 597)

Ceteris paribus Other things being equal—all other relevant things remaining the same. (p. 24)

Change in demand A change in buyers' plans that occurs when some influence on those plans other than the price of the good changes. It is illustrated by a shift of the demand curve. (p. 58)

Change in supply A change in sellers' plans that occurs when some influence on those plans other than the price of the good changes. It is illustrated by a shift of the supply curve. (p. 63)

Change in the quantity demanded A change in buyers' plans that occurs when the price of a good changes but all other influences on buyers' plans remain unchanged. It is illustrated by a movement along the demand curve. (p. 61)

Change in the quantity supplied A change in sellers' plans that occurs when the price of a good changes but all other influences on sellers' plans remain unchanged. It is illustrated by a movement along the supply curve. (p. 64)

Classical A macroeconomist who believes that the economy is self-regulating and always at full employment. (p. 664)

Classical growth theory A theory of economic growth based on the view that the growth of real GDP per person is temporary and that when it rises above subsistence level, a population explosion eventually brings it back to subsistence level. (p. 555)

Coase theorem The proposition that if property rights exist, if only a small number of parties are involved, and transactions costs are low, then private transactions are efficient, and it doesn't matter who has the property rights. (p. 396)

Collusive agreement An agreement between two (or more) producers to form a cartel to restrict output, raise the price, and increase profits. (p. 346)

Command system A method of allocating resources by the order (command) of someone in authority. In a firm a managerial hierarchy organizes production. (pp. 106, 229)

Common resource A resource that is rival and nonexcludable. (p. 372)

Comparative advantage A person or country has a comparative advantage in an activity if that person or country can perform the activity at a lower opportunity cost than anyone else or any other country. (p. 40)

Competitive market A market that has many buyers and many sellers, so no single buyer or seller can influence the price. (p. 56)

Complement A good that is used in conjunction with another good. (p. 59)

Constant returns to scale Features of a firm's technology that lead to constant long-run average cost as output increases. When constant returns to scale are present, the *LRAC* curve is horizontal. (p. 262)

Consumer equilibrium A situation in which a consumer has allocated all his or her available income in the way that, given the prices of goods and services, maximizes his or her total utility. (p. 181)

Consumer Price Index (CPI) An index that measures the average of the prices paid by urban consumers for a fixed basket of consumer goods and services. (p. 525)

Consumer surplus The excess of the benefit received from a good over the amount paid for it. It is calculated as the marginal benefit (or value) of a good minus its price, summed over the quantity bought. (p. 109)

Consumption expenditure The total payment for consumer goods and services. (p. 493)

Consumption function The relationship between consumption expenditure and disposable income, other things remaining the same. (p. 674)

Contestable market A market in which firms can enter and leave so easily that firms in the market face competition from *potential* entrants. (p. 354)

Cooperative equilibrium The outcome of a game in which the players make and share the monopoly profit. (p. 352)

Core inflation rate The Fed's operational guide is the rate of increase in the core PCE deflator, which is the PCE deflator excluding food and fuel prices. (p. 759)

Cost-push inflation An inflation that results from an initial increase in costs. (p. 711)

Council of Economic Advisers The President's council whose main work is to monitor the economy and keep the President and the public well informed about the current state of the economy and the best available forecasts of where it is heading. (p. 731)

Crawling peg An exchange rate that follows a path determined by a decision of the government or the central bank and is achieved in a similar way to a fixed exchange rate. (p. 632)

Creditor nation A country that during its entire history has invested more in the rest of the world than other countries have invested in it. (p. 637)

Credit risk The risk that a borrower, also known as a creditor, might not repay a loan. (p. 479)

Cross elasticity of demand The responsiveness of the demand for a good to a change in the price of a substitute or complement, other things remaining the same. It is calculated as the percentage change in the quantity demanded of the good divided by the percentage change in the price of the substitute or complement. (p. 92)

Crowding-out effect The tendency for a government budget deficit to raise the real interest rate and decrease investment. (p. 581)

Currency The notes and coins held by individuals and businesses. (p. 591)

Currency drain ratio The ratio of currency to deposits. (p. 601)

Current account A record of receipts from exports of goods and services, payments for imports of goods and services, net interest income paid abroad, and net transfers received from abroad. (p. 634)

Cycle The tendency for a variable to alternate between upward and downward movements. (p. 507)

Cyclical surplus or deficit The actual surplus or deficit minus the structural surplus or deficit. (p. 745)

Cyclical unemployment The higher than normal unemployment at a business cycle trough and the lower than normal unemployment at a business cycle peak. (p. 521)

Deadweight loss A measure of inefficiency. It is equal to the decrease in total surplus that results from an inefficient level of production. (p. 114)

Debtor nation A country that during its entire history has borrowed more from the rest of the world than it has lent to the rest of the world. (p. 637)

Default risk The risk that a borrower, also known as a creditor, might not repay a loan. (pp. 479, 577)

Deflation A persistently falling price level. (p. 524)

Demand The entire relationship between the price of the good and the quantity demanded of it when all other influences on buyers' plans remain the same. It is illustrated by a demand curve and described by a demand schedule. (p. 57)

Demand curve A curve that shows the relationship between the quantity demanded of a good and its price when all other influences on

consumers' planned purchases remain the same. (p. 58)

Demand for loanable funds The relationship between the quantity of loanable funds demanded and the real interest rate when all other influences on borrowing plans remain the same. (p. 575)

Demand for money The relationship between the quantity of real money demanded and the nominal interest rate when all other influences on the amount of money that people wish to hold remain the same. (p. 605)

Demand-pull inflation An inflation that starts because aggregate demand increases. (p. 709)

Depository institution A financial firm that takes deposits from households and firms. (p. 593)

Depreciation The decrease in the value of a firm's capital that results from wear and tear and obsolescence. (p. 494)

Deregulation The process of removing regulation of prices, quantities, entry, and other aspects of economic activity in a firm or industry. (p. 313)

Derived demand Demand for a factor of production—it is derived from the demand for the goods and services produced by that factor. (p. 421)

Desired reserve ratio The ratio of reserves to deposits that banks *plan* to hold. (p. 601)

Diminishing marginal rate of substitution The general tendency for a person to be willing to give up less of good y to get one more unit of good x, while at the same time remaining indifferent as the quantity of good x increases. (p. 206)

Diminishing marginal returns The tendency for the marginal product of an additional unit of a factor of production to be less than the marginal product of the previous unit of the factor. (p. 251)

Diminishing marginal utility The tendency for marginal utility to decrease as the quantity consumed of a good increases. (p. 180)

Direct relationship A relationship between two variables that move in the same direction. (p. 18)

Discouraged worker A marginally attached worker who has stopped looking for a job because of repeated failure to find one. (p. 519)

Discretionary fiscal policy A fiscal action that is initiated by an act of Congress. (p. 744)

Diseconomies of scale Features of a firm's technology that make average total cost rise as output increases—the *LRAC* curve slopes upward. (p. 262)

Disposable income Aggregate income minus taxes plus transfer payments. (pp. 656, 674)

Dominant strategy equilibrium An equilibrium in which the best strategy for each player is to cheat *regardless of the strategy of the other player*. (p. 345)

Dumping The sale by a foreign firm of exports at a lower price than the cost of production. (p. 164)

Duopoly An oligopoly market in which two producers of a good or service compete. (p. 342)

Economic depreciation The *fall* in the market value of a firm's capital over a given period. (p. 225)

Economic efficiency A situation that occurs when the firm produces a given output at the least cost. (p. 227)

Economic growth The expansion of production possibilities. (pp. 38, 540)

Economic model A description of some aspect of the economic world that includes only those features of the world that are needed for the purpose at hand. (p. 11)

Economic profit A firm's total revenue minus its total cost, with total cost measured as the opportunity cost of production. (p. 224)

Economic rent Any surplus—consumer surplus, producer surplus, or economic profit. (p. 306)

Economics The social science that studies the *choices* that individuals, businesses, governments, and entire societies make as they cope with *scarcity* and the *incentives* that influence and reconcile those choices. (p. 2)

Economies of scale Features of a firm's technology that make average total cost fall as output increases—the *LRAC* curve slopes downward. (pp. 238, 262)

Economies of scope Decreases in average total cost that occur when a firm uses specialized resources to produce a range of goods and services. (p. 239)

Efficient Resource use is efficient if it is *not* possible to make someone better off without making someone else worse off. (p. 5)

Efficient scale The quantity at which average total cost is a minimum—the quantity at the bottom of the U-shaped *ATC* curve. (p. 328)

Elastic demand Demand with a price elasticity greater than 1; other things remaining the same, the percentage change in the quantity demanded exceeds the percentage change in price. (p. 86)

Elasticity of supply The responsiveness of the quantity supplied of a good to a change in its price, other things remaining the same. (p. 94)

Employment-to-population ratio The percentage of people of working age who have jobs. (p. 518)

Entrepreneurship The human resource that organizes the other three factors of production: labor, land, and capital. (p. 4)

Equilibrium expenditure The level of aggregate expenditure that occurs when aggregate *planned* expenditure equals real GDP. (p. 680)

Equilibrium price The price at which the quantity demanded equals the quantity supplied. (p. 66)

Equilibrium quantity The quantity bought and sold at the equilibrium price. (p. 66)

Excess capacity A firm has excess capacity if it produces below its efficient scale. (p. 328)

Excess reserves A bank's actual reserves minus its desired reserves. (p. 601)

Exchange rate The price at which one currency exchanges for another in the foreign exchange market. (p. 620)

Excludable A good or service or a resource is excludable if it is possible to prevent someone from enjoying the benefit of it. (p. 372)

Expansion A business cycle phase between a trough and a peak—a period in which real GDP increases. (p. 499)

Expected utility The utility value of what a person expects to own at a given point in time. (p. 471)

Expected wealth The money value of what a person expects to own at a given point in time. (p. 470)

Exports The goods and services that we sell to people in other countries. (pp. 152, 494)

Externality A cost or a benefit that arises from an action that falls on someone other than the person or firm choosisng the action. (p. 392)

Factors of production The productive resources used to produce goods and services. (p. 3)

Federal budget The annual statement of the outlays and receipts of the government of the United States, together with the laws and regulations that approve and support those outlays and taxes. (p. 730)

Federal funds rate The interest rate that the banks charge each other on overnight loans. (pp. 593, 760)

Federal Open Market Committee The main policymaking organ of the Federal Reserve System. (p. 597)

Federal Reserve System (the **Fed**) The central bank of the United States, a public authority whose main role is the regulation of banks and money. (pp. 572, 597)

Final good An item that is bought by its final user during the specified time period. (p. 492)

Financial capital The funds that firms use to buy physical capital and that households use to buy a home or to invest in human capital. (p. 568)

Financial institution A firm that operates on both sides of the market for financial capital. It borrows in one market and lends in another. (p. 570)

Firm An economic unit that hires factors of production and organizes those factors to produce and sell goods and services. (pp. 44, 224)

Fiscal imbalance The present value of the government's commitments to pay benefits minus the present value of its tax revenues. (p. 742)

Fiscal policy The use of the federal budget, by setting and changing tax rates, making transfer payments, and purchasing goods and services, to achieve macroeconomic objectives such as full employment, sustained economic growth, and price level stability. (pp. 656, 730)

Fiscal stimulus The use of fiscal policy to increase production and employment. (p. 744)

Fixed exchange rate An exchange rate the value of which is determined by a decision of the government or the central bank and is achieved by central bank intervention in the foreign exchange market to block the unregulated forces of demand and supply. (p. 631)

Flexible exchange rate An exchange rate that is determined by demand and supply in the foreign exchange market with no direct intervention by the central bank. (p. 631)

Foreign currency The money of other countries regardless of whether that money is in the form of notes, coins, or bank deposits. (p. 620)

Foreign exchange market The market in which the currency of one country is exchanged for the currency of another. (p. 620)

Four-firm concentration ratio A measure of market power that is calculated as the percentage of the value of sales accounted for by the four largest firms in an industry. (p. 234)

Free-rider problem The problem that the market would provide an inefficiently small quantity of a public good. (p. 374)

Frictional unemployment The unemployment that arises from normal labor turnover—from people entering and leaving the labor force and from the ongoing creation and destruction of jobs. (p. 521)

Full employment A situation in which the unemployment rate equals the natural unemployment rate. At full employment, there is no cyclical unemployment—all unemployment is frictional and structural. (p. 521)

Full-employment equilibrium A macroeconomic equilibrium in which real GDP equals potential GDP. (p. 661)

Game theory A set of tools for studying strategic behavior—behavior that takes into account the expected behavior of others and the recognition of mutual interdependence. (p. 344)

Generational accounting An accounting system that measures the lifetime tax burden and benefits of each generation. (p. 742)

Generational imbalance The division of the fiscal imbalance between the current and future generations, assuming that the current generation will enjoy the existing levels of taxes and benefits. (p. 743)

Gini ratio The ratio of the area between the line of equality and the Lorenz curve to the entire area beneath the line of equality. (p. 449)

Goods and services The objects that people value and produce to satisfy human wants. (p. 3)

Government debt The total amount that the government has borrowed. It equals the sum of past budget deficits minus the sum of past budget surpluses. (p. 734)

Government expenditure Goods and services bought by government. (p. 494)

Government expenditure multiplier The quantitative effect of a change in government expenditure on real GDP. It is calculated as the change in real GDP that results from a change in government expenditure divided by the change in government expenditure. (pp. 696, 747)

Government failure A situation in which government actions lead to inefficiency—to either underprovision or overprovision. (p. 370)

Government sector balance An amount equal to net taxes minus government expenditure on goods and services. (p. 638)

Gross domestic product (GDP) The market value of all final goods and services produced within a country during a given time period. (p. 492)

Gross investment The total amount spent on purchases of new capital and on replacing depreciated capital. (pp. 494, 568)

Growth rate The annual percentage change of a variable—the change in the level expressed as a percentage of the initial level. (p. 540)

Herfindahl–Hirschman Index A measure of market power that is calculated as the square of the market share of each firm (as a percentage) summed over the largest 50 firms (or over all firms if there are fewer than 50) in a market. (p. 234)

Hotelling Principle The idea that traders expect the price of a nonrenewable natural resource to rise at a rate equal to the interest rate. (p. 434)

Human capital The knowledge and skill that people obtain from education, on-the-job training, and work experience. (p. 3)

Hyperinflation An inflation rate of 50 percent a month or higher that grinds the economy to a halt and causes a society to collapse. (p. 524)

Implicit rental rate The firm's opportunity cost of using its own capital. (p. 224)

Import quota A restriction that limits the maximum quantity of a good that may be imported in a given period. (p. 160)

Imports The goods and services that we buy from people in other countries. (pp. 152, 494)

Incentive A reward that encourages an action or a penalty that discourages one. (p. 2)

Incentive system A method of organizing production that uses a market-like mechanism inside the firm. (p. 229)

Income effect The effect of a change in income on buying plans, other things remaining the same. (p. 211)

Income elasticity of demand The responsiveness of demand to a change in income, other things remaining the same. It is calculated as the percentage change in the quantity demanded divided by the percentage change in income. (p. 91)

Indifference curve A line that shows combinations of goods among which a consumer is *indifferent*. (p. 205)

Individual transferable quota (ITQ) A production limit that is assigned to an individual who is free to transfer (sell) the quota to someone else. (p. 404)

Induced expenditure The sum of the components of aggregate planned expenditure that vary with real GDP. Induced expenditure equals consumption expenditure minus imports. (p. 678)

Inelastic demand A demand with a price elasticity between 0 and 1; the percentage change in the quantity demanded is less than the percentage change in price. (p. 85)

Inferior good A good for which demand decreases as income increases. (p. 60)

Inflation A persistently rising price level. (p. 524)

Inflationary gap An output gap in which real GDP exceeds potential GDP. (p. 660)

Inflation rate targeting A monetary policy strategy in which the central bank makes a public commitment to achieve an explicit inflation rate and to explain how its policy actions will achieve that target. (p. 775)

Interest The income that capital earns. (p. 4)

Interest rate parity A situation in which the rates of return on assets in different currencies are equal. (p. 628)

Intermediate good An item that is produced by one firm, bought by another firm, and used as a component of a final good or service. (p. 492)

Inverse relationship A relationship between variables that move in opposite directions. (p. 19)

Investment The purchase of new plant, equipment, and buildings, and additions to inventories. (p. 493)

Keynesian A macroeconomist who believes that left alone, the economy would rarely operate at full employment and that to achieve full employment, active help from fiscal policy and monetary policy is required. (p. 664)

Keynesian cycle theory A theory that fluctuations in investment driven by fluctuations in business confidence—summarized by the phrase "animal spirits"—are the main source of fluctuations in aggregate demand. (p. 705)

Labor The work time and work effort that people devote to producing goods and services. (p. 3)

Labor force The sum of the people who are employed and who are unemployed. (p. 517)

Labor force participation rate The percentage of the working-age population who are members of the labor force. (p. 519)

Labor productivity The quantity of real GDP produced by an hour of labor. (p. 550)

Labor union An organized group of workers that aims to increase the wage rate and influence other job conditions. (p. 428)

Laffer curve The relationship between the tax rate and the amount of tax revenue collected. (p. 741)

Land The "gifts of nature" that we use to produce goods and services. (p. 3)

Law of demand Other things remaining the same, the higher the price of a good, the smaller is the quantity demanded of it; the lower the price of a good, the larger is the quantity demanded of it. (p. 57)

Law of diminishing returns As a firm uses more of a variable factor of production with a given quantity of the fixed factor of production, the marginal product of the variable factor of production eventually diminishes. (p. 251)

Law of supply Other things remaining the same, the higher the price of a good, the greater is the quantity supplied of it; the lower the price of a good, the smaller is the quantity supplied. (p. 62)

Legal monopoly A market in which competition and entry are restricted by the granting of a public franchise, government license, patent, or copyright. (p. 298)

Lemons problem The problem that in a market in which it is not possible to distinguish reliable products from lemons, there are too many lemons and too few reliable products traded. (p. 476)

Lender of last resort The Fed is the lender of last resort—depository institutions that are short of reserves can borrow from the Fed. (p. 600)

Limit pricing The practice of setting the price at the highest level that inflicts a loss on an entrant. (p. 355)

Linear relationship A relationship between two variables that is illustrated by a straight line. (p. 18)

Loanable funds market The aggregate of all the individual markets in which households, firms, governments, banks, and other financial institutions borrow and lend. (p. 573)

Long run The time frame in which the quantities of *all* factors of production can be varied. (p. 248)

Long-run aggregate supply The relationship between the quantity of real GDP supplied and the price level when the money wage rate changes in step with the price level to maintain full employment. (p. 650)

Long-run average cost curve The relationship between the lowest attainable average total cost and output when the firm can change both the plant it uses and the quantity of labor it employs. (p. 261)

Long-run macroeconomic equilibrium A situation that occurs when real GDP equals potential GDP—the economy is on its long-run aggregate supply curve. (p. 658)

Long-run Phillips curve A curve that shows the relationship between inflation and unemployment when the actual inflation rate equals the expected inflation rate. (p. 718)

Lorenz curve A curve that graphs the cumulative percentage of income or wealth against the cumulative percentage of households. (p. 447)

M1 A measure of money that consists of currency and traveler's checks plus checking deposits owned by individuals and businesses. (p. 591)

M2 A measure of money that consists of M1 plus time deposits, savings deposits, money market mutual funds, and other deposits. (p. 591)

Macroeconomics The study of the performance of the national economy and the global economy. (p. 2)

Margin When a choice is made by comparing a little more of something with its cost, the choice is made at the margin. (p. 10)

Marginal benefit The benefit that a person receives from consuming one more unit of a good or service. It is measured as the maximum amount that a person is willing to pay for one more unit of the good or service. (pp. 10, 36)

Marginal benefit curve A curve that shows the relationship between the marginal benefit of a good and the quantity of that good consumed. (p. 36)

Marginal cost The *opportunity cost* of producing *one* more unit of a good or service. It is the best alternative forgone. It is calculated as the increase in total cost divided by the increase in output. (pp. 10, 35, 254)

Marginal cost pricing rule A rule that sets the price of a good or service equal to the marginal cost of producing it. (p. 313)

Marginal external benefit The benefit from an additional unit of a good or service that people other than the consumer enjoy. (p. 406)

Marginal external cost The cost of producing an additional unit of a good or service that falls on people other than the producer. (p. 394)

Marginally attached worker A person who currently is neither working nor looking for work but has indicated that he or she wants and is available for a job and has looked for work some time in the recent past. (p. 519)

Marginal private benefit The benefit from an additional unit of a good or service that the consumer of that good or service receives. (p. 406)

Marginal private cost The cost of producing an additional unit of a good or service that is borne by the producer of that good or service. (p. 394)

Marginal product The increase in total product that results from a one-unit increase in the variable input, with all other inputs remaining the same. It is calculated as the increase in total product divided by the increase in the variable input employed, when the quantities of all other inputs remain the same. (p. 249)

Marginal propensity to consume The fraction of a *change* in disposable income that is spent on consumption. It is calculated as the *change* in consumption expenditure divided by the *change* in disposable income. (p. 676)

Marginal propensity to import The fraction of an increase in real GDP that is spent on imports. It is calculated as the *change* in imports divided by the *change* in real GDP, other things remaining the same. (p. 677)

Marginal propensity to save The fraction of a *change* in disposable income that is saved. It is calculated as the *change* in saving divided by the *change* in disposable income. (p. 676)

Marginal rate of substitution The rate at which a person will give up good *y* (the good measured on the *y*-axis) to get an additional unit of good *x* (the good measured on the *x*-axis) while at the same time remaining indifferent (remaining on the same indifference curve) as the quantity of *x* increases. (p. 206)

Marginal revenue The change in total revenue that results from a one-unit increase in the quantity sold. It is calculated as the change in total revenue divided by the change in quantity sold. (p. 272)

Marginal social benefit The marginal benefit enjoyed by society—by the consumer of a good or service (marginal private benefit) plus the marginal benefit enjoyed by others (marginal external benefit). (p. 406)

Marginal social cost The marginal cost incurred by the producer and by everyone else on whom the cost

falls—by society. It is the sum of marginal private cost and marginal external cost. (p. 394)

Marginal utility The *change* in total utility resulting from a one-unit increase in the quantity of a good consumed. (p. 179)

Marginal utility per dollar The marginal utility from a good that results from spending one more dollar on it. It is calculated as the marginal utility from the good divided by its price. (p. 182)

Market Any arrangement that enables buyers and sellers to get information and to do business with each other. (p. 44)

Market failure A situation in which a market delivers an inefficient outcome. (p. 114)

Market income The wages, interest, rent, and profit earned in factor markets and before paying income taxes. (p. 446)

Markup The amount by which the firm's price exceeds its marginal cost. (p. 329)

Means of payment A method of settling a debt. (p. 590)

Microeconomics The study of the choices that individuals and businesses make, the way these choices interact in markets, and the influence of governments. (p. 2)

Minimum efficient scale The *smallest* quantity of output at which the long-run average cost reaches its lowest level. (p. 263)

Minimum wage A regulation that makes the hiring of labor below a specified wage rate illegal. The lowest wage at which a firm may legally hire labor. (p. 131)

Monetarist A macroeconomist who believes that the economy is self-regulating and that it will normally operate at full employment, provided that monetary policy is not erratic and that the pace of money growth is kept steady. (p. 665)

Monetarist cycle theory A theory that fluctuations in both investment and consumption expenditure, driven by fluctuations in the growth rate of

the quantity of money, are the main source of fluctuations in aggregate demand. (p. 705)

Monetary base The sum of currency and reserves of the depository institution deposits. (p. 598)

Monetary policy The Fed conducts the nation's monetary policy by changing interest rates and adjusting the quantity of money. (p. 656)

Monetary policy instrument A variable that the Fed can directly control or at least very closely target. (p. 760)

Money Any commodity or token that is generally acceptable as a means of payment. (pp. 44, 590)

Money income Market income plus cash payments to households by the government. (p. 446)

Money multiplier The ratio of the change in the quantity of money to the change in the monetary base. (p. 602)

Money price The number of dollars that must be given up in exchange for a good or service. (p. 56)

Monopolistic competition A market structure in which a large number of firms make similar but slightly different products and compete on product quality, price, and marketing, and firms are free to enter or exit the market. (pp. 233, 324)

Monopoly A market structure in which there is one firm, which produces a good or service that has no close substitutes and in which the firm is protected from competition by a barrier preventing the entry of new firms. (pp. 233, 298)

Monopsony A market in which there is a single buyer. (p. 429)

Moral hazard A tendency for people with private information, *after entering into an agreement*, to use that information for their own benefit and at the cost of the less-informed party. (p. 476)

Mortgage A legal contract that gives ownership of a home to the lender in the event that the borrower fails to meet the agreed loan payments (repayments and interest). (p. 569)

Mortgage-backed security A type of bond that entitles its holder to the income from a package of mortgages. (p. 569)

Multiplier The amount by which a change in autonomous expenditure is magnified or multiplied to determine the change in equilibrium expenditure and real GDP. (p. 682)

Nash equilibrium The outcome of a game that occurs when player A takes the best possible action given the action of player B and player B takes the best possible action given the action of player A. (p. 345)

National saving The sum of private saving (saving by households and businesses) and government saving. (p. 573)

Natural monopoly A market in which economies of scale enable one firm to supply the entire market at the lowest possible cost. (p. 298)

Natural monopoly good A good that is nonrival and excludable. When buyers can be excluded if they don't pay but the good is nonrival, marginal cost is zero. (p. 372)

Natural unemployment rate The unemployment rate when the economy is at full employment—natural unemployment as a percentage of the labor force. (p. 521)

Negative externality An externality that arises from either production or consumption and that imposes an external cost. (p. 392)

Negative relationship A relationship between variables that move in opposite directions. (p. 19)

Neoclassical growth theory A theory of economic growth that proposes that real GDP per person grows because technological change induces an amount of saving and investment that makes capital per hour of labor grow. (p. 555)

Net borrower A country that is borrowing more from the rest of the world than it is lending to it. (p. 636)

Net exports The value of exports of goods and services minus the value of imports of goods and services. (pp. 494, 638)

Net investment The amount by which the value of capital increases—gross investment minus depreciation. (pp. 494, 568)

Net lender A country that is lending more to the rest of the world than it is borrowing from it. (p. 636)

Net taxes Taxes paid to governments minus cash transfers received from governments. (p. 573)

Net worth The market value of what a financial institution has lent minus the market value of what it has borrowed. (p. 572)

Neuroeconomics The study of the activity of the human brain when a person makes an economic decision. (p. 193)

New classical A macroeconomist who holds the view that business cycle fluctuations are the efficient responses of a well-functioning market economy bombarded by shocks that arise from the uneven pace of technological change. (p. 664)

New classical cycle theory A rational expectations theory of the business cycle in which the rational expectation of the price level, which is determined by potential GDP and *expected* aggregate demand, determines the money wage rate and the position of the *SAS* curve. (p. 705)

New growth theory A theory of economic growth based on the idea that real GDP per person grows because of the choices that people make in the pursuit of profit and that growth will persist indefinitely. (p. 556)

New Keynesian A macroeconomist who holds the view that not only is the money wage rate sticky but also that the prices of goods and services are sticky. (p. 665)

New Keynesian cycle theory A rational expectations theory of the business cycle that emphasizes the fact that today's money wage rates were negotiated at many past dates, which means that *past* rational expectations of the current price level influence the money wage rate and the position of the *SAS* curve. (p. 705)

Nominal GDP The value of the final goods and services produced in a given year valued at the prices that prevailed in that same year. It is a more precise name for GDP. (p. 497)

Nominal interest rate The number of dollars that a borrower pays and a lender receives in interest in a year expressed as a percentage of the number of dollars borrowed and lent. (p. 574)

Nonexcludable A good or service or a resource is nonexcludable if it is impossible (or extremely costly) to prevent someone from enjoying its benefits. (p. 372)

Nonrenewable natural resources Natural resources that can be used only once. (p. 420)

Nonrival A good or service or a resource is nonrival if its use by one person does not decrease the quantity available for someone else. (p. 372)

Normal good A good for which demand increases as income increases. (p. 60)

Normal profit The return to entrepreneurship is normal profit and it is the profit that an entrepreneur earns *on average*. (p. 225)

Official settlements account A record of the change in official reserves, which are the government's holdings of foreign currency. (p. 634)

Offshore outsourcing A U.S. firm buys finished goods, components, or services from firms in other countries. (p. 165)

Oligopoly A market structure in which a small number of firms compete. (pp. 233, 342)

Open market operation The purchase or sale of government securities—U.S. Treasury bills and bonds—by the Federal Reserve System in the *loanable funds market*. (p. 598)

Opportunity cost The highest-valued alternative that we must give up to get something. (pp. 9, 33)

Output gap The gap between real GDP and potential GDP. (pp. 522, 660)

Payoff matrix A table that shows the payoffs for every possible action by each player for every possible action by each other player. (p. 344)

Perfect competition A market in which there are many firms each selling an identical product; there are many buyers; there are no restrictions on entry into the industry; firms in the industry have no advantage over potential new entrants; and firms and buyers are well informed about the price of each firm's product. (pp. 233, 272)

Perfectly elastic demand Demand with an infinite price elasticity; the quantity demanded changes by an infinitely large percentage in response to a tiny price change. (p. 85)

Perfectly inelastic demand Demand with a price elasticity of zero; the quantity demanded remains constant when the price changes. (p. 85)

Perfect price discrimination Price discrimination that occurs when a firm sells each unit of output for the highest price that anyone is willing to pay for it. The firm extracts the entire consumer surplus. (p. 310)

Pigovian taxes Taxes that are used as an incentive for producers to cut back on an activity that creates an external cost. (p. 397)

Political equilibrium The situation in which the choices of voters, firms, politicians, and bureaucrats are all compatible and no group can see a way of improving its position by making a different choice. (p. 371)

Pooling equilibrium The equilibrium in a market when only one message is available and an uninformed person cannot determine quality. (p. 479)

Positive externality An externality that arises from either production or consumption and that creates an external benefit. (p. 392)

Positive relationship A relationship between two variables that move in the same direction. (p. 18)

Potential GDP The value of production when all the economy's labor, capital, land, and entrepreneurial ability are fully employed; the quantity of real GDP at full employment. (p. 498)

Poverty A state in which a household's income is too low to be able to buy the quantities of food, shelter, and clothing that are deemed necessary. (p. 451)

Predatory pricing Setting a low price to drive competitors out of business with the intention of setting a monopoly price when the competition has gone. (p. 358)

Preferences A description of a person's likes and dislikes and the intensity of those feelings. (pp. 9, 36, 179)

Price cap A regulation that makes it illegal to charge a price higher than a specified level. (p. 128)

Price cap regulation A rule that specifies the highest price that the firm is permitted to set—a price ceiling. (p. 315)

Price ceiling A regulation that makes it illegal to charge a price higher than a specified level. (p. 128)

Price discrimination The practice of selling different units of a good or service for different prices. (p. 299)

Price effect The effect of a change in the price of a good on the quantity of the good consumed, other things remaining the same. (p. 209)

Price elasticity of demand A units-free measure of the responsiveness of the quantity demanded of a good to a change in its price, when all other influences on buyers' plans remain the same. (p. 84)

Price floor A regulation that makes it illegal to trade at a price lower than a specified level. (p. 131)

Price level The average level of prices. (p. 524)

Price taker A firm that cannot influence the price of the good or service it produces. (p. 272)

Principal–agent problem The problem of devising compensation rules that induce an *agent* to act in the best interest of a *principal*. (p. 229)

Principle of minimum differentiation The tendency for competitors to make themselves similar to appeal to the maximum number of clients or voters. (p. 376)

Private good A good or service that is both rival and excludable. (p. 372)

Private information Information about the value of an item being traded that is possessed by only buyers or sellers. (p. 476)

Private sector balance An amount equal to saving minus investment. (p. 638)

Producer surplus The excess of the amount received from the sale of a good or service over the cost of producing it. It is calculated as the price of a good minus the marginal cost (or minimum supply-price), summed over the quantity sold. (p. 111)

Product differentiation Making a product slightly different from the product of a competing firm. (pp. 233, 324)

Production efficiency A situation in which goods and services are produced at the lowest possible cost. (p. 33)

Production possibilities frontier The boundary between those combinations of goods and services that can be produced and those combinations that cannot. (p. 32)

Production quota An upper limit to the quantity of a good that may be produced in a specified period. (p. 139)

Profit The income earned by entrepreneurship. (p. 4)

Progressive income tax A tax on income at an average rate that increases as income increases. (p. 459)

Property rights The social arrangements that govern the ownership, use, and disposal of anything that people value. Property rights are enforceable in the courts. (pp. 44, 395)

Proportional income tax A tax on income at a constant rate, regardless of the level of income. (p. 459)

Public choice A decision that has consequences for many people and perhaps for the entire society. (p. 370)

Public good A good or service that is both nonrival and nonexcludable. It can be consumed simultaneously by everyone and no one can be excluded from enjoying its benefits. (p. 372)

Public production The production of a good or service by a public authority that receives its revenue from the government. (p. 407)

Purchasing power parity A situation in which the prices in two countries are equal when converted at the exchange rate. (p. 628)

Quantity demanded The amount of a good or service that consumers plan to buy during a given time period at a particular price. (p. 57)

Quantity supplied The amount of a good or service that producers plan to sell during a given time period at a particular price. (p. 62)

Quantity theory of money The proposition that in the long run, an increase in the quantity of money brings an equal percentage increase in the price level. (p. 608)

Rate of return regulation A regulation that requires the firm to justify its price by showing that its return on capital doesn't exceed a specified target rate. (p. 314)

Rational choice A choice that compares costs and benefits and achieves the greatest benefit over cost for the person making the choice. (p. 9)

Rational expectation The best forecast possible, a forecast that uses all the available information. (p. 714)

Real business cycle theory A theory of the business cycle that regards random fluctuations in productivity as the main source of economic fluctuations. (p. 705)

Real exchange rate The relative price of U.S.-produced goods and services to foreign-produced goods and services. (p. 630)

Real GDP The value of final goods and services produced in a given year when valued at the prices of a reference base year. (p. 497)

Real GDP per person Real GDP divided by the population. (pp. 498, 540)

Real income A household's income expressed as a quantity of goods that the household can afford to buy. (p. 203)

Real interest rate The nominal interest rate adjusted to remove the effects of inflation on the buying power of money. It is approximately equal to the nominal interest rate minus the inflation rate. (p. 574)

Real wage rate The money (or nominal) wage rate divided by the price level. The real wage rate is the quantity of goods and services that an hour of labor earns. (p. 547)

Recession A business cycle phase in which real GDP decreases for at least two successive quarters. (p. 499)

Recessionary gap An output gap in which potential GDP exceeds real GDP. (p. 661)

Regressive income tax A tax on income at an average rate that decreases as income increases. (p. 459)

Regulation Rules administered by a government agency to influence prices, quantities, entry, and other aspects of economic activity in a firm or industry. (p. 313)

Relative price The ratio of the price of one good or service to the price of another good or service. A relative price is an opportunity cost. (pp. 56, 203)

Rent The income that land earns. (p. 4)

Rent ceiling A regulation that makes it illegal to charge a rent higher than a specified level. (p. 128)

Rent seeking The lobbying for special treatment by the government to create economic profit or to divert consumer surplus or producer surplus away from others. The pursuit of wealth by capturing economic rent. (pp. 167, 306)

Required reserve ratio The minimum percentage of deposits that depository institutions are required to hold as reserves. (p. 600)

Resale price maintenance A distributor's agreement with a manufacturer to resell a product *at or above a specified minimum price*. (p. 357)

Reserves A bank's reserves consist of notes and coins in its vaults plus its deposit at the Federal Reserve System. (p. 593)

Risk aversion The dislike of risk. (p. 470)

Rival A good, service, or a resource is rival if its use by one person decreases the quantity available for someone else. (p. 372)

Rule of 70 A rule that states that the number of years it takes for the level of any variable to double is approximately 70 divided by the annual percentage growth rate of the variable. (p. 541)

Saving The amount of income that is not paid in taxes or spent on consumption goods and services. (p. 568)

Saving function The relationship between saving and disposable income, other things remaining the same. (p. 674)

Scarcity Our inability to satisfy all our wants. (p. 2)

Scatter diagram A graph that plots the value of one variable against the value of another variable for a number of different values of each variable. (p. 16)

Screening Inducing an informed party to reveal relevant private information. (p. 479)

Search activity The time spent looking for someone with whom to do business. (p. 128)

Self-interest The choices that you think are the best ones available for you are choices made in your self-interest. (p. 5)

Separating equilibrium The equilibrium in a market when signaling provides full information to a previously uninformed person. (p. 479)

Short run The time frame in which the quantity of at least one factor of production is fixed and the quantities of the other factors can be varied. The fixed factor is usually capital—that is, the firm uses a given plant. (p. 248)

Short-run aggregate supply The relationship between the quantity of real GDP supplied and the price level when the money wage rate, the prices of other resources, and potential GDP remain constant. (p. 651)

Short-run macroeconomic equilibrium A situation that occurs when the quantity of real GDP demanded equals the quantity of real GDP supplied—at the point of intersection of the *AD* curve and the *SAS* curve. (p. 658)

Short-run market supply curve A curve that shows the quantity supplied in a market at each price when each firm's plant and the number of firms remain the same. (p. 278)

Short-run Phillips curve A curve that shows the tradeoff between inflation and unemployment, when the expected inflation rate and the natural unemployment rate are held constant. (p. 718)

Shutdown point The price and quantity at which the firm is indifferent between producing the profit-maximizing output and shutting down temporarily. The shutdown point occurs at the price and the quantity at which average variable cost is a minimum. (p. 276)

Signal An action taken by an informed person (or firm) to send a message to uninformed people. (p. 332)

Signaling A situation in which an informed person takes actions that send information to uninformed persons. (p. 478)

Single-price monopoly A monopoly that must sell each unit of its output for the same price to all its customers. (p. 299)

Slope The change in the value of the variable measured on the y-axis divided by the change in the value of the variable measured on the x-axis. (p. 22)

Social interest Choices that are the best ones for society as a whole. (p. 5)

Social interest theory A theory that the political and regulatory process relentlessly seeks out inefficiency and introduces regulation that eliminates deadweight loss and allocates resources efficiently. (p. 313)

Stagflation The combination of inflation and recession. (pp. 663, 712)

Stock A certificate of ownership and claim to the firm's profits. (p. 570)

Stock market A financial market in which shares of stocks of corporations are traded. (p. 570)

Strategies All the possible actions of each player in a game. (p. 344)

Structural surplus or deficit The budget balance that would occur if the economy were at full employment and real GDP were equal to potential GDP. (p. 745)

Structural unemployment The unemployment that arises when changes in technology or international competition change the skills needed to perform jobs or change the locations of jobs. (p. 521)

Subsidy A payment made by the government to a producer. (pp. 140, 407)

Substitute A good that can be used in place of another good. (p. 59)

Substitution effect The effect of a change in price of a good or service on the quantity bought when the consumer (hypothetically) remains indifferent between the original and the new consumption situations—that is, the consumer remains on the same indifference curve. (p. 212)

Sunk cost The past expenditure on a plant that has no resale value. (p. 248)

Supply The entire relationship between the price of a good and the quantity supplied of it when all other influences on producers' planned sales remain the same. It is described by a supply schedule and illustrated by a supply curve. (p. 62)

Supply curve A curve that shows the relationship between the quantity supplied of a good and its price when all other influences on producers' planned sales remain the same. (p. 62)

Supply of loanable funds The relationship between the quantity of loanable funds supplied and the real interest rate when all other influences on lending plans remain the same. (p. 576)

Symmetry principle A requirement that people in similar situations be treated similarly. (p. 118)

Tariff A tax that is imposed by the importing country when an imported good crosses its international boundary. (p. 157)

Tax incidence The division of the burden of the tax between the buyer and the seller. (p. 133)

Tax multiplier The quantitative effect of a change in taxes on real GDP. It is calculated as the change in real GDP that results from a change in taxes divided by the change in taxes. (p. 747)

Tax wedge The gap between the before-tax and after-tax wage rates. and returns to other factors of production. (p. 738)

Technological change The development of new goods and of better ways of producing goods and services. (p. 38)

Technological efficiency A situation that occurs when the firm produces a given output by using the least amount of inputs. (p. 227)

Technology Any method of producing a good or service. (p. 226)

Time-series graph A graph that measures time (for example, years, quarters, or months) on the x-axis and the variable or variables in which we are interested on the y-axis. (p. 506)

Total cost The cost of all the productive resources that a firm uses. (p. 253)

Total fixed cost The cost of the firm's fixed inputs. (p. 253)

Total product The maximum output that a given quantity of labor can produce. (p. 249)

Total revenue The value of a firm's sales. It is calculated as the price of the good multiplied by the quantity sold. (pp. 88, 272)

Total revenue test A method of estimating the price elasticity of demand by observing the change in total revenue that results from a change in the price, when all other influences on the quantity sold remain the same. (p. 88)

Total surplus The sum of consumer surplus and producer surplus. (p. 112)

Total utility The total benefit that a person gets from the consumption of all the different goods and services. (p. 179)

Total variable cost The cost of all the firm's variable inputs. (p. 253)

Tradeoff A constraint that involves giving up one thing to get something else. (p. 9)

Tragedy of the commons The absence of incentives to prevent the overuse and depletion of a commonly owned resource. (p. 401)

Transactions costs The opportunity costs of making trades in a market. The costs that arise from finding someone with whom to do business, of reaching an agreement about the price and other aspects of the exchange, and of ensuring that the terms of the agreement are fulfilled. (pp. 115, 238, 396)

Trend The tendency for a variable to move in one general direction. (p. 507)

Tying arrangement An agreement to sell one product only if the buyer agrees to buy another, different product. (p. 357)

Unemployment rate The percentage of the people in the labor force who are unemployed. (p. 518)

Unit elastic demand Demand with a price elasticity of 1; the percentage change in the quantity demanded equals the percentage change in price. (p. 85)

U.S. interest rate differential The U.S. interest rate minus the foreign interest rate. (p. 625)

U.S. official reserves The U.S. government's holdings of foreign currency. (p. 634)

Utilitarianism A principle that states that we should strive to achieve "the greatest happiness for the greatest number of people." (p. 116)

Utility The benefit or satisfaction that a person gets from the consumption of goods and services. (p. 179)

Value of marginal product The value to the firm of hiring one more unit of a factor of production. It is calculated as the price of a unit of output multiplied by the marginal product of the factor of production. (p. 421)

Velocity of circulation The average number of times a dollar of money is used annually to buy the goods and services that make up GDP. (p. 608)

Voucher A token that the government provides to households, which they can use to buy specified goods and services. (pp. 383, 407)

Wages The income that labor earns. (p. 4)

Wealth The value of all the things that people own—the market value of their assets—at a point in time. (pp. 448, 568)

Working-age population The total number of people aged 16 years and over who are not in jail, hospital, or some other form of institutional care. (p. 517)

Abatement technology, **395**
Abe, Shinzo, 168
Ability-to-pay principle, 138
Above full-employment equilibrium, **660**
Absolute advantage, **40**
Absolute poverty, 451
Absolute value, 85
Accounting profit, 224
Acemoglu, Daron, 561
Actual aggregate expenditure, 679
Adidas, 324
Adverse selection, **476**, 478, 479–480
Advertising
    brand names, 333
    digital, 240–241
    efficiency of, 333
    expenditures in, 330–331
    market battles, 240–241
    in monopolistic competition, 330–332
    quality signaled through, 332–333
Affordable quantities, 185, 202
Aggregate demand, **654**. *See also*
    Aggregate supply–aggregate
    demand model
    aggregate expenditure and, 687,
      688–689
    changes in, 655–657
    cost-push inflation and, 712
    fiscal stimulus and, 747
    fluctuations in, 662–663, 664–665
    increase in, 709
    in long run, 690–691
    in short run, 690
    substitution effect and, 655, 687–688
    wealth effect and, 654–655
    wealth effect and curve in, 687
Aggregate demand curve
    real GDP demanded and, 655
    shifts in, 657
    substitution effects in, 655
    wealth effects in, 654–655, 687
Aggregate expenditure, 494–495
    actual, 679
    aggregate demand and, 687, 688–689
    components of, 765
    consumption function in, 694
    import function in, 694
    real GDP and, 674, 692–693
    schedule and curve in, 678
    slope, 684
Aggregate income, 493
Aggregate labor market, 546–547
Aggregate planned expenditure, **674**,
    678–679
Aggregate production function, **546**
Aggregate supply
    changes in, 652–653
    decrease in, 711
    fiscal stimulus and, 748
    fluctuations in, 663
    long-run, 650
    response, 664, 665
    short-run, 651
Aggregate supply–aggregate demand
    model (*AS-AD* model), 650, 658
    business cycle in, 660–661
    economic growth in, 659

    inflation in, 659
    price level and, 687
    RBC theory and, 727
Agricultural Revolution, 53
Ahrendts, Angela, 462–463
Airbus, 353, 657
Airline industry, 308–310
Airplanes, 154
Air pollution, 393, 400
Alic, Lejla, 46
Allocative efficiency, **35**, 37
Almunia, Joaquín, 316
Alternative price indexes, 528
Amazon.com, 575
American Beverage Association, 194
American Dream, 452
American Recovery and Reinvestment
    Act of 2009 (2009 Fiscal Stimulus
    Act), 746
American Society of Civil Engineers, 385
Anarchy, State, and Utopia (Nozick), 118
Android, 291
Antitrust law, **356**, 358
    Clayton Act, 356
    price fixing and, 357
    Sherman Act, 356
AOL, 326
Apple, 166, 239, 290–291, 351, 462
Appreciation, 620, 627
Arbitrage, **628**
AS-AD model. *See* Aggregate supply-aggre-
    gate demand model
Asia, 545
Asics, 324
Assets
    cash, 593
    depository institution's types of,
      593–594
    of Fed, 598
    liquid, 592
    prices, 572
Assortive mating, 458
Asymmetric information, **476**
Athey, Susan, 176
AT&T, 359, 360–361
Attainability, 32
Auerbach, Alan, 742
Australia, 141, 405
Australian school, 595
Automatic fiscal policy, **744**
Automatic stimulus, 745
Autonomous consumption, 674
Autonomous expenditure, **678**, 686, 689
Autonomous tax multiplier, **696**
Auto production, 263, 554
Average cost, 254–255
Average cost pricing rule, **314**
Average fixed cost, **254**
Average product, **249**, 252, 258
Average product curve, 252
Average total cost, **254**–255
Average total cost curve, 254–255
Average variable cost, **254**
Axes, 15, 18

Babolat, Eric, 334
Babolat's Play Pure Drive, 334–335

Baby boomers, 742
Backward-bending labor supply curve,
    424–425
Balanced budget, **732**, 745
Balanced budget multiplier, **697**
Balance of payments accounts, **634**–635
    borrowers and lenders, 636
    exchange rate and, 639
Balance of trade, 635
Balance sheet, 598, 599
Baltimore Ravens, 470
Banana Republic, 329
Bananas, 74–75
Bank of America, 166, 593, 598–600
Bank of Japan, 627
Banks, 7. *See also specific banks*
    central, 597
    commercial, 570, 593, 596
    crisis event influencing, 772
    interest rates and, 610–611
    loans, 765
    money created by, 600–602
    100 percent reserve, 595
    reserves, 596, 766, 768
    run on, 772
    savings, 593
Bardaro, Katie, 427
Barnard, Bobby, 285
Barriers to entry, **298**
    firms, 236
    legal, 298–299
    monopoly created by, 306
    natural, 298
    oligopoly and, 342
    ownership, 298
Barro, Robert, 430, 581, 648, 748–749
Barry, David, 98
Barter, 590
BEA. *See* Bureau of Economic
    Analysis
A Beautiful Mind (film), 345
Behavioral economics, **192**
Beige Book, 759, 762
Below full-employment equilibrium, **661**
Benefits, **9**
    from depository institution, 594
    economic, 594
    external, 115, 373, 406, 407
    marginal, 10, 36, 58, 113, 121, 406
    marginal private, 406
    marginal social, 108–109, 129, 137,
      374, 378, 402, 406
    private, 406
    of public goods, 374
    underestimate, 378
    unemployment, 522
Benefits principle, 138
Bentham, Jeremy, 116, 221
Bernanke, Ben, 516, 759
Best affordable choice, 208–209, 210
Best affordable point, 208–209
Biased CPI, 527
Big Mac index, 629
Big tradeoff, **117**, **460**–461
Bilateral monopoly, **429**
Bill rates, 764
Biocom, 6

Black market, 128–129
Blockbuster, 210
Bloomberg, Michael, 133–134, 194–195
BLS. *See* Bureau of Labor Statistics
Board of Governors, 597
Boeing, 164, 353
Bond markets, 569
Bond rates, 764
Bonds, 569, 582–583
Boorstin, Daniel J., 175
Borrowers
　international, 636
　lenders and, 636
　net, 636
　women as, 552
Borrowing
　for consumption, 637
　lowering cost of, 594
Boston Lighthouse, 373
Bounded rationality, 192
Bounded self-interest, 192–193
Bounded willpower, 192
Boyd, Aaron, 462
Brand names, 333
Brazil, 453
Break-even point, 274
Brunner, Karl, 665
Budget. *See also* Federal budget
　balanced, 732, 745
　balanced multiplier, 697
　government deficits of, 580–581
　in historical perspective, 732–734
　local, 736
　state, 736
　structural balance of, 746
　U.S. government, 736
Budget deficit, 732
Budget equation, 203
Budget line, 178, **202**, 209
Budget surplus, 580, **732**
Bureaucrats, 371
　government and inefficiency of,
　　408–409
　objectives of, 377
Bureau of Economic Analysis (BEA),
　495, 508
Bureau of Labor Statistics (BLS), 525
Bush, George W., 166, 538
Business cycle, 499
　in *AS-AD* model, 660–661
　expansion, 540–542
　inflation and, 714
　mainstream theory on, 704–705
　RBC theory, 705–708, 727
　real GDP and, 499
　turning points in, 686
　in U.S., 660–661
Business organizations
　corporations as, 231–232
　partnership as, 231
　proprietorship as, 230–232
　types of firms, 230–231
Buyers, 67, 134–135, 142–143, 307–308

CAB. *See* Current account balance
Caballero, Ricardo J., 728
Canada, 544
Cap-and-trade, 398

Capital, 4. *See also* Human capital
　debt and, 734
　financial, 4, 568–570
　marginal product of capital, 260
　physical, 551, 568
　quantity of, 652
　rental markets and rates, 432
　value of marginal product of, 432
Capital accumulation, 38
Capital and financial account, 634
Capital gains, 231, 568
Capital losses, 568, 772
Capital rental markets, 432
Capital services, 420
Capture theory, 313
Carbon dioxide, 393
Carbon emissions, 7, 398–400, 410–411
Card, David, 132
Carney, Mark, 595
Cartel, 343
Cash assets, 593
Casual labor, 420
Causation, 18
CBO. *See* Congressional Budget Office
CBS, 431
Celler-Kefauver Act, 356
Cellphones, market for, 361
Centers for Medicare & Medicaid Services
　(CMS), 117
Central bank, 597
Centrally planned socialism, 8
CEO. *See* Chief executive officer
Ceteris paribus, **24**
Chained CPI, 528
Chained-dollar Real GDP, 508–509
Change in demand, 58–59
　influence of, 68
　for loanable funds, 577–579
　marginal utility and, 186
　quantity demanded change and, 60–61
　short-run market equilibrium and, **279**
　for U.S. dollars, 624–625
Change in quantity demanded, 61, 186
Change in quantity supplied, 64–65
Change in supply, 63
　expected future prices in, 64
　factors of production and, 63
　influence of, 70
　prices of related goods produced
　　and, 63
　quantity supplied changes and, 64–65
　state of nature in, 64
　suppliers and technology in, 64
Charter schools, 409, 436–437
Chetty, Raj, 490
Chicago School, 783
Chief executive officer (CEO), 229
China
　exchange rate management of, 633
　fixed exchange rate policy of, 632
　real GDP per person growth in,
　　542, 545
　standard of living in, 500
　trade with, 152
Choices, 2, 288
　best affordable, 208–209, 210
　consumer, 192–194, 208–213
　consumption, 178–180

household, 221
public and private, 370–371, 379
rational, 9
as tradeoff, 9
with uncertainty, 472
Chrome, 299
Chrysler, 258
Circular flows
　of expenditure and income, 492–494
　through markets, 44–45
　model, 493
Citibank, 166, 600
Citicorp, 229
Citigroup, 593, 610
CK, 329
Clarida, Richard H., 538
Classical growth theory, 555
Classical macroeconomics, 664
Clayton Act, 356
Clean Air Act, 393, 397
Clean technology, 396–397
Climate change, 7
Close substitutes, 207
CMS. *See* Centers for Medicare &
　Medicaid Services
Coal, 411
Coase, Ronald, 373, 396
Coase theorem, 396
Coca Cola, 332–333
Cocoa, 34
Coffee, 71, 98–99
College education, 69
College majors, 427
Collision insurance, 473
Collusion, 324, 347
Collusive agreement, 346, 348–349
Command system, 106, 229
Commercial banks, 570, 593, 596
Commodity markets, 420
Commodity prices, 420
Commodity substitution bias, 527
Common resources, 115, 372
　efficient use of, 404
　inefficient use of, 402–403
　ITQs and, 404–405
　tragedy of the commons, 401–405
　unsustainable use of, 401
Comparative advantage, 40
　in international trade, 152, 165
　national, 152
　opportunity cost and, 40, 42
　U.S. and, 153–154
Compensation, of employees, 496
Competition. *See also* Monopolistic
　competition; Perfect competition
　efficiency and, 288–289
　single-price monopoly compared to,
　　304–306
Competitive environment, 233–238
Competitive equilibrium, 112
Competitive market, 56, 116–119
Complements, 59, 93–94, 207–208
Complements in production, 63, 455
Compound interest, 438
Concentration measures, 234–237
Congress, U.S., 730
　fiscal stimulus passed by, 746
　monetary policy role of, 760

Congressional Budget Office (CBO), 667, 746, 777
Constant returns to scale, **262**
Constants, 26
Constraints, 226, 249–252
Consumer choices, 192–194, 208–213
Consumer equilibrium, **181**
Consumer Financial Protection Bureau, 571
Consumer Price Index (CPI), 523, **525**, 759. *See also* Alternative price indexes
biased, 527
calculating, 525–526
chained, 528
inflation rate and, 526–527
reading numbers of, 525
Consumer surplus, **109**, 189, 288, 305, 473
Consumption, 504
autonomous, 674
borrowing for, 637
choices, 178–180
induced, 674
PCE deflator and, 528, 759
personal, 495
positive and negative externalities of, 392
possibilities, 178, 202–204
as real GDP function, 677
savings plans and, 674–675
U.S. function of, 677
Consumption expenditure, **493**, 765
Consumption function, **674**–675, 694
Contestable market, **354**
Contests, 106, 457–458
Contracts, long-term, 230
Convergence, to equilibrium, 681
Cook, Tim, 462
Cooperative equilibrium, **352**
Coordinates, 15
Coordinating decisions, 45
Copyright, 298
Core inflation rate, **529**, **759**
Corporate income taxes, 731
Corporate profit, 496
Corporations, 231–232
Correlation, 18
Cost curves
auto plant average, 263
long-run average, 261–262
product curves and, 256
shifts in, 258–259
short-run costs, 256–258
store checkouts with, 256–257
technology and, 258–259
total, 253
Cost-push inflation, **711**–713
Costs. *See also specific costs*
compact glossary of, 259
of insurance, 474
long-run, 260–263
opportunity, 32–34
selling, 331–332
short-run, 253, 260–261
total, 253, 274, 331
total fixed, 253
total variable, 253, 256
transaction, 115, 238, 396
Council of Economic Advisors, **731**
CPI. *See* Consumer Price Index

CPI basket, 525
CPS. *See* Current Population Survey
Crawling peg, **632**–633
Credit
financial crisis of, 570–571
sub-prime crisis of, 480
Credit cards, 592
Creditor nation, **637**
Creditors, 637
Credit risk, **479**
Credit Union, 593
Cross elasticity of demand, 92–94, 97
Crowding-out effect, **581**
Currency, **591**, 598
drain, 772
Euro, 620
foreign, 620
trading, 620
Yen, 620, 621
Yuan, 620, 621
Currency drain ratio, **601**, 612–613
Current account, **634**
Current account balance, 638
Current Employment Survey (CES), 531
Current Population Survey (CPS), 517, 531
Cycle, **507**
Cyclical surplus or deficit, **745**
Cyclical unemployment, **521**, 522

Daimler-Benz, 359
Dales, Paul, 640
Darwin, Charles, 489, 555
Deadweight loss, 114, **131**, 314
minimum wages and, 131
monopoly and, 305
from overfishing, 403
rent ceiling and, 129
tariffs and, 159
Debt
capital and, 734
government, 734–735
interest, 732
international, 743–744
of Japan, 750–751
Debtor nation, **637**
Debtors, 637
Decisions
coordinating, 45
Fed strategies in making, 761–762
firm's output, 274–277
long run, 248
output, 248, 274
perfect competition and firm's, 273
price, 302–303
rent-*versus*-buy, 432, 438–439
short run, 248
shutdown, 276
single-price monopoly, 300–303
supply's time-frame for, 96
temporary shutdown, 276
uncertainty and, 470–472
Deductible, 480
Default risk, **479**
Deficits
balance of trade and, 635
budget, 732
cyclical, 745
government budget, 580–581

Japan's, 736
structural, 745–746
Deflation, **524**
causes of, 715–717
consequences of, 717
ending, 717
in Japan, 716
problem of, 524
quantity theory and, 715
Degree of substitutability, 207–208
Dell, 283, 324
Delta, 22
Demand, **57**, 273
all possible changes in, 72–73
changes in, 186, 279, 284–285
consumer surplus and, 109
cross elasticity of, 92–94, 97
decreasing, 68, 72–73
derived, 421
elastic, 85–86
elastic and inelastic, 85–86
for factors of production, 421–423
in foreign exchange market, 621
of human capital, 455
income and, 60
income elasticity of, 91–92, 97
increasing, 59, 68, 72–73
individual, 108–109
labor supply and, 428
law of, 57, 60
for loanable funds, 575–576
loanable funds market increase in, 577–579
long-run growth of, 579
marginal benefit and, 58
market, 108–109
for money, 621
of oil, 433
preferences and, 60
prices and, 59–60
prices of related goods and, 59
schedule, 57–58
selling costs and, 332
U.S. dollar changes in, 624–625
for U.S. dollars, 622–623
U.S. exports, 624
U.S. import, 625
willingness to pay and value in, 108
Demand curve, 57–58
elasticity along linear, 87
equation of, 76
income effect and, 211
for labor, 422
movement along, 61
for movies, 211
price change and, 211
price effect and, 209
shift of, 61
straight line in, 76
Demand for labor, 421
in aggregate labor market, 546–547
curve, 422
firm's changes in, 423
Demand for loanable funds, **575**
Demand for money, **605**
Demand-pull inflation, **709**
in Kalamazoo, 710–711
in U.S., 711

Department of Commerce, U.S., 235
Depository institution, 593, 595–596
    asset types in, 593–594
    economic benefits from, 594
    regulation of, 594
    reserves of, 598
    types of, 593
Deposits, 591
    Fed policies influencing, 610–611
    loans creating, 600–601
    as money, 592
Depreciation, 224, **494**, 620
    of dollar, 627
    economic, 225
Deregulation, 313
Derived demand, 421
Desired reserve ratio, 601
Developing countries, 552, 559
Diadora, 324
Diesel, 329
Digital advertising, 240–241
Diminishing marginal product
    of capital, 260
**Diminishing marginal rate
    of substitution, 206**
**Diminishing marginal returns,
    251**, 402
Diminishing marginal utility, 179–180
Diminishing returns, 260
    law of, 251, 254, 547
    technological change and, 555
Dimon, Jamie, 230
Direct relationships, 18
Discounting, 438–439
Discount rate, 600
Discouraged workers, 519
The Discoverers (Boorstin), 175
Discretionary fiscal policy, 744
Discretionary fiscal stimulus, 747
Discrimination, 130
    economic inequality and, 456–457
    perfect price, 310, 311
    price, 299, 307–311
Diseconomies of scale, 262–263
Disney Corporation, 311
Disposable income, 576, 656, **674**
Dissaving, 675
Divisible goods, 202
Division of labor, 53
Djokovic, Novak, 457
DKNY, 329
DNA decoding, 287
Doha, Qatar, 163
Doha Development Agenda, 163
Doha Round, 163
Dollar index, 640
Dollars, U.S.
    appreciating, 627
    chained-, 508–509
    changes in demand of, 624–625
    changes in supply of, 625–626
    demand for, 622–623
    depreciating, 627
    exchange rate changes and, 626, 631
    exchange rate of, 621
    foreign exchange market and, 620
    marginal utility per, 182–188, 195
    supply curve for, 623

Domestic jobs, 164
Domestic products, 494
Dominant-strategy equilibrium, 345
Double coincidence of wants, 590
Double counting, 492
Draghi, Mario, 720
Drugs, 142
Duflo, Esther, 54, 409
Dumping, 164
Duopolists' dilemma, 349–350
Duopoly, 342, 352–354
Duranton, Gilles, 120
Dusunceli, Fazil, 74
DVDs, 210

Earl Jackets, 329
Earnings sharing regulation, 315
East Point Seafood, 372
eBay, 175
e-Books, 214–215
ECB. *See* European Central Bank
Economic accounting, 225
Economic coordination, 44–45
Economic depreciation, 225
Economic efficiency, 227–228
Economic growth, 38, 540.
        See also Gross domestic product
    in *AS-AD* model, 659
    basics of, 540–542
    business cycle expansion and, 540–542
    causes of, 558
    cost of, 38
    education stimulating, 559
    influences on, 559
    long-term trends in, 543–545
    perpetual motion in, 557
    policies for achieving faster, 558–559
    RBC theory and, 708
    rule of 70 and, 541–542
    savings and, 558
    sources of, 553
    sustainability of, 555–559
    sustained growth in, 541–542
    in U.S., 38–39, 543, 666–667
Economic inequality
    discrimination and, 456–457
    globalization and, 455–456
    poverty and, 451
    sources of, 455–458
    technological change and, 455
    trends in, 449–450
    in U.S., 446–452
    wealth and, 448–449, 458
Economic model, 11, 18–21
Economic profit, 224
    firm's, 224
    in long run, 281–282
    maximizing, 273, 302
    revenue and, 272
    in short run, 279–280
    total cost and revenue in, 274
    zero, 327
Economic rent, 306
Economic Report of the President (Council
    of Economic Advisers), 731
Economics, 2. *See also* Keynesian
    economics; Macroeconomics
    firm's problems with, 224–226

    graphing data in, 15–18
    of healthcare, 378–383
    Industrial Revolution beginning
        of, 53
    microeconomics, 2
    as policy tool, 11
    scatter diagrams in, 16–17
    scope of, 9
    as social science, 11
    voodoo, 741
    way of thinking in, 9
The Economics of School Choice
    (Hoxby), 409
Economies of scale, 238–239, 262–263
Economies of team production, 239
Economy
    exchange rate and world, 656
    mixed, 8
    model, 32
    perpetual motion, 557
    real GDP and world, 544–545
    of South Africa, 560–561
    underground, 501
    unemployment and recovery in, 776
    U.S., 504
    U.S. struggles in, 770
    well-being of, 503
    world, 453–454, 544–545, 656
Education
    charter schools and, 409
    college, 69
    external benefits of, 373
    income and, 451
    jobs and, 69
    public production from, 407
    to stimulate economic growth, 559
Efficiency
    of advertising and brand names, 333
    allocative, 35, 37
    common resources, 404
    competition and, 288–289
    of competitive equilibrium, 112
    of competitive markets, 112–115
    economic, 227–228
    equilibrium and, 288
    fair rules and, 118
    of market equilibrium, 396
    of monopolistic competition, 329
    obstacles to, 114
    of perfect competition, 288–289, 305
    with price discrimination, 311
    product development and, 330
    production, 33, 35
    public good quantity and, 375
    of public provision, 375–376
    of resource allocation methods,
        106–107
    resources used with, 35–37, 288
    taxes and, 137–138
    technological, 227
Efficiency wage, 522
Efficient, 5
Efficient scale, 328
Elastic demand, 85–86
Elasticity
    compact glossary of, 97
    along linear demand curve, 87
    marginal revenue and, 301

minus sign and, 85
total revenue and, 88
Elasticity of demand
   cross, 92–94, 97
   expenditures and, 90
   factors influencing, 86–87
   income, 91–92, 97
   in monopoly, 301
   for peanut butter, 90
   price, 84–85, 89, 97, 99
   tax incidence and, 135
Elasticity of supply, 94, 97
   calculating, 94–95
   factors influencing, 95–96
   tax incidence and, 136–137
Elastic supply, 94–95, 136–137
Electronic Road Pricing (ERB), 12
Employee compensation, 496
Employment
   full, 521, 548, 650, 652, 660–661, 737
   to population ratio, 518
   real GDP and, 524
   unemployment and, 516–520
   U.S. growth in, 530
Employment Act of 1946, 730–731
Endowment effect, 193
Energy bars, 60–68, 70
England, 553
Entrepreneurship, 4, 225
Entry, 281–283, 325
Environment
   carbon emissions in, 7
   climate change in, 7
   competitive, 233–238
   quality of, 501
   standards, 165
Environmental Protection Agency (EPA),
   397, 410–411
EPA. *See* Environmental Protection Agency
Equality of opportunity, 118
Equal value of money, 628
Equations
   budget, 203
   of demand curve, 76
   of exchange, 608, 715
   linear, 26
   of straight lines, 26–27
   of supply curve, 76
Equilibrium
   above full-employment, 660
   below full-employment, 661
   consumer, 181
   convergence to, 681
   cooperative, 352
   dominant-strategy, 345
   efficiency and, 288
   full-employment, 661
   inefficiency of pooling, 479
   labor market, 425, 547–548
   loanable funds market, 577
   long-run, 282–283, 606–607
   long-run macroeconomic, 658–659
   market, 66–67, 77
   minimum wages below, 145
   money market, 606
   Nash, 345, 349–350, 400
   oil price, 434
   overfishing, 402–403

in perfect competition, 304
   political, 371
   pollution and, 394–395
   production quotas and, 139
   real GDP, 689–691
   rent seeking, 306–307
   short run, 279, 606–607
   short-run macroeconomic, 658
Equilibrium expenditure,
   680–681, 695
Equilibrium price, 66, 128, 131
Equilibrium quantity, 66
Equity
   competitive market efficiency
     and, 112–115
   of resource allocation methods,
     106–107
Essay on the Principle of Population
   (Malthus), 489
Ethnicity, 451
Etonic, 324
Euro, 620
European Central Bank (ECB), 720–721
European Commission, 316
Eurozone, 720–721
Excess capacity, 328
Excess reserves, 601
Exchange rate, 641
   arbitrage and, 628
   balance of payments and, 639
   changes in, 626, 631
   China's management of, 633
   crawling peg as, 632–633
   expected future, 625, 626, 629
   fixed, 631–632
   flexible, 631
   fluctuations in, 764–765
   market, 500
   one-year forward, 628
   policy, 631–633
   as price, 620–621
   real, 630
   of U.S. dollars, 621
   volatility of, 630
   world economy and, 656
Excite@Home, 326–327
Excludable, 372, 373
Exit, 281–283, 325
Expansion, 499, 540–542
Expectations, 655
Expected future exchange rate,
   625, 626, 629
Expected future income, 60, 576
Expected inflation, 713–714, 718
Expected profit effect, 622
Expected utility, 471–472
Expected wealth, 470
Expenditures, 684
   actual aggregate, 679
   in advertising, 330–331
   aggregate, 494–495
   aggregate planned, 674, 678–679
   autonomous, 678
   circular flow of, 492–494
   consumption, 493, 765
   elasticity of demand and, 90
   equilibrium, 680–681, 695
   fixed prices and, 674–677

GDP and, 495
   on goods and services, 732
   government, 494, 495
   government multiplier, 696, 747
   induced, 678, 682
   monetary policy and plans for, 765
   personal consumption, 495
   taxes on, 738
   U.S. healthcare, 379–381
Exploitation, of developing countries, 165
Exports, 152, 494
   effect, 622
   gains and losses from, 156
   markets with, 154, 156
   net, 494, 495, 638–639, 765
   subsidies, 163
   of U.S., 152–154
   U.S. airplane, 154
   world demand for U.S., 624
External benefits, 115, 406
   of education, 373
   resource allocation with, 407
External cost, 115, 394, 402
Externalities, 392
   global, 400
   market failures and, 115
   negative, 392, 394–400
   negative consumption, 392
   negative production, 392
   pollution as negative, 394–400
   positive, 392, 406–409
   positive consumption, 392
   positive production, 392
   types of, 392

Facebook, 12, 240–241, 299
Factor markets, 44
   anatomy of, 420
   for capital services, 420
   inequality, uncertainty and, 489
   services of land in, 420
Factors of production, 3
   change in supply and, 63
   demand for, 421–423
   natural resources and, 3
   prices and, 56, 63, 259, 423
Fair Labor Standards Act, 132
Fairness
   of competitive market, 116–119
   of minimum wages, 131–132
   poor people and ideas of, 117
   principles of, 116
   of rent ceiling, 130
   social interest and, **5**–6
   symmetry principle and, 118
   taxes and, 138
Fair results, 130
Fair rules, 130
FDA. *See* Food and Drug Administration
FDIC. *See* Federal Deposit Insurance
   Corporation
Federal budget, 730
   balancing, 735
   global perspective of, 736
   historical perspective of, 732–734
   institutions and laws, 730–731
   2013 highlights of, 731–732
   U.S., 736

Federal Deposit Insurance Corporation (FDIC), 594
Federal funds rate, 593, 760
　loose links in, 771
　monetary policy and, 763
Federal Home Loan Mortgage Corporation (Freddie Mac), 570–571
Federal National Mortgage Association (Fannie Mae), 570–571
Federal Open Market Committee (FOMC), 597, 760, 762, 774, 776
Federal Reserve Act, 758, 760
Federal Reserve Banks, 597
Federal Reserve System (the Fed), 572, 597
　assets of, 598
　balance sheet of, 598, 599
　bank reserves and, 596
　Board of Governors, 597
　decision-making strategy of, 761–762
　deposits influenced by policies of, 610–611
　dollar index and, 640
　fighting inflation, 768–769
　fighting recession, 766–767
　financial crisis of 2008-2009 and, 772–773
　inflation rates and, 761–762
　liabilities of, 598
　loose links and time lags of, 769–771
　low interest rates from, 776–777
　monetary policy of, 656
　policy actions of, 773
　policy free lunches and, 783
　policy tools of, 598–600
　quantitative easing, 603
　structure of, 597
　Taylor rule of, 775
　unemployment rate and, 762
Federal Trade Commission, 316, 359
Feldstein, Martin, 741
Fila, 324
Final good, 492
Finance, 568
Financial assets, 572
Financial capital, 4, 568
Financial capital markets, 569–570
Financial crisis, 578, 599, 611
　of credit, 570–571
　key elements of, 772
　persistently slow recovery from, 773
　policy actions after, 773
　sub-prime credit crisis, 480
　Third World debt crisis, 637
　of 2008-2009, 772–773
Financial innovation, 596, 604
Financial institutions, 570
　commercial banks, 570
　financial capital and, 568
　financial markets and, 568–572
　physical capital and, 568
　stock markets, 570
Financial markets, 568–572
Financial property, 44
Financial Stability Oversight Council, 571
Finland, 453
Firestorm Wildlife Suppression, 375–376

Firms, 44, 224
　barriers to entry and, 236
　business organization types of, 230–231
　collusive agreements of, 348–349
　constraints, 226
　coordination, 238
　cutting taxes, 740
　demand for labor changes of, 423
　demand for labor of, 421–422
　demand for products of, 272–273
　economic activities coordinated by, 238–239
　economic problems of, 224–226
　economic profit of, 224
　GDP and, 493
　goals of, 224
　information and organization of, 229–231
　information constraints of, 226
　market constraints of, 226
　in monopolistic competition, 367
　monopolistic competition and number of, 324
　output decisions of, 274–277
　in perfect competition, 273
　pros and cons of types of, 231
　with short-run costs, 261
　short-run outcomes of, 280
　short-run output of, 326
　short-run technology constraints of, 249–252
　small number of, 343
　supply curve of, 277
　technology constraints of, 226
First-come, first-served, 106–107, 115, 130
Fiscal imbalance, 742
Fiscal policy, 656, 730
　automatic, 744
　discretionary, 744
　generational effects of, 742–744
　supply-side, 737–741
Fiscal stimulus, 744–745
　aggregate demand and, 747
　aggregate supply and, 748
　Congress passing, 746
　discretionary, 747
　magnitude of, 748–749
　multipliers, 748–749
Fisher, Franklin, 358
Fisher, Irving, 595
Fisher, Richard, 774, 776
Fish stock, 401–404
Fixed exchange rate, 631–632
Fixed prices, 674–677
Flexible exchange rate, 631
FOMC. *See* Federal Open Market Committee
Food, 89
Food and Drug Administration (FDA), 163
Food stamps, 459
Force, 107
Ford, 258, 263
Foreign currency, 620
Foreign exchange market, 620, 625–626
　demand in, 621
　exchange rate as price in, 620–621

　exports effect in, 622
　law of demand for, 621–622
　law of supply for, 623
　market equilibrium in, 624
　money demand and supply, 621
　People's Bank of China and, 632–633
　supply in, 623
　trading currencies in, 620
　U.S. dollar demand curve, 622
　U.S. dollar questions and, 620
　U.S. dollar supply curve, 623
Foreign labor, 164–165
Forster, E. M., 727
Four-firm concentration ratio, 234, 235
Fracking. *See* Hydraulic fracturing
Fractional-reserve banking, 595
France, 738, 741
Free lunches, 783
Free market, for drugs, 152
Free-rider problem, 374, 375, 400
Free trade, 157, 159–161, 164, 167
Frictional unemployment, 521
Friedman, Milton, 595, 665, 783
Fujimaki, Takeshi, 750
Full employment, 521, 548, 650
　above equilibrium of, 660
　below equilibrium of, 661
　potential GDP and, 737
　quantity of labor, 652
Full Employment and Balanced Growth Act of 1978, 731
Full-employment equilibrium, 661
Fundamental determinant of demand, 434
Furman, Jason, 530
Future amounts
　discounting, 438–439
　present value of sequence of, 439

Gains
　capital, 231, 568
　from exports, 156
　global market trade, 155–156
　from imports, 155
　from insurance, 475
　producer, 159
　from trade, 40–43
Gallegos, Hector, 46
Games
　chicken, 351
　features of, 344
　oligopoly, 344–351
　price fixing, 346–350
　price wars and, 354
　prisoner's dilemma, 344–345
　repeated, 352–355
　repeated duopoly, 352–354
　sequential, 352–355
　sequential entry, 354
Game theory, 344
Gap, 329
Gasoline, 398
Gates, Bill, 7
Gateway, 283
GATT. *See* General Agreement on Tariffs and Trade
GDI. *See* Gross domestic income

GDP. *See* Gross domestic product
GDP deflator, 528
General Agreement on Tariffs and Trade (GATT), 158
General Motors (GM), 258, 263
General Theory of Employment, Interest and Money (Keynes), 516, 727
Generational accounting, 742
Generational imbalance, 743
Geographical scope of markets, 236
German Bund, 582
Gini ratio, 449, 454
Global inequality, 454
Globalization, 6, 455–456
Global markets
    foreign labor in, 164–165
    net gain from trade in, 155–156
    for oil, 435
Global warming, 393
GM. *See* General Motors
GNNP. *See* Green Net National Product
Gokhale, Jagadeesh, 742
Goods and resources. *See also* Common resources
    classification of, 372
    divisible and indivisible, 202
    information as, 481
    price discrimination of, 308
Goods and services, 3
    expenditures on, 732
    final, 492
    of government, 370
    government expenditure on, 495
    net exports of, 495, 638
    range of, 239
Goods markets, 44
Google, 241, 299, 316–317
Government
    bonds, 582–583
    budget deficits, 580–581
    budget surplus, 580
    bureaucratic inefficiency and, 408–409
    goods and services of, 370
    insurance provided by, 380–382
    license, 298
    in loanable funds market, 580–581
    mortgage lenders sponsored by, 570
    purchases of, 372–373
    subsidies, 140–141, 314
    U.S. budget, 736
Government debt, 734–735
Government expenditure, 494, 495
Government expenditure multiplier, 696, 747
Government failure, 370, 377
Government sector balance, 638, 639
Government securities, U.S., 598
Graphs
    creating, 15–16
    of economic data, 15–18
    economic models using, 18–21
    insurance analysis and, 474
    misleading, 18
    with more than two variables, 24–27
    time-series, 506–507
Great Depression, 166, 516, 647, 686, 730, 783

Green Net National Product (GNNP), 502, 503
Greenspan, Alan, 576, 759
Grisham, John, 40
Gross domestic income (GDI), 692
Gross domestic product (GDP), 492, 770. *See also* Potential GDP; Real GDP
    circular flow of expenditure and income in, 492–494
    defined, 492, 494
    deflator, 528
    expenditure approach to, 495
    final goods and services in, 492
    firms and household, 493
    in given time period, 492
    GNNP replacing, 502
    income approach to, 496
    market value and, 492
    measuring U.S., 495–497
    nominal, 497
    produced within country, 492
    real, 497
Gross investment, 494, 568
Gross private domestic investment, 495
Gross profit, 494
Growth rate, 540

Hamermesh, Daniel, 132
Harbaugh, John, 470
Harley-Davidson, 281
Harris, Jay M., 482
Harvard College, 482–483
Harvard University, 176
HDI. *See* Human Development Index
Healthcare, 373, 735
    economics of, 378–383
    inefficiency and, 381
    market failure, 378–379
    MSB of, 378
    Obamacare and, 382
    universal coverage in, 380
    U.S. expenditures in, 379–381
Health insurance
    subsidized, 382–383
    vouchers in, 383
Health regulations, 163
Herfindahl-Hirschman Index (HHI), 234
    industries and, 235
    merger guidelines and, 359
    in monopolistic competition, 325
    oligopoly and, 343
Holiday Inn, 333
Home price bubble, 578
Honey Run Honey, 392
Hong Kong, 39, 545, 620
Horizontal price fixing agreement, 357
Hotelling, Harold, 434, 489
Hotelling principle, 434, 435, 489
Households
    choices of, 221
    GDP and, 493
    income of, 450–451
    production of, 501
Housing market, 128–130
Housing shortage, 128
Hoxby, Caroline M., 409, 418
Hubbard, Thomas, 368

Human capital, 3, 568, 637
    demand/supply/wage rates in, 455
    growth, 552
    lost, 516
    potential GDP and, 652
Human Development Index (HDI), 503
Hume, David, 537
Humphrey-Hawkins Act, 731
Hurricane Katrina, 118, 119
Hydraulic fracturing (fracking), 46–47, 399
Hyperinflation, 524

IBM, 283, 354
Iceland, 405
Ignorance, rational, 377
Illegal goods markets, 142–143
Illiquidity, 572
Impact lag, 749
Implicit rental rate, 224
Import function, 677, 694
Import quotas, 160–161
Imports, 152, 494
    decrease in, 158
    effect, 623
    function, 677
    gains and losses from, 155
    marginal propensity to, 677
    markets with, 153
    multiplier size and, 685
    U.S., 152–154
    U.S. demand for, 625
    U.S. T-shirt, 153
Incentive, 2
    for cheating, 140
    for overproduction, 140
    principal-agent problem and, 229
Incentive system, 229
Income. *See also* Poverty; Wages; Wealth
    aggregate, 493
    changes in, 204, 211
    circular flow of, 492–494
    corporate taxes on, 731
    countries distribution of, 453
    demand and, 60
    differences in, 4
    disposable, 576, 656, 674
    distribution of, 446
    education and, 451
    expected future, 60, 576
    GDP and, 496
    gross domestic, 692
    of households, 450–451
    inelastic demand, 91–92, 97
    inequality in, 450
    labor markets with differences in, 455–458
    Lorenz curve, 447–448
    lost, 516
    maintenance programs, 459
    market and money, 446, 460
    mean, 446
    median, 446
    mode, 446
    money, 446, 460
    net domestic, 496
    proportion spent on goods of, 86–87

Income (*continued*)
    proprietors', 496
    real, 203
    redistribution of, 459–461, 524
    rental, 496
    rise in, 188
    Supplementary Security, 459
    U.S. average, 454
    U.S. distribution of, 446, 452–453
    wealth compared to, 448–449
Income effect, 57, 425
    demand curve and, 211
    substitution effect and, 212–213
Income elasticity of demand, **91**–92, 97
Income taxes
    corporate, 731
    investment and, 739
    multiplier size and, 685
    progressive, 459
    proportional, 459
    regressive, 459
    supply-side fiscal policy and, 737–738
    U.S. rates of, 459
Indifference curve, **205**, 207–209
Indirect tax, 496, 731
Individual demand, 108–109
Individual Retirement Accounts (IRAs), 558
Individual supply, 110
Individual transferable quota (ITQ),
    404–405
Indivisible goods, 202
Induced consumption, 674
Induced expenditure, **678**, 682
Industrial Revolution, 53, 553
Industries
    airline, 308
    HHI and, 235
    infant, 164
    market correspondence to, 236–237
    publishing, 214–215
    revenues of, 232
Inefficiency, 140, 378
    of bureaucrats, 408–409
    common resources and, 402–403
    healthcare and, 381
    of minimum wages, 132–133
    of monopolies, 305
    of overproduction, 141
    of pooling equilibrium, 479
    of private provision, 375
    of public overprovision, 377
    of rent ceiling, 129
Inefficient overproduction, 395
Inelastic demand, **85**–86, 91–92
Inelastic supply, 94–95, 136–137
Inequality, 453–454, 489.
    See also Economic inequality
Infant industry, 164
Inferior goods, **60**, 92, 213
Inflation, **524**
    in *AS-AD* model, 659
    business cycle and, 714
    cost-push, 711–713
    cycles in, 709–714
    demand-pull, 709–711
    expected, 713–714, 718
    Fed fighting, 768–769
    forecasting, 714

    money growth and, 608–609
    price levels and, 527
    problem of, 524
    sources of, 709
Inflationary gap, **660**, 762, 768
Inflation rate
    core, 529, 759
    CPI and, 526–527
    Fed and, 761–762
    measuring, 526
Inflation rate targeting, **775**
Information
    asymmetric, 476
    firms and organizations, 229–231
    firms constraints on, 226
    as goods, 481
    invisible hand in uncertainty and, 481
    organization and, 229–231
    private, 476–480
Information-age monopoly, 7, 299
Infrastructure, 384–385
Innovation
    financial, 596, 604
    patents and, 298–299
Insolvency, 572
Institutions and laws, 730–731
Insurance
    collision, 473
    companies, 473–474, 570
    costs of, 474
    gains from, 475
    government providing, 380–382
    graphical analysis of, 474
    markets, 473–474, 480
    Obamacare and, 382–383
    in U.S., 380–382, 475
    value and costs of, 474
Intel Corporation, 354
Intellectual property, 44
Intellectual property rights, 553
Interdependence, 343
Interest, **4**
    bounded self-, 192–193
    compound, 438
    debt, 732
    forgone, 225
    self-, 5, 10, 481
    social, 5–6, 108, 481
    social theory on, 313
Interest rate parity, **628**
Interest rates, 572, 774
    banks and, 610–611
    changes in, 763–764
    from Fed, 776–777
    long-term real, 765
    nominal, 574, 604
    real, 574, 765
    real after-tax, 739
    U.S. and differentials in, 625, 764–765
    U.S. relative to foreign, 624–625
Intergenerational transfers, 458
Intermediate good, **492**
Internal Revenue Service (IRS), 117
International aid, 559
International borrower, 636
International debt, 743–744
International Harvester, 283
International lender, 636

International substitution, 687
International trade
    comparative advantage in, 152, 165
    exploitation in, 165
    financing, 634–639
    losers compensated in, 167
    restrictions to, 157–163, 166–167
    to stimulate economic growth, 559
    surplus in, 156
    tariff revenue influencing, 166–167
    U.S. airplane exports in, 154
International Trade Commission (ITC), 164
Internet
    advertising market battles on, 240–241
    regional access to, 12
Intertemporal substitution effect,
    655, 687, 707
Inventions, 299
Inverse relationships, **19**–20
Investment, **493**, 765
    gross and net, 494, 568
    gross private domestic, 495
    income taxes and, 739
    net, 568
Invisible Hand, 6, 8, 53, 113, 481
iPhone, 239, 290–291

Japan, 544
    debt of, 750–751
    deficit of, 736
    deflation in, 716
    trade of, 169
Jevons, William Stanley, 192
Jobs
    domestic, 164
    education and, 69
    offshore outsourcing of, 165–166
    prospects, 427
    zones, 560
Johnson, Dwayne "The Rock," 4
Johnson, Simon, 561
Joint unlimited liability, 231
JPMorgan Chase, 230, 570, 593, 610
Just-affordable combinations, 181

Kalamazoo
    cost-push inflation in, 713
    demand-pull inflation in, 710–711
Karns, Scott, 90
Kay's Kloset, 357
Kershaw, Clayton, 4
Key money, 128
Keynes, John Maynard, 516, 576, 664,
    674, 686, 727, 730
Keynesian cycle theory, **705**
Keynesian economics
    aggregate expenditure in, 694
    algebra of, 694–697
    autonomous tax multiplier, 696
    balanced budget multiplier, 697
    equilibrium expenditure in, 695
    government expenditure multiplier,
    696, 747
    multipliers in, 695
Keynesian macroeconomics, **664**–665
Keynesian model, 674
Kimberly-Clark, 350
Kiva.org, 552

KLM, 622
Knowledge, 406–409
Known oil reserves, 434
Kotlikoff, Laurence, 382–383, 742
Krueger, Alan, 132
Kyagalanyi Coffee, Ltd., 98
Kydland, Finn, 705
Kyoto Protocol, 393

Labor, 3
   backward-bending, 424–425
   casual, 420
   demand and supply of, 428
   demand curve for, 422
   demand for, 421–422
   division of, 53
   foreign, 164–165
   full employment and, 652
   market demand for, 424
   productivity and advances, 552–553
   services, 225, 420
   supply of, 547, 548–549
   technology and demand for, 423
   underemployed, 519
Labor force, 517, 548–549
Labor force participation rate, 519
Labor markets, 426–427, 430–431
   aggregate, 546–547
   competitive, 424–425
   employment-to-population ratio in, 518
   equilibrium, 425, 547–548
   income differences in, 455–458
   indicators of state of, 517–519
   minimum wages in, 131–132
   monopsony in, 429
   potential GDP and, 548
   in RBC, 707
   unemployment rate in, 517–519
   with unions, 428
Labor productivity
   growth of, 551–553
   increase in, 550–551
   technological advances and, 552–553
Labor union, 428
Laffer, Arthur B., 741
Laffer curve, 741
Land, 3
   rental markets and rates of, 432–433
   services, 420
   value of marginal product of, 432–433
Last resort loans, 600
La Vorgna, Marc, 194
Law-making lag, 749
Law of demand, 57, 60, 621–622
Law of diminishing returns, 251, 254, 547
Law of one price, 628
Law of supply, 62, 65, 623
Learning-by-doing, 164
Lee, Dwight R., 430
Legal barriers to entry, 298–299
Legal monopoly, 298
Legal system, 107
Lehman Brothers, 570, 596
Leisure time, 501
Lemons problem, 476–477
Lender of last resort, 600
Lenders, 570, 636
Levanon, Gad, 504

Levi's, 329
Levitt, Steven, 221–222
Liabilities
   of Fed, 598
   joint unlimited, 231
   limited, 231
   unlimited, 230
Lieb, Rebecca, 240
Life-cycle savings patterns, 458
Life Technologies Corp., 287
Limited liability, 231
Limit pricing, 355
Linear equations, 26
Linear relationships, 18–19, 26
Line-item veto, 730
Liquidity, 592, 594
Loanable funds
   changes in demand for, 575–576
   changes in supply of, 576–579
   demand and supply of, 575–576
   home price bubble and, 578
   quantity of, 575–576
   in RBC, 707
   supply of, 575, 576–577
   wealth and, 576
Loanable funds market, 573–574,
   766, 768
   demand increase in, 577–579
   equilibrium, 577
   global, 636–637
   government in, 580–581
Loans, 594
   bank, 765
   deposits created by, 600–601
   last resort, 600
   market, 479
   money creation through, 602
Local budgets, 736
Lomborg, Bjørn, 399
Long, John, 705
Long run, 248
   aggregate demand in, 690–691
   decisions, 248
   output, price, and profit in, 281–282
   zero economic profit in, 327
Long-run aggregate supply, 650
Long-run average cost curve, 261–262
Long-run costs
   economies and diseconomies of scale, 262–263
   production functions in, 260
   short-run costs and, 260–261
Long-run equilibrium, 282–283, 606–607
Long-run macroeconomic equilibrium, 658–659
Long-run Phillips curve, 718
Long-run supply, 96
Long-term bond rate, 764
Long-term contracts, 230
Long-term growth trends, 543–545
Long-term real interest rate, 765
Loose links, 769–771
Lorenz curve, 446, **447**–448, 453
Losses
   capital, 568
   comparisons of, 276
   from exports, 156
   from imports, 155

profit maximizing and, 326–327
   in short run, 279–280
   social, 158–161
Lottery, 107, 130
Lucas, Robert E., Jr., 498, 705, 728
Lucas wedge, 498–499
Luxuries, 86, 91–92

M1, 591–592, 601
M2, 591–592, 601
Macroeconomics, 2
   classical view of, 664
   fluctuations in, 658–663
   Keynesian view of, 664–665
   long-run equilibrium in, 658–659
   monetarist view of, 665
   new classical view of, 664
   new Keynesian, 665
   performance in, 537
   policy tradeoffs and, 783
   real variables in, 529
   schools of thought in, 664–665
   short-run equilibrium in, 658
   trends in, 647, 658–663
Mad cow disease (BSE), 163
Mainstream business cycle theory, 704–705
Major, Steven, 582
Majority rule, 106, 115
Malthus, Thomas Robert, 489, 555
Malthusian theory, 555, 558
Mankiw, N. Gregory, 166
Manning, Peyton, 470
Margin, 10
Marginal analysis, 184
Marginal benefit, 10, 36, 113, 121, 406
   decreasing, 36
   demand and, 58
   preferences and, 36
Marginal benefit curve, 36
Marginal cost, 10, 35, 113, **254**
   average cost and, 254–255
   calculating, 35
   increasing, 62, 140
   lowest price is, 63
   marginal revenue and, 275, 302, 304
   PPF and, 35
   short-run costs, 254
   supply and, 109–110
Marginal cost pricing rule, 313
Marginal external cost, 394, 402
Marginally attached workers, 519–520
Marginal private benefit, 406
Marginal private cost, 394, 402
Marginal product, 249, 251
   average product and, 252, 258
   of capital, 260
   value of, 421, 432–433
Marginal product curve, 250–251
Marginal propensity to consume (MPC), 676
Marginal propensity to import, 677
Marginal propensity to save, 676, 684
Marginal rate of substitution (MRS), 206, 209
Marginal returns
   diminishing, 251, 402
   increasing, 250–251

Marginal revenue, 272
elasticity and, 301
MC and, 275, 302, 304
price and, 300
Marginal social benefit,
108–109, 137, 406
common resources and, 402
of healthcare, 378
of housing, 129
of public goods, 374
Marginal social cost, 121, **394**
common resources and, 402
of housing, 129
of public goods, 375
supply curve and, 110
taxes and, 137
Marginal utility, 179, 182, 185, 187–191
change in demand and, 186
diminishing, 179–180
positive, 179
Marginal utility per dollar, 182–188, 195
Markets, 44
for bananas, 75
for bank reserves, 766, 768
bond, 569
for cellphones, 361
circular flows through, 44–45
for coffee, 71, 99
for college education, 69
commodity, 420
competitive environment of, 233–238
contestable, 354
coordinating decisions and, 45
coordination, 238
demand in, 108–109
efficiency of competitive, 112–115
equilibrium, 66–67, 77
exit and entry in, 281–283
with exports, 154, 156
fairness of competitive, 116–119
financial capital, 569–570
firm's constraints in, 226
geographical scope of, 236
for illegal goods, 142–143
with import quotas, 160–161
with imports, 153
industry correspondence of, 236–237
insurance, 473–474, 480
legal system for, 107
for loans, 479
for oil, 435
prices and, 56
for real GDP, 767–768
rental, 420
for school teachers, 437
structure, 236
with tariffs, 157, 159
understanding, 175
U.S. competitiveness of, 237
for used car, 476–479
U.S. rice, 169
Market capitalism, 8
Market demand, 424
Market equilibrium, 279
efficiency of, 396
in foreign exchange market, 624
Market exchange rate, 500
Market failure, 114–115

Market fundamentals, 434, 630
Market income, 446, 460
Marketing, 240
in monopolistic competition, 324–325
product development and, 330–333
Market price, 106, 496
Market supply, 110, 278
Market supply curve, 110, 425
Market value, 225, 492
Markup, 329
Marriage, wealth concentration and, 458
Marshall, Alfred, 175
Marshall, Bob, 176
Marshall, Mary Paley, 175
Marx, Karl, 8
Mathews, Timothy, 93
Maximum points, 20–21
Mayer, Marissa, 462–463
Mazumdar-Shaw, Kiran, 6
McKenzie, Richard B., 430
Mean income, 446
Means of payment, 590, 592
Median income, 446
Medicaid, 380–381, 459, 460
Medicare, 380–381, 460, 742
Medium of exchange, 590
Mergers and acquisitions, 359
Merrill Lynch, 570
Mexico, 164–165
MGM, 431
Michigan, 522
Microeconomics, 2
Microloan, 552
MicroPlace.com, 552
Microsoft, 7, 9, 227, 299, 312, 358
Mill, John Stuart, 116, 664
Minimum efficient scale, 263
Minimum points, 20–21
Minimum wage, 131, 522
below equilibrium, 145
deadweight loss and, 131
fairness of, 131–132
inefficiency of, 132–133
in labor markets, 131–132
monopsony and, 431
states raising, 144–145
unemployment and, 131, 132
Mitsubishi Bank, 622
Mixed economy, 8
Mode income, 446
Model economy, 32
Momentary supply, 96
Monetarism, 783
Monetarist cycle theory, 705
Monetarist macroeconomics, 665
Monetary base, 598
Monetary policy, 597, 656
achieving goals of, 758
conduct of, 760–762
Congress' role in, 760
exchange rate fluctuations in, 764–765
expenditure plans and, 765
of Fed, 656
federal funds rate and, 763
fighting recession, 766–767
free lunches and, 783
macroeconomics and, 783

objectives of, 758–760
operational maximum employment goal in, 759
operational price stability goal in, 759
president's role in, 760
responsibilities in, 760
strategies for, 775
transmission of, 763–771
Monetary policy instrument, 760–761
Monetary stimulus, 770, 772–775
Money, 44, 590
appreciating U.S. dollars, 627
bank loans and, 765
banks creating, 600–602
creation process, 601–602, 612–613
demand and supply of, 621
demand for, 605
deposits v. checks as, 592
depreciating U.S. dollars, 627
equal value of, 628
finance, and, 568
growth, not quantity of, 717
holding, 604
inflation and growth of, 608–609
key, 128
loans creating, 602
nominal, 604
nominal interest rate, 574, 604
official measures of, 591–592
price level and, 604, 630
quantity demanded of, 604
quantity of, 665
quantity theory of, 608–609
real, 604
real GDP and, 604
as store of value, 591
supply of, 621
U.S. multiplier and, 613
in U.S. today, 591
wage rate, 653, 710
Money income, 446, 460
Money market, 604–605, 607, 766
equilibrium, 606
mutual funds, 593
Money multiplier, 602, 612–613
Money price, 56
Money wage rate, 653, 710
Monopolistic competition, 233, 324, 335
advertising in, 330–332
efficiency of, 329
entry and exit in, 325
examples of, 325
firms in, 367
HHI and, 325
marketing in, 324–325, 330–332
number of firms in, 324
output in, 326–329
perfect competition compared with, 328–329
price in, 326–329
product development and, 330–332
Monopoly, 115, **233**. *See also* Cartel; Oligopoly
barriers to entry creating, 306
bilateral, 429
creating and buying, 306
deadweight loss and, 305

elasticity of demand in, 301
inefficiency of, 305
information-age, 7, 299
legal, 298
natural, 298, 313–315, 342
natural good, 372
output and price decisions of, 300–303
price discrimination and, 307–311
price-setting strategies of, 299
pros and cons of, 430
reasons for, **298**
regulation, 313–315
single-price, 299, 304–306
uncertainty and, 481
Monopsony, **429**, 431
Monthly price survey, 525
Moral hazard, **476**, 478, 480
Morgan, J. P., 356
Morgenstern, Oskar, 344
Mortgage, **569**, 570
Mortgage-backed security, **569**, 571, 598
Motorola, 237
MSN, 326
Multifiber Arrangement, 164
Multiplier, **682**
    aggregate expenditure curve slope
        and, 684
    autonomous tax, 696
    balanced budget, 697
    business cycle turning points and, 686
    effect, 682–683
    fiscal stimulus, 748–749
    government expenditure, 696, 747
    in Great Depression, 686
    greater than 1, 683
    imports and, 685
    income taxes and, 685
    in Keynesian economics, 695
    money, 602, 612–613
    price levels and, 687–691
    process, 685
    size of, 683, 695
    tax, 747
    U.S. money, 613
Murphy, Kevin, 132
Mutual funds, 593

Nadal, Rafael, 457
NAFTA. *See* North American Free Trade
    Agreement
NASA space program, 683
Nash, John, 345
Nash equilibrium, **345**, 349–350, 400
National Collegiate Athletic Association
    (NCAA), 430
National comparative advantage, 152
National Income and Product Accounts,
    495, 638
National saving, **573**
Natural barriers to entry, **298**
Natural monopoly, **298**, 313–315, 342
Natural monopoly good, **372**
Natural oligopoly, 342
Natural resources. *See also* Oil
    factors of production and, 3
    nonrenewable, 3, 420, 433, 434
    renewable, 401
Natural unemployment rate, **521**, 718

Nautica Clothing Corporation,
    326, 328–329
Navistar International, 283
NBC, 431
NCAA. *See* National Collegiate Athletic
    Association
NEC, 283
Necessities, 86, 91–92
Needs-tested spending, 745
Negative consumption externalities,
    392
Negative externality, 392, 394–400
Negative production externalities, 392
Negative relationships, **19**–20, 27
Neoclassical growth theory, **555**–556
Nestlé, 70
Net borrower, **636**
Net domestic income, 496
Net exports, **494**, 495, **638**–639, 765
Net investment, **494**, 568
Net lender, **636**
Netscape Navigator, 358
Net taxes, **573**
Net worth, **572**
Neuroeconomics, **193**
New Balance, 324
New classical cycle theory, **705**
New classical macroeconomics, **664**
New Deal, 516, 742
New goods bias, 527
New growth theory, **557**, 558
New Keynesian cycle theory, **705**
New Keynesian macroeconomics, **665**
New Zealand, 141, 405
Nike, 166, 324, 331
Nixon, Richard, 760
No-claim bonus, 480
Noise, 392
Nokia, 351
Nolan, Patty, 90
Nominal interest rate, **574**, 604
Nominal money, 604
Nonexcludable, **372**, 373
Nonrenewable natural resources, 3, **420**,
    433, 434
Nonrival, **372**, 373
Normal goods, **60**
Normal profit, **225**, 253
Normative statement, 11
North American Free Trade Agreement
    (NAFTA), 167
Nozick, Robert, 118

OASDHI. *See* Old Age, Survivors,
    Disability, and Health Insurance
Obama, Barack, 11, 69, 166, 168, 735
Obamacare. *See* Patient Protection and
    Affordable Care Act
Obstfeld, Maurice, 11
Occupy Wall Street, **8**
Official settlements account, **634**
Offshore outsourcing, **165**–166
Oil
    demand and supply of, 433–434
    equilibrium price of, 434
    global markets for, 435
    known reserves of, 434
    OPEC, 713

production, 46–47
    trade services for, 152
    U.S. markets of, 435
Old Age, Survivors, Disability, and Health
    Insurance (OASDHI), 459
Oligopoly, **233**, **342**
    barriers to entry and, 342
    games, 344–351
    game theory and, 344
    HHI and, 343
    Nash equilibrium and, 345, 349
    natural, 342
    price-fixing game in, 346–350
    repeated games, 352–355
    sequential games, 352–355
    small number of firms and, 343
100 percent reserve banking, **595**
One-year forward exchange rate, 628
OPEC. *See* Organization of the Petroleum
    Exporting Countries
Open Market Committee, 640
Open market operation, **598**
Open market purchase, 598–599
Open market sale, 599
Operational maximum employment
    goal, 759
Operational price stability goal, 759
Opportunity cost, **9**, **33**, 272
    comparative advantage and, 40, 42
    of goods, 128
    increasing, 33
    of leisure, 425
    PPF and, 32–34
    prices and, 56
    of production, 224
    as ratio, 33
    of wire hanger, 162
Organization of the Petroleum Exporting
    Countries (OPEC), 713
Organizations
    business, 230–232
    information and, 229–231
Origin, 15
Outcomes, 280
Outlays, 731–732, 734
Outlet substitution bias, 528
Output
    decisions, 248, 274
    external cost and, 394
    firm's decisions on, 274–277
    firm's short-run, 326
    in long run, 281–282
    in monopolistic competition,
        326–329
    price compared to, 304
    price decisions and, 302–303
    profit-maximizing, 275
    in short run, 278–280, 326
    single-price monopoly decisions for,
        300–303
Output gap, **522**, **660**, 759, 762
Outsourcing, offshore, 165–166
Overfishing equilibrium, 402–403
Overproduction, 114
    incentives for, 140
    inefficiency of, 141, 395
Ownership, 229
Ownership barriers to entry, **298**

Pandl, Zach, 582
Paradox of value, 189
Parkhouse, Albert J., 162
Partnership, 231
Patent, 298–299
Patient Protection and Affordable
    Care Act (Obamacare),
    370, 382, 504
Payoff matrix, **344**–345, 349–350
Peanut butter, 90, 93
Pension funds, 570
People's Bank of China, 632–633
Pepsi, 332, 650–653
Percentages and proportions, 85
Perfect competition, **233**, 235, **272**
    economic profit and revenue in,
        272–273
    efficiency of, 288–289, 305
    equilibrium in, 304
    firm's decisions in, 273
    firm's output decisions in, 274–277
    monopolistic competition compared
        with, 328–329
    output, price, and profit in long run,
        281–282
    output, price, and profit in short run,
        278–280
    price takers in, 272
    temporary shutdown decision in, 276
Perfectly elastic demand, **85**, 136
Perfectly elastic supply, 136–137
Perfectly inelastic demand, **85**, 135
Perfectly inelastic supply, 136–137
Perfect price discrimination, **310**, 311
Perfect substitute, 273
Perpetual motion economy, 557
Personal characteristics, 107
Personal computers, 283
Personal consumption expenditure deflator
    (PCE deflator), 528, 759
Personal consumption expenditures, 495
Personal Responsibility and Work
    Opportunities Reconciliation
    Act, 461
Phillips curve
    long-run, 718
    short-run, 718
    in U.S., 719
Physical capital, 551, 568
Pigou, Arthur Cecil, 397
Pigovian taxes, **397**
Piketty, Thomas, 463
Plosser, Charles, 705, 774, 776
Policy actions, 773
Policy tools, 598–600
Political equilibrium, **371**
Political marketplace, 370–371
Politicians, 370–371
Pollution
    cap-and-trade on, 398
    equilibrium and, 394–395
    as negative externality, 394–400
    produce less and, 395
    regulation of, 396–397
    taxes on, 397–398
    U.S. air, 393, 400
Pooling equilibrium, **479**
Pool risk, 594

Population, 60
    age distribution of, 521–522
    CPS and, 517
    employment ratio to, 518
    growth, 549–550
    neoclassical theory on growth of, 555
    working-age, 517
Positive consumption externalities, 392
Positive externalities, 392, 406–409
Positively skewed distribution, 446
Positive marginal utility, **179**
Positive production externalities, 392
Positive relationships, **18**–19, 27
Positive statement, 11
Postal Service, U.S., 299
Potential entry, 236
Potential GDP, **498**, 540–541
    changes in, 652
    determining, 546–548
    forces causing growth in, 548–551
    full employment and, 737
    growth of, 498
    human capital and, 652
    labor markets and, 548
Poverty, **451**
PPP. *See* Purchasing power parity
Predatory pricing, **358**
Pre-existing conditions, 382
Preferences, **9**, **179**–180, 184
    demand and, 60
    indifference curve and, 205
    map, 205
    marginal benefits and, 36
Premiums, 473
Prescott, Edward, 705, 738
Present value, 438, 439, 742
President, 730, 760
Price cap regulation, **315**
Price ceiling, **128**
Price discrimination, **299**
    of airlines, 308
    among buyers, 307–308
    efficiency and rent seeking with, 311
    of goods and resources, 308
    monopoly and, 307–311
    perfect, 310, 311
    rent seeking with, 311
    travelers and, 309–310
Price effect, **209**
Price elasticity of demand, **97**
    calculating, 84–85
    for coffee, 99
    for food, 89
    percentages and proportions in, 85
Price fixing. *See also* Collusion
    antitrust law and, 357
    game, 346–350
    horizontal agreements on, 357
    vertical agreements on, 357
Price floor, **131**
Price gap, **128**
Price gouging, 119
Price level, **524**
    in *AS-AD* model, 687
    equilibrium real GDP and, 689–691
    inflation and, 527
    money and, 604, 630
    multiplier and, 687–691

one-time fall in, 715
one-time rise in, 711
persistently falling, 715
real GDP and fixed, 678–681
short-run aggregate supply and, 651
Prices, 273, 324
    adjustments of, 67
    asset, 572
    average quantity and, 84–85
    of bananas, 75
    Big Mac index and, 629
    change in, 203–204, 209
    commodity, 420
    demand and, 59–60
    exchange rate as, 620–621
    expected future, 59–60, 64
    factors of production and, 56, 63,
        259, 423
    firms short-run output and, 326
    fixed, 674–677
    of gasoline, 398
    in long run, 281–282
    marginal revenue and, 300
    market fundamental, 434
    markets and, 56
    in monopolistic competition, 326–329
    oil equilibrium, 434
    opportunity cost and, 56
    output compared to, 304
    output decisions and, 302–303
    predicting changes in, 68–75
    production quotas influencing, 140
    regulation of, 114, 115
    as regulator, 66–67
    of related goods, 59
    relative, 56, 203, 209, 655
    rise and fall of, 140
    in short run, 278–280
    single-price monopoly decisions for,
        300–303
    stability of, 758, 759
    supply, 63
    surplus influencing, 67
    time since change in, 87
Price takers, **272**
Price wars, 354
Princeton, 482
Principal–agent problem, **229**
    incentive pay and, 229
    long-term contracts and, 230
    ownership and, 229
    in production, 229
Principle of increasing marginal cost, 402
**Principle of minimum
    differentiation**, **376**
The Principles of Economics (Marshall, A.),
    175
Prisoner's dilemma, 344–345, 400
Private benefit, 406
Private good, **372**
Private information, **476**–480
Private property, 404
Private provision, 375
Private sector balance, **638**, 639
Private subsidies, 408–409
Producer gains, 159
Producer surplus, **111**, 288, 305,
    308, 473

Product curves
    average, 252
    cost curves and, 256
    marginal, 250–251
    short-run costs, 256–258
    in short-run technology constraints, 249
    total, 250
Product development, 330–333
Product differentiation, **233**, **324**
Production. *See also* Factors of production
    aggregate function, 546
    auto, 263, 554
    complements in, 63, 455
    economies of team, 239
    efficient, 33, 35
    equilibrium and quotas in, 139
    of households, 501
    incentive systems in, 229
    of iPhone, 239
    in long-run costs, 260
    lost, 516
    negative externalities in, 392
    oil, 46–47
    opportunity cost of, 224
    Pepsi, 650–653
    positive externalities in, 392
    principal–agent problems in, 229
    public, 407, 408
    resources diverted from, 524
    substitutes in, 63, 455
    techniques in, 227
    technological advances and, 286
Production efficiency, **33**, 35
Production functions, 260
Production possibilities frontier (*PPF*),
    32, 41, 546
    MC and, 35
    opportunity costs and, 32–34
    total product curve and, 250
    tradeoffs in, 33
Production quota, **139**–140, 404
Product schedules, 249
Profit-maximizing output, 275
Profits, **4**
    accounting, 224
    collusion maximizing, 347
    corporate, 496
    expected effect and, 622
    gross, 494
    long run, 281–282
    and losses, 279–280
    loss minimizing and, 326–327
    normal, 225, 253
    no round-trip, 628
    producer surplus and, 308
    short run, 278–280
    zero economic, 327
Progressive income tax, **459**
Prohibition, 143
Property, private, 404
Property rights, **44**, **395**–396, 404, 553
Proportional income tax, **459**
Proprietorship, 230–232
Proprietors' income, 496
Protection, argument against, 164–167
Public choice, **370**
    alternate solutions in, 379
    political marketplace and, 370–371

Public franchise, 298
Public goods, 115, **372**, 556
    benefits of, 374
    efficient quantity of, 375
    excludable and rival, 372
    MSB of, 374
    MSC of, 375
    providing, 374–377
Public overprovision, 377
Public production, **407**, 408
Public provision, 375–376
Public school teachers, 436–437
Publishing industry, 214–215
Puma, 324
Purchasing power parity (PPP),
    500, **628**–629

QE. *See* Quantitative easing
Quality, 324
    advertising and, 332–333
    change bias, 527
    of environment, 501
Quantitative easing (QE), 603
Quantity
    affordable and unaffordable, 185, 202
    average prices and, 84–85
    of capital, 652
    deflation and theory of, 715
    equilibrium, 66
    full employment and labor, 652
    of loanable funds, 575–576
    of money, 665
    of money demanded, 604
    money growth, not, 717
    public good and efficient, 375
    regulation of, 114
Quantity demanded, **57**
    change in demand vs change in, 60–61
    changes in, 61, 186
    of money, 604
    of real GDP, 654, 655
Quantity supplied, **62**, 64–65
    of real GDP, 650
Quantity theory of money, **608**–609
Quintiles, 446–447, 452
Quota
    import, 160–161
    ITQ, 404–405
    production, 139–140, 404

Railroads, 553
Ralph Lauren, 329
Rate of return regulation, **314**
Rational choice, **9**
Rational ignorance, 377
Ratio scale, 507
Rawls, John, 117
RBC theory. *See* Real business cycle theory
R&D. *See* Research and development
Reagan, Ronald, 538, 741
Real business cycle (RBC) theory,
    705–708, 727
Real exchange rate, **630**
Real GDP, **497**, 504–505
    actual and planned expenditure and, 679
    aggregate demand curve and, 655
    aggregate expenditure and,
        674, 692–693

business cycle and, 499
    calculating, 497
    chained-dollar, 508–509
    consumption as function of, 677
    employment and, 524
    equilibrium, 689–691
    with fixed price level, 678–681
    fluctuations of, 498–499
    leisure time and, 501
    limitations of, 501–503
    market for, 767–768
    money holding and, 604
    quantity demanded, 654, 655
    quantity supplied, 650
    unemployment over cycle and, 522–523
    uses and limitations of, 498
    U.S. growth in, 666–667
    world economy growth of, 544–545
Real GDP per person, **498**, **500**, **540**,
    542, 545
Real income, **203**
Real interest rate, **574**, 765
Real money, 604
Real property, 44
Real-time ad platform, 240
Real wage rate, 522, 529, **547**
Receipts, 731, 733
Recession, **499**, 599, 766–767, 772
Recessionary gap, 656, **661**, 746, 762
Recognition lag, 749
Recorded music, 190–191
Redbox, 210
Redistribution
    of income, 459–461, 524
    of surplus, 306
    of wealth, 524
Reebok, 324
Reference base period, 525
Regressive income tax, **459**
Regulation, **313**
    of depository institution, 594
    earnings sharing, 315
    health and safety, 163
    of natural monopoly, 313–315
    of pollution, 396–397
    price cap, 315
    of prices, 114, 115
    rate of return, 314
Reinhart, Carmen M., 11
Relative price, **56**, **203**, 209, 655
Rent, **4**
Rental income, 496
Rental markets
    capital, 432
    land, 432–433
    vehicle, 420
Rental rate, 420
    of capital, 432
    implicit, 224
    of land, 432–433
Rent ceiling, 129, 130
Rent seeking, **167**, **306**
    equilibrium, 306–307
    with price discrimination, 311
Rent-*versus*-buy decisions, 432, 438–439
Repeated duopoly game, 352–354
Repeated games, 352–355
Required reserve ratio, **600**

Resale price maintenance, 357
Research and development (R&D),
    350–351, 559
Reservation wage, 424
Reserve ratio, 612
Reserves, 593, 600
    banks, 596, 766, 768
    commercial banks with, 596
    of depository institution, 598
    desired, 601
    excess, 601
    known oil, 434
    100 percent bank, 595
    U.S. official, 634
Resources. *See also* Common resources;
    Goods and resources; Natural
    resources
    allocation methods for,
      106–107, 407
    common, 115
    efficient use of, 35–37, 288
    production and diversion of, 524
    substitution possibilities of, 95–96
    technological change and, 38, 62
Restoring American Financial Stability
    Act of 2010, 571
Revenue
    economic profit and, 272
    elasticity and total, 88
    of industries, 232
    from tariffs, 158, 166–167
    total and marginal, 272
    total cost and, 274
Ricardo, David, 555, 581, 664
Ricardo-Barro effect, 581
Risk
    buying and selling, 473–475
    credit, 479
    default, 479
    pool, 594
    supply, 74–75
    trading, 474
Risk aversion, 470
Rival, 372
Robinson, James, 561
Robinson-Patman Act, 356
Robots, as skilled workers, 554
Rockefeller, John D., 356, 358
Romer, Christina, 748–749
Romer, Paul, 556
Roosevelt, Franklin D., 516
Rosen, Sherwin, 458
Rule of 70, 541–542
Rule of law, 107
Russell, Bertrand, 727
Ryan, Paul, 735

Sachs, Jeffrey, 648
Saez, Emmanuel, 450
Safety regulations, 163
Sala-i-Martin, Xavier, 648
Samsung, 86
Saudi Arabia, 636
Saving function, 674–675
Savings, 568
    bank, 593
    consumption and, 674–675
    economic growth and, 558

    life-cycle patterns in, 458
    national, 573
    taxes and, 739
Savings and loan association (S&L), 593
Scarcity, 2, 32
Scatter diagrams, 16–17, 659
Schiefsky, Mark J., 482
Schmalensee, Richard, 358
Schmitt-Grohé, Stephanie, 784
Schott, Jeffrey, 168
Schumpeter, Joseph, 556, 647
Screening, 479
Search activity, 128
Search engines, 317
Securities, 594, 598
Self-interest, 5, 10, 192–193, 481
Sellers, 67, 133–135, 142–143
Selling costs, 331–332
Separating equilibrium, 479
Sequential entry games, 354
Sequential games, 352–355
Shephard, William G., 237
Shepperson, John, 119
Sherman Act, 356, 358
Shoes, 331
Shortages, 67
Short run, 248
    aggregate demand in, 690
    decisions, 248
    equilibrium, 279, 606–607
    outcomes in, 280
    output, price, and profit in,
      278–280, 326
    profits and losses in, 279–280
Short-run aggregate supply, 651
Short-run costs
    average cost, 254
    average total cost curve, 254–255
    cost curves, 256–258
    firms with, 261
    long-run costs and, 260–261
    marginal cost, 254
    product curves, 256–258
    shifts in cost curves, 258–259
    TC and, 253
    total cost, 253
Short-run macroeconomic
    equilibrium, 658
Short-run market supply curve, 278
Short-run Phillips curve, 718
Short-run supply, 96
Short-run technology constraints
    average product curve, 252
    marginal product curve, 250–251
    product curves in, 249
    product schedules in, 249
    total product curve, 259
Short-term bill rate, 764
Shutdown decisions, temporary, 276
Shutdown point, 276
Signal, 332
Signaling, 478
SilkySkin, 357
Simon, Julian, 489
Singapore, 121, 545
Single-price monopoly, 299
    competition compared to, 304–306
    output and price decisions in, 300–303

Skilled workers, robots as, 554
S&L. *See* Savings and loan association
Slope
    aggregate expenditure, 684
    across arc, 23–24
    of curved line, 23–24
    of line, 26–27
    marginal propensities and, 676
    at point, 23
    of relationship, 22–24
    of straight line, 22–23
Smart phone, 290–291
Smetters, Kent, 742–743
Smith, Adam, 8, 53, 54, 113, 537, 555,
    558, 664
Smith, Thomas M., 436
Smoot-Hawley Act, 158, 166
Social interest, 5–6, 108, 481
Social interest theory, 313
Social loss, 158–161
Social networking, 241
Social science, 11
Social Security
    programs, 459
    taxes, 133, 135, 138, 731
    time bomb of, 742–743
Solow, Robert, 555
South Africa, 453, 560–561
Specialization, 40, 457
Speculation, 629
SSI. *See* Supplementary Security Income
Stafford, Penny, 343
Stagflation, 663, 712
Stagnation, 720
Standard of living, 38
    in China, 500
    across countries, 500
    over time, 498
    U.S., 498
Standard Oil, 358
Starbucks, 264, 343
State budgets, 736
State of nature, 64
Statistical discrepancy, 496
Statute of Monopolies of 1624, 553
Steam technology, 553
Stern, Nicholas, 399
Stevenson, Betsey, 11
Stevenson, Robert, 553
Stiglitz, Joseph, 502
Stimulus. *See also* Fiscal stimulus
    automatic, 745
    monetary, 770, 772–775
Stock, 570
Stock markets, 570
Store checkouts, 256–257
Store of value, 591
Straight line equations, 26–27
Strategies, 344
    dominant-strategy equilibrium, 345
    Fed's decision-making, 761–762
    game theory, 344
    for monetary policy, 775
    monopoly price-setting, 299
    tit-for-tat, 352, 354
    trigger, 352
Structural change, in unemployment,
    521–522

Structural surplus or deficit, 745–746
Structural unemployment, 521, 522
Stuit, David, 436
Sub-prime credit crisis, 480
Subsidies, 114, **407**, 496
　export, 163
　government, 140–141, 314
　in health insurance, 382–383
　private, 408–409
　services from, 459–460
　in U.S., 141
Substitutability, degree of, 207–208
Substitutes, 59
　close, 207
　closeness of, 86
　cross elasticity of demand and, 92–93
　monopolies and no close, 298
　perfect, 273
　in production, 63, 455
Substitution
　diminishing marginal rate of, 206
　income effect and, 212–213
　international, 687
　marginal rate of, 206, 209
　possibilities, 95–96
Substitution bias
　commodity, 527
　outlet, 528
Substitution effect, 57, **212**, 425
　aggregate demand and, 655, 687–688
　in aggregate demand curve, 655
　income effect and, 212–213
　intertemporal, 655, 687, 707
Sugary drinks, 194–195
Sundance Records & Tapes, 285
Sunk cost, 248
Supplementary Security Income (SSI), 459
Supply, 62, 621
　all possible changes in, 72–73
　bananas at risk and, 74–75
　changes in, 64–65, 284–285
　decision time-frame, 96
　decrease in, 70, 72–73, 139–140
　elastic and inelastic, 94–95
　in foreign exchange market, 623
　of human capital, 455
　increase in, 64, 70, 72–73, 140
　individual, 110
　of labor, 547, 548–549
　labor demand and, 428
　law of, 62, 65, 623
　for loanable funds, 575, 576–577
　loanable funds changes in, 576–579
　long-run, 96
　long-run growth of, 579
　market, 110, 278
　market curve of, 110
　MC and, 109–110
　minimum price and cost of, 63, 110
　momentary, 96
　of money, 621
　of oil, 433–434
　perfectly elastic, 136–137
　perfectly inelastic, 136–137
　prices, 63
　producer surplus and, 111
　risk, 74–75

　schedule, 62
　short-run, 96
　technology changing, 286
　U.S. dollars changes in, 625–626
Supply curve, 62–63
　backward-bending labor, 424–425
　equation of, 76
　of firms, 277
　market, 110, 425
　MSC curve and, 110
　short-run market, 278
　straight line in, 76
　for U.S. dollars, 623
Supply of loanable funds, 575, **576**–577
Supply-side fiscal policy, 737–741
Supply-siders, 737
Surplus
　budget, 580, 732
　consumer, 109, 189, 288, 305, 473
　cyclical, 745
　in international trade, 156
　prices influenced by, 67
　producer, 111, 288, 305, 308, 473
　redistribution of, 306
　structural, 745–746
　total, 112, 113, 288
Sustainable Fishing Act, 405
Sustained growth, 541–542
Sweden, 453
Symmetry principle, 118

Taiwan, 545
Talking with
　Caroline M. Hoxby, 418
　Esther Duflo, 54
　Raj Chetty, 490
　Ricardo J. Caballero, 728
　Richard H. Clarida, 538
　Stephanie Schmitt-Grohé, 784
　Steven D. Levitt, 222
　Susan Athey, 176
　Thomas Hubbard, 368
　Xavier Sala-i-Martin, 648
TANF. *See* Temporary Assistance for Needy Households
Tariffs
　deadweight loss and, 159
　influence of, 157–159
　international trade and, 166–167
　markets with, 157, 159
　revenue from, 158, 166–167
　social loss from, 158–159
　two-part, 313
　in U.S., 158
　winners and losers from, 159
TARP. *See* Troubled Asset Relief Program
Taxes, 114
　autonomous multiplier for, 696
　buyer and seller equivalency of, 134–135
　on buyers, 134–135
　on carbon emissions, 398
　consumers paying, 138
　corporate income, 731
　on drugs, 143

　efficiency and, 137–138
　on expenditures, 738
　fairness and, 138
　firms cutting, 740
　income, 459
　indirect, 496, 731
　MSC and, 137
　multiplier, 747
　net, 573
　perfectly elastic demand and, 136
　perfectly inelastic demand and, 135
　Pigovian, 397
　on pollution, 397–398
　prohibition and, 143
　savings and investments with, 739
　on sellers, 133–134
　Social Security, 133, 135, 138, 731
　U.S. firms cutting, 740
Tax incidence, 133, 135–137
Tax multiplier, 747
Tax revenues, 744–745
Tax wedge, 738
Taylor rule, 775
Team production, economies of, 239
Technological change, 38
　diminishing returns and, 555
　economic inequality and, 455
　resources and, 38, 62
Technological efficiency, 227
Technology, 64, 226
　abatement, 395
　advancing, 284–287, 653
　clean, 396–397
　cost curves and, 258–259
　firm's constraints of, 226
　labor demand and, 423
　labor productivity and advances in, 552–553
　short-run constraints of, 249–252, 259
　steam, 553
　supply changed by, 286
Temperature analogy, 190
Temporary Assistance for Needy Households (TANF), 459, 461
Temporary shutdown decisions, 276
Tennis racquets, 334–335
A Theory of Justice (Rawls), 117
Third World debt crisis, 637
Three sector balances, 639
Thrift institutions, 593
Time lags, 749, 769–771
Time-series graphs, 506–507
Tit-for-tat strategy, 352, 354
T-Mobile, 359, 360–361
Toshiba, 239
Total cost curves, 253
Total costs, 253, 274, 331
Total factor productivity, 706
Total fixed cost, 253
Total product, 249, 251, 256
Total product curve, 250, 259
Total revenue, 88, **272**, 274
Total revenue test, 88
Total surplus, 112, 113, 288
Total utility, 179–181, 189
Total variable cost, 253, 256
TPP. *See* Trans Pacific Partnership

Trade
  balance of, 635
  cap-and-, 398
  with China, 152
  free, 157, 159–161, 164, 167
  gains from, 40–43
  global market, 155–156
  net gain from, 155–156
  protection in, 164–167
  in risk, 474
  of services for oil, 152
  U.S. and Japan's, 169
  wars, 166
Trade books, 214–215
Tradeoff, 9
  big, 117, 460–461
  choices as, 9
  policy, 783
  along PPF, 33
Traffic congestion, 120–121
Tragedy of the commons, 401–405
Transactions costs, 115, 238, 396
Transfer payments, 495, 731
Trans Pacific Partnership (TPP), 168
Transportation, 384–385
Treasury bills, 764
Trends, 507
  in economic growth, 543–545
  in economic inequality, 449–450
  in macroeconomics, 647, 658–663
  in wage rate, 426
Trigger strategy, 352
Troubled Asset Relief Program
    (TARP), 773
T-shirts, 153, 157–161
Turner, Matthew, 120
2009 Fiscal Stimulus Act, 746
Two-part tariffs, 313
Tying arrangement, 357–358

Uhlig, Harald, 748–749
Unaffordable quantities, 202
Unattainability, 32
Uncertainty
  buying and selling risk, 473–475
  choices with, 472
  decisions facing, 470–472
  expected utility and, 471–472
  expected wealth and, 470
  factor markets, inequality and, 489
  information and invisible hand in, 481
  monopoly and, 481
  risk aversion and, 470
  utility of wealth and, 470–471
Underemployed labor, 519
Underemployment rate, 520
Underestimate benefit, 378
Underground economy, 501
Underproduction, 114
Unemployment, 721
  alternative measures of, 520
  benefits, 522
  compensation, 459
  cyclical, 521, 522
  defining, 519
  economic recovery and, 776
  employment and, 516–520
  Fed and, 762

  frictional, 521
  labor markets indicators and, 517–519
  marginally attached workers in,
    519–520
  in Michigan, 522
  minimum wage causing, 131, 132
  most costly, 520
  natural rate of, 521, 718
  problem of, 516–517
  real GDP and, 522–523
  rise in, 530
  structural, 521, 522
  structural change in, 521–522
Unemployment rate, 507, 518, 762
Unemployment-to-population ratio, 518
Unions, 428–431
United Kingdom, 738, 741
United States (U.S.). *See also* Dollars, U.S.
  airplane exports of, 154
  air pollution in, 393, 400
  appreciating and depreciating dollar
    in, 627
  average income in, 454
  borrowing for consumption of, 637
  budget in historical perspective of,
    732–734
  business cycle in, 660–661
  comparative advantage and, 153–154
  concentration measures in, 235,
    236–237
  Congress, 730, 746, 760
  consumption function in, 677
  cost-push inflation in, 713
  as debtor nation, 637
  demand changes in dollar of, 624–625
  demand for dollar, 622–623
  demand-pull inflation in, 711
  Department of Commerce of, 235
  dollar exchange rate in, 621
  dollar questions and, 620
  dollar supply curve of, 623
  economic growth in, 38–39, 543,
    666–667
  economic inequality in, 446–452
  economic struggles in, 770
  economy of, 504
  employment growth in, 530
  exports demand, 624
  federal budget of, 736
  financial crisis of 2008-2009 and,
    772–773
  firms cutting taxes, 740
  flexible exchange rate in, 631
  foreign interest rates relative to,
    624–625
  Gini ratio in, 449
  government budget of, 736
  government securities of, 598
  Great Depression in, 166
  healthcare expenditures of, 379–381
  illegal drugs in, 142–143
  import demand, 625
  import function in, 677
  import quotas and, 160–161
  imports and exports of, 152–154
  income distribution in, 446, 452–453
  income tax rates in, 459
  infrastructure in, 384–385

  insurance in, 380–382, 475
  interest rate differential in,
    625, 764–765
  international debt of, 743–744
  Japanese trade with, 169
  marginal utility per dollar in,
    182–188, 195
  market competitiveness in, 237
  measuring GDP of, 495–497
  money in, 591
  money multiplier in, 613
  as net borrower, 636
  official reserves of, 634
  oil markets of, 435
  Phillips curve in, 719
  Postal Service, 299
  poverty in, 451
  RBC impulse for, 706
  real GDP growth in, 666–667
  rice market in, 169
  stagflation in, 663
  standard of living in, 498
  structural budget balance of, 746
  subsidies in, 141
  supply changes in dollar of, 625–626
  tariffs in, 158
  tax wedge in, 738
  underground economy in, 501
  wage rates in, 426
  world demand for exports of, 624
Unit elastic demand, 85
Unit of account, 590–591
Units-free measure, 85
Universal coverage, 380
Unlimited liability, 230
Uribe, Martin, 784
U.S. *See* United States
Used car market, 476–479
U.S. interest rate differential, 625
U.S. official reserves, 634
Utilitarianism, 116–117
Utility
  expected, 471–472
  marginal, 179–180, 182, 185–191
  maximizing, 181–184
  recorded music with, 190–191
  total, 179–181, 189
  of wealth, 470–471

Value, 108. *See also* Present value
  absolute, 85
  insurance costs and, 474
  market, 225, 492
  money's equal, 628
  paradox of, 189
  present, 438, 439, 742
  store of, 591
Value of marginal product, 421
  of capital, 432
  of land, 432–433
Vanderbilt, W. H., 356
Variable cost, 308
Variables
  having maximum and minimum
    points, 20–21
  in macroeconomics, 529
  more than two, 24–27
  moving in opposite directions, 19–20

moving in same direction, 18–19
    unrelated, 21
Vehicle rental markets, 420
Velocity of circulation, 608
Vertical price fixing agreement, 357
VF Corporation, 326
Vietnam War, 711
Voluntary export restraint, 163
von Neumann, John, 344
Voodoo economics, 741
Voters, 370
Vouchers, 383, 407
    advantages of, 409
    in health insurance, 383

Wage rate, 555
    of human capital, 455
    money, 653, 710
    real, 522, 529, 547
    trends in, 426
    in U.S., 426
Wages, 4. *See also* Minimum wage
    efficiency, 522
    reservation, 424

Wal-Mart, 44, 166, 620
Walton, Sam, 44
Warranties, 478–479
Wealth, 448, 568
    aggregate demand curve and,
        654–655, 687
    distribution of, 448
    economic inequality and,
        448–449, 458
    effect, 654–655
    expected, 470
    income compared to, 448–449
    loanable funds and, 576
    marriage and concentration of, 458
    redistribution of, 524
    unequal, 458
    utility of, 470–471
Wealth of Nations (Smith), 53
Web browsers, 358
Welch, Finis, 132
Welfare, 459, 461
Wells Fargo, 593
Westinghouse, 236
Willingness to pay, 108

Women
    as borrowers, 552
    in labor force, 548–549
    wage rates and, 555
    welfare and, 461
Woolf, Virginia, 727
Working-age population, 517
World Economic Forum, 560
World economy, 453–454,
    544–545, 656
World Trade Organization
    (WTO), 163
Wright, Frank Lloyd, 392
Writers Guild of America, 431
WTO. *See* World Trade Organization

Yahoo!, 241
Yale College, 482
Yellen, Janet, 597, 774, 776
Yen, 620, 621
Yuan, 620, 621

Zero economic profit, 327
Zuckerberg, Mark, 12, 229

Chapter 1: p. 1: Monkey Business/Fotolia; p. 2: Frank Modell/The New Yorker Collection/The Cartoon Bank; p. 6 (top): ADEK BERRY/Stringer/AFP/Getty Images; p. 6 (bottom): STR New/Reuters Pictures; p. 7 (right): Snap Happy/Fotolia; p. 7 (left): Christian Prandl/image-BROKER/Alamy; p. 8 (left): Brendan McDermid/Reuters Pictures; p. 8 (right): Pictorial Press Ltd/Alamy; p. 12: karelnoppe/Fotolia.

Chapter 2: p. 31: Jim West/Alamy; p. 53: Alamy; p. 54: Eric Fougere/VIP Images/Corbis.

Chapter 3: p. 55: Patti McConville/Alamy; p. 69: AP Photo/Reed Saxon; p. 71: wavebreakmedia/Shutterstock.

Chapter 4: p. 83: Kike Calvo/National Geographic/Corbis.

Chapter 5: p. 105: Roza/Fotolia; p. 113 (left): Mike Twohy/The New Yorker Collection/The Cartoon Bank; p. 113 (right): Stephen Coburn/Shutterstock; p. 119: A.J. Sisco/Newscom; p. 121: Bloomberg/Contributor/Bloomberg/Getty Images.

Chapter 6: p. 127: DOL Photo/Alamy.

Chapter 7: p. 151: Matt Mawson/Eureka/Corbis; p. 162: Justin Sullivan/Staff/Getty Images News/Getty Images; p. 166: Terry Vine/ Blend Images/Alamy; p. 175: Stock Montage, Inc./Historical Pictures Collection.

Chapter 8: p. 177: Moxie Productions/Blend/Corbis.

Chapter 9: p. 201: Corbis; p. 208: Robert Weber/The New Yorker Collection/The Cartoon Bank; p. 210 (right): Justin Sullivan/Staff/Getty Images News/Getty Images; p. 210 (left): Cardinal/Corbis; p. 214: Newscom; p. 221: Bettmann/Corbis.

Chapter 10: p. 223: Jurgen Ziewe/Alamy; p. 230: AFP/Staff/Getty Images; p. 233 (left insert): Michael Newman/PhotoEdit; p. 233 (left): Robert Glusic/Getty Images; p. 233 (right insert): George Widman/AP Images; p. 233 (right): Alastair Miller/Bloomberg via Getty Images; p. 239: Oliver Leedham/Alamy; p. 241: Source: Based on Google, Yahoo, Facebook financial reports, "Profit Comparison" https://investor.google.com/earnings.html, https://investor.yahoo.net/annuals.cfm , http://investor.fb.com/annuals.cfm.

Chapter 11: p. 247: Tim Thompson/Corbis; p. 257 (left): Paul Burns/Blend Images/Alamy; p. 257 (right): Dennis Wall/MCT/Newscom; p. 263: Jim West/Alamy.

Chapter 12: p. 271: PhotoEdit/Alamy; p. 281: Rena Schild/Shutterstock; p. 283 (left): Digital Vision/Photodisc/Getty Images; p. 283 (right): Elena Elisseeva/Shutterstock; p. 285: Landis Images; p. 290: Iain Masterton/Alamy.

Chapter 13: p. 297: Kristoffer Tripplaar/Alamy; p. 311: William Hamilton; p. 312: Bloomberg via Getty Images; p. 317: Source: Based on Google financial reports: "Google's Revenue, Cost, and Profit" http://www.google.com/finance?fstype=bi&cid=694653.

Chapter 14: p. 323: Julian Finney/Getty Images; p. 331: Michael Blann/Digital Vision/Getty Images.

Chapter 15: p. 341: Cunaplus/Fotolia; p. 353 (bottom): Stephen Brashear/AP Images; p. 353 (top): Photo courtesy of Airbus S.A.S.; p. 356 (left): Source: Based on The Sherman Act of 1890, U.S. Department of Justice, http://www.justice.gov; p. 356 (right): Source: Based on The Clayton Act and Its Amendments, U.S. Department of Justice, http://www.justice.gov; p. 361: Source: Based on Market Shares in Cellphone Service" http://www.verizon.com/about/investors/annual-reports/; http://investor.t-mobile.co/CorporateProfile.aspx?iid=4091145; http://www.att.com/gen/investor-relations?pid=9186; http://investors.sprint.com/QuarterlyResults.aspx?iid=4057219; p. 367: Topham/The Image Works; p. 368: Evanston Photographic Studio.

Chapter 16: p. 369: Nancy Kennedy/Shutterstock; p. 370: "Source: Based on Bureau of Economic Analysis, "What Governments Buy" http://www.bea.gov/"; p. 373: Kenneth C. Zirkel/Photodisc/Getty Images; p. 376: A. T. Willett/Alamy; p. 379: "Source: Based on World Health Organization, "Healthcare Expenditures in 14 Countries" http://www.who.int/en/"; p. 381: Source: Based on Bureau of Economic Analysis, "Sources of Expenditure on Healthcare" http://www.bea.gov/; p. 382 (left): Lawrence Kotlikoff; p. 382 (right): Kotlikoff, Laurence J., The Healthcare Fix: Universal Insurance for All Americans, Cover, © 2007 Massachusetts Institute of Technology, by permission of The MIT Press; p. 385: ZUMA Press, Inc./Alamy.

Chapter 17: p. 391: Jeff Haller/Keyhole Photo/Corbis; p. 393: Danita Dellmont/Gallo Images/Getty Images; p. 398: Source: Based on Energy Information Administration, "The Price of Gasoline in Four Countries" http://www.eia.gov/; p. 399 (left): David pearson/Alamy; p. 399 (right): Patrick Jube/Getty Images; p. 400: Source: Based on United States Environmental Protection Agency, "The Global Distribution of CO2 Emissions" http://www.epa.gov/; p. 403 (left): Marten Ryckaert/Bridgeman Art Library; p. 403 (right): Source: Based on United Nations Food and Agriculture Organization, "The Atlantic Cod Catch: 1850–2005" http://www.fao.org/home/en/; p. 409: David Grossman/Alamy; p. 417: David Joel Photography Inc.

Chapter 18: p. 419: MBI/Alamy; p. 427: Javier Larrea/AGE Fotostock America Inc.; p. 430 (left): Susana Gonzalez/Getty Images; p. 430 (right): Jamie Squire/Getty Images.

Chapter 19: p. 445: Bloomberg via Getty Images.

Chapter 20: p. 469: Rawpixel/Fotolia; p. 480: Source: Based on Interest data from the Federal Reserve Bank of St Louis, FRED database, and author's calculations and assumptions, "The Price of Commercial Credit Risk" http://research.stlouisfed.org/fred2/; p. 489: World History Archive/Alamy.

The Pearson Series in Economics

Abel/Bernanke/Croushore
*Macroeconomics**

Acemoglu/Laibson/List
*Economics**

Bade/Parkin
*Foundations of Economics**

Berck/Helfand
The Economics of the Environment

Bierman/Fernandez
Game Theory with Economic Applications

Blanchard
*Macroeconomics**

Blau/Ferber/Winkler
The Economics of Women, Men, and Work

Boardman/Greenberg/ Vining/ Weimer
Cost-Benefit Analysis

Boyer
Principles of Transportation Economics

Branson
Macroeconomic Theory and Policy

Bruce
Public Finance and the American Economy

Carlton/Perloff
Modern Industrial Organization

Case/Fair/Oster
*Principles of Economics**

Chapman
Environmental Economics: Theory, Application, and Policy

Cooter/Ulen
Law & Economics

Daniels/VanHoose
International Monetary & Financial Economics

Downs
An Economic Theory of Democracy

Ehrenberg/Smith
Modern Labor Economics

Farnham
Economics for Managers

Folland/Goodman/Stano
The Economics of Health and Health Care

Fort
Sports Economics

Froyen
Macroeconomics

Fusfeld
The Age of the Economist

Gerber
*International Economics**

González-Rivera
Forecasting for Economics and Business

Gordon
*Macroeconomics**

Greene
Econometric Analysis

Gregory
Essentials of Economics

Gregory/Stuart
Russian and Soviet Economic Performance and Structure

Hartwick/Olewiler
The Economics of Natural Resource Use

Heilbroner/Milberg
The Making of the Economic Society

Heyne/Boettke/Prychitko
The Economic Way of Thinking

Holt
Markets, Games, and Strategic Behavior

Hubbard/O'Brien
*Economics**

*Money, Banking, and the Financial System**

Hubbard/O'Brien/ Rafferty
*Macroeconomics**

Hughes/Cain
American Economic History

Husted/Melvin
International Economics

Jehle/Reny
Advanced Microeconomic Theory

Johnson-Lans
A Health Economics Primer

Keat/Young/Erfle
Managerial Economics

Klein
Mathematical Methods for Economics

Krugman/Obstfeld/Melitz
*International Economics: Theory & Policy**

Laidler
The Demand for Money

Leeds/von Allmen
The Economics of Sports

Leeds/von Allmen/ Schiming
*Economics**

Lynn
Economic Development: Theory and Practice for a Divided World

Miller
*Economics Today**

Understanding Modern Economics

Miller/Benjamin
The Economics of Macro Issues

Miller/Benjamin/North
The Economics of Public Issues

Mills/Hamilton
Urban Economics

Mishkin
*The Economics of Money, Banking, and Financial Markets**

*The Economics of Money, Banking, and Financial Markets, Business School Edition**

*Macroeconomics: Policy and Practice**

Murray
Econometrics: A Modern Introduction

O'Sullivan/Sheffrin/Perez
*Economics: Principles, Applications and Tools**

Parkin
*Economics**

Perloff
*Microeconomics**

*Microeconomics: Theory and Applications with Calculus**

Perloff/Brander
*Managerial Economics and Strategy**

Phelps
Health Economics

Pindyck/Rubinfeld
*Microeconomics**

Riddell/Shackelford/ Stamos/ Schneider
Economics: A Tool for Critically Understanding Society

Roberts
The Choice: A Fable of Free Trade and Protection

Rohlf
Introduction to Economic Reasoning

Roland
Development Economics

Scherer
Industry Structure, Strategy, and Public Policy

Schiller
The Economics of Poverty and Discrimination

Sherman
Market Regulation

Stock/Watson
Introduction to Econometrics

Studenmund
Using Econometrics: A Practical Guide

Tietenberg/Lewis
Environmental and Natural Resource Economics Environmental Economics and Policy

Todaro/Smith
Economic Development

Waldman/Jensen
Industrial Organization: Theory and Practice

Walters/Walters/Appel/ Callahan/Centanni/ Maex/O'Neill
Econversations: Today's Students Discuss Today's Issues

Weil
Economic Growth

Williamson
Macroeconomics

Macroeconomic Data

These macroeconomic data series show some of the trends in GDP and its components, the price level, and other variables that provide information about changes in the standard of living and the cost of living—the central questions of macroeconomics. You will find these data in a spreadsheet that you can download from your MyEconLab Web site.

	NATIONAL INCOME AND PRODUCT ACCOUNTS	1968	1969	1970	1971	1972	1973	1974	1975	1976	1977
	EXPENDITURE APPROACH										
the sum of	1 Personal consumption expenditures	557.4	604.5	647.7	701.0	769.4	851.1	932.0	1,032.8	1,150.2	1,276.7
	2 Gross private domestic investment	156.9	173.6	170.1	196.8	228.1	266.9	274.5	257.3	323.2	396.6
	3 Government expenditures	226.8	240.4	254.2	269.3	288.2	306.4	343.1	382.9	405.8	435.8
	4 Exports	47.9	51.9	59.7	63.0	70.8	95.3	126.7	138.7	149.5	159.4
less	5 Imports	46.6	50.5	55.8	62.3	74.2	91.2	127.5	122.7	151.1	182.4
equals	6 Gross domestic product	942.5	1,019.9	1,075.9	1,167.8	1,282.4	1,428.5	1,548.8	1,688.9	1,877.6	2,086.0
	INCOME APPROACH										
	7 Compensation of employees	532.1	586.0	625.1	667.0	733.6	815.1	890.3	950.2	1,051.3	1,169.0
plus	8 Net interest, rent, and profit	221.7	228.1	222.0	246.6	279.5	317.3	323.3	357.1	405.4	456.8
equals	9 Net domestic product at factor cost	753.8	814.1	847.1	913.6	1,013.1	1,132.4	1,213.6	1,307.3	1,456.7	1,625.8
plus	10 Indirect taxes less subsidies	72.2	79.4	86.6	95.8	101.3	112.0	121.6	130.8	141.3	152.6
	11 Depreciation	113.3	124.9	136.8	148.9	160.9	178.1	206.2	237.5	259.2	288.3
equals	12 GDP (income approach)	939.3	1,018.4	1,070.5	1,158.3	1,275.3	1,422.5	1,541.4	1,675.6	1,857.2	2,066.7
plus	13 Statistical discrepancy	3.2	1.6	5.3	9.5	7.1	6.1	7.4	13.2	20.5	19.3
equals	14 GDP (expenditure approach)	942.5	1,019.9	1,075.9	1,167.8	1,282.4	1,428.5	1,548.8	1,688.9	1,877.6	2,086.0
	15 Real GDP (billions of chained 2009 dollars)	4,569.0	4,712.5	4,722.0	4,877.6	5,134.3	5,424.1	5,396.0	5,385.4	5,675.4	5,937.0
	16 Real GDP growth rate (percent per year)	4.9	3.1	0.2	3.3	5.3	5.6	−0.5	−0.2	5.4	4.6
	OTHER DATA										
	17 Population (millions)	200.7	202.6	205.0	207.6	209.8	211.9	213.8	215.9	218.0	220.2
	18 Labor force (millions)	78.7	80.7	82.8	84.4	87.0	89.4	92.0	93.8	96.2	99.0
	19 Employment (millions)	75.9	77.9	78.7	79.4	82.1	85.1	86.8	85.8	88.8	92.0
	20 Unemployment (millions)	2.8	2.8	4.1	5.0	4.9	4.4	5.2	7.9	7.4	7.0
	21 Labor force participation rate (percent of working–age population)	59.6	60.1	60.4	60.2	60.4	60.8	61.3	61.2	61.6	62.2
	22 Unemployment rate (percent of labor force)	3.6	3.5	5.0	6.0	5.6	4.9	5.6	8.5	7.7	7.1
	23 Real GDP per person (2009 chained dollars per year)	22,770	23,254	23,036	23,497	24,468	25,603	25,237	24,945	26,034	26,963
	24 Growth rate of real GDP per person (percent per year)	3.9	2.1	−0.9	2.0	4.1	4.6	−1.4	−1.2	4.4	3.6
	25 Quantity of money (M2, billions of dollars)	545.3	578.7	601.4	674.4	758.1	831.8	880.7	963.7	1,086.6	1,221.4
	26 GDP deflator (2009 = 100)	20.6	21.6	22.8	23.9	25.0	26.3	28.7	31.4	33.1	35.1
	27 GDP deflator inflation rate (percent per year)	4.3	4.9	5.3	5.1	4.3	5.4	9.0	9.3	5.5	6.2
	28 Consumer Price Index (1982–1984 = 100)	34.8	36.7	38.8	40.5	41.8	44.4	49.3	53.8	56.9	60.6
	29 CPI inflation rate (percent per year)	4.2	5.4	5.9	4.2	3.3	6.3	11.0	9.1	5.8	6.5
	30 Current account balance (billions of dollars)	1.6	1.6	3.7	0.3	−4.1	8.9	6.0	19.9	7.1	−10.9

	1978	1979	1980	1981	1982	1983	1984	1985	1986	1987	1988	1989	1990
	1,426.2	1,589.5	1,754.6	1,937.5	2,073.9	2,286.5	2,498.2	2,722.7	2,898.4	3,092.1	3,346.9	3,592.8	3,825.6
	478.4	539.7	530.1	631.2	581.0	637.5	820.1	829.6	849.1	892.2	937.0	999.7	993.5
	477.4	525.5	590.8	654.7	710.0	765.7	825.2	908.4	974.5	1,030.8	1,078.2	1,151.9	1,238.4
	186.9	230.1	280.8	305.2	283.2	277.0	302.4	303.2	321.0	363.9	444.6	504.3	551.9
	212.3	252.7	293.8	317.8	303.2	328.6	405.1	417.2	452.9	508.7	554.0	591.0	629.7
	2,356.6	2,632.1	2,862.5	3,211.0	3,345.0	3,638.1	4,040.7	4,346.7	4,590.2	4,870.2	5,252.6	5,657.7	5,979.6
	1,320.3	1,481.1	1,626.3	1,795.4	1,894.5	2,014.1	2,217.6	2,389.2	2,545.6	2,725.7	2,950.9	3,143.9	3,345.0
	526.1	563.6	575.7	669.6	683.5	767.4	921.4	982.9	987.1	1,058.8	1,174.8	1,242.1	1,258.4
	1,846.4	2,044.7	2,202.0	2,465.0	2,578.0	2,781.5	3,139.0	3,372.1	3,532.7	3,784.5	4,125.7	4,386.0	4,603.4
	162.0	171.6	190.5	224.1	225.9	242.0	268.7	286.7	298.5	317.2	345.0	371.5	398.0
	325.1	371.1	426.0	485.0	534.3	560.5	594.3	636.7	682.2	728.0	782.4	836.1	886.8
	2,333.5	2,587.4	2,818.5	3,174.1	3,338.2	3,584.0	4,002.0	4,295.5	4,513.4	4,829.7	5,253.1	5,593.6	5,888.2
	23.2	44.8	43.9	36.7	6.8	54.2	38.7	51.3	76.7	40.6	-0.5	64.2	91.4
	2,356.6	2,632.1	2,862.5	3,211.0	3,345.0	3,638.1	4,040.7	4,346.7	4,590.2	4,870.2	5,252.6	5,657.7	5,979.6
	6,267.2	6,466.2	6,450.4	6,617.7	6,491.3	6,792.0	7,285.0	7,593.8	7,860.5	8,132.6	8,474.5	8,786.4	8,955.0
	5.6	3.2	-0.2	2.6	-1.9	4.6	7.3	4.2	3.5	3.5	4.2	3.7	1.9
	222.5	225.0	227.6	229.9	232.1	234.2	236.3	238.4	240.6	242.8	245.0	247.3	250.0
	102.2	105.0	107.0	108.7	110.2	111.5	113.5	115.5	117.8	119.9	121.7	123.9	125.9
	96.0	98.8	99.3	100.4	99.5	100.8	105.0	107.2	109.6	112.4	115.0	117.3	118.8
	6.2	6.1	7.7	8.3	10.7	10.7	8.5	8.3	8.2	7.4	6.7	6.5	7.1
	63.2	63.7	63.8	63.9	64.0	64.0	64.4	64.8	65.2	65.6	65.9	66.4	66.5
	6.1	5.9	7.2	7.6	9.7	9.6	7.5	7.2	7.0	6.2	5.5	5.3	5.6
	28,164	28,738	28,338	28,783	27,964	28,995	30,829	31,851	32,671	33,502	34,594	35,531	35,813
	4.5	2.0	-1.4	1.6	-2.8	3.7	6.3	3.3	2.6	2.5	3.3	2.7	0.8
	1,322.4	1,425.8	1,540.4	1,679.6	1,831.4	2,054.8	2,219.3	2,416.7	2,613.5	2,783.8	2,933.4	3,056.1	3,223.6
	37.6	40.7	44.4	48.5	51.5	53.6	55.5	57.2	58.4	59.9	62.0	64.4	66.8
	7.0	8.3	9.0	9.3	6.2	3.9	3.5	3.2	2.0	2.5	3.5	3.9	3.7
	65.2	72.6	82.4	90.9	96.5	99.6	103.9	107.6	109.7	113.6	118.3	123.9	130.7
	7.6	11.3	13.5	10.4	6.2	3.2	4.4	3.5	1.9	3.6	4.1	4.8	5.4
	-12.7	-1.2	8.5	3.4	-3.3	-35.1	-90.1	-114.3	-142.7	-154.1	-115.8	-92.4	-74.9